W9-ANQ-366

PRINCIPLES OF BUSINESS LAW

PRENTICE-HALL INTERNATIONAL, INC., LONDON
PRENTICE-HALL OF AUSTRALIA, PTY., LTD., SYDNEY
PRENTICE-HALL OF CANADA, LTD., TORONTO
PRENTICE-HALL OF INDIA (PRIVATE) LTD., NEW DELHI
PRENTICE-HALL OF JAPAN, INC., TOKYO
PRENTICE-HALL DE MEXICO, S.A., MEXICO CITY

PRINCIPLES OF BUSINESS LAW

Alternate Seventh Edition

UNIFORM COMMERCIAL CODE

ESSEL R. DILLAVOU
Professor of Business Law, Emeritus
University of Illinois

CHARLES G. HOWARD
Professor of Law, Emeritus
University of Oregon

PAUL C. ROBERTS
Professor of Business Law
University of Illinois

WILLIAM J. ROBERT
Professor of Business Law
University of Oregon

ROBERT N. CORLEY
Associate Professor of Business Law
University of Illinois

Prentice-Hall, Inc.
Englewood Cliffs, N.J.

LIBRARY OF CONGRESS CATALOG CARD NUMBER: 64–12852

Second printing.........August, 1964

PRINTED IN THE UNITED STATES OF AMERICA
70684-C

PREFACE

In preparing the manuscript for the Alternate Seventh Edition, Uniform Commercial Code, the authors have been especially mindful of two factors: first, current thinking as to content which should be included in a course or courses in Business Law; and second, the needs of students in those states which have adopted the Uniform Commercial Code.

There are many teachers of business law who feel that room must be made in the basic business law course for an understanding of the social significance of law and the part it has played in the development of our economic life. To assist the student in appreciating the value and use of basic rules of law in our complex society—and to assist them in understanding their application to particular legal fields such as contracts, negotiable instruments, and business associations—the introductory chapters include materials on business and its relation to society; the nature of law; basic legal concepts of property; law as ordered society; the evolution of business and the emergence of the free enterprise system; governmental limitation on free enterprise; bigness in business, labor and government; and automation.

The role of the businessman in modern society is becoming more and more significant. In order to understand more readily the rules of law that create "the legal tools"—contracts and other legal instruments—material included in the Introduction outlines the social, economic, and political history out of which such tools evolved. A presentation of the present political, social, and economic climate within which business is conducted is also included.

There are many teachers who still believe that the traditional approach to Business Law is sound. The teacher in his personal presentation considers, as text and cases are presented, the purpose of law in our complex society and its function in resolving business and social conflicts. It has been the intent of the authors to so organize this text that the instructor may select the approach he desires to follow. By inclusion or deletion of particular portions of the material, he may use whatever approach he feels best fits the needs of his particular students.

Two additional aspects of the text should be noted. First, at several points in Book II on Contracts, moral and ethical issues are pointed up, providing the teacher who desires to do so an opportunity to emphasize ethical considerations in the area of business. Second, although the court decision to each of a number of the case problems found at the end of each chapter has been indicated, the student is asked to discuss the soundness of the decision. Opportunity is thus afforded to discuss a decision from the viewpoint of accepted principles of law, morals, and ethics and from that of its impact upon our industrial society.

The Uniform Commercial Code has been adopted by over half of the states and others are giving it serious consideration. (See the list immediately following this preface.) This text includes a discussion of all of the pertinent provisions of the Code and contains selected cases, decided to date, which interpret the Code or explain its principles. The Code repeals most of the uniform legislation affecting business—the Negotiable Instruments Law, the Sales Act, and others. However, students in Code states should be familiar with the provisions of such repealed uniform legislation, just as students in Noncode states should be familiar with the Commercial Code. For these reasons, this text includes discussions of both the Uniform Acts and the Uniform Commercial Code, with the primary emphasis on the Code especially where it has modified the existing law.

As has been true of previous editions, the authors use the combination text-case method of presentation, selecting cases, as far as possible, that are free from complicated procedural questions but which introduce the student to current problems and procedures confronting business. Many new cases have been inserted to meet this objective and to keep abreast of current law, especially the Uniform Commercial Code.

The authors are indebted to many current and past users of the text for helpful suggestions. These suggestions have been of substantial assistance to the authors in the preparation of this alternate edition and in helping to produce a text which they feel is an unusually effective teaching tool. Special acknowledgment is made to Professor Hollis K. Martin of the University of Arizona for his constructive review and comment on the final manuscript.

The authors wish to express their appreciation to Mrs. Jack Dearth, Mrs. Lowell Edwards, and Mrs. Charles G. Howard of Eugene, Oregon, and Miss Ann Dodd of Urbana, Illinois for their able assistance in the preparation, checking, and editing of the manuscript.

The authors also acknowledge their indebtedness to the Columbia University Press, New York 27, N.Y., for permission to reprint excerpts from Cardozo, *The Paradoxes of Legal Science;* Stevens and Sons Limited, 11 New Fetter Lane, London E. C. 4, for permission to reprint excerpts from Friedman, *Legal Theory* (3rd Edition); The University of Nebraska Press, Lincoln 8, Nebraska, for permission to reprint excerpts from Beutel, *Experimental Jurisprudence;* Southern Methodist University Press, Dallas 22, Texas, for permission to reprint excerpts from Harding, *The Ghost of Herbert Spencer: A Darwinian Concept of Law;* The Fund of the Republic, Inc., Box 4068, Santa Barbara, California, for permission to reprint excerpts from Kerr, *Unions and Union Leaders of Their Own Choosing,* and Berle, *Economic Power and the Free Society;* the Foundation Press, Inc. for permission to reprint excerpts from Handler, *Cases and Materials on Trade Regulations;* Yale University Press for permission to reprint excerpts from Cardozo, *The Growth of the Law;* John E. Balint, Industrial Engineer, Eugene, Oregon, for contributing material on the subject of automation; and Professor Robert S. Summers, School of Law, University of Oregon, Eugene, Oregon, for contributing materials on the subject of judicial reasoning.

Acknowledgment is made of the courtesy of the National Conference of Commissioners on Uniform State Laws and The American Law Institute in granting us permission to reproduce in part the copyrighted Official Comments to the Code.

The following is a list of states which have adopted the Uniform Commercial Code.

State	Effective	State	Effective
ALASKA	January 1, 1963	NEBRASKA	Sept. 2, 1965
ARKANSAS	January 1, 1962	NEW HAMPSHIRE	July 1, 1961
CALIFORNIA	January 1, 1965	NEW JERSEY	January 1, 1963
CONNECTICUT	October 1, 1961	NEW MEXICO	January 1, 1962
GEORGIA	January 1, 1964	NEW YORK	Sept. 27, 1964
ILLINOIS	July 2, 1962	OHIO	July 1, 1962
INDIANA	July 1, 1964	OKLAHOMA	January 1, 1963
KENTUCKY	July 2, 1960	OREGON	Sept. 1, 1963
MAINE	Dec. 31, 1964	PENNSYLVANIA	July 1, 1954
MARYLAND	Feb. 1, 1964	RHODE ISLAND	January 2, 1962
MASSACHUSETTS	October 1, 1958	TENNESSEE	July 1, 1964
MICHIGAN	January 1, 1964	WEST VIRGINIA	July 1, 1964
MISSOURI	July 1, 1965	WISCONSIN	July 1, 1965
MONTANA	January 2, 1965	WYOMING	January 2, 1962

The Uniform Commercial Code was presented to the legislatures in four states—Hawaii, Minnesota, Texas, and Washington—but was not adopted in these states. Eight other states, including Florida, Idaho, Iowa, Kansas, Nevada, North Carolina, South Carolina, and South Dakota are studying the Code for possible adoption.

CONTENTS

BOOK ONE / INTRODUCTION

BOOK TWO / CONTRACTS

BOOK FIVE / BUSINESS ORGANIZATIONS

BOOK SIX / PERSONAL PROPERTY

BOOK SEVEN / SECURED TRANSACTIONS

BOOK EIGHT / REAL PROPERTY

TABLE OF CASES

PRINCIPLES OF BUSINESS LAW

BOOK I

INTRODUCTION

1

Business and Its Relation to Society and the Law

1-1. Business and society. Business activity, like any other human conduct, operates within the framework of organized society and is subject to its pressures and controls, whether they be economic, political, social, or governmental. Activity by nongovernmental organizations creates much of the atmosphere within which business is conducted. Trade and manufacturing associations, political parties, labor unions, chambers of commerce, granges, and similar groups function much like government. They have their own legislative assemblies which make by-laws and rules, and establish official positions which give the officers power not only to regulate and control their members, but to influence others who are not members. These private bodies by their collective action help to create the climate within which business is conducted. The nature and purpose of the influence, with its resulting climate, depend upon the economic, social, and political ideology of such pressure groups. Out of these conflicting interests come legal rules which also regulate and control business activity. Only by studying how law has evolved from such conflicts and has been made to function as a means of social and business control can we understand the role of law in its relation to business.

Therefore, in order to understand the relationship between law and business, in Book I we discuss the nature and origin of law; basic legal concepts of property; business and the free enterprise system; the evolution of law in relation to business; freedom of contract and limitation on freedom of contract; monopolies; and government regulation of business. With this background, the application of particular rules of law to particular areas of business conduct is better understood, and such legal instruments as business contracts, negotiable instruments, and sales contracts have greater significance. The organization, purpose, and function of business associations, such as corporations and partnerships, are more apparent. The reason for security transactions and man's duty to abide by his promise has meaning and the necessity of courts as instruments of government to settle controversies and protect persons and property is better appreciated.

Business conduct as a human activity is broad and comprehensive. It has to do with supplying human wants. People must be fed, clothed, housed, transported, entertained, secured, and supplied with a multiplicity of goods and services. This task must be performed within a framework or organization, subject both to internal regulation and to social control.

As distinct from other legal problems, business legal problems are ever-present, urgent, and vital. "Doing business" is an everyday affair. A businessman daily enters into a multiplicity of legal relations, arising out of contracts, title to goods, security transactions, insurance, labor relations, and business institutions. When a decision has to be made, the proper one is more likely to follow if the businessman has some idea of the implications of the law applicable to the problem. Judgment resting on a previous study of law, its history, and its evolution is more likely to produce a correct decision than one made without this background.

Only in an ordered society can business function. Controls that make an ordered society and are enforced by government are *legal* controls. As stated above, there are many non-legal controls and sanctions arising out of organized group action, as well as ethical considerations, that influence the climate within which business operates.

The businessman, in conducting his business, is always faced with the "dilemma of the times." The uncertainty of the economy, influenced day by day and week by week by domestic and international strife, competition, monopolistic power, government regulation, artificially stimulated consumer demands, and price fluctuation, make flexibility a necessity. In making the adjustments necessitated by changing conditions, the businessman is influenced and regulated by the rules of law under which he must operate. These rules change and increase in number and complexity with changes in economic, political, and social growth. Business operating in a simple, rural economy was less affected and restrained than business operating in our present complex, technological age. Large populations living in an urban society under centralized government, with mass communication and rapid transit, have greatly affected business activity. Whether the law as an instrumentality of social control is affected by changes in man's way of living, or whether man's way of living is affected by the law, is not always easy to determine. But the law, with which we are concerned, is the final authority.

1-2. What is the law? It is not possible to give a simple definition of the law. The literature about law—its source, its definition, and its purpose—is voluminous. The following generally recognized authoritative definitions illustrate different ideas about the law:

1. ". . . all law is originally formed in the manner in which in ordinary, but not quite correct, language, customary law is said to have been

formed, i.e., that it is first developed by custom and popular faith, next by jurisprudence, everywhere therefore by internal silently operating powers, not by the arbitrary will of a law-giver." –Savigny, Friedman, *Legal Theory*, 136 (1953).

2. "Law emanates from the sovereign not from its creatures. The sum total of all those rules of human conduct for which there is a state sanction. . . . Law in its essence is made up of those rules of human conduct which are made mandatory by the state upon all its citizens and without which social order and well-being could not exist." –Justice Stone.

3. Law is "a rule of conduct arising out of the natural relations of human beings established by the creator, existing prior to any positive precept, discovered by right, reason and the rational intelligence of man." –Kent.

4. "The prophecies of what the courts will do in fact and nothing more pretentious are what I mean by the law." "Law is a statement of the circumstances in which the public force will be brought to bear upon men through courts." –Oliver Wendell Holmes.

5. "Law is an experimental process in which the logical factor is only one of many leading to a certain conclusion. . . . Law is a means to an end. . . . The law is both a result of social forces and an instrument of social control." –W. Friedman.

Thus, it may be seen that definitions of the law depend largely upon which particular aspect, feature, or relationship the author thinks important, significant and worthy of emphasis. Each of the definitions listed above rests upon, and is sustained by, predetermined, definite, fixed, nonlegal concepts and beliefs about the nature of man, religion, ethics, philosophy, economics, politics, and forms of government.

These beliefs have been roughly classified into different schools of legal thought. The most important of these schools are designated as the historical, the analytical, the natural, and the sociological. A general sketch of each of these four schools of legal thought is given in the following sections.

1-3. Schools of legal thought. *Historical.* If the scholar in his definition gives weight to the evolutionary process of ideas and formalizes them into rules of conduct resting on custom and tradition, then the historical aspect has been emphasized and made important. From primitive times community living has required order. Hence, as society developed, there evolved customary and traditional rules of conduct. Law was found in these rules, not handed down, but evolved. Custom results from repeated approved usage, and when such usage by common adoption and acquiescence justifies each member of society in assuming that every other member of society will conform thereto, a rule of conduct has been formulated. When such a rule is adopted by a court as controlling in a particular case, or is enacted into legislation, law has been made. An illustration of such historical development is the "law merchant." Here a system of commercial customs about bills of exchange, bills of lading, sales, partnerships, and other business transactions evolved. These customs were in time recognized by the law courts and became a part of the common law. Cardozo in his book, *The Paradoxes of Legal Science*,[1] speaks of the evolution of law in this way:

Law defines a relation not always between fixed points, but often, indeed oftenest, between points of varying position. The acts and situations to be regulated have a motion of their own. There is change whether we will or not. . . . There is need to import some of this same conception of relativity into our conception of the development of the law. . . . Constancy consists in fitting our statement of the relation to the new position of the objects and the new interval between them. I find an illustration of my thought in the development of the law governing ocean bills of lading. At first, a bill of lading imported the delivery of merchandise on board a designated ship. The time came, however, with the upheavals of the great war when the goings and comings of ships were too uncertain to be known or stated in advance. Goods were left at the dock and all that the steamship company would undertake was to send them forward when it could. During the war the old routine of trans-oceanic shipments was destroyed and no steamship company was able to predict even within months when it would be able to ship goods or on what steamer. The documents issued to its shippers conformed to these necessities. They no longer acknowledged receipt on a designated vessel. The acknowledgment was merely that the goods had been received for shipment on a named vessel and/or on a following steamer. When the war was over the change that had thus been born of necessity was continued for convenience. . . . The old form of document thus came to be supplanted by a new one which omitted an acknowledgment once recognized as vital. The question was still open as to the extent to which the courts would effectuate the change. A bank was to pay for goods against a draft and a bill of lading. Was a document in the new form a bill of lading against which payment might be made? To have said no, would have kept the law consistent with ancient definitions. To have said yes kept it consistent with the realities of usage and the needs of ocean commerce. In this dilemma the courts preferred to say yes (*Victor v. National City Bank*, 237 N.Y. 538). The truth of course was that there had been a change in methods of transportation which necessitated a revision of the legal formula if the relation defined by law was to maintain its former correspondence with the regulation to be regulated, i.e., the relation known to business. Refusal to change the statement of the rule would have given to the change of events an exaggerated movement. . . .

When changes of manners or business have brought it about that a rule of law which corresponded to previously existing norms or standards of behavior corresponds no longer to the present norms or standards but on the contrary departs from them, then those same forces or tendencies of development that brought the law into adaptation to the old norms and standards are effective, without legislation, but by the inherent energies of the judicial processes, to

[1] Cardozo, *The Paradoxes of Legal Science*, 11 (1927) (New York, Columbia University Press).

restore the equilibrium. My illustrations have been drawn from changing forms of business. . . . Manners and customs (if we may not label them as law itself) are at least a source of law. The judge, so far as freedom of choice is given to him, tends to a result that attaches legal obligation to the folkways, the norms or standards of behavior exemplified in the life about him.

Such has been the history of the law of negotiable instruments, partnership, sales, and many other areas of commercial law. Although the evolution of the law by judicial process may have been somewhat arrested by the legislative enactment of many uniform laws in the commercial field, development has not stopped. Business necessity has brought about amendment and revision, as evidenced by the recent drafting and codification of the Uniform Commercial Code, parts of which are to be considered in later portions of this text.

Friedman summarizes the historical school of thought as follows:

(1) Law is found, not made. A pessimistic view is taken of the power of human action. The growth of law is essentially an unconscious and organic process; legislation is therefore of subordinate importance as compared with custom.

(2) As law develops from a few easily grasped legal relations in primitive communities to the greater complexity of law in modern civilization, popular consciousness can no longer manifest itself directly, but comes to be represented by lawyers, who formulate the technical legal principles. But the lawyer remains an organ of popular consciousness, confined to the task of bringing into shape what he finds as raw material. Legislation follows as the last stage; the lawyer is therefore a relatively more important law making agency than the legislators.

(3) Laws are not of universal validity or application. Each people develops its own legal habits, as it has its peculiar language, manners and constitution.[2]

Analytical. If the scholar in his definition gives weight to the need for certainty and to a system of positive rules logically deduced from fundamental principles dictated by a sovereign state, with power to command, then law is defined from an analytical point of view. Law here is a rule laid down by a superior power, to guide and regulate those under the power. Under this concept, ideals of justice and morals are not of paramount importance. The state as the lawgiver hands down the law and as sovereign is bound by no overriding superior divine law or principle. Thus, law is a system of principles or rules in the nature of commands. Such commands may be orders of a monarch, or of a totalitarian authority, or they may be legislative enactments, administrative orders, or judicial pronouncements of a democratic state.

This legal theory presupposes a highly organized government limited to the particular purpose of keeping order. Under this philosophy, business activity in the United States has been given considerable latitude.

[2] Friedman, *Legal Theory,* 137 (1953) (London, Stevens & Sons Ltd).

With such security, the individual, free to carry on economic, social, political, and other activities not inconsistent with ordinary police sanction, cares for himself. Providing for public welfare and controlling business are considered outside the province of government. During the nineteenth century this concept, aided by natural law ideas, gave free reign to individualism in business and economy, thus undergirding and stimulating free enterprise. Such terms as *liberty of contract, free competition, individualism,* and *absence of government control* conveyed ideas, defined activities, and expressed policies entitled to protection under the Constitution of the United States.

Natural law. If the author in his definition gives significance to the idea that man by nature seeks an ideal of absolute right and justice as a higher law by which to measure all other rules of conduct, then an aspect based on natural law has been emphasized and made important. From very early times ethical values—good, right, reason, and justice—have been elements in the law. Justinian in the Roman Institutes in 528 A.D. spoke of law as that which is "good and equitable," a "theory of right and wrong," a standard of conduct—namely, "to live honestly, to hurt nobody and give everyone his due."

Law, when set against a background of Divine principles, becomes a rule of reason, pronounced by reasonable men for the benefit of mankind and the establishment of the good community. Man as a reasonable being is able to distinguish between good and evil. Above him there exists law resting on reason and divine authority, which validates man-made law. Thus, when the state by legislation or by judicial process lays down rules of conduct that are unfair, unreasonable, or inimicable to the common good, they are in violation of natural and divine law.

Blackstone, in his commentaries, says: "This law of nature being coeval with mankind and dictated by God himself, is of course superior in obligation to any other. It is binding all over the globe in all countries and at all times; no human laws are of any validity if contrary to this . . ."

Natural law, nurtured by the church, softened the rigid common law of England; became the basis of equity; and, finding its way to America, is expressed in the Declaration of Independence in the words "certain unalienable Rights, . . . Life, Liberty and the pursuit of Happiness."

Sociological. If the writer in his definition seeks to find and describe law by what it does, its method, its purpose, and how it functions in balancing conflicting social interests, then many aspects of society will be emphasized and made important. In order to find how the law is made, what it is, and how it functions, investigation into many areas of society is required. The lawmakers, legislators, and judges in making laws are necessarily influenced by their previous predilections, economic theories, political bias, and such social considerations as are significant at the time. Under the pressure of conflict of interests, legislators and courts make law. Thus, law, when enacted by the legislature or pronounced by the courts, is, in the end, the result of finding an equilibrium between conflicting interests.

The law will be what the legislature has said, or what the court has said about what the legislature has said, or what the court says the law is, if the legislature has not spoken.

Law is not only generalization deduced from a set of facts, a recognized tradition, a prescribed formula for determining natural justice, but it also consists of rules for social control growing out of the experiences of mankind. Current social mores, political ideologies, international situations and conditions, and present economic and business interests are all elements to be investigated and evaluated in making the law and in determining how it operates. In order to find and define the law, facts must be ascertained by an ordered or scientific method. It is advocated that by this method law may be determined, simplified, and better adapted to social needs. Such techniques will permit a determination of what motivates legislators in making legislation and judges in deciding cases. Such emphasis leads to a consideration of statistical studies as to how and what law regulates, what should be regulated and why, and what new rules are required.

By such studies the strength, the extent, and the importance of different conflicting interests can be measured, and from such data appropriate laws for adjusting conflicts of interest can be formulated. The conflicting interests have been described as follows: "The rich want to avoid taxes and obtain security by means of high unearned incomes, and the ability to bequeath their advantages to their children. The poor want security in the form of pensions, unearned incomes, and confiscation of wealth in order to give their own children equality of opportunity."[3] Other conflicting interests may be enumerated. Isolationists want tariff protection and "fortress America." Internationalists demand free trade and world order. Private-power adherents vie with public-power advocates, management and automation are set against labor, big business conflicts with big government, and overproduction and the affluent society conflict with old established economic principles. In modern society, juvenile delinquency, divorce, marketing, criminal law, housing, and public health all seek for attention. It is believed that these concerns and pressures can be measured "in terms of numbers, volume, and power and the law makers can settle them by fitting and appropriate rules, ascer-

[3] Beutel, *Some Potentialities of Experimental Jurisprudence As A New Branch of Social Science,* 33 (1957) (Lincoln, Neb., University of Nebraska Press).

tained by scientific investigation into what is required to adjust the conflicts."[4]

It is alleged that ". . . lawyers are still relying upon ancient theories, institutions and dogmas about the nature of man fomented by clerics and philosophers in that simple state of society just antedating the emergence of the scientific method. What the law is depends upon the rationalization of ethics, politics, sociology, psychology, religion, the judicial hunch, history, traditions, logic, all influenced by how law makers, the legislators and judges interpret the Bible, Aristotle, Plato, Thomas Aquinas, Mansfield, Adam Smith, Rousseau, Kent, Hegel, Montesquieu, Bentham, Blackstone, Marshall, Story, Holmes, Cardozo, Pound and Marx. In light of the scientific method and what it has to offer for the future, there is need to re-examine the basic postulates of social control and the legal system. . . ."[5] Under an extended sociological and experimental theory, it is suggested that law as a means of social control can be determined and implemented by scientific and statistical studies into areas of human activity.

In conclusion it may be said that any attempt to find or give a fixed and certain definition of the law is impossible. The law is defined by scholars, judges, legal writers, lawyers, and legislators according to what to them seem the most important, dominant, and significant elements in its nature and purpose.

Thus, in studying law, it is necessary to look behind each definition at the circumstances and conditions which gave rise to its formulation; only then can one understand the author's meaning. In reading legislation, judicial opinions, and other legal materials, an understanding of what jurisprudential theory motivated the writer is of great assistance in determining what idea an author wishes to convey, the intention of a legislature, and why and how a judge reached his decision.

Whatever school of thought dominates in defining law, the historical, the analytical, the natural, or the sociological, it is submitted that some aspect of the natural-law concept plays a part and continues to have relevance. Whether the state by legislation lays down a rule or the courts hand down a principle, it is very likely to be tested by some general moral and ethical proposition such as: "whether it is fair, proper, reasonable and honest, such as a reasonable, honest and fair-minded man would adopt."

Friedman, in his book on legal theory, speaking of the influence of natural law, remarks:

> Natural law thinking in the United States undoubtedly inspired the fathers of the Constitution and it has dominated the Supreme Court more than any

[4] Beutel, supra, n.3, 11.
[5] Beutel, supra, n.3, 12.

other law court in the world. Such thinking has not prevented the court from vacillating from the unconditional condemnation of legislative regulation of social and economic conditions to its almost unrestricted recognition, from the recognition of almost unrestricted freedom of speech and assembly to virtual outlawing of a political party, and, on the other hand, from the toleration of the most blatant discrimination against negroes to the strong protection given in recent judgments. Yet the American Constitution gives as near an approach to the unconditional embodiment of natural rights as can be imagined.[6]

1-4. Law and business ethics. Since natural law plays an important part in our law, the issues of whether all that is legal must be moral, or the converse, merit discussion. If an act is legal, is it *ipso facto* moral? If an act is immoral, is it *ipso facto* illegal? These questions have more than one answer. "Laws are of course, not the only rules of conduct which govern man's actions. People conform also to fashions, to manners, to customs, to conventional standards, to precepts of morality."[7] Through group pressures people are subject to all kinds of economic ideologies and political theories. These ideologies and theories may express both moral principles and rules of law. Some may be moral rules outside of and unconcerned with rules of law, and some moral rules may be partially within and partially outside of rules of law. For example, the moral principle, "Thou shalt not steal," is not only a moral rule but a legal rule. Stealing is a crime, which, depending on the value of the property stolen, may be either grand or petty larceny. Such conduct as gossiping, indolence, and intemperance may be immoral but not necessarily illegal. However, if by gossip slanderous statements are made which injure another, then gossiping becomes illegal. Whether illegal conduct is moral, or moral conduct is illegal, becomes a close question.

What conduct is considered legal and moral or illegal and immoral changes from time to time. Formerly the ownership of slaves and the employment of child labor were regarded by many as neither immoral nor illegal. However, as such conduct took on strong moral implications and met with public disapproval, it likewise became illegal. Segregation and the sale of fireworks offer striking examples of what formerly were considered both moral and legal but now are illegal, although by many not considered immoral. Gambling is by some considered immoral, yet some aspects of gambling are not illegal, though other aspects may be both immoral and illegal. Standards of morality vary from place to place and from time to time. The manufacture and sale of intoxicating liquor is another illustration of conduct that has at different times been moral and legal, immoral and illegal, illegal and moral, and to some immoral although legal. Another illustration of how changing moral standards affect

[6] Friedman, supra, n.2, 67.
[7] Vinogradoff, *Common Sense in Law,* 19.

legal standards is found in the law of the sale of goods. In early, less complex society, trading and sales transactions were face-to-face affairs. The seller and buyer, standing before each other with equal bargaining capacity, dickered over the specific article before them. The deal was a duel of cleverness and wits. Equality of bargaining power was always assumed, leaving room for much talk. Out of this "dealers' talk" developed the legal doctrine of *Caveat Emptor*—"let the buyer beware." Extravagant statements, overreaching, and "pulling a fast deal," as in a horse trade, were considered accomplishments rather than vices. The range of what was considered fair play was wide, and, as between equally clever parties, fraud and deceit were hard to uncover.

In today's complex technological and machine age, with its great productive capacity accompanied by mass marketing and distributing systems, the uninformed buyer-consumer does not stand in an equal bargaining position with trained sellers and producers. Many buyers today, even upon inspection of the desired article, understand little of the quality, character, construction, and operational capacity of complicated merchandise such as refrigerators, washing machines, television and radio sets, and automobiles; or the content and quality of drugs, cosmetics, and other synthetic materials. By the very nature of the case, equal bargaining power is impossible. Therefore, purchase order forms and printed devices containing schemes to evade liability by way of disclaimer of warranties hidden in fine print in standardized sales contracts take on moral consideration.

The regular seller of merchandise by implication warrants the merchantability and general fitness of the article sold. Automobile manufacturers and dealers have sought to eliminate this liability by substituting in the contract of a sale a warranty which is less effective in protecting the buyer. In discussing this narrow warranty, Judge Francis in *Henningsen v. Bloomfield Motor, Inc.*,[8] states:

> The terms of the warranty are a sad commentary upon automobile manufacturers' marketing practices. Warranties developed in the law in the interest of and to protect the ordinary consumer who cannot be expected to have the knowledge or capacity or even the opportunity to make adequate inspection of mechanical instrumentalities like automobiles and to decide for himself whether they are reasonably fit for the designed purpose. . . . But the ingenuity of the Automobile Manufacturers Association by means of its standardized form has metamorphosed the warranty into a device to limit the maker's liability. . . .
>
> Under modern conditions the ordinary layman on responding to the importuning of colorful advertising has neither the opportunity nor the capacity to inspect or to determine the fitness of an automobile for use; he must rely on the manufacturer who has control of its construction, and to some degree on the

[8] (N.J.) 161 A.2d 69, 78, 86 (1960).

dealer who to a limited extent called for by the manufacturer's instructions, inspects and services it before delivery. In such marketing milieu his remedies and those of persons who properly claim through him should not depend upon the intricacies of the law of sales. The obligation should not be based alone on the privity of contract. It should rest . . . upon the demands of social justice. . . .

The traditional contract is the result of free bargaining of parties who are brought together by the play of the market, and who meet each other on the footing of approximate economic equality. In such a society there is no danger that freedom of contract will be a threat to the social order as a whole. But in the present day commercial life the standardized mass contract has appeared. It is used primarily by enterprises with strong bargaining power and position. "The weaker party in need of the goods or services is frequently not in position to shop around for better terms, either because the author of the standard contract has a monopoly (natural or artificial) or because all competitors use the same clauses. His contractual intention is but a subjection more or less voluntary to terms dictated by the stronger party terms whose consequences are often understood in a vague way, if at all.". . . Such standardized contracts have been described as those in which one predominant party will dictate its law to an undetermined multiple rather than to an individual. They are said to resemble a law rather than a meeting of the minds. . . . The gross inequality of bargaining position occupied by the consumer in the automobile industry is thus apparent. Such control and limitation of his remedies are inimical to public welfare and at the very least call for great care by the courts to avoid injustice through the application of strict common-law principles of freedom of contract.

Dealers' talk and contractual arrangements between sellers and buyers, formerly considered moral and legal, may now be considered deceitful, fraudulent, overreaching, immoral, and illegal. Consumers, no longer equal with sellers, are vulnerable to all types of deceptive merchandising practices, price manipulation, false advertising, mislabelling, extravagant statements about additives in miracle drugs, cosmetics, and food products, undisclosed interest rates and financial charges in installment contracts, and extreme promotional schemes. Consequently, legal obligations and duties are being attached to processors, distributors, and sellers under the doctrine of *Caveat Venditor*. The old doctrine of *Caveat Emptor* is passing from the scene.

Although there is definitely a relation between law and morals, it is not always easy to equate morals with law. There is no fixed standard of morals. "Morality points toward high idealism, law toward what will work. . . . The laws of men do not primarily aim at promoting virtue, but only at securing a peaceful living together; they do not forbid all that is evil, but only that which imperils society; they do not command all that is good, but only that which pertains to the general welfare."[9] As society becomes more complex and equal bargaining power less available, moral standards begin to have influence on that which is legal or

[9] d'Entreves, *Natural Law,* 86 (1955).

illegal. In some cases of wrongdoing, it is obvious that the immoral act is illegal; in other cases, the wrongdoing may be obviously immoral but not illegal. If a fixed and definite public opinion has not been reached concerning what conduct is immoral, it is not likely that a legislative or judicial determination will be made that such conduct is illegal. As stated by a learned judge, "Law is rough business at best, and can never be a substitute for morals, religion, art, culture or science. It merely makes straight the road and safe the highway for the coming of better influences. Even intelligent people expect too much and know too little of the law."[10]

1-5. Basic legal concepts about property. All life is concerned with and affected by property. It is the motive for economic activity, the subject matter of succession and inheritance, the substance with which debts are settled, and the mark of prestige. It is that with which businessmen deal and is the measure of wealth.

Property, whether communal or private, can exist only in an ordered society. Property depends upon the economic pattern and social structure of the community. In a communistic society, communal property predominates and individual interests are subordinated to the interests of the group. In an individualistic society, private property predominates and group interests are subordinate. Private property is made secure by rules of law which impose duties upon people not to interfere with the liberty, person, or property of the individual.

In Anglo-American law, the right of private property and freedom of contract stimulated by the ideals of individualism became the bases of the dominant economic philosophy of western civilization. The security of personal liberty and private property was the principal function of common law. Government under common law was limited to the preservation of order, thus permitting the pursuit of business and liberty of contract to enjoy unhampered activity. Property became more than things: it became rights created by contract. Contract rights—enforceable promises—became valuable and represented wealth. Thus, the contract in the free enterprise system was the effective instrument by which property was created.

Since our economic structure rests upon various concepts of property, some consideration of its history, nature, and function is of primary importance. During the course of its history, the term *property* has had different meanings. In one context the word means things—land and movables—and in another the word means rights or claims that are invisible, that "can neither be seen nor handled; are creatures of the mind and exist only in contemplation." The term may also mean the union of both physical and non-physical concepts. The term *property* is also said to

[10] Crane, "Judge and Jury," 15 *Am. Bar Assoc. Jour.*, 201, 202 (1929).

connote an aggregate of legal relationships existing between persons with respect to or concerning physical things like land and automobiles, and intangibles such as contract rights, debts, wave-lengths, news, patent rights, and weather expectations. In order that businessmen may communicate accurately and have a "meeting of the minds" when dealing in the area of property law, it is important that the term *property* mean the same thing to different persons at different times. It will be the purpose of this section to set out in detail some of the variant meanings given to the term *property.*

The term *property* or property itself is meaningless except as it is associated with individuals. The terms used in expressing this association are *ownership, title,* and *possession.*

Ownership is a word signifying degrees; it is a "more or less" word. To *own* is to have. But the question is, what must one have to be an owner? Ownership denotes the *quantum* of property interest one has. An owner may have all the legal relations or interests concerning the subject matter of property, or an owner may have less than all the legal interests in a particular thing, tangible or intangible, while at the same time another may have legal interests in the same thing. Thus, a lessor has an interest in land which is limited by the interest held by the lessee. The lessor is said to hold the fee and the lessee the leasehold. Both own property and are in a position under the proper circumstances to exclude the other.

The word *title* is often used synonymously with *ownership.* The word signifies the method by which ownership is acquired, whether by gift, by purchase, or by other methods. It also indicates the evidence by which the claim of ownership is established—the deed or other written instrument. It includes not only the method and the evidence, but the result. The result which obtains from the method, the evidence, and the documents used is characterized by such words as *legal title, equitable title, good title, marketable title, tax title, fee simple title,* and so forth.

The word *possession* is difficult to define precisely. It links together the concept of physical control or dominion by a person over property with his personal and mental relationship to it. It is distinguished from mere custody, since the latter is limited to physical control only, without any interest therein, adverse to the true owner. Possession, however, means not only physical control or the power to have physical control, but also legal sanctions therewith to enforce continued relation with the thing, or, if deprived of such relation, to have the same restored.

In determining whether the legal consequence "possession" is present, the court must examine in each particular case the claimant's intent and physical relation to the thing in question. Possession may be actual; that is, physically held by the owner, or physically held by one over whom the owner has control, such as a servant or agent. Possession may be constructive; that is, physical custody may be in one person while another has a better right. *X* finds *B*'s watch, knowing it to be *B*'s watch. *X* appropriates it to his own use, and sells and delivers it to *C*. *X* is guilty of larceny because he dispossessed *B* of the watch, although at the time *B* was not in physical possession of the watch. Possession is said to be some evidence of ownership and "nine points of the law." This statement is not accurate, although under some circumstances custodial possession does endow one with an exclusive right against others. A finder, as against the true owner, has no property right but as to all others he has a better right.

The meanings found in the word *possession* depend upon the fact situation involved and the end to be achieved. Thus, the fact situation and policy reasons resulting in possession in a finder case, abandoned property, acquisition of wild animals, delivery in gift and bailment situations, trespass, crimes, attachments by sheriffs, and illegal holding under statutes are all different.

Property as things. In early law it was difficult to understand how there could be ownership, possession, and transfer of rights, with respect to things, without possessing and transferring the thing itself. A thing could be seen, touched, possessed, and delivered; hence the thing was the property. Rights to the thing were embodied in the physical object, so that the handing over of the physical object was essential to endowing another with property, ownership, title, possession, and all the other attributes one could have in a thing. Things owned and possessed were of two kinds: land and chattels. Land, a fixed, immovable thing, could not be handed over or delivered. In England under the feudal system, in order to satisfy the requirement of physical delivery, land was transferred by a symbolic process called *feoffment,* by which a twig or clod taken from the land by the grantor was delivered to the grantee. This symbol is said, in the proper case, to have seised the grantee with fee simple title. This historical symbolism is reflected in our present method of conveying land. Today the transfer of land is accomplished by the execution, delivery, and recording of a thing—a written instrument—called a *deed.*

No difficulty was experienced in owning, possessing, and manually delivering a movable thing. The most significant movable things in early civilization were cattle. Their mobility facilitated their use as a medium of exchange. From the term *cattle* is derived the word *chattel.* These two types of things, land and chattels, became known as two different kinds of property. Land became real property and chattels became personal property. Such designation arose out of the types of remedies developed to protect rights with respect to land and chattels.

One seeking a remedy against interference with the land, such as eviction or dispossession, brought an action to recover the land itself;

that is, the ousted plaintiff sought to recover the thing—the *res*. The action was called an action *in rem*, or a real action. Thus, the thing protected—land—derived its name *real property*.

Since a movable thing—a chattel—could be stolen, destroyed, or transferred away, a remedy other than the recovery of the thing or *res* was necessary. An action against the wrongdoer for restitution by way of damages was instituted. This action was against the wrong-doing person, and was called an action *in personam*, or a personal action. Thus, the things protected—movable chattels—derived their name, *personal property*.

Land has a fixed location. Therefore, its title, ownership, method of transfer, inheritance, and succession are governed by the law of the place where it is located. The law which controls movables, however, is highly influenced by the law of the domicile of the owner of the chattels.

Land and chattels as "things" are designated as "property" not only in common parlance, but also in court opinions, legal texts, and statutes. The following examples are illustrative. "The term 'property' as commonly used denotes an external object over which the right of property is exercised." "A man's property consists of lands, buildings, automobiles, and so on." "Property is of a fixed and tangible nature, capable of being had in possession and transmitted to another, such as houses, lands and chattels." By statutes in many states, "dogs are hereby declared to be personal property."

There are physical things incapable of being included within the term "property" as here considered. Such things as light, air, clouds, running water, and wild animals by reason of their nature are not subject to exclusive dominion and control and hence are not property. However, wild animals when caught and reduced to possession as physical things are included within the term *property*. Although the owner of land has no natural rights to "light" and "air," he may acquire, by way of easement, the right to have light and air come onto his land from that of an adjacent owner. Likewise, an owner of land has the right that the air over his land be free from pollution. Property rights in running water may be acquired by agreement, hence changing the natural rights to water.

Commercial necessities and historical considerations have endowed many printed and written instruments, such as commercial paper, bills of lading, warehouse receipts, and certificates of stock, with attributes of a thing or chattel. Thus, as things, their physical delivery is essential to serve as objective evidence of transfer.

Property as non-physical or incorporeal. The concept that only things were the subject of property and that property was more than the thing itself developed during the days of feudal land tenure in England. Out of the English feudal land system there developed many intangible and invisible inheritable rights called "incorporeal hereditaments." "These rights grew out of, touched or concerned the land, but they were not the substance of the thing itself." Among such rights were the right to use common pasture land and parks, called "the commons," and rights to annuities and rents. Such incorporeal interests are recognized in our law today. A lease granting the right to explore for oil accompanied by a duty to pay royalties, if oil is found, creates no property in a thing, but an invisible, intangible right concerning the land. Such right is property. For example, easements, leases, and various types of restrictive covenants which touch and concern land are property interests protected by the courts.

Property as relationships. In the preceding paragraphs land, chattels, commercial paper, bonds, negotiable instruments, and written and printed documents are considered things, called *property*.

In order to have a more complete idea of the meaning of the term *property*, we shall in this section refer to things—land, chattels, commercial paper, bonds, written and printed documents, contracts, debts, and choses in action—not as property, but as the subject matter of property. The term *property* as here used means a part or the totality of relationships existing between persons with respect to physical things, or with respect to non-physical fact situations such as contracts, debts, choses in action, patent rights, news, and pensions. The particular relationships with which we are concerned are "rights," "powers," "privileges," and "immunities."

These legal relations are defined by the Restatement of the Law of Property[11] as follows:

"A right is a legally enforceable claim of one person against another, that the other shall do a given act or shall not do a given act." For every right there is a corresponding duty. *A*'s right concerning the ownership, possession, and use of his land, home, and chattels places *B* under a duty not to interfere with or deny *A* his rights.

"A power is an ability on the part of a person to produce a change in a given legal relation by doing or not doing a given act." For every power there is a corresponding liability. *A* gives *B*, his agent, authority to transfer his, *A*'s, land. *B* has the power to change *A*'s legal relation with respect to the land; thus *A* is under a liability that such change will be made. *Liability* here does not mean duty. One often says "liability to pay money." What is meant is in this situation, duty to pay money.

"A privilege is a legal freedom on the part of one person as against another to do a given act or legal freedom not to do a given act." For

[11] American Law Institute, *Restatement of Property*, Sec. 1–5 (1936).

every privilege there is an absence of a right. *A* has the privilege of painting his house; all others have no right or concern with his privilege.

"An immunity is a freedom on the part of one person against having a legal relation altered by a given act or omission to act on the part of another person." For every immunity on one side there is a disability on the other. *A* owes *B* money, secured by a mortgage. *A* pays *B*. *A* is now immune from any legal right of *B*'s to foreclose, and *B* is under a disability.

If a person has all the rights, powers, privileges, and immunities that one is capable of having with one person or with all the persons in the world with respect to or concerning land or chattels, tangible and intangible, then such aggregate of legal relations constitutes *property.*

One may, however, have property with respect to a thing or intangible situation and not have all the relationships. These relationships are continually changing. If *A* exercises a power and mortgages his land to *B*, *A* has cut down his right relations and endowed *B* with right relations concerning the land. Again, if the state passes restrictive legislation concerning the use of *A*'s land, his legal relations have been diminished.

In order to identify the relationships termed "property" concerning things, the Restatement of the Law of Property uses the word *interest.* "The word interest includes . . . varying aggregates of legal rights, powers, privileges, and immunities and distributively [means] any one of them." Thus, rights, powers, privileges, and immunities with respect to land are "interests in land," or likewise, interests in things.

In order to make more vivid what is meant by "legal relations" called property and to illustrate how such relations exist and function, the following well-known fact situation is appropriate. Our story is about Robinson Crusoe. Two assumptions are necessary. First, let it be assumed that the island occupied alone is not within the jurisdiction of any government. Under these conditions, there could be relationships, but no legal relationships, no ordered society—hence, no property. No legal relationships of any kind cluster about Crusoe, his picked bananas, the land on which he stands, or his collected chattels. The land and the things are just things, capable of being subjects of property if there were persons present and a government representing persons.

When Friday comes upon the scene, the situation is changed. Relationships with respect to things come into existence. Crusoe could say to Friday, "These bananas are mine." Crusoe has rights, powers, privileges, and immunities concerning the bananas, and his right to them places Friday under a duty not to interfere. Friday, however, can well say, "How will you enforce my duty?" Unless Crusoe can enforce Friday's duty not to interfere, Crusoe's right will be of little consequence. Under these circumstances, Crusoe's power to enforce the claimed relationship rests merely upon self-help. Since there is no government, no societal agent, such as a sheriff, and no courts to come to the aid of Crusoe, his relationships with respect to the things are not "legal relationships" or "property interests." If Crusoe has anything, it is by virtue of his own power, under the "doctrine of self-help."

On the other hand, let it be assumed that the island occupied by Crusoe is under the jurisdiction of the United States Government. By discovery, occupation, or purchase, the United States has acquired the island. By this is meant that the United States Government has the totality of all the rights, powers, privileges, and immunities with respect to the island. When Crusoe entered upon the land, he was a trespasser upon public lands, unless the public lands were of such character as to give Crusoe a privilege to enter. To pursue the hypothetical situation further, let it be assumed that Crusoe, through the proper public officials, secures a patent from the United States for a portion of the island. The United States by this process exercised a power relation by which it divested itself of relations concerning the land and endowed Crusoe with relations of rights, powers, privileges, and immunities with respect to the land. Subject to limitations in the patent, Crusoe now has "the property" in that portion of the island described in the patent. Crusoe is now in relation with all the Fridays in the world, so that, when the particular Friday arrives and crosses Crusoe's boundary, our wandering Friday enters either as a trespasser or invitee. By reason of Crusoe's rights in respect to the land, Friday is under a duty not to trespass. If Friday trespasses and continues to do so, Crusoe can call in societal agents, and go to the courts and enforce Friday's duty not to trespass. He can compel Friday to cease trespassing and make restitution for any damages. Thus Crusoe has an enforceable legal right-duty relation called "property."

Crusoe has a power of destroying his own relation and creating relations in others. Thus, he has the power to enter into contracts and transfer all his legal interests by sale or by gift. Or Robinson may part with some of his interests and reserve to himself those which remain. Thus, he may lease his land and chattels or borrow money and give a mortgage to secure the loan. In each case, he has divided his legal interests by creating legal interests in a lessee and mortgagee and retaining legal interests in himself. Upon termination of the landlord-tenant relationship and the mortgagor-mortgagee relationship, Crusoe will be immune from the interests of the lessee and mortgagee.

If Crusoe has a totality of all the relationships regarding the land, he then has complete ownership or property. He may, however, from time to time have less than all the relationships or interests in land. When he leases the land, grants an easement over the land, or dedicates portions to the city for streets, he diminishes his legal relationships. Likewise, Crusoe may have his relationships reduced by the government through its exercise of the police power by way of zoning or its power of eminent domain or of taxation.

Just how few relationships Crusoe may have and still have property cannot be definitely ascertained. If a court gives a judgment in favor of the particular relationships asserted, then it may be said that a "property interest" exists. As we have seen, the term *property* connotes a multiplicity of rights, duties, powers, and immunities. The term may include all or some of the relationships. One may have or create all of these elements in another, or one may have or be endowed with a very limited number of these elements and still have a property interest. Thus, a person in possession of illegal goods as against the state may have no property; however, he may have a property interest as against third persons. Even though a statute makes ownership and possession of slot machines illegal, "there yet exists certain rights [sic: privileges] in the individual who may possess such a contraband article as against any one other than the state. The owner [sic: person in possession] at least has the privilege of destroying the machine, he also has the right to surrender it to the authorities. It is true his right to the possession of the slot machine is by law very limited; nevertheless, he has certain claims and powers not possessed by any other, which invests in him something real and tangible. . . . There are no property rights innate in objects themselves. Such rights as there are are in certain persons as against others with respect to the particular objects in question. Since property or title is a complex bundle of rights, duties, powers, and immunities, the taking away of some or a great many of these elements does not entirely destroy the title [sic: property]."[12]

The right to be free from fear and from the noise of low-flying planes and the privilege of quiet use and enjoyment of land are forms of property. The "continuing and frequent low flights over the appellant's land constituted a taking of property. . . . Property in a thing consists not merely in its ownership and possession, but in the right of its use, enjoyment and disposal."[13]

The change of the grade of a street which lessens the enjoyment of an easement of ingress and egress by abutting property owners is the taking of property.[14]

Injunctive relief has been granted to restrain the chemical seeding of clouds, because such seeding dissipated and scattered the clouds, prevent-

[12] People v. Walker (Cal. App.), 90 P.2d 854, 855 (1939).
[13] Ackerman v. Port of Seattle (Wash.), 348 P.2d 664, 666 (1960).
[14] In re Forsstrom et ux., 44 Ariz. 472, 38 P.2d 878 (1934), page 25.

ing rain. Such conduct is an interference with a property right, namely, the right to a possibility that it may rain.[15]

As mentioned above, just how many relationships concerning a thing or situation are necessary to create property is not easily determined. The problem may be illustrated in the distinction made between what is called an easement and a license. An easement is property because it is an interest in another's land, that is, a privilege to enter, use, and enjoy accompanied by a no-right of the owner to interfere. A license, on the other hand, even though it may be called a privilege to enter another's land, does not include a protected interest in the land. A license is a mere authority to enter, revocable at pleasure in the absence of certain equitable considerations. Thus, since it does not include relationships which give an interest in the land, it is not property. For example, members of the traveling public have only a license to use the public highways. Such license-privilege, freedom, or whatever it may be called does not constitute a property right. Therefore, an injunction may not be issued against traffic officials for enforcing traffic regulations.[16] However, an abutting property owner has a privilege of unhampered ingress and egress, which is property. It is a nice question as to whether the privilege of traveling upon the public highway and the no-right of others to interfere are relations which constitute property with respect to the highway. Of course, most of one's freedom to use the public highway is protected by duties imposed by the law of tort and traffic regulations.

Which legal relations in the total bundle are most significant, important, and decisive cannot be given a uniform fixed determination. The relationship concept of the term *property* is used by the court as a tool to solve the particular problem before it. Whether particular relations are legally protected interests and called "property" or the "thingified" concept of property is used will depend upon the circumstances, the purpose and intention of the parties, and the result sought to be obtained by the court.

Thus, in construing statutes involving crimes and tort liability, the court may emphasize a "thingified" concept of property. In our technological and complex society, new relationships are continually being established and asserted which demand protection. When these new relationships are given judicial protection, they become legal interests or property. For example, in advertising and marketing, when ideas expressed in word, form, shapes, or modes of packaging acquire an economic value, the right to use and exploit such ideas becomes a property interest protected by the courts. By such protection the courts do not create property: they

[15] Southwest Weather Research v. Rounsaville (Texas Civ. App.), 327 S.W.2d 417 (1958), page 27.

[16] Cicchetti v. Anderson (R.I.), 155 A.2d 64 (1959).

merely recognize that which already exists. The right to exclude others from the use of collected news items, the rebroadcasting of radio and television programs, the right to have unimpaired the rain potential of clouds over one's land, and the privilege of unhampered entrance to and from the street by an abutting landowner are illustrations of newly created property interests.

1-6. Law as ordered society. In the sections above, law has been presented from the standpoint of definitive rules with consideration given to the non-legal origins or background out of which such rules develop. In thinking about law, it is natural to consider law as a mass of detailed rules which regulate conduct and are found in constitutions, judicial decisions, and legislative enactments. The term *law* does connote rules, but "The Law" is something more. In a broad and significant sense, "The Law" represents an established way of thinking and acting which results in an ordered society. "The Law" is recognized as collective conduct which ends in a result—an adjusted social condition. In such social condition, universally approved ideas and controlled behavior are the "alternative to chaos." The specific rules called laws are the means by which the result—ordered society—is obtained. "Laws are nothing more than rules promulgated by government as a means to an ordered society."[17] "The Law," then, is a regulated, established "mode of conduct made obligatory," either by universal consent or because non-compliance with specific rules will bring sanctions into operation by the enforcing machinery of the state. The state is a viable organism endowed with sovereign power which enforces the detailed rules. Each member of society has a right to expect that every other member of society will conduct himself in compliance with the understood mode. In an effective legal order, members of society believe in and have faith that conduct is certain, reasonable, and predictable. Not only is the present orderly and under the rules capable of being made so, but also, the future can be reliably predicted. Within an ordered society there is always an approved system or an "important persistent element," "rules" which keep people regulated by defining an ascertainable standard of conduct against which non-conforming conduct is measured and judged. In a broad sense, "The Law" includes not only the rules, the instrumentalities for enforcing the rules—the courts—but also the result—an ordered society or "way of living." "The Law" is all-pervading; it is an atmosphere or climate. It overlays and operates in all areas of society—in the home, religion, recreation, education, travel, communication, citizenship, ownership, and business. Even at night when one sleeps, "The Law" is present. It is the orderly behavior of others which contributes to the undisturbed occupation of

[17] Miami Laundry Co. v. Florida Dry Cleaning & Laundry Board (Fla.), 183 So. 759, 764 (1938).

one's home. During the morning drive to work, the conduct of others in exercising due care and caution for the "use of the traffic and way" assures safe arrival. However, if there is non-compliance with the prescribed traffic pattern, the machinery of control and enforcement imposes sanctions by way of fines and imprisonment. Such control is essential in order that the goal, orderly traffic movement, may be achieved. Where non-compliance occurs, the detailed rules concerning specific conduct—rules of law—come into play. In a traffic accident, not only will speed rules and other motor vehicle regulatory rules be involved, but many other legal rules concerning ownership, due care, negligence, agency, insurance, and so forth, also have relevance. The goal sought is traffic order; it is obtained by compliance with the rules.

In order to distinguish between "The Law" as social order and the detailed rules which produce the social order, an illustration from our national pastime, "the baseball game," will be informative. In order to produce a desired result—"the game"—predetermined rules which make for a controlled activity are essential. These are the "rules of the game." The rules, however important, are not the most significant element. The most significant feature is "the game." "The game," the totality of all thoughts, rules, and prescribed activity, is a regulated spectacle. Spectators do not carry rule books; umpires do. The spectators are concerned with a performance; they go to see "the game"—not to check whether the pitcher's mound is so many feet from the home plate. "The game" is a living, progressive, regulated spectacle, the conduct of which may be relied upon and predicted. The spectator can expect with certainty that during the game the left fielder will not throw the ball over the fence, the hitting batter will not run to third base, nor the pitcher throw the ball into the grandstands. Such conduct would not produce a "ball game," but only chaos.

Thus, a "ball game" in its totality is a controlled and ordered activity, operating under baseball rules. On a greater scale, our social order is "The Law" operating under rules. The important difference is the sanctions imposed for the breach of the rules. There is no appeal from a decision of a baseball umpire to a state court. However, the baseball game is conducted within the orbit of legal order. If a player or spectator commits assault and battery upon the umpire, not only baseball rules but legal rules are violated.

As pointed out in Section 1 above, private groups, fraternities, chambers of commerce, unions, trade associations, country clubs, churches, and baseball leagues organize and become entities and by rules regulate and control their members. The "cohesive and coercive rules" which regulate the unit or entity are not rules of law. The sanction for breach lies within the unit, by way of expulsion or fines, and not with the state. However, legal rules may arise out of contract or other relations between individual members and the group. Such rules are rules of law.

Law as a social order has been discussed in order that rules of law may be understood, may be made more purposeful and meaningful. As man becomes more civilized and society more organized and complex, there will be more rules of law. It is true that one cannot know all the rules; yet one can know some of the rules and their purpose. Keeping in mind the end result, an ordered society, it will be our purpose in this book to present and discuss specific rules of law as they are applicable to commercial transactions and controversies which arise out of contract relations; the creation and operation of unincorporated and incorporated institutions; the marketing of goods and services; the extension of credit; agency; labor-management relations; and other business conduct.

IN RE FORSSTROM et ux.
1934, 44 Ariz. 472, 38 P.2d 878

LOCKWOOD, Judge. The question is solely one of law, and the facts may be briefly stated as follows: The main tracks of the Southern Pacific Railroad cross North Stone Avenue near an intersection of Sixth Street at the present grade of said Avenue. The authorities of the City of Tucson, believing that such grade crossing is a menace and hazard to public travel on the street, determined to abolish it by the construction of an underpass or subway below the tracks. . . . [By so doing] ingress and egress to the premises of the abutting property owners will be made more difficult. . . .

We come then to the question as to whether the proposed action of the City of Tucson, insofar as it affects petitioners at all, is a ["taking of property"] within the meaning of the statute. . . .

In order that we may understand the better what is meant by a "taking" of property, we should have a clear knowledge of what property really is. The word is used at different times to express many varying ideas. Sometimes it is taken in common parlance to denote a physical object, as where one says an automobile or a horse is his property. On careful consideration, however, it is plain that "property" in the true and legal sense does not mean a physical object itself, but certain rights over the object. A piece of land in an unexplored and uninhabited region which belongs to no one does not necessarily undergo any physical change merely by reason of its later becoming the property of any person. A wild animal may be exactly the same physically before and after it is captured, but, when it is running free in the forest, no one would speak of it as property. We must therefore look beyond the physical object itself for the true definition of property. Many courts and writers have attempted to define it, using different words, but meaning in essence the same thing. One of the great writers on jurisprudence says:

"Property is entirely the creature of the law. . . . There is no form, or color, or visible trace, by which it is possible to express the relation which constitutes property. It belongs not to physics, but to metaphysics; it is altogether a creature of the mind." Bentham: *Works* (Ed. 1843), Vol. 1, p. 308.

[Other authorities say] ". . . Property itself, in a legal sense, is nothing more than the 'exclusive right of possession, enjoying and disposing of a thing.' . . ." *Chicago & Western, etc., R.R. Co. v. Englewood, etc. Co.*, 115 Ill. 375, 4 N.E. 246, 249, 56 Am. Rep. 173.

"Property, in its broader and more appropriate sense, is not alone the chattel or the land itself, but the right to freely possess, use, and alienate the same; and many things are considered property which have no tangible existence, but which are necessary to the satisfactory use and enjoyment of that which is tangible." *City of Denver v. Bayer*, 7 Colo. 113, 2 P. 6.

"It is used in the constitution in a comprehensive and unlimited sense, and so it must be construed. . . . It need not be any physical or tangible property which is subject to a tangible invasion. . . . The right to light and air, and access is equally property. . . ." *State v. Superior Court*, 26 Wash. 278, 66 P. 385, 388.

It would follow from these definitions and explanations of the meaning of the term "property" that since it consists, not in tangible things themselves, but in certain rights in and appurtenant to them, it would logically follow that, when a person is deprived of any of these rights, he is to that extent deprived of his property, and that it is taken in the true sense, although his title and possession of the physical object remains undisturbed. Any substantial interference, therefore, with rights over a physical object which destroys or lessens its value, or by which the use and enjoyment thereof by its owner is in any substantial degree abridged or destroyed, is both in law and in fact a "taking" of property. It is apparently only of recent years that the meaning of the word "taking," when used in regard to eminent domain, has been properly understood by the majority of the courts, although it would seem obvious that a careful analysis of the true nature of "property" would have shown it long since. . . .

From the very nature of these rights of user and of exclusion, it is evident that they cannot be materially abridged without, ipso facto, taking the owner's property. If the right of indefinite user is an essential element of absolute property or complete ownership, whatever physical interference annuls this right takes "property"—although the owner may still have left to him valuable rights (in the article) of a more limited and circumscribed nature. He has not the same property that he formerly had. Then, he had an unlimited right; now, he has only a limited right. His absolute ownership has been reduced to a qualified ownership. Restrictings *A's* unlimited right of using one hundred acres of land to a limited right of using the same land, may work a far greater injury to *A* than to take from him the title in fee simple to one acre, leaving him the unrestricted right of using the remaining ninety-nine acres. Nobody doubts that the latter transaction would constitute a "taking" of property. Why not the former? . . .

"Property in land must be considered, for many purposes, not as an absolute, unrestricted dominion, but as an aggregation of qualified privileges, the limits of which are prescribed by the equality of rights, and the correlation of rights and obligations necessary for the highest enjoyment of land by the entire community of proprietors. . . ."

. . . The changing of the street grade which lessens the enjoyment of the easement of ingress and egress is within the true meaning of the constitutional provision (and a "taking") which injuriously affects the value of adjoining property (and) is "damage." The damage is to the easement of ingress and egress.

SOUTHWEST WEATHER RESEARCH v. ROUNSAVILLE

1958, (Tex. Civ. App.) 320 S.W.2d 211 Affirmed (1959) 327 S.W.2d 417

Per Curiam. This is an appeal from an injunction issued by the Eighty-third District Court, Jeff Davis County, Texas, which said injunction commands the appellants "to refrain from seeding the clouds by artificial nucleation or otherwise and from in any other manner or way interfering with the clouds and the natural conditions of the air, sky, atmosphere and air space over plaintiffs' lands and in the area of plaintiffs' lands to in any manner, degree or way affect, control or modify the weather conditions on or about said lands. . . ."

Appellees are ranchmen residing in West Texas counties, and appellants are owners and operators of certain airplanes and equipment generally used in what they call a "weather modification program" and those who contracted and arranged for their services.

It is not disputed that appellants did operate their airplanes at various times over portions of lands belonging to the appellees, for the purpose of and while engaged in what is commonly called "cloud seeding." Appellants do not deny having done this, and testified through the president of the company that the operation would continue unless restrained. He stated, "We seeded the clouds to attempt to suppress the hail." The controversy is really over appellants' right to seed clouds or otherwise modify weather conditions over appellees' property. . . .

We have carefully considered the voluminous record and exhibits that were admitted in evidence, and have concluded that the trial court had ample evidence on which to base his findings and with which to justify the issuance of the injunction. . . .

Appellants maintain that appellees have no right to prevent them from flying over appellees' lands; that no one owns the clouds unless it be the state, and that the trial court was without legal right to restrain appellants from pursuing a lawful occupation; also that the injunction is too broad in its terms. . . .

Appellees urge here that the owner of land also owns in connection therewith certain so-called "natural rights," and cites us the following quotation from *Spann v. City of Dallas,* III Tex. 350, 235 S.W. 513, 514, in which Chief Justice Nelson Phillips states:

"Property in a thing consists not merely in its ownership and possession, but in the unrestricted right of use, enjoyment and disposal. Anything which destroys any of these elements of property, to that extent destroys the property itself. The substantial value of property lies in its use. If the right of use be denied, the value of the property is annihilated and ownership is rendered a barren right. . . .

"The very essence of American constitutions is that the material rights of no man shall be subject to the mere will of another." *Yick Wo v. Hopkins,* 118 U.S. 356, 6 S.Ct. 1064, 30 L.Ed. 220.

In Volume 34, *Marquette Law Review,* at page 275, this is said:

Considering the property right of every man to the use and enjoyment of his land, and considering the profound effect which natural rainfall has upon the realization of this right, it would appear that the benefits of natural rainfall should come within the scope of judicial protection, and a duty should be imposed on adjoining landowners not to interfere therewith.

In the *Stanford Law Review,* November 1948, Volume 1, in an article entitled, "Who Owns the Clouds?", the following statements occur:

The landowner does have rights in the water in clouds, however, the basis for these rights is the common law doctrine of natural rights. Literally, the term "natural rights" is well chosen; these rights protect the landowner's use of his land in its natural condition. . . .

All forms of natural precipitation should be elements of the natural condition of the land. Precipitation, like air, oxygen, sunlight, and the soil itself, is an essential to many reasonable uses of the land. The plant and animal life on the land are both ultimately dependent upon rainfall. To the extent that rain is important to the use of land, the landowner should be entitled to the natural rainfall.

In *California Law Review,* December 1957, Volume 45, No. 5, in an article, "Weather Modification," are found the following statements:

"What are the rights of the landowner or public body to natural rainfall? It has been suggested that the right to receive rainfall is one of those 'natural rights' which is inherent in the full use of land from the fact of its natural contact with moisture in the air. . . .

"Any use of such air or space by others which is injurious to his land, or which constitutes an actual interference with his possession or his beneficial use thereof would be a tresspass for which he would have remedy." *Hinman v. Pacific Air Transport,* 9 Cir. 83 F.2d 755, 758.

Appellees call our attention to various authorities that hold that, although the old ad coelum doctrine has given way to the reality of present-day conditions, an unreasonable and improper use of the air space over the owner's land can constitute a trespass; *Guity v. Consumers Power Co.*, D.C., 36 F. Supp. 21; Restatement of the Law of Torts, paragraph 194 etc.; *United States v. Causby,* 328 U.S. 256, 66 S.Ct. 1062, 90 L.Ed. 1206. Other cases are cited, also, and apparently hold that the landowner, while not owning or controlling the entire air space over his property, is entitled to protection against improper or unreasonable use thereof or entrance thereon. . . .

We believe that under our system of government the landowner is entitled to such precipitation as nature deigns to bestow. We believe that the landowner is entitled, therefore and thereby, to such rainfall as may come from clouds over his own property that nature in her caprice may provide. It follows, therefore, that this enjoyment of or entitlement to the benefits of nature should be protected by the courts if interfered with improperly and unlawfully.

Review Questions and Problems

1. Name and discuss the school of legal thought reflected in each of the following judicial statements:
   a. "If a debtor obtains a discharge under an insolvent act, a subsequent promise to pay the debt is regarded as a new contract, supported by the pre-existing moral obligation, as a consideration for the new promise." Mr. Justice Harns, *Carshore v. Huyck,* 6 Barb. 583 N.Y. (1849).
   b. "We must weigh the purpose to be served, the desire to be gratified, the excuse for the deviation from the letter, the cruelty of enforced adherence." Mr. Justice Cardozo, *Jacob & Youngs v. Kent,* 230 N.Y. 239, 129 N.E. 889 (1921).
   c. "There must be power in the states and the nation to remould through experience our economic practices and institutions to meet changing social and economic needs. I cannot believe that the framers of the Fourteenth Amendment, or the States which ratified it, intended to deprive us of the power to correct the evils of technological unemployment and excess productive capacity which have attended the progress of useful arts." Mr. Justice Brandeis dissenting in *New State Ice Co. v. Liebman,* 285 U.S. 262, 276 (1932).

d. "The principle embodied in this exception was established by the old custom of merchants, which 'before the end of the thirteenth century was already conceived as a body of rules which stood apart from common law.' . . . at that stage these rules were applied merely as the general custom of commercial transactions . . . but later became a part of the common law." Leventritt, Referee, *Brown et al. v. Perera,* 176 N.Y. Supp. 215, 219 (1918).

e. "The word 'law' imports a general rule of conduct with appropriate means for its enforcement declared by some authority possessing sovereign power over the subject; it implies command and not treaty." Opinion of the Justices, 262 Mass. 603, 160 N.E. 439, 440 (1928).

2. Distinguish between rules of law, and "The Law" as an institution.
3. Does man's way of living create and change the law, or does the law influence and change man's way of living? Discuss from the standpoint of historical and analytical schools of thought.
4. *P* was injured by a fall down an unlighted stairway in a church building. *P* believed the fall was caused by the negligence of the church officials. At the time of the fall and injuries, the church officials had a contract of liability insurance in full force with the *N* and *N* Casualty Company. After the injuries, an agent of the insurance company promised *P* to pay all of her expenses, incurred by reason of the fall, if she would refrain from suing on the policy. *P* refrained and claimed $1,500.00 damages under the policy. The insurance company refused to pay and *P* sued on the agent's promise. The insurance company claimed that organizations like churches and charitable institutions are not liable in torts, and that by her promise not to sue she gave up nothing of value. Therefore, the promise of the agent to pay was without consideration. *Ralston v. Matthew,* 173 Kan. 550, 250 P.2d 841 (1952). Decide the case. Does it have any moral implications?
5. In 1910 the town of *X* had a population of 3,500 persons. *Y* purchased for $900.00 a corner lot near the center of the town. In 1962 the town has a population of 45,000 persons. *Y*'s lot is now valued at $30,000.00. Is the significant feature about *Y*'s lot the fact that it is a thing, or the fact that it is the subject of a multiplicity of relationships?
6. Can there be a trespass upon land without government?
7. *A* and *B* were skating on a municipally owned pond. *C* forcibly ejected them from the pond. Has *C* invaded *A*'s and *B*'s property rights?
8. Upon what theories may it be argued that low-flying airplanes interfere with an owner's land?
9. Illustrate by hypothetical situations different kinds of pressures brought upon business that create the climate within which it operates.

2

Law and the Evolution of Business

1-7. Epochs of industrial development in relation to the state. No attempt will be made here to write an economic history. However, a simple outline of the beginning and development of our present industrial and free enterprise system and its relation to the state will assist in making clear the climate in which business operates and the necessity for legal control. From the time of primitive man to the present, the methods and procedures for the production and distribution of goods and services have evolved by epochs or stages. No clear division for each era is possible, for each period merges into the next. For the purpose of presenting the material, the evolution of business may be divided into the following epochs: the primitive, the domestic or shop, the merchant middleman, the factory-wage earner; the epochs of unlimited free enterprise, of government regulation and limited free enterprise; the epoch of bigness—big business, big unions, big government; and the epoch of technology and automation.

The primitive epoch. Primitive man as a hunter and limited agriculturist had little, if any, industry, no distribution and market system, and little government. He made his own implements for the chase and his clothes and simple household utensils.

The domestic or shop epoch. After long years of evolution, man ceased his nomad existence, and upon becoming attached to a particular parcel of land, began to develop better agricultural techniques and more utensils and implements. Permanent location and lack of mobility led to a division of labor. Craftsmen began to process goods out of iron, to weave cloth, and to manufacture other articles, first in the home and then in local shops. The production of more goods than the local manufacturers could consume led to the exchange of different articles between craftsmen. Out of this trading developed a market.

The merchant middleman epoch. Increased population and a demand for goods and services brought about the next stage of development. In order for the local craftsmen to get their articles to the consumer, the merchant middleman became a necessity. During this period, roughly prior to 1760, industry was operated and controlled by small, independent master craftsmen who employed a few employees, classified by experience and trade as apprentices and journeymen. These master craftsmen manufactured merchandise themselves and also processed materials furnished them by merchants. Such was the business system that prevailed in medieval times, sustained, upheld, regulated, and controlled by the state.

The factory-wage earner epoch. The next stage in the evolution of business, known as the *industrial revolution,* produced the factory-wage earner system. Out of this system arose the capitalistic free enterprise economy with which we are familiar.

The invention of the steam engine in 1760, the power loom in 1776, and other technological developments, colonial expansion, improved transportation, the development of a money economy, and the creation of financial institutions and the corporation brought about great changes in production and distribution methods and in employer-employee relationships and fostered new economic ideas. Spurred by new concepts of freedom introduced by Adam Smith, and by natural law, medieval restrictions on industry and commerce were loosened, permitting the free enterprise system to come into being.

Industrialization in the United States, however, did not begin to develop until after the Revolution. In Colonial America, the craft system and the idea of guild and state controls operated, but not to the same extent as in England. Early Massachusetts and New York statutes fixed prices of bread, regulated the wages and hours of carpenters, bricklayers, and other laborers, and set limits upon the percentage of profit. It was not until 1840 that textiles in the New England States and coal and steel in the Middle States set the pattern for the great industrial growth in the United States that took place after the Civil War.

The epoch of unlimited free enterprise. After the Civil War liberty of contract and free enterprise, sustained by a *laissez-faire* philosophy, brought about unrestricted competitive conduct that led to the construction of thousands of miles of railroads, the exploitation of natural resources, and the expansion to the west. As a result, vast fortunes were amassed and large corporations, trusts, and monopolies developed. From 1870 to 1890 the industrialization of the United States grew at a rapid pace. During these two decades, the population (aided by immigration) increased to twenty-four million, business enterprises invested capital, and the number of wage earners doubled. Professor Handler in his book, *Cases and Materials on Trade Regulations* (1937), at page 208, describes this epoch in the following picturesque language:

> It was a swash-buckling age of feverish money making activity, of fortunes rapidly made and lost, of Alger-like careers of lowly clerks who rose to be cap-

tains of industry, of titanic battles among robber-barons, an era of corruption, of exploitation and of rapid national growth.

The financial scandals attending the construction of our railroads, the fraudulent manipulations of insiders, of which those of Gould, Fisk and Drew are most familiar, the wide-spread and persistent discriminations in rates, the arrogant attitude of railroad management aroused much hostility and culminated in the Granger movement in the west. These conditions were brought to light in a series of legislative inquiries. . . .

Out of these legislative inquiries came the first significant federal regulatory legislation, the Interstate Commerce Act of 1887 and the Sherman Anti-Trust Act of 1890.

The epoch of government regulation. The character of the national economy in 1885 and the inability of the states to control and regulate interstate industrial and commercial life led to a demand for Congress to enact federal regulatory legislation. Thus, in 1887, under its Constitutional power to regulate commerce between the states, it passed the Interstate Commerce Act providing for an Interstate Commerce Commission, which became the first quasi-executive, quasi-legislative, and quasi-judicial regulatory administrative board.

Three years later in 1890, in order "to protect trade and commerce against unlawful restraints and monopolies," Congress passed the Sherman Anti-Trust Act, which declared that "every contract, combination in the form of a trust or otherwise, or conspiracy in restraint of trade or commerce among the several states or with foreign nations is hereby declared illegal." Congress by this legislation meant to preserve competition by eliminating the evils resulting from contracts and combinations which stifled competition and hampered free enterprise. From 1890 to the present, this Act has been variably enforced. Court decisions have dealt with the application of this legislation to many aspects of restraints upon interstate commerce, such as combinations, controlling and fixing prices, resale, the control of the source and the flow of goods, geographical limitation of trade areas, price maintenance, the allocation of business, and labor restraints. From 1890 to 1930, not only did federal economic regulatory legislation begin and expand, but state regulatory legislation also was enacted. The extent and constitutional validity of such legislation since 1890 have ebbed and flowed, depending upon the stability of the economy, the forcefulness of the President of the United States, and the political, philosophical, and economic backgrounds of the members of the Supreme Court of the United States. In the sections to follow, the struggle between laissez-faire economy and the growth of governmental interference will be discussed.

The Great Depression in 1930 gave impetus to an extensive intrusion of government into business activity. The depression did not cure itself.

Both national and state legislation affecting almost every aspect of business was enacted to meet the national emergency. The constitutionality of much of the legislation has been sustained by changing the meaning of the "due process of law" clause in the 5th and 14th Amendments from a due process that implemented the laissez-faire economic doctrine which sustained liberty of contract and held inviolable property rights, to the premise that

> so far as due process is concerned . . . a state is free to adopt what ever economic policy may reasonably be deemed to promote public welfare . . . to enforce that policy by legislation adopted for that purpose. . . . If the laws passed are seen to have a reasonable relation to a proper legislative purpose and are neither arbitrary nor discriminatory, the requirements of due process are satisfied. Upon proper occasions and by appropriate measures the state may regulate a business in any of its aspects, including the prices to be charged for the products it sells.[1]

Thus, government today, is no longer limited to enforcing contracts, protecting property, and maintaining order.

The growth, expansion, and bigness of

> the modern corporate system with its concentration of power in a limited number of gigantic corporations, its inflexible prices, its mal-distribution of income, its mechanization and displacement of labor, its separation of ownership and control, and its insecurity has robbed the economic system of its capacity for automatic adjustment. The old economy of petty trade, free competition, flexible prices, freedom of opportunity and equality of bargaining power required a minimum of state intervention to keep it functioning. . . . Unlimited freedom of contract and economic action for the dominant group in American business meant the economic enslavement and destruction of the opportunities and liberties of their less powerful rivals and customers. Governmental intervention was thus necessary to preserve competition.[2]

The epoch of bigness. The big corporation. Over seventy years have passed since Congress enacted the Sherman Anti-Trust Act to control monopolies; yet in spite of this act, corporations have become larger and larger. As late as 1948, Justice Douglas in his dissenting opinion restated the purpose of the act of 1890 and comments on "size" in the case of *United States v. Columbia Steel Co.*[3] as follows:

> Size is the measure of the power of a handful of men over our economy. That power can be utilized with lightning speed. It can be benign or it can be dangerous. The philosophy of the Sherman Act is that it should not exist. For all power tends to develop into a government in itself. Power that controls the economy should be in the hands of the elected representatives of the people,

[1] Nebbia v. New York, 291 U.S. 502, 506 (1934).

[2] Handler, *Cases and Materials on Trade Regulation,* 14 (1937) The Foundation Press, Chicago, Ill.

[3] 344 U.S. 495 (1948).

not in the hands of an industrial oligarchy. Industrial power should be decentralized. It should be scattered into many hands so that the fortunes of the people will not be dependent on the whim or caprice, the political prejudices, the emotional stability of a few self-appointed men.

Whether the Sherman Act and its accompanying amendments have served the purpose for which they were intended is open to question. Since Congress set no standards by which to determine what contracts and combinations brought about restraints in interstate commerce, it was left to the court to find tests and give meaning to the words. Justice Jones, in *Apex Hosiery Co. v. Leader*,[4] said,

> The prohibitions of the Sherman Act were not stated in terms of precision or of crystal clarity, and the act itself does not define them. In consequence of the vagueness of its language, perhaps not uncalculated, the courts have been left to give content to the statute, and in the performance of that function it is appropriate that the courts should interpret its words in the light of its legislative history and of the particular evils at which the legislation was aimed.

Over the years, the Courts have filled the gaps by determining what is and what is not interstate commerce, and by limiting the words "every contract" to include only those contracts that make possible combinations which unreasonably and unduly restrain trade. Contracts in restraint of trade are not *per se* illegal, even though the combinations created by them potentially have the power to monopolize trade and commerce. Mere "bigness" itself is not proscribed, it is only when bigness is coupled with the intention to unreasonably restrain trade that "bigness" comes under the prohibition of the act. The judicial approval of vertical combinations of corporations operating on different levels, the recognition of price differentials resting on extensive advertising, and the creation of new commodities through research have brought about great corporations which are permissible. New inventions, complicated techniques, and mass production have made bigness a necessity. Whether bigness permits competition to be more open and free between both large and small units; whether price differentials rest on quality, quantity, extensive advertising, or agreements; and whether the economic facts of today require enforced competition are unanswered questions.

Professor Berle, writing about corporate Bigness, under the title "Economic Power and the Free Society," states:

> Today approximately 50 per cent of American manufacturing—that is everything other than financial and transportation—is held by about 150 corporations, reckoned, at least, by asset values. If finance and transportation are included, the total increases. If a rather larger group is taken, the statistics would probably show that about two-thirds of the economically productive assets of the United States, excluding agriculture, are owned by a group of not more

[4] 310 U.S. 469, 471 (1940).

than 500 corporations. This is actual asset ownership. (Some further statistical analysis is called for if financial corporations be included, for these, of course, double up. One of the largest and most plainly oligarchically controlled corporations in the United States, the Metropolitan Life Insurance Company, duplicates assets because it holds securities of other corporations.) But in terms of power, without regard to asset positions, not only do 500 corporations control two-thirds of the non-farm economy but within each of that 500 a still smaller group has the ultimate decision-making power. This is, I think, the highest concentration of economic power in recorded history. Since the United States carries on not quite half of the manufacturing production of the entire world today, these 500 groupings—each with its own little dominating pyramid within it—represent a concentration of power over economics which makes the medieval feudal system look [insignificant]. In sheer economic power this has gone far beyond anything yet seen.

We can talk about the various alleged legal controls which somehow or other, when the chips are down, neither control nor even seek to control. We can point out the fear of "monopoly" and "restraint of trade" and say that from time to time this fear has checked the process. True, our law has prevented any one of these power groups from becoming a monopoly, but it has not seriously prevented the concentration of power as power, though it has prevented certain ultimate results. The question is then: Why has concentrated economic power in America not got completely out of hand? Many of these corporations have budgets, and some of them have payrolls, which, with their customers, affect a greater number of people than most of the ninety-odd sovereign countries of the world. American Telephone & Telegraph, for example, based on combined population and wealth, would be somewhere around the thirteenth state of the union in terms of budget, and certainly larger than many of the countries of South America. Some of these corporations are units which can be thought of only in somewhat the way we have heretofore thought of nations.

Whether we like it or not, this is what has happened. As noted, it is not the product of evil-minded men. I believe that we must try to work with the system. The dangers are obvious. But history cannot usually be reversed. Until engineers and economic forces give us a way by which a man can manufacture an automobile in his back yard, we will continue to have organizations the size of General Motors or Ford—as long as people want Chevrolets or Fords. We will have railroads the length of the Union Pacific as long as people want to go across the continent by railroad. In other words, until a combination of technique and organization can be invented permitting individuals to do the job, we are bound to try to make the best we can out of the situation. To my mind most of the results are rather surprisingly good.

This does not mean, however, that I am not afraid. I am. I believe it is the content of these systems rather than their form that matters. Their power can enslave us beyond present belief, or perhaps set us free beyond present imagination. The choice lies with the men who operate the pyramids, and with the men affected who can demand what they really want. Our Anglo-Saxon democratic liberties, after all, were beaten out, not against the framework of the personal possessory property regime, but against the background of two of the most brutal despotisms in Western history. Both the Angevin dynasty in Normandy and the Tudor dynasty in England were rank despotisms. The content of our democratic liberties from Magna Carta down was pumped in by extraneous moral processes. Our institutionalized liberties present the case of an institution conscripted into utility, rather than something that emerged full-armed from the head of Jove. It was probably better that way; the democracy of the Greeks did not work so very well.

We have to accept this power situation as, let us call it, a neutral mechanism subject to the control of the body politic as long as we keep it subject to that control. That control, I believe, will be essentially intellectual and philosophical, capable of being translated into legal rules when necessity arises. . . .[5]

Big unions. The large and powerful labor union is a recent development. The factory system, with its mass-production methods, brought about a huge concentration of labor. Yet the laborer was left in the unfair position of having to deal as an individual for his terms of employment with the corporate employer, who had huge power.

Acting alone and having little bargaining power, he was forced to accept the employer's terms. Under the doctrine of freedom of contract, the laborer, if he willed to work, was not only bound by such terms, but was also subject to dismissal at will. He had no job security, no right to recover for overtime, no power to limit hours, and no right to compel safety measures; if injured, he had no medical or hospital care. His right to recover damages was limited by the fellow-servant rule. He enjoyed no vacations with pay and anticipated no pension to comfort his declining years. In his early attempts to organize his fellow workers to better his condition, he was often convicted and jailed for criminal conspiracy. Later, employees who engaged in union activities were enjoined, were held in contempt of court, and were subject to imprisonment for civil conspiracy.

With such conditions of employment, unionization of labor was inevitable. Only through an effective labor organization with power to bargain collectively with the organized employers could the laborer's economic status be improved. For years, labor organizations struggled to survive. They were strenuously opposed by employer groups. In an attempt to gain bargaining power, labor unions were organized to picket and to conduct strikes and boycotts. Employers countered by discharging those who became union members, imposed the "yellow-dog contract," secured labor-restrictive legislation, and were aided by the courts through the use of the court injunction.

Continual industrial strife, the Great Depression of the 1930's, the excessive use of the court injunction, the inability of labor to gain equality of bargaining power, proper wages, and conditions of employment brought about government intervention. If freedom of contract, which permitted solution of industrial problems by the bargaining process, was

[5] A. A. Berle, Jr., *Economic Power and the Free Society,* 14 (1960) (New York, Fund for the Republic).

to be preserved, equality of bargaining power on behalf of the laborer must be established. The only alternative to industrial strife was to enforce terms of employment by legislative fiat and compulsory arbitration. Such extensive governmental encroachment was avoided in 1932 when Congress, under its power to "ordain and establish" courts, enacted the "Norris-La Guardia Anti-injunction Act," which limited the power of the federal courts and made strikes and peaceful picketing free from court injunctions. The act provides that "no court of the United States . . . shall have jurisdiction to issue any restraining order or temporary or permanent injunction in a case involving or growing out of a labor dispute. . . ." In order to aid unionization for collective bargaining purposes, the act states the public policy of the United States to be:

> Whereas under prevailing economic conditions, developed with the aid of governmental authority for owners of property to organize the corporate and other forms of ownership association, the individual unorganized worker is commonly helpless to exercise actual liberty of contract and to protect his freedom of labor and thereby to obtain acceptable terms and conditions of employment, wherefore, though he should be free to decline to associate with his fellows, it is necessary that he have full freedom of association, self-organization and designation of representatives of his own choosing, to negotiate the terms and conditions of his employment, and that he shall be free from interference, restraint or coercion of employers of labor or their agents, in the designation of such representatives or in self-organization or in other concerted activities for the purpose of collective bargaining or other mutual aid or protection; therefore, limitations upon the jurisdiction and authority of the courts of the United States are hereby enacted.

In 1933 Congress enacted the National Industrial Recovery Act. Although in 1935 declared unconstitutional, it nevertheless became recognized as the Declaration of the Rights of Labor.

In 1935 the Byrnes Anti-Strikebreaker Act was passed to free labor from the effective use of strikebreakers by making unlawful their transportation in interstate commerce.

In spite of governmental assistance to labor through legislation, industrial strife was not eliminated. Congress had not yet provided methods and procedures to implement its policy of securing equal bargaining power for labor, to the end that industrial peace would be obtainable through free collective bargaining.

"The denial by the employers of the right of the employees to organize, and the refusal of employers to accept the procedure of collective bargaining lead to strikes and other forms of industrial strife or unrest. . . ." In order to meet this situation, Congress in 1935, under the authority of the commerce clause, passed the National Labor Relations Act, known as the "Wagner Act," 49 Stat. 449. The Findings and Policy of the Act set out in part in Section 1 are that:

. . . The inequality of bargaining power between employees who do not possess full freedom of association or actual liberty of contract and employers who are organized in the corporate or other forms of ownership association substantially burdens and affects the flow of commerce and tends to aggravate recurrent business depressions by depressing wage rates and the purchasing power of wage earners in industry and by preventing the stabilization of competitive wage rates and working conditions within and between industries. Experience has proved that protection by law of the right of the employees to organize and bargain collectively safeguards commerce from injury . . . and promotes the flow of commerce by removing certain recognized sources of industrial strife and unrest, by encouraging practices fundamental to the friendly adjustment of industrial disputes arising out of differences as to wages, hours, or other working conditions and by restoring equality of bargaining power between employers and employees.

The Federal Anti-Labor Injunction Act of 1932 and the National Labor Relations Act of 1935 established a policy of "governmental protected freedom of employees" to organize and bargain collectively. The National Labor Relations Act sets forth the right of employees to organize and to bargain collectively through representatives of their own choosing. It defines "unfair labor practices" of the employer. It creates a Board empowered to prevent the defined unfair labor practices of employers which affect interstate commerce and outlines the procedure for determining and ending such conduct. The act, specifically drafted to assist labor, provides that the act shall not be construed so as to interfere with the right to strike.

The act was challenged in its entirety as an attempt to regulate all industry by invading the reserved power of the states. It was claimed that it was not a true regulation of commerce or of matters affecting interstate commerce, but that it had as its object compulsory supervision by the federal government of all industrial labor relations. Its constitutionality was upheld in 1937 in the case of *National Labor Relations Board v. Jones and Laughlin Steel Corporation*,[6] wherein the court states:

The term "affecting commerce" means in commerce, or burdening or obstructing commerce or the free flow of commerce, or having led or tending to lead to a labor dispute burdening or obstructing commerce or the free flow of commerce.

This definition is one of exclusion as well as inclusion. The grant of authority to the Board does not purport to extend to the relationship between all industrial employees and employers. Its terms do not impose collective bargaining upon all industry regardless of effects upon interstate or foreign commerce. It purports to reach only what may be deemed to burden or obstruct that commerce and, thus qualified, it must be construed as contemplating the exercise of control within constitutional bounds. It is a familiar principle that acts which directly burden or obstruct interstate or foreign commerce, or its free flow, are within the reach of the Congressional power. Acts having that effect are not

[6] 301 U.S. 1 (1937).

rendered immune because they grow out of labor disputes. . . . The Congressional authority to protect interstate commerce from burdens and obstructions is not limited to transactions which can be deemed to be an essential part of a "flow" of interstate or foreign commerce. Burdens and obstructions may be due to injurious actions springing from other sources. The fundamental principle is that the power to regulate commerce is the power to enact "all appropriate legislation" for its "protection or advancement, . . . to promote its growth and insure its safety, . . . to foster, protect, control and restrain, . . . no matter what the source of dangers which threaten it.". . . Thus "if Congress deems certain recurring practices, though not really part of interstate commerce, likely to obstruct, restrain or burden it, it has the power to subject them to national supervision and restraint."

Since the end sought by the act was the prevention of interference with interstate commerce by strikes and labor disputes caused by an employer's unfair labor practices as set out in the act, an employer not primarily using interstate transportation was "subject to the act if as a consequence of labor disputes in his plant, the stopping of manufacturing necessarily resulted in a cessation of the movement of manufactured goods in interstate commerce."

Such broad interpretation brought within the protection of the act the employees of most industrial units. Under the stimulus of this federal protective legislation, labor organizations grew and prospered. Labor has not only exerted influence at the federal level but has also achieved protective legislation on the state level. Following the adoption of the Federal Employers Liability Act of 1909, which gave a remedy to the injured worker by taking from interstate employers the defenses of the fellow-servant rule, assumption of risk, and contributory negligence by the employee, similar statutes were adopted by several states. Such legislation, however, proved inadequate because of expensive litigation and delays. Therefore, to secure adequate protection and compensation for injured employees in hazardous employment, State Workmen's Compensation laws were enacted. Compensation for injuries to employees under these acts is now a charge on industry, which has led to the installation of many safety devices and improvements in the conditions of employment. Within the past forty years, labor has secured legislation limiting hours of labor, setting minimum wages, providing social security and unemployment insurance, and other remedial legislation. By 1947 organized labor, as an institution of economic power and influence, began to create contentions which indicated that it had more than achieved bargaining power and was itself engaged in unfair labor practices and coercive conduct toward employers. Thus was enacted the Labor-Management Act of 1947, known as the Taft-Hartley Act, which has for its purpose "equalizing" and "balancing" the opportunities and legal responsibilities of employers and employees. The Act recognizes not only the legitimate rights of labor and management, but also their duties: namely, that "neither have the right to engage in any practice which will interfere with the free flow of commerce or jeopardize public health and safety." In order to balance labor-management collective bargaining power, the act grants protection and privileges to the employer not included within the National Labor Relations Act of 1935. Employers are granted the right to sue unions for breach of contract, given a wider latitude for persuasion, and freed from certain coercive union activities declared to be unfair labor practices.

In the last decade labor organizations and industrial corporations have grown to enormous size and great power. Through collective bargaining not only have wages increased and conditions of employment improved, but many fringe benefits such as medical care, vacation with pay, and pensions, have been achieved. A national labor policy founded upon collective bargaining through strong and vigorous unions and the development of a strong independent labor movement as part of our American institutions have made possible the possession, exercise, and control of great economic power by labor leaders. These leaders, it is charged, "sit behind lordly desks in glass and marble headquarters of giant unions . . . command huge treasuries; . . . have a controlling voice in investments of billions of dollars of pensions and welfare funds; their strike calls can plunge vital industries into long periods of idleness; their political machinery can influence the democratic process by persuading hundreds of thousands of workers and their families to register and vote."[7] It is asserted also that the abuse of power "by union officers for personal financial advantage under cover of conflicts of interest has corrupted, undermined and weakened the labor movement. . . . The government which vests in labor unions the power to act as exclusive bargaining representatives must make sure that the power is used for the benefit of the workers and not for personal benefit."[8]

In order to correct these abuses, Congress in 1959 amended the Labor-Management Act of 1947 by passing the Labor Management Reporting and Disclosure Act, known as the "Landrum-Griffin Act" (29 U.S.C.A. Sec. 141–187), "to provide for the reporting and disclosure of certain financial transactions and administrative practices of labor organizations and employers, to prevent abuses in the administration of the trusteeships by labor organizations, to provide standards with respect to the election of officers of labor organizations, establish an advisory committee on ethical practices and permit relationships between the National Labor Relations Board and state agencies. . . ."

The joint House and Senate Committee, in its conference report

[7] Raskin, *The Squeeze on Unions,* Atl. Mthly. 207:55 (1961).
[8] 2 U.S. Code Congressional and Administrative News 2331 (1959).

recommending the above legislation, made the following observations concerning labor organizations:

The problems of . . . [labor organizations,] now large and relatively strong institutions, are not unlike the difficulties faced by other groups in American society which aspire to live by the same basic principles and values within their group as they hold for the whole community. But equal rights, freedom of choice, honesty, and highest ethical standards are built into changing institutions only after struggle. Trade unions have grown well beyond their beginnings as relatively small closely knit associations of workmen where personal, fraternal relationships were characteristic. Like other American institutions some unions have become large and impersonal; they have acquired bureaucratic tendencies and characteristics.[9]

The role of the big union as an American institution in our democratic society is discussed by Clark Kerr, a labor economist, in an article entitled "Unions and Union Leaders of Their Own Choosing,"[10] as follows:

A quarter of a century ago in the United States the great issue in industrial relations was "unions of their own choosing." The country was in the depths of a profound depression and a great ferment was in process. A new orientation of the American economy was in the making—an orientation toward full employment, government sponsored security for workers and farmers, government regulation of business practices and the creation of workers' organizations to balance the power of employers in the industrial labor markets of the nation. The American economy, previously largely monistic in the management-labor area, in a few short years became pluralistic. Ranged alongside the power of the private employer was now the power of the state and the power of the union.

As it turned out, this new balance of power made less difference than once supposed, for the employers generally adapted quite well to the new situation and found they could prosper within it; but there was a new environment largely set by government, and within this new environment the employer faced the union as well as the individual employee. New unions came into being and old ones found new life. Workers could vote unions and collective bargaining into their plants and they did so on a mass basis. They chose to have unions and they got them.

A quarter of a century later—today—unions are well established and secure in most major industries of the nation. Their members number eighteen million. They can close down even the giants of American industry—General Motors and United States Steel. They negotiate 100,000 contracts covering the working rules that guide and govern important aspects of the life of industrial men in nearly every trade and every industry and nearly every town. Income, leisure, job security, retirement, pace of work, job opportunities, discipline—all are affected by union participation in the rule-making process. And Union influence extends outside the industrial government of the nation into its political processes too. Unions affect the selection and the election of candidates. They are intimately woven into much of our economic and political life.

This quarter century has seen the great change in the power structure of our

[9] 2 U.S. Code, supra, n.8, 2322 (1959).

[10] *Unions and Union Leaders of Their Own Choosing*, 3–5, 21 (1957) (New York, Fund for the Republic).

economy from monism to pluralism. It has seen new wealth, new security, new satisfaction for nearly all the people. It has seen the creation of a "modern capitalism" which can stand as a vital alternative in the great ideological, economic, scientific, and military contest that enthralls and engulfs the world—an alternative that has amply produced both goods and freedom. These developments in the United States have resulted in an acceptance of the surrounding society by its members which can hardly be matched in our earlier history or elsewhere in the world at any time in history. It is a society with consensus.

This consensus and the great achievements of the recent period should not obscure the fact that our society is still changing. Industrialization is new to the United States and to the world. The final form of the industrial society cannot yet be clearly seen. In particular, the ultimate adjustments between institutional power and individual choice within the state, the private economic organizaion and the economic process (such as the labor market) are not yet settled and, of course, may never be in any final way. Many large and open, and even more small and silent, battles will be waged in the process of adjustment. Nor should this consensus and these achievements obscure the fact that all is not for the best even in "the best of all possible worlds." There are no really dramatical internal crusades today either existing or needed; but there are reforms which are both needed and in the making. This discussion relates to one of them.

American government has been under critical scrutiny almost since the founding of the nation. American industry was subjected to an intensive national review particularly in the 1930's. It had become big and powerful and sometimes corrupt. The Great Depression was laid at its doorstep since it was the most prominent doorstep around at the time. American unions are today undergoing similar scrutiny. They, in turn, have become big and powerful and sometimes corrupt.

It is said by some, that only the unions can scrutinize themselves; that it is not the proper business of anybody else because they are private, voluntary associations. The corporations said this once too and they were scrutinized. And the unions will be too. For, though they are private, their actions are clothed with the public interest; they affect the levels of wages and prices, the access of individuals to jobs, the volume and continuity of production, and many other important aspects of society. Also, they are seldom really voluntary. Even in the absence of the closed or union shop, social pressure often assures membership. Along with this external scrutiny, the unions should scrutinize themselves, and the more effectively they undertake this scrutiny (and they are doing surprisingly well), the less need there is for external examination and external reform. Our pluralistic system has three main organized elements, the state, the corporation, and the union. It is essential that each element function effectively, and consequently that each of them be subject to both internal and external criticism. . . .

Unions, like many other institutions, often seek to extend their sphere of activity until it covers more and more of the life of their members, not only as workers but also as consumers and citizens. If the limited-function corporation and the limited-function state and the limited-function church are desirable, so also is the limited-function union. Union paternalism (housing projects, vacation resorts, recreation facilities) has little more to recommend it than employer paternalism. Union political activity, while inevitable and often desirable, should not infringe on the rights of the member as a citizen. He should not be required to support, financially or otherwise, a political party or candidate not of his own choice. The union should find its primary function in relating to the worker as worker, not also as consumer and as citizen.

Trade unions have historically been fighting organizations. They have emphasized unity within their own circles and the "standard rate" in the labor market. But now they are established, secure, and accepted. Full employment in the economy and grievance machinery in the plant give the individual worker a status largely unknown twenty-five years ago. The union attitude of limited class warfare directed at the surrounding society and of discipline directed at the individual member is no longer required by the new situation.

Might the unions turn their attention from the old slogans and the old dogmas, and undertake a new orientation toward their role in industrial society? This new role might well be that of a liberating force in industrial society, of a force helping to build a type of industrialization which would meet the desires of the single individual as well as of the organized group. This would be a mission the employers might well join, for they too have pressed for conformity and against individuality among the workers.

Big government. It has been the traditional policy in the United States that government has for its object to maintain law and order, so that the greatest freedom will be permitted to its citizens. It is argued that, since government operates under a system of checks and balances, it cannot be an effective instrument for carrying on business. On the other hand, since business has for its prime purpose the efficient, economical production and distribution of goods and services, it is asserted that business can, when left free to function, care for the needs of society.

Such, however, has not been the effect. Monopolistic control of wealth and national emergencies such as wars, economic depressions, and public disasters have brought about great public needs which required government intervention for solution. Since World War I government has assumed many functions previously limited to private organizations and individuals, and in addition many new ones previously thought unnecessary. Government now operates directly, or regulates and controls activities in the fields of land management, transportation, agriculture, manufacturing, distribution, credit, insurance, construction, health, welfare, education, and other areas.

The bigness of government is illustrated by data shown in the *Statistical Abstract of the United States 1960*, at page 387, wherein the following information is given concerning the operation of "Federal Business-Type Activities." The principal assets and liabilities involved in carrying out such activities for the year 1959 were 112 billion, 448 million dollars. Of these assets, "Public enterprise funds" equal 24 billion, 935 million dollars. These are administered by the Department of Agriculture, Farm Credit Corporation, Housing and Home Finance Agency, Federal Savings and Loan Insurance Corporation, Small Business Administration, Export-Import Bank, Tennessee Valley Authority, Panama Canal Company,

Veterans Administration, General Services Administration, Treasury Department, the Post Office, and the Interior Department.

In addition, the assets and liabilities of other activities including the Farm Home Administration, the Rural Electric Administration, the Corps of Engineers, the Atomic Energy Commission, and the Department of Health, Education and Welfare, plus intra-governmental deposit and revolving trust funds, amount to 87 billion, 613 million dollars.

The total funds involved in the operations of "Federal Business-Type Activities" have increased from 36 billion, 153 million dollars in 1953 to 112 billion, 448 million dollars in 1959. In carrying out these activities, the United States Government owns land, structures, and equipment valued at 28 billion, 964 million dollars.

"The federal government as a large proprietor owns 718,600,000 acres of land, and employed as of December, 1960, 2 million 665 thousand persons with an annual payroll of 1 billion, 234 million dollars. The Federal government operates under a yearly budget of 78 billion 367 million dollars and carries a gross public debt of 286 billion 330 million dollars."[11]

An understanding of the size and extent of government interference, regulation, and control of business, local, state and federal, can be obtained by a survey of the rules, regulations, and restraints found in the indices of local, state, and federal statutes, and in the indices of the administrative rules and orders of various government administrative boards.

On the local level, a business in selecting a site is affected by zoning laws, building and construction specifications, safety, sanitary, and fire requirements, taxes, improvement assessments, and police regulations.

On the state level, the nature and types of business organizations—corporate, partnership, or other—are regulated by the business association laws. Even the name, fictitious or personal, may be limited and required to be filed. Financing by stock issues and security methods are regulated by Blue Sky laws, usury laws, and other financial restrictions.

Not only are manufacturing businesses regulated, but regulation and control by licenses also extend to persons engaged in businesses which require personal capacity, which render services, and which distribute wares like food, feed, and dangerous instruments. A license has as its purpose the setting of standards of personal technical competence, character and honesty, and quality and safety. One may find in state statutes as many as seventy different professions, occupations, and business operations, from accountants to weighmasters, subject to state regulation and control. Banks, building and loan associations, financial institutions, in-

[11] *The World Almanac*, 1961, pp. 277, 739. *Federal Employment Bulletin*, December 1960.

surance, and foreign corporations must observe regulatory laws and comply with orders of state administrators. Public utilities, such as railroads, communications, gas and electric corporations, and trucking companies, cannot operate without a certificate of convenience and necessity from the proper state authority. The manufacture, conveyance, sale, and distribution of gas and electricity; the rates, services, and facilities; the improvements and extensions; the capital stock and bonded indebtedness; the expenses and dividends, are all subject to the supervisory powers of state administrators.

The circumstances and conditions under which production and marketing are conducted are subject to regulation and control. Safety requirements—restrictions on the hours, place, and conditions under which employees work—are prescribed. Laws provide for aid and assistance for loss caused by accidents and sickness. Pensions, minimum wages, nondiscrimination rules of employment, and other employment standards are required.

Marketing is controlled and regulated by a multiplicity of rules concerning quality, weights, measures, adulteration, merchandising, trade marks, infringement, unfair competition, and false advertising.

On the Federal level, it would not be possible to list all the Federal boards and agencies that bear upon business conduct. The few mentioned above were found in the *Statistical Abstract of the United States* for 1960. The *United States Government Organization Manual* for 1960–1961 lists alphabetically by initial 71 different federal commissions, boards, and agencies.

Over the past fifty years there has been a progressive expansion of government regulations and control of business consistent with the growth and expansion of the big corporations and big unions. This partial survey of big government is enough to give some idea of the extent of government bigness and its intrusion into business activity. The combined impact of big business, big unions, and big government on the political, economic, and social structure raises doubts as to whether the competitive system can be preserved. It is asserted that competition is the chief regulator of our economic order and must be preserved. Although it is a spur for efficient and effective business for the benefit of the consumer, it can nevertheless be dangerous and destructive.

Since the Sherman Anti-Trust Act of 1890, much legislation has been enacted to protect and aid the competitive process and at the same time to regulate and control its destructive features. Whether competition as traditionally understood can be a regulatory factor in an epoch of bigness is yet to be seen.

The epoch of technology and automation. Man spent 10,000 years moving from primitive agriculture to an industrial civilization. It has taken only 150 years to move from one industrial revolution to a technological age which may be a second industrial revolution. Since 1945, or within the space of less than twenty years, mankind has been affected more rapidly by technological developments—instrumentation and automation—than during any previous period. Automation is creating an accelerated industrial pace out of which arise problems that will require the combined efforts of business, labor, and government. Therefore, some consideration of its nature and its implications seems essential.

Automation is "the mechanization of sensory and control processes." The term refers to more than "automatic controls" like those used in regulating temperature and tensions, and making selections in machine operations. Automation is a technological trend of revolutionary force and consequence made possible by recent technical advances.

Although its economic, political, and social implications are not yet determined, its effect on production and labor-management relationships is already evident. Its use in diverse industries in the United States now represents expenditures amounting to millions of dollars.

In a factory, automation starts with some step of the manufacturing process; it is expanded to other steps, and ends by uniting into one automatic process all manufacturing procedures, so that only supervisory human labor is necessary. In the manufacture of ball-bearings, for instance, the raw material entering the factory is returned completely processed and packaged for shipment. Movement of the raw material, testing, processing, re-testing, packaging, storing, inventory control, order processing, and shipment are carried out by automatic means.

Automation is sometimes limited to isolated groups of steps in the manufacturing process, as illustrated in the manufacture of automobile engine blocks. Blocks are conveyed, placed and turned automatically for the drilling of holes, then tested and gauged, and defective units are rejected and worn-out drills replaced entirely, all by the push of an electric control switch. Other portions of the automobile are similarly manufactured, and the automatic steps are then correlated by human intervention into a finished automobile.

Automatic control equipment consists of many small devices. The technology of electronics, pneumatics, and hydraulics is used to make and operate a complex controlled manufacturing system.

Numerical control automation is part of a long-term general industrial program for the purpose of obtaining more efficient and economical production. Numerical control is applied to more than 90 per cent of present-day metal-working operations, as well as to assembling, batching, testing, inspection, and packing of many types of materials. Numerical control automation is most significant in its capacity to reduce machine time, labor, and costs while increasing production and quality. In electrical manufacturing, machine time has been reduced from 60 hours to 45 minutes, and the rejection rate of defective units has dropped from 50 per cent with human operation to 2 per cent with numerical control. Cost reduction in aircraft manufacturing has been reduced from $18,500 per particular unit to $1,950, with a saving of 85 per cent in manpower.

Automatically controlled diesel engines, electronic computers, automatic switches, power-lift trucks, and conveyors have greatly reduced the number of transportation and warehouse workers. Bakeries and food-processing plants are now equipped with machinery by which one man can do in one-half the time that which formerly required 24 men. Automation not only displaces the laborer and the blue-collar workers, but also office employees. Banks and financial institutions with electronic computers do more work with one-third fewer employees.

The effect of automation on the political, social, and economic environment of the United States has been evaluated differently. It is said that "American industry could not have achieved the measure of success it enjoys today without the rapidly expanding new technologies of instrumentation and automation. The constant improvement of manufacturing techniques and processes, the creation of new and better job opportunities, the introduction of thousands of new and improved products in the past ten years, reflect the widespread introduction of new advances in instrumentation and automation."

On the other hand, automation's "liberation of the worker" has also led to large displacement of labor, with unemployment, shorter workweek, and no return after a layoff.

> Indications are plentiful that automation is drying up the fields of historic union strength. . . . The march of technology is like a pincer movement in its impact on unions. It eliminates large numbers of blue-collar jobs in manufacturing and transportation, thus chipping away the bedrock of union enrollment. To the extent that new jobs are created, they involve hard-to-organize engineers, technicians and white-collar workers. . . .
>
> [Another effect of automation] is the degree to which automation makes business invulnerable to strike harassment. When push buttons and electronic control devices regulate every operation from receipt of raw materials to the loading of the finished goods, a handful of non-union supervisors and clerks will be able to keep acres of machines producing in the face of a total walkout by unionized factory crews.[12]

There has also developed from the shorter workweek a new economic phenomena called "moonlighting," that is, the holding of two jobs by one laborer. Such activity increases unemployment, creates fatigue, and is objected to because usually the second job pays less and is not under union control.

[12] Raskin, supra, n.7, 55, 56 (1961).

Solutions to the problem are sought in job increases in the automated plant and in adjustment by collective bargaining agreements. Older workers are retired early with long-term severance pay. School programs are established to prepare the displaced worker for other skilled jobs. Automation funds are set up under joint management-labor committees to determine how best to train and replace displaced workers. An elaborate agreement was negotiated in 1960 between the Pacific Maritime Association and the International Longshoremen's and Warehousemen's Union. The agreement, signed for six years, recognizes the manpower-reduction problem in automation and provides an adjustment for displaced labor.

The extent of the displacement of employees; the need for their retraining, relocation, and re-employment; the rapidity of plant obsolescence; and the distribution of surpluses brought about by automation, create problems of national magnitude. The solution of these problems will no doubt require participation and intervention by the United States Government.

If businessmen and labor leaders are successfully to meet international and national competition and are to operate under a free enterprise system, they must have the capacity to adapt themselves to the accelerated changes that occur in an automated age. Controls, both legislative and judicial, are inevitable. What they will be depends upon the businessmen's understanding of the problem.

Legislative protection of small business. Bigness, as evidenced by large corporations and their dominance in particular technological fields, has made it difficult for small business concerns to compete. In order to preserve free competitive enterprise, government has found it necessary to assist "small business." To accomplish this, Congress passed the Small Business Act of 1953. The act provided for the establishment of a Small Business Administration with the following functions: (1) to make loans to small business and to make disaster loans; (2) to enter into procurement contracts with other Federal agencies and to perform under these contracts by subcontracting with small business; (3) to provide technical and managerial aids to small business; and (4) to assist small business in obtaining government contracts. The administration was to terminate in 1955. However, the agency was extended to 1957, and by Public Law 85-536, 1958, the 1953 act was amended and continued to be known as the "Small Business Act." 15 U.S.C.A. Sec. 631–647 (1961). It is stated in the act as a declaration of policy that:

> The essence of the American economic system of private enterprise is free competition. Only through full and free competition can free markets, free entry into business and opportunities for the expression and growth of personal initiative and individual judgment be assured. The preservation and expansion

of such competition is basic not only to the economic well-being but to the security of this nation. Such security and well-being cannot be realized unless the actual and potential capacity of small business is encouraged and developed. It is the declared policy of the Congress that the government should aid, counsel, assist and protect, insofar as is possible, the interests of small business concerns in order to preserve free competitive enterprise, to insure that a fair proportion of total purchases and contracts for property and services for government (including but not limited to contracts for maintenance, repairs and construction) be placed with small business enterprises, to insure that a fair proportion of the total sales of government property be made to such enterprises, and to maintain and strengthen the small economy of the nation.

In order to carry out its objectives, the administration is authorized to obtain as a revolving fund from the Treasury of the United States a sum not to exceed $975,000,000 outstanding at any one time. Additional capital is appropriated to the fund from time to time. The act defines a small business concern and creates a Loan Policy Board to govern the granting and denial of applications for financial assistance. Under certain restrictions, "the administration is empowered to make loans to enable small business concerns to finance plant construction, conversion, or expansion, including the acquisition of land; or to finance the acquisition of equipment, facilities, machinery, supplies or materials; or to supply such concerns with working capital to be used in the manufacture of articles, equipment, supplies or materials for war, defense, or civilian production or as may be necessary to insure a well balanced economy. . . ."

In order to assist small business concerns in technological development, the administrator is authorized to consult with representatives of small business concerns. He would assist and encourage such firms to set up joint programs of development and research by constructing and operating laboratories, and by collecting and disseminating research information to participating members. The hope is that such a program "will maintain and strengthen the free enterprise system and the economy of the nation."

Since the Small Business Administration loan program is limited to short-term loans, Congress found it necessary to come to the assistance of small business by passing in 1958 the Small Business Investment Program, Public Law 85-699. 15 U.S.C.A. Sec. 661–696 (1961), which provides for setting up a program to supply long-term and equity-type financing to small business. In order "to improve and stimulate the national economy in general and small business in particular," it has been necessary to establish a program "to stimulate and supplement the flow of private equity capital and long-term loan funds which small business concerns need for the sound financing of their business operations and for their growth, expansion and modernization and which are not available in adequate supply." It is stated that the program shall be carried out in such manner "as to insure the maximum participation of private financing services."

The Small Business Administration may also establish a Small Business Investment Division. This Division has power to create small business investment corporations with $300,000 paid-in capital surplus and such corporations are organized to provide a source of equity capital for incorporated small business concerns.

In order to encourage the formation of small business investment corporations, the Small Business Administration is authorized to provide a maximum of $150,000 to each such corporation formed. This is done by the purchase of $150,000 worth of subordinate debentures from the newly organized corporations. National and state banks are also authorized to purchase a certain number of the shares of these new corporations. The small business investment corporations so organized are authorized to purchase convertible debentures of small business concerns on terms and at interest rates fixed by the Small Business Administration. It is hoped that by such governmental aid the "potential capacity of small business will be encouraged and developed as a means of preserving the competitive process."

1-8. The emergence of the free enterprise system. The term *free enterprise* has become a cliché with many meanings. Businessmen set the term against almost every type of restrictive government legislation. Government legislates to give competition greater freedom, wider scope, broader application, and more significance. In order to understand the phrase "free enterprise" and its accompanying phrase, "liberty of contract," a brief history of the economy out of which the doctrine emerged is necessary. The free enterprise system arose as a protest against the governmental, mercantile planned economy of the sixteenth and seventeenth centuries.

The mercantile system. The mercantile system followed the economy of the Middle Ages, a period in which business and trading activity was not worthy of respect. The Middle Ages was a period of rigid class distinction; "the saint and the noble" lived upon the labor of the lowly, who led a miserable life. Trading was considered an unholy pursuit, and if man sought profit, he did so for the benefit of the common good. This meant supporting the lord and bishop to furnish largesse for their almoners.

The discovery of new lands and precious metals in the sixteenth century made possible the extensive use of money as a medium of exchange. The feudal economy of the Middle Ages, resting principally on the exchange of goods in kind, gradually disappeared. Money, in the form of national currencies, became the measure of wealth, facilitated trade and commerce, and brought about competition among the nations to maintain a balance of trade. Powerful states developed. Spain, Holland, France, and England vied politically and economically for trade, wealth, power, and prestige. In order to secure money for armies, court expense, and colonial exploitation, it was necessary to stimulate industry and trade. Government became the chief promoter of business. In order to gain for the state the largest possible income, manufacturing and trade were kept under governmental patronage and were subject to an elaborate system of regulation and control. Tariffs were imposed, and for a fee the state issued special privileges and monopolies to corporations and trading companies. As a source of income, the right to conduct monopolistic markets was granted by the crown to individuals, churches, and towns. The grantees exacted tolls from traders, issued rules, and secured legislation to protect the monopoly. It was illegal for unlicensed traders to bring to the market for sale or to buy "merchandise, victuals or other things." Also, it was illegal to spread rumors to enhance prices or to dissuade others from coming to the market. Such conduct was called forestalling. Legislation forbade the act of acquiring possession of commodities for sale within certain geographical areas. It was illegal to engross, that is, by contract, to control and regulate the supply and demand of future goods. In addition to marketing privileges, royal charters were granted, giving monopolies to manufacture and process nearly every consumer commodity, such as salt, iron, powder, leather, cloth, bread, wool, and beer. Government statutes controlled price and regulated weights and measures. Labor was rigidly regulated by a guild system which set workers' wages and bound them to a particular task at a particular place under a long period of apprenticeship.

Justice Frank in *Hume v. Morse-McCormack Lines*[13] describes the mercantile period as follows:

> When trade increased, and, under the impact of many factors, the national, dynastic, territorial State arose, in the days of the Tudors and the first two Stuarts, to take the place of local and relatively self-sufficient units, a new set of attitudes (which had begun to emerge in the 13th and 14th centuries) found full expression in a rigorous economic nationalism which historians were later to call "mercantilism." A rising merchant class was released by centralized government from most of the ancient hampering restrictions imposed by the local governing units. The result was a vast liberation of the energies of alert individuals engaged in the pursuit of gain. This meant a substantial departure from the moral ideal of the medieval period, an ideal not always matched by the realities, which had condemned the striving of the individual for wealth as one of the seven deadly sins. But the adventurous merchant was still not free to think primarily of his own advancement. The scheme of government was totalitarianoid. The highly conscious dominant notion was the welfare of the nation, regarded as an entity, to be secured by an intensive state regulation of all phases of agriculture and industry. The energies of the striving individual

[13] 121 F.2d 336 (1941), at p. 338.

were canalized so as to foster the wealth of the nation; there was a strong note of disapproval of any man who sought his own selfish advantage at the expense of public advantage. Self-interest was not, as yet, considered the prime mover; the material interests of the State were paramount. The "mercantilist" system was profoundly paternalistic (or maternalistic). Particularly was that true as to laborers. No one in Elizabeth's reign would have dreamed of suggesting that there was a complete right of freedom of contract between master and servant; as to such undertakings, notions of status, of non-contractual rights and duties, were still operative. An elaborate labor code was an integral part of the Elizabethan plan of government; employers could not, at will, discharge their workers, nor depress their wages unduly; reciprocal obligations were imposed on workers; unemployment relief was accorded by the State, as a matter of right, with no obloquy to the recipient.

It is not possible to do so here, but to compare the extent of regulation and control of business during the mercantile period with present United States federal and state regulatory control would be revealing. Such a study might well justify an inference that "statism" has made a complete circle. (See Sec. 1-7 on big government, p. 44.)

Laissez-faire and free enterprise. Resentment against limitation of trade between cities, objection to special privileges and monopolistic controls granted by the crown, rebellion of the apprentice against the master, the invention of machinery, the development of the factory system, and the influence of natural law, particularly in the seventeenth and eighteenth centuries, brought an end to the mercantile system. The proponents of natural law, beginning in the seventeenth and eighteenth centuries, asserted that man is guided by a principle, that he is part of nature, and that, as a rational and intelligent man, he acts in conformity with all of his desires and impulses. Conduct based on these ideas creates rules and regulations for a good society. Such moral and just principles are above any rules of law that may be pronounced by government. Thus, legislation and royal decrees inconsistent with natural law are invalid. This concept of freedom and individualism opened the way for the industrial revolution. The doctrine declared that a man is a free agent and that it is just as natural to be unbound as it is to be bound. This ideology ran counter to the paternalistic mercantile system which controlled and regulated all business for the benefit of the crown.

Governmental, mercantile planned economy was also challenged by Adam Smith, who expounded the doctrine "that each man when seeking selfish advantage is led by an invisible hand to promote an end which is no part of his intention; so that individual selfishness is the best means of fostering social welfare." Thus, business and economic progress limited only by the pursuit of each man's selfish interest would better serve society than would regulation and control by the state.

It was recognized as a basic rule of natural law that if man's acquisitive instinct was given free play in trade, and if business and government restraints were reduced to a minimum, the inevitable result would be competitive conduct between free men. Competitive conduct, stimulated by ". . . personal interest. . . . [the profit motive] compels each man vigorously and continuously to perfect and multiply the things he sells." The operation of such economic theory would automatically lead, in a free system, to the stabilization of prices, to the improvement of techniques to make better goods, and to increased production. This would bring about full employment and would equalize the distribution of goods and services, thus creating harmony between capital and labor.

The term *laissez-faire* applied to these principles is attributed to a French manufacturer who in response to a government official's inquiry as to what the government could do for industry replied, "Laissez-nous faire," which translated means "let us alone." "Laissez-faire" or "let alone-ism" as an economic and political doctrine required minimum government interference in business affairs. It ended mercantilism, and as the dominant controlling economic philosophy in the the United States after the Civil War, brought about great industrial growth and the accumulation of wealth.

The section to follow will discuss how the doctrine of laissez-faire found its way into the Constitution of the United States, and after the Civil War sustained free enterprise, brought about liberty of contract, motivated industrial development and influenced legislation and judicial opinion.

1-9. Constitutional protection of laissez-faire and liberty of contract—Due process. Freed from mercantilism and state control, the eighteenth and nineteenth centuries were conspicuous for the industrial revolution, exploration, colonization, and the exploitation of natural resources. The law resting on natural justice and broad ideas of freedom protected men from interference by the government in the free exercise of their acquisitive instinct.

Freedom of contract became a natural right; an agreement between the parties with few limitations. The contract became the law which the courts must respect and enforce. The liberty of one person was limited only by the principle of like liberty of other persons.

In the United States, after the Civil War, industry and business, stimulated by a laissez-faire economic doctrine and unlimited free enterprise, had an enormous growth. Liberty of contract and private property enjoyed constitutional protection from restrictive federal and state legislation, through a new meaning given to the Fifth and Fourteenth Amendments. Although the Declaration of Independence does not use the word *property* as an "inalienable right," it is used in the Fifth and Fourteenth Amendments. The Fifth Amendment, as applicable to federal legislation, states: "nor be deprived of life, liberty or property without due process of law," and the Fourteenth Amendment, as applicable to state legislation, states: "nor shall any state deprive any person of life, liberty or property without due process of law. . . ."

Prior to 1850 the words "due process of law" were limited in meaning to judicial procedural methods. That is, "they [due process of law] mean a course of legal proceedings according to those rules and principles which have been established in our system of jurisprudence for the enforcement and protection of private rights . . . according to the law of the land." The idea that every citizen shall not be condemned before trial, and that his life, liberty, and property shall enjoy the protection of the general "law of the land" had its origin in the Magna Charta of 1215, which states that "no freeman shall be taken or imprisoned or disseised or exiled or in any way destroyed . . . except by lawful judgment of his peers and by the law of the land."

The Statutes of Westminster of 1354, which enacted into legislation the principles of the Magna Charta, use the words "due process of law." These words having been interpreted to be identical with "the law of the land," were incorporated into Colonial charters and later found their way into state and federal constitutions.

The meaning of the words "due process of law" did not remain limited to procedural due process but, under the influence of individualism and the prevalent laissez-faire doctrine, the words took on a broader meaning, known as "substantive due process."

In adjudicating individual controversies, the English and American courts of the nineteenth and twentieth centuries applied and created a common law, based on natural law. The common law, as it developed out of the industrial revolution of England, had for its purpose in economic and business life the protection of the individual, the security of private property, and the enforcement of contract promises as property. The contract thus became the most important legal instrument or device by which the free enterprise system developed.

The concept of liberty of the individual to contract, upheld by laissez-faire economic doctrine, became the ideal for Western civilization and American democracy and set the standard by which the validity of legislative restraints and limitations was determined.

The federal Constitution reflects such ideology in Article I, Section 10, which provides that "No state shall . . . pass . . . [any] law impairing the obligation of contracts." The first case involving this Constitutional provision was *Fletcher v. Peck*,[14] which arose in 1810. Although a legislative enactment, authorizing certain contracts, had been obtained by bribery,

[14] 10 U.S. (6 Cranch) 87.

nevertheless an attempted repeal of the act was held invalid, as an impairment of the obligation of contracts. Likewise, in the famous *Dartmouth College v. Woodward* case,[15] Justice Marshall held a corporate charter to be a contract and a New Hampshire statute which attempted to change such charter, unconstitutional. Although the Fifth and Fourteenth Amendments were more often used to shield contracts from legislative interference, the "obligation-of-contracts clause" gave stability to business corporations' charters.

Two other clauses of the Constitution used to safeguard freedom of contract and protect private property from legislative encroachment are the Fifth and Fourteenth Amendments. Although these amendments do not use the words "liberty of contract" or express an economic doctrine, the phrase "due process of law," used therein, has been expanded beyond procedural due process by judicial decisions to what is known as "substantive due process." Such expansion permitted "liberty of contract" and the right to private property to be included as fundamental freedoms entitled to constitutional protection.

"Substantive due process" was a judicial theory used to test the constitutional validity of state and federal legislation, which legislation had for its purpose the regulation and control of private property and business enterprises. The doctrine maintained that when two parties enter into an agreement, or negotiate to enter into an agreement, the legislature has no right to interfere with the negotiation nor to prescribe the terms or the conditions under which the agreement is made or performed. The limits or boundaries of substantive due process have never been definitely determined. However, it was early declared by the Supreme Court of the United States, as a judicial policy, that the determination of the legality of state and federal regulatory legislation was a judicial function, not a legislative function. Legislation to meet the requirements of substantive due process had to be reasonable; that is, reasonable in its purpose, reasonable in its means, not arbitrary, and of such character as not to impose unreasonable or arbitrary limitations on freedom of contract, or to unduly restrict the use of private property. Whether legislation was reasonable or unreasonable or "unduly restricted individual life, liberty or property rights more severely than an advantage to the community can possibly justify" was sometimes determined, not by any specific constitutional provision or basic principle of law, but by the judge's historical, economic, political, and social ideas as to what seemed to him reasonable, sensible, and most advantageous for the public good.

The first significant pronouncement of "substantive due process" is found in the case of *In re Jacobs*.[16] Judge Earl, in holding invalid a law

[15] 17 U.S. (4 Wheat) 518.
[16] 98 N.Y. 98, 110 (1885).

forbidding the manufacture of cigars or the preparation of tobacco in tenement houses in cities having a population exceeding 500,000, states:

> Generally it is for the legislature to determine what laws and regulations are needed to protect the public health and secure the public comfort and safety. . . . But they must have some relation to these ends. Under the mere guise of police regulations, personal rights and private property cannot be arbitrarily invaded, and the determination of the legislature is not final or conclusive. If it passes an Act, ostensibly for the public health, and thereby destroys or takes away the property of a citizen, or interferes with his personal liberty, then it is for the courts to scrutinize the Act and see whether it really relates to and is convenient and appropriate to promote the public health. It matters not that the legislature may in the title to the Act, or in its body, declare that it is intended for the improvement of the public health. Such a declaration does not conclude the courts, and they must yet determine the fact declared and enforce the supreme law.
>
> It is plain that this is not a health law, and that it has no relation whatever to the public health. Under the guise of promoting the public health the legislature might as well have banished cigar-making from all the cities of the State, or confined it to a single city or town, or have placed under a similar ban the trade of a baker, of a tailor, of a shoemaker, of a woodcarver, or of any other of the innocuous trades carried on by artisans in their homes. The power would have been the same, and its exercise, so far as it concerns fundamental, constitutional rights, could have been justified by the same arguments. Such legislation may invade one class of rights today and another tomorrow, and if it can be sanctioned under the Constitution, while far removed in time we will not be far away in practical statesmanship from those ages when governmental prefects supervised the building of houses, the rearing of cattle, the sowing of seed, and the reaping of grain, and governmental ordinances regulated the movements and labor of artisans, the rate of wages, the price of food, the diet and clothing of the people and a large range of other affairs long since in all civilized lands regarded as outside of governmental functions. Such governmental interferences disturb the normal adjustments of the social fabric, and usually derange the delicate and complicated machinery of industry and cause a score of ills while attempting the removal of one.

In tracing the development of "substantive due process," we note that the language used by Mr. Justice Field in his dissenting opinion in the Slaughter-House cases of 1873, concerning the privileges and immunities clause of the Fourteenth Amendment, is similar to that later used by the court in giving meaning to the phrase "due process of law." Justice Field declares that the term "privileges and immunities" in the Fourteenth Amendment "comprehended protection by the government; the enjoyment of life and liberty with the right to acquire and possess property of every kind and to pursue and obtain happiness . . . that these were the great fundamental rights set forth in the act . . . 'as appertaining to every freeman' . . . and it is to me a matter of professional regret that its validity [a statute confirming a twenty-five year monopoly upon a domestic corporation] is recognized by a majority of this court for by it the right of free labor, one of the most sacred and imprescriptible rights of man, is violated. . . ."

Substantive due process as a judicial doctrine and standard resting on laissez-faire philosophy by which to invalidate restrictive legislation constitutionally is illustrated by Mr. Justice Peckham in the following cases.

In 1897 Mr. Justice Peckham, in *Allgeyer v. Louisiana*,[17] holding that a state statute which interfered with the pursuit of interstate insurance business was not due process of law and was unconstitutional, used the following language:

> The supreme court of Louisiana says that the act of writing within that state, the letter of notification, was an act therein done to effect an insurance on property then in the state, in a marine insurance company which had not complied with its laws, and such act was therefore prohibited by the statute. As so construed, we think the statute is a violation of the fourteenth amendment of the federal Constitution, in that it deprives the defendants of their liberty without due process of law. The statute which forbids such act does not become due process of law, because it is inconsistent with the provisions of the Constitution of the Union. The "liberty" mentioned in that amendment means, not only the right of the citizen to be free from the mere physical restraint of his person, as by incarceration, but the term is deemed to embrace the right of the citizen to be free in the enjoyment of all his faculties; to be free to use them in all lawful ways; to live and work where he will; to earn his livelihood by any lawful ways; to earn his livelihood by any lawful calling; to pursue any livelihood or avocation; and for that purpose to enter into all contracts which may be proper, necessary, and essential to his carrying out to a successful conclusion the purposes above mentioned.
>
> It was said by Mr. Justice Bradley, in *Butchers' Union Slaughter-House Co. v. Crescent City Live-Stock Landing Co.* . . . in the course of his concurring opinion in that case, that "the right to follow any of the common occupations of life is an inalienable right. It was formulated as such under the phrase 'pursuit of happiness' in the Declaration of Independence."
>
> It is true that these remarks were made in regard to questions of monopoly but they well describe the rights which are covered by the word "liberty," as contained in the fourteenth amendment.
>
> . . . The main proposition advanced by the defendant is that his enjoyment upon terms of equality with all others in similar circumstances of the privilege of pursuing an ordinary calling or trade, and of acquiring, holding, and selling property, is an essential part of his rights of liberty and property, as guaranteed by the fourteenth amendment. The court assents to this general proposition as embodying a sound principle of constitutional law.
>
> . . . In the privilege of pursuing an ordinary calling or trade, and of acquiring, holding, and selling property, must be embraced the right to make all proper contracts in relation thereto . . .

Justice Peckham, declaring unconstitutional a statute limiting a work day for bakers to ten hours in *Lochner v. New York*,[18] reaffirms his posi-

[17] 165 U.S. 578 (1897).
[18] 198 U.S. 45 (1905).

tion expressed in the Allgeyer case and defines the limits of "substantive due process":

The statute necessarily interferes with the right of contract between the employer and employees, concerning the number of hours in which the latter may labor in the bakery of the employer. The general right to make a contract in relation to his business is part of the liberty of the individual protected by the fourteenth amendment of the federal Constitution. *Allgeyer v. Louisiana,* 165 U.S. 578, 17 S.Ct. 427, 41 L.Ed. 832. Under that provision no state can deprive any person of life, liberty, or property without due process of law. The right to purchase or to sell labor is part of the liberty protected by this amendment, unless there are circumstances which exclude the right. . . .

The state, therefore, has power to prevent the individual from making certain kinds of contracts, and in regard to them the federal Constitution offers no protection. If the contract be one which the state, in the legitimate exercise of its police power, has the right to prohibit, it is not prevented from prohibiting it by the fourteenth amendment. Contracts in violation of a statute, either of the federal or state government, or a contract to let one's property for immoral purposes, or to do any other unlawful act, could obtain no protection from the federal Constitution, as coming under the liberty of person or of free contract. Therefore, when the state, by its legislature, in the assumed exercise of its police powers, has passed an act which seriously limits the right to labor or the right of contract in regard to their means of livelihood between persons who are sui juris (both employer and employee), it becomes of great importance to determine which shall prevail—the right of the individual to labor for such time as he may choose, or the right of the state to prevent the individual from laboring, or from entering into any contract to labor, beyond a certain time prescribed by the state.

It must, of course, be conceded that there is a limit to the valid exercise of the police power by the state. . . . Otherwise the fourteenth amendment would have no efficacy and the legislatures of the states would have unbounded power, and it would be enough to say that any piece of legislation was enacted to conserve the morals, the health, or the safety of the people; such legislation would be valid, no matter how absolutely without foundation the claim might be. The claim of the police power would be a mere pretext—become another and delusive name for the supreme sovereignty of the state to be exercised free from constitutional restraint. This is not contended for. In every case that comes before this court, therefore, where legislation of this character is concerned, and where the protection of the federal Constitution is sought, the question necessarily arises: Is this a fair, reasonable, and appropriate exercise of the police power of the state, or is it an unreasonable, unnecessary, and arbitrary interference with the right of the individual to his personal liberty, or to enter into those contracts in relation to labor which may seem to him appropriate or necessary for the support of himself and his family? Of course the liberty of contract relating to labor includes both parties to it. The one has as much right to purchase as the other to sell labor. . . .

There is no reasonable ground for interfering with the liberty of person or the right of free contract, by determining the hours of labor, in the occupation of a baker. There is no contention that bakers as a class are not equal in intelligence and capacity to men in other trades or manual occupations, or that they are not able to assert their rights and care for themselves without the protecting arm of the state, interfering with their independence of judgment and of action. They are in no sense wards of the state. . . .

It is a question of which of two powers or rights shall prevail—the power of the state to legislate or the right of the individual to liberty of person and freedom of contract. The mere assertion that the subject relates, though but in a remote degree, to the public health, does not necessarily render the enactment valid. The act must have a more direct relation, as a means to an end, and the end itself must be appropriate and legitimate, before an act can be held to be valid which interferes with the general right of an individual to be free in his person and in his power to contract in relation to his own labor. . . .

We think the limit of the police power has been reached and passed in this case. There is, in our judgment, no reasonable foundation for holding this to be necessary or appropriate as a health law to safeguard the public health, or the health of the individuals who are following the trade of a baker. If this statute be valid, and if, therefore, a proper case is made out in which to deny the right of an individual sui juris, as employer or employee, to make contracts for the labor of the latter under the protection of the provisions of the federal Constitution, there would seem to be no length to which legislation of this nature might not go. . . .

. . . It is unfortunately true that labor, even in any department, may possibly carry with it the seeds of unhealthiness. But are we all, on that account, at the mercy of legislative majorities? A printer, a tinsmith, a locksmith, a carpenter, a cabinetmaker, a dry goods clerk, a bank's, a lawyer's, or a physician's clerk, or a clerk in almost any kind of business, would all come under the power of the legislature, on this assumption. No trade, no occupation, no mode of earning one's living could escape this all-pervading power, and the acts of the legislature in limiting the hours of labor in all employments would be valid, although such limitation might seriously cripple the ability of the laborer to support himself and his family.

. . . Under such circumstances the freedom of master and employee to contract with each other in relation to their employment, and in defining the same, cannot be prohibited or interfered with, without violating the federal Constitution. . . .

The doctrine of judicial supremacy, as pronounced by Justice Peckham in the above cases, rests on the two theories: the court's acceptance of Adam Smith's assumption "that realization of private pecuniary motives will result in public gain," and the theory that the will of the people, having been expressed in written constitutions which it is the duty of the court to interpret, is superior to the popular will of the people expressed through legislation. The great advocate of this doctrine was Judge Cooley.

An analysis of Cooley's influence on Constitutionalism and the United States Supreme Court by Arthur L. Harding[19] is here presented (footnotes omitted):

In the first half of the nineteenth century the principal concern of the evolving American constitutionalism was the proper delimitation of the possibly

[19] Harding, *The Ghost of Herbert Spencer: A Darwinian Concept of Law, Origins of the Natural Law Tradition,* Southern Methodist University, Studies in Jurisprudence: I, pp. 81–90 (1954).

overlapping functions of the state and federal governments. There was little occasion to come to the defense of those human liberties derived from the neoclassical doctrines of Hooker, Coke, and Locke, for those liberties were little challenged. In the second half of the century, however, such issues did come to the fore, and the proper delimitation of the powers of government with respect to individuals became the principal task. The authoritative thesis for this age was supplied in 1868 with the publication by Thomas M. Cooley of his *Treatise on the Constitutional Limitations* . . . [which] abounds in reference to Burlamaqui, to Locke, to Lieber, to Jefferson. The influence of Blackstone's Book I and of the writings of Lord Coke is evident. In formulating his doctrine of natural rights, Cooley departed little from the accepted statement. He adopted Locke's concept of organized society antedating government and conferring rights which are superior to government. His strong individualism was essentially that of Bentham, but was colored somewhat by the Spencerian concept of the inevitability of the struggle of individual man against other men. Cooley's concept of the role of the political state, of the legal order, was essentially the negative one of [Herbert] Spencer: to maintain a certain minimum of public order, to protect individuals seeking to further their individual interests in society, and to enforce economic bargains.

Cooley's significant contribution to the course of American law was to be found in the doctrine of implied limitations upon the powers of the state governments, and of an implied power in the courts to make these limitations effective. Notwithstanding that the state constitutions specified with considerable particularity the natural rights of individuals, Cooley asserted that there were other and implied limitations on legislative power which were to be found in the ethical concepts of previously existing organized society. The implied limitations so read into the written constitution were to share with the written constitution the prestige of being the direct expression of the will of the people. The popular will so directly expressed was to be considered at all times paramount to the popular will as expressed indirectly through legislation. It was, therefore, the duty of the courts to strike down such legislation as would exceed the implied limitations upon the legislative power, even though no specific constitutional prohibition appeared to have been impinged.

Cooley accepted from Adam Smith the laissez-faire assumption that the realization of private pecuniary motives will result in the public gain. The realization of monetary gain through economic activity was to be strictly a private affair from which government was to be barred, either as entrepreneur or as regulator. The struggle for economic advantage of individual over individual was strictly a private matter to which government could be only a bystander. . . . His strong bias in favor of laissez-faire economics undoubtedly facilitated the popular acceptance of Spencerism by seeming to give it the support of constitutional law. More importantly, his theory of implied limitations upon the power of government, and an implied power in the courts to make these limitations effective, set the stage for the next development which was undoubtedly Spencerian in its content.

LIBERTY OF CONTRACT

It has been seen that Spencerism or Social Darwinism came to America close on the heels of Darwinism. It came at a time when America was in an economic revolution. Sparked by the needs of the Civil War, industrialization was going forward at a rapid rate. The strains of readjustment were great. The accelerated growth of cities created new problems and brought forth demands for new legislation. The new industrialists, drinking for the first time the heady wine of economic power, were pushing forward relentlessly, sometimes ruthlessly, toward the realization and extension of that power. By the same token the newly developing laboring class, apprehensive of some courses of events, was turning to government for what was believed to be essential protection. Farmers, seeing their own power slip away, reacted similarly.

Quite naturally Spencerism was well received by the new industrialists, who could find therein an ethical justification for the necessity of ruthless competitive practices, resulting in the destruction of weaker competitors, or even in the near impoverishment of workers. Such things were thought of as contributing to the economic development of the nation. Andrew Carnegie was prominent in sponsoring Spencer and Spencerism in this country. Others such as James J. Hill and the elder Rockefeller advanced Spencerism as justifying the moral necessity of publicly criticized business practices. Such, however, was the pervasiveness of the individualist faith and the gospel of the inevitability of human progress, that the acceptance of Spencerism was not confined to those who stood to gain by its adoption but extended to many whose interests would not be served thereby.

What economic interests were asserted in the name of Spencerism? They were several: a right to enter freely into any economic activity or vocation free of governmental restriction; a right to buy and sell goods and services on a free market without governmental interference; a right to borrow and lend money on a free market on whatever terms that market might establish; a right to combine or to associate with others to realize economic ends. These claims were not particularly new. Jeremy Bentham had advocated them as a key to human happiness under his Utility principle. In Bentham's system, however, these claims were not unlimited; rather they were subject to limitation in the protection of the happiness of others and for the public good. Spencer's contribution was to remove the limitations. According to the savage interpretation of Darwinism adopted by Spencer, the public good was not served by the protection of the economically weak against the economically strong. To the contrary, the economic welfare of the community would be enhanced by removing from the field of economic activity those less fitted to engage therein, just as the quality of the race as a whole would be improved by eliminating from the race its weaker members. Corollary propositions were that the power of taxation would not be used to take gains from the economically successful for the benefit of the economically unsuccessful; that the powers of government would not be used to aid one individual or class of individuals in economic dealings with other individuals or classes; and that government would not occupy any field of economic activity so as to impair the ability of an individual to enter that field.

Supporters of this Spencerian view found in Judge Cooley's theory of constitutional limitations what they thought to be legalistic support. The next task was to establish Cooley's theory as the law of the land. By coincidence, 1868, the year that saw the first publication of Cooley's work, saw also the adoption of the Fourteenth Amendment to the United States Constitution with its injunction that no state should deprive any person of his life, liberty, or property without due process of law. Only four years after the adoption of that Amendment a brilliant lawyer, John A. Campbell, was to argue to the United States Supreme Court in the first of the Slaughterhouse cases that the Fourteenth Amendment embodied both the Spencerian concept of a natural liberty of economic activity and the Cooley doctrine of implied limitations upon legislative power. Attacking the validity of a Louisiana statute establishing a slaughterhouse monopoly in the New Orleans area, Campbell contended that barring others from entering the slaughtering business was a violation of the natural liberties of the individual; and then that the Fourteenth Amendment clothed the United States Supreme Court with the power and duty to strike down the Louisiana statute. Campbell lost his battle but in the long run won the war. Two important Justices of the Court were converted to his view, Justice Brandley largely on the basis of arguments derived from Spencer and Cooley, and Justice Field largely on the basis of arguments derived from Adam Smith. Thereafter in other cases these two were to advance Campbell's argument unceasingly until it prevailed as the doctrine of the majority of the court. The development, however, extended over a period of years.

Campbell's argument, which had failed in its initial appearance in the United States Supreme Court, was carried by others to the state courts and there met with considerable success. Thus, vindicating Campbell's contention, now bearing the label of Liberty of Right of Contract, state courts invalidated state legislation designed to fix the hours of labor, to require the payment of wages in cash in lieu of orders on a company store, to prohibit employers from interfering with membership in labor unions by their employees, to prohibit contracts by railway workers purporting to release the company in advance from any liability for injury to the workers, to prohibit the imposition of fines on employees, and other purposes.

Finally in 1905, in a case involving the validity of a New York law limiting the workday of bakers to ten hours, Campbell's Spencerian-Cooley theory prevailed with a majority of the Justices of the Supreme Court and the statute was stricken down. This was too much for Mr. Justice Holmes, whose own legal philosophy contained a substantial Darwinism. In a caustic dissent Holmes referred bitingly to the "inarticulate major premises" of the majority opinion. He declared his belief that the case was "decided upon an economic theory which a large part of the country does not entertain" and asserted that "the Fourteenth Amendment does not enact Mr. Herbert Spencer's Social Statics."

The comparatively late date of the inclusion of Liberty of Contract among the natural rights of men is interesting. By 1905 Spencer was generally discredited as a philosopher. Among sociologists Spencer's tooth-and-claw sociology had been supplanted by Lester Ward's sociology of co-operation and intelligent control. Certainly by 1905 Spencer had lost a considerable part of his popular following, and the idea of legislative regulation had gained support. Nevertheless the Court set forth to graft onto the older tradition of Natural Law an increasingly unacceptable concept of a natural right of contract supposedly derived from the laws of organic existence. . . .

Applying the theory the court in 1915 invalidated a state statute outlawing the "yellow dog" contract, and in 1923 rejected wagefixing by statutory authority. Also in 1923 was stricken down a minimum wage statute applicable to the District of Columbia, and again in 1936 a state minimum wage statute fell. The gulf between Court and the people appeared to be ever widening, with ever increasing criticism of the Court by those advocating legislative protection against claimed economic abuses. The final result of course was the courtpacking controversy of 1937 and a possible reorientation of American legal theory.

In any event the Supreme Court in 1937 sustained the validity of a Washington statute fixing a minimum wage for women workers of $14.50 for a forty-eight-hour week. The opinion by Chief Justice Hughes reaffirmed the Court's support of certain cases decided prior to the 1905 adoption of the Liberty of Contract theory, and repeated the 1898 statement that

> the fact that both parties are of full age, and competent to contract, does not necessarily deprive the state of the power to interfere, where the parties do not stand upon an equality, or where the public health demands that one party to the contract shall be protected against himself. . . . The state still retains an interest in his welfare, however reckless he may be. The whole is no greater than the sum of all the parts, and when the individual health, safety and welfare are sacrificed or neglected, the state must suffer.

The Court concluded by overruling the 1923 decision which had nullified a minimum wage statute for the District of Columbia.

That the 1937 case was decided upon a reappraisal of the Spencerian doctrine may be seen by examining the dissenting opinion of Justice Sutherland, with its reliance upon Cooley's Constitutional Limitations and its reiteration of language from a 1908 opinion that

> the right of a person to sell his labor upon such terms as he deems proper is, in its essence, the same as the right of the purchaser of labor to prescribe the conditions on which he will accept such labor from the person offering to sell. . . . In all such particulars the employer and employee have equality of right, and any legislation that disturbs that equality is an arbitrary interference with the liberty of contract which no government can legally justify in a free land.

1-10. Legislative control of liberty of contract—a new application of due process. In discussing limitations on liberty, a distinction must be made between freedoms. Freedoms are not all of equal value and significance. There are liberties, "implicit in the concept of ordered society" and "so rooted in the traditions and conscience of the American people as to be ranked as fundamental and absolute." These liberties are set out in the First Ten Amendments to the Constitution of the United States. These amendments restate the historically established natural rights of man; recognize his worth as an individual; prescribe the procedures for protecting him from mental and physical restraint, unlawful search, seizure and arrest, and oppression by the majority; and "afford him an opportunity to grow in mind and spirit." These particular liberties are called civil liberties, basic to western culture and American democracy. During the past half-century, they have been carefully guarded by the courts, and by "procedural due process" have been given protection under the Fifth and Fourteenth Amendments. At the same time, legislative limitations have been placed on other freedoms thought to be fundamental and absolute but considered by some jurists to be qualified and of lesser value. These freedoms are concerned with economic and business activity. Freedom to contract, the right of private property, and the unhampered pursuit of business are no longer considered free from legislative impairment.

By the end of the nineteenth century and the beginning of the twentieth century the inevitable consequence of unrestrained free competitive conduct reached its climax. The economic strong became stronger; and the economic weak, weaker. The recognition of the impersonal corporation as a person within the protection of the Fifth and Fourteenth Amendments, and the judicial determination that liberty of contract and the right of property were fundamental absolute rights under the due process clauses, both brought about a condition of inequality of bargaining power by which the economically strong had an excess of liberty of contract and the economic weak had little, if any, liberty of contract. Under the Spencerian doctrine of the "survival of the fittest," this condition of economic unbalance was justified and tolerated, both politically and legally. However, public reaction to such inequality manifested itself in the early 1900's in vigorous and strong agrarian and labor movements. The laborer, the farmer, the small businessman dominated by monopolies, the dispossessed, and the overreached consumer, all sought legislation as a method to equalize unequal bargaining power. It was argued that if "substantive due process" had for its purpose the protection of the liberty of contract, it must necessarily protect liberty of contract for the weak as well as the strong.

Legislation limiting freedom of contract was not new. In order to safeguard the general welfare, and aid the overreached, it had long been considered within the police power to prevent by legislation fraudulent, usurious, immoral, and illegal contracts. Such contracts had never been sanctioned under the "due process" clause of the Fourteenth Amendment. Whether these particular contracts were detrimental to the safety, health, morals, and general welfare of the community and were under the police power was recognized as a matter for legislative judgment. It was soon discovered that unemployment, long hours of work, low wages, unsafe and unhealthful working conditions, price irregularities, overreaching the consumer, and monopolistic controls of commodities, had a deleterious effect upon the general welfare and were a matter of public concern that could be effectively ameliorated only by legislation. By 1937 it was realized "that freedom of contract is a qualified and not an absolute right. There are no absolute rights to do as one wills or to contract as one chooses. The guarantee of liberty does not withdraw from legislative supervision that wide department of activity which consists in making contracts, nor does it deny to government the power to provide restrictive safeguards. Liberty implies absence of arbitrary restraint, not immunity from reasonable regulations and prohibitions imposed in the interests of the community." Mr. Justice Hughes in *West Coast Hotel Co. v. Parrish.*[20]

New tests were being found for "due process of law." New meaning was given to the words by evaluating what the legislature was actually attempting to do, not what the Supreme Court thought it had a right to do. Police power through legislative encroachment on business was expanding and constitutional protection of freedom of contract, retreating Legislation equalizing bargaining power became recognized as a proper function of the state. Whether the legislation was justified and reasonable was a matter for the state and "not the function of the court to nullify because in the court's judgment the legislation might be outside the 'vague contours of due process.'" Mr. Justice Frankfurter, *American Federation of Labor v. American Sash and Door Co.*[21]

The question whether social and economic regulatory legislation impinges upon freedom of contract and business activity and is in violation of due process of law, is no longer an exclusive function of the judiciary. Whether such legislation is reasonable, whether it concerns itself with a fit subject, whether it is economically sound and socially desirable, is up to the legislative branch of government.

The above doctrine was recognized, and a full explanation of its implication is set out by Justice Roberts in the case of *Nebbia v. People of the State of New York,*[22] in the following language:

> . . . Under our form of government the use of property and the making of contracts are normally matters of private and not of public concern. The general rule is that both shall be free of governmental interference. But neither property rights nor contract rights are absolute; for government cannot exist if the citizen may at will use his property to the detriment of his fellows, or exercise his freedom of contract to work them harm. Equally fundamental with the private right is that of the public to regulate it in the common interest.
>
> The Fifth Amendment, in the field of federal activity, and the Fourteenth, as respects state action, do not prohibit governmental regulation for the public welfare. They merely condition the exertion of the admitted power, by securing that the end shall be accomplished by methods consistent with due process. And the guaranty of due process, as has often been held, demands only that the law shall not be unreasonable, arbitrary, or capricious, and that the means selected shall have a real and substantial relation to the object sought to be attained. It results that a regulation valid for one sort of business or in given circumstances, may be invalid for another sort, or for the same business under

[20] 300 U.S. 379, 380 (1937).
[21] 335 U.S. 538, 542 (1949).
[22] 291 U.S. 502 (1934).

other circumstances, because the reasonableness of each regulation depends upon the relevant facts.

The reports of our decisions abound with cases in which the citizen, individual or corporate, has vainly invoked the Fourteenth Amendment in resistance to necessary and appropriate exertion of the police power.

The court has repeatedly sustained curtailment of enjoyment of private property, in the public interest. The owner's rights may be subordinated to the needs of other private owners whose pursuits are vital to the paramount interests of the community. The state may control the use of property in various ways; may prohibit advertising bill boards except of a prescribed size and location, or their use for certain kinds of advertising; may in certain circumstances authorize encroachments by party walls in cities; may fix the height of buildings, the character of materials, and methods of construction, the adjoining area which must be left open, and may exclude from residential sections offensive trades, industries and structures likely injuriously to affect the public health or safety; or may establish zones within which certain types of buildings or businesses are permitted and others excluded. And although the Fourteenth Amendment extends protection to aliens as well as citizens, a state may for adequate reasons of policy exclude aliens altogether from the use and occupancy of land.

Laws passed for the suppression of immorality, in the interest of health, to secure fair trade practices, and to safeguard the interests of depositors in banks, have been found consistent with due process. These measures not only affected the use of private property, but also interfered with the right of private contract. Other instances are numerous where valid regulation has restricted the right of contract, while less directly affecting property rights.

The Constitution does not guarantee the unrestricted privilege to engage in a business or to conduct it as one pleases. Certain kinds of business may be prohibited, and the right to conduct a business, or to pursue a calling, may be conditioned. Regulation of a business to prevent waste of the state's resources may be justified. And statutes prescribing the terms upon which those conducting certain businesses may contract, or imposing terms if they do enter into agreements, are within the state's competency.

Legislation concerning sales of goods, and incidentally affecting prices, has repeatedly been held valid. In this class fall laws forbidding unfair competition by the charging of lower prices in one locality than those exacted in another, by giving trade inducements to purchasers, and by other forms of price discrimination. The public policy with respect to free competition has engendered state and federal statutes prohibiting monopolies, which have been upheld. On the other hand, where the policy of the state dictated that a monopoly should be granted, statutes having that effect have been held inoffensive to the constitutional guarantees. Moreover, the state or a municipality may itself enter into business in competition with private proprietors, and thus effectively although indirectly control the prices charged by them. . . .

So far as the requirement of due process is concerned, and in the absence of other constitutional restriction, a state is free to adopt whatever economic policy may reasonably be deemed to promote public welfare, and to enforce that policy by legislation adapted to its purpose. The courts are without authority either to declare such policy, or, when it is declared by the legislative arm, to override it. If the laws passed are seen to have a reasonable relation to a proper legislative purpose, and are neither arbitrary nor discriminatory, the requirements of due process are satisfied, and judicial determination to that effect renders a court functus officia. "Whether the free operation of the normal laws of competition is a wise and wholesome rule for trade and commerce is an economic question which this court need not consider or determine." *Northern Securities Co. v. United States,* 193 U.S. 197, 337, 338, 24 S.Ct. 436, 457, 48 L.Ed. 679. And it is equally clear that if the legislative policy be to curb unrestrained and harmful competition by measures which are not arbitrary or discriminatory it does not lie with the courts to determine that the rule is unwise. With the wisdom of the policy adopted, with the adequacy or practicability of the law enacted to forward it, the courts are both incompetent and unauthorized to deal. The course of decision in this court exhibits a firm adherence to these principles. Times without number we have said that the Legislature is primarily the judge of the necessity of such an enactment, that every possible presumption is in favor of its validity, and that though the court may hold views inconsistent with the wisdom of the law, it may not be annulled unless palpably in excess of legislative power.

The lawmaking bodies have in the past endeavored to promote free competition by laws aimed at trusts and monopolies. The consequent interference with private property and freedom of contract has not availed with the courts to set these enactments aside as denying due process. Where the public interest was deemed to require the fixing of minimum prices, that expedient has been sustained. If the lawmaking body within its sphere of government concludes that the conditions or practices in an industry make unrestricted competition an inadequate safeguard of the consumer's interests, produce waste harmful to the public, threaten ultimately to cut off the supply of a commodity needed by the public, or portend the destruction of the industry itself, appropriate statutes passed in an honest effort to correct the threatened consequences may not be set aside because the regulation adopted fixed prices reasonably deemed by the Legislature to be fair to those engaged in the industry and to the consuming public. And this especially so where, as here, the economic maladjustment is one of price, which threatens harm to the producer at one end of the series and the consumer at the other. The Constitution does not secure to any one liberty to conduct his business in such fashion as to inflict injury upon the public at large, or upon any substantial group of the people. Price control, like any other form of regulation, is unconstitutional only if arbitrary, discriminatory, or demonstrably irrelevant to the policy the Legislature is free to adopt, and hence an unnecessary and unwarranted interference with individual liberty.

Tested by these considerations we find no basis in the due process clause of the Fourteenth Amendment for condemning the provisions of the Agriculture and Markets Law here drawn into question.

That freedom for master and servant to contract as they please is not a fundamental absolute right but subject, under the proper circumstances, to legislative control, was recognized as early as 1905 by Mr. Justice Holmes, in his famous dissenting opinion in the case of *Lochner v. New York:*[23]

[23] Lochner v. New York, 198 U.S. 45 (1905).

This case is decided upon an economic theory which a large part of the country does not entertain. If it were a question whether I agreed with that theory, I should desire to study it further and long before making up my mind. But I do not conceive that to be my duty, because I strongly believe that my agreement or disagreement has nothing to do with the right of a majority to embody their opinions in law. It is settled by various decisions of this court that state Constitutions and state laws may regulate life in many ways which we as legislators might think as injudicious, or if you like as tyrannical as this, and which, equally with this, interfere with the liberty to contract. Sunday laws and usury laws are ancient examples. A more modern one is the prohibition of lotteries. The liberty of the citizen to do as he likes so long as he does not interfere with the liberty of others to do the same, which has been a shibboleth for some well-known writers, is interfered with by school laws, by the post-office, by every state or municipal institution which takes his money for purposes thought desirable, whether he likes it or not.

The fourteenth amendment does not enact Mr. Herbert Spencer's Social Statics. The other day we sustained the Massachusetts vaccination law. *Jacobson v. Massachusetts,* 197 U.S. 11, 25 S.Ct. 358, 49 L.Ed. 643, 3 Ann.Cas. 765. United States and state statutes and decisions cutting down the liberty to contract by way of combination are familiar to this court. *Northern Securities Co. v. United States,* 193 U.S. 197, 24 S.Ct. 436, 48 L.Ed. 679. Two years ago we upheld the prohibition of sales of stock on margins, or for future delivery, in the Constitution of California. *Otis v. Parker,* 187 U.S. 606, 23 S.Ct. 168, 47 L.Ed. 323. The decision sustaining an eight-hour law for miners is still recent. *Holden v. Hardy,* 169 U.S. 366, 18 S.Ct. 383, 42 L.Ed. 780. Some of these laws embody convictions or prejudices which judges are likely to share. Some may not. But a Constitution is not intended to embody a particular economic theory, whether of paternalism and the organic relation of the citizen to the state or of laissez-faire. It is made for people of fundamentally differing views, and the accident of our finding certain opinions natural and familiar, or novel, and even shocking, ought not to conclude our judgment upon the question whether statutes embodying them conflict with the Constitution of the United States.

General propositions do not decide concrete cases. The decision will depend on a judgment or intuition more subtle than any articulate major premise. But I think that the proposition just stated, if it is accepted, will carry us far toward the end. Every opinion tends to become a law. I think that the word "liberty," in the fourteenth amendment, is perverted when it is held to prevent the natural outcome of a dominant opinion, unless it can be said that a rational and fair man necessarily would admit that the statute proposed would infringe fundamental principles as they have been understood by the traditions of our people and our law. It does not need research to show that no such sweeping condemnation can be passed upon the statute before us. A reasonable man might think it a proper measure on the score of health. Men whom I certainly could not pronounce unreasonable would uphold it as a first instalment of a general regulation of the hours of work. Whether in the latter aspect it would be open to the charge of inequality I think it unnecessary to discuss.

The doctrine expressed in Mr. Justice Holmes's dissenting opinion was gradually adopted. That liberty of contract and the right to use one's property as one pleases, even though admitted to be fundamental rights, became amenable to social needs was illustrated in the state case of *Miami Laundry Co. et al. v. Florida Dry Cleaners & Laundry Board:*[24]

Liberty of contract and the right to use one's property as he wills are fundamental constitutional guarantees, but the degree of such guarantees must be determined in light of social and economic conditions that prevail at the time the guarantee is proposed to be exercised rather than at the time the constitution was approved securing it; otherwise, the power of the legislature becomes static and helpless to regulate and extend them to new conditions that constantly arise.

Thus, Justice Holmes's dissenting opinion finally became the law of the land. It is ably reviewed by Mr. Justice Frankfurter in the case of *American Federation of Labor v. American Sash and Door Company:*[25]

The coming of the machine age tended to despoil human personality. It turned men and woman into "hands." The industrial history of the early Nineteenth Century demonstrated the helplessness of the individual employee to achieve human dignity in a society so largely affected by technological advances. Hence the trade union made itself increasingly felt, not only as an indispensable weapon of self-defense on the part of workers but as an aid to the well-being of a society in which work is an expression of life and not merely the means of earning subsistence. But unionization encountered the shibboleths of a pre-machine age and these were reflected in juridical assumptions that survived the facts on which they were based. Adam Smith was treated as though his generalizations had been imparted to him on Sinai and not as a thinker who addressed himself to the elimination of restrictions which had become fetters upon initiative and enterprise in his day. Basic human rights expressed by the constitutional conception of "liberty" were equated with theories of laissez-faire. The result was that economic views of confined validity were treated by lawyers and judges as though the Framers had enshrined them in the Constitution. This misapplication of the notions of the classic economists and resulting disregard of the perduring reach of the Constitution led to Mr. Justice Holmes' famous protest in the Lochner case against measuring the Fourteenth Amendment by Mr. Herbert Spencer's Social Statics. 198 U.S. 45, 75. Had not Mr. Justice Holmes' awareness of the impermanence of legislation as against the permanence of the Constitution gradually prevailed, there might indeed have been "hardly any limit but the sky" to the embodiment of "our economic or moral beliefs" in that Amendment's "prohibitions." *Baldwin v. Missouri,* 281 U.S. 586, 595, 50 S.Ct. 436.

The attitude which regarded any legislative encroachment upon the existing economic order as infected with unconstitutionality led to disrespect for legislative attempts to strengthen the wage-earner's bargaining power. With that attitude as a premise, *Adair v. United States,* 208 U.S. 161, 28 S.Ct. 277, and *Coppage v. Kansas,* 236 U.S. 1, 35 S.Ct. 240, followed logically enough; not even *Truax v. Corrigan,* 257 U.S. 312, 42 S.Ct. 124, could be considered unexpected. But when the tide turned, it was not merely because circumstances

[24] (Fla.) 183 So. 759, 762 (1938).
[25] 335 U.S. 538, 542 (1949).

had changed and there had arisen a new order with new claims to divine origin. The opinion of Mr. Justice Brandeis in *Senn v. Tile Layers Union,* 301 U.S. 468, 57 S.Ct. 857, shows the current running strongly in the new direction—the direction not of social dogma but of increased deference to the legislative judgment. "Whether it was wise," he said, now speaking for the Court and not in dissent, "for the State to permit the unions to [picket] is a question of its public policy—not our concern." Id. at 481. Long before that, in *Duplex Printing Press Co. v. Deering,* 254 U.S. 443, 488, 41 S.Ct. 172, he had warned:

> All rights are derived from the purposes of the society in which they exist; above all rights rises duty to the community. The conditions developed in industry may be such that those engaged in it cannot continue their struggle without danger to the community. But it is not for judges to determine whether such conditions exist, nor is it their function to set the limits of permissible contest and to declare the duties which the new situation demands. This is the function of the legislature which, while limiting individual and group rights of aggression and defense, may substitute processes of justice for the more primitive method of trial by combat.

Even where the social undesirability of a law may be convincingly urged, invalidation of the law by a court debilitates popular democratic government. Most laws dealing with economic and social problems are matters of trial and error. That which before trial appears to be demonstrably bad may belie prophecy in actual operation. It may not prove good, but it may prove innocuous. But even if a law is found wanting on trial, it is better that its defects should be demonstrated and removed than that the law should be aborted by judicial fiat. Such an assertion of judicial power deflects responsibility from those on whom in a democratic society it ultimately rests—the people. . . .

But there is reason for judicial restraint in matters of policy deeper than the value of experiment: it is founded on a recognition of the gulf of difference between sustaining and nullifying legislation. This difference is theoretical in that the function of legislating is for legislatures who have also taken oaths to support the Constitution, while the function of courts, when legislation is challenged, is merely to make sure that the legislature has exercised an allowable judgment, and not to exercise their own judgment, whether a policy is within or without "the vague contours" of due process. . . .

Courts can fulfill their responsibility in a democratic society only to the extent that they succeed in shaping their judgments by rational standards, and rational standards are both impersonal and communicable. Matters of policy, however, are by definition matters which demand the resolution of conflicts of value, and the elements of conflicting values are largely imponderable. Assessment of their competing worth involves differences of feeling; it is also an exercise in prophecy. Obviously the proper forum for mediating a clash of feelings and rendering a prophetic judgment is the body chosen for those purposes by the people. Its functions can be assumed by this Court only in disregard of the historic limits of the Constitution.

Judicial restraint and deference to legislative judgment enlarged the scope of police power, and ushered in a new concept of due process.

Mr. Justice Black, in *Lincoln Federal Labor Union v. Northwestern Iron & Metal Co.*,[26] speaking of due process of law, states:

This Court beginning at least as early as 1934, when the Nebbia case was decided, has steadily rejected the due process philosophy enunciated in the Adair-Coppage line of cases. In doing so it has consciously returned closer and closer to the earlier constitutional principle that states have power to legislate against what are found to be injurious practices in their internal commercial and business affairs, so long as their laws do not run afoul of some specific federal constitutional prohibition, or of some valid federal law. See *Nebbia v. New York*, 291 U.S. 502, 506 (1934) and *West Coast Hotel Co. v. Parrish*, 300 U.S. 379, 380 (1937). Under this constitutional doctrine the due process clause is no longer to be so broadly construed that the Congress and state legislatures are put in a strait jacket when they attempt to suppress business and industrial conditions which they regard as offensive to the public welfare.

Appellants now ask us to return, at least in part, to the due process philosophy that has been deliberately discarded. Claiming that the Federal Constitution itself affords protection for union members against discrimination, they nevertheless assert that the same Constitution forbids a state from providing the same protection for non-union members. Just as we have held that the due process clause erects no obstacle to block legislative protection of union members, we now hold that legislative protection can be afforded non-union workers.

Not only has state police power been enlarged under a new application of due process, but there has also developed a like power in the federal government. In the exercise of powers granted to it by the Constitution, the federal government also exercises powers that are concerned with the welfare, safety, health, and morals of the people.

In the exercise of its power to regulate and control commerce among the several states, Congress has not only power to protect interstate commerce, but authority to adopt measures "to promote its growth, insure its safety, foster, protect, control, restrain and remove burdens and obstructions at its source" which may interfere with its flow. The burdens and obstructions which interfere with its flow are concerned with the health and safety of labor, the welfare of the community, and the economy of the state. In sustaining the Federal Fair Labor Standards Act setting standards for hours and wages by excluding from interstate commerce goods manufactured in violation of the Act, Mr. Justice Stone, in *United States v. F. W. Darby Lumber Co.*,[27] comments:

There remains the question whether such restriction [shipment in interstate commerce of lumber manufactured by employees paid less than the minimum wage] on the production of goods for commerce is a permissible exercise of the commerce power. The power of Congress over interstate commerce is not con-

[26] 335 U.S. 526, 527 (1949).
[27] 312 U.S. 100, 105 (1941).

fined to the regulation of commerce among the states. It extends to those activities intrastate which so affect interstate commerce or the exercise of the power of Congress over it as to make regulation of them appropriate means to the attainment of a legitimate end, the exercise of the granted power of Congress to regulate interstate commerce.

Likewise, the Court has upheld statutes requiring inspection and treatment of diseased cattle in infected areas, the inspection and grading of tobacco, and the exclusion of convict-made goods and adulterated milk, to prevent shipment in interstate commerce.

The Sherman Act, the National Labor Relations Act, the Railway Labor Act, the Public Utilities Holding Company Act of 1935, the Agriculture Market Agreement Act of 1937, and the Agriculture Adjustment Act of 1938 (1941) are illustrations of the use of the commerce power to promote health, safety, and the welfare of the economy.

The enlargement of the scope of federal regulatory powers under the extension of the commerce clause covers nearly every aspect of business. National baseball has not yet come within the purview of federal regulation even though teams travel across state lines. Traveling is not the important thing; playing, which occurs intrastate, is. "That which in its consummation is not commerce does not become commerce among the states because the transportation that we have mentioned takes place." *Federal Baseball Club v. National League.*[28] However, for a different opinion that casts some doubt on the above, see *Gardella v. Chandler.*[29]

The above are examples of federal regulation of trade and business under the commerce clause. They illustrate the breadth of governmental intrusion into business activity. Such is a far cry from the judicial policy advocated by the United States Supreme Court in 1888, in the case of *Kidd v. Pearson.*[30] Mr. Justice Lamar, speaking for the Court, says:

> If it be held that the term [interstate commerce] includes the regulation of all such manufactures as are intended to be the subject of commercial transactions in the future, it is impossible to deny that it would also include all productive industries that contemplate the same thing. The result would be that Congress would be invested, to the exclusion of the states, with the power to regulate not only manufacturing, but also agriculture, horticulture, stock raising, domestic fisheries, mining—in short every branch of human industry.

In the exercise of the taxing power, Congress has exercised a police power to prevent misrepresentation and fraud in the sale of commodities. The Court, in the case of *McCray v. United States,*[31] sustained a federal statute imposing a tax of 10 cents per pound on all oleomargarine

[28] 259 U.S. 200 (1922).
[29] 172 F.2d 402 (1949).
[30] 128 U.S. 1, 21 (1888).
[31] 195 U.S. 27 (1904).

colored to resemble butter, and one-fourth of a cent on uncolored oleomargarine. Although the statute was a revenue measure, it operated as a police regulation to prevent the sale of an article that looked like butter.

Under its power to tax for the general welfare set out in Article 1, Sec. 8, Par. 1 of the Constitution, Congress enacted in 1935 the Social Security Act. It was assailed on the ground that the act permitted the federal government to invade the reserve powers of the states, and engage in a function limited to them. The constitutionality of the act was upheld in *Steward Machine Co. v. Davis.*[32] The court in its opinion found that:

> during the years 1929 to 1936, when the country was passing through a cyclical depression, the number of unemployed mounted to unprecedented heights. . . . The fact developed that the states were unable to give requisite relief and the problem had become national in area and dimension. . . . In the presence of this urgent need for some remedial expedient, the question is to be answered whether the expedient adopted has overleaped the bounds of power.

The court recognized "that every tax is in some measure regulatory" and imposes an economic burden on the activity taxed, and that even though general welfare may be a local burden, the Social Security Act "is an attempt to find a method by which all public agencies may work together for a common end." Said the court, "It is too late today for the argument to be heard with tolerance that in a crisis so extreme the use of moneys of the nation to relieve the unemployed and their dependents is a use for any other purpose narrower than the promotion of the general welfare."

In the second Social Security case, *Helvering v. Davis,*[33] the court upheld the tax provisions which sustain the Old Age and Survivors Insurance Benefits. The court broadly construed the power of Congress to tax for "the general welfare," saying that "the line must be drawn between one welfare and the other, between the particular and the general," and what that is, is to be decided by Congress and not by the court.

1-11. Control of business conduct by judicial intervention—Business tort. The businessman, in his competitive practice, is curbed by three forces: first, by his own moral concepts as influenced by the reaction of his business associates; second, by some positive law, legislative or otherwise, making particular conduct a crime and imposing penalties; and third, by his duty not to injure others in the conduct of his business, for fear of having to pay damages. We are concerned with the third sanction in this section. In addition to the duty imposed by the traditional law of

[32] 301 U.S. 548 (1935).
[33] 301 U.S. 619 (1937).

torts, this field of the law includes the duty not to inflict injury by unfair competitive practices. Not only is the tort defined by common law, but it is also a wrong, made so by legislation and administrative orders. Such torts are called business torts and are found within conduct labeled as unfair competition, disparagement, inducing breach of contract, and infringement on trademarks and trade names. (See Sec. 1-16 of Chapter 3, Book I.)

Competition. *Right to compete.* In general, the right to enter into a business as a competitor of others in the same field is not denied by our economic or political order. Even though the opening of a new enterprise will do serious harm to existing and established businesses, freedom of competition has not been denied. If insufficient demand exists to insure the economic life of all, the law sanctions the economic death of those unable to survive. The facts that old customers are enticed to a new business, that prospective sales dwindle, or that similar wares are offered at lower prices give no cause of action to the old entrepreneur against the new. "The right of a seller to lower his price in good faith to meet the equally low price of a competitor in a sale of goods of like grade and quality is, in reality, the right to compete."[34] Even though one has a sale almost consummated, a competitor, with knowledge of that fact, is at liberty to tempt the customer with a lower price on similar goods.

However, price discrimination that has for its purpose the elimination of competition is illegal. It may take either of two forms. It may be such as to eliminate competition on the level at which the seller is doing business, or it may be such as to aid the buyer to eliminate competition in his field. Price discrimination in either area that tends to restrict competition is illegal and subject to such penalties as the law provides. Illustrative of the first type is the producer who sells his product at a certain price in one area but cuts that price materially in another locality in an attempt to drive out competitors. It is permissible to discriminate in price to meet competition or to care for difference in transportation costs, but it is no longer proper to use price reductions to destroy a competitor.

It is likewise improper for a producer to offer attractive prices to one buyer in a given area and not to make those prices available to other dealers in the same territory. To give one retailer a material advantage over his competitors, thus making it possible for him to undersell them, tends to force the competitors out of the market. But the manufacturer or producer is allowed to make price concessions in certain instances. He may make different prices to different classes of customers. A jobber may obtain a lower price than a retailer, although the latter is willing to

[34] Balian Ice Cream Co. v. Arden Farms Co., page 85.

buy as much as the former. It is also proper to make quantity concessions to the large user, provided those concessions are also available to other customers who are willing to purchase in similar quantities. The producer must be in a position to justify the discrimination in price because of the difference in the cost of servicing the quantity user over the cost of supplying the occasional buyer. The question remains pertinent in all price discrimination cases: Has the reduced price a tendency to eliminate competition?

Competition for the primary purpose of injuring another without an intention to benefit himself is illegal.

If a person enters into a competing business for the express purpose of driving his competitor out of business and, having accomplished his purpose, intends to withdraw from the enterprise, he commits an actionable wrong.[35] It is also true that, if one conducts his business in such a manner as to embarrass or harass unduly a competitor without correspondingly promoting his own interests, he may be enjoined from indulging in such tactics. One who injures a competitor commits a wrong unless he can justify it as the lawful exercise of a right.

To these general principles the legislatures have from time to time added further exceptions in the case of public utilities. Those industries in which the public has a peculiar interest and which competition most seriously hampers by duplication of facilities and increased costs have been relieved of competition.

Retail price control. Attempts have often been made by producers to control the price at which their article is sold at the retail level. A contract between the producer and retailer to the effect that the article will not be sold for less than a certain price is illegal at common law. Such an agreement was thought to be contrary to public policy because it eliminated price as a factor in competition between the retailers selling identical products and, hence, robbed society of potentially lower prices. It was also inconsistent to say that title to the article sold passed to the retailer and at the same time permit the seller to have control of the article sold.

Although a contract containing a retail price-maintenance clause was illegal, manufacturers were able to control prices by selling only to those who maintained the advertised price, since the sellers were at liberty to select their own buyers. If a retailer was discovered cutting the retail price, the manufacturer, by refusing him the privilege of making further purchases, cut off his supply of commodities, thus exercising power to control the resale price. If, however, manufacturers by organization provided for a scheme that caused all price cutters to be reported to a central

[35] Tuttle v. Buck, page 89.

office and maintained a list of such retailers, such organization was an illegal combination and subject to criminal prosecution.

It is alleged that price cutting has an injurious effect upon the public as well as upon the good will achieved by the manufacturer's product; thus, the states have passed what are generally called *fair-trade* or *price-maintenance* statutes, which protect the distributors and the public against the unfair trade practice of price cutting in the distribution of articles of standard quality having a trade-mark, patent, or name. The acts have for their purposes the regulation of such unfair competition as price cutting and the elimination of price wars. The remedy authorized by these statutes to protect sellers creates a cause of action in tort for unfair competition. Damages or injunctive relief is given against buyers who sell commodities at a price less than that stipulated between the vendor and the vendee.

These fair-trade laws usually provide as follows:

No contract relating to the sale or resale of a commodity that bears, or the label or content of which bears, the trade-mark, brand, or name of the producer or owner of such commodity, and that is in fair and open competition with commodities of the same general class produced by others, shall be deemed in violation of any law of the state by reason of any of the following provisions which may be contained in such contract:

1. That the buyer will not re-sell such commodity except at the price stipulated by the vendor.

2. That the producer or vendee of a commodity requires upon the sale of such commodity to another, that such purchaser agree that he will not, in turn, re-sell except at the price stipulated by such producer or vendee. Such provisions in any contract shall be deemed to contain or imply conditions that such commodity may be re-sold without reference to such agreement in the following cases:

a. In closing out the owner's stock for the purpose of discontinuing delivery of any such commodity: provided, however, that such stock is first offered to the manufacturer of such stock at the original invoice price, at least ten (10) days before such stock shall be offered for sale to the public.

b. When the goods are damaged or deteriorated in quality, and notice is given to the public thereof.

c. By an officer acting under the orders of any court.

Also, most fair-trade laws prohibit "wilfully and knowingly advertising, offering for sale or selling any commodity at less than the prices stipulated in any contract entered into pursuant to the provisions of the act whether the person so advertising, offering for sale or selling is or is *not a party to such contract.*" This so-called "nonsignor" clause adopted in most state price-fixing acts binds persons who are not parties to the contract to control resale prices. Thus, a distributor and one or more retailers may conspire or agree to combine to fix a minimum price; they may by such agreement impose the minimum price fixed upon other retailers in the trade even though such retailers are not parties to the contract.

State fair-trade laws which impose a duty upon "nonsignors" to comply with resale price maintenance agreements on trade-marked goods in interstate trade were held in the case of *Schwegmann Brothers et al. v. Calvert Distillers Corporation,* 1951, 341 U.S. 384[36] to be illegal, in violation of the Sherman Anti-Trust Act, and not within the protective provisions of the Miller-Tydings Act. The Miller-Tydings Act, it was held, does not by its provisions make legal price control contracts against persons who have not signed the agreement. In order to avoid the consequences of the Schwegmann case, Congress in 1952 passed what is known as the McGuire Act, which provides that unfair methods of competition in commerce, and unfair or deceptive acts or practices in commerce are unlawful, but that the anti-trust acts shall not render unlawful any contracts or agreements prescribing minimum or stipulated prices, or that require a vendee to enter into contracts prescribing minimum prices for resale of a commodity which bears the trade-mark, brand, or name of the producer or distributor of such commodity, provided such contracts are lawful as applied to intra-state transactions under the statutes of the state.

The purpose of the McGuire Act is to protect the rights of states under the Constitution to regulate their own affairs. It permits states to enact statutes that make legal the contracts prescribing minimum prices for the resale of commodities, and to extend the provisions of such contracts to cover persons who are not parties to such contracts.

This federal legislation has not solved the problem of price control maintenance. At common law and by statute, price-fixing contracts are deemed monopolistic and in restraint of trade. However, under the McGuire Act and state legislation (the fair-trade act), "contracts or agreements" between distributors and one or more retailers to fix prices are legal. These contracts are not regarded as monopolistic schemes of price-fixing. Such contracts are designated as *vertical* price maintenance agreements, that is, "between producers or manufacturers of a particular commodity and those handling the product, in a straight line down to and including the retailer." Such contracts are to be distinguished from what is termed "horizontal agreements." These are "cross agreements between competitors or between the same class of persons, such as manufacturers, producers, wholesalers or concerns in competition with each other with

[36] Schwegmann Brothers et al. v. Calvert Distillers Corporation, page 90.

like commodities." These agreements are monopolistic, restrain trade, and reduce competition.

"Vertical price-fixing maintenance contracts," resting on the voluntary consent of the parties, were made exempt from federal anti-trust laws, and valid under state statutes, for the purpose of stimulating "fair and open competition with commodities of the same class." Whether this result has been attained is doubtful. Price-fixing by contract in order to stimulate competition presupposes there are sufficient manufacturers and dealers to make competition a reality. Such, however, has not been the case. With the control of trade-marked specialty articles in the hands of a few large corporations, price-fixing agreements limit rather than stimulate competition. (See Sec. 1-7 of Chapter 2, Book I, "Big Corporations.")

Also, the effectiveness of the fair-trade acts to stimulate competition and regulate prices has been limited because that portion of the McGuire Act which requires nonsigners to be bound by prices agreed upon between the vendor, manufacturer, distributors, and retailer has met with constitutional objections. In 18 states the nonsigner clause has been held unconstitutional.[37] In 17 states the courts have held the nonsigner clause constitutional.[38]

The reasons given for holding the nonsigner statute invalid are:

(1) The statute is an illegal restriction upon the right of contract and disposition of one's own property. Without any purport to declare the business clothed or affected with a public interest, it destroys the property right of retailers to fix the prices at which they will sell their goods. (2) it stigmatizes as unfair an act that is untainted by deceit, oppression or unfair dealing and involves no assault upon the good will of the manufacturer. (3) It ignores the motivating purpose of the retailer, which may be merely to shave his margin of profit or otherwise and compels the consuming public to pay tribute to a retailer who, as an alert and efficient merchant, does not want to charge the fixed prices, the effect of which goes well beyond what has been called "predatory price cutting." (4) It grants special privileges and is an attempt to delegate power to fix prices, a power which the Legislature itself does not have in general, and this is done without laying down any standard or yardstick to be used. (5) It tends to establish a monopoly as it is in restraint of fair trade rather than in promotion of it. (6) It offends constitutional guaranties of a right of personal liberty and private property and allows a citizen to be deprived of his property without due process of law. (7) The right to contract or not contract is a property right protected by constitutional demand of due process of law. (8) It constitutes an unlawful exercise of the police power because the imposition upon a nonsigner to a price fixing contract bears no reasonable relationship to public health, safety, morals or the general welfare.[39]

[37] General Electric Co. v. American Buyers Cooperative, page 93.
[38] General Electric Co. v. Telco Supply, page 96.
[39] General Electric Co. v. American Buyers Cooperative, supra.

Some of the reasons given in support of the constitutionality of the nonsigner clause are:

(1) The primary object of the statute is to prevent willful assaults upon the manufacturer's good will. (2) The enactment is within the police power of the state to promote the general welfare and does not offend due process or equal protection provisions of the constitutions nor impair freedom of contract. (3) A nonsigner dealer, by virtue of voluntarily deciding to buy and sell the commodity on which a minimum price is fixed by a contract with other parties, elects to be bound by the contract. (4) It is not monopolistic in effect and does not offend constitutional provisions condemning monopolies, for it automatically ceases to operate where there is no competition with commodities of the same general class produced by others. (5) It does not delegate legislative power or power to fix a resale price on another's property so as to violate due process.[40]

Threats or intimidation. Injury to one's business resulting from threats to customers or intimidation of prospective purchasers is recoverable in damages. If the threats are made by one in good faith who thinks they are legally sound, no tort has been committed, but an injunction will be issued restraining such conduct in the future. Thus, if the owner of a patent honestly believes that another is infringing on his patent, he may threaten potential purchasers with a lawsuit in case they purchase. Should a court later determine that no infringement existed, the party who threatened the buyers is not liable for damages. His threat was made in good faith for the purpose of protecting his own interest.

Disparagement. One who disparages or belittles the goods of another may be enjoined from future misconduct, and in certain instances may be compelled to pay damages to the injured party. There appear to be four distinct elements of disparagement:

1. An express or implied misstatement of fact—as distinguished from words of comparison which indicate merely an opinion. Such expressions as "good" or "bad," "better" or "best" are in effect opinions.

2. The statement must concern the injured party's goods. Merely misrepresenting favorably one's own goods never constitutes disparagement. Some misstatement must be made about goods offered for sale by another.

3. The motive that prompts the statement must be bad. In other words, the statements must be made for the deliberate purpose of injuring the other party.

4. The injured party must allege and show special—as distinct from general—damages. That is, he must be able to prove loss of specific sales as a result of the statements. A general allegation and demonstration that business had declined a certain amount would not be enough.

[40] General Electric Co. v. American Buyers Cooperative, supra.

All four elements must be present in order to recover damages. A showing of the first two elements, however, will entitle one to an injunction against a repetition of such statements.

Disparagement is a business tort that has arisen out of the tort of libel and slander. The defamatory statements concerning the goods may also impute dishonesty, fraud, and questionable business methods to the owner of the goods. If such is the case, then a "libel per se" has been committed. A libellous statement concerning goods alone is called trade libel, and as such is not a "libel per se." In the case of trade libel, special damages must be alleged and proven.[41] Disparagement is recognized as a method of unfair competition which entitles the injured person to a remedy through the Federal Trade Commission or relief in the courts.

Inducing breach of contract. To induce one person to breach his contract with another is to commit a tort. The effect is the same even though the one who induced the breach did so in order to sell his own goods or services.

Mere passive presentation of the merits of one's products which has the net result of causing one to breach a contract and to purchase the goods of another is not actionable. It is only where one is active in persuading another to violate one agreement in order to be free to make another that a tort is committed.

Closely akin to inducing breach of contract are those cases involving boycotts. In general it can be said that an agreement to boycott a certain individual or group of individuals is legal only as long as it is in furtherance of some justifiable objective. Thus, an agreement by retail coal dealers whereby no purchaser may purchase on credit so long as he owes another dealer is legal, because of the protection such an agreement accords all parties to it.

APPROPRIATION OF COMPETITOR'S TRADE VALUES

Trade dress or wrapper. Wrappers and trade dress used to make merchandise more attractive and convenient to display do not of themselves have an exclusive trade value. No one has an exclusive right to the use of color combinations and package methods. Wrappers and color designs to be protected must be so distinctive as to entitle them to registration under the copyright or trade-mark law. However, if a distinctive wrapper

[41] Rosenberg v. J. C. Penney Co., et al., page 98.

or color design accompanying a distinctive name has by usage acquired a secondary meaning by becoming so identified with the goods that it distinguishes them from others and identifies the origin of the goods, the owner has an exclusive right to their use, and others may be enjoined from the use of the wrapper as an act of unfair competition.

Trade-mark or name. Technically a trade-mark is supposed to be some mark or stamp imprinted upon the product, whereas a name does not have to be attached to the product. So far as the legal rights of the owner are involved, there is practically no difference between the two.

The first user of a trade-mark or name has a right to its exclusive use. The second user of such a mark or name, or of one which is deceptively similar, may be enjoined from its further use. Just how similar the mark, name, or trade dress must appear before relief will be granted presents an interesting problem. In general, it can be said that, whenever the casual observer, as distinct from the careful buyer, tends to be misled into purchasing the wrong article, an injunction is available to the injured party.

Descriptive, geographical, and proper names. A name or mark which is descriptive of the nature of the article sold may not be exclusively appropriated by any one concern. Such terms as "Always Closed" for revolving doors and "Rubberoid" for roofing fall in the descriptive class and may be used by anyone. However, if the words used are so fanciful and remote from a description of the subject matter, such as "floating power" for engine mountings and "stronghold" for ribbed nails, it is appropriate for trade-mark use.

Geographical or place names indicating a specific origin cannot be technical trade-marks. Such words are in the public domain. Every manufacturer or producer has a right to indicate upon his product or article where it is produced. The same is true in the case of proper names. Every individual has a right to make use of his name in connection with his business. Any good will or favorable reputation that attaches to it should not be denied to him. Consequently, one generally cannot exclusively appropriate another's proper name.

The three rules indicated above are subject to one well-recognized exception. If a descriptive, geographical, or proper name has been used so long as to become identified with a certain product, thus having a secondary meaning, the first user will be protected in its use on the principles of unfair competition. Newcomers in the field who desire to use a descriptive term, a geographical location of their plant, or their names in identifying their products will have to qualify the use in such a manner as to avoid possible injury to the first user's good will. The latest cases indicate that such names cannot be identified as the name of the product by the second user, but that the maker's name or location may be placed on the product in some inconspicuous manner. Thus, it is clear that no one by the name of Ford could manufacture an automobile and call it Ford, although the name Ford could undoubtedly be used by the manufacturer in his business.

Limited protection only. An important question in the use of trade-marks and names is: In what territory will the first user be protected in their use? In reply to this question, two rules can definitely be indicated, while a third has aroused considerable conflict in those states which have passed on the problem.

1. If two parties in different localities and at different times innocently create and use the same name or mark, each user will be protected in that territory which he first penetrated with the name or mark. The first user cannot deny the second user the benefit of the good will which the latter has innocently built up. Each will be protected in the territory which he has pre-empted by prior use.

2. A second user, although innocent, will not be protected in territory where the first user has conducted any business, regardless of how slight or trifling those business transactions are.

3. If the first user's good will has penetrated into new territory, but no business has been transacted there, a second user may adopt the name or mark and intentionally profit by the good will which the first user has built up. However, a second user will be guilty of unfair competition if he adopts and uses the name, trade-mark, or design with knowledge that it has acquired a secondary meaning elsewhere, and that the first user intends to invade the territory and expand his business.[42]

The only merit in registering a trade-mark or name is that a presumption immediately arises that the party registering the mark or name is the first user. This presumption can be rebutted by another's proof of prior use. The first user is always protected regardless of registration.

A trade-mark or name is protected only against infringement on articles of the same class. A first user cannot enjoin a second user from use of a mark or name on an article of an entirely different character. Three tests have been applied by the courts in determining whether articles are of the same class.

1. Are the articles so similar that one can be substituted for the other, as cocoa or chocolate?

2. Are the articles allied products, or are they used together, such as automobiles and automobile tires?

[42] Triangle Publications, Inc. v. Central Pub. Co., Inc., page 100.

3. An association of ideas test: Does one article call the other to mind? Are they usually associated together in retail establishments? Hats and shoes offer an illustration of this group.

Through the adoption of these tests the courts attempt to prevent the confusion of goods by consumers, attempt to make possible the expansion of a line to include new articles similar in nature, and attempt to protect the good will of a business concern from the assault of a predatory competitor or one attempting to profit from the efforts of another.

Effect of wrongful use of name or mark. A second user who makes an improper use of a trade-mark, name, or wrapper can always be enjoined from using it in the future. In addition, if the user is an intentional wrongdoer—if he intentionally profits from the use of another's good will—the injured party may recover damages or the profits of the wrongdoer. In some courts, including the federal courts, the first user may recover both profits and damages. It should be borne in mind, however, that damages or profits can be recovered only in case of intentional wrongdoing. If the second user copies the mark or name exactly or so nearly as to indicate bad faith, damages or profits are recoverable. If the second user has no knowledge of the first user's name or mark, an injunction is the only remedy available in most of the states.

Federal registration. The first user of a trade-mark, which is used in interstate commerce, may have it registered with the federal government, and after it has been registered and used for a period of five years without protest on the part of another user, it then becomes conclusively presumed that the registered user was the first in point of time to make use of the mark. The marks are registered for use with the specific types of merchandise indicated in the application for registration. Descriptive and geographical names which have been used in business for at least one year may receive a limited amount of protection by registering the name with the government. Registration continues for a period of twenty years unless the user or his assignee has abandoned the use of the mark or it has been canceled. Procedure is also made available for having the registration renewed for an additional twenty years.

Trade information and advertising. Information about one's trade, customers, processes, or manufacture is confidential in nature. If a competitor can discover this information fairly through research, study, or observation, he may use it freely in the absence of a patent or a copyright. However, if he obtains such information by bribery of an employee of the first concern or by engaging an employee of the first concern with the understanding that he will use this information, the second party may be enjoined from making use of it.

In this connection it should be emphasized that an idea once exposed to the public may thereafter be used by anyone. The forward march of civilization is dependent upon the freedom with which new ideas are adopted. A book or magazine article containing new ideas may be copyrighted, but the ideas set forth therein may be used by anyone so long as the language used is not published by another. One who unfolds to an interested party a plan for financing his product or for merging several industries may discover later that the interested party has made use of these ideas without compensating the originator of them. To forestall such a possibility, the originator of the idea should, before explaining his idea, obtain a promise of payment in case his plan is adopted.

BUSINESS TORTS CASES

BALIAN ICE CREAM CO. v. ARDEN FARMS CO.

1952, 104 F. Supp. 796

YANKWICH, C. J. Before me are fifteen actions brought by various plaintiffs, ice cream manufacturers, against a group of defendants. Originally the complaints were directed against certain corporate and individual defendants,—who were the officers and directors of the corporations. At the conclusion of the plaintiff's case, the court dismissed the cases as to the individual defendants. The cases then proceeded against nine corporation defendants, all of which are wholly-owned subsidiaries of Arden Farms Co., a corporation. The litigation has been the subject of two prior opinions by the writer. In these opinions, the chief facts underlaying the cases are given. The proof at the trial narrowed the issue to one single act of the defendants on which the claims under the various federal and state statutes were based,—namely, the drastic reduction by the defendants of the wholesale price of ice cream in the Los Angeles area on November 21, 1949.

The reduction was to $1.06 per gallon for the wholesale base price of "Flavor Fresh" ice cream from $1.44 per gallon. The reduction did not apply to other states in which it was alleged these products were sold, such as Arizona, Oregon, Washington, Idaho and Montana. Other monopolistic practices were alleged in the complaint in this and the other cases,—such as misuse of patented products, unlawful discounts and the like. They need not concern us, as the entire case was built around the price reduction. On it, in the cause in which this opinion is written, were based seven claims or causes of action.

The first is based on § 1 of the Sherman Anti-Trust Act, and alleges that the defendants combined to monopolize trade by selling and distributing ice cream in the Los Angeles area at reduced prices for the purpose of eliminating competition.

A second cause of action under § 2 of the Sherman Act charges an attempt to monopolize trade and inter-state commerce by selling ice cream in Los Angeles at prices lower than sold in places in the adjoining states already mentioned.

A third cause of action restates the same facts as a violation of § 3 of the Clayton Act by exclusive requirement agreements aimed at lessening competition.

Another course of action is grounded on § 1 of the Robinson-Patman Price Discrimination Act. It alleges discrimination in price between customers in the Los Angeles area and those in the localities above mentioned. Another cause of action is under § 3 of the Robinson-Patman Price Discrimination Act and charges the sale of ice cream at unreasonably low prices.

A final cause of action is based on the California Cartwright Act. It charges a combination (a) to create and carry out restrictions in trade and commerce (b) to reduce the price of ice cream, and (c) to prevent competition in ice cream and kindred products.

Damages are asked in the present case in the sum of $72,934.35 with demand to treble the amount as to the causes of action arising under the Sherman, Clayton and Robinson-Patman Acts and to double it under the State Act.

These actions are unique in that they concern acts not between a group of corporations which are strangers to one another but acts of a parent corporation and its subsidiaries wholly owned and controlled by it. They are maintainable only because the Supreme Court in some very recent cases has held that a corporation dealing with its subsidiaries may be guilty of violations of the anti-trust statutes.

The philosophy behind the Anti-Trust Laws has been discussed in detail by the writer in the prior opinions in these cases. Their aim is: "To suppress combinations to restrain competition and attempts to monopolize by individuals and corporations."

In this manner they seek to maintain the freedom of commerce between the States.

. . . Price discrimination is also condemned by § 1 of the Robinson-Patman Act, except when made in good faith to meet a competitor's law prices, as provided in § 2 (b) of the Act. Any sales made at unreasonably low prices are distinctly forbidden by § 3 of the Robinson-Patman Act, when made for the purpose of destroying competition or eliminating a competitor. As stated in one of the prior opinions, two conditions must concur before prices may be condemned under this section of the Act: (a) the prices must be found to be unreasonably low, and (b) they must be found to have been established with the design and purpose to destroy competition.

The California Cartwright Act specifically prohibits restrictions in trade and commerce.

. . . the problem, in the last analysis, reduces itself to what I stated it to be toward the conclusion of the argument; was the price reduction justified by business and economic considerations of the type which would govern reasonable persons, confronted with diminishing sales in an endeavor to keep their customers or gain others?

The answer to this question requires us to consider the problem of competition and what it entails. When we do this, we must bear in mind that the aim of all anti-trust statutes, from their very inception, and the aim of the state statutes which have followed them, was to prevent monopoly by fostering competition. Too often, at the present time, especially in actions instituted by individuals to recover treble damages, the contrary aim of the various state "Fair Trade" Acts is attempted to be injected into anti-trust litigation. It has no place there. For, as a recent writer has stated, the object of the States and of some of the Federal Regulatory Commissions, such as the Federal Trade Commission, seems to be to establish a "soft" competition,—a competition that does not hurt much.

> . . . In any competitive economy we cannot avoid injury to some of the competitors. The law does not, and under the free enterprise system it cannot, guarantee businessmen against loss. That businessmen lose money or even go bankrupt does not necessarily mean that competition has been injured . . . We cannot guarantee competitors against all injury. This can only be accomplished by prohibiting competition.

It is of the essence of competition that it must, of necessity injure others. For, as a three-judge court once wrote:

> Competition is, in its very essence, a contest for trade.

In such contest, differences in (a) the quality of goods offered, and (b) their prices are accepted means of competition. Reputable concerns constantly advertise, "We will not be knowingly undersold." And no case exists in which the courts have held that a price reduction, in itself, not having as its purpose the destruction of a competitor or the monopolization of trade or commerce, but made to meet competition in the field or to retain trade or custom or to gain new custom, is illegal as such.

. . . The right of a seller to lower his price in good faith to meet the equally low price of a competitor in the sale of goods of like grade and quality, is in reality, the right to compete. For to deny a seller the right to meet his competitor's lower price to his customer is in effect to deny him the right to compete with that competitor.

. . . The heart of our national economic policy long has been faith in the value of competition.

. . . It is enough to say that Congress did not seek by the Robinson-Patman Act either to abolish competition or so radically to curtail it that a seller would have no substantial right of self-defense against a price raid by a competitor. For example, if a large customer requests his seller to meet a temptingly lower price offered to him by one of his seller's competitors, the seller may well find it essential, as a matter of business survival, to meet that price rather than to lose the customer.

. . . When a business concern is confronted with a set of economic conditions prevailing in a market, and, after long and mature consideration, decides upon a policy of price reduction, which, in its effect, was not so drastic as some of its competitors had offered in particular instances, should it be penalized because it decided to solve the problem by giving to all its customers the benefit of prices which its competitors had given to special customers only?

The answer is obvious. In an industry shot through with favoritism, euphemistically called "inducements," is a concern compelled to participate in the freezing of a partial discrimination when it affects its entire business under penalty of damages? There is no principle of law or policy that requires the Court to make itself the instrument of so grave an injustice. To repeat,—the object of the anti-trust law is to encourage competition. Lawful price differentiation is a legitimate means for achieving the result. It becomes illegal only when it is tainted by the purpose of unreasonably restraining trade or commerce or attempting to destroy competition or a competitor, thus substantially lessening competition, or when it is so unreasonable as to be condemned as a means of competition. The price reduction here has none of these stigmata. And if the tests of reasonableness, which the writer laid down in one of the prior opinions, be applied, it is apparent that the price reduction here was (a) long in contemplation; (b) it bore a realistic relation to previous changes by others in the field, either in the locality or elsewhere; (c) it corresponded to factors relating to cost of production and demand for the article and to continuous shrinkage of Arden's custom,—all of which, after long and mature consideration, called for the reduction. These are legitimate criteria for legal price reduction.

. . . If the plaintiffs suffered any injury, it is that which flows naturally and irrevocably from competition. This is not actionable under any of the Federal and State statutes involved.

Judgment will, therefore, be for the defendants.

TUTTLE v. BUCK
1909, 107 Minn. 145, 119 N.W. 946

Action by Edward C. Tuttle against Cassius M. Buck.

For more than 10 years last past he has been and still is a barber by trade, and engaged in business as such in the village of Howard Lake, Minn., owning and operating a shop. The defendant is possessed of large means, and is a banker in the village of Howard Lake and is nowise interested in the occupation of a barber. For the sole purpose of injuring the trade of the plaintiff and of accomplishing his threats of ruining the plaintiff's business and driving him out, the defendant fitted up and furnished a barber shop in said village for conducting the trade of barbering. Failing to induce any barber to occupy said shop on his own account, the defendant has hired a barber to occupy said shop, and to serve so many of plaintiff's patrons as said defendant has been or may be able to direct from plaintiff's shop.

Elliott, J. . . . To divert to one's self the customers of a business rival by the offer of goods at lower prices is in general a legitimate mode of serving one's own interest, and justifiable as fair competition. But when a man starts an opposition place of business, not for the sake of profit to himself, but regardless of loss to himself, and for the sole purpose of driving his competitor out of business, and with the intention of himself retiring upon the accomplishment of his malevolent purpose, he is guilty of a wanton wrong and an actionable tort. In such a case he would not be exercising his legal right, or doing an act which can be judged separately from the motive which actuated him. To call such conduct competition is a perversion of terms. It is simply the application of force without legal justification, which in its moral quality may be no better than highway robbery.

Nevertheless, in the opinion of the writer this complaint is insufficient. It is not claimed that it states a cause of action for slander. No question of conspiracy or combination is involved. Stripped of the adjectives and the statement that what was done was for the sole purpose of injuring the plaintiff, and not for the purpose of serving a legitimate purpose of the defendant, the complaint states facts which in themselves amount only to an ordinary everyday business transaction. There is no allegation that the defendant was intentionally running the business at a financial loss to himself, or that after driving the plaintiff out of business the defendant closed up or intended to close up his shop. From all that appears from the complaint he may have opened the barber shop, energetically sought business from his acquaintances and the customers of the plaintiff, and as a result of his enterprise and command of capital obtained it, with the result that the plaintiff, from want of capital, acquaintance, or enterprise, was unable to stand the competition and was thus driven out of business. The facts thus alleged do not in my opinion, in themselves, without reference to the way in which they are characterized by the pleader, tend to show a malicious and wanton wrong to the plaintiff.

A majority of the Justices, however, are of the opinion that on the principle declared in the foregoing opinion, the complaint states a cause of action.

Judgment for plaintiff affirmed.

SCHWEGMANN BROTHERS et al. v. CALVERT DISTILLERS CORPORATION

1951, 341 U.S. 384

MR. JUSTICE DOUGLAS delivered the opinion of the Court.

Respondents, Maryland and Delaware corporations, are distributors of gin and whisky. They sell their products to wholesalers in Louisiana, who in turn sell to retailers. Respondents have a price-fixing scheme whereby they try to maintain uniform retail prices for their products. They endeavor to make retailers sign price-fixing contracts under which the buyers promise to sell at not less than the prices stated in respondents' schedules. They have indeed succeeded in getting over one hundred Louisiana retailers to sign these agreements. Petitioner, a retailer in New Orleans, refused to agree to the price-fixing scheme and sold respondents' products at a cut-rate price. Respondents thereupon brought this suit in the District Court by reason of diversity of citizenship to enjoin petitioner from selling the products at less than the minimum prices fixed by their schedules.

It is clear from our decisions under the Sherman Act (July 2, 1890, 26 Stat. 209, ch. 647) that this interstate marketing arrangement would be illegal, that it would be enjoined, that it would draw civil and criminal penalties, and that no court would enforce it. Fixing minimum prices, like other types of price fixing, is illegal per se. *United States v. Socony-Vacuum Oil Co.*, 310 U.S. 150, 84 L.Ed. 1129, 60 S.Ct. 811; *Kiefer-Stewart Co. v. Joseph E. Seagram & Sons, Inc.*, 340 U.S. 211, ante, 186, 71 S.Ct. 259. Resale price maintenance was indeed struck down in *Dr. Miles*

Medical Co. v. John D. Park & Sons Co., 220 U.S. 373, 55 L.Ed. 502, 31 S.Ct. 376. The fact that a state authorizes the price fixing does not, of course, give immunity to the scheme, absent approval by Congress.

Respondents, however, seek to find legality for this marketing arrangement in the Miller-Tydings Act enacted in 1937 as an amendment to par. 1 of the Sherman Act. (Aug. 17, 1937) 50 Stat. 673, 693, ch. 690, 15 USC par. 1. That amendment provides in material part that "nothing herein contained shall render illegal, contracts or agreements prescribing minimum prices for the resale" of specified commodities when "contracts or agreements of that description are lawful as applied to intrastate transactions" under local law.

Louisiana has such a law. La. Gen. Stat. par 9809. 1 et seq. It permits a "contract" for the sale or resale of a commodity to provide that the buyer will not resell "except at the price stipulated by (the) vendor." The Louisiana statute goes further. It not only allows a distributor and retailer to make a "contract" fixing the resale price, but once there is a price-fixing "contract" known to a seller, with any retailer in the state, it also condemns as unfair competition a sale at less than the price stipulated even though the seller is not a party to the "contract." In other words, the Louisiana statute enforces price fixing not only against parties to a "contract" but also against non-signers. So far as Louisiana law is concerned, price fixing can be enforced against all retailers once any single retailer agrees with a distributor on the resale price. And the argument is that the Miller-Tydings Act permits the same range of price fixing. . . .

The argument at first blush has appeal. But we think it offends the statutory scheme.

We note to begin with that there are critical differences between Louisiana's law and the Miller-Tydings Act. The latter exempts only "contracts or agreements prescribing minimum prices for the resale." On the other hand, the Louisiana law sanctions the fixing of maximum as well as minimum prices, for it exempts any provision that the buyer will not resell "at the price stipulated by the vendor." We start then with a federal act which does not, as respondents suggest, turn over to the states the handling of the whole problem of resale price maintenance on this type of commodity. What is granted is a limited immunity—a limitation that is further emphasized by the inclusion in the state law and the exclusion from the federal law of the nonsignor provision. The omission of the nonsignor provision from the federal law is fatal to respondents' position unless we are to perform a distinct legislative function by reading into the Act a provision that we meticulously omitted from it.

A refusal to read the nonsigner provision into the Miller-Tydings Act makes sense if we are to take the words of the statute in their normal and customary meaning. The Act sanctions only "contracts or agreements." If a distributor and one or more retailers want to agree, combine, or conspire to fix a minimum price, they can do so if state law permits. Their contract, combination, or conspiracy—hitherto illegal—is made lawful. They can fix minimum prices pursuant to their contract or agreement with impunity. When they seek, however, to impose price fixing on persons who have not contracted or agreed to the scheme, the situation is vastly different. That is not price fixing by contract or agreement; that is price fixing by compulsion. That is not following the path of consensual agreement; that is resort to coercion.

Much argument is made to import into the contracts which respondents make with retailers a provision that the parties may force nonsigners into line. It is said that state law attaches that condition to every such contract and that therefore the Miller-Tydings Act exempts it from the Sherman Act. Such a condition, if implied, creates an agreement respecting not sales made under the contract, but other sales. Yet all that are exempted by the Miller-Tydings Act are "contracts or agreements prescribing minimum prices for the resale" of the articles purchased, not "contracts or agreements" respecting the practices of noncontracting competitors of the contracting retailers.

It should be noted in this connection that the Miller-Tydings Act expressly continues the prohibitions of the Sherman Act again "horizontal" price fixing by those in competition with each other at the same functional level. Therefore, when a state compels retailers to follow a parallel price policy, it demands private conduct which the Sherman Act forbids. See *Parker v. Brown*, 317 U.S. 341, 350, 87 L.Ed. 315, 325, 63 S.Ct. 307. Elimination of price competition at the retail level may, of course, lawfully result if a distributor successfully negotiates individual "vertical" agreements with all his retailers. But when retailers are forced to abandon price competition, they are driven into a compact in violation of the spirit of the proviso which forbids "horizontal" price fixing. A real sanction can be given the prohibitions of the proviso only if the price maintenance power granted a distributor is limited to voluntary engagements. Otherwise, the exception swallows the proviso and destroys its practical effectiveness.

The contrary conclusion would have a vast and devastating effect on Sherman Act policies. If it were adopted, once a distributor executed a contract with a single retailer setting the minimum resale price for a commodity in the state, all other retailers could be forced into line. Had Congress desired to eliminate the consensual element from the arrangement and to permit blanketing a state with resale price fixing if only one retailer wanted it, we feel that different measures would have been adopted—either a nonsigner provision would have been included or resale price fixing would have been authorized without more. Certainly the words used connote a voluntary scheme. Contracts or agreements convey the idea of a cooperative arrangement, not a program whereby recalcitrants are dragged in by the heels and compelled to submit to price fixing . . .

Reversed. Plaintiffs denied injunctive relief against defendant Schwegmann Brothers selling plaintiffs' product at cut-rate price.

GENERAL ELECTRIC COMPANY v. AMERICAN BUYERS COOPERATIVE
(Ky. 1958) 316 S.W.2d 354, 358

STANLEY, Commissioner. The appeal brings before us the constitutionality of the statute which regulates the resale price of commodities, generally called the Fair Trade Act. The trial court held the first section of the act constitutional and the second section of the act (nonsigner provision) unconstitutional. The validity of the entire act was debated on appeal.

. . . The General Electric Company brought this suit against American Buyers Cooperative, Inc. to enjoin it from doing what is charged to be in violation of the statute and to recover damages therefor. The court sustained the defendant's motion for a summary judgment on the ground of unconstitutionality of the second section of the statute, KRS 365.090 and dismissed the complaint.

General Electric Company (hereinafter GE), as is well known, manufactures small electric household utilities and appliances that are trademarked and bear the brand "General (GE) Electric." The articles are sold by GE to franchised wholesale distributors who in turn sell them to retail dealers. The appliances are in fair and open competition in Louisville and elsewhere throughout the country with commodities of the same general class produced and sold by others. GE has expended large sums of money in the development of its appliances of a high quality and in promoting and advertising them and its trade-mark.

. . . GE has entered into agreement with many retail dealers in Louisville and elsewhere in Kentucky, which agreements provide that GE appliances shall not be advertised, offered for sale or sold by the dealer at less than the minimum retail resale prices stipulated by GE.

. . . The defendant, now appellee, American Buyers Cooperative, Inc. (hereinafter ABC), is engaged in the general business of selling merchandise, including electric appliances, at retail in Louisville, Kentucky. ABC has never signed a Fair Trade Agreement with GE and occupies the position of a nonsigner. GE notified ABC on several occasions of the existence of its Fair Trade Agreements in effect in Kentucky and of the minimum retail prices stipulated pursuant to such agreements. ABC received such notices and thereafter sold GE appliances at less than the minimum retail prices so stipulated.

. . . A significant feature of the present statute is that it is confined to products bearing a trade-mark, brand or name. The enactment of such statutes and the decisions upholding them rest in a large measure upon the concept that good will of the owners of the trade-mark, brand or name continues to adhere to the commodity until it reaches the ultimate consumer and that the owner is entitled to protect its good will by controlling the price of the product.

Beyond that concept, particularly with respect to the section relating to persons who are parties to such contracts, the courts have upheld the law as having a constitutional objective that is within the police power of a state in order to preserve the general welfare of the people and as not delegating legislative power or depriving a person of his property without due process of law.

. . . We are not concerned with the economic and social philosophy of such laws or the wisdom of the legislation. We are concerned only with the question of whether it is within the power of the Legislature under the Kentucky constitution to enact a statute which sanctions the fixing of minimum retail prices as described. The question is divisible. One part relates to the approval of an express contract made with a retailer directly or indirectly. The other relates to a retailer who is not a party to such a contract. The right to judicial relief from violation of such a contract and such a prohibition is, of course, implicit in the legal question.

First section. This part of the statute declares that a contract of the kind described shall not be deemed to be in violation of any law of this state. It is apparent, therefore, that the premise of the statute is that such a contract might or would otherwise be monopolistic, or an illegal restraint of trade. Section 198, Kentucky Constitution, imposes the duty upon the General Assembly to enact such laws as it deems necessary to prevent trusts and other combinations formed "to depreciate below its real value any article, or to enhance the cost of any article above its real value." This constitutional provision is not self-executing. The General Assembly is left to its discretion to determine the need for legislation upon the subject. Various statutes dealing with trade practices are embraced in Chapter 365 of the Kentucky Revised Statutes.

. . . We agree that these contracts are not to be regarded as a monopolistic scheme of price fixing. The economists and the courts recognize a difference between what are termed "horizontal" and "vertical" price maintenance agreements. The former are cross-agreements between competitors or between the same class of persons, such as producers and wholesalers, or persons or concerns in competition with each other with like commodities. The latter are agreements between a producer or manufacturer of a particular commodity and those handling the product, in a straight line down to and including the retailer. The present scheme is regarded as "vertical" price fixing. In *Commonwealth v. Grinstead,* 111 Ky. 203, 63 S.W. 427, 56 L.R.A. 709, we held that a contract of this character was not within the purview of the Kentucky anti-monopoly statute (since repealed). However, the Congress seems to have regarded it necessary to enact the Miller-Tydings Act in 1937 and declare that nothing contained in the Sherman Anti-Trust Act, 15 U.S.C.A. 1, should render illegal vertical agreements which prescribe minimum prices for the resale of trade-marked commodities when contracts or agreements of that description are lawful as applied to intrastate transactions under local law.

. . . Our Bill of Rights declares as one of "the great and essential principles of liberty and free government" and as "inherent and inalienable * * * the right of acquiring and protecting property." This is free enterprise. Our economic system is founded upon competition—"the life of trade." It is an established principle that the constitutional guaranty of the right of property protects it not only from confiscation by legislative edicts and from the physical taking for public or private use, but also (subject to reasonable regulation based upon some reasonable ground for the public good) from any unjustifiable impairment or abridgement of this right, such as depriving the owner of any of its essential attributes or such as restricts or interrupts its common, necessary or profitable use. The right of the owner to fix the price at which his property shall be sold is an inherent attribute of the property itself.

Supplemental to this property right provision is sec. 2 of the Constitution which forbids the exercise of arbitrary power of government over the "property of free men."

This statute, we think, is a legislative invasion of the broad constitutional liberty of the people to acquire and protect their property and engage in free trade.

. . . Although the action authorized by the statute sounds in tort, it rests upon the legislative fiat that a nonsigner by force of law is bound by a contract of strangers. It would destroy the fundamental principle that the obligation of a contract is, in general, limited to the parties making it and cannot be imposed upon one not a party or in privity with a party or who has not in some legal way assented to the contract. One cannot be held liable for the breach of a contract of other parties merely because he knows of its existence. See *Johnson v. Coleman,* Ky., 288 S.W.2d 348.

While the term "freedom of contract" does not appear in the federal or state constitutions, it is always embraced in the meaning of "liberty" as employed in those instruments, and is safeguarded by the constitutional guaranty of "pursuit of happiness," so one has the right to refuse to accept a contract or to assume such liability as may be proposed. [See Sec. 1-9, Chapter 2, Book I, on "Constitutional Protection of Laissez-Faire and Liberty of Contract—Due Process."]

Our conclusion is that the second section of the Act, that is KRS 365.090, is unconstitutional and the judgment to that effect is affirmed. We hold, as did the circuit court, that the first section of the statute, that is KRS 365.080, is constitutional.

The judgment is affirmed.

GENERAL ELECTRIC COMPANY v. TELCO SUPPLY
(1958) 84 Ariz. 132, 325 P.2d 394

PHELPS, J. This is an appeal from a judgment of the trial court declaring unconstitutional the Arizona Fair Trade Act of 1936, being A.R.S. 44–1421 to 44–1424 inclusive.

The facts are that General Electric Company, a corporation, hereinafter designated as plaintiff, brought an action against Telco Supply, Inc., a corporation, hereinafter designated as defendant, seeking to enjoin it from selling commodities produced by plaintiff at prices less than those stipulated in contracts plaintiff had with other Arizona retail dealers which plaintiff claimed was in violation of the Arizona Fair Trade Act. Plaintiff had contracts with a number of retail merchants in Arizona who handled its products fixing a minimum price at which such products bearing its trade-mark or brand name, "General (GE) Electric," were permitted to be sold. Defendant is a "nonsigner" or in other words, it had not entered into such an agreement with plaintiff.

Defendant raised in its pleadings the constitutionality of the Fair Trade Act and specifically alleged that said act violates numerous provisions of the federal and state constitutions as hereinafter enumerated.

On appeal plaintiff has assigned but one error: that the court erred in awarding defendant judgment based upon the ground that the Fair Trade Act is unconstitutional. . . .

The legislatures of forty-five states have adopted fair trade acts which differ but slightly from their Arizona counterpart, and the courts of some thirty odd states are almost equally divided on the question of their constitutionality. . . .

It is first urged that the act violates the provisions of art. 14, sec. 15 of the Arizona Constitution which provides that:

> Monopolies and trusts shall never be allowed in this State and no incorporated company, co-partnership or association of persons in this State shall directly or indirectly combine or make any contract . . . to fix the prices, limit the production, or regulate the transportation of any product or commodity. . . .

An exclusive privilege or right is indispensable to the existence of a monopoly. Its primary characteristic is to stifle competition so as to give to a person, association, corporation or combination thereof the control over prices of the commodity sought to be monopolized . . . the act here involved cannot possibly be construed as creating a monopoly. It not only does not stifle or prohibit competition, but expressly provides that the act cannot become operative unless the commodity involved is in free and open competition with commodities of the same general class produced by others. The classification of the commodities affected are perfectly legitimate and have a reasonable relation to the object of the legislation. The act clearly is designed to protect the brand, name or trade-mark of a producer. It is in no sense of the word a price fixing law. . . .

With respect to the right of the legislature to declare the economic policy of the state reasonably deemed to promote the general welfare and the lack of power of the courts to interfere therewith, we said in *State of Arizona v. Walgreen Drug Co.,* 57 Ariz. 308, 113 P.2d 650, in considering the constitutionality of the Unfair Sales Act of this state, that we approved language used in *Nebbia v. People of State of New York,* 291 U.S. 502, at page 537, 54 S.Ct. 505, at page 516, 78 L.Ed. 940, which reads as follows:

> . . . [A] state is free to adopt whatever economic policy may reasonably be deemed to promote public welfare, and to enforce that policy by legislation adapted to its purpose. The courts are without authority either to declare such policy, or, when it is declared by the legislature, to override it. . . . With the wisdom of the policy adopted, with the adequacy or practicability of the law enacted to forward it, the courts are both incompetent and unauthorized to deal.

In *General Electric Co. v. Klein,* Del., 106 A.2d 206, 211, in discussing the constitutionality of the non-signer clause of the Delaware Fair Trade Act, the court said:

> . . . The question before us is not the wisdom of this legislation; it is whether the situation presents a reasonable necessity for the protection of the public welfare, and whether the means bear a reasonable relation to the end sought. . . . And if these questions are fairly debatable, the legislative judgment must control. . . .

The McGuire Amendment to the Sherman Anti-Trust Act expressly provides that the enforcement of the fair trade acts of the states as it relates to nonsigners shall not constitute an unlawful burden or restraint upon or interference with commerce. There is no conflict between the Arizona Fair Trade Act and any federal law. Therefore, there is no aspect of the supremacy of laws involved in this case.

Furthermore, we are not impressed with the argument that because the Arizona Fair Trade Act came into existence during the depression of the 1930's it is now invalid. It is a sufficient answer to observe that the act was re-enacted in 1956 in the Arizona Revised Statutes. Its enactment was and is a proper exercise of the police power of the state in the establishment of a public policy relating to the economy and public welfare of the state. Whether the nation is in the midst of a depression or an era of prosperity, the principle involved is the same.

We therefore hold that the Arizona Fair Trade Act, A.R.S. Sec. 44–1421 to 44–1424 inclusive, is constitutional.

Judgment of the trial court is reversed and remanded with directions to render judgment not inconsistent with this decision.

ROSENBERG et al. v. J. C. PENNEY CO. et al.

1939, 30 Cal. App. 609, 86 P.2d 696

Libel action by Rosenberg against J. C. Penney Co. and others. A judgment for $25,000.00 was entered against the defendant J. C. Penney Co. and the defendant appealed.

Rosenberg and J. C. Penney operated similar stores on opposite sides of the street, and were competing for the sale of "gym pants" to the local high school. J. C. Penney Co. placed in its store window samples of "gym pants," those offered for sale by the plaintiff and those offered for sale by J. C. Penney Co. This display consisted of placards comparing the garments. The placards attached to the samples offered for sale by the plaintiffs stated: "Rosenbergs garments are poorly made seconds or prison made merchandise. Seams crooked. Slovenly made. Long loose stitches. Notice the shoddy appearance, the wrinkled waist and hems of the garment." On a board at the right of the display of the plaintiff's goods, the defendant stated concerning its "gym pants": "Note the fine workmanship, fullness of cut, etc. We think it no more than fair that the Shoddy Garments of Rosenberg & Bush be replaced free of charge by them, and that they make good their loud and vociferous boast of selling only first grade merchandise."

These placards remained in the window of J. C. Penney Company during all of the day of September 27th.

PULLEN, J. . . . It is next contended that the window display was not libelous per se. Section 45 of the Civil Code defines a libel as follows: "Libel is a false and unprivileged publication by writing, printing, picture, effigy, or other fixed representation to the eye, which exposes any person to hatred, contempt, ridicule, or obloquy, or which causes him to be shunned or avoided, or which has a tendency to injure him in his occupation."

. . . Ir. determining whether or not there is a libel per se [the Court] must place itself in the position of a reader under the circumstances of the publication.

In examining the placards together and separately, in the light of the foregoing authorities, the trial court was correct in its conclusion that such published matter must be accepted as libelous per se.

We are unable to reproduce in this opinion photographs in evidence, which are before us in the brief of respondents. In this exhibit, however, on one side is shown garments taken from the stock of Rosenberg & Bush. On the other side of the window is a garment on sale by the J. C. Penney Company, and affixed to these garments were descriptive legends endeavoring to make invidious comparisons with plaintiffs' goods. Appellants argued that these placards amounted to mere legitimate criticism of a competitor's stock, and did not therefore constitute libel. However, from an examination of the legends hereinbefore set forth, the public would naturally infer from such inspection that the firm of Rosenberg & Bush was selling as first grade merchandise, garments which were shoddy, poorly made seconds, and prison made merchandise, which was being offered to the public as first grade merchandise. It is also charged that these garments sold by Rosenberg & Bush as first grade merchandise were so defective and contained so much starch and filler that they lost 25 per cent of weight after laundering, and that its customers had been defrauded by purchasing as preshrunk garments, those which were not preshrunk, and that the seams were crooked; that they had long stitches and were slovenly made; and that they were offered for sale despite the loud and vociferous boast of Rosenberg & Bush that they were selling only first grade merchandise. From the foregoing it is clearly apparent that Rosenberg & Bush were accused of fraud and deception and unfair dealing with their customers. Charges of this nature are libelous per se.

. . . There are two classes of statements concerning the goods of a competitor, first, where the statement is made with reference to goods or products, but there is also included libelous words concerning the seller, which impute to him, in connection with the sale of such goods, fraud, dishonesty, or questionable business methods; and, secondly, statements that go no further than to criticize the goods of a competitor, which criticism is based upon or appeals to a personal taste or preference of the buyer, but contains no imputation against the honesty or integrity of the merchant in the sale of the goods.

It is the claim of appellant that the window display in question falls under the second class and was merely legitimate competition.

. . . It needs but a reading of the placards to show that appellants went far beyond this legitimate comparison.

. . . *Judgment of $25,000 against defendant will be reduced to $5,000.00 compensatory damages and $5,000 for exemplary damages.*

TRIANGLE PUBLICATIONS, INC. v. CENTRAL PUB. CO., INC.

1954, 117 F. Supp. 824

REEVES, CIRCUIT JUDGE. This controversy arises from a business that originated early in the development of television and has endeavored to expand (in the wake of television development) a business that, in a way, accompanied the advance of television development, and it then sought to utilize the opportunities attending the development of television in Kansas City and its environs.

The plaintiff and its predecessors or constituents within the last two or three years in most eastern cities began the issuance of magazines designed to serve the public in connection with approaching or coming television displays or programs. As the number of television channels increased in the Midwest, it followed such increases and supplied its service and helpful magazines to the public. And for that purpose it expended large sums of money to promote and advertise its service magazines.

As a preliminary, in the year 1953, it caused its magazines prominently designated as TV Guide to be sold and distributed in the Kansas City area. Toward the end of that year it definitely planned and definitely arranged to open a place of business in Kansas City and to issue and distribute its localized magazine giving to the public advance television programs.

The cover of its magazine displayed in prominent and conspicuous lettering or insignia "TV Guide."

On the other hand, the defendant (incorporated late in 1951) had been issuing in Kansas City a magazine which conspicuously advertised or displayed on its front cover the design or insignia "TV Preview." It furnished to the public locally, substantially the same information the plaintiff had furnished elsewhere and which it was planning to supply in the Kansas City area with a cover magazine containing the letters and word "TV Guide."

That the plaintiff in the very nature and course of business would expand and did expand into Kansas City was anticipated by the defendant.

. . . On December 4, 1953, after the plaintiff had leased property and had made its definite arrangement to open offices in Kansas City, defendant issued its magazine containing conspicuously on its front cover the insignia or designation "TV Guide." This was done after it was known that the plaintiff had entered the Kansas City area.

. . . This suit was filed on December 21, 1953, and a preliminary restraining order was issued without notice.

. . . The controversy does not involve an infringement of a trademark, It is not contended that such exists but the contention is that the defendant is unfairly competing with the plaintiff. The sole and only question is whether plaintiff had acquired a secondary meaning in the use of the descriptive words "TV Guide."

. . . The plaintiff relies upon the rule that a trade-name, as in this case, may acquire a secondary meaning. This is a familiar doctrine. A secondary meaning identifies the product with the proprietor in the minds of the public.

However, a second user will be guilty of unfair competition if he adopts the name, mark or design with knowledge that it has acquired a secondary meaning elsewhere and that the first user intends to invade the territory and expand his business.

The fact that a trade mark or trade name may have acquired a secondary meaning in one locality does not mean that it has acquired such meaning in an entirely different trade area where the public is unfamiliar with such name or mark.

It should be stated here that, as announced above, the public, through advance information and otherwise of plaintiff's magazine, had become familiar with the name employed by the plaintiff.

. . . The rule announced by the Supreme Court of the United States in *Hanover Star Milling Co. v. Metcalf,* 240 U.S. 403, loc. cit. 415 and 419, 36 S.Ct. 357, 361, 60 L.Ed. 713, followed the common law:

> But where two parties independently are employing the same mark upon goods of the same class, but in separate markets wholly remote the one from the other, the question of prior appropriation is legally insignificant; unless, at least, it appear that the second adopter has selected the mark with some design inimical to the interests of the first user, such as to take the benefit of the reputation of his goods, to forestall the extension of his trade, or the like.

. . . It is unnecessary to multiply authorities. Quite clearly the defendant was advised and understood that the plaintiff was extending its operations into the Kansas City area. In fact, plaintiff's magazine had already been introduced in Kansas City and its area and the defendant was apprised of that fact. It knew, moreover, not only of the expanding business of the plaintiff, but that it was on the moment of extending its operations into Kansas City, and after it had actually established headquarters in Kansas City, the defendant, for the first time, issued a magazine clearly imitative of the name and mark used by the plaintiff on the cover of its magazines. The defendant abandoned an equally descriptive and significant mark, "TV Preview" and adopted that of the plaintiff.

Under all of the authorities this was unfair competition even though the plaintiff had not fully entered the area.

It follows that the plaintiff is entitled to a temporary injunction.

Review Questions and Problems

1. The meaning of "due process of law" in the Fourteenth Amendment is now fundamentally different from that in 1905. Illustrate by appropriate cases how this difference came about.
2. "Under our form of government where the written constitution, by its own terms is the supreme law, some agency of necessity must have the power to say the final word as to the validity of a statute assailed as unconstitutional. The constitution makes it clear that the power has been entrusted to the court. . . . But to say that the words of the constitution mean today what they did not mean when written—that is, that they do not apply to a situation now to which they applied then—is to rob that instrument of the essential element which continues it in force as the people have made it. . . ." Discuss the above statement from the standpoint of legal philosophy and economics.
3. During a national emergency the legislature of state *A* passed an act which authorized the district courts of the counties to extend the period of redemption from foreclosure sales, "for such additional time as the court may deem just and equitable." How can this legislation be harmonized with the obligations of contract and due process clauses of the Fourteenth Amendment? *Home Building & Loan Assn. v. Blaisdell,* 290 U.S. 398 (1934).
4. An independent contractor enters into a contract to clean windows and do janitor work for a manufacturer who produces articles, part of which are shipped in interstate commerce. The window-washing contractor's employees are employed under conditions less than the minimum required by the Fair Labor Standards Act. A suit is brought to enjoin the contractor from violating the act. Decide the case. *Tobin v. Johnson,* 198 F.2d 130 (1952).
5. "Price control is one of the means available to the states and Congress in their respective domains for the protection and promotion of the welfare of the economy." It is important to determine what commodity is subject to price controls. Who determines whether its production and distribution affect the health, safety, and welfare of the people? *Sunshine Anthracite Coal Co. v. Adkins,* 310 U.S. 381 (1940).
6. "It has never been supposed, since the adoption of the Constitution, that the business of the butcher, the baker, the tailor, the woodchopper, the mining operator, or the miner was clothed with such public interest that the price of his conduct or his wages could be fixed by state regulation." Justify this statement by an economic theory.

7. "The state has power to prevent the individual from making certain kinds of contracts, and in regard to them the Federal Constitution offers no protection." May a state in the exercise of its police power prohibit gambling contracts, contracts for the sale of narcotics, tobacco, fireworks, oleomargarine, birth-control devices, obscene literature, and contracts which include waiver of the warranty for fitness, use and purpose of commodities offered for sale?
8. "Declaring such statutes unconstitutional under the due process clause of the Fourteenth Amendment, these decisions elevated liberty of contract to the status of fundamental property rights . . . and formulated the then-prevailing philosophy of social Darwinism." What does the statement "under the philosophy of social Darwinism" mean?
9. The words "due process" cannot be defined with exactness. It is certain that these words imply a conformity with natural and inherent principles of justice. To what authority is left the task of determining what are "natural and inherent principles of justice"?
10. "The United States is as much bound by its contracts as are individuals." If this statement is true, upon what theory could Congress abrogate the gold clause in all of the government's obligations? *Perry v. United States*, 294 U.S. 330 (1935).
11. "Our pluralistic system has three main organized elements, the state, the corporation, and the Union." Discuss what effect these three elements have upon the operation of the free enterprise system.
12. What similarity may be found between mercantilism and modern capitalism?
13. The steam engine accelerated the Industrial Revolution. Discuss the effect of automation on the present economic system.
14. Sunbeam Corporation, a manufacturer, entered into a contract with its wholesalers, which had for its purpose the control of resale prices. Under the contract the wholesalers promised not to sell Sunbeam commodities below certain stipulated prices and to refrain from selling commodities to retailers who refused to sign price maintenance contracts. *X* induces these wholesalers who signed contracts with Sunbeam, to sell Sunbeam commodities below the stipulated price to non-signer retailers. Has *X* breached any duty? Has he committed a tort?
15. *A*, the only grocer in Centerville, quarrelled with *B*. *B* rented a building and made plans to enter the grocery business in the same community. Under what conditions, if any, will *A* be able to enjoin *B*?
16. *X* Co. was engaged in selling farm wagons in a certain state when *Y* Co. entered the state with a competitive make. *X* Co. instructed a representative to follow the sales agent of *Y* Co. and to harass or threaten until the sales agent left the territory. What recourse, if any, has *Y* Co.?
17. *A*, the owner of a certain make of car, is asked by *F*, a friend, how he likes the car. *A* replies that it has a very weak transmission. Assuming that the statement is untrue, will the manufacturer or retailer of the car have an action against *A*?
18. *A* used a "Good Housekeeping" certification seal to indicate approval of certain consumer items and a guarantee. Can *B* later use as a trademark on items of an identical nature, "Good Housekeeper"?

19. W. Parker desires to manufacture fountain pens and to give the pens of his manufacture his name. Assuming there is at present a pen by that name, has he a right to do so?
20. Elgin Watch Co., located at Elgin, Illinois, manufactures watches, giving them the name of Elgin. Will a competitor be able to apply that name to its watches if they are made in Elgin?
21. *X* Co. sells dresses under the trade name of "Sweet Sixteen." He has been engaged in the business for many years in the eastern and middle western states. *Y* Co., with knowledge of the good will attached, proposes to sell dresses under the same name in Washington, Oregon, and California. May *Y* Co. be enjoined at the request of *X* Co.?
22. Yale Lock Co. manufactures locks of all kinds under the name "Yale." *X* Co. desires to manufacture bricks and sell them under the same name. Should it be able to do so?
23. *X* Co. manufactures Stetson hats. *Y* Co. desires to manufacture and sell Stetson shoes. Should it be permitted to do so?
24. The Mahogany Association objected to the use by *X* of the term Philippine Mahogany to wood which *X* imports. The association published to *X*'s customers that *X*'s product was "an inferior wood and not comparable to mahogany, that it would not stand up, is a counterfeit, a substitute and a fraud." May *X* enjoin the use of similar statements in the future and recover damages for disparagement of goods?
25. *A* sells his restaurant together with good will to *B*. Six months later *A* opens a competing restaurant across the street. There was no covenant in the contract that *A* would not open another restaurant. May *B* enjoin *A*? If there was a promise by *A* not to compete for 3 years, may *B* enjoin *A*? May *A* use his own name in the business four years later?

3

Formal Sources of the Law

1-12. Historical background. As stated in Section 1-2, it is not possible to give a simple definition of law or tell exactly from whence it came. Law does not just happen. It does not spring into existence in full form. Law in its beginning was associated with religion. Its source was in God or gods. The earliest code appearing over four thousand years ago in Babylon was handed down by the City God. Likewise, a thousand years later the Hebrew God gave the Ten Commandments to Moses. In Rome the priests were the givers of law, its custodians and adjudicators of its application. Law also developed out of custom and is said to be man made in compliance with the Law of Nature.

These indirect or "informal sources" furnished the law which later became formalized into statutes and court decisions. As society became more complex, man found it necessary to make or write his law—this was done by legislative bodies. Such formal law is called *written law.* Law developed by the courts, or judge-made law, is formal law although called "unwritten" in order to distinguish it from statutory law. Unwritten law in this sense is called *common law.* The term is also used, probably in its largest sense, to distinguish between the English system of law and the systems of law developed in other sections of the world.

The sources of the American common law are found, for the most part, in the English law. The American colonists were governed by charters granted by the king of England. These charters were general in their nature and left much to be worked out by the people of the colonies. Since most of the colonists were of English origin, they naturally were controlled by the customs of their mother country. In Louisiana, and to some extent in Texas and California, the Civil law or the Roman law is the basis of the legal system, because these states were founded by French and Spanish peoples. The law of Continental Europe is based more directly upon the Roman law.

1-13. Formal sources of the law. The court, by its decision, lays down a principle based upon custom or convenience and thus creates a precedent that will be controlling in similar future controversies. The reports of such controversies are published in books known as "reported cases." Legislative bodies enact statutes and the body of law thus formulated is called statutory law. Another source of law is the rulings and decisions of administrative boards and commissions.

Written or statutory law. The Constitution of the United States and the constitutions of the various states are the fundamental written law. Article VI of the Constitution of the United States provides: "This Constitution and the laws of the United States which shall be made in pursuance thereof; and all treaties made, or which shall be made under the authority of the United States, shall be the supreme law of the land; and the judges in every state shall be bound thereby, anything in the Constitution or laws of any state to the contrary notwithstanding." All other law must conform to, or be in harmony with, these constitutions. The constitutions define and limit the powers of government for the purpose of giving protection to the individual who lives under government, and for whose benefit government is formed. Each state has its own constitution which is the fundamental written law of the state. Legislative enactments by Congress, by the various state legislatures, by cities and towns, and by other smaller governmental units must conform to the constitutions and find in them their authority, either expressed or implied.

The doctrine of the supremacy of the Constitution was established at an early date in our country's history in the celebrated case of *Marbury v. Madison.*[1] Chief Justice Marshall stated: "Certainly, all those who have framed written constitutions contemplated them as forming the fundamental and paramount law of the nation, and consequently, the theory of every such government must be, that an act of the legislature, repugnant to the constitution, is void. This theory is essentially attached to a written constitution and is, consequently, to be considered by this court, as one of the fundamental principles of our society."

Many of the cases in Chapter 2 deal with the constitutionality of statutes. It was there noted that in more recent times the courts have upheld the constitutionality of many regulatory statutes and the power of the states to legislate against practices felt to be injurious in their commercial and business affairs.

The statutes which are enacted by legislative bodies comprise the largest source of written law. Such statutes cover a wide range of subject matter. Many of these statutes directly affect business and commercial transactions. Each state has its own statutes and as a consequence the statutory law is not uniform among the states. While many legislative enactments relate to specific problems of a particular state, there are others which are of a more general application. In the field of business law it is particularly desirable that the laws of the various states be the same.

[1] 1 Cranch 137, 2 L.Ed. 60 (1803).

Uniform legislation. A great portion of the written law—state legislation—which affects or concerns business had its inception with the National Conference of Commissioners on Uniform State Laws. The National Conference of Commissioners on Uniform State Laws is made up of commissioners appointed by the governors of the states. This national body has for its purpose: "(1) The promotion of the uniformity in state laws on all subjects where uniformity is deemed desirable and practicable; (2) to draft model acts on (a) subjects suitable for interstate compacts, and (b) subjects in which uniformity will make more effective the exercise of state powers and promote interstate cooperation; and (3) to promote uniformity of judicial decisions throughout the United States." Subjects approved for consideration by the commissioners are referred to special committees with instructions to prepare and report a draft of acts. Expert draftsmen are employed to assist in drafting acts. Tentative drafts are submitted yearly to the conference for discussion, criticism, and correction. When approved by the National Conference, the Uniform Acts are recommended to the state legislatures for adoption. The National Conference within the last sixty years has drafted and approved one hundred and fourteen acts. Some of the more important acts are: The Uniform Negotiable Instruments Act; The Uniform Partnership Act; The Uniform Sales Act; The Uniform Warehouse Receipts Act, with amendments; The Uniform Limited Partnership Act; The Uniform Bills of Lading Act; The Uniform Principal and Income Act; The Uniform Stock Transfer Act; The Uniform Trust Receipts Act; The Insurers Liquidation Act; and the Uniform Act Governing Secured Creditors Dividends in Liquidation Proceedings. The above acts have been adopted by some or all the states.

The most significant recent development in the field of uniform state legislation is the *Uniform Commercial Code.* This was prepared under the auspices of the National Conference of Commissioners on Uniform State Laws in cooperation with the American Law Institute. It is the stated purpose of the Code to collect in one body the law that "deals with all the phases which may ordinarily arise in the handling of a commercial transaction from start to finish." "The concept of the present act is, that 'commercial transaction' is a single subject of the law notwithstanding its many facets."

The Uniform Acts become effective when adopted by the legislative body of a state. The statutes of each state must be examined to determine which particular Uniform Acts have become state law. Some of them have been adopted by a large number of states while others have been less widely adopted. The Uniform Commercial Code which received final approval in 1952 has currently been adopted in over twenty-five states.[2]

[2] See page viii following the preface for a listing of states which have adopted the Uniform Commercial Code.

The first state to enact it as law was Pennsylvania which adopted it in 1953. The legislative bodies of many other states are considering its adoption.

The role of the court in the field of statutory law is important. We have noted that when brought into question, the constitutionality of a statute is a matter for court determination. Also, the courts interpret the meaning of statutes, determine their application to specific situations, and handle matters relating to their enforcement. In the final analysis it is what the court says that a statute means that determines its effect.

The common law—stare decisis. While statutes are an increasingly important source of law in modern times, the common law is the primary source of law in this country.

Probably the most significant difference between the Civil law system and the common law system is that the former is based upon a codification of the law while in the latter, rules and principles of law are derived from cases decided by the courts. Thus the common law is comprised of those legal principles which are enunciated by the courts in the process of deciding controversies.

When a court of competent jurisdiction has decided a controversy and has in a written opinion set forth the rule or principle which was the basis for its decision, that rule or principle will be followed by the court in deciding subsequent cases. Likewise, subordinate courts in the same jurisdiction will be bound by the rule of law set forth in the decision. This reliance upon precedent is basic to the common law and has resulted in the development of a great body of law which is to be found in the reports of cases decided by the courts over the years. The doctrine whereby rules established in prior cases are regarded as binding precedents is called *stare decisis* which means "to stand by decisions and not to disturb what is settled."

This adherence to judicial precedents gives a degree of certainty and stability to the law which would otherwise be lacking. People enter into contracts and create property rights that are established in reliance upon principles of law established by the cases. As stated in *American Mortgage Co. of Scotland v. Hopper:*[3] "To overrule precedents which have become recognized rules of property and the basis of contract relations, unsettles titles, disturbs business transactions, and introduces an element of uncertainty into the administration of justice from which the public suffer great inconvenience."

However, the doctrine of *stare decisis* has not been applied in such a fashion as to render the law rigid and inflexible. If a court should find that the prior decision was "palpably wrong" it may overrule it and decline to follow the rule enunciated by that case. By the same token, if the court should find that a rule of law established by a prior decision is

[3] 64 Fed. 553.

no longer sound because of changing conditions, it would not consider the rule to be a binding precedent. This accommodation of the law to changing conditions is expressed in the case of *Carroll v. Local 269 International Brotherhood of Electrical Workers:*[4] "It is the peculiar genius and strength of the common law that no decision is *stare decisis* when it has lost its usefulness in our social evolution; it is distinguished, and if times have sufficiently changed, overruled. Judicial opinions do not always preserve the social status of another generation."

The balance between certainty of the law and flexibility of the law is expressed by the United States Supreme Court in the case of *Helvering v. Hallock.*[5] The Court states: "We recognize that *stare decisis* embodies an important social policy. It represents an element of continuity in law and is rooted in the psychologic need to satisfy reasonable expectations. But *stare decisis* is a principle of policy and not a mechanical formula of adherence to the latest decision, however recent and questionable, when such adherence involves collision with a prior doctrine more embracing in its scope, intrinsically sounder and verified by experience."

When judicial opinions unduly "preserve the social status of another generation" remedy by way of legislation is necessary. *Stare decisis* again functions in aiding the court in giving meaning to the corrective statute or passing upon its meaning.

Administrative law. An increasingly important source of law in recent times is that which is derived from rulings and decisions of administrative bodies. During the past fifty years there has been a noticeable increase in the use of administrative boards and commissions to perform quasi-judicial functions. The agencies, created by legislative enactment, are charged with the administration of laws that are general in character. Such laws demand interpretation when applied to specific situations and, as a consequence, numerous hearings are held to determine the rights and duties of various parties who may be protected by, or are subject to, their provisions. Based upon evidence submitted to the administrative unit, appropriate orders are issued. These orders have the effect of law and may be enforced in court, and in many instances, at the request of an aggrieved party, may be reviewed by the courts.

The rules of procedure for hearings before such administrative bodies are usually formulated by the administrative bodies themselves and are made available to those who may be interested in them. The hearings are often informal in character, but on the whole they follow the pattern set by the courts in hearing and weighing evidence, as well as in the initiation of the action. A hearing normally originates with the filing of a petition or complaint, and the interested parties are then notified that a

[4] 133 N.J.Eq. 144, 31 A.2d 223 (1943).
[5] 309 U.S. 106 (1940).

hearing will be held at a stated time, that the interested parties are given an opportunity to file pertinent documents in the interim, and that they will have an opportunity to present evidence at the time of hearing.

The board often appoints a person to conduct the hearing, listen to the evidence, submit his findings of the facts, and make his recommendations to the board regarding the disposition to be made in the case. The board studies the report and issues such orders as the law in the case appears to demand.

The rules of procedure differ among the various administrative agencies, and any interested party should obtain a copy of them before enlisting the aid of a particular board. It should be emphasized that the goal of such boards, including the utility commissions, labor boards, and trade commissions, is to see that a general law which controls a certain area of economic activity is complied with and the boards may adopt whatever reasonable procedure for hearings best accomplishes their objective.

Review Questions and Problems

1. What is the basic difference between common law and Civil law systems?
2. What different meanings are attached to the term *common law?*
3. Give illustrations of situations in which a court has declared a law to be unconstitutional.
4. Why would it be desirable to have uniformity of laws among the states in the field of commercial law?
5. Does the common law vary from one state to another?
6. What is the role of the court in connection with state or federal statutes?
7. Is a court absolutely bound to follow precedents established in earlier cases?
8. "The common law judges are dead but they rule us from their graves." What is the meaning of this old adage?
9. How do you account for the growth of administrative bodies in the last half-century?

4

Classification of the Law

1-14. Substantive and adjective law. It is possible to classify the law in many different ways. Many of these classifications are overlapping and interrelated. One of the basic differentiations is *substantive law* as opposed to *adjective* or *procedural law*. *Substantive law* is the substance of the law—the rules and principles which are applied by the courts in resolving conflicts. It has been defined as that part of the law which creates, defines, and limits rights as contrasted with that branch of the law which establishes the procedures whereby such rights are enforced and protected. Thus, as noted in Chapter 1, the rights which a person has in land are determined by the substantive rules of the law of property. If his rights in the land are invaded, the procedural law would prescribe the method for obtaining redress for such invasion.

Adjective law provides the legal machinery whereby substantive rules are given effect. Included in this category are procedures for instituting legal action and determining the issues to be decided at the trial of a case, the conduct of a trial, the appeal to a higher court, and the enforcement of judgments and decrees issued by the court. The material in Chapter 5 treats these legal procedures in more detail.

1-15. Private law. Anglo-American law may be divided into two main divisions—*private law* and *public law*. Private law is that body of law which pertains to the relationships between individuals in organized society. It may be separated into certain fields, such as contracts, agency, sales, negotiable instruments, business organizations, and others. The law in these areas and others pertaining to business law is fully treated in the main text material of this book. The balance of this section deals briefly with another field of private law which is less directly related to business, namely, the law of torts.

The law of torts. The law of contracts deals with the enforcement of rights and duties arising out of agreements created by the mutual assent of the parties. The law of crimes deals with the enforcement of duties imposed by the state. The law of torts deals with the enforcement of duties existing between individuals as members of society. A breach of such duties may be both a tort and a crime, for example, assault and battery, trespass, and nuisances. Each member of society is entitled to have certain interests protected. Some of these interests are: (1) Freedom from bodily harm or apprehension of bodily harm. Invasions of these interests are called assault, battery, and false imprisonment. (2) Freedom from injury to property. Invasions of this interest are called trespass to goods, conversion of chattels, and trespass to land. (3) Freedom from disparagement of reputation. Invasions of this interest are called defamation, libel, and slander. (4) Freedom from invasion of the right of privacy. (5) Freedom from interference with business relationships. Invasions of this interest are called deceit, threats and intimidations to customers, inducement of breach of contract, and slander of title and trade name. For a more complete discussion of the law of business torts, see Book I, Chapter 2, Section 1–11. If any member of society invades such protected interests of another, the party injured has a right to be reimbursed in damages for the wrong committed. This wrong is called a tort.

Conduct is tortious if any of the following elements are present: (1) If it is intentional; that is, if the actor intends his conduct to result in injury to another. *A* strikes *B* accidentally while mingling in a crowd. *A* here intends no harm. *A*'s conduct is not tortious. *A* must intend harm. (2) If it is in such "reckless and wanton disregard of the safety of others" that the actor should know or should have reason to know that harm will likely result. *A* recklessly and knowingly drives through a stop light. *B* is injured. *A*'s conduct is tortious. (3) If it is negligent; that is, if there is failure to exercise due care. Due care is what a reasonable man, guided by those circumstances which ordinarily regulate the conduct of human beings, would do or would not do under the circumstances. *A*, a garage owner, or his employees, leave oil-soaked rags and waste near *B*'s stored cars. The rags ignite and burn the cars and adjacent buildings. *A* is liable for loss of the cars and adjacent buildings. *A* was negligent in leaving the highly inflammable material where it might cause damage. *A*'s lack of knowledge of the dangerous quality of the oily rags is immaterial. Manufacturers of chattels which are likely to be dangerous because of hidden defects are liable for injury caused by reason of the defective materials used. *B* is injured by reason of the collapse of an automobile wheel. The manufacturer of the car is liable because he was negligent in using defective material and in providing improper inspection. (4) Conduct is tortious under certain unusual situations where absolute liability is imposed, even though the actor is innocent and exercises reasonable care. Harm caused by dangerous or trespassing animals, blasting operations, and escape of fire are examples. Strict liability is also imposed by workmen's compensation statutes. (5) "The unreasonable and unlawful use by a person of his own property, either real or personal, or from his own unlawful, improper, or indecent activity, which causes harm to another's person, or the use of his property, or the public generally" is tortious conduct. This conduct is generally described as a nuisance. Nuisances may be either private or public. A private nuisance is one that disturbs the interest of some private individual, whereas the public nuisance disturbs or interferes with the public in general, is in violation of some penal statute, and hence is a crime.

"An owner of property, although conducting a lawful business thereon, is subject to reasonable limitations and must use his property so as not to unreasonably interfere with the health and comfort of his neighbors, or to their right to the enjoyment of their property." Trade, business, and industrial activities are often nuisances by reason of their location, and liability is imposed even in the absence of negligence. For example, slaughter-houses, stables, chemical works, refineries, and tanneries, because of their offensive odors, may interfere with the peaceful enjoyment of property of adjacent landowners. Also, garages, filling stations, rock crushers, and skating rinks may be nuisances because of noise; factories and smelters, by reason of the escape of noxious gases. Whether a particular trade, business, or industrial activity constitutes a nuisance depends upon the locality in which it is conducted and the nature and extent of the harm resulting from its operation. The principle of law here involved is the basis of the zoning ordinances by which cities regulate the location of business enterprises. Under the state's power to protect the health, morals, and general welfare of its citizens—known as the police power—the legislature may declare what activities of a trade or business constitute a nuisance and may prohibit or limit such activities.

The unlawful interference by one person with the control and possession of the personal property of another is a trespass. One is entitled to have exclusive possession and control of his personal property and may recover for any physical harm to his goods by reason of the wrongful conduct of another. Conversion is the wrongful disposition and detention of goods of one person by another. A party in possession of the goods of another, who upon demand wrongfully or for insufficient cause refuses to return the same, is guilty of conversion. Any exercise of dominion by another of the true owner's goods is a tortious act entitling the owner to recover either the goods or damages. For example, the wrongful sale of goods by a bailee, by an agent, or by a pledgee of goods is trespass to goods.

The one in exclusive possession of land is entitled to enjoy the use of the land free from interference of others, either by direct interference or by indirect interference through instrumentalities placed upon the land. Entry upon the land of another is a trespass even though the one who enters is under the mistaken belief that he is the owner by purchase, or has a right, license, or privilege to enter thereon. Intention to enter or invade the premises of another, without consent of the owner, is a trespass. In the absence of negligent conduct, no trespass is committed if a person or his goods are accidentally placed upon another's land; thus, property placed upon another's land without negligence on the part of the owner does not make the owner of the property a trespasser.

At common law, the owner owns the air space above the land. Consequently, stretching telephone and high-tension wires above his property without consent is a trespass. Whether airplanes flying over the land of another is a trespass raises some doubt. The interference with the right of exclusive possession is the basis of trespass. It is doubtful whether an owner of land has exclusive possession of the atmosphere above the land. The United States Air Commerce Act of 1926 and the Regulations of the Secretary of Commerce, 1928, as well as the Uniform State Law for Aeronautics, provide that the "navigable air space" above the "minimum safe altitudes of flight" shall be "subject to a public right of freedom of interstate and foreign air navigation." The Uniform State Law for Aeronautics provides that "the ownership of the space above the land and waters of this state is declared to be vested in the several owners of the surface beneath, subject to the right of flight. . . . Flight in aircraft over the lands and waters of this state is lawful, unless at such a low altitude as to interfere with the then existing use to which the land or water, or space over the land or water, is put by the owner, or unless so conducted as to be imminently dangerous to persons or property lawfully on the land or water beneath." Landing aircraft on another's land is unlawful, except where a forced landing is necessary. Although such forced landing is not a trespass, nevertheless, the owner of the aircraft is liable for all damages caused by such landing. (For a detailed discussion of property rights in space, see Book I, Chapter 1, Section 1-5.)

1-16. Public law. Whereas *private law* deals with relationships between individuals, *public law* is the law pertaining to the public as a whole. *Public law* may be divided into three general classes: (1) Constitutional law concerns itself with the powers of the federal and state governments which are exercised through legislation and executive orders. The extent of the powers of Congress and state legislatures to pass laws, and of the executives of the federal government and the states to issue orders, involves questions of constitutional law. (2) Administrative law is concerned with officials, boards, and commissions created by legislatures. Orders and decrees of administrative boards, such as the Interstate Commerce Commission, the Federal Trade Commission, the National Labor Relations Board, and so forth, fall within the field of administrative law. The term also includes the remedies granted to an individual who is injured by the illegal acts of administrative officers, boards, and commissions. (3) Criminal law consists of statutes and general maxims that forbid certain conduct as detrimental to the welfare of the state and provide punishment therefor. Criminal actions are prosecuted by the state as the moving party (plaintiff) against any citizen for the violation of a duty prescribed by the common or statutory law. Crimes are either common law crimes or statutory crimes, and in states where a criminal code has been adopted, all crimes are statutory in character. Conduct that violated custom or Christian principles and shocked the community sense of propriety constituted a crime at common law. Blasphemy, murder, rape, riot, adultery, and conspiracy are illustrations. By statute, "a crime or public offense is an act or omission forbidden by law, and punishable upon conviction by either of the following punishments: (1) Death; (2) Imprisonment; (3) Fine; (4) Removal from office; (5) Disqualification to hold and enjoy any office of honor, trust, or profit under the constitution or laws of this state." In the absence of complete codification, common law crimes are still recognized, and incomplete statutes are supplemented by common law as to mode of indictment and punishment. Crimes against the United States are enumerated and defined by federal statute.

Crimes are classified as treason, felonies, and misdemeanors. Treason is defined by the federal constitution as follows: "Treason against the United States shall consist only in levying war against them, or in adhering to their enemies, giving them aid and comfort." A like provision is found in state constitutions.

Felonies are offenses usually defined by statute to include all crimes punishable by death or by imprisonment in the state prison. Examples are murder, grand larceny, arson, and rape.

Crimes of lesser importance than felonies, such as petty larceny, simple assault, drunkenness, trespass, disorderly conduct, and vagrancy, are called misdemeanors and are usually defined as any crimes not punishable by death or by imprisonment in the state prison, but punishable by fine or confinement in the local jail. It is sometimes said that every statute for the breach of which there is a penalty by way of fine or imprisonment in the local jail is a criminal statute. There is a difference of opinion as to whether acts in violation of city ordinances that provide for fine and imprisonment as a penalty are crimes. Violation of traffic ordinances, building codes, and similar municipal ordinances where prosecution takes place before a city magistrate are sometimes termed petty offenses, or public torts, and are not included within the term crime.

1-17. Law and equity. The term equity is peculiar to Anglo-American law. Equity arose because of the failure of the law to give adequate and proper remedy. In early English law the courts could not give remedies for injuries received unless the king's original writs covered the particular remedy sought. Consequently, the proceedings at law were so limited that it was often impossible to obtain justice in the king's courts.

In order that justice might be done, the person seeking a remedy sought redress from the king in person. Since the appeal was to the king's conscience, he referred such matters to his spiritual adviser, the chancellor. Such an individual was usually a church official, and in giving a remedy he usually favored the Ecclesiastical law and the Civil law.

By such method there developed a new system of procedure and new rules. Actions involving these rules were said to be brought in "chancery" or in "equity," in contradistinction to suit "at law" in the king's courts.

Many rights not recognized in the common law were created and enforced. For example, trusts in lands were recognized; rescission was allowed on contracts created through fraud; injunction and specific performance were developed.

Law as a remedy gives only money damages, whereas equity gives the plaintiff what he bargains for. Thus, *A*, by contract, agrees to deliver to *B*, for a consideration, a very valuable article, something that cannot be duplicated. Upon *A*'s breach, *B*'s only remedy in law is money damages, which are not adequate, because it is the specific article that *B* desires. In equity, however, *B* can, by specific performance, force *A* to deliver the article.

Again, if *A* persists in trespassing upon *B*'s land, *B*'s remedy in law is damages for injury done. *A* may pay the damages and trespass again. In equity, however, *B* may enjoin *A* from going on his land, and, if *A* continues, he is subject to arrest for contempt of court.

Further, a trustee, having legal title and the right to manage and control an estate, may sell the estate or employ it for his own use. By a bill in equity, however, the beneficiary may enjoin the trustee from further misuse and may force him to give an accounting.

In a few states, courts of equity are separate and distinct from courts of law. In most states the equity and law courts are organized under a single judge who has two dockets—one in law, the other in equity. Whether the case is in equity or in law is determined by the remedy desired. Modern Civil Practice Acts have abolished the common law names heretofore used to distinguish different forms of actions at law and in equity. The first pleading in civil actions, whether at law or in equity, is usually called the "complaint." The first pleading by the defendant is called the "answer."

Review Questions and Problems

1. *A* hits and slightly injures *B* during a friendly scuffle. Is *A* guilty of a tort? *A* throws a brick in a crowded street intending to break *B*'s window, but hits and injures *C*. Is *A* liable to *B* and *C*? Has *A* committed both a tort and crime?

2. *A*, a patent medicine manufacturer, without *B*'s permission, publishes an advertisement including *B*'s picture, with laudatory statements by *B* of the value of the medicine. *B* is a doctor. Is *A* liable to *B*?
3. *A* is invited as a guest to come upon *B*'s land. *C* without invitation enters *B*'s land with *A*. Is *C* a trespasser?
4. *B* has *A*'s permission to place his automobile upon *A*'s lot for three weeks. After three weeks have elapsed, *B* goes upon *A's* lot to get his car. Is *B* guilty of trespass?
5. *A*, while engaged in blasting stumps upon his land, exercises every reasonable caution, places warning signs, and so forth. However, rocks and debris are thrown upon *B*'s adjoining land. Is *A* liable to *B*?
6. *A*, driving his car in a reckless manner, collides with *B*, causing *B*'s car to enter *C*'s yard throwing out *D*, who lands in *C*'s yard, causing damage to *C*'s property. Is *A* liable to *B*? Is *B* liable to *C*? Is *D* liable to *C*?
7. *A* parks his car without parking lights upon a dark street. *B*, while negligently driving down the street, hits and damages *A*'s car. Has *B* a defense in an action by *A*?
8. *A*, an aviator, while flying above the prescribed statutory height over *B*'s land, is compelled because of engine trouble to land upon *B*'s property. Is *A* liable as a trespasser? In landing, *A* damages growing crops. What liability has the owner of the aircraft?
9. *A* has owned and operated for a number of years a smelter and foundry. A large residential district has developed near the factory. A small stream adjacent to the factory passes through a park created within the residential district. Pollution of this stream by the factory has become obnoxious to the residents. Fumes and noises from the factory are harmful and disturbing to the people of the vicinity. What remedy, if any, has a resident of the community against *A*?
10. Where did equity have its origin? When are the laws of equity applicable? Who usually presides at the equity courts?

5

The Judicial System

1-18. Classification of courts. In the United States there are two large classes of courts, state courts and federal courts.

State courts. The state courts, authough not subject to uniform classification, may be grouped as follows: supreme courts, intermediate courts of appeal, and trial courts. The trial courts are called courts of first instance because it is here that an action at law or a suit in equity is started. Trial courts are also named according to the governmental unit of which they are a part. A circuit court usually has the geographical limitations of a county and is located at the county seat. It is called a circuit court because in early times a single judge sitting as a court travelled from one county to another. Other county courts are chancery courts, county courts, district courts, and justice's courts, often limited to townships. Courts with jurisdiction limited to a city are called municipal courts.

Courts are also named according to the subject matter with which they deal. Probate courts deal with wills and the estates of deceased persons; domestic relations courts, with divorces, family relations, juveniles, and dependent children; criminal and police courts, with violators of state laws and municipal ordinances; and traffic courts, with traffic violators. For an accurate classification of the courts of any state, the statutes of that state should be examined.

United States courts. The courts of the United States are created by the authority of the Constitution, and their jurisdiction is limited by the grant of power given to the federal government by the states through the Constitution The Constitution of the United States provides in Section 1, Article III, that "The judicial power of the United States shall be vested in one Supreme Court and in such inferior courts as the Congress may from time to time ordain and establish. The judges both of the Supreme and inferior courts shall hold their offices during good behavior, and shall, at stated times, receive for their services, a compensation which shall not be diminished during their continuance in office."

The courts of the United States that are inferior to the Supreme Court are the United States Courts of Appeal and the United States District Courts and other special courts such as the Court of Customs and Patent Appeals, the Court of Claims, and the Court of Tax Appeals. The district courts are the trial courts of the federal judicial system. The great majority of the cases heard in the federal courts originate in the district courts. There are 95 United States District Courts presided over by 230 United States District Judges. The number of judges in each judicial district is determined by statute, and it depends upon the volume of business. The district courts have original jurisdiction, exclusive of the courts of the states, over all offenses against the laws of the United States. Federal crimes—offenses against the laws of the United States—can be prosecuted only in the federal courts. The accused shall be entitled to a trial by a jury in the state and district where the crime was committed. The same facts may constitute a crime against both state and federal authority. Robbery of a federal bank is a crime against both sovereigns. The robber may be tried by both the federal and state courts.

In civil actions the district courts have jurisdiction where the matter in controversy exceeds the sum or value of $10,000, exclusive of costs or interest, and is between: (1) citizens of different states or (2) citizens of a state and foreign states, or citizens or subjects thereof. Jurisdiction here rests on a controversy in excess of $10,000 and "diversity of citizenship," i.e., the plaintiff and defendant must be citizens of different states. This does not prevent the plaintiff from bringing his suit in a state court, but if the defendant is a citizen of another state, the defendant has the right to have the case removed to the federal court. A defendant, by having the case removed to the federal court, has an opportunity of having a jury selected from a larger area than the county where the cause arose, thus avoiding the possibility of jurors prejudicial to the plaintiff. For the purpose of suing in a federal court a corporation is considered a citizen of the state where it is incorporated. The United States District Courts have jurisdiction to try cases involving more than $10,000, even though diversity of citizenship is not involved, if the law suit arises out of rights granted by the Constitution, laws, or treaties of the United States. For example, a district court has jurisdiction to try a suit in equity brought by persons engaged in sheep raising and living in the same state if the matters in controversy exceed $10,000 and the relief sought is to test the constitutionality of the Taylor Grazing Act, which regulates and controls sheep grazing on federal lands.

The district courts may also hear cases arising under the Constitution or federal laws and treaties that involve personal rights without reference to the money value of the controversy. For example, the amount of the controversy is not a jurisdictional question when the suit is brought by the United States or an officer thereof and arises under the Constitution or federal laws and treaties. The civil actions involving personal rights concern admiralty, bankruptcy, setting aside orders of administrative boards—like the Interstate Commerce Commission—matters relating to patents, copyrights and trademarks, taxes, elections, restraint of trade, federal lands, regulating commerce, the rights of freedom of speech, press and religion, the liberty of the individual protected by the Fifth Amendment, also those rights secured to individual citizens by the Fourteenth Amendment to the Constitution of the United States. District courts have concurrent jurisdiction with the Court of Claims in suits against the United States for sums not exceeding $10,000. By statutes the district courts now have original jurisdiction to try tort cases involving damages to citizens caused by officers or agents of the federal government. District courts have power to issue writs of habeas corpus and to grant injunctions in a variety of cases. In cases where injunctions are sought, three judges must hear the case. The variety of actions and suits over which the United States district courts have jurisdiction are numerous. For a complete listing see 28 U.S.C.A., § 1331–1441 (1949), (Supp. 1955).

Direct appeals from the decisions of the district courts to the United States Supreme Court may be made in several situations, such as: (1) In criminal cases where the decision of the lower court is based upon the invalidity or construction of a statute upon which the indictment or information was founded. (2) Where the lower court has held an Act of Congress unconstitutional, and an agency of the government is a party. (3) Where the lower court consisting of three judges has either granted or denied after notice an interlocutory or permanent injunction.

The intermediate courts of appeal from the United States District Courts are called the United States Courts of Appeals. In 1891 because of the heavy burden placed upon the United States Supreme Court, Congress established the Courts of Appeals. The 95 federal judicial districts are divided into 11 circuits, and Courts of Appeals have been established for each circuit. These courts are not trial courts and are limited to appellate jurisdiction only. After a case has been decided by a district court, a dissatisfied party may appeal to the Courts of Appeals of the circuit in which the district court lies.

In most cases the decisions of the Courts of Appeals are final. The jurisdiction of the court is determined by Congress and it may be changed from time to time. Cases in the Courts of Appeals may be reviewed by the Supreme Court by a writ of certiorari granted upon a petition of any party to any civil or criminal case before or after a judgment or decree in the Courts of Appeals. The writ of certiorari to review a judgment of the Courts of Appeals is within the discretion of the Supreme Court. The writ will be issued where necessary to secure uniformity of decision or to bring cases of grave public concern to the court of last resort for decision.

Cases in Courts of Appeals may also be reviewed by the Supreme Court in which a state statute has been held unconstitutional and a federal question is presented. Also, the Courts of Appeals may by certification seek instructions from the Supreme Court on any question of law in any civil or criminal case.

The United States District Court and the Courts of Appeals cannot review, retry, or correct the judicial errors charged against a state court. Final judgments or decrees rendered by the highest court of a state are reviewed by the Supreme Court of the United States. State cases appealed to the United States Supreme Court must concern the validity of a treaty or statute of the United States or must present a question involving the validity of a state statute on the grounds that the statute is repugnant to the Constitution, treaties, or laws of the United States and that the state decision is in favor of the statute's validity. Where a case involves the constitutionality of a state statute or treaty, or when a citizen's rights, privileges, or immunities under the constitution or laws are impaired, the case may be brought to the United States Supreme Court by writ of certiorari.

The Supreme Court has original and exclusive jurisdiction in all controversies between two or more states, all proceedings against ambassadors, public ministers, consuls, and domestics of foreign states, all controversies between the United States and a state, and all actions by a state against citizens of another state or country.

1-19. The jurisdiction of courts. "Jurisdiction means the power given to a court by the constitution or the legislature to adjudicate concerning the subject and parties, to determine the cause, to render a judgment, and to carry such judgment into effect." For example, "probate courts shall have the original jurisdiction of all probate matters, namely, the settlement of estates of deceased persons, the appointment of guardians and conservators, the settlement of their accounts, the regulation of all matters relating to apprentices and the supervision of the sale of real estate of deceased persons for the payment of debts."

Jurisdiction over the subject matter. In order that a court may act, it must have jurisdiction over the subject matter coming before it. That is, the subject matter of the case must come within the limits of the court. For example, a probate court would not have jurisdiction to determine questions of law involving a civil suit for damages. Likewise a court has certain geographical limits within which it must act. A circuit court in one county would have no jurisdiction to determine title to the land lying within the boundaries of another county. Likewise a court in one state would have no jurisdiction to hear a case upon an actionable cause arising in another state.

Courts are also limited in their jurisdiction as to the amount of money involved in the suit. For example, a "justice of the peace shall have jurisdiction in all actions on book accounts where the amount of the balance owing to the plaintiff shall not exceed $200."

Jurisdiction over the person. In order to render a binding judgment, a court must have jurisdiction, not only over the subject matter, but also over the person of the defendant.

This jurisdiction is accomplished by a summons that issues out of the court in which the case is to be tried and is delivered to the sheriff to be served upon the individual made defendant in the suit.

Every person sued is entitled to such notice, either by personal service or by publication, in order that opportunity to defend may be given.

The summons must be served within the geographical limits of the court because the officers of one governmental unit have no authority to serve a summons outside their particular county or state. A sheriff of a county in Illinois would have no authority to serve a person in the state of Missouri. By statute in some states, a summons issuing out of an equity court in one county can be served by a sheriff of another county in the same state. In other instances the summons can be served only by the sheriff of the county in which the court sits and which is within its jurisdiction. If a person comes into the state or county, as the case may be, and is served with a summons by the sheriff, such person is then under the authority and jurisdiction of the court.

In case the defendant is a nonresident of the place where the suit is brought, service may be had by publication. This situation, however, does not give the court authority to render a personal judgment for damages. Accompanied by proper attachment proceedings, service by publication does bring under the court's jurisdiction all attached property of a nonresident which lies within the territorial limits of the court, so that such attached property is liable for the judgment debt and may be used to satisfy the judgment.

Review Questions and Problems

1. Name and classify the various federal courts. By what authority is the United State Supreme Court created? How does it differ from the lower federal courts?
2. Name four state courts. What jurisdiction does the justice's court have?
3. Over what must the courts have jurisdiction in order to render a judgment? Has one court any jurisdiction over a matter arising in another county? May a court render a judgment against a person who is not found in the county?

6

Legal Procedures for Resolving Conflicts

1-20. Instituting suit. A legal proceeding is initiated when the plaintiff files with the clerk of the court a complaint, a declaration, or a petition, as the case may be, depending upon the jurisdiction. This paper, called the *first pleading,* has for its purpose the statement of alleged facts upon which the plaintiff rests his cause of action. The pleading indicates the remedy he desires and serves to inform the defendant of the nature of the lawsuit. Upon the filing of the complaint or petition, a summons is issued out of the office of the sheriff and served upon the defendant. Sometimes, particularly if the remedy sought is in equity, a copy of the complaint or petition is delivered to the defendant.

Suits at law or in equity under Modern Practice Acts are called *civil actions,* as distinguished from criminal actions. Proceedings in attachment, ejectment, eminent domain, forceable entry and detainer, and claim and delivery, are statutory remedies, and the proceedings are regulated by special statutes. Civil actions arising out of injuries to property or persons are called *tort actions.* Also suits for damages arising out of breach of contract are included within the term civil actions. Suits which seek specific performance of contracts, bills for accounting against trust officers, and also suits to prohibit injurious conduct and continuing trespass upon real property are called *equitable actions.*

1-21. The summons. The clerk of the court issues the summons, which the sheriff of the county serves upon the defendant.

The following is the usual form of a summons:

COURT SUMMONS

In the Name of the People of the State of Illinois. In the .... Court of .... County, Illinois.

John Doe
Plaintiff
vs. } No. ....
Richard Roe
Defendant

To the above named defendants:

You are hereby summoned to answer the complaint in the above entitled cause.

Take notice that you must file your answer or otherwise make your appearance in said court held in the court house in the city of ...., Illinois, on or before the first (or third) Monday in the month of ...., 19...., provided this writ shall be served upon you not less than 20 days prior to said date.

If this writ shall be served upon you less than 20 days before said date, you will file your answer or otherwise make your appearance in said court on or before the third (or first) Monday in the month of ...., 19.....

If you do not appear according to the command of this writ, plaintiff may take judgment against you by default.

This summons must be returned by the officer or other person to whom it was given for service, with indorsement thereon with service and fees, if any, not later than 5 days after service thereof and in no event later than the date first above named.

WITNESS .... the clerk of said court and the seal thereof, at ...., Illinois, this .... day of ...., 19.....

(Seal)

....

Clerk

Plaintiff's attorney (or plaintiff, if he be not represented by attorney)

....

Address

....

1-22. Service of the summons. The sheriff, upon receipt of a summons, proceeds at once to search out the defendant. The defendant must be served personally, that is, the sheriff must leave a copy of the summons with the defendant in person. A corporation is served with process when a copy of the summons is left with its president if he can be found in the county in which the suit is brought; if the president cannot be found in the county, then service may be had when a copy of the summons is left with any agent of the corporation found in the county. The method of service is not always the same in the various states. In a few jurisdictions the summons may be left with an adult member of the defendant's household or with some person at the defendant's place of business.

A defendant may waive service of process and enter his appearance, or he may authorize his attorney to accept service for him. Such entry of appearance must be in writing and must be made a part of the record in order that jurisdiction may be had over the person of the defendant.

1-23. Return of summons. A definite period of time is prescribed by statute within which a sheriff must make service and return the summons to the clerk. For example, in some jurisdictions service must be had twenty days before the court convenes. Otherwise, the suit goes over to the next term for want of service. When the summons is served, the sheriff indorses the summons when, where, and upon whom served, with a statement of his fees. This procedure is called the sheriff's "return."

1-24. Judgment by default. After the return of the summons by the sheriff, the court has jurisdiction over the person of the defendant. The defendant must show why judgment should not be entered against him. If the defendant fails to defend his case by filing proper pleadings or fails to appear within a definite period of time, a judgment will be given against him for want of plea or of appearance. This judgment is called a judgment by default. The plaintiff may then proceed to prove his damages and to secure judgment for damages and costs. After proof, the court enters the amount of damages and costs upon the court docket, which stands as a judgment against the defendant as shown by the record of the court.

1-25. Framing the issues. As heretofore stated, the first pleading must clearly and accurately allege facts sufficient to give a right of action to the plaintiff. The purpose of such a pleading is to inform the defendant of the charge that the plaintiff has against him. The defendant's attorney, after studying the complaint, may choose one of several different ways to meet it. On motion to the court the defendant may object to the complaint, pointing out specifically its defects. If such defects be true, the court may dismiss the action or give the plaintiff an opportunity to amend. The defendant's attorney, through such motion, may admit all of the facts alleged in the complaint by arguing that those facts are not sufficient to give the plaintiff a cause of action. Such motion, called a demurrer, raises a question of law, not a question of fact. If the court finds the complaint sets forth facts sufficient to give the plaintiff a cause of action, it will overrule the demurrer. The court will then grant leave to the defendant to answer the complaint, or, on the defendant's failure to do so, enter a judgment by default for the plaintiff. If the court finds, however, that the complaint fails to state facts sufficient to give the plaintiff a cause of action, the court will sustain the demurrer or motion and grant leave to the plaintiff to amend.

After the determination of the sufficiency of the complaint, the defendant will file his pleading, called an answer, which may admit certain facts and deny others. By this process, called pleading, the issues of the suit are determined by arriving at some point of law or fact, affirmed by one party and denied by the other party, by which the court and jury will know what questions of law and of fact are to be decided.

1-26. The trial. The issues having been framed, the case is ready for trial. The judge will set a day for the trial at which jurymen will be present, unless the parties agree to have the case heard by the court rather than by a jury. The jury is selected by the lawyers from the existing panel. The witnesses are then called, each one being sworn before testimony is received from him. No evidence will be permitted to come before the jury unless it has a direct bearing upon the issues raised by the pleadings. The witnesses for the plaintiff are heard first; then the witnesses for the defendant are called. After all the evidence is in, the lawyers argue the case and try to convince the jury of the merits of their clients' positions. The court, at the close of the arguments, instructs the jury as to the law, whereupon the jury retires to make its decision. The foreman of the jury, usually the first person approved by both attorneys, reads a verdict in some such form as follows: "We, the jury, find the issues for plaintiff (or defendant as the case may be) and assess the damages that he is entitled to recover at ____ dollars."

1-27. A suit in equity. The first pleading in equity, as in law, is generally called a complaint, however, in other jurisdictions the first pleading may be called a bill or petition. The chronological method of procedure in equity is similar to a suit at law. But a law action is tried before a jury, whereas a suit in equity is generally before the judge only. Equity suits arise when there is no adequate remedy at law. Since law gives only money damages and they may be insufficient to make the injured party whole, equity gives the plaintiff what he bargained for. (See Book I, Chapter 4, Section 1–17.)

Proof and hearings. Usually a suit in equity is tried before the judge without a jury. By statute in some states a jury may be had to hear the evidence, as in divorce cases. The verdict of the jury in these cases is advisory only and is not binding on the court. The judge passes upon questions of both law and fact and may decide the case upon the bill and answer without the introduction of oral testimony. If the facts are voluminous and complicated, the judge often refers the case to another person, called a master, to take the testimony. This is the usual procedure where an accounting is required. The master hears the evidence and reports back to the judge his conclusions of fact and law. Sometimes the master's duty is confined only to the hearing and reporting of testimony.

Decrees. The decision of the court in equity is called a decree. A judgment in a court of law is measured in damages, whereas a decree of a court of equity is said to be "in personam," that is, it is directed to the defendant, who is to do, or not to do, some specific thing.

If the remedy sought is not damages but some affirmative act on the part of the defendant, that is, specific performance of contract or other equitable remedy, and the defendant fails to file an answer, or if the filed answer is stricken and an amended answer is not filed within a period prescribed by statute, the plaintiff is entitled to a decree "pro confesso." Such decree is like a judgment by default in a court of law.

Decrees are either final or interlocutory. A decree is final when it disposes of the issues in the case, reserving no question to be decided in the future. A decree quieting title to real estate, granting a divorce, or ordering specific performance is final. A decree is interlocutory when it reserves some question to be determined in the future. A decree granting a temporary injunction, appointing a receiver, and ordering property to be delivered to such a receiver would be interlocutory.

Contempt of court. Failure upon the part of the defendant to obey a decree of a court of equity is contempt of court. Any person in contempt of court may be placed in prison or fined by order of the court.

1-28. Remedies. It has been previously noted that a person may bring an action at law to recover money damages for the breach of a contract or for injury to his person or property and that a suit in equity may be brought for relief other than money damages. Equity affords remedies such as injunction, rescission of a contract for fraud, and specific performance of a contract in situations where the remedy at law by way of money damages is not regarded as an adequate one.

If a person has obtained a judgment or decree there remains the question of how such judgment or decree may be enforced in the event that the losing party does not voluntarily comply. The failure to comply with the terms of an equity decree renders the party in contempt of court and subjects him to fine or imprisonment should he continue in default. If a person against whom a judgment at law is rendered does not satisfy it the person who has obtained the judgment may apply for a writ of execution. This will direct the sheriff to seize the property of the judgment debtor and to sell enough thereof to satisfy the judgment and to cover the costs and expenses of the sale. If the judgment debtor's property does not sell for enough to pay the judgment and costs, the judgment creditor may at a later date have execution issued for the deficiency against such property as the debtor may then own. Execution may also be levied against intangible property, such as bank accounts, which may be taken in satisfaction of the judgment. Wages may be garnisheed in satisfaction of a judgment but statutes closely regulate the amount of wages that can be garnisheed and otherwise restrict the use of this remedy. It should be noted that certain property of a judgment debtor is by statute exempt from execution. Thus, the statutes provide for a homestead exemption and necessary household items, clothing, and the tools used by a person in his trade are also exempt.

In many states the unsatisfied judgment becomes a lien upon the real property owned by the judgment debtor at the time of the judgment, or any real property acquired by him during the life of the judgment. Thus the debtor could not convey a clear title to such property unless the judgment lien were satisfied.

In addition to the remedies available to obtain enforcement of a judgment, other remedies are available to give assurance to a plaintiff that the defendant will be able to satisfy a judgment rendered against him and to prevent the defendant from disposing of his property so as to defeat the collection of a judgment. The most common of these remedies is attachment. The plaintiff at the time of the issuance of the summons may have the property of the defendant seized pending the outcome of the trial. Likewise, any obligations owing to the defendant may be garnisheed by serving proper notice upon the person indebted to the defendant—employer, bank, and so on—that the money owed shall not be paid to the defendant until the court shall so order. Attachment is governed by statute and these vary among the states. The attaching creditor must file a bond for the protection of the defendant, and the statutes provide methods whereby the attachment may be discharged.

Other remedies which are available prior to judgment include civil arrest and receivership.

1-29. Nonjudicial methods for resolving conflicts. There are situations in which it is not advantageous to settle business disputes by judicial proceedings. The amount involved, the necessity for a speedy decision, the nature of the contest, the uncertainty of a legal remedy, the unfavorable publicity, and the expense entailed are factors in avoiding a court trial.

Since proceedings in judicial tribunals are by law the authorized legal method to adjudicate controversies, other methods are few and limited. Compromise by accord and satisfaction (see Book II, "Contracts," Chapter 13, Section 2-127), self-help, and arbitration are possible remedies. Accord and satisfaction are inadequate to avoid litigation unless satisfaction is obtained. If the agreement for an accord is broken, resort to the court is necessary to enforce the promise. Self-help is not satisfactory because the aggressor is likely to create more difficulties than he settles. Arbitration as an extra-judicial procedure is the most inexpensive, speedy, and amicable method of settling disputes and avoiding litigation. Arbitration has been defined as "a contractual proceeding, whereby the parties to any controversy in order to obtain an inexpensive and speedy final disposition of the matter involved select judges of their own choice and by consent submit their controversy to such judges for determination in place of tribunals provided by ordinary process of law."[1]

Arbitration, as a contractual method or as a proceeding prescribed by statute, is distinguished from *appraisement*. *Arbitration* presupposes a dispute to be tried and decided by disinterested third parties. An *appraisement* is a proceeding agreed upon in advance for the determination of a value, damages, a loss, a quantity, or a measure, and not for the purpose of finding liability. It has for its purpose preventing disputes, not settling differences. Since appraisers are experts in their particular field, they are permitted large discretion in their choice of proceeding. In

[1] Alderman v. Alderman (Tex. Civ. App.), 296 S.W.2d 312, 314, (1956).

performing their duties they act on their own knowledge and investigation and are not required to hear evidence. In absence of fraud, collusion, or mistake, their decision is binding on the parties. Since arbitration has for its purpose settling a controversy, its proceedings are different. Arbitration may be called a quasi-judicial proceeding. Its rules and regulations are set by statute or stipulated by contract. Upon notice, a hearing is held, testimony taken, deliberations had, and a decision rendered by the arbitrators called an award, without the necessity for written pleadings, motions, rules of evidence, and other formal requirements of a law suit.

Arbitration has long been recognized at common law. Its use and effectiveness, however, have been limited by a negative attitude on the part of the courts. Agreements to submit existing and future controversies to arbitrators have met judicial opposition, because it is alleged such agreements "oust the courts of jurisdiction." It is argued that disputes are not private matters, but matters of public concern; courts are public institutions to settle controversies; citizens ought not be permitted to deprive themselves or others of the protection of public tribunals and well established procedures. Furthermore, the opposition to arbitration contends that to permit individuals to create tribunals and to provide for their procedures by contract in order to settle their disputes, constitutes an indirect repeal of that legislation which provides for judicial process. This is particularly true as to future disputes, because a person should not bind himself in advance to remove his right to judicial process and appeal before he is aware of the nature of the controversy. Courts are institutions to redeem wrongs and settle controversies and their power to function ought not be contracted away.

Such ideas, however, have not prevailed. It is contended that there never "have been any factual basis for holding that an agreement to arbitrate 'ousted' jurisdiction. It has no effect upon the jurisdiction of any court. Arbitration simply removes a controversy from the arena of litigation. It is no more an ouster of judicial jurisdiction than is a compromise and settlement . . . or a covenant not to sue. Each disposes of issues without litigation. One no more than the other ousts the court of jurisdiction."

Even though arbitral agreements may not "oust" the court's jurisdiction, at common law they are not a very effective method for settling controversies. There are several reasons. First, since it is assumed that arbitrators are the agents of the parties, their authority can be cancelled at any time, thus making the stability of the arbitral procedure rest upon the continued consent of the parties. Second, either party at any time may revoke the agreement by giving notice of refusal to comply, leaving only a remedy for damages for the breach of contract. Since a party always has the power to breach a contract, an arbitral agreement is no different from any other agreement for which a judicial proceeding is necessary to recover for a breach. A defendant who has broken a contract to arbitrate is not precluded from defending the action thereon, for he can insist that the plaintiff is entitled to nominal damages only.

The inadequacy of common law arbitration led to remedial legislation. In nearly all states, arbitration is now subject to statute. These statutes vary greatly, depending upon their purpose. Some come to the aid of the common law, some set up new and complete methods of procedure. Where a statute recognizes the existence of common law arbitration, failure to comply strictly with the statutory procedure will not avoid the proceedings. However, when the statute provides for a definite complete procedure, strict compliance is necessary, otherwise the proceedings are null and void. It is held that even though strict statutory compliance has not been made, a proceeding at common law may be conducted, provided the parties have not previously contracted what particular method shall be used.

In many states, statutes are merely declaratory of the common law. In others, statutes are enacted to make arbitral proceedings more effective. They eliminate the necessity for a suit on the award, by allowing the award to be entered as a judgment in the court, upon which an execution may issue; by removing the common law right of revocation; by compelling specific performance of the agreement to arbitrate and by the enforcement of the award. Some jurisdictions have statutes which provide for compulsory arbitration. Nevertheless, it is held that statutes compelling parties to submit to arbitration are in violation of the constitutional right to trial by jury. Moreover, they violate the Fourteenth Amendment of the Federal Constitution, if the statute makes the decision of the arbitrators final and closes the courts to litigants. However, if there is an appeal to the courts from the arbitrator's award, no constitutional rights have been denied.

Since statutes vary widely, no attempt will be made to discuss these differences. By way of illustration, however, some of the provisions of a typical statute are here listed:

1. Persons may submit any controversy to commercial arbitration except disputes concerning the title to real estate, and conditions of employment under collective bargaining agreements.

2. By written contract there may be arbitration of any controversy arising from a contract, or from a refusal to perform the whole or any part of a contract. Likewise, an agreement in writing may be made to submit to arbitration any controversy existing between the parties.

3. Any party aggrieved by the failure, neglect, or refusal of the other

party to perform under a contract, or to submit a dispute to arbitration, may petition the court for an order directing that the arbitration be carried out according to the terms of the agreement. Upon hearing, if the court finds that making the contract to arbitrate or submission to arbitrate is not an issue, the court shall direct the parties to proceed to arbitrate according to the terms of the agreement.

4. If, however, there is doubt as to the making of the contract or submission, the court shall try the issue, either with or without a jury. If it is found that no contract was made, the petition shall be dismissed. If it is found that a contract to arbitrate or to submit was made, and there was a default, the court will issue an order directing the parties to proceed with arbitration according to the contract.

5. After an award has been made, it is filed with the clerk of the court and after twenty days, if no exceptions are filed, it shall become a judgment upon which an execution may be issued for satisfaction, as if a judgment had been entered in a civil action.

6. Exception to an award may be made for the following causes: corruption, fraud, partiality, misconduct, exceeding power, and mistake, or upon an award resting on matters not within the statute.

7. Appeals from the judgment may be taken as in any legal action, and such appeals cannot be denied by contractual provisions.

8. If it appears that the award should be vacated, the court may refer it back to the arbitrators, with instructions for correction and rehearing. If the arbitrators do not act, the court has jurisdiction to try the case.

Arbitration as a "substitute for the courts for settling controversies" is an excellent procedure if it works. But if it does not work and there is resort to the courts, the very end sought is not accomplished. In spite of the uncertainty of the law about arbitration, the procedure for arbitration has been a successful method for settling differences within trade groups and associations. There has been sufficient experience in the field for the publication of standard contract clauses, rules, and procedures.

The previous attitude of the courts, the question of whether arbitration is a matter of contract concerned with substantive law, or a matter of procedure regulated by contract or statute, makes for conflict both at common law and in statutes. Therefore, the student is advised to refer to local decisions and statutes for complete information.

1-30. Appeals. Most of the material in this chapter under the heading "Court Procedure" relates to what occurs at the trial of a case in the lower court. After the trial, the defeated party may not be satisfied with the judgment of the court or the verdict or the jury. A dissatisfied party to a suit has a right of appeal to a higher court. The cases collected and abstracted in this text, except those taken from the Federal Supplement, which reports cases tried in United States District Courts, and some cases from the New York Supplement, have been tried in a lower court and had an appeal taken to a higher court. Since appellate procedures are not uniform in the several states, state statutes and court rules should be consulted.

In preparation for and during the trial, attorneys are careful to point out what seem to them errors of procedure, of introduction of testimony, or of instructions to the jury. In taking exceptions to the rulings of the court and noting errors, the attorney at the trial is laying a foundation for an appeal. Whether plaintiff or defendant, the person who appeals is called the appellant, the opposite party on the appeal is called the respondent or appellee. If the defendant appeals, his name will usually appear first in the reported case although his name appeared last in the case below. Care must be used in reading a reported case in order to ascertain the relationship of the parties. In order to perfect an appeal, the dissatisfied party must comply with the statutes, either state or federal as the case may be, and with such rules as are prescribed by the appellate court.

A party to a judgment, decree, or appealable order, may by himself or by attorney give notice in open court at the time the judgment or decree is rendered that he intends to appeal from such judgment, decree, or order, or from some specific part. The court will enter in his docket the fact that such notice was given. Statutes provide that appeals must be taken within a certain number of days from the entry of the judgment, usually 30, 60, or 90 days. The party desiring the appeal must give notice to the opposing party within a time prescribed by statute that such appeal is taken. The filing of the notice of appeal and its entry upon the journal of the court where the trial was held give the appellate court jurisdiction of the case. After the appellate court has acquired jurisdiction, it may dismiss the appeal upon its own motion or that of the respondent if there are any statutory omissions in perfecting the appeal.

Within at least ten days after giving notice of appeal, the appellant serves on the adverse party an undertaking (surety-bond) to the effect that the appellant will pay all damages, costs, and disbursements that may be awarded against him on the appeal. This is to protect the respondent so that he may collect his judgment if the appellant loses on appeal. Upon no objection or upon acceptance of the bond or surety by the respondent, the appeal is said to be perfected.

Within at least 30 days (time varies in different states) after the appeal is perfected, the appellant shall file with the clerk of the appellate court what is known as a *transcript*. The transcript consists of a copy of the judgment, decree, or order appealed from, the notice of appeal, the proof of service upon the respondent, the undertaking (bond) and such other papers as are required by the rules of the court. If the appeal is from a decree in equity, and if the cause is to be tried anew on the evidence by the appellate court, the clerk of the lower court forwards, together with a copy of the evidence heard, all depositions (written testimony) and other papers filed with the clerk in the lower court. The respondent, if he so desires, is entitled to a copy of the evidence. Such evidence is considered a part of the "transcript."

The bill of exceptions. A bill of exceptions is a written instrument in which are set out the objections or exceptions made and taken by the attorneys during the trial to the decisions, rulings, and instructions of the trial judge. The rulings excepted to are stated with an enumeration of as much evidence as is necessary to explain the exceptions. Sometimes the bill of exceptions may include all of the testimony, including the exhibits offered, received, or rejected, and the instructions for the jury, given or refused. The bill of exceptions must be agreed to by the parties, "settled" or "allowed," signed by the trial judge, and filed with the clerk of the trial court. When this is done, it becomes a part of the record of the case.

In order to present the case to the appellate court, the appellant must prepare and file a "brief." The brief will contain a statement of the case and, in an action at law, a list of the assignment of errors upon which the appellant has based his reasons for appeal. The assignment of errors found in the "bill of exceptions" and set out in the "brief" may contain any of the following:

1. The court upon the examination of witness *X* erred in failing to sustain the objection to the admission of testimony in response to the following questions: (Here in the brief are set forth the questions, the objections, the answers given, and so forth.)
2. The court erred in denying the motion for a nonsuit or directed verdict. (Here are set out the exact motion and the court's ruling.)
3. The court erred in giving or in failing to give the following instructions: (Here are set out the instructions, the objections made, and so forth.)
4. The court erred in its decision because the statute under which the action was brought is unconstitutional. (Here are set out the statute and the reasons for its unconstitutionality.)

The next division of the "brief" sets out the points and authorities relating to the particular assignments of error. Here the attorney presents the particular propositions he seeks to have sustained. Previously decided cases will be cited as authority for the propositions proposed.

The next division of the "brief" contains the arguments on both fact and law by which the attorney attempts to show how the court committed the errors alleged. The respondent or appellee files a brief of like character setting out his side of the case with points, authorities, and arguments. By such procedure the case on the issues raised gets to the court of appeals for decision.

The court of appeal upon receipt of the case will place it on the calendar for hearing. The attorneys will be notified of the time and will be given an opportunity for oral arguments. After deliberation by members of the court, an opinion will be written stating the law involved and giving the court's reasons for its decision. The court by its decision may affirm or reverse the court below, or the court may send the case back for a new trial. At the end of each published opinion found in the reports, there will appear in a few words the result of the court's decision. Such words may be "affirmed," "reversed," "reversed and remanded," and so forth, as the case requires.

1-31. Judicial reasoning. After a court of review decides a case, the court prepares and publishes an opinion which states the reasoning on which the decision is based. In many cases, the general character of such reasoning is deceptively simple; the court has determined that some rule or rules of law are applicable, and has decided the case accordingly.

Such reasoning has been characterized as syllogistic in form. According to this view, the applicable rule of law is stated as the major premise, the facts to which the rule applies as the minor premise, and the court's determination as the conclusion. Thus, to illustrate from an actual case: "No woman is entitled to recover damages against a party who has seduced her spouse" (major premise), "the plaintiff is a woman" (minor premise), "therefore the plaintiff is not entitled to recover" (conclusion).

Although the structure of most judicial opinions may be cast in syllogistic form, the student must not conclude that legal reasoning which exhibits this form is sound reasoning. Reasoning may be syllogistic, and "logical," but at the same time quite unsound as a basis for practical decision. Thus, in the foregoing illustration, the reasoning is "logical," but is not sound because the major premise is based on what Justice Cardozo called an "assumption of a bygone inequality. . . ." Early in the development of the common law, women occupied a lower status than men. This was reflected in decisions establishing the rule that a man could recover damages for the seduction of his wife because, it was said, a man had a property interest in the body of his wife. But a woman could not recover for the seduction of her husband, since she had no such property interest in the body of her husband. However, as Justice Cardozo said in the case of *Appenheim v. Kridel*, by 1920, "Social, political, and legal reforms [have] changed the relations between the sexes, and put woman and man upon a plane of equality. Decisions founded upon the assumption of a bygone inequality [are] unrelated to present-day realities, and ought not to be permitted to prescribe a rule. . . ."

Obviously, judicial reasoning must be sound as well as "logical." That is, both major and minor premises must be true in the light of "present-day realities." The most difficult task an appellate court confronts in each case is to establish sound premises for a decision. However, judicial opinions seldom reflect any effort by judges to ascertain the existence of some valid formal relationship between premises and conclusion such as that exemplified in the syllogism. Justice Cardozo has described the role of the appellate judge as follows:

> The judge is to scrutinize the aggregate of social facts of which "the juridical norm" is to be regarded as a product. Chief among these are "the positive laws, the usages actually obeyed, the economic needs, the aspirations toward the realization of the just." But the scrutiny, though an essential part of his function, is not the whole. The judge interprets the social conscience, and gives effect to it in law, but in so doing he helps to form and modify the conscience he interprets. Discovery and creation react upon each other.

In most cases, the pertinent legal rule or rules (major premise) have been authoritatively formulated. Accordingly, most judicial reasoning revolves around establishment of what, in syllogistic terms, is called the minor premise. Consider the following reasoning: "An offer and an acceptance are required to form a contract" (major premise), "*D*'s statement to *P* did not constitute an acceptance" (minor premise), "therefore no contract was formed" (conclusion). Here, the principal task of the court was to determine whether *D*'s statement to *P* constituted an acceptance of *P*'s offer. By establishing the minor premise that it did not, the court by the application of the major premise formulated and applied a legal rule that an offer and an acceptance must coincide in order to form a contract.

Several kinds of reasoning ordinarily influence a court in determining the application of a legal rule or rules. A court may base its determination upon the literal meaning of words appearing in the rule, upon the purpose of the rule, upon similarities between the facts of the case to be decided and the facts of decided cases, or upon considerations of social policy. Thus, reasoning is literal, purposive, precedent-oriented, or policy-oriented. Adherents of the schools of jurisprudence discussed in Sec. 1-3 above may be identified in terms of which of these "approaches" to judicial decision they emphasize or prefer. Thus, members of the historical school would emphasize precedent-oriented analysis. Some positivists would emphasize the literal approach. Adherents of sociological and natural law jurisprudence would prefer the purposive and policy-oriented approaches.

Literal reasoning, or what has also been characterized as the literal approach, may be illustrated by the following hypothetical case: Congress, having jurisdiction over the District of Columbia, passed a law providing that vehicles should not be taken into parks in Washington, D.C. Pursuant to this law, appropriate signs were posted at park entrances. *D* entered one of the parks pushing his bicycle, and was arrested and convicted of violating the law. *D* appealed, and his conviction was upheld on the basis that, as *D*'s bicycle had all the physical characteristics of a vehicle, it constituted a "vehicle"; therefore, *D* had violated the statute.

A court adopting a "purposive approach" to the issue presented by the foregoing hypothetical case might have decided *D*'s appeal differently. If, upon inquiry into the purpose of the law, it appeared that Congress was only attempting to reduce risk of harm to pedestrians in the park, such a court might have refused to uphold *D*'s conviction upon the basis that as he did not ride the bicycle into the park, he did not expose pedestrians to any significant risk of harm, and therefore did not violate the statute.

Purposive reasoning may also be illustrated by the following hypothetical case. *P* sent *D* an offer of wheat seed by mail; *D* accepted by mail, but shortly after depositing the letter of acceptance in the letter box, learned of another offer at a lower price, and accepted it. *D* then wired *P* that he was not accepting *P*'s offer, although he had a few moments earlier mailed a letter of acceptance. *P* attempted to hold *D* to a contract, citing the well-established rule that an acceptance by mail is effective upon mailing. The court stated that this rule was not applicable because its primary purpose was to protect the accepting party in cases in which he justifiably acted in reliance on what he considered to be a contract at the time of mailing. In this case there was no such reliance, and therefore no basis for applying the rule.

Few principles are more firmly established in Anglo-American law than the principle of *stare decisis*, which requires that like cases be decided in like manner. Accordingly, many judicial decisions are precedent-oriented, and in nearly every case lawyers and judges expend considerable time and energy analyzing and discussing similarities and differences between the facts of decided cases and the facts of the case to be decided.

The great mass of cases are decided within the confines of *stare decisis*. Yet there is a steady evolution, for it is not quite true that there is nothing new under the sun; rarely is a case identical with the one that went before. Courts have a creative job to do when they find that a rule has lost its touch with reality and should be abandoned or reformulated to meet new conditions and new moral values. And in those cases where there is no *stare decisis* to cast its light or shadow, the court must hammer out new rules that will respect whatever values of the past have survived the tests of reason and experience and anticipate what contemporary values will best meet the tests. The task is not easy—human relations are infinitely complex and subtlety and depth of spirit must enter into their regulation. Often legal problems elude final solution and courts there can do no more than find what Cardozo called the least erroneous answer to insoluble problems.[2]

Policy considerations influence the decision of many cases. Such considerations often influence a court to apply or refuse to apply an existing rule, and are usually of paramount significance in those relatively infrequent cases in which a court is called upon to resolve problems not heretofore adjudicated by that court. Policy-oriented reasoning may be illustrated as follows: *P* claimed damages for harm to an eye due allegedly to *D*'s negligent failure to place safety guards over a grindstone. Immediately after the harm to *P* occurred, *D* placed safety guards over the grindstone. At the trial, *P* sought to introduce evidence of *D*'s action for the purpose of showing that *D* had, by placing the guards over the grindstone, admitted that he had been careless. *D* objected to the admission of this evidence, but the court overruled his objection, and the jury rendered a verdict for *P*. On appeal, the appellate court decided that admission of this type of evidence was error. The court stated that there was a strong policy to encourage employers to establish and maintain optimum safety conditions at all times. The admission of the proffered evidence would frustrate this policy because an employer would, after an accident, hesitate to improve safety conditions for fear that this might be used against him in a lawsuit by the injured employee.

The literal, the purposive, the precedent-oriented, and the policy-oriented approaches to determining the application of legal rules may each influence the decision of a particular case. Sometimes these approaches point in different directions. Thus, in those cases in which the courts refused to apply the doctrine that the consumer of defective food could recover for breach of warranty only against the seller and not against the manufacturer, the courts adopted a policy-oriented approach and chose to protect the health of consumers rather than follow the precedents which had established the non-liability of manufacturers.

When a court decides a case primarily upon the basis of what is here called policy-oriented reasoning, a choice between conflicting policies is often required. Thus, the immediately preceding illustration may also be viewed as posing a conflict between the policy of protecting consumer health and the policies underlying the doctrine of *stare decisis*. The cases in which one party claims that another has infringed a trademark usually pose a conflict between the policy of protecting an established property right and the policy of fostering competition. The illustrations could be multiplied by numerous cases in which the courts carefully weigh all factors in determining which approach is to be decisive.

Occasionally, a case arises presenting issues that have been decided

[2] Traynor, Judge, 2 *Univ. of Ill. Law Forum* 232 (1956).

differently by different courts. The court must then choose between conflicting precedents. This choice is frequently made primarily on the basis of an evaluation of the policy considerations supporting each precedent. Often, courts also consider other factors, such as the standing of the tribunals which decided the conflicting precedents.

When reading assigned cases, the student should attempt to analyze the court's reasoning in terms of the discussion in this section. The student will thereby enhance his comprehension of the cases and also improve his own reasoning powers.

1-32. How to study a case. In order to understand a case, it is necessary to know how a legal issue is presented by the use of the rules of procedure called adjective law, and how this legal issue is resolved by the application of the rules of substantive law.

The case of *Levitz Furniture Company v. Fields,* Court of Common Pleas of Lebanon County, Pa., 1958, 6 Leb. 385, is here used to illustrate the problem.

The plaintiff, Levitz Furniture Company, entered into a contract to sell a television set to the defendant, Harold Fields. The contract contained a provision for a confession of judgment whereby the plaintiff was authorized to obtain a judgment against the defendant if he should be in default of any terms of the contract. The defendant stopped making payments under the contract and the plaintiff applied for and obtained a judgment against him. An execution was issued on the judgment and the sheriff has levied upon defendant's property. The defendant filed a petition to set aside the judgment and to be allowed to defend the case. He alleged that the set had never performed properly and that there was a warranty that the set would perform satisfactorily. At the hearing on the petition he testified that the plaintiff had been unable to make the set work after repeated efforts, and that he had therefore attempted to cancel the contract. The contract contained another provision that "no warranties of any kind with respect to the property have been made by the seller."

Ehrgood, P. J. . . . The defendant contends that under the evidence produced and heretofore referred to, and under the law of Pennsylvania, that there is an implied warranty that the sale and installation of the Spartan TV set as contracted for under the installment agreement between the parties, was suitable and would function for the purpose for which it was sold, wherefore, parol evidence is admissible and properly received by the court at the hearing in this matter.

It also seems clear to the court that inasmuch as the installment contract is dated December 29, 1956, the question involved is controlled by the provisions of the Commercial Code which became effective July 1, 1954. Article 2 of said Code pertains to sales, being Section 315, relating to implied warranties being Title 12-a, P.S., 2-315, and provides as follows:

"Where the seller at the time of contracting has reason to know any particular purpose for which the goods are required and if the buyer is relying on seller's skill or judgment to furnish suitable goods, there is, unless excluded or modified under the next section, an implied warranty that the goods shall be satisfactory for such purpose."

The plaintiff contends that the court erred in admitting testimony of the defendant and wife with respect to alleged warranties, either expressly or implied, because the best evidence thereof was the writing itself which contained the following:

"Buyer acknowledged that he has received delivery of the property, having first examined and tested it, and found it to be in first class condition, and as represented by seller. No warranties of any kind with respect to the property and this transaction have been made by the seller (except that seller hereby warrants that it has a right to enter into this contract), unless endorsed hereon by writing."

Plaintff cites *Kull v. General Motors*, 311 Pa. 508, in which the court held, inter alia:

"Where the parties have integrated their understanding and agreements into a formal, explicit contract, and excluded from the contract all previous communications not contained in the contract and provide that no modification shall be binding unless in writing, it cannot be permitted, in a suit brought on the contract, to prove parol modification of that contract in the absence of an averment of fraud, accident, or mistake in omitting from the writing sued upon on the terms afterwards offered in evidence."

In the instant case there was no averment of fraud, accident, or mistake, nor was there any evidence of fraud, accident, or mistake submitted at the time of the hearing. However, the plaintiff has overlooked the provisions of the Commercial Code hereinafter referred to by the court. Wherefore, the court will now refer to the court decisions and authorities applicable to the oral evidence produced by the defendant and the law relating thereto.

The aforesaid Section of the Commercial Code replaced and restated Section 15 of the Uniform Sales Act of 1915 (69 P.S. 124), relating to implied warranties, and which provides as follows:

"Where a buyer, expressly or by implication, makes known to the seller the particular purpose for which the goods are required, and it appears that the buyer relies on the seller's skill or judgment, (whether he be the employer or manufacturer or not), there is an implied warranty that the goods shall be reasonably fit for the purpose."

. . . Wherefore, it seems clear to the court, after considering the foregoing evidence produced by defendant and his wife, and the law applicable thereto, that the defendants have been diligent and timely in presenting their petition to open judgment and that they have produced sufficient evidence to indicate a meritorious defense to the plaintiff's claim in that there is an implied warranty created by operation of law, which was not fulfilled by the plaintiff, notwithstanding the provisions in the contract that any changes of warranty had to be in writing.

. . . Further, it seems clear to the court that the defendants were unfamiliar with the construction and operation of TV sets and relied upon the judgment of the plaintiff and his employees that they would receive a set which was in a reasonably good condition to be usable for the purpose for which they agreed to purchase the same. The question as to whether or not the TV set which the plaintiff sold to the defendant complied with such requirements is a question of fact for a jury or a fact finding body to determine.

The first step in case analysis is a statement of the facts.

Statement of facts: Fields, the defendant, purchased a TV set from Levitz Furniture Company, the plaintiff. The sales agreement provided that no warranties were made by the seller and that if the buyer defaulted the seller could confess a judgment against him. The set did not perform satisfactorily, and the defendant stopped making payments. The plaintiff took judgment against him. The defendant seeks to have the judgment set aside.

Legal procedure by which is raised the question of law: The defendant filed a petition asking that the judgment obtained by confession be set aside and that he be allowed to defend the action and introduce evidence of breach of warranty by way of defense.

Question of law: By this process an issue of substantive law was raised. Does a retail seller of goods impliedly warrant the goods that are sold?

Plaintiff's argument: The plaintiff contended that the agreement disclaims any warranties and that since the best evidence of warranty is the writing the court should not admit the defendant's testimony.

Defendant's argument: The defendant claims that despite the disclaimer an implied warranty exists under the law of the state and that he should be allowed to introduce evidence of breach of warranty by way of defense.

The opinion and holding of the court: The court held that under the Commercial Code there was an implied warranty created by operation of law. This warranty existed notwithstanding the contract provision that any changes of warranty had to be in writing. The defendant justifiably relied on the plaintiff to furnish a set that would be usable for the purpose for which it was purchased. Therefore, the judgment was set aside and the defendant may introduce evidence to a jury or fact finding body to establish that the warranty was breached.

This case was decided in 1958 by the Court of Common Pleas of Lebanon County, Pennsylvania. The case can be found in Volume 6 of the reports of the courts of that county at page 385. This is a trial court opinion and does not appear in other case reports.

Most of the cases in this book are decisions of appellate courts. Decisions of state courts are generally reported in two sources. One of these is the state reports and the other the regional reporters published by the West Publishing Company, St. Paul, Minnesota. The latter is a collection of cases decided in the appellate courts of the states in a particular region of the country.

For example, at page 25 of the text will be found the case of *In re Forsstrom et ux.* (1934), 44 Ariz. 472, 38 P.2d 878. This case which was decided in 1934 can be found in Volume 44 of the Arizona reports at page 472. The same case can be found in the second series of the Pacific Reporter, Volume 38 at page 878. The letter "P" here means Pacific Reporter. This reporter includes cases decided by the courts in the states of California, Oregon, Washington, Idaho, Montana, Colorado, Utah, Arizona, New Mexico, Nevada, Wyoming, Kansas, Oklahoma, Alaska, and Hawaii. The figure "2d" after the letter "P" indicates that the Pacific Reporter is now in a second series.

In addition to the above reporter, there are the Atlantic, cited as Atl. or A.2d; the South Eastern cited as S.E. or S.E.2d; the South Western cited as S.W. or S.W.2d; the Southern cited as So. or S.2d; the North Western cited as N.W. or N.W.2d; the North Eastern cited as N.E. or N.E.2d. In addition to these reporters there is a special reporter for the State of New York called the New York Supplement, cited N.Y.S. and N.Y.S.2d. In this reporter are found trial court cases and cases decided by the intermediate appellate courts of the State of New York.

Cases decided by United States courts are found in the West's National Federal Reporter System. U. S. district court cases are found in the Federal Supplement Reporter, cited as F. Supp. or F. Supp.2d. United States Court of Appeals cases are found in the Federal Reporter, F. or F.2d. Cases decided by the United States Supreme Court are found in the Supreme Court Reporter, cited S.Ct. Also, cases decided by the United States Supreme Court are found in the official U. S. Reporter, published by the U. S. Government Printing Office, cited as U.S. In addition, special United States courts and administrative boards, such as the Court of Tax Appeals, Courts of Claims, Referees in Bankruptcy, the National Labor Relations Board, and others have their own special bound volumes for the publication of their cases.

Review Questions and Problems

1. What is the first step in a suit at law? What is a court summons? Who serves it? Must he find the party served?
2. What is meant by a judgment by default or a decree "pro confesso"?
3. What is meant by the term "framing the issues"? Describe the steps used in framing the issues.
4. What relationship exists between the framing of the issues and the introduction of evidence? Why?
5. What may the party, against whom the court has sustained a motion by way of demurrer, do? Who renders the verdict?
6. What is the difference between a final and an interlocutory decree in a court of equity?
7. What is administrative law and who administers it?
8. Who is an appellant, an appellee?
9. Give the steps by which a case is appealed from a trial court to a court of appeals.
10. What is a "transcript"? A "bill of exceptions"?
11. What does an attorney include in his brief?
12. Distinguish between the "remedies" used in equitable suits and law actions.
13. Illustrate by an appropriate example hypothetical syllogistic form in legal reasoning.
14. Describe "literal," "purposive," "precedent-oriented" types of judicial reasoning.
15. What are nonjudicial methods for resolving conflicts?

7

The Uniform Commercial Code: Typical Business Situations—Transactions to Litigation

1-33. Purpose and theory. In our mercantile economy commercial law is more generally used than other areas of the law. Commerce is not organized along state lines. Conflicting laws of the several states confuse, burden, and inhibit legitimate business enterprise. Uniformity throughout American jurisdictions is essential for the efficient and effective operation of the "commercial transaction." The National Conference of Commissioners on Uniform State Laws, the American Law Institute, Merchants Associations, bankers and various Bar Associations have united in drafting and presenting to state legislative bodies the Uniform Commercial Code.

The Code is divided into ten articles which relate to the different aspects of a commercial transaction. The stated purpose of the Code is "to simplify, clarify, and modernize the law governing commercial transactions; to permit the continued expansion of commercial practices through custom, usage, and agreement of the parties; and to make uniform the law among the various jurisdictions."

1-34. The commercial transaction. Law designated "business or commercial law" as developed by the judicial process and codified by legislatures has heretofore been classified into separate independent parts, even though the "commercial transaction" out of which each part arose has been a single related process. The law concerned with each separate part has been given its own particular name. The National Conference of Commissioners on Uniform State Laws has prepared and recommended over the past years uniform laws dealing with the different aspects of the "commercial transaction." These laws are The Uniform Negotiable Instruments Law; The Uniform Warehouse Receipts Act; The Uniform Sales Act; The Uniform Bills of Lading Act; the Uniform Stock Transfer Act; The Uniform Conditional Sales Act; and The Uniform Trust Receipts Act.

The Uniform Negotiable Instruments Act and The Uniform Sales Act were finally adopted by every state in the Union. The other Acts, while not adopted by all the states, are nevertheless generally accepted as authoritative statements of the law.

It is to be noted that each Act is a statement of the law applicable to a particular part of a total "commercial transaction." The drafters of The Uniform Commercial Code have predicated it upon the "concept . . . that (a) 'Commercial Transaction' is a single subject of law notwithstanding its many facets." It is the purpose of The Uniform Commercial Code not only to "integrate" or bring together into one Act each of the above related Acts, but also—since the earliest of the above Uniform Acts was drafted in 1896 and the latest in 1933—to make such revisions and additions as "modern commercial practice" dictates.

Enactment of the Code replaces the above enumerated Uniform Acts and, in addition, makes statutory a considerable body of law formerly "covered by case law and custom." Although its enactment has repealed *in toto* these Uniform Acts, much of the law included within these repealed Uniform Acts has been retained.

Commenting on the related fields of law involved in a single transaction, the drafters state:

> A single transaction may very well involve a contract for sale, followed by a sale, the giving of a check or draft for a part of the purchase price, and the acceptance of some form of security for the balance.
>
> The check or draft may be negotiated and will ultimately pass through one or more banks for collection.
>
> If the goods are shipped or stored, the subject matter of the sale may be covered by a bill of lading or warehouse receipt or both.
>
> Or it may be that the entire transaction was made pursuant to a letter of credit either domestic or foreign.
>
> Obviously, every phase of commerce involved is but a part of one transaction, namely, the sale of and payment for goods.
>
> If, instead of goods in the ordinary sense, the transaction involved stocks or bonds, some of the phases of the transaction would obviously be different. Others would be the same. In addition, there are certain additional formalities incident to the transfer of stocks and bonds from one owner to another.
>
> This Act purports to deal with all the phases which may ordinarily arise in the handling of a commercial transaction, from start to finish.
>
> Because of the close relationship of each phase of a complete transaction to every other phase, it is believed that each Article of this Act is cognate to the single broad subject "commercial transaction" . . .

The "commercial transaction" is comprised of the total process—the production and collection of raw materials, the assembly, the manufacture, the sale of the goods, and the finances involved and the final distribution of the goods to the ultimate consumer.

The means and methods by which "commercial transactions" are carried out and the evidence of the legal relationships of the parties are the contract, shipping orders, bills of lading, warehouse receipts, insurance policies, bank deposits, checks, certificates of deposit, letters of credit, loans, notes, chattel mortgages, trust receipts, security devices of all kinds, investments, and numerous other legal instruments.

CLASSIFICATION OF THE SUBJECT MATTER OF A TRANSACTION

Goods which are the subject matter of a commercial transaction may be classified into two groups: *industrial goods* and *consumer goods*. Such classification is determined largely by the character of buyers. In order to better understand the "legal functional classification of goods" made by the Commercial Code a situation which involves the marketing of a manufactured product will be analyzed. Beginning with "raw materials" each step thereafter will be traced until a finished product has been placed in the hands of the consumer. The first steps are the production, collection, and assembly of "raw materials" which consist of products of the forest, farm, sea, and mine. Such material may be called *industrial goods*. Included within this class may be machinery, fabricating items, accessories, parts, capital, equipment, and operating supplies for service activities. Sellers here are the producers of raw materials, and buyers are processors, manufacturers, distributors, and vendors of services. Sales are in large quantities and involve large sums of money. Financing is often on credit, and transactions are repeated. Such transactions usually do not include wholesalers or middle men. Since the subject matter—raw material, machinery, equipment, and parts—must be suitable for a particular purpose, technical knowledge and understanding by sellers and buyers with equal bargaining powers may justifiably be presumed. This professional competence among businessmen will therefore make for a somewhat different application of the law to such transactions, than that which is applied to transactions between the retailer and ultimate consumer.

In the analysis of the commercial transaction, the second class of goods is called *consumer goods*. Transactions involving goods of this character are the most numerous.

In order to make vivid the "close relationship in each phase of a complete transaction to every other phase," different types of transactions will be illustrated. The "dealer, retailer—ultimate consumer" relationship will be presented first.

1. *Consumer Goods: Retailer, Dealer—Ultimate Consumer Transactions, Illustrations.* The goods which are the subject matter of this type of transaction are legion—watches, diamonds, automobiles, washing machines, choses in action, combination radio, hi-fi, and television sets, to name but a few.

(a) *A consumer installment purchase transaction—warranties. B* purchased from S, at S's retail store, a Saturn combination twenty-one inch,

63 model television, hi-fi, and radio set. At the time of the purchase S gave *B* a short demonstration. While trying different stations, the control knobs fell off the instrument. S said to *B*, "Don't worry; it will be right when it is delivered."

S filled out some forms and asked *B* to sign. *B* signed, but did not read the forms, which consisted of white, yellow, and pink copies. *B* was given the pink copy. *B* thought he was signing a sales slip calling for "payment in ninety days." Upon signing the papers, *B* gave S a check for $26.60. In addition to the cost of the merchandise, *B* was charged $29.95 for installation and a one-year service policy. The set was delivered to *B*'s home. Upon first operation the knobs dropped off, voices were heard, but no picture was produced. The knobs continued to drop off, and within one month the serviceman was called six times. At the end of a month, *B* stopped making payments, set the machine aside, and purchased another set.

S demanded payment and *B* refused to pay. The paper *B* had signed was an installment contract for a second-hand Saturn set. It contained a confession of judgment clause which provided that if *B* did not pay the installments S could apply to the court for a judgment against him. Accordingly, S took a judgment against *B* for $226.60. The installment contract, which was on the second yellow sheet, set forth that *B* had purchased the set for $190.05; installation $29.95; total $220.00; tax $6.60, total $226.60. On the reverse side of the yellow copy was an installment lease contract under the heading "Additional Provisions." In addition to the confession of judgment clause, the yellow copy also contained a clause, "[There are] no warranties of any kind with respect to the property."

B sought to have the judgment set aside and to establish that there had been a breach of warranty. He admitted that he knew that the set was a demonstrator and that he did not have a written warranty. The court opened the judgment for the admission of oral testimony to prove an implied warranty under the terms of the Uniform Commercial Code. The court stated: ". . . the plaintiff has overlooked the provisions of the Commercial Code hereinafter referred to by the court. Wherefore the court will now refer to the court decisions and authorities applicable to the oral evidence produced by the defendant and the law relating thereto."[1] The Commercial Code section (2–315) to which the court referred provides: "When the seller at the time of contracting has reason to know any particular purpose for which the goods are required and if the buyer is relying on seller's skill or judgment to furnish suitable goods,

1 Levitz Furniture Company v. Fields, Pa. Court of Common Pleas, 1958, 6 Leb. 385. Del Duca and King, *Commercial Code Litigation,* Dickinson School of Law, 55 (1960).

there is, unless excluded or modified under the next section, an implied warranty that the goods shall be satisfactory for such purposes."

(b) *A sale contract: manufacturer-dealer-ultimate consumer transaction—warranties. B* purchased from S, an automobile dealer, a car manufactured by *M. W, B*'s wife, was injured while driving the car. The car was a gift from *B* to *W*. Shortly after the delivery of the car, and while she was driving it, *W* heard a loud noise "from the bottom by the hood." She said, "It felt as if something cracked." The steering wheel spun in the driver's hand, the car veered sharply and crashed into a brick wall, damaging the car and injuring *W*. As a result of the impact, the front of the car was so badly damaged that it was impossible to determine if any of the parts of the steering wheel mechanism, workmanship, or assembly were defective or improper prior to the accident. The insurance inspector testified "something went wrong with the steering wheel down at the front wheels." There was not sufficient evidence to make out a prima facie case of negligence on the part of either the dealer or the manufacturer.

B had signed a printed purchase order at the time of the sale. On the face it contained blanks to be filled in describing the car, the accessories, and details of financing. The type used in the printed part became smaller in size toward the bottom of the page where the purchaser placed his signature. The fine print stated in part: "The front and back of this order comprises the entire agreement . . . no other agreement will be recognized . . . I have read the matter printed on the back hereof and agree it is part of this order."

B testified that he did not read the fine print on front or back. No one called the matter to his attention.

The back of the purchase order contained a paragraph expressly stating there were no warranties, expressed or implied, other than as to material and workmanship, and that this warranty was expressly in lieu of all other warranties.

B sued both the manufacturer and dealer for damages to the car, medical and hospital expenses, and loss of his wife's society and services. Since negligence could not be proven, the case was given to the jury solely on the theory of breach of warranty of fitness for a particular purpose and merchantability.

Francis, J. in deciding this case states:

The normal pattern that a manufacturer-dealer relationship follows relegates the position of the dealer to the status of a way station along the car's route from maker to consumer. This is indicated by the language of the warranties. The words "original purchaser" taken in their context signify purchaser as a member of the public . . . (U.C.C. Section 2–314, 315)

The uniform act (sales) codified, extended, and liberalized the common law of sales. The motivation in part was to ameliorate the harsh doctrine of caveat emptor, and in some measure to impose a reciprocal obligation on the seller to beware. The transcendent value of the legislation, particularly with respect to implied warranties, rests in the fact that obligations on the part of the seller were imposed by operation of law, and did not depend for their existence upon express agreement of the parties. And of tremendous significance in a rapidly expanding commercial society was the recognition of the right to recover damages on account of personal injuries arising from a breach of warranty . . .

The particular importance of this advance resides in the fact that under such circumstances strict liability is imposed upon the maker or seller of the product. Recovery of damages does not depend upon proof of negligence or knowledge of the defect . . .

As the Sales Act and its liberal interpretation by the courts threw this protective cloak about the buyer, the decisions in various jurisdictions revealed beyond doubt that many manufacturers took steps to avoid these ever increasing warranty obligations. Realizing that the act governed the relationship of buyer and seller, they undertook to withdraw from actual and direct contractual contact with the buyer. They ceased selling products to the consuming public through their own employees and making contracts of sale in their own names. Instead, a system of independent dealers was established; their products were sold to dealers who in turn dealt with the buying public, ostensibly solely in their own personal capacity as sellers. In the past in many instances, manufacturers were able to transfer to the dealers burdens imposed by the act and thus achieved a large measure of immunity for themselves . . .

The manufacturer agrees to replace defective parts for 90 days after the sale or until the car has been driven 4,000 miles, whichever is first to occur, if the part is sent to the factory, transportation charges prepaid, and if examination discloses to its satisfaction that the part is defective. It is difficult to imagine a greater burden on the consumer, or less satisfactory remedy. Aside from imposing on the buyer the trouble of removing and shipping the part, the maker has sought to retain the uncontrolled discretion to decide the issue of defectiveness. Some courts have removed much of the force of that reservation by declaring that the purchaser is not bound by the manufacturer's decision . . .

Then Chrysler urges that since it was not a party to the sale by the dealer to Henningsen, there is no privity of contract between it and the plaintiffs, and the absence of this privity eliminates any such implied warranty . . .

The limitations of privity in contracts for the sale of goods developed their place in the law when marketing conditions were simple, when maker and buyer frequently met face to face on an equal bargaining plane and when many of the products were relatively uncomplicated and conducive to inspection by a buyer competent to evaluate their quality. See, *Freezer, Manufacturer's Liability for Injuries Caused by His Products,* 37 Mich. L. Rev. 1 (1938). With the advent of mass marketing, the manufacturer became remote from the purchaser, sales were accomplished through intermediaries, and the demand for the product was created by advertising media. In such an economy it became obvious that the consumer was the person being cultivated. Manifestly, the connotation of "consumer" was broader than that of "buyer." He signified such a person who, in the reasonable contemplation of the parties to the sale, might be expected to use the product. Thus, where the commodities sold are such that if defectively manufactured they will be dangerous to life or limb, then society's interests can only be protected by eliminating the requirement of privity between the maker and his dealers and the reasonably expressed ultimate consumer . . .

We see no rational doctrinal basis for differentiating between a fly in a bottle of beverage and a defective automobile. The unwholesome beverage may bring illness to one person, the defective car, with its great potentiality for harm to the driver, occupants, and others, demands even less adherence to the narrow barrier of privity . . .

Accordingly, we hold that under modern marketing conditions, when a manufacturer puts a new automobile in the stream of trade and promotes its purchase by the public, an implied warranty that it is reasonably suitable for use as such accompanies it into the hands of the ultimate purchaser. Absence of agency between the manufacturer and the dealer who makes the ultimate sale is immaterial . . .

Public policy at a given time finds expression in the Constitution, the statutory law and in judicial decisions. In the area of sale of goods, the legislature will have imposed an implied warranty of merchantability as a general incident of sale of an automobile by description. The warranty does not depend upon the affirmative intention of the parties. It is a child of the law; it annexes itself to the contract because of the very nature of the transaction. *Minneapolis Steel & Machinery Co. v. Casey Land Agency*, 51 N. D. 832, 201 N. W. 172 (Sup. Ct. 1924). The judicial process has recognized a right to recover damages for personal injuries arising from a breach of that warranty. The disclaimer of the implied warranty and exclusion of all obligations except those specifically assumed by the express warranty signify a studied effort to frustrate that protection. True, the Sales Act authorizes agreements between buyer and seller qualifying the warranty obligations. But quite obviously the Legislature contemplated lawful stipulations (which are determined by the circumstances of a particular case) arrived at freely by parties of relatively equal bargaining strength. The lawmakers did not authorize the automobile manufacturer to use its grossly disproportionate bargaining power to relieve itself from liability and to impose on the ordinary buyer, who in effect has no real freedom of choice, the grave danger of injury to himself and others that attends the sale of such a dangerous instrumentality as a defectively made automobile. In the framework of this case, illuminated as it is by the facts and the many decisions noted, we are of the opinion that Chrysler's attempted disclaimer of an implied warranty of merchantability and of the obligations arising therefrom is so inimical to the public good as to compel an adjudication of its invalidity . . .

Section 2–318 of the Uniform Commercial Code proposes that the warranty be extended to "any natural person who is in the family or household of his buyer or who is a guest in his home if it is reasonable to expect that such person may use, consume or be affected by the goods and who is injured in person by breach of the warranty." And the section provides also that "A seller may not exclude or limit the operation" of the extension. A footnote thereto says that beyond this provision "the section is neutral and is not intended to enlarge or restrict the developing case law on whether the seller's warranties, given to his buyer, who resells, extend to other persons in the distributive chain." Uniform Commercial Code . . .

Under all of the circumstances outlined above, the judgments in favor of the plaintiffs and against the defendants are affirmed.[2]

[2] Henningsen v. Bloomfield Motors, Inc. and Chrysler Corporation, 32 N. J. 358, 161 A.2d 65 (1960). See text page 146.

(c) *Dealer—ultimate consumer—third party transaction; security. B* purchased an automobile from S, a dealer. *B* traded in his old car, made a cash payment of $28.50 and executed a conditional sales contract and promissory note for the sum of $1,928.40, balance due on the purchase price, payable in 24 monthly installments of $80.35 each. These instruments were immediately indorsed and assigned for value before maturity to *A* Discount Corporation.

Before the purchase *B* examined the car and made a test drive. *B* testified he understood S to say, "With your automobile and $28.50 cash there will be a balance of $900 plus carrying charges and interest." S asked whether *B* was familiar with a contract which S had previously executed with *B*'s brother. *B* answered in the affirmative and signed the contract without reading it.

B took delivery of the car. While on the way home he examined the papers and found the balance due to be $1,928.40 and not $900.00. *B* made no complaint for two weeks. The complaint was made when *B* brought the car in to have the wheels aligned. S informed *B* that it was now out of his hands, for he had sold the contract to *A* Discount Corporation.

The financing data on the contract showed the list price of the car as $1,564.32. Added charges for freight, power-glide, undercoat, optional equipment, two-toned paint, taxes, insurance, finance charges, interest, etc. brought the total "time price" to $2,601.90, less $645.00 for the old car and $28.50 cash, and left a balance of $1,928.40.

B now seeks to rescind the contract, recover his money, and secure damages for deceit. In deciding whether *B*, the purchaser of the car, could rescind the contract and recover his down payment from a good faith purchaser of the note and conditional sale contract, the *A* Discount Corporation, the court discussed the negotiability of conditional sale contracts. The court cited *Tuscaloosa Motor Co. v. Cockrell,* Ala. Appeals, 132 S.2d 736 (1957), which case held that the note and the conditional sale contract were negotiable instruments. The court relied upon a previous Alabama case, *Commercial Credit Co. v. Seale,* 30 Ala. App. 300, 8 S.2d 199 (1942), in which case an assignee, a purchaser for value before maturity of a conditional sale contract and a note attached, recovered possession of a car sold by a dealer to a defaulting buyer. Concerning the right of a third party—a purchaser of a conditional sale contract—to take free from defenses as if the conditional sale contract were a negotiable instrument, SIMPSON, J. in the *Seale* case states:

> The instrument in suit (the conditional sale contract) appears to have all the lineaments and characteristics of a negotiable instrument when tested by the foregoing rules of law (NIL). In fact, the question posed for our decision seems to have been conclusively settled by the holding in the Parks case, supra, where it was observed: "The fact that a negotiable paper retains title

to property therein described as security for the debt does not destroy its negotiability. Such retention of title gives a better security for the note, partakes of the nature, and is entitled to the same protection as the secured debt. Plaintiff therefore is in as favorable a position as if the suit were upon the note."

The conditional sale contract, therefore, partaking of the same nature and entitled to the same protection as the negotiable note, was not subject to the defense interposed in a suit by an innocent holder thereof in due course. It is axiomatic, of course, that such paper in the hands of a bona fide purchaser for value, before maturity, is immune from the defenses which might be available against it when suit is by the original holder, unless it be shown that such purchaser had notice of such defenses . . .

Another error which militates against affirmance is the ruling of the trial court as regards the admissibility of testimony of the oral warranty claimed by the defendants. The contract for the purchase of the automobile (in the form of a purchase order) was in writing, duly signed by both parties and purports to express the entire agreement.

The case held that the purchaser of the conditional sale contract took the paper free of the defenses which the buyer had against the seller. Thus the case illustrates how law has evolved to meet the best interest of commerce and how, by usage and trade, the "commercial meaning" intended by the parties has been made effective.

The ultimate consumer transaction takes many forms and is always changing. It may be manufacturer direct to the consumer by way of door-to-door selling; or manufacturer to retail store to consumer; or by mail order, supermarket, or road-side stand. The consumer's legal rights vary with each situation. Thus a consumer injured by an explosion of a bottle of catsup in a supermarket stands in a different relationship to the retailer than a purchaser of a defective product purchased by way of a mail order catalogue.

2. *The Industrial Goods Transaction—Illustrations.* The commercial transaction concerned with industrial goods differs considerably from transactions dealing with consumer goods. The difference is reflected primarily in the type of buyer and the purpose for his purchase. Buyers are fewer and they are more familiar with the commodity; quantities are larger, financing is different; and sales are less frequent. The transaction is most generally direct from the producer to the processor—distributor or service operator. The transaction may be executed by intermediaries, distributors, agents, or middlemen. Each particular type of transaction involves the application and creation of different legal relations, depending upon the nature of the contract of sale, the financial plan, remedies, warranties, and other factors.

(a) *Manufacturer—dealer, distributor transaction. M* Company delivered five automobiles to *D* Company, dealer and distributor, by common carrier. The carrier, in violation of instructions, delivered the automobiles to *D* Company without receipt of payment in full either by way of cash or certified check. The automobiles were delivered by the carrier upon receipt of an uncertified check for three cars and no payment for two cars. The checks were subsequently dishonored. *D* Company became insolvent and the automobiles were taken by receivers of *D* Company. *M* Company, the manufacturer, demanded surrender of the five automobiles from the receivers. The receivers refused to surrender the cars.

M Company and *D* Company, the dealer, were parties to a written contract which reads as follows:

Title to each company product shall be and remain with the company until receipt by the company in cash of the full purchase price therefor, together with all charges provided in paragraph 4, unless the sale is on credit, in which event title shall pass on delivery to carrier or to dealer, whichever first shall occur, and that the company shall have the right to retake possession of and resell each company product until title to such product shall have passed to the dealer.

In commenting upon the theory and purpose of the Uniform Commercial Code concerning the financial consequences flowing from the relationship of the parties in the type of transaction set out above and discussing how the rights of the parties are determined "irrespective of location of legal title," the court in *Girard Trust Bank v. Lepley Ford*, Common Pleas Court in Philadelphia County, Pa., 1957, 12 D. & C.2d 351, states:

Petitioner (*M* Company) alleges that since the title to the five automobiles did not pass from it nor vest in Warren Lepley Ford, Inc. (*D* Company) petitioner is still owner and entitled to the immediate possession of the said automobiles.

There can be no doubt that this matter comes within the scope of the Uniform Commercial Code of April 6, 1953, P. L. 3, 12A PS Section 1–101, which is intended to encompass commercial transactions within this Commonwealth. After a careful study of the Code, we conclude that we are compelled to find against petitioner.

One of the changes brought about by the code is in reference to title to property. The common law and the Sales Act of May 19, 1915, P. L. 543, 69 PS Section 1 et seq., made the right of the parties to a transaction depend upon the location of the legal title. The Code, however, provides for the rights of parties irrespective of the location of legal title: Introductory Comment, Pennsylvania Bar Association Notes, 12A PS page 62. The first sentence of Section 2–401 of the Code provides:

Each provision of this Article with regard to the rights, obligations and remedies of the seller, the buyer, purchasers or other third parties applies irrespective of title to the goods except where the provision refers to such title.

The reason for the rule is to be found in the Uniform Commercial Code Comment, 12A PS page 63, wherein it is stated:

The arrangement of the present Article is in terms of contract for sale and the various steps of its performance. The legal consequences are stated as following directly from the contract and action taken under it without resorting to the idea of when property or title passed or was to pass as being the determining factor. The purpose is to avoid making practical issues between practical men turn upon the location of an intangible something, the passing of which no man can prove by evidence, and to substitute for such abstractions proof of words and actions of a tangible character.

The article on secured transactions removes any doubt of the lack of importance of where legal title rests. Section 9–202 provides:

Each provision of this Article with regard to rights, obligations and remedies applies whether title to collateral is in the secured party or in the debtor.

The petitioner argues in its brief that Section 1–102 (3) (e) of the Code permits a variance, by agreement, from the effect of the provisions of the Code and thus title remains of importance by the terms of the contract. The section relied on by the petitioner provides:

Section 1–102 (3) (e):

Subject to the foregoing subsections and except as otherwise specifically provided in this Act, the effect of provisions of this Act may be varied by agreement.

However, a foregoing subsection, 1-102 (3) (b) provides:

Except as otherwise provided by this Act the rights and duties of a third party may not be adversely affected by an agreement to which he is not a party or by which he is not otherwise bound;

Therefore, any contractual agreement between petitioner and Warren Lepley Ford, Inc. cannot vary the rights of the receivers in this case, as provided for in the Code.

In order to ascertain the rights of the parties in this case, it is necessary to determine their status or classification under the Code. The status of the receivers is that of a lien creditor from the time of their appointment: Section 9–301 (3). The status of petitioner, the goods having been delivered to the buyer, is that of a holder of a security interest. Section 2–401 (1) (a) provides that any reservation by a seller of the title (property) in goods delivered or otherwise identified to a contract for sale is limited in effect to reservation of a security interest. The status and classification of the petitioner may also be determined from Section 1–201 (37), which defines security interest as follows:

Security interests mean an interest in property which secures payment or performance of an obligation. The reservation by a seller or consignor of property notwithstanding identification of goods to a contract for sale or notwithstanding shipment or delivery is a security interest. The term also includes the interest of a financing buyer of accounts, chattel paper, or contract rights.

Having determined the petitioner's status as the holder of a security interest we turn to Article 9 of the Code which regulates security interests in personal property and sets forth the rights of the parties in regard thereto.

The rights of the parties to a security transaction are set forth in Article 9 and are made dependent upon whether or not the security interest has been perfected. Section 9–302 requires the filing of a financing statement to perfect a security interest, with certain exceptions listed therein not applicable in the case at bar. It is agreed that petitioner filed no financing statement. Petitioner argues that it was not necessary to perfect its security interest by filing a financing statement because the transaction comes within Section 9–302 (1) (d), which exempts from filing a purchase money security interest in consumer goods. Section 9–302 provides:

(1) a financing statement must be filed to perfect all security interests except those covered in Subsection (2) and the following: . . .

(d) a purchase money security interest in consumer goods; but filing is required if the goods are part of the realty under Section 9–313 or a motor vehicle required to be licensed;

We cannot agree with petitioner's contention that this was a sale of consumer goods. Section 9–109 (1) defines consumer goods as follows:

(1) Consumer goods if they are used or bought for use primarily for personal, family, or household purposes;

The nature of this transaction clearly shows that *D* Company, as a dealer, purchased these automobiles for the purpose of resale. This places the goods in the classification of inventory and as such the Code required the petitioner to file a financing statement to perfect its security interest. Section 9–109 (4) defines inventory as:

(4) inventory if they are held or are being prepared for sale . . .

The exception with respect to consumer goods does not, therefore, apply to this transaction. There is another exception found in Section 9–302 to the requirement that security interests be perfected. Section 9–302, subsections (2) and (2) (b) provides:

(2) the filing provisions of this Article do not apply to the assignment of a perfected security interest, or to a security interest . . .

(b) in property subject to a statute of this state which provides for central filing of, or which requires indication on a certificate of title of, such security interests in such property.

Compliance with any such statute is equivalent to filing under this Article.

These provisions indicate that if a statute of the state requires that a lien or encumbrance be noted on a certificate of title, then filing is not required under Section 9–302. The Vehicle Code of May 1, 1929, P.L. 905, 75 PS Section 284, requires certain types of liens and encumbrances to be noted on the title, it is certain, under Section 31 (b) of the Vehicle Code, that manufacturers and dealers, until resale of the vehicles, are not required to obtain certificates of title for new motor vehicles. It seems clear, therefore, that the automobiles here involved do not fall within the provisions of Section 9–302 (2) as goods, a security in which is not required to be perfected.

It follows from the foregoing that the petitioner is the holder of an unperfected security interest.

Its rights as such are determined by Section 9–301, which provides:

(1) Except as otherwise provided in Subsection (2), an unperfected security interest is subordinate to the rights of . . .

(c) a lien creditor who becomes such without knowledge of the security interest and before it is perfected;

It is agreed by the parties that the receivers had no knowledge of the existence of a security interest in the petitioner. It is clear that as lien creditors without knowledge of any existent unperfected security interest the receivers take priority over the holder of such unperfected security interest.

For the reasons given, the court held since the receivers had no knowledge of the manufacturer's claimed security interest, the receivers should prevail over *D* Company and *M* Company, notwithstanding the manufacturer's claim of "title."

3. *Classification of Goods Under the Commercial Code.* The classifications of goods discussed above as the subject matter of a transaction are called "consumer goods" and "industrial goods." The terms "consumer goods" and "industrial goods" are general and have application and meaning only when it is ascertained to whom the goods are sent and the purpose for which they are used. The methods and reasons for the transfer of different kinds of goods from one person to another involve and create many different kinds of legal relationships. In order to better understand the "legal functional classifications of goods" set out in the Code, it is necessary to appreciate the classification of goods as "consumer goods" and "industrial goods," for it is these goods that constitute the subject matter of the "Commercial Transaction." The Uniform Commercial Code, which has for its purpose encompassing the entire "commercial transaction," has codified all the law governing the transaction. Thus to answer legal questions concerning the rights of the parties involved in any particular phase, the Code must be considered as a whole. Goods have therefore been classified under the Code according to the relationship of the parties in light of the purpose for which the goods are to be used, their mobility, and the means and methods by which the goods are transferred.

Under Article 2, Sales, Section 2–105 (1) "goods" means:

> All things (including specially manufactured goods) which are movable at the time of identification to the contract for sale other than the money in which the price is to be paid, investment securities (Article 8), and things in action. Goods also includes the unborn young of animals and growing crops and other identified things attached to realty as described in the section on goods to be severed from realty (Section 2–107).

The concept of "movability" or negotiability of goods rather than the idea of the thing—personal property, merchandise, or chattels—is employed by the Code. For a discussion of basic legal concepts about "things" as property see Section 1–5, page 14 of the text. Under Article 2, "unborn young of animals," "growing crops," and "things attached to realty" are included. Money, investment securities, choses in action, and real estate are not "things or goods" under this Article. Although investment securities are expressly excluded by Article 3, Sales, the drafters state "it is not intended by this exclusion . . . to prevent the application of Article 3, Sales, to choses in action, securities, etc., when the case makes such application sensible and the situation involved is not covered by Article 8."

Under Article 7, Documents of Title, Section 7–102 (e) "goods" means all things—personal property, chattels, merchandise—which are treated as movable for the purpose of a contract of storage or transportation.

Under Article 9, Secured Transactions, Section 9–105 (f) "goods" includes "all things which are movable at the time the security interest attaches or which are fixtures (Section 9–313) but does not include money, documents, instruments, accounts, chattel paper, general intangibles, contract rights, and other things in action. "Goods" also includes the unborn young of animals and growing crops."

For the purpose of making effective the security interest in security transactions, under Section 9–109 "goods" are classified as "consumer goods, equipment, farm products, inventory," as follows:

(1) consumer goods if they are used or bought for use primarily for personal, family, or household purposes;
(2) equipment if they are used or bought for use primarily in business (including farming or a profession) or by a debtor who is a nonprofit organization or a government subdivision or agency or if the goods are not included in the definition of inventory, farm products, or consumer goods;
(3) farm products if they are crops or livestock or supplies used or produced in farming operations or if they are products or crops or livestock in their unmanufactured states (such as ginned cotton, wool clip, maple syrup, milk, and eggs), and if they are in the possession of a debtor engaged in raising, fattening, grazing or other farming operations. If goods are farm products they are neither equipment nor inventory;
(4) inventory if they are held by a person who holds them for sale or lease or to be furnished under contracts of service or if he has so furnished them, or if they are raw materials, work in process, or materials used or consumed in a business. Inventory of a person is not to be classified as his equipment.

Comment 1 to the above section indicates the importance of such classification thusly:

This classification is important in many situations: it is relevant for example in determining the rights of the persons who buy from a debtor goods subject to a security interest (Section 9–307); in certain questions of priority (Section 9–312); in determining the place of filing (Section 9–401); and in working out rights after default (Part 5).

The Code has set up "special rules applicable to different classes of collateral." Comment 5 to Section 9–102 contains an index of these rules. This classification is mutually exclusive.

Property—an automobile for example—cannot at the same time and as to the same person, be both equipment and inventory. In borderline cases—a physician's car or a farmer's jeep which might be either consumer goods or equipment—the principal use to which the property is put should be considered as determinative. Goods can fall into different classes at different times; a radio is inventory in the hands of a dealer and consumer goods in the hands of a householder.[3]

1-35. General provisions; rules of construction; variation by contract. *Rules of construction.* The Code is to be "liberally construed and applied to promote its purposes and policies"; namely, "to amplify, clarify, and modernize the law governing commercial transactions; to permit

[3] Comment, paragraph 1 and 2, Uniform Commercial Code, 1958 Official Text, p. 616.

the continued expansion of commercial practices through custom and usage and agreement of the parties; and to make uniform the law among the various jurisdictions."

The Code is drafted as a "general act intended as a unified coverage of the subject matter, a commercial transaction." It is a uniform codification of "permanent character," and since it covers an "entire field of the law," it is not vulnerable to implied repeal, "if such can reasonably be avoided."

The Code, however, is not so rigid that courts may not, in order to carry out its policies and purposes, recognize new developments and commercial situations, even though such situations are not included within its express language. This principle of inclusion is illustrated and was adopted in the case of *Agar v. Agar*, 264 N. Y. 248, 190 N.E. 479 (1934), wherein the court limited the seller's remedy to damages for the breach of an executory contract of the sale of a stock certificate—chose in action—not covered by the Uniform Sales Act.

For the sake of uniformity and to comply with business experience, the court construed the word "goods" in the Sales Act to include "choses in action." The drafters of the U.C.C. not only intend that the Code shall cover matters not expressly included therein, where reasonable, but they also intend not to unduly limit "freedom of contract."

Section 1–102 (3) of the Code provides that it

> may be varied by agreement, except as otherwise provided in this Act and except that the obligations of good faith, diligence, reasonableness, and care prescribed by this Act may not be disclaimed by agreement but the parties may by agreement determine the standards by which the performance of such obligations is to be measured if such standards are not manifestly unreasonable.

There are some limitations upon the extent to which "the effect of the Code may be varied by agreement."

Limit on variation by contract. The meaning of the statute and the definition cannot be varied by agreement. Thus an instrument non-negotiable in form cannot by agreement be made negotiable. Thus contracts of employment, documents of title, security transactions, and informal written claims for money, even though they recite upon their face "This instrument shall be negotiable," are not negotiable instruments if they do not comply with the formal requisities set out in Section 3–104, Article 3. But, such instruments may be negotiable under the provisions of other articles of the Code. However, this does not mean that the parties cannot by contract or conduct arrive at a result similar to negotiability by estoppel. That is, an obligor by his conduct or agreement may be precluded from setting up defenses against a good faith purchaser of an instrument that does not comply with formal requirements of the Code.

However, subject to any statute [see Motor Vehicle Finance Act, Pa. Stat. Section 615 (g) discussed in *First National Bank of Milville v. Horwatt,* 192 Pa. Super, 581, 162 A.2d 60 (1960), see Article 3–103 (27), Article 9–206] or decision which establishes a different rule for buyers of consumer goods, an agreement by a buyer that he will not assert against an assignee any claim or defense which he may have against the seller, is enforceable by an assignee who takes his assignment for value in good faith and without notice of a claim or defense, except as to defenses of a type which may be asserted against a holder in due course of a negotiable instrument under Article 3 on Commercial Paper.[4]

This limitation makes it impossible to cut off by waiver "real defenses as in the law of Negotiable Instruments." The execution of a negotiable note in connection with a security agreement is given like effect as the execution of an agreement containing a waiver of defense clause.

The "agreement" includes within it the effect given to course of dealings and usage of the trade as set out particularly in Section 1–205. The Code, by the words "usage of trade," seeks to give to the agreement the "commercial meaning" intended by the parties. "The language used by the parties is to be interpreted as meaning what it may fairly be expected to mean to the parties involved in the particular transaction and in a given locality or in a given vocation or trade." The Commercial Code draws a distinction between professional business people and the consumer. Such professional business people are subject to higher standards of conduct because of experience and knowledge.

It is the intention of the drafters that the Code be interpreted in light of "commercial meaning" in such a manner as to avoid "interference with evolutionary growth" as occurred in *Manhattan v. Morgan,* 242 N.Y. 38, 15 N.E. 594 (1926), where under the formal requisites set out by the Negotiable Instruments Act in Sections 20, 23, and 24, a certificate issued by a banker in the following form:

> This is to certify that the bearer is entitled to receive a bond for one thousand dollars . . . of the kingdom of Belgium . . . upon the surrender of and in exchange for this certificate . . . every taker and holder of this certificate . . . and the undersigned agree to treat the bearer of the certificate owner thereof . . .

was held nonnegotiable, denying the good faith purchaser the right to collect the bonds because of notice of theft.

Although this instrument would not be negotiable under Article 3 of the Code—"Commercial Paper"—it is believed the results of negotiability could have been obtained under Article 8 of the Code.

Territorial application of the Code (U.C.C. Section 1–105). Where the

[4] Anglo-California Trust Co. v. Hall, p. 439.

transaction covers two or more states, the parties may agree that the law of either state or a particular state shall govern the rights and duties of the parties. Concerning failure to so contract, the Code provides that a court in a Code state shall apply the Code, if the transaction "bears an appropriate relation to the state." What is an appropriate relation to the state is not specified. In *Atlas Credit Corporation v. Dolbow,* 193 Pa. Super. 649, 165 A.2d 704 (1961), a Delaware resident purchased a boat in Delaware for $5,980, making a down payment of $500. A Credit Corporation advanced to the seller $5,480 and took therefore as security an assignment of the sale contract, under an agreement called an *equipment lease.* The agreement was accompanied by a promissory note containing a confession of judgment clause. The contract was not filed and did not contain an agreement as to the application of the law of any particular state. The agreement called for performance in Pennsylvania. After default by the buyer, the boat was repossessed, brought to Pennsylvania, and sold. The court held, "This is sufficient to warrant the application of Pennsylvania law as bearing a reasonable relationship to the transaction."

Remedies to be liberally construed (U.C.C. Section 1–106). The purpose of this section is:

> . . . to negate the unduly narrow or technical interpretation of some remedial provisions of prior legislation by providing that the remedies in this Act are to be liberally administered to the end stated in the section. Second, to make it clear that compensatory damages are limited to compensation. They do not include consequential or special damages, or penal damages; and the Act elsewhere makes it clear that damages must be minimized.

Waiver or renunciation of claim or right after breach (U.C.C. Section 1–107). The purpose of this section as stated by the comment is:

> This section makes consideration unnecessary to the effective renunciation or waiver of rights or claims arising out of an alleged breach of a commercial contract where such renunciation is in writing and signed and delivered by the aggrieved party. Its provisions, however, must be read in conjunction with the section imposing an obligation of good faith (Section 1–203). There may, of course, also be an oral renunciation or waiver sustained by consideration but subject to Statute of Frauds provisions and to the Section of Article 2 on Sales dealing with the modification of signed writings (Section 2–209). As is made express in the latter Section this Act fully recognizes the effectiveness of waiver and estoppel.

This changes the common law rules which required consideration in order to make a release binding. (For discussion of the common law doctrines of consideration, release, accord and satisfaction, and renunciation as applied to other areas of the law, see pp. 199, 334, and 335.)

Review Questions and Problems

1. Mr. *X*, a commission merchant, engaged in buying stock, purchased 25 head of hogs from Farmer *Y*. Farmer *Y* delivered the animals to a nearby shipping point. Trace the legal relations arising from the contracts involved in the various facets of the total "commercial transaction" from live hogs to sausage wrapped in plastic and purchased by housewife *W* at an urban supermarket.
2. Name several legal instruments that are used in a "commercial transaction," and explain the purpose of each.
3. Describe and illustrate by appropriate hypotheticals the different types of subject matter—goods—to which the term "commercial transaction" has meaning.
4. *P* entered into an oral contract with *D* whereby *D* agreed to purchase a Keystone stoker boiler unit for *P* and install it as a part of a heating system to be used in a four-unit apartment house owned by *P*. For a consideration of $1400, *D* orally agreed to secure the heater and adapt it to the appurtenances in the apartment in order to convert the system from steam to hot water. *D* is not a dealer in heating units. He is a handyman and on occasions installs heating systems which he purchases from others. *P* had previously hired *D* as a plasterer but not as a plumber. *P* told *D* that he was relying on *D*'s skill and knowledge to furnish and install a Keystone unit that would fit and be proper and suitable to heat the building. It was understood between the parties that *D* could not "guarantee" the "Keystone Unit."

   After installation, the unit would not heat *P*'s apartment. *D* unsuccessfully attempted to correct the difficulty. *P*, at a cost of $2,232.50, found it necessary to install a larger boiler and do other work in order to adequately heat the apartment. *P* sues *D* for damages. What result? *Victor v. Barzaleski*, Court of Common Pleas of Luzerne County, Pa., 19 D. & C. 698, 14 Luzerne 150 (1939), Del Duca & King, Commercial Code Litigation, Dickinson School of Law, (1960).
5. *A*, nursery operator, desired to purchase an automatic electric heating system for his greenhouse. He explained his needs to the *X* Heating Company and the latter agreed to install a heating system for $2500. The nurseryman signed a note and conditional sale contract for this amount. *X* sold the paper to *Y* Bank. The heating system failed to maintain proper temperature and *A*'s plants died. The bank seeks to collect on the note. What are the rights of the parties?
6. Illustrate how the Uniform Commercial Code makes allowance for new developments in commercial situations even though such situations are not included within the express language of the Code.
7. What are the reasons for drawing a distinction between "consumer goods" and "industrial goods"?
8. If a contract is entered into between *A*, a citizen of a non-Code state and *B*, a citizen of a Code state, what law will determine the rights and duties of the parties to the contract and the remedies available for breach?

BOOK II

CONTRACTS

8

Nature of a Contract

2-1. Introduction. The law of contracts forms the oldest branch of the law relating to business or to commercial transactions. In one form or another it has existed from the beginning of organized society. Just as the safety of person and of property depends upon the rules of criminal law, so the security and stability of the business world are dependent upon the law of contracts. It is the legal mechanism by which the free enterprise capitalistic system has developed and been made to operate. It is the tool by which promises are made and expectations created to the end that there will be a continuous flow of goods and services to meet man's economic needs.

To a very high degree, our whole philosophy of personal liberty, with its concept of private property—the right to acquire and to dispose of property freely with provision for individual business enterprise—has as one of its main structural supports the law of contracts. The freedom to contract as well as the sanctity of and respect for contracts form a highly important feature of our cultural life.

Capital and wealth are evidenced by promises. The greater the number of enforceable promises, the greater the wealth. In order for a contract to serve as an instrument to create wealth and enhance the economic good, freedom to contract, accompanied by legal machinery for the enforcement of promises, is essential.

By contract the parties, by mutual assent either expressed or implied, "fix their own terms and set bounds upon their liabilities." Thus, it may be said that the parties freely create for themselves their own law, leaving it only to the state to set up the machinery for the interpretation of the contract and the enforcement of the promises.

Although the parties to a contract "fix their own terms and set bounds upon their liabilities," they are subject to limitations. To create a valid contract, there must be compliance with specific rules of law. The expression of "the terms" must be promissory in character and must create a legal obligation. What promises are legally binding depend upon how and to whom they are expressed and whether there are present other elements, such as consideration, exchange of value, reliance, capacity of the parties, and other aspects concerned with social policy and public morals. In addition to the traditional formal requirements, a contract is no longer exclusively a private individual affair between the parties. It has become a matter of public concern. The unequal distribution of economic power has brought about inequality in bargaining; hence, in many areas such as marketing, labor relations, insurance, and corporations, the parties must "fix their terms and set bounds on their liabilities" within the requirements of legislative control.

Legislation as a source of law is not limited to these areas however. Legislation provides the framework of the law in the areas of sales, commercial paper, partnerships, corporations, and secured transactions. To provide uniformity among the states, uniform statutes were developed in many of these areas. However, many states modified the Uniform Acts or did not adopt them. In recent years, there has been a movement to unite the law applicable to commercial transactions in one uniform statute known as the Uniform Commercial Code. The complete history of the Code was discussed in Chapter five.

The Code, which has now been adopted in over twenty-five states, is limited in its application. It does not apply to noncommercial transactions such as the sale of real estate or contracts involving services. The Code incorporates by reference the basic principles of law and equity including the law relating to voidable contracts and agency. The student is cautioned to keep the limited applicability of the Code clearly in mind.

Since the law of contracts furnishes the foundation for other branches of commercial law, a study of the general rules applicable to contract law material precedes the invasion of other fields. The particular rules of law pertaining to agency, sales, negotiable instruments, corporations, partnerships, and security transactions are all superimposed upon the general principles of contract law.

Contracts are made so frequently and have become so much a part of our everyday life that we often fail to realize when they are made or, once made, when they are performed. Purchasing groceries, dropping money in the coin box of a bus, paying for a ticket to the theatre, and signing a written agreement to buy real estate are each equally illustrative of the myriad of daily contract transactions.

2-2. Classification. For certain purposes it is desirable to classify contracts according to characteristics which they possess. They may well be classified as follows:

1. Formal or simple.
2. Executed or executory.
3. Express or implied (in fact or in law).

4. Bilateral or unilateral.
5. Valid, voidable, or unenforceable.[1]

2-3. Formal or simple contracts. During the early history of the law, some prescribed formality had to accompany a promise or transfer to make it enforceable. Early English law enforced only those promises which were written, signed, and sealed. The seal was usually a waxen impression placed on the document immediately after the signature. Later the doctrine of consideration—more fully developed in a later chapter—was substituted for the seal. For most transactions, consideration is now required in the majority of the states even though a seal is used. In some states, a seal creates a presumption of consideration but is not conclusive, being rebuttable by the presentation of evidence to the contrary. Those contracts which do not require or bear a seal are designated *simple* or *informal* contracts.

In most of our states, certain documents, such as deeds, powers of attorney, and formal corporate acts, must be accompanied by a seal, and are known as *formal* contracts. It has become customary on many instruments to use the word "SEAL" or the initials "L.S." in place of the more formal waxen or mechanical impression.

2-4. Executed and executory contracts. An executed contract is one that has been fully carried out by the contracting parties. An executory contract is one that is yet to be performed. An agreement may be executed on the part of one party and executory on the part of the other. A contract for the purchase of a suit of clothes on credit, followed by the delivery of the suit, is executed on the part of the dealer and executory on the part of the purchaser.

2-5. Express or implied. A contract may result from an agreement in which all of the detailed terms are clearly set forth either in writing or orally, in which event it is said to be an *express* contract. On the other hand, a contract may be entirely implied from facts such as acts of the parties, the acts being such that a contract may be inferred from them. In other instances, the contract may be, and often is, partially expressed and partially implied. Thus, an employee may be engaged to perform certain work without any clear agreement as to the compensation to be received. When the service has been rendered, the courts impose a duty upon the employer to pay a reasonable sum for the benefit received. This duty to pay is implied from the nature of the situation and the type of service rendered.

A contract is also implied in fact whenever one person, without protest, knowingly accepts a benefit at the expense of another under circumstances which negate the possibility of a gift. The person who accepts the

[1] To be discussed in detail in chapters which follow.

benefit implicitly promises to pay the fair value of the benefit that he receives, but no implied promise to pay arises where the person who receives a benefit is totally unaware that such a benefit is being conferred. It is the acceptance of benefits at a time when it is possible to reject them that raises the implied promise to pay for them. To illustrate, *A*, by mistake, and during the absence of *B* on a fishing trip, made certain repairs on *B*'s residence. Upon his return *B* was under no duty to pay for the repairs, although he of necessity made use of them in connection with his occupancy of the property. The use of the house created no implied promise to pay for the repairs, since *B* had never had the opportunity to reject them. However, where *B* is present and watches the repairs being made, his silence may well be deemed an acceptance of an offer, obligating him to pay the reasonable value of the improvement.

2-6. Quasi contract. A contract implied in fact must be distinguished from a contract implied in law, generally known as quasi contract. The former is a true contract, created by inference from facts and circumstances which show the assent and intention of the parties. The latter arises in situations in which courts, to do justice and to avoid unjust enrichment, impose a duty upon a party and consider the duty as arising from a contract for the purpose of establishing the existence of a legal remedy. The remedy of quasi contract is a legal fiction dictated by reason, justice, and equity to prevent one person from being unjustly enriched at the expense of another. The law presumes a promise by a party to do what in equity and good conscience he ought to do even though he does not want or intend to do it. The remedy of quasi contract is generally not available where there is an action for breach of an express contract.

Quasi contract, as a remedy, is used in several types of situations where one person, unofficiously and without fault or misconduct, confers a benefit upon another, for which the latter in equity and good conscience ought to pay.[2] Among such situations are those in which money is improperly paid or received, property is wrongfully appropriated or converted, money or property is obtained by trespass, fraud, or duress, or necessities of life are furnished a person under legal disability. In each of these situations, there is no contract but one person would be unjustly enriched if he were not required to pay for the benefits received.

2-7. Bilateral or unilateral contracts. As stated in the section which follows, a contract grows out of an offer made by one party to another and accepted by the latter. A bilateral contract involves two promises, one made by each of the parties to the agreement. To illustrate, let us assume that *A* offers to sell to *B* certain merchandise at an established price. *B*, after receiving the offer, communicates his acceptance to *A* by

[2] Misisco v. La Maita, page 167.

promising to buy the merchandise and to pay the price set forth in the offer. After the promises are exchanged, it becomes the duty of each party to carry out the terms of the agreement. Most contracts are bilateral in character.

A *unilateral* contract consists of a promise for an act, the acceptance consisting of the performance of the act requested rather than the promise to perform it. An unsolicited order for merchandise sent by a retailer to a manufacturer, asking for prompt shipment of the goods ordered, best illustrates a unilateral offer. The buyer requests and desires shipment, rather than a promise to ship. Until the goods are shipped, the retailer is at liberty to withdraw his offer. Further discussion of these contracts will be found in the later chapter dealing with offer and acceptance.

2-8. Elements of a contract. A contract has been defined as "an agreement enforceable by law." A more complete definition follows: A contract is an agreement between two or more competent persons, having for its purpose a legal object, wherein each of the persons acts in a certain manner or promises to act or to refrain from acting in such a manner. This definition breaks up logically into four component parts:

1. Agreement—offer and acceptance.
2. Mutuality—consideration.
3. Competent parties.
4. Legal object.

These elements are all essential in an enforceable agreement and will be considered in detail in the chapters that follow. In addition to the discussion of these matters, each chapter will contain a discussion of the Code provisions relating to contracts for the sale of personal property.

NATURE OF A CONTRACT CASE

MISISCO v. LA MAITA
1963 (Conn.) 192 A(2) 891

MURPHY. The plaintiff was awarded a judgment for damages of $4500 representing the increase in value of certain real property owned by the defendant on which the plaintiff had expended time and money in improvements under a repudiated oral agreement of the defendant to convey the property to the plaintiff at a specified time. . . .

The defendant in 1955 offered and agreed to sell, when he retired at age sixty-five, a two-family house and garage which he owned in Stratford to the plaintiff, his nephew, for $14,500. At the time, the two apartments brought in rent of $62.40 a month. The plaintiff moved into the second-floor apartment, for which he paid $30 a month rent, and subsequently took over the entire house and garage, for all of which he paid the defendant $100 per month. Thereafter, the plaintiff made substantial alterations and improvements to the property and created a third apartment. He expended approximately $4885 in so doing, excluding the value of his own time. After increasing the rent to $120 per month, the defendant repudiated his agreement to sell and instituted eviction proceedings which caused the plaintiff to vacate the premises in March, 1961. The alterations and improvements to the property were made with the knowledge, acquiescence and encouragement of the defendant and in reliance on his agreement to sell the property to the plaintiff. . . .

Upon these facts, the court concluded that the agreement, not being in writing, was . . . (unenforceable), that the property had been enhanced in value in the amount of $4500, and that under the circumstances the defendant should not be permitted to retain, without compensation, the benefits obtained unjustly by his repudiation of the agreement. . . .

The cause of action stated is not for breach of contract but is to recover for the loss which the plaintiff has incurred as a result of making, to the enrichment of the defendant, expenditures for and the improvements to the property in reliance on a course of conduct by the defendant which led the plaintiff to believe that the defendant would sell the property to him. *Fischer v. Kennedy*, 106 Conn. 484, 492, 138 A. 503. It is an action in quasi contract, i.e., an obligation, arising by law, on which the same remedy is given as would be given if the obligation arose out of contract. *Bartlett v. Raidart*, 107 Conn. 691, 694, 142 A. 398. Although the right of recovery is based on equitable principles, it is nevertheless an action at law, the purpose of which is to prevent unjust enrichment.

There is no error. In this opinion the other judges concurred.

9 Offer and Acceptance

FORMATION OF AN OFFER

2-9. Definition. As noted in the previous chapter, one of the first steps in the formation of any contract lies in arriving at an agreement between the contracting parties. This agreement is sometimes spoken of as "a meeting of the minds" but is better known as *offer and acceptance.* An agreement can be reached only after one of the parties has made a definite proposal to the other. Such a proposal constitutes an offer.

An *offer* is the communication by one party, known as the *offeror,* to another party, called the *offeree,* of the former's willingness to act or to refrain from acting as specified if the latter will act or promise to act or refrain from acting as requested.

2-10. Communication. No offer becomes effective until it has been communicated to the offeree. The unexpressed desire to enter into an agreement can never constitute an offer. The writing of a letter embodying a definite proposition will also prove futile unless the letter is mailed and reaches the offeree.

An offer is effectively communicated only by the offeror or his duly authorized agent. If the offeree learns of the offeror's intention from some outside source, no offer results because it must be communicated through the medium or channel selected by the offeror.

An offer to the public may be made through the newspapers[1] or the posting of notices, but it is not effective so far as a particular individual is concerned until he learns that the offer has been made.

2-11. Meeting of minds. The minds of the contracting parties must meet on the subject matter of the contract or no true agreement has been reached. When Jones offers to sell his used Chevrolet car to Brown for $750 and Brown agrees to buy it, no contract results if Jones, who has two such cars, was thinking of one and Brown had in mind the other. In reality they failed to reach an agreement; their negotiations resulted in no bargain because Jones offered to sell Car *X* and Brown promises to buy Car *Y*. The rule that the minds of the parties must be in accord is limited

[1] Lefkowitz v. Great Minneapolis Surplus Store, page 179.

in one important respect; namely, that the intention of the parties is to be determined by their individual conduct—and what each leads the other reasonably to believe—rather than by their innermost thoughts, which can be known only to themselves. It is the objective manifestation of intent rather than the subjective which controls. Thus, the courts hold the minds of the parties to have met when a written agreement is signed. Each person who signs a written document with the idea of entering into a contract is presumed to know the contents thereof. Since the act of signing manifests a person's intention to be bound by the terms contained in the writing, he is in no position at a later date to contend effectively that he did not mean to enter into the particular agreement. All contracts should be read carefully before they are signed.

Offers clearly made in jest or under the strain or stress of great excitement are usually not enforced, as one is not reasonably justified in relying on them.

2-12. Offer definite. Not all communications that invite future business transactions are so worded as to constitute offers. Many are of a preliminary character, being transmitted primarily for the purpose of inducing the person to whom they are addressed to respond with an offer.[2] Within this class of communications fall most catalogs, circulars, advertisements, estimates, proposals in which major terms are not included, and oral statements of general terms, where it is understood that the detailed terms will be reduced to writing and signed before the agreement is to be binding.

The chief reason why proposals of the kind indicated do not qualify as offers is that the parties making them have no intention of entering into an agreement on the basis of the terms expressed. The party making the statement, as the other party should reasonably understand, never intends any legal consequences to flow from his action, sometimes because major terms are lacking and sometimes because of the circumstances under which the statements are made. An offer must be definite, and the proposal must be made under such circumstances that the person receiving it has reason to believe that the other party is willing to deal on the terms indicated.

One of the reasons why terms must be definite is that courts may have to determine at a later date if performance is in compliance with the terms. Consequently, if the terms are vague or impossible to measure with some precision, or if major terms are absent, no contract results.[3] Time for performance is not necessarily a major term, since in the absence of a time clause, the court assumes performance is to take place within a reasonable time. Price is usually a major term, although where one person has performed under the agreement, the court will assume that a rea-

[2] Courteen Seed Co. v. Abraham, page 182.
[3] Trammel v. Morgan, page 183.

sonable price was intended. An executory agreement, however, in which price is absent, will normally not be enforced.

The Code recognizes that parties often do not include all of the terms of the contract in their negotiations. It provides that even though one or more terms are left open, a contract for sale of personal property does not fail for indefiniteness if the parties have intended to make a contract and there is a reasonably certain basis for giving an appropriate remedy. It further provides that an agreement which is otherwise sufficiently definite to be a contract is not made invalid by the fact that it leaves particulars of performance to be specified by one of the parties. The specification must be made in good faith and within limits set by commercial reasonableness. Unless otherwise agreed, specifications relating to assortment of the goods are at the buyer's option and those relating to shipment are at the seller's option.

2-13. Auctions and advertisements for bids. When articles are sold at public auction, the offer is said to be made by the bidder and accepted by the seller at the drop of the auctioneer's hammer. Because of this rule, the seller can withdraw his article from sale at any time during the auction. The purchaser may withdraw his bid at any time before the auctioneer has concluded the sale. Naturally, the seller may, by statements in the circulars relating to the sale or by statements made on the part of the auctioneer, prescribe the conditions under which the contract is to be concluded. Thus, an auction advertised "without reserve" means that the property will be sold to the highest bidder. In such a case each bid is an acceptance unless or until a higher bid is received or the bid is retracted. A retraction of a bid does not revive a previous bid.

Unless it is announced before the sale, the seller has no right to bid at his own sale. For him to bid or have an agent do so would amount to fraud, the potential buyers having the right to presume that the sale is held in good faith. If an auctioneer knowingly accepts a bid on the seller's behalf or the seller makes or procures such a bid without giving notice of such bidding, the buyer may at his option avoid the sale or take the goods at the price of the last good faith bid prior to his bid.

When one advertises that bids will be received for construction work, it is held that the person calling for bids makes no offer, but that the party who submits a bid is the offeror. The one calling for the bids may reject any or all of them, and in the absence of some statute, the bidder is free at any time to withdraw his bid until it has been accepted. The same is true of public construction. Although the statutes of many states provide that public work must be let to the lowest and best bidder, most courts hold that all bids may be rejected. However, in these states, any contract for public work that is consummated must be let to the lowest responsible bidder.

2-14. Tickets. Tickets purchased for entrance into places of amusement or as evidence of a contract for transportation often contain matter in small print that attempts to limit or define the rights of the holder. Some conflict exists relative to the effectiveness of these stipulations, but it is generally held that they become a part of the offer and are accepted by the holder if he is aware of the printed matter even though he does not read it. There are some cases, such as those involving steamship tickets, in which the purchaser is presumed to know about the printed matter even though his attention is not called to it at the time the ticket is delivered.

If a ticket is received merely as evidence of ownership and is to be presented later as a means of identification, the provisions are ineffective unless the recipient's attention is directed to them at the time the ticket is accepted.[4] Thus, tickets given at checkrooms or repair shops are received usually as a means of identifying the article to be returned rather than with any idea of the ticket embodying the terms of a contract.

Printed material often found on the back of contract forms and occasionally on letterheads, unless embodied in the contract by reference thereto, generally is not considered to be a part of any contract set forth on such a form or letterhead.

DURATION OF OFFER

2-15. Duration. An offer that has been properly communicated continues as such until it lapses, is revoked, is rejected, or is accepted. The offer continues until one of the above takes place.

2-16. Lapse of offer after reasonable time. An offer does not remain open indefinitely, even though the offeror fails to withdraw it. If the offer stipulates the period during which it is to continue, it automatically lapses at the end of that period. An attempted acceptance after that date can amount to no more than a new offer being made by the offeree of the original offer. An offer that provides for no time limit remains open for a reasonable time—a reasonable time being such period as a reasonable person might conclude was intended. Whether an offer has lapsed because of the passage of time is usually a question of fact for the jury after it has given proper weight to all related circumstances, one such being the nature of the property. An offer involving property the price of which is constantly fluctuating remains open a relatively short time in comparison with property the price of which is more stable.[5] Other factors that should be considered are: the circumstances under which the offer is

[4] Kergald v. Armstrong Transfer Exp. Co., page 1840.

[5] Minnesota Linseed Oil Co. v. Collier White Lead Co., page 1850.

made, the relation of the parties, and the means used in transmitting the offer. For example, an offer made orally usually lapses when the conversation ends unless the offeror clearly indicates that the proposal may be considered further by the offeree.

2-17. Death or insanity. The death or adjudication of insanity of the offeror or the offeree causes an offer to terminate, even though the other party has no notice of the death or insanity. It should be emphasized at this point, however, that the death or the insanity of one of the parties does not cause a rescission of a contract that has previously been formed.

To illustrate, assume that Adams offers to sell to Barnes a certain electronic computer for $15,000 and that Barnes, after, but without knowledge of Adams' death, mails his acceptance to Adams and immediately enters into a contract to resell the computer to Curtis for $17,000. The estate of Adams has no duty to deliver the machine, even though Curtis may have a claim against Barnes for breach of contract if Barnes fails to deliver it to Curtis. Had the acceptance of Barnes become effective before the death of Adams, the executor of Adams' estate would have been obligated to deliver the computer.

2-18. Revocation. Generally speaking, an offeror may revoke his offer at any time before it has been accepted. Even though the offeror has promised to hold his offer open for a definite period, the right to revoke it remains. As long as it is a mere offer, it can generally be withdrawn legally even though morally or ethically such action seems unjustified in many instances.

A few recent decisions, however, have held that it is too late to withdraw an offer after the offeree, in reliance on it, has changed substantially his position; particularly if a promise to hold it open for a certain period is involved. This situation is well illustrated by general contractors who submit bids for improvements in reliance upon offers made to them by subcontractors or suppliers of material. The case of *Drennan v. Star Paving Company*[6] illustrates the application of this doctrine, commonly referred to as the doctrine of *promissory estoppel.*

The Code contains a provision which tends to achieve the same result in all cases under it as is achieved by those courts which have applied the doctrine of promissory estoppel to the contractor situation. The provision stipulates that an offer to sell or to buy goods, which is made by a merchant and which includes the statement that the offer will remain open for a stated period, cannot be withdrawn within a reasonable time or within the stated period, provided such period does not exceed three months. The offer must be a signed written offer and in the event the offer is on a form supplied by the offeree, it must be separately signed by

[6] Drennan v. Star Paving Company, page 186.

the offeror. Thus, within certain limits, a promise to hold an offer to buy or sell goods open for a stated period is treated as if it were an option.

The revocation of an offer becomes effective only when it has been communicated to the offeree. The mere sending of a notice of revocation is insufficient. It must be received by the offeree or have reached a destination where it would have been available to him.

Communication of a revocation is effective regardless of how or by whom it is conveyed. If the offeree obtains knowledge from any source of the offeror's conduct clearly showing an intent to revoke, the offer is terminated. Direct notice of revocation is not required because it would be unjust to let the offeree knowingly take advantage of the offeror's position. To illustrate: an offeree who learns from a neighbor of the offeror that an industrial site offered for sale has been sold by the offeror to a third party cannot thereafter accept the offer. The offer is revoked as soon as the offeree learns of the sale, regardless of the source of his information.

2-19. Revocation of public offers. It would be impossible for the offeror of a public offer to give personal notice of revocation to all persons who may have learned of the offer. Because of this fact, the offeror may withdraw his offer by giving the same general publicity to the revocation as he gave to the offer. A public offer made through the newspapers in a certain locality may be withdrawn through the same medium. As a result, it is possible for such an offer to be withdrawn without the offeree's having learned of the withdrawal.

2-20. Option contracts. An option contract is an agreement based upon some consideration to hold an offer open for an agreed period of time. Quite often the offeree pays, or promises to pay, money in order to have the offer remain open, but the consideration may be any other thing of value. The significant fact is that the offer has been transformed into a contract of option based upon consideration supplied by the offeree. It is now irrevocable for the period of the option, even by death.

Frequently an option is part of another contract.[7] A lease may contain a clause that gives to the tenant the right to purchase the property within a given period at a stated price, or a sale of merchandise may include a provision that obligates the seller to supply an additional amount if ordered by the purchaser. Such options are enforceable, since the initial promise to pay rent serves as consideration for both the lease and the right to buy, and the original purchase price of goods serves as consideration for the goods purchased and the option to buy additional goods.

2-21. Rejection. Rejection by the offeree causes an offer to terminate even though the original offer was to have remained open for a longer

[7] Mathieu v. Wubbe, page 188.

period. The offeree cannot, after his rejection, change his mind and accept the offer. An attempt to do so will, at best, amount to a new offer that, to form a contract, must be accepted by the original offeror. If *B* has paid S for a ten-day option to purchase property at a given price, but on the seventh day tells S that he does not want it, S is immediately free to sell to another buyer. A rejection of an offer contained in an option contract may terminate the option prior to its normal expiration date. This is particularly true if the offeror relies upon the rejection and changes his position.

Except in those cases where the Code is applicable, an attempted acceptance that departs from the terms of the offer is in effect a rejection of the offer. (See Section 2–27.) Such an acceptance is deemed a *counteroffer*, which may or may not be accepted by the original offeror. By making a counteroffer, one rejects the original offer[8] unless the offeree uses language making it clear that he is still considering the original offer. A counteroffer is a rejection because it implies that the original terms are not acceptable to the offeree.

An acceptance embodying terms other than those contained in the offer should be distinguished from a request for additional information. This distinction is especially necessary when the request for further information suggests that the original offer is still being considered.

Rejection of an offer is not effective until it has been communicated to the offeror[9] by the offeree or his chosen agent. Consequently, a telegram of rejection sent but withdrawn before delivery to the offeror does not bar a later acceptance.

ACCEPTANCE

2-22. Definition. An agreement consists of an offer by one party and its acceptance by the person or persons to whom it is made. Figuratively speaking, an offer hangs like a suspended question, and the acceptance should be a positive answer to that question. The offeror, in effect, says, "I will sell you this article for $200. Will you buy it?" The acceptor answers the question in the affirmative. An acceptance is an indication by the offeree of his willingness to be bound by the terms of the offer. It may, if the offer permits, take the form of an act, the signing and delivering of a written instrument, or a promise communicated to the offeror.

2-23. Acceptance of unilateral offer. As indicated in the previous chapter, contracts are either unilateral or bilateral, depending upon whether the offer must be accepted by an act or whether a promise to

[8] Morrison et al. v. Parks, page 190.
[9] Diebel v. Kaufman, page 191.

perform will create the contractual relation. Most contracts are bilateral in nature, and, in case the offer is ambiguous, the courts tend to construe them as bilateral. The fact remains, however, that many contracts are unilateral in form. The offeror in such cases does not require, in fact does not desire, a promise or assurance of performance, but insists on completion of the act requested before a contract is created.

Since a unilateral offer is not accepted until completion of the requested act, the offeror is at liberty to withdraw his offer at any point prior to the time when substantial performance has been completed. If only partial performance has occurred prior to withdrawal, and if it has benefited the offeror, he must pay for the benefit conferred, but he is not obligated to permit the offeree to complete performance. If substantial completion of performance has occurred prior to withdrawal, the offeror has lost his right to withdraw. However, expense incurred in preparation for performance does not affect the offeror's right to revoke his offer. If the offer is continuous in character, envisaging a series of contracts resulting from a series of acts, it may be withdrawn at any time, as to future acts.[10] A promise of continuous guaranty made to a creditor to insure payment of future purchases by a debtor is of this kind. It may, by proper notice, be terminated at any time, thus relieving the guarantor of liability for debts contracted thereafter.

To distinguish further between bilateral and unilateral contracts, let us illustrate by the following typical situations. A hardware merchant is approached by a salesman of a manufacturer and signs a purchase order for certain goods, the order being subject to the approval of the manufacturer's home office. The acceptance is effective as soon as that approval has been communicated to the merchant, because the offer was bilateral in nature, and was to be accepted by a promise to ship. Until notice of approval is received, the offeror is at liberty to withdraw his offer. On the other hand, if a merchant is immediately in need of several items of merchandise and mails a letter to a certain concern asking for immediate shipment of the articles listed, the offer would clearly be unilateral in states which have not adopted the Code. The acceptance is effective as soon as the goods are placed with the carrier for shipment, even though the buyer has no knowledge of that fact. Until they are placed with the carrier, the buyer is free to revoke his offer even though the manufacturer has incurred expenses in anticipation of delivery. In general, no contract is created until the act requested in the unilateral offer has been performed.

Under the Code, such an offer may be treated as a unilateral offer and accepted by shipment or it may be treated as a bilateral offer and accepted by a promise to ship. However, the buyer may treat the offer as

[10] Butchers' Advocate Co. v. Berkof et al., page 192.

having lapsed unless notification of acceptance is made within a reasonable length of time. Commencing performance is a reasonable mode of acceptance, but notice may still be required.

2-24. Bilateral offer. A bilateral offer is accepted by a promise to do the things requested in the offer.[11] The promise must be communicated to the offeror and may consist of any conduct which unequivocally evinces an intention to be bound by the conditions prescribed in the offer.[12] Such intention must be communicated to the offeror. The acceptance may take the form of a signature to a written agreement or a nod of the head. No formal procedure is required by the laws of acceptance. If the offer is made to a group of people in the aggregate, the acceptance is not complete until each person of the group has indicated his acceptance. Until then the offeror is at liberty to withdraw.

Where the agreement takes the form of a written instrument, the acceptance is effective only when the document has been signed and delivered, unless it was clearly the intention of the parties that the earlier verbal agreement be binding and that the writing act merely as a memorandum or better evidence of their oral contract.

2-25. Silence as assent. As a general rule, the offeror cannot force the offeree to speak. In most cases, therefore, *mere* silence by the offeree never amounts to acceptance, although the offeror in his offer may have stated that a failure to reply would constitute an acceptance. A previous course of dealing between the parties or the receipt of goods under certain circumstances might well raise a duty upon the part of the offeree to speak in order to avoid contractual relationship.[13] Silence of *itself* never constitutes an acceptance, but silence with intent to accept may do so. For example, the receipt of a renewal fire insurance policy retained by the insured with intent to keep and pay for it constitutes acceptance of the offer to insure for the new period. Mailing out the renewal policy constituted the offer to insure and the retention of the policy was the acceptance if so intended.

The Code provides that a buyer has accepted goods when he fails to make an effective rejection or does any act inconsistent with the seller's ownership. Failure to reject will not be construed as an acceptance until the buyer has a reasonable opportunity to examine the goods.

2-26. Acceptance by offeree. Only the person to whom the offer is made can accept the offer. An offer cannot even be assigned to a third party. Quite often goods are ordered from a firm that has discontinued business, and the goods are shipped by its successor. In such case the offeror is under no duty to accept the goods. If he accepts the goods know-

[11] Hill's Inc. v. William B. Kessler, Inc., page 193.
[12] Lewis and Lewis v. Root and Root, page 194.
[13] Hendrickson v. International Harvester Co. of America, page 195.

ing that they were shipped by the successor, he then by implication agrees to pay the new concern for them.

Offers to the public may be accepted by any member of the public who is aware of the offer. Option contracts, although containing an offer, are usually assignable.

2-27. Acceptance must follow offer. In contracts which do not come within the provisions of the Code, an acceptance to be effective must conform to the terms of the offer. As was discussed in Section 2–21, if the acceptance contains new terms or conditions or deviates in any manner from the terms of the offer, it becomes a counteroffer and a rejection of the original offer, unless it states that it is not to be considered a rejection. A stipulation in an offer relating to time, place, or manner of acceptance must be strictly complied with by the offeree. Any deviation in these terms will be construed to be a counteroffer and a rejection.

Under the Code, an expression of acceptance or a confirmation which adds new or different terms may be an acceptance, but the new terms, if material, are not included. If the new terms are minor, they are included unless the offeror promptly rejects them or the offer states that the acceptance is limited to the terms of the offer. A counteroffer is still not an acceptance, but one who attempts to accept but makes a minor change or adds a few new terms does not lose the effect of his acceptance. The effect of the Code is to say that additional terms are construed as proposals or additions to the contract.

The Code further recognizes that conduct by the parties which recognizes the existence of a contract is sufficient to establish the contract for sale even though the writings do not establish the contract. In such a case, the terms on which the writings agree are part of the contract together with the other agreements of the parties.

2-28. Time of taking effect. In contracts not subject to the provisions of the Code, an acceptance of a bilateral offer becomes operative when communicated to the offeror. Whether the communication is effected when deposited with the medium of communication, or only when it reaches the offeror, turns on the medium used. If the offeror indicates the means to be used, as "reply by telegram," the acceptance is completed as soon as it is deposited with that agency. Usually the offeror does not specify a means to be used, so in such a case the courts presume the offeree is authorized to use the same medium as was used in transmitting the offer. Thus, when an offer is received by mail, a contract is formed as soon as an acceptance is deposited in the mail if it is properly addressed and stamped. However, if an offer by mail is accepted by telegram, the acceptance dates only from the time it is received by the offeror.[14] Whenever the offeree uses an unauthorized medium, the ac-

[14] Lucas v. Western Union Telegraph Co., page 195.

ceptance is delayed until it reaches its destination. If no particular medium is indicated, as in the case of an offer made in conversation, the mail is deemed the authorized medium.

The ultimate effect of these rules is to place upon the offeror, where an acceptance is involved, any possible loss resulting from a failure on the part of his communicating agency. A contract may exist although a letter of acceptance is lost in the mails. The offeror, in such cases, is duty bound to perform even though he may have entered into other contracts as a result of his failure to receive a reply. He can avoid this result only by stating in his offer that the acceptance shall be ineffective until it is actually received by him.

An offer is effective even though it be delayed in reaching the offeree. Since the delay normally results from the negligence of the offeror's agent or his chosen means of communication, he should bear the loss resulting from the delay. However, if the delay is apparent to the offeree, his acceptance will be good only if it becomes effective within a reasonable time after the offer would normally have been received.

In those contracts under the Code, acceptance by any reasonable means of communication is effective as soon as placed with the communicating agency unless the offeror in the offer specifies a particular means to be used at the time of acceptance. An offer is construed as inviting acceptance in any manner and by any medium reasonable under the circumstances. As was discussed in Section 2–23, an order to buy goods for prompt or current shipment may be accepted either by a prompt promise to ship or by the prompt shipment of the goods. In the event the goods shipped do not conform to the order, the seller may reasonably notify the buyer that the shipment is not an acceptance but is only offered in accommodation to the buyer.

A written contract is formed only when it has been signed by both parties and is delivered. Even in such a case, delivery may be conditioned upon the happening of some event.

OFFER AND ACCEPTANCE CASES

LEFKOWITZ v. GREAT MINNEAPOLIS SURPLUS STORE

1957, (Minn.) 86 N.W.2d 689

Murphy, J. . . . This case grows out of the alleged refusal of the defendant to sell to the plaintiff a certain fur piece which it had offered for sale in a newspaper advertisement. It appears from the record that on April 6, 1956, the defendant published the following advertisement in a Minneapolis newspaper:

Saturday 9 A.M. Sharp
3 Brand New
Fur
Coats
Worth to $100.00
First Come
First Served
$1
Each

On April 13, the defendant again published an advertisement in the same newspaper as follows:

Saturday 9 A.M.
2 Brand New Pastel
Mink 3-Skin Scarfs
Selling for $89.50
Out they go
Saturday. Each $1.00
1 Black Lapin Stole
Beautiful,
worth $139.50. . . .$1.00
First Come
First Served

The record supports the findings of the court that on each of the Saturdays following the publication of the above-described ads the plaintiff was the first to present himself at the appropriate counter in the defendant's store and on each occasion demanded the coat and the stole so advertised and indicated his readiness to pay the sale price of $1. On both occasions, the defendant refused to sell the merchandise to the plaintiff, stating on the first occasion that by a "house rule" the offer was intended for women only and sales would not be made to men, and on the second visit that plaintiff knew defendant's house rules.

The trial court properly disallowed plaintiff's claim for the value of the fur coats since the value of these articles was speculative and uncertain. The only evidence of value was the advertisement itself to the effect that the coats were "Worth to $100.000," how much less being speculative especially in view of the price for which they were offered for sale. With reference to the offer of the defendant on April 13, 1956, to sell the "1 Black Lapin Stole . . . worth $139.50 . . ." the trial court held that the value of this article was established and granted judgment in favor of the plaintiff for that amount less the $1 quoted purchase price.

The defendant contends that a newspaper advertisement offering items of merchandise for sale at a named price is a "unilateral offer" which may be withdrawn without notice. He relies upon authorities which hold that, where an advertiser publishes in a newspaper that he has a certain quantity or quality of goods which he wants to dispose of at certain prices and on certain terms, such advertisements are not offers which become contracts as soon as any person to whose notice they may come signifies his acceptance by notifying the other that he will take a certain quantity of them. Such advertisements have been construed as an invitation for an offer of sale on the terms stated, which offer, when received, may be accepted or rejected and which therefore does not become a contract of sale until accepted by the seller; and until a contract has been so made, the seller may modify or revoke such prices or terms. (Cases cited.) . . .

The defendant relies principally on *Craft v. Elder & Johnston Co. supra.* In that case, the court discussed the legal effect of an advertisement offering for sale, as a one-day special, an electric sewing machine at a named price. The view was expressed that the advertisement was (38 N.E.2d 417, 34 Ohio L.A. 605) "not an offer made to any specific person but was made to the public generally. Thereby it would be properly designated as a unilateral offer and not being supported by any consideration could be withdrawn at will and without notice." It is true that such an offer may be withdrawn before acceptance. Since all offers are by their nature unilateral because they are necessarily made by one party or on one side in the negotiation of a contract, the distinction made in that decision between a unilateral offer and a unilateral contract is not clear. On the facts before us we are concerned with whether the advertisement constituted an offer, and, if so, whether the plaintiff's conduct constituted an acceptance.

There are numerous authorities which hold that a particular advertisement in a newspaper or circular letter relating to a sale of articles may be construed by the court as constituting an offer, acceptance of which would complete a contract. (Cases cited.)

The test of whether a binding obligation may originate in advertisements addressed to the general public is "whether the facts show that some performance was promised in positive terms in return for something requested." 1 Williston, *Contracts* (Rev. ed.), § 27.

The authorities above cited emphasize that, where the offer is clear, definite, and explicit, and leaves nothing open for negotiation, it constitutes an offer, acceptance of which will complete the contract. The most recent case on the subject is *Johnson v. Capital City Ford Co.*, La. App., 85 So.2d 75, in which the court pointed out that a newspaper advertisement relating to the purchase and sale of automobiles may constitute an offer, acceptance of which will consummate a contract and create an obligation in the offeror to perform according to the terms of the published offer.

Whether in any individual instance a newspaper advertisement is an offer rather than an invitation to make an offer depends on the legal intention of the parties and the surrounding circumstances. Annotation, 157 A.L.R. 744, 751; 77 C.J.S., Sales, 25b; 17 C.J.S., *Contracts,* § 389. We are of the view on the facts before us that the offer by the defendant of the sale of the Lapin fur was clear, definite, and explicit, and left nothing open for negotiation. The plaintiff having successfully managed to be the first one to appear at the seller's place of business to be served, as requested by the advertisement, and having offered the stated purchase price of the article, he was entitled to performance on the part of the defendant. We think the trial court was correct in holding that there was in the conduct of the parties a sufficient mutuality of obligation to constitute a contract of sale.

The defendant contends that the offer was modified by a "house rule" to the effect that only women were qualified to receive the bargains advertised. The advertisement contained no such restriction. This objection may be disposed of briefly by stating that, while an advertiser has the right at any time before acceptance to modify his offer, he does not have the right, after acceptance, to impose new or arbitrary conditions not contained in the published offer.

Judgment affirmed for plaintiff.

COURTEEN SEED CO. v. ABRAHAM

1929, 129 Ore. 427, 275 P. 684

Defendant, Abraham, had certain clover seed for sale and sent out samples to a number of dealers in which it was stated he was asking 24 cents per pound. Plaintiff requested a firm offer and a lower price and defendant's reply is indicated in the opinion below. The lower court gave judgment for plaintiff and defendant appealed.

BROWN, J. . . . Contracts in general are reached by an offer on the one side and acceptance on the other. . . . So it becomes necessary to determine whether the defendant actually offered to sell the clover seed to the plaintiff corporation, and whether it was defendant's intention that contractual relations should exist between them on plaintiff's acceptance.

The writing upon which the plaintiff relies to show an offer is a telegram sent by defendant to plaintiff on October 8, 1927, which reads: "I am asking 23 cents per pound for the car of red clover seed from which your sample was taken. No. 1 seed, practically no plantain whatever. Have an offer 22¾ per pound, f.o.b. Amity."

Plaintiff's acceptance of the alleged offer reads: "Telegram received. We accept your offer. Ship promptly, route care Milwaukee Road at Omaha."

A contract should be construed to effect the intention of the parties thereto, as gathered from the entire writings constituting the contract. It is this intent that constitutes the essence of every contract. *Lochmund v. Lope Sing*, 54 Or. 106, 111, 102 P. 598. . . . Giving due consideration to every word contained in the defendant's telegram to plaintiff, we are not prepared to say that that telegram constituted an express offer to sell. It would be poor reasoning to say that the defendant meant to make the plaintiff an offer when he used this language: "I am asking 23 cents per pound for the car of red clover." That does not say, "I offer to you at 23 cents per pound the car of red clover," nor does it say, "I will sell to you the carload of red clover at 23 cents per pound." The writer of the telegram used the word "offer" with reference to some other person when he concluded by saying: "Have an offer of 22¾ per pound, f.o.b. Amity." Each of the words "offer" and "asking" has its meaning; and we cannot assume that the writer of the telegram meant to use these words in the same sense, nor can we eliminate the word "asking" from the writing. . . .

It is laid down by eminent authority that information or invitation to negotiate does not constitute an offer. Perhaps one of the most comprehensive discourses on the subject appears in 1 Page on the Law of Contracts, and . . . we set out the following interesting excerpts from section 84 thereof:

> The commonest examples of offers meant to open negotiations and to call forth offers in the technical sense are the advertisements, circulars and trade letters sent out by business houses. While it is possible that offers made by such means may be in such form as to become contracts, they are often merely expressions of a willingness to negotiate. . . .

From a review of the decisions, and of the law governing the question at issue in the instant case, we are of the opinion that the motion for a nonsuit should have been sustained.

This cause is reversed and remanded, with directions to enter a nonsuit. [*For defendant*]

TRAMMEL v. MORGAN
1957, (Ohio), 158 N.E.2d 541

The defendant Morgan was a boxer and agreed to let plaintiff manage him for five years for a certain fee provided that plaintiff was to purchase for defendant a home "suitable for his family, at a fair price to be paid out of Morgan's earnings as a boxer." The defendant in violation of the agreement obtained contracts through other promoters and plaintiff sues to recover damages arising from the breach. The lower court gave judgment for plaintiff and defendant appealed, insisting there was no contract.

PER CURIAM. . . .

Defendant claims that the findings of the trial judge are manifestly against the weight of the evidence and contrary to law; that the judgment of the trial court is not sustained by sufficient evidence and is against the manifest weight thereof and contrary to law, in which claims we concur.

We have hereinabove said that the consideration for the so-called second contract had not been paid. The Probate Court held that plaintiff had a reasonable time to purchase the home provided for. We hold the provisions for such purchase are too indefinite for enforcement, and that the contract never became effective because the purchase of the home by plaintiff was a requirement precedent to the agreement becoming effective as a binding contract, *no other* consideration therefor appearing.

There being no enforceable consideration for such contract the trial court should have rendered final judgment declaring the same void and unenforceable, and this court coming now to render the judgment which the trial court should have rendered final judgment is entered for defendant.

KERGALD v. ARMSTRONG TRANSFER EXP. CO.

1953, (Mass.) 113 N.E.2d 53

LUMUS, J. This is an action of contract, begun by writ dated August 26, 1949, in which the plaintiff sues for the loss of her trunk and its contents. The defendant is an intrastate common carrier. There was evidence that the plaintiff arrived with her trunk at the South Station in Boston late in an evening in May, 1949, and went to the defendant's office there. She was not asked the value of her trunk, but was given a small pasteboard check by the defendant which was not read to her and which she did not read, but put in her purse. The trunk was to be delivered at her home in Boston. The defendant failed to deliver her trunk, and admitted that it had been lost. The small check had on one side the order number and the words "Read contract on reverse side," and on the other the words, "The holder of this check agrees that the value of the baggage checked does not exceed $100 unless a greater value has been declared at time of checking and additional payment made therefor . . ."

The judge instructed the jury, over the exception of the defendant, that the plaintiff is bound by that limitation if she had knowledge of it when she took the check, and otherwise is not. The jury returned a verdict for the plaintiff for $1,700, and the defendant brought the case here.

Where what is given to a plaintiff purports on its face to set forth the terms of a contract, the plaintiff, whether he reads it or not, by accepting it assents to its terms, and is bound by any limitation of liability therein contained, in the absence of fraud. . . .

On the other hand, where as in this case what is received is apparently a means of identification of the property bailed, rather than a complete contract, the bailor is not bound by a limitation upon the liability of the bailee unless it is actually known to the bailor. (Cases cited.)

The cases in this Commonwealth so clearly show the law applicable to the facts of this case that we need not discuss decisions elsewhere. But we may say that our conclusions are supported by well-reasoned cases in New York as well as other jurisdictions.

Judgment for plaintiff affirmed.

MINNESOTA LINSEED OIL CO. v. COLLIER WHITE LEAD CO.

1876, Fed. Cas. No. 9,635, 4 Dill. 431

The defendant, Collier White Lead Co., is being sued for $2,150 which it admits is owing to the plaintiff for linseed oil previously shipped. It has refused to pay because it maintains the plaintiff failed to ship oil under a second contract, thus causing it damages which should be deducted from the $2,150. The facts regarding the second contract are that on July 31, plaintiff by telegram offered to sell a certain amount of linseed oil to defendant at a certain price. Although this telegram was transmitted late in the evening of July 31, it was not delivered to defendant until the morning of August 2. On August 3 defendant accepted plaintiff's offer by depositing a telegram with the telegraph office in his city and shortly thereafter upon the same day defendant received a telegram from the plaintiff revoking plaintiff's offer. The market price on linseed oil was very unstable.

Nelson . . . In the case at bar the delivery of the message at the telegraph office signified the acceptance of the offer. If any contract was entered into, the meeting of minds was at 8:53 of the clock, on Tuesday morning, August 3rd and the subsequent dispatches are out of the case. . . . Conceding this, there remains only one question to decide, which will determine the issues: Was the acceptance of defendant deposited in the telegraph office Tuesday, August 3rd, within a reasonable time so as to consummate a contract binding upon the plaintiff? . . .

The better opinion is, that what is, or is not, a reasonable time, must depend upon the circumstances attending the negotiation, and the character of the subject matter of the contract, and in no better way can the intention of the parties be determined. If the negotiation is in respect to an article stable in price, there is not so much reason for an immediate acceptance of the offer, and the same rule would not apply as in a case where the negotiation related to an article subject to sudden and great fluctuations in the market. *Parson on Contracts* (Volume 1, p. 482) says: ". . . If no definite time is stated, then the inquiry as to a reasonable time resolves itself into an inquiry as to what time it is rational to suppose the parties contemplated; and the law will decide this to be that time which as rational men they ought to have understood each other to have had in mind." Applying this rule, it seems clear that the intention of the plaintiff, in making the offer by telegram, to sell an article which fluctuates so much in price, must have been upon the understanding that the acceptance, if at all, should be immediate, and as soon after the receipt of the offer as would give a fair opportunity for consideration. The delay, here, was too long and manifestly unjust to the plaintiff, for it afforded the defendant an opportunity to take advantage of a change in the market and to accept or refuse the offer as would best subserve its interests.

Judgment will be entered in favor of the plaintiff for the amount claimed. The counterclaim is denied. Judgment accordingly.

DRENNAN v. STAR PAVING COMPANY
1958, (Cal.) 333 P.2d 757

Drennan, the plaintiff, was a general contractor and in preparation for submitting a bid on a school job requested the defendant to submit a bid for certain paving which was involved. The defendant offered to do the work for $7,131.60, and the plaintiff used this subcontractor's offer in making his bid. The contract was awarded to plaintiff, but as he approached the defendant, he was notified that it could not perform as it had made an error in its calculations. The plaintiff got another to do the work at a cost of $10,948.60 and seeks to recover this difference of the defendant. The lower court gave judgment for plaintiff in the amount of $3,817.00.

TRAYNOR, J. . . . There is no evidence that defendant offered to make its bid irrevocable in exchange for plaintiff's use of its figures in computing his bid. Nor is there evidence that would warrant interpreting plaintiff's use of defendant's bid as the acceptance thereof, binding plaintiff, on condition he received the main contract, to award the subcontract to defendant. In sum, there was neither an option supported by consideration nor a bilateral contract binding on both parties.

Plaintiff contends, however, that he relied to his detriment on defendant's offer and that defendant must therefore answer in damages for its refusal to perform. Thus the question is squarely presented: Did plaintiff's reliance make defendant's offer irrevocable?

Section 90 of the Restatement of Contracts states: "A promise which the promisor should reasonably expect to induce action or forbearance of a definite and substantial character on the part of the promisee and which does induce such action or forbearance is binding if injustice can be avoided only by enforcement of the promise." . . .

Defendant's offer constituted a promise to perform on such conditions as were stated expressly or by implication therein or annexed thereto by operation of law. (See 1 Williston, *Contracts* [3rd ed.], § 24a, p. 56, § 61,

p. 196.) Defendant had reason to expect that if its bid proved the lowest it would be used by plaintiff. It induced "action * * * of a definite and substantial character on the part of the promisee."

Had defendant's bid expressly stated or clearly implied that it was revocable at any time before acceptance we would treat it accordingly. It was silent on revocation, however, and we must therefore determine whether there are conditions to the right of revocation imposed by law or reasonably inferable in fact. In the analogous problem of an offer for a unilateral contract, the theory is now obsolete that the offer is revocable at any time before complete performance. Thus section 45 of the Restatement of Contracts provides: "If an offer for a unilateral contract is made, and part of the consideration requested in the offer is given or tendered by the offeree in response thereto, the offeror is bound by a contract, the duty of immediate performance of which is conditional on the full consideration being given or tendered within the time stated in the offer, or, if no time is stated therein, within a reasonable time." In explanation, comment *b* states that the "main offer includes as a subsidiary promise, necessarily implied, that if part of the requested performance is given, the offeror will not revoke his offer, and that if tender is made it will be accepted. Part performance or tender may thus furnish consideration for the subsidiary promise. Moreover, merely acting in justifiable reliance on an offer may in some cases serve as sufficient reason for making a promise binding (see § 90)."

Whether implied in fact or law, the subsidiary promise serves to preclude the injustice that would result if the offer could be revoked after the offeree had acted in detrimental reliance thereon. Reasonable reliance resulting in a foreseeable prejudicial change in position affords a compelling basis also for implying a subsidiary promise not to revoke an offer for a bilateral contract.

The absence of consideration is not fatal to the enforcement of such a promise. It is true that in the case of unilateral contracts the Restatement finds consideration for the implied subsidiary promise in the part performance of the bargained-for exchange, but its reference to section 90 makes clear that consideration for such a promise is not always necessary. The very purpose of section 90 is to make a promise binding even though there was no consideration "in the sense of something that is bargained for and given in exchange." (See 1 Corbin, *Contracts* 634 et seq.) Reasonable reliance serves to hold the offeror in lieu of the consideration ordinarily required to make the offer binding. . . .

When plaintiff used defendant's offer in computing his own bid, he bound himself to perform in reliance on defendant's terms. Though defendant did not bargain for this use of its bid neither did defendant make it idly, indifferent to whether it would be used or not. On the contrary it is reasonable to suppose that defendant submitted its bid to obtain the subcontract. It was bound to realize the substantial possibility that its bid would be the lowest, and that it would be included by plaintiff in his bid. It was to its own interest that the contractor be awarded the general contract; the lower the subcontract bid, the lower the general contractor's bid was likely to be and the greater its chance of acceptance and hence the greater defendant's chance of getting the paving subcontract. Defendant had reason not only to expect plaintiff to rely on its bid but to want him to. Clearly defendant had a stake in plaintiff's reliance on its bid. Given this interest and the fact that plaintiff is bound by his own bid, it is only fair that plaintiff should have at least an opportunity to accept defendant's bid after the general contract has been awarded to him.

It bears noting that a general contractor is not free to delay acceptance after he has been awarded the general contract in the hope of getting a better price. Nor can he reopen bargaining with the subcontractor and at the same time claim a continuing right to accept the original offer. See *R. J. Daum Const. Co. v. Child*, Utah, 247 P.2d 817, 823. In the present case plaintiff promptly informed defendant that plaintiff was being awarded the job and that the subcontract was being awarded to defendant. . . .

Judgment for plaintiff affirmed.

MATHIEU v. WUBBE

1951, 330 Mich. 408, 47 N.W.2d 670

BUTZEL, J. . . . Clara Noble [Mathieu], plaintiff, * * * [was the lessee] . . . of property owned by Bernard Wubbe, defendant.

The original lease was for one year, from August 1, 1947 to July 31, 1948, at a monthly rent of $100. It contained the following provisions:

> It is further expressly understood and agreed between the parties hereto that the tenant shall have the option at the expiration of the term hereof, to renew this lease under the same terms and conditions hereinbefore and hereinafter set forth for an additional term of one year, upon written notice.
>
> It is further understood and agreed between the parties hereto that during the term hereof or the extension thereof by virtue of the provisions of the paragraph next above set forth, that the tenant shall have the option to purchase the demised premises at the agreed price of $16,500.00 including the furniture now on the said premises, or for the agreed price of $15,000.00 not including the furniture now on the premises . . .

The lease further provided that if the option to purchase were exercised the down payment would be one-half of the purchase price, "after deducting any indebtedness by way of mortgage."

Plaintiff exercised the option to renew the lease for one year, and remained in possession under the lease until July 31, 1949, on which day, a

Sunday, at about 8:30 in the evening, she sent the following telegram:

Bernard Wubbe, Request Ans.
Ready to close deal on 108 Winder Street. Please call me Monday morning.
Clara Mathieu.

The telegram was received very early in the morning of August 1 by defendant. . . .

After plaintiff sent the telegram there was a telephone conversation between the parties, and it was agreed that they would meet at the office of defendant's attorney at 10:30 on Monday morning (August 1, 1949). At the meeting, according to the plaintiff's own testimony, the defendant refused to recognize the option as still binding, although his attorney advised him to the contrary. The plaintiff insisted on exercising the $15,000 option provision. The defendant offered to sell the premises for $16,500, including the furniture, with an $8,000 down payment, but this was refused. The plaintiff's attorney was given an abstract of title, but when he called shortly thereafter for an extension of time for its examination, it was refused, and he was told all dealings were off. This suit for specific performance of the option followed. The plaintiff was denied relief by the trial court and has taken this appeal.

The plaintiff makes two contentions, first, that the telegram taking up the option was effective when sent, and second, if there were any defects in the acceptance they were waived by the defendant's subsequent actions. The appellant's first contention ignores a more basic question: Was the telegram a legally effective acceptance of the continuing offer of the option? The telegram was an indication of willingness to make some agreement, but it did not specify which was contemplated.

In *Beecher v. Morse,* 286 Mich. 513, 282 N.W. 226, 227, we said:

"It is well settled by the decisions that an option is a mere offer, and that acceptance thereof must be made within the time allowed or the optionee's rights thereunder will be lost. It is also apparent that substantial compliance with the terms of the option is not sufficient to constitute an acceptance of the offer. . . .

"An option is but an offer, strict compliance with the terms of which is required; acceptance must be in compliance with he terms proposed by the option both as to the exact thing offered and within the time specified; otherwise the right is lost." *Bailey v. Grover,* 237 Mich. 548, 213 N.W. 137, 139. . . .

Before there can be a legally enforceable obligation there must be an offer and an acceptance. When there is a single offer, a simple assent might be sufficient, but when there are alternatives, definiteness is required. To hold otherwise would be to bind the defendant to some contract, but to allow the plaintiff complete freedom of choice. The telegram of July 31, 1949, was not a sufficient acceptance of the defendant's offer.

In view of the foregoing we need not decide when the telegram became effective as an acceptance, or what effect C.L. 1948, § 435.1, Stat. Ann. § 18.851, dealing with Sunday contracts, had on this telegram.

The appellant's second contention arises out of a misconception as to the legal status of the parties when they met on August 1, 1949. When the option expired on July 31, the defendant was relieved of any obligation he might have owed to the plaintiff prior to that time. He could, if he wished, sell the property in question to any one and this included the plaintiff. Therefore he could deal with the plaintiff, and no legal effect would arise from these dealings in the absence of some new contractual relation.

The decree of the trial court dismissing the bill is affirmed.

MORRISON et al. v. PARKS

1913, 164 N.C. 197, 80 S.E. 85

This is an action by plaintiff, Morrison and others, to recover damages from Parks for failure to deliver lumber. The offer follows:

> Gentlemen: I have about 80,000 feet of oak left yet, for which I will take $16 per M delivered on cars at Bridgewater "log run." I will take $8 per M for the mill culls I have at Bridgewater, as that is what it cost me, cut and deliver the same.

The plaintiff replied as follows:

> Dear Sir: Your letter of the 20th received and would say we will take your 4/4 oak at $16, mill culls out, delivered on cars at Bridgewater. We will handle all your mill culls, but not at the price you are asking. We are buying from A.L. & Co. for $4.50 on board the cars. We should be glad to handle yours at this price. How soon will you have some 4/4 ready to load? We will take the 80,000 feet and will depend on this, and will load it out as soon as you can put it on the railroad. Please write us at once how soon you will have some of this stock ready to load.

Clark, C. J. . . . The alleged contract being in writing, the construction of this written evidence was a matter for the court. In order to make the offer and reply a contract, the acceptance must be "(a) absolute and unconditional; (b) identical with the terms of the offer; (c) in the mode, at the place, and within the time expressly or impliedly required by the offeror." The plaintiff Morrison testified that "4/4" means lumber "an inch thick, of any length or width," and that "log run" means "any thickness with culls out." He further testified that the market price of 4/4 lumber of that character, at that place and time, was $18.50.

It is apparent that the reply was not an acceptance of the terms of the offer of the defendant. (1) The defendant offered to take $8 per M for mill culls. The plaintiff replied, offering $4.50. (2) The defendant offered

80,000 feet of oak, "log run," at $16. The plaintiff replied, offering $16 per M for 4/4 oak—an entirely different article and which he himself testified was then worth in the market $18.50 at the same place.

There was no contract. The offer of the defendant was not accepted, but a counter offer of an entirely different nature was made. The minds of the parties never met.

Judgment for defendant affirmed.

DIEBEL v. KAUFMAN
1945 (Ohio App.) 62 N.E.2d 770

MILLER, J. This is an appeal on question of law and fact from the Common Pleas Court of Franklin County, Ohio.

The action is one for specific performance of a contract for the purchase and sale of 30 shares of stock in The Modern Tool, Die and Machine Company, which is being held by the defendant [Kaufman] as executor of the estate of Mary E. Cain, and which, under the terms of her will, he is authorized to sell. The regulations of the company contain the provision that a stockholder desiring to sell must first offer the stock at the market price to the company which shall have an option of purchase for thirty days.

On May 18, 1943, the defendant made an offer in writing to The Modern Tool, Die and Machine Company to sell the 30 shares involved herein at a price of $175 per share. On May 28, 1943, a special directors' meeting was called and a resolution was duly passed authorizing the acceptance of the offer by the company. A special stockholders' meeting was held on June 4th and a motion to approve the purchase was lost for the want of a two-thirds majority. The defendant then sought to sell the stock and announced through his attorney that sealed bids would be accepted up to 12:00 o'clock noon, June 7th, at which time the highest bid would be accepted. At ten minutes to 12:00 N., June 7th, the plaintiff and his attorney called at the office of Henry S. Ballard, attorney for the executor, and who had made the offer to sell, and attempted to deliver to Mr. Ballard a sealed bid for the purchase of this stock. Mr. Ballard refused to accept the bid, stating that he had just been served with a copy of pleadings being filed in a suit in the Common Pleas Court in which this stock was involved. The offer was one of $180 per share, making a total of $5,400.00 for the same. A cash tender was made several days later and the same was refused.

We are of the opinion that the defendant was justified in refusing to sell this stock to the plaintiff for two reasons: First, an offer unless given for a valuable consideration can be withdrawn at any time before acceptance, which was done in the instant case; second, according to the conditions as contained in the company regulations, when an offer was made to the company by the stockholder to sell stock, the company had an option for thirty days in which to accept. During this period of time the holder of the stock could not legally sell to a third person, for although the stockholders at one meeting might refuse to accept the offer, they might well reconsider their action within the thirty day period and decide to purchase the stock. It will be noted that the company at no time notified the defendant that the offer had been rejected by the company. Had this been done, it would seem that the defendant, having given notice to the company, with an offer to sell at a definite price, and this offer being rejected by the company, would then be at liberty to dispose of the same. Since the defendant had no right to offer the stock for sale as he did on June 7, the plaintiff acquired no right to purchase it. The plaintiff was secretary of the company and was fully informed as to its bylaws and regulations.

Judgment for the defendant.

BUTCHERS' ADVOCATE CO. v. BERKOF et al.

1916, 158 N.Y. Supp. 160, 94 Misc. 299

Action by the Butchers' Advocate Company, plaintiff, against Jacob W. Berkof and another. From a judgment for plaintiff, and an order denying defendants' motion for a new trial, defendants appeal.

LEHMAN, J. The defendants, on or about August 1, 1914, signed a paper which reads as follows:

Brooklyn, N.Y., August 1, 1914.

Undersigned hereby authorizes the publishers of the Butchers' Advocate to insert our ad. to occupy ¼ page in Butchers' Advocate for one year and thereafter until publishers have order to discontinue the ad., for which we agree to pay $8 (eight dollars) per insertion.

Safety Auto Trolley,
J. W. Berkof.

The plaintiff proceeded under this authorization to publish advertisements for the defendant. Some time in September the defendants notified the plaintiff to discontinue the advertisement, but the plaintiff continued to insert same in each issue, and has recovered a judgment for the sum of $416, the price named for insertion of advertisement for one year. . . .

. . . In this case the defendant in the written agreement merely authorizes the plaintiff to publish his advertisement for one year. The defendant at that time did not expressly or impliedly in any form agree to do anything. It was evidently a mere offer or unilateral promise on the part of the defendant, which could ripen into a mutual contract only when the offer was accepted . . . by performance. . . .

In this case . . . the offer was merely to pay a certain sum per insertion, which was authorized for one year, and in such cases the past performance implied only an acceptance of the offer to pay according to the insertions. It follows that the plaintiff is entitled to no recovery for insertions made after the defendants had notified it to cease publications.

Judgment should therefore be reversed. . . .

HILL'S, INC. v. WILLIAM B. KESSLER, INC.

1952, (Wash.) 246 P.2d 1099

Action by Hill's, Inc., against William B. Kessler, Inc., for breach of contract. The Superior Court, King County, Hugh C. Todd, J., rendered the judgment for plaintiff, and defendant appealed.

MALLERY, J. The plaintiff, Hill's, Inc., ordered thirty-four men's suits from the defendant, using a printed form supplied by defendant through its salesman.

The printed form provided that the order would not become a binding contract until it had been accepted by an authorized officer of the defendant at its office in Hammonton, New Jersey.

The defendant's salesman procured the order on May 16, 1950, and on May 23, 1950, the defendant by form letter, advised the plaintiff that "You may be assured of our very best attention to this order." What occurred next is shown by the trial court's finding of fact:

> . . . but notwithstanding, on or about July 18, 1950, defendant intentionally and deliberately, at the instigation of a large retail store selling defendant's clothing in the downtown Seattle area, wrongfully cancelled said order and breached its agreement with plaintiff to deliver said suits as ordered, or at all. That at the time defendant cancelled said order and breached its agreement, the period for placing orders for delivery of fall suits had passed, and it was impossible for plaintiff to thereafter procure comparable suits from any other source to meet its fall trade. . . .

Thereupon, plaintiff brought this action for loss of profits in the amount of a 66⅔ per cent markup aggregating $815.83.

From a judgment in favor of the plaintiff, the defendant appeals.

The defendant contends that its letter of May 23, 1950, in which it said "You may be assured of our very best attention to this order," was not an acceptance of the plaintiff's order.

In *Bauman v. McManus*, 75 Kan. 106. 89 P. 15, 18, 10 L.R.A., N.S., 1138, the court said:

. . . The promise that the order shall receive prompt and *careful* attention seems to imply something more than that the manufacturers will quickly and cautiously investigate the advisability of accepting it. The care they might expend in that direction—in looking up defendants' financial standing, for instance—is not presumably a matter in which any one but themselves would be greatly interested. The engagement to use care seems more naturally to relate to the manner of filling the order than to the settling of a doubt whether to fill it at all. The expression of thanks for the favor has some tendency in the same direction. We incline strongly to the opinion that the letter standing by itself was as effectual to close a contract as though in set phrase it had said that the goods would be shipped; that to permit any other construction to be placed upon it would be to countenance the studied use of equivocal expressions, with a set purpose, if an advantage may thereby be derived, to keep the word of promise to the ear and break it to the hope.

Judgment is affirmed for plaintiff.

LEWIS AND LEWIS v. ROOT AND ROOT
1959, (Wash.) 337 P.2d 52

Plaintiff, Lewis and Lewis, placed an order, through a broker for 1,000 squares of No. 1-5x green centigrade shingles at $11.75 per square, the purchaser requiring a minimum of one truck load a week and preferably two. The defendant received the order which said "please confirm this order with Lewis and Lewis." The defendant did not confirm the order but in time made three shipments at the price indicated. It now, having refused to make further shipments, denies there was any acceptance of the offer. The lower court awarded damages to the plaintiff in its suit to recover on the contract.

HUNTER, J. . . . In the case of *Pillsbury Flour Mills, Inc. v. Independent Bakery, Inc.*, 1931, 165 Wash. 360, 5 P.2d 517, 8 P.2d 430, 10 P.2d 975, which is similar on the facts to the instant case, we said:

This appeal presents for determination only one question, which we state as follows: Where an order for a quantity of goods to be delivered in installments is given to a salesman subject to the seller's written approval, does that order become a binding contract on the seller's delivery of a number of the installments, without communication by the seller to the buyer of acceptance of the order? The question was answered in the affirmative, and we stated:

The contracts were for delivery by installments. One contract was for the shipment of fifteen hundred barrels of flour; the other for four hundred and fifty barrels of flour. It was not contemplated—in fact, it was agreed otherwise—that all of the flour would be delivered in one shipment. Under that arrangement, as soon as one installment of flour was delivered and accepted the contracts became binding on the parties. Thereafter the appellant was bound to perform by delivering the remainder of the flour called for in the contracts. A corresponding obligation was imposed upon the respondent of accepting the remainder of the flour under the contract. Failure of performance on the part of either would entitle the other party to recover for the damages suffered by the breach of the contract.

In the present case, as soon as the first shipment of shingles was delivered by the appellants and accepted by the respondents, in pursuance of the order of July 7, 1955, the contract became binding upon the parties. By their failure to deliver the balance of the shingles, as called for in the purchase order, the appellants were answerable to the respondents for their damages suffered as a result of the breach . . .

Finding no error in the record, the judgment of the lower court is affirmed.

HENDRICKSON v. INTERNATIONAL HARVESTER CO. OF AMERICA

1927, 100 Vt. 161, 135 Atl. 702

Action by Peter Hendrickson against the International Harvester Company of America to recover damages on account of the defendant's failure to deliver to him a broadcast seeder. The defendant's agent took the order for the machine, which order was retained by the defendant an unreasonable time and, until this controversy arose, without indicating that it either accepted or rejected the offer of the plaintiff to buy the seeder mentioned.

POWERS, J. . . . The order was subject to approval. . . . The fact that the defendant kept the order without approving it or notifying the plaintiff of its disapproval would amount to an acceptance.

True it is that it takes two to make a bargain, and that silence gives consent . . . only when there is a duty to speak. And true it is that it is frequently said that one is ordinarily under no obligation to do or say anything concerning a proposition which he does not choose to accept; yet we think that, when one sends out an agent to solicit orders for his goods, authorizing such agents to take such orders subject to his (the principal's) approval, fair dealing and the exigencies of modern business require us to hold that he shall signify to the customer within a reasonable time from the receipt of the order his rejection of it, or suffer the consequences of having his silence operate as an approval.

Judgment for plaintiff.

LUCAS v. WESTERN UNION TELEGRAPH COMPANY

1906, 131 Iowa 669, 109 N.W. 191

Lucas, the plaintiff, had received one evening by mail an offer from Sas to exchange certain real properties at given terms, saying he would have to know at once as other deals were involved. The next morning at 9:10 A.M. he deposited a telegram of acceptance with defendant, which was not sent until 4:41 P.M., reaching Sas at 6:03. Sas sold the property to another at 3:30 P.M., and the plaintiff sues the defendant for damages arising from the delay. The defendant contends the acceptance was effective as soon as the telegram was deposited with it, the delay thus causing the plaintiff no loss. The lower court gave judgment for the defendant.

LADD, J. . . . The proposition of an exchange was made to plaintiff by letter. In communicating it, properly addressed, to the mails for transmission, the post office became the agent of Sas to carry the offer, he taking the chances of delays in transmission. . . . Having sent the proposition by mail he impliedly authorized its acceptance through the same agency. Such implication arises (1) when the post is used to make the offer and no other mode is suggested, and (2) when the circumstances are such that it must have been within the contemplation of the parties that the post would be used in making the answer. . . . The contract is complete in such a case when the letter containing the acceptance is properly addressed and deposited in the United States mails. . . . This is on the ground that the offeror, by depositing his letter in the post office, selects a common agency through which to conduct the negotiations, and the delivery of the letter to it is in effect a delivery to the offeror. . . . But plaintiff did not adopt this course. On the contrary he chose to indicate his acceptance by transmitting a telegram to Sas by the defendant company. Sas had done nothing to indicate his willingness to adopt such agency and the defendant in undertaking to transmit the message was acting solely as the agent of the plaintiff. The latter might have withdrawn the message or stopped its delivery at any time before it actually reached Sas. It is manifest that handing the message to his own agent was not notice to the sendee of the telegram. The most formal declaration of an intention of acceptance of an offer to a third person will not constitute a contract. A written letter or telegram, like an oral acceptance, must be communicated to the party who has made the offer or to someone expressly or impliedly authorized to receive it, and this rule is not complied with by delivering it to the writer's own agent or messenger even with direction to deliver it to the offeror. . . . It is very evident on authority and principle that in the absence of any suggestion, one transmitting an offer by mail cannot be bound by an acceptance returned in some other way until it is received or he has notice thereof. The plaintiff then did not accept the offer of Sas until the telegram was received by the latter.

The case was sent back for retrial with the instructions to ascertain whether the acceptance was delivered to the offeror within a reasonable time.

Review Questions and Problems

1. W Co. agreed to publish a manuscript for *H*, royalties payable to *H* to be agreed upon after costs of publication were ascertained. At the

time the printing had reached the page-proof stage, differences and misunderstandings developed and the work ceased. *H* seeks to obtain the return of the manuscript without payment for any work done, urging that no contract was formed because major terms were not agreed upon. What result?

2. *A*, a retailer, placed a boat in a display window, and some clerk, in error, placed a price tag of $95 on it. *B* entered the store and indicated his willingness to buy at the $95 figure, but *A* refused to sell because the tag should have been $125. Is *A* obligated to sell?
3. *A*, sales agent of *S*, took an order from *B* for a television set at a price of $500, the printed order providing that it did not bind *S* until approved by him at the Chicago office. The order also provided that *B* could not cancel it without the approval of *S*. Before the order had reached *S*, *B* changed his mind and mailed a letter to *S*, withdrawing his offer, the letter reaching *S* before he received the order. Disregarding *B*'s letter, *S* shipped the set, but *B* refused to accept it. *S* sued *B* for breach of contract and the court denied recovery. Was this a sound decision? Why?
4. *A* offered to sell his house to *B* for $5,000. *B* offered to give him $4,500, which *A* refused to accept. Later *B* tendered *A* $5,000, which was refused. Had the offer been rejected before the tender?
5. Potter purchased ice of Citizens Ice Co. by placing a card in his window, and the company responded by filling the ice box. Boston Ice Co. purchased the business of Citizens Ice Co., whose window card was used, and gave service to Potter, who assumed Citizens Ice Co. was servicing the box. When billed for ice, he refused to pay, contending no contract with Boston Ice Co. What result?
6. On March 13, *A* offered by mail to sell his grocery store to *B* for $3,000. On March 15 *B* mailed his acceptance, which reached *A*'s office on March 18. On March 17 *A* died. May *A*'s executor recover from *B* in case he fails to perform?
7. *X* submitted a bid for certain brick work to *C*, who used it as a basis for a general contract bid on a certain job. *C*'s bid was accepted, and he notified *X* he had been successful and would have a form contract ready soon. When the form arrived, it contained two or three new terms and *X* refused to sign or to perform. Is *X* liable to *C*?
8. *A* wrote a letter to *B* offering to sell a certain diamond ring for $300. He added that, unless he heard from *B* within the next ten days, he would conclude that *B* had accepted. *B* failed to make any reply. Was there a contract?
9. *A* advertised for bids on a certain construction job. *B* submitted the lowest bid. *A* wrote to *B*, saying: "You are the lowest bidder. Come on down." Was this an acceptance of the bid?
10. *B* Co.'s base bid on a school construction project was $197,670 but his bid included costs on additional alternatives and additions. *B* Co.'s bid was low and School Board notified him that it accepted the bid at a cost of $209,081.37, apparently including base bid and unspecified alternates and additions. *B* Co. could find nothing in its list to total this amount and refused to perform. The court held there was no contract. Was this a sound decision? Give reasons.

11. *N* leased property to *R* which lease gave *R* the right of first refusal of a new lease at expiration of the existing lease. The court held this clause unenforceable because it was too indefinite. In your opinion, was this a sound decision?
12. A certain school board advertised for bids on a new high-school building. A statute in that state provided that all contracts for public works should be let to the lowest and best bidder. *A*, a responsible bidder, submitted the lowest bid, but the board rejected all of the bids. Has *A* a good cause of action against the school board?
13. On May 15 at 8:30 A.M., *B* received a telegram from *S*, offering to sell 500 summer suits at designated prices. *B* replied by telegram at 4:30 P.M. accepting the offer, but the telegram did not reach *S* until the next morning at 9:15 A.M. On May 15 at 3:30 P.M., *S* telegraphed to *B* his withdrawal, but this telegram did not reach *B* until 8:30 A.M. the next day. Is there a good contract?
14. *X* Co., engaged in the development of a real estate project, needed a good construction foreman. It employed *A*, promising to pay him $125 a week and a fair share of the profits made on the project. *X* Co. later refused to pay any of the profits. The court held the agreement to be unenforceable. Was this a good decision? Why?
15. *O* parked his car in a parking lot, paid 35 cents and received a ticket which stated the operator of parking lot was not liable for contents. *O* did not notice the ticket provision; the car was stolen, but was later found without contents. Has *O* a good cause of action against the operator?
16. *O* offered in writing to lease property to *T* for three years at a monthly rental of $700. *T* accepted in writing with three minor modifications to the offer and mailed his check of $700 for the first month's rent. *O* cashed the check, and *T* moved in at considerable expense. *O* now contends the contract is unenforceable because of changed terms. What result?
17. *F* contracted to sell *D* certain described real estate for $11,000, payable as follows: "assume loan, pay cash difference, and purchaser would execute and deliver money security deed covering balance that may be due vendor." The court refused to enforce the contract because the terms were uncertain. Do you agree with it? Why?

10

Consideration

2-29. Definition. While there are a few instances in which courts are enforcing written promises without consideration, a promise standing alone and unsupported by consideration is generally unenforceable.[1] Although defined in various ways, consideration is best expressed as the surrender of or promise to surrender a legal right at the request of another. Actually, it is the price for which the promisor bargains in exchange for his promise. The thing bargained for may be something of detriment to the promisee or something of benefit to the promisor. In either case, if it is the thing requested, the performance or the promise to perform the act requested supplies the consideration needed to make the promise of the promisor enforceable. Whenever a right has been surrendered or a promise to surrender a right has been made at the request of another, the other's promise then becomes enforceable.

2-30. Adequacy of consideration. The value of any given consideration is usually unimportant. So long as the promisee gives the consideration demanded by the promisor, the courts are satisfied. Although the act requested is of little value and the promise given is relatively of much greater value, the courts seldom give any attention to that fact, except as it may be some evidence of fraud. Nevertheless, it should be remembered that a promise unsupported by any consideration and exacting no action or promise by the promisee is unenforceable. Some consideration must exist. A promise in the nature of a gratuity is unenforceable. The fact that the recipient of a proposed gift must take certain steps to place himself in a position to receive it cannot be substituted for consideration, but if, however, the promisee is requested to act in a certain manner and the action is considered to be the price paid for the promise, the taking of such action as is requested will function as consideration. Care must be used in determining whether the offeree's conduct acted as consideration or merely as a move to meet the conditions for a gift. Thus, a promise to make a donation to a charitable or civic organization is enforceable only if made in furtherance of a particular objective and the

[1] Stelmack et al. v. Glen Alden Coal Co., page 206.

organization to be benefited takes some action in reliance upon the promise before it is withdrawn.

A gift, once it has been executed, cannot be set aside by the donor because of the lack of consideration. Once a gift has been completed, the property involved belongs to the donee.

A statement that a nominal consideration exists or is promised is not consideration unless it is the thing bargained for and performance is expected. Quite often a promise is made stating that it is given for $1 in hand paid and other good and valuable consideration, there never having been any intention to pay the dollar. Under the circumstances, no consideration is present unless, in fact, some other consideration was provided.[2] The statement that consideration was given is a mere pretense and without foundation in fact or in contemplation of the parties.

2-31. Performance of statutory duty. The performance of some duty imposed by statute will not constitute a valid consideration for another's promise. Thus, a promise to appear as a witness at a trial or a promise by a public officer to make an arrest will not support a promise to pay money therefor. If the party promises to go beyond what the law demands, then he has waived a legal right and consideration has been given.

2-32. Modification of contractual obligations. As a general rule, an agreement that offers for its consideration the performance of an existing contractual duty by one of the parties is unenforceable, performance being nothing more than the courts would compel him to do.[3] He has surrendered no legal right. Hence, an owner who promises a contractor an additional sum to complete a job already under contract is not legally bound to pay the additional sum. If, however, the promisee agrees to do anything other than, or different from, what the original contract demanded, ample consideration is provided. The contractor who agrees to complete his work at a different date or in a different manner may always recover on a promise of the owner to pay an additional amount. The cancellation of the original contract and the formation of an entirely new agreement is always possible.

Some conflict exists in those cases in which a third party promises added compensation to one of two contracting parties if the latter will complete his contract. The majority of the courts hold that a promise made to a third party to perform an existing contractual obligation offers no consideration although the more recent judicial decisions appear to favor the promisee. Thus, a promise by a third party to a contractor to pay an additional sum upon the latter's completion of a certain construction job is unenforceable in most of the states. It is unenforceable even

[2] American Handkerchief Corp. v. Frannat Realty Co., page 209.

[3] Reynolds v. Hancock, page 210.

when the contractor fulfills his contract only because of the promise of the additional sum. Here also, if anything new or different is requested, the contract becomes binding because of the new consideration.

The Uniform Commercial Code has eliminated consideration as a requirement to modify a contract for the sale of personal property. In such contracts, terms favorable to one party may be changed to more burdensome provisions by mutual agreement without any consideration being given by the other party. However, a signed agreement which excludes modification or rescission except by another writing cannot be otherwise modified or rescinded. Except as between merchants, a requirement preventing modification on a form supplied by a merchant must be separately signed by the other party.

The fact that the Code does not require consideration to modify a contract involving the sale of personal property, while consideration is required to modify other contracts, raises serious social issues and illustrates the effect of changing public attitudes toward the law. The strict requirements of contract law are yielding to moral and ethical considerations. Why should additional consideration be required if the additional promise is made voluntarily and in good faith? On the other hand why should the original contract not be considered sacred? Some courts, in their desire to reach a just result, will examine the reason for the change of terms and conclude that additional consideration was not required under the circumstances of the particular case. The next section illustrates this approach.

2-33. Unforeseeable difficulties. A promise to pay additional compensation for the completion of a contract is usually deemed binding where unforeseen difficulties are encountered after the original agreement is entered into.[4] In such a case the result is most often justified on the theory that, in effect, the parties rescinded the old agreement, because of the new circumstances, and formed a new one. Even in such cases, however, it is safest for the contractor—the party under duty to perform—to have some new consideration provided for or to rescind the old agreement and execute a new one. Unforeseen difficulties are those which seldom occur and are extraordinary in nature. Price changes, strikes, bad weather, and shortage of material are of frequent occurence and are not unforeseeable. Even though difficulties are unforeseen, the promisor is obligated to perform at the original contract price unless the other party indicates a willingness to make an adjustment.

2-34. Payment of a lesser sum. There is one exception to the general rule relating to adequacy of consideration. If the consideration on each side involves money—money given to satisfy a money debt or to support a promise to pay money in the future—the consideration given must

[4] Pittsburgh Testing Laboratory v. Farnsworth & Chambers Co., Inc., page 211.

equal in value the promise made. Because of this rule, an agreement between a debtor and his creditor to have the debt discharged upon the payment of a sum less than the amount agreed to be owing is unenforceable.[5] In most states, even though the lesser sum has been paid, the unpaid portion is collectible. The payment of the lesser sum is the performance of an existing obligation and cannot act as consideration for a release of the balance. Naturally, if there is evidence that the creditor made a gift of the balance to the debtor, no recovery may be had by the creditor. A receipt which states that the payment is in full satisfaction of the account is in many states an indication that a gift was intended. Furthermore, where the debt consists of a note or written agreement, the cancellation and return of the evidence of indebtedness will act to discharge the debt.

2-35. Lesser sum and other consideration. Payment of a lesser sum, where accompanied by additional consideration, will discharge a larger sum. Since the value of consideration is ordinarily unimportant, the added consideration may take any form. Because the general rule recorded in the previous section has proved to be unpopular, the courts have seized upon almost any act as supplying the needed consideration. Payment in advance of the due date, payment at a place other than that agreed upon, surrender of the privilege of bankruptcy, and the giving of a *secured* note for less than the face of the debt have all been found sufficient to discharge a larger amount than that paid.

The mere giving of a negotiable note for a lesser sum than the entire debt will not release the debtor of his duty to pay the balance. The note is merely a promise to pay, and consequently the mere promise to pay less than is due will not discharge the debt.

2-36. Disputed claims. In a good faith controversy between two parties over the amount of indebtedness owing, it is possible to compromise at any figure which is not less than both parties admit to be correct.[6] That is if *A* denies that he owes over fifty dollars, while *B* insists that *A* owes him one hundred dollars, a settlement at fifty dollars or more is binding. Even if at a later date *B* offers convincing evidence that the amount was in excess of the agreed figure, no recovery can be had. The consideration for *B*'s promise to settle for less than one hundred dollars was *A*'s surrender of the right to enter court in an attempt to reduce the figure below that amount.

2-37. Composition of creditors. When the creditors agree with each other and with their debtor to accept a certain percentage of their claims in full satisfaction thereof, the agreement is binding. This combined

[5] Monroe v. Bixby, page 213.

[6] Nardine v. Kraft Cheese Co., page 214.

agreement is known as a composition of creditors and bars them from enforcing the balance of their claims. Under our Bankruptcy Act, a composition of creditors may take place before or after bankruptcy proceedings have been instituted.

2-38. Forbearance to sue. Forbearance to sue or a promise to forbear, where requested, will support a promise by another. Surrender of the right to bring suit acts as the consideration. Should the promisor want assurance that the promisee will not institute legal proceedings, there must be a promise to forbear. Mere inaction in such a case will not suffice since the promisor wants a bilateral agreement rather than a unilateral one. Perhaps in most cases involving the surrender of suit a bilateral agreement is desired; in such case refraining is inadequate to support the promise.

A claim must be made in good faith for its surrender to act as consideration. Consequently, if one makes a claim in bad faith without any intention of prosecuting suit, the waiver of suit will not make the promise of the other party to settle for a certain sum enforceable. Forbearance to sue constitutes consideration only if the party forbearing thinks he has a genuine cause of action. Whether he could win in court is unimportant so long as he thinks he has cause for action.

2-39. Mutuality of engagement or illusory promises. A promise for a promise may, and usually does, constitute sufficient consideration, but each party must be bound by his promise or neither is bound. Therefore, an agreement that gives to one of the parties the right to cancel the contract at any time prior to the time for performance is not binding. If the right to cancel is not absolute, but is conditioned upon the happening or nonhappening of some event, the contract is such that neither party may avoid it unless the condition occurs.

Promises that appear to assure something of value, but when fully understood, *do not* embody such an assurance, are called illusory promises because real mutuality is lacking.[7] Let us consider the following agreement: *B*, a trucker, promises to purchase from S all he wants of regular triple-X (XXX) gasoline at 20 cents a gallon plus taxes, and S promises to sell all that *B* wants at that price. Careful analysis of this agreement makes it clear that *B* has not agreed to buy any gasoline. He has promised to purchase only in case he wants it, which is equivalent to no promise at all. Since *B* has thus given S no consideration for his promise, *B*'s promise being illusory, S is at liberty to withdraw, and his withdrawal becomes effective as soon as notice thereof reaches *B*. Until withdrawn by S, the above agreement stands as a continuing offer on his part, and any order received prior to revocation must be filled at the quoted price.

In the above case, if *B* had agreed to buy, when required, S's gasoline, rather than XXX gasoline, for a period of one year the agreement would have been binding. Whenever the buyer is certain to have needs or requirements, an agreement to purchase all of one's needs or requirements will support the promise to supply them even though the amount is uncertain, since past experience will, in a general way, aid the seller in estimating the amount required. The Code provides that a term which measures the quantity by the output of the seller or the performance of the buyer, means such actual output or requirements as may occur in good faith. In addition, no quantity unreasonably disproportionate to any stated estimate or in the absence of a stated estimate to any normal or otherwise comparable prior output or requirement may be tendered or demanded. In other words, quantity must bear a reasonable relationship to estimates given or to past outputs or requirements.

Often a buyer purchases a limited amount of goods and obtains a guaranteed price on other goods of like character that are ordered within an agreed time. Such an agreement constitutes an option as to the future goods, the consideration for the option being the purchase of some of the goods. The seller in these cases is under a duty to deliver the ordered goods within the agreed period.

2-40. Past or moral consideration. Past or moral consideration is insufficient to support a present promise. The consideration must consist of some present surrender of a legal right. Some act that has taken place in the past will not suffice. Hence, an express warranty concerning goods or property sold, when made after the sale has taken place, is unenforceable,[8] and a promise to pay for a gift previously received cannot be enforced.

A seeming exception to this rule exists in those cases in which one person requests another to perform some work for him without definitely specifying the compensation to be paid. After the work is completed, the parties agree upon a certain sum to be paid for the work. It appears as if the work done in the past furnishes the consideration to support the promise made later to pay a definite sum. This assumption is scarcely correct. As soon as the work is completed, the party performing it is entitled to reasonable compensation. Later he surrenders this right in consideration of a promise to pay a definite sum.

The heading of this section suggests a matter of morals or ethics. Law often lags somewhat behind what may be good ethics. *A*'s brother has been out of work for some time and has a substantial bill for groceries with *X* Co. *A* voluntarily promises *X* Co. to pay the bill but neglects to

[7] Streich v. General Motors Corp., page 216.

[8] James v. Jacobsen, page 218.

do so. There may be, in the minds of some, a moral obligation on A's part to pay but no legal obligation arises. Similarly, in the case of a warranty made concerning goods after the contract of sale is completed. It may be good morals and good business to respect the warranty but legally it is unenforceable.

2-41. Exceptions to past and moral consideration rules. A new promise to pay a debt that has been discharged in bankruptcy is enforceable without any added consideration. The promise to pay must be expressed. Acknowledgement or part payment cannot import a promise to pay the creditor. Most states by statute require the new promise to be in writing, which promise may be to pay only a part of the debt or to pay it only when certain conditions are satisfied.

A creditor who has given a voluntary and binding release of part of a debt may not enforce a later promise by his debtor to pay the balance. The release of the unpaid portion is considered in the nature of a gift, and promise to pay for a gift previously received is unenforceable.

There is, however, a decided trend in current authority to enforce a promise to pay for a gratuity knowingly received under circumstances where there is a strong moral obligation to pay.[9] Illustrative are those instances in which stockholders pay money to an insolvent corporation to restore solvency. A liability to repay cannot well be shown because the corporation would by that fact continue to be insolvent. After the corporation has weathered the storm, a promise to repay the amount received appears to be enforceable.

2-42. Reliance on promise—substitute for consideration. As referred to previously from time to time, there has been in the process of development during the past few years a rule of law which protects those who rely upon a promise even though no consideration has been given. The new principle provides that a promise which the promisor reasonably expects may induce action or forbearance substantial in character, is binding if required to avoid injustice. Before the rule comes into play, the promisee must have changed his position substantially because of the promise, and such reliance must have been reasonably foreseen by the promisor. The promise must have been of such a nature as to induce the particular action involved.

Notes, given to a bank by a stockholder or officer to strengthen its financial position, although supported by no consideration, have been enforced where the bank continued to operate and insolvency later occurred. Bailees who gratuitously accept property of others for safekeeping are required to exercise a certain degree of care over the property even though nothing is received for their services. Cases in these two areas support the rule indicated in the previous paragraph.

[9] Old American Life Ins. Co. v. Biggers, page 219.

CONSIDERATION CASES

STELMACK et al. v. GLEN ALDEN COAL CO.
1940, 339 Pa. 410, 14 A.2d 127

Barnes, J. This is an appeal from the order of the court below entering judgment for the defendant [Glen Alden Coal Company] in an action of assumpsit brought by plaintiffs to recover the cost of repairs to their building which was damaged as a result of mining operations conducted by the defendant. The suit is upon an oral agreement, and the sole question involved is whether the contract is supported by consideration.

On July 3, 1922, plaintiffs purchased a certain lot of ground situated in the city of Scranton, upon which was erected a building containing stores and residential apartments. The deed to them incorporated by reference, and was made subject to, certain reservations, conditions and releases respecting the mineral rights in the land, which appeared in prior conveyances in the chain of title. Among these was the following provision: "It is also expressly understood and agreed by and between the parties to this deed that the right to surface support to the said surface or right of soil is not hereby conveyed. . . . That in no event whatever shall the parties of the first part, their heirs or assigns, be liable for any injury or damage that may be caused or done to the said surface or right of soil, or to the building or improvements that are now or hereafter may be put thereon, by reason of the mining and removing of said coal and minerals." The original grantor reserved the right to remove coal and other minerals, with the express understanding that "the exceptions and reservations aforesaid have materially reduced the amount of consideration of his Indenture, and that any damages of any nature whatsoever, that may occur by reason of the mining and removing of all of said coal and other minerals have by such reduction, been fully liquidated and paid and satisfied. . . ."

The defendant company is the present owner of the coal and mineral rights in the premises, and is actively engaged in mining operations. The plaintiffs aver that they were informed in 1927 by a duly authorized agent of the defendant that mining was about to begin under their property which would cause a subsidence of the soil. He is alleged to have made an oral agreement with them, on behalf of defendant, that if they would permit the coal company's employees to enter upon their land and prop up their building to prevent its collapse, or to minimize any damages which might occur, the company would make all repairs necessary to restore the property to its original condition.

Plaintiffs permitted the ties and supports to be erected about their building which rendered it "unsightly" and resulted in some loss of rents, although it is not contended that the work was performed negligently. As the operations continued during the period from 1928 to 1935, it became necessary, according to plaintiffs, to reconstruct the building, due to the further subsidence of the surface. From time to time the defendant made repairs to the property, but later refused to restore it to its previous condition.

In the present action for the breach of the alleged oral agreement, plaintiffs seek to recover the sum of $3,185, representing the amount expended by them for the repair and restoration of their property. The court below excluded all evidence of the oral agreement, upon the ground that plaintiffs had failed to show that it was supported by a consideration, and directed a verdict in favor of the defendant. From the order of the court in banc refusing a new trial, and entering judgment for the defendant, plaintiffs have taken this appeal.

Plaintiffs contend that (1) there was consideration for the oral agreement because of the detriment suffered by them in permitting the defendant to enter upon their land and place props and ties about their building; (2) the promise to repair was supported by a "moral consideration"; and (3) they are entitled to recover under the doctrine of promissory estoppel.

That consideration is an essential element of an enforceable contract is one of our fundamental legal concepts, and there are but few exceptions to the rule. "Consideration is defined as a benefit to the party promising, or a loss or detriment to the party to whom the promise is made." *Hillcrest Foundation, Inc. v. McFeaters,* 332 Pa. 497, 503, 2 A.2d 775, 778. The terms "benefit" and "detriment" are used in a technical sense in the definition, and have no necessary reference to material advantage or disadvantage to the parties.

It is not enough, however, that the promisee has suffered a legal detriment at the request of the promisor. The detriment incurred must be the "quid pro quo," or the "price" of the promise, and the inducement for which it was made. "Consideration must actually be bargained for as the exchange for the promise." Restatement, Contracts, Section 75, Comment (b); and see *Union Trust Co. v. Long,* 309 Pa. 470, 475, 164 A. 346. If the promisor merely intends to make a gift to the promisee upon the performance of a condition, the promise is gratuitous and the satisfaction of the condition is not consideration for a contract. . . .

In the present case it clearly appears that the defendant's offer to repair the plaintiff's building was entirely gratuitous. The permission to enter upon the land and erect props and ties was sought by defendant merely for the purpose of conferring a benefit upon plaintiffs as a voluntary act, and not as the price or consideration of its alleged promise to restore the building to its original condition. The placing supports about the structure was of no conceivable advantage to the defendant, for, as we have seen, it had no liability whatever "for any injury or damage that may be caused or done to the said surface or right of soil, or to the buildings or improvements" under the provisions of the deeds in plaintiff's chain of title. The interest of plaintiffs alone was served by the defendant's efforts to prevent the collapse of the structure and to minimize the damages resulting from the mining operations. As this was done at the expense of the defendant, and solely for the protection of the plaintiffs, we are unable to see how it could have constituted a consideration for the defendant's promise, and have converted a purely gratuitous undertaking into a binding contract.

Here there was no pre-existing legal or equitable obligation which could serve as the foundation of a moral obligation. The plaintiffs and their predecessors in title were fully compensated, as expressly stated in the original deed, for any loss which might result from the withdrawal of surface support by the owner of the mining rights. The possibility of damage was reflected in the reduced purchase price paid for the property. Plaintiffs acecpted the deed with full knowledge of the reservations and waiver of damages, and with the express stipulation that defendant should have no liability whatsoever for a subsidence of the land.

Nor can plaintiffs' final contention that the defendant should be estopped from repudiating its promise be sustained. The doctrine of promissory estoppel, upon which they rely, may be invoked only in those cases where all the elements of a true estoppel are present, for if it is loosely applied, any promise, regardless of the complete absence of consideration, would be enforceable. The principle involved is defined in the Restatement, Contracts, Section 90, in the following terms:

> A promise which the promisor should reasonably expect to induce action or forbearance of a definite and substantial character on the part of the promisee and which does induce such action or forbearance is binding if injustice can be avoided only by enforcement of the promise. . . .

Here no action was taken by plaintiffs in reliance upon the defendant's promise which resulted in disadvantage to them. They did not alter their position adversely or substantially. They have suffered no injustice in being deprived of a gratuitous benefit to which they have no legal or equitable right. We are satisfied there is nothing in the present record to bring this case within any recognized exception to the well established principle of contract law, that a promise unsupported by consideration is nudum pactum, and unenforceable.

The judgment of the court below is affirmed.

AMERICAN HANDKERCHIEF CORP. v. FRANNAT REALTY CO.

1954, N.J., 109 A.2d 793

The plaintiff, American Handkerchief Corp., initiated this action to recover damages for wrongful eviction from leased premises. The plaintiff's lease with defendant was to expire in the near future and it desired to renew, if it could locate satisfactory sub-tenants for part of the space. In the interim it obtained an option agreement that provided as follows: "For one dollar and other good and valuable consideration, said Tenant is hereby given the right to renew or extend said leases for two years." The terms of the new lease were also stipulated, but the defendant shortly thereafter notified plaintiff that it would not renew the lease and that it was withdrawing the offer. The lower court gave judgment for the defendant, and the plaintiff appealed.

VANDERBILT, C. J. . . . The defendant has consistently claimed that the writing in question was a mere offer without valid consideration that never ripened into a binding option-contract between the parties because it was withdrawn prior to any acceptance by the plaintiff. The writing purported to give the plaintiff the "right to renew" the two leases upon the terms therein provided. If based upon consideration it is an option-contract, and as such irrevocable. . . .

On the other hand, if the quoted draft was not supported by consideration, it is a mere offer only. . . . Since the defendant-offeror sought to revoke the offer prior to its acceptance by the plaintiff, the pertinent question is whether this writing was without consideration and thus a mere offer, or whether it was an option supported by valid consideration.

The draft in question provides that the right to renew the leases was given "for One Dollar ($1.00) and other good and valuable consideration." Insofar as the one dollar is concerned, the plaintiff admits that it was never paid. And although it is an elementary principle that the law will not enter into an inquiry as to the adequacy of the consideration, . . . it is equally well settled that consideration, no matter how small, must be the "price bargained for and paid for a promise," . . . and "an inquiry whether the dollar was really bargained for as the consideration will always be pertinent, for where a promise of value is stated to have been made for a small money consideration there is often reason to doubt whether a bargain to exchange the sum mentioned for the promise was really intended by the parties," 1 Williston, *supra,* sec. 115. It is clear that not only was the one dollar never paid, but it was not the consideration bargained for between the parties.

We also fail to discover any proof in the record of "other good and valuable consideration" and counsel has not directed our attention to anything which could properly qualify as such. . . . We therefore conclude that there was no consideration for the offer and therefore it was effectively revoked by the defendant in September 1951, prior to acceptance by the plaintiff.

The judgment of the lower court is affirmed.

REYNOLDS v. HANCOCK
1959 (Wash.) 335 P.2d 817

Plaintiff, Reynolds, sued Hancock because the latter withdrew an offer to purchase real estate which had been listed by the owner with the plaintiff, causing the plaintiff to lose his potential commission.

MALLERY, J. . . . The plaintiffs brought this suit against the defendant buyers on the theory that printed paragraph seven of the earnest-money receipt constituted a contract between them and the defendants, which the defendants breached by withdrawing their offer. They prayed for the amount of their commission as the measure of damage suffered by reason of the defendants' breach. Paragraph seven provides:

"Purchaser offers to purchase the property in its present condition, on the terms noted. This offer is made subject to approval of the seller by midnight of March 27, 1957. *In consideration of agent submitting this offer to seller, purchaser agrees with the agent not to withdraw this offer* during said period, or until earlier rejection thereof by seller. Purchaser agrees that written notice of acceptance given to agent by seller shall be notice to purchaser. If seller does not accept this agreement within the time specified, the agent shall refund the earnest money upon demand." (Italics ours.)

The trial court, holding there was no consideration to the defendants for their promise not to withdraw the offer, granted judgment for the defendants, and the plaintiffs appeal.

The trial court's conclusion of law was correct. The appellants were not the respondents' agents. At the intermediate stage of the negotiations relating to the air-mail letter, it would have been a breach of duty to the owners not to transmit to them the specific offer in question. It was not a consideration for the promise of the respondents with whom they were dealing at arm's length.

This is a conclusive answer to appellants' contentions.

There is another independent answer equally conclusive upon the matter. Only the owners would owe the appellants any commission to which they might become entitled under the agency agreement. If for any reason the respondents became obligated to the appellants for breach of some contract between them, the measure of damages would not be the agreed commission under the real-estate agency to which respondents were not privy. See *Giovannoni v. Waple & James, Inc.*, 70 App.D.C. 229, 105 F.2d 108.

Assuming then that a breach of contract did exist, the amount of damages would be the cost of mailing the air-mail letter. For this no remedy is available.

The judgment is affirmed.

PITTSBURGH TESTING LAB. v. FARNSWORTH & CHAMBERS CO., INC.

1958, 251 F.2d 77

MURRAH, C. J. This is an appeal from a judgment of the District Court invalidating, for lack of consideration, an oral contract to pay additional compensation for services rendered in connection with the performance of an antecedent written contract. Jurisdiction is based upon diversity of citizenship and requisite amount in controversy.

According to the unchallenged findings of the trial court, the appellant, Pittsburgh Testing Laboratory, entered into a written subcontract with the appellee, Farnsworth & Chambers, Inc., under the terms of which the Testing Company agreed to do all of the testing and inspection of materials required under a master contract between Farnsworth and the Douglas Aircraft Corporation for the construction of concrete ramps and runways at Tulsa, Oklahoma. The consideration for the performance of the service was $24,450, to be paid in seven monthly installments, less ten percent retainage until completion of the contract. In the preliminary negotiations, Farnsworth estimated that the job would be completed in seven months, or October 15, 1952, on the basis of a ten-hour day, sixty-hour work week, and that the Testing Company's work would be concluded about November 1. While these representations undoubtedly formed the basis for Pittsburgh's proposal and for the lump sum compensation in the contract, there was no guarantee of a completion date or hour work week. Before the end of the seven months period, and in September 1952, it became manifest that the contract would not be completed within the estimated time, due principally to the necessity of moving 1,200,000 tons of dirt or material instead of the estimated 600,000 tons. A controversy thereupon arose between the parties as to Pittsburgh's obligation under the written contract and Farnsworth's liability for overtime compensation to Pittsburgh's personnel for work in excess of the sixty-hour week. Pittsburgh was told by Farnsworth's representatives that if it would continue to perform its services, it would be compensated. When, however, no payments were made in December 1952, Pittsburgh refused to proceed unless a new contract was entered into providing payment for the remaining work at the rate of $3,492.85 per month from November 1 until the completion of the work, plus time and one-half for all man hours worked over sixty hours per week. On December 20, the parties entered into an oral contract to that effect and Pittsburgh continued to perform the same service and to submit invoices for the monthly compensation, and separate invoices for overtime pay in excess of the sixty hours per week. Although Farnsworth did not remit for the invoices or reply to Pittsburgh's persistent statements, it made no protest or objection to either the statements for the stipulated additional compensation or the separate statements for the overtime. After the work was completed in the Spring of 1953, and Pittsburgh had been paid the balance of the retainage under the original contract, Farnsworth finally repudiated the oral agreement and this suit followed.

The trial court specifically found that at the time of making the oral contract to pay additional compensation, plus overtime, a bona fide dispute existed between the parties concerning their respective obligations under the written contract. The trial court also specifically found, however, that the Testing Company performed no services pursuant to the oral contract which it was not already bound to do by the terms of the written contract. Based on these findings, the trial court finally concluded that the oral contract was unenforceable for want of consideration, and that Farnsworth was not estopped to defend on that basis.

It is the general rule, followed in Oklahoma where this contract was made and performed, that a promise to pay additional compensation for the doing of that which the promisee is already legally bound to do or perform, is insufficient consideration for a valid and enforceable contract. . . .

Another more widely accepted exception might properly be called the "unforeseeable difficulties exception," under which the courts have recognized the equities of a promise for additional compensation based upon extraordinary and unforeseeable difficulties in the performance of the subsisting contract. In these circumstances, the courts generally sustain the consideration for the new promise, based upon standards of honesty and fair dealing and affording adequate protection against unjust or coercive exactions. . . .

As far as we can determine, Oklahoma courts have not had occasion to embrace or reject what seems to us a salutary exception to the rule. But, there can be no doubt that the oral contract was made in the face of unforeseen and substantial difficulties—circumstances which were not within the contemplation of the parties when the original contract was made, and which were recognized when the subsequent oral contract was entered into. The performance of the contract took more than twice as long as the parties estimated. Pittsburgh's primary cost was expensive skilled labor, and the consideration for the contract was necessarily based upon the estimated time required for performance. We should be content to sustain the contract on the assumption that the Oklahoma courts would recognize and apply the so-called unforeseen difficulties exception in a case like ours. But the contract need not rest upon that ground alone. There can be no doubt that an agreement which compromises a bona fide dispute concerning duties and obligations under a subsisting contract, is supported by valid consideration and is enforceable. . . . The trial court's specific finding in that regard is amply supported by the evidence, and we hold the contract valid and enforceable. The judgment is accordingly reversed.

MONROE v. BIXBY

1951, 330 Mich. 353, 47 N.W.2d 643

BOYLES, J. Plaintiff, Monroe, the owner of a house and lot on Clancy Street in the city of Grand Rapids, on September 1, 1937, entered into a written land contract to sell it to her daughter, the defendant, for $4,000. $60.60* was paid on the purchase price and the balance of $3,039.40,* with interest at the rate of 6 per cent per annum, was to be paid in monthly instalments of $30 or more per month the first year, then $35 or more each month. Defendant's then-husband was also named as a vendee but some time later defendant and her husband were divorced and assignment of his interest in the contract was made to the defendant. Plaintiff shows that some time later defendant asked to have the monthly payments and the interest reduced. Plaintiff drew up a purported agreement which is as follows:

Agreement

First party, Anna V. Wiley Monroe; Second party, Hazel May Bixby;

First party agrees to accept 5% interest on contract. The first party agrees to accept Thirty ($30.00) Dollars a month payment instead of Thirty-five ($35.00) Dollars a month. The first party agrees to give the second party a deed when the first party has received Twenty-Five Hundred ($2,500.00) Dollars from September 1, 1939.

The second party is not to transfer the contract unless the first party agrees to the transfer.

(s) Mrs. Anna V. Wilev Monroe

Subscribed and sworn to
before me this 5th day
of November, 1940.

(s) Catharine M. May,
Notary Public,
My comm. expires
Nov. 23, 1940

(Seal)

This paper was signed by plaintiff but not by defendant. After it was executed by the plaintiff, the defendant made monthly payments until

* Apparently an error in the record.

January 25, 1950, when defendant refused to make further payment.

Plaintiff claims when the $2,500 was paid upon the contract she was to give a deed and have a mortgage to secure her for the balance of the $4,000 purchase price. Defendant claims that she was entitled to a deed after paying the $2,500 upon the contract and was under no obligation to pay the balance of the $4,000 purchase price.

When the contract showed an unpaid balance of $1,178.08, defendant refused to pay more, and plaintiff filed the instant bill of complaint praying for a foreclosure of the land contract and an accounting for certain furniture. She claimed that the aforesaid "agreement" was invalid because of lack of consideration and failure to comply with the statute of frauds. After a hearing on the merits, the court entered a decree dismissing plaintiff's bill of complaint but decreeing that there was $32.08 still due her on the contract and directing plaintiff to execute a deed to defendant upon payment of that amount, as prayed for by the defendant in her cross bill. Plaintiff appeals.

Assuming that defendant's position was supported by the proofs, and that the plaintiff had agreed to accept less than the full amount of the purchase price, such an agreement must be considered as unenforceable for lack of consideration. Plaintiff's claim of $1,178.08, balance of the purchase price and interest, was a liquidated demand, and any agreement to accept less than the full amount could not be considered as a compromise and settlement of an unliquidated or doubtful claim.

Under the law in this state there is no doubt that a payment of less than the full amount of a past-due liquidated and undisputed debt, although accepted and receipted for as in full satisfaction, is only to be treated as a partial payment, and does not estop the creditor from suing for and recovering the balance. *People for use of Zeeland Brick Co. v. Fidelity & Deposit Co.*, 195 Mich. 738, 162 N.W. 338, 340.

We have many times held that part payment of a past-due, liquidated and undisputed claim, even though accepted in full satisfaction thereof, does not operate to discharge the debt, but constitutes a payment *pro tanto* only. *Aston v. Elkow*, 279 Mich. 232, 271 N.W. 742, 743. . . .

We conclude that the claimed "agreement" to accept less than the amount due for principal and interest on the contract, being without consideration, was void. That being true, there is no occasion to consider the claim that it also was void because of the statute of frauds.

Judgment for plaintiff.

NARDINE v. KRAFT CHEESE CO.

1944, (Ind. App.) 52 N.E.2d 634

FLANAGAN, J. For several years prior to August 24, 1941, the appellant, Lattie Nardine, a resident of Vincennes, Indiana, had operated a grocery in Lexington, Kentucky, under the name of Standard Market. During that time she had been an open account customer of appellee. In July 1941 she purchased from appellee 515¾ pounds of longhorn cheese. After a short time a dispute developed as to this cheese. Appellant said it was spoiled when received and that appellee should take it back. Appellee said that appellant spoiled it trying to force cure it and therefore it could not be returned. This dispute continued until after appellant closed her business on August 24, 1941.

Thereafter letters were exchanged between the parties concerning settlement of appellant's account, whereby it developed that there were other differences as to items in the account. About October 1, 1941, appellee's Lexington manager went to Vincennes to discuss the account with appellant but they were unable to agree as to the amount appellant owed. The dispute concerning the shipment of longhorn cheese above referred to was continued at that conference.

On October 30, 1941, appellant wrote appellee the following letter:

> Enclosed please find check in the amount of One Hundred Forty Six Dollars and one cent ($146.01) which according to our records pays my account in full.
>
> You will notice that I have taken a 10¢ per lb. deduction on the 515¾ lb. bad longhorn cheese, that I received from you. We are still at quite a loss on this cheese, as we really had to sacrifice it to get rid of it.
>
> In regard to the balance on your statement of overcharges and deductions, I wish to advise that I find it impossible to check upon this as they are so old. I feel that if the deductions were not in order, that I should have been notified at the time they were taken from the checks. As you told me, these were left over from before the time you took over this account.
>
> We are sorry to have had to make the above deductions, but I really feel that it is a just one. It has been a pleasure to do business with the Kraft Cheese Company at Lexington, and I want to thank you for all past favors.
>
> With best regards to you, I remain,

Enclosed with the letter was a check for $146.01, marked, "This pays my account in full to date." After receiving the letter and check appellee mailed the check to the Vincennes bank on which it was drawn for certification. The bank certified the check and returned it to appellee who still retains it.

Thereafter appellee brought this action against appellant seeking to recover on account for the balance it claimed due after deducting the sum of $146.01. Appellant answered among other things that there had been an accord and satisfaction. Trial resulted in judgment for appellee in the sum of $87.88 and this appeal followed. The sufficiency of the evidence is properly challenged.

When the holder of a check has it certified by the bank on which it is drawn, the drawer is discharged and the debt becomes that of the bank. . . . If it was tendered in full payment of a claim which was unliquidated or concerning which a bona fide dispute existed, the acceptance of the check discharged the debt. . . .

Appellee says that there was no dispute because the trial court found that the longhorn cheese which appellant claims was spoiled when it arrived was in fact spoiled by appellant in trying to force cure it. The trial court could, and undoubtedly did, find that appellant spoiled the cheese. But in determining whether there was an accord and satisfaction we are not concerned with the question as to who was right and who was wrong in an existing dispute. We are concerned only with the question as to whether a good faith dispute existed at the time the check was tendered in full payment. *Neubacher v. Perry, supra.* The evidence on this question by both parties was all to the effect that such a dispute did exist.

It is true as appellee contends that the question of accord and satisfaction is ordinarily a question of fact, but where the controlling facts requisite to show accord and satisfaction are undisputed the question becomes one of law. . . .

Our conclusion is that the facts in this case show an accord and satisfaction of the claim sued upon.

Judgment for defendant Nardine.

STREICH v. GENERAL MOTORS CORP.

1955, 5 Ill. App.2d 485, 126 N.E.2d 389

The plaintiff, Streich, as seller sues for breach of what he contends is a contract to supply the defendant with its requirements for certain air magnet valves from September 1, 1948 to August 31, 1949. This would have been approximately 1,600 units based on previous requirements. The so-called contract consisted of a purchase order reading as follows:

> This Purchase Order is issued to cover shipments of this part, to be received by us from September 1, 1948, to August 31, 1949, as released and scheduled on our 48 'Purchase Order release and Shipping Schedule.'

It described the valves and set a price of $13.50 each, and on the reverse side the order said it constituted the final agreement between buyer and seller. It called itself a contract, but said, "Deliveries are to be made both in quantities and at times specified in schedules furnished by Buyer."

The defendant contended there was no contract since no goods had been ordered, although the plaintiff spent considerable sums of money for machinery and tooling in preparation for production.

McCormick, J. . . . There is no question but that under the law a contract properly entered into whereby the buyer agrees to buy all its requirements of a commodity for a certain period, and the seller agrees to sell the same as ordered, is a valid and enforceable contract and is not void for uncertainty and want of mutuality. . . . The contract in the instant case is not such a contract. Purchase Order No. 11925 states that it is issued to cover "shipments of this part, to be received by us from Sept. 1, 1948 to August 31, 1949 as released and scheduled on our series 48 'Purchase Order release and Shipping Schedule' No. 478412 attached and all subsequent Purchase Order releases." . . . Reading and construing the two documents together, notwithstanding the detailed provisions contained on the reverse side of the purchase order, the result is an agreement on the part of the seller to sell a certain identified valve at a certain fixed price in such quantities as the buyer may designate, when and if it issues a purchase order for the same. The word "release" as used throughout these documents is treated by both parties as equivalent to "order."

In *Corbin on Contracts,* Vol. 1, § 157, the author says:

> In what purports to be a bilateral contract, one party sometimes promises to supply another, on specified terms with all the goods or services that the other may order from time to time within a stated period. A mere statement by the other party that he assents to this, or 'accepts' it, is not a promise to order any goods or to pay anything. There is no consideration of any sort for the seller's promise; and he is not bound by it. This remains true, even though the parties think that a contract has been made and expressly label their agreement a 'contract.' In cases like this, there may be no good reason for implying any kind of promise by the offeree. Indeed, the proposal and promise of the seller has the form of an invitation for orders; and the mode of making an operative acceptance is to send in an order for a specific amount. By such an order, if there has been no previous notice of revocation, a contract is consummated and becomes binding on both parties. The standing offer is one of those that empowers the offeree to accept more than once and to create a series of separate obligations. The sending in of one order and the filling of it by the seller do not make the offer irrevocable as to additional amounts if the parties have not so agreed.

See also *Williston on Contracts,* Rev. Ed., Vol. 1, 104A.

Here, the buyer proffers purchase order 11925, with its twenty-five or more clauses, to the seller for acceptance. In the instrument it makes no promise to do anything. On the surface it appears to be an attempt to initiate a valid bilateral contract. The seller accepts, and as by a flash of legerdemain the positions of the buyer and the seller shift. The buyer now becomes the promisee and the seller the promisor. The promise of the seller to furnish identified items at a stated price is merely an offer and cannot become a contract until the buyer issues a release or order for a designated number of items. Until this action is taken the buyer has made no promise to do anything, and either party may withdraw. The promise is illusory, and the chimerical contract vanishes. "An agreement to sell to another such of the seller's goods, wares, and merchandise as the other might from time to time desire to purchase is lacking in mutuality because it does not bind the buyer to purchase any of the goods of the seller, as such matter is left wholly at the option or pleasure of the buyer. . . ."

The agreement in question is an adaptation of what was termed an "open end contract," which was used extensively by the federal government during the late war. However, it was used only in cases where the commodities dealt with were staples and either in the possession of or easily accessible to the seller. In this case the use of the contract is shifted and extended to cover commodities which must be manufactured before they are available for sale. According to the admitted statements in the complaint, special tools had to be manufactured in order to produce the item herein involved. The seller here, misled by the many and detailed provisions contained in purchase order No. 11925 and ordinarily applicable to an enforceable bilateral contract, undoubtedly, as he alleged in his complaint, did go to considerable expense in providing tools and machines, only to find that by the accepted agreement the buyer had promised to do absolutely nothing. A statement of expectation creates no duty. Courts are not clothed with the power to make contracts for parties, nor can they, under the guise of interpretation, supply provisions actually lacking or impose obligations not actually assumed. . . .

The agreement contained in purchase order No. 11925 was artfully prepared. It contains, in print so fine as to be scarcely legible, more than twenty-three clauses, most of which are applicable to bilateral contracts. It has all the indicia of a binding and enforceable contract, but it was not a binding and enforceable contract because the promise was defective. Behind the glittering facade is a void. This agreement was made in the higher echelons of business, overshadowed by the aura of business ethics. To say the least, the agreement was deceptive. In a more subterranean atmosphere and between persons of lower ethical standards it might, without any strain of the language, be denominated by a less deterged appellation.

Nevertheless, as the law is today, on the pleadings in the instant case, the trial court could do nothing but sustain the motion to dismiss the complaint. The judgment of the Circuit Court is affirmed.

Judgment for defendant affirmed.

JAMES v. JACOBSEN

1956, (Ga. App.) 91 S.E.2d 527

Jacobsen brought an action against James, defendant, to recover for alleged breach of warranty to the effect that the property purchased was free of termites. The warranty was given after the contract of sale had been signed.

GARDNER, J. The record reveals that this is an action ex contractu and not ex delicto. This leads us to consider first whether or not the instrument regarding termite infestation was a legal and binding contract with sufficient consideration to vary the terms of the original contract of sale and contract of purchase. It is our understanding of the law that where the vendor of realty stipulates the terms upon which the property is offered for sale and such offer is accepted by a proposed purchaser, such contract between them is executed within the terms of the agreement. The contract of sale set up certain specifications, all of which were fulfilled by the vendor and the purchaser within the specified time. Before the consummation of the sale there was executed an instrument in which the seller guaranteed to the purchaser, in writing, that the premises in question were free of termite infestation and free of damage due to any previous termite infestation. . . .

The original contract was based on legal consideration and was valid and enforceable. The original contract of sale here, as the record reveals, was executed on January 14, 1955 and the express warranty with regard to termites was given by the defendant on February 10, 1955. The sale had not taken place and no delivery of the property had been made and the parties had not yet done what the original contract obligated them to do. See *Woodruff v. Graddy & Sons,* 91 Ga. 333, 17 S.E. 264. Where, as here, the termite instrument is relied upon as a part of the original contract of sale, there are decisions to the effect that such a reliance is not tenable but is nudum pactum. . . .

Judgment for defendant.

OLD AMERICAN LIFE INS. CO. v. BIGGERS
1949, 172 F.2d 495

This is an action by the Insurance Company to cancel a contract or to limit the recovery under the contract to $22,443.36. The defendant Biggers had from time to time advanced money to the plaintiff in order to keep it in good standing, but the amounts could not be set up as a loan because the company would not then be considered financially sound. Defendant finally refused to make additional advances, so the company entered into a written agreement with one Bozeman, agent of Biggers, whereby it promised, in consideration of past services and a release from any claims against the company, to pay to Bozeman 10 per cent of all gross premiums received thereafter, although there was an oral understanding with Biggers that payments would cease when the sum of $22,443.36 had been paid. Under new management the company prospered and had paid

$15,460.19, offering to pay the balance of $6,983.17 if Biggers would release any claim thereafter. He refused to do so, hence this action.

PHILLIPS, C. J. It is clear that Bozeman did not render to the Insurance Company any of the personal services provided for in the contract. We think it may be reasonably inferred from the evidence that Biggers did not render the Insurance Company any personal service under the contract. In fact, counsel for Biggers states in his brief that the parties did not contemplate that any of such services would be rendered.

The Insurance Company contends that, since no limitation as to time is expressed in the contract, either it is terminable at the will of either party, or it will terminate at the time when the parties intended it should cease to operate.

We do not think the contract should be regarded as one for personal services and, therefore, terminable by either party on reasonable notice. The parties did not contemplate that either Biggers or Bozeman would render any personal services under the contract. The advances which Biggers had made to the Insurance Company were donations and created no express or implied legal obligation of the Insurance Company to repay them. The release by Biggers of any claim which Biggers had against the Insurance Company for such donations did not constitute a legal consideration for the contract, because the relinquishment of a claim which is wholly without merit or foundation does not constitute a legal consideration. It follows that the contract must be supported, if at all, by the moral obligation which arose from the donations made by Biggers. We think it may be said that, while it was not intended that such donations should create a legal obligation on the part of the Insurance Company to repay them, Biggers expected that, if the Insurance Company prospered, through the control he was able to exercise over it, he would eventually be indirectly repaid through the payment of salaries or commissions. Made under those circumstances, we think the donations created a moral obligation on the part of the Insurance Company sufficient to support a future executory promise.

While the authorities are not in agreement, the trend of modern authorities is to the effect that where services or other consideration moving from the promisee conferred an actual, material, or pecuniary benefit on the promisor, and not merely a detriment to the promisee, and the promisee expected to be compensated therefor and did not intend it as mere gift or gratuity, and the benefit received had not constituted the consideration for another promise already performed or still legally enforceable, a moral obligation arises which will support a subsequent executory promise where there was originally no contract, perfect or imperfect, obligating the promisor.

We, therefore, conclude that the donation made by Biggers to the Insurance Company constituted a consideration in the nature of a moral obligation for the promise of the Insurance Company to pay Biggers 10 per cent of its gross premiums, but only to the extent of such obligation and no further, and that, when payments made under the contract equal the amount of the donation, the contract will terminate.

The judgment is reversed and the cause remanded for further proceedings in accordance with this opinion.

Review Questions and Problems

1. *H* offered to sell a residence to *S* at an agreed price and *S* promised to purchase it, but it was also agreed that if *S* had not sold his presently owned residence by March 1, he could rescind the agreement to purchase from *H*. *S* sold the property but refused to take *H*'s property. The court held that there was no contract, the agreement lacking mutuality. Was this a sound decision?
2. An uncle promised to pay his nephew $5,000 on his 21st birthday if the latter would refrain from smoking, drinking, and gambling until he reached that age. The nephew conformed to his uncle's request, but the latter refused to pay, alleging no consideration as a defense. Is the uncle liable?
3. *M* contracted to purchase from *H* certain real estate at a given price, the sale being conditioned upon *M* finding satisfactory tenants. Later *H* refused to perform, contending that there was no mutuality since *M* was not bound. Did *M* supply any consideration for *H*'s promise to convey?
4. Mrs. *B* promised the pastor of *X* Church that she would donate to the trustees of the church $2,500 with which to pay off a mortgage if they would obtain subscriptions for the balance of the mortgage. The balance was subscribed, but Mrs. *B* refused to pay her share. Were the trustees entitled to recover on the promise?
5. *C* engaged *H* to act as a pilot during a strike and told *H* that it would employ him as long as it continued in business. *H* did not agree to work for any particular period and, some time after the strike ended, he was discharged. *C* urged that no consideration was given for its promise to employ *H* for the long period. The court held that no contract existed and that *H* had no claim based upon his dismissal. Was the decision sound?
6. *B*, being insolvent and faced with the possibility of bankruptcy, called all his creditors together and agreed to refrain from bankruptcy and to pay each one of them 10 cents on the dollar if they would release him. All the creditors agreed to the proposition. The payment was made. Later, *B* became prosperous, and *C*, one of the creditors, attempted to recover the balance of his claim. Had *C* any basis for recovery?
7. *O* borrowed $4,000 of *C* and gave his note for the amount to fall due six months later. Two weeks after the note was given, *O* persuaded

S to sign his name to the note. When the note fell due, *O* was unable to pay it, and *C* seeks to recover of *S*. Has *S* a good defense?

8. *A* contracts to build a barn for *B* at a cost of $1,000. Because of an increase in the cost of labor and materials, *A* refused to perform. *B* promises to pay *A* an additional $300 if the barn is completed. May *A* recover on this promise, assuming that the barn is completed? Suppose *A* had agreed to complete the barn within a certain date at the time the second promise was made. Would the result have been the same?
9. *V* Co. agreed in writing to deliver to *J* Co. all coal mined at a particular mine at specified prices and *J* Co. agreed to accept "all coal which our equipment will permit us to process to best advantage and which market conditions will permit us to handle" for the term of one year. *V* Co. later refused to deliver, claiming no contract because there was no mutuality. The court held that no contract existed. In your judgment, is this a sound decision?
10. *W*'s brother had been seriously ill and had incurred a substantial bill while in the hospital. As he was being released from the hospital, *W* promised to pay the bill, but later refused to do so. The court held he was not obligated to pay. Was this a sound decision?
11. *A* owed *B* $500, which was past due, and, since *B* was having difficulty in collecting the account, he accepted $400 in full satisfaction, at the same time giving *A* a receipt in full of the account, which stated that the $100 balance had been forgiven. At a later date, *A* was able to pay, and *B* brought suit to recover the balance. Should he have been allowed to recover?
12. A building and loan company agreed with an insurance company to purchase of the insurance company all the insurance it needed during the next ten years, and the latter agreed to supply all insurance needed at local current rates at the time the insurance was needed. Was this an enforceable contract?
13. *O* and *B* entered into a written agreement whereby *O* agreed to sell certain real estate to *B* for $8,500, and *B* agreed to purchase at that price, but was to be released if not able to finance it so as to pay cash. *O* later refused to perform, contending no mutuality and therefore no consideration. What result?
14. *O* contracted to sell to *B* property upon which *O* had recently completed a new house, the price being $17,500. After the contract was signed, but prior to payment, *B* became concerned about the possibility of water in the basement. *O* then promised that the basement would be dry treated and free from water. *B* then settled for the property and received title. Water later caused damage. Is *O*'s promise enforceable?

11 Voidable Contracts

2-43. Voidable contracts. A voidable contract is one that, for some reason satisfactory to the court, may be set aside at the request of one of the parties. It differs from a contract that is void in that the latter cannot be enforced by either party, whereas the former is binding unless the injured party sees fit to avoid the agreement.

The Uniform Commercial Code incorporates the law relative to capacity to contract, fraud, misrepresentation, duress, and mistake as supplementary to its provisions. Therefore, the materials contained in this chapter are applicable to all contracts including those under the Code.

CAPACITY OF PARTIES

2-44. Competent parties. Our definition of a contract provides that the agreement must be entered into between competent parties. All persons are presumably competent to contract without restriction—except infants, insane persons, intoxicated persons, married women, and corporations. The power of a corporation to contract is limited by its charter and will be considered later under the subject of corporations. By legislation in most states, married women today are accorded the same right to contract that is granted to anyone else. Under the common law, unmodified by statute, they had few contractual powers.

The law concerning insane persons and drunkards is similar to that which governs the rights of infants. It will be considered separately only in those cases in which the rules differ.

2-45. Infants' contracts are voidable. An infant normally reaches his majority at the age of twenty-one, although some states have provided that women become of age at eighteen. A contract between an infant and an adult is voidable only by the infant; the adult finds his obligation enforceable unless the infant desires to disaffirm.

The right to avoid contracts is granted to a minor in order to protect him from those who would otherwise be led to take advantage of his immaturity and inexperience. Although the right to avoid is absolute, the court not taking time in most states to inquire if a contract is fair or favorable, a minor of high ethical standards would seldom use the law to take advantage of an adult. Although on occasion he may be tempted to do so, it is wiser ethically to use the right only when it is needed to avoid a contract through which an adult has imposed upon the minor or has persuaded him to make an improvident or unsound agreement.

It is said by many courts that the appointment of an agent by an infant is absolutely void, contracts entered into by such an agent being no effect. The tendency of the courts at present, however, seems to be to place contracts of this nature in the same category as any other agreement of the minor, thus requiring the infant to avoid contracts made by his agent in order to evade liability.

If an infant has entered into a partnership agreement, he may withdraw from the partnership at any time, regardless of the terms of the agreement, and avoid liability in damages to his partners. The capital which he has invested is nevertheless subject to firm debts; therefore, to the extent of the capital which he has invested, he cannot avoid the payment of firm creditors. Legislation in many states has altered in a limited way the right of minors to avoid their contracts. Some take away the minor's right to avoid after he marries, and a few give the courts the right to approve freedom of contract upon a showing of maturity. These and other exceptions to the general rule may be found in one state or another, but in most states the rule gives the minor the right to avoid any contracts made during his minority.

Where the contract is purely executory—not performed on either side—the matter is quite simple, for any act on the part of the infant that clearly indicates an intent to disaffirm the agreement will have that effect. After such conduct on the part of the infant, any attempt by the adult to recover damages for breach of the agreement would be utterly futile.

2-46. Executed contracts. The fact that both parties to the contract have fulfilled their promises does not affect the right of the infant to avoid the agreement. If he is in possession of the consideration that has passed to him, he must return it to the other party, as he cannot disaffirm the contract and at the same time retain the benefits. Any burdens imposed by the contract upon the infant must continue to be met until he decides to disaffirm the agreement. If the minor has the consideration received by him but in a different form—for example, if he has traded it for something else—he is probably bound to return the consideration which he has, as a basis of his disaffirmance.

The right of an infant to disaffirm a contract differs from other voidable contracts in that an infant who has sold goods to an adult may demand the return of goods from innocent third persons who in turn have purchased from his immediate transferee. In those states which have adopted the Uniform Sales Act this procedure is no longer possible in the case of personal property. In all other instances, however, an infant may disaffirm as against innocent third parties.

The states are somewhat in conflict concerning those cases in which the infant has spent or squandered what he received and is, therefore, unable to return it. The majority of the states hold that the infant may disaffirm the contract and demand the return of the consideration with which he has parted, even though he is unable to return that which he received. Hence, an infant may purchase an automobile, and, after driving it for a year or two, rescind his contract and demand the full amount which he paid for it,[1] or, after having an accident that demolishes it, he may follow the same procedure. A few of the courts, however, hold that if the contract is advantageous to the infant and the adult has been fair in every respect, the contract cannot be disaffirmed unless the infant returns the consideration which he received.

A provision in a contract wherein the minor states he is of age does not deprive him of the right to rescind, nor does the fact that he is in business, has all the appearances of an adult, or possesses a business acumen beyond that of the average adult, except as these situations may have been modified by statute in an occasional state.

A minor is not permitted to avoid a contract in part only, as disaffirmance must be in total or not at all.

2-47. Time of disaffirmance. With the exception of sales of real estate by a minor, an infant may avoid his contract and demand the consideration with which he has parted at any time during his minority. This right continues until a reasonable time after he becomes of age, a reasonable time depending on the nature of the article involved and on the surrounding circumstances. In the case of real estate sold by the infant, it may consist of several years.

A minor cannot disaffirm a sale of his real estate until after he reaches his majority. This provision is said to result from the fact that the land will always be there; he cannot be materially injured by being forced to wait until he becomes of age. He may, however, prior to disaffirmance, enter into possession and take over the management of the property, thus appropriating to himself the income from it while title rests in the adult. Where the minor does not avail himself of this protection, many states permit him at the time of disaffirmance of the sale of real estate to recover from the adult for the use of the property while he has been out of possession.

2-48. Ratification. An executed contract is ratified by the minor when he retains the consideration received for an unreasonable time after

[1] Wooldridge v. Hill, page 233.

reaching his majority, by acceptance of benefits incident to ownership, such as rents, dividends, or interest, by selling the property received[2] or by any other act after becoming of age which clearly indicates satisfaction with the bargain made during minority. A contract which is wholly executory is disaffirmed by continued silence or inaction by the minor.

A majority of the states hold that ratification is impossible unless the minor knows of his right to disaffirm at time of the alleged act of ratification. In no state is ratification possible until the minor reaches his majority, since action prior to that date could always be avoided.

2-49. Liability for necessaries. It is often said that an infant is liable on his contracts for necessaries. Such a statement, technically speaking, is not true, for he is liable in quasi contract only for the reasonable value of necessaries received by him after proper consideration is given to his station in life. Hence, a contract of an infant to buy so-called necessaries is never enforceable. It is only after they have been delivered that the question of liability arises. Furthermore, an infant is not liable for the contract price, but only for the reasonable value of the necessaries which he receives, after his station in life is properly considered.

Before goods can be considered as necessary, it must be established that the infant is in need of them and that they have been delivered to him. If an infant is already possessed of four suits of clothes and his station in life does not demand more, or if he is adequately supplied with necessaries by a parent or a guardian, another suit cannot be considered a necessary, although, as a general rule, clothing falls within the list of necessaries.

Necessaries consist of such things as clothing, food, lodging, medical attention, and a certain amount of education. Although other things may occasionally be deemed necessaries, the majority of the courts closely limit the list to those enumerated. Contracts relating to the minor's estate, property, or business do not involve necessaries.[3] Thus, insurance contracts, agreements for the repair of property, or the employment of people to look after property or business may be avoided by the minor. Such agreements should be made with his guardian. Money borrowed and used to purchase necessaries need not be repaid unless the lender supervises its spending.

2-50. Parent's liability for infant's contract. Many people seem to labor under a misapprehension concerning the parent's liability for the contracts of an infant. The parent is liable on a contract made by a minor only when the minor is acting as his agent or when the parent joins the minor in making the contract. It should also be noted that the parent has

[2] Camp v. Bank of Bentonville, page 235.

[3] Pelham v. Howard Motors, Inc., page 236.

a duty to support his minor children, and having failed in this duty, he is responsible for any necessaries furnished the infant by third parties. At the same time it should be noted that the parent is entitled to any compensation which an infant earns unless he has in some manner surrendered this right. Payment to the infant does not discharge this duty owed to his parent unless the parent has authorized the payment or has left the minor to support himself. This latter is known as emancipation and the minor, having assumed the obligation to support himself, is entitled to the compensation earned by his services.

2-51. Infant's torts. An infant is liable for his own torts. If, considering his age, an infant negligently injures the person or property of another, he thereby creates a legal liability in favor of that person. For this reason an infant who, by misrepresenting his age, induces an adult to enter into a contract, may rescind the agreement, but, in a strong minority of states, he is liable for any resulting damage in an action of deceit. Such conduct possesses all the elements of fraud, but a majority of states deny any recovery against the minor because enforcement of the tort liability has the indirect effect, in many respects, of enforcing the contract.[4]

The parent is responsible for his children's torts if they are committed at his direction or in his presence when the children should have been controlled.[5]

2-52. Contracts of insane persons. Contracts of insane persons, according to the view of most courts, are voidable much the same as those of infants. There is a tendency to go a step further and hold that, provided the contract is reasonable and no advantage has been taken of the disabled party's condition, an insane person cannot disaffirm unless he can return the consideration received. The appointment of a conservator for an insane person vests the conservator with full control over the property of his charge. For this reason any contracts made by a lunatic after such an appointment are absolutely void and not merely voidable.

2-53. Drunkard's contracts. If a person becomes so far intoxicated as to be incapable of understanding the effect of his action, he is thereby incapacitated, and his contracts are voidable. They differ from those of the infant and the insane person in that they could not be disaffirmed if the disaffirmance would injure a third party who had subsequently in good faith purchased the property involved. Drunkards, like infants, are liable in quasi contract for necessaries.

[4] Lesnick et al. v. Pratt, page 237.
[5] Gissen v. Goodwill, page 238.

FRAUD

2-54. Definition. Since misrepresentation and fraud are similar in most respects, they will be treated together. An intentional misstatement concerning an existing material fact that induces another to act thereon to his damage is fraud. From this it will be seen that the chief elements of fraud are intention to mislead, misstatement, material fact, reliance upon the statement, and injury to the defrauded party. Misrepresentation is alike in all particulars except the first; intention to mislead is not a requisite of misrepresentation. An unintentional misstatement of fact, made honestly and in good faith, gives the injured party remedies that are in all respects, save one, identical with those arising in case of fraud. Consequently, the material in the sections that follow is applicable to both unless otherwise indicated.

2-55. Untrue statement. The very gist of fraud or misrepresentation is an untrue statement. The statement may involve an oral or a written expression that is clearly untrue,[6] or the untruth may be the result of a series of statements, the net result of which is to mislead. Although each statement, taken alone, may be true, there is fraud if all of them, taken together, tend to mislead the party to whom the statements are made. A partial truth, when information is requested, becomes an untruth whenever it creates a false impression and is designed to do so.

2-56. Failure to disclose as misrepresentation. In the absence of a *fiduciary* relationship—one of trust and confidence, such as exists between principal and agent or guardian and ward—one party is under no duty to inform the other party to an agreement of special facts and circumstances that vitally affect the value of the subject matter under consideration and are known only to him.[7] In other words, silence, of and by itself, does not constitute fraud. To this rule two exceptions exist: first, it is the duty of the vendor of property which has a known latent defect—one not apparent upon inspection—to inform the purchaser of the defect; and second, a person who has misstated an important fact at some previous occasion is obligated to correct the statement when negotiations are renewed.

The gist of these exceptions is that one of the parties rests under the impression that certain things are true, whereas the other party is aware that they are not true and also knows of the misunderstanding. There is a tendency to hold that fraud exists under these circumstances. A typical illustration involves the sale of farm land for a lump sum when the buyer indicates that he thinks there are 80 acres in the tract. If the seller knows

[6] Kotz et al. v. Rush, page 240.

[7] Balogh v. Sacks, page 242.

there are only 60 acres in the particular property, he is duty-bound to notify the buyer of that fact. Similarly, if there had previously been a house on the tract, but unknown to the buyer, it had been destroyed, the seller, provided he is in possession of the information, should make known such fact to the buyer. This does not mean that a potential seller or buyer has to disclose all the factors about the value of property that are in his possession. It is only where he knows that the other party to the agreement is harboring a misunderstanding relative to some vital matter that the duty to speak arises.

2-57. Physical concealment of facts. A misrepresentation may be made by conduct as well as by language. Any physical act which has for its ultimate object the concealment of the true facts relating to the property involved in a contract is in effect a misstatement. One who turns back the speedometer on a car, fills a motor with heavy grease to keep it from knocking, or paints over an apparent defect—in each case concealing an important fact—asserts an untrue fact as effectively as though speaking. Such conduct, if it misleads the other party, amounts to fraud and makes rescission possible.

2-58. Material facts. To constitute fraud the misstatement must relate to some material existing fact—one that has a moving influence upon the conduct of the contracting party. Statements of opinion are not statements of fact and as a rule do not justify one in relying thereon. A statement of fact relates to something that exists at present or that has taken place in the past,[8] whereas a statement of opinion is usually qualified, directly or indirectly, by such terms as "I think" or "I believe" and merely purports to be the impression or present understanding of the speaker. Statements of value or of the manner in which an article will act or react in the future are usually considered to be expressions of opinion. An expert—one who by experience or position is better qualified to judge than another—who intentionally misstates his opinion misstates a fact, his opinion being the fact. Many of the courts have gone beyond this in holding that all who intentionally misstate their opinion are guilty of fraud.

A promise to perform some act in the future is not a misstatement of a present fact, and a rescission of the agreement will be denied, even though the promisor fails to perform. In such cases the injured party is limited to an action to recover damages for breach of the contract. However, if the promisor never intended to carry out his promise at the time he made it, he misstated his intention and fraud resulted.[9]

An intentional misrepresentation of existing local or state law affords no basis for rescission, since the law is presumably a matter of common

[8] Leece v. Griffin, page 251.
[9] Channel Master Corporation v. Aluminum Limited Sales, Inc., page 246.

knowledge, open and available to all who desire to explore its mysteries. A misstatement as to the law of another state or nation, however, is one of fact and may be used as a basis for redress.

2-59. Reliance by injured party. Clearly, if the party to whom the misrepresentations are made does not rely upon them but, after pursuing his own investigation, makes his decision as a result of information obtained by himself, fraud is lacking. Most states go a step further and hold that, if all the information is readily available for ascertaining the truth of statements, reliance upon the misrepresentation is not justified. In such a case the party is said to be negligent in not taking advantage of the facilities available for confirmation of the statement. Extreme care should be exercised in the application of this rule to limit it to cases in which no substantial effort or expense is required to determine the true facts.

In order to establish fraud, the party relying upon the misstatement must offer proof of resulting damage, although normally such damage is proved by evidence which indicates that the contract would have been more valuable provided the statements had been true.

2-60. Effect of fraud. Fraud gives to the injured party several remedies in addition to those available for nonfraudulent breach. If the contract is executory, he may plead fraud as a defense in the event action is brought against him. Where the contract has been executed, he may demand a rescission and a return of the consideration parted with, in which case he must offer to restore the consideration which he has received. If the injured party desires to do so, he may carry out the terms of the contract and bring a tort action of deceit to recover the damages he has suffered by reason of the fraud.

It should be noted that rescission is permitted only in case the defrauded party acts with reasonable promptness after he learns of the fraud. Undue delay on his part effects a waiver of his right to rescind, thus limiting the defrauded party to recovery of damages. Under the Code, neither rescission of the contract for sale, nor rejection or return of the goods, shall bar or be deemed inconsistent with a claim for damages or other remedy.

2-61. Unintentional misrepresentation. Occasionally one unwittingly makes a misrepresentation because of a mistaken conception on his part as to existing facts. Although no fraud results, a contracting party who has relied upon such a statement is as effectively injured as though the statement had been intentionally made. The remedy in such a case is rescission—the right to sue and recover damages for misrepresentation usually is denied.

In the case of fraud, an action to recover damages may be prosecuted successfully against one who misrepresents intentionally, even though he is not a party to the contract. Generally, if the statement is made with no intention to mislead, no action can be maintained against the third party. However, if one makes a statement of fact as being true, with reckless disregard for whether it is true or false, and it is later proved to be false, an action for damages by one who relied on the statement will lie. A person should not make a statement as true when he is uncertain concerning its truth or knows it to be true only with certain qualifications. Although the person making such a statement is not a contracting party, he will be liable to anyone injured by reliance upon the statement if the disclosure is expected to be relied upon.[10]

MISTAKE

2-62. Bilateral mistake. Although it is difficult to state rules of law that will apply to every conceivable set of circumstances in which mistake is involved, the general law relative to mistake is fairly well established. Bilateral mistake arises when the contracting parties reach an agreement based on the mutual assumption that a certain material fact exists when such is not actually the case. Mutual mistake may be either of two distinct types: first, one in which the minds of the parties fail to meet, resulting in no contract; and second, one which merely makes the agreement more onerous for one of the contracting parties and therefore voidable at his option.[10]

Typical of the first type are those cases in which the subject matter of the contract has been destroyed prior to the date of the agreement or in which language used is clearly subject to two interpretations and each party construed it differently. Under either set of circumstances, no contract was made, the agreement being void at the time it was made. The second type may well be illustrated by the sale of floor covering for a certain room at a lump-sum figure on the assumption that only a certain number of square feet was involved. If the area is greater than both parties thought to be true, the contract is voidable at the instance of the injured party.

In ordinary business, it is customary upon many occasions to dispose of property about which the contracting parties willingly admit that all the facts are not known. In such instances, the property is sold regardless of the quality or characteristics that it possesses. The agreement may not be rescinded where it later appears that the article contains certain properties which neither of the parties had reason to suspect. Under such conditions, the property forms the subject matter of the agreement, regardless of what its nature happens to be. Thus, *A* sells *B* a farm, and

[10] Wire & Textile Machinery, Inc. v. Robinson, page 245.

shortly thereafter a valuable deposit of ore is discovered on it. Such an agreement could not be rescinded on the ground of mutual mistake.

2-63. Unilateral mistake. A contract entered into because of some mistake or error on the part of one of the contracting parties usually affords no basis for relief. The majority of such mistakes result from carelessness or lack of diligence on the part of the injured party, and should not, therefore, affect the rights of the other party who, without any misconduct, entered into the agreement.

This rule is subject to one well-recognized exception.[11] Where a mistake has been made in the calculation or transmission of the figures which form the basis of a contract and prior to acceptance such mistake is clearly apparent to the offeree, the contract may be avoided. Hence, a contractor who arrives at, or transmits his estimates for a bid on construction work, using the wrong figure, may be relieved of his contract if the error was so great as to become apparent to the offeree prior to the latter's acceptance. The courts, in such a case, refuse to allow one party knowingly to take advantage of another's mistake.

2-64. Reformation of written agreements. All written contracts should be carefully read before they are signed. Normally, the parol evidence rule forbids the introduction of any evidence to vary the terms of a written agreement. The writing is the best evidence of the nature of the contract entered into between the parties; however, if it can be established definitely that a mistake has been made in reducing an agreement to writing, the injured party may demand that the writing be reformed by a court of equity, in order to conform to the intention of the parties.[12] In such a case the evidence must clearly indicate that the scrivener made an error, and that the agreement as written did not represent the intention of either of the parties. Occasionally a mistake is made in the execution of a contract, such as an error in the description of land conveyed by a deed. If the deed does not convey the land called for by the contract, it may, upon petition, be altered to conform to the agreement, unless the rights of innocent third parties have intervened.

DURESS

2-65. Nature of duress. Every agreement presupposes that the parties thereto are free to enter into the agreement or not, as their best judgment dictates. Therefore, if the will of one of the parties is coerced through fear of the other, the contract is not a voluntary one and may be avoided by the injured party. The essence of duress is the inability freely to exercise one's will at the time of the formation of an agreement because of

[11] Rushlight Auto. Sprinkler Co. v. City of Portland, page 246.

[12] Metropolitan Life Insurance Company v. Henriksen et al., page 248.

fear, usually the result of misconduct on the part of the other party.

Such fear may result from a threat of bodily injury, or it may be induced by a threat of criminal prosecution of the contracting party or some close relative. The guilt or innocence of the party charged with the crime has no bearing on the rescission unless the person guilty of the crime is asking the rescission. A contract made by him for the purpose of adjusting the effect of his crime is enforceable even though induced by threat, but if the contract is made by some close relative who had no part in the crime, it is voidable. Threat of a civil suit—one to recover a debt or property or for some injury—has never been held to constitute duress.

Unlawful retention of, a threat to retain wrongfully, or a threat to destroy the property of another, if used to compel the owner's consent to the terms of an unfavorable contract, is duress.[13] Such pressure robs the owner of the property of the free exercise of his will and gives him the right to avoid the agreement. Thus, if a lease has expired and the tenant threatens to destroy the property unless the lease is renewed, a renewal contract can be rescinded.

VOIDABLE CONTRACTS CASES

WOOLDRIDGE v. HILL

1953, (Ind. App.) 114 N.E.2d 646

The plaintiff, Wooldridge, sued to recover from the defendant $530 which he had paid the latter on the price of an automobile, the plaintiff being 17 years of age at the time of sale. Six months after the purchase he notified defendant of his desire to rescind and returned the auto. The lower court gave plaintiff judgment for $280 only and he appealed.

Crumpacker, J. . . . A careful examination of the record reveals testimony to the effect that at the time of the occurrences in question the appellant was a hired hand on the appellee's farm. He was still in high school and during the school year the appellee paid him $10 per week, room, board and laundry. During vacations in the summer his cash wages were increased to $20 per week. He had, on occasions, told the appellee of his desire to buy an automobile so that "I wouldn't have to depend on the other fellows to take me all the time." As a result of these conversations the appellant and appellee, on October 4, 1950, went to the place of business of a man named Alexander who owned the automobile here involved. The appellee told the appellant on the occasion that if he wanted the car he would buy it for him and that he could pay for it at the rate of $5 per week and when he got it paid for he, the appellee, would transfer title to him but in the meantime he would retain title in

[13] Kolias v. Colligan, page 250.

himself. That was agreeable to the appellant and the appellee bought the car from Alexander for $1,350 and delivered it to the appellant under the above arrangement. The appellant thereupon gave the appellee his check in the sum of $400, designated "car payment," which the appellee subsequently cashed. Thereafter the appellant made weekly payments aggregating $130 to April 7, 1951, when he left the appellee's employ and delivered the car into his possession. On May 5, 1951, he gave the appellee written notice of his disaffirmance of the contract between them and demanded his money back. . . .

This brings us to the consideration of appellant's right to a new trial because of the contention that the amount of his recovery was too small or because there is no evidence upon which the court could fix his damage at $280. It was held in *McKee v. Harwood Automotive Co.*, 1932, 204 Ind. 233, 183 N.E. 646, that where an infant 19 years old rescinded his contract to purchase an automobile and returned the same to the seller, in the absence of any evidence showing that it was a "necessary" or used in gaining a livelihood, the infant's liability to pay the contract price was thereby extinguished and the court approved the infant's recovery of all monies paid on the contract.

There is no contention in this case that the automobile involved was a "necessary" or that it was used by the appellant in gaining his livelihood, and, in view of the fact that there is no dispute that he paid the appellee $530 under the purchase agreement, it is difficult to understand the basis upon which the court assessed his damages at $280. There is no evidence in the record, direct or inferential, upon which such a recovery can be sustained. We suspect, however, that the court concluded that these proceedings, though brought in law, should be determined under equitable principles and as the appellant had had the use of the automobile for approximately six months he ought, in good conscience, to pay something for its use and the natural wear and tear incidental thereto as in no other way could both parties be placed in statu quo. Equitable as such a decision may be it is not sanctioned by the law of Indiana. This court, in *Story & Clark Piano Co. v. Davy*, 1918, 68 Ind. App. 150, 119 N.E. 177, 180, quoted with approval the following excerpt from *McCarthy v. Henderson*, 1885, 138 Mass. 310:

> It is clear that, if the plaintiff had made no advance, the defendants could not maintain an action against him for the use of the property. The contract, express or implied, to pay for such use is one he is incapable of making, and his infancy would be a bar to such suit. We cannot see how the defendants can avail themselves of and enforce, by way of recoupment, a claim which they could not enforce by a direct suit.

It is our considered judgment that the decision of the court in this case is contrary to law. It is therefore reversed and the cause remanded to the Rush Circuit Court with instructions to sustain the appellant's motion for a new trial.

CAMP v. BANK OF BENTONVILLE

1959, (Ark.) 323 S.W.2d 556

McFADDIN, J. Jerry Lee Camp appeals from a decree of the Chancery Court which found that Camp, now of lawful age, had ratified a debt which he made while a minor. The question is whether Camp's acts under the circumstances here shown were sufficient to support the decree holding that there had been ratification.

On January 9, 1957, Camp executed his note to A. V. Bright, doing business as "Bright's Used Cars," for $3,000 [probably for truck], payable $125 per month until paid in full. The note was secured by a chattel mortgage covering: (a) one 1952 2-ton Chevrolet truck; (b) one 1954 Plymouth sedan; (c) miscellaneous stock of automotive parts valued at $500; and (d) eleven cows and increase. Bright immediately and unconditionally transferred the note and mortgage to the appellee, Bank of Bentonville (hereinafter called "Bank"). The payments made to the Bank on the note were:

Date	*Amount*	*Nature of Payment*
2/25/57	$ 50.00	Cash.
3/20/57	100.00	Cash.
4/20/57	800.00	Proceeds of sale of Plymouth car.
5/ 1/57	47.52	Return of insurance premium cancelled when Plymouth car was sold.
7/ 1/57	51.00	Probably cash.
11/ 8/57	102.00	To be discussed later in this opinion.
12/ 9/57	100.00	To be discussed later in this opinion.
12/13/57	56.00	To be discussed later in this opinion.

When Camp defaulted, the Bank filed suit for judgment and foreclosure of the mortgage. Camp's defense was: that he was not 21 years of age until August 19, 1957; that the three payments credited on the note thereafter (i.e. November 8th, December 9th, and December 13th) were not sufficient to constitute ratification; and that he now disaffirmed the entire transaction. The said three payments came about in this manner: each was made to the Bank by A. V. Bright from money due by him to Camp, and each payment was made with Camp's implied consent. The $100 on December 9, 1957, was part of the proceeds of the sale of a car. The payments of November 8th and December 13th were for money that Bright owed Camp for work. Camp was doing considerable hauling of some kind for Bright, and Bright, with Camp's implied consent, made the two payments on the dates mentioned.

The Chancery Court held that Camp, after reaching full age, had ratified the note and mortgage; and under all the facts and circumstances here existing, we cannot say that the Chancery Court was in error. . . .

From our own cases, and from all of the foregoing [cases in other states], we are not willing to hold that payment after reaching full age is, in itself, sufficient to constitute ratification as a matter of law: rather, we think the better rule is, to examine each case on its own facts and determine whether payment, along with all the other facts and circumstances, constitutes ratification. We have done that in the case at bar. There is no claim of any kind that Bright ever imposed on Camp when the note and mortgage were executed on January 9, 1957. Camp was working for Bright all along; and thought he was of full age, as he considered eighteen to be the lawful age. It was not until after this suit was filed and he had consulted an attorney that he ever had any idea of disaffirmance of any part of the trade. This is the case of a man who was doing his own work, carrying on his own business, making trades in which there is no claim that he was imposed on, and who, after reaching 21, continued to make payments on the obligation, with no thought of disaffirming the transaction. Under all these facts and circumstances, we reach the conclusion that Camp, after reaching full age, ratified the particular transaction here involved.

Affirmed.

PELHAM v. HOWARD MOTORS, INC.

1959, (Ill. App.) 156 N.E.2d 597

Kiley, J. This is an action by Pelham to recover the down payment a minor made in the purchase of an automobile. The trial court, without a jury, found that the automobile was a "necessary" and entered judgment for defendant's costs. Plaintiff has appealed.

The minor bought the automobile on May 21, 1956, under a conditional sale contract for $2,075.60, and paid $500 down. At that time, he was 20 years and three months old, but in the Bill of Sale he certified that he was "21 years of age or over," and he told the seller he was 22 years of age, because he "wanted to buy a car and I could not buy it at the age of twenty." He drove the car home and brought it back to the seller the next evening for repairs. He "picked it up" the next day, but "they had not done anything." He left it with the seller May 26, and on May 29 his attorney wrote defendant "repudiating" the contract and demanding return of the down payment. The demand was refused and this suit followed.

The question is whether the automobile was a "necessary." If it was, the court's judgment was right because "it is well established, as a general rule, that an infant or his estate may be held liable for necessaries furnished him," *Zazove v. Minneapolis, St. P. & S. Ste. Marie Ry. Co.*, 218 Ill. App. 534. The fact of emancipation is not relevant, nor is the question of misrepresentation.

Our Supreme Court in 1871, in *McKanna v. Merry*, 61 Ill. 177, 179, said "The articles furnished, or money advanced, must be actually necessary, in the particular case, for use, not mere ornament, for substantial good, not mere pleasure. . . . The courts have generally excluded from the term 'necessaries,' horses. . . ." But the court pointed out that if riding was necessary for the minor's health a horse would not be excluded. In 1915 this court, in *Lein v. Centaur Motor Co.,* 194 Ill. App. 509, affirmed judgment for the minor in recovering a down payment on an automobile, despite the defense that the automobile was intended for use in, and was necessary to, the business of passenger service. The court stated that the doctrine of "necessaries" was not to be extended to the minor's trading contracts. . . .

The only testimony adduced to show that the automobile was a "necessary" was in cross-examination of plaintiff. He stated he worked at Anna's Flower Shop, had worked there for five years as a porter, and never made deliveries. The plain inference that the automobile was for pleasure is also indicated by the answer "pleasure" to the question, in the Conditional Sales Contract, "Will the car be used for Pleasure, Business, Taxicab or Hire?" We think the car was not a "necessary," as a matter of law.

An automobile for a minor for pleasure is not an article of a kind for which a minor is liable. The trial court's finding was erroneous and the judgment is reversed and the cause remanded with directions to enter judgment for plaintiff.

Reversed and remanded with directions.

LESNICK et al. v. PRATT
1951, (Vt.) 78 A.2d 487

CLEARY, J. . . . This is an action of tort for fraud and deceit involving the sale of an automobile to the plaintiff by the defendant (Pratt). The defendant pleaded infancy. Trial was by the court with judgment for the plaintiffs. Both parties excepted.

The findings of fact show that at the time of the sale on January 20, 1949, the defendant falsely and fraudulently represented that the automobile was fully paid for and was free of liens and encumbrances and on September 13, 1949, the plaintiffs were obliged to pay the balance owing on a conditional sale contract which the defendant had signed when he purchased the automobile on January 10, 1949. The defendant was born on July 29, 1928, so when he bought the automobile and when he sold it to the plaintiffs he was a minor.

Thus it is clear that the cause of action arises out of a contract and, as this court said in *West v. Moore,* 14 Vt. 447, 450: "It is for us to declare the law as we find it." In that case, which was trespass on the case for false warranty in the sale of a horse, this Court held: "Though an infant is liable for positive wrongs, and constructive torts, or frauds, yet, to charge him, the fraudulent act must be wholly tortious. If the matter arises from contract, though the transaction is infected with fraud, it cannot be turned into a tort to charge the infant by a change in the form of action."

In *Gilson v. Spear*, 38 Vt. 311, another case for deceit, or fraudulent concealment of unsoundness in the sale of a horse, and a plea of infancy, where both the English and American cases on the subject are collected and discussed, this Court held 38 Vt. at page 315: "We think that the fair result of the American as well as of the English cases is that an infant is liable in an action *ex delicto* for an actual and wilful fraud only in cases in which the form of action does not suppose that a contract has existed; but that where the gravamen of the fraud consists in a transaction which really originated in contract the plea of infancy is a good defense. For simple deceit on a contract of sale or exchange, there is no cause of action unless some damage or injury results from it, and proof of damage could not be made without referring to and proving the contract. An action on the case for deceit on a sale is an affirmance by the plaintiff of the contract of sale, and the liability of the defendant in such an action could not be established without taking notice of and proving the contract." That case then repeats and adopts the principle as stated in *West v. Moore, supra*. . . .

We are governed by the law we have quoted. If modern youth has become so sophisticated that he no longer needs protection from his contracts or public opinion demands that the long recognized rule be changed, it can be done by statute. We are constrained to hold that the plea of infancy in the present case was a full defense. Therefore, it is unnecessary to consider other questions raised by the exceptions.

Judgment reversed and judgment for the defendant to recover his costs.

GISSEN v. GOODWILL

1955, (Florida) 80 S.2d 701

Gissen, the plaintiff and appellant, sued the defendant for injuries sustained from acts of the defendant's daughter. The lower court gave judgment for defendant and plaintiff appealed.

KANNER, J. . . . It is averred in the second amended complaint that at the time of the appellant's injury, he was employed as a clerk at the Gaylord Hotel in the City of Miami Beach, Florida, and the appellees were residing as business invitees at the same hotel; that the minor child, Geraldine Goodwill, 8 years of age, "did wilfully, deliberately, intentionally and maliciously" swing a door "with such great force and violence against the plaintiff so that the middle finger on plaintiff's left hand was caught in the door and a portion of said finger was caused to be instantaneously severed and fell to the floor. . . ."

It is a basic and established law that a parent is not liable for the tort of his minor child because of the mere fact of his paternity. 39 Am. Jur., sec. 55, p. 690; and 67 C.J.S., Parent and Child, § 66, p. 795. However, there are certain broadly defined exceptions wherein a parent may incur liability: 1. Where he intrusts his child with an instrumentality which, because of lack of age, judgment, or experience of the child, may become a source of danger to others. 2. Where a child, in the commission of a tortious act, is occupying the relationship of a servant or agent of its parents. 3. Where the parent knows of his child's wrongdoing and consents to it, directs or sanctions it. 4. Where he fails to exercise parental control over his minor child, although he knows or in the exercise of due care should have known that injury to another is a probable consequence. 39 Am. Jur., secs. 56, 57, 58, 59, pp. 692–697; 67 C.J.S., Parent and Child, § 67, 68, pp. 797–800; and *Steinberg v. Cauchois,* 249 App. Div. 518, 293 N.Y.S. 147.

Analyzing this problem in the light of the exceptions for parent liability enumerated, one may note that the exceptions relating to instrumentality intrusted to a child, to master and servant or agent relationship, and to parental consent or sanction of a tortious act by the child do not bear upon the circumstances here involved. It is only the fourth category which may be logically analyzed for the purpose of determining whether legal culpability might be attached to the parents of the child here concerned, and it is on this exception to the general rule that the appellant relies. . . .

An analysis of cases related to or bearing upon the type of case that we have here is necessary in order to determine whether the second amended complaint states a cause of action or whether it is deficient for the reason urged by the appellees.

In the case of *Bateman v. Crim,* D.C. Mun. App., 34 A.2d 257, the question concerned the liability of the parents of two boys, 10 and 12 years of age, who, while playing on the sidewalk with a football, collided with plaintiff, injuring her. The court instructed verdict for the parents, which verdict was affirmed on appeal. Plaintiff claimed that a parent's failure to exercise proper supervision, notwithstanding lack of evidence of prior unrestrained conduct, renders liability to parents for acts of a minor which would have been averted through adequate supervision and that whether proper supervision had been employed was in such case a question of fact for the jury. Nevertheless, the court stated that there was no evidence that either boy had previously played with a football on public streets or conducted himself in a disorderly manner; and that in order to attribute to a parent responsibility for injuries resulting from his minor child's wrongful deed, parent's negligence in exercising parental restraint must have some *specific relation to the act complained of,* and that such was lacking in this case. . . .

One common factor from the foregoing case appears salient in the assessment of liability to the parents, that the child had the habit of doing the particular type of wrongful act which resulted in the injury complained of. In the instant case, the cause of action sought to establish fails in that the negligence charged with relation to parental restraint is not claimed to flow from the commission of an act or course of conduct which the child habitually engaged in and which led to the appellant's injury. It is nowhere claimed that the child here involved had a propensity to swing or slam doors at the hazard of persons using such doors. The deed of a child, the enactment of which results in harm to another and which is unrelated to any previous act or acts of the child, cannot be laid at the door of the parents simply because the child happened to be born theirs. However, a wrongful act by an infant which climaxes a course of conduct involving similar acts may lead to the parents' accountability. A deed brought on by a totally unexpected reaction to a situation which is isolated in origin and provocation could not have been foretold or averted and hence could not render the parents responsible.

Therefore, from the allegations of the second amended complaint, it is not made to appear that the injury claimed to have been sustained by the appellant was a natural and probable consequence of negligence on the part of the appellee parents.

The judgment of the court below is affirmed.

KOTZ et al. v. RUSH
1951, (Ark.) 238 S.W.2d 634

MILLWEE, J. Appellants, E. W. Kotz and wife, plaintiff, owned and operated a business known as "White River Camp" located at one end of the bridge over White River on U.S. Highway 62 in Carroll County, Arkansas. The camp consists of a cafe, store building, garage, apartment and several cabins and boats. . . .

A contract was entered into in March, 1949 whereby appellee agreed to purchase the property at a price of $26,750. Appellee exchanged a lot in Dallas, Texas and paid $1,000 cash on the purchase price leaving a balance of $14,837.50, to secure the payment of which she executed a note and mortgage of the camp property to appellants payable at $150 per month. After making six monthly payments appellee defaulted. Appellants instituted this suit to foreclose the mortgage on April 15, 1950.

Appellee filed an answer and cross-complaint alleging that appellants made certain false and fraudulent representations as to profits earned in the business in 1947 and 1948 and the number of reservations for "float" trips for the 1949 season. Appellee asked that the mortgage be cancelled and for recoupment of damages sustained by reason of said false representations to the extent of the balance of the purchase price alleged due.

The chancellor found for appellee on her cross-complaint and directed that $8,000 be deducted from the balance due on the mortgage because of false representations by appellants which induced the execution of the contract and mortgage. Appellants were awarded judgment for $5,965.43 after allowing the credit of $8,000 and foreclosure was ordered.

To sustain the allegations of her cross-complaint appellee introduced several witnesses who were present during the negotiations between the parties. Appellee and others present testified that appellant E. W. Kotz told appellee that he realized a net income of $6,500 per year from the operation of the camp during the seasons of 1947 and 1948. When appellee asked him to produce some record evidence of such earnings, Kotz stated that he did not keep accurate records, that he did very little banking business and facetiously remarked that he just kept his books in his hip pocket. . . .

She testified that at the time of the negotiations Kotz also told her that he already had reservations for all cabins and boats for the first thirty days of the 1949 fishing season, and that only one reservation was turned over to her. She lost money in the operation of the business in 1949.

Gerden Whitner testified that he worked for both the appellants and appellee in their respective operations of the camp; that both parties did about the same volume of business and that he had heard Kotz say that he was not making any money out of the business. . . .

Appellant E. W. Kotz admitted that he represented to appellee that he made approximately $6,500 out of the business in 1947, but stated that he told her he did not make that much in 1948. Although he filed an income tax return in 1947, he could not remember whether he reported an income of $6,500 from the business that year, nor could he remember how many reservations he turned over to appellee for the 1949 season. There was some evidence by appellants to the effect that appellee did not operate the camp efficiently.

The authorities seem to recognize the rule that false representations by the seller as to present or past income of the property sold or conveyed will, if relied upon by the purchaser, constitute actionable fraud. . . .

The remedies of a purchaser in cases of this kind are set forth in *Danielson et al. v. Skidmore, et al.*, 125 Ark. 572, 189 S.W. 57, 58, as follows: "He may rescind the contract, or by returning or offering to return the property purchased within a reasonable time entitle himself to recover whatever he has paid upon the contract. Again, he may elect to retain the property and sue for the damages he has sustained by reason of the false and fraudulent representations, and in this event the measure of his damages would be the difference between the real value of the property in its true condition and the price at which he purchased it. Lastly, to avoid circuity of action and a multiplicity of suits, he may plead such damages in an action for the purchase money, and is entitled to have the same recouped from the price he agreed to pay. . . ."

Appellee chose the last remedy mentioned above and the only issue is whether the chancellor's findings are against the preponderance of the evidence. We think the greater weight of the evidence supports the conclusion that appellants wilfully misrepresented their past income from the property; that appellee made a diligent effort to ascertain the truth or falsity of such representations, which were within the peculiar knowledge of the appellants; and that appellee relied on such false representations to her damage in the amount fixed by the court.

The decree is, therefore, affirmed.

BALOGH v. SACKS

1954 (Ohio App.) 123 N.E.2d 37

Suit by purchaser to rescind a contract to purchase a lot. The trial court entered judgment as matter of law for vendor, and purchaser appealed.

DOYLE, J. Fred Sacks, the owner of a lot in a recorded allotment, entered into an option agreement with one Steve Balogh, Jr., for its purchase. Balogh exercised the option, and, in pursuance of the agreement, paid $485 as partial payment, in addition to $15 which he had theretofore paid as consideration for the option.

Later, Sacks tendered a deed to Balogh, who transmitted it to his attorney for examination. Soon thereafter Balogh learned of an 18-inch gas line which crossed his lot, by virtue of a right-of-way or easement given the East Ohio Gas Company many years prior, and concealed three or four feet deep into the earth. Balogh thereupon brought suit to rescind the contract and to recover back the money paid.

Upon trial the court entered judgment as a matter of law for the defendant, Sacks. This judgment is now before this court on appeal. Error is claimed in the court's ruling.

The purchaser, as shown by the evidence, exercised the option which contained the following specific stipulation:

> That if this option be duly exercised by the optionee, . . . the optioner agrees to convey said lot to the optionee by a duly executed deed of general warranty, with release of dower, . . . free from all encumbrances, except . . . *easements*, reservations, and conditions of record. . . .

It is claimed that Balogh, the plaintiff, was a builder of houses, and he negotiated for the purchase of the lot for the purpose of building a home thereon for resale to the public; that although the defendant "did not make any positive misrepresentations that a gas line did not exist, . . . after the plaintiff had stated his business and his intent to construct a dwelling house, the defendant, knowing of the impossibility of constructing such house in a proper location, remained silent, although he knew of the location of the gas line; . . . that concealment of these materials facts was equivalent to positive misrepresentations; that there was a duty on the part of the defendant to disclose the gas line, under the situation existing between the parties at the time of negotiation; and that defendant's concealment was fraud because the gas line was concealed and a latent defect not discoverable upon examination of the premises. . . ."

In the light of the facts and the general rules of law, we believe the following statement appropriate: A party can commit a legal fraud in a business transaction with another by fraudulent misrepresentations of material fact, or by such conduct or artifice, for a fraudulent purpose, as will mislead the other party, or throw him off his guard, and cause him to omit inquiry or examination, which he would otherwise make. However, when there is no relation of trust or confidence between the parties as imposes upon one an obligation to give full information to the other, the latter cannot proceed blindly, omitting all inquiry and examination, and then complain that the other did not volunteer to give the information he had. Ignorance of a fact not essential to a contract, but which, if known, might have influenced the action of a party, is not per se such a mistake as will afford legal or equitable relief. . . .

We do not think the claim is sound in law. The parties dealt at arms length. There was no legal duty to speak of the easement. The vendee was warned in the option of such an encumbrance, and it was easily discoverable by a prudent person. The law does not make a vendor the guardian of a purchaser dealing at arms length with him, nor does the law, under these circumstances, create a sword of Damocles to threaten, under the guise of fraud, the legal security of a vendor.

Judgment for defendant affirmed.

CHANNEL MASTER CORPORATION v. ALUMINUM LIMITED SALES, INC.

1958, 4 N.Y. 2d 403, 151 N.E.2d 833

FULD, J. On this appeal, here on questions certified by the Appellate Division, we are called upon to determine the sufficiency of a complaint in a tort action for damages based on fraud and deceit.

The plaintiff, a manufacturer and processor of aluminum, requires for its business a dependable supply of aluminum ingot in large quantity. The defendant is engaged in the business of selling that metal. The amended complaint states two causes of action.

In the first cause of action, the plaintiff alleges that in April, 1954, the defendant represented that "its available and uncommitted supplies and productive capacity of aluminum ingot, then existing, were such as rendered it then capable of selling to the plaintiff 400,000 pounds per month and that it had entered into no binding commitments with other customers which could in the future reduce such available and uncommitted supplies and productive capacity." The complaint then recites that such representations were made "with the intention and knowledge that plaintiff should rely thereon and in order to induce the plaintiff to refrain from entering into commitments with other suppliers and to purchase the greater part of its requirements from the defendant," that the plaintiff acted in reliance on the representations and that they were false and known by the defendant to be so. In truth and in fact, the complaint further asserts, the defendant had previously entered into long-term contracts with other customers which committed all of the defendant's supplies and productive capacity for many years to come. By reason of the defendant's fraudulent misrepresentations and the plaintiff's reliance thereon, the complaint continues, the plaintiff refrained from securing commitments for future supplies from others and was thereby injured in its business. . . .

To maintain an action based on fraudulent representations, whether it be for the rescission of a contract or, as here, in tort for damages, it is sufficient to show that the defendant knowingly uttered a falsehood intending to deprive the plaintiff of a benefit and that the plaintiff was thereby deceived and damaged. . . .

The essential constituents of the action are fixed as representation of a material existing fact, falsity, *scienter*, deception and injury. . . . Accordingly, one "who fraudulently makes a misrepresentation of . . . intention . . . for the purpose of inducing another to act or refrain from action in reliance thereon in a business transaction" is liable for the harm caused by the other's justifiable reliance upon the misrepresentation. 3 Restatement, Torts, § 525, p. 59.

As examination of the complaint demonstrates, it contains all the necessary elements of a good cause of action, including statements of existing fact, as opposed to expressions off future expectation. The representations allegedly made, that the defendant had "available and uncommitted supplies and productive capacity of aluminum ingot" sufficient to render it then capable of selling to the plaintiff 400,000 pounds a month and that it had entered into no binding commitments which could in the future reduce such available and uncommitted supplies and productive capacity and that it was its intention to make available and to sell to the plaintiff the number of pounds specified for a period of five years, related to the defendant's present intention. A person's intent, his state of mind, it has long been recognized, is capable of ascertainment and a statement of present intention is deemed a statement of a material existing fact, sufficient to support a fraud action.

Judgment for plaintiff.

WIRE & TEXTILE MACHINERY, INC. v. ROBINSON

1955 (Mass.) 125 N.E.2d 403

The plaintiff, acting through Kenner, its president, sold to Mohawk Wire Co., acting through Robinson, its president, certain machinery at a price of $6,000. The buyer paid only $1,000 in cash and the conditional sale contract provided that plaintiff retain title to the machinery as security for the balance payable in installments. For the security to be good at bankruptcy it was necessary to record it in the city where the business was located. Plaintiff asked Robinson for the address and was told, "Court Street Road, Syracuse, N.Y." The contract was recorded there, but the true address was Salina, N.Y., a city adjacent to Syracuse. Mohawk became a bankrupt, the plaintiff lost its security because of improper recording, and plaintiff sued the defendant in tort for fraud. Robinson contends he made the statement in good faith believing it to be true. The lower court gave judgment for plaintiff and defendant appeals.

SPALDING, J. . . . The defendant argues that the plaintiff has not made out a case because the evidence would not warrant a finding that his representations were consciously false. It is true that the evidence does not show that the defendant knowingly stated what was false. On the contrary such evidence as there was on that issue tends in the opposite direction. The defendant testified that he was executive vice president of a corporation which had its principal place of business in Brooklyn, New York, and visited the Mohawk plant only once or twice a month; that the post office address of Mohawk had always been Syracuse; that Syracuse had always been designated for freight and other shipments; that he had never heard of Salina until the conditional sale agreement was questioned in the bankruptcy court; and that the street on which Mohawk's plant is located runs into the downtown section of Syracuse and is called Court Street in Salina and Court Street in Syracuse. This testimony, of course, might be disbelieved but such disbelief would not establish scienter.

But proof that the representations were consciously fraudulent was not essential to the plaintiff's case. The rule deducible from the New

York decisions is that a representation made as of one's own knowledge when knowledge there is none, a reckless misstatement, or an opinion based on grounds so flimsy as to lead to the conclusion that there was no genuine belief in its truth, are all sufficient upon which to base liability for deceit. . . . Tested by these principles we are of opinion that the evidence was sufficient to warrant a finding for the plaintiff on the count for deceit. The judge could have found that when the defendant made the representation to Kenner he was making a statement of fact of his own knowledge concerning a matter that was susceptible of knowledge with the intention that it would be used in connection with the drafting and recording of the conditional sale agreement. In fact the statement was not true. The evidence amply warranted a finding that the defendant had never ascertained and did not know the location of Mohawk. Despite what he believed, he ran the risk of liability for deceit if he did not know and spoke as if he did. Giving the appearance of knowledge where there is none, without heed to the consequences, would, as we read the New York decisions, support, a finding for deceit. As stated above the judge found that the plaintiff relied on the defendant's representation concerning Mohawk's address. . . .

Judgment for plaintiff affirmed.

RUSHLIGHT AUTO SPRINKLER CO. v. CITY OF PORTLAND

1950, 189 Or. 194, 219 P.2d 732

The plaintiff, in submitting its bid to the defendant City of Portland for a certain sewage and disposal project, hurriedly submitted a bid of $429,444.20 and issued its certified check of $21,472.21 to be retained by the city in event plaintiff failed to enter a contract after notice that his bid had been accepted. When the bids were opened, it was discovered that the next lowest bid was $671,600. All were quite concerned because plaintiff's bid was exceedingly low and plaintiff discovered that it had omitted an item for steel of $99,225.68. Plaintiff requested that its bid be withdrawn, but it was accepted and the certified check was cashed when plaintiff refused to proceed with the work, the contract being let to another. Plaintiff seeks to recover the amount of the check. The lower gave judgment for plaintiff and defendant appealed.

Rossman, J. . . . As we said, the City concedes the mistake concerning the steel item which the plaintiff's officers, to their manifest embarrassment, described. The plaintiff prays that its mistake be deemed excusable; the City insists that the error was a culpable one. . . .

So far as we can ascertain, the plaintiff's bid was compiled by an adequate staff of estimators. No one challenged the competence of the estimators nor questioned the methods they pursued. The record shows that one of the estimators, after having calculated the amount of earth that would have to be moved in one phase of the construction work, called upon a member of the City Board of Engineers for the purpose of comparing his estimate with that made by the board. He found that the two were virtually the same. That fact and an occasional other one mentioned in the record tend to show that the estimators were careful. . . .

We believe that it is manifest from the evidence that the difference between the plaintiff's bid and the next higher was so large that all of those concerned with the undertaking were rendered uneasy. The plaintiff's officers at once returned to their work sheets, fearing that they must have committed a mistake. The City Engineer, according to his own words, found the variation so great that it "scared us to death." A member of the Board of Engineers, who seemingly expressed himself in wary words, described the plaintiff's bid as "a very low" one and termed the difference between it and the City's estimate "a very decided difference." The bid aroused suspicion in all minds. We think that the difference apprised the City that a mistake had probably occurred.

It is true, as already indicated, that the steel item accounts for only $99,225.68 or 41 per cent of the total disparity of $242,155.80 between the plaintiff's and the next higher bid. Therefore, it alone did not provoke the misgivings. The $99,225.68 was a substantial part of the total difference. The variation between the second and third high bids was only $2,232.06. The difference between the second and the fourth high bids was $13,291.50. The material fact is that the omission of the steel was a substantial factor in reducing the bid to such a low amount that the city officials surmised that it was too good to be true. . . .

From *Williston on Contracts* (rev. ed), § 1573, the following is taken:

> In two classes of cases, mistake of one party only to a contract undoubtedly justifies affirmative relief as distinguished from a mere denial to enforce the contract specifically against him;
>
> (1) Where the mistake is known to the other party to the transaction. . . .

Section 503, Restatement of the Law, Contracts, says: "A mistake of only one party that forms the basis on which he enters into a transaction does not of itself render the transaction voidable; . . ."

The Reporters' Notes to that section cites many illustrative decisions and some treatises. From the notes, we take the following: "Where one party knows or has reason to know that the other party has made a basic mistake (see Comment *c*) restitution is granted. This situation has frequently arisen where there has been an error in the price given. In this case rescission is ordinarily allowed. . . ."

We believe that in this State an offer and an acceptance are deemed to effect a meeting of the minds, even though the offeror made a material mistake in compiling his offer, provided the acceptor was not aware of the mistake and had no reason to suspect it. But if the offeree knew of the mistake, and if it was basic, or if the circumstances were such that he, as a reasonable man, should have inferred that a basic mistake was made, a meeting of the minds does not occur. The circumstances which should arouse the suspicions of the fairminded offeree are many, as stated in § 94 of Williston on Contracts (rev. ed.): ". . . And the same principle is applicable in any case where the offeree should know that the terms of the offer are unintended or misunderstood by the offeror. The offeree will not be permitted to snap up an offer that is too good to be true; no contract based on such an offer can then be enforced by the acceptor. . . ."

It is unnecessary to state once more that the proof in cases of this kind must possess a high degree of cogency. The bidder must prove, not only that he made a material mistake, but also that the offeree was aware of it. In this case, the facts which we have mentioned are unchallenged.

It is our belief that although the plaintiff alone made the mistake, the City was aware of it. When it accepted the plaintiff's bid, with knowledge of the mistake, it sought to take an unconscionable advantage of an inadvertent error. Equity is always prepared to grant relief from such situations.

The decree of the Circuit Court is affirmed.

METROPOLITAN LIFE INSURANCE COMPANY v. HENRIKSEN et al.

1955, 8 Ill. App.2d 127, 126 N.E.2d 736

The plaintiff, insurer, brought an action against insured and beneficiary to reform a $1,000 life policy which erroneously gave insured the option at end of 20 years to receive an annual annuity of $1,051 instead of $10.51. The Superior Court of Cook County, Frank M. Padden, J., entered a decree reforming the policy, and the beneficiary and the insured appealed.

LEWE, J. The defendants, who are the insured and named beneficiary in a life insurance policy issued by plaintiff, appeal from a decree reforming the policy and perpetually enjoining them or anyone claiming through them from maintaining any action on the policy except for the amount of it as reformed.

There was evidence that: On February 29, 1932, the defendant Everett N. Henriksen, aged twelve, applied to plaintiff by written application for an ordinary life insurance policy under a plan of insurance known as "Life with Premium Reduced" L.P.R. The pertinent provisions of the signed application read:

No. 14. Amount of insurance desired $1,000, ordinary premium payable annually.

No. 15. Plan of insurance as designated in rate book L.P.R.

The letters "L.P.R." are an abbreviation for a plan of insurance called Life Premium Reduced after twenty years. Under this plan the annual premium was $16 for the first 20 years and, if the policyholder elected to continue the policy, the annual premium would be $10 thereafter until death. At the end of 20 years the insured, in lieu of continuing the policy, had a right to elect any one of the four plans of settlement:

(1) To receive the total Cash Surrender Value of One Hundred Ninety Dollars; or

(2) To receive a Paid-up Participating Life Policy for Five Hundred Forty Two Dollars; or

(3) To receive an Annuity Contract providing for the yearly payment of Ten Dollars and Fifty One Cents during the lifetime of the Insured, the first payment of the annuity to be made one year from date of issue of the Annuity Contract; or

(4) To receive in cash Sixty Three Dollars and to continue the Policy as as a Whole Life Policy by the payment of Thirteen Dollars and Twenty Nine Cents, and a like amount annually thereafter during the lifetime of the Insured; the Policy to be endorsed to that effect by the Company.

March 4, 1932, the plaintiff issued the policy here in controversy. Through a clerical mistake the terms of settlement in number "(3)" of the policy read "To receive an Annuity Contract providing for the yearly payment of $1051 during the lifetime of the Insured, the first payment of the annuity to be made one year from date of issue of the Annuity Contract." As a result of this clerical error, the defendant Everett N. Henriksen would appear to be entitled, upon maturity of the policy, to receive benefits amounting to one hundred times those afforded him under the policy applied for.

After its issuance the policy in question was in the hands of the plaintiff on four different occasions for the purpose of making a change of beneficiary and noting a loan and repayment. On these occasions those clerks whose function it was to change the beneficiary and note loans and their repayment were not required to, and did not, examine the face of the policy to check the options of settlement. Plaintiff did not keep a copy of the policy here involved, nor does it retain any copies of policies issued by it. There was also evidence tending to prove that this is the general practice among insurance companies.

April 3, 1950, the plaintiff, through one of its agents, learned for the first time that the policy provided for an annuity contract of $1,051 annually for the lifetime of the insured. Immediately upon discovering the mistake the plaintiff tendered a corrected policy to the defendant

Everett N. Henriksen, providing for an annuity contract of $10.51 a year, which was refused. . . .

This record leaves no doubt that one of the plaintiff's clerks, in copying the modes of settlement described on the rate card onto the policy brief, left out the decimal point in the third settlement, thus making it read $1051 instead of $10.51.

The law seems well settled that a court of equity may reform an insurance policy where the contracting parties make a mistake and the policy fails to express the real contract between them. . . .

For the reasons given the decree is affirmed.

Decree affirmed.

KOLIAS v. COLLIGAN

1959, (Cal. App.) 342 P.2d 265

DRAPER, J. This action arises out of a construction contract. Knowing that a commercial concern desired to lease a building built to its specifications, defendant Colligan negotiated with plaintiff, who owned vacant land in an industrial section of San Francisco. By letter, Colligan offered to plan, build, finance and lease a building for plaintiff for $67,500. Plaintiff accepted the offer. Long-term financing in the sum of $50,000 would not be available until completion of the building. As part of his "package deal" Colligan arranged for Mrs. Waegemann (named as a defendant herein but not served) to provide the interim financing, and also to loan $17,500 on security of a second deed of trust. To secure Mrs. Waegemann's advances for the interim financing, plaintiff's property was transferred to her, to be reconveyed to plaintiff when the building was completed and the long-term loans were made. Plaintiff asked that the location of the building on the lot be changed somewhat from that planned by Colligan. The latter notified plaintiff that this would require additional work and, some four months before completion, sent a letter advising plaintiff of this fact and specifying the amounts to be charged for a portion of this extra work. Plaintiff did not sign an approval of this letter until shortly after completion of the building. At about the time of this acceptance, Colligan sent plaintiff a bill detailing all extras, in an amount totalling some $9,000. Seven months later, plaintiff paid the charges for extras in full. One day less than two years after payment, he brought this action to recover $8,455.74 paid for extra work. Defendant cross-complained for interest and rents amounting to $3,431.80 which he claims was erroneously omitted from his bills to plaintiff. After trial without a jury, the court awarded plaintiff $2,629 on the complaint, granted cross-complainant $1,271, and entered judgment in favor of plaintiff for the net amount of $1,358. Defendant appeals.

Appellant next asserts error in the admission of any evidence relating to the reasonable value of the extra work. The argument is that respondent voluntarily paid these charges, and that payments voluntarily made are not recoverable. But in overruling appellant's single objection to such evidence, the court pointed out that he would be allowed to offer evidence as to the claimed voluntary character of the payment. Much evidence on this issue was in fact introduced by both parties. At most, the objection raised a question as to the order of proof. We find no abuse of discretion in the ruling. In any event, appellant was in no way prejudiced, since the issue was fully tried and was determined against him.

There is substantial evidence that neither respondent's acknowledgment of the charges nor his payment of them was voluntary. Appellant's joint venturer, Mrs. Waegemann, held title to respondent's property. There is evidence that she and appellant would not reconvey to respondent until he acknowledged and paid the charges for extra work. It follows that the acknowledgment and payment here were made under compulsion, and were not voluntary. Whether respondent, as a reasonably prudent person, acted under compulsion is a question of fact for the trier of fact, which has, on substantial evidence, resolved it against appellant. . . .

Judgment in favor of plaintiff affirmed.

LEECE v. GRIFFIN
1962 (Colo.) 371 P.2d 264

Moore, J. We will refer to plaintiff in error as Leece, and to defendants in error as defendants or as Griffin, Hedrick, or United where the reference is to them individually.

The action was brought by Leece to recover damages for fraud. She alleged that she was induced to buy certain real estate in Mesa county by the false representations of defendants concerning improvements on, and the productivity of, the land. Griffin was the owner of the property involved; United was the real estate broker employed by Griffin to effect a sale of the premises; and Hedrick was the salesman employed by United with whom Leece dealt in making the contract of purchase. . . .

The trial court granted the motion of defendants for a directed verdict, and judgment entered accordingly.

Reduced to essentials the allegations of the complaint attempt to state a claim for actionable fraud based on four alleged misrepresentations: . . . Second. That the land sold to the plaintiff was fraudulently represented as producing land capable of providing an income of $2300 but was not.

With reference to this alleged misrepresentation the trial court commented:

She said that she asked about what the income would be and he took out a piece of paper and made computations on this little piece of paper and then told her that the income should be $2,300, $1,500 from the fruit, so it's clear that she knew that he wasn't representing that this had been the income. She made no further inquiry, apparently, from him as to how he computed it. Obviously, that would be conjectural, a prediction of annual profit in the–future income.

From the opinion of this court in *Bell Press, Inc. v. Phillips,* 147 Colo.–, 364 P.2d 398, we quote the following pertinent language:

It is well settled in Colorado that one of the essential elements of fraud and deceit is that there be a false representation of a material fact, which fact either exists in the present or has existed in the past; and, conversely, that a mere expression of an opinion in the nature of a prophecy as to the happening or nonhappening of a future event is not actionable. *Morrison v. Goodspeed,* 100 Colo. 470, 68 P.2d 458, 71 P.2d 154; and *Ginsberg v. Zagar,* 126 Colo. 536, 251 P.2d 1080. . . .

The trial court correctly applied this rule to the evidence before it at the close of plaintiff's case. . . .

The trial court committed an error in directing a verdict for the defendants, and the judgment accordingly is affirmed.

Hall and Pringle, JJ., concur.

Review Questions and Problems

1. *M,* a minor, purchased and paid $93 on a diamond engagement ring, *J* being the seller. The engagement was later terminated but the girl refused to return the ring to *M. M,* nevertheless, seeks to avoid his contract with *J* and recover the down payment. Is he entitled to do so?
2. A minor purchased a car by giving his age as 23. After making one payment in addition to the down payment, he defaulted and the seller repossessed. May the minor rescind and recover the payments made?
3. *W,* a minor, traded his car to *S* on a later model, *S* promptly selling the car to *F,* an innocent party. *W* desires to rescind and obtain the return of his old car from *F.* Has he the right to do so?
4. *M,* a minor, shortly before reaching his majority purchased some corporate stock. Three years later, the stock having paid no dividends, he desires to rescind, although he has been of age for two years. Has he the right to do so?
5. An infant purchases an overcoat for which he promises to pay $125. What are the factors to be considered in determining his liability? Would the result be the same if the overcoat had not been delivered?
6. *M,* a minor, purchased a car to drive to and from work. May he avoid the contract upon reaching his majority?
7. *M,* a married minor who was under guardianship and had always been adequately supplied with food by the guardian, contracted for

groceries in the amount of $150. He later refused to pay for them, and when sued, claims his minority as a defense. Is the defense good?

8. A partner purchased the interest of his copartner in a small business for $900, refraining from disclosing to the copartner that he had a ready buyer for the business at $2,500. Was fraud present?
9. *A* procured from *B* a deed to certain land upon the strength of *A*'s promise to erect a factory upon the land. *A* failed to erect the factory. May the deed be set aside because of fraud?
10. *R* sold a motel to *D* by stating that he paid $66,000 for it and had earned a net profit of $6,000 during the previous year. Both statements were substantially incorrect, but *D* made no attempt to verify them until after the transaction was completed. The court held the contract to be voidable. Was this a sound decision?
11. *A* traded a used car to *B* Co. on a new one, but before doing so he added certain chrome to his car to make it appear to be a much later model than it was. Even though he made no statement concerning the model, did he commit fraud?
12. *A* submitted a bid to the City of *B* on the construction of a water main. Being hurried in his bid, he figured the weight of the pipe per foot instead of the price per foot. When his bid was received, the city engineer called attention to the fact that the bid proposed to install the pipe for less than the pipe could be purchased. Nevertheless, the city council immediately notified *A* of its acceptance. May *A* avoid the contract because of the mistake?
13. *W* took a stone to *B*, a jeweler, for inspection. *W* did not know the nature of the stone, but had been informed that it was probably a topaz. *B* examined the stone, but was also uncertain as to its nature. He offered to purchase it, such as it was, for $1, and the sale was consummated. It appeared later that the stone was an uncut diamond worth about $700. *W* brings an action to rescind. What should be the result?
14. *K* sold to *B* a farm, each being under the impression that it had a 14.3-acre tobacco base under the Agriculture Adjustment Act, whereas it had only a 9.2-acre base. *K* sued to recover part of purchase paid because of mutual mistake. The court allowed recovery. Was this a sound decision?
15. A person from a rural area and inexperienced in city values sought to purchase a residence. In trying to sell one to him, the owner stated that the property was worth between $6,000 and $7,000, knowing that its value was not in excess of $3,000. The sale was completed and the buyer, having later discovered the true value, desires to rescind. Was fraud present?
16. An elderly lady was offered $500 an acre for land near a city. She wired her daughter for advice and received a telegram which read "price adequate." She then contracted to sell to buyer at $500. Actually the telegraph company erred, and the telegram should have read "price *inadequate*." May the sale be set aside because of mistake, the buyer having no knowledge of the error?
17. *O* sold real estate to *A*, *B*, *C*, and *D* for $16,000, each purchaser paying $4,000 for his undivided interest. The property was of little value and, unknown to *D*, *O* had agreed to give a rebate of $3,000 to

A, B, and *C.* When this was discovered by *D,* he alleged fraud and sought to rescind. Was he entitled to rescission?

18. *S* and *D,* owners of the stock of a closed corporation, had a contract that upon the death of one, the other would purchase the shares of the deceased owner. *S* died, leaving only this stock and other stock pledged to secure this corporation's debts. While *S's* widow was without means, *D* refused to buy the stock at a fair price or to have the corporation pay its debts so the other stock could be released. Finally, in desperation, she sold the stock to *D,* at much less than its value, obtaining the release of the other stock at that time. She now sues to recover damages, alleging duress. What result?
19. *P,* a prospective purchaser of land presently leased for a long time to the government at rather nominal rental, knew that the government was to terminate the lease in the near future. Since this fact was unknown by *H,* the owner, *P* was able to purchase the property much cheaper than would otherwise have been possible. If *H* had made inquiry of the government he could have known of its intention. *P* had acted as the agent of *H* in managing the property. The court held that no fraud was present. Was this a sound decision?
20. *S* sold goods on credit to *B,* the latter being asked to indicate how he stood financially. He said he had $3,000 in his business assets but neglected to say he had liabilities of $2,100. *S* seeks to avoid the contract and recover the goods sold. Has he a right to do so?
21. *W* contracted to purchase a lot of *M* Co. and to have the latter build a house according to specifications for $24,000, $2,400 being the down payment. Work progressed, but *W* wanted to be released. *W* said, if he was forced to perform, he would resell the house to an undesirable character and ruin *M* Co.'s subdivision development. *M* Co. appeared to agree to *W's* release and resold the property elsewhere but did not repay the $2,400. *W* sued for the $2,400 and *M* Co. asserts contract based on duress, and the court so held. Do you agree?

12

Unenforceable Contracts

2-66. Nature of Unenforceable Contracts. A court may refuse to enforce agreements possessing those essentials normally required in the formation of a contract for three reasons: (1) the agreement is a contract for the sale of personal property and is subject to the provisions of the Code which provide that if an agreement or a clause thereof is found by the court to be unconscionable as a matter of law at the time of making, it is unenforceable; (2) the object sought to be accomplished by the agreement is illegal; or (3) the parties have failed to reduce the agreement to writing, as required by the Statute of Frauds. In these situations, judicial processes are not available to assist in the enforcement of the agreement.

In those cases under the Code where it is contended that a contract or a clause is unconscionable, the court is given a wide latitude in reaching a decision. The term unconscionable has no exact definition, but evidence as to the commercial setting, purpose, and effect of the contract or clause may be used by the court in making the determination. *Campbell Soup Co. v. Wentz,*[1] while not decided under the Code, illustrates the type of contract likely to be held unconscionable.

An illegal agreement is one which calls for the performance of an illegal act by one of the parties. A contract may be illegal (1) because it is definitely forbidden by statute or (2) because it is inimical to the best interests of society. Since the character of the laws differs from state to state, certain contracts may be legal in one state and illegal in another. Those agreements which are more or less uniformly held to be illegal are considered in the following sections.

ILLEGALITY

2-67. Wagering contracts. The essence of a wagering agreement is that one of the parties is to win at the expense of the other, the winner

[1] Campbell Soup Co. v. Wentz, page 267.

being determined largely by chance. England, from a very early date, has continued to regard such agreements as legal. In this particular the United States has failed to follow the precedent established by her mother country; therefore, in the majority of the states, wagering contracts are considered illegal and unenforceable except as modified by statute.

To the extent that it is not forbidden by legislation, a contract to purchase grain futures or corporate securities on margin is legal if the agreement is so drawn that delivery must be accepted if tendered. However, if the agreement and the transactions between the parties indicate an intention on the part of the parties to the effect that one is to pay the other a certain sum, dependent upon the rise or fall of the market price, the agreement is illegal. Such an agreement is merely a wager as to the future course of the market, and is unenforceable. Where the contract makes it possible for one of the parties to demand delivery—and is thus legal—a subsequent agreement made at the time for performance, whereby the parties agree to settle on the basis of the change in price level, is legal. In effect, the new agreement merely establishes the damages for failure to perform the original contract. All transactions on the stock exchanges or boards of trade provide for ultimate delivery and are, therefore, legal.

2-68. Usurious contracts. Most states limit the amount of interest that may be charged upon borrowed money or for the extension of the maturity of a debt. Any contract by which the lender is to receive more than the maximum allowed by the statute is illegal. In the majority of the states the lender is denied the right to collect any interest in such cases, although a few of the states permit recovery of the legal rate. The law against usury is not violated by collection of the legal maximum in advance; by making, in addition to the maximum interest charge, a service fee that is no larger than reasonably necessary to cover the incidental costs of making the loan—inspection, legal, and recording fees; or by the latter principle, which makes it possible for a seller to add a finance or carrying charge on long-term credit transactions even though the charge exceeds the maximum interest rate.

The purchase of a note or bill of exchange at a discount greater than the maximum interest is not usurious, unless the maker of the note is the person who is discounting it.[2] A note or bill of exchange is considered the same as any other personal property and may be sold for whatever it will bring upon the market. There are some courts, however, which hold that if the seller indorses the negotiable paper and thus remains personally liable on it, a discount greater than the legal rate of interest is usurious. This is particularly true if the paper is considered worthless except for the indorsement. In such a case the sale of the paper merely amounts to a loan for the period the note has yet to run.

[2] Lydick v. Stamps, page 270.

As long as one lends the money of others, he may charge a commission in addition to the maximum rate. A commission may not be legally charged when one is lending his own funds, even though he has to borrow the money with which to make the loan and expects to sell the paper shortly thereafter. The various states have also enacted laws governing the operations of pawnshops, credit unions, and small-loan companies, which, under certain well-defined limitations, may charge a much higher rate of interest than is permitted on ordinary loans. An exception to the general rule is also made in favor of corporations; bonds or notes of incorporated companies may in most states bear any rate the particular industry is willing to pay.

2-69. Sunday contracts. The validity of contracts entered into on Sunday or to be performed on Sunday is dependent upon the law of the particular state in which they are made. In many states, all such contracts are legal; in others, almost all of them are illegal. The western states are very liberal in such matters, whereas the eastern states are more conservative and often refuse to enforce Sunday contracts.

2-70. Limitation of liability. Public utilities and other quasi-public enterprises—those holding out their services to the general public and which are more or less essential to satisfy everyday needs—are denied the right by contract to relieve themselves of responsibility for their own carelessness.[4] To permit them to do so would leave the public at their mercy. Therefore a public carrier or a public parking lot, which in its contract provides that it will not be liable for loss or damage to property entrusted to it even though caused by its own negligence, is nevertheless liable. The provision, being contrary to public policy, is illegal and unenforceable.

2-71. Contracts in restraint of trade. Competition, usually relied upon to encourage maximum production and to maintain reasonably low prices, can produce that result only if it is permitted to operate. Consequently, the courts hold contracts that provide for the restraint of trade or the limitation of competition to be illegal. A person who has agreed not to compete with another is free to disregard his contract, or a retailer who has agreed with others to maintain a certain retail price for a specific article of merchandise is not bound, because such agreement is illegal and void. The contract of a retailer to maintain prices established by the producer is treated in the text under a discussion of Fair Trade laws.

Contracts which have as their primary purpose the restraint of free competition may take many forms. Agreements not to compete, to divide the market, to maintain prices, to limit production, to pool the business,

[3] Miller's Mutual Fire Ins. Ass'n. of Alton, Ill. v. Parker, page 271.

to divide the profits, for exclusive dealing, or for tie-in sales are all of this character. Unless they fall within the exceptions noted later, they are considered contrary to public policy and are unenforceable.

2-72. Exceptions. Contracts in partial restraint of trade are valid if such restraint has reference to and is ancillary to the sale of property, a business, or a profession, or to the discontinuance of employment, and if such restraint is reasonably necessary for the protection of the purchaser or the employer. For example, a contract in which *A* sells his grocery business to *B* and as part of the consideration *A* promises not to enter the grocery business in the same locality for a period of three years is a legal contract even though there is a partial restraint of trade. Since the purchaser of good will has very limited protection as such, it has become customary to insert certain restrictions upon the seller by contract. Any restriction upon the future conduct of the seller that is essential to protect fully the buyer in the fruits of his purchase is legal. The restriction should be no greater in time or territory than is required to protect the buyer. If the restriction exceeds what is reasonably necessary, a few courts will reform the contract so as to contain reasonable restrictions,[5] but most courts hold the entire limiting clause illegal, thus leaving the buyer without protection.[6] In the absence of an effective restrictive agreement, one who sells his good will limits his future business conduct only slightly. He must not thereafter directly or by circular solicit business from his old customers, although he may advertise generally.

An employee in his contract of employment may agree that, at the termination of his employment, he will not enter into business for himself or with a competitor in the territory where he has built up his acquaintance in the service of the principal. Such a contract forbids him to carry away from his principal that good will which he builds up in his principal's service.

Similar restrictions are often imposed in leases and sales of real estate. So long as the vendor or lessor does not desire to have competition on property that he controls, he may avoid such competition by contract. Since other property in the community may be used for competitive purposes, the agreement is binding. If a lease is made, however, for the express purpose of taking an industry out of competition, the lease is unenforceable in that it limits competition.

2-73. Contracts to influence governmental action. A contract, except for strictly professional services, whereby one proposes to use his influence to secure executive, legislative, or judicial action, is illegal. Pressure group lobbying in support of, or opposition to, certain legislation is generally conceded to be legal, but contracts to compensate a group for

[4] Thomas v. Parker, page 272.
[5] Donahue v. Permacel Tape Corporation, page 273.

its influence are illegal. For this reason an agreement whereby one is to use his influence to bring about the election or appointment of another to public office is unenforceable.

A contract whereby one agrees in any manner to obstruct the wheels of justice falls under the same heading. To illustrate: *A* agrees to pay *B* one thousand dollars if the latter will absent himself from the state during the time a certain case is being tried. *B* upon his return cannot legally recover the money promised. His only possibility of recovery rests upon a voluntary payment by *A*.

Contracts quite similar to those involving the relation of one to his government are those which involve the relation of an employee to his employer. Any attempt by contract to persuade an employee to violate his duty to his employer is illegal. Likewise, any agreement whereby one person is to injure the person or property of another in any manner is illegal.

2-74. Effect of illegal contracts. It is incorrect to say that illegal contracts are void. They are merely unenforceable. The courts, in such cases, simply refuse to grant any relief. Although one of the parties has fully carried out his part of the agreement, he may neither demand performance nor force a return of his consideration. The court leaves the parties just as it finds them; fully or partially executed contracts are left undisturbed.

2-75. Exceptions. To this general rule there are at least three exceptions. If the refusal to grant affirmative relief has the indirect effect of enforcing an illegal contract, the court will give the necessary aid to relieve the injured party from further performance of the illegal agreement. Again, where the situation is such that the best interests of a large portion of the public demand that the contract be enforced, the court will see that the terms of the agreement are carried out. Thus, a contract whereby a bank loans to a customer more than the law permits is illegal; however, the interests of other depositors being involved, the borrower must repay what he has borrowed. Where certain contracts are made illegal to protect society, or a certain segment of it, the injured party is usually granted relief if he is one of the group which the law was designed to protect.

A party who performs an illegal contract, in ignorance of the fact that it is illegal because certain important facts are not revealed to him, may recover for his performance.

2-76. Contracts illegal in part. Contracts that contemplate the performance of various acts, some legal and some illegal, may be enforced to the extent that they are legal. This is true only in those cases in which the contract, by nature, may be so divided that the legal portion can be segregated from the illegal portion.

STATUTE OF FRAUDS

2-77. Written contracts. As a general rule, contracts are enforceable although not reduced to writing. An oral agreement, if proved, is as effective as a written one. A written agreement signed by the parties, however, possesses at least two distinct advantages over an oral one. In the absence of a writing, it often becomes difficult to prove the existence of a contract. Thus, if one of the parties denies the existence of an agreement, and no outside witness was present when the contract was formed, it becomes quite difficult to persuade a jury that a contract exists. Unless convincing evidence of its existence is available, a contract is of little value. Contracts that are reduced to writing and expressed with clarity leave few matters open to dispute.

Too often an oral agreement leaves much to conjecture, with the inevitable result that disagreements occur and the courts are called upon to settle the dispute. Although a written agreement is not always essential, it is generally desirable,[6] particularly for executory contracts.

As a general rule, written agreements may not be varied by parol evidence. This principle of law commonly referred to as "the parol evidence rule" means that oral evidence may not be introduced concerning pre-existing or contemporaneous agreements which are in conflict[7] with the written contract. The written contract is the only evidence of the agreement since all matters which were agreed upon prior to its execution are presumed to have been incorporated in the written agreement. All negotiations are said to have merged in the agreement. Since the rule is based on the concept of merger, parol evidence is admissible to establish modifications agreed upon subsequent to the execution of the written agreement as well as to establish cancellation of the contract by mutual agreement. However, it is best to modify or cancel a written agreement by another writing. Moreover, if the agreement falls under the provisions of the Statute of Frauds, the modification or cancellation is required to be in writing. To illustrate, let us assume a written agreement has been made for the erection of a certain building, in accordance with specifications, for $50,000. Parol evidence would not be admitted later to show that the original specifications or price were other than those shown in the writing. However, it would be possible to present oral evidence that the specifications and price had been changed after the original agreement had been entered into. On the other hand, a contract for the sale of real estate that had been reduced to writing could not be altered by a later oral agreement, because such contracts are required by the Statute of Frauds to be in writing.

[6] Federal Security Insurance Company v. Smith, page 276.
[7] Silverstein v. Dohoney, page 276.

There are several exceptions to the parol evidence rule which find their basis in equity, good conscience, and common sense. Evidence of fraudulent misrepresentation, lack of delivery of an instrument where delivery is required to give it effect, intention of the parties, and errors in drafting or reducing the contract to writing are admissible under some of the many exceptions to the rule.

The Code recognizes that terms of an agreement may be explained or supplemented by a course of dealing, or usage of trade, or by a course of performance. Where a contract of sale involves repeated occasions of performance by either party with knowledge of the nature of the performance and opportunity for objection to it by the other, any course of performance accepted or acquiesced in, without objection, is relevant in determining the meaning of the agreement. If there is an inconsistency, express terms control course of performance and course of performance controls both course of dealing and usage of trade. In addition, the Code allows the admission of oral evidence of consistent additional terms unless the court finds the writing to have been intended also as a complete and exclusive statement of the terms of the agreement.

2-78. Statute of Frauds. At an early date in English history there was enacted what is known as the Statute of Frauds. This statute provided that certain contracts could not be enforced unless they were reduced to writing and signed by the parties sought to be bound thereby. It was designated the Statute of Frauds because its purpose was to prevent fraud on the part of those who attempted to establish a valuable contract by the false testimony of their friends.

It certainly never was intended that the Statute of Frauds be used as an instrument of fraud or as an escape from the effect of contracts freely and fairly entered into, although such may be the result in certain cases. In the areas covered by the Statute of Frauds, it is possible for an oral contract to be made in good faith and liability for its breach to be avoided because written evidence is lacking. The Statute of Frauds ethically is best used as a defense when the oral contract itself or its major terms are in dispute. If the parties are unable to reach a settlement in such a case, use of the Statute of Frauds may be justified.

Because of the abuse made of the Statute of Frauds, there may be some question as to whether it should be retained in our laws. However. until our legislatures are persuaded to remove it, attention must be given to its effect. The law varies somewhat from state to state, and only those provisions that are fairly uniform in the various states and which relate primarily to business are discussed in detail in the sections that follow. In addition to these, many states require the following to be in writing:

1. The appointment of an agent to sell real estate.
2. The creation of a trust.

3. The promise to pay a debt that has been outlawed by the Statute of Limitations or that has been barred by bankruptcy.

4. An agreement to bequeath property to someone under the terms of a will.

2-79. Debt of another. Contracts whereby one becomes responsible for the debt, default, or miscarriage of a third person must be reduced to writing. Such agreements are called *contracts of guaranty*, and are not enforceable if made orally. To illustrate: *A* orally agrees to become secondarily responsible for *B*'s grocery bill at *C*'s store during the next six months. *B* purchases $300 worth of groceries and fails to pay for them. Although *A*, in a sense, is morally bound to make good his promise, it cannot be enforced, as it was not in writing.

A contract of guaranty exists only where the promise of the guarantor is collateral or secondary to the promise of some other party and a guarantor is liable only if the principal debtor fails to perform. If the agreement is such that the promise of the principal debtor is cancelled or merges in the present agreement or the promise is to pay out of money held for, or owing to, the principal debtor, no guaranty results. The promise is an original one and no writing is required. Thus, in the previous illustration, if the credit had been extended directly to *A*—the goods being charged to his account—or had been extended to both *A* and *B* jointly, the oral agreement would have been binding. In such a case, *B* merely becomes an agent of *A*, with power to purchase groceries. There is no other debt or promise in favor of *C* to which *A*'s promise is collateral. Although *A* may recover from *B* the amount expended, so far as the grocer is concerned, the debt is that of *A*.

An agreement which has for its object the substitution of one debtor for another does not fall within the statute. No writing is required in such a case. Thus, if *A* says to *Y*, "If you will release *B* from his liability to you, I will pay the same," and *Y* consents, the agreement is binding, although made orally, because it is a primary promise of A and not secondary to *B*'s promise, as in a guaranty contract.

In case a guarantor agrees to become responsible for the default or debt of another because of some material advantage that he may gain from the transaction, no writing is required. Thus, an oral guaranty by a *del credere agent*—a consignee who sells consigned goods on credit, but who guarantees to the consignor that the buyers will pay for the goods purchased—is enforceable. Since the agent obtains a commission for selling the merchandise, his pecuniary interest in the consignment disposes of the necessity of a writing, and the consignor may collect from the consignee on the oral guaranty if the purchaser fails to pay.

2-80. Contracts of executors. Agreements entered into by those administering estates, whereby they agree to become liable out of their own property for the debts of the estate, must be in writing. In such a case, the executor or administrator is in reality agreeing to become responsible for the debts of another, namely, the estate.

2-81. Sale of real estate. Contracts for the sale of real estate have always been deemed very important by the law. From the time when people first aspired to become owners of land, certain formalities were required at the time of its transfer. The Statute of Frauds provides that all agreements for the sale of any interest in or concerning real estate shall be in writing. The language is broad enough to include an estate for life, a mortgage, an easement, an assignment of a contract to sell realty, or a lease, as well as an absolute estate in fee simple. The statute in most states excludes from its operation leases of short duration; thus, in almost all states, a lease for one year requires no writing. Although timber, wild grass, minerals, and fixtures permanently attached to real estate are considered part of the realty, an oral contract for their sale will be enforced, provided the agreement indicates that title is to pass after they are severed from the land.[8] A contract that imposes a duty upon the seller to sever and deliver rather clearly suggests that title is to pass later, and the contract will be considered a contract for the sale of goods with no sale of real property involved. Where the buyer is to enter, sever, and effect delivery, the courts are somewhat in conflict. If the right to enter and take is one that can be exercised in a relatively short period of time, it is likely to indicate an intention to sell personal property as distinct from realty. To illustrate: *A* orally contracts to deliver to *B* 100 twelve-inch trees from certain timber land. Later he refuses to deliver the trees and denies any liability. Inasmuch as it is apparent that title was to pass only after the trees were severed from the land, the agreement is enforceable without any written evidence, unless the price is enough to bring the case under the personal property rule.

2-82. Part performance. Although part performance may be helpful in obtaining court aid in other oral contracts, such as sales of personal property, part performance by the buyer of real estate does not make the contract enforceable. The writing is not dispensed with merely because the buyer has made a down payment. If the seller refuses to carry out the oral agreement, the buyer has as his only remedy the right to recover all payments made and the reasonable value of all improvements that have been added by him. If the *buyer* refuses to perform, he may not recover the payments he has made or the value of the improvements.

A buyer may progress to a point where mere return of payments made by him and compensation for improvements added by him prove unfair and inequitable. Courts of equity, to handle such situations fairly, often

[8] Sutton v. Wright & Sanders, page 278.

disregard this section of the Statute of Frauds and enforce the oral contract. The courts are not entirely in agreement as to what is required to remove the case from the Statute, but mere part payment or mere entry into possession, standing alone, is not enough. Where both take place and cannot be explained on any basis other than a contract for sale, courts will enforce the oral agreement. This is also true if, in addition, the buyer makes substantial improvements or has placed himself in a position where he cannot be restored to his prior condition, such as when health has been undermined by partial performance or previous important employment opportunities have been terminated.

2-83. Contracts of long duration. A contract that by its terms must continue for a period longer than one year from the making thereof must be reduced to writing. Thus, an agreement to work for another for a period of years or a contract by a manufacturer that gives to a retailer exclusive territory for eighteen months is not enforceable if made orally. Where the contract is possible of completion within a year, no writing is essential although actual performance is spread over a period of years.[9] For illustration, assume that *A* contracted orally to sell to *B* 15,000 tons of steel at $185 a ton, *B* being free to order it out as he saw fit within a period of fifteen months. One thousand tons were ordered out and paid for, after which *A* refused to ship the balance. The contract was enforceable even though the remaining balance was ordered out fourteen months after the contract was made, completion having been possible within one year at the time the contract was made. The real test is: Do the terms of the agreement permit of its performance within the period of one year? If so, no writing is essential, regardless of when the performance is completed. Thus, if the time for performance is of uncertain duration, being dependent upon the happening of a contingency such as death, the act of one of the parties, the arrival of a certain ship, or the sale of certain property, no writing is required, despite the fact that actual performance extends over several years. Since it is possible for such contingencies to occur within a year, the contract falls outside of the statute. Attention should also be called to the fact that the year is figured from the date of the agreement, and not from the time performance is to begin. A contract to work for one year at a certain salary, employment to begin two days later, would have to be in writing.

In contracts that provide for performance over a period in excess of one year, full performance of all obligations by one of the parties, which has been accepted by the other, makes the agreement enforceable. Thus, if a present sale of goods is made, followed by delivery, the oral agreement is binding although the buyer is to make his payments over a period of 18 months. Some few states go even further and hold that where

[9] Joseph v. Sears Roebuck & Co., page 280.

the contract calls for complete performance by one of the parties within a year, the oral agreement is effective.

2-84. Sale of personal property—in general. The old English Statute of Frauds provided that any contract for the sale of personal property involving more than ten pounds sterling should be in writing.[10] This provision, in modified form, has become part of the law of every state and varies only as to the amount. In one state, any sale involving over $30 must be written, whereas in another state any sale of personal property for less than $500 is enforceable though oral. In determining whether the value of property is such as to cause it to fall within the statute, it often becomes necessary to decide how many contracts have been entered into. Thus, *A* orders from *B* fifteen bushels of potatoes to be delivered at once and ten barrels of apples to be delivered ten weeks later. Either item considered alone is worth less than $50; both items total over $50. If the parties intended only one contract, the Statute of Frauds is applicable; however, if two contracts were entered into, no writing is required. The intention of the parties in these cases is gleaned from such factors as the time and the place of the agreement, the nature of the articles involved, and other surrounding circumstances. The Code contains several Statute of Frauds provisions which are discussed in the next section.

2-85. Sale of personal property—Code states. The Code contains Statute of Frauds provisions specifically applicable to the sale of goods and to the sale of securities. In addition, there is a general provision that covers contracts for the sale of personal property which do not fall within the other categories. This general provision provides that a contract for the sale of personal property is not enforceable by way of action or defense beyond $5,000 in amount or value of remedy unless there is some writing which indicates that a contract for sale has been made between the parties at a defined or stated price, reasonably identifies the subject matter, and is signed by the party against whom enforcement is sought or by his authorized agent.

The provision relating to sale of goods is applicable to contracts involving $500 or more. Such contracts are unenforceable unless there is some writing sufficient to indicate that a contract for sale has been made between the parties and signed by the party against whom enforcement is sought or by his authorized agent or broker. A writing is not insufficient because it omits or incorrectly states a term agreed upon but the contract is not enforceable beyond the quantity of goods shown in such writing. It further provides that: (1) in a contract between merchants, a confirmation sent by one of the parties to the other need not be signed by the latter if he neglects to object to it within 10 days; (2) goods to be specially manufactured (not suitable for sale to others in the ordinary

[10] Ozier et al v. Haines, page 282.

course of the seller's business) where work has been started or a commitment is made before withdrawal, fall outside the statute; (3) goods received or paid for make a contract enforceable only to the extent they are paid for or received and accepted; and (4) such contracts are enforceable in the quantity admitted if a party admits in his pleadings or testimony that a contract for sale was made. This latter provision will eliminate the defense where the contract was actually made as most courts allow one party to call the other party to the witness stand for purposes of cross-examination about the transaction. Thus, the Code eliminates the Statute of Frauds as a dilatory defense in contracts for the sale of goods, but gives protection in those cases required to prevent fraud.

The provision of the Statute of Frauds pertaining to securities applies to all sales of securities. It requires written evidence signed by the party to be charged or his authorized agent or broker, or delivery of the security or payment before a contract for sale is enforceable. This statute also contains a provision on confirmations and a provision for establishing the contract by the use of pleadings or testimony similar to the provisions in the sale of goods section.

2-86. Sale of personal property—Noncode states. In states which have not adopted the Code, the Statute of Frauds provisions relating to personal property are usually found as a part of the law of sales. In most states, the statute is so worded or construed as to include a contract of sale or to sell both tangible and intangible personal property. These statutes usually provide that a contract involving the sale of personal property in excess of a stipulated amount shall not be enforceable by action unless: (1) the buyer accepts the goods or a part of them and actually receives the same (2) the buyer gives something in earnest to bind the bargain by way of payment or part payment, or (3) there is sufficient written evidence of the agreement. In addition, the statutes generally do not apply where the contract involves goods that are to be specially manufactured by the seller for the buyer and are not readily resaleable in the ordinary course of the seller's business.

2-87. A contract involving two or more sections of statute. A single contract often involves two or more sections of the statute. In such a case, all sections of the statute that are involved must be complied with or the contract is unenforceable. Thus, an indivisible oral contract may involve an agreement to sell both real and personal property, followed by delivery of some of the personalty. Since only one contract is involved and real property requires a written memorandum, no part of the contract is enforceable.

An oral contract for the sale of personal property may be so drawn that it cannot be completed within a period of one year, in which case receipt and acceptance of part of the property does not eliminate the necessity for a writing. All sections of the Statute of Frauds must be complied with when a contract involves two or more of them.

2-88. Nature of the writing. The writing required by the Statute of Frauds is not a formal written document signed by both parties. The law merely requires that some note or memorandum concerning the transaction be signed by the party sought to be bound by the agreement. A situation exists in which one party may be bound by an agreement although the other party is not bound. Such a result may be explained on the theory that the agreement is legal in all respects, but proper evidence of such an agreement is lacking unless the person sought to be charged with the contract has signed a writing. Any kind of note or memorandum that describes the property involved, that sets forth the major terms, and that indicates the parties to the agreement is sufficient.[11] If one memorandum is incomplete, but it is clear that two or more writings relate to the same subject matter, they may be joined to supply the necessary written evidence. This is true only if it is clear that the writings relate to the same agreement.

The signature may be quite informal and need not necessarily be found at the close of the document. It may be in the body of the writing or elsewhere, so long as it identifies the writing with the signature of the person sought to be held. See Section 2-85 for Code requirements.

2-89. Effect of no writing. It is said that a contract that requires a writing dates from the time of the oral agreement but is unenforceable until written evidence of it is available. The agreement is valid in every respect except that proper evidence is lacking. However, if, at any time before suit is started, the party sought to be held signs any statement that indicates the existence of such a contract, he furnishes the necessary evidence. Other evidence, regardless of how authentic and preponderant it is, cannot be substituted. The Statute of Frauds is complied with only by the securing of some note or memorandum in writing signed by the proper party. Of course, the Code provision concerning pleadings and testimony greatly reduces the use of the defense in cases involving personal property.

UNENFORCEABLE CONTRACTS CASES

CAMPBELL SOUP CO. v. WENTZ

1949, 172 F. 2d 80, (Third Circuit)

GOODRICH, C. J. These are appeals from judgments of the District Court denying equitable relief to the buyer under a contract for the sale

[11] Wozniak v. Kuszinski, page 283.

of carrots. The defendants in No. 9648 are the contract sellers. The dedendant in No. 9649 is the second purchaser of part of the carrots which are the subject matter of the contract.

The transactions which raise the issues may be briefly summarized. On June 21, 1947, Campbell Soup Company (Campbell), a New Jersey corporation, entered into a written contract with George B. Wentz and Harry T. Wentz, who are Pennsylvania farmers, for delivery by the Wentzes to Campbell of all the Chantenay red cored carrots to be grown on fifteen acres of the Wentz farm during the 1947 season. Where the contract was entered into does not appear. The contract provides, however, for delivery of the carrots at the Campbell plant in Camden, New Jersey. The prices specified in the contract ranged from $23 to $30 per ton according to the time of delivery. The contract price for January, 1948 was $30 a ton.

The Wentzes harvested approximately 100 tons of carrots from the fifteen acres covered by the contract. Early in January, 1948, they told a Campbell representative that they would not deliver their carrots at the contract price. The market price at that time was at least $90 per ton, and Chantenay red cored carrots were virtually unobtainable. The Wentzes then sold approximately 62 tons of their carrots to the defendant Lojeski, a neighboring farmer. Lojeski resold about 58 tons on the open market, approximately half to Campbell and the balance to other purchasers.

On January 9, 1948, Campbell, suspecting that Lojeski was selling it "contract carrots," refused to purchase any more, and instituted these suits against the Wentz brothers and Lojeski to enjoin further sale of the contract carrots to others, and to compel specific performance of the contract. The trial court denied equitable relief. We agree with the result reached, but on a different ground from that relied upon by the District Court.

. . . A party may have specific performance of a contract for the sale of chattels if the legal remedy is inadequate. Inadequacy of the legal remedy is necessarily a matter to be determined by an examination of the facts in each particular instance.

We think that on the question of adequacy of the legal remedy the case is one appropriate for specific performance. . . . We think if this were all that was involved in the case specific performance should have been granted.

The reason that we shall affirm instead of reversing with an order for specific performance is found in the contract itself. We think it is too hard a bargain and too one-sided an agreement to entitle the plaintiff to relief in a court of conscience. For each individual grower the agreement is made by filling in names and quantity and price on a printed form furnished by the buyer. This form has quite obviously been drawn by skillful draftsmen with the buyer's interests in mind.

Paragraph 2 provides for the manner of delivery. Carrots are to have their stalks cut off and be in clean sanitary bags or other containers approved by Campbell. This paragraph concludes with a statement that Campbell's determination of conformance with specifications shall be conclusive.

(7) The defendants attach this provision as unconscionable. We do not think that it is, standing by itself. We think that the provision is comparable to the promise to perform to the satisfaction of another and that Campbell would be held liable if it refused carrots which did in fact conform to the specifications.

The next paragraph allows Campbell to refuse carrots in excess of twelve tons to the acre. The next contains a covenant by the grower that he will not sell carrots to anyone else except the carrots rejected by Campbell nor will he permit anyone else to grow carrots on his land. Paragraph 10 provides liquidated damages to the extent of $50 per acre for any breach by the grower. There is no provision for liquidated or any other damages for breach of contract by Campbell.

The provision of the contract which we think is the hardest is paragraph 9, set out in the margin. It will be noted that Campbell is excused from accepting carrots under certain circumstances. But even under such circumstances the grower, while he cannot say Campbell is liable for failure to take the carrots, is not permitted to sell them elsewhere unless Campbell agrees. This is the kind of provision which the late Francis H. Bohlen would call "carrying a good joke too far." What the grower may do with his product under the circumstances set out is not clear. He has covenanted not to store it anywhere except on his own farm and also not to sell to anybody else.

(8) We are not suggesting that the contract is illegal. Nor are we suggesting any excuse for the grower in this case who has deliberately broken an agreement entered into with Campbell. We do think, however, that a party who has offered and succeeded in getting an agreement as tough as this one is, should not come to a chancellor and ask court help in the enforcement of its terms. That equity does not enforce unconscionable bargains is too well established to require elaborate citation.

(9) The plaintff argues that the provisions of the contract are separable. We agree that they are, but do not think that decisions separating out certain provisions from illegal contracts are in point here. As already said, we do not suggest that this contract is illegal. All we say is that the sum total of its provisions drives too hard a bargain for a court of conscience to assist.

This disposition of the problem makes unnecessary further discussion of the separate liability of Lojeski, who was not a party to the contract, but who purchased some of the carrots from the Wentzes.

The judgments will be affirmed.

LYDICK v. STAMPS
1958, (Tex.) 316 S. W. 2d 107

One Cloke approached Stamps, defendant, for a loan of $15,000 which was refused, whereupon Cloke referred him to Lydick, the plaintiff, who appeared willing to help Cloke obtain the loan. The parties later met in the plaintiff's office where Cloke made an $18,000 note to run four months at 5 per cent interest to the order of plaintiff. The plaintiff then indorsed the note to the defendant who gave him only $15,000, which the plaintiff turned over to Cloke, this being the only amount received by Cloke. The plaintiff, as indorser, paid $18,300 to defendant, and is now trying to recover $6,600 from the defendant under a statute which allows recovery of double the amount of usurious interest paid. The defendant contends there was no usury present but that it was merely discounting commercial paper. The plaintiff contends that the loan was in reality made to Cloke, and that the defense of usury is good against any holder of the note. Several other notes were likewise discounted, Cloke in each case getting only the net amount.

The lower court gave judgment for defendant and plaintiff appealed.

Boyd, J. . . . We think there was usury in each note, and although the jury found that appellees did not make any loans but were merely purchasers of the notes from appellant, we think all the contracts were void as to interest, and valid only as to the amount paid by appellees for the respective notes. . . .

Under the English rule and the Spanish law, by which a contract to secure the payment of usury is absolutely void, a note given for usurious consideration is void in the hands of an innocent indorsee for a valuable consideration. In Texas also a usurious contract gathers no vitality by its circulation, and is void as to interest in the hands of an innocent holder. It is now settled that there can be no innocent purchaser of a usurious note, either before or after maturity, and it is immaterial that there is nothing on the face of the note or the security to put the transferee on notice. 42 Tex. Jur., p. 1000, sec. 99, citing cases. See, also, 27 R.C.L., p. 244, sec. 47; *National Bond & Investment Co. v. Atkinson,* Tex. Civ. App., 254 S. W.2d 885. . . .

We agree with appellees that a note may be sold at a discount of more than ten per cent without thereby becoming tainted with usury. 42 Tex. Jur., p. 903, sec. 22. Such a transaction, however, does not purge a note of the usury which is already in the contract. . . .

Judgment for plaintiff.

than ten per cent without thereby becoming tainted with usury. 42 Tex. Jur., p. 903, sec. 22. Such a transaction, however, does not purge a note of the usury which is already in the contract. . . .

Judgment for plaintiff.

MILLER'S MUT. FIRE INS. ASS'N OF ALTON, ILL. v. PARKER
1951, (N.C.) 65 S.E.2d 341

Defendant, Parker, operates an automobile parking lot in Charlotte in connection with one of his filling stations. A Mrs. Jenkins contracted for the parking of her automobile on said lot on a monthly basis under an agreement that the defendant should not be liable for the loss of said vehicle by fire or theft.

The automobile was stolen while parked on defendant's lot. Plaintiff, insurance carrier, paid Mrs. Jenkins the loss sustained, took an assignment, and now sues under the doctrine of subrogation. In its complaint it alleges want of due care on the part of the defendant in protecting the automobile against theft and particularizes the acts of alleged negligence on his part. The defendant, answering, denies negligence or want of due care on his part and pleads the contract with the owner in bar of plaintiff's right to recover. The lower court gave judgment for defendant.

BARNHILL, J. A provision in a contract seeking to relieve a party of the contract from liability for his own negligence may or may not be enforceable. It depends upon the nature and the subject matter of the contract, the relation of the parties, the presence or absence of equality of bargaining power and the attendant circumstances.

Under our system of government, freedom of contract is a fundamental, basic right of every citizen. Even so, the public interest is paramount. If the provision is violative of law or contrary to some rule of public policy, it is void and unenforceable. . . .

It is a well-recognized rule of law that in an ordinary mutual benefit bailment, where there is no great disparity of bargaining power, the bailee may relieve himself from the liability imposed on him by the common law so long as the provisions of such contract do not run counter to the public interest. *Hanes v. Shapiro & Smith.* . . . This rule is applied with practical unanimity where the public neither has nor could have any interest whatsoever in the subject matter of the contract, considered either as a whole or as to the incidental covenant in question, and the agreement between the parties concerns their private affairs only. In respect to such contracts the public policy of freedom of contract is controlling.

Respecting other types of bailment, there are various shades of opinion. Many courts hold that where the bailee makes it his business to act as bailee for hire, on a uniform and not an individual basis, it is against the public interest to permit him to exculpate himself from his own negligence. And the decided trend of modern decisions is against the validity of such exculpatory clauses or provisions in behalf of proprietors of parking lots, garages, parcel check rooms, and warehouses, who undertake to protect themselves against their own negligence by posting signs or printing limitations on the receipts or identification tokens delivered to the bailor-owner at the time of the bailment. In such cases, the difference is the difference between ordinary bailees, on the one hand, and what may be called professional bailees, on the other. They hold themselves out to the public as being possessed of convenient means and special facilities to furnish the service offered for a price. They deal with the public on a uniform basis and at the same time impose or seek to impose predetermined conditions which rob the customer of any equality of bargaining power.

While there is authority contra, we are persuaded this rule is founded on reason and common sense and should prevail in respect to contracts such as the one relied on by the defendant.

The complexity of today's commercial relations and the constantly increasing number of automobiles render the question of parking a matter of public concern which is taxing the ingenuity of our municipal officials. People who work in the business sections of our cities and towns and who rely on automobiles for transportation find it difficult—sometimes impossible—to locate a place on the public streets where daily parking is permitted. They are driven to seek accommodation in some parking lot maintained for the service of the public. There they are met by predetermined conditions which create a marked disparity of bargaining power and place them in the position where they must either accede to the conditions or else forego the desired service. . . .

Judgment for defendant was reversed and new trial ordered.

THOMAS v. PARKER

1951, (Mass.) 98 N.E.2d 640

COUNIHAN, J. This is a suit in equity in which the plaintiffs seek to enjoin the defendant from engaging in the bakery business in violation of a negative covenant in a bill of sale of a bakery business given by the defendant to the plaintiffs. The evidence is not reported, but the judge made voluntary findings of facts which he adopted as findings of material facts. . . .

Facts admitted in the pleadings and those found by the judge are as follows: On October 15, 1949, the defendant (Parker) by a bill of sale sold the plaintiffs the bakery business conducted by him at No. 136 Hudson Street, Boston, "together with good will and bakery machinery in said bakery." In this bill of sale the defendant "agrees that he will not engage in the baker business directly or indirectly for a period of seven years within a radius of seven miles of Boston." The defendant during the year 1950 entered the employ of the Boston Syrian Baking Co. in Boston as a baker at a weekly salary. There was then and is now only one other baker of handmade Syrian bread in Boston. The defendant has at no time interfered with customers of the plaintiffs by way of solicitation and has not actively participated in the management or control of his employer's business.

The judge found the limitations of seven years in time and of seven miles in area unreasonable. He found, however, it reasonable to restrict the defendant from engaging in the "baker business directly or indirectly," within a radius of four miles of No. 136 Hudson Street, Boston, for a period of four years from October 15, 1949. He further found that the defendant, in violation of this restriction, is and has been engaged in the "baker business directly or indirectly," and ordered the entry of a decree enjoining the defendant from continuing in such business. From a decree to this effect the defendant appeals. There was no error in the entry of the decree.

It is well settled that a covenant of the sort here in question may be enforced by injunction "if the interest to be protected is consonant with public policy and if the restraint is limited reasonably in time and space. What is reasonable depends upon the facts." *Becker College of Business Administration & Secretarial Science v. Gross*, 281 Mass. 355, 358, 183 N.E. 765, 766. Here the judge found the original limitations to be unreasonable and modified them to the extent necessary to protect the plaintiffs. We are of opinion that the restrictions as modified are justifiable and enforceable. . . .

Decree affirmed with costs.

DONAHUE v. PERMACEL TAPE CORPORATION

1955, (Ind. Sup. Ct.) 127 N.E.2d 235

ACHOR, J. Appellee (plaintiff) is engaged in the manufacture and sale of adhesive tapes. Appellant was formerly a sales representative for appellee. During such employment the parties entered into a written contract, the pertinent sections of which are as follows:

> . . . 2. Employee for a period of three (3) years after leaving Company's employment for any reason whatsoever, shall not, in the United States or Canada without first obtaining Company's written permission, engage in or enter the employment of or act as a sales agent or broker for the products of or as an advisor or consultant to any person, firm or corporation engaged in or about to become engaged in the manufacture of adhesive or adhesive tapes.

Thereafter appellant (Donahue) terminated his employment with appellee and, without the consent of appellee, became a sales representative for a competitor. An action for temporary and permanent injunctive relief followed. A temporary restraining order was issued and it is from that decree that this appeal is prosecuted.

In support of his appeal, appellant contends among other things that whereas, the scope of his employment with appellee was limited to northern Indiana, the restrictive covenant contained in the contract was unreasonably restrictive in that the restricted territory (United States and Canada) encompassed too large an area, and that therefore the contract in its entirety was contrary to public policy and void. The cause was submitted to the trial court upon the verified pleadings which were admitted into evidence. It is upon these facts that the validity of the restrictive covenant in issue must be determined. . . .

We proceed to analyze the second class of cases which state that covenants in restraint of trade will be enforced if limited to the "area of the business involved"—those related to (2) *the sale of a business or profession.* The rule is well established that a vendor may enter into a valid covenant not to compete within the area of the business or profession *sold.* . . .

It must be noted that these cases relate to the good will, which is "the interest to be protected" in the business or profession *sold,* and they do not relate to the scope of the business of the buyer. For example, if the seller operated stores in cities *A, B,* and *C,* and he sells the store in city *A,* the cases do not hold that a negative covenant may be enforced prohibiting seller from continuing business in cities *B* and *C,* neither do they hold that the mere fact that the *buyer* operates a business throughout the state of Indiana that he may preclude a seller whose business was limited to a single county, from operating elsewhere within the State of Indiana. In fact the contrary rule is true. *Consumers' Oil Company v. Nunnemaker, supra.* The "good will" must be related to the particular transaction between the parties. As stated in 2 Page on Contracts 1389, § 789, as follows: "If for any reason the restraint is greater than is necessary to protect the good will, the contract is invalid."

By clear analogy the precedent of these cases, when applied to employer-employee covenants, clearly supports the conclusion that such covenants will be upheld, if limited to the area in which operation of the employee's activity was related to the good will of the employer's business. . . .

As heretofore stated, the facts before us present a case of first impression in this state. It is therefore our opportunity and responsibility to decide the case upon those principles which most fully do justice to both the parties themselves and to the public.

The general principles governing the legality of a contract in restraint of trade have been stated by *Williston on Contracts*, § 1636, pp. 4580–4581:

> It is everywhere agreed that in order to be valid a promise imposing a restraint in trade or occupation must be reasonable. The question of reasonableness is for the court, not the jury; and in considering what is reasonable, regard must be paid to (a) the question whether the promise is wider than is necessary for the protection of the covenantee in some legitimate interest, (b) the effect of the promise upon the covenantor, and (c) the effect upon the public. . . .
>
> To what conclusion do we arrive when we apply the first above stated test to the facts in this case? Was (a) the covenant wider than was necessary for the protection of the covenantee (appellee) in some legitimate interest? There was no evidence from which the court could assume that the "confidential sales information, including ideas, customer lists and the like . . . made available" to appellant, were related (except in a general way) to appellee's business outside the limited area of his employment with appellee in northern Indiana. Therefore, the case clearly fails to meet the first test of "necessity for the protection of the covenantee" in the area prescribed,—"the United States and Canada. . . ."
>
> . . . We conclude therefore that when measured by each of the above three criteria (a), (b) and (c), that the covenant of the contract before us was unreasonable to the extent that it attempted to restrict the gainful employment of appellant beyond the area of his former employment with appellee.

The above conclusion gives rise to the final issue in the case. It is asserted that even though the covenant of the contract may not be enforceable as to all the area interdicted, that the equities of the case require enforcement in the area of appellant's former actual employment. In support of this position the following cases are cited involving the sale of a business, in which restrictive contracts have been held divisible and have been enforced as to the area of the business sold although they have been held invalid as to the extended area beyond which the business operated: *Bennett v. Carmichael Produce Co., supra; Beard v. Dennis,* 1855, 6 Ind. 220; *Wiley v. Baumgardner, supra.* However, we are not permitted to consider that question or the equities which might support such a decision in this case. In each of the above cited cases the contracts specifically described or referred to both the area of the business sold as well as the extended area interdicted. Whereas the contract before us does not describe the area of appellee's former employment but, on the contrary, the restricted territory is described in one indivisible whole—"The United States and Canada." We cannot rewrite the contract made by the parties and add to it matters which it does not contain and then use the contract as rewritten as a basis for litigation, however justifiable equitable interference under the circumstances might seem to be. We conclude, therefore, the covenant of contract upon which this action is predicated, is unenforceable in its entirety. *Consumers' Oil Company v. Nunnemaker, supra.*

Therefore, the temporary restraining order heretofore issued is ordered dissolved. (Decision for defendant, Donahue.)

SILVERSTEIN v. DOHONEY
1954 (N.J. Sup. Ct.) 108 A.2d 451

Silverstein and Silverstein brought suit to recover on a three-year lease of space in defendant's business building where cigarette vending machines might be placed. The contract was in writing and provided for commissions to defendant, but failed to indicate the amount of the commissions. The lower court gave judgment for the defendant and plaintiff appealed, contending an enforceable contract.

SCHETTINO, J. S. C. . . . For a period prior to the execution of the writing, plaintiffs had a machine upon defendant's premises and paid commissions on cigarette sales. . . .

Unless a requirement exists that an agreement be in writing, the parties may bind themselves contractually by writing or oral understanding or by a combination of both. The parol evidence rule inhibits additions to or variations from a writing intended to constitute the entire agreement and as well contradictions of so much of an agreement as may have been reduced to written form. But it is clear that parol evidence as to the rate of commission does not offend these principles. The writing on its face evidences that a commission was intended. Proof of the rate does not add to the obligations of the parties under the writing, but rather expounds the obligation which the writing recognizes to be a part of the agreement. Nor, of course, does the oral testimony contradict or vary any written term. Perhaps to express it another way, the writing does not purport to be the entire understanding and, on its face, it is apparent that something was left out, and hence the admission of the testimony squares with the rule as stated in *Ross v. Orr*, 3 N.J. 277, 282, 69 A.2d 730, 732, (1949):

> . . . it is equally true that if the written contract purports to contain the whole agreement, and it is not apparent from the writing itself that something is left out to be supplied by extrinsic evidence, parol evidence to vary or add to its terms is not admissible. . . .

Judgment reversed, costs to abide the result of the retrial.

FEDERAL SECURITY INSURANCE COMPANY v. SMITH
1958, 259 Fed.2nd 294

PICKETT, J. Joseph L. Smith brought this action for an accounting of insurance commissions alleged to be due him from the defendant, Federal Security Insurance Company, under the provisions of an oral General

Agency insurance contract. The Insurance Company admitted in its pleadings that it entered into a verbal contract whereby plaintiff was to sell its policies in the State of Idaho, but denied that the commission schedule as claimed by the plaintiff was agreed to or that plaintiff was to act as a General Agent. . . . Judgment was entered for the plaintiff in the sum of $38,346.60. . . .

The trial court found that on or about January 1, 1953 the parties entered into a verbal agreement by the terms of which plaintiff agreed to sell insurance for the defendant in the State of Idaho and to serve as Exclusive General Agent for the defendant's insurance business in that state; that on all policies sold by the plaintiff he was to receive a commission of 90 per cent of the first year's premiums, 17½ per cent of the second year's renewal premiums, and 7½ per cent of the renewal premiums from three to ten years; that on policies sold within the State of Idaho for the defendant by other persons, the plaintiff was to receive 10 per cent of the first year's premiums and 2½ per cent on renewal premiums from two to ten years. The court also found that the agreement was effective as of January 1, 1953, and was terminated on the 8th day of February, 1954. The question presented is whether there is substantial evidence to sustain these findings.

While it is agreed that there was a verbal arrangement whereby plaintiff was to represent the defendant in Idaho, there was a sharp conflict between the parties as to some of the terms. The plaintiff testified that early in January, 1953, he met A. A. Timpson, Vice-president and General Manager of the defendant company, in Salt Lake City, Utah, for the purpose of negotiation with defendant company a General Agency contract for the State of Idaho. After stating to Timpson that he would not accept any contract except that of a General Agent, he was advised to return later for a decision. The gist of plaintiff's testimony is that upon his return a few days later, Timpson agreed to a General Agency contract with commissions as stated in the Court's findings.

The plaintiff stated that the contract was to commence immediately and was to be reduced to writing and forwarded to him in Idaho. . . . In March, the plaintiff, with the consent of Timpson, opened a bank account in Idaho for the company. Timpson testified that the plaintiff was the only agent working for the company throughout its various territories who was authorized to withdraw funds from the company's bank account. After obtaining an Idaho license, plaintiff and agents selected by him sold and continued to sell defendant's insurance in Idaho. Timpson testified that it was quite likely that the company advised the Idaho Insurance Commissioner that plaintiff was the designated person to hire and discharge its agents in Idaho. In July of 1953 Timpson forwarded a form of contract to plaintiff, which was substantially different from that which Smith testified had been agreed upon. Plaintiff did not sign it and there was no change in his method of handling the company's business prior to the termination of his services in February of 1954. The trial court accepted plaintiff's version of the contract, which satisfies the substantial evidence rule.

The fact that the parties intended that their agreement should later be reduced to writing does not affect the validity of the oral arrangement. It is quite evident that the parties did not intend that the effectiveness of the contract was to be delayed until reduced to writing as actual performance began and continued for several months before a written form was submitted, which admittedly was not the same as the original understanding. The rule is that the mere intention to reduce an oral or informal agreement to writing is not of itself sufficient to show that the parties intended that until such formal writing was executed the contract should be ineffective. In the absence of a contrary intention, where the terms of a contract have been agreed upon, the failure to later execute a contemplated written instrument does not prevent the contract from becoming an obligation of the parties. . . .

As to the date upon which the contract was to become effective, we do not believe that the evidence supports the finding that it was to be effective as of January 1, 1953. It is without conflict that negotiations between Smith and Timpson began after the first of the year and continued for several days. The record does not disclose the date upon which Smith arrived in Idaho. An Idaho license was obtained by plaintiff about February first. . . .

The case is remanded for determination of the date upon which plaintiff qualified as an agent for defendant in Idaho, for an accounting from that date, and a modification of the judgment accordingly.

SUTTON v. WRIGHT & SANDERS
1926, (Tex. Civ. App.) 280 S.W. 908

This suit was instituted by Sutton to recover damages because the defendant failed to take and pay for 100,000 cubic yards of sand at 12½ cents a yard. The plaintiff owned land upon which there was a substantial deposit of sand and gravel, and the defendant contracted to buy the amount indicated, being given license to enter on the land and remove it. The buyer was to have five years in which to remove it, but was to remove not less than 1,000 cubic yards a month. The plaintiff alleged it was possible for the defendant to have removed all of the sand within one year. The defendant set up the Statute of Frauds as a defense, and the lower court ordered the jury to return a verdict for the defendant.

Cobbs, J. . . . In this case it will be noted by the oral contract there was no intention, express or implied, to sell land per se, but the sale of gravel thereon only. There was no intention to pass ownership or title to the land, and only a permission was given to enter thereupon in order to excavate and remove 100,000 cubic yards of gravel therefrom. Of course, a contract for any interest in land is widely different from a contract to remove a commodity therefrom, because a sale of the land, as such, would carry the gravel with it, but sale of the gravel, as such, would not include or pass title to the land in which it was situated, or any part thereof. *Anderson v. Powers*, 59 Tex. 214.

It is urged that the gravel could be moved in one year, and a proper construction of the contract so indicated. If such was the effect to be given to the contract or intention of the parties, and was so found by the jury, it would not be in violation of the statute of frauds. It may be that the issue as to the time of performance should go to the jury. If the contract was to be performed within one year, that would not take beyond the time provided for in the statute of frauds, and the contract would be in harmony therewith. Does the option to perform the contract to remove the gravel all in five years bring it within the statute, and thus subject it to be denounced by the statute?

The evidence showed no limit was fixed as to the time within which all the gravel should be removed. It did provide that some should be removed each month, and it was agreed that not less than 1,000 cubic yards should be taken out per month, and the "pay to be not less than $125 a month as a minimum."

The contract on its face does not show that it was not to be performed within one year, but was ambiguous in that particular. It was a question of fact whether it was to be and could be performed within one year, which, if so, would not on its face render it void per se. If two constructions to a contract can be given, one legal and the other illegal, the court will give that construction to the contract that will make it legal. It was ambiguous in the particulars referred to, and was not determinable on its face as a question of law. It is true that the testimony showed a verbal contract for the sale of an interest in land, but a severance of the commodity within a year would not render it obnoxious to the statute of frauds. Clearly it was a contract for the sale of gravel, a merchantable commodity, such as trees or other products of the land, and is real estate only by an arbitrary construction of a rule of law. The title to the land itself did not pass, and the land, as such, still remained in its locus, and title to the land upon which the gravel lay was not affected. We hardly think that five years, given as the ultimate date for removal, will have much effect in the determination of the question as to performance. As stated, we think gravel on the natural soil stands with the same relation to it as the growing trees. . . .

The court's charge created fundamental error, as the record showed the existence of controverted material facts, and for the reasons given *the judgment is hereby reversed and the cause remanded for another trial.*

(The amount involved did not violate the Texas statute concerning the sale of personal property.)

JOSEPH v. SEARS ROEBUCK & CO.

1953, (S.C.), 77 S.E.2d 583

OXNER, J. This is an action (by Joseph) to recover damages for breach of an alleged oral warranty by appellant with respect to the safety of a pressure cooker sold to respondent. The trial resulted in a verdict for respondent in the sum of $2,500. The major question for determination is whether the Court below erred in not granting a motion by appellant for a nonsuit, and later for a directed verdict, upon the ground that the alleged warranty was unenforceable because not in writing as required by the 5th clause of the 4th section of the Statute of Frauds, Section 11–101(5) of the Code of 1952, which provides that no action shall be brought to charge any person upon any oral agreement "that is not to be performed within the space of one year from the making thereof."

Although the record contains the entire testimony taken at the trial, we need only state the facts pertinent to the questions raised by the exceptions. In January, 1949, respondent bought a pressure cooker from appellant for $16.95, which was paid in cash. Among the representations which respondent alleged were made to and relied upon by her at the time of the sale, were that appellant's saleslady stated that said pressure cooker "was safe in every respect" for use in cooking; "that there was no danger whatever" in using it; and that in view of the safety devices thereon, "no explosion was possible." In support of the foregoing allegations in the complaint, respondent testified that having heard conflicting reports as to the safety of pressure cookers, she specifically inquired whether there was any danger in such a utensil exploding, to which the saleslady replied: "There is no possible danger in these things exploding." She further testified that the saleslady told her that it was impossible for the cooker to "blow up because Sears had this device on it that would go off at 35 lbs. pressure, that there was no way, shape or form for it to explode." She said that she was wholly unfamiliar with the operation of pressure cookers and relied on the foregoing representations and warranties in making the purchase.

Respondent used this utensil rather regularly until November 23, 1950. While cooking dinner on that day, it exploded and as a result, respondent was burned, her stove demolished, and the house considerably damaged. No question is raised as to the amount of the verdict. . . .

The only question for our determination is whether the oral warranty upon which this action is based is within the 5th provision of the 4th section of the Statute of Frauds. Appellant contends that the statute applies because the alleged warranty was impossible of performance within a year. In support of this contention, appellant offered testimony to the effect that with proper use, one of these pressure cookers would last for ten to fifteen years. However, one of its witnesses admitted that it was "possible for one to wear out in a year," and another that she had heard of explosions occurring within a year.

The question of whether a warranty as to the quality or condition of a chattel must be in writing when the life of such article ordinarily extends beyond a year is an important one. If appellant's view is accepted, most oral warranties would be unenforceable. Although cases are legion sustaining a recovery of damages for breach of an oral warranty with respect to the condition or quality of chattels sold, no decision has been cited, and we have found none, holding that such warranty was unenforceable because it constituted an oral agreement which was not to be performed within one year from its making. The fact that the Statute of Frauds has never been raised in any of these cases is significant.

If there is a possibility of performance within a year, the agreement is not within the statute. The fact that performance within a year is highly improbable or not expected by the parties does not bring a contract within the scope of this clause. Accordingly, it has been held that a contract to employ another "for an indefinite period (of time) so long as plaintiff's work was satisfactory" was not within the statute. *Cline v. Southern Railway Co., supra,* 110 S.C. 534, 96 S.E. 532. A similar conclusion has been reached as to an agreement which was construed by the Court as being one to "employ the plaintiff for the rest of his natural life as long as he did his work in a satisfactory manner." *McGehee v. South Carolina Power Co.,* 187 S.C. 79, 196 S.E. 538, 541. . . .

It is also uniformly held that the statute does not apply when by the happening of a contingency the defendant may be required to perform his contract within a year.

In *Gadsden v. Lance,* McMul. Eq. 87, the Court said: "It is equally well settled that when the agreement is to be performed on a contingency which may or may not happen within the year, a note in writing is not necessary, unless it appears from the agreement that it is to be performed after the year. To the same effect, see *Thompson v. Gordon,* 3 Strob. 196; *Walker v. Wilmington, C. & A. Railroad Co.,* 26 S.C. 42, 196 S.E. 535. It is on this principle that it has been held that an oral contract of insurance, although extending beyond a period of one year, is not within the statute because the liability of the insurer thereon may occur within the year by the happening of the contingency insured against. . . .

The oral warranty in the instant case will now be considered in the light of the foregoing principles. In effect, appellant said to respondent: "The pressure cooker is not dangerous and will not explode. If it does explode, we shall indemnify you or be responsible in damages." The testimony shows that it was possible for the explosion to have occurred within a year. The fact that it did not occur in the instant case until almost two years does not affect the question. If the warranty sued on is within the statute, it would be unenforceable whether the breach occurred the day after the sale or ten years thereafter. We think the warranty was one subject to a contingency which might occur within one year after its making and therefore not within the statute. . . .

All exceptions are overruled and the judgment below affirmed.

OZIER et al. v. HAINES

1951, 343 Ill. App. 400, 99 N.E.2d 395

O'CONNER, J. Plaintiffs (Ozier and Others) filed complaint in the Circuit Court of Piatt County, which alleged in substance that the plaintiffs operated a grain elevator, that the defendant was a farmer who came to the elevator and verbally sold plaintiff 5,000 bushels of corn for $1.24 per bushel. While the defendant was in the office, the plaintiffs, relying upon the contract of sale, called a grain broker on the telephone and resold the grain. The complaint alleged that the defendant knew that the plaintiffs resold the grain, and knew that the plaintiffs resold the grain in reliance upon the defendant's agreement, and that the defendant is estopped to defend against his acts, representations and contract.

The complaint further alleged that it was the custom of the trade, which custom was well known by all the parties and relied upon by them, to buy and sell grain upon verbal contracts, and for the purchasing elevator company to resell said grain to grain brokers immediately upon such verbal sale being made.

Thereafter the defendant refused to deliver the corn and the plaintiffs had to purchase corn on the open market at a higher price and bring this suit to recover the difference in price at which the corn was purchased on the open market and the price at which the defendant had agreed to sell to the plaintiffs.

Defendants filed a motion to dismiss, which trial court granted. The plaintiffs elected to stand by the complaint and a final judgment was entered for the defendant. Plaintiffs appeal from this ruling of the trial court.

The defendant in his motion pleaded the Statute of Frauds. Plaintiffs contend the defendant is estopped from relying on the Statute.

A situation similar to this was before this court in the case of *Ludlow*

Cooperative Elevator Company v. Burkland, 338 Ill. App. 255, 87 N.E.2d 238. In that case we held that the Statute of Frauds, as set forth in Section 4 of our Sales Act, Chap. 121½ Ill. Rev. Stats. 1947, was a good defense and the plaintiff could not recover. We recognized that one may be estopped under certain circumstances from asserting the Statute of Frauds, but pointed out that the moral wrong of refusing to be bound by an agreement because such an agreement does not comply with the Statute of Frauds, does not authorize the application of the doctrine of equitable estoppel.

The section of the Sales Act quoted in the *Ludlow* case, *supra*, is still in force and unchanged (Chap. 121½, Ill. Rev. Stats. 1949, Sec. 4).

Our Supreme Court laid down the rule in *Lowenberg v. Booth*, 330 Ill. 548, 162 N.E. 191, 195, that in order to invoke the principle of equitable estoppel six elements must appear, the first of which is: "Words or conduct by the party against whom the estoppel is alleged, amounting to a misrepresentation or concealment of material facts."

We cannot find a misrepresentation or concealment of material facts by the defendant. Promises as to future action are not misrepresentations of existing fact. Action taken in reliance on such promises, as distinguished from action taken in reliance on a misrepresentation of existing facts, cannot raise an estoppel. While it is true that equity will not allow the Statute of Frauds to be a shield to shelter a fraud, the breach of a promise which the law does not regard as binding, is not a fraud. There does appear to be a moral wrong, but if we attempted to right this moral wrong under these conditions, the Statute would be rendered nugatory. The plaintiffs are presumed to know the law, and they could easily have protected themselves by making a part payment on the contract, or by preparing a written memorandum of the contract.

We have carefully examined all the cases cited by the plaintiffs. No one of them sustains the position taken by the plaintiffs here. It may well be that this section of the Statute is an anachronism, but this argument should be addressed to the legislature and not to this court.

The judgment of the trial court is affirmed.

WOZNIAK v. KUSZINSKI

1959 (Mich.) 90 N.W.2d 456

The plaintiff, Wozniak, brought this suit for specific performance of a contract to sell real estate. The plaintiff had made a down payment of $300 and defendant signed a receipt which stated the price of $6,050 and terms of payment, describing the property as "Prop. known as 1503 Joy." The city and state were not mentioned but the property was in Jackson, Mich., where the defendant lived. The defendant refused to perform and contended the writing was inadequate. The lower court entered decree for defendant and plaintiff appealed.

Black, J. There can be no doubt that the cases relied upon by the chancellor, if presently authoritative, fully support his opinion. The trouble is that this Court has "recently evidenced" a disposition "to liberalize its interpretation of the statute of frauds" (*Goldberg v. Mitchell*, 318 Mich. 281, 286, 28 N.W.2d 118), reference on the disposing occasion having been made to *Cramer v. Ballard*, 315 Mich. 496, 24 N.W.2d 80. In Cramer our majority concluded its opinion this way (315 Mich. at page 511, 24 N.W.2d at page 86, of report):

> To the extent that our previous decisions may be considered inconsistent with this opinion, on the specific question as to admissibility of extrinsic testimony to supplement a description in a memorandum for sale of real estate, or an interest therein, for the purpose of identifying the property, not contradictory or inconsistent with the memorandum description, but merely to show that no other property could have been in contemplation, it must be understood that the court now declines to follow such decisions.

What was done in Cramer is quite consistent with the trend of modern authority. Professor Grismore, noting this new course of the judiciary in his "Principles Of The Law Of Contracts" (1947, Bobbs-Merrill), § 261, p. 449, said:

> Preliminary to this discussion (of the statute of frauds) it is worthy of observation that the tendency, in general, has been to interpret the statute in such a way as to narrow the scope of its operation as much as possible. This result has been accomplished not only by resolving all ambiguities in the phraseology of the statute in such a way as to exclude as many cases as possible from its operation, but also by excluding cases which are within the language, on the ground that they are not within the purpose or spirit of the statute. In fact, in recent years there has been a tendency to doubt the wisdom of the statute as applied to modern conditions and to advocate its outright repeal.

It is not to be gainsaid that our quoted commitment to the rule of evidentiary supplementation, of an otherwise insufficient memorandum relating to sale of real estate, partially eviscerates § 8 of our statute of frauds (C.L. 1948, § 566.108) as once understood and interpreted. Such being the case, it is advisable that the fact and effect be openly heralded, and that we firmly announce that which is to be in this field of law relating to rights in and titles to land. Whether the old interpretation of said § 8, or the new one, is best for society remains and will remain debatable. The change having taken place, we can only say that equity can and will, given appealing equities arrayed against perfidy or fast dealing, prevent most of the frauds that section 8 of this venerable statute was intended to frustrate. . . .

Since the street address of the home is given correctly in the memo-

contended the writing was inadequate. The lower court entered decree for defendant and plaintiff appealed.

tending to deal with respect to it and no other, we are constrained to hold that the description given in the memorandum was appropriately supplemented according to Cramer's said rule. . . .

Reversed and remanded for entry of decree in favor of the plaintiffs, conditioned on due payment by them of the agreed purchase price.

Review Questions and Problems

1. *A* and *B* were two contractors engaged primarily in road construction work, and two jobs in their area were to be let at public bids. They agreed that each would bid on one of the jobs only, it being understood on which one each was to bid. When the bids were opened, it was discovered that *B* bid on both jobs and was the successful bidder at each opening. Since *A* would have been the successful bidder on one of the jobs, except for *B*, he sues *B* for damages resulting from the breach of contract. Should *A* recover?
2. *M* was purchasing a residence from *S* on installments at a price of $20,000. After payment of $5,000, *M* needed money, so *W* paid the remaining $15,000 to *S*, took title and resold the property to *M* for $21,000 on installments. *M* is now in default and *W* seeks to foreclose the contract of sale. *M* insisted that the resale was nothing more than a loan to *M* of $15,000 and the $6,000 added was in reality usurious interest and that there is no contract for the sale of real estate but rather a loan, secured by real estate which is involved. The court held it to be a loan at usurious interest. Was this a sound decision in your judgment?
3. *H* contracted through his broker for grain futures, it being known that he had no need for grain, but expected to sell and make a profit. The market fell and he suffered substantial losses for which he gave notes. He is now sued, and as a defense urges that the consideration was illegal. What result?
4. *X* Council of Boy Scouts of America admitted boys to its summer camp program only if the boys and their parents signed an agreement releasing the camp of all liability for injury even though camp officials were careless. *F* was injured and brought suit, the court holding the camp liable. It found the exculpatory clause to be illegal. Do you agree with the decision?
5. *P* contracted to do certain construction work for *G*, the written contract providing that no additional work was to be done unless agreed to in writing. Later *G* made several requests for added work at specified rates orally, but after the work was completed, he refused to pay because the requests were not in writing. The court permitted *P* to recover. Was the decision sound?
6. *A* held a claim against *B* and *C* for $500. He was threatening to sue them when *F*, the father of *B*, promised to pay the amount if the firm failed to do so, provided that *A* would refrain from bringing suit for 8 months. No suit was brought during that period, and *A* now desires to recover from *F*. Assuming that the agreement was not in writing, is it enforceable?
7. *S* contracted orally to make a speedboat for *B*, according to specifications, at the price of $650. Upon completion, *S* tendered the boat, but *B* rejected it, urging the Statute of Frauds as a defense. Is the defense good?

8. *A* made an oral contract with *B* whereby *A* was to convey certain real estate to *B* for the price of $6,000. In reliance upon the oral agreement, *B* hauled certain fertilizer to the farm, piped water to the feed lots, and made cement platforms for feeding livestock. Under these conditions was the oral agreement enforceable?
9. *P* orally employed *A* to train skilled workmen and agreed to retain *A* as an employee as long as they retained any of the employees trained by *A*. After three years, *P* released *A* although several employees trained by *A* were still in *P*'s employment. Is the Statute of Frauds a good defense for *P*?
10. A finance company loaned money directly to the buyer of a car and added to the loan a finance or carrying charge which was greatly in excess of the legal rate of interest. Was usury present?
11. A cotton compress company accepted cotton for baling and provided in the contract that it was not to be liable for loss of the cotton by fire or other causes even though the loss resulted from its negligence. A loss arose because of carelessness, and the cotton owner seeks to recover for his loss. Is the compress company liable?
12. An injured employee entered into an oral contract with his employer to surrender any claim he might have, in consideration of the employer's promise to employ him at a certain job as long as the employee lived or his work was satisfactory. Was the oral agreement enforceable?
13. A mortgagee charged the mortgagor $3,750, in addition to the maximum interest, as an expense of refinancing a mortgage of $75,000. Will the mortgagee be able to collect the interest?
14. *O* contracted in writing to sell real estate to *B*. The contract called for designated payments, which, if not made on time, permitted *O* to rescind the agreement. There was a later oral agreement to extend the time of payment. Was the oral agreement binding?
15. *O* sold his filling station to *B*, along with numerous assets, including accounts receivable. As part of the oral contract, he guaranteed that the accounts would be paid. Some failed to pay their accounts, and *B* seeks to recover of *O*, who desires to use the Statute of Frauds by way of defense. Is it available?
16. *P* orally employed *A* as manager of his bowling alleys and agreed to pay him one-half the profits, further orally agreeing to sell a one-half interest in the business within two years for $10,000. He later refused to sell to *A*, selling the entire business to *X* for $29,000. Has *A* any recourse against *P*?
17. *O* sued *W* for injuries resulting from the carelessness of *W* in failing to maintain the premises leased to *O*. The lease contained language relieving the landlord of liability for any negligence on his part. The court held this provision to be enforceable. Was the decision sound?
18. Suit was brought by *S* against *R* to enjoin *R*, a former employee, from competing in the sale of seismographing and core-bit drilling equipment to the oil industry in New Mexico, Texas, and Oklahoma, in violation of an employment contract restricting competition in those states for five years after employment ceased. *R* contended the contract was illegal because the period was too long and the territory too broad, since S had been represented by *R* in only parts of the three states. The court approved the time period but enjoined *R* only in those parts of the three states in which *R* had previously represented S. Is this a sound decision?

13

Performance of Contracts

CONDITIONS

2-90. Failure to perform. For every breach of contract, regardless of how small or trifling the provision violated, the injured party, usually called the *obligee,* is entitled to some relief. For a violation of minor significance, he has as his only remedy the right to recover damages. However, in an executory contract where the provision is one of vital importance and the breach is material, rescission of the agreement may be demanded. To illustrate: *A* agrees to build a brick house for *B*, according to agreed specifications, for $20,000 and to have it completed by a certain date. *A* is ten days late in finishing the house. The breach being of minor importance, *B* must accept and pay the contract price less any damages sustained by reason of the delay. On the other hand, let us assume that the breach consisted in building a five-room house instead of a seven-room house called for by the contract. Unquestionably, the breach of such an important provision would justify *B* in rescinding the agreement.

Those terms of a contract, the breach of which justifies rescission, are called *conditions*. Conditions may be *precedent, concurrent,* or *subsequent*. For purposes of our discussion, only the first two will be considered in detail. *Conditions subsequent* establish events, the occurrence of which take away otherwise vested rights. An insurance policy which takes away the right to recover for a fire loss, unless notice of the loss is given to the insurer within a stated period, has included a condition subsequent. Failure to give notice causes the insured to lose his right to recover.

2-91. Conditions precedent. Most contracts are so drawn that one of the parties must perform some duty before he obtains a right against the other party. The performance of this duty is called a *condition precedent.* In other words, the promise to perform by the second party is dependent upon performance by the first party. To take a simple illustration: *A* agrees to work for *B* one month for $400. *A's* work for the month is a condition precedent to his right to recover the $400.

Not all of the terms which impose a duty of performance on a person are of sufficient importance to constitute conditions precedent. If a provision is relatively insignificant, its performance is not always required to precede recovery from the second party. In such cases, the party who was to receive performance merely deducts damages for the breach before performing on his part. Judging whether a provision is breached, or whether the breach of a particular provision is so material as to justify rescission, often presents a problem.[1] If damage caused by the breach can be readily measured in money, or if the nature of the contract has not been so altered as to defeat the justifiable expectations of the party entitled to performance, the clause breached is not considered a condition precedent. To illustrate, assume that *R*, a retail grocer, contracts to buy from S 10,000 pounds of Ole's oleo at 15 cents a pound, *R* to pay for the oleo within thirty days and S to send a salesman to display and assist in selling the oleo. If S fails to send a salesman and the oleo fails to sell, must *R* pay for it? Was the provision for sending a salesman a condition precedent to *R*'s duty to pay? Whether the provision is an important one would doubtless depend on whether *R* had previously sold oleo and upon whether Ole's brand was new to the trade. If the brand is a new one and needs special promotion, and if *R* is a somewhat inexperienced grocer, it seems likely that the breach is so substantial as to justify rescission. It would be difficult to measure with any degree of accuracy the money damage resulting from the breach.

Whenever there has been substantial performance of the condition precedent, the promisee becomes obligated to perform, less damages for minor deficiencies.

2-92. Time as a condition. What is the result of a failure to perform within the time set forth in a contract? May the agreement be rescinded? The answer to these questions depends upon the type of contract involved. The time provision establishing the exact time for performance of a contract that involves primarily the expenditure of labor and materials or the production of a commodity of little value to anyone other than the contracting party is normally not considered of major significance. Thus, the failure of a contractor to complete a house by the date set in the contract would not justify rescission by the owner. He could, however, deduct from the contract price such damages as resulted from the delay.

A clause calling for performance within a certain time found in a contract for the sale of marketable goods is usually held to be a condition precedent[2] to the extent that substantial compliance is required.

[1] Bonadelle Construction Co. v. Hernandez, page 299.
[2] Sunshine Cloak & Suit Co. v. Roquette et al., page 300.

In contracts whereby retailers purchase goods that are normally bought and sold in the market, performance by the seller on the exact date specified is considered quite important. Sales promotion campaigns and provisions for the normal needs of customers are built around delivery dates. To replace merchandise not received promptly, other sources must be tapped. Failure to comply in detail with the time provisions of such contracts usually justifies the buyer in rejecting an offer to perform at a later date.

An extended delay eventually becomes material in the performance of any contract and ultimately justifies rescission. If partial performance has not taken place, a relatively short delay may justify rescission, whereas if performance is under way and time is not of the essence, a delay of some time may be required before rescission is justified. In those cases that provide no specific date for performance, it is implied that performance will take place within a reasonable time, the length of time being dependent upon the nature of the commodity involved and the surrounding circumstances.

In those contracts in which time for performance normally is deemed not to be a condition precedent, performance on time may be made a condition precedent by adding a clause that "time is of the essence in this agreement." The parties may stipulate that something shall be important in a particular contract which ordinarily is not considered so. In such a case, failure to perform on time affords ground for rescission, unless the court construes the time clause to be a penalty provision and therefore unenforceable.

2-93. Concurrent conditions. Many contracts are so drawn that the parties thereto are to act simultaneously as to certain matters. An agreement that calls for a conveyance by *A* of a certain farm upon payment of $60,000 by *B* is illustrative of such a situation. The deed is to be delivered at the time payment is made. Those terms of a contract that require both parties to the agreement to perform contemporaneously are designated *concurrent conditions*. Under the terms of such an agreement, neither party is placed in default until the other has offered to perform. Such offer on his part is called a *tender*, and actual performance is unnecessary to place the other party in default. For this reason *B* could not successfully sue *A* for failure to deliver the deed until he had offered to make the payment required. Actual payment is not required unless *A* offers to deliver the deed; tender of payment is sufficient.

The Code makes it clear in contracts for the sale of personal property, that the buyer, unless otherwise agreed, must tender payment as a condition to the seller's duty to tender and complete delivery. Tender may be made by any means or in any manner current in the ordinary course of business unless the seller demands payment in legal tender and gives a reasonable extension of time to procure it.

2-94. Money tender and its effect. A valid tender of money owing to a creditor has certain rather important effects. Although it does not discharge or pay the debt, it extinguishes any security that protects the debt and stops interest from accruing thereafter, and, in case the creditor later brings suit recovering no more than the amount tendered, he must pay his own court costs. Thus, any mortgage or pledge of property is discharged by a tender of the debt, the debt itself remaining an unpaid and unsecured obligation until it is paid.

A valid tender consists of an unconditional offer to pay in legal tender the proper amount at the proper time to the creditor or his agent. A tender before the maturity of an obligation is not a proper tender, and the creditor rests under no duty to accept it. Tender of payment in something other than legal tender—such as a check—is good unless the creditor refuses it because it is not legal tender. If he refuses it for some other reason, a proper tender has been made.

2-95. Divisible and installment contracts. While many contracts are completely performed at one time, there are many situations where the contract is to be performed in stated installments. In addition, installment contracts are created by clauses providing that each delivery is a separate contract. Where a contract is to be performed on more than one occasion, two important questions arise: (1) Is the contract divisible on both sides, such that the second party is under a duty to perform in part after the first party performs an installment? (2) Does material breach of any installment justify a rescission of the balance of the agreement? The Code contains provisions relevant to both inquiries. These provisions provide that unless otherwise agreed, all of the goods called for by the contract must be tendered in a single delivery at which time payment is due, but where the circumstances give either party the right to make or demand delivery in lots, the price, if it can be apportioned, may be demanded for each lot. Thus if the price can be determined for each lot, the buyer must pay for each lot as it is delivered and the contract is treated as divisible.

Insofar as Question 2 is concerned, the Code allows a buyer, unless the seller gives adequate assurance that the breach will be corrected, to reject nonconforming goods where the value of the installment is impaired to the extent that it cannot be cured. If the default is so substantial as to impair the value of the whole contract, the buyer may treat the breach as a breach of the whole and rescind the whole contract. The value would be impaired where the breach indicates the seller's inability to perform, or his unreliability. A buyer will be held to have reinstated the agreement by accepting a nonconforming installment without giving notice of cancellation or by demanding performance of the agreement. Thus, in a divisible contract, a buyer may waive a breach and demand full performance or may rescind the agreement on substantial breach of an installment. The same questions are present in states which have not adopted the Code but the answers and legal principles are not as clear as those stated in the Code and difficult questions are presented.

2-96. Anticipatory breach. The majority of the contracts that are not fully performed are breached during the period of performance or after the time for performance has arrived. It is possible, however, for one party by his conduct to give the other party a cause of action before the time for performance has arrived. This situation is known as *anticipatory breach*. Thus, if one party to an agreement should directly inform the other that he will not perform, the latter may take him at his word and terminate the agreement. This termination may be immediately followed by an action to recover damages, although the time for performance has not yet arrived,[3] or the other party has said that he would wait for performance and has urged retraction of the breach. An anticipatory breach may be retracted unless the other party cancels the contract, materially changes his position, or indicates that he considers the repudiation final. If a buyer of goods "covers" the contract by purchasing other goods, this is deemed a material change of position. The above principles are contained in the Code. In those contracts which do not come within the Code, an anticipatory breach may be retracted unless the other party had changed his position in reliance on the breach. In such cases, the breaching party is estopped to change his mind and is prevented from attempting to carry out the original agreement.

The rule of anticipatory breach is not applicable to a promise to pay a money debt, such as a note, bond, or book account. Although the debtor before maturity denies that he will pay the debt when it falls due, the creditor must wait until maturity before bringing suit. In such cases it is not essential that he take action immediately in order to reduce the damages that might otherwise accrue; whereas, in the case of a contract for the erection of a building, it is necessary for the injured party to make another contract as soon as possible after he is informed that the contractor has refused to proceed with the contract.

EXCUSES FOR NONPERFORMANCE

2-97. In general. Even though the contract is silent on the point, a party may be relieved from performing a provision of the contract in-

[3] Whitley Construction Co. v. Va. Supply & Well Co., page 301.

cluding conditions precedent, or his liability for breach of contract may be eliminated, on the ground that he is excused from performing the contract as agreed upon. The law generally has eliminated liability for breach of contract where (1) one party has waived performance by indicating that he does not intend to hold the party to the terms; (2) one party has prevented the other party from carrying out the agreement or he or someone else has frustrated performance of the contract; or (3) the contract itself has become impossible of performance as contrasted with merely becoming more burdensome. In addition, the Code allows substituted performance where the agreed carrier or other facilities become unavailable or the agreed manner of delivery becomes commercially impracticable, and where the agreed means or manner of payment fails because of some governmental regulation. In either case, a reasonable substitute or equivalent method of performance will discharge the contract. The Code also gives sellers an excuse if performance has become impracticable by the failure of presupposed conditions.

2-98. Waiver. The essence of waiver is conduct that indicates an intention not to enforce certain provisions of the agreement. It usually occurs after a breach and is established by some statement or conduct indicating a willingness to forgive the breach. In contracts for the sale of personal property, a waiver must be in writing and delivered to the party in breach. In addition, a waiver may be retracted by reasonable notice unless the retraction would be unjust because of a change of position in reliance on the waiver.

2-99. Prevention and frustration. There arises in every agreement an implied condition that neither party will interfere with the other in his performance or with his normal expectations growing out of the agreement.[4] Should such interference take place, the one attempting performance is relieved of performing and may bring an action to recover damages because of the other's breach of this implied condition. Assume that *A* agrees to sell a house to *B* for a certain sum, it being understood that *A* did not own the house but expected to buy it at a public sale. If, when the public sale takes place, *B* bids against *A*, he is clearly guilty of prevention, and *A* is justified in refusing to perform. Furthermore, *A* may immediately sue *B* for such damages as resulted from the latter's wrongful act.

2-100. Additional hardship. It is customary for those who desire to be relieved of performance in the event unusual circumstances later intervene, to provide therefor in their contract. To this end, the contracts of many industrial concerns provide that the manufacturer shall be relieved from performance in case of fire, strikes, difficulty in obtaining raw ma-

[4] Seggerbruch v. Stosor, page 302.

terials, or other incidents over which it has no control. To be effective, however, it is generally held that such provisions must be included in the body of the agreement. The mere fact that such a statement appears at the top of a letterhead upon which the agreement is written does not affect the rights of the parties unless attention is directed to it at some place in the agreement.

In this connection, it should be emphasized that conditions arising to make performance more difficult or burdensome never, in the absence of a contract clause, afford ground for rescission. Thus, if a contractor has engaged to complete a structure according to specifications for a given sum and has not shifted the risk to the owner by contract, destruction of the partially completed building by a tornado will not relieve him of liability. It is his duty to rebuild, and he should have covered any such loss by insurance.

2-101. Impossibility of performance—generally. True impossibility of performance stems from the nature of the thing promised, rather than from the inability of the particular party to carry out his agreement, except in those cases involving personal services. Thus, one who contracts to sell to *B* 5,000 items manufactured by *X Co.* is not relieved because *X Co.* reduces its production to the point where it refuses to supply more than 2,000 of the items to the seller. The failure of some third party to aid in performance does not excuse the primary obligor of his duty to perform. Real impossibility normally relieves a promisor of his duty to perform, but if such impossibility develops out of negligence or lack of diligence on his part, no release is granted to him. Furthermore, in some cases the ability to perform is the essence of the contract, it having been contemplated at the time of the agreement that performance may or may not have been possible. A promisor who knowingly accepts the risk of performance under such circumstances is in no position to ask for relief when it is later determined that he will be unable to perform.

Let us assume that *A* contracts to sell and deliver 500 bales of cotton from a *certain* plantation, delivery of cotton from any other source not being permitted by contract terms. *A* actually raises only 200 bales, and seeks to be released of his duty to deliver the balance. Naturally, if his inability to deliver has developed out of the fact that he failed to plant a sufficient acreage or was careless in his planting, cultivation, or harvesting of the crop, *A* should not be relieved of his duty to deliver. However, if he planted enough to have produced 800 bales under normal conditions, but the weather or other factors were such as to decrease the yield materially below that which was normally grown, failure to perform would be excused. In such a case, he is obligated to deliver the 200 bales at the contract price, providing the buyer desires such partial performance. Had the parties at the time of making the contract taken into account such contingencies and *A* had nevertheless promised performance, impossibility could not be effectively urged by him as a defense. It is because people seldom take such factors into consideration when making a contract that relief is provided when impossibility develops.

2-102. Impossibility of performance—specific cases. There are four groups of cases in which impossibility of performance may properly be offered as an excuse for nonperformance. The first of these deals with situations in which performance becomes illegal because of the enactment of some law or some act on the part of the government. Illustrative of this situation are instances in which a manfacturer is prevented from making delivery of merchandise because the armed forces make a superior demand for it. In this connection it should be noted that governmental action which merely makes an agreement more burdensome than was anticipated does not afford a basis for relief.

The second is death or incapacitating illness of one of the contracting parties. This is not deemed to be a form of impossibility unless the nature of the contract is such as to demand the personal services of the disabled person. Ordinary contracts of production, processing, and sale of property are unaffected by the death or illness of one or both of the parties. In the event of death, it is assumed that the contract will be carried out by the estate of the deceased.

However, if a contract is one for personal services or is of such a character as clearly to imply that the continued existence of the contracting party is essential to performance, death or illness will excuse nonperformance.[5] If an artist contracts to paint a portrait or an architect agrees to draw plans and specifications for a building, the death or illness of the artist or architect concerned renders performance impossible. The nature of the service to be rendered by them is such as to demand their personal attention. Performance by someone else could not be substituted without the approval of both parties. In contracts for personal services, illness excuses a laborer for his inability to perform, but it does not bar the employer from terminating the contract of employment, provided the employee's absence constitutes a material breach. In such cases, the employee is merely relieved of paying damages for the breach.

In a contract for personal services—one in which the employer-employee relationship exists—death of the employer, as well as of the employee, terminates the relation. His estate is not liable to the employee in damages for prematurely terminating the contract in such a case.

Many agreements involve certain subject matter the continued existence of which is essential to the completion of the contract. As a result, we have the third rule that destruction of any subject matter that is es-

[5] Wasserman Theatrical Enterprise, Inc. v. Harris, page 304.

sential to the completion of the contract will operate to relieve the parties from the obligations assumed by their agreement. Another somewhat analogous situation arises where property that one of the parties expected to use in performance is destroyed. If a factory from which the owner expected to deliver certain shoes is destroyed by fire, performance is not excused, inasmuch as performance is still possible, although an undue hardship may result. But, had the contract stipulated that the shoes were to be delivered from this particular factory, its destruction would have operated to excuse a failure to perform. Stated in other language, the destruction of the source from which one of the parties *expects* to make performance does not relieve him. He is still under duty to obtain the property from some other source. A destruction of the source from which he has *agreed* to make delivery will excuse him, for he is not at liberty to use any other source.

A few of the states have been more liberal in holding that where both parties *understood* delivery was to be made from a certain source, even though it was not expressly so agreed, destruction of the source of supply will relieve the obligor from performing. In these few states the courts read in an implied term to the effect that delivery is to be made from the anticipated source.

The last form of impossibility is where there is an essential element lacking. It has never been very satisfactorily defined. Apparently, where some element or property which the parties assumed existed or would exist is in fact lacking, the agreement may be rescinded. Mere additional burden or hardship is not sufficient to relieve the party from the duties imposed by the agreement, but it must be definitely proved that performance is substantially impossible because of the missing element. A contracts to build an office building at a certain location. Because of the nature of the soil, it is utterly impossible to build the type of building provided for in the agreement; the agreement must therefore be terminated. The missing element is the proper condition of the soil. In other words, from the very beginning the contract terms could not possibly have been complied with, and in such cases the courts are prone to release the contracting party.

2-103. Impracticability. As was mentioned in section 2-97, the Uniform Commercial Code allows substituted performance in shipment or payment in certain situations. In addition, the Code has rejected the strict requirements of the law of impossibility and has recognized that parties to a contract do make certain basic assumptions which, if they later prove to be incorrect, result in one party as a practical matter being unable to perform the agreement. The Code provides that failure of a seller to deliver, or to deliver on time, is not a breach of contract if his performance has been made impracticable by the occurrence of a contingency, the nonoccurrence of which was a basic assumption on which the contract was made. He is also excused if performance is made impracticable by compliance with governmental regulations. If only a portion of the seller's capacity is affected, he must allocate his production in a reasonable manner among his customers. Sellers are required to notify buyers of the delays and the allocations. Buyers are allowed to terminate the whole contract upon receipt of notice of allocation, or they are allowed to negotiate modifications of the agreement. Failure to modify within 30 days of the notice causes the contract to lapse insofar as affected deliveries are concerned.

2-104. Right to recover for part performance—impossibility. Often impossibility of performance becomes apparent only after the agreement has been partially performed. One coat of paint is placed upon a house before it is destroyed. In such cases, is the loss of the work already completed to fall upon the one doing the work or upon the party who was to have the benefit of the labor? Most states permit the person who has partially performed to recover for the value of the benefit the other party would have received had impossibility not arisen. This is simply another way of saying that the recipient of the work must pay for all labor and material expended up to the date of impossibility, provided the labor and material had attached to the property of the one for whom the work was being done.[6]

Care should be taken in such cases, however, to differentiate between impossibility and mere additional burden. The destruction of a partially completed building does not make recovery possible for the work done. Performance is still possible by starting construction anew, although the cost will be greater than was anticipated. The additional cost in the latter case must be borne by the contractor.

2-105. Willful breach—recovery for benefits. Contracts that are willfully and substantially breached after part performance has taken place may or may not confer some benefit on the promisee. Even though a benefit has been conferred, it may be such a one as the promisee may or may not be able to return to the other party. In construction contracts and other contracts of a similar nature, in which the benefit received from partial performance cannot be returned, the person entitled to performance is not required to pay for the benefit conferred upon him.[7] The other party is penalized to that extent because of his failure to perform. Where the breach is unintentional–resulting from a mistake or a misunder-

[6] Carrol v. Bowersock, page 307.

[7] Johnson et al. v. Fehsefeldt, page 308.

standing—the party must pay for the net benefit which he has received. However, such net benefit is automatically taken into account if the damages are computed on the cost of completing the contract.[8]

In those contracts where partial performance confers benefits of such a nature that they can be returned, the recipient must either return the benefits or pay for their reasonable value. In contracts for the sale and purchase of goods, the buyer who receives only a portion of the goods contracted for and still has them when he learns of the breach must either pay their reasonable value, less the damages resulting from the failure to receive the balance of the goods, or return the goods received. He cannot keep the goods and at the same time refuse to pay for the benefits received from them.

DAMAGES

2-106. Specific performance distinguished. As stated before, every breach of a contract that has not been waived, regardless of how trivial in nature, gives rise to a cause of action by the injured party. He is in all cases permitted to recover a judgment which will compensate for the damages sustained. In addition, there are a few instances in which a court of equity will compel the promisor to carry out the express terms of the contract. The remedy is known as specific performance, and it can be insisted upon only in exceptional cases—situations in which the recovery of damages does not fully compensate the injured party.[9] That line of cases, in which the contract calls for the delivery of unique property having some peculiar or intrinsic value, furnishes the most typical illustration of contracts that may be specifically enforced. An agreement which calls for the delivery of a relic of ancient days, a family heirloom, or shares of stock in a closed corporation, may be specifically enforced. A more common type of contract, which is often the subject of specific performance, involves contracts for the sale of real estate. The courts have always held that a certain piece of real estate may have intrinsic worth; therefore, recovery of damages may not fully compensate. Specific performance may usually be demanded whenever the grantor refuses to deed real estate as provided by agreement, or when the buyer refuses to carry out the agreement of purchase.

2-107. Measure of damages. The amount of damages recovered in any case is usually a matter for the jury to determine after proper in-

[8] Bainum v. McGrady, page 308.
[9] Hogan v. Norfleet, page 309.

structions have been received from the court. The recovery allowed is dependent largely upon the evidence presented to the jury. The amount of the judgment varies directly with the proof concerning the injury. It is the duty of the jury to compensate the plaintiff for the loss he has suffered; therefore, if the evidence discloses that no material injury resulted from a breach, only nominal damages are allowed—nominal damages being some small and inconsequential sum allowed merely to denote that a cause of action existed. However, assuming that the breach causes actual loss, it becomes the duty of the jury to place the plaintiff in as good a position as he would have enjoyed—as far as the payment of money can do so—had performance taken place. The judge accepts the conclusion reached by the jury, unless he feels that it has given improper weight to the evidence, in which case he may set aside the verdict of the jury and order a new trial.

2-108. Damages must result from breach. The damages that the jury find to be sustained in any case must be such as the parties contemplate would normally arise from the breach.[10] Unusual and unexpected damage resulting from peculiar facts unknown to both parties at the time the agreement was entered into should not influence the amount of the recovery.

The plaintiff in a cause of action is not entitled to recover the amount which he expends for attorney's fees, unless the contract so provides or special legislation permits it in the particular case. Court costs, however, which include witness fees, filing costs, and so forth, are assessed against the defendant in the event judgment is rendered against him.

2-109. Duty to mitigate damages. As soon as a contract has been breached, it becomes the duty of the party suffering damages to reduce the actual loss to the lowest possible point. He cannot add to his injury or permit the damages to be enhanced when it is reasonably within his power to prevent such occurrence.[11] An employee who has been wrongfully discharged cannot sit idly by and expect to draw his pay. A duty is imposed upon him to seek other work of the same general character.

2-110. Liquidated damages. In order to avoid the expense of litigation, it is customary in certain types of contracts to provide for the amount of damages to be paid for the breach of particular terms. These provisions are legal and will be enforced as long as the court does not consider the stipulation to be a penalty for failure to perform, rather than compensation for damages. Should the court find the term to have been inserted primarily to force actual performance and not to compensate for probable injury, it will not be enforced. In order to be construed as liquidated damages, the amount of recovery agreed upon must bear a close

[10] Brandtjen & Kluge, Inc. v. Hughes, page 311.
[11] Clark v. Marsiglia, page 312.

relation to the probable damage to be sustained by the breach. Once having arrived at the conclusion that the parties intended to compensate for possible damages, the court will not permit either of them to introduce evidence showing the amount of actual damages; recovery is allowed for the amount agreed upon by the parties, although actually the damages suffered may vary somewhat from those agreed upon in the contract.[12]

The Code also seeks to avoid the fixing of unreasonably large liquidated damages by declaring them to be void as a penalty. To be valid, a liquidated-damages clause must be reasonable in light of the anticipated or actual harm caused by the breach, the difficulties of proof of loss, and the inconvenience or nonfeasibility of otherwise obtaining an adequate remedy. The Code further attempts to avoid penalties by allowing a buyer who is in breach of contract to obtain from a seller who has rescinded the contract because of the buyer's breach, restitution of part of his payments if they exceed (1) the amount stated in the liquidated damage clause or (2), if there is no liquidated damage clause, 20 per cent of the contract or $500, whichever is smaller. Thus, a buyer who has made part payment will not be penalized by breaching the contract, and the seller is prohibited from receiving a windfall in excess of $500 or the amount stated as liquidated damages of the seller and any benefit actually received by the buyer.

PERFORMANCE OF CONTRACTS CASES

BONADELLE CONSTRUCTION CO. v. HERNANDEZ

1959 (Cal. App.) 337 P.2d 85

GRIFFIN, J. This is an action for specific performance or damages. On January 9, 1957, respondents (a young war veteran and his wife) signed a deposit receipt for the purchase of a described lot and a house to be erected thereon, according to "Plan 3-H" (corner). The foundation had already been laid. It was orally agreed it would be in accord with the requirements of the Veterans' Administration and similar in appearance to a model house located near-by which was shown to defendants by plaintiff's agent. . . . "Seller hereby agrees with the purchaser that the proposed construction shall be completed in accordance with the plans and specifications submitted to the V.A. under Master C.R.V." Application for the loan was made by defendants and it was duly processed and the house was constructed. Plaintiff executed a grant deed to the property

[12] Smith v. Lane, page 313.

which was placed in escrow about March 15, 1957. Within two days after the exterior color coat stucco of the house had been applied by means of a spray gun, defendants noticed it was streaked and blotched over a great area. Defendants notified the salesman of plaintiff company who negotiated the deal that the house was unsatisfactory and not acceptable to them in that condition. The agent told them to wait about a week and it would dry out in even color. They waited and it was still streaked and blotched. No steps were taken by plaintiff to correct the condition. Several demands were made by defendants to have them do so and each time plaintiff insisted defendants take possession and they would correct the condition afterwards. . . . Defendants refused to accept and orally rescinded the contract. Plaintiff then brought this action. After trial, the court found generally in accordance with the defendants' evidence, as above related, and found, in addition, that the defect was a material one; that plaintiff had ample time and ample notice to correct it, and the failure to do so was willful and intentional. . . .

In this connection it is argued that the failure of a building contractor to comply strictly with construction specifications in some minor matter is not necessarily such failure of performance as would warrant rescission by the owner, and that there is no evidence of plaintiff's failure to perform being willful or intentional. . . .

As said in *Connell v. Higgins, supra* (170 Cal. 541, 150 P. 775), relied upon by plaintiff, "The definition of substantial performance is difficult to give in general terms. It is usually a question to be determined in each case with reference to the existing facts and circumstances." And quoting from 2 *Elliott on Contracts,* Par. 1607, it is said at page 912: " 'Substantial performance means that there has been no willful departure from the terms of the contract, no omission of any of its essential parts, that the contractor has in good faith performed all of its substantive terms. . . . Whether, in any case, such defects or omissions are substantial, or merely unimportant mistakes that have been or may be corrected, is generally a question of fact."

A partial failure of consideration resulting from the willful failure of plaintiff to perform a material part of the contract is sufficient to justify defendants' rescission. . . . The judgment in favor of defendants was justified. The motion for new trial was properly denied.

Judgment affirmed.

SUNSHINE CLOAK & SUIT CO. v. ROQUETTE et al.

1915, 30 N.D. 143, 152 N.W. 259

Sunshine Cloak & Suit Company brought an action to recover $173.25 alleged to be due for certain ladies' cloaks and coats. The evidence indicated that defendant ordered the goods with the understanding that they were to be shipped by August 15, they being fall goods. They were shipped on September 28 and arrived October 12. They were immediately returned to the plaintiff. Lower court gave judgment for the plaintiff.

CHRISTIANSON, J. . . . It is doubtless true, as appellant contends, that time is never considered as the essence of a contract, unless by its terms it is expressly so provided. . . . But, although it is true that time is never considered as the essence of the contract, unless it is so provided by the terms thereof, still it is not necessary to declare in so many words "that time is of the essence of the contract," but it is sufficient if it appears that it was the intention of the parties thereto that time should be of the essence thereof.

The Supreme Court of Iowa, in considering this question in *Bamberger Bros. v. Burrows*, 145 Ia. 441, 450 said: "In the law of sales it is a settled rule that time may be of the essence of the contract; and, when a time for delivery is fixed it is generally so regarded. Therefore, if the seller fails to make delivery on the date so fixed, the buyer may rescind or recover damages for the seller's breach of contract." . . .

In *Cleveland Rolling Mill Co. v. Rhodes*, 121 U.S. 255, that court said: ". . . In the contracts of merchants time is of the essence. The time of shipment is the usual and convenient means of fixing the probable time of arrival, with a view of providing funds to pay for the goods, or of fulfilling contracts with third parties." . . . We are satisfied that the agreement to ship on August 15th was a condition precedent.

Judgment reversed.

WHITLEY CONSTRUCTION CO. v VA. SUPPLY & WELL CO.

1959, (Ga.) 108 S. E.2d 819

QUILLIAN, J. As against general demurrer the truth of all properly pleaded allegations of a petition is to be presumed; . . . and, where in an action, brought in the Civil Court of DeKalb County, to recover the sum of $2,125.67, it is alleged that on a date prior to August 5, 1957, the plaintiff and the defendant, both corporations, entered into an oral agreement, the defendant corporation acting through its duly authorized president, by the terms of which the plaintiff corporation agreed to drill, on the defendant's property, an eight-inch well for water, at the all-inclusive price of $6 per foot drilled, the drilling not to exceed a maximum depth of 600 feet, and the defendant agreed to assume the risk of the depth required to reach water and the risk of the quantity of water encountered; and, where it is further alleged that the plaintiff promptly began drilling operations pursuant to the terms of the agreement; reduced the agreement to writing, asking the defendant to sign and return it, to which request the defendant replied that it had no intention of signing the writing and would not be responsible for the payment for drilling the well unless the well produced 40 gallons per minute at a depth of approximately 400 feet; and, on September 10, 1958, after having drilled to a depth of 354 feet and after another fruitless effort to have the defendant sign the written memorandum, the plaintiff, as a result of the defendant's actions, ceased work on the well, having complied with the terms of the *agreement insofar as it was permitted to do so by the defendant,* the petition stated a cause of action for damages for an anticipatory breach of an executory contract containing mutual promises which was accepted by the plaintiff, and the trial court did not err in overruling the defendant's general demurrer to the petition. The plaintiff alleged the terms of the contract, its performance of the work in compliance with the terms of the contract "insofar as it was permitted to do so by the defendant," the defendant's absolute repudiation of the entire contract prior to the plaintiff's full performance, the prompt acceptance of such repudiation by the plaintiff by its cessation of its drilling operation, and the extent of its damage, measured by the number of feet drilled at the contract rate, plus an item of sales tax due on materials used. These allegations, properly construed most strongly against the pleader, established the defendant's anticipatory breach of the oral contract, accepted by the plaintiff, and the plaintiff's legal excuse for its failure to fully perform. . . .

The defendant's refusal after the inception of the work, to be bound by the original oral contract unless the plaintiff agreed to certain terms different from and entirely repugnant to the provisions of the original contract, constituted an absolute and unequivocal renunciation of the original agreement. *Jordan v. Madsen*, 69 Utah 112, 252 P. 570; *Borochoff v. William Muirhead Const. Co.*, 56 Ga. App. 519, 193 S. E. 118.

As indicated above, the trial court properly overruled the defendant's general demurrer to the petition.

Judgment for plaintiff affirmed.

SEGGERBRUCH v. STOSOR

1941, 309 Ill. App. 385, 33 N. E.2d 159

O'CONNOR, J. . . . March 6, 1940, plaintiff, Grace Turner Seggerbruch, filed a "Separate Action in Chancery" in which, among other things, she alleged that a short time prior to May 1, 1939, defendant, intending to cheat and defraud plaintiff, acquired adjoining real estate and erected a gasoline station thereon; that since May 1, 1939, defendant had refused to have an attendant at the gasoline station located on plaintiff's premises, except that he sold about 200 gallons of gasoline a month from that station while prior to May 1, he had sold approximately 12,000 gallons a month; that defendant was financially insolvent and plaintiff was without an adequate remedy at law; that she was entitled to recover the reasonable rental of the premises which was $150 a month; that the lease be cancelled and plaintiff be given a decree for the amount found due.

Defendant filed his answer in which he alleged he kept an attendant who operated the gasoline station on plaintiff's premises every day, substantially as alleged in his answer to the forcible detainer suit; admitted he sold approximately 12,000 gallons of gasoline per month prior to May 1, 1939; alleged he had asked plaintiff to "enclose the grease and oil rack so that he could more completely service his customers," which plaintiff refused to do, and thereupon he was compelled to erect a gasoline station on the adjoining premises; denied he was insolvent; denied that the reasonable rental value of the premises was $150 per month, and denied that plaintiff was entitled to recover damages.

April 23, 1940, the case was heard before the court without a jury and a decree entered which found the equities in favor of plaintiff; that defendant had maliciously failed and refused to operate the gasoline station on plaintiff's premises for the purpose of defrauding her; that there was due and owing plaintiff $147.50 a month from May 1, 1939, to the date of the entry of the decree. The decree further found the court had theretofore entered judgment at law in the forcible detainer case in plaintiff's favor and against defendant that she recover possession of the premises and it was decreed that plaintiff recover from defendant $1,696.25. Defendant appeals from that part of the decree awarding plaintiff $1,696.25. No appeal was taken from the judgment entered in the forcible detainer case.

Defendant contends he had a right to construct and conduct a station on the adjoining premises because, as stated by counsel, "No minimum rental is fixed and there is no agreement that the defendant will not conduct the same business at any other address"—that since the lease contained no provision on this question defendant was at liberty to conduct the gasoline station on the adjoining premises.

In deciding the case the chancellor said:

> The parties hereto entered into a written lease for the premises and as a rental it is provided that defendant would pay plaintiff 1¾ cents for each gallon of gasoline "sold from the premises each month during the term." . . . During the term created by the lease the defendant built another station immediately adjoining this particular station and began to operate the new place.
>
> The pleadings admit that prior to his occupation of the new station there was sold an average of 12,000 gallons of gas at the station operated under the lease and that immediately after the new station began to be operated the sale

of gas in the old place dropped to some 200 gallons a month. The defendant on the witness stand admits there was no change in the volume of sale at the place so that since the operation of the new station the sales in the two places have reached about the same as the sales in the old place when it was operated alone.

In an undertaking such as we have here the lessee undertakes to operate the premises in such a way as to reasonably produce the rental contemplated by the parties at the time the contract was entered into, and that he will not by his own act deprive the plaintiff of her share of the bargain to which she would be reasonably entitled if the premises continued in the condition in which it was rented without hindrance on the part of the defendant.

Here the defendant willfully and deliberately and purely with the intention of injuring the plaintiff built himself a station right next door and transferred to the new place. Now he stands before the Court and says there is nothing in my contract that I will not cheat the plaintiff by building my own station next door thereby depriving her of income under the lease. Of course, there is not. Certainly the plaintiff could not foresee such a possibility and the law will not stand by and allow such an evident wrong to be committed without finding some remedy. The law will treat the income from the new place as belonging to the old, especially since the evidence clearly shows there was no change in the volume.

We agree with the statement of the chancellor and while there was no express covenant in the lease, it was clearly implied that defendant would use reasonable diligence in operating the gas station on plaintiff's premises. . . .

Judgment for plaintiff.

WASSERMAN THEATRICAL ENTERPRISE, INC. v. HARRIS

1950, 137 Conn. 488, 77 A.2d 329

BROWN, C. J. The plaintiff brought this action to recover damages for the defendant's failure to produce a theatrical performance as provided in a written contract between the parties. The court rendered judgment for the defendant and the plaintiff has appealed.

These facts are not in dispute: On October 30, 1946, the plaintiff entered into a contract with the defendant (Harris) whereby the latter agreed to present Walter Huston in a theatrical performance entitled "The Apple of His Eye" at Worcester, Massachusetts, on the night of December 16, 1946. The contract contained this provision: "(T)his agreement and the terms hereof shall be subject to the customs governing uncontrollable circumstances, such as . . . illness of any of the chief artists of the said attraction and the like, and . . . upon the happening of any such events no claim for compensation or damages shall be made by either party as against the other." The plaintiff which had been engaged in theatrical productions in Worcester for some eleven years, had reason to anticipate a profit from the production and went to considerable expense and effort in preparing to stage it. On December 12, 1946, the defendant canceled the performance on the ground of Huston's illness. At the same time, bookings for Ithaca, Springfield and Rochester, scheduled to follow that for Worcester, were also canceled. The plaintiff has received nothing for its loss incident to the cancellation of the performance and has been at all times ready, able and willing to perform its obligations under the contract. The show, with Huston as leading man, had been on the road since the early fall of 1946. After eight performances a week had been given for four weeks in Boston, it opened in New Haven on December 12, 1946, for four performances and closed on December 14. As scheduled, the show opened for a month in Chicago on December 25. Huston participated in every performance given and had no understudy.

The defendant alleged as a special defense the provision of the contract quoted above, that Huston was the chief artist and essential performer in the production, and that by reason of his illness performance of the contract on December 16, 1946, was rendered impossible on the part of the defendant. Whether the court was warranted in sustaining this defense and, in reliance thereon, rendering judgment for the defendant is the question for determination. "One who engages for performance of such personal character that it can be performed only by a particular person is excused from liability by the physical incapacity of that person, before breach of the contract unless he has clearly assumed the risk of such incapacity. . . . Generally it is the promisor himself who is to render the personal services, but the principle is applicable to contracts where the promisor has agreed that a third person shall render such services and the latter becomes physically unable to do so. . . ." 6 Williston, Contracts (Rev. Ed.) § 1940. The quoted provision of the contract therefore is substantially declaratory of the condition which arises by implication in an agreement of this nature. An agreement for personal services, in the absence of a manifested contrary intention, is always subject to the condition, implied by law, that the person who is to render the services shall be able to perform at the appointed time. . . .

In the view which we take of the case, the only conclusion of the court requiring consideration was that Huston's apprehension as to the state of his health was reasonable and reasonably justified the defendant in canceling the performance. The rule quoted is amplified by this further principle: "Where a promisor apprehends before . . . the time for performance of a promise in a bargain . . . that performance will seriously jeopardize his own life or health or that of others, he is not liable, unless a contrary intention is manifested or he is guilty of contributing fault, for failing to begin . . . performance, while such apprehension exists, if the failure to begin . . . performance is reasonable. . . ." Restatement, 2 Contracts Section 465. "Out of regard for human welfare the rule is often applicable . . . though performance is not only practicable but is not increased in difficulty. The possible consequences of performing may be so injurious as to free the promisor; and the fact that it later appears that no harmful consequences would have ensued does not alter the rule. The promisor is not bound to perform so long as failure to perform is reasonable because of existing ground for apprehension. . . ."

The further facts established by the finding as corrected and material upon this issue, which is sufficiently raised by the special defense, may be thus summarized: While playing in Boston, Huston, for some two weeks prior to December 12, experienced a tickling sensation in his throat, and during this time the condition became progressively worse. As often as two or three times during a performance he experienced a tightening of his throat. Although use of a medication afforded him temporary relief, he had similar difficulty while performing on the stage in New Haven on December 12, 13, and 14. His throat condition was a continuous and increasing cause of worry to him for he was constantly in fear during a performance that he would be unable to finish it. This fear did not affect him in social intercourse off the stage, but because of his apprehension that he could not go on with the show in the face of the recurring throat sensation he wanted to find out definitely the nature of his ailment. Had he kept the engagement in Worcester, and had his throat tightened, he probably could have completed the performance with the aid of lozenges. He had consulted a doctor in New York three or four times in the spring of 1946. The only doctor Huston consulted during November and December, 1946, was Dr. Loyal Davis, his personal friend, who, after hearing his symptoms, though no examination was made, advised him to go to Chicago for a complete and thorough examination and to have the condition attended to. Huston's throat attacks were becoming more frequent and he felt impelled to do something about them without delay. While he believed he could complete the New Haven engagement, he insisted upon canceling all performances for the week of December 16 in order to look after his throat condition immediately, for he believed it would be impossible for him to continue after concluding in New Haven. He was gravely concerned over the consequences of any delay in procuring medical attention.

From New Haven he proceeded to Chicago. A minor operation was performed on his throat at a hospital there and specimens of tissue were taken. The report that these disclosed no malignant condition relieved his mind, and he was able to resume his next scheduled performances in Chicago, where he played every performance. Huston was a man with a sincere desire to carry out his obligations. During his entire theatrical career of forty-five years, the only request which he had made for the cancellation of a performance was for the one at Worcester. The court's conclusion that Huston's fear and apprehension that his illness was of such a nature that it would, in the absence of immediate expert medical attention, seriously jeopardize his health and particularly his voice was a reasonable one and was warranted upon the facts set forth in the preceding paragraph.

There is no error. Judgment for defendant affirmed.

CARROL v. BOWERSOCK

1917, 100 Kan. 270, 164 Pac. 143

This action by Carrol was brought to recover for the part performance of a contract to construct a reinforced concrete floor in a warehouse. It appears that a fire destroyed the warehouse after the old floor had been cut away and some forms built and a few concrete footings poured. Certain floor rods were also in place but not permanently attached.

Burch, J. . . . The contractor cannot give and the owner cannot obtain that which they have contracted about. Neither one can complain of the other on that account, and the law must deal with the new situation of the parties created by the fire. The owner cannot be called upon to reimburse the contractor merely because the contractor has been to expense in taking steps tending to performance. . . . The owner must be benefited. He should not be enriched at the expense of the contractor. That would be unjust, and to the extent that the owner has been benefited, the law may properly consider him as resting under a duty to pay. The benefit which the owner has received may or may not be equivalent to the detriment which the contractor has suffered. . . .

The test of benefit received has been variously stated. Sometimes it is said that benefit accrues whenever the contractor's material and labor, furnished and performed according to the contract, have been attached to the owner's realty. . . . "In whatever way the principle may be stated, it would seem that the liabilty of the owner in a case like this should be measured by the amount of the contract work done which, at the time of the destruction of the structure, had become so far identified with it as that but for the destruction it would have inured to him as contemplated by the contract." 186 Mass. 520.

. . . The test is whether or not the work would have inured to his benefit as contemplated by the contract if the fire had not occurred. . . .

(Recovery was allowed for cutting away old floor and concrete footings, but not for form work or rods in place which had not been attached.)

JOHNSON et al. v. FEHSEFELDT

1908, 106 Minn. 202, 118 N. W. 797

Plaintiffs were owners of a threshing outfit and entered into an agreement to thresh Fehsefeldt's grain. They abandoned the work after completing only part of it. They now seek to recover for the portion completed. The lower court directed a verdict for the plaintiffs for the work they had done at the agreed price per bushel. Defendant appeals.

JAGGARD, J. . . . The essential question is whether the contract was entire and indivisible, in the sense that the plaintiffs could not recover upon a quantum meruit or upon the contract to the extent to which it had been performed. On principle we are of the opinion that plaintiffs could not recover. When they found that they were operating at a loss, they had the option to complete the contract, recover the contract price, and submit to the loss, or to abandon the contract, lose the work they had done, and be subject to whatever damages might be recoverable for the breach of the contract. The fact that plaintiffs had rendered services, the value of which the defendant retained, did not entitle plaintiffs to recover on quantum meruit because of the contract and of the inability of the defendants to return the services. . . .

It would be obviously inconsistent with common justice that plaintiffs should recover pro tanto on the contract which they had substantially violated. They were in the wrong. They were not in a position to say to the defendant: "We will perform the contract we have agreed to if it proves profitable. If we find it unprofitable, we will abandon it." That would be to contradict the contract.

Judgment reversed.

BAINUM v. McGRADY

1955, (M.Ct. of App. D. C.) 117 A.2d 462

CAYTON, C. J. Bainum was the contractor on a school building project and McGrady was his electrical subcontractor. Following a dispute between them, the subcontractor left the job. The contractor later sued him for the difference between the amount of the subcontract and the actual cost of completing the work. The subcontractor defended on the ground that he had left the project because of plaintiff's breach and he demanded by way of counterclaim the value of labor and materials supplied on the job prior to the cancellation. The trial judge found that there was "no material breach of the contract by the plaintiff" and that defendant was not justified in leaving the job uncompleted. He awarded plaintiff $1,500 but from that award made a deduction of $650 by way of credit to defendant for work and materials furnished prior to the breach. Both parties have appealed.

Plaintiff's appeal is based on the contention that he was entitled to the full amount of $1,500 and that it was [an] error to allow a credit against that amount. . . .

Plaintiff's appeal: The question is as to the right of one who has improperly breached a contract to recover for such benefit as he may have conferred on the other party by part performance. While there has been some difference of opinion among courts on this subject, most courts have allowed recovery where the breach, though wrongful, was not shown to have been willful and deliberate. (See *Williston on Contracts,* 3d ed. Section 1475, p. 4123, and cases cited therein.) But such recovery has generally been restricted to situations where the benefit conferred by the defaulting party exceeds the damage sustained by the innocent party on account of the breach.

In *Restatement, Contracts,* p. 357, it is said: ". . . Where the defendant fails or refuses to perform his contract and is justified therein by the plaintiff's own breach of duty or nonperformance of a condition, but the plaintiff has rendered a part performance under the contract that is a net benefit to the defendant, the plaintiff can get judgment . . . for the amount of such benefit in excess of the harm that he has caused to the defendant by his own breach . . . if (a) the plaintiff's breach or nonperformance is not willful and deliberate. . . ." (Emphasis supplied.) This position has been accepted as the rule in the federal courts. See *Amtorg Trading Corp. v. Miehle Printing Press & Mfg. Co.,* 2 Cir., 1953, 206 F.2d 103.

In this case, even if we assume that the subcontractor was guilty of no conscious moral fault in leaving the project and that his breach was not willful and deliberate, the fact remains that he did not confer a "net benefit" on the plaintiff prior to the breach. It is clear that plaintiff sustained actual damage in the amount of $1,500, representing the difference between the amount of his original contract with defendant and of the second contract for completion of the job. It is true that defendant did work on the job amounting to $650. But that did not result in a net benefit to plaintiff, because proceeding from that point plaintiff had to spend $1,500 to have the work completed. *Consequently, plaintiff* (Bainum) *was entitled to a judgment for that amount.*

HOGAN v. NORFLEET

1959 (Fla. App.) 113 S.2d 437

Moody, J. Appellant, plaintiff below, brought a suit for specific performance after exercising his option to purchase a franchised bottled gas business. The appellee, defendant below, filed a motion to dismiss and, upon hearing, the court dismissed the complaint, or in the alternative, granted plaintiff leave to file a suit on the law side of the court. To this order plaintiff filed interlocutory appeal.

Defendant is the owner of Norfleet Gas and Appliance, a bottled gas business based on a franchise covering a particular territory. The complaint alleges that in October, 1951, defendant induced the plaintiff to enter his business stating that he needed help in his business and planned to retire; that if the plaintiff would work for him the defendant would sell his business to the plaintiff and that in furtherance thereof, in December 1952, the parties signed a written option setting forth the price and terms under which the plaintiff could purchase said business if such option were exercised. The complaint further alleges plaintiff exercised his option in October, 1957, but that the defendant has failed and refused to transfer said business to the plaintiff; that said business is prosperous; that it is the type of business and franchise which cannot be obtained in the open market; that the plaintiff fully performed his part of the agreement, and, that defendant should be required to convey all of the assets of said business including the franchise and privileges of such business.

The sole point argued on appeal and the only point covered in this opinion is whether or not specific performance should be granted for the sale of the business as set forth in the complaint. The general rule is that, although the remedy of specific performance is available to enforce contracts for the sale of realty, specific performance of contracts relating to personal property will not be enforced for the reason that ordinarily compensation for breach of contract may be had by way of an action at law for damages. Such an action would be regarded as fully adequate.

The apparent reluctance of equity to grant specific performance of (a) contract relating to personalty does not arise from any less regard for contracts involving contracts for personalty than for those involving realty, but is simply a corollary of the principle upon which equity acts in decreeing specific performance, namely, the inadequacy of the remedy at law for damages. . . .

Our Florida courts have held that specific performance of a contract is a matter of equitable cognizance as applied both to real and personal property, and where, in the case of personal property, it is of a peculiar character and value, specific performance will be granted. . . .

In the case now before us, it appears the contract of sale involves a going business including good will and an operating franchise covering a particular territory. Obviously, such a franchise would not be available in the open market and its value would be very difficult, if not impossible, to ascertain. The value of good will or of a going business is an intangible asset of an indefinite, speculative or uncertain value. The contract executed in 1952 provides the method of determining the purchase price.

However, the measure of damages in an action at law would entail the determination of the *present* value of such business which involves elements of going business value, good will and prospective profits. Certainly these are matters which cannot be readily ascertainable or fixed and could not conform with the rule in a law action that any recoverable damages must be susceptible to reasonable ascertainment.

For the reasons stated the decree is reversed and the cause is remanded for further appropriate proceedings.

BRANDTJEN & KLUGE, INC. v. HUGHES

1951, (Tex. Civ. App.), 236 S.W.2d 180

COLLINGS, J. This case was brought by Jack Hughes, plaintiff, doing business as Hughes Printing & Office Supply Company, against appellant, Brandtjen & Kluge, a corporation, claiming damages for the breach of a written contract. Hughes alleged that on October 25, 1945 appellant, by and through its duly authorized agent, entered into a written contract by which appellant agreed to sell and he agreed to buy a 12 x 18 four roller Kluge Automatic Platen Press for a stated consideration of $1,785.00; that by the terms of the contract such amount was to be paid $50.00 at the time of the execution of the contract, $307.00 upon delivery of such printing press and the balance in 29 monthly installments, beginning 30 days after the installation of the press. . . .

Hughes filed suit on September 9, 1948. He alleged the reasonable value of the press at that time to be $4,000.00 and asked judgment for the difference in such reasonable value and the contract price. He also alleged that by reason of appellant's failure to deliver the press, which operated automatically without a press feeder, it has been necessary for him to employ an experienced printer to feed his old presses for 104 weeks at $60.00 per week, or a total $6,240.00 and asked judgment for such amount.

On January 20, 1949, appellant, as shown by its pleading, tendered said printing press to Hughes and the tender was accepted. Hughes alleged, however, in his amended pleading that the acceptance of such tender in no way compensated him for the special damages suffered because of appellant's failure to deliver the press for a period of more than three years; that appellant knew that the press it contracted to deliver was automatic and could be operated without the necessity of being fed by an experienced printer; that appellant could have delivered such press on or before January 1, 1947, but failed and refused to do so until the tender on January 20, 1949; that because of such failure and refusal to deliver the automatic press, appellee was required to pay a skilled printer $60.00 per week for 104 weeks to feed his old presses and that the loss and damages resulting therefrom was $6,240.00, for which sum he prayed judgment.

The jury, in answer to special issues, found: (1) that under the circumstances appellant delayed an unreasonable time in delivering the press; (2) that appellee Hughes suffered special damages in the sum of $3,120.00 as money paid for extra help as a direct result of such delay; (3) that appellant knew that an unreasonable delay in delivery would result in special damages; (4) that appellant's delay was not caused by priority regulations issued by the Civil Production Administration; and (5) that such delay was not the result of a condition over which defendant had no control. Based upon such jury findings, judgment was entered for Hughes in the sum of $3,120.00. Brandtjen & Kluge bring this appeal.

It is contended in appellant's first point that since there was "no proof of notice of special damages accruing to plaintiff" the court erred in refusing to give an instructed verdict for appellant. In our opinion, there was proof of notice to appellant of such special damages. The evidence shows that appellant was a manufacturer of printing presses; that the press decribed in the contract was automatic and required no one to feed it. It was built for the purpose of eliminating a press feeder. Hughes testified that this was the "main selling point" urged by appellant's agent. The presses which Hughes owned and used in his printing business prior to the purchase and delivery of the press in question, were not automatic and required the presence of a printer to feed them when they were in operation. Appellant's agent inspected Hughes' shop and at the time of making the contract knew the kind of equipment and presses that he had. There is no question but that the agent who sold the press was acting within the course of his employment with his principal when he made the sale. It was on this occasion that he acquired such knowledge. Appellant accepted and endorsed the contract as provided and required by the contract to fix its liability. Under these facts appellant was charged with knowledge that delay in delivery of the press would result in damages to Hughes. . . .

The jury found there was an unreasonable delay in delivering the press and that the damages suffered by Hughes by reason of such delay was $3,120.00. These findings are supported by both pleadings and evidence and are the basis of the judgment rendered. . . .

The judgment of the trial court is affirmed.

CLARK v. MARSIGLIA

1845, 1 Den. (N.Y.) 317

Assumpsit by Clark for work, labor, and material. The defendant delivered to the plaintiff a number of paintings to be cleaned and repaired at an agreed price. After the work was begun, the defendant directed the plaintiff to stop, but the latter persisted and is now attempting to recover the full contract price. The lower court charged the jury that, as the plaintiff had begun work, he had a right to finish and that the defendant could not revoke the order.

PER CURIAM. The question does not arise as to the right of the defendant below to take away these pictures, upon which the plaintiff had performed some labor, without payment for what he had done, and his damages for the violation of the contract, and upon that point we express no opinion. The plaintiff was allowed to recover as though there had been no countermand of the order; and in this the court erred. The defendant, by requiring the plaintiff to stop work upon the paintings, violated his contract and thereby incurred a liability to pay such damages as the plaintiff should sustain. Such damages would include a recompense for the labor done and materials used, and such further sum in damages as might, upon legal principles, be assessed for the breach of the contract; but the plaintiff had no right by obstinately persisting in the work to make the penalty upon the defendant greater than it would otherwise have been.

To hold that one who employs another to do a piece of work is bound to suffer it to be done at all events would sometimes lead to great injustice. . . . In all such cases the just claims of the party employed are satisfied when he is fully recompensed for his part performance and indemnified for his loss, in respect to the part left unexecuted; and to persist in accumulating a larger demand is not consistent with good faith toward the employer.

Judgment reversed.

SMITH v. LANE

1951, (Tex. Civ. App.), 236 S.W.2d 214

W. O. MURRAY, C. J. This suit was instituted by Blaze H. Lane against Pinkie Smith, seeking to recover the amount of liquidated damages provided for in two contracts in the total sum of $780.00. Defendant, though served with citation, did not answer and judgment by default in that amount was rendered. From that judgment this appeal has been prosecuted by Pinkie Smith, through the means of a writ of error.

By the terms of the first contract sued on Lane agreed to loan to Smith the sum of $500.00. Smith agreed to seek, permit and provide a suitable place for the operation of Lane's Juke Boxes and Coin-operated Music Machines "at 628 E. Commerce Street, at the place of business now owned and operated by Smith in the City of San Antonio and being known as Deluxe Cafe, also at 106 Sycamore Street and at any other place that Smith might open or engage in a business." No other Juke Boxes were to be permitted to operate upon such premises for a violation of which the sum of $500.00 was agreed upon as "liquidated damages, because of the inconvenience of ascertaining the actual damages and the uncertainty thereof." Smith was to receive one-half of all funds and money deposited in the Juke Boxes, but such payment was first to be applied to the payment of the loan until it was completely paid back to Lane.

The second contract was exactly the same as the first, except the loan was for the sum of $280.00 and the liquidated damages was for the same amount.

A breach of these two contracts was alleged and a default judgment was rendered, as above stated, for the stipulated liquidated damages in the sum of $780.00.

Appellant's first contention is that the provisions for damages in the event of a breach, were for penalties and not for liquidated damages, as such. It will be borne in mind that the defendant did not file an answer herein or in any way raise the issue at the trial, but, on the other hand, wholly made default. The provision not only referred to the damages as "liquidated damages" but further gave the reason why liquidated damages were agreed upon, to wit, "because of the inconvenience of ascertaining the actual damages and the uncertainty thereof." It is true the courts are inclined to construe such provision as one for a penalty rather than as for liquidated damages, as such, but this is true only where the defendant appears and by both allegation and proof raises the issue. Under such circumstances the burden of proof is upon the defendant. 13 Tex. Jur., Damages, §§ 46 and 54. . . .

Here the damages were indefinite and uncertain and, in view of the language of the contracts and the default of appellant, the trial court properly construed the contracts as providing for liquidated damages and not for penalties.

Appellant next contends that the contracts were void because their provisions seek to establish a monopoly and are in restraint of trade, thereby violating § 26 of Art. 1, of the State Constitution, Vernon's Ann. St.

The provisions of the contract only granted to appellee the exclusive right to place on the premises of appellant the Coin-operated Music Machines belonging to appellee and in consideration thereof to allow appellant to participate in one-half of the revenue produced by the machines. There is nothing in the record to indicate that these contracts tended to establish a monopoly or were in restraint of trade and the point is overruled.

Appellant's third point presents the contention that the contracts were void in that they did not provide for a specified duration or time of performance. The contracts were silent as to when they should terminate. Under such circumstances they are not necessarily void. They may be construed as lasting for a reasonable time or during the life of the promisee, or so long as he may continue in business. *Schlag v. Johnson,* Tex. Civ. App., 208 S.W. 369; *Langever v. United Advertising Corp.,* Tex. Civ. App., 258 S.W. 856. We overrule appellant's third and last point.

The judgment is affirmed.

Review Questions and Problems

1. A Co. installed and leased to E at his restaurant a burglar alarm system for five years at a certain rental, A Co. to maintain and repair said system as needed. The state condemned E's property for public use. A Co. sued for rental falling due thereafter, and E claimed impossibility as a defense. The court denied any recovery by A Co. In your judgment, was this a good decision?
2. A contracts to paint a picture of B's wife and to have it completed by October 1. He fails to complete the picture until the following January. May B rescind the agreement?
3. S Co. on October 15 contracted with G to care for him for life for $8,500, care to begin on November 1. G paid the money but died two days before November 1, and his executor seeks to recover the $8,500 paid by G. The court permitted recovery. Does this seem to you to be a fair decision?
4. C contracted to build a residence for O according to specifications at a stipulated cost. He departed substantially from specifications at several points, reducing his costs materially. O refused to pay anything, and C brought suit. Is C entitled to recover anything for work done?
5. S sold a line of greeting cards to B and agreed that the latter could have the exclusive agency in a medium-sized community. The cards were shipped; B learned that S sold the same line to other dealers, and he refused to pay for cards received. The court held that he must pay for them, less $1 in damages, concluding that the exclusive dealership clause was relatively unimportant. Was the decision sound?
6. A, a schoolteacher, is hired by the B School Board for a term of eight months at $300 a month. After school has been in progress for two months, the school building is destroyed by fire. The Board refuses to pay any further salary to A. May he recover?
7. S contracted to sell and deliver to B 500 bales of cotton at a later date. The cotton crop of S was seriously reduced by pests and unfavorable weather conditions, and he raised only 200 bales. He delivered the 200 bales to B but refused to deliver an additional 300 bales. B brought suit for damages. Should he have succeeded?
8. C contracted to do a considerable amount of work on improving O's residence, part of the work involving the addition of millwork. After some of the work had been done, the residence was destroyed by fire, leaving C with $2,000 of millwork on hand that he was to use on the

job but that has little value for use elsewhere. *C* seeks to recover of *O* for the value of the millwork. Should he succeed?

9. *S* contracted to sell and deliver to *B* 300,000 gallons of molasses produced by *X* Company during a certain year, the price being agreed upon. *X* Company reduced its output and refused to let *S* have as much as he needed to fill his contracts. Because of this fact, *S* claims to be released of his liability to *B* on the basis of impossibility. Was impossibility present?
10. *A* contracted to perform certain excavation work for the city of Chicago. After he had completed about one-half the work, he refused to continue, because of the pressure of other work. The city procured another contractor to complete the work at approximately one-half the original contract price. Has the original contractor a right to recover for the work performed by him? Ethically is it wiser to penalize *A* for his wilful breach, or it is sounder to make the city pay for the net benefit it receives?
11. *G* promised to sell *A*, an employee of United Cleaning Company, 75 shares of its stock for $7,500, the corporation being a small one whose shares were not readily available. *G* refused to carry out the agreement and *A* filed a bill for specific performance. Should he recover?
12. *S* contracted to sell to *B* 365,000 yards of certain cloth at 8.9375 cents per yard. War intervened before time for shipment and the O.P.A. established a maximum price of 8.037 cents for such cloth. *S* refused to deliver any cloth under the contract. Has *B* a cause of action against *S*?
13. *H* Co. agreed to repair the refrigeration system on *M*'s ship and to test it for effectiveness at cost of $4,700. The work was done but before *H* Co. could test it, *M* took ship on trip. *M* claims to have suffered damages because work was not effective. In spite of this, the court allowed recovery by *H* Co. What defense did *H* Co. have against *M*'s claim of poor workmanship?
14. *M*, who had given to *H* a mortgage on certain property as security for a loan of $3,000 and interest, offered at maturity the proper amount in payment of the debt. *H*, being mistaken as to the amount of interest due, refused to accept the payment. He later began foreclosure proceedings. Had he a right to foreclose?
15. *W* sued *S* for loss of value of a boat which *S*, an experienced operator in salvaging submerged boats, had agreed to raise and keep afloat until it reached harbor. Before *S* could begin operation the boat slipped off the reef and sank in deep water, making it impossible to raise it. The court held this did not relieve *S* of liability. Is the decision sound?
16. *O* leased property to *T* for five years, which the latter expected to use in sale of automobiles. War intervened, automobiles were not available, and *T* desires to be released of his contract. Is the contract binding?

14

Rights of Third Parties

ASSIGNMENT

2-111. Nature of assignment. A contract creates both rights and duties. It gives to the contracting parties certain rights protected by law and at the same time imposes upon them prescribed duties. An *assignment* consists of some act whereby one party transfers his rights under a contract, or some portion of them, to a third party. The transferor is known as the *assignor,* whereas the one receiving the assignment is called the *assignee.* Where contract rights are conditioned upon the performance of certain duties, it is customary to say that the contract as a whole has been assigned.

2-112. Requisites of assignment. No particular formality is essential to an assignment. Consideration, although usually present, is not required. However, an assignment without consideration, where the right involved has not been realized through the collection of money or receipt of other performance, may in most states be rescinded by the assignor by notice to the debtor or obligor.

Unless the contract assigned deals with real or personal property covered by the Statute of Frauds, an assignment may be either oral or written, although it is better to have a written assignment. Any contract, including the rights arising therefrom, may be assigned provided both parties to the agreement are willing. The more important question deals with the effect of an assignment where the other party to the original contract refuses to respect it. In the sections immediately following, an attempt is made to suggest the particular legal principles which are helpful in determining those rights and contracts that may be assigned even over the protest of the other party.[1]

2-113. Personal rights. Contracts often grant rights which are quite personal or confidential in character, the very nature of which seems to forbid their transfer. Clearly, such rights may not be assigned effectively without the consent of the person against whom the right is to be enforced. Illustrative of such rights are (1) the right to services of a particu-

[1] Hubbard v. Goode, page 323.

lar employee or agent;[2] (2) the right to have a particular artist paint a portrait; and (3) the right to purchase goods of a particular manufacturer and to resell them at retail in an agreed area. Agreements of the character mentioned are so personal in nature or involve so high a degree of trust and confidence between the parties that their transfer may not be perfected without the approval of all interested parties. The Code provides that rights cannot be assigned where the assignment would materially change the duty of the other party, or increase materially the burden or risk imposed on him by his contract, or impair materially his chance of obtaining return performance.

2-114. Purchases on credit. If the assignment of a contract right places an additional burden or risk upon the obligor that was not contemplated at the time he made the agreement, the assignment is not effective unless he assents to it. Such appears to be true of sales of merchandise on credit. Although there is some conflict on the matter, most states appear to hold that one who has agreed to purchase goods on credit may not assign to a third party his right to purchase the goods, since the latter's credit may not be as good as that of the original buyer. Although upon delivery of the goods to the assignee and his failure to pay, the seller could nevertheless look to the assignor for payment, the courts incline to the view that an assignment of the right to buy on credit is not enforceable by the assignee against the seller. In those contracts involving the sale of real estate or personal property on installments secured by a mortgage or retention of title, the seller is fairly well secured regardless of the credit standing of the buyer. Consequently, the right to buy in such cases is generally held to be assignable.

2-115. Claims for money. All claims for money, due or to become due under existing contracts, may be assigned. In this connection, it should be borne in mind that an assignment is more than a mere authorization or order directed to the debtor since an authorization or order leaves the option of payment to the debtor.

A question often arises concerning the liability of the assignor in case the assignee is unable to collect from the debtor. If the assignee takes the assignment merely as security for a debt owing from the assignor to the assignee, it is clear that, if the assigned claim is not collected, the assignor is still liable to pay his debt. On the other hand, it should be equally plain that if the assignee purchases a claim against a third party, he should have no recourse against the assignor unless the claim proves invalid for some reason or unless the claim is sold expressly with recourse.

In any event, the assignor warrants that the claim which he assigns is a genuine claim. In case there is a defense available to the third party

[2] Wetherell Bros. Co. v. United States Steel Co., page 325.

debtor and the claim cannot be collected, the assignor must return the amount which he has received from the assignee.

2-116. Rights of the assignee. Unless the contract being assigned provides otherwise, the assignee receives the identical rights of the assignor. Since the rights of the assignee are neither better nor worse than those of the assignor, any defense of the third party available against the assignor is available against the assignee.[3] Part payment, fraud, duress or incapacity can be set up against the assignee as well as against the assignor. Because of this fact it is becoming customary to insert a clause in a contract of sale that the buyer waives any defense he may have against the seller in case the seller assigns the contract to a third party. Thus far, the courts seem inclined to enforce such a clause, although installment sale contracts by statute in several states may not effectively include such a clause.

If the assignee buys a claim which is subject to a defense, the assignee has a claim against the assignor. The assignor of a claim impliedly warrants that the claim assigned is a genuine one and free from defenses.

It is customary for certain contracts to contain a provision that they are nonassignable. The majority of the states strictly enforce such a provision. A few hold an assignment of such a contract to be valid, although allowing damages to be recovered for a breach of this provision. Under the Code, a prohibition of assignment of "the contract" is construed as only prohibiting the delegation of the assignor's duties, unless the circumstances of the case clearly indicate that the rights are also not assignable even though the agreement is to the contrary. The Code takes the position that a claim for damages for breach of the whole contract ought always to be assignable.

2-117. Wages. An employee entitled to wages under a contract of employment can make a binding assignment of his wages to be earned with that particular employer. In case the wages have been earned, the assignee has the right immediately to collect them. If they have not been earned, the assignment is nevertheless valid, the right to collect being deferred until they are earned.

The power to assign wages is limited in one particular. A mere expectancy cannot be assigned, since only existing contract rights may be assigned. Therefore, an assignment of future wages to be earned at a certain profession or trade when the assignor at the time is not employed is ineffective. A wage assignment is valid, provided the assignor is employed, although the duration of his employment depends upon the will of the employer.

Recently a tendency has been observed to enact legislation which

[3] American Bridge Co. et al. v. City of Boston, page 327.

limits the portion of future wages that may be effectively assigned. Many states now provide that an assignment of more than one-fourth of future wages shall not be enforceable, and have indicated the method for determining the priority where various assignees are involved. Other safeguards have been established to protect the employee against unusual and unsuspected assignments being included in ordinary contracts of sale.

2-118. Delegation of duties. Certain duties imposed by contract are so personal and confidential in character that it is unreasonable to assume that any person can perform them except the contracting party. If the duties are not of this type and may be performed as well by one person as another, it is said that they can be *delegated.* Contracts which call upon a party to perform such nonpersonal duties may be assigned in such a way as to give the assignee the privilege of performing the duties which are conditions precedent to the right he seeks to enforce. To illustrate: a building contractor is not expected to do all the work on any particular building, it being understood that he will delegate responsibility for certain portions of the structure. If the construction is to be done according to agreed specifications, the agreement to build is assignable. It is presumed that all contractors are able to follow specifications, and since the duties are mechanical in nature, the owner is bound to permit the assignee to build. However, if the assignee fails to do a good job, the assignor is liable to the same degree as if he were performing. In some respects it is as if two rights were being assigned, the right to build and the right to collect the contract price. When and if the building is properly completed, the assignee is entitled to collect the contract price.

2-119. Responsibility for performance. Failure on the part of the assignee to perform the duties gives rise to a cause of action by the obligee. In the majority of the states he can elect to sue either the assignor or the assignee, provided the assignee has agreed, expressly or by implication, to assume the burdens of the contract. Except in those contracts under the Code, the mere assignment, with nothing more, of a contract which calls for the performance of affirmative duties by the assignor, does not impose those duties upon the assignee, although there is a decided trend to hold that an assignment of an entire contract carries an implied assumption of the liabilities. It is only where the assignee undertakes to perform as a condition precedent to enforcement of the rights, or has promised to perform as part of the contract of assignment, that he has any true liability for failure to perform. To illustrate: if a tenant assigns a lease, the assignee is not liable for future rents after he vacates the property unless he expressly assumes the burdens of the lease at the time of the assignment. This is true even though he vacates the property before the lease expires. To the extent that an assignee accepts the benefits of a contract that are predicated upon the performance of duties later to be undertaken, he becomes obligated to perform those duties. However, if he merely receives the assignment of a right to purchase or to lease, he is not liable for the purchase price or the rental unless he demands title to, or possession of, the realty.

Under the Code, an assignment of a contract or of all the rights under a contract is a delegation of duties which the assignee assumes unless the contract provides otherwise or the assignment is given as security.

The assignor, of course, is not released by an agreement on the part of the assignee to assume the burdens of the contract. In such a case, the third party has his choice of holding either the original contracting party or the assignee. He cannot be denied his claim against the assignor without his consent.

2-120. Notice. Immediately after the assignment, the assignee should notify the third party of his newly acquired right. This notification is essential for two reasons:

1. In the absence of any notice of the assignment, the third party is at liberty to perform—pay the debt or do whatever else the contract demands—for the original contracting party. In fact, he has no knowledge of the right of anyone else to require performance. Thus, the right of the assignee to demand performance can be defeated by his failure to give notice. The assignor who receives performance under such circumstances becomes in turn a trustee of funds or of property received and can be compelled to turn them over to the assignee. As soon as notice is given, however, the third party must perform for the assignee.[4]

2. The notice of assignment is for the protection of innocent third parties. The assignor has the power, although not the right, to make a second assignment of the same subject matter. If notice of the assignment has been given, it has much the same effect as the recording of a mortgage. It furnishes protection for the parties who may later consider taking an assignment of the same right. One taking an assignment should, therefore, always confirm the existence of the right by communicating with the debtor. If the debtor has not been notified of a previous assignment, and if the assignee is aware of none, the latter can, in many states, feel free to take the assignment, but should immediately give notice to the debtor. In other words, the first assignee to give notice, provided he has no knowledge of a prior assignment, has, in what is probably the majority of the states, a superior claim to the right assigned.[5]

In many other states, it is held that the first party to receive an assign-

[4] Russell v. Fred G. Pohl Co., page 328.
[5] Adamson v. Paonessa et al., page 329.

ment has a prior claim, regardless of which one gives notice first. In all states, however, the party who is injured by reason of the second assignment has a cause of action against the assignor to recover the damages which he has sustained.

CONTRACTS FOR BENEFIT OF THIRD PARTIES

2-121. Nature of such contracts. Contracts are often made with the express purpose of benefiting some third party. The most typical example of such agreements is the contract for life insurance in which the beneficiary is someone other than the insured. The insured often does not others who may have an interest in his life.

Another illustration may be taken from mortgages. Real property is often conveyed with an outstanding mortgage against it, and in such cases it is customary for the purchaser to assume and agree to pay the mortgage debt. Indirectly, at least, the holder of the mortgage stands in a position to benefit from this promise.

It should be noted that these examples illustrate two entirely different situations. In the first case, the party to be benefited is a mere donee; in the second case, he is a creditor of the party to whom the promise is made.

2-122. Donee beneficiary. Has a donee who is to be benefited by the terms of a contract a right to succeed in a suit against a promisor who fails to perform? The early law limited recovery to those instances in which the third party was a close relative of the promisee. Recovery was denied in other cases, because no privity of contract existed between the parties; the third party had no contractual relation with the promisor. Gradually the rule permitting recovery has been extended until today a majority of the states allow the third party donee, in all cases, to bring suit against the promisor for failure to perform.[6] The chief reason advanced for the extension of this doctrine is that to deny the third party a recovery would be to bar substantial recovery by anyone. The promisee could not recover substantial damages, because he was not to benefit by performance and, therefore, would not be materially damaged by failure of performance. Nevertheless, a few states deny recovery by the third party in such cases, unless there is a close relationship. In all states, by statute or otherwise, the beneficiary of a life insurance contract is permitted to recover from the insurer.

2-123. Benefit must be direct. A donee beneficiary is entitled to recover only where the contract is expressly made for his benefit. If he is

[6] Wesley v. Electric Auto-Lite Co., 330.

to benefit only incidentally, the contract gives him no right. Thus, an action by an orphanage was not sustained when it was based on the breach of an agreement between several parties to close their places of business on Sunday; and, in case any one or more of them kept open on Sunday, each one keeping open was to pay one hundred dollars to the orphanage. The contract was entered into primarily to benefit the contracting parties, and the orphanage was only indirectly to be a beneficiary. Contracts of guaranty which assure the owner of performance of construction contracts by contractors have been held in many states to benefit the material men and laborers. A few states have held otherwise, indicating their belief that the agreement was made primarily to protect the owner.

In many states, a contract made for the express purpose of benefiting a third party may not be rescinded without the consent of the beneficiary. The latter has a vested interest in the agreement from the moment it is made. In these states, an insurance company has no right to change the named beneficiary in a life insurance policy without the consent of the beneficiary, unless the contract itself gives this right.

2-124. Creditor beneficiary. The person who buys mortgaged real estate and assumes the mortgage debt enters a contract made for the benefit of a third party who is a creditor. It has been urged by the courts of several states that the third party in such cases should not be allowed to sue. The reasons given are the following: (1) a proper analysis of the situation indicates that the contract is not made primarily for the benefit of the creditor, but in reality it is expected to benefit the debtor in that it transfers the burden of performing; (2) failure to perform on the part of the promisor does materially damage the promisee, and a suit by him would result in a judgment for substantial damages. Despite this rather sound reasoning, a majority of the states allow the third party creditor beneficiary to recover.

RIGHTS OF THIRD PARTIES CASES

HUBBARD v. GOODE

1959, (N. Mex.) 335 P.2nd 1063

Hubbard, the plaintiff, leased two trucks with well drilling equipment on them to Goode at a rate of $900 a month for one year. At any time during the first nine months, Goode had an option to purchase for $15,000 less 90 per cent of rental paid to date. Two months later Goode assigned this lease to Hair and Russell and plaintiff immediately demanded possession, claiming the lease to be nonassignable. After suit was filed, pending the hearing, plaintiff repossessed the property without notice and refused to return it. Hair and Russell demand damages for this wrongful conduct. The lower court gave judgment for defendants and allowed them damages.

COMPTON, J. . . . The principal question on appeal is whether the lease was assignable, appellant contending that it was non-assignable without his consent, since "the equipment covered by the lease sale agreement here involved was of a highly specialized nature and required special skill for its operation, that appellant relied upon the experience and ability of the defendant Goode."

The refusal of appellant's tender of proof on this issue is made a point for a reversal of the judgment. The argument cannot be sustained. Such restrictions or limitations as would render a lease nonassignable must appear from the written agreement itself. Of course there are exceptions to the rule, for instance, where the act to be performed is personal in its character, one to be done by the person named only, or where personal confidence may be inferred as the basis of the agreement. . . . Turning to the lease, we find nothing therein to indicate that it was limited to the parties thereto, or to distinguish it from the ordinary lease transaction.

There was a finding that appellees had complied with all the terms of the lease, both at the time the action was instituted and when appellant repossessed the equipment, and that as a result, appellees had sustained damages in amount of $3,000, the consideration paid for the lease, $840 expended by appellees in enlarging and remodeling the equipment, and $3,000 as loss of profit by being deprived of its use. This finding is strongly challenged, but we think the finding has ample support. There is evidence that appellees complied with all the provisions of the lease; that they paid Goode $3,000 for the assignment and that they enlarged and remodeled the drilling rig so as to better use it in their drilling activities.

Appellees were engaged in drilling wells and had contracted with two drilling companies to do extensive drilling for them, and the breach by appellant of the agreement deprived them of the opportunity to fulfill their contract. Appellees testified as to the number of wells to be drilled, etc., and the profit from each well. While the loss was not established with exactness, loss of profit was established with reasonable certainty and that was a sufficient basis to measure the damages. Where it is certain that damages have resulted, mere uncertainty as to the amount will not preclude the right of recovery. (Cases cited.)

It is asserted that remodeling the drilling rig did not afford a basis for damages; the claim being that appellees did this on their own accord. This theory cannot be sustained as this loss was a direct result of appellant's wrongful act. The court merely reimbursed appellees for the loss caused by the breach. 32 Am. Jur. (Landlord & Tenant) § 276, expresses the rule in this respect thusly:

> In addition to the value of the unexpired term or lost profits, the tenant may recover compensation for any other loss which results to him as a direct and natural consequence of the landlord's wrongful act, and which is not attributable to his own fault or want of care. * * *

The judgment will be affirmed. It is so ordered.

WETHERELL BROS. CO. v. UNITED STATES STEEL CO.
1952, 105 F. Supp. 81

Wetherell Bros. Co., a Massachusetts corporation, had held a contract since 1930 with the defendant whereby it had the exclusive right in the New England states to sell cold, rolled steel strips on a 5 per cent commission and stainless steel products on a 7 per cent commission. The contract was to run indefinitely except as it might be terminated by two years notice. On March 1, 1950, the Massachusetts corporation liquidated and ceased to function, but sold some assets to Penn Seaboard Iron Co., a Pennsylvania corporation, and so far as possible sought to assign to the latter their right to represent United States Steel Co. in New England. The Pennsylvania corporation changed its name to Wetherell Bros. Co., but refrained from giving notice of the assignment to the defendant. Learning of the new arrangement, however, the defendant notified the parties of the immediate termination of the sales relationship. Plaintiff, the Pennsylvania corporation, brings suit for breach of contract.

McCarthy, D. J. . . . The plaintiff seeks to hold the defendant liable because of its action in terminating the contract between it (defendant) and Wetherell-Massachusetts. Since admittedly no contract was ever entered into between the plaintiff and the defendant, the question of law is whether the duties of the Wetherell-Massachusetts under the contract could be effectively assigned to plaintiff without the consent of the defendant. The conclusion is inescapable: the assignment to the plaintiff of the duties of Wetherell-Massachusetts under its sales agency contract without the consent of the defendant was ineffective for the purpose of substituting the plaintiff for the "assignor" corporation with whom the defendant contracted.

This was a contract for a sales agency within a particular geographical area, an exclusive agency in that only the principal could compete with Wetherell-Massachusetts in obtaining customers for the defendant's products.

In a contract for a sales agency the personal performance of the agent is practically always a condition precedent to the duty of the principal and employer. The performance of the agent's duty cannot be delegated to a substitute. The assignee of the agent's right must fail, therefore, in his attempt to enforce it if he merely tenders a substituted performance. IV Corbin, *Contracts* (1951) 865, p. 444. . . .

The Court later expanded on the reasons underlying the New York Bank Note decision in *Brighton Packing Co. v. Butchers' Slaughtering & Melting Association,* 211 Mass. 398, 403, 97 N.E. 780, 782.

The claim has been made also that it is only in a technical sense that these two companies could be called distinct entities. They had the same capital stock and practically the same stockholders, officers and agents; the Maine company had taken over all the assets and assumed all the liabilities of the other, and was carrying on the same business, at the same stand, in the same manner and under the same management. The master has found that for practical purposes the two companies were the same. Accordingly, the plaintiff claims that an agreement with the one is the same as an agreement with the other, that the defendant's ignorance of their separate identity was immaterial, that the agreement may be treated as made with either company indifferently, was capable of enforcement by either or at least by the Maine company, and is valid in the hands and for the benefit of the plaintiff. But we cannot assent to this reasoning. These are two distinct corporations, created by the laws of two different states. The powers of each corporation are limited and controlled by the statutes of the state which created it, and it is scarcely conceivable that the statutes of the two states are the same or that the franchises and powers of the two corporations are identical. But if this were so, it would remain true that they are the creation of two different governments, the offspring of different parents, and not only distinct legal entities, but having separate and distinct existences. . . .

The contract in this case is one requiring a relationship of particular trust and confidence, and such a contract cannot be assigned effectively without the consent of the other party to the contract. The grant of an exclusive agency to sell one's goods presupposes a reliance upon and confidence in the agent by the principal, even though the agent be what is frequently called a large "impersonal" corporation. It is apparent that the principal in this case must have relied upon the "legal equation" represented by the corporation which it chose as its sole sales representative in a large area; otherwise, the surrender of the right to grant additional agencies is illogical.

The plaintiff has argued that the fact that the assignment is made from one corporation to another alters the rule of non-assignability of the agent's duties under the contract. The New York Court of Appeals met this argument in an early phase of the *New York Bank Note Com-*

pany litigation. See *New York Bank Note Co. v. Hamilton Bank Note E. & P. Co.,* 180 N.Y. 280, 73 N.E. 48, 51–52:

The plaintiff was not only technically but substantially a different entity from its predecessor. It is true that in dealing with corporations a party cannot rely on what may be termed the human equation in the company. The personnel of the stockholders and officers of the company may entirely change. But though there is no personal or human equation in the management of a corporation, there is a legal equation which may be of the utmost importance to parties contracting with it. In dealing with natural persons in matters of trust and confidence, personal character is or may be a dominant factor. In similar transactions with a corporation, a substitute for personal character is the charter rights of the corporation, the limits placed on its power, especially to incur debt, the statutory liability of its officers and stockholders. These are matters of great importance when, as at present, many states and territories seem to have entered into the keenest competition in granting charters; each seeking to outbid the other by offering to directors and stockholders the greatest immunity from liability at the lowest cash price. . . .

Judgment must be entered for the defendant.

AMERICAN BRIDGE CO. et al. v. CITY OF BOSTON

1909, 202 Mass. 374, 88 N.E. 1089

The plantiffs had received an assignment of all money due or to become due by the City of Boston to one Coburn under two contracts and now seek to recover the amount authorized by two architects' certificates. Shortly after they were issued Coburn defaulted, and the city desires to recoup the damages resulting from the breach and deduct it from the amount of the two certificates. The default took place, however, after the city had received notice of the assignment. This is an action by the assignee to recover.

HAMMOND, J. . . . The assignment of a chose in action conveys, as between assignor and assignee, merely the right which the assignor then possesses to that thing; but as between the assignee and the debtor it does not become operative until the time of notice to the latter, and does not change the rights of the debtors against the assignor as they exist at the time of the notice.

It becomes necessary to consider the exact relation between the defendant and Coburn, the assignor, at the time of notice. The auditor has found that written notice of the assignments were given to the defendant on November 14, 1902, before the service of any trustee process. At that time there does not seem to have been any default on the part of Coburn. At the time of the notice what were the rights between him and the defendant, so far as respects this contract? He was entitled to receive these sums, but he was also under an obligation to complete his contract. This right of the defendant to claim damages for the nonperformance of the contract existed at the making of the contract and at the time of assignment and of notice, and the assignees knew it, and they also knew that it would become available to the defendant the moment the assignor should commit a breach. Under these circumstances it must be held that the assignees took subject to that right. . . . Even if the sums were due and payable in November, 1902, at the time of notice, still if this action had been brought by the assignor after the default, there can be no doubt but that the defendant would have had the right to recoup the damages suffered by his default. And the assignees who seek to enforce this claim can stand in no better position in this respect than the assignor.

Judgment for defendant.

RUSSELL v. FRED G. POHL CO.

1951, 7 N.J. 32, 80 A.2d 191

The plaintiff Russell obtained a judgment against the defendant in the amount of $7,169.28. A writ of attachment was issued, which in effect sought to gain for plaintiff the amount respondent, American Type Founders, Inc., owed the defendant. The garnishee, American Type Founders, Inc., admitted that it owed the defendant in excess of $7,169.28 but stated that after the attachment it paid all it owed to Title Guarantee and Trust Company, to whom the amount had been assigned by Pohl and Co. prior to plaintiff's attachment. The lower court held the payment to the assignee to be a proper one, and the plaintiff appealed.

HEHER, J. . . . The contention is that where a garnishee in attachment "pays over funds of the defendant to a third party asserting a claim to said funds by virtue of assignment," the "payment being made after attachment and contrary to R.S. 2:42-27 (N.J.S.A.) and Rule 3:72-3," the garnishee is guilty of a contempt of court and is liable for the payment of plaintiff's judgment in attachment, "irrespective of the merits of the claim of the third party." . . .

But the fallacy of this argument lies in the unwarranted assumption that the assigned credits remained the property of the defendant in attachment. When the writ of attachment issued, there had been an absolute assignment of the rights and credits in question by the defendant in attachment to the Title Guarantee and Trust Company, with notice of the assignment to the debtor. . . .

By force of the assignments, the relation of debtor and creditor had ceased to exist between the respondent and the defendant in attachment when the writ issued, and there was no property of the defendant in attachment in respondent's hands upon which the writ could operate, and so the respondent is not chargeable as garnishee. There was nothing in respondent's possession belonging to the principal debtor which was subject to garnishment. . . .

The general rule is that priority in time determines priority between an attachment or garnishment and an assignment of a chose in action. . . . By a valid and effective assignment, the title to the chose in action vested in the assignee; and payment after notice of the assignment to any person other than the assignee will not relieve the debtor of his duty to the assignee. . . . Notice of the assignment charges the debtor with the duty of payment to the assignee. . . .

The judgment is affirmed.

ADAMSON v. PAONESSA et al.

1919, 180 Cal. 157, 179 Pac. 880

Interpleader suit by John Z. Adamson, treasurer of the city of Calton, against Geo. C. Paonessa, Charles W. Lloyd, and the National Surety Company. It appears that Paonessa was to do certain street work for the city and as such secured a bond for faithful performance with the National Surety Company as surety. In order to obtain the surety, Paonessa agreed that all payments were to be withheld until completion and then paid to the surety company. Following completion of construction and final payment to the surety, it was to return the money to Paonessa if the surety had incurred no liabilitities. This agreement between Paonessa and the surety was, under the circumstances, found to be an assignment. Later because of loans made to him, Paonessa made an assignment of his claim to one Lloyd, who immediately served notice on the city clerk of the assignment. The city had no notice of the prior assignment. The treasurer was just ready to make the payment in bonds to Lloyd when the surety company intervened, as they had been compelled to pay material-men some $10,000.

Lawlor, J. . . . The surety company neglected to give immediate notice of the assignment to it, and before it gave such notice Lloyd had taken as assignment for a valuable consideration without notice or knowledge of the prior assignment, and had given notice of his own assignment. The rule is well established in such a case. It is thus stated in *Widenmann v. Weiniger*, 164 Cal. 667: ". . . As between successive assignees of a chose in action, he will have a preference who first gives notice to the debtor, even if he be a subsequent assignee, providing at the time of taking it he had no notice of a prior assignment."

The judgment of the lower court, therefore, in directing the delivery of the bonds to Lloyd, was correct and to that extent is affirmed. . . .

WESLEY v. ELECTRIC AUTO-LITE CO.

1959, (Common Pleas, Ohio) 155 N.E. 2nd 713

LEIS, J. This is an action brought by Ransom Wesley against the Electric Auto-Lite Company for wages allegedly due him from the defendant. Plaintiff is an employee of the defendant and is a member of the Local 68, Metal Polishers, Buffers, Platers and Helpers International Union. Plaintiff stands in the shoes of a third party beneficiary to a contract entered into between defendant and plaintiff's bargaining unit, said Local 68, and for his claim avers that defendant corporation has breached said contract, thereby resulting in a loss to plaintiff of some fifty-six hours or work at $2.60½ per hour.

The demurrer of the plaintiff to defendant's amended answer having been overruled, the case was tried before the Court, a jury having been waived. . . . By way of background, it should be stated that the defendant corporation was engaged in the manufacture of various electric auto accessories, including automotive lamps. While defendant produced for various customers, the Chrysler Corporation accounted for approximately eighty-five per cent of the volume of production (R. 49). The evidence shows that beginning in December of 1955, the orders to defendant from its chief customer, Chrysler, were cut severely by what counsel for defendant aptly described as a "blizzard of cancellations." . . . At the time of the cancellations, the plant was working a five day week. Due to the order cancellations, the decision was made by defendant corporation to cut down to a four day week without a reduction in working force. (R. 72.) As a result, plaintiff was laid off seven consecutive Fridays from February 10, 1956 to March, 1956, although he reported for work each of the seven Fridays in question. (R. 39–40.) Therein lies the crux of this lawsuit.

It is the claim of plaintiff that being third man in seniority in his union (R. 39), he was entitled under Local 68's contract with defendant corporation, to continue his full time work week, until probationary employees, and those employees with less seniority than he were laid off first.

Both parties cite the agreement of July 11, 1955, between the Electric Auto-Lite Company Lamp Division and the Metal Polishers, Buffers, Platers and Helpers International Union in support of their positions.

There are three pertinent parts of this Agreement to which the Court will refer.

The first part is Article III (A) "Working Hours":

(A) *Eight* (8) *consecutive hours, except for the lunch period, shall constitute a normal work day, and forty* (40) *hours of five consecutive days* (Monday, Tuesday, Wednesday, Thursday, and Friday) *shall constitute a normal week's work* except when a holiday occurs on these days, in which event thirty-two (32) hours shall constitute a week's work. [Emphasis added.]

The next part is Article VI (G) which the Court will label the "seniority clause":

(G) *When it becomes necessary to reduce the working force of a department, probationary employees will be laid off first. Thereafter, layoffs will be made according to seniority to provide normal eight* (8) *hours per day and forty* (40) *hours per week for employees in the polishing and buffing departments;* . . .

To put it simply, plaintiff says that under the seniority clause he is entitled to a forty hour week until all those with less seniority than he are laid off first. . . .

Upon the evidence and law, the Court finds that plaintiff is a third party beneficiary to the contract of July 11, 1955, between The Electric Auto-Lite Company Lamp Division and the Metal Polishers, Buffers, Platers and Helpers International Union; that plaintiff being third man on the seniority list has a contractual right under the seniority clause VI(G) to have those with less seniority laid off first; that plaintiff's employment was reduced contrary to the provisions of the seniority clause and that plaintiff is entitled to recover therefor.

Judgment for the plaintiff.

Review Questions and Problems

1. *P* employed *A* to work, the latter agreeing to a reasonable restraint from competing when employment terminated. *P* sold his business to *T*, and assigned the contract. *A* quit and began to compete immediately in the area. Has *T* a good cause of action against *A*, who urged such a contract could not be assigned?
2. *C*, a contractor with wide experience in organizing and building canning factories, contracted with *A* and *B* to form a corporation and construct a canning factory to fit their needs. He assigned the contract to *H*, who knew nothing about canning factories. Are *A* and *B* bound to permit *H* to carry out the agreement?

3. *R*, working for *L* Railway, owed *A* $75 and assigned to *A* future wages as security for the debt. *R* had no contract of employment which would run for a definite period, but was employed at the time of assignment. His employer paid the money to *A*, but *R* is seeking to recover the amount of *L*, contending wages earned under such circumstances were not assignable. Is *L* liable to *R*?
4. Suppose that *A* contracts to build a house for *B* at a certain contract price. *A* later assigns the contract to *C*, who agrees to complete the building. What right has *B* against *A* if *C* fails to build the house?
5. *M*, who held a $30,000 interest in the estate of an uncle, made an assignment of one-half of his interest to his wife, without receiving any consideration therefor. Later he assigned all of his interest to the *X* Company. The company immediately notified the executor of the estate of the assignment. *M*'s wife had failed to give notice until some time after the second assignment. Whose claim is superior?
6. Bank sued on a conditional sales contract for equipment signed by *C*, the contract providing that, in event it was later assigned by the seller, *C* waived any defenses he might have had against the seller. Seller assigned the contract to Bank, and *C* refused to pay because the equipment was defective. The court gave judgment for Bank. Was this a good decision?
7. Home Co. agreed to make loans to Shaw up to a total of two and one half million dollars on properties to be built with guaranteed loans under the Serviceman's Readjustment Act. Shaw assigned this contract to Ott, and Home Co. refused to accept the loan commitment. The court held the contract to be nonassignable. Was this sound?
8. *A* gave a mortgage to *B* to secure a loan of $10,000. Later *A* sold the property to *C*, who assumed and agreed to pay the mortgage debt. Does this give to *B* an action against *C* if he fails to pay the debt at maturity? Does the agreement release *A* from further liability?
9. *H* held a life insurance policy in *N* Company which had lapsed but which carried a cash surrender value of $500. *H* assigned the policy right to *M*. *M* demanded payment from *N* Co., but it paid *H*. May *M* recover of *N* Co.?
10. *S* sold a truck to *B* for $2,500, the contract reciting the wrong serial numbers. *B* was called in to sign a new contract in which the correct serial number was indicated. Both contracts included the promise to pay for the delivered truck. *B* neglected to have the first contract canceled and returned to him, and *S* assigned both contracts to innocent third parties. Will the assignee of the contract containing wrong serial numbers be able to recover of *B*?
11. *A* was engaged by a milk producers' association for one year to pick up and deliver milk of the members to a certain dairy company, the compensation being an agreed amount for each 100 pounds delivered. *A* assigned the contract to *B*. Was the association bound to permit *B* to pick up and deliver the milk?
12. *A* deeded land to *B*, who agreed, as part of the consideration, to pay *C* $1,500 upon death of *A*. Later *A* and *B* agreed that *B* should not pay *C* any amount. In the interim, *C*, a donee, learned of the first deed. Later, when *A* died, *C* sued *B* on his signed promise. Is *B* liable?

13. *L* Co. issued a life insurance policy upon the life of *A*, it providing that the policy could not be assigned without the consent of *L* Co. The right to money under the policy had matured, and *A* assigned the money claim to *M*. When the company refused to pay, *M* brought suit. The court allowed *M* to recover. Is this a sound decision?

15

Discharge of Contracts

2-125. Performance. The customary manner of obtaining a discharge of a contract is by complete performance. After all the terms of the agreement have been fully complied with by both parties, the contract no longer exists.

Executory agreements may be discharged by mutual agreement of the parties; the release of one party to the contract furnishes the consideration for the release of the other. An agreement which is fully performed on one side and executory on the other may not be discharged in this manner. The agreement to discharge the party under duty to perform is, in such a case, without consideration to support it, unless there is a clear indication of an intention to make a gift.

2-126. Payment. The final act of performance in many contracts consists in the payment of a money debt, and there are at least three features of payment that deserve special treatment. These features are suggested in the form of the following questions: What constitutes payment? Which of several items has been paid? What is good evidence of payment?

In answer to the first question, there is no doubt that the transfer of money acts as payment, but the receipt of the debtor's check, his note, or an endorsed check[1] or note of someone else is not payment unless the creditor expressly receives such items as payment. They are considered as conditional payment, payment becoming final only when the instruments are honored. The same appears to be true of the assignment of an account receivable. Unless indicated otherwise, the assignment is received as collateral for the principal indebtedness, and unless the assigned claim is collected, the debtor must pay his indebtedness.

A debtor who owes several obligations to his creditor is free at the time of payment to stipulate which of the several obligations he is paying, and the creditor who receives such payment is obligated to follow the instructions given. In the absence of any instructions, the creditor may apply the payment on any of several obligations that are due or he may credit a portion of the payment upon several obligations. The

[1] Tuckel et al. v. Jurovaty, page 316.

creditor, in the absence of instructions, may apply a payment against a claim that has been outlawed, but this will not cause the outlawed claim to revive where other obligations existed against which the payment could have been applied. A claim based upon an illegal consideration may not be credited where legal claims exist. Furthermore, if the source of a payment is someone other than the debtor and this fact is known to the creditor, the payment must be applied in such a manner as to protect the party responsible for payment. Hence, if a surety supplies the money for the payment and the creditor knows it, he is bound to apply the payment on the obligation for which the surety was secondarily liable. Finally, if the creditor fails to make a particular application prior to the time the issue is raised in court, the payment is applied against the debtor's obligations in the order of their maturity, except where the creditor holds both secured and unsecured obligations, in which event the courts are inclined to apply it on an unsecured obligation which is matured. Similarly, if both principal and interest are due, the court considers the interest to be paid first, any balance being credited to the principal.

A receipt is acceptable evidence of payment, although it may be rebutted by evidence showing it to be in error or to have been given under mistake. A check is evidence of payment, but the evidence is more conclusive where the purpose for which it is given is stated on the check.

2-127. Accord and satisfaction. An accord consists of an agreement between contracting parties whereby one of them is to do something different from that called for by the contract. This accord is satisfied when the terms of the new agreement are fully performed. Both accord and satisfaction must take place before the old obligation is discharged, unless the new agreement expressly states that it is being substituted for the old.[2] The new agreement of itself does not terminate the old agreement. To illustrate: *A* purchased a used car from *B* and agreed to pay him $600 within sixty days. *A* failed to pay *B* at the end of the period, and a new agreement was entered into whereby *A* was to deliver two used cars, accurately described, in full payment of the debt. At any time before the used cars are delivered, *B* may recover upon the original contract. The delivery of the cars constitutes the satisfaction of the accord, and thus discharges the old contract.

2-128. Novation. *Novation* is an agreement whereby an original party to a contract is replaced by a new party. In order for the substitution to be effective, it must be agreed to by all of the parties. The remaining contracting party must agree to accept the new party and at the same time consent to release the withdrawing party.[3] The latter consents to

[2] Virginia-Carolina Electrical Works, Inc. v. Cooper et al., page 346.
[3] Strunk Chain Saws, Inc. v. Williams, page 348.

withdraw and permits the new party to take his place. The new party agrees to assume the burdens and duties of the retiring party because of some consideration which he receives. Provided none of these essentials are missing, the withdrawing party is discharged from the old agreement. To illustrate: *A* purchases an automobile from *B*, and after making a small down payment, agrees to pay the balance of $400 within six months. Finding times somewhat hard, *A* sells the car to *C*, who agrees to pay the balance to *B*. Both parties notify *B* of this arrangement. As yet no novation is completed because *B* has not agreed to release *A* and to look to *C* for payment. If *B* releases *A*, then *A* is discharged from any duty arising under the original agreement, and a novation is created.

2-129. Cancellation and alteration. An intentional cancellation or alteration of the written evidence of an agreement will have the effect of discharging it. This situation arises most frequently with negotiable instruments. An intentional material alteration of a note or check avoids the instrument.

2-130. Statute of Limitations. The Statute of Limitations prescribes a time limit within which suit must be started after a cause of action arises. An action for breach of any contract for sale of personal property must be commenced within four years. The Code further provides that the original agreement may reduce the period of limitation to not less than one year but may not extend it. In contracts which do not fall under the Code, and in those states which have not adopted the Code, there is a wider variety of limitation periods, the most common being six years. Some states distinguish between oral and written contracts, making the period longer in the latter. The purpose of this legislation is to bar the possibility of action being brought long after evidence is lost or important witnesses have died. Any contract action must be brought within the prescribed period after the obligation matures or after the cause of action arises, as the case may be.

Any voluntary[4] part payment made on a money obligation tolls the statute, starting it to run anew, unless made under circumstances such as to negate an intent to pay the balance. Similarly, any new promise or clear acknowledgment[5] of the indebtedness renews the obligation and starts it to run anew even though it had been entirely outlawed, no new consideration being required to support the promise. If the old obligation has expired, a new promise may be partial or conditional. Since there is no duty to pay the debt, the debtor may attach such conditions to his new promise as he sees fit. A few states require the new promise or acknowledgment to be in writing particularly where the original obligation

[4] Nilsson et al. v. Kielman et al., page 350.
[5] Whale Harbor Spa, Inc. v. Wood, page 351.

was in writing. The Code does not alter the law on tolling of the Statute of Limitations.

The period during which a debtor removes himself from the state or the period when the debtor or creditor is incapacitated by minority or insanity is usually totally or partially eliminated from the period prescribed by statute. In other words, the debtor's absence from the state extends the period within which an action may be brought against him, and a minor usually has a short time in which to bring action after he reaches his majority, although the full period set by statute has expired earlier.

BANKRUPTCY[6]

2-131. Kinds of bankruptcy. The federal government has by statute —the Bankruptcy Act—provided a procedure whereby, under certain conditions, one may be discharged of his obligations. He is permitted to start his business life anew, unfettered by weighty obligations assumed in the past. The filing of a voluntary petition in bankruptcy usually accomplishes this result. The federal court, through its designated officers, takes control of all property involved, turns it into cash, pays all expenses, and uses the balance to pay off creditors as far as possible.

At the same time the Bankruptcy Act has made it possible for a creditor of an insolvent debtor to get his full share of the insolvent's estate by filing an involuntary petition in bankruptcy against the debtor. A person cannot be forced into involuntary bankruptcy unless his liabilities equal at least $1,000. If twelve or more creditors exist, the petition must be signed by at least three of them—otherwise, only one need sign. The petitioning creditors as a group must also own definite unsecured claims totalling $500 or more. Relatives, persons holding fully secured claims, and other biased creditors are not counted in determining the number of creditors required to sign the petition. If there are only eleven creditors other than relatives, one creditor may bring about involuntary bankruptcy regardless of the total number of creditors involved.

2-132. Who may become bankrupts. Any person, firm, or corporation may become a voluntary bankrupt, with the exception of five types of corporations. Railway, banking, insurance, municipal, and building and loan corporations may not become voluntary bankrupts, but an insolvent railway may petition a bankruptcy court for confirmation of a reorganiza-

[6] A number of the sections included under bankruptcy do not bear on the subject of discharge of contracts, but because of those that do, the subject is treated at this point for the sake of convenience.

tion plan, provided the plan has first been approved by the Interstate Commerce Commission.

Any natural person, except a farmer or wage earner, any partnership, and any moneyed business or commercial corporation except the five previously mentioned, may be adjudged an involuntary bankrupt for proper cause. It should be noted that three new groups are exempt from involuntary bankruptcy, namely, farmers, wage earners, and nonbusiness corporations.

A farmer is defined as anyone engaged in the tillage of the soil, raising poultry or livestock and their products, or operating a dairy. If he spends most of his time on the farm and expects to derive most of his income from it, he is deemed a farmer although he is incidentally engaged in other enterprises.[7] A wage earner is one who works for another at a rate of pay of $1,500 a year or less.

2-133. Acts of bankruptcy. The purpose of involuntary bankruptcy is to force an equal distribution of an insolvent debtor's assets. In this connection it should be noted that mere insolvency affords no basis for a petition in involuntary bankruptcy. Unless a debtor has committed some act which indicates an intention to abuse or to prefer certain creditors, or has done something which shows a willingness to have his assets distributed, involuntary bankruptcy is impossible. The Bankruptcy Act sets forth six acts, one of which must be committed within four months prior to the petition before involuntary bankruptcy proceedings are possible.

Acts of bankruptcy by a person shall consist of his having:

1. Conveyed, transferred, concealed, or removed, or permitted to be concealed, or removed, any part of his property with intent to hinder, delay, or defraud his creditors, or any of them;

2. Transferred, while insolvent, any portion of his property to one or more of his creditors with intent to prefer such creditors over his other creditors;[8]

3. Suffered or permitted, while insolvent, any creditor to obtain a lien upon his property through court action and not having vacated or discharged such lien within thirty days from the date thereof or at least five days before the date set for any sale or other disposition of such property;

4. Made a general assignment for the benefit of creditors;

5. While insolvent or unable to pay his debts as they mature, procured, permitted, or suffered voluntarily or involuntarily the appointment of a receiver or trustee to take charge of his property;

6. Admitted in writing his inability to pay his debts and his willingness to be adjudged a bankrupt.

[7] Rice v. Bordner, page 352.

[8] In re Stovall Grocery Co., page 353.

Attention should be called to the fact that the second, third, and fifth acts must be accompanied by insolvency at the time they are committed. With respect to the first, fourth, and sixth acts, insolvency is not required. Another provision of the act, however, makes solvency at the time the petition is filed a good defense to the first act of bankruptcy. In none of the other acts is solvency at the time the petition is filed important. In the first three instances mentioned, it is a matter of insolvency at the time the act is committed. *Insolvency,* as used in bankruptcy, refers to a situation in which the debtor's assets valued on the basis of a voluntary sale fail to equal his liabilities.

It should be emphasized, concerning the third act, that it is not the lien which constitutes the act of bankruptcy, but it is the failure to vacate it within the time allotted to the debtor.

The petition in involuntary bankruptcy must be filed within four months of some act of bankruptcy. Whenever recording is required in order to render a transfer fully effective, the four months' period is calculated from the date of recording and not from the date of the transfer.

2-134. Officers of the court. The bankruptcy petition is filed with the clerk of the Federal District Court and is then referred to the referee, who is appointed by the court to hear the evidence and to submit his findings to the court. All dividends are ordered paid by the referee, he being a semiadministrative and judicial officer.

A trustee is elected by the creditors at the first meeting, a majority in number and amount of claims held by those present at the meeting being necessary for election. The trustee then takes title to all property, both real and personal, owned by the bankrupt at the time the petition was filed. It becomes his duty to dispose of the property as best he can, under the supervision of the court, for the benefit of creditors. Personal property, purchased by an innocent party from the bankrupt after the filing of the petition but before the trustee or receiver takes possession, remains with the purchaser. Any property received by the bankrupt after the filing of the petition belongs to his new estate, except that all devises, bequests, or inheritances received within six months thereafter belong to the trustee. Executory contracts may be accepted or rejected within 60 days after the petition in bankruptcy has been passed upon. If the trustee chooses to reject a long-term contract, the other party is then permitted to file a claim for damages against the bankrupt estate. In case of leases, however, the landlord may file a claim for all past due rentals and for damages caused by breach of the lease agreement, but the latter claim shall not be in excess of one year's rental.

A receiver is a temporary officer appointed by the court to take charge of a bankrupt's property until a trustee is appointed. He is appointed only when someone is required to care for the property in this intervening period in order to avoid waste or loss.

2-135. Recoverable preferences. Any transfer of property by an insolvent person to a particular creditor that has the effect of preferring that creditor above the others constitutes a preference. A preferential transfer may be recovered by the trustee if it took place within the four months preceding the filing of the bankruptcy petition, and if the creditor, at the time of the transfer, knew, or had cause to believe, that he was obtaining a greater percentage of his claim than other creditors could recover.[9] The transfer may consist of the payment of money or the transfer of property as payment of, or as security for, a prior indebtedness. A mortgage or pledge may be set aside as readily as payment, providing it is received by the creditor with knowledge of the debtor's insolvency. Such pledge or mortgage can be avoided, however, only if it was received within the immediate four months prior to the filing of the petition of bankruptcy and was obtained as security for a previous debt. In the case of the mortgage, the four months' period dates from the recording of the mortgage rather than from its signing.

If the property received by a preferred creditor has been sold to an innocent third party, recovery of the property may not be had, but its value may be obtained from the creditor. A creditor, however, who in good faith extends additional credit after having received a preference, may deduct from the recoverable preference the amount of any new unpaid credit items. In this manner, a creditor who attempts to help an insolvent debtor out of his financial difficulties is not penalized if, after obtaining payment, he extends no greater credit than the old claim amounted to.

Any judgment lien obtained within the four months' period is void, irrespective of knowledge, so long as it continues to maintain the character of a lien at the time the petition in bankruptcy is filed, if the judgment was obtained while the debtor was insolvent.

2-136. Exceptions to recoverable preference rule. Payment of a fully secured claim does not constitute a preference and, therefore, may not be recovered.

Transfers of property for a present consideration may not be set aside. A mortgage given to secure a contemporaneous loan is valid although the mortgagee took the security with knowledge of the debtor's insolvency. An insolvent debtor has a right to extricate himself, as far as possible, from his financial difficulty.

Any debtor of a bankrupt may set off against the amount he owes the

[9] Marks, Trustee v. Goodyear Rubber Sundries, Inc., page 354.

bankrupt estate any sum which the estate owes him.[10] To the extent of his set-off against the estate, he becomes a preferred creditor, legally entitled to his preference. This rule is not applicable where the claim against the bankrupt has been purchased or created with the express purpose of set-off. A bank that has loaned a bankrupt $2,000 and happens to have $1,500 of the bankrupt on deposit at the time of bankruptcy, is a preferred creditor to the extent of the deposit. This set-off must be allowed, unless the evidence discloses that the deposit was made with the express purpose of preferring the bank. In such a case the deposit becomes part of the bankrupt estate.

2-137. Provable claims. Not all claimants against a bankrupt may share in his assets. Those claims upon which dividends are paid are called provable claims and must be filed within six months after notice of the first creditors' meeting. All judgments, workmen's compensation awards, and claims founded upon a contract are provable; thus, any debt or claim for damages because of breach of contract may be filed. Disputed contract claims that have not been made definite at the time for filing are made certain by court decree or agreement prior to the payment of dividends by the trustee.

Tort claims—demands made because of injury to person or property—are not provable unless they have been reduced to contract or judgment prior to the petition in bankruptcy, except that, in torts involving negligence, the injured party may prove his claim if he has instituted suit prior to the filing of bankruptcy proceedings. Thus, *A*, who has an action against *B* because of an assault by the latter, is deprived of any share in *B*'s bankrupt estate, provided the petition in bankruptcy is filed before *A* has reached an agreement with *B*. As noticed in the succeeding section, however, the claim is not discharged, and may be enforced against any new assets *B* may acquire.

Claims for costs in suits started against the bankrupt or in cases started by him and abandoned by the trustee are also provable. Taxes also represent provable claims.

A claim by a creditor who has received a recoverable preference is not allowed until he has returned the preference. If a creditor has knowingly received payment of a claim from an insolvent debtor within four months of bankruptcy, he is not entitled to prove other claims until he has surrendered the preference that he received.

2-138. Claims that are discharged. All provable claims, with a few exceptions, are discharged by a discharge in bankruptcy. The most important of these exceptions are claims for taxes, losses resulting from

10 Frank v. Mercantile Nat. Bank, page 355.

breach of trust by one acting in a fiduciary capacity,[11] liability resulting from willful or malicious tort,[12] wages earned within three months of filing of the petition in bankruptcy, and liabilities for property or money obtained under false pretenses or by fraudulent representations. Nonprovable claims, not being discharged, also continue as claims against the bankrupt after his discharge.

It becomes the duty of the bankrupt, as soon as a petition in bankruptcy is filed, to schedule all his creditors and the amount due each. The claim of any creditor who is not listed and who does not learn of the proceedings in time to file his claim is not discharged. The bankrupt, under such circumstances, remains liable.

In addition to providing that certain claims are not discharged, the Bankruptcy Act provides a number of circumstances under which the bankrupt may not obtain a discharge. In such a case the assets of his present estate are distributed among his creditors, but he remains liable out of future assets for that portion of the claims that remains unpaid after all assets have been liquidated and distributed. The Bankruptcy Act states the following about the discharge of bankrupts:

> The court shall grant the discharge unless satisfied that the bankrupt has (1) committed an offense punishable by imprisonment as provided under this Act; or (2) destroyed, mutilated, falsified, concealed, or failed to keep or preserve books of account or records, from which his financial condition and business transactions might be ascertained, unless the court deems such acts or failure to have been justified under all the circumstances of the case; or (3) while engaged in business as a sole proprietor, partnership, or as an executive of a corporation, obtained for such business money or property or credit, or obtained an extension or renewal of credit, by making or publishing or causing to be made or published, in any manner whatsoever, a materially false statement in writing respecting his financial condition or the financial condition of such partnership or corporation; or (4) at any time subsequent to the first day of the twelve months immediately preceding the filing of the petition in bankruptcy, transferred, removed, destroyed, or concealed or permitted to be removed, destroyed, or concealed, any of his property, with intent to hinder, delay, or defraud his creditors; or (5) has within six years prior to bankruptcy been granted a discharge . . . ; or (6) in the course of a proceeding under this Act refused to obey any lawful order, or to answer any material question approved by the court; or (7) has failed to explain satisfactorily any losses of assets or deficiency of assets to meet his liabilities.

Any of the circumstances mentioned may be set up by a creditor as a bar to a discharge, or they may be set up by the trustee, when he has been authorized to do so by the creditors. Furthermore, if any creditor can show reasonable cause for believing that the bankrupt has done any

[11] Airo Supply Co. v. Page, page 355.
[12] Wegiel v. Hogan, page 357.

of the things mentioned, the burden shifts to the bankrupt to show that he has not committed an act that will bar discharge. In addition, it should be suggested that the discharge of a partnership does not aet as a discharge of the individual members of the firm. They are discharged only upon action of the court in their behalf as individuals.

The third ground for barring the discharge has been recently limited to businessmen. Prior to 1960, persons not in business who furnished false financial statements to obtain property or credit would also be denied a discharge. Because of the fact that false financial statements are frequently submitted to short-term lending institutions which loan relatively small amounts of money, Congress decided that such action should not bar discharge but should only prevent discharge of the debt which arose out of the transaction in which the fraudulent financial statement was submitted. Therefore, a false financial statement by a businessman is a complete bar to a discharge but a false financial statement by a person not engaged in business is only a bar to discharge of the debt involved.

2-139. Exemptions. The bankrupt is allowed the exemptions provided by the law of the state in which he resides. Such laws usually provide for a certain sum in cash or personal property and, if the bankrupt owns his homestead, some additional amount.

2-140. Priority of claims. Since the trustee's title to property is only the title previously held by the bankrupt, any valid lien against the property continues after bankruptcy and must be paid first if the trustee desires to dispose of the property free of encumbrances; otherwise, the lienholder merely enforces his lien. Should a sale of the property fail to pay the entire secured debt, the creditor then becomes an unsecured creditor for the deficit.

The Bankruptcy Act provides a definite order for the payment of provable claims as follows:

1. Costs of preserving and administering the bankrupt estate.
2. Claims of wage earners not exceeding $600 to each claimant, provided the wages have accrued within the three months preceding bankruptcy.[13]
3. Claims for money expended in defending against or setting aside arrangements of the bankrupt debtor.
4. Claims for taxes.
5. Claims for rent granted priority by state statute and any claims allowed priority by federal law. Many of the claims held by the federal government have been given priority under this provision.
6. Claims of general creditors.

In case funds are insufficient to pay in full any particular class of creditors, the funds available for such group are distributed in proportion

[13] United States v. Munro-Van Helms Company, Inc., page 359.

to the amount of each claim, all classes falling lower in the list receiving no payment. For example, if the assets are insufficient to pay in full the claims of wage earners amounting to $600 per person and earned within the previous three months, the wage earners would share proportionately the amount available, but the claims for taxes and general creditors would not share, no payment being made on them.

2-141. Fraudulent conveyances. Conveyances of property to relatives or friends that are made for the purpose of hindering, delaying, or defrauding creditors may usually be set aside by the creditors.[14] This rule applies whether or not bankruptcy has intervened. In any case where the conveyance leaves the transferor without sufficient assets with which to pay his debts, the transfer is said to be fraudulent. The courts insist that one must be "just before he is generous."

If property has been fraudulently transferred to an innocent third party, it can be avoided only if the consideration given for it was inadequate, and then only if the third party is reimbursed to the extent he gave consideration for it. Property may be taken from a person who receives it with knowledge of the fraud, in which case the person becomes an ordinary creditor of the debtor.

The states usually impose no time limit in which an action may be brought by creditors to set aside a fraudulent conveyance. Whenever creditors discover that such a transfer has been effected, they are free to institute an action for the purpose of restoring the property to the debtor's estate, in which it may be attached and sold by his judgment creditors or used by a bankruptcy court in paying creditors.

2-142. Reorganizations. At one time the law made it possible for a small minority of creditors to jeopardize the interests of the majority whenever a debtor became financially embarrassed. They could force the debtor into bankruptcy and insist upon liquidation at unfavorable times; they could demand, in many instances, foreclosure of mortgages or threaten lengthy and expensive receiverships unless the other creditors purchased their claims at exorbitant figures; or they could effectively block any plan for rehabilitation of the debtor until their demands had in large measure been satisfied. Amendments to the Bankruptcy Act were made to relieve this situation and have been woven together in such a way as to meet several distinct needs. In general, the method chosen by this legislation is to coerce the minority interests to follow a plan that has been approved by a large group and sanctioned by the court.

The reorganization chapters of the Bankruptcy Act provide for four distinct situations: (1) an arrangement which modifies only the claims of unsecured creditors; (2) one which alters only the claims held against debtors other than corporations of creditors secured by real estate; (3)

[14] Cross v. Commons et al., page 360.

one by which wage earners who earn no more than $3,600 a year may reorder their affairs; or (4) a complete reorganization of a corporation which is in financial difficulty. In this latter situation, the corporation is usually permitted to continue operation under court supervision until some plan of reorganization is approved or it is determined that no plan can secure the requisite support for its approval. If such support cannot be obtained, the court proceeds to liquidate the corporation as in any other case of bankruptcy.

The procedure for reorganization is somewhat similar in each of the four types, since the plan must be approved by the court and by a stipulated percentage of the creditors who are affected by the plan. The percentage varies from a simple majority in number and amount to two-thirds of the claims in each class affected, depending on the type of arrangement which is involved.

DISCHARGE OF CONTRACTS CASES

TUCKEL et al. v. JUROVATY
1954 (Conn.) 109 A. 2d 262

BALDWIN, J. The plaintiffs brought suit to recover the balance due on sale of a television set to the defendant. They have appealed from a judgment for the defendant.

Stated briefly, the facts are these: the plaintiffs were engaged in the business of selling radio and television sets. On November 30, 1950, they sold a television set to the defendant (Jurovaty) for the agreed price of $340. The defendant paid $85 in cash, took the set and agreed to pay the balance of the purchase price within thirty days. On December 22, 1950, the defendant gave to the plaintiffs' agent an additional $85 in cash and indorsed to the plaintiffs and delivered to their agent a check for $170, drawn to the order of the defendant by Joseph Irving. The plaintiffs presented the check to the bank for payment but it was returned for insufficient funds. Three to four weeks later the plaintiffs notified the defendant that the check had not been honored. The question presented is whether the acceptance of the check and the marking of the bill as paid discharged the defendant's obligation.

In the absence of a special agreement to the contrary, the giving of a check by a debtor to his creditor does not discharge the debt until the check is paid. *Borst v. Ruff*, 137 Conn. 359, 361, 77 A.2d 343; *Kossover v. Willimantic Trust Co.*, 122 Conn. 166, 168, 187 A. 907, 107 A.L.R. 693. In the case at bar, the defendant was the indorser and not the drawer of the check. This does not alter the situation. The dishonored check leaves the defendant's obligation to the plaintiffs still outstanding. The indorsement of the check made it negotiable in the hands of the defendant but it did not convert it into money. 40 Am. Jur. 766, § 76. The check still retained its character as a written promise to pay in accordance with its terms.

The decision of this case turns upon whether the facts found spell out a special agreement by the parties that acceptance of the check and $85 in cash, representing the balance due on the purchase price, constituted payment in full. The defendant argues that the court has so found. We do not so interpret the finding. The court concluded from the subordinate facts found that "[t]he acceptance of the check . . . and the marking of the defendant's bill 'paid in full' constituted payment of the $170.00 balance due the plaintiffs." This was no more than a conclusion drawn from subordinate facts. It is not a finding that there was a special agreement. In the giving and acceptance of a check to pay a debt, it is presumed that the parties intended only a conditional payment. "Ordinarily the parties act, and the great volume of trade proceeds, upon the assumption that the condition will in due course be fulfilled. Thus the merchant who sells goods and receives a check therefor often credits the amount upon his books and perhaps issues a receipt purporting to show that the charge for them has been paid; or the holder of a note upon receipt of a check or draft offered in payment of it may surrender the note; but these and like facts in themselves will not destroy the presumption that only conditional payment has been made. They are the results of the assumption that the check or draft will ultimately be paid, rather than the evidence of its acceptance in absolute payment." *Bassett v. Merchants' Trust Co.*, 118 Conn. 586, 595, 173 A. 777, 780, 93 A.L.R. 1008; *Sperandeo v. Aetna Casualty & Surety Co.*, 131 Conn. 407, 410, 40 A.2d 280; 40 Am. Jur. 766, § 76. Something more than the facts found is required to demonstrate that the intention of the parties was otherwise. Nor does the fact that the plaintiffs retained the check three to four weeks after it had been returned unpaid alter the presumption that the check was accepted only as a conditional payment of the amount it represented. The plaintiff is not suing the defendant on the check. He is suing upon the defendant's promise to pay for the television set.

There is error, the judgment is set aside and a new trial is ordered.

VIRGINIA-CAROLINA ELECTRICAL WORKS, INC. v. COOPER et al.

1951, (Va.), 63 S.E.2d 717

BUCHANAN, J. The appellant, plaintiff below, filed its notice of motion for judgment against the defendants (Cooper and Others), trading as Ocean View Enterprises, for a balance of $468.30, alleged to be due for work and materials at Ocean View Amusement Park operated by the defendants. The defendants filed a plea of the general issue and a special plea of accord and satisfaction. The trial court heard the evidence offered on the special plea, sustained it and dismissed the plaintiff's action. We granted plaintiff a writ of error. . . .

It appears that the plaintiff, on July 31, 1947, sent the defendants a statement of their account, composed of 14 invoices, totaling $790.33. On November 3, 1947, Ocean View Improvement Corporation, whose connection with the matter is not explained, wrote to plaintiff saying, "We are enclosing a check for $322.03 in settlement of our account to date which is contrary to your statement of July 31, which shows a balance due of $799.33 (*sic*). The difference of $468.30 covers the below items." Four items were then listed, totaling $468.30, which the letter stated were for repairs to a motor, improperly done. The letter concluded, "We regret this bit of unpleasantness but trust you will see our position in its proper light and will accept the settlement as submitted." No check was enclosed in this letter.

November 5, 1947, plaintiff wrote to the sender acknowledging receipt of the letter of November 3, saying, "You failed to enclose the check, but this omission is unimportant as we would have returned same to you. . . . Please be advised that we are expecting you to pay the full amount of our account and that we are prepared to go into court to prove our case."

November 14, 1957, Ocean View Improvement Corporation wrote the plaintiff, referring to its letter of November 5, and saying, so far as here material, "We failed to enclose our check for $323.03 and are, in spite of the statement that you would not accept it, enclosing it never-the-less and if you wish to retain it or return it, it is unimportant to us. . . . If you feel, under the circumstances, that it is necessary to take this matter to court there is no other choice for us except to acquiesce."

The check enclosed was for $323.03, dated November 13, 1947, signed by Ocean View Enterprises, bearing no notation other than the words "Per letter."

By letter of November 19, 1947, plaintiff replied, "We have deposited your check for $323.03 as part payment of the amount you owe us. We expect you to pay the full amount of the balance due."

On its first assignment of error the plaintiff contends that these transactions did not constitute an accord and satisfaction. We agree with this contention.

"Accord and satisfaction is a method of discharging a contract or cause of action, whereby the parties agree to give and accept something in settlement of the claim or demand of the one against the other, and perform such agreement, the 'accord' being the agreement, and the 'satisfaction' its execution or performance." 1 C.J.S., Accord and Satisfaction, § 1, p. 462. *Owen v. Wade,* 185 Va. 118, 124, 37 S.E.2d, 759, 762.

"The thing agreed to be given or done in satisfaction must be offered and intended by the debtor as full satisfaction, and accepted as such by the creditor." 1 C.J.S., Accord and Satisfaction, § 6, p. 476. *Mercury Insurance Co. v. Griffith,* 178 Va. 9, 20, 16 S.E.2d 312, 316; *McGuire v. Martin,* 152 Va. 453, 356, 147 S.E. 265, 266.

Thus an accord and satisfaction is founded on contract embracing an offer and acceptance. The acceptance of course, may be implied, and as a general rule, where the amount due is unliquidated, i.e., disputed, and a remittance of an amount less than that claimed is sent to the creditor with a statement that it is in full satisfaction of the claim, or is accompanied by such acts or declarations as amount to a condition that if accepted, it is accepted in full satisfaction, and the creditor accepts it with knowledge of such condition, then accord and satisfaction results. 1 Am. Jur., Accord and Satisfaction, § 19, p. 221; § 23, p. 224; § 24, p. 225. Annotations, 34 A.L.R. at p. 1044, 75 A.L.R. at p. 916. . . .

These exchanges constituted no offer and acceptance and hence no accord and satisfaction. The burden was on the defendants to prove their plea. *Standard Sewing Machine Co. v. Gunter,* 102 Va. 568, 574, 46 S.E. 690, 692. Their evidence failed to show that they intended the check to be in satisfaction of the plaintiff's demand, but rather the contrary; and if they did so intend it was not made known to the plaintiff in any clear manner, nor was there on the check or in the correspondence any condition that if the check was accepted it was to be in full settlement. To the contrary, before the check was sent the plaintiff wrote it would not be so accepted, and thereafter the check was sent with no condition as to its use, but with what amounted to an expression of willingness that the balance be litigated. *Cf. Thomas & Cross v. Brown,* 116 Va. 233, 237, 81 S.E. 56, 57; *County of Campbell v. Howard & Lee,* 133 Va. 19, 112 S.E. 876.

The plea of accord and satisfaction was no bar to the plaintiff's action and should have been overruled. The judgment below is reversed and the case will be remanded for a trial on its merits under the defendants' plea of the general issue.

Reversed and remanded.

STRUNK CHAIN SAWS, INC. v. WILLIAMS

1959, 111 S.2d 195

This is an action against defendant, Williams, to collect $500, the balance of an account. The defendant asserts novation as a defense. The plaintiff had difficulty collecting a $2430.72 account from defendant for merchandise sold when a partnership, S & F Repair Service, offered to take defendant's assets and assume the obligation, payable in monthly installments. It paid $500 on account and gave its notes for the balance, defendant's name not appearing on the notes. S & F became insolvent, leaving $500 of the amount unpaid, and plaintiff seeks to recover of the defendant. The lower court gave judgment for defendant, implying that the taking of another's note indicated a release of the original party.

GLADNEY, J. . . . The only defense urged herein is a plea of novation, in which it is contended defendant's obligation was extinguished by plaintiff's substitution of a new obligation for the original debt, and a new debtor for the defendant. The plea was sustained by the trial judge.

Novation is defined and explained in the following articles of the LSA-Civil Code:

"Art. 2185 Novation is a contract, consisting of two stipulations; one to extinguish an existing obligation, the other to substitute a new one in its place."

"Art. 2189 Novation takes place in three ways:

"1. When a debtor contracts a new debt to his creditor, which new debt is substituted to the old one, which is extinguished.

"2. What a new debtor is substituted to the old one, who is discharged by the creditor.

"3. When by the effect of a new engagement, a new creditor is substituted to the old one, with regard to whom the debtor is discharged.

"Art. 2192 The delegation, by which a debtor gives to the creditor another debtor who obliges himself towards such creditor, does not operate a novation, unless the creditor has expressly declared that he intends to discharge his debtor who has made the delegation."

Counsel for appellant earnestly insists novation does not take place by the substitution of one debtor for another unless there is an express declaration by the creditor to discharge the debtor who has made the delegation. The evidence as presented, it must be admitted, does not show that by oral or written expression plaintiff stipulated the release of the defendant from his original obligation. But we are of the opinion our jurisprudence has accorded a more liberal construction to the above-quoted articles and a debtor may be discharged where the intent of the creditor to novate is clearly indicated. . . .

We deem it unnecessary to attempt a review of the jurisprudence relating to the application of Articles 2189 and 2192, LSA-C.C. This has been excellently done in an article entitled "The Requisites and Effects of Novation: A Comparative Survey," written by Walter L. Nixon, Jr., *Tulane Law Review*, Volume 25, page 100. The author therein, page 113, concluded:

"Despite the fact that Article 2192 of the Louisiana Civil Code provides that express intention on the part of the creditor is requisite to novation by the substitution of a new debtor for the old one, the Louisiana jurisprudence indicates that acts tanamount [sic] to an express declaration will suffice. * * *"

As observed above, our courts have not adhered to the strict construction contended for by appellant but have ruled a release or discharge can be evidenced by acts of a creditor clearly disclosing an intent to no longer look to the original debtor for payment.

For the reasons herein assigned, the judgment from which appealed is affirmed at appellant's cost.

NILSSON et al. v. KIELMAN et al.

1945, 70 S.D. 390, 17 N.W.2d 918

Action by M. T. Nilsson and E. P. Nilsson against Ethel E. Kielman and L. T. Nilsson on a note. The note matured in 1926 and the statute of limitations had run against it unless certain payments indorsed thereon had extended the life of the note. One payment resulted from the sale of certain property pledged as security and a second payment was the result of the collection of a note which had been assigned as collateral. Ethel E. Kielman made no payments and the security for the note had been given plaintiff many years before the money was realized and the credit given on the note.

ROBERTS, J. . . . It appears from the provisions of SDC33.0213 that an acknowledgment or promise to be effectual to interrupt the running of the statute of limitations must be in writing and signed by the party to be charged, but this requirement does not alter or take away the effect of a part payment. It is the settled law of this state that a part payment to be effectual to interrupt the running of the statute must have been made voluntarily and must have been made and accepted under circumstances consistent with an intent to pay the balance. . . . Payments made by a joint debtor bind only the person making the payments and do not operate to interrupt the running of the statute as to the other debtors not participating or acquiescing in the payments. . . . The principle on which part payment operates to take a debt without the statute is that the debtor by the payment intends to acknowledge the continued existence of the debt.

The agreement with reference to the amount of credit on January 19, 1940, constitutes neither a new promise in writing nor a part payment as of that date. It is the fact of voluntary payment made by the debtor, and not entry of credit, that interrupts the running of the statute. Nor did the collection of the account amounting to $74.40 give new life to the debt.

Plaintiffs were authorized to collect the accounts and apply the proceeds to payment of the debt, but this did not have the same effect as if made personally by the defendants. There is no vital distinction between such a case and one where money received by the payee of a note from collateral security such as notes and mortgages of third parties pledged by the maker is credited on the principal note. Such payment does not interrupt the running of the statute. . . . The underlying reason for the doctrine is that a creditor is not an agent of the debtor to such an extent as to make an act done by him in the name of the debtor operate as a new promise to himself without which element the payment cannot operate to interrupt the statute.

Judgment for defendant affirmed.

WHALE HARBOR SPA, INC. v. WOOD

1959, 266 Fed. 2nd 953

JONES, J. The appellant, Whale Harbor Spa, Inc., is a Florida corporation. Its stock was owned in equal shares by Dorothy W. Wood and Al B. Luckey. The corporation was managed by Luckey. The Luckey and Wood families had been close friends over a period of many years. Between May 1, 1946, and October 14, 1948, Mrs. Wood made six open loans aggregating $24,750 to the corporation. These loans were not evidenced by promissory notes or other written obligation. On July 10, 1950, Mrs. Wood loaned the corporation $5,000 upon its demand note. On April 7, 1947, the corporation paid Mrs. Wood $3,000 on account. The amount of the advances unpaid remains at $26,750. The indebtedness was set up on the corporation's books and was carried as a liability of the corporation to Mrs. Wood. On July 10, 1950, the corporation, by an endorsement on a letter from Mrs. Wood's agent, acknowledged the existence of the indebtedness and the amount of it. From at least as early as November, 1952, and at intervals of never more than six months, the bookkeeper of the corporation, at the direction of Luckey, sent to Mrs. Wood or her agent profit and loss statements and balance sheets of the corporation. The balance sheets showed an indebtedness to Mrs. Wood of $26,750. After the death of both Mrs. Wood and Luckey, the executor of Mrs. Wood brought suit against the corporation for the amount of the unpaid advances. The corporation did not deny that the loans had been made nor did it contend that payment had been made. Its sole defense is that the indebtedness is barred by the Florida statute of limitations. The plaintiff, as executor of Mrs. Wood's estate, contended that the balance sheets were written acknowledgments of the debt sufficient to toll the statute, and further contended that the corporation was equitably estopped to plead the statute of limitations. The court, after a trial without a jury, determined that no part of the debt was barred by the statute of limitations and entered judgment against the corporation. It has appealed.

It is not questioned that the period of limitation has run and that the statute of limitations is a bar to decovery unless the statute has been tolled or the corporation is estopped to assert it. The Florida statute requires that "Every acknowledgement of or promise to pay a debt barred by the statute of limitations, must be in writing and signed by the party to be charged." F.S.A. § 95.04. This statute does not apply to promises made before the expiration of the period of limitations, and verbal promises made before the cause of action had run will take the cause of action out from the operation of the statute. . . . Where there is a distinct acknowledgment in writing of the debt, a promise to pay it will be inferred. . . .

The precedents of the decided cases point to a rule, which we think is sound in principle, that the requirement of an acknowledgment of an indebtedness which will interrupt the running of the statute of limitations is met by a balance sheet of a corporate debtor where the obligations in question are listed as liabilities of the corporation.

No error is shown in the judgment of the district court for the appellee. That judgment is affirmed.

RICE v. BORDNER

1905, 140 Fed. 566

Petition in involuntary bankruptcy filed by Rice against the defendant.

ARCHIBALD, J. . . . But, passing that by, the proofs that have been submitted lead to the same result. They show that in a small way the respondent may be said to have had several occupations. He had a store, was agent for the sale of fertilizers, and he ran a farm. The question is: In which business was he chiefly engaged? This is to be determined by which was of paramount importance to him, or on which he depended for a living . . . about which there can be no serious question. No doubt at one time he had a store of considerable local importance; the election district being named after it. But that was many years ago, and the business had been so eaten into by other stores which have started up about him at no great distance that what he was doing in that line at the time these proceedings were instituted was insignificant. . . . From this, as he swears, his income was about $60 or $70 a year; and it is difficult to see how it could be more. In addition he sold $200 or $300 worth of fertilizers as agent for a phosphate company. . . .

In contrast to this is shown that the respondent had two farms, aggregating 240 acres, which he managed himself, employing but one man regularly besides his son; others being called in as occasion required. From this land he raised wheat, oats, corn and hay, besides having a number of cows and selling milk; the total farm products being valued at from $1,000 to $1,200, out of which he realized about $600, and the sales of milk alone amounting to some $200 to $250. That it was upon the farm that he depended for a livelihood is evident; what is called his store being the merest excuse for one, and yielding him but a pittance. . . . The petition is therefore dismissed at the cost of the petitioning creditor.

In re STOVALL GROCERY CO.

1908, 161 Fed. 882

NEWMAN, J. . . . The bankrupt firm is alleged to have been composed of M. E. and C. C. Stovall, which firm, according to the petition, did business at different times under the name of Stovall Grocery Company. . . . The first ground of bankruptcy is that on the 25th day of January, 1908 (this petition having been filed on February 1, 1908), the firm committed an act of bankruptcy by paying to one H. L. Singer a note for $3 in full of Singer's claims, and that this was a preference, and intended to be a preference. I do not think that the payment of $3 to a creditor a week before the bankruptcy proceedings was instituted could be classed as a preference. It is not such a substantial transaction as would, of itself, justify the institution of a proceeding in bankruptcy. . . . It would be difficult to draw a line and say what amount would be sufficient, and what would not, made in payment of a debt, to make a substantial preference. This would depend more or less on the character of the business, whether large or small.

The other ground of bankruptcy relied upon is this: "That on the 24th day of December, 1907, said C. C. Stovall, a member of said firm, conveyed and transferred his undivided half interest in and to a certain lot . . . in the city of Atlanta, to Mattie E. Stovall, his wife, without consideration, with intent to hinder, delay, and defraud his creditors and the creditors of said firm. . . ."

It will be perceived that the act of bankruptcy alleged here is the transfer by an individual member of a firm of property with intent to defraud individual creditors and firm creditors. That is not an act of bankruptcy on the part of the firm. The partnership entity must act, and what is relied upon must be its act.

As neither of the grounds of bankruptcy contained in the petition are sufficient, the demurrer to the petition is sustained.

MARKS, TRUSTEE v. GOODYEAR RUBBER SUNDRIES, INC.
1956, 238 Fed. 2nd 533

This was a suit instituted by Marks, trustee in bankruptcy, to recover of the defendant an alleged preferential payment.

SWAN, J. This appeal presents a narrow issue, namely, whether the defendant, a creditor of the bankrupt, had reasonable cause to believe that its debtor was insolvent at the time when merchandise purchased from it was returned for credit against the bankrupt's account.

The facts are not in dispute. On December 27, 1954, one week before filing a voluntary petition in bankruptcy, the bankrupt returned to defendant goods having an invoice value of $2,903 which defendant had sold to the bankrupt on credit on November 19, 1954. After credit was given for the returned merchandise, there was still due and owing from the bankrupt to defendant $5,799.61. The returned merchandise was accompanied by a letter reading:

"Finding ourselves financially embarrassed, we are returning this date the merchandise shipped to us per your invoice No. 19289 consisting of 5806 lbs of film." . . .

It is obvious that return and acceptance of the merchandise was a preferential transfer, as defined in § 60, sub. a of the Bankruptcy Act, and the only question for decision is whether it was a voidable preference, as defined in § 60, sub. b, 11 U.S.C.A. § 96. This turns on whether defendant had reasonable cause to believe that its debtor was insolvent when the merchandise was returned.

The district judge concluded that the defendant did not have such reasonable cause and that the plaintiff had failed to sustain his burden of proof. With these conclusions we are constrained to disagree.

In determining what constitutes "reasonable cause" it is well settled that notice of facts which would incite a man of ordinary prudence to an inquiry under similar circumstances is notice of all the facts which reasonably diligent inquiry would have disclosed. Payment by the return of merchandise may in certain circumstances be sufficient to indicate reasonable cause for belief of the buyer's insolvency. However, where a buyer returned goods because his inventory was too large and business was bad, the seller was held not to have received a voidable preference. Thus acceptance of goods returned by a buyer is not of itself proof that the seller had reasonable cause to believe the buyer insolvent. In the case at bar the goods were returned because, as stated in bankrupt's letter, the partnership found themselves "financially embarrassed," and the defendant in its letter of January 3rd, interpreted that phrase as meaning "financially unable to meet your obligations." Also it not only asked what the buyer could do "in the retirement of your overdue account," but demanded "some positive schedule of payments from you in the next few days," "in order to prevent our factors from stepping in to take action on this account." Furthermore, Mr. Lake, the defendant's credit man, testified that after getting the letter of December 27th and the return of the goods, he would not have extended further credit without further explanation from the debtor. Appendix 29a. We think that the foregoing facts would "incite a man of ordinary prudence to an inquiry." . . .

Judgment of dismissal is reversed and judgment awarded to the plaintiff for $2,903 plus interest from December 27, 1954.

FRANK v. MERCANTILE NAT. BANK

1905, 182 N.Y. 264, 74 N.E. 841

This was an action by Frank, the trustee in bankruptcy, to recover a certain deposit in National Broadway Bank, which the defendant had assumed as part of the liabilities of said bank. The defendant desired to set off certain notes signed by the bankrupt which were taken from the plaintiff contended the right of set-off did not arise as most of the notes had not matured.

CULLEN, C. J. . . . Section 68 of that law (bankruptcy act) provides that "in all cases of mutual debts or mutual credits between the estate of the bankrupt and a creditor the account shall be stated and one debt shall be set off against the other, and the balance only shall be allowed or paid. . . ." The argument is that, as unmatured claims against the bankrupt are provable against his estate they necessarily are the subject of set-off under the provisions of section 68. We think that this position is well taken, but we shall refrain from entering into any discussion of the question, as the proposition seemed to be settled by decisions of the federal courts. The uniform current of authority in the District and Circuit Courts of the United States, is to that effect, and the law is so stated in the textbooks on bankruptcy.

Judgment for defendant.

AIRO SUPPLY CO. v. PAGE

1954, (Ill. App.) 119 N.E.2d 400

The defendant Page had acted as plaintiff's bookkeeper over a period of three years, during which he embezzled $14,775.77. Some time later he filed a voluntary petition in bankruptcy and obtained a discharge. Thereafter he began to work for Automatic Electric Company where his wages are now the subject of a garnishment proceeding. The lower court denied garnishment concluding that the claim was discharged by bankruptcy. Plaintiff appealed.

FRIEND, J. . . . Upon this state of the record the question presented is whether plaintiff's claim for the recovery of funds which defendant, its former employee, admittedly embezzled or misappropriated, is released by defendant's discharge in bankruptcy. Section 35, title 11, U.S.C.A. reads as follows: "A discharge in bankruptcy shall release a bankrupt from all of his provable debts, whether allowable in full or in part, except such as . . . (4) were created by his fraud, embezzlement, misappropriation or defalcation while acting as an officer or in any fiduciary capacity." There can be no doubt that the debt, which was reduced to judgment by agreement of the parties, was created by defendant's fraud, embezzlement, misappropriation or defalcation; this charge is not denied. It is conceded that the defendant was not acting as an officer of the corporation; the inquiry is thus narrowed to whether he was acting in any fiduciary capacity. He argues that the phrase "in any fiduciary capacity," as used in the Bankruptcy Act, embraces only technical trusts and not trusts which are implied in a contract or in the position of the parties. . . .

Was defendant, as a bookkeeper, and in sole charge of plaintiff's cash accounts, acting in a fiduciary capacity? Plaintiff cites various decisions which we regard as in point and controlling. In *Citizens Mut. Automobile Ins. Co. v. Gardner*, 315 Mich. 689, 24 N.W.2d 410 plaintiff obtained a judgment against defendant, an insurance agent, for premiums which defendant had collected and failed to remit. Garnishment proceedings were then instituted on the judgment, which defendant moved to dismiss, based on a discharge in bankruptcy which he had obtained after the entry of the judgment. The court held that his discharge in bankruptcy did not prevent the enforcement of the judgment, since it clearly appeared from the record in the case in which judgment was entered that defendant's obligation to the plaintiff arose from his failure to remit the insurance premiums that he had collected. The court concluded that this constituted a defalcation within the meaning of the act; and with respect to a contention similar to defendant's in the instant proceeding, the court said that "for the purposes of this case it may be assumed that defendant was not shown to have been guilty of fraud, embezzlement or misappropriation, but it does not follow that there was no defalcation on his part within the meaning of the term as used in the bankruptcy act. It has been repeatedly held that one who, acting in a fiduciary capacity, fails to observe his duty to make payment of money coming into his possession in such capacity, places himself, by such failure, within the scope of the term 'defalcation.' . . ."

All the circumstances of record clearly indicate that defendant occupied a position of trust. He handled plaintiff's funds and admits that he embezzled and wrongfully "converted"' them while he was occupying this position. As plaintiff's counsel point out, defendant was not the "honest debtor" whom the Bankruptcy Act was intended to aid; both the letter of the law and every consideration of justice and public policy require that he be compelled to repay the money he misappropriated.

Accordingly, we hold that the court erred in abating and dismissing the garnishment proceeding. The judgment of the Superior Court is therefore reversed, and the cause remanded with directions that judgment be entered on the garnishment in favor of plaintiff.

Judgment reversed and cause remanded with directions.

WEGIEL v. HOGAN

1953, (N.J. Sup. Ct.) 100 A.2d 349

Wegiel, plaintiff, seeks to enforce a $5,000 judgment obtained against the defendant, the latter contending the claim was discharged by bankruptcy. Judgment was originally obtained under wrongful death statute by next of kin. It appeared that Vincent Wegiel was walking on the highway pulling or pushing a wagon containing wood while accompanied by his son pushing a bicycle. Although the evidence was essentially circumstantial, it appeared they were hit by the defendant and the boy dragged for at least a block. The defendant, failing to stop, continued for another ten blocks when the car jumped the curb, hit a street sign and came to a stop, the bicycle being found near where the car stopped. The lower court disregarded bankruptcy and permitted action on the judgment, and the defendant appealed.

Ewart, J. A. D. The principal question presented for determination by this appeal is whether or not defendant's discharge in bankruptcy operates to release and discharge a judgment theretofore secured by plaintiff in her representative capacity against the defendant.

The pertinent section of the National Bankruptcy Act upon which defendant relies reads:

"A discharge in bankruptcy shall release a bankrupt from all of his provable debts, whether allowed in full or in part, except such as . . . ; (2) are liabilities for obtaining money or property by false pretenses or false representations, *or for willful and malicious injuries to the person or property of another*, . . ." 11 U.S.C.A. § 35. (Emphasis supplied.) . . .

In the case at bar, there were no eyewitnesses to the happening of the accident in which the plaintiff's intestates lost their lives, but the proofs at the trial were wholly circumstantial. However, circumstantial evidence may suffice, indeed often is more certain, satisfying and persuasive, than direct evidence. In re *Lewis, supra*, 11 N.J. at page 221, 94 A.2d at page 330.

In the light of the foregoing decisions and definitions, may it be said that the defendant was guilty of inflicting wilful and malicious injuries to the persons of the plaintiff's intestates in the absence of any proof of any positive intent or purpose by the defendant to run them down? Here we have the circumstances that the defendant drove and propelled his automobile on a public highway in the City of Bayonne; struck and killed the decedent Vincent Wegiel and his 14-year-old son, Michael; the body of Michael was apparently carried on the defendant's automobile for a distance of approximately a block beyond the point where the accident occurred; defendant failed to stop and render assistance to the injured persons, but, on the contrary, continued driving for a distance of some 10 blocks (from 42nd to 32nd Streets) where he lost control of his car; the car jumped the curb, struck and bent the post of a street sign and overturned; and the broken bicycle found by the officer at the scene where the defendant's car overturned offered mute but persuasive evidence of the manner in which the defendant must have been operating his car. In addition, while the defendant denied at the police station that he had been involved in an accident and even denied having been in the vicinity of the place where the accident occurred, yet in the "Agreed Statement in Lieu of Record" presented on this appeal, it is frankly stated that defendant Hogan was the operator of the automobile on the public highway known as Avenue E at or near its intersection with East 42nd Street in the City of Bayonne on December 24, 1931 and that his automobile had struck decedents Vincent and Michael Wegiel, both of whom died as a result of the injuries suffered thereby. And of course, the jury found against him at the trial.

The act of the defendant in driving his automobile in the manner in which he did drive it on the occasion in question was deliberate, voluntary and intentional. In the sense that it was voluntary and intentional, it was wilful. There is no proof that he was actuated by personal malevolence or personal malice toward the two people he killed, but it is not necessary that such elements exist to constitute malice in its legal sense. Where one, with reckless indifference to consequences, performs a deliberate act in the face of known circumstances and the high degree of probability of producing harm, the law imputes to the actor a constructive intention to inflict the injuries resulting therefrom and stamps the act as willfully injurious rather than as mere negligence. *King v. Patrylow, supra;* In re *Lewis, supra.*

In driving his automobile upon a public highway in the City of Bayonne at about the hour of 7:50 in the evening, defendant Hogan should have anticipated the existence of other vehicles or traffic upon the street; notwithstanding, he apparently drove and propelled his automobile in a wanton and reckless manner and with an utter disregard of the rights and safety of others; after striking two people on the highway, and carrying the body of one of them for a distance of approximately a block, he failed to stop and render assistance but continued on his way for a distance of some ten blocks until he lost control of his car which jumped the curb and upset. We find that the circumstances of this case support the conclusion that the defendant Hogan, with knowledge that injury would probably result from his conduct and with reckless indifference to the consequence, deliberately drove and propelled his car upon a public highway in such a manner as to inflict death upon two people and was therefore guilty of inflicting "willful and malicious injuries to persons," and that hence his discharge in bankruptcy does not operate to release the judgment against him or to bar further proceedings thereon. . . .

For the reasons stated, the order appealed from will be affirmed.

UNITED STATES v. MUNRO-VAN HELMS COMPANY, INC.
1957, 243 Fed. 2nd 10

Munro-Van Helms Company, Inc. is involved in a bankruptcy proceeding during which a question is raised as to the priority to be given, if any, of claims by laborers for vacation pay which had been earned over a period of a year based upon a percentage of their earnings, the vacation pay for the year having been accrued within the past three months. The lower court allowed the vacation pay for the full year, while creditors contended that only that portion of the vacation pay actually earned within the last three months was entitled to priority.

JONES, J. . . . Vacation pay is, by all of the decisions, regarded as wages. 6 Remington on Bankruptcy, 382, § 2807. The courts are not in accord as to extent of the priority which claims for vacation pay should be accorded by courts of bankruptcy. It has been held that full priority should be given to claims for vacation pay which accrued during the three months' period even though part of the services upon which the right to the pay is conditioned was rendered prior to the beginning of the three months' period. In re *Kinney Aluminum Co.*, D.C.S.D. Cal. 1948, 78 Supp. 565; Supp. Vol. 3 Moore's Collier on Bankruptcy, 192, § 64.203. This theory is based upon the assumption that the purpose of the priority granted to wage claimants is to benefit those who have lost employment by reason of the bankruptcy and need the protection of the statute. In re *Kinney Aluminum Co., supra.* It has been said, however, that the priority was intended to provide that those who created assets immediately prior to the filing of the petition and had not received payment for such creations should be set apart in a privileged class. In re *Raiken*, D.C.N.J. 1940, 33 F. Supp. 88. This purpose would not be served by allowing priority for the full amount of vacation pay.

The better reasoned rule is, we think, that announced by the Ninth Circuit where Judge Healy, speaking for the court, said:

"Under the terms of the statute the compensation claimed must have been earned within the three months' period and also must be due. If any employee here had not, prior to bankruptcy, completed a year's continuous service no compensation for vacation time would have been due him, regard being had to the wage agreement. All having completed the required year's service prior to bankruptcy, vacation compensation may fairly be regarded as due even though the vacation was not to be taken until some later time; but the vacation had been earned by the performance of the entire year's service, and only one-fourth of it earned during the three months preceding bankruptcy. We see no more justification for giving priority to vacation pay conditionally accruing prior to such three months' period than for giving priority to straight wages earned prior thereto." Division of Labor Law Enforcement, *State of Cal. v. Sampsell*, 9 Cir., 1949, 172 F.2d 400, 401.

We decide that the vacation pay of those entitled to it under the contract constituted wages earned over the period of a year but such wages are entitled to priority only to the extent of one-fourth of the annual vacation pay. In reaching this conclusion we are aware that some of the employees will perhaps have put in more time during the yearly period than others whose vacation pay would be the same, and we recognize the possibility that some, perhaps all, will have worked more in some of the quarter-annual periods than in others. Vacations, and their equivalents in vacation pay, result from arrangements to secure the well-being of employees and are factors in maintaining harmonious employer-employee relations. Each employee's status as such, under the vacation article of the agreement, continues even though there is an illness, a lay-off or other work interruption, and while continuing the inchoate vacation right accumulates. (Priority allowed for only that portion earned during the last three months.)

CROSS v. COMMONS et al.

1953, Mich., 59 N.W.2d 41

This suit was initiated by plaintiff Cross, trustee in bankruptcy of defendant, to recover part of the value of property alleged to have been conveyed in fraud of creditors. The lower court gave judgment for defendant, and plaintiff has appealed.

Butzel, J. George D. Commons was purchasing the home in which he resided in the township of Laketon, county of Muskegon, State of Michigan, on land contract. From time to time he had borrowed sums of money from Mark Jones who, on November 10, 1950, loaned him an additional amount so as to make the aggregate owing $5,000, which amount Commons agreed to pay to Jones in one year, with interest at 6 per cent. As security for the loan, Commons pledged his vendee's interest in the land contract to Jones. The debt became due on November 10, 1951. Commons was unable to pay and in lieu of foreclosure he assigned his equity in the property to Jones. At the time of the transfer there was $5,300 due Jones and $2,756.62 still owing to the vendors in the land contract, so that the total indebtedness was $8,056.62. It is conceded that the fair market value of the property was $10,000. Jones thereupon paid off the balance due the land contract vendors and transferred the premises to Charles O. White and Martha White, his wife, who sold the property for $10,000.

On November 23, 1951, an involuntary petition in bankruptcy was filed against Commons, and six days later he was adjudged a bankrupt. George H. Cross, as trustee in bankruptcy, brought the instant suit against Commons, Jones and wife, and White and wife, to recover the sum of $1,943.38, the difference between the $10,000 realized from the sale of the property and the sum of $5,300 due Jones and $2,756.38 due the vendors on the land contract. Plaintiff claims recovery on the theory that the transfer to Commons' equity in the property to Jones and wife and by them to White and wife was either a preference under the bankruptcy act or an unlawful, fraudulent conveyance, without consideration and in fraud of creditors. No consideration is shown to have been paid by White and wife to Jones and wife. The record indicates that over $500 was paid out for taxes, repairs and improvements after Commons assigned the contract and prior to the sale to third parties. The trial judge did not deem it necessary to consider additional amounts but based his opinion and decrees on the ground that Commons owned a homestead interest in the property at the time he conveyed to Jones and, as his equity was of a value of less than $2,500, the amount of homestead interest exempt under the law, such interest was immune from the claims of his creditors and his trustee in bankruptcy. He held that Commons had a right to do whatever he saw fit with his exempt property.

In our discussion we view the facts as found by the trial judge. He found that Commons was insolvent at the time he assigned the contract; that Jones and his wife knew of his financial condition notwithstanding the fact that bankruptcy proceedings had not been begun; that the fair value of the property was $10,000; and that Commons' equity, after deducting the amount due Jones and the balance still owing the vendors on the contract, was $1,943.38 for the recovery of which amount only suit was brought. . . .

In 6 Am. Jur., Bankruptcy, § 1102, it is said that:

Creditors cannot complain of transfers of exempt property. A transfer of such property, although made within four months of bankruptcy and made while the debtor is insolvent, does not deplete the assets available for administration by the trustee in bankruptcy for the benefit of the general creditors. Therefore, a transfer of exempt property cannot constitute a preference.

. . . The Bankruptcy Act § 6, as amended, 11 U.S.C.A. § 24, provides as follows:

Sec. 6. Exemptions of bankrupts. This title shall not affect the allowance to bankrupts of the exemptions which are prescribed by the laws of the United States or by the State laws in force at the time of the filing of the petition in the State wherein they have had their domicile for the six months immediately preceding the filing of the petition, or for a longer portion of such six months than in any State. . . .

The trial judge also based his opinion on *Kleinert v. Lefkowitz,* 271 Mich. 79, 259 N.W. 871, 875, wherein the history of the homestead exemption and the rights of the trustee in bankruptcy are carefully considered and where we said:

. . . The homestead exemption did not pass to the trustee in bankruptcy. Defendants could do with it what they pleased. Creditors were not defrauded by reason of any dealings therewith. By the terms of the bankruptcy statute the bankruptcy courts and the state courts have concurrent jurisdiction. Homestead exemptions are governed by the law of the state. The exemption involved is not necessarily the exemption of the bankrupt, but involves the right of his wife to claim a homestead exemption. The trustee in bankruptcy authorized by the referee to institute this suit invoked the jurisdiction of the state court, and in the courts of the state he has available to him the remedies conferred by the laws of the state. Defendants are entitled to the homestead rights of the real estate used and occupied by them as such.

. . . *The decree of the lower court, dismissing the bill, is affirmed, with costs to defendants.*

Review Questions and Problems

1. *M* and *X* were co-makers of a note. After maturity, *M* made some payments, and a question arose as to whether the payments extended the period of *X*'s liability. Is the liability of *X* outlawed, or was it extended by the payments of *M*? Is one who owes a debt ever morally justified in using the Statute of Limitations to evade payment?
2. *L & B,* a partnership, sued *W* for services rendered and *W* urged accord and satisfaction as a defense. *W* claimed the bill to be excessive and mailed a check for a lesser amount marked "in full of account." *L&B* drew a line through the statement and cashed the check. Was this an accord and satisfaction?
3. *A* sold a printing machine to *B* on the installment plan. *B* sold the machine to *C*, who agreed to pay the balance of the purchase price. Both parties notified *A* of the arrangement. *C* failed to make the payments, and *A* now seeks to hold *B*. May he do so?

4. On April 1, *B* purchased a typewriter on credit at a price of $150 and on July 1 he purchased bookkeeping machines at a cost of $325, both items being purchased of *C*. On August 1 *B* mailed his check of $200 to *C* and instructed him to apply it on the $325 item. Assuming a five-year Statute of Limitations, how much will *C* be able to recover of *B* as of June 1 five years after the typewriter was purchased?
5. *D* owed Bank a $4,000 note, and long after it was due the bank credited a small bank balance of $1.41 owing to *D* on the note. Did this toll the Statute of Limitations?
6. *A* is a farmer and earns by the operation of the farm the sum of $4,500 a year. As a result of some unwise investments, he becomes insolvent and gives a mortgage on his farm to secure one of his creditors. May other creditors force him into involuntary bankruptcy?
7. *C* sued *T* to recover on an indebtedness of $500, which *T* claimed was discharged in bankruptcy. *K* had sold the goods to *T* but had assigned the $500 claim to *C* and *T* had received notice of the assignment to *C*. *T* listed *K* as a creditor and notice of bankruptcy was sent to *K* but not to *C*. Consequently, *C*, not learning of bankruptcy, failed to file a claim. Because of this, *C* contends the claim is not discharged. Is *C* correct in his contention?
8. *A*, while insolvent, paid an obligation for $300 in favor of *B*. Although *A* was insolvent at the time, he was clearly unaware of the fact. Has he committed an act of bankruptcy?
9. A petition in involuntary bankruptcy was filed against *K* on Nov. 29. On Nov. 30 *K* sold to *M* $16,000 in accounts receivable for $15,600, *M* knowing of the petition in bankruptcy. *K* used these funds to meet payroll and taxes. On Dec. 10, *K* was adjudicated a bankrupt, and the trustee sought to obtain the return of the accounts. The court allowed the trustee to recover. Was this decision sound?
10. *B* owed *C* a past due indebtedness of $500 and induced the latter to extend the maturity of the indebtedness three years at 6 per cent interest by giving a chattel mortgage as security. Sixty days after the mortgage was given, *B* filed a petition in voluntary bankruptcy. Under what conditions, if any, will the trustee in bankruptcy be able to avoid the mortgage?
11. *A* became a voluntary bankrupt. At the time the petition was filed, he owed *B* the sum of $2,000, which was to fall due 60 days later. *B* owed *A* on a separate transaction the sum of $1,000, which was due at the time the petition was filed. May the trustee collect the $1,000 and force *B* to become an ordinary creditor as to the $2,000?
12. An insurance agent collected premiums but failed to remit to the company. The agent became a bankrupt and obtained his discharge. Is he still liable to the company for the premium? Was the agent a fiduciary?
13. *B* Co. supplied materials to *K* Co., the materials being used by the latter in a certain building. He received payments from time to time when *K* Co. was known to be insolvent and when *B* Co. could, under the mechanics lien law, have filed a lien to secure the balance due if payments were not made. *K* Co. is in bankruptcy and the trustee

seeks to recover the payments from *B* Co. The court held these payments were not voidable. Why?

14. In 1927, *A* deeded certain property to his wife's uncle in order to avoid the payment of large obligations maturing in 1930. In 1931, *A* was declared a bankrupt. May the trustee recover the property conveyed to the uncle?
15. *B* owed his bank a note for $15,000 and, at a time when he was insolvent, arranged to deposit all receipts with the bank. He was not to draw any checks until the balance exceeded the note owing to the bank. He became a bankrupt at a time when the bank balance was $10,500. May the bank set off the balance against the note and file a claim for the difference?
16. *E* Co., now in bankruptcy, had failed prior to bankruptcy to make contractual payments to the union welfare fund. The court held that the default in payments for the three months immediately prior to bankruptcy should not be treated as wages. Is this a sound decision?
17. *A* filed a petition in voluntary bankruptcy and was adjudicated a bankrupt on March 1, 1954. Three months later, his aunt died and bequeathed him $15,000. Will he be able to retain this amount or will it revert to the trustee in bankruptcy?
18. *E*, now in bankruptcy, had given checks for wages shortly before it ceased to do business, and the checks were dishonored by the bank. The employees sold and assigned the checks to *S*. The court permitted *S* to have priority as if he were a wage earner. Was this sound?
19. *B* became a bankrupt but failed to list *S*, a surety on one of his obligations, as a creditor. Does *S*, who did not learn of the bankruptcy until later, still have a good claim against *B*?

BOOK III

AGENCY

16

Creation of the Agency

3-1. Definition. In the broad sense agency is the relation created by employment. Strictly defined, however, agency is the relationship that arises when one party authorizes another to create, to modify, or to terminate contractual relations between the former and third parties. The one granting the authority is known as the *principal,* whereas the one to whom the power is given is called the *agent.* Agency as defined in this limited sense excludes the relationship of master and servant, for the latter has no power to create contractual relations. For an agent to act, three parties are necessary: the principal, the agent, and a third party with whom contracts may be formed. To create the master and servant relation, only two parties are necessary. However, since many of the laws relating to master and servant are analogous to those governing principal and agent, and since the two relations often merge, as when an agent performs the duties of a servant and vice versa, the rules of agency herein set forth will be deemed to apply to either situation unless otherwise stipulated.

An agent is not necessarily an employee subject to social security and withholding tax. Local fire insurance agents and commission houses are usually agents but not employees.

3-2. Agent distinguished from independent contractor. A person may contract for the services of another in such a way as to have full and complete control over the manner in which the latter conducts the work, or he may contract for a certain end result. If the agreement provides merely that the second party is to accomplish a certain result and has full control over the manner and methods to be pursued in bringing about the result, he is deemed an independent contractor, and the one receiving the benefit of his services is in no sense responsible to third parties for his actions. On the other hand, if the second party places his services at the disposal of the first in such a manner that the action of the second is controlled by the former, an agency relation is established.[1] To illustrate: *A* contracts to build a boat for *P* at a cost of $1,000 and according to cer-

[1] King v. Young, Brown, and Beverly, Inc., page 344.

tain specifications. In such a case it is clear that *A* is an independent contractor with the completed boat as the result, and *P* in no sense becomes responsible for lumber or other material purchased. However, had *P* engaged *A* by the day to build the boat and had authorized *A* to purchase the necessary materials, it is equally clear that an agency would have been created.

APPOINTMENT OF AGENT

3-3. Proper parties. It is generally stated that anyone who may act for himself may act through an agent. To this rule there is one fairly well-recognized exception. An infant may enter into a contract, and so long as he does not disaffirm, the agreement is binding. There is considerable authority to the effect that any appointment of an agent by an infant is void. Therefore, under this theory any agreement entered into by such an agent would be ineffective, and an attempted disaffirmance would be superfluous. Most recent cases hold, however, that the act of the agent is voidable only, being subject to rescission or ratification by the minor.

Nevertheless, an infant may act as an agent for someone else, and any agreement which he makes while acting for his principal is binding. Although the infant has a right to terminate his contract of agency at his will, as long as he continues in the employment his acts within the scope of the authority conferred become those of his employer.

Contracts that delegate authority to an agent, like any other agreements, must have for their purpose a legal object. As in the case of other illegal contracts, the courts would not force the parties to carry out an agency agreement with an illegal purpose, but would leave the parties without any legal redress.

3-4. Express delegation of authority. The usual procedure followed in the creation of an agency is for the principal expressly to confer certain authority upon the agent. The agreement may be explicit, setting forth in detail the rights and duties of the respective parties, or it may consist of general terms, in which event the extent of the authority conferred depends upon various factors, such as general custom, business usage, and past practices of the particular principal.

Usually no particular formalities are essential to the appointment of an agent; it may be either written or oral, with two exceptions. First, where the purpose of the agency can be exercised only by the signing of a formal document under seal, the agency must be created under seal. Where a formal sealed instrument is used for the conferring of authority upon the agent, he is said to possess a power of attorney. A formal power of attorney may be general, giving the agent authority to act in all respects as the principal could act, or it may be special, granting to the agent very restricted authority. It is customarily acknowledged before a notary public whose seal is attached thereto. Second, the law in the majority of the states requires that any agent who is given power to sell or to convey any interest in or concerning real estate must obtain such power by a written authorization from the principal. The ordinary real estate broker, however, in most states would not need a written agreement, as his authority is merely to find a buyer with whom the seller is willing to contract. Normally, he has no authority to enter into a binding contract to convey the property.

A further exception exists in a few states where it is required that the authority must possess the same dignity as the act to be performed. In these states an agent who possesses authority to sign a contract which is required to be in writing must receive his appointment by an instrument in writing. Such is not the law in most states.

3-5. Authority by estoppel. No agency ever arises without some action or conduct on the part of the principal. The proposed agent cannot by his own conduct alone establish the relationship, and no statement of his, standing alone, can justify a third party in believing an agency exists. An agency is a matter to be proved, and third persons dealing with an agent do so at their peril. A duty rests upon the third party to ascertain the nature and extent of the agent's authority. Generally speaking, if the agent has no authority or it is insufficient to authorize the particular act involved, the principal is not bound.

Nevertheless, conditions often develop under which the principal, because of his conduct, is estopped to deny the existence of an agency. An agent under such conditions is called an ostensible agent, and the agency is said to arise by estoppel. (1) The principal must conduct himself in such a manner as to lead third parties reasonably to believe that an agency exists. (2) The third party must know of such conduct and act in reliance thereon. No estoppel can arise except where the third party relies upon facts known to him at the time he transacts business with the agent, which facts would have led a reasonably prudent person to assume that an agency existed.

An agency by estoppel may arise from a course of dealing on the part of the agent, which is constantly ratified by the principal,[2] or it may result from the agent's holding himself out as such without any dissent on the part of the principal and under conditions where the principal owed a duty to speak. To illustrate: Upon several occasions A indorses his principal's name to checks and has them cashed at the bank. The principal has never given the agent such authority, but no protest is lodged with the

[2] Pettinger v. Alpena Cedar Co., page 374.

bank until the agent appropriates to his own use the proceeds from one of the checks. The principal then attempts to recover from the bank. By ratification of the agent's previous unauthorized action, the principal has led the bank reasonably to assume that the agent possesses such authority.

3-6. Agent's power to appoint subagents. Agents are usually selected because of their personal qualifications. Owing to these elements of trust and confidence, a general rule has developed that an agent may not delegate his duty to someone else and clothe the latter with authority to bind the principal.[3] An exception has arisen to this rule in those cases in which the acts of the agent are purely ministerial or mechanical. An act that requires no discretion and is purely mechanical may be delegated by the agent to a third party. Such a delegation does not make the third party the agent of the principal or give him any action against the principal for compensation. The acts of such third party become in reality the acts of the agent and bind the principal only so long as they are within the authority given to the agent. Acts which involve the exercise of skill, discretion, or judgment may not be delegated without permission from the principal.

The case of authorized salesmen for local insurance agents seems to offer a slight exception to this rule. The local agent of an insurance company often authorizes his salesmen to accept fire insurance risks. Even though such action seems to involve a certain amount of judgment and discretion, the insurance companies are bound by the subagent's act, although they are in no respect obligated to compensate him, for the salesman must obtain his compensation from the local agent.

An agent may, under certain circumstances, have the implied authority to appoint other agents for the principal, in which case they become true employees of the principal and are entitled to be compensated by him. Such a power on the part of the agent is not often implied, but if the situation is such that the major power conferred cannot be exercised without the aid of other agents, the agent is authorized to select such help as is required. Thus, a manager placed in charge of a branch store may be presumed to possess authority to hire the necessary clerks and sales force demanded by the size of the business.

RATIFICATION

3-7. Definition. Contracts entered into by an agent who lacks authority are ineffective unless they are subsequently adopted by the principal. Ratification consists of conduct which approves an act performed by one party for another without authority. Such approval cures the defect

[3] State ex rel. Kendrick v. Thormyer, page 375.

of lack of authority, and the relation of the parties assumes the status that would have existed had authority been granted before the act took place.

3-8. Conditions required for ratification. Various conditions must exist in order that ratification be effective and bring about a contractual relation between the principal and the third party. It should be remembered in this connection that ratification is used only where no authority, either actual or otherwise, can be shown. Furthermore, the authority reverts back and becomes effective as of the date of the act performed by the agent. Because of this fact, ratification can be effective only where both the principal and the agent were capable of doing the act at the time it was performed and are still capable at the time of ratification. For this reason a corporation may not ratify contracts made by its promoters before the corporation was formed. For the corporation to be bound by such agreements a novation or assumption of liability must be shown. Ratification is impossible because the corporation was not in existence when the agreement was formed and could not possibly have entered into a contract at that date.

3-9. Other conditions. An agent's act may be ratified only when he holds himself out as acting for the one who is subsequently charged with the agreement. In other words the agent must have professed to act as an agent. A person who professes to act for himself and who makes a contract in his own name does nothing that can be ratified even though he intends at the time to let another have the benefit of his agreement.

The states are slightly in conflict as to whether the third party—the one with whom the agent dealt—may withdraw before ratification takes place. The better view, and that which apparently has the support of most of the states, is to the effect that the third party may withdraw from the transaction at any time before it is ratified by the principal. If not permitted to withdraw, he would be unable to hold the principal and at the same time would not be free to act with others concerning the subject matter until the principal had exercised his option. It seems only fair, therefore, to permit the third party to withdraw at any time before the principal has indicated his adoption of the transaction. However, it should be pointed out that ratification does not require notice to the third party. As soon as conduct constituting ratification has been indulged in by the principal, the third party loses his right to withdraw.

Furthermore, as a general principle, ratification does not bind the principal unless he acts with full knowledge of all the important facts. Of course, where ratification is expressed and the principal acts without any apparent desire to know or to learn the facts involved, he may not later defend himself on the ground that he was unaware of all the material facts. Where, however, ratification is to be implied from the conduct of the principal, it must be apparent that he acts with complete understanding of all important details. *A*, a salesman with authority only to solicit orders, having no authority to sell, contracts to sell certain of his principal's goods to *T*, and signs *P*'s name to the order. As an inducement to *T* to enter into the agreement, *A* sells all of the articles at a 10 per cent discount. *A* informs *P* of the sale, and files the duplicate sales slip without *P* having an opportunity to inspect it. At the time the order is ready to be shipped, it is noted for the first time that the discount is to be allowed. It would seem to be improper to impute ratification under such circumstances.

3-10. Conduct constituting ratification. What conduct on the part of the principal will amount to ratification? Ratification may be either express or implied. Where certain formalities, such as a writing or an authorization under seal, are required to create a particular agency, the ratification must follow the form required for the creation of the agency. Aside from this, any conduct which definitely indicates an intention on the part of the principal to adopt the transaction will constitute ratification. It may take the form of words of approval to the agent, a promise to perform, or actual performance, such as delivery of the product called for in the agreement. Accepting the benefits of the contract or basing a suit on the validity of an agreement clearly amounts to ratification.

At this point it should be mentioned that an unauthorized act may not be ratified in part and rejected in part.[5] The principal cannot accept the benefits and refuse to assume the obligations. Because of this fact it is said that a principal, by accepting the benefits of an authorized agreement, ratifies the means used in procuring the agreement unless, within a reasonable time after learning of the true facts, he takes steps to return, so far as possible, the benefits which he has received.[6]

Some conflict exists as to whether silence or inaction on the principal's part can be construed as ratification. Where the situation is such that failure to speak misleads the third party, causing him to rely upon the validity of the agent's acts, it seems that a duty to speak develops. As soon as a principal learns of an unauthorized act by his agent, it is usually his duty to repudiate it with promptness.

CREATION OF THE AGENCY CASES

KING v. YOUNG, BROWN, AND BEVERLY INC.

1958, (Fla. App.) 107 S.2nd 751

King, the plaintiff, brought suit against Young, a trucker, Brown, a transportation broker, and Beverly, Inc., a supplier of vegetables, to re-

[5] Casady v. Manchester Fire Ins. Co., page 376.
[6] Kessler et ux. v. Troast et ux., page 376.

cover for losses sustained in a two tractor-trailer collision caused by the negligence of Young's driver. The plaintiff alleged that Young was the agent of the other defendants. Beverly, Inc. called Brown to obtain transportation for a load of beans to a destination in Georgia and Brown in turn called Young. Young picked up the beans and upon the return of the receipted bill of lading was to receive from Brown $234.79, less a brokerage commission of 7%. Brown and Beverly, Inc. both contend that Young was an independent contractor and that no agency relationship existed. The lower court found in their favor and King appealed so far as his claim against Brown was concerned. Young was held liable and no appeal was taken from that judgment.

KANNER, J. . . . The term *agency* may be defined as "a contract either express or implied upon a consideration, or a gratuitous undertaking, by which one of the parties confides to the other the management of some business to be transacted in his name or on his account, and by which that other assumes to do the business and render an account of it." 2 Am. Jur., Agency, section 2, p. 13. In an agency relationship, the party for whom another acts and from whom he derives authority to act is known and referred to as a principal, while the other party who acts for and represents the principal and who acquires his authority from him is known and referred to as an agent. Thus, the agent steps into the shoes of his principal and acts for him pursuant to the grant of authority vested in him by the principal. 2 Am. Jur., Agency, section 2, p. 13.

In the instant case, Brown was merely the intermediary in the transaction between the shipper and the transportation medium. What he did was to procure transportation for the shipper through the trucker Young, for which he, Brown, was to receive as his brokerage commission a percentage of the total transportation price. Although Brown arranged for Young to haul the beans, Young was to pay his own expenses; he had the control and choice of routes to follow; and he was completely independent of Brown after the load was arranged, except that Young had to bring back a receipt so as to show delivery of the beans before he could collect his freight charge.

The status of an independent contractor, as distinguished from that of an agent, consists of a contractual relationship by one with another to perform something for him, but the one so engaged is not controlled or subject to the control of the other in the performance of the engagement but only as to the result. Conversely, a principal in an agency relationship retains the right to control the conduct of an agent in regard to the engagement intrusted to him. It may be said that the recognized distinction between an agent and an independent contractor relationship is determined by whether the person is subject to or whether he is free from control with regard to the details of the engagement. . . .

The position assumed by appellant is inconsistent, because the agency relationship as applied to the instant case can only contemplate that one person, that is, the principal, is superior and that the other person, the agent, is subordinate. There is no indication whatever that Brown was a principal to either the shipper of the commodity or of the trucker. He was called upon by the shipper as a transportation broker to procure transportation and he then arranged with the trucker to haul the load, for which he was only to receive a commission for his services. . . .

Judgment affirmed.

PETTINGER v. ALPENA CEDAR CO.
1913, 175 Mich. 162, 141 N.W. 535

One James H. Wade purchased from plaintiff, John Pettinger, numerous camp supplies for his lumbering outfit. After considerable credit had been extended to Wade, the plaintiff demanded payment and Wade appealed to one Gannon for assistance. Gannon approved the account and told the plaintiff to send it to the defendant. This procedure was followed and the bill was paid. Gannon also told the plaintiff to continue to furnish supplies and the bills would be paid by the defendant. (Wade carried blank labor orders which he used to pay laborers, and which were drawn on the defendant. The plaintiff had often cashed these and they were always honored by the defendant.) The defendant refused to pay subsequent bills for supplies and denied that Gannon or Wade possessed any authority to bind it, but offered evidence indicating that they were in charge of the lumbering interests of one Gustin, who happened to be the president of the defendant company.

Bird, J. . . . Inasmuch as there was no proof that Gannon had any actual authority to act for the defendant the question here raised is one of agency by estoppel. . . . In *Clark v. Dillman*, 108 Mich. 625, 66 N.W. 570, it was said:

> It is undoubtedly the law that a person may be bound by the representations and acts of another, as agent, where there has been such a holding out as reasonably to lead one dealing with him to believe in the existence of such agency. But all the elements of estoppel must be present. There must be conduct calculated to mislead and it must be under circumstances which justify the claim that the alleged principal should have expected that the representations would be relied and acted upon; and, further, it must appear that they were relied and acted upon, in good faith, to the injury of innocent party.

The plaintiff claims to have parted with his merchandise in the belief that the defendant was interested in the lumbering which Wade was carrying on, and that Gannon was acting for it, and that it would pay for such supplies as he furnished the camp. This belief was induced by the fact that Gannon had approved of an account which he held against Wade, and the defendant had paid it as he was advised by Gannon it would do. . . . A check for $100, drawn by the Alpena Cedar Company to order of Gannon and indorsed by him to Wade, was accepted by plaintiff as a payment on Wade's account, and this check was honored by the defendant. This incident, in connection with other evidence, helped to confirm the belief of plaintiff that Gannon was acting for the defendant.

Judgment for the plaintiff affirmed.

STATE ex rel. KENDRICK v. THORMYER
1958, (Ohio App.) 155 N.E. 2nd 66

This was a mandamus action brought against the defendant, Thormyer, by Kendrick to compel reinstatement of the latter as a state employee. Kendrick had been released by a notice signed with Thormyer's name by one Reiners, his assistant. By statute power of appointment and dismissal rested in the head of the department Thormyer, and plaintiff alleges that the dismissal was ineffective because action was taken without the personal knowledge of Thormyer.

MILLER, J. . . . The question presented is whether or not the suspension was by Thormyer, who had no personal knowledge of the transaction, even though his name appeared on the letter to the relator, which in fact was signed by his alleged authorized agent, Fred G. Reiners. Now, if there had been a proper delegation of authority to Reiners, clearly, the suspension order would have been that of Thormyer, but it is our opinion that such powers may not be delegated for the reason that the authority imposed upon Thormyer involved personal judgment or discretion. We are supported in our conclusion by 2 O. Jur. 2d, 134, which says:

> It is a well-established general rule that when authority delegated to an agent involves personal trust or confidence reposed in the agent, and especially when the exercise of that delegated authority involves personal judgment, skill, or discretion, such authority cannot be delegated by the agent to another as subagent to represent the principal, unless the principal has given express authority to the agent to delegate the authority conferred upon him. Ordinarily authority to conduct a transaction does not include authority to delegate the performance of the acts incidental to that transaction which involve the agent's discretion or skill, unless it is otherwise agreed as between the principal and the agent.

And in 9 C. Jur. 2d, 420, it is said:

> Where the whole power of appointment to, and removal or suspension from, a particular position rests in one officer, an order of suspension issued by another officer is absolutely void and of no effect. An action for wrongful suspension of a civil service employee must be brought against the employing

authority who made the actual suspension and not against a supervisor who caused the suspension.

In our case the sole power of appointment was in Trormyer who also possessed the sole power of suspension or removal under Section 143.26, Revised Code. . . .

For the foregoing reasons we hold that the order of suspension was void and since the relator has no adequate remedy at law the writ of mandamus will be allowed in accordance with the prayer of the petition.

Judgment for the plaintiff.

CASADY v. MANCHESTER FIRE INS. CO.
1899, 109 Iowa 539

Action by Casady for money had and received. The plaintiff's father was an agent for the defendant. He defaulted and disappeared. The defendant asked one Palmer to investigate and report immediately. Palmer accepted payment of the shortage from the plaintiff, but agreed to see that the plaintiff was appointed agent in the place of his father. The company cashed the check but appointed someone else as agent. They contended that Palmer had no authority to make the contract.

LADD, J. It may be conceded that Palmer did not have authority to make such a contract. Neither was he empowered by the telegram to adjust the father's accounts and receive the plaintiff's check in settlement. But he did so, and the company approved his course by retaining the money. It cannot be permitted to ratify a part of this transaction without being held to have confirmed the whole. It could not retain the money without approving the method resorted to by its agent, Palmer, in procuring it. . . . These [the facts] were learned shortly afterwards and then, at least, it was bound either to return the check, or to carry out Palmer's contract, purporting to have been made in its behalf. Having refused to ratify the making of the contract by Palmer for plaintiff's appointment as agent to succeed his father, the consideration failed, and the plaintiff became entitled to recover for money had and received.

KESSLER et ux. v. TROAST et ux.
1927, 101 N.J. EQ. 536, 138 Atl. 371

This was a bill to set aside a deed and mortgage. The plaintiff agreed to purchase certain land from the defendants providing they were able to secure municipal permission to construct a clothing store on the premises. The defendants' agent represented that the permission had been granted and caused a deed to be executed to the plaintiff, the latter paying $1,000 and giving a purchase money mortgage for the balance of the price. The municipality refused to permit the construction of the store, the representation of the defendants' agent having been fraudulent.

BENTLEY, VICE CHANCELLOR. . . . It is difficult to determine whether or not it is intended to be urged that the defendant Troast is not responsible for the fraudulent representation of his agent, who was his father. Pom. Eq. Jur. Sec. 909 says:

> An express ratification, however, is not necessary. If the principal received and retains the proceeds of the agent's fraud—the property, money and the like obtained through an executed transaction—or claims the benefit of or attempts to enforce an executory obligation thus procured, he renders himself liable for the fraudulent acts of his agent.

Rescission allowed.

Review Questions and Problems

1. *P* orally appointed *H*, her husband, as her agent to sell certain real estate. *H* signed *P*'s name to a contract to sell. Is the contract binding?
2. *M*, driving a gasoline truck, negligently ran into and killed *Z*. *M* was driving the truck for his brother, a distributor of *T* oil and gas products, the contract with *T* Co. providing that the truck carry the words *T* Co. at certain places, that it be used for delivery of *T* Co. products to designated filling stations and that the driver, in collecting for deliveries made, sign the receipt in name of *T* Co. For these services *M*'s brother received a commission. When sued by *Z*'s executor for wrongful death, *T* Co. claimed *M*'s brother was an independent contractor rather than an agent. The court held the brother was an agent of *T* Co. Was the decision sound?
3. *A*, an insurance salesman for *X* Company without authority to adjust losses, learned that *T*'s car had been badly damaged in an accident, and because he knew it was covered by insurance, he had it towed to *G*'s garage for immediate repairs. Some time later, the adjuster for *X* Company visited the garage to see the car and noticed that *G* was engaged in repairing it. He made no comment, and the company later refused to pay the repair bill, alleging lack of authority by *A*. Is *X* Company liable?
4. *G*, engaged by *F* Co. at 10¢ a mile to deliver a new truck to a buyer and to pick up a used one, was instructed to drive by the shortest route, not to drive on gravel roads, to check the oil on arrival and to replace any oil loss. *G*, while en route, was injured in an accident but *F* Co.'s workmen's compensation insurer refused to pay, insisting that *G* was an independent contractor. The court held *G* was an employee. Was the court sound in its decision?
5. *A*'s mother loaned him $400 to start a meat market, but without her knowledge, he opened it in his mother's name. She received all promotional literature, and signed all checks, *A* telling her he did this to be certain not to use the money for other purposes. The business failed, and one of the creditors who had relied upon the mother's credit, brought suit against her. Is she liable?

6. *P* became seriously ill of tularemia from eating rabbits purchased at the market of *D* and brought suit to recover damages. The defendant contended he had sublet that department to *A*, although all advertisements were in the name of *D* and purchases were made in reliance on them. Was *D* liable on basis of agency by estoppel?
7. *A* entered into a contract with *T* for *P* for the purchase of 300 bushels of potatoes at 50 cents a bushel. *A* possessed no authority to represent *P*, and *T* attempted to withdraw from the contract before it was ratified by *P*. Was the rescission effective?
8. *A*, an employee of *P* School, contracted in his own name and without authority to buy certain school books from *T*. Later *P* School took action ratifying the contract, but thereafter it refused to accept the books. When sued by *T*, *P* School asserts that the ratification did not bind it. Is this true?
9. *A*, a soliciting agent for *C* Ins. Co., sold to *S* two policies of life insurance and over a period of fourteen years collected and forwarded the premiums to the company, although the policy said that all premiums were to be sent direct to *C* Co. *S* also paid to *A* $5,000 as a fund to use in case he failed to pay any premium on time. *A* disappeared with the fund, and the company denies liability, insisting that its soliciting agent had no authority to collect premiums. The court held *C* Co. liable. Discuss the soundness of this decision.

17

Principal and Third Party

LIABILITY OF PRINCIPAL

3-11. General liability. The principal is liable only for those acts of his agent which fall within the actual or apparent scope of his authority.[1] His actual authority consists of that expressly conferred or which is incidental thereto. Incidental powers are those required for, or reasonably anticipated in, carrying out the major purpose for which the agency was created. Apparent authority is that which results from estoppel and gives the agent power to bind his principal in many cases where he has no right to do so. Because of the position which the principal has permitted his agent to assume, third parties are justified from appearances in believing he possesses authority.

3-12. Custom and usage. The incidental powers of an agent often vary with local or general custom or usage. To illustrate: *P* appoints *A* as his agent to sell a certain used automobile for $900. As an incident to his authority to sell, *A* has authority to enter into a written contract with the purchaser and to sign *P*'s name to the contract. Whether he has implied or incidental authority to sell on credit instead of cash or to warrant the condition of the car sold turns upon general or local custom. If it is customary for other agents in this locality to make warranties or sell on credit, this agent may assume he possesses such authority in the absence of different instructions.

Customs often vary between different lines of business and between employers engaged in the same kind of endeavor. Where these customs are well established and known, third parties are bound to respect them. Illustrating these general principles, let us assume that it is not customary for so-called departmental buyers in the department stores to buy, but merely to list needs. In such case, the purchasing office contracts for goods. This limitation being general, third parties would be bound by it. However, it might be customary for a particular department store to give agents authority to buy. In the latter case, any new employee named as buyer has power to make binding contracts to purchase.

[1] Krantz v. Oak Park Trust & Savings Bank, page 386.

3-13. Secret limitations. It is said that secret limitations imposed upon the powers of an agent do not bind third parties unless their attention has been drawn to them. In other words, the third party, having established that an agency exists and having determined in a general way the limits of the authority, is not bound to explore for unexpected and unusual restrictions. He is justified in assuming, in the absence of contrary information, that the agent possesses those powers which like agents customarily have.

An instruction to a sales agent not to sell to a certain individual or not to sell to him on credit, when credit sales are customary, cannot affect the validity of a contract made with this individual unless the latter was aware of the limitation at the time the contract was made. The principal, by appointing an agent normally possessed of certain authority, is estopped to set up the limitation as a defense, unless the limitation is made known to the third party prior to the making of the contract.

3-14. Powers enlarged by emergency. An existing emergency which necessitates immediate action on the part of the principal or his representative may add sufficiently to the agent's powers to enable him to meet the situation. However, if time permits and the principal is available, any proposed remedy for the difficulty should be submitted to the principal for approval.[2] It is only when the principal is not available that the powers of the agent are extended. Furthermore, the agent receives no power greater than that sufficient to solve the difficulty. Thus, the power of an agent to borrow money on the strength of his principal's credit is rarely implied. Suppose, however, that a C.O.D. shipment arrives for the principal during his absence and money is not available to pay for the goods. Clearly, his representative in charge of the business may borrow sufficient funds to pay for the goods and avoid demurrage charges and other possible losses. The principal would not be liable for any excess borrowed beyond that required to pay for the particular shipment.

3-15. Notice to agent. Notice or knowledge acquired by an agent while acting within the scope of his authority binds the principal. This fact is true because the agent is the principal's other self, and, therefore, what one knows, the other knows. For the principal to be bound, the notice must have been acquired by an agent who represented the principal in regard to the particular subject matter involved.[3] An agent who is acquiring property for his principal and has knowledge of certain unrecorded liens against the property takes the property for his principal subject to those liens. Knowledge of some other agent who had never represented the principal in the particular transaction and who did not

[2] Carlson v. Hannah et al., page 388.
[3] People ex rel. Carr v. Gullborg, page 390.

receive the notice definitely for his principal could not affect the principal's interest.

Considerable dispute has arisen as to whether notice acquired by an agent before he became such can affect the principal. The better view is that notice which is acquired before the creation of the agency and is later retained by the agent while representing his principal is notice to the latter.

Notice to the agent, when he is under a duty to some third party not to disclose the information, does not affect the principal. Furthermore, notice to the agent, combined with collusion or fraud between him and the third party that would defeat the purpose of the notice, would not bind the principal. Thus, an agent who receives notice of an unrecorded mortgage from the mortgagor, with the request that the fact not to be made known to the principal, has not received notice which is binding on the principal. If he purchases the property, it will not be subject to the mortgage.

PECULIAR POWERS

3-16. Real estate broker. The ordinary real estate broker possesses no authority, implied or apparent, in the absence of an express grant, to enter into a contract for the sale of property listed with him. It is his business to find a party who is willing to purchase the property upon the proposed terms. The owner reserves the right to contract, or not as he sees fit, at the time the broker's prospective buyer is presented.

The same is true of many solicitors—often called salesmen—whose authority is limited to obtaining orders for merchandise that are subject to approval by the principal. If such a limitation conforms to the custom or usage, the buyer's contract is ineffective until it has been approved by the seller.

3-17. Right to collect. The power of an agent to collect a bill owed to his principal may not readily be implied. It has been held that possession of a statement upon the principal's billhead and in the principal's handwriting did not justify an assumption of such authority.

A question of considerable difficulty is encountered concerning the apparent or implied power of a salesman to collect. Clearly the agent behind the counter or other agent who sells the goods has, under most circumstances, an implied power to collect for them at the time of the sale but not at a later date.[4] If, however, the sale is on credit, no power

[4] Zazzaro v. Universal Motors, page 391.

exists to collect at a later date unless the business is a relatively small one in which the agent performs a rather general service.

The agent who delivers goods which have been sold for cash undoubtedly has a right to collect all payments due at the time of delivery. Otherwise, the ordinary delivery boy has no authority to collect unless it is expressly conferred or arises through custom.

The traveling salesman who covers certain designated territory and solicits orders for his principal has no authority to collect as payments fall due except those payments that are to be made at the time the order is obtained. In the absence of express authority, payments made to such agents, which fail to find their way into the principal's possession, may again be collected from the debtor.

Authority to collect gives the agent no authority to accept anything other than money in payment. He is not empowered to accept negotiable notes or property in settlement of an indebtedness unless expressly authorized. It is customary to accept checks as conditional payment. Under such circumstances the debt is not paid unless the check is honored. If the check is not paid, the creditor is free to bring suit on the contract which gave rise to the indebtedness or to sue on the check, at his option.

3-18. Purchase on credit. An agent who is given special authority to purchase is limited to the quantity and quality of goods set forth by the principal. Such limitations imposed upon a general purchasing agent at a particular occasion would, however, amount to secret limitations and would not, therefore, be effective against innocent third parties. A general agent placed in charge of a business presumably has power to purchase either on credit or for cash. If the principal provides a special purchasing agent with cash and instructs him not to purchase on credit, the majority holds that the principal is not liable for goods purchased on credit. This rule is true only where the agent has not in some manner been held out as possessing greater authority.

3-19. Written agreements—how executed. The principal is liable upon all contracts made by the agent so long as they relate to matters within the scope of his authority and are properly executed.[5] So far as simple contracts are concerned, although the signature does not indicate definitely who the real contracting party is, most of the states permit the use of parol evidence to show the intention of the agent and the third party. Without question this is true whenever the signature is ambiguous. It is possible, however, for the third party to desire to contract with the agent alone and one the strength of his credit. Where such is true, the principal is not liable.

There is a rule of law relating to negotiable instruments to the effect

[5] Goodenough v. Thayer et al., page 392.

that no one can be held thereon unless his name is attached thereto. Because of this fact, the agent should exercise care to see that any negotiable paper executed by him bears his principal's name and his own, preceded by "by" or "per," following his principal's. If this procedure is not followed the ultimate holder of the paper may be able to hold both the principal and the agent, or the agent alone. Although considerable conflict exists, according to the law of most states parol evidence may be introduced to explain a signature to negotiable paper that is clearly ambiguous. Some states hold that unless the instrument as a whole explains the signature, the agent shall be held liable.

UNDISCLOSED PRINCIPAL

3-20. Undisclosed principal's contracts. For various reasons a principal often desires to hide his identity. In such instances he appoints an agent to act for him; the agent enters into all contracts in his own name, leaving the third party unaware of any principal. Such agreements are always entered into on the strength of the agent's credit, as no principal is disclosed. Although such is the case, the third party, upon learning of the principal's identity, may elect to enforce the contract against the principal rather than against the agent.[6] The principal is responsible for all contracts entered into by the agent within the scope of the agent's authority. Furthermore, even though the agent has been definitely limited, the courts hold the principal liable for acts which would have been within the apparent scope of the agent's authority had the principal been known.

The undisclosed principal is never liable upon a negotiable instrument signed by his agent since his name does not appear thereon. It is possible in many such cases for the third party to waive the note and sue upon the agreement that furnished the consideration therefor, avoiding the difficulty encountered by a suit on the note or bill of exchange.

3-21. Settlement between principal and agent. In the preceding section it was indicated that the third party, after learning of a principal's interest in any transaction, might elect to look to the principal for performance. Suppose, in such a case, that the principal supplied the agent with money to purchase the goods, but they were delivered to the agent on the strength of his own credit. What should be the result? It is clear, under such circumstances, that the principal is relieved of all responsibility. A slightly different problem arises where the principal settles with the agent after the contract is made and the goods are de-

[6] Kayton et al. v. Barnett et al., page 393.

livered, but before his disclosure to the third party. Any bona fide settlement between principal and agent before disclosure apparently relieves the principal. A settlement cannot have this effect, however, when it is made after the third party has learned of the existence of the principal and the principal is aware of that fact.

The general rule seems to be fair to the third party, in that it gives him all the protection which he originally bargained for, and at the same time it helps the principal, in that it protects him against a second demand for payment.

3-22. Election. Election means choice, and a choice becomes possible only when the third party learns of the existence of a principal. If a settlement has taken place previously, no election is possible; otherwise, the third party who learns the identity of an undisclosed principal may look either to the agent or to the principal for performance until such time as he definitely elects to hold one or the other. No conduct on his part which precedes the disclosure of the principal can constitute an election. Because of this rule, it has been held that an unsatisfied judgment obtained against the agent before disclosure of the principal will not bar a later action against the principal.[7]

After disclosure, the third party may evidence his election by obtaining a judgment against one of the parties, or by making an express declaration of his intention. It has been held that the sending of a statement to one of the parties does not indicate an election. Most states also hold that the receipt of a negotiable instrument from one of them does not show an election. The mere starting of a suit against one of the parties has been held insufficient to cause an election, but if the case proceeds to the point where a judgment is obtained against either the agent or the principal, election has taken place although the judgment remains unpaid. From these illustrations it can be seen that very definite action is essential to constitute an election. The third party is usually free at any time to sue the particular party whose credit is best.

LIABILITY FOR AGENT'S TORTS

3-23. Negligent acts. The principal becomes liable to third parties for any damage occasioned them by the negligence of the agent so long as the latter is acting in the course of his employment.

Should the agent be engaged in his own busness when the tort is committed, having left temporarily his principal's business, the principal is relieved of any liability. The fact that he may have been in the possession of his employer's vehicle does not extend the liability of the

[7] Lindquist v. Dickson, page 394.

principal.[8] The real test is: was the agent about his principal's business when the tort was committed? The fact that he has combined his own with the principal's business does not release the principal, unless the agent has quite definitely departed from his principal's business at the time of the accident.

The principal cannot avoid liability by showing that he has instructed the agent not to do the particular act complained of. Neither is he released by evidence that the agent was not doing the work his principal had instructed him to do, where the agent had misunderstood the instruction. As long as the agent is attempting to follow out his principal's business, the principal is liable.

A large number of states have adopted what has become known as the family car doctrine. Under it, any member of the family is considered to be an agent of the parent-owner when using it for his or her convenience or amusement, if the car is made available generally for family use.[9]

3-24. Willful acts. Thus far attention has been given to a situation in which the third party is damaged by negligent conduct of the agent. Suppose, however, the agent willfully and deliberately injured the third party. Is the principal liable? Clearly, if the wilfull misconduct of the agent has nothing to do with his principal's business and is animated entirely by hatred or a feeling of ill-will toward the third party, the principal is in no respect liable. Where the predominant motive is not to work off a personal grudge, but rather to advance his principal's interests, it has been held that the principal is liable.[10]

It should be stressed at this point that an agent is always liable to any third person who is injured as a consequence of the agent's tort. This is true even though the tort is committed while the agent is about his principal's business and is acting in the utmost good faith, having no reason to believe he is committing a tort. An agent who commits a tort innocently while following instructions of the principal and who is compelled to pay the injured party, may demand reimbursement from his principal. Similarly, if a tort grows out of the agent's carelessness or willful act and the principal is compelled to settle with the third party, he may seek recovery from the agent.

LIABILITY OF THIRD PARTY

3-25. Contracts for disclosed principal. The disclosed principal may sue the third party upon any contract made by the agent for the former's

[8] Nelson v. Broderick & Bascom Rope Company, page 394.
[9] Jones v. Cook, page 396.
[10] Lockhart v. Friendly Finance Co., page 397.

benefit. This rule applies to all simple contracts in which the principal is the real party in interest, despite the fact that they are made in the agent's name. Furthermore, any contract made for the benefit of the principal, although the agent acted outside the scope of his authority, entitles the principal to performance, provided the contract has been properly ratified before withdrawal.

3-26. Undisclosed principal. The undisclosed principal is entitled to performance by third parties of all simple contracts made for his benefit by the agent. In the ordinary case, it is no defense for the third party to say that he had not entered into no contract with the principal. When, however, the contract is one which involves the skill or confidence of the agent and which would not have been entered into but for this skill or confidence, its performance may not be demanded by the principal. In other words, whenever a contract made for the benefit of an undisclosed principal is such that it cannot be assigned or its duties delegated, the principal cannot demand its benefits.

In all cases, the principal takes over the contract subject to all defenses which the third party could have established against the agent. If the third party contracts to buy from such an agent and expects to be able to set off an acount which he has against the agent, he has this same right to set off against the undisclosed principal.

PRINCIPAL AND THIRD PARTY CASES

KRANTZ v. OAK PARK TRUST & SAVINGS BANK
1958, (Ill. App.) 147 N.E.2nd 881

Krantz, the plaintiff, drew several checks on the defendant bank in favor of 661 Sheridan Apartments, Inc. These were cashed by the bank after being indorsed with the corporation's name by its president, who used the money for his personal needs. The plaintiff contends that the president had no express authority to cash checks and the indorsement being ineffective, payment by the bank was improper. This is an appeal from a lower court judgment in favor of the defendant.

FRIEND, J. . . . Under the settled rule in this State, the president of a corporation, by virtue of his office, is the business head thereof, and any contract pertaining to the corporate affairs, within the general powers of the corporation, will, when executed by the president and in the absence of proof to the contrary, be presumed to have been executed by the authority of the corporation, as one of the powers incident to the office of president. *Green v. Ashland*, Sixty-Third State Bank, 346 III.

174, 178 N.E. 468. It was held in that case that the presumed authority of the president of a corporation to contract on its behalf and so bind the corporation in respect of matters pertaining to corporate affairs is unaffected, in so far as the public is concerned, by any instructions given to the president, or by limitations upon authority imposed through corporate by-laws. These are matters solely between the corporation and its officers; the by-laws and the special instructions, alike, are binding upon none but the officers and the members of the corporation. The rationale of the rule is that the corporation entrusts the chief executive office of president to a person known to and selected by its board of directors, and so entrusts general control of its affairs to its president. Accordingly, the general public dealing with the person in whom the corporate body avowedly reposes such confidence ought not to be required to search for the precise authority of the president to fulfill each ordinary and usual function of his office; if the president is unworthy of trust in the execution of the ordinary business affairs of the corporation, then it seems more equitable that the corporation, rather than persons dealing with it, should suffer. In the case here under consideration, the president of the payee corporation, in the exercise of his presumed authority, on five occasions endorsed checks payable to the order of a building corporation, all being drawn on defendant bank.

In order to conduct its business, the authority to endorse checks must be placed in some officer of a corporation, and in the absence of express authority to endorse checks, implied authority is given to the president, who is vested with general direction of the affairs of the corporation. *Corn Belt Bank v. Forman,* 264 Ill. App. 589. In the latter case it was held that the authority so implied is an actual authority, in keeping with commercial usage, arising from the business nature of the corporation, and that commercial transactions must be construed in accordance with commercial usage.

The allegation that the president of the corporate payee lacked express authority to endorse checks payable to the order of the corporation did not state that the defendant bank had notice or knowledge of such lack of authority. The mere allegation of the lack of express authority does not negate the presumed authority of the president; for even were the president of the corporation denied authority, by the by-laws, to endorse checks, yet, unless knowledge or notice of such lack of authority were communicated to the bank, it would be entitled to rely upon the presumed authority of the chief executive officer to endorse checks.

We think the court properly allowed defendant's motion to strike the complaint and dismiss the suit. The judgment order of February 27, 1957, in favor of defendant and against plaintiff for costs is therefore affirmed.

CARLSON v. HANNAH et al.
1951, 6 N.J. 202, 78 A.2d 83

During the year 1940 Carlson and Galler Beverages, Inc. entered into a contract whereby the former was to act as distributor for "7-Up" in Paterson and certain territory north of the city. He was to supply his own truck, and was not to assign his contract without the approval of Galler. In 1942 Carlson, the plaintiff, was called into the service of the United States Army, so he made an agreement with the defendant to operate his route, with a certain amount being paid to the plaintiff for use of his truck. He then gave one McHugh power of attorney to act for him in those matters requisite and necessary to the distributorship. Business increased and the company demanded an additional truck, and a driver was found for it, he being given the outside city route. In 1944, the defendant threatened to quit unless he were protected when the plaintiff returned from the service, so McHugh agreed that the northern route was to be his upon the plaintiff's return, the latter being limited to the city route. This agreement had the approval of Galler. After plaintiff's return, he refused to approve the contract made by McHugh and demanded his entire territory although the defendant continued to operate the northern route as though it were his own. The plaintiff then instituted this suit to determine the effect of McHugh's contract and for an accounting. The lower court determined that McHugh exceeded his authority and gave plaintiff a judgment of $4,000.

ACKERSON, J. . . . The power of attorney which accompanied the contract made between Carlson personally and Hannah on May 22, 1942, conferred upon McHugh authority to act for the plaintiff during his absence ". . . in all matters pertaining to my distributorship of a carbonated beverage known as '7-Up', . . . giving my said attorney full power to do everything whatsoever, requisite and necessary to be done in said distributorship, . . ." McHugh's authority with respect to the operation of the accompanying contract itself is expressed in paragraph 8 thereof, hereinabove quoted, giving him power "to alter" the contract when deemed necessary with the consent of the other party thereto.

Attorneys in fact created by formal letters of attorney are merely agents and their authority and the manner of its exercise are governed by the principles of the law of agency. 2 Am. Jur. (Agency), § 26, p. 29. The power of an agent to bind his principal is limited to such acts as are within his actual or apparent authority. *Baurhenn v. Fidelity, etc. of Maryland,* 114 N.J.L. 99, 104, 176 A. 137 (E. & A. 1934). Such actual authority may be express or implied. Implied authority may be inferred from the nature or extent of the function to be performed, the general course of conducting the business, or from the particular circumstances of the case.

Implication is but another term for meaning and intention; express authority given to an agent includes by implication, whether the agency be general or special, unless restricted to the contrary, all such powers as are proper and necessary as a means of effectuating the purposes for which the agency was created. *Sibley v. City Service Transit Co.*, 2 N.J. 458, 463, 66 A.2d 864 (1949); 2 Am. Jur. (Agency) § 86, p. 70. Accordingly, it is well settled that, unless otherwise agreed, the authority of an agent to manage a business extends no further than the direction of the ordinary operations of the business, including authority to make contracts which are incidental to such business, are usually made in it, or are reasonably necessary in conducting it. But prima facie, authority to manage a business does not include authority to dispose of it in whole or in part. Restatement (Agency) § 73, Title F.

What, then, was the purpose of the instruments executed by plaintiff on the eve of entering the armed forces? Obviously he desired to preserve his business intact until his return and appointed McHugh to supervise it during his absence. Logically it is impossible to imply from the evidence before us any authority in the agent McHugh to dispose of any part of his principal's business by gift, sale or otherwise, and thereby defeat the very purpose for which such instruments were created. The grant of power was intended to aid and facilitate the operation of the distributorship during plaintiff's absence and not to authorize its partition upon his return. Restatement (Agency) § 73, Comment (b). . . .

Appellant further contends that McHugh's authority to contract for the assignment of the territory in question was implied under the doctrine of "emergency power." This principle is defined in the Restatement (Agency) § 47, as follows:

> Unless otherwise agreed, if after the authorization is given, an unforeseen situation arises for which the terms of the authorization make no provision and it is impracticable for the agent to communicate with the principal, he is authorized to do what he reasonably believes to be necessary in order to prevent substantial loss to the principal with respect to the interests committed to his charge.

It is important to note, however, that this rule is expressly qualified in the Restatement as applicable only where it is "impracticable for the agent to communicate with the principal" and ascertain his wishes before acting. *Sibley v. City Service Transit Co., supra*, 2 N.J. at page 463, 66 A.2d 864.

The claimed emergency relied upon the invocation of the foregoing rule is said to be the choice with which McHugh was confronted of either abandoning the entire route because of the uncertainty of replacing Hannah due to war time shortage of manpower, or acceding to his demand for a part of the territory on plaintiff's return. We find no merit in this contention. Emergency in this connection means "a sudden or unexpected occurrence or condition calling for immediate action." *Frank v. Bd. of Education of Jersey City*, 90 N.J.L. 273, 278, 100 A. 211, 213, L.R.A. 1917D, 206 (E. & A. 1916). The evidence discloses that continuous pressure to procure the questioned contract had been exerted on McHugh by both Hannah and Galler for upwards of two months before it was finally signed. During all of this period of resistance, however, no attempt was made to communicate with Carlson and it was not impracticable to have done so. Furthermore there is no proof that Hannah could not have been replaced. While McHugh testified that he did not know where he could have picked up another driver, nevertheless it does not appear that he made any effort to do so. Significantly, only a month before the execution of the questioned contract, another driver was procured to help Hannah service the territory. No immediate urgency or necessity was presented other than an opportunity to demand a part of plaintiff's capital and that situation was of Hannah's own making.

We therefore conclude that the defendant McHugh was not authorized to make the executory assignment of territory attempted to be accomplished by the agreement of September 2, 1944. . . .

Judgment of the lower court affirmed.

PEOPLE ex rel. CARR v. GULLBORG

1927, 324 Ill. 438, 155 N.E. 324

THOMPSON, J. This appeal is from a judgment of the county court of Cook county overruling objections to taxes extended against an apartment building at 1549 Fargo Avenue, Chicago, and ordering a sale of the property. . . .

In 1925 the board of assessors continued the valuation of $80,250, but the board of review raised it to $110, 250. Appellant paid the taxes based on a full valuation of $80,250 and filed objections to the balance on the ground that he had not received notice of the hearing before the board of review and that it was without jurisdiction to increase the valuation. The records of the board of review show that notice of the hearing was sent to George P. Adams. Appellant testified that he is a manufacturer and that Adams is employed in his office; and that in 1925 Adams occupied one of the apartments in his building at 1549 Fargo Avenue and was authorized to receive the rent from the other tenants; that Adams was not a leasing agent nor an agent having general supervision of the property; and that this authority was limited to receiving the rent and delivering it to him at his office. . . .

The law is well settled that, when notice to an agent is relied upon to bind a principal, the nature of the agency must be such that the law will presume that the agent carried the notice to his principal, or it must be established as a fact that he did communicate to his principal such notice. Notice to or knowledge of an agent while acting within the scope of his authority and in reference to a matter over which his authority extends is notice to or knowledge of the principal, but, in order to be binding upon the principal, the knowledge must be acquired while his agent is acting within the scope of his authority and in reference to a matter over which his authority extends. . . . Conceding that Adams received the notice of the hearing before the board of review, it was not binding upon appellant because it was not a matter over which Adams' authority extended. . . .

Judgment for defendant, Gullborg.

ZAZZARO v. UNIVERSAL MOTORS
1938, (Conn.) 197 Atl. 884

This was an action by Anthony T. Zazzaro to recover possession of an automobile. The defendant had given one Horwitz special authority to sell it for $400 net. The plaintiff signed a contract to purchase, and gave his check for $100 and note for $300 in settlement. Horwitz, to induce the sale, promised personally to hold the note for a few days until the plaintiff could borrow $300 on his insurance. The note, however, was immediately turned over to the defendant. When the check arrived from the insurance company, the plaintiff indorsed and delivered it to Horwitz, who failed to surrender it to the defendant. The defendant, under the conditional sale contract, repossessed the car and plaintiff now seeks to recover it on the theory that he had paid for it in full.

BROWN, J. . . . The court has stated the implied powers incident to the agency relationship in these words: "The creation of an agency carries with it the usual and appropriate means of accomplishing its object and clothes the agent with such authority as is proper to effectuate its purpose." *Kearns v. Nickse,* 80 Conn. 23, 25. . . . The American Law Institute, in dealing with the question as to the circumstances under which incidental authority is inferred, says: "Unless otherwise agreed, authority to conduct a transaction includes authority to do acts which are incidental to it, or are reasonably necessary to accomplish it." Restatement Agency, § 35, p. 89. And under Comment (a), it is further stated that "conversely to the rule . . . prima facie, an agent is not authorized to do acts not incidental to the transaction, nor usually done in connection therewith, nor reasonably necessary." The application of this principle to the undisputed facts in this case make evident that the court was warranted in concluding that Horwitz had no authority to accept payment of the note. As the defendant's agent for this isolated transaction only and pursuant to express instructions, he sold this car known by the plaintiff to belong to the defendant for $100 cash plus his note to its order for $300 due thirteen days later and secured by the conditional bill of sale, both of which instruments were forthwith turned over to the defendant, which kept them. Horwitz collected the note before maturity. Under these circumstances, authority in Horwitz to accept payment of the note was neither proper nor reasonably necessary to do the act directed or to accomplishing the result specified by the defendant. Nor was the acceptance of the payment either a usual or an appropriate means to that end.

Judgment for defendant affirmed.

GOODENOUGH v. THAYER et al.

1882, 132 Mass. 152

This was an action by plaintiff, Goodenough, to recover damages for breach of contract. The plaintiff entered into a contract for space in the steamer Atrato for shipment from Boston to London of certain livestock. The steamer was to put on board a condenser capable of supplying sufficient water. The agreement stated that it was between Thayer and Lincoln, agents of the steamer Atrato, and H. B. Goodenough. It was signed merely Thayer and Lincoln, Agents. Several sheep and hogs died en route because of a shortage of water. The defendants, Thayer and Lincoln, contend that the contract was with the owner of the steamer and they are not personally liable.

ENDICOTT, J. . . . The defendants in the body of the agreement disclose their principal, for they describe themselves as agents of the steamship Atrato, and they do not sign the instrument personally, but as agents. The case does not fall, therefore, within that class of cases cited by the plaintiff, where the instrument does not disclose the name of the principal; nor within the other class of cases cited, where, although in the body of the instrument it appears, or is to be inferred that the party signing is agent, or is acting in behalf of other persons, the instrument is signed by his name only. In these cases it was held that there was a personal undertaking by the defendant.

Nor can it be said that the recitals in the body of the instrument, that the defendants were agents of the steamship Atrato, and their signatures thereto, describing themselves as agents were mere discriptio personarum. . . . The agreement contains express stipulations on the part of the steamship Atrato, and express provisions touching the liability of her owners, as where it recites, "steamer agreeing to put on board a condenser capable of supplying the stock with water in sufficient quantities," etc. . . .

Taking all of the provisions of the special agreement together, it appears that it was not the intention of the parties that the defendants should be bound personally, but that it was the intention to bind the shipowners. And the intention is so plainly apparent that it is not to be controlled by the words, "agents of the steamer Atrato," instead of for the steamer Atrato.

Judgment for defendant.

KAYTON et al. v. BARNETT et al.
1889, 116 N.Y. 625, 23 N.E. 24

This action was brought to recover a balance of the purchase price for certain property. On the 17th day of March, 1881, the plaintiffs sold and delivered to William B. Bishop several machines. All but $1,500 was paid before Bishop died in an insolvent condition. Plaintiffs, Kayton and another, having learned that he acted for the defendants, instituted this action.

FOLLETT, CH. J. When goods are sold on credit to a person whom the vendor believes to be the purchaser and he afterwards discovers that the person credited bought as agent for another, the vendor has a cause of action against the principal for the purchase price. The defendants concede the existence of this general rule, but assert that it is not applicable to this case, because, while Bishop and the plaintiffs were negotiating, they stated they would not sell the property to the defendants, and Bishop assured them he was buying for himself and not for them. It appears by evidence, which is wholly uncontradicted, that the defendants directed every step taken by Bishop in his negotiations with plaintiff; that the property was purchased for and delivered to the defendants, who ever since retained it. . . . Notwithstanding the assertion of the plaintiffs that they would not sell to the defendants, they, through the circumvention of Bishop and the defendants, did sell the property to the defendants, who have had the benefit of it, and have never paid the remainder of the purchase price pursuant to their agreement. Bishop was the defendants' mind, and so the minds of the parties met, and the defendants having, through their own and their agent's deception, acquired the plaintiffs' property by purchase, cannot successfully assert that they are not liable for the remainder of the purchase price because they, through their agent, succeeded in inducing the plaintiffs to do that which they did not intend to do, and, perhaps would not have done had the defendants not dealt disingenuously.

Judgment for plaintiffs.

LINDQUIST v. DICKSON

1906, 98 Minn. 369, 107 N.W. 958

Action by Lindquist to recover from the defendant, as an undisclosed principal, for labor and material performed and furnished by the plaintiff in decorating and repairing her house. It appeared that the plaintiff entered into the contract with defendant's husband, assuming at the time that he was the owner; that later the plaintiff obtained a judgment against the husband on this claim, ignorant of the fact that the property was owned by defendant. The defendant contends that such an unsatisfied judgment is a bar to this action.

START, C. J. . . . The general rule is that where a simple contract, by parol or writing, is made by an authorized agent without disclosing his principal, and the other contracting party subsequently discovers the real party, he may abandon his right to look to the agent personally and resort to the principal. . . .

Election implies full knowledge of the facts necessary to enable a party to make an intelligent and deliberate choice. . . . We, therefore, hold upon principle what seems to be the weight of judicial opinion that, if a person contracts with another, who is in fact an agent of an undisclosed principal, and, after learning all the facts, brings an action on the contract and recovers judgment against the agent, such judgment will be a bar to an action against the principal. But an unsatisfied judgment against the agent is not a bar to an action against an undiscovered principal when discovered, if the plaintiff was ignorant of the facts as to the agency when he prosecuted his action against the agent.

Judgment for plaintiff.

NELSON v. BRODERICK & BASCOM ROPE COMPANY

1958, (Wash.) 332 P.2nd 460

OTT, J. September 6, 1955, Tom Verhoef, an employee of Broderick & Bascom Rope Company, and Ardelle Nelson were engaged in a lover's quarrel. They had discussed their differences at some length in a telephone conversation that morning. Shortly thereafter, at approximately twelve o'clock noon, while Verhoef was driving a company automobile out of the driveway from a parking area, he was intercepted head on by Ardelle Nelson, driving her Cadillac automobile. Having blocked the exit, she forced Verhoef to back his car into the lot. She pursued him around the parking lot until she cornered his car with hers in such a manner that he could not escape without making a sharp turn to either the right or left.

When both cars were stopped, Ardelle Nelson left her car and approached the car in which Verhoef was sitting. He locked the doors and rolled down the left-door window a few inches. The conversation between them relating to their love affair continued for approximately twenty minutes. When Ardelle Nelson could not gain entrance to the company car operated by Verhoef, she picked up a rock and broke the glass window in the door on the driver's side. Violent argument ensued for about five minutes. While Ardelle Nelson was at the driver's side of the automobile (and, as she stated, was preparing to return to her automobile), Verhoef started the company car in motion and turned it sharply to the left to miss the Cadillac. The evidence is in dispute as to whether Ardelle Nelson hung on to the company car as Verhoef turned it to the left, or whether she was dragged along the side of the automobile some twenty feet, in her effort to avoid being struck. She fell to the ground when Verhoef stopped the car, and was injured.

Ardelle Nelson commenced this action for damages against Broderick & Bascom Rope Company, the employer, contending that she was injured by its employee, Verhoef, while he was engaged in the performance of his master's duties. At the close of the plaintiff's evidence, the court sustained a challenge to its sufficiency and dismissed the action.

From the judgment of dismissal, the plaintiff has appealed.

Appellant contends that, considering the evidence most favorably for appellant, it established that (1) respondent owned the offending vehicle, (2) Verhoef was an employee of respondent and was driving the company vehicle, (3) the incident occurred within the working hours of the employee, (4) the moving of the offending car was in furtherance of the master's business, (5) the incident occurred on the master's property, and that this evidence established a presumption of the employer's liability which was sufficient to submit the issue to the jury.

Assuming that these elements establish a presumption of employer liability, the presumption is rebuttable and may be overcome by the plaintiff's testimony. . . .

Further, the doctrine of *respondeat superior* provides, generally, that the master is liable for the acts of his servant committed within the scope or course of his employment. The general rule, however, has several exceptions, one being that, when a servant engages on a mission in furtherance of his master's business and, thereafter, completely forsakes the purpose of the employment and engages on an escapade of his own that results in an injury to another, the master is not liable. . . .

In the instant case, the injury occurred during a lovers' quarrel. Neither of the parties was engaged in any other activity. Verhoef did testify that, at the time he started the company automobile in motion and drove it some twenty feet, he intended to drive to Renton on company business. However, he had not yet returned to the place, in furtherance of his master's business, from which appellant's wrongful interference had driven him. Appellant's evidence established that the escapade in which they were then engaged had not terminated, and that she intended the break in the affair to be only temporary. At the moment of the injury, Verhoef was attempting to extricate himself from the situation developed by the appellant. In applying the law to the facts, the trial court properly found that Verhoef was not furthering his master's business or acting in any manner pursuant to his master's authority at the time the injury was inflicted upon the appellant.

The judgment is affirmed.

JONES v. COOK

1922, 90 W.Va. 710, 111 S.E. 828

An action by C. N. Jones to recover damages resulting from a collision with defendant's automobile, which was negligently driven by defendant's stepdaughter. The stepdaughter, Ivol Hickman, was returning from a football game with numerous friends, but no other member of defendant's family was in the car. Defendant introduced no evidence but asked a directed verdict. It was granted and plaintiff appeals.

Meredith, J. . . . But there arises a more serious question on the record. It can fairly be inferred from the evidence that defendant's automobile was a "big closed Hudson 'family car' "; that it was acquired by him for the use and pleasure of his family, including his stepdaughter; that she was accustomed to drive it with his knowledge and consent, not only generally, but also with his permission on this particular occasion. . . . Therefore, the question for decision is whether the defendant is liable for an accident occurring by reason of the proved negligence of his stepdaughter, while driving his automobile acquired for the purposes mentioned. . . .

It necessarily follows that, unless the driver of defendant's car at the time of the injury was in his service, the defendant is not liable. The authorities cannot be reconciled. In the leading case of *Doran v. Thompsen* (76 N.J.L. 754), a case very similar to the case at bar, the court held the owner not liable. In that case the daughter, who was the driver, was the only member of defendant's family in the automobile. In the later case of *Missell v. Hayes* (86 N.J.L. 348), a son of the defendant was driving the automobile, and with him at the time of the accident were the defendant's wife and daughter, and two guests. The court differentiates that case from the case of *Doran v. Thompsen,* in that in the *Missell* case there were members of the defendant's family in the automobile, other than the driver, and held that it was a question for the jury to determine whether the son, while driving the automobile, was the father's servant on the father's business; and affirmed a judgment in favor of the plaintiff.

We see no possible ground of difference concerning the owner's liability, whether there be but one member of the family or all members of the family in the automobile at the time of the negligent injury. . . . The doctrine of agency is not confined to merely commercial business transactions, but extends to cases where the father maintains an automobile for family use, with a general authority, expressed or implied, that it may be used for the comfort, convenience, pleasure, and entertainment or outdoor recreation of members of the owner's family. This view accords with the great weight of authority.

Judgment reversed.

LOCKHART v. FRIENDLY FINANCE CO.

1959, (Fla.) 110 S.2nd 478

The plaintiff, Lockhart, purchased a television set from a third party, after which the defendant claimed to have security interest in it. It was orally agreed between plaintiff and defendant that plaintiff would pay $100 at the rate of $15 a week. The plaintiff failed to pay so the defendant sent its agent out to collect the account or repossess. Plaintiff, when approached by the agent and two detectives, told them not to enter since his wife was ill and very nervous. Nevertheless, they entered and threw a small radio and lamp on the floor, breaking them, and slamming a door so hard the glass in it was broken. They carried the television set away, and the plaintiff sued for trespass and damages sustained. The lower court directed a judgment for the plaintiff, but later ordered a new trial because he thought he erred. The plaintiff appealed from the order for a new trial.

Wiggington, J. . . . We are now called upon to determine whether the undisputed facts recited above, construed in a light most favorable to the defendant, were reasonably susceptible of but the single conclusion that defendant was liable as a matter of law.

The problem here presented has been passed upon by our Supreme Court on many occasions. Basically it has been held that the determination of this question must turn upon the facts and circumstances of each case.

Actions for trespass committed by an agent are based upon the doctrine of respondeat superior. The master's liability does not arise unless the tortious act was committed as an incident to the master's business and while acting within the range of employment, or that the master directed the wrongful act or ratified it afterwards. The test of liability is whether the act constituting the trespass was within the general scope of the servant's employment while engaged in the employer's business, and was done with the view of furthering that business.

The latest decisions on this subject have followed the modern view that the liability of the master for intentional acts which constitute legal wrongs can only arise when that which is done is within the real or apparent scope of the master's business. It does not arise where the servant has stepped aside from his employment to commit a tort which the master neither directed in fact nor could be supposed, from the nature of his employment, to have authorized or expected the servant to do.

It is appellee's contention that the issues of whether its agent's act of trespass was committed within the real or apparent scope of defendant's business; whether the agent stepped aside from his employment to commit the act complained of; and whether defendant directed or could be supposed to have authorized or expected the agent to commit the tortious act, were all questions for the jury to determine. It is upon this premise that appellee insists the trial court committed error in directing a verdict on these issues in plaintiff's favor, and that the court's subsequent order granting a new trial because of such error is correct and should be sustained. . . .

The manager's instruction to the agent to go to plaintiff's house and get the television receiver, knowing as he did that the agent was not then armed with judicial process entitling him to lawfully take the security claimed by defendant, is susceptible of but one reasonable interpretation. These instructions, unqualified as they were, contemplated that the agent would take such action as he deemed necessary in order to carry them out. That the agent did not misinterpret these instructions is evidenced by the fact that he reinforced himself with the assistance of two city detectives before arriving at plaintiff's home with the obvious intention of retaking the receiver by whatever means appeared necessary. Defendant's manager knew, or is presumed to have known, that television receivers are customarily, if not invariably kept inside people's homes, and cannot be seized by a lienor over the objection of the owner without the commission of a trespass. Defendant accepted and benefited from its agent's activities by retaining the receiver without offering to return it to its owner, knowing or being presumed to have known the manner in which possession of the instrument was obtained.

It is our view that the undisputed evidence established defendant's liability for the tortious act of its agent, and any contrary view that may have been taken by the jury could not have been sustained. There was no genuine issue of any material fact touching upon defendant's liability in this case, and the trial court was correct as a matter of law in directing a verdict in plaintiff's favor. It therefore follows that the court committed error by entering its order granting a new trial. . . .

The order granting a new trial is reversed.

Review Questions and Problems

1. For what acts of the agent is the principal responsible? What is the effect of custom and usage on the powers of the agent?
2. Mrs. *G* owned a store and placed her son in general charge thereof. She gave him very definite instructions not to enter into any contracts for advertising without her consent. Nevertheless, he entered into a contract for advertising that would compare favorably with advertising in other stores of like size. Is the mother liable?
3. *A* operated a department store, in which for each department there was a party known as the buyer although he possessed no actual authority to purchase. The duty of each buyer was to select the goods and submit his choice to the management for approval. *T* sold an order of goods to one of the buyers and the goods were shipped without the approval of the management. Was *A* liable?
4. *A* was *O*'s agent in charge of a lumber yard and of loading and unloading lumber. He had been instructed never to pile lumber outside the lumber yard, but because of ease in unloading, he piled some outside and near a sidewalk. Some of it fell on *C*, who was passing by on the sidewalk. Was *O* liable to *C*? If *O* was liable to *C*, did he have an action against *A*? Could *C* have recovered of *A*?
5. *A* was a traveling salesman for *P*. He sold and delivered to *T* goods amounting to $300. At the time of delivery, he collected the sale price, but failed to turn it in to *P*. Will *T* have to pay again? Would the result be the same if *P* had shipped the goods and *A* had collected at the end of the month? Suppose *A* had sold the goods in exchange for groceries and had used the groceries. Would *P* have been able to collect again of *T*?
6. *A*, while acting as traveling salesman for *B*, is informed of the dissolution of the firm *X* and *Y*. Later *A*, being now employed by *P*, sells goods to *Y*. *P* assumes that *X* is still a partner, inasmuch as the same firm name is continued. Is *P* charged with notice of the dissolution?
7. *X* Railway Co., in operating a train late at night, severely injured *A*, a brakeman on the train. The conductor took him immediately to a local doctor and told the doctor the railroad would care for the bill. *X* Co. refused to pay, stating the conductor had no authority to select its medical staff. What result if the doctor sues *X* Co.?
8. *A* was authorized by *P* to purchase bowling alley equipment on credit. He told the seller he was acting as an agent, but was not at liberty to disclose his principal's name. The bill remaining unpaid and *P* being now disclosed, may the seller recover of *A*?
9. *A*, acting as the appointed agent of *F*, took title to certain property and in payment *A* gave his note to *S*, secured by a mortgage on the property. Default arose and foreclosure took place, out of which a deficiency arose. *F* denied any liability for the deficiency because only *A*'s name appeared on the note. The court held *F* was not liable. Was this a sound decision?

10. *A* was the purchasing agent of *P* for the purpose of buying poultry and farm produce. In all his transactions with the farmers, *A* acted as the principal and purchased on the strength of his own credit. *A* failed to pay for certain of the produce purchased. The farmers, having ascertained that *P* was the true principal, seek to hold him. May they do so? Suppose *P* had previously settled with *A*?
11. *P* engaged *A* to operate a retail lumber business in the latter's name. *A* sold merchandise to *T* on credit. Later *P* notified *T* that *A*'s agency was terminated and directed *T* to pay the debt to *P*. *T* later disregarded instructions and paid the obligation to *A*, who failed to account to *P*. May *P* collect from *T*?
12. *M* was a collection agent for *C* and in payment of an account, *X* Co. made a check to *C* for $7,000 and handed it to *M*. *M* indorsed *C*'s name on the check and cashed it without remitting to *C*. *C* is now attempting to recover from *X* Co., contending that the authority to collect gave no authority to indorse. What decision?
13. *S*, a bus driver for *X* Co., was operating his bus when it was struck by a truck of *T* Co., driven by *F*. *S* stopped the bus and attempted to get name of the truck driver and license number of the truck. At this point, *F* kicked and beat him up very badly. *S* sued *T* Co. for damages and the court held the latter was not liable, as the agent was motivated by anger and was not acting for his principal. Do you think this is sound?
14. *A*, an employee of Bank, purchased substantial quantities of supplies from *T* in *A*'s name, although actually he was purchasing for Bank with proper authority. *A* failed to pay for some of the supplies, and *T* obtained a judgment against him but was unable to collect. Having learned that the purchases were made for Bank, *T* now seeks to recover of Bank. Should he recover?
15. *Q* was the sales and collection agent for *C* Dairy Co., and as such he sold dairy products to *T* Co., often billing and collecting for items not delivered, spurious tickets having apparently been signed in error by an agent of *T* Co. The fraud has now been discovered, and *T* Co. has sued to recover the payments improperly made. *C* Co. claims that *Q* was acting outside the scope of his authority in collecting for spurious items. The court held *C* Co. liable. Discuss the soundness of this decision.

18

Principal and Agent

DUTIES AND LIABILITIES OF AGENT

3-27. Classification. The extent of the duties imposed upon the agent are governed largely by his contract of employment. In addition to the duties expressly assumed by the agent, certain others are implied by the nature of the relationship. These duties divide themselves roughly into five groups. The agent is: (1) to be loyal to his principal; (2) to obey all reasonable instructions; (3) not to be negligent; (4) to account for all money or property received for the benefit of the principal; and (5) to inform the principal of all facts which materially affect the subject matter of the agency. A duty arising under any specific circumstances will usually be found to fall within one of these groups.

3-28. Duty to be loyal. As an organic part of every contract of employment, an implied duty arises on the part of the agent to be loyal to the interests of his principal, and broadly interpreted, the duty to be loyal encompasses all the other duties outlined above. Because of the duty of loyalty it is held that he should undertake no business venture that competes or interferes in any manner with the business of his employer or make any contract for himself when he should have made it for his principal. The same rule forbids a sales agent to sell his principal's property to himself, unless the principal assents to the sale. The rule also prevents a purchasing agent from buying his own property or that in which he has an interest. Transactions violating these rules may always be rescinded by the principal, despite the fact that the agent acted for the best interests of his principal and the contract was as favorable as could be obtained elsewhere. The general rule is applied without favor in order that every possible motive or incentive for unfaithfulness may be removed.

In any case in which the agent obtains the consent of the principal to deal with himself, the agent must disclose fully all facts which materially influence the situation. In such a case, they do not deal at "arm's length," and the circumstances demand the utmost good faith on the part of the agent.

Because of the loyalty demanded of an agent, a broker is denied the right to represent both the seller and the buyer in the same transaction unless both have been informed of his dual relationship.[1] His desire to earn the commission is apt to cause him to disregard the best interests of one of his principals.

If a contract is entered into between the two principals, it may be avoided when it is learned that one agent represented both parties. Even though the agreement is fully performed, the agent who, unknown to the parties, acted in a dual capacity is denied the right to compensation for his services. He should have notified the parties of his peculiar relationship.

3-29. Use of confidential information. Loyalty demands that information of a confidential character acquired while in the service of the principal shall not be used by the agent to advance his interests in opposition to those of the principal. An employee who learns of secret processes or formulas or comes into possession of lists of customers may not use this information to the detriment of his employer.

An employee who, having learned of a valuable lease held by his employer, leases the property for himself may be forced to hold the lease in trust for his employer. If the agent "steals a march" on his principal, the profit belongs to the principal and not to the agent. The rule is applied with equal severity whether the agent acts before or after he severs his connection with the principal. An employee who copies a list of his employer's customers may not circularize such a group after he enters business for himself. A distinction must be drawn, however, between the use of secret information and the use of skill acquired at a certain employment. The latter may be used, although it affects injuriously his former employer. For this reason there is nothing to hinder a person who has made the acquaintance of his employer's customers from later circularizing those whom he can remember. His acquaintanceship is part of his acquired skill. The employer may protect himself in the latter case by a clause in the employment agreement to the effect that the employee will not compete with the employer or work for a competitor for a limited period of time after his employment is terminated.

3-30. Profits from violation of duty. All profits made by an agent out of transactions conducted for his principal or resulting from violation of his duty of loyalty belong to, and may be recovered by, the principal. Such profits include rebates, bonuses, commissions, or divisions of profits received by an agent for dealing with a particular third party. Here again the contracts may have been favorable to the employer, but the result is the same, since the agent should not be tempted to abuse the confidence reposed in him.

[1] Standard Realty & Development v. Ferrera, page 409.

An agent is presumed to give all his time wholeheartedly to furthering his principal's cause. Suppose, however, that he takes part of his time, unknown to his employer, to perform work for someone else and obtains compensation for it. Clearly, such compensation belongs to the principal. Thus, a traveling salesman who, without the consent of his employer, carries a sideline which he sells to customers of his employer may be compelled to turn over his sideline commissions to his principal.

This duty of the agent refers only to the time which the contract demands be spent on the principal's business. Any money made after hours, or during a period when he is not expected to be working for his principal, unquestionably remains the property of the agent.

3-31. To obey instructions. It becomes the duty of an agent to obey all instructions issued by his principal as long as they refer to duties contemplated by the contract of employment. Burdens not required by the agreement cannot be indiscriminately imposed by the employer. An instruction may not be regarded lightly merely because it departs from the usual procedure and seems fanciful and impractical to the employee. It is not his business to question the procedure outlined by his superior. Any loss which results while he is pursuing any other course makes him absolutely liable for the result.

Furthermore, an instruction of the principal does not become improper merely because the motive is bad. He may be well aware of the agent's distaste for certain tasks, yet, if those tasks are such as may be called for under the employment agreement, it becomes the agent's duty to perform them. Failure to perform often results in proper grounds for his discharge.

This obligation on the part of the agent to follow carefully his principal's orders applies to an agent who acts gratuitously, as well as to one who receives pay for his services. Although the former is under no duty to perform, even though he has promised to do so, yet if he undertakes to carry out his commission, he must follow explicitly the instructions received.

Closely allied to the duty to follow instructions is the duty to remain within the scope of the authority conferred. Because of the doctrine of estoppel, it often becomes possible for an agent to exceed his authority and still bind his principal. In case of such a violation of his contract, the employee becomes responsible for any resulting loss. He is in this instance failing to follow the instructions set forth in his contract with his employer. These instructions must be fully complied with, as well as those issued later by the principal.

3-32. Unusual circumstances. Occasionally circumstances arise that nullify instructions previously given. Because of the new conditions, the old instructions would, if followed, practically destroy the purpose of the agency. Whenever such an emergency arises, it becomes the duty of the agent, provided the principal is not available, to exercise his best judgment in meeting the situation.

An instruction to do an illegal or immoral act, or an act that will impair the security or position of the agent, may be disregarded. To illustrate: A factor has a lien on goods in his possession for all money advanced to his principal. An order from the principal to return the goods or to sell them on credit could be disregarded until such time as all advances had been paid.

3-33. Duty not to be negligent. All agents are presumed to exercise that degree of skill and diligence ordinarily expected of those who perform like undertakings. An agent who agrees to perform a particular task implies that he possesses the requisite skill and training. His duty is to exercise only a reasonable degree of care, and he is not liable for a failure to use the highest degree of care possible.[2] An agent may be intrusted to loan the money of another. If he exercises ordinary prudence in ascertaining the state of the title to property securing the loan and reasonably estimates its value, he cannot be held liable upon nonpayment of the loan at its maturity. In a previous chapter it was observed that the negligence of an agent might, under certain conditions, make the principal liable to third parties. Where the agent is clearly responsible for the damage, the principal may recover from the agent the amount paid by him to the third party. The burden of loss in such cases may, if the principal desires, be shifted to the negligent party.

3-34. Duty to account. Money or property intrusted to the agent must be accounted for to the principal. Because of this fact, the agent is required to keep proper records showing receipts and expenditures, in order that a complete accounting may be rendered. Any money collected by an agent for his principal should not be mingled with funds of the former. If they are deposited in a bank, they should be kept in a separate account and so designated that a trust is apparent. Otherwise, any loss resulting from an insolvent bank must be borne by the agent.

The principal may follow any funds misappropriated by the agent until they fall into the hands of a third party. Even then the principal may follow the proceeds and impress a trust upon them, so long as they have not reached an innocent third party. Furthermore, if such proceeds can be shown to have increased the estate of the agent, a trust may be imposed upon the agent's estate to that extent.

3-35. To give notice. It becomes the duty of an agent to tell his principal all facts which vitally affect the subject matter of the agency and which are obtained within the scope of the employment. Matters learned

[2] Robbins v. Roumel, page 410.

while outside the scope of employment and which the agent never expects to use need not be communicated to the principal.

This rule extends beyond the duty to inform the principal of conflicting interests of third parties in a particular transaction, and it imposes upon the agent a duty to give all information which materially affects the interest of the principal. Thus, knowledge of facts which have greatly advanced the value of property placed with an agent for sale should be communicated before the property is sold at a price previously established by the principal.

DUTIES AND LIABILITIES OF PRINCIPAL

3-36. To employ. First and foremost, it becomes the duty of the principal to employ the agent in accordance with their agreement and to pay him the agreed compensation. If no definite compensation has been agreed upon, there arises a duty to pay the reasonable value of such services. Whenever the party performing the services is a stranger to the employer, the obligation to compensate exists. However, where relatives are working for one another and no express agreement has been formulated, the courts are likely to infer that the services so rendered should be considered as gratuitous.

Whether the agent is entitled to have actual work to perform in addition to his compensation is questionable. Where, however, his skill depends upon constant practice, it is doubtful whether the employer fulfills his agreement merely by paying the agreed compensation without offering him any work to do.

3-37. Real estate broker's commission. In the absence of an express agreement, the real estate broker earns his commission at either one of two times. As soon as he finds a buyer who is ready, willing, and able to meet the terms outlined by the seller, he has earned his commission. The owner cannot rob him of his compensation by refusing to deal with the prospective purchaser or by withdrawing the property from sale. He cannot relieve himself of the duty to pay the commission by terminating the agency and later contracting directly with the broker's prospect. The fee is earned if it is shown that the broker was the inducing cause of the sale.[3]

The commission is also earned as soon as the owner contracts with the purchaser, even though it later develops that the buyer is unable to meet the contract's terms. The owner assumes the risk of performance if he is willing to, and does, contract with the buyer presented by the broker. The broker's commission is contingent on payment by the purchaser only when his contract of employment so states.[4] An owner who

[3] Haymes v. Rogers, page 412.

[4] Richard v. Falleti et ux., page 414.

lists property with several brokers is obligated to pay the first one to find a satisfactory purchaser, at which time the agency of other brokers is automatically terminated.

There are three distinct types of real estate listings—placing of property with real estate brokers for sale. First is the simple listing of the property for sale on the terms set forth by the seller, in which case the listing may be with several brokers and the right to withdraw or terminate the relationship at any time is reserved by the seller. Under such circumstances, the seller pays the commission to the first broker who finds a buyer. The second type consists of an exclusive listing which usually gives to the broker the exclusive right to find a buyer for an agreed period of time. In this case the seller is not free to list the property with other brokers and a sale through other brokers would be a violation of the contract of listing, although the seller, himself, is free to find a buyer of his own. Third, a listing in which the broker is given an exclusive right to sell. In this case even the seller is not free to find a buyer of his own choosing. If the seller does sell on his own behalf, he is obligated to pay a commission to the broker holding an exclusive right to sell.

3-38. Compensation of sales representatives. Salesmen who sell merchandise on a commission basis have problems confronting them that are similar to those of the broker, unless the employment contract is specific in its details. Let us assume that *X* Co. appoints *A* as its exclusive sales representative in a certain territory on a commission basis and that the employer is engaged in producing and selling electrical equipment. *T*, a businessman in the area involved, sends in a large order for merchandise directly to the home office of *X* Co. Is *A* entitled to a commission on the sale? It is generally held that such a salesman is entitled to a commission only on sales solicited and induced by him, unless his contract of employment gives him greater rights.

The salesman usually earns his commission as soon as an order from a responsible buyer is obtained, unless his contract of employment makes payment contingent upon delivery of the goods or collection of the sale's price. If payment is made dependent upon performance by the purchaser, the employer cannot deny the salesman his commission by terminating the agency prior to collection of the account. When the buyer ultimately pays for the goods, the seller is obligated to pay the commission.

An agent who receives a weekly or monthly advance against future commissions is not obligated to return the advance if commissions equal thereto are not earned. The advance, in the absence of a specific agreement, is considered by the courts as a minimum salary.

3-39. Reimbursement and indemnity. Money expended by the agent in behalf of the principal may be recovered. It must appear that the money was reasonably spent and that its expenditure was not necessitated by the misconduct or negligence of the agent.

The agent is justified in presuming that instructions given by the principal are such as he lawfully has a right to give and that performance resulting from such instructions will not injuriously affect third parties. Where this is not the case, and the agent incurs a liability to some third party because of trespass or conversion, the principal must indemnify the agent against loss.[5] In like manner, it becomes the duty of the principal to make possible performance by the agent whenever the latter has entered into a contract in his own name for the former's benefit. The undisclosed principal must fully protect his agent.

TERMINATION OF AGENCY

3-40. By act of the parties. An agency may be terminated by an act of the parties or by operation of law. An agency which is created to continue for a definite period of time ceases, by the original agreement, at expiration of that period. If the parties consent to the continuation of the relationship beyond such period, the courts imply the formation of a new contract of employment. The new agreement contains the same terms as the old one and continues for a like period of time, except that no implied contract can run longer than one year.

An agency created to accomplish a certain purpose automatically ends with the completion of the task assigned. In such a case third parties are not entitled to notice of the termination. Furthermore, when it is possible for one of several agents to perform the task, such as selling certain real estate, it is held that performance by the first party terminates the authority of the other agents.

Any contract may be terminated by mutual agreement; therefore, the agency relationship may be severed in this manner. Furthermore, either party to the agreement has full power to terminate it whenever he desires although he possesses no right to do so. Wrongful termination of the agency by either party subjects him to a suit for damages by the other party. An exception to these rules exists in the case of so-called agencies coupled with an interest. Such agencies cannot be terminated without the consent of the agent, and a full discussion of them will be found in a subsequent section.

3-41. Wrongful termination and its effect. An employment at the will of the parties may be terminated by either party at any time. On the other hand, if the employer wrongfully terminates a contract which was

[5] Hoggan v. Cahoon, page 415.

to continue for an agreed period, he becomes liable for damages. If the agent is discharged for cause, such as failure to follow instructions or to exercise proper care or for nonperformance of various other duties, he may not recover damages from his employer.

The employee who has his employment wrongfully cut short is entitled to recover his compensation for work done before his dismissal and an additional sum for damages. Most of the states permit him to bring an action either immediately following the breach, in which he recovers prospective damages, or after the period has expired and thus recover the damages actually sustained. In the latter case, he is compelled to deduct from the compensation called for in the agreement the amount which he has been able to earn during the interim. Under such circumstances, the employee is held to a duty to exercise reasonable diligence in finding other work of like character. Apparently this rule does not require him to seek employment in a new locality or to accept work of a different or more menial character. His duty is to find work of like kind, provided it is available in the particular locality.

3-42. Termination by law. Certain acts are held by law to terminate the agency. Among these are death, insanity, or bankruptcy of either of the parties. Bankruptcy has such an effect only in case it affects the subject matter of the agency.

It is said of such cases that the agency is immediately terminated and that no notice need be given to either the agent or the third parties. However, with reference to insanity, unless the principal has been publicly adjudged insane, it is believed that his agent's contracts are binding on the principal unless the third party is aware of the mental illness.

3-43. Agency coupled with an interest. It is said that an agency coupled with an interest cannot be terminated without the consent of the agent. Such agencies are of two classes: those in which the agent has a legal or equitable interest in the subject matter; and those in which the agency is created as a source of reimbursement to the agent because of money owed him by the principal. This latter type is most often called an *agency coupled with an obligation.* Although it cannot be terminated by the principal during his lifetime, it is terminated by death. A true agency coupled with an interest is not terminated in either case. To illustrate: a mortgagee who receives a mortgage in which is included a provision giving him the right to sell in case of default could not have this right taken away during the lifetime or by the death of the principal On the other hand, an agent who is given the right to sell a certain automobile and to apply the proceeds on a claim against the principal has his right cut off by the death of his principal.

Under either type of agency, it should be clear that the interest in the subject matter must be greater than the mere expectation of profits to be realized.[6] In other words, a principal who has appointed an agent to sell certain goods on commission could certainly terminate the agency at any time he desired although his conduct might constitute a breach of the agreement.

3-44. Notice in event of termination. Termination of the agency, as explained above, may take place by act of the parties or by operation of law. If the parties by their own action have terminated the agency, it is the duty of the principal to notify all third parties who have learned of the existence of the agency of its termination.[7] Those entitled to such notice may be divided into two groups: (1) those who have previously relied upon the agency by dealing with the agent; and (2) those who have never previously dealt with him, but who, nevertheless, have learned of the agency. The principal's duty to the first class can be satisfied only by the actual receipt of notice by the third party. He satisfies his duty to the second group by giving public notice, such as newspaper publicity, in the location involved. If any one of the second group, not having seen the newspaper account of the termination, relies upon the continuation of the agency to his detriment, he has no cause of action against the principal. If a member of the first group has not received direct notice from the principal, but has learned indirectly of the severance of relation or of facts sufficient to place him on inquiry, he is no longer justified in extending credit to the agent.

Where the agency is terminated by action of law, such as death, insanity, or bankruptcy, no duty to notify third parties devolves upon the principal. Such matters receive publicity through newspapers, official records, and otherwise, and third parties normally become aware of the termination without the necessity for additional notification. If the death of the principal occurs before an agent contracts with a third party, the third party has no cause of action against either the agent or the principal unless the agent is acting for an undisclosed principal. In the latter case, since the agent makes the contract in his own name, he is liable to the third party. Otherwise, the third party is in as good a position to know of the death of the principal as is the agent.

PRINCIPAL AND AGENT CASES

STANDARD REALTY & DEVELOPMENT v. FERRERA

1957, (Cal. App.) 311 P.2nd 855

The plaintiff, Standard Realty & Development Company, contacted McEvoy, a real estate broker, to see if he could aid it in obtaining certain property owned by the defendant. The broker approached the defendant

[6] Flanagan v. Brown, page 416.
[7] Meeker v. Mannia, page 417.

and persuaded him to list the property with him for sale and, a few days later had a "straw" man pay defendant $500 for an option to purchase the property for $32,500, the option being assigned to the plaintiff. The defendant later learned that a new industrial plant was to be located nearby and refused to carry out the contract, alleging fraud because the broker was acting as an agent for both parties without defendant's knowledge. Plaintiff brought a suit for specific performance and the lower court gave judgment for defendant. The plaintiff appealed.

Fourt, J. . . . Appellant contends that granted arguendo the trial court was correct in its finding that McEvoy was acting in a dual capacity as agent for plaintiff and defendants, nonetheless, it is not grounds for a rescission of the contract even though he made no disclosure of this fact to the defendants. There is persuasive authority to the contrary in the recent Supreme Court case of *McConnell v. Cowan,* 44 Cal.2d 805, 285 P.2d 261. In that case the court discusses a factual situation similar to the one presented in this case, where there was dual representation, the agent assuming to act in a double capacity without disclosing this fact to one principal. At page 809 of 44 Cal.2d, at page 264 of 285 P.2d, the court says:

> * * * Such conduct is a fraud upon his principal, and not only will the agent not be entitled to compensation for services so rendered, but the contract or dealings made or had by the agent, while so acting also for the other party without the knowledge or consent of the principal, are not binding upon the latter, and if they still remain executory, he may repudiate them on that ground, or, if they have been executed in whole or in part, he may by acting promptly and before the rights of innocent parties have intervened, restore the consideration received, rescind the contract and recover back the property or rights with which he has parted under it.* * *

The defendants in the case before us followed the prescribed procedure exactly, and the trial court did not err in finding that the defendants had a right to rescind the contract. Thus the defendants could not be required to specifically perform the option agreement, nor is plaintiff entitled to recover damages. See *Vice v. Thacker,* 30 Cal.2d 84, 90, 180 P.2d 4; 9 Cal. Jur.2d 198.

This Court having found defendants justified in rescinding the contract, the other points raised by appellant on appeal become immaterial and it is unnecessary to discuss them.

Judgment affirmed.

ROBBINS v. ROUMEL

1957, (D.C. App.) 138 A.2nd 922

Plaintiff, Roumel, brought an action against Robbins for rent collected by the latter, Robbins being resident manager of an apartment building owned by plaintiff. Plaintiff had opened a bank account in a nearby bank and rented a night depository for use by the defendant in handling deposits. Defendant's defense is that the money was solen from an unlocked desk drawer in the living room of her apartment where rents were collected. No deposits had been made over a two week period although rents had been collecting during this period. The lower court gave judgment for the plaintiff and defendant appealed.

ROVER, C. J. . . . The standard of care imposed upon an agent to protect his principal's property is that of reasonable care and skill. Where the property involved is the money of a principal, the agent is required to keep it in a safe place, and unless supplied with proper facilities for the safe-keeping of the funds he is both privileged and required to deposit the money in a bank.

Procedurally, when a principal sues his agent for an accounting or for money had and received, a prima facie case is established by the principal's proof or the agent's admission that a sum of money has come into the agent's possession. He need go no further, for the burden is then on the agent to negate his liability either by showing that he has accounted for the money or by offering some sufficient reason why he cannot. In accordance with the foregoing principles, while an agent may allege theft as an affirmative defense, he may not rest on this alone. The law will impose liability if the money was stolen as a result of the agent's failure to follow his principal's instructions with respect to the handling and custody of the receipts, or if the agent neglected to perform some duty which rested on him independently of his instructions and the omission under the circumstances amounted to a failure to exercise reasonable care. The burden of proving that the principal's instructions were followed or that reasonable care was exercised is upon the agent alleging theft as an affirmative defense.

In the instant case, appellant admits in her answer collection of the funds and alleges that the money was presumably stolen. The evidence, however, was such that the trial court could have found that reasonable care was not exercised in protecting the money. The receipts were kept in an unlocked desk drawer in her apartment where tenants and workers had frequent access. Though banking facilities were readily available for day and night deposits, appellant concedes that a daily accounting and depositing of the receipts was not made; the money was in fact kept in the unlocked drawer over a period of two or three weeks. The agent offered no proof that the principal had knowledge of or consented to this manner of keeping the receipts, and in view of the evidence we must hold that the trial court could have found that appellant failed to sustain the burden of showing that reasonable safety precautions were taken. . . .

Judgment for plaintiff affirmed.

HAYMES v. ROGERS
1950, (Ariz.) 222 P.2d 789

DECONCINI, J. In our former opinion, June 12, 1950, 70 Ariz. 257, 219 P.2d 339, we held that as a matter of law there was bad faith shown on the broker's part which precluded him from recovery of his commission. In the light of the motion for rehearing and a re-examination of the evidence and instructions we are constrained to change our view.

Kelley Rogers, hereinafter called appellee, brought an action against L. F. Haymes, hereinafter referred to as appellant, seeking to recover a real estate commission in the sum of $425.00. The case was tried before a jury which returned a verdict in favor of appellee. The said appellant owned a piece of realty which he had listed for sale with the appellee, real estate broker, for the sum of $9,500. The listing card which appellant signed provided that the commission to be paid appellee for selling the property was to be five (5%) per cent of the total selling price. Tom Kolouch was employed by the said appellee as a real estate salesman, and is hereinafter referred to as "salesman."

On February 4, 1948 the said salesman contacted Mr. and Mrs. Louise Pour, prospective clients. He showed them various parcels of real estate, made an appointment with them for the following day in order to show them appellant's property. The salesman then drew a diagram of the said property in order to enable the Pours to locate and identify it the next day for their appointment. The Pours, however, proceeded to go to appellant's property that very day and encountering the appellant, negotiated directly with him and purchased the property for the price of $8,500. The transcript of evidence reveals that the appellant knew the Pours had been sent to him through the efforts of appellee's salesman, but whether he knew it before they verbally agreed on a sale and appellant had accepted a $50 deposit was in dispute. Upon learning that fact he told the Pours that he would take care of the salesman.

Appellant makes several assignments of error and propositions of law directed against the appellee's requested instructions given by the trial court and the court's refusal to grant his requested instructions and a motion for an instructed verdict in favor of the defendant.

The trial court correctly refused defendant's motion for an instructed verdict in his favor, because the matter of bad faith on the part of the appellee broker should have been submitted to the jury.

The important proposition of law relied upon by the appellant is as follows:

The law requires that a real estate broker employed to sell land must act in entire good faith and in the interest of his employer, and if he induces the prospective buyer to believe that the property can be bought for less, he thereby fails to discharge that duty and forfeits all his right to claim commission and compensation for his work.

There is no doubt that the above proposition of law is correct. A real estate agent owes the duty of utmost good faith and loyalty to his principal. The immediate problem here is whether the above proposition is applicable to the facts in this instance.

The facts here are as follows: The salesman informed the purchasers that he had an offer of $8,250 for the property from another purchaser which he was about to submit to appellant. He further told them he thought appellant would not accept the offer, but they might get it for $8,500.

Mr. Rogers, the appellee broker, testified that appellant phoned him after he had accepted the $50 deposit from the purchasers and informed him that he had closed the deal himself and felt that he owed no commission but would split the commission with him, which he, the appellee, refused to do. He further testified that the appellant told him that if their other offer from a third person had been $8,500 he would have accepted it and paid a full commission.

The evidence in this case presents a close question as to good or bad faith on the part of the broker. The trial court should have submitted that matter for the jury to decide. This court has held in negligence cases where the question is close or is in the "shadow zone" that the trial court should not as a matter of law decide those things but rather submit the question to the jury. *Dillow v. City of Yuma*, 55 Ariz. 6, 97 P.2d 535. We feel that while the facts are not analogous, yet the principle of law is the same and decline to decide what is bad faith as a matter of law because that is within the province of the triers of fact. The appellant is entitled to have the jury weigh the evidence and inferences therefrom as to whether or not appellee acted in bad faith in the light of the foregoing.

We wish to reiterate that a broker or salesman owes the utmost good faith to his principal as does any other person acting as agent or in a fiduciary capacity. If an agent betrays his principal, such misconduct and breach of duty results in the agent's losing his right to compensation for services to which he would otherwise be entitled. . . .

In this case the appellant sold the property to a purchaser whom he knew was sent to him by the appellee's salesman. Therefore, in the absence of bad faith the broker is entitled to his commission when he is the procuring cause of sale. . . .

Judgment is reversed and the case remanded for a new trial with directions to submit the question of bad faith on the part of the appellee to the jury.

Judgment reversed.

RICHARD v. FALLETI et ux.
1951, 13 N.J. Super. 534, 81 A.2d 17

Bigelow, J. A. D. The appellant, Richard, a real estate broker, sues for the unpaid half of a commission earned on the sale of land. The trial court held that plaintiff's right was contingent on delivery of the deed and rendered judgment for defendants inasmuch as the deed had not been delivered.

By the contract between the parties to the action, the defendant agreed to pay a commission of $750 "in consideration of services rendered in connection with the sale" of defendants' premises; "said commission to be paid one-half on signing agreement for sale of property and the balance on delivery of deed." The agreement of sale was signed the same day and $3,000 on account of the purchase price was paid. At the same time, the defendants paid plaintiff $375, being one-half the stipulated commission. Two and one-half months later—time having been made of the essence—defendants tendered the deed, but the buyer failed to pay the purchase price, "stating that he did not have in hand funds necessary to perform on his part." And so there was no delivery of deed.

It is familiar law that in the absence of a special agreement, a broker earns his commission when he produces a customer able and willing to buy the property upon the seller's terms. The broker is entitled to a commission if the seller accepts the broker's customer and enters into a binding contract with him, even though the buyer eventually proves to be financially unable to carry out the purchase. *Freeman v. Van Wagenen,* 90 N.J.L. 358, 101 A. 55 (Sup. Ct. 1917); *Matz v. Bessman,* 1 N.J. Misc. (Sup. Ct. 1923); *Brindley v. Brook,* 160 A. 398, 10 N.J. Misc. 612 (Sup. Ct. 1932). The rule is the same in other jurisdictions. 12 C.J.S., Brokers, § 85, p. 188. The broker and his employer may, however, by the use of appropriate language, make the broker's right to a commission depend upon a future happening, such as the actual passage of title from vendor to purchaser. . . .

Where a debt has arisen, liability will not be excused because, without fault of the creditor and due to happenings beyond his control, the time for payment, as fixed by the contract, can never arrive. Restatement, Contracts, § 301; Williston, *Contracts,* § 799; *Goldfarb v. Cohen,* 92 Conn. 277, 102 A. 649 (Conn. 1917). . . .

In the instant appeal, the broker completed performance on his part when he induced the purchaser to sign the agreement of sale. He was under no duty to assist at the closing of title. The promise to pay him a commission was not in form conditional: "We hereby agree to pay to Carmine Richard a commission in the amount of $725." The clause fixing the time for payment is independent, separated by a semicolon from the agreement to pay, ______ "said commission to be paid one-half on signing of Agreement of Sale and the balance on delivery of deed." We are satisfied that the obligation to pay was not made contingent on delivery of the deed. The commission fell due when it became evident that the buyer could not or would not pay for the land.

The judgment is reversed.

HOGGAN v. CAHOON

1903, 26 Utah 444, 72 Pac. 512, 99 A.S.R. 837

This action was commenced by Hoggan to recover the sum of $290.35 and interest, the same being the amount of damages and costs paid by the plaintiff. It appears that the plaintiff was made agent of the defendant to take possession of certain property upon which the latter claimed to have a chattel mortgage. Because the defendant had no right to the goods, one S. S. Johnson obtained judgment against the plaintiff for wrongfully taking his goods. The lower court gave judgment for defendant, and plaintiff appeals.

BARTCH, J. We will, in the first instance, consider the question whether the complaint states a cause of action. . . . Therefrom [the facts] it appears that the defendant appointed the plaintiff as his agent for the purpose of transacting certain specific business, which was to take into possession certain goods and chattels, and transport them to a particular place named. The agent proceeded to, and did transact the business of the agency at the special instance and under the direction of the principal; and, although the goods and chattels were covered by a mortgage held by the principal, the agent was not aware that the taking and carrying away of them constituted a tort. He, as appears, acted in good faith, and upon the faith of representations and assurances of the principal that such taking was lawful and proper. . . .

If the allegations are in fact true, the plaintiff has a right of recovery. The facts stated are such as to characterize the case as an exception to the rule that tort feasors or wrongdoers cannot have redress against each other. That rule applies to cases where he who seeks redress knew or must be presumed to have known that the transaction which resulted in the damages he was compelled to pay was tortious and unlawful. But where, as appears from the allegations in this case, an agent acts in good faith for his principal, under the principal's direction, and relies upon his representations that the transaction is lawful, and the same is not manifestly unlawful, the law implies indemnity, for damages of third parties, to the agent from the principal. . . .

The agent has the right to assume that the principal will not call upon him to perform any duty which would render him liable in damages to third persons. Having no personal interest in the act, other than the performance of his duty, the agent should not be required to suffer loss from the doing of an act apparently lawful in itself, and which he has undertaken to do by the direction and for the benefit and advantage of the principal. . . . Wherever, then, the agent is called upon by his principal to do an act which is not manifestly illegal and which he does not know to be wrong, the law implies a promise on the part of the principal to indemnify the agent for such losses and damages as flow directly and immediately from the execution of the agency. . . . *Mechem on Agency*, § 653.

We are of the opinion that the court erred in sustaining the demurrer. *Judgment reversed.*

FLANAGAN v. BROWN

1886, 70 Cal. 254

This is an action upon a note for $27,000. The owner, who had purchased it from an insolvent bank for $32, made an agreement with the plaintiff, Flanagan, whereby the note was to be placed with the plaintiff to sell, dispose of or collect. The proceeds were to be divided equally between the parties. After this agreement the owner released his claim at the request of the defendant. The plaintiff contends that he has an agency coupled with an interest and the owner had no power to surrender his claim.

SULLIVAN, J. . . . If Flanagan has any standing, it must result from something else than his mere custody of the paper; he is not the owner of it; he is a mere agent entrusted with its custody; was he such an agent that his principal had not the right to revoke his authority? . . . The term "power, coupled with an interest" is well understood, and is discussed and defined in the very cases cited by the code commissioners under the section above referred to. These cases lay down the rule that a power coupled with an interest is where the grantee has an interest in the estate as well as in the exercise of the power. It is determined to exist or not according as the agent is found to have such estate or not before the execution of the power. If his interest is only a right to share the proceeds which result from the execution of his power, the agent has not a power coupled with an interest.

The case of *Brown v. Pforr*, 38 Cal. 550, recognizes the rules as to power coupled with an interest.

There the agents had an interest to the extent of $750 in the execution of the power conferred within the time named in their contract of agency, but they had no interest in the real estate which was the subject of the agency. Accordingly, the principal, even within the time limited in the contract, was held to be at liberty to revoke.

. . . Flanagan, in the sense of the rule here laid down, and of the rule laid down by section 2356 of the code, was not a holder of a power coupled with an interest. If not, by the terms of this section his power was revocable, and his principal's release is a good bar to this action.

Judgment for defendant.

MEEKER v. MANNIA
1896, 162 Ill. 203, 44 N.E. 397

A bill by Mannia for specific performance of a contract involving the purchase of real estate. The defense was that the full purchase price had not been paid. It appeared that the plaintiff paid some $200 to one Liebner, who was apparently acting for Frey & Schlund, who were in turn the agents of the defendant. Frey & Schlund made Liebner their agent to aid in disposing of real estate in this particular section of Chicago because he could speak the Polish language. Various neighbors of Mannia, the plaintiff, testified to having paid various sums to Liebner, and later receiving deeds for the property, all of which plaintiff was well aware. Liebner failed to account for this particular $200 and the defendant contends that the agency was terminated about a month before the transaction took place.

CRAIG, J. But it is said in the argument that Liebner was discharged as agent before he collected the money. There is some evidence in the record that Frey & Schlund discharged him between the 1st and 10th of September, 1891. . . . Moreover, if they had terminated the agency, it was their duty to give these Polish people, with whom he had been dealing and doing business as their agent, notice that the agency was terminated. But this was not done or attempted to be done until October 26, 1891, after the money in question had been paid, when a notice was published in a newspaper.

Mechem on Agency (§ 229), in speaking on this subject, says:

> Where general authority is once shown to have existed, it may be presumed to continue until it is shown to have been revoked, and persons who have dealt with the agent as such, or who have had notice of his authority, may very properly expect that if the authority be withdrawn, they will be given reasonable and timely notice of that fact, and that they may therefore lawfully presume, in the absence of such notice, that the authority still continues.

Specific performance decreed.

Review Questions and Problems

1. *P* appointed *A* his agent to look after all *P*'s insurance needs, compensating *A* at the rate of $50 a month for this service. *A* obtained fire

insurance for *P*, and because he was a member of the local underwriters group, he obtained a rebate of 10 per cent on all insurance premiums. Must *A* hold this rebate for *P*'s benefit?

2. *P* listed business property for sale by *B*, a broker. *B* discovered a buyer willing to purchase the property if a long-term tenant could be obtained. *T* had appointed *B* as a broker to find a long-term lease for him. The lease was given, the sale completed, and the commissions paid to *B* by both *P* and *T*. The tenant now discovers for the first time that *B* obtained two commissions, and seeks to rescind the long-term lease. The court allowed rescission. Was this sound?
3. *P* employed *A* as manager of his business and authorized him to buy such supplies and merchandise as was needed. Being a member of CO-OP, *A* purchased all of his supplies through it. At the end of the year, he received a personal dividend of $900 because of the purchases. Is he entitled to retain it? Assume that he purchased the supplies as advantageously as he could have at any other place.
4. *P* Co. was engaged in a wholesale business supplying goods to hospitals and novelty stores, *A* being its manager. *A*, while still working for *P* Co., agreed with a salesman of *P* Co. and a third party to enter a competing business and arranged to handle two lines for which *P* Co. previously held the exclusive agency. *A* quit and entered the competing business but *P* Co. seeks to enjoin them from operation. If the court refuses to enjoin them, do you consider its decision a sound one?
5. *A* collects money for *P*, but deposits it in *X* bank in his own name. The bank becomes insolvent and is expected to pay about 40 cents on the dollar. Who must bear the loss?
6. *W* gave *M* money to loan for him, and the latter loaned to an insolvent person, the loan being secured by a second mortgage on property which was scarcely worth the amount of the two mortgages. *W* was unable to recover when the debt fell due and sued *M* for the loss. Do you feel *M* should be held liable?
7. *P* takes *A* into his home and treats him as a child of his own, furnishes him with the necessities of life, and makes possible his education. After *A* becomes of age, may he recover the reasonable value of various services rendered to *P* while he was a minor?
8. *A*, while employed by *P*, decided to enter into business in competition with *P*. While working for *P*, he informed many customers of his decision and solicited their business. He also persuaded certain of the employees to quit and work for him when he opened his business. *P* later discovered this and sued *A* for damages. Is *A* liable?
9. *B*, appointed to sell merchandise in a certain area for *S*, was to receive a commission of 2 per cent on all sales. He received a weekly advance of $75 for ten weeks but his commissions only averaged $40 a week. Does he owe *S* the $350 difference?
10. *A* had for several years worked in his father's feed store and had often purchased feed from *T*, the father making payment in the regular course of business. The father refused to pay for the last shipment, claiming the son had never been authorized to purchase, and that if he had, the father had dismissed him prior to the purchase, and that

if he had, the father had dismissed him prior to the purchase in question. Is *T* entitled to recover of the father for the grain delivered?

11. *P* listed his property with *A*, a real estate broker, for sale at a price of $20,000. *A* located a buyer at that figure and *P* entered into a contract with the buyer, but the buyer was unable to finance the purchase, so the contract was rescinded by mutual agreement. If *A* sues *P* for his commission, is he entitled to it?

19

Agent and Third Party

LIABILITY OF AGENT TO THIRD PARTY

3-45. Liability on contract. The agent seldom incurs any liability to the third party upon contracts entered into for a known principal. In such cases he negatives any personal responsibility by a proper execution of the contract. Only if the agent carelessly executes a written agreement may he find himself bound by its terms. To use an illustration suggested previously, the agent who signs a negotiable instrument for his principal, but fails to indicate clearly the principal's existence and his relation to the instrument, is personally liable.

It often happens that the third party, for certain reasons, desires to add the credit of the agent to that of the principal or to contract with the agent alone. The credit of the principal may be weak, or his credit rating may be unknown. Under such circumstances, the third party, who is well acquainted with the agent, is perfectly willing to contract with the latter but not with the former. Where, therefore, the agent voluntarily assumes the burden of performance in his personal capacity, he unquestionably becomes liable in the event of nonperformance by his principal.

In addition to the above situation, the agent of an undisclosed principal always assumes personal liability.[1] So far as the third party is informed, the contract is made with the agent, and he takes on full responsibility for its performance. It should be noted in this connection, however, that the third party has an option. He may elect to hold either the agent or the principal, provided he acts within the proper time after he learns of the existence of the undisclosed principal. If the agent is held liable, he in turn has recourse against the principal.

3-46. Warranty of authority. Occasionally an agent attempts to act for a principal when he possesses no power to bind the latter. In such instances he may or may not be aware of the limitation of his power; he may honestly think his authority extends to the act complained of, or he may be well aware that he was never appointed an agent. In either event he becomes liable to third parties for the damages resulting from his

[1] Datko v. Gieb, page 423.

failure to bind the principal. His liability is said not to rest upon the contract itself, but to result from breach of an implied warranty. Every agent impliedly warrants to third parties that he possesses power to affect the contractual relations of his principal.[2] If in any particular transaction he fails to bear such a relation to his principal, he violates this implied warranty. In addition, an agent who intentionally misrepresents his authority may be liable in an action of deceit. In such a case all the elements of fraud are present. Presumably, in either event, the damages would be those suffered because the agent failed to possess the authority that he attempted to exercise.

The agent may escape liability for damages arising from lack of authority by a full disclosure to the third party of all facts relating to the source of his authority. Where all the facts are available, the third party is as capable of judging the limits of the agent's powers as is the agent. In other words, the third party must rely upon the warranty in order to hold the agent for its breach. Where he has full knowledge of all particulars, he relies upon his own judgment and not upon the agent's representation of authority.

The liability of the agent is qualified in one other respect. He is not liable when, unknown to him, his agency has been cut short by the death of his principal. Such an event as death is usually accompanied by sufficient publicity to reach third parties. As indicated in an earlier section, the facts are equally available to both parties, so no warranty arises.

3-47. Competent principal. Every agent who deals with third parties warrants that his principal is capable of being bound. Consequently, an agent who acts for a minor or a corporation not yet formed may find himself liable for the nonperformance of his principal. The same rule enables the third party to recover from the agent where his principal is an unincorporated association.[3] In such a case, since there is no entity capable of being bound, a breach of the warranty results. The third party has a right to insist that the principal be a person, a firm, or a corporate entity capable of entering into an enforceable agreement. An unincorporated body has no legal entity, and only those voting for the particular transaction, or later adopting it, are liable.

Where, however, the third party is fully informed that the principal is an unincorporated organization, and he agrees to look entirely to it for performance, the agent is relieved. The evidence must clearly indicate such an agreement, as the normal presumption is that the third party expects to look to one party and not to the membership for performance.

In case the principal is a corporation, the agent does not warrant that his principal has legal capacity to enter into the particular transaction. In

[2] Boelter v. National Mfrs. Bank et al., page 424.
[3] Codding v. Munson, page 425.

other words, the agent is not responsible if the contract made by him exceeds the authorized powers of the corporation. The limits of a corporation's powers are governed by its charter. Since charters are usually made a matter of public record, the powers of the corporation are equally available to the agent and to the third party.

3-48. To account for money received. An agent who, in the course of his employment, receives money from third parties for the benefit of the principal owes no duty to account to the third parties. If such money does not find its way into the principal's hands, it may be recovered in an action by the principal against the agent. This rule adequately protects all parties. On the other hand, money paid to an agent who has no authority to collect it, and not turned over to the principal, may be recovered in an action by the third party. To illustrate: a traveling salesman normally has no authority to collect for his principal. Should he do so and surrender the money to his principal, the debtor has no cause of action. A failure on his part to account to his principal, however, subjects him to an action by the third party.

A different problem is presented when money is paid to an agent in error, such as occurs by overpayment of an account. If the agent has passed the money on to his principal before the mistake is discovered, it is clear that only the principal is liable. Nevertheless, money which is still in the possession of the agent when he is notified of the error should be returned to the third party. The agent does not relieve himself of this burden by subsequently making payment to his principal.

Any payment made in error to an agent and caused by his mistake or misconduct may always be recovered from him, although he may have surrendered it to his principal. Also, any overpayment may be recovered from the agent of an undisclosed principal. In such a case the agent is dealt with as the principal.

LIABILITY OF THIRD PARTY TO AGENT

3-49. On contract. Normally the agent possesses no right to bring suit on contracts made by him for the benefit of his principal. It is only where the agent binds himself to the third party, either intentionally or ineptly by a failure properly to express himself, that he may maintain an action. An agent of an undisclosed principal always binds himself. As a result, he may, in his own name, sue the third party in the event of nonperformance by the latter. Under the circumstances outlined, either the agent or the principal might bring suit. But in case of a dispute the right of the principal is superior.

Custom has long sanctioned an action by the agent based upon a contract in which he is interested because of anticipated commissions. As a result, a factor may institute an action in his own name to recover for goods sold. He may also recover against a railroad for delay in shipment of goods sold or to be sold.

Similarly, an agent who has been vested with title to commercial paper may sue the maker thereof. The same is true of any claim held by the principal that he definitely places with the agent for collection and suit where such is necessary. In all cases of this character, the agent retains the proceeds as a trust fund for his principal.

3-50. In tort. Most torts committed by third parties give rise to a cause of action irrespective of an agency. There are two distinct cases, however, in which the employment becomes important. First, any third party who maliciously influences the principal to terminate his agent's employment thereby commits a tort. He must compensate the agent for any damages which result from such conduct.[4] Second, any third person who influences another in breaching a contract in which the agent is interested thereby renders himself liable to the agent. To illustrate: The agent has sold goods to *T* upon which he is entitled to a commission. Anyone who causes *T* to refuse to carry out the agreement thereby damages the agent and is correspondingly liable.

AGENT AND THIRD PARTY CASES

DATKO v. GIEB
1953, (Oh. App.), 113 N.E.2d 672

Per Curiam. The plaintiff, a minor, entered into an agreement to purchase a motor vehicle from defendant, paying the said defendant the full purchase price of $1,500. After he took delivery of the car he offered to return it to defendant and demanded the return of his money on the ground that he was a minor both on the date of the purchase and at the time of his disaffirmance of the purchase. The fact that he was then a minor is not in dispute. The record shows that the plaintiff conducted his negotiations with the defendant, believing him to be the owner of said automobile and paid to him the full purchase price. After the purchase of the automobile, the plaintiff learned for the first time that the certificate of title was in the name of Robert Beckett, said certificate of title being signed by Beckett in blank and delivered to plaintiff in such form by the defendant at the time the transaction was completed.

[4] Loughery et al. v. Huxford et al., page 426.

Upon trial, after the foregoing evidence was introduced, upon defendant's motion for judgment at the conclusion of plaintiff's case the court granted said motion for reason that the defendant did not have the certificate of title to the automobile in his name. That the rule relating to an undisclosed agent did not apply and that because of the provisions of Section 6290-4, G.C., the plaintiff could not maintain an action for return of his money against the defendant because the defendant did not have the registered title to the car in his name and in so holding the court committed prejudicial error to the rights of the plaintiff.

The motor vehicle title law is not concerned or involved in this proceeding. If the defendant acted for an undisclosed principal, making the contract in his own name, he is bound by his contract and an infant with whom he deals has the right to look to him for the return of the money upon disaffirmance of the purchase agreement during his minority or within a reasonable time after becoming of age.

Judgment reversed and cause remanded for further proceedings according to law. Exceptions noted.

BOELTER v. NATIONAL MFRS. BANK et al.

1927, 194 Wis. 1, 215 N.W. 436

Action by Paul Boelter against the National Manufacturers' Bank and H. C. Hilton. It appeared from the evidence that plaintiff was seeking for a house which he might rent. He learned that a house belonging to one Verbeck was for rent at $35 a month and that the key was with the defendants. He, through his agent, obtained the key from Hilton, cashier of defendant bank. He desired to rent the house and asked the rental. Hilton informed him that the previous parties paid $35 a month. He asked to deposit $5 and send the balance down the next day. This was done and in each case the defendant gave a duplicate deposit slip in favor of Verbeck. Plaintiff moved in, but was soon ejected by Verbeck, as the defendants had no authority to lease—their only authority being to collect the rent. This is an action to recover the damages.

ROSENBERRY, J. . . . The question is, Does this amount on the part of Hilton to a representation that he was authorized by Verbeck to rent the premises in question? There is no dispute as to the fact that he had no such actual authority. *Oliver v. Morawetz*, 97 Wis. 333, 72 N.W. 877, establishes the proposition that a person who represents to another that he has authority to do an act as agent, when in fact he has no such authority, is liable on an implied warranty, or in an action of deceit, according to the facts of the particular case. . . .

The defendant Hilton personally or as cashier of the bank neither did nor said anything that was not in accord with the truth. If he was guilty of a breach of duty to anyone, it was to Verbeck, a depositor, when he handed out the key to the Verbeck property without ascertaining the authority of the party to whom he handed it to receive it. But he owed the plaintiff no duty in that respect. . . . Plaintiff's agents conceded that, when they went to the bank to ask for the key, they were already apprized of all the facts that they ever ascertained, and that was that the premises were for rent, the former tenant had paid $35 per month, that the key was in the custody of the bank, and that the rent would be received by the bank on behalf of Verbeck. There was no inquiry whatever as to the right of the bank or Hilton to make a lease of the premises. . . .

If the defendant Hilton is liable at all, it must be upon an implied warranty. All of the cases which we have been able to find are cases in which the agent expressly represented himself as having authority from his principal to act. We find no case where an agent has been held liable under circumstances such as are presented here, either upon deceit or assumpsit. It is apparent here that every word which Hilton said and every act which he did was consistent with the performance of his duty as cashier of the bank. . . . We search in vain for any circumstance in this which warrants a finding that Hilton held himself out as the agent of Verbeck.

Judgment for defendant.

CODDING v. MUNSON

1897, 52 Nebr. 580, 66 A.S.R. 524

Munson sued Codding, alleging that he had sold and conveyed land for the price of $10,000 but had only received the sum of $9,750, and prayed a judgment for the remaining $250. The plaintiff, having been promised $10,000 for the property, transferred it to the defendant as trustee. The contract of sale was signed for the Mothers' Jewels Home by the defendant. Since the Home was an unincorporated institution, the plaintiff contends that the defendant is individually liable for the unpaid balance.

The evidence discloses that meetings were held in New York by some of its citizens for the purpose of securing a location there for an institution for orphans under the patronage of the Woman's Home Missionary Society of the Methodist Episcopal Church. Both plaintiff and defendant attended the meetings and it was agreed that $10,000 was essential. Donations in the form of negotiable notes were to be taken and defendant was made trustee. This land was transferred to defendant upon the reecipt of $9,750 in notes properly indorsed. The plaintiff contends that defendant is individually liable for the balance. The lower court gave the following instruction: "If you find from the evidence that Codding was in this transaction only agent and trustee for the Mothers' Jewels Home, and that all his transactions as such agent have been performed in good faith, then you should find for the defendant." Judgment thereupon rendered for the defendant.

IRVINE, J. . . . It is the general rule that one who assumes to act as agent for a principal who has no legal status or existence renders himself individually liable on contracts so made. . . . This doctrine receives its most frequent application in cases like the present, where a person or committee incurs obligations as the result of instructions given by a body gathered together informally for a special purpose, and possessing no definite membership or continued power of existence. The rule is founded upon a presumption of fact, and is not the expression of any positive or rigid legal principle. The presumption referred to is that the parties to a contract contemplate the creation of a legal obligation capable of enforcement, and that, therefore, it is understood that the obligation shall rest on the individuals who actively participate in the making of the contract, because of the difficulty in all cases, the impossibility in many, of fixing it upon the persons taking part in or submitting to the action of the evanescent assemblage. If, however, the person with whom the contract is made expressly agrees to look to another source for the performance of its obligations, or if the circumstances be such as to disclose an intention not to charge the agent, as where the other agrees to accept the proceeds of a particular fund, there is no longer reason to indulge the presumption, and it may be rebutted by proof of such facts.

Applying these principles to the case at bar, the evidence would raise prima facie the presumption upon which the general rule is based. On the other hand, it was sufficient to justify the inference that the plaintiff did not look to the defendant personally, but was to receive merely the subscription notes or their proceeds. The instructions should have stated the law as we have indicated it and submitted to the jury the issues bearing thereon. Instead . . . the instruction was erroneous, because it made Codding's release from liability depend upon his action as agent for the home. . . . (Case sent back for retrial because of improper instruction.)

LOUGHERY et al. v. HUXFORD et al.

1910, 206 Mass. 324, 92 N.E. 328

Plaintiffs, Loughery and others, claimed that on or about March 24, 1904, plaintiffs orally contracted with the Lange Canning Co. of Eau Claire, Wis., and with the Reedsburg Canning Co. of Reedsburg, Wis., by which the plaintiffs were to be their general agents for the year 1904 for the sale on commission in New England of their goods. The defendants, with knowledge of such contracts, persuaded the canning companies to rescind and break the agreements. The result was that defendants obtained the agency while the plaintiffs were denied it. The plaintiffs, for loss of commissions and other damages, obtained a judgment of $1,549.20. The defendants filed objections.

HAMMOND, J. The rulings requested were rightly refused. While the evidence as to sales made by the plaintiffs or defendants before the year 1904, and by the defendants in 1904, was not admissible as showing the rule of damages, or even as conclusively showing the damages, still it was admissible as having some bearing upon the value to the plaintiffs of the contract and the amount of the damages suffered by the breach.

Exceptions overruled. Judgment for plaintiff.

Review Questions and Problems

1. *B*, the secretary-treasurer of *C* Co., gave a company note to Bank, typed the signature of *C* Co. and immediately followed it with his own signature, there being no "by" or "per" or anything to indicate that he signed as agent. The bank sought to hold him as a co-maker and the court gave judgment for the bank. Was this decision sound?
2. *A*, thinking he had authority to do so, signed *P*'s name to a contract whereby *T* was to drill an oil well for $7,000. It developed later that *A* had no authority to act for *P*. Is *A* liable if the contract was signed "*P* per *A*"?
3. *A*, acting for a corporation which is soon to be formed, orders two delivery trucks from *T*. The corporation is formed, but refuses to ratify the contract. Under what circumstances is *A* liable to *T*?
4. *T*, by reason of an error on the part of *A*, an agent for *P*, overpays to the extent of some $300 his account with *P*. Before *A* pays the money over to *P*, *T* discovers the error and demands the excess from *A*. Is *A* under a duty to return the money to *T*, or may he turn it over to *P*?
5. *A* signed his mother's name to an application for a loan to be made by *T*. At that time, he made full disclosure to *T* as to the basis for his authority. *A* actually had no authority to act for his mother, and *T* sued *A* because the loan was not made. Was *A* liable?
6. Name two instances in which the agent may sue the third party for breach of a contract, the contract being made for the benefit of the principal.
7. *T*, because of his dislike of *A*, persuades *P* to discharge *A*. Assuming that *A* does not have a contract for any definite period, may he recover damages from *T*?

BOOK IV

COMMERCIAL PAPER

20

Introduction to the Law of Commercial Paper

4-1. Definition of the term "negotiable." The commercial world has for many years used the term *negotiable* as an adjective describing a certain type of written contract designated as a vehicle to represent credit and to function as a substitute for money.

The term negotiable is of Latin origin. It is derived from the Latin word *negotiatus*, consisting of the prefix, *neg*, meaning *not* or *negation*, plus the root *otium*, meaning leisure—making the combination *not-leisure* or *non-leisure*—plus the suffix *able*, meaning capable of. The idea as expressed by the Latin words was easily applicable to business. It was further developed to mean the capacity of certain kinds of paper to pass, like money, from person to person. The paper so designated was soon used as a medium of exchange.

It has been noted previously that law is closely related to the financial aspects of a business enterprise; the contract is the basis for commercial transactions. We now consider a specialized application of the contract concept to those devices which provide a means of extending credit and obtaining funds for business operations. It is obvious that business could not expand and develop its full potential if it were necessary to rely only upon money—coin and currency—for its transactions. Thus, the check is used in settling about nine-tenths of all business transactions. Accumulations of wealth in the form of commercial paper far exceed wealth represented by actual money. "Commercial paper" plays such an important role in the field of business that it is essential to the efficient operation of our modern economy.

4-2. History. Negotiable instruments, now called "commercial paper," are of two main types, the *promissory note* and the *draft* (bill of exchange). The Uniform Commercial Code also lists the *certificate of deposit* and the *check* under the title commercial paper. Each type has its own particular history, and each took on the characteristics of negotiability for the same reasons. Today the promissory note, the bill of exchange (draft), and the check are specifically included within the Uniform Commercial Code. Article 3 of the Uniform Commercial Code designates negotiable instruments as *drafts, checks, certificates of deposit,* and *notes.*

It is not possible to give an extensive historical background of the promissory note and the bill of exchange. However, a short comment upon the early English origins and sources of these two significant instruments seems pertinent.

The promissory note. The origin of the modern promissory note may be traced to an early writing called *scripta obligatoria* or *writing obligatory.* The debtor made a promise, formally under seal or informally without a seal, to pay a sum of money to the creditor, his attorney, or a nominee. Thus the attorney or nominee could sue the debtor. Sometimes the paper would read "payable to the creditor or the producer of the document." Early cases tried in the "Fair Courts" in England in the sixteenth century disclose suits by persons other than the original creditor, such as an attorney or assignee or the "bearer or producer of the paper." Thus the idea of a transferable writing, either as order or bearer paper, was conceived. In buying and selling goods and wares from overseas, *bills of debt,* or *billes obligatorie* were given for merchandise by one merchant to another merchant. By transferring the "billes obligatorie," the merchant as creditor could empower another to collect a debt, or the merchant as debtor could use the paper to pay a debt owed by him to another. Thus these notes served as a medium of exchange and to discharge debts. The following is a description of how such writings were used to pay debts: "In 1445 a foreign merchant made out a 'bill' to John Felde for wool sold; the bill was originally delivered to Louis Fycham, Felde's attorney, who in his turn passed it to Laurence Parke. He delivered it to John Petite. The latter then bought with it certain goods from Jacob Flemming."[1] By statute and a recognition of the law merchant by the king's court these written obligations took on many of the present characteristics of negotiable promissory notes.

Bills obligatory were not only used to pay for goods, but they were issued by goldsmiths to merchants who left their surplus funds for safe keeping with the goldsmiths. These instruments were transferable; it may be said that they were the forerunners of our modern bank notes.

Bank notes issued by an individual goldsmith as a banker were subject to the risk of the bankruptcy of the goldsmith. It was not until 1694 when the Bank of England was established that a quasi-government institution gave credit to bank notes. The Bank of England was authorized to issue "bills obligatory and of credit"—bank notes—which would pass from one person to another, by assignment or indorsement, for the payment of debts.

[1] J. Milnes Holden, *The History of Negotiable Instruments in English Law* (London: University of London, The Athalone Press, 1955), pp. 4, 12, 66. The quoted material of this section is printed by permission of the publishers.

However, in the famous case of *Clerke v. Martin* (1702), Lord Holt, C. J., held that such *bills obligatory,* promissory notes, issued by the Bank of England were not, within the custom of merchants, transferable by indorsement as inland bills of exchange. Merchants and bankers were much disturbed by this decision, and two years later in 1704 Parliament passed the Statute of 3 and 4 Anne c.IX entitled, "An Act for giving like remedy upon promissory notes as is now used upon bills of exchange for the better payment of inland bills of exchange." This statute, known as the Promissory Note Act, recognized notes as order and bearer paper like inland bills of exchange and gave to promissory notes the attributes of negotiability according to the custom of merchants.

Another early source of modern promissory notes now recognized as government obligations, such as bonds and paper money, was the English Exchequer Bill. The English government was authorized by statute in 1696 to borrow money and issue interest-bearing demand bearer bills therefor. The act authorized that these bills pass from one person to another and be accepted for the payment of debts. Soon, by necessity, these instruments—as government paper money—took on all the attributes of negotiability.

The bill of exchange. The origin or source of the bill of exchange rests in antiquity. There is evidence of its use in ancient Assyria, Egypt, Greece, and Rome. The bill of exchange was invented for the purpose of effecting an exchange of money—coin, silver, and gold—in distant parts without running the risk of its physical transportation. Italian merchants are said to have introduced the efficient use of modern bills of exchange. As trade and commerce increased, a safe and effective method for the exchange of money became a necessity. Goldsmiths and money exchangers in the different countries established a system whereby a merchant, who owed money in a foreign country, could pay his debt. The merchant delivered his money to his local exchanger, and the local exchanger drew a bill upon his foreign correspondent, directing that the creditor merchant be paid or that the foreign merchant collect from the foreign correspondent exchanger. The exchangers met from time to time at the local merchant fairs and settled the accounts. The type of instrument used by the exchangers is the ancestor of our modern bill of exchange, bank draft, and check.

Not only were drafts drawn on money exchangers, acting as bankers, but merchants in foreign countries also became drawees when their credit was well established. The following situation illustrates how the modern trade acceptance developed: *D*, a silk merchant in London, had his purchasing agent *A*, in Brussels, purchase silk from a merchant in Brussels. In order to pay for the silk, *A* drew a bill of exchange on *D* in London, payable to the order of the Brussels merchant. The Brussels merchant cashed the bill with a money exchanger, who sent it, in turn, to London for collection. Instead of making the seller in Brussels the payee, A might, "by way of exchange, as is done by common custom of merchants," cash the bill of exchange with an exchanger and pay the Brussels seller with coin. By the close of the seventeenth century, these instruments were in general use but not yet recognized by the common law courts of England. An examination of the very early English law reports discloses no reference to commercial paper.

Disputes between merchants were adjudicated in special courts set up by the merchants themselves. The decisions were reached after applying the usage and custom of the merchants. Out of this system arose a very definite form of what is known as the *lex mercatores*, or law merchant. The greater part of commercial activity in England was conducted at great fairs, to which all merchants came, both foreign and local, to display their wares. At each of these fairs a court sat to adjust differences between buyers and sellers. The very nature of the situation demanded speedy and permanent termination of the disputes. These special mercantile courts were called the Courts of Piepoudres (pieds poudrés), so called because justice was administered as the dust still fell from the litigants' feet. These courts were later created by statute and continued as separate bodies until about 1756. Through royal prerogative, the king's court, by this time jealous of the administration of justice by others, gradually won its way and absorbed the merchants' courts. However, in deciding commercial cases, the king's court applied the law merchant. When determining suits between merchants, or when a merchant was a party to the suit, before the court would recognize the law merchant, the party pleading such custom and usage was under a duty to show himself to be a merchant. This rule prevailed until about two hundred years ago.

The absorption of these merchants' courts by the king's courts over a period of thirty years, under Lord Mansfield, wove the law merchant into, and made it part of, the common law. The practice of permitting the proof of custom and usage of the merchants in the common law courts made possible the development of separate rules which became established rules of law. The union of these mercantile customs with the legal system already in operation resulted in the formation and further development of the law merchant by judicial action.

Until 1882 in England, and until a still later date in all of the states in the United States except California, the law merchant was found largely in the reports of judicial decisions. In these judicial decisions, previous usage and custom were interpreted and applied according to the prevailing and established usage of the particular community. This situation led to varying interpretations and a consequent lack of uniformity. In order to find the law, it was necessary to examine many decisions. The result of such a search was often futile, owing to the conflicts and contradictions of important rules.

Consequently, in England, in 1882, Parliament enacted what is known as the Bills of Exchange Act. The Act completely codified the law as found in the decisions, and harmonized the existing rules in as complete and comprehensive a manner as possible.

In 1895, in the United States, under the leadership of the American Bar Association and the American Bankers Association, a commission was appointed for the purpose of revising and codifying the law merchant in the United States. This committee, taking the English Bills of Exchange Act as a model, derived, with modifications, the Uniform Negotiable Instruments Law (NIL). This Act was completed in 1896, and was submitted to the legislatures of the various states with recommendations for adoption. The Act was adopted by every state, with some changes being made in states seeking to make the Act more suitable for their purposes.

The Uniform Commercial Code was promulgated in 1952. Since that date, twenty-eight states have repealed the NIL and have adopted the Commercial Code. It is being considered for adoption by other states. Article 3 of the Code—Commercial Paper—replaces the Uniform Negotiable Instruments Law (referred to as the NIL) in those states which have adopted the Code.

Article 3 of the Code both revises and modernizes the NIL. While many of the basic concepts of the law of negotiable instruments are common to both, there are many significant changes and additions contained in the Code. During the years subsequent to the promulgation of the NIL, there have been substantial changes in the practices of business in connection with negotiable instruments. Article 3 of the Code recognizes these changes and brings the law up to date in keeping with modern commercial practices.

Quotations in this book are from the Uniform Commercial Code, 1958, Official Text.

4-3. Miscellaneous paper evidencing "monetary obligations." The right to money that one person may have against another may arise from many situations. The right may arise out of a contract for the sale of goods, for a loan of money, for services rendered, or for injuries received. The evidence of such claims may be simple contracts, either written or oral. Consequently, the words and the language used in simple contracts and in other claims for money will vary with the particular circumstance. Claims for money evidenced by "commercial paper," however, must comply with certain formalities as these are expressed in the language of Article 3 of the Code. It is not necessary that the same words be used in the same place in each instrument, but it is necessary that the same meaning be expressed. A discussion of the language which must appear upon the face of an instrument to give it the character of negotiability required by Article 3 will be taken up in the following chapter.

Another distinguishing feature separating commercial paper, "drafts" (bills of exchange), "checks," "certificates of deposit," and "notes" from other forms of claims for money is the method of transferring title from one person to another. Nonnegotiable commercial paper is transferred by assignment, whereas, negotiable contract rights are transferred by negotiation.

4-4. Difference between negotiation and assignment. In Book Two on Contracts, we learned that contract rights were transferable by a legal process called assignment. Suppose *A* owed *B* $100 for goods sold by *B* to *A*, or for services rendered by *B* for *A*. *B* has a right that *A* pay him $100. *A* is under duty to *B* to pay this $100. This type of contract right owned by *B* is called a *chose in action.* Under the early common law, this type of right for money due was not transferable. Under modern law, this right is transferable by the process of assignment. *B* may sell to *C* his right to collect $100 from *A*. Let us suppose that for any number of reasons *A* had a counterclaim against *B* for $35, either because the goods sold were not as required by contract or that the contract was induced by fraud on the part of *B*. If so, then the right that *C* purchased from *B* would be subject to *A's* defense of fraud or failure of consideration. *C*, the assignee, would secure no better right against *A* than the original right held by *B*, the assignor.[2]

In the example given above, let the situation be changed, so that the evidence of the debt is not a simple contract for money, but a negotiable promissory note given by *A* to *B*. Under the law merchant codified by the Commercial Code, the right that *B* now has against *A* is superior to the right *B* had as evidenced by the simple contract right. The distinguishing feature of the latter is its unique capacity of transferability. *B* sells and negotiates the note to *C*. Assuming that *C* is a purchaser in good faith and that he is otherwise qualified, *C* will get a better title as purchaser of the commercial paper than as purchaser of the simple contract right; that is, *C*, as holder of a right evidenced by commercial paper, takes title free from the personal defenses that are available against the original party to the paper. This feature is the very essence of negotiability. Business convenience requires this characteristic; it is the very reason for which the paper is created. A businessman is not willing to take a note,

[2] Universal C.I.T. Corporation v. Hudgens, page 451.

a check, a draft, or certificate of deposit from a payee if he thereby incurs all of the risk of an assignee of an ordinary contract right. Under the Code, negotiability eliminates all personal defenses between the original parties as against a holder in due course, thus making commercial paper free to pass as money from person to person, fulfilling the purpose for which it was created.

4-5. The negotiation of special types of paper evidencing monetary obligations—nonnegotiable instruments. The limiting of the transfer of paper by negotiation to negotiable instruments is not always consistent with business practice. The Code, therefore, by Section 3-805 expands Article 3 by permitting instruments which satisfy all the requirements of negotiability, but which do not use the words "or order," or "bearer," to be transferred by negotiation as follows:

> This Article applies to any instrument whose terms do not preclude transfer and which is otherwise negotiable within this Article but which is not payable to order or to bearer, except that there can be no holder in due course of such an instrument.

The official comment following Section 3-805 states:

> It refers to a particular type of instrument which meets all requirements as to form of a negotiable instrument except that it is not payable to order or to bearer. The typical example is the check reading merely "Pay to John Doe." Such a check is not a negotiable instrument under this Article. At the same time it is still a check, a mercantile specialty which differs in many respects from a simple contract. Commercial and banking practice treats it as a check, and a long line of decisions before and after the original Act have made it clear that it is subject to the law merchant as distinguished from ordinary contract law . . .
>
> Such a check passes by indorsement and delivery without words of assignment, and the indorser undertakes greater liabilities than those of an assignor. This section resolves a conflict in the decisions as to the extent of that undertaking by providing in effect that the indorser of such an instrument is not distinguished from any indorser of a negotiable instrument . . .
>
> In short, the 'nonnegotiable instrument' is treated as a negotiable instrument, so far as its form permits. Since it lacks words of negotiability there can be no holder in due course of such an instrument.

Since the Code has specially enumerated the draft, the check, the certificate of deposit, and the note as the only negotiable "commercial paper" under Article 3, it is necessary to look to other portions of the Code to determine negotiable attributes for other types of "monetary obligations."

The negotiable aspects of "monetary obligations" not strictly negotiable, such as "chattel paper" which is defined as "a writing or writings which evidence both a monetary obligation and a security interest in, or a lease of, specific goods," create varying rights and duties, depending upon the course of business and the kind of holder. When a transaction is evidenced by a security agreement or a lease *and* by a note or other instrument or a series of instruments, the group of writings taken together constitutes chattel paper. The negotiability of documents of title, investment securities, and other instruments in writing used in the ordinary course of business and transferred by delivery, is determined by the "rules of holding in due course" applicable to the particular type of paper in question. (Section 9-308, Purchase of Chattel paper, and Section 9-309, Protection of Purchasers of Instruments and Documents, text p. 986).

Accounts, contract rights, and all types of written instruments—*choses in action*—evidencing claims for money which are not involved in a "security transaction" are transferable under the common law rules of assignment.

4-6. The development of negotiability by court decisions and the business reasons for the integration of the law of commercial paper with other business transactions. Although the Uniform Negotiable Instruments Law (NIL) as originally drafted was apparently limited in its application to the historical types of negotiable paper—promissory notes and bills of exchange—three problems, relating to other types of commercial paper, developed by reason of codification.

Did codification mean that other types of credit instruments, generally accepted in commerce and shown by the usage of business to have the characteristics of negotiability, remain nonnegotiable unless such instruments comply strictly with the terms of the NIL? Should the language of the Negotiable Instruments Law be broadly interpreted to cover new instruments that have developed in commerce and that pass freely in trade? Or should the Negotiable Instruments Law be strictly limited to application to bills of exchange, promissory notes, and checks, leaving other instruments, by custom and usage or legislative enactment, to acquire their own particular attributes of negotiability?

The following instruments illustrate types of credit paper which were not defined by the Negotiable Instruments Law, but which carried some characteristics of negotiability: corporate bonds, registered bonds, municipal warrants, interim certificates, interest coupons, trading stamps, conditional sale contracts, insurance policies, warehouse receipts, stock certificates, and bills of lading. To meet business needs, Uniform Acts were adopted specifically to give negotiable character to such instruments as bills of lading, warehouse receipts, and certificates of stock. If legislatures did not enact statutes giving negotiable attributes to instruments other than bills of exchange, promissory notes, and checks, partial negotiability was given to such instruments by contract and court decisions.

In the absence of fraud in the execution, it was possible for the parties, by express provisions in written instruments, to waive defenses and give protection to bona fide purchasers. Even though the language of the instrument did not comply with the formal requisites of the Negotiable Instruments Law, if the parties by contract expressed their intention that the instrument be negotiable, the courts have recognized such intention to the extent that a bona fide purchaser would take the paper free from the defenses of failure or lack of consideration, fraud in the inducement, set-offs, and breach of warranty. Such development is illustrated in the case of *Anglo-California Trust Co. v. Hall*, 1922, 61 Utah 223, 211 Pac. 991. The case is as follows:

On May 23, 1920, the defendant Hall entered into a conditional sales contract with the Ritchie Motor Company for the purchase of a tractor and a plow for the sum of $1,195. Four hundred dollars was paid by Hall at the signing of the agreement, the balance of $795 to be paid in six months. The tractor and plow were delivered to Hall, and the Ritchie Motor Company assigned the conditional sales contract to the plaintiff, Anglo-California Trust Co. Hall, the defendant, defaulted on the contract, and at the time of the suit there was due $871.85, together with $100 attorney's fees.

Hall sets up as a defense a breach of warranty in that the tractor and plow would not perform as represented . . . the conditional sales contract contained the following clause:

"It is agreed that in the event the seller shall assign and transfer this agreement and his rights and the moneys payable hereunder to a third party, then the purchaser shall be precluded from in any manner attacking the validity of this agreement on the ground of fraud, duress, mistake, want of consideration, or failure of consideration, or upon any other ground, and the moneys payable hereunder by the purchaser shall be paid to such assignee or holder without recoupment, set-off, or counterclaim of any sort whatsoever."

The lower court found that Hall was estopped to set up the defense of breach of warranty.

Weber, J. . . . Appellant Hall contends that the above paragraph, upon which respondent relies as precluding the defense interposed by defendant, is void and contrary to public policy. The law will not give effect to a stipulation intended to grant immunity to fraud and iniquity. When the execution of a contract is produced by fraud, a party is not bound by any claim therein precluding him from setting up false and fraudulent representations within a proper time. 13 C.J. 394. In the answer, it is averred:

"That at the time of entering into said contract the said Ritchie Motor Company falsely represented and warranted to the defendant that said tractor would pull the plows sold therewith in usual and ordinary plowing at a depth of 10 inches in the soil, and that this defendant, believing and relying wholly upon the representations and warranties so made entered into the agreement aforesaid."

What constitutes a warranty is defined by section 5121, Comp. Laws, Utah 1917:

"Any affirmation of fact or any promise by the seller relating to the goods is an express warranty if the natural tendency of such affirmation or promise is to induce the buyer to purchase the goods, and if the buyer purchases the goods relying thereon, no affirmation of the value of the goods, nor any statement purporting to be a statement of the seller's opinion only, shall be considered as a warranty."

The demarcation between breach of warranty and fraud is clearly defined in Black on Rescission and Cancellation. Par. 23. The author says:

"Fraud is distinguished from breach of warranty in this respect: That, in the case of fraud, there is a guilty knowledge of the falsity of the representation on the part of the party making it, while in a breach of warranty there is not this guilty knowledge. The same transaction cannot be characterized as a warranty and a fraud at the same time."

It therefore appears that the allegation quoted from the answer is not a charge of fraud. Nor does the record contain any evidence whatever tending to prove fraud. In harmony with the undisputed evidence, the trial court found:

That the tractor would not pull the plows sold in usual and ordinary plowing at a depth of 10 inches in the soil, so represented and warranted by said Ritchie Motor Company.

The question now arises whether defendant could in his contract waive, as against the assignee, the breach of warranty. The statute provides that:

"In the case of an assignment of a thing in action, an action by the assignee is without prejudice to any set-off or other defense existing at the time or before notice of the assignment. Comp. Laws, Utah 1917, Par. 6496."

May the provisions of the statutes referred to be waived by one who enters into a written contract for the purchase of goods? It cannot be said that it is against public policy for a purchaser to waive warranty and thus estop himself from complaining of a breach of warranty. It will be noticed that paragraph 8 of the contract between defendant and plaintiff's assignor not only provides that in event of its assignment the purchaser shall be precluded from in any manner attacking its validity on the ground of fraud, duress, mistake, want or failure of consideration, or upon any other ground; but it is in addition provided that the moneys thereunder payable by the purchaser "shall be paid to such assignee or holder without recoupment, set-off or counterclaim of any sort whatever."

In the absence of fraud or duress, a purchaser may certainly in a written contract waive any set-off or counterclaim that he may have. Waiver is defined as a voluntary abandonment of some known right or advantage, and does not necessarily depend upon any new or additional consideration. (Cases cited.)

If a purchaser desires to waive the warranty that had been given him, why can he not do so, and that for the benefit of the seller or assignee, or both, or either? For a purchaser to sign a contract containing such a stipulation may not be a wise thing to do, but courts cannot rewrite contracts into which parties have seen fit to enter, and unless fraud or duress, or something against public policy, enters into the transaction, a purchaser who waives defenses, as the defendant has done, cannot obtain relief from an improvident contract, into which he enters without care and foresight . . .

The judgment for the plaintiff Trust Company is affirmed.

The drafters of the Uniform Commercial Code, recognizing the problems involved in the codification of the law in a single limited area such as the Uniform Negotiable Instruments Act, the desires of the businessman to make business paper more vendable as illustrated in the above case, and recognizing also the business necessity for the development of the "mobility" of commercial paper, have drafted the Uniform Commercial Code.

In order to make certain what specific paper should serve as a substitute for money, Article 3 of the Code specifies what is "commercial paper." This Article is far more limited than was the Negotiable Instruments Law. Article 3 of the Code specifically designates what is commercial paper and deals with no other instruments. "The Article does not apply to money, documents of title, or investment securities." (U.C.C. 3-103) Article 3 "Commercial Paper" is limited to the "draft," "check," "certificate of deposit," and the "note."

Instruments within the scope of Article 3 may also be subject to the provisions of Article 4, "Bank Deposits and Collections"; Article 7, "Documents of Title"; Article 8, "Investment Securities"; and Article 9, "Secured Transactions." If the instruments specified in Article 3 are used as collateral, in the course of bank collections or as investment paper, and are in fact negotiable under Article 3, Article 3 may nevertheless be applicable, unless there is a conflict between Article 3 and other provisions of the Code. If there is a conflict with other provisions of the Code, such provisions will prevail over the provisions of Article 3. (U.C.C. 9-201, 9-202) Also, it must be noted that Article 3 does not prevail if there exist rules of law or regulations governing usury, small loans, and installment sales contracts. (U.C.C. 9-201, 9-203)

Some of the legal implications of Article 3 are illustrated in the case of *First National Bank of Millville v. Horwatt,* 192 Pa. Super. 581, 162 A.2d 60 (1960) wherein a buyer purchased a motor vehicle from a dealer, executing an installment sales contract with an *attached note.* The note standing alone satisfied all the requirements of a negotiable instrument —"commercial paper." The contract and note were assigned to a bank by the dealer. The buyer defaulted and the bank entered a judgment on the note. The buyer moved to open the judgment, alleging fraud by the dealer in that the dealer upon tender of payment by the buyer, neither had the automobile nor the certificate of title.

After he had purchased the car, the buyer had returned it to the dealer for repair at which time another bank seized the car, claiming the right of possession under a floor-plan financing scheme with the dealer. The buyer tendered payment for the car, demanding title. The seller (dealer) could not furnish a certificate of title.

The court ordered the judgment in behalf of the assignee bank reopened in order to permit the buyer to introduce evidence of the dealer's fraud and insolvency. Three reasons for opening the judgment were given by WOODSON, J.

Section 15 (G) of the Motor Vehicle Sales Finance Act (of June 28, 1947, P.L. 1110) 69 P. S. Section 615 (g), provides as follows:

"G. No installment sale contract shall require or entail the execution of any note or series of notes by the buyer, which when separately negotiated, will cut off as to third parties any right of action or defense which the buyer may have against the original seller."

The plaintiff argues that it is a holder in due course of a negotiable instrument and this precludes the defendant from introducing his defense against it which he may have had against the seller (assignor). To lend credence to such an argument would defeat the very purpose of Section 15 (G) and would afford a purchaser of a motor vehicle no remedy whatsoever particularly, as in the case here, where the judgment note is attached to the motor vehicle installment sale contract. The note being attached to the sales contract, of itself, gives notice to any assignee that the transaction is subject to Sec. 15 (G) of the Motor Vehicle Sales Finance Act. So that it is not necessary to decide whether this note is negotiable in that the assignee has notice that the entire transaction is subject to the Motor Vehicle Sales Finance Act and, of course, Section 15 (G) thereof.

In addition, the sales contract to which the note is physically attached recites that . . . the assignee shall have all rights and be subject to all obligations of the seller hereunder. Are we now to treat the note separately from the sales contract and consider it negotiable and the assignee holder in due course? The words "obligations of the seller" connotes any defense the purchaser may have against the seller. To come to any other conclusion would be contrary to sound reasoning, and particularly when the note was entered of record, the sales contract was part and parcel thereof. For this reason as well as the first, the defendant should be permitted to introduce his defense of failure of consideration and fraud.

There is also a third reason why this judgment should be opened. The facts are that on July 14, 1958, defendant tendered to plaintiff assignee a money order for the full amount due on said sales contract and requested the certificate of title to the motor vehicle, which the plaintiff did not and could not produce. See Section 30 of the Motor Vehicle Sales Finance Act, 69 P.S. Section 630, which provides that:

"When the final payment on an installment sale contract is made in cash, money order, or equivalent tender by the buyer, or his authorized representative, at the designated licensed office of the holder, the certificate of title, showing satisfaction of this encumbrance, shall be delivered at the time of such tender of payment . . ."

The appellant contends that "the Motor Vehicle Sales Finance Act is repealed in a large part by the Uniform Commercial Code," of April 6, 1953, P.L. 3, 12A P.S. Section 1-101 and particularly with respect to the rights of the assignee of an installment sales contract and accompanying note.

The Finance Act is not among those acts specifically repealed by the Commercial Code, 12A P.S. Section 10-102, which, in addition to the specific repealers, contains the usual provision that "all acts and parts of acts inconsistent with this Act are hereby repealed." 1953 P.L. 181, 12A P.S. Section 10-103 . . .

Article 9 of the Uniform Commercial Code, relating to Secured Transactions, provides in Section 9-201 that nothing in that article "validates any charge or practice illegal under any rule of law or regulation governing . . . retail installment sales . . ." and in Section 9-203 that a transaction although subject to the Article must also comply with the Motor Vehicle Sales Finance Act. 12A P.S. Sections 9–201 and 9–203.

The legislature did not intend to repeal the Motor Vehicle Sales Finance Act by the passage of the Uniform Commercial Code.

The appellant argues that under Section 3-302 of the Code it is a holder in due course and that under Section 3-305 it is insulated from the defenses which could be made against the dealer-payee. Pressing the argument under the Uniform Commercial Code further, appellant argues that even if it were subject to the defenses which the buyer has against the original seller in a case where it attempts to repossess the financed vehicle or to collect the debt through a levy upon that vehicle, it is not subject to the defenses when, as here, it enters a general judgment against the payee of the note. It quotes from paragraph 2 of the Uniform Commercial Code Comments of Section 9-203 as follows: "In lieu of the type of cut-off clause discussed in the preceding paragraph, a negotiable note is frequently executed in connection with a conditional sale contract or purchase money chattel mortgage. This section allows the note to have its normal operation except when secured by consumer goods. Where consumer goods are involved, sub-section (1) makes even a holder in due course of the note subject to defenses if he seeks to enforce the security agreement or levies on the goods. Thus a holder may be entitled to judgment on the note, but may become subject to a total or partial defense by making a subsequent levy on the goods." . . .

If the appellant were a holder in due course of a *separate note* (italics ours) without knowledge that the note originated in connection with the financing of a motor vehicle sale, its contention that it is insulated from the defenses raised here might have merit. If this were the case, the provisions of the Uniform Commercial Code alone might control, and the Motor Vehicle Sales Finance Act would do no more than impose criminal liability upon the dealer for requiring of the buyer a note which could be separately negotiated, in violation of Section 15 (G) of the Act. But, that is not this case. The note here was not separately negotiated. It was connected to and a part of the installment sales contract. The plaintiff knew, as the court below pointed out, that by virtue of Section 15 (G) supra, the transfer from the dealer to it could not cut off, as to it, any right of action or defense which the buyer has against the original seller.

As pointed out above, commercial necessity has made it necessary for paper to develop with attributes of negotiability even though such paper does not satisfy the formal requisites of the Negotiable Instruments Law. Remedial and descriptive language, called "luggage," often made the promise or order conditional, destroyed negotiability, and subjected the bona fide purchasers to the defenses of the primary obligors and the claims of ownership of previous holders. Efforts to avoid such difficulty by contract, legislation, and court decisions have not been completely successful.

Articles 7 and 8 of the Code have set up new categories for business instruments which are not intended to be used as a substitute for money.

(U.C.C. 8-102, 7-501) Investment securities, bonds, stock certificates, bills of lading, warehouse receipts, interim certificates, other types of documents of title, and security devices are thus excluded from Article 3.

Under Article 3 which sets out the requisites of negotiability (U.C.C. 3-104) *form* is the test. The words that appear on the face of the paper determine negotiability. Such paper is "short-term" paper payable in money, and is to be used as a medium of exchange. On the other hand "a security" (U.C.C. 8-102) although an engagement to pay money is "long-term" paper and is "functional" in nature and has for its purpose the *investment of money*. Drafts, checks, certificates of deposit, and notes will continue to be "couriers without luggage" and serve as a substitute for money passing freely from person to person "free from equities." "Security," by definition, is a broad term and is inclusive enough "to cover anything which security markets such as the organized exchanges as well as the 'over-the-counter' markets are likely to regard as suitable for trading." The negotiable attributes of such business paper are determined by Sections 8-102 and 8-105. Section 8-105 calls such paper negotiable instruments. The comment to the Section under the title "Purposes" states: "This Article gives to bona fide purchasers of securities rights greater than those they would have if the things bought were chattels and simple contracts." (For a discussion of the rights of purchasers and assignees of simple contract claims for money, see Sections 4-3, 4-4 above.)

4-7. Kinds of commercial paper—definitions. Section 3-104 (2) limits "commercial paper" to the draft (bill of exchange), the check, the certificate of deposit, and the note. A writing which complies with the requirements of this section is:

(a) a "draft" (bill of exchange) if it is an order;
(b) a "check" if it is a draft drawn on a bank and payable on demand;
(c) a "certificate of deposit" if it is an acknowledgment by a bank of receipt of money with an engagement to repay it;
(d) a "note" if it is a promise other than a certificate of deposit.

The instrument must contain either an order or promise. An order is defined as . . . "a direction to pay and must be more than an authorization or request. It must identify the person to pay with reasonable certainty. It may be addressed to one or more such persons jointly or in the alternative but not in succession."

A promise is defined as "an undertaking to pay and must be more than an acknowledgment of an obligation."

Commercial paper under this Article as under the Negotiable Instruments Law may be classified according to the number of parties required to create the paper.

The draft (bill of exchange) and the check are three-party paper. The note is two-party paper.

The nature of the draft (bill of exchange)—the check. A draft presupposes a debtor-creditor relationship between the drawer and drawee. The drawee is the debtor, the drawer the creditor. The drawer-creditor orders the drawee-debtor to pay money to a third party who is the payee and who may be a creditor of the drawer. The creator or issuer of a draft (bill of exchange) is called the drawer. He issues the order to his debtor, the drawee, to pay another person called the payee. It is necessary to note here that "issue" is the first delivery of the instrument. This is in most cases made to the payee. Under the Negotiable Instruments Law "issue" meant "first delivery of the instrument complete in form to a person who takes as *holder*." This seemed to exclude persons not payees. The Code permits delivery to a person whose name does not appear on the paper and who is called a *remitter*. Historically the bill of exchange was often four-party paper—the drawer, the payee, the drawee, and the remitter. Often a person will procure a check or draft (particularly in the case of foreign bills) drawn by a third party, to be used in paying a debt due from the person procuring the draft to the person to whom the debtor has the draft made payable. The person procuring the bill is called the "remitter." His name does not appear on the bill. The payee who takes the bill from the *remitter* for value is held in the proper case to be a holder in due course. The debtor-creditor situations in which the drawer of an instrument delivers it to a third party—a remitter—for delivery to the payee vary greatly. (For illustrations see U.C.C. 3-302, Comment 2.)

When the order issued by the drawer is formally accepted in writing by the drawee, the drawee thereafter is called an *acceptor*. "An acceptance is the drawee's signed engagement to honor the draft as presented." By acceptance the drawee becomes the primary obligor and his liability is similar to the liability of the maker of a promissory note. Thus the parties to a draft are the drawer, the drawee-acceptor, the payee, and, under the proper circumstances, the remitter. If a draft is not bearer paper, but payable to the order of a payee, an indorsement is necessary for negotiation. When the payee indorses he is called an indorser, and the person entitled to payment an indorsee.

A check is a draft (a bill of exchange, three-party paper) drawn on a bank (drawee-debtor) by a depositor (drawer-creditor) to the order of the payee. The payee may be a person thus creating order paper, or the payee may be "cash" thus creating bearer paper.

Checks serve a particular purpose; therefore, there are significant legal differences between checks as drafts and drafts drawn on persons not banks. (See Article 4, U.C.C. Bank Deposits and Collections; text page 646).

A check drawn by a bank upon itself is a *cashier's check.* Since the drawer and drawee are the same, the instrument may have some of the attributes of a promissory note. A *certified check* is a check which has been accepted by the drawee bank. (U.C.C. 3-411 and 3-802)

Traveller's checks are like cashier's checks in that the financial institution issuing such instrument is both the drawer and the drawee. Such instruments are negotiable instruments under Article 3 when they have been completed by the payee-holder, who identifies himself by his signature. (See Comment 4, Section 3-104)

Other types of drafts. Drafts (bills of exchange) other than checks may be designated or classified according to the situation in which they are used and the purpose sought to be accomplished. Drafts may be called bank drafts, banker's acceptances, and trade acceptances.

Bank draft. A bank draft is a banker's check; that is, it is a check drawn by one bank on another bank, payable on demand. Ordinarily a bank draft is used because the credit of a bank makes it more acceptable than a check drawn by an individual. If, for example, *A*, a businessman, from Eugene, Oregon, plans a buying trip in New York, he may purchase a bank draft from a Eugene bank, which draft is drawn by the Eugene bank on its correspondent bank in New York. *A* thus has an instrument which enables him to make purchases in New York because it is readily acceptable by merchants in that city as payment for goods.

Banker's acceptances. A draft is often used as an instrument to secure prompt payment for goods shipped by manufacturers to distributors in large quantities. The draft used in such transactions is involved with security arrangements and is often given a name that refers to the type of security arrangement. Drafts of this character are called *documentary drafts* under the Code and defined by Section 5-103 (b) as follows:

> A documentary draft or a documentary demand for payment is one honor of which is conditioned upon the presentation of a document or documents. Document means any paper including documents of title, security, invoice, certificate, note of default, and the like.

A draft accompanying security instruments may be under proper circumstances negotiable commercial paper, controlled by Article 3, or it may be so related to the security transaction that its negotiable attributes will be determined by Article 9.

The business situation in which a banker's acceptance is used may be described as follows: The seller of goods often refuses to deliver to the buyer upon the buyer's credit alone; or the seller of the goods may wish to secure in payment for his goods a negotiable instrument that has a ready sale. A draft accepted by a bank would have stronger credit than a check or a trade acceptance. *B* informs his banker that he expects to purchase goods from S and requests the bank to accept a draft drawn on it by S. *B* presents collateral to the bank or agrees to keep a certain amount on deposit in order that the bank will be assured of funds at the time of payment. The collateral may consist of other notes, shipping documents, warehouse receipts, and bills of lading. By this means the bank does not make a loan, but merely lends its credit to the buyer and thus gives selling capacity to the paper. S can dispose of his paper more readily and on better terms than if the negotiable instrument were a trade acceptance accepted only by the original buyer, *B*.

Acceptance of such draft must be written on the draft. A separate acceptance in writing before or after the creation of the paper was proper under the Negotiable Instruments Law but is no longer valid under the Code. However, a draft drawn by the seller in reliance upon a paper previously given by the bank, called a *letter of credit,* creates a binding obligation of the bank. *Letters of credit,* although used in domestic trade, are more frequently employed in international trade. In domestic commerce, letters of credit are employed in automobile marketing to assure the manufacturer of prompt payment by the distributor. Such paper is also used to assist in securing credit to finance the manufacture of articles which are made for a particular buyer.

Federal banks are authorized by the Federal Reserve Act, 41 Stat. 378 (1919) as amended 12 U.S.C. Section 615 (1946) to issue letters of credit in foreign trade and accept time bills of exchange, either by writing on the face thereof, or by letter of credit. Letters of credit are regulated by Article 5 of the Code.

Trade acceptance. The trade acceptance is another type of draft used largely by manufacturers and merchants. A trade acceptance is taken by the seller as payment for goods purchased at the time of the sale. The seller draws on the purchaser to his own order for the goods sold. When the draft is accepted by the purchaser, it becomes his primary obligation. The buyer, having acknowledged the debt by his acceptance, cannot later dispute the debt as against a holder of the trade acceptance. The seller often *discounts* trade acceptances at the bank or uses them as collateral for loans.

The process of discounting is extremely important in business and commercial transactions. Typically it involves the situation in which the holder of a trade acceptance desires to obtain money on the strength of the instrument prior to the time when it matures. Thus, the holder may be in need of funds presently, and if he is the owner of a trade acceptance which matures six months in the future, he may by discounting obtain funds for his present needs. If the trade acceptance is discounted at a bank, for example, the bank would compute the interest that would accrue during the life of the trade acceptance, subtract this amount from the face of the instrument, and pay the borrower the net sum.

This instrument, to the extent that it complies with Article 3, may be "commercial paper." However, if it is closely related to documents of title involved in a security transaction, which is usually the case, it will be controlled by Article 9.

Drafts classified as to time. Sight drafts are bills of exchange, payable at sight. This type of paper is termed call paper. Time drafts are drafts payable at a future time (such as 30 or 60 days after date of acceptance, for example).

Classification of promissory notes. Promissory notes, which comply strictly with the formal requisites of negotiability as well as those which do not comply with such requirements of Article 3 (U.C.C. 3-104 (3)), may be used in many different ways. The purpose for which they are used and the nature of the security for the promise given by the maker to support his promise, are often used to designate the type or kind of note. A note which on its face carries only the promise of the maker and is limited to his personal security, may be called a simple promissory note. However, business convenience often requires a high degree of certainty that the money promised will be paid, hence the personal promise of the maker is often supported by other contracts which make available property as collateral security or contracts which enumerate various remedies that may be used by the payee or holder in case of default by the primary obligor. In addition to property as security, the payee may require the promise of another person. Such person may be a cosigner or an accommodation party. Thus notes may be called personal notes, collateral notes, judgment notes, conditional sale notes, real estate mortgage notes, and bonds. The extent to which such additional contracts affect negotiability will be discussed in sections to follow. Added language which does not affect negotiability is specifically set out in Section 3-112 of the Code.

Whatever the commercial instrument is called, it is controlled by the terms of the Code. Thus a bond—a promise to pay money—although not a negotiable instrument within Article 3, is negotiable under Article 8. Descriptions of different kinds of "promises to pay money" are given in the following sections.

Collateral note. A note may be secured by personal property in the nature of other notes, bonds, stock certificates, chattel paper, and other security devices, temporarily placed within the control of the payee or holder. The property transferred is called collateral, and such a note a collateral security note. For a list of different kinds of property which may be used as collateral security for a note, see U.C.C. Section 9-102.

The note secured by such collateral may or may not be controlled by Article 3.

Judgment note. The maker may sign a contract as additional security, which contract gives a remedy to the payee or holder to take a judgment against the defaulting maker, primary obligor, or sureties, without a trial. This form of note is called a judgment note. (See text p. 463.)

Conditional sale note. In order to secure the payment of a note given for the sale of merchandise, the contract of sale may be set forth upon the face of the note. The contract usually provides that title to the chattel sold shall remain with the payee-vendor until the note given is paid in full, and, in addition, that in case of default in payments as shown upon the note, the vendor may repossess the chattel. A note in this form is called a conditional sale note.

Such a note may be attached to the conditional contract and be an integral part of the instrument, or the note may be a "commercial specialty promise," negotiable in form, separate and apart from the sale contract. (For a discussion of the rights of a holder of a note attached to a conditional contract see *First National Bank of Millville v. Horwatt,* p. 441.) It is believed that a holder for value of a separate note, who has no knowledge that it arose out of a conditional sale contract, takes free from defenses. Whether such paper would be controlled by Article 3 or Article 9, or both, depends upon the circumstances, the relation of the parties, and the extent to which the security is significant. (U.C.C. 3-103) In addition to pertinent Code provisions, the student should check local statutes concerned with the sale of automobiles and other consumer goods.

Mortgage notes, chattel and real. A security contract separate from the simple promissory note is illustrated by the mortgage. There are two kinds of mortgages, depending upon the character of the property used as security. When the maker conveys to the payee as security a right in the title of chattels, the note so secured is called a chattel mortgage note. When the right in the title conveyed is in real property, the note so secured is called a real estate mortgage note.

Article 9 of the U.C.C. (except for transactions excluded by Section 9-104, which include matters regulated by federal and local statutes concerned with public policy) governs all secured transactions involving personal property. All former security devices such as pledges, chattel mortgages, conditional sales, etc. are now consolidated into the "security transaction." However, the conditional sale, the chattel mortgage, and other well-known security devices will likely continue to be used as security for the promissory note, which note may or may not accompany the paper.

The negotiable attributes of the chattel note will be determined by

Article 3, unless it conflicts with Article 9, in which case the whole security transaction must conform to the requirements of Article 9.

Article 9 of the Code is not applicable to a real estate mortgage as a security interest. Article 3 is applicable to the note which is secured by the real estate mortgage. If the mortgagee uses the note and real estate mortgage to secure his own obligation, then Article 9 becomes pertinent. The following illustration is given in the comment to Section 9-102 of the Code:

> The owner of Blackacre borrows $10,000 from his neighbor, and secures his note by a mortgage on Blackacre. This Article is not applicable to the creation of the real estate mortgage. However, when the mortgagee in turn pledges this note and mortgage to secure his own obligation to *X*, this Article is applicable to the security interest thus created in the note and the mortgage. Whether the transfer of the collateral for the note, i.e., the mortgagee's interest in Blackacre, requires further action (such as recording an assignment of the mortgagee's interest) is left to real estate law. See Section 9-104 (j).

Certificate of deposit. The classification of different types of promises to pay money is sometimes controlled by the character of the maker. This is true of the certificate of deposit and of the bond. A certificate of deposit is given by a bank to a depositor, as a receipt for the deposit, the bank engaging to repay the amount to the depositor. Care must be taken to distinguish certificates of deposit from the usual receipt given by the bank when a depositor deposits sums to his checking account. This receipt is called a "deposit slip," which evidences the contract of deposit. There is no uniformity in this type of paper. The language used does not satisfy the requirements for negotiable paper; consequently such deposit slips are not negotiable.

A bond. A bond under the Negotiable Instruments Law was designated as a promissory note, a bearer instrument, issued under seal by a corporation, public or private. The negotiable attributes of a bond are covered by Article 8 of the Code. A bond is a very formal instrument and in general is so worded as to satisfy the requirements of negotiability. However, since the bond is used as an investment instrument for the purpose of loaning money over a long term, it necessarily carries on its face much language referring to the nature of security and the remedies permitted in case of default. Under the old Negotiable Instruments Law such language usually impaired its negotiability.

A bond may be secured by a mortgage on personal property or real property. When real estate is used as security for a bond, the security instrument is called a trust deed. The mortgagee is a trustee who holds the mortgage in trust for the benefit of all the bond holders. Such trust instrument is usually long and complicated in that there is set out therein the powers of the trustee and the remedies for foreclosure in case of default.

Bonds may be registered. The registration also affects the rights of the parties. (For the rights of issuers with respect to registered owners, see U.C.C. 8-207.)

For the requirements of a bond and its negotiable attributes, see Article 8—Investment Securities. Article 3—Commercial Paper, does not cover bonds or other investment securities.

INTRODUCTION TO THE LAW OF COMMERCIAL PAPER CASES

UNIVERSAL C.I.T. CREDIT CORPORATION v. HUDGENS

1962, 234 Ark. 668, 356 S.W.2d 658

George Rose Smith, J. On May 21, 1959, the appellees, Anson Hudgens and his daughter, bought a used Ford car from E. W. Mack, doing business as West Memphis Auto Sales. The conditional sales contract executed by the purchasers was transferred by Mack to the appellant finance company the next day. None of the monthly payments were made by the purchasers, who insist that they were defrauded. The appellant brought this action in replevin to recover the car. The case was transferred to equity, where the chancellor canceled the contract for fraud in its procurement and for usury. We do not reach the issue of usury, for we have concluded that the decree must in any event be affirmed upon the finding of fraud.

It should be stated at the outset that the appellant does not and cannot invoke the protection afforded to the holder of a negotiable instrument. No promissory note is involved, and the conditional sales contract is not negotiable, as it does not contain an unconditional promise payable to order or bearer. *Gale & Co. v. Wallace*, 210 Ark. 161, 194 S.W.2d 881. Hence, as we held in the case cited, the appellant holds the contract subject to defenses available against the original seller.

If the execution of the contract was induced by fraud it was properly canceled. *Gentry v. Little Rock Road Mach. Co.*, 232 Ark. —, 339 S.W.2d 101. Here, as in the Gentry case, the purchasers testified that the seller represented the vehicle to be in good condition, when in fact it needed extensive repairs. Mack's salesman gave the appellees a signed memorandum stating that the seller had given a 30-day guarantee on the motor, transmission, and rear end; but when the dissatisfied purchasers brought the car back within a few days Mack refused to repair it unless the buyers would bear half the expense.

A more serious charge of fraud is the appellees' assertion that Mack's salesman, Harris, induced them to sign the contract in blank and then filled it in for $300 more than the agreed purchase price of $1,095. As a witness for the appellant, Harris admitted that the contract was signed in blank and was left with him for completion, but he insisted that the figure which he inserted as the purchase price, $1,395, was in accordance with the parties' agreement.

No useful purpose would be served by a detailed discussion of the conflicting testimony. Hudgens, his daughter, and his son were all present when the car was bought, and all three testified to facts amply supporting the charge of fraud. Their version of the matter is contradicted only by the salesman, Harris. After studying the record we cannot say that the evidence adduced by one side is essentially more credible than that adduced by the other. The chancellor had the great advantage of observing the witnesses as they testified. His findings do not appear to us to be against the weight of the evidence.

Affirmed.

Review Questions and Problems

1. *M* executed a nonnegotiable note to *P* and also gave *P* a letter stating that he had no defenses on the note. The bank in reliance upon the letter purchased the note from *P*. Can the bank enforce the note against *M* if *M* has a defense against *P*?
2. The words "This note is negotiable" were placed on a note which did not otherwise qualify as a negotiable instrument. Should the note be treated as a negotiable instrument?
3. *A* purchased an automobile from *B* under a conditional sale contract which called for a usurious rate of interest. The contract stipulated that it should be treated as a negotiable instrument and that *A* waived all defenses. Can *A* assert the defense of usury against a purchaser of the contract?
4. *M* drew a check which recited "Pay to *P* $500." *P* indorsed the check to *A*. If the check is dishonored would *A* have recourse against *P*?
5. What is meant by the statement: "Form is the test of negotiability under Article 3—Commercial Paper"?
6. *A* purchased a chattel from *B* and gave a note in payment. The note provided that title would remain in *B* until the note was paid. If the chattel were destroyed prior to the maturity of the note would *A* be relieved of liability?
7. *M* executed a note in favor of *P* and also delivered certain collateral to *P*. What may *P* do if *M* fails to pay the note at maturity?
8. A note contained a provision allowing a confession of judgment against the maker if he should fail to pay an installment. How does this benefit the holder of the note?

9. *A*, a wholesaler, sold *B*, a retailer, some roofing material for resale to *B*'s customers. In connection with the transaction *A* drew an instrument payable to *A*'s order. The instrument was addressed to *B* and accepted by him. *A* transferred it to *X*. What is this type of instrument usually called?
10. S, a dealer, sold an automobile to *B* on a conditional sale contract. *B* signed the contract and also a note which was attached to the contract. S detached the note and indorsed it to *X* Bank for its discounted value. S then sold the conditional sale contract to *Y* Bank. The automobile did not function properly and the motor and transmission must be replaced. S, who is now insolvent, refused to replace the defective motor and transmission. Both banks seek to collect from *B*. What are their respective rights against *B*?

21

Creation of Commercial Paper

LANGUAGE AND WORDS REQUIRED TO CREATE NEGOTIABLE PAPER

4-8. Requirements of a negotiable instrument. In order that an instrument may be negotiable it must conform to certain requirements. As a general proposition, if it does not satisfy these requirements, it will not be negotiable and will not have the attributes which attach to negotiable instruments. The Code provides that in order to qualify as a negotiable instrument within the framework of Article 3—Commercial Paper, a writing must (a) be signed by the maker or drawer; (b) contain an unconditional promise or order to pay a sum certain in money; (c) be payable on demand or at a definite time; and (d) be payable to order or to bearer. These are the basic requirements; but it is important to note that in connection with requirement (b), there is a restriction to the effect that there must be "no other promise, order, obligation, or power given by the maker or drawer except as authorized by this Article." The Code does permit some powers to be given without impairing negotiability. Thus, for example, if collateral has been given as security for the instrument, the right to sell the collateral, if there is a default on the instrument, may be granted without impairing negotiability. Each of the requirements for negotiability will now be considered in more detail.

4-9. Writing and signature. The requirement of the Code is simply that there be a writing signed by the maker or drawer. It is not required that any particular type or kind of writing be used, nor is it necessary that the signature be at any particular place upon the instrument. The instrument may be in any form which includes "printing, typewriting, or any other intentional reduction to tangible form." A symbol is a sufficient signature if it was "executed or adopted by a party with present intention to authenticate a writing." These provisions are somewhat broader than their counterparts in the NIL. The use of the word "authenticate" in the definition of "signed" makes it clear that a complete signature is not required. The authentication may be printed or written and may be placed on the instrument by stamp.

4-10. The necessity of a promise or order. One of the basic requirements of a negotiable note is that it must contain a *promise* to pay. It is not required that the exact word "promise" be used; it is necessary, however, that in absence of the word promise, the language used shall manifest an undertaking or promise. A promise must be derived from the language, not from the fact that a debt exists. For example, the words in an instrument "due *X*, $500 for value received" would not satisfy the requirement of a promise. A mere acknowledgment of a debt in writing is not promissory. The simplest form of an instrument which merely acknowledges a debt is an I.O.U. Though such written memorandum is sufficient to evidence and create a valid enforceable instrument upon which recovery may be had by the creditor or his assignee against the debtor, such instruments are not negotiable notes. In order to constitute a promise, there must be an undertaking to pay and the mere acknowledgment that an obligation exists would not be sufficient.

A draft must contain an *order* to pay. The purpose of the instrument is to order the drawee to pay money to the payee, and it is therefore necessary that plain language be used to show an intention to make an order. The language must signify more than an authorization or request. It must be a direction to pay. Thus, an instrument in the following form would not be negotiable: "To John Doe. I wish you would pay $1,000 to the order of Richard Roe. (Signed) Robert Lee." This would nevertheless be a valid authorization for John Doe to make payment to Richard Roe.

4-11. The promise or order must be unconditional. Negotiable instruments serve a dual purpose and the law is designed to facilitate the usefulness of such instruments. There is not enough currency to satisfy the needs of business and commerce and the negotiable instrument serves in a sense as a substitute for money. By far the greater number of transactions use negotiable instruments rather than money—currency. The other useful purpose served by negotiable instruments is to serve as a basis for short-term credit. Negotiable instruments thus stand for money which is to be paid in the future. If these purposes are to be served, it is essential that the intruments be readily accepted and that they be freely transferable. Conditional promises or orders would defeat these purposes for it would be necessary to make a determination with regard to whether or not the condition had been performed. The instruments would therefore not circulate rapidly, and would be transferred at extremely high rates of discount. In recognition of the functions which are served by negotiable instruments, and the need for certainty if the instruments are to serve as a substitute for money and a basis for credit, the Code requires that the promise or order be unconditional. If the promise or order is a conditional one, the instrument would not be negotiable even though it satisfied all of the other requirements.

The question of whether or not the promise or order is conditional arises when the instrument contains language in addition to the promise or order to pay. The Code specifies those situations in which the additional language renders the promise or order conditional, and also sets forth a number of situations in which the additional language does not impair negotiability. The promise or order is not unconditional if it is stated to be controlled by or subject to the terms of some other agreement. Likewise a promise or order is conditional, with certain exceptions, if the instrument contains a provision that it is to be paid only out of a particular fund or source.

Reference to other agreements. The Code provides that a mere reference in an instrument to a separate agreement will not impair negotiability. Such recitals are informative rather than restrictive. Under the NIL some cases had held that if the language disclosed an executory promise as the return for which an instrument was given, there was then an implied condition that the promise must be performed before liability would arise. The Code clearly resolves this problem by stating that implied or constructive conditions do not render a promise or order conditional.[1]

Clearly a promise or order is conditional if reference to some other agreement is required in order to determine the conditional or unconditional character of the promise or order. If it is stated in the instrument that the promise or order is *subject to* the terms of a certain contract, it would be necessary to refer to such contract in order to determine whether the promise or order is conditioned or restricted. This would render the promise or order conditional. However, a mere *reference* to some other contract or agreement does not condition the promise or order. A distinction, then, is to be drawn between additional language which imposes the terms of some other agreement and that which simply gives information as to the transaction which gave rise to the instrument. Thus, the use of the words *subject to contract* conditions the promise or order while the words *as per contract* would not render the promise or order conditional.[2]

Statements of the consideration for which the instrument was given and statements of the transaction out of which the instrument arose are simply informative and are not conditional. A draft may have been drawn under a letter of credit and a reference to this fact does not impose a condition. Notes frequently contain a provision that some sort of security has been given, such as a mortgage on property or that title to goods has been retained as security for the payment of the note. In either case the purpose

[1] Park National Bank v. Motyl, page 471.
[2] United States v. Farrington, page 473.

is to make clear to the holder that the promise to pay is secured by something in addition to the general credit of the maker and as a consequence a mere reference to the security does not destroy negotiability. Some cases under prior law had reached a different conclusion.

Notes given in payment for property purchased on installment often provide that title to such property shall not pass to the maker of the note until all payments called for have been made. A statement to this effect in a note does not condition the promise to pay.

The particular fund concept. A statement that an instrument is to be paid only out of a particular fund imposes a condition. Such an instrument does not carry the general personal credit of the maker or drawer and is contingent upon the sufficiency of the fund on which it is drawn. An illustration of such promise or order is as follows: "To *A.* Pay to *B* or order $500 out of the proceeds of the sale of my store building. (Signed) *Y.*" Even though there is a sufficient fund in existence when the instrument falls due, the instrument is nonnegotiable because this is a fact which could not be ascertained from the face of the instrument.

There are two exceptions to the foregoing rule with regard to a limitation to payment out of a particular fund. An instrument issued by a government or government agency is not deemed nonnegotiable simply because payment is restricted to a particular fund. Second, an instrument issued by or on behalf of a partnership, unincorporated association, trust, or estate may be negotiable, although it is limited to payment out of their entire assets. These provisions are new under the Code.

The Code provides that a *mere reference* to a particular fund does not impair negotiability. Such references are often made for purposes of record keeping and accounting, and do not in any way limit liability to the fund mentioned. Thus, a check which provides "charge to agent's disbursing account" would not be deemed to contain a conditional order, but would simply indicate the account to be debited.[3]

4-12. The sum must be certain. The language used in creating commercial paper must be certain with respect to the amount of money promised or ordered to be paid. Otherwise, its value at any period could not be definitely determined. If the principal sum to be paid is definite, negotiability is not affected by the fact that it is to be paid with interest, in installments, with exchange at a fixed or current rate, or with cost of collection and attorney's fee in case payment shall not be made at maturity.[4] If at any point of time during the term of the paper its full value can be ascertained with certainty, the requirement that the sum must be certain is satisfied. The obligation to pay costs and attorney's fees

[3] National Deposit Bank of Owensboro v. Ohio Oil Co., page 476.
[4] Gramatan National Bank & Trust Co. v. Montgomery, page 477.

is part of the security contract, separate and distinct from the primary promise to pay money and does not, therefore, affect the requirement as to a sum certain. The certainty of amount is not affected if the instrument specifies different rates of interest before and after default; neither is the certainty affected by a provision for a stated discount for early payment or an additional charge if payment is made after the date fixed.

4-13. Instruments must be payable in money. An instrument, to be negotiable, must be payable in money. Instruments payable in chattels, such as one hundred bushels of wheat or one ounce of gold, are therefore not negotiable. "Money" is defined under the Code as "a medium of exchange authorized or adopted by a domestic or foreign government as a part of its currency." The amount payable may be stated in foreign as well as domestic money, provided the medium specified has government approval. The Code provides that "an instrument is payable in money if the medium of exchange in which it is payable is money at the time the instrument is made." Thus, the amount payable may be stated in sterling, francs, lire, or other foreign currency. If the sum payable is stated in foreign currency, the instrument may be satisfied by payment of the dollar equivalent, that is, the number of dollars that could be purchased by the foreign currency at the "buying sight rate" on the day payable, or if it is demand paper at the rate on the date of demand. However, if it is specified in the instrument that a foreign currency is the medium of payment, payment would have to be made in that currency. Under the Code an instrument expressed in terms of foreign currency but payable in dollars is negotiable, even though the exchange rate fluctuates. It might be argued that the sum is not certain since the number of dollars required to satisfy the instrument could not be determined until the date of payment or demand.

Negotiable instruments are sometimes made payable in "currency" or "current funds." Under the Code such terms mean that the instrument is payable in money.

TIME OF PAYMENT MUST BE CERTAIN

4-14. In general. As a substitute for money, negotiable instruments would be of little value if the holder were unable to determine at what time he could demand payment. It is necessary, therefore, that there be certainty as to the time of payment. The law, codified by Article 3 of the Uniform Commercial Code, requires that a negotiable instrument be payable on demand or at a "definite time." The NIL provided that an instrument must be payable on demand or "at a fixed or determinable future time."

4-15. Demand paper. An instrument is payable on demand when it so states, when payable at sight or on presentation, or when no time of payment is stated. In general, the words "payable on demand" are used in notes and the words "at sight" in drafts. If nothing is said about the due date, the instrument is demand paper.[5] A check is a good illustration of such an instrument. The characteristic of demand paper is that the holder of such paper can require payment at any time by making a demand upon the person who is obligated on the paper.[6]

4-16. Payable at a definite time. In order to be negotiable an instrument must be either payable on demand or payable at a definite time. This is in keeping with the necessity for certainty in instruments. It is important that the value of an instrument at any given time be capable of determination. This value will be dependent upon the ultimate maturity date of the instrument. The Code specifies that if an instrument is payable only upon an act or event which is uncertain as to when it will occur it is not payable at a definite time even though the act or event has occurred. Thus, an instrument payable "thirty days after my father's death" would not be negotiable under the Code. Such an instrument would have been negotiable under the NIL.

The requirement of certainty as to the time of payment is satisfied if it is payable on or before a specified date. Thus, an instrument payable on June 1, 1965, is payable at a definite time as is one payable "on or before" June 1, 1965. In the latter situation the obligor on the instrument has the privilege of making payment prior to June 1, 1965, but is not required to pay it until the specified date. An instrument payable at a fixed period after a stated date, or at a fixed period after sight, is payable at a definite time. The expressions "one year after date" or "sixty days after sight" would thus be proper.

Acceleration provisions. A type of provision often found in a negotiable instrument that hastens or accelerates the maturity date of an instrument is called an accelerating clause. One type of accelerating provision which is in common use provides that in case of default in payment of interest or of an installment of the principal, the entire note shall become due and payable.[7] Another type is one giving the holder an option to declare the instrument due and payable when he feels insecure. These and many other types of accelerating provisions are being used increasingly in instruments by the commercial world. The Code provides that an in-

[5] Liberty Aluminum Products Company v. John Cortis et ux, page 477.
[6] Cassiano v. Bellino, page 479.
[7] *Ibid.*

strument payable at a definite time subject to any acceleration may be negotiable. If, however, a provision allows the holder to declare the instrument due when he feels insecure, it is to be noted that such person must act, in good faith, in the belief that the likelihood of payment is indeed impaired. The presumption is that he has acted in good faith, placing the burden on the other party to show that such was not the case. Under the NIL this sort of accelerating provision destroys negotiability.

Extension clauses. Extension clauses are the converse of acceleration provisions. They provide for the extension of the time for payment beyond that specified in the instrument. Thus, a note payable in two years might provide that the maker has the right to extend the time of payment six months. The Code provides that an instrument is payable at a definite time if it is payable "at a definite time subject to extension at the option of the holder, or to extension to a further definite time at the option of the maker or acceptor, or automatically upon or after a specified act or event." It is to be noted that in an extension at the option of the holder, no time limit is required. The holder always has the right to refrain from undertaking collection. An extension at the option of the maker or acceptor, or an automatic extension, must provide for a definite time for payment.

PAYABLE TO ORDER OR BEARER

4-17. Words of negotiability. Both the NIL and the Code require words of negotiability. Such words clearly express the intention to create negotiable paper. The words of negotiability are "order" and "bearer." These exact words are not required; words of equivalent meaning may be used. However, it is desirable to use the words "order" or "bearer" so as to avoid questions as to whether the words used import negotiability. In the absence of words of negotiability, an instrument will ordinarily lack the capacity to pass current as money. The Code contains a provision not found in the NIL to the effect that an instrument which is not payable to order or bearer, but which satisfies the other requirements of negotiability, will be treated in most respects as though it were negotiable. In the foregoing situation, however, the holder cannot be a holder in due course. The reason for the recognition granted to such instruments—that is, instruments lacking words of negotiability—is to bring the law into conformity with commercial and banking practice. Thus, a check which provides "Pay to A" is recognized as a check under Article 3.

The maker of a note, made payable to *X* or order, may be said to make two promises. The maker promises to pay *X* if *X* holds the paper; he also promises to pay any other person that *X* may order him to pay. A drawer of a draft orders the drawee to pay the named payee, or any person named by the payee.

4-18. Order paper. The distinguishing characteristic of order paper is that it requires indorsement for negotiation whereas bearer paper is negotiated by delivery. The Code provides that "an instrument is payable to order when by its terms it is payable to the order or assigns of any person therein specified with reasonable certainty, or to him or his order, or when it is conspicuously designated on its face as 'exchange' or the like and names a payee."

The Code follows the NIL in providing that an instrument may be payable to the order of the maker or drawer, the drawee, or a payee who is not a maker, drawer, or drawee. It may be payable to two or more payees together or in the alternative. An instrument payable to the order of "*A* or *B*" may be negotiated by the indorsement of either of the parties. It may be drawn payable to the order of "*A* and *B*" in which event the indorsement of both would be required.

The Code removes uncertainties which existed under the NIL by providing that an instrument may be payable to the order of:

An estate, trust, or fund, in which case it is payable to the order of the representative of such estate, trust, or fund or his successors; or
An office, or an officer by his title as such in which case it is payable to the principal but the incumbent of the office or his successors may act as if he or they were the holder; or
A partnership or unincorporated association, in which case it is payable to the partnership or association and may be transferred by any person thereto authorized.

There were decisions under the NIL that an instrument payable to the order of the estate of a decedent was bearer paper. The Code recognizes that such paper is intended to be payable to the order of the estate representative. Likewise, if an instrument is payable to the order of the "Development Fund," for example, it is payable to the representative thereof, or his successors. An instrument payable to the order of the "Treasurer of the Traffic Club" runs to the present treasurer or his successors in that office. An instrument payable to the order of a partnership or an unincorporated association, such as a labor union, may be indorsed or transferred by an authorized person.

Cases decided under the NIL had held that an instrument which was not payable to order would nevertheless be order paper if it contained a statement such as "payable upon return of this certificate properly indorsed." The Code recognizes that the purpose of such language was usually to have the indorsement serve as a receipt. Hence the addition of such clauses does not make the instrument payable to order under the Code.

The Code provides that "an instrument made payable both to order and to bearer is payable to order unless the bearer words are handwritten or typewritten." It sometimes happens that in filling in a printed form a person will execute an instrument in such a form as "Pay *to the order of A* or bearer." Under the Code this is considered as order paper because the insertion of the name of the payee is held to be controlling. On the other hand, if the word "bearer" is added either in typewriting or handwriting, this indicates an intent that the instrument is payable to bearer. The next section treats another ambiguous instrument, i.e., one which is payable to "order of bearer."

4-19. Bearer paper. The Code specifies that an instrument is payable to bearer and can be negotiated by delivery if it is payable to:

(a) bearer or the order of bearer; or

(b) a specified person or bearer; or

(c) "cash" or the order of "cash," or any other indication which does not purport to designate a specific payee.

The basic characteristic of bearer paper as distinguished from order paper is that it may be negotiated by delivery—that no indorsement is required. Under the Code, bearer paper is determined by what appears on the face of the paper and by indorsements. The Code largely follows the NIL, except that some uncertainties have been resolved as, for example, when an instrument is made payable to "order of bearer." The Code makes such paper, bearer paper since the word, "bearer," is the significant word and necessarily controls. The provision included in the NIL that an instrument is payable to bearer, "when payable to the order of a fictitious or nonexisting person," has been omitted; under the Code such paper is order paper and an indorsement is necessary for negotiation. Even though an impostor—one impersonating another—has been designated as payee, or an instrument is made payable to one who is not intended to have any interest in it, indorsement is necessary for negotiation.

The Code section which defines bearer paper omits the NIL designation as bearer paper, paper on which "the only or last indorsement is in blank," and eliminates the rule that an instrument which is bearer on its face remains bearer paper even though a special indorsement appears thereon. Under the Code *any* negotiable instrument specially indorsed becomes payable to order. Paper which is on its face payable to order and indorsed in blank is payable to bearer until specially indorsed.

Paper is bearer paper when it "does not purport to designate a specific payee." This language means an impersonal or inanimate designation of a payee such as "cash," "bills payable," "Ship Fortune," or "Twenty Tons of Steel." Since such designated payee cannot indorse the paper, the maker clearly intended title should pass by delivery only.

FACTORS NOT AFFECTING NEGOTIABILITY

4-20. Terms and omissions not affecting negotiability. The Code sections previously discussed set out the formal requisites for negotiability and specify the kind of paper that shall pass current as money. Under the Code it is the "draft," the "check," the "certificate of deposit," and the "note" that are created to perform this function. Such paper, by reason of its purpose, must necessarily be expressed in a few words.

Thus additional words giving an option to the holder to require something to be done in lieu of the payment of money would impede the currency of commercial paper. However, some language may be omitted from, or added to, the formal words which create negotiable paper without affecting its negotiability. The Code permits certain omissions or the insertion of certain specific promises and obligations, in addition to the payment of money, which do not affect negotiability. Such additional language usually pertains to security, or gives other privileges and options to the holder.

Negotiability is not affected by the inclusion of statements relating to collateral given as security for an instrument. Thus the power to sell the collateral in case of default, or "a promise or power to maintain or protect collateral or to give additional collateral," does not impair negotiability. The statement quoted is new under the Code. The NIL provided for sale of collateral if the instrument was not paid at *maturity*. Under the Code any default such as failure to pay interest or an installment may be made the basis for selling the collateral.

The inclusion of a provision authorizing a confession of judgment does not impair negotiability. As under the NIL such confession is authorized only if the instrument is not paid when due.[8] In many states judgment clauses are not permitted.[9] The Code does not purport to change the state law, but merely provides that the inclusion of such a clause does not affect negotiability.

Other terms which are allowable under the Code include a waiver of rights given by statute to an obligor and a "term in a draft providing that the payee by indorsing or cashing it acknowledges full satisfaction of an

[8] Atlas Credit Corp. v. Leonard, page 480.
[9] Gramatan National Bank & Trust Co. v. Montgomery, page 477.

obligation to the drawer." The latter is new under the Code and is intended to clarify the prior law which was uncertain as to the effect of such a clause.

The Code suggests certain formal language to be used in order to give an instrument its negotiable character. Nevertheless, the instrument need not include the exact language of the Code, but may use any terms that clearly indicate an intention to conform to the requirements of the Code. Many words which would appear to be essential are, in fact, nonessential. The validity and negotiable character of an instrument otherwise negotiable are not destroyed by the fact that it is not dated, that the words "value" or "value received" are omitted, or that it does not state what consideration was given for it. Neither is it necessary that a negotiable instrument bear a seal. If it bears a seal, its negotiability will not be affected.

An instrument is negotiable even though it does not specify the place where it is drawn or the place where it is made payable.

4-21. Date, antedating, postdating. The Code emphasizes the immateriality of dating as an essential element of negotiability. Whether there is no date, an antedate, or a postdate is not important. The date appearing on the instrument is presumed correct until evidence is introduced to prove a contrary finding. Even though the date on the instrument is not proper, it has no effect on the negotiability. This portion of the Code is comparable to like provisions of the NIL governing the negotiability of an instrument. Any fraud or illegality connected with the date of the instrument does not affect its negotiability, but merely gives defenses to the parties as provided for under other Code sections.

An undated instrument is an incomplete instrument; the date may be inserted by the holder under the rules provided for in the next section.

If an instrument is payable on demand or at a fixed period after date, the date which is put on the instrument is the date of the instrument even though it is antedated or postdated.

4-22. Incomplete instruments. The Code contains special provisions relating to incomplete instruments. Under the law prior to the Code it was presumed that only a holder could properly fill in a date. Such conclusion no longer follows since the absence of a date is just another kind of incompleteness and should be treated like any other blank place in the paper. The Code states the law concerning incompleteness as follows:

> (1) When a paper whose contents at the time of signing show that it is intended to become an instrument is signed while still incomplete in any necessary respect it cannot be enforced until completed, but when it is completed in accordance with authority given it is effective as completed.[10]

[10] Sun Oil Co. v. Redd Auto Sales, page 482.

(2) If the completion is unauthorized the rules as to material alteration apply (Section 3-407), even though the paper was not delivered by the maker or drawer; but the burden of establishing that any completion is unauthorized is on the party so asserting.

The language "signed while still incomplete in any necessary respect" used in the Code is used in place of the expression "wanting in any material particular" as set out in the NIL. The purpose of this change as stated in the comment to this Section is "to make it entirely clear that a complete writing which lacks an essential element of an instrument and contains no blanks or spaces or anything else to indicate that what is missing is to be supplied, does not fall within this Section." "Necessary" means "necessary to a complete instrument." Such an instrument will always include the promise or order, the designation of the payee and the amount payable. The paper under this section must contain enough formal words at the "time of signing" to show "that it is intended by the creator that by completion it will become a negotiable instrument."

A blank paper bearing only a signature cannot later be completed for the purpose of creating negotiable paper. However, a person signing a blank form and delivering the same, cannot meet the burden of establishing that such form signed by him in blank was completed improperly as to amount when it is accompanied by other documents relevant to the same transactions.[11]

When the completion of an incomplete instrument is unauthorized, such completion is treated as a material alteration. (U.C.C. 3-407) Lack of authority to complete may be shown against a holder, but a holder in due course, or a holder through a holder in due course, will take free from the defense of nondelivery of an incomplete instrument. Under the NIL nondelivery of an incomplete instrument was a real defense which could be asserted even against a holder in due course.[12]

It is recommended that incomplete instruments be issued only on rare occasions. If commercial convenience dictates such issuance, caution requires that authority for completion be set forth in writing at the time of signing. Such written evidence will overcome the problem of whether the completion was authorized or unauthorized.

4-23. Instruments payable to two or more persons. The Code resolves the problems which arise when two or more persons are named as payees. When it is necessary to make an instrument payable to the order of any one of several payees, such are called *alternative payees;* thus "payable to the order of *A* or *B* or *C*" means pay to any of the three. However, when it is intended to make the instrument payable to *A* and

[11] Century Appliance Company v. Groff, page 484.
[12] Newark Trust Co. v. Herr, page 486.

B and *C* together, such instrument is payable to a *unit* or *joint payees.* An instrument payable in the alternative designates the payee with reasonable certainty, and an endorsement and delivery by any one of the payees passes title. Much difficulty arises when one of the payees dies. Does the survivor or the deceased payee's personal representative succeed to the deceased payee's interest? The question here is not one of negotiability or who is holder, but who is the owner of the paper. To assure the right of survivorship, the relationship should be spelled out thus: "pay to *A* or *B* or the survivor."

An instrument payable to the order of joint payees can be negotiated only by the indorsement of all of the payees or by the authorization of one to sign for the other.[13] Payment by the obligor to one of the payees will not otherwise discharge the obligation toward the others.

Reference is here made to U.C.C. 3-110 which provides that "an instrument is payable to order, when payable to two or more payees together or in the alternative." The drafter's comment to this section states:

> It eliminates the word "jointly" used in the NIL which has carried a possible implication of a right of survivorship. Normally an instrument payable to "*A*" and "*B*" is intended to be payable to the two parties as tenants in common and there is no survivorship in the absence of express language to that effect.

If an instrument is payable to *A* and/or *B* it is payable to *A* or to *B*, or to *A* and to *B* together, and it may be negotiated, enforced, or discharged by any one payee or by both the payees.

4-24. Instruments payable with words of description. By Section 3-110 of the Code an instrument is payable to order when by its terms it is payable to the order of "an office or an officer by his title as such in which case it is payable to the principal, but the incumbent of the office or his successors may act as if he or they were the holder." Thus, an instrument payable to the "Secretary-Treasurer of *B* Corp." runs to the officer and his successors, and may thereafter be indorsed by them. Section 3-117 goes further; it purports to comply with the commercial usage of limiting the words identifying the payee officer or office to a mere description only and makes the paper payable to the principal. The occupier of the office as an agent is the holder and his function as described payee is limited to the negotiation of the paper.

Thus, the words, "Henry Rose, Treas. of the West Coast Insurance Company," merely describe Henry Rose as Treasurer. The real payee, or party in interest is "The West Coast Insurance Company," the principal.

Care must be used to distinguish between the legal significance of the

[13] Gill Equipment Co. v. Freedman, page 487.

additional descriptive words. The additional words, "Treasurer," "President," "Agent," "Cashier," may merely describe the person acting as agent or officer. The named principal is the payee-owner. However, additional words describing a named payee as a "fiduciary for a specified person or persons" such as "Henry Roe, Executor under the will of Mary Brown" or "John Smith, Trustee of the Ford Trust," are more than descriptive words.

In such cases, the significant person by reason of the law of trusts, trustees, and fiduciaries is the individual named. He is the real party in interest. He has power to negotiate, enforce, or discharge the paper. As a trustee he is liable for breach of trust, but this does not impinge upon his power to negotiate.

It should be noted here that purchasers of paper which discloses on its face a trust situation, are put on notice of the fiduciary position of the payee. Such purchasers may not be holders in due course, thus they are subject to the rights of the beneficiary if the trustee negotiated the instrument in breach of trust and they have notice of such breach.

Where descriptive words such as Henry Roe, "Agent," "Treasurer," "President," or "Executor" do not disclose a principal or beneficiary, the person named is the payee and real party in interest. Such person may negotiate, enforce, or discharge the paper.

4-25. Ambiguous terms and rules of construction. Since negotiable commercial paper passes current as money, it must mean the same thing to different persons at different times and in different places. The language should be clear, distinct, and unambiguous. A holder should feel free to negotiate and takers encouraged to accept. In order to eliminate as much as possible the use of parol evidence in case of doubt or ambiguity, except to reform the paper as created, the rules of the Code are so drafted as to give faith to holders and purchasers that valid negotiable paper has been made and can circulate free from defenses. The rules are:

(a) Where there is doubt whether the instrument is a draft or a note the holder may treat it as either. A draft drawn on the drawer is effective as a note.

(b) Handwritten terms control typewritten and printed terms, and typewritten control printed.

(c) Words control figures except that if the words are ambiguous, figures control.

(d) Unless otherwise specified a provision for interest means interest at the judgment rate at the place of payment from the date of the instrument, or if it is undated from the date of issue.

(e) Unless the instrument otherwise specifies two or more persons who sign as maker, acceptor or drawer or indorser and as a part of the same transaction are jointly and severally liable even though the instrument contains such words as "I promise to pay."[14]

(f) Unless otherwise specified consent to extension authorizes a single extension for not longer than the original period. A consent to extension, expressed in the instrument, is binding on secondary parties and accommodation makers. A holder may not exercise his option to extend an instrument over the objection of a maker or acceptor or other party who in accordance with Section 3-604 tenders full payment when the instrument is due.

A meaning cannot be given the paper which is inconsistent with these rules.

These rules are self-explanatory. However the phrase "extension of time" merits some consideration. In order to retain and continue the liability of primary and secondary parties, co-makers, and indorsers, the following clause is often found in commercial paper, particularly in notes: "The makers, indorsers, and other secondary parties of this note consent that it may be extended without notice to them." Under suretyship law, extension of an obligation by a creditor without the consent of the sureties discharges the sureties. (U.C.C. 3-606) Consent to such extension binds the secondary parties. Only one extension is permitted, and it is limited to a period no longer than that of the original paper. If payment is tendered on the due date and not accepted, no extension can be made and all prior parties are discharged.

4-26. Other writings affecting instrument. Commercial paper as a method of payment often arises out of many types of written collateral contracts. The Code refers to the effect such separate written collateral agreements have on the commercial paper. Separate written agreements may be a conditional sale contract for consumer goods, a contract for the purchase of a house by way of a cash down payment accompanied by a note for the balance secured by a mortgage, or the purchase of heavy industrial machinery. Such contracts are legion and out of them arise promises to pay money.

Notes, drafts, and checks are also contracts. The effect of these contracts on each other under the NIL was confusing and indecisive. The Code attempts to simplify the problem by providing:

(1) As between the obligor and his immediate obligee or any transferee the terms of an instrument may be modified or affected by any other written agreement executed as a part of the same transaction, except that a holder in due course is not affected by any limitation of his rights arising out of the

[14] Roller v. Jaffe, page 489.

separate written agreement if he had no notice of the limitation when he took the instrument.

(2) A separate agreement does not affect the negotiability of an instrument.

The Code gives guidance for the drafting of commercial paper so that written agreements will not control the negotiability of the commercial paper accompanying the separate writing.

The Code clearly states that a separate writing between the original parties may modify or affect the promise, except "that a holder in due course is not affected by any limitation of his rights arising out of such separate written agreement if he had no notice of the limitation when he took the instrument."

The Code assumes the premise that "A separate agreement does not affect negotiability." A separate contract, which states the consideration that gives rise to the instrument, will not of itself affect the commercial paper. Likewise, mere reference to some contract which is part of the total transaction will not affect the paper. As between the immediate parties, the contract and its accompanying note may be one entire agreement to be read together. This does not mean that one is necessarily modified or affected by the other. Thus, security arrangements, title reservations in conditional sale contracts, reference to chattel and real estate mortgages may not affect the paper. On the other hand, the separate instrument may subject the maker of the commercial paper to conditions which make the promise conditional and nonnegotiable (U.C.C. 3-105).

Third persons who are not parties to the agreements are not affected. Thus, a purchaser of a note secured by a conditional sale contract, even with knowledge of such security contract, may be a holder in due course. However, a purchaser with knowledge of any defenses arising out of the separate agreement would not be a holder in due course. (See U.C.C. 3-302 concerning holders in due course.)

4-27. Instruments "payable through" a bank and instruments "payable at" a bank. The Code seeks to clarify the confusion arising by reason of the different authority conferred upon banks in the collection process when the words "payable through a bank" and "payable at a bank" are used.

Countless numbers of checks, drafts, and notes, representing insurance payments, pension checks, dividends, payroll checks, and other types of instruments used to transfer credit are "made payable through" a particular bank. Is the bank by these words ordered to draw the money out of the drawee's account? Is a collecting bank under the responsibility of making proper presentment? The Code provides:

An instrument which states that it is "payable through" a bank or the like designates that bank as a collecting bank to make presentment but does not of itself authorize the bank to pay the instrument.

The words, "payable through," do not make the bank the drawee; they do not authorize or order the bank to pay the instrument out of funds in the account of the drawee, neither do they order or require the bank to take the paper for collection. The bank's agency authority is extremely limited; it is merely a funnel or collecting means by which the paper is to be properly presented to the drawee. An instrument payable "through" a designated bank has been held not to be payable by such bank.

If it is intended that payment should be made by a designated bank through which the instrument passes, clear and appropriate language to that effect should be used.

Different results are obtained when the language used is "payable *at* a bank." Under Section 87 of the NIL "where the instrument is made payable at a bank it is equivalent to an order to the bank to pay the same for the account of the principal debtor thereon." By this language bills and notes payable at a bank had been held to be like postdated checks. Thus, where a note was made payable at a bank, and the holder transmitted the note to the bank for collection and remittance with directions from the maker to charge his account, the maker was discharged and the holder lost if the bank failed before any book entries were made. The nonpayment was due to the negligence of the bank, the holder's agent.

On the other hand, other courts have held that NIL Section 87 did not make a note payable at a bank equivalent to a check; that Section 87 was only intended to settle the difficult question of the bank's right, without specific authority, to pay such an instrument and charge the same to the account of the principal debtor.

The Code provides two alternatives either of which may be adopted by a state:

Alternative A—A note or acceptance which states that it is payable at a bank is the equivalent of a draft drawn on the bank payable when it falls due out of any funds of the maker or acceptor in current account or otherwise available for such payment.

Alternative B—A note or acceptance which states that it is payable at a bank is not of itself an order or authorization to the bank to pay it.

The Code limits the duty of the bank to that of notifying the maker or acceptor that the instrument has been presented and to ask for instructions. Without such instructions the words "payable at Bank *X*" do not require or authorize the bank to pay.

The Code accepts either of two positions, namely, that a note "payable at a bank" *is* like a draft, and upon its due date the bank is authorized, without consultation, to make the payment out of any available funds of the maker; or, such words are *not* an order, but a mere direction to the bank to ask for instructions. Either of these positions may be selected by the state legislature upon the adoption of the Code.

CREATION OF COMMERCIAL PAPER CASES

PARK NATIONAL BANK OF HOLYOKE v. MOTYL

1957, 13 Mass. App. Dec. 67

RILEY, P. J. The plaintiff bank is the holder of a promissory note dated July 31, 1952 signed by the defendants and endorsed to it by the Bell Building Utilities, Inc., the payee of said note.

The evidence shows that the note was executed simultaneously with a conditional sale agreement for the sale of aluminum windows with screens by the Bell Co. to the defendants and that the agreement and the note were on one sheet of paper, the note being separated from the agreement by a perforation so that the note could be detached from the agreement and that the note was detached for the purpose of this suit although the agreement was assigned to the plaintiff on July 31, 1952 at the time the note was endorsed to it. The printed form of the note and conditional sale agreement were furnished to the Bell Company by the plaintiff. The agreement contained the following words at the top in large type,

THE PARK NATIONAL BANK OF HOLYOKE
HOLYOKE, MASSACHUSETTS
CONDITIONAL SALE CONTRACT

Directly beneath this title were the words,

> Contract made . . . between the undersigned Buyer, . . . and the undersigned Seller, . . . which term shall be deemed to include any assignee of Seller's interest.

In the agreement was also the following provision:

> Buyer agrees to pay to Seller or order at the office of THE PARK NATIONAL BANK OF HOLYOKE the Balance Due (Item 6) in 30 consecutive monthly installments of $17.00

The following words were also contained in the conditional sale contract:

> A Promissory Note was executed by the Buyer in connection with this Contract setting forth the Balance Due and was given as evidence thereof and not as payment therefor.

The printed form of the note also contained this provision:

> Payable at THE PARK NATIONAL BANK OF HOLYOKE, Holyoke, Mass.

There was evidence that the Bell Company installed the storm windows in the defendants' home late in October, 1952; that the first installment on the note became due on February 1, 1953 and was not paid; that on March 10, 1953 the plaintiff wrote the defendants a letter demanding payment; that the defendants refused payment because the storm windows were not satisfactory and did not fully serve the purpose for which they were sold; that the plaintiff acknowledged it had received a complaint from the defendants and that it would bring it to the attention of the Bell Company and that the storm windows were defective. The defendants testified that they voluntarily signed the conditional sale contract and the note attached thereto but did not read the contents of either; that they did not receive a copy of the conditional sale agreement and the plaintiff admitted it was its general practice to accept the entire agreement, the conditional sale contract and the attached note and that it knew the note contained on its face the following writing:

If paid on or before February 1, 1953 Bell Building Utilities will pay interest charges.

The defendants, in addition to a general denial, denied that the plaintiff was a holder in due course and a bona fide purchaser of the note for value before its maturity and say that the note was executed and delivered through the fraudulent representations of the plaintiff or its agent; that the note was not negotiable; that there was a failure of consideration for said note; that the plaintiff or its agent failed through negligence to comply with the provisions of Section 13 of Chapter 255 of the General Laws in not furnishing the defendants a copy of the conditional sale contract and that the plaintiff or its agent warranted the goods to be free from all defects but that said goods were defective and not merchantable.

It appears from the evidence that the contract was negotiated by a salesman of the Bell Building Utilities, Inc. and that this salesman and a Mr. Attridge of the Bell Company secured the signatures of the defendants to the sale contract and note; that during the course of the transaction various questions pertaining to the male defendant's finances were asked of him and his answers were written down on the back of the sale agreement upon a blank thereon entitled "Credit Application" which appeared above the assignment of the contract and which assignment had printed in it *as assignee* the name of the plaintiff in large type. There is no evidence that any of the agents of the plaintiff had anything to do with the sale of the personal property or in the negotiations which culminated in the execution of the note and sale agreement.

The trial judge found for the plaintiff and, among others, made the following findings of fact:

I find that the defendants signed the conditional sales contract and the attached note and that they knew the contents of both; that the note was then detached from the conditional sales contract and the conditional sales contract was then delivered to the plaintiff for the sole purpose of allowing the plaintiff to make a credit investigation from information contained on the back of the conditional sales contract.

I find as a fact that when the plaintiff discounted the note on August 7, 1952, it had no knowledge, direct or indirect, that the storm windows were in any way defective, I find that the note was complete and regular on its face and was negotiated before maturity and before any installment payment was due. I find upon all the facts that the instrument declared upon was a negotiable promissory note and that the plaintff was a holder in due course and for value. Upon all the evidence I find that in the transaction between the plaintiff and the seller of the storm windows, Bell Building Utilities, Inc., that there was no relation of principal and agent and that there was no evidence of any conspiracy between them to defraud the defendants. I also find that when the plaintiff discounted the note it had no knowledge that the storm windows had not been installed.

It was a question of fact for the judge to determine whether the plaintiff had proven the elements necessary to entitle it to recover in this action. In many aspects it resembles the case of *Commercial Credit Co. v. M. McDonough Co.*, 238 Mass. 73. His findings of fact show that his denial of the defendants' requests and his granting of the plaintiff's requests were not made as rulings of law but as findings of fact. We cannot say that these findings of fact were not permissible upon the evidence. . . .

Judgment for plaintiff affirmed.

UNITED STATES v. FARRINGTON
1959, 172 F. Supp. 797

The maker, Davis Aircraft Engineering, Inc., executed two notes to a bank as payee. On the face of the printed-form notes there appeared in ink a statement that collateral securities had been deposited to secure the obligation and that "this note evidences a borrowing made under and is *subject to* the terms of loan agreement dated January 3, 1952, between the undersigned and the payee thereof. . . ." On the back of the notes were the signatures of Davis, one Atkinson and the defendant, Farrington. The loan agreement called for a revolving credit arrangement for the benefit of Davis Aircraft and provided that all borrowings are to be personally indorsed or guaranteed by Davis, Atkinson, and Farrington. This was signed by Davis and Atkinson but not by Farrington. The notes were restrictively indorsed to the plaintiff. The defendant claims that he did not know the nature of the instruments which he signed and that he was told that it was a mere formality to satisfy the bank that the company's stockholders knew "what was transpiring." Davis Aircraft is now in bankruptcy.

ALDRICH, D. J. . . . If these notes were negotiable there is no defense; the defendant is liable as an endorser. Mass. G.L. c. 107, Sections 39(6), 52, 86, 87.* He contends that they were not negotiable because making the obligation subject to the terms of the loan agreement caused it to lack "certainty." Mass. G.L. c. 107, Section 23(2), provides that for an instrument to be negotiable it "Must . . . contain an unconditional promise or order to pay a sum certain in money." Defendant does not and cannot point to anything in the loan agreement which would have, in fact, imposed any contingency upon the obligation had the terms of the loan agreement been included on the face of the note itself. Cf. *City Nat. Bank v. Adams*, 266 Mass. 239, 165 N.E. 470. His position is that as a matter of law an instrument is conditional if it incorporates by reference a separate document making it imposible to know whether the obligation is certain or not until that document is examined. The Massachusetts cases upon which defendant relies, with the possible exception of *Costelo v. Crowell*, 127 Mass. 293, all involved separate agreements that in fact imposed contingencies when read into the instrument. Whether the instrument becomes nonnegotiable because on its face it is subject to an agreement which may impose contingencies even though it in actual fact does not, is quite a different matter, leading to policy questions of large compass. Although this precise question is often left undiscussed by the cases, see *National Bank of Newbury v. Wentworth*, 218 Mass. 30, 105 N.E. 626, there is a considerable body of authority to the effect that if the instrument contains the phrase, "subject to" the terms of another document, or words to that effect, the reference is fatal to negotiability regardless of the actual provisions of the other document** (cases cited).

This principle has apparently been modified in some jurisdictions, particularly with regard to corporate bonds, to the extent of permitting the incorporation of terms of a mortgage or deed of trust designed to secure the obligation of the primary instrument. In such cases it is said that making the note or bond subject to the provisions of what is clearly an agreement regarding collateral security in no way "restricts, or burdens with conditions, the absolute promise to pay" contained in the instrument (cases cited). But see *Brannan, Negotiable Instruments Law* 256–259 (7th Ed., Beutel 1948), criticizing many of the cases upholding negotiability and stating that the "cases on the point are now in hopeless confusion." Id. at 257. See also the Uniform Commercial Code, Mass. G.L. c. 106, comparing Section 3-105(1)(e) with Section 3-105(2)(a), and Massachusetts Commercial Code and Uniform Commercial Code Comments thereon.

In the case at bar it could be argued from the placement of the handwritten words that the note was described as subject to the loan agreement for the purpose of indicating the circumstances under which it was executed, and setting forth more fully the undertaking with respect to collateral security, and not in order to limit the promise to pay. However, I believe this is not the only and necessary interpretation, and that the ambiguity can be resolved only by examination of the loan agreement. It is true that inspection of this agreement will resolve the ambiguity in favor of the plaintiff, but I rule that that is not enough to make the instrument negotiable.

If the instrument is not negotiable because of the reference to the loan agreement, neither is it a promissory note within the meaning of the law merchant. Therefore the defendant cannot be held liable as a co-maker under a line of Massachusetts cases antedating the Negotiable Instruments Law. See *Gloucester Mutual Fishing Ins. Co. v. Boyer*, 294 Mass. 35, 38, 200 N.E. 557. But under the Boyer case he will be liable as a guarantor of the corporation's promise. . . .

It is not open to the defendant to claim that he was defrauded by Davis. As against an innocent third party, either the payee or the plaintiff, he must be ruled to have acted too negligently to permit him to use such fraud as a shield. The defendant admitted that he knew that loans to the Company were being arranged, that he "probably did know" that the instruments he was signing were notes, and that he was being asked to indicate his knowledge as a stockholder of "what was transpiring." He must be charged with knowledge that his signature had all the appearance of being an endorsement or subjecting him to liability in some manner, or at the least was capable of being so construed. (cases cited) . . . It would be expected for the bank to assume a knowledge of the loan agreement on his part as it was an integrated part of the transaction with which he understood the bank wanted him to be acquainted. Since at the least the loan agreement resolves an ambiguity for which defendant must be charged, I rule under the circumstances that he is liable on the instrument even though it is not negotiable.

The amounts due have been stipulated.

Judgment is ordered for plaintiff in the amount of $350,683.35. . . .

[The case was decided under the NIL, but the Court included the following footnotes with reference to the U.C.C.:

* All the provisions of the Negotiable Instruments Law cited in this opinion have been repealed, effective October 1, 1958, by the enactment of the Uniform Commercial Code, Acts 1957, c. 765, Sections 2, 21, M.G.L.A. c. 106 following Section 9-507; c. 106 Section 1-101 et seq., 3-402, 3-415. They remain of course applicable as the law of this case.

** Such would also seem to be the meaning of the Uniform Commercial Code, Mass. G.L. c. 106, Section 3-105(2) (a). See Massachusetts Commercial Code Comment (appearing in M.G.L.A.) and particularly the Uniform Commercial Code Comment No. 8, stating that "an instrument is not negotiable unless the holder can ascertain all of its essential terms from its face."]

NATIONAL DEPOSIT BANK OF OWENSBORO v. OHIO OIL CO.
1933, 250 Ky. 288, 62 S.W.2d 1048

On July 18, 1928, the National Deposit Bank of Owensboro cashed the following check, which was indorsed by the payee, C. A. Libs, and placed the proceeds to his credit:

Marshall, Ill. July 18, 1928 No. 112

The Dulaney National Bank 70–559

Pay to the order of C. A. Libs $9,200.00 Nine Thousand Two Hundred Dollars *Agent's disbursing account.*

Roy F. Keown

Roy F. Keown was an agent of the Ohio Oil Co. and had been authorized to draw checks on the account of the Ohio Oil Co. On July 26, 1928, the plaintiff received notice from the Dulaney National Bank (drawee) that the defendant (Ohio Oil Co.) had stopped payment on the check. In the meantime Libs had drawn against his account. The defendant contended that it was not liable because Keown's agency had been revoked and that the check was drawn against "Agent's disbursing account," which was a particular fund. From a judgment in favor of the plaintiff, defendant appealed.

CLAY, J. . . . It is insisted that the check was not negotiable because it was drawn upon a particular fund. One of the requirements of a negotiable instrument is that it must contain an unconditional promise or order to pay a sum certain in money. Section 3720b-1, Kentucky Statutes. When an order or promise to pay is unconditional or not unconditional is determined by Section 3720b-3, Kentucky Statutes, which reads as follows:

> An unqualified order or promise to pay is unconditional within the meaning of this Act, though coupled with it:
> (1) An indication of a particular fund, out of which reimbursement is to be made, or a particular account to be debited with the amount; or
> (2) A statement of the transaction which gives rise to the instrument.
> But an order or promise to pay out of a particular fund is not unconditional.

The check is not an order or promise to pay out of a particular fund. It imports absolute liability, and merely indicates a particular account to be debited with the amount. We are therefore constrained to the view that it is a negotiable instrument.

Judgment in favor of plaintiff bank affirmed.

[This case was decided under the NIL.]

GRAMATAN NATIONAL BANK & TRUST CO. OF BRONXVILLE v. MONTGOMERY
1961. (Mass.) 177 N.E.2d 577

WILKINS, C. J. . . . The defendants in this action of contract to recover upon a promissory note were defaulted when the case was called for trial. Later at a hearing for the assessment of damages the defendants' counsel made the limited contention that the plaintiff was not entitled to attorney's fees. The judge denied the defendants' requests for rulings, and found for the plaintiff for the amount due on the note with interest and attorney's fees. The defendants excepted.

Reasonable attorney's fees may be recovered on an overdue note which so provides. *Leventhal v. Krinsky,* 325 Mass. 336, 341, 90 N.E.2d 545, 17 A.L.R.2d 281. See G.L. (Ter. Ed.) c. 107, Section 24;* 17 A.L.R.2d 288. The underlying question is whether the note in the case at bar contains such a provision.

The note, dated November 26, 1954, is for the amount of $2,663.40 payable in sixty monthly installments "with interest from maturity at the highest lawful rate. If any installment of this note is not paid when due the entire unpaid amount hereof shall immediately become due and payable, and if permitted by law, undersigned jointly and severally authorize any attorney at law to appear in any court of record in the United States for undersigned, and confess judgment for such amount as may appear to be unpaid hereon at maturity, together with interest and attorney's fees, in favor of the holder hereof. . . ."

There has been no confession of judgment. Indeed such a stipulation in a note or contract is prohibited by statute in this Commonwealth. G.L. (Ter. Ed.) c. 231, Section 13A. See *McDade v. Moynihan,* 330 Mass. 437, 441–442, 115 N.E.2d 372, 39 A.L.R.2d 1223. The provision for attorney's fees appears only in the part of the note authorizing the confession of judgment. The item of attorney's fees should not have been allowed, and the defendants' requests should have been granted.

Exceptions sustained . . .

[The case was decided under the NIL. The following footnote appears in the opinion:

* For notes delivered beginning October 1, 1958, see Uniform Commercial Code, G.L. c. 106, Section 3-106(e), inserted by St. 1957, c. 765, Sections 1, 21.]

LIBERTY ALUMINUM PRODUCTS COMPANY v. JOHN CORTIS ET UX.
1958 (Pa.) 38 Wash. 223, 14 D. & C.2d 624.

CUMMINS, J. On January 16, 1957, the Liberty Aluminum Products Company, creditor, caused the Prothonotary of Washington County, Pennsylvania, to enter a note in the face amount of $3,400.00, executed by John Cortis and Julia Cortis, his wife. Defendants moved to strike the judgment and assigned as reasons the facts: (1) the note did not contain a schedule of installments; (2) set out no date of maturity; and (3) no default of payment was alleged at or prior to the entry of the said judgment.

The defendants' motion to strike is based primarily on two alleged deficiencies, to wit: The lack of a maturity date or installments and the failure to show a default prior to the entry of judgment.

The Act of February 24, 1906, 12 P.S. 739, specifically authorizes the Prothonotary to enter judgment without declaration or affidavit of default and for this reason it is submitted that the entry of judgment without declaration was proper.

The first alleged deficiency is the one which must be explored a little further. The defendants' motion to strike completely overlooks the Uniform Commercial Code (Act of April 6, 1953, P.L. 3; 12 (A) P.S. 3–108). This Code states categorically that "instruments payable on demand include those payable at sight or on presentation and *those in which no time for payment is stated*" (italics added)—that under the Commercial Code this instrument is a demand note by virtue of its tenor.

Even if this were not so, the logic of the situation compels this conclusion. The parties have the right to use a blank and tailor it to their needs. And the failure to include installment payments simply and clearly means that none were intended.

The next question relates to the demand or default necessary prior to the entry of judgment on a demand note. The answer to that is simple: None. The entry of the note itself is sufficient demand for payment: *Haydt v. Kohler*, 11 Lehigh 150.

It has always been clear as a matter of fact that a note payable on demand may be entered *without* default and even before the note becomes due. *Chubb v. Kelly*, 80 Pa. Super. 487; *Salas v. Curzon*, 73 Pa. Super. 170.

In addition to this, the inference of the lack of payment is possible from the possession of the note by the judgment creditor. *Drey v. Nevling*, 106 Pa. Super. 42.

It is perfectly proper to enter a judgment on a demand note at any time and no demand other than the entry of the note is necessary as a prerequisite of the judgment.

The argument can be made that there is question as to the amount of the judgment. This is answered for us by *National Finance Company v. Hickman*, 62 York 13, which states that the Prothonotary may enter judgment for the face of the amount due and that the defendant is free to show any credits to which he is entitled at or before execution.

It is our opinion that the motion to strike the judgment should be denied for the reason that it must be decided solely on the face of the record, as is indicated by the cases and the statutes cited above. The face of the record will support the judgment.

CASSIANO v. BELLINO

1959, 338 Mass. 765, 157 N.E.2d 409

The plaintiff is the indorsee of a note executed by the defendants. The note contained a clause providing that if the principal or interest were in default for 30 days, the entire balance would become immediately due and payable at the option of the holder. The plaintiff in notifying the defendants by letter of the transfer requested payment of interest then due. No payment was made and two months later plaintiff brought suit. The defendants argued that after default the principal was not due without a demand for payment of the accelerated amount. The lower court ruled for the plaintiff, indorsee-holder.

WILKINS, C. J. . . . The acceleration clause is valid. *A-Z Servicenter, Inc. v. Segall*, 334 Mass. 672, 676, 138 N.E.2d 266. The note was negotiable notwithstanding that clause. G. L. c. 107, Section 24. *Star Brewing Co. v. Higgins*, 248 Mass. 480, 481, 143 N.E. 332. To enforce a note payable on demand, the bringing of suit is in itself a sufficient demand (cases cited).

As we said as to the institution of another type of suit, "A more definite and insistent form of 'written demand' could hardly be imagined." *Standard Oil Co. of New York v. Y-D Supplies Co.*, 288 Mass. 453, 455, 193 N.E. 66, 67.

The defendants also argue that after default the principal was not due without a demand for payment of the accelerated amount. They point out that the plaintiff's letter asked only for the payment of interest. This point is of first impression in this Commonwealth. The views of other courts are divided. The only citation made by the defendants is *Parker v. Mazur*, Tex. Civ. App., 13 S.W.2d 174, which is representative of the judicially declared law of Texas that in the circumstances general equitable principles require presentment and demand for payment of the accelerated amount. See *Griffin v. Reilly*, Tex. Civ. App., 275 S.W. 242; *Ross v. Isaacs*, Tex. Civ. App., 54 S.W.2d 182, 186; *Faulk v. Futch*, 147 Tex. 253, 257, 214 S.W.2d 614, 5 A.L.R.2d 963. Another case holding that demand upon the maker is necessary to accelerate the payment of the entire debt is *Berkowitz v. Kasparewicz*, 121 Conn. 140, 146, 183 A. 693, 104 A.L.R. 1326.

To the contrary and to the effect that a demand for the full amount, or notice of an intention to exercise the option to collect it, is not a condition precedent to bringing suit, are cases in many jurisdictions. Some are of long standing. (Cases cited).

The interpretation of the acceleration clause is governed by the law of contracts and was not covered by the negotiable instruments law, which was in effect at the time of the transaction. See *Shapiro v. Weber*, supra, 220 App. Div. 667, 669, 222 N.Y.S. 421. In the existing state of the authorities, we have a free choice of the rule which, to our thinking, is better suited to negotiable instruments and commercial practice. Ours is now the decision whether the signer of a note containing an acceleration clause upon default optional with the holder is, after default, entitled to a special notice, as a condition precedent to suit, that the holder has elected to avail himself of the benefits of that clause. A maker must be held to know what he signed. We do not favor placing this unnecessary burden upon the recovery of the loan. We are aware of no policy in this Commonwealth which would handicap the enforcement of a contract, freely made, for the repayment of cash borrowed. We are not informed of any reason why the defendants should be given the advantage of the defense asserted. It cannot be denied that before suit presentment for payment and demand for the full amount of the note would have precluded this deference. Such presentment and demand could have preceded service of the writ by the briefest period of time.

Order dismissing report affirmed.

[This case was decided under the NIL.]

ATLAS CREDIT CORP. v. LEONARD

1957, Court of Common Pleas of Lancaster County, Pa. 15 D. & C.2d. 292
56 Lanc. Rev. 57

JOHNSTONE, J. On July 5, 1956, judgment was entered in the office of the prothonotary in favor of plaintiff and against defendants in the sum of $3,510.08. This judgment was entered on the warrant of attorney contained in a note dated July 2, 1956, given by defendants to National Home Developers, Inc. The note, which was payable one day after date, was assigned to plaintiff on July 2, 1956, according to a stipulation filed by counsel for all parties.

Defendants presented their petition to this court praying that the judgment be opened and they be allowed to enter a defense. The petition recites that defendants entered into a written contract with the National Home Developers, Inc., on June 26, 1956, under which National agreed to furnish the labor and materials necessary to cover completely the exterior walls of defendants' dwelling with aluminum siding. Defendants executed the note in question in blank and the note was subsequently completed in its present form. This note was delivered by defendants in payment of the labor and materials called for in the contract. It is further averred by defendants that National did not do the work called for in the contract in a workmanlike manner and never completed the contract in accordance with its terms. In order to remedy the inferior workmanship of National, it will be necessary for defendants to remove all of the siding installed by National and replace it with new materials at a cost of $3,500. Defendants further aver that the note in question is not a negotiable instrument and that any defense which they have against National is available to them against plaintiff.

A petition to open a confessed judgment is addressed to the equitable ear of the court, and on appeal the only question to be considered is whether the court abused its discretion in granting or refusing the petition: *Kuntz v. Landbar Hotel Co., Inc.*, 380 Pa. 90. However, the court has no discretionary power to open a judgment where the petition does not set forth facts which are sufficient at law to sustain a verdict in favor of petitioners: *Shinn v. Stemler*, 158 Pa. Superior Ct. 350. From the facts averred in defendants' petition to open the judgment in this case, it is obvious that a good legal defense has been stated, which would sustain a verdict in favor of defendants, provided that defense can be made against plaintiff. This defense is only available to defendants if plaintiff in this action is not a holder in due course of the note upon which judgment was entered. If plaintiff is a holder in due course, the defense averred by defendants is not available to them since they had no dealings with plaintiff and they have not averred facts which would bring them within the exceptions set forth in Section 3-305 of the Uniform Commercial Code of April 6, 1953, P. L. 3, 12A PS Section 3-305.

An examination of the note in question discloses that it is dated July 2, 1956, and is payable one day after date. The confession of judgment incorporated in the note authorized the prothonotary or any attorney of any court of record of Pennsylvania, or elsewhere, to appear and enter judgment against the signers of the note, without any limitation as to the time when the confessed judgment may be entered. Under Section 3-112(1) (d) the negotiability of an instrument is not affected by a term authorizing a confession of judgment on the instrument if it is not paid when due. However, Section 3-104(1) (b) of the code provides that any writing to be a negotiable instrument must contain an unconditional promise or order to pay a sum certain in money and no other promise, order, obligation or power except as is authorized by the code. The note in question does include the power to confess judgment, and that power is not limited to a confession of judgment if the note is not paid when due. The negotiability of the note was destroyed by the addition of the power to confess judgment at any time: *Miners State Bank v. Aukszto-kalnis,* 283 Pa. 18; *Shinn v. Stemler,* supra; *Burger v. Freedom Township,* 13 D. & C. 539. This was the uniform holding of our appellate courts under the Negotiable Instruments Law, 56 PS Section 7 (a)) and the Uniform Commercial Code, while worded slightly differently, has the same meaning: 12A PS Section 3-112(1) (d).

Since the note in question has been determined to be nonnegotiable, plaintiff is not a holder in due course and takes the note subject to any defense available to defendants against the original payee. It having been determined that defendants have stated a good defense which would support a verdict in their favor, the judgment should be opened and defendants allowed into a defense.

. . . *Defendants' petition is granted.* . . .

SUN OIL CO. v. REDD AUTO SALES, INC.

1959 (Mass.) 159 N.E.2d 111

The plaintiff was the supplier of gasoline and oil to a filling station operated by one Lawrence Mulkern. The defendant was engaged in a "used car business" next door to the filling station. The reported evidence indicated that it was a practice that whenever the plaintiff made a delivery of gas and oil to Mulkern, the latter would go next door and obtain from Romeo Aiello, the president and treasurer of defendant, a corporation check signed by Aiello, but left blank as to date, amount, and payee. Mulkern would then fill in and deliver the check to plaintiff's driver in payment. Mulkern would later reimburse the defendant in the amount of the check. (Other facts are set forth in the opinion.)

RONAN, J. . . . Mulkern's purchases from the plaintiff were on the consignment system, payment for a shipment being made at the next following delivery. On October 22, 1956, a delivery was made to Mulkern, and payment was made in the usual way, with a corporation check signed in blank by Aiello and completed by Mulkern. The amount of this check, however, was eventually paid to the plaintiff by Mulkern. On October 29, 1956, the plaintiff ceased operating with Mulkern under the consignment system and made one last delivery to him.

The plaintiff's assistant credit manager, one Grant, spoke to Mulkern and demanded payment for the gasoline and oil delivered that day and for the dishonored check of October 22 and the protest fee. Mulkern went to Aiello and obtained a signed corporation check, blank as to date, amount, and payee. In Grant's presence he completed the check for $1,180.71 (for the delivery that day and for the dishonored check plus charges). He made it payable to the Sun Oil Company, as requested by Grant. When Grant received the check, it was complete. When it appeared later that Mulkern was unable to reimburse the defendant, Aiello caused payment on the check to be stopped.

At the time of the instant transaction G.L. c. 107 (the Negotiable Instruments Law) was the applicable statute. The defendant, as an accommodation party, was liable under Section 52 of c. 107* to a holder in due course despite the holder's knowledge at the time of his taking the instrument that the maker was only an accommodation party (cases cited). It is clear that the plaintiff was a holder in due course. See G.L. c. 107, Section 75.** A payee may be a holder in due course, *Leonard v. Woodward,* 305 Mass. 332, 334–335, 25 N.E.2d 705, 127 A.L.R. 999; *Johnson v. Favazza,* 325 Mass. 627, 629, 91 N.E.2d 780, and this is so even though the instrument was incomplete when signed by the maker. *Russel v. Bond & Goodwin, Inc.,* 276 Mass. 458, 463, 177 N.E. 627. Here the instrument was complete when delivered by Mulkern to Grant. The fact that it was completed in his presence is unimportant. Mulkern had actual authority to complete the instrument, as Aiello himself testified. And see G.L. c. 107, Section 36.***

The only substantial issue is whether the delivery of the check was an ultra vires act for which the defendant corporation cannot be held. It has been said that "our cases . . . make a distinction between the exercise by a corporation of powers manifestly outside the general authority granted by its charter, and the exercise of powers which, although of the sort which in general the corporation possesses, have been abused in the particular case. In the latter case if the abuse of corporate authority is unknown to the party dealing with the corporation the defence of ultra vires is not available." *Wiley & Foss, Inc. v. Saxony Theatres, Inc.,* 335, Mass. 257, 261, 139 N.E.2d 400, 402. The giving of accommodation paper may be within the express chartered powers of a trading corporation, *Bennett v. Corporation Finance Co., Inc.,* 258 Mass. 306, 154 N.E. 835, or reasonably related to the purposes for which the business was incorporated. *American Surety Co. of New York v. 14 Canal St., Inc.,* 276 Mass. 119, 125, 176 N.E. 785. *Wasserman v. National Gypsum Co.,* 335 Mass. 240, 139 N.E.2d 410. Whether the defendant's acts were within its corporate purposes was a question of fact. In the instant case the judge impliedly found that the practice was not ultra vires. We are not disposed to upset that finding. The reported evidence on the point is meager, and while it may be that the issuance of accommodation paper was beyond the corporate power of this defendant, we cannot assume such to be a fact from the mere assertion that it was engaged in the "used car" business. What evidence there was indicated that relations between the defendant and Mulkern were on a commercial as well as a friendly basis. Mulkern testified that he would recommend business to the defendant; that the defendant was permitted to park some of its automobiles at Mulkern's station; that Mulkern "sold gas to the defendant at a discount and that the defendant owed him about seventy . . . dollars." On the present record we cannot say that the act was "manifestly outside" the defendant's powers.

There is no allegation that the defendant was insolvent or threatened with insolvency at the time, or that the rights of creditors were affected (cases cited). . . .

Order dismissing report affirmed. . . .

[The court included the following footnotes. The case was decided under the NIL.

* See now G.L. c. 106, Section 3-415 (1,2) Uniform Commercial Code, St. 1957, c. 765).

** See now G.L. c. 106, Section 3-302.

*** See now G.L. c. 106, Section 3-112(1) and Section 3-407(3).]

CENTURY APPLIANCE COMPANY v. GROFF

1958, (Pa.) Court of Common Pleas of Lancaster County, 56 Lanc. Rev. 67

The defendant executed an installment note which contained a confession of judgment clause and was payable to the order of the Fulton National Bank. The note was given for the purchase of a soft water system from the Century Appliance Company. The bank indorsed the note to the plaintiff who obtained a judgment thereon. The defendant seeks to open the judgment and contends that he had been told that the amount of the installation would not exceed $350; that the note was blank as to amount at the time he signed it; and that it was not until after the judgment was confessed that he learned that the real debt was $538.55.

WISSLER, P. J. . . . The deposition consisted of the testimony of defendant and plaintiff and one witness for plaintiff. Defendant testified, inter alia, as follows: ". . . (Q) Did you at any time prior to the installation of this water softener sign a judgment note? (A) Not prior. (Q) After the system was installed did you sign a note? (A) Yes. (Q) Do you know how long after did you sign? (A) A few days later. (Q) What was on the note? (A) The note was blank. He said he would have the Fulton Bank fill it out; he did not have the right amount as he did not know what the costs were going to be. (Q) Did he say it would exceed $350.00? (A) He said it would not. (Q) Was there any writing on the note before you signed it? (A) No. (Q) When did you first find out that the amount of the job was $538.55? (A) Some time later he called by phone. (Q) Did Mr. Lehman ever furnish you with an itemized bill for this job? (A) No. (Q) Did you ask him for one? (A) Yes, several times. (Q) When he told you the bill was $538.55, what did you tell him? (A) That was not what the agreement was. (Q) Mr. Groff, do you know whether this note was ever discounted at the bank? (A) Clifford was taking it to the Fulton Bank. I had to call at the bank at a later date."

. . . Clifford C. Lehman testified, inter alia, as follows: "(Q) Your name? (A) Clifford C. Lehman. (Q) You are the owner of Century Appliance Company? (A) President. (Q) Will you tell us why this note was signed by Mr. Groff in blank? (A) The job was completed and I inspected the job. Mr. Groff was satisfied. The amount of the credit asked for was on the upper left hand of the application, written in. Mr. Groff agreed with this and then signed the note which he duly returned to the Fulton Bank. (Q) The note was blank when you had Mr. Groff sign? (A) That is correct. (Q) He knew it? (A) That is correct. (Q) Did you tell him why he had to sign it in blank? (A) That is correct. Due to the interest charges and insurance charges I did not know the amount, and the bank would fill them in which they duly did. He was notified by the bank as the amount of the note would be. (Q) The night that the note was signed was that the night the job was finished? (A) Not to the best of my knowledge. It was several nights after the job was finished. . . ."

The gravamen of the defendant's contention is that he signed the note in blank; that the whole amount would not exceed $350.00; and that the job was unsatisfactory.

As to the contention of signing the note in blank, the Uniform Commercial Code of April 6, 1953, P.L. 3, 12A PS 3-115, provides as to incomplete instruments as follows: "(1) When a paper whose contents at the time of signing show that it is intended to become an instrument is signed while still incomplete in any necessary respect it cannot be enforced until completed, but when it is completed in accordance with authority given it is effective as completed; (2) if the completion is unauthorized the rules as to material alterations apply (Section 3-407) even though the paper was not delivered by the maker or drawer; but the burden of establishing that any completion is unauthorized is on the party so asserting." Section 1-201, paragraph 8 of the Uniform Commercial Code, supra. "Burden of establishing" a fact means the burden of persuading the triers of fact that the existence of the fact is more probable than its nonexistence.

The work for which the note was given was completed February 26, 1957. On the same date defendant signed an application for a property improvement loan to be made by the Fulton National Bank of Lancaster, Pennsylvania, and the amount of credit sought was $500.00, which amount was written in the upper left part of the application and approved by the defendant. Defendant then on February 27, 1957, signed the note in question in blank which was later filled in by the Fulton National Bank in the amount of $538.55 after it had ascertained the correct amount of the loan, including interest and insurance charges. Defendant also signed a Borrower's Completion Certificate whereby he certified that all articles and materials had been furnished and installed and the work satisfactorily completed on premises indicated in his application to the Fulton National Bank. It is not denied by defendant that in March, 1957, the Fulton National Bank sent him a Payment Coupon Book which indicated the amount of the note as being $538.55 and which he returned to the bank with a memorandum stating that Clifford C. Lehman would take care of this. All of this clearly indicates that the note in question was completed in accordance with authority given and that the defendant has not met the burden of establishing that the completion of the note was unauthorized. . . .

The rule to show cause why judgment should not be opened . . . is discharged.

NEWARK TRUST CO. v. HERR
1954, (Pa.) 54 Pa. Lanc. L.R. 31

The defendants executed a note to Jim Miller and Company for the installation of storm windows. The note contained certain blanks which were filled in by Miller. The note was indorsed to plaintiff. The defendants resist payment on the ground that the storm windows were defective.

Wissler, J. . . . The gravamen of the defendants' contention is that the note in question was signed in blank by the defendants upon the representation of an agent of Jim Miller and Company that the paper which they were signing was an order blank for eleven aluminum combination storm windows and screens and two combination aluminum doors for a cash price, the total order being $446.00, and that plaintiff is not a holder in due course because of Section 15 of the Uniform Negotiable Instrument Act which provides as to an incomplete instrument not delivered, as follows: "Where an incomplete instrument has not been delivered it will not, if completed and negotiated, without authority, be a valid contract in the hands of any holder, as against any person whose signature was placed thereon before delivery." It is obvious that this section relates only to cases where there has been no delivery of the instrument by the person signing, as is further evidenced by the following Section 16 in reference to delivery, when effectual, and when presumed: "Every contract on a negotiable instrument is incomplete and revocable until delivery of the instrument for the purpose of giving effect thereto. As between immediate parties, and as regards a remote party other than a holder in due course, the delivery, in order to be effectual, must be made either by or under the authority of the party making, drawing, accepting, or indorsing, as the case may be; and in such case the delivery may be shown to have been conditional, or for a special purpose only, and not for the purpose of transferring the property in the instrument. But where the instrument is in the hands of a holder in due course, a valid delivery thereof by all parties prior to him so as to make them liable to him is conclusively presumed. And where the instrument is no longer in the possession of a party whose signature appears thereon, a valid and intentional delivery by him is presumed until the contrary is proved."

This section has been held by the Delaware courts to mean that conditional delivery may be shown as between the immediate parties and as against persons not holders in due course: *Wilmington Trust Co., et al. v. Morgan,* 92 Atl. 988, 5 Boyce, Del., 261.

It is true that by Section 14 of the Uniform Negotiable Instruments Act, Volume 5 of Uniform Laws Annotated, any incomplete instrument must be filled up strictly in accordance with the authority given and within a reasonable time, but this same section also provides that if any such instrument, after completion, is negotiated to a holder in due course, it is valid and effectual for all purposes in his hands, and he may enforce it as if it had been filled up strictly in accordance with the authority given and within a reasonable time.

The difficulty with defendants' position is that all the acts of infirmity alleged in the petition to open the judgment existed between the immediate parties to the note and not between the parties and the plaintiff as a holder in due course, and as there is no allegation that plaintiff had notice of any infirmities at the time it was negotiated to it, the defendants cannot avail themselves of such alleged infirmities as against the plaintiff as a holder in due course.

The rule to show cause why the judgment should not be opened and defendants let into a defense is discharged. . . .

[This case was decided under the NIL.]

GILL EQUIPMENT CO. v. FREEDMAN

1959, 339 Mass. 303, 158 N.E.2d 863

The defendant was attempting to sell a large, used, diesel-operated, 50-ton shovel for one Forte. He met with Gill, the president of plaintiff, a company engaged in selling new and used construction equipment. Gill decided to buy and signed a contract which he gave to the defendant along with a check for $15,000 as part payment, payable to Forte. Payment was stopped on the check when Forte reported he had lost it, and another check was issued. It was then learned that Forte had found the check and cashed it and that the shovel was encumbered by a previous conditional sale agreement. Another $15,000 check was drawn, this time to Forte *and* the defendant. The check was indorsed by both and cashed, Forte retaining all of the money. Ultimately, it developed that Forte could not give clear title to the shovel as he had previously sold it to another party. Plaintiff now sought to recover the money represented by the check from the defendant. The lower Court ruled for the plaintiff and defendant took exceptions.

Cutter, J. . . . At the close of the arguments the defendant requested rulings (1) that there was no evidence that the defendant ever received any proceeds of the January 30 check, and (2) that in the absence of such evidence the judge must find for the defendant. Both of these requests were denied. . . .

The judge's ultimate finding for the plaintiff must stand if there was evidence to warrant such a finding and if by his action on requests for rulings he correctly instructed himself as to the applicable law. Upon this record, he could find that the defendant was acting here as a broker or agent of Forte, the purported owner of the shovel; that the defendant may have represented himself as owner initially; and that he had effected a contract between the plaintiff and Forte, who claimed to be the owner, or at least to have an interest in the shovel sufficient to authorize him to sell it. The judge would also have been warranted in finding, or in inferring from the facts which he could have found, (1) that there had been confusion with respect to two deposit checks given to Forte, including the purported loss and later cashing of the first check by Forte; (2) that there had been belated revelation or discovery of the outstanding conditional sale agreement; (3) that, following these events, Cragun, the plaintiff's lawyer, and Gill, its president, undertook to give Forte and the defendant a new deposit check without getting title to the shovel; (4) that this was done to enable Forte and the defendant to go through with the transaction; and (5) that the defendant in substance agreed to assume responsibility for supervising the proper application of the check to expedite and complete the transaction, from which the defendant expected to get a commission.

The check was payable to both the defendant *and* Forte. A receipt for the check was required in behalf of both of them. The indorsement of both of them was necessary to cash the check or otherwise to transfer it.

See G.L. C. 107, Section 64 (recently repealed by St. 1957, c. 765, Section 2, and, under Section 1, supplanted by G.L. c. 106, Section 3-116); D.C. Code (1940 Ed.) Section 28-312. See also cases cited in annotations to Section 41 in Beutel's *Brannan, Negotiable Instruments Law* (7th Ed.) 631–634. Once the check was delivered to the defendant, the defendant had complete control of the check and could control the expenditure of the proceeds. Cragun's testimony would warrant the inference that the check in effect was impressed with a trust or fiduciary obligations requiring the defendant to see to its application to discharge liens and encumbrances on the shovel to the extent that there were any.

It is argued that receipt of the check without more under these circumstances does not warrant a finding that the defendant appropriated the check to his own use, and that without such a finding . . . the plaintiff cannot recover. If Cragun's testimony be believed, the receipt of the check payable to the defendant and Forte jointly had been made a joint act upon which the defendant had assumed "personal responsibility." (Cases cited.) The effect of this, in a matter in which the defendant had a financial stake at least for a commission, was to make any use of the check or its proceeds use by and for the benefit of the defendant, so far as the plaintiff was concerned. The transaction with respect to the shovel never was carried out and the consideration for the check failed. Neither the check uncashed nor $10,000 of its proceeds were restored to the plaintiff. The defendant cannot be heard, in the face of his receipt and of his indorsement of the check, to say that he did not receive the benefit of it and of the proceeds as contemplated by his explicit arrangement with Cragun. See *Atzinger v. Atzinger*, 325 Mich. 78, 84, 37 N.W.2d 764. A finding was warranted that the receipt and indorsement by the defendant of the check, later cashed, was for his benefit and upon his responsibility. . . .

Exceptions overruled. . . .

[This case was decided under the NIL.]

ROLLER v. JAFFE

1957, 387 Pa. 501, 128 A.2d 355

The defendants, husband and wife, executed a note for $10,000. The note read: ". . . after date *I* promise to pay to the order of Caroline Roller." Mrs. Jaffe, one of the defendants, contends that she never received any consideration for the note and that no consideration was ever intended to pass from the plaintiff to her. She contends that she signed only for the accommodation of her husband. The lower count entered an order denying the plaintiffs motion for judgment on the pleadings.

BELL, J. . . . Plaintiff filed a motion for judgment on the pleadings which was overruled by the lower Court. The lower Court based its action on two grounds: (1) the pleadings raised factual questions requiring a jury trial, and (2) the wife-defendant's plea of want of consideration raised an adequate defense to a suit of an unsealed note. We do not agree with this conclusion; the plea of want of consideration was not a legal defense to the note.

The general rule is that when two or more persons execute a promissory note, they are jointly and severally liable. Negotiable Instruments Law of May 16, 1901, P.L. 194, Ch. 1, Art. I, Section 17, 56 P.S. Section 22;* Uniform Commercial Code of April 6, 1953, P.L. 3, Section 3-118; 12A P.S. Section 3-118(e); *Heffner v. First National Bank*, 311 Pa. 29, 32, 166 A. 370, 87 A.L.R. 610.

Chapter 1, Art. II, Section 29 of the Negotiable Instruments Law of 1901, supra, 56 P.S. Section 67, provides with respect to an accommodation maker: "Such a person is liable on the instrument to a holder for value, notwithstanding such a holder at the time of taking the instrument knew him to be only an accommodation party." In *Delaware County Trust, Safe Deposit & Title Ins. Co. v. Haser*, 199 Pa. 17, at page 25, 48 A. 694, at page 696, this Court stated:

> It may now be considered as well settled in this state that one who signs a note as maker, though he does it merely for the accommodation for the payee or the indorser, thereby places himself in the situation of a principal and will not be allowed to escape the consequences of his action by subsequently alleging that he was but a surety. . . . The relation created by the maker is that of principal debtor, and his rights and liabilities are the same whether the accommodation is for the payee in the note or for the third person. The liability of the maker does not depend upon the person for whose accommodation the note is made, but upon the situation in which the maker has placed himself by assuming the position of a principal debtor. . . .

On the question of interest, defendants' position is equally untenable. The note clearly specifies that it is payable "with interest." Unless the note provides otherwise, interest is due on a promissory note, not from the due date, but from the date of execution. Section 17 (2) of the Negotiable Instruments Law of 1901, supra, provides:

> 2. Where the instrument provides for the payment of interest, without specifying the date from which interest is to run, the interest runs from the date of the instrument, and if the instrument is undated from the issue thereof.**

Order reversed. The record is remanded to the lower Court with directions to enter judgment on the pleadings in favor of the plaintiff and against the defendants in the sum of $8,955.98 with interest from April 30, 1954. . . .

[The Court in two footnotes to the opinion stated:

* The Negotiable Instruments Law of 1901, although repealed by the Uniform Commercial Code, 12A P.S. Section 1-101 et seq., is applicable in the case at bar since the note was executed prior to the enactment of the Uniform Commercial Code. This provision we note was re-enacted in the Code.

** The Code has a similar provision: Uniform Commercial Code of April 6, 1953, P.L. 3, Section 3-118 (d) 12A P.S. 3-118 (d).]

Review Questions and Problems

1. The three major stockholders of *X* Corporation signed their names on the back of a note executed by the Corporation under the phrase, "waiving demand and notice." The note contained reference to a loan agreement with the payee. The corporation defaulted on the note and *H*, the holder, seeks to impose liability on the stockholders. Should *H* succeed?
2. A note contained a provision: "This note is given to take up the freight and rehandling of N.P. car 43607, and proceeds from resale of said car shall apply on this note." Is this note negotiable?
3. *M* entered into a conditional sale agreement in connection with a purchase of goods from *P*. *P* supplied the printed form of agreement which contained a detachable note. The note was signed by *M* with the understanding that it was given merely as evidence of the balance due and not as payment. *P* indorsed the detached note to the bank. *P* defaulted on the sale contract. Can the bank hold *M*?
4. *M* entered into a contract to purchase 25 typewriters from *P* and executed a note payable to *P*'s order for the purchase price. The contract provided that the typewriters were to be delivered at the end of the month. The note contained a clause, "This note is given for payment as per contract for the purchase of goods of even date, maturity being in conformity with the terms of such contract." *P* indorsed the note to *A*. When *A* attempted to collect on the note *M* refused to pay on the ground that the typewriters were defective. Must *M* pay?
5. *M*, a stockholder, indorsed a note of *X* Corporation, prior to delivery of the note to the payee. The note stated that it was "subject to" the terms of a loan agreement. The loan agreement did not contain any terms which impair negotiability. *X* Corporation became bankrupt. The note was indorsed to *H* for value. Can *M* assert the defense that the Corporation had failed to live up to its agreement with him which furnished the consideration for his indorsement?
6. *M* executed a demand note which provided for 6 per cent interest. Is this note negotiable?
7. *M* purchased an automobile from *P*. *P* was willing to sell for $900 cash or $1000 on a time purchase. *M* executed a $1000 note payable in six months with a provision that if the entire amount of $900 were paid within three months the note would be discharged. *P* indorsed the note to *H*. *H* sues on the note at maturity and *M* defends on the ground that the car was defective. What result?

8. *A* of Seattle, Washington, drew a draft on *B* of Vancouver, B. C., payable in Seattle for 100 Canadian dollars. Is this draft negotiable?
9. *M* executed a note payable to the order of *P* on a printed form which contained blank spaces to be filled in, setting forth a schedule of installment payments. These spaces were left blank. No maturity date was specified. Three days after delivery of the note *P* indorsed to *H* who made a demand for payment the next day. *M* refused to pay and contended that he had been defrauded by *P*. Should *H* be allowed to recover from *M*?
10. *M* executed a note payable to the order of *P*. The note provided that it was payable "one year after the end of the war." Is the note negotiable?
11. A draft provided: "Pay to Albert Prince $250 on return of this instrument properly indorsed." Prince indorsed to Harold Boyd for value. Boyd sought to recover from the maker who alleged a defense. Should Boyd prevail?
12. A note was drawn payable to the "Cuban Consulate." Ricardo, the Consul at the time of the issue of the note, was recalled to Havana and replaced by Ken Kennedy. Can Kennedy negotiate the note?
13. An instrument was drawn "Payabe to Sam Sampson on return of this instrument properly indorsed." Sam indorsed to Ralph, who presented the note to the maker for payment. The maker refused to pay and alleged a defense good against Sampson. Is Ralph subject to this defense?
14. An instrument is drawn "Pay to the order of cash." Is it negotiable? How could it be negotiated?
15. S Furniture Co. agreed to install wall-to-wall carpeting in *P*'s house and also to pay off *P*'s debts and add the amount to the bill for the carpet. The amount of the note was left blank. *P* contends that S Furniture Co. inserted an amount in excess of that owed. Can *P* have a confessed judgment on the note set aside?
16. A check was drawn payable to "Smith and/or Jones or order." Smith cashed the check at the bank after indorsing his name only. Smith then departed with the money and Jones seeks recovery from the bank. Should he succeed? What would your answer be if the check were payable to "Smith and Jones."
17. *M* executed an undated note payable to the order of *P* "with interest." How much, if any, interest is *P* entitled to receive?
18. A note and mortgage were executed at the same time and the note provided that it was given "as per" a mortgage of even date. May the note be negotiable?
19. *X* Corporation issued dividend checks "payable through the First National Bank." What is the function of the bank? Would it make a difference if the instrument were a note "payable at the First National Bank"?

22

Transfer and Negotiation

4-28. In general. As noted in Section 4-4 of this book, the rights which a person has in an instrument may be transferred to another by "negotiation" or "assignment." Transfer is an encompassing word which means the process by which the owner of property delivers it to another intending thereby to pass his rights in it to the other.[1] The Code provides that "The transfer of an instrument vests in the transferee such rights as the transferor has therein . . ." (U.C.C. 3-201). Negotiation is defined in Section 3-202 as a specific type of transfer which is in such form that the transferee becomes a "holder." The importance of determining whether the transfer is a negotiation lies in the fact that this is determinative of whether the transferee is a holder. A "holder" is a person who is in possession of an instrument "drawn, issued, or indorsed to him or to his order or to bearer or in blank."

A person must first qualify as a holder before he can be a holder in due course. A holder in due course, as noted in the next chapter, occupies a preferred status and must satisfy other requirements in addition to being a holder. Thus, the distinction between negotiation and assignment is a significant one under the Code as it was under the NIL.

Since a transferee obtains the rights of a transferor, a person who derives his title through a holder in due course has the same rights as a holder in due course. This is often referred to as the "shelter provision." This is subject, however, to the limitation that a person who formerly held the paper cannot improve his position by later reacquiring it from a holder in due course. If a former holder was himself a party to any fraud or illegality affecting the instrument, or if he had notice of a defense or claim against it as a prior holder, he cannot claim the rights of a holder in due course by taking from a later holder in due course. This continues the NIL philosophy that though a holder in due course should have a free market for his paper, one who was a party to any fraud or who had notice of a claim or defense against an instrument should not be allowed to improve his status by repurchasing from a later holder in due course. A person should not be allowed "to wash the paper clean by passing it into the hands of a holder in due course and then repurchasing it" (U.C.C. Comment Section 3-201). The following examples are given to

[1] In re Hackenbroch's Estate, page 502.

illustrate this Section: (1) *P* fraudulently induces *M* to execute a note payable to the order of *P*. *P* indorses to *A* who takes in good faith and otherwise satisfies the requirements of a holder in due course. *A* indorses to *H* who has notice of the fraud but did not participate in it. *H* obtains the rights of *A* and cuts off the defense of fraud. (2) *P* indorses to *A* who has notice of the fraud. *A* negotiates it to *B* who takes without notice of the fraud and is a holder in due course. *A* repurchases the note from *B*. *A* remains subject to *M*'s defense of fraud and does not acquire *B*'s rights as a holder in due course.

A transfer may be made of a security interest in an instrument. In such event the transferee acquires the rights of the transferor in the limited interest given. This provision in the Code follows the NIL provision in this regard.

It sometimes happens that an order instrument, or one which is specially indorsed, is transferred without indorsement.[2] Thus a purchaser may pay for an instrument in advance of the time when it is delivered to him and the seller either inadvertently or fraudulently may fail to indorse the paper. Of course, an indorsement would be necessary for negotiation. If the transferee has given value for the instrument, and if there was no contrary agreement between the parties, the transferee has a specifically enforceable right to an indorsement. However, the negotiation is not effective until the indorsement is given. The transferee is not a holder and cannot qualify as a holder in due course if he receives notice of a defense or claim prior to such indorsement. The Code follows the NIL in this connection and makes it clear that until the indorsement is given the transferee is not entitled to the presumption that he is the owner. This means that he must establish his right to the unindorsed paper by proof of the transaction by which he acquired it.

4-29. Negotiation. There are two methods of negotiating an instrument so that the transferee will become a holder. If the instrument is payable to order, it is negotiated by indorsement and delivery. If it is payable to bearer, it is negotiated by delivery alone which means that a thief or finder can negotiate this bearer paper. The Code follows the NIL with regard to the basic concepts of negotiation but clarifies certain situations in which there were conflicting decisions under the NIL.

The indorsement in the case of order paper must be written on the instrument itself or on a paper so firmly affixed to it as to become a part thereof. Such paper is called an *allonge*. The indorsement must be made by the holder or by some one who has the authority to do so on behalf of the holder.

The indorsement must be for the entire amount of the instrument. A

[2] Colozzi v. Bevko, Inc., page 502.

cannot indorse to *B* $50 out of a $100 check; he must indorse the whole amount to *B* or it is not a negotiation. If it is not for the entire amount, such transfer is effective only as a partial assignment. The rights of a partial assignee are to be determined under local law. An indorsement "Pay *A* one-third and *B* two-thirds" is not effective as a negotiation and neither *A* nor *B* are holders. However, an indorsement to "*A* and *B*" is effective. The only instance in which a negotiation of a part interest can be made is when such part interest is the entire remaining unpaid balance of the instrument. In case part of an instrument has been paid, it can be indorsed as to the *residue.*

Sometimes an indorser will add words to his indorsement such as "I hereby assign all my right, title, and interest in the within note." Some decisions under the NIL held that such language created an assignment and not an indorsement. The Code rejects these decisions on the theory that such language was not intended to have a limiting effect. Section 3-202 (4) of the Code provides: "Words of assignment, condition, waiver, guaranty, limitation or disclaimer of liability, and the like accompanying an indorsement do not affect its character as an indorsement." Thus, if an indorser adds the words "I guarantee payment" to his indorsement, he is nevertheless negotiating the instrument.

A special provision of the Code (Section 3-203) takes care of the situation in which the name of the payee is misspelled. The payee may negotiate by indorsing either in the name appearing on the instrument or in his true name, or both. A person who pays the instrument or gives value for it may require that both names be indorsed. The desirable practice is to indorse in both names.

NEGOTIATION BY INDORSEMENT

4-30. Kinds of indorsement. The NIL provided that an indorsement could be either special or in blank and that it could also be restrictive, qualified, or conditional. The Code provides specifically for special and blank indorsements and restrictive indorsements. Conditional indorsements are included under the heading of restrictive indorsements. Recognition of the qualified indorsement "without recourse" is found in the chapter of the Code dealing with the liability of parties. (See Section 4-58.)

4-31. Blank indorsement. A blank indorsement consists of the indorser's name written on the instrument, or the paper firmly affixed thereto for that purpose, and is a form of indorsement commonly used.

It does not specify any particular indorsee. If an instrument has been drawn payable to order and is indorsed in blank, it becomes payable to bearer and may be negotiated by delivery, without indorsement. However, if such instrument is thereafter indorsed specially, it reverts to its status as order paper and the indorsement is required for further negotiation. The blank indorsement thus changes order paper to bearer paper when it is the only or last indorsement. For example, a check on its face payable to "Henry Smith or order," if indorsed "Henry Smith," carries a blank indorsement. By this indorsement and delivery, Henry Smith relinquishes all rights to the instrument even though he has not directed payment to any particular person. Consequently, as long as it is bearer paper, it can be negotiated by mere delivery and a thief or finder could by such delivery pass title to the instrument. On the other hand, if the person to whom Henry Smith had indorsed the paper in blank had himself indorsed it specially, a further indorsement would be required for negotiation.

The NIL, like the Code, provided that a blank indorsement of order paper made the paper payable to bearer. However, there were conflicting decisions under the NIL as to whether an order instrument once indorsed in blank continued to be bearer paper even though subsequently specially indorsed. The Code clarifies this by expressly providing that a later special indorsement controls.

4-32. Special indorsement. The Code provides in Section 3-204 (1): "A special indorsement specifies the person to whom or to whose order it makes the instrument payable. Any instrument specially indorsed becomes payable to the order of the special indorsee and may be further negotiated only by his indorsement." Thus an indorsement "Pay to Henry Smith" or "Pay to the order of Henry Smith" is a special indorsement and requires the further indorsement by Henry Smith for negotiation.

As noted in Section 4-31, a blank indorsement of order payable makes it payable to bearer. Under the NIL a special indorsement of paper, which was *on its face* payable to bearer, did not affect its status as bearer paper. The Code has reversed this rule of the NIL and provides that the special indorsement of a bearer instrument requires further indorsement by the indorsee. The underlying philosophy of this provision is that the special indorser is the owner of the paper and, even though the paper on its face is payable to bearer, the owner has the right to require the indorsement of his indorsee as evidence of the satisfaction of his own obligation.

The Code continues the rule of the NIL that the holder of an instrument may convert a blank indorsement into a special indorsement by writing above the blank indorser's signature "any contract consistent with the character of the indorsement." Thus, Richard Roe, to whom an instrument has been indorsed in blank by John Doe, could write above Doe's signature "Pay to Richard Roe." The paper would now require Roe's indorsement for further negotiation.

4-33. Restrictive indorsements. A person who indorses an instrument may impose certain restrictions upon his indorsement. This was true under the NIL and the Code continues this concept with certain changes and modifications as to the effect of restrictive indorsements. The Code in Section 3-205 provides: "An indorsement is restrictive which either

(a) is conditional; or

(b) purports to prohibit further transfer of the instrument; or

(c) includes the words "for collection," "for deposit," "pay any bank," or like terms signifying a purpose of deposit or collection; or

(d) otherwise states that it is for the benefit or use of the indorser or other persons."

Under the NIL there was provision for a conditional indorsement. Such an indorsement is not frequently used. An indorser could add to his indorsement a statement such as "Pay to the order of W. J. Robert upon delivery of one Ford car No. 79643 on June 1, 1964." The payor may nevertheless pay the instrument on its due date and receive a discharge even though the condition has not been discharged. However, under the NIL, the conditional indorser did have protection to the extent that the funds received by the holder had to be held for the indorser until the condition had been fulfilled. The Code includes the conditional indorsement within the classification of restrictive indorsements and the law, as it developed under the NIL, has been somewhat changed. The comment to Section 3-206 states: "Contrary to the original Section 39 (of the NIL), Subsection 3 (of the Code) permits a transferee under a conditional indorsement to become a holder in due course free of the conditional indorser's claim." A conditional indorsement does not affect negotiability so a conditional indorsee can qualify as a holder in due course.

The Code has revised the law as it relates to restrictive indorsements. Section 3-206 provides:

(1) No restrictive indorsement prevents further transfer or negotiation of the instrument.

(2) An intermediary bank, or a payor bank which is not the depositary bank, is neither given notice nor otherwise affected by a restrictive indorsement of any person except the bank's immediate transferor or the person presenting for payment.

(3) Except for an intermediary bank, any transferee under an indorsement which is conditional or includes the words "for collection," "for deposit," "pay any bank," or like terms (subparagraphs (a) and (c) of Section 3-205) must pay or apply any value given by him or on the security of the instrument con-

sistently with the indorsement and to the extent that he does so he becomes a holder for value. In addition such transferee is a holder in due course if he otherwise complies with the requirements of Section 3-302 on what constitutes a holder in due course.

(4) The first taker under an indorsement for the benefit of the indorser or another person (subparagraph (d) of Section 3-205) must pay or apply any value given by him for or on the security of the instrument consistently with the indorsement and to the extent that he does so he becomes a holder for value. In addition such taker is a holder in due course if he otherwise complies with the requirements of Section 3-302 on what constitutes a holder in due course. A later holder for value is neither given notice nor otherwise affected by such restrictive indorsement unless he has knowledge that a fiduciary or other person has negotiated the instrument in any transaction for his own benefit or otherwise in breach of duty (Subsection (2) of Section 3-304).

It is to be noted that under the Code a restrictive indorsement does not prevent further negotiation. This changes the law as it existed under the NIL to the extent that a restrictive indorsee or one who takes from him could not be a holder in due course. An indorsement "Pay A only" does not prohibit further negotiation under the Code.

Sections 3-205 and 3-206 of the Code should be considered together. The first two Subsections of 3-206 apply to all four of the types of restrictive indorsements. Subsection (3) applies to conditional indorsements, indorsements for deposit, and indorsements for collection. Trust indorsements are subject to the provisions of subsection (4).

Reference must be made to Article 4—Bank Deposits and Collections—for the definitions relative to banks. A *payor* bank is the bank upon which a check is drawn. An *intermediary bank* is one to which an item is transferred in the course of collection. A *depository* bank is the first bank to which an item is transferred for collection.

Section 3-206 (2) significantly changes the law by providing that intermediary banks and payor banks may disregard any restrictive indorsements except that of the immediate transferor. This provision is justified by virtue of the fact that banks handle a large number of items each day and do not have an opportunity to scrutinize and consider the restrictive indorsement. However, a depository bank and persons who are not involved in the collection process must pay or apply the value given for the instrument consistently with the indorsement.

Subsection 3-206 (3) relates to conditional, deposit, and collection indorsements. The restrictive indorsement must be respected by any transferee other than an intermediary bank. Such transferee must pay or apply any value given by him for the instrument consistently with the indorsement. The most frequent application of this subsection is to instruments which are intended to be lodged in a bank for collection.

Subsection 3-206 (4) establishes a rule similar to the one above, except that the duty to act consistently with the indorsement is limited to the first taker under it. Thus if an instrument is indorsed by *A* "Pay to *B* in trust for *C*" and delivered to *B*, the latter becomes a trustee for *C*. As a trustee *B* is liable to *C* for any breach of his fiduciary obligation. If *B* sells the instrument to *D*, *D* can be a holder in due course. *D* does not have to see that *B* fulfills his duty as a trustee. If *D* had actual notice that *B* was violating his fiduciary obligation, he would not be a holder in due course, but the trust indorsement as such does not put him on notice. A trustee commonly has the power to sell trust assets in transactions which are not related to the bank collection process.

4-34. Rescission of negotiation. The NIL provided that the indorsement of an instrument by a corporation or by an infant was effective to transfer the instrument even though the corporation or infant lacked capacity and might incur no liability.[3] However, the power of an infant to pass the property in the instrument by indorsement does not affect his power to disaffirm his indorsement. Likewise a corporation has only those powers given to it by its charter or such as are necessary and incident to carrying out the purposes for which it was created. A corporation cannot be held for acts done by its officers outside the scope of its corporate powers. Like an infant, a corporation may pass title to negotiable paper even though the transaction was made outside the powers given by the charter. This concept is extended to other situations by Section 3-207 of the Code which provides:

(1) Negotiation is effective to transfer the instrument although the negotiation is
- (a) made by an infant, a corporation exceeding its powers, or any other person without capacity; or
- (b) obtained by fraud, duress, or mistake of any kind; or
- (c) part of an illegal transaction; or
- (d) made in breach of duty.

(2) Except as against a subsequent holder in due course such negotiation is in an appropriate case subject to rescission, the declaration of a constructive trust or any other remedy permitted by law.

By the above provision, when an instrument has been negotiated, the taker is a holder until the instrument has been recovered from his possession. A person who negotiates an instrument gives up all his rights until he recovers it. This Section does not impose liability on the infant or other party negotiating the instrument. He may take advantage of the defenses which are afforded to him by Sections 3-305, 3-306, and 3-307.

4-35. Reacquirer. When an instrument is returned to or reacquired

[3] Snyder v. Town Hill Motors, page 500.

by a person who formerly held the same, such holder is a *reacquirer,* and he may reissue or further negotiate the instrument. He is not, however, entitled to enforce payment against any intervening persons to whom he was liable. Such intervening indorsers are also discharged as to subsequent parties except subsequent holders in due course. A person may reacquire an instrument for the purpose of eliminating the liability of an intervening party and this is usually accomplished by striking out such party's indorsement. If the indorsement is so stricken, that indorser will be discharged even as against a subsequent holder in due course. The Code clarifies the law under the NIL but does not alter the basic concepts regarding reacquirers.

TRANSFER AND NEGOTIATION CASES

SNYDER v. TOWN HILL MOTORS, INC.

1960, 193 Pa. Super. 578, 165 A.2d 293

MONTGOMERY, J. . . . This was an action of assumpsit in which minor appellant sought to recover $1,000.00 from appellees on three theories. . . (c) the right of an infant to rescind the negotiation of an instrument under Section 3-207 of the Uniform Commercial Code of 1953, April 6, P.L. 3 (12A P.S. Section 3-207). The jury returned a verdict for defendants (appellees). . . .

The minor (Snyder) contracted with his friend, Rhea, to purchase the latter's 1955 Chrysler automobile for $1,000 and the trade of his 1946 Pontiac automobile. Thereafter they went to the place of business of the Town Hill Motors, Inc. (hereinafter referred to as Motor Company), where Rhea negotiated with Abbamondi, the Motor Company's salesman, for the purchase of a Lincoln automobile. Thereupon, Rhea instructed Snyder to assign the title of the Pontiac to the Motor Company and to endorse and deliver to it the check for $1,000 made to Snyder's order and in his possession, as the down payment by Rhea on the Lincoln. Snyder intended to use the check in payment for the Chrysler. Snyder complied with Rhea's instructions, delivered the check and title to Abbamondi as agent for the Motor Company, and demanded a receipt from Rhea, who gave it in the following form:

"Received of Richard Snyder one-thousand dollars and 1946 Pontiac coupe in exchange for a 1955 Chrysler Windsor."

Snyder accepted delivery of the Chrysler; but one month or more later he returned it to the Motor Company and, contending that the amount of an encumbrance on the Chrysler was more than Rhea had represented it to be, demanded the return of the Pontiac and $1,000. Having deposited the check and received the proceeds thereof, the Motor Company refused Snyder's demand, Rhea disposed of the Chrysler and applied the proceeds of the sale on the encumbrance. . . .

Appellants' third theory is, likewise, without merit. The rescission of a negotiable instrument by an infant against a subsequent holder in due course is not permitted by Section 3-207 of the Uniform Commercial Code, on which appellant relies. Having received the instrument by negotiation from Rhea for value, in good faith, and without notice that it was overdue or had been dishonored or that there was any defense against it, the Motor Company was a subsequent holder in due course. Section 3-302 of the Code. The jury has found that there were no dealings between Snyder and the appellees.

Appellant's argument that the Motor Company was not a "subsequent" holder in due course is not supported by the evidence. The fact that the check was not manually transferred from Snyder to Rhea and then to the Motor Company would be immaterial under the definition of "delivery" contained in Section 191 of the Negotiable Instruments Law of 1901, Act of May 16, 1901, P.L. 194, 56 P.S., Section 491 et seq., which provides that transfer of possession may be actual or constructive. Although the Uniform Commercial Code repealed the Negotiable Instruments Law, it nevertheless did not prescribe any new definition of the term delivery. We are of the opinion, therefore, that the established definition should prevail. The generally recognized meaning of "delivery" set forth in Corpus Juris Secundum is as follows: "What constitutes delivery depends largely on the intent of the parties. It is not necessary that delivery should be by manual transfer. A constructive delivery is sufficient if made with the intention of transferring the title, and this rule is recognized by the definition of delivery in Negotiable Instruments Act, Section 191 as the transfer of possession, 'actual or constructive.'" 10 C.J.S. Bills and Notes Section 78d.

The facts previously stated show clearly the intention of these parties. Together, Snyder and Rhea took the check to the Motor Company, where it was exhibited and where Rhea exercised dominion over it by directing Snyder to hand it over to the Motor Company. Snyder agreed to this and accepted Rhea's receipt, which acknowledged that Rhea had received the proceeds of the check. This was sufficient to constitute constructive delivery from Snyder to Rhea and "subsequently" from Rhea to the Motor Company.

Orders affirmed. . . .

IN RE HACKENBROCH'S ESTATE

1962, 35 Ill. App.2d 155, 182 N.E.2d 375

Decedent gave his nephew, Lawrence Hackenbroch, a brown package on his birthday and said: "Here, Lawrence, this is yours, this is your gift." After the decedent's death, the administrator of his estate claimed that the contents of the package—negotiable instruments (unindorsed) belonged to the estate. The lower court held in favor of the administrator.

MURPHY, P. J. At the conclusion of the testimony and after an extended discussion of the facts and the law with the attorneys, the court found there was not sufficient evidence to indicate a valid gift, because the evidence was not clear and convincing, and that the assets in controversy belong to the estate of the decedent. . . .

Respondent contends that uncontradicted proof of delivery by donors of unindorsed certificates of stocks and bonds, accompanied by expressions of donative intent, and acceptance by donee, establishes a gift *inter vivos;* that possession of unindorsed certificates of stocks and bonds by respondent is evidence of a gift *inter vivos;* and that in a citation proceeding to recover property from a claimant in possession, the burden is on the administrator to prove title in the estate. We have examined the authorities cited in support of these contentions, but we are not persuaded that their application to the undisputed facts here results in a different conclusion from that of the trial court.

Negotiable instruments can be the subject of a valid gift without endorsement or written assignment by the payee, if delivered to the donee by the payee with intent to transfer the title. The burden of proof of the gift is on the donee to prove all essential facts of a valid gift. The essential facts are the delivery of property by the donor to the donee with intent to pass title, and the proof to sustain the gift must be clear and convincing. Mere possession by one claiming property as a gift, after the death of the owner, is insufficient to prove a valid gift. . . .

Affirmed.

COLOZZI v. BEVKO, INC.

1954, 17 N.J. 194, 110 A.2d 194

The plaintiff, Colozzi, had obtained a judgment against Alrich, O'Hara, and Corson. These proceedings involved execution on the judgment. The property being levied upon was in the hands of Blumberg, a Pennsylvania resident. The property consisted of notes, made by Bevko, Inc., a New Jersey corporation, to defendants, Alrich, O'Hara, and Corson. Blumberg claimed that he had held the notes as collateral security for an indebtedness of the three defendants and that such notes were therefore not subject to execution. The lower court ruled in favor of Blumberg and vacated restraints upon his sale of the notes. (Other facts appear in the opinion.)

BURLING, J. . . . The facts disclosed during reception of evidence on these motions were that Alrich, O'Hara and Corson were principal stockholders of Bevko, Inc., a New Jersey corporation. Bevko, Inc. required financing for a project undertaken by it, and Alrich, O'Hara and Corson obtained the necessary funds from Blumberg. Blumberg, called as a witness by the receiver, testified that on February 25, 1953, at his office in Philadelphia, Pennsylvania, he met with Alrich, O'Hara, and Corson, Sidney Bookbinder, their attorney, and William Schwab, Blumberg's attorney. He testified that the three Bevko, Inc. notes ($20,000 each) were prepared and signed at that meeting, were delivered to him (Blumberg) then and were held by him thereafter. He testified that at the same meeting a written financing contract was entered into between him (Blumberg), Alrich, O'Hara, and Corson. The financing contract was identified and placed in evidence. The gist of the financing contract was that Blumberg agreed to loan $25,000 each to Alrich, O'Hara and Corson; each of the latter was immediately to invest $5,000 in Bevko, Inc. and loan $20,000 to Bevko, Inc., and receive a corporate note therefor. Each was to "give to Blumberg an individual note to be secured by their issued shares (i.e., 25% each), of the said corporation." Paragraph 11 of the agreement provided that in event of liquidation of Bevko, Inc. prior to its fulfillment of contracts (attached to the agreement), the assets should be distributed according to their investment, the investment of each of Alrich, O'Hara and Corson being identified as $5,000. Blumberg testified that Alrich, O'Hara and Corson delivered their individual notes to him on the same day. Mr. Bookbinder, called as a witness by the receiver, testified that the Bevko, Inc. notes were pledged to Blumberg as collateral for the three $25,000 loans. The Bevko, Inc. notes were not indorsed by Alrich, O'Hara and Corson. Mr. Bookbinder testified the individual notes (as distinguished from the Bevko, Inc. notes) were made by Alrich, O'Hara and Corson on February 26, 1953. He predicated the statement upon the date written on the individuals' notes and did not expressly deny the making thereof on February 25, 1953. Each of the individuals' respective $25,000 notes referred to the delivery of Bevko, Inc. stock to Blumberg as collateral security, and these individuals' notes also provided "The Above Collateral Security and any heretofore or which may hereafter" be deposited with Blumberg "and any other property of maker in (Blumberg's) possession, . . . shall stand as one general continuing collateral security . . ." for the individuals' obligations to Blumberg. The receiver asserted that "This being executed in Pennsylvania, Pennsylvania law will control." The receiver introduced evidence of pertinent Pennsylvania law. Blumberg did not object to the introduction of Pennsylvania law into the case, and on this appeal concedes generally its applicability.

The superior Court, Law Division, determined on the evidence that the Bevko, Inc. notes in question had been validly pledged to Blumberg as collateral security. . . .

The final question involved is whether the absence of indorsement of the Bevko, Inc. notes by, respectively, Alrich, O'Hara and Corson, defeats the pledge.

The pertinent Pennsylvania statutory provision expressly negatived the necessity of indorsement. 56 P.S. Section 101 (1901, May 16, P.L. 194, Ch. 1, Art. III, Section 49) provided:

> Where the holder of an instrument, payable to his order, transfers it for value without indorsing it, the transfer vests in the transferee such title as the transferer had therein; and the transferee acquires, in addition, the right to have the indorsement of the transferer; but for the purpose of determining whether the transferee is a holder in due course, the negotiation takes effect as of the time when the indorsement is actually made. . . .

A negotiable note is transferred for "value" when it is transfered to the holder as and for collateral security. (Cases cited.) "Value," under the Pennsylvania negotiable instrument statutes applicable at the time of the transactions involved herein, was defined as "any consideration sufficient to support a simple contract," including an antecedent or pre-existing debt. (Cases cited.) There is little doubt that under Section 25 of the Uniform Negotiable Instruments Law one who has taken a negotiable instrument in payment of or as collateral security for a debt, including a pre-existing debt, is a holder for value. See 45 Mich. L. Rev. 214 et seq. (1947). The Pennsylvania statutes further provided: "Where the holder has a lien on the instrument, arising either from contract or by implication of law, he is deemed a holder for value to the extent of his lien." 56 P.S. Section 64. Cf. R. W. 7:2–27, N.J.S.A. Compare *Blaney v. Mellor Co.*, supra.

We find that under the pertinent principles of Pennsylvania law, hereinbefore discussed, the trial court's determination that there was a valid pledge of the Bevko, Inc. notes in question, without indorsement, by delivery to Blumberg on February 25, 1953, was not erroneous. . . .

[This case was decided under the NIL]

Review Questions and Problems

1. *P* induced *M* by fraudulent representations to execute a note payable to *P*. *P* indorsed the note to *A* who had no notice of the fraud when he first acquired the note but subsequently learned of the fraud and

thereafter indorsed to *B*, a holder in due course. *A* then repurchased the note from *B*. Can *A* enforce the note against *M*?

2. *A* contracted to purchase a note from *P*, the payee. *A* paid in advance for the note with the understanding that *P* would obtain the note from his safety deposit box and deliver it to *A* on the following day. The next day *P* indorsed the note "Pay *A*, without recourse, *P*." What is *A*'s position?
3. *A* borrowed $10,000 from *B* and executed to *B* a note in that amount secured by notes payable to *A* as collateral. *A* did not indorse the pledged notes. Is the pledge valid?
4. *P*, the payee of a note given in payment for a TV set, indorsed it "without recourse" to a bank. The bank sought to recover from *M*, the maker of the note. *M* refused to pay and contended that *P* had never delivered the set. Is this a good defense?
5. The payee of a check indorsed it in blank and delivered it to *A*. *A*, by mistake and believing that the check had been paid, delivered the check to the drawer. Is the payee-indorser discharged of liability?
6. A check was drawn payable to *A* and *B*. It was indorsed by *B*, but *A*'s indorsement was forged. The bank paid the check and *A* seeks to recover from the bank. Should he succeed?
7. *M* made a note payable to the order of *P*. *P* indorsed to *A* by writing his name "*P*" on the back of the note. *A* transferred the note to *B* without indorsement. Is *B* a holder?
8. *H* received a note by blank indorsement. Why might he wish to transform this into a special indorsement? Could he do this if the note were payable to bearer on its face?
9. A check is indorsed "for deposit and collection" with *X* bank. What are the bank's rights and duties with regard to this check?
10. *M*, a minor, purchased a car from a friend and gave a check in payment. The friend indorsed the check and used it in part payment for another car from a dealer. *M* now wishes to rescind and to recover his check from the dealer. Can he do so?

23

Holders and Holders in Due Course

4-36. Who is a holder. A "holder" is defined in general terms by Section 1-201 (20) of the Code to mean "a person who is in possession of a document of title or an instrument or an investment security drawn, issued, or indorsed to him or to his order or to bearer or in blank." The Code following the NIL specifies that one who is the holder of an instrument may transfer or negotiate it and with certain exceptions may discharge it or enforce payment. A person may be a holder even though he does not own the instrument. A person in possession of a negotiable instrument may occupy two very different positions. A holder may be in no better position than the assignee of any simple contract right. That is, he may be subject to any personal defenses that the maker or drawer or other parties prior to him may have against the payee. Again he may be a holder free from such personal defenses where his rights against the primary party are superior to those possessed by the former holder or owner of the instrument. Such a holder is said to be a *holder in due course.* Both the NIL and the Code require that for a holder to occupy such a position he must satisfy very definite requirements.

4-37. Requirements for a holder in due course. Such a holder must have taken the instrument for value and in good faith. In addition he must not have notice that the instrument is overdue, that it has been dishonored, that any other person has a claim against it, or that any other person has a defense to it. If a holder can satisfy all of these requirements, he will be able to qualify as a holder in due course. These basic requirements were contained in the NIL, but are somewhat revised under the Code.

Payee may be a holder in due course. The Code in Section 3-302 (2) expressly provides that a payee of an instrument may be a holder in due course.[1] Under the NIL there was a conflict as to whether a payee could have this status because of the requirement in Section 52 (4) of the NIL, "that at the time it was *negotiated* to him he had no notice of any infirmity in the instrument or defect in the title of the person *negotiating*

[1] Mellen v. Gora, page 519.

it." (Emphasis supplied.) The word "negotiated' has been eliminated by the Code.

Since the payee of an instrument usually deals directly with the primary party, he ordinarily has notice of any defense against it.[2] However, if the payee is able to satisfy the requirements set forth in Section 3-302, he may become a holder in due course in the same fashion as any other holder. There are a variety of situations in which the payee may qualify as a holder in due course.

To illustrate, assume that *M* signs his name to an instrument complete except for the amount, payable to the order of *P*, and directs his agent, *A*, to purchase a certain quantity of merchandise from *P* and pay for the same by filling in the proper amount. The agent, *A*, in violation of this authority, completes the check in a larger sum than authorized, delivers it to *P* complete and regular upon its face, obtains the merchandise, and appropriates the balance. *P* is not immediate to *M* in the transaction and has no knowledge of the unauthorized act of *M*'s agent. *P* has satisfied all of the requirements of a holder in due course in that he has taken the check in good faith, for value, and without notice.

4-38. When a holder does not become a holder in due course. Section 3-302 (3) of the Code provides:

> A holder does not become a holder in due course of an instrument:
> (a) by purchase of it at judicial sale or by taking it under legal process; or
> (b) by acquiring it in taking over an estate; or
> (c) by purchasing it as part of a bulk transaction not in regular course of business of the transferor.

The foregoing is a codification of the law as it stands under existing cases. The person purchasing or acquiring the paper is merely succeeding to the interest of the prior holder and acquires only the rights of such prior holder. However, if the prior holder was a holder in due course the purchaser may acquire that status under Section 3-201 which provides that "Transfer of an instrument vests in the transferee such rights as the transferor had therein. . . ."

Examples of Subsection (a) are purchases at execution sales and bankruptcy sales. Subsection (b) applies to an executor or administrator who takes over the instrument as part of an estate. Subsection (c) is illustrated by the situation in which as a part of a corporate consolidation one corporation takes over all of the assets of the other corporation. In all of these situations the Code recognizes that circumstances do not warrant granting to the holder the status of a holder in due course.

[2] L & N Sales Company v. Stuski, page 520.

Purchaser of a limited interest. Section 3-302 (4) provides that "A purchaser of a limited interest can be a holder in due course only to the extent of the interest purchased." This is similar to the provision in the NIL. The import of this Subsection of the Code is that the purchaser of a limited interest does not have protection as a holder in due course to the full value of the paper. Thus if a negotiable instrument is transferred to a holder by way of a pledge, the pledgee-holder may be a holder in due course, but he takes the instrument free of defenses only to the extent of the debt which is secured by the pledge. The following sections cover the requirements of a holder in due course in greater detail.

4-39. Must take for value. As noted previously, the Code requires that a holder take for value in order to qualify as a holder in due course. The Code continues the requirement of the NIL in this regard and one who receives an instrument as a donee, for example, is thus not a holder for value. Section 3-303 of the Code provides:

> A holder takes the instrument for value
> (a) to the extent that the agreed consideration has been performed or that he acquires a security interest in or a lien on the instrument otherwise than by legal process; or
> (b) when he takes the instrument in payment of or as security for an antecedent claim against any person whether or not the claim is due; or
> (c) when he gives a negotiable instrument for it or makes an irrevocable commitment to a third person.

Under the Code an executory promise to give value does not make the holder a holder for value. Except as qualified in paragraph (c) it is required that the consideration agreed upon by the parties must actually have been given. This requirement clarifies the situation as it existed under the NIL where there was an apparent conflict on this question. If a purchaser has not yet paid value when he becomes aware of a defense to the instrument, he does not have to pay for it but is free to rescind the transaction. Accordingly, there is not the same necessity to give him the standing of a holder in due course, free from claims and defenses, as in the case of a holder who has actually parted with value. A holder who purchases an instrument for less than its face value can be a holder in due course to the full amount of the instrument; but, if the discount is exceedingly large, it may, along with other factors, be evidence of bad faith on the part of the holder.

The provision that a mere promise to pay for negotiable paper does not make one a holder for value is of particular importance in banking transactions. A bank will often give provisional credits to its customers on items which are deposited, pending collection of such items. If the bank learns of defenses to these items before they are collected and before the customer has withdrawn the funds represented by the deposits, the provisional credits will not be regarded as value. The bank will not be free of claims and defenses in connection with the paper so deposited. Of course, if the bank has collected an item and the customer has withdrawn the funds for which provisional credit was given, the bank could qualify as a holder for value.

Both under the Code and under the NIL it becomes necessary to determine the point of time at which the customer has been paid the proceeds of an item left with the bank for collection. The courts have applied different theories in making this determination and in tracing the funds against which payment has been made. In many cases the courts in determining whether the item arising from the deposited paper has been drawn upon, apply the "first in, first out" theory. Under this theory the earliest credits are deemed to have been absorbed by the earliest debits. The Code does not spell out the tracing rules which are to be applied, and it would appear that the common law on this subject is still applicable.

The Code retains the NIL rule that a holder who takes an instrument in payment of an antecedent claim is a holder for value. The same is true of a holder who takes the instrument as security for an antecedent debt. Thus if *A* owed *B* $500 on a past due account and transferred a negotiable instrument to *B* in payment of such account or as security for its payment, *B* would qualify as a holder for value. In this regard it is to be noted that "value" is not synonymous with consideration. Consideration is significant in determining whether an obligation can be enforced against a party (Section 3-408 of the Code) whereas value is relevant on the question of the qualification of a holder as a holder in due course.

As noted above a mere promise to pay for negotiable paper does not make one a holder for value. If the promise to pay is negotiable in form, however, the purchaser immediately becomes a holder for value. For example, a drawer who issues his check in payment for a negotiable note becomes a holder for value even before his check is cashed. The reason for this rule is that there is a possibility that the check or other negotiable instrument might be negotiated to a holder in due course in which event the party giving it could not refuse to pay. By the same token an irrevocable commitment to a third person would leave the holder no alternative but to live up to his commitment. In these circumstances the holder has placed himself in a position where he could be required to perform and is thus in much the same position as a person who has actually paid.

4-40. Must be a taker in good faith and without notice. In order that a person may qualify as a holder in due course he must have taken the instrument in good faith.[3] This was a requirement under the NIL and is continued under the Code. The Code has combined and reworded provisions of the NIL and has added specific provisions for the purpose of removing some uncertainties in the existing law.

In the Code definition of a holder in due course, it is specified not only that the holder must have taken in good faith but also that he must have taken:

1. Without notice that the instrument is overdue.
2. Without notice that it has been dishonored.
3. Without notice of any defense against the instrument.[4]
4. Without notice of any claim against it.

If a person has notice of any of the foregoing, he would not be a holder in due course.[5] The Code defines notice in Section 1-201 in part as follows: "A person has notice of a fact when (a) he has actual knowledge of it; or (b) he has received a notice or notification of it; or (c) from all the facts and circumstances known to him at the time in question he has reason to know that it exists."[6]

Notice of claim or defense. The NIL included in the definition of a holder in due course a requirement that a holder must have taken an instrument complete and regular on its face. The Code handles this requirement somewhat differently by including in Section 3-304 (1) a provision: "The purchaser has notice of a claim or defense if (a) the instrument is so incomplete, bears such visible evidence of forgery or alteration, or is otherwise so irregular as to call into question its validity, terms, or ownership or to create an ambiguity as to the party to pay." Thus this requirement is related to the good faith provision of the Code rather than as a separate component in the definition of a holder in due course. Contrary to the NIL a purchaser who buys incomplete paper or takes paper with knowledge that it has subsequently been completed can qualify as a holder in due course unless the circumstances are such as to arouse suspicion which would require him to make an investigation.[7]

Also, the Code provides in Section 3-304 (1) (b) that notice of a claim or defense is given if "the purchaser has notice that the obligation of any party is voidable in whole or in part, or that all parties have been discharged." The comment to this Subsection states, that the "voidable" obligation does not refer to a set-off or counterclaim but is limited to a situation in which a party has the right to avoid his original obligation on

[3] Budget Charge Accounts v. Mullaney, page 521.
[4] Fidelity Trust Co. v. Gardener, page 522.
[5] Potter Bank & Trust Co. v. Henneforth, page 523.
[6] Elbar Realty Inc. v. City Bank & Trust Co., page 525.
[7] First National Bank of Philadelphia v. Anderson, page 527.

the instrument. Notice that one party has been discharged is not notice of any lack in the obligation of the remaining parties.

"The purchaser has notice of a claim against the instrument when he has knowledge that a fiduciary has negotiated the instrument in payment of or as security for his own debt or in any transaction for his own benefit or otherwise in breach of duty." (U.C.C. 3-304 (2)) Thus, if a trustee negotiates a trust instrument in payment of his own personal debt, this would give notice of misappropriation of the funds. However, the mere fact that a purchaser has knowledge of the fiduciary relation would not in itself prevent him from being a holder in due course. One is entitled to assume that the fiduciary acted properly in the absence of the circumstances set forth in the above section.

Notice that an instrument is overdue. A holder in due course must be a holder who has purchased the paper before it is due. The law presumes that every person under a duty will perform on the date that performance is due, and, if such person fails to perform—that is, fails to pay the instrument—it is presumed that he has some defense or valid reason for not performing. Consequently, a purchaser of overdue paper would be charged with knowledge that some defense may exist. Where an instrument is payable on a fixed date, any purchaser thereafter would not be a holder in due course.

Where the instrument is due upon a fixed date, but subject to an early maturity by reason of an accelerating clause, the instrument would not be overdue until the option to mature the paper had been exercised by the holder. Under the Code, if an acceleration of the instrument has been made, the purchaser with notice of such fact is a purchaser of overdue paper. A notice that acceleration of the instrument has been made is notice that an instrument is overdue. However, a purchaser may take accelerated paper as a holder in due course if he takes without notice of the acceleration.

If the instrument is payable on demand, it is said to be overdue an unreasonable length of time after issue. The Code provides that a purchaser has notice that an instrument is overdue if he has reason to know "that he is taking a demand instrument after demand has been made or more than a reasonable length of time after its issue." (U.C.C. 3-304 (3) (c)) Thus under the Code a purchaser may take, as a holder in due course, a demand instrument on which a demand has actually been made if he takes without notice that the demand has been made. What is a reasonable or an unreasonable time is determined by a consideration of the nature of the instrument, the usage of the trade or business, and all of the circumstances and facts involved in each case. With regard to a check, however, the Code provides: "A reasonable time for a check drawn and payable within the states and territories of the United States and the District of Columbia is presumed to be thirty days." (U.C.C. 3-304 (3) (c)) "Presumption" or "presumed" as these expressions are used in the Code mean that "the trier of fact must find the existence of the fact presumed unless and until evidence is introduced which would support a finding of its nonexistence." (U.C.C. 1-201 (31)) The thirty day presumption in the case of a check was not included in the NIL.

If an instrument is payable in installments it may be transferred at a time when one or more of the installments is past due. There was some uncertainty under the NIL as to the status of one who took paper when an installment was overdue. The Code resolves this uncertainty by providing that a purchaser who has reason to know of an overdue installment or other part of the principal amount has notice that the instrument is overdue and therefore could not be a holder in due course. Past due interest, on the other hand, does not impart notice of any defect in the instrument. It is recognized that interest payments are frequently in arrears.

Factors which do not impart notice of defense or claim. Section 3-304 (4) sets forth a number of situations in which knowledge of certain facts does *not* of itself give the purchaser notice of a defense or claim.

Knowledge that an instrument is antedated or postdated does not prevent a holder from taking in due course. Some prior decisions had held to the contrary.

Subsection (b) provides that notice of a defense or claim is not imparted by virtue of knowledge "that it was issued or negotiated in return for an executory promise or accompanied by a separate agreement unless the purchaser has notice that a defense or claim has arisen from the terms thereof." The import of the Subsection is that while mere notice that there is an executory promise or separate agreement will not deprive one of holder-in-due-course status, if he has notice of a default in connection therewith which raises a defense or claim against the instrument, he is on notice to the same degree as would be furnished by any other information.

Knowledge that an incomplete instrument has been completed does not give notice of a defense or claim. However, if the purchaser has notice that the completion was improper, he cannot be a holder in due course.

As noted previously, knowledge that the person negotiating is a fiduciary and knowledge "that there has been default in payment of interest on the instrument or in payment of any other instrument except one of the same series" (U.C.C. 3-304 (4) (f)) does not impart to a purchaser notice of a defense or claim.

Miscellaneous. The final provisions of Section 3-304 provide:

(5) The filing or recording of a document does not of itself constitute notice

within the provisions of this Article to a person who would otherwise be a holder in due course.

(6) To be effective notice must be received at such time and in such manner as to give a reasonable opportunity to act on it.

Both of these Subsections are new. Subsection (5) clarifies the law under the NIL by providing that filing or recording does not impart constructive notice to a holder. Subsection (6) is explained in the comment to the Code as follows: "It means that notice must be received with a sufficient margin of time to afford a reasonable opportunity to act on it, and that a notice received by the president of a bank one minute before the bank's teller cashes a check is not effective to prevent the bank from becoming a holder in due course."

4-41. Rights of a holder in due course. The holder in due course occupies an exalted position as described in Section 3-305 of the Code. This Section applies not only to one who is himself a holder in due course but also applies to a transferee who acquires the rights of a holder in due course.

The holder in due course takes the instrument "free from (1) all *claims* to it on the part of any person." (Emphasis added.) This broad language encompasses freedom from both legal and equitable claims.

Likewise, Section 3-305 (2) of the Code provides that to the extent that a holder is a holder in due course he takes the instrument free from:

(2) all *defenses* of any party to the instrument with whom the holder has not dealt except (emphasis added)

(a) infancy, to the extent that it is a defense to a simple contract; and
(b) such other incapacity, or duress, or illegality of the transaction, as renders the obligation of the party a nullity; and
(c) such misrepresentation as has induced the party to sign the instrument with neither knowledge nor reasonable opportunity to obtain knowledge of its character or its essential terms;[8] and
(d) discharge in insolvency proceedings; and
(e) any other discharge of which the holder has notice when he takes the instrument.

The term "all *defenses*" includes nondelivery of an instrument and a qualified delivery of an instrument. Under NIL, Section 15 it was provided: "Where an incomplete instrument has not been delivered it will not, if completed and negotiated without authority, be a valid contract in the hands of any holder, as against any person whose signature was placed thereon before delivery." This rule is abrogated by the Code through this Section and Section 3-115 dealing with incomplete instru-

[8] Equitable Discount Corp. v. Fischer, page 529.

ments and Section 3-407 dealing with alteration. Thus the defense of non-delivery of an incomplete instrument cannot be asserted against a holder in due course.

Infancy. The Code follows the decisions under the NIL to the effect that the defense of infancy may be asserted against a holder in due course. The laws of the various states differ with regard to the degree of protection afforded an infant and the Code does not attempt to state the conditions under which infancy is available as a defense. These questions are to be resolved under local law in accordance with each state's policy with regard to protecting infants.

Incapacity. Incapacity, as the word is used in this Section of the Code, relates to any incapacity other than infancy. It includes mental incompetence, guardianship, ultra vires acts of a corporation, or lack of corporate capacity to do business. As in the case of infancy, state laws determine the effect of contracts entered into by persons lacking capacity to contract. In some states the law merely renders the obligation of the instrument voidable at the election of the obligor. In such states the defense of incapacity cannot be asserted against a holder in due course. In other states the effect is to render the obligation of the instrument null and void in which event the defense may be asserted against a holder in due course.

Duress. As stated in Comment 6 to this Section: "Duress is a matter of degree. An instrument signed at the point of a gun is void even in the hands of a holder in due course. One signed under threat to prosecute the son of the maker for theft may be merely voidable so that the defense is cut off." Thus in each case it will be necessary to determine the degree of duress in order to decide whether or not the person imposed upon can assert the defense against a holder in due course.

Illegality. There are many state statutes relating to illegal transactions and the effects thereof. Gambling and usury are two of the most common. Contracts involving usury in particular are treated quite differently in different jurisdictions. If the local law makes obligations of a usurious nature null and void, the defense of usury can be asserted against a holder in due course. If the statute does not have this effect, the defense would be cut off.

Misrepresentation. The decisions under the NIL recognized a distinction between fraud in the inducement or consideration and fraud in the inception. The former pertains to the consideration for which an instrument is given.[9] The primary party intended to create an instrument, but

[9] Bancredit v. Bethea, page 532.

was fraudulently induced to do so. Such a defense is not available against a holder in due course. Fraud in the inception exists where a negotiable instrument is procured from a party when circumstances are such that the party does not know that he is giving a negotiable instrument. The NIL recognized that in some situations this defense can be asserted even against a holder in due course. The Code likewise recognizes fraud in the inception, sometimes called fraud in the *factum,* as being available as a defense against a holder in due course. The theory is that since the party primarily to be bound has no intention of creating an instrument, none is created. For example: *A,* intending to sign a lease at the request of *B,* unknowingly, and by trickery on the part of *B,* signs a negotiable instrument. *B* negotiates the instrument to *C,* a bona fide purchaser. Upon presentation of this instrument by *C* to *A* for payment, *A* may have a real defense against *C*. Carelessness on the part of the maker which facilitates the fraud will deprive him of this defense against a holder in due course.[10] Thus, in the above illustration, if *A* had signed the so-called lease without reading it and had allowed himself to be deceived into thinking the negotiable instrument he signed was a lease, he would have been liable to a holder in due course of the instrument. In such a case he cannot throw the loss occasioned by his negligence on the holder in due course.

A person who is unable to meet his obligations may become involved in bankruptcy or other insolvency proceedings. " 'Insolvency proceedings' include any assignment for the benefit of creditors or other proceedings intended to liquidate or rehabilitate the estate of the person involved." (U.C.C. 1-201 (22)) The Code makes it clear that a discharge in bankruptcy or other insolvency proceedings will be available as a defense against a holder in due course. Thus, if *A* owed *B* $500 on a negotiable note and thereafter filed a petition in bankruptcy and received his discharge, *A* could assert his discharge in bankruptcy as a defense against a holder in due course to whom *B* had negotiated the note.

Other discharge of which holder has notice. As noted previously, a purchaser is not a holder in due course if he has notice that all the parties to an instrument have been discharged. However, if the notice does not include all of the parties, the holder may still be a holder in due course. Suppose that *M* has made a note payable to the order of *P*. *P* has indorsed to *A*, *A* has indorsed to *B*, and *B* has indorsed to *C*. If *C* discharges *B* from his liability as an indorser and then negotiates the paper to *H*, *H* could be a holder in due course and could hold the maker and prior indorsers liable. If he does not have notice of the discharge of *B*, such discharge would not be effective against him.

[10] First National Bank of Philadelphia v. Anderson, page 527.

4-42. Rights of one not a holder in due course. Section 3-306 of the Code provides:

> Unless he has the rights of a holder in due course any person takes the instrument subject to
>
> (a) all valid *claims* to it on the part of any person; and
>
> (b) all *defenses* of any party which would be available in an action on a simple contract; and
>
> (c) the *defenses* of want or failure of consideration, non-performance of any condition precedent, non-delivery, or delivery for a special purpose (Section 3-408); and
>
> (d) the *defense* that he or a person through whom he holds the instrument acquired it by theft, or that payment or satisfaction to such holder would be inconsistent with the terms of a restrictive indorsement. The *claim* of any third person to the instrument is not otherwise available as a defense to any party liable thereon unless the third person himself defends the action for such party. (Emphasis added.)

This Section does not substantially change the law under the NIL, but it does resolve some uncertainties which existed thereunder. It provides for *claims* and *defenses* which can be asserted against one who is not a holder in due course, or who has not become entitled by transfer to the rights of a holder in due course. Thus, if *A* purchases an instrument from *B* in good faith, but with knowledge that it is overdue, he would be subject to the claims and defenses enumerated in this Section.

(a) One who is not a holder in due course or a transferee from a holder in due course takes subject to the *rights of other persons* in the paper. Comment 2 to this Section provides: "'All valid claims to it on the part of any person' includes not only claims of legal title, but all liens, equities, or other claims of right against the instrument or its proceeds. It includes claims to rescind a prior negotiation and to recover the instrument or its proceeds."

(b) Section 58 of the NIL provided in part that: "In the hands of any holder other than a holder in due course, a negotiable instrument is subject to the same defenses as if it were nonnegotiable." The Code continues this concept in this Subsection. Thus, fraud in the inducement or consideration is a defense which is not available against a holder in due course but which is available against a holder who does not have the rights of a holder in due course. For example, *A* is induced by *B*, through fraud, to purchase shares of stock in a corporation. *A*, in settlement therefor, executes and delivers a note payable to the order of *B*. *B* indorses the note to *C*. *A*, upon learning that the stock is valueless, can set up this defense against *C* on the date of maturity if *C* does not have the status of a holder in due course. Of course, if *C* were a holder in due course or a transferee from a holder in due course, he would take free of this defense.

(c) Lack of consideration and failure of consideration are quite common defenses. For example, *A* gives *B* his note in payment for merchandise. The merchandise does not meet the requirements of the contract or it is never delivered. *B* negotiates the note to *X*, who has knowledge of the breach. *X* negotiates the note to *C*, a holder in due course. *C*, the holder in due course of *A's* note, may recover on the same, free from *A*'s defense, but *X* had he retained the note would have been subject to the defense.

The defenses of nondelivery, conditional delivery, or delivery for a special purpose may be asserted against one who is not a holder in due course. A holder in due course takes the instrument free of these defenses. For example, *A* executed a note in favor of *B* intending to deliver it to *B* only after *B* had performed certain services. *B* managed to obtain possession of the note without *A*'s knowledge and negotiated it to *C*. *A* can assert the defense of nondelivery against *C* if *C* is not a holder in due course. As between immediate parties and parties other than holders in due course, the delivery may be shown to be conditional or for some special purpose only. To illustrate: *A* drew a check in favor of *B* and delivered it to him with the express understanding that it was to be negotiated only on condition that *B* first redecorate the main floor of *A*'s department store. *B* negotiates the check to *C* in violation of this understanding. If *C* is not a holder in due course, *A* can assert the conditional delivery and *B*'s failure to perform as a defense against *C*.

(d) A person who is not a holder in due course is subject to the defense that he acquired the instrument by theft or that a person through whom he holds the instrument acquired it by theft. Of course, a person who acquired by theft could not be a holder in due course. One who is a holder in due course is free of the defense that a person through whom he holds acquired the instrument by theft. Also a holder who does not have the rights of a holder in due course takes subject to the defense that there is a restrictive indorsement on the paper and that payment would not conform to such indorsement.

As to *claims* of a *third person* to the instrument, the Code provides that they are not available as a defense unless the third person who has the claim to the instrument defends the action in which enforcement of the instrument is sought. The reasons for the foregoing provisions are set forth in Comment 5 to Section 3-306 of the Code: "The contract of the obligor is to pay the holder of the instrument and the claims of other persons against the holder are generally not his concern. He is not required to set up such a claim as a defense, since he usually will have no satisfactory evidence of his own on the issue; and the provision that he may not do so is intended as much for his own protection as for that of the holder. The claimant who has lost possession of an instrument so payable or indorsed that another may become a holder has lost his rights on the instrument, which by its terms no longer runs to him."

Comment 5 further provides:

> Nothing in this Section is intended to prevent the claimant from intervening in the holder's action against the obligor or defending the action for the latter, and asserting his claim in the course of such intervention or defense. Nothing here stated is intended to prevent any interpleader, deposit in court, or other available procedure under which the defendant may bring the claimant into court or be discharged without himself litigating the claim as a defense.

Thus the claimant is given an opportunity to establish his claim without burdening the defendant with the duty to assert and establish it on his behalf.

4-43. Burden of establishing signatures, defenses, and due course.

(1) Unless specifically denied in the pleadings each signature on an instrument is admitted. When the effectiveness of a signature is put in issue

(a) the burden of establishing it is on the party claiming under the signature; but

(b) the signature is presumed to be genuine or authorized except where the action is to enforce the obligation of a purported signer who has died or become incompetent before proof is required.

(2) When signatures are admitted or established, production of the instrument entitles a holder to recover on it unless the defendant establishes a defense.[11]

(3) After it is shown that a defense exists a person claiming the rights of a holder in due course has the burden of establishing that he or some person under whom he claims is in all respects a holder in due course. (U.C.C. 3-307)

The above Section treats the procedural aspects of commercial paper litigation with regard to problems of pleading and proof. Basically, the foregoing rules are in conformity with the Code policy to encourage the free movement of commercial paper. Maximum protection is given to the holder of the paper yet the basic rights of a defendant are also protected. It is to be noted there is a general presumption that a signature is genuine or authorized;[12] that the defendant has the burden of establishing any and all defenses; and that when a defense has been established, the holder has the burden of proving his holder-in-due-course status—that he is himself a holder in due course or that some person through whom he claims is a holder in due course.[13] Unless a defense is shown to exist, the holder-in-due-course question is not in issue.

[11] Bachman v. Brubaker, page 534.

[12] Altex Aluminum Supply Co. v. Asay, page 537.

[13] First Pennsylvania Banking and Trust Co. v. DeLise, page 540.

HOLDERS AND HOLDERS IN DUE COURSE CASES

MELLEN et al. v. GORA

1956 (Pa.) 70 York Leg. Rec. 1

ANDERSON, J. . . . In this action in assumpsit based on a series of promissory notes, aggregating over four thousand ($4000.00) dollars, the plaintiffs have moved for judgment on the pleadings, alleging that the pleadings indicate that:

1. The plaintiff is a holder in due course of the notes executed and delivered by the defendant and as such, the defense of failure of consideration is not available to the defendant. . . .

The notes in question are signed by the defendant Gora and are all made payable to plaintiff's decedent, John F. Mellen, and are not under seal. Plaintiff's first contention raises a somewhat novel question. May the named payee in a note be a holder in due course? Since the adoption of the Uniform Commercial Code in Pennsylvania there is no doubt about this query, for the Act of April 6, 1953, P.L. 3, Section 3-302, specifically provides "(2) A payee may be a holder in due course." Prior to the adoption of the Code the law in Pennsylvania was to the same effect although some jurisdictions held to the contrary. *Johnston v. Knipe* 260 Pa. 504; *Glassport Trust Co. v. Feightner*, 300 Pa. 317. Do the pleadings in the instance case show unequivocally that John F. Mellen, payee, was a holder in due course? We do not so conclude. Defendant in his answer denies indebtedness to Mellen and pleads failure of consideration and prior knowledge on the part of Mellen of the infirmities inherent in the notes and sets out a quite involved and complicated business transaction between and among Mellen, Gora, and two incorporated business concerns as the source of the notes. Defendant further asserts that Mellen was not only present during the aforesaid business transactions but that he participated therein, had full knowledge of, and personally signed one of the three agreements involved as president of one of the participating corporations. Assuming the truth of these assertions, as we must for the purpose of this motion, it is clear that a question of fact is presented for the determination of a jury as to the "good faith" and "without notice" features constituting a holder in due course. See *Johnston v. Knipe* supra, as reported originally in 33 Montgomery County Law Reporter 280. . . .

Plaintiff's motion for judgment on the pleadings is overruled.

L. & N. SALES COMPANY v. STUSKI
1958, 188 Pa. Super. 117, 146 A.2d 154

WATKINS, J. . . . This appeal is from the refusal of the court below to open a judgment, entered by confession, under power given in a note executed by the defendant in favor of the plaintiff. The note was executed in conjunction with a conditional sales contract which was a purchase money security agreement for the purchase of 123 Bev-Flo pourers from the sales outlet of the manufacturer of the pourers. . . .

The defendant after solicitation by an agent of Beverage Control Sales Co. of Philadelphia, Inc., manufacturer of Bev-Flo pourers, agreed to purchase 123 pourers. The pourers were held out by the manufacturer as being an attachment for the bottles used in dispensing alcoholic drinks which would measure and count each drink dispensed, thereby enabling the owner to dispense uniform size drinks, and secure an accurate inventory of drinks dispensed and gain complete control over this phase of his business. Defendant purchased the pourers for these exact reasons. The pourers were installed on September 21, 1955. On September 28, 1955, a purchase contract was signed, which contract did not release or limit any warranties by the seller. . . .

The defendant, according to the uncontradicted testimony, experienced difficulty with the pourers shortly after their installation in that the meters did not register accurately, the drinks poured were not consistent in that one would be large, another small, and that it was impossible to have any control over the business or inventory under these circumstances. The seller's service man attempted to correct the defects and prevent the mechanism from sticking by use of lubricating oil and other means, but was apparently unsuccessful. The defendant after making one monthly payment defaulted and judgment was confessed for the unpaid balance, plus collection fees.

That the plaintiff is not a holder in due course as payee of the note is obvious, since it was a distributor, under control of the manufacturer seller, and subject to the defense of breach of warranty of fitness for a particular purpose. *Sisemore & Kierbow Co. v. Nicholas,* 1942, 149 Pa. Super. 376, 27 A.2d 473. This transaction having been consummated subsequent to the enactment of the Uniform Commercial Code is therefore governed thereby (cases cited). . . .

The order of the court below is reversed, the judgment directed to be opened and the defendant let into a defense. . . .

BUDGET CHARGE ACCOUNTS, INC. v. MULLANEY

1958, 187 Pa. Super. 190, 144 A.2d 438

The defendant signed a note on February 17, 1956, to the order of Rowland Agency, Inc. The payee indorsed the note to Associated Acceptance Corporation, a Philadelphia firm, which then indorsed to Budget Charge Accounts, Inc., a New York firm, on February 20, 1956. A judgment was entered against the defendant by confession. The defendant applied for an order opening the judgment on the ground that the signatures on the note were secured by false representations made by an agent for the payee of the note. An order was granted and the plaintiff appealed.

WATKINS, J. . . . The defense in this case is fraud in the inception. The action being based on a negotiable instrument, the defense is as to the original payee. The testimony discloses that the appellees' defense was that the signatures to the note were obtained by false representations of the payee; that these representations were that they had won a free clothes dryer and were to be paid the sum of $20 each for interviews they obtained for the payee with prospective purchasers; that the signatures were obtained by these representations and that they had no knowledge that they were signing a judgment note; that the note was signed on February 14, 1956; that the dryer was delivered several days later and connected in March, 1956, and that it was defective; that they learned by television that the payee had been exposed as a fraudulent company; that they tried to reach the payee by letters and by personal visits but found the office closed; that their first knowledge that a claim was being made on a note was the receipt of the monthly payment book from the appellant; and that they never made any payments and wrote to the appellant stating that they had been defrauded and asked that the dryer be removed.

The fraud whereby the original note was obtained was not denied at the hearing. The appellant seeks to circumvent this defense by proving that it is a holder in due course. The defense appearing to be meritorious as to the payee, the burden of showing it was a holder in due course is then on the one claiming to be such. *Colonial Finance Company v. Hoover*, 112 Pa. Superior Ct. 60, 170 A. 338 (1934).

A holder in due course, as defined under the Uniform Commercial Code, 1953, April 6, P. L. 3, Section 3-302, 12A PS Section 3-302, is a holder who takes the instrument for value; and in good faith including observance of the reasonable commercial standards of any business in which the holder may be engaged; and without notice that it is overdue or has been dishonored or of any defense against or claim to it on the part of any person. Ordinarily a showing of the above requirements is largely one of fact which together with the credibility of those seeking to show same, is for a jury.

There is some merit in the contention of the appellees that the negotiation of this note, executed on February 17, 1956, to the Associated Acceptance Corporation and then to the appellant on February 20, 1956, even before the installation of the dryer, might well raise a jury question as to whether the negotiation was for the purpose of cutting off the defense of fraud in the inception and so affecting the good faith of the holder. . . .

Order affirmed.

FIDELITY TRUST CO. & GARDENER
1959, 191 Pa. Super. 17, 155 A.2d 406

The defendants, husband and wife, were the owners of a home. They were called upon by one Alex Di Santis who posed as an agent for "Reliable Home Improvement." He induced them to sign a contract for $1500 to have aluminum siding installed on their home. He told them that his company wanted a "model home" and that they would secure credits amounting to between $600 and $900 so that they would not have to make any payments for 12 to 14 months. Di Santis clipped the heading, "Reliable Home Improvement," from the original contract and in its place stamped "Premier Insulation Sales." Subsequently, the defendants signed a note to Premier and a completion certificate although they were led to believe that they were signing a loan application. The note was subsequently indorsed by Premier "without recourse" to the plaintiff bank. The lower Court held for the plaintiff.

HIRT, J. . . . The note, by the confession contained in it, authorized the entry of judgment for the whole principal sum "at any time" and judgment was entered by the plaintiff on July 24, 1956, before any alleged default in defendants' obligation. The note therefore was nonnegotiable, and, unless defendants are estopped, it is open to the same defenses which defendants would have had against Premier Insulation Sales. The assignee of a nonnegotiable note takes it subject to all equities with which it was affected in the hands of the assignor and may not enforce payment unless the maker is estopped from asserting a defense (cases cited). . . .

The date appearing on the note is the date of the completion certificate quoted above, which was secured at a later time. Normally of course the note and application for credit would be executed on a date prior to the completion of the work—in fact even before the work was commenced, since under plaintiff's own theory the purpose of the loan application and note was to provide funds to pay for the work. Accordingly the fact that the note in the instant case bore the same date as the completion certificate of itself was such a significant irregularity as to put upon the bank the duty of inquiry. We are not impressed by the completion certificate. The defendants clearly were imposed upon when their signatures to it were obtained. And even on its face, under the circumstances it does not have the legal effect of a certificate of no defense to the note in this action by the bank. Its purpose was to raise money for Premier and not for the benefit of the defendants. It is only where the purpose of the note, which the certificate of no defense accompanies, is to raise money by the sale of it *for the benefit of the original obligors* that they cannot defend against a purchaser for value without notice (cases cited). . . .

Under the facts here presented the defendants are entitled to the benefit of legal rules governing Incomplete Instruments (Uniform Commercial Code of April 6, 1953, P.L. 3, 12A P.S. Section 3-115) and Alteration of Instruments (Uniform Commercial Code, 12A P.S. Section 3-407). Cf. *Smith v. Weld,* 2 Pa. 54; *McComsey v. McGowan,* 325 Pa. 484, 486, 190 A. 884. In our view, for the reasons above stated, the bank cannot claim as a matter of law that it was a bona fide holder, without actual or constructive notice of Premier's fraud. Defendants are entitled to have a jury pass upon the factual issues involved and raised in their petition to open the judgment; defendants' rule to open judgment should have been made absolute.

The order is reversed. . . .

POTTER BANK AND TRUST COMPANY v. HENNEFORTH

1958 (Pa.) Court of Common Pleas of Montgomery County, 74 Montg. 420

The defendant executed a note in favor of a named payee who discounted the note with the plaintiff bank. The note contained a confession of judgment of clause. The bank obtained a judgment and the defendant sought to have the judgment set aside. In the proceedings to set aside the judgment, the defendant sought to obtain information from the plaintiff through interrogatories to be answered by the plaintiff. The plaintiff objected to the interrogatories.

Gerber, J. . . . Before considering the plaintiff's objections to specific interrogatories it should be noted that the principal theory of the defendant assumes that the plaintiff is not a holder in due course of the note because the plaintiff did not exercise good faith in discounting same for the original payee.

The Uniform Commercial Code describes a holder in due course as ". . . a holder who takes the instrument . . . in good faith including observance of the reasonable commercial standards of any business in which the holder may be engaged; and without notice . . . of any defense against . . . it on the part of any person": Act of April 6, 1953, P.L. 3, Section 3-302 (I) (b) (c), 12A P.S. 3-302.

The case law in this instance imposed a rather heavy burden upon the defendants. "To defeat the rights of one dealing with negotiable instruments is not enough to show that he took them under circumstances which ought to excite the suspicions of a prudent man and cause him to make inquiry, but that he had knowledge of an infirmity or defect, or of such facts that his failure to make further inquiry would indicate a deliberate desire on his part to evade knowledge because of a belief or fear that investigation would disclose a vice in the transaction": *First National Bank v. Goldberg*, 340 Pa. 337, 340 (1941).

Despite the fact that the framers of the Uniform Commercial Code consider Section 3-302 to be an expression of the case law holdings, the comment to 3-302 (1) (b) (c) of said Code appears to soften the effect of the foregoing quotation from the *Goldberg* case. The comment states: "A businessman engaging in a commercial transaction is not entitled to claim the peculiar advantages which the law accords to the good faith purchaser—called in this context holder in due course—on a bare showing of 'honesty in fact' when his actions fail to meet the generally accepted standards current in his business, trade, or profession."

However, whether or not the effect of the code is to ease the burden resting upon the party questioning the good faith of the holder, the defendants must prove what knowledge of the transaction was had by the plaintiff. The proof of such knowledge necessitates the production of evidence peculiarly within the control of the plaintiff. A rather wide latitude should therefore be allowed to the defendants to elicit that information.

The plaintiff objects to interrogatories one through five on the theory that they refer to other transactions and are irrelevant. This objection is without merit. It is incumbent upon the defendants to prove the plaintiff "had actual knowledge . . . of such facts that his failure to make further inquiry would indicate a deliberate desire on his part to evade knowledge because of a belief or fear that investigation would disclose a vice in the transaction": *First National Bank v. Goldberg, supra.* Evidence which tends to show that the plaintiff had such knowledge is relevant and necessary for the defendants to prove in order to carry their burden. Such knowledge on the part of the plaintiff can properly be shown by evidence of prior transactions all of which are similar in context, and subject matter and involved the original payee and the holder of this note. The knowledge gained by the plaintiff from any prior transactions had with the payee of this note is extremely pertinent in this case. . . .

The plaintiff objects to interrogatories six, seven, nine, ten, and eleven on the grounds that the defense implied in the question is not a valid one as against a holder in due course. All these questions go to the good faith of the plaintiff and are therefore relevant and pertinent to the issue here involved. . . .

Plaintiff is directed to answer all the interrogatories in accordance with this opinion except interrogatory four. . . .

ELBAR REALTY, INC. v. CITY BANK & TRUST CO.
1961 (Mass.) 173 N.E.2d 256

The plaintiff, Elbar, seeks to recover from the defendant (City Bank) for the alleged conversion of a United States Treasury certificate of indebtedness. The jury found for Elbar in the sum of $101,633.33. The certificate in question was stolen from Elbar. The thief obtained the services of a disbarred attorney to "peddle" the certificate. The attorney contacted a fellow club member, Goldman, and "asked him if he knew anyone who would buy or loan on a $100,000 certificate . . . at a discount–that he wanted to borrow $90,000 for a client." Goldman contacted one Marks who knew the president of City Bank and arranged a meeting with the attorney, Goldman, and the bank president in attendance. The City Bank discounted the certificate and paid the money to the attorney.

CUTTER, J. . . . This action is governed by G.L. c. 107. See especially Section 82.* City Bank contends, upon the basis of *Filosi v. Crossman*, 111 Conn. 178, 184–185, 149 A. 774, that Section 82 does not apply where the action is for conversion of the certificate rather than upon the instrument itself. The Filosi case seems contrary to the result reached in *Fillebrown v. Hayward*, 190 Mass. 472, 481–482, 77 N.E. 85, and to general authority elsewhere. We do not follow it (cases cited). . . .

General Laws c. 107, Section 82, reads, "Every holder is deemed prima facie to be a holder in due course; but when it is shown that the title of any person who has negotiated the instrument was defective the burden is on the holder to prove that he or some person under whom he claims acquired the title as holder in due course. . . ." In Massachusetts, under Section 82, the party contending that a defect in title exists has the burden of establishing the existence of the defect (cases cited). Where such a defect is established, then the holder has the burden, in the sense of the ultimate burden of persuasion (and not merely the burden of going forward with evidence), "of proving that he was a holder in due course" (cases cited). If the jury believed, as they obviously did, the ample evidence that the certificate had been stolen, the thief had a defective title. Under Section 82, the thief was a person "who . . . [had] negotiated the instrument." Thus, City Bank then had the ultimate burden of proof that it was a holder in due course. . . .

We accept these decisions as establishing the possibility that upon occasion a verdict may be ordered for the holder where, upon all rational views of a fully described transaction, no inference of bad faith can reasonably be drawn (case cited).

The crucial issue is whether City Bank took the certificate of indebtedness in good faith so that it became a holder in due course under G.L. c. 107, Sections 75, 79 (NIL Sections 52, 56). In *Fillebrown v. Hayward,* 190 Mass. 472, 480, 77 N.E. 45, 46, it was said, "[N]either knowledge or suspicious circumstances, nor doubts as to the genuineness of the title, nor gross negligence on the part of the taker either singly or together are sufficient to defeat the holder's recovery, unless amounting to proof of want of good faith." This court (at page 482, 77 N.E. at page 47) indicated that the test on this issue of fact was whether the taker of the instrument "knew, or in the face of facts sufficient to put her upon inquiry purposely refrained from knowing[,] of the fraud" affecting the instrument. See *Smith v. Livingston,* 111 Mass. 342, 343 (where the trial judge, in a charge which this court regarded as correct in general, said "that there might be such recklessness as would be inconsistent with honesty of purpose"); *Reynolds v. Park Trust Co.,* 245 Mass. 440, 446, 139 N.E. 785, 787, (although an "investigation . . . would have shown . . . [fraud, the holder was] not bound to make" one); *Russell v. Bond & Goodwin Inc.,* 276 Mass. 458, 463–464, 177 N.E. 627, 629 ("suspicion . . . was not the equivalent of knowledge which would show bad faith"); *Standard Acceptance Corp. v. Chapin,* 277 Mass. 278, 282, 178 N.E. 538, 540 (that "the would-be seller of a negotiable instrument is unscrupulous and has been concerned in . . . illegal transactions is not enough"); *Macklin v. Macklin,* 315 Mass. 451, 455, 53 N.E.2d 86, 88 ("[t]he rights of a holder . . . are to be determined by the simple test of honesty and good faith, and not by a speculative issue as to his diligence or negligence"); *Gramatan National Bank & Trust Co. v. Moody,* 326 Mass. 367, 371, 94 N.E.2d 771, 773. In view of these decisions, the test in the present case, based upon the language of the Fillebrown case at page 482, 77 N.E. at page 47 is whether the jury could reasonably infer that the group acting for City Bank knew "facts sufficient to put . . . [it] upon inquiry and purposely refrained" from inquiring or from knowing about other facts which would have revealed the lack of title in Shapiro's client.

City Bank was not entitled to a directed verdict. Assuming that City Bank was a holder in due course to the extent of amounts already paid to Shapiro from the "Special" account before it learned of the theft, it was not one with respect to the amounts then remaining in the checking account (cases cited).

We do not, however, place our approval of the trial judge's refusal to direct a verdict solely upon the narrow ground just mentioned. There was sufficient evidence to warrant submitting to the jury the issue whether City Bank took the bond in good faith. . . .

Exceptions sustained. . . .

[This case was decided under the NIL.

* Section 82, which is Section 59 of the Uniform Negotiable Instruments Law (NIL), was repealed by St. 1957, c. 765, Section 2, and the enactment (by Section 1) of the Uniform Commercial Code, effective October 1, 1958. See c. 765, Section 21. The present comparable provision is G.L. c. 106, Section 3-307(3). See comment on 1957 Official Text of the Code, p. 282.]

THE FIRST NATIONAL BANK OF PHILADELPHIA v. ANDERSON

1956 (Pa.) Court of Common Pleas of Bucks County, 7 D. & C.2d 661, 6 Bucks 287.

The defendant entered into a contract with the Atlantic Storm Window Co. for the installation of twelve jalousie windows. A judgment note signed by the defendant appeared on the same sheet of paper as the contract. The note was indorsed for value to the plaintiff bank. The defendant claims that the note was signed in blank; that it was to be in the amount of $744; that it was completed in the amount of $895.32; and that the work was improperly done and the windows were not as represented. When the bank notified the defendant that payments on the note were to be made to it, he complained of the defective work and refused to pay. The bank entered judgment against him and defendant seeks to have it set aside on the above grounds, asserting also that he did not have sufficient opportunity to examine the note and contract before signing.

BIESTER, P. J. . . . It is the position of plaintiff that it was a holder in due course for value, without notice, and that it is, therefore, not subject to the various defenses and objections raised by petitioners.

Our first inquiry must be of determination of the question of whether, under the facts revealed by the record before us, plaintiff is a holder in due course.

Section 3-302 of the Uniform Commercial Code of April 6, 1953, P. L. 3, the provisions of which govern the proceeding before us, states that:

> (1) A holder in due course is a holder who takes the instrument
> (a) for value; and
> (b) in good faith including observance of the reasonable commercial standards of any business in which the holder may be engaged; and
> (c) without notice that it is overdue or has been dishonored or of any defense against or claim to it on the part of any person.

It is our understanding that, as to these provisions, defendant contends that the bank was not a holder in due course in that it did not take the instrument in good faith, on the theory that it became incumbent upon plaintiff to communicate with the payee and/or the makers of the note to determine whether the work had been satisfactorily completed before accepting the note. We find no merit in this contention. (The court cites pre-Code cases.) . . .

Although these cases are decided under the Negotiable Instruments Law of May 16, 1901, P. L. 194, we find no provision in the Uniform Commercial Code making any change in the good faith concept. True, Section 1-201 defines good faith as being honesty in fact and under Section 3-302 good faith includes the observance by reasonable commercial standards of any business in which the holder may be engaged. No evidence was presented, however, indicating that the failure to make inquiry of the payee or the maker of the note as to the satisfactory completion of the contract was in any sense a divergence from common banking or commercial practice. On the contrary, if a holder of an instrument were required to investigate in each instance whether the contract had been completed satisfactorily before accepting it, the burden placed on the free flow of negotiable paper would be almost insurmountable.

We, therefore, find that plaintiff bank accepted the paper in good faith and is a holder in due course. . . .

As to the alleged alteration of the judgment note in that it is said to have completed contrary to the original agreement of the parties, Section 3-407 of the Uniform Commercial Code appears to clearly control the situation. It provides, inter alia, that when an incomplete instrument has been completed, the subsequent holder in due course may enforce it as completed. Without holding that there was a material alteration of the instrument, we do find that even if there was such an alteration it would not be effective as a defense against the holder in due course.

As was said in the recent and remarkably similar case of *Newark Trust Co. v. Herr*, 54 Lanc. pp. 31, 34:

The difficulty with defendants' position is that all the acts of infirmity alleged in the petition to open the judgment existed between the immediate parties to the note and not between the parties and the plaintiff as a holder in due course, and as there is no allegation that plaintiff had notice of any infirmities at the time it was negotiated to it, the defendants cannot avail themselves of such alleged infirmities as against the plaintiff as a holder in due course.

Petition to open the judgment is refused.

EQUITABLE DISCOUNT CORP. v. FISCHER

1957 (Pa.) Court of Common Pleas at Lancaster County, 12 D. & C. 2d 326., 55 Lanc. 381

JOHNSTONE, J. The plaintiff seeks to recover in this action in assumpsit the sum of Six Hundred ($600.00) Dollars, together with interest, on three trade acceptances, each in the sum of Two Hundred ($200.00) Dollars, executed and delivered by the defendant to Sterling Materials Company, Inc., and transferred by indorsement to the plaintiff. At the close of the trial of this case, the court entered a directed verdict in favor of the plaintiff and against the defendant on motion of counsel for the plaintiff. The defendant has filed a motion for a new trial and assigned two reasons in support thereof. Argument was heard by the court *en banc* and counsel for the parties have submitted briefs.

The testimony reveals that the defendant admittedly signed three trade acceptances, each in the sum of Two Hundred ($200.00) Dollars, all dated July 25, 1955, all payable to the order of Sterling Materials Company, Inc., at The First Columbia National Bank at Columbia, Pa., and serially due on December 1, 1955, January 1, 1956, and February 1, 1956. These trade acceptances were delivered by the defendant to Sterling Materials Company, Inc., in payment of certain roofing materials, which the defendant later refused to accept. On August 10, 1955, in the regular course of its business, the plaintiff purchased the three trade acceptances from Sterling Materials Company, Inc., for the sum of Four Hundred Twenty ($420.00) Dollars and they were transferred to the plaintiff by unrestricted indorsements. Notice of the purchase of the three trade acceptances by the plaintiff from Sterling Materials Company, Inc., was given to the defendant by the plaintiff by letter dated August 10, 1955. Subsequently, the three trade acceptances were forwarded through regular channels to the paying bank on their respective due dates and payment was refused. Purchase of the trade acceptances was made by the plaintiff without knowledge of any defense on the part of the defendant and without knowledge that the defendant had not received the materials purchased.

The defendant, an electrical contractor, agreed to purchase a quantity of roofing materials from a representative of Sterling Materials Company, Inc., and to pay therefor the sum of Six Hundred ($600.00) Dollars. The defendant was requested to pay cash for the materials but he arranged to make three monthly payments of Two Hundred ($200.00) Dollars each. The Sterling representative had the defendant sign the three trade acceptances, telling him they were in the nature of a note and would be put through a bank. The record discloses that the defendant had had no experience with trade acceptances and did not know what they were, but had experience in writing checks. No effort was made by the defendant to obtain any advice before signing the trade acceptances and he knew when he signed them that he would have to pay them on their respective due dates. The day after signing the trade acceptances the defendant went to his bank and asked the bank to check Dun & Bradstreet on the reputation of Sterling Materials Company, Inc. Following the receipt from the bank of the report, the defendant cancelled the order and refused to take delivery of the materials. No testimony was offered as to the method used to cancel the order or the time of the cancellation.

The question to be determined here is whether the court properly directed a verdict for the plaintiff or should have permitted the jury to pass on whether the defendant had a defense under Section 3-305 (2) (c) of the Uniform Commercial Code (12 A. P. S. Section 3-305). The record clearly discloses the plaintiff to be a holder in due course of the three trade acceptances. They were purchased for value, before their due dates and in the regular course of business. The trade acceptances had not been dishonored and the plaintiff had no notice of any defense on the part of anyone, including the defendant. Under these circumstances, the plaintiff meets the requirement of a holder in due course as defined by the Code. As such a holder, the plaintiff took the trade acceptances free from all defenses on the part of the defendant, with whom the plaintiff had no dealings, except those set forth in Section 3-305 of the Code. In the present case, the only possible defense available to the defendant is set forth in Section 3-305 (2) (c). This section of the Code reads, a holder in due course takes the instrument free from all defenses of any party to the instrument with whom the holder has not dealt except "(c) such misrepresentation as has induced the party to sign the instrument with neither knowledge nor reasonable opportunity to obtain knowledge of its character or its essential terms." By directing a verdict for the plaintiff, the court determined at the time of the trial that the defendant had not produced testimony which justified submitting to the jury the question of whether the defendant had brought himself within the exception to the general rule. After further deliberation and careful study of the record, we are convinced that the defendant failed to show he was induced to sign the trade acceptances by misrepresentations, with neither knowledge nor reasonable opportunity to obtain knowledge of their character or essential terms and that the directed verdict was proper.

This particular part of the section of the Code is new but follows the majority of the decisions which recognized the defense of fraud in the essence or fraud in the factum against a holder in due course. The circumstances of the present case do not bring it within the class of cases where the maker is tricked into signing. In *Resh v. First National Bank of Allentown*, 93 Pa. 397, the defendant signed a note but was told he was signing a receipt and there the court held the instrument invalid even in the hands of a holder in due course. Here the defendant signed the three trade acceptances after being told they were in the nature of a note and would be put through a bank. The defendant knew he was signing three obligations which he would be required to pay on their several due dates. The record is devoid of any testimony that any misrepresentations were made by the Sterling representative before or at the time the defendant signed. The defendant knew that he had agreed to purchase certain roofing materials and that he would have to pay for the materials at the rate of Two Hundred ($200.00) Dollars per month for three months. He said he thought he was signing something in the nature of a check and he could hardly have been more correct.

However, paragraph (c) of subsection (2) of Section 3-305 of the Code extends the defense to an instrument of which the signer had neither knowledge nor reasonable opportunity to obtain knowledge of its character or its essential terms. In other words, was the defendant excusably ignorant of the contents of the writing he signed and had he no opportunity to obtain such knowledge. In our opinion the defendant was not ignorant of what he signed. He knew the three trade acceptances were obligations which required him to pay definite amounts of money on certain dates. He admitted being told the trade acceptances were like a note and would be put through a bank. He testified he thought he was signing something in the nature of a check, which he was accustomed to signing, and knew or must have known that a check is an order to pay money to some named person. It is true that he did not know the meaning of the word negotiable but he knew that checks which he issued might get into the hands of someone other than the payee. The defendant may have given no thought at the time of signing to the possibility of the instruments getting into the hands of someone other than Sterling Materials Company, Inc. but he knew he had promised to pay definite sums of money on definite dates. The defendant was not only aware of the character of the instruments signed but also understood the essential terms of the three trade acceptances.

The defendant made no effort to ascertain from any outside source the meaning or implications of the instruments he signed. The Sterling representative did not refuse to permit the defendant to make inquiries, since no such request was made and the defendant apparently understood what he was doing and needed no help. It was the defendant who suggested that payment for the materials be spread over a three months' period. The defendant also testified that he never saw the Sterling representative before and had no reason to place any confidence in anything he said. The defendant had been in business for almost forty years and obviously considered himself capable of transacting business without the aid or assistance of anyone else.

The facts of this case are even weaker than those in *First National Bank vs. Anderson,* 7 D. & C. 2d, 661, where the court refused to open a judgment entered on a warrant of attorney signed by three persons who had not read the contract and note and made no effort to seek advice before signing.

The motion for a new trial is dismissed.

BANCREDIT, INC. v. BETHEA
1961, 65 N.J. Super. 538, 168A. 2d 250

Bethea and his son executed a note and conditional sales contract—leaving the amount blank—for the purchase of an automobile from Chippy's Auto Mart, Inc. The note and contract were purchased by the plaintiff. The defendants asserted that the note had been procured by fraud—that material misrepresentations had been made as to the nature and character of the instrument they signed and that the condition of the automobile was falsely represented. The lower court ruled as a matter of law that the note was negotiable, that plaintiff was a holder in due course, and that the defendants had not produced sufficient evidence to support their defenses. The defendants appealed.

FREUND, J. A. D. . . . Defendants contend that a jury question was presented as to their defenses of fraud and the claim of infancy raised by Lynn Bethea. They also argue that plaintiff has not shown itself to be a holder in due course and is therefore subject to all defenses, real and personal, which defendants may have with respect to the instrument.

In regard to the latter contention we note that defendants have not produced any evidence to rebut the *prima facie* presumption that every holder is a holder in due course. R.S. 7:2–59, N.J.S.A. Having failed to offer proof that any of the statutory conditions of a holder in due course, R.S. 7:2–52, N.J.S.A., did not exist at the time plaintiff received the instrument, they cannot successfully contest Bancredit's status in this respect. *Crown Capital Corporation v. Broderick,* 130 N.J.L. 198, 32, A.2d 289 (Sup. Ct. 1943). Even if defendants could ultimately show that the payee's title was defective, thereby shifting the burden of proof to plaintiff (cases cited); see New Jersey, Study of the Uniform Commercial Code (Nov. 1960), Section 3-307(2), especially comment (1), the latter's uncontradicted evidence of the regularity of its acceptance of an instrument complete in all material respects constituted an adequate discharge of that burden (cases cited). . . .

As a holder in due course plaintiff is, of course, immune to all personal defenses of the maker against the payee, including that of fraud in the inducement. *Davis v. Clark,* 85 N.J.L. 696, 698–699, 90 A. 303 (E. & A. 1914). Therefore, to the extent that defendants' assertion of fraud is grounded in the alleged misrepresentations of the payee's agent with respect to the quality and condition of the automobile, it cannot successfully be raised against plaintiff.

Defendants, however, relying on *New Jersey Mortgage and Investment Co. v. Dorsey,* 60 N.J. Super. 299, 158 A.2d 712 (App. Div. 1960), affirmed 33 N.J. 448, 165 A. 2d 297 (1960), urge the real defense of fraud in the *factum* and insist that the evidence is sufficient to warrant a jury finding that they were unaware that the instrument they were signing was a negotiable note. We consider the contrary inference to be the compelling one. The proofs leave no doubt that defendants knew they were signing a negotiable instrument and that their misconception, if any, was as to the amount of their obligation. The testimony of Tony Bethea is illustrative:

Q. What agreement did you enter into? A. My son went down to buy a car. Chippy asked me to sign papers to borrow $500. He needed $500 to pay down on the car. That afternoon I went down there and he said . . .

Q. (Mr. Gehrie interrupting) How do you know Chippy? A. I have been doing business with him for 15 years. He said "Will you sign the papers so your son will get $500?" I signed a paper to get $500 from Beneficial Loan. It was for Lynn to get a car.

Q. When you signed this paper you thought you were signing for a loan? A. I know I signed it for one loan but not this one here. . . .

The defense of fraud in the *factum* is not available to a maker who knowingly creates a negotiable instrument but leaves the amount blank on the understanding that a lesser sum will be inserted than subsequently appears on the note in the hands of a holder in due course. The maker has not, in this situation, been misled as to the character of the instrument he is creating, but only as to the extent of his obligation. His defensive assertions are grounded in deception as to the terms of his commitment, not in ignorance of its quality. *New Jersey Mortgage and Investment Co. v. Dorsey,* supra, 60 N.J. Super., at p. 302, 158 A.2d, at p. 714. His defense is one of fraud in the inducement, effective only against the misleading payee and those successors to his interest who do not occupy the protective status of holder in due course (cases cited).

The condition of the proofs was such as not to present a jury issue on either the nature of the fraud, or the negligence of the maker of the note. The defense of fraud in the *factum* was properly rejected by the trial judge as a matter of law.

The aforementioned conclusions are grounded in our Negotiable Instruments Law, under which unauthorized completion of a partially blank instrument which is delivered to the payee or holder is only a personal defense. R.S. 7:2–14, N.J.S.A.; *Cinema Circuit Corp. v. Merrill Amusement Corp.*, 121 N.J.L. 216, 2 A.2d 43 (Sup. Ct. 1938) The anomalous rule that nondelivery of an incomplete instrument constitutes a real defense, R.S. 7:2–15, N.J.S.A.; see *Budget Corp. of America v. De Felice,* supra. 46, N.J. Super., at p. 493, 135 A.2d, at p. 33; also see criticism of this rule and proposed change in New Jersey, Study of Uniform Commercial Code, supra, Section 3-305, comment (1), Section 3-115, especially comments (2) and (3), Section 3-407 (3), is not here applicable, as the note and contract were undoubtedly delivered by defendants to the payee, Chippy's. Defendants' interposition at this point, to the effect that the payee's fraud was such as to preclude effective delivery of the incompleted instrument, thereby invoking R.S. 7:2–15, N.J.S.A., was considered and rejected in *New Jersey Mortgage and Investment Co. v. Dorsey,* supra, 60 N.J. Super., at p. 306, 158 A.2d at p. 716. Failure of the maker to establish either fraud in the execution or freedom from negligence debases entirely the merit of such a contention.

Since the blanks were filled in by the payee, the question of the latter's authority to do so becomes irrelevant in a suit against the maker by a holder in due course. Not only did the instant plaintiff have the right to assume that the payee filled in the blanks in accordance with its authority, but even knowledge, if such existed, on the part of Bancredit that the instrument contained blanks when executed did not impose on the latter a duty to make further inquiry as to the payee's authorization (cases cited).

We therefore consider defendants' own proofs to demonstrate conclusively that there was an utter absence of fraud in the execution of the note under consideration . . . *Judgment for plaintiff.*

[This case was decided under the NIL.]

BACHMAN & CO. INC. v. BRUBAKER

1958 (Pa.) Court of Common Pleas of Lancaster County, 56 Lanc. 289

WISSLER, P. J. The defendants, Charles C. Brubaker and Gladys Mae Brubaker, purchased a Jordon combination upright freezer from

Wholesale Frozen Foods, Inc. and executed and delivered to Wholesale Frozen Foods, Inc., a judgment note dated January 10, 1956, in the amount of $902.40, payable to the order of said Wholesale Frozen Foods, Inc., and payable in 24 monthly installments of $37.60 each, the first payment to become due on February 25, 1956, and the balance of payments to be made on even date of each succeeding month thereafter until paid, and in case payments shall not be made at maturity of the payments at Bachman and Co., Inc., 131 Chestnut Street, Harrisburg, Pennsylvania, then defendants authorize judgment to be entered thereon for the payments which shall not have been made.

On December 23, 1957, plaintiff, the transferee of the note, caused judgment to be entered in the amount of $526.40 in the Prothonotary's Office of Lancaster County on the warrant of attorney to confess judgment contained in said note to No. 3604, Confessed Judgments 1957.

The defendants, on January 3, 1958, filed a petition to open the judgment and a rule was granted thereon on the same day. The plaintiff filed an answer to said petition on January 28, 1958, but no reply was filed to the answer. The basis of the petition to open was the defective condition of the self-defroster as well as the freezing unit. Plaintiff averred, inter alia, in its answer: "The plaintiff has been advised that the averments contained in Paragraphs 4 through 12, both inclusive, of the Petition to Open Judgment need not be answered by it. However, if the defendants mean to say by the averments contained in said paragraphs that they have a full, just and complete defense to the judgment of the plaintiff, a holder in due course, they shall be deemed to be denied. The plaintiff avers that it is holder in due course of said judgment note, having discounted said note on January 18, 1956, for value prior to default, without notice of any defense to said note on the part of the defendants, and that it accepted negotiation of said note in good faith without notice of any infirmity."

The deposition consists of the testimony of defendants and their witnesses, but none on the part of the plaintiff, although upon being asked by counsel for defendants, he denied that he had received a letter from Gladys Mae Brubaker, one of the defendants, complaining of these defects and further stated that plaintiff took over the contract on January 18, 1956. Defendants' testimony was to the effect that about a week after the purchase of the freezer they called Mr. Hogan, owner of the Wholesale Frozen Foods, Inc., from whom the purchase was made, complaining of its defects and he replaced the entire freezer within a month. Defendants experienced the same or similiar trouble with the second freezer, but continued to make the payments until October, 1956. Said Gladys Mae Brubaker testified on re-direct examination as follows: (BY MR.

COHEN): (Q) Mrs. Brubaker, at any time did you contact Bachman and Co., Inc. (A) Yes, I wrote to tell them why we weren't sending a payment because the refrigerator wasn't working properly. (Q) Did you get a reply? (A) No. (Q) Do you remember when you sent it? (A) After October of 1956. (Q) Did you address it to any one particular person? (A) I don't remember. I took it off the payment book. (Q) Did anybody from Bachman and Co. come down to look at the freezer? (A) No. (Q) You made payments to Bachman and Co. prior to contacting them? (A) Yes.

Accepting this testimony as true, the first notice of the defect was given to plaintiff in October, 1956, which was practically ten months after January 18, 1956, the date of transfer from Wholesale Frozen Foods, Inc.

It is the contention of defendants that plaintiff offered no testimony as to its being holder in due course and rely on Section 3-307 of the Uniform Commercial Code of April 6, 1953, P.L. 3, 12A P.S. Section 3-307, which provides as follows: "After evidence of a defense has been introduced a person claiming the rights of a holder in due course has the burden of establishing that he or some person under whom he claims is in all respects a holder in due course."

The difficulty with this contention is that it ignores plaintiff's answer which specifically states that "it is a holder in due course of said judgment note, having discounted said note on January 18, 1956, for value prior to default, without notice of any defense to said note on the part of the Defendants, and that it accepted negotiation of said note in good faith without notice of any infirmity." The defendants not only failed to reply to plaintiff's answer, but also from their own testimony first gave notice in October, 1956, ten months subsequent to the transfer of the note to plaintiff. In Vol. 7 *Standard Pennsylvania Practice*, Section 116, Page 102, it is stated with cited cases: "In proceedings to open a judgment, a replication should be filed if it is intended to deny facts which are stated in the answer. Where no replication is filed, the facts stated in the answer will be taken to be true pro confesso and the application to open the judgment will be refused in such case if the answer to the petition is responsive and no testimony is introduced. Sometimes such a result is produced by express local rules of court." See also *M. A. Long Co. v. Keystone Portland Cement Co.*, 302 Pa. 308. An application to open a judgment confessed upon a warrant of attorney is in the nature of an equitable proceeding addressed to the sound discretion of the court. There must be more than an oath against an oath or a mere conflict of testimony to justify certification of the issue for jury trial, and the evidence must carry such conviction of truth as to convince the judge that the judgment should be opened and a jury trial awarded. The weight of the evidence and the credibility of the witnesses are for the judge who sits as a chancellor: *Mutual Building and Loan Association of Shenandoah v. Walukiewicz,* 322 Pa. 240. A court has no discretionary power to open a judgment where the petition does not set forth facts which are sufficient at law to sustain a verdict in favor of the petitioner. *Sferra et al., v. Urling et al.,* 324 Pa. 344, 347; *Shinn et al., v. Stemler,* 158 Pa. Superior Ct. 350.

This court feels that the answer filed is responsive to the defendants' petition to which no replication has been filed. This answer shows the plaintiff a holder of a negotiable note for value and without notice of any defects prior to January 18, 1956, the date of the transfer of the note to plaintiff, defendants' own testimony revealing that the first and only notice, if any, given to plaintiff was in October, 1956, approximately ten months thereafter.

The petition to open the pleadings and the testimony on the rule are insufficient to justify the submission of the question to the jury and are wholly inadequate to sustain a verdict in favor of petitioners.

The rule to show cause why the judgment should not be opened and the defendants let into a defense is discharged.

ALTEX ALUMINUM SUPPLY CO. v. ASAY

1962, 72 N.J. Super. 582, 178 A. 2d 636

Home Specialists, Inc. was payee of a note executed by the defendant. The payee by its president indorsed the note to plaintiff, Altex Aluminum Supply. The defendant contends that Home Specialists, Inc. had agreed to hold the note and that defendant was to pay off the note by giving additional business to the payee. He testified that he did secure a siding job for Home Specialists, Inc. and that his share of the contract price was more than sufficient to pay the note. The lower Court ruled in favor of the plaintiff.

SULLIVAN, J. A. D. . . . Defendant, testifying in his own behalf, admitted signing the note and delivering it to Home Specialists, Inc., the payee. He said, however, that the payee was supposed to hold the note and "to do nothing with the note," and that defendant would give the payee additional business to pay off the note. He further testified that he did secure a siding job for Home Specialists, Inc., and that his share of the contract price was more than sufficient to pay the note. The payee, however, refused to return the note to him although he made repeated demands for it. Defendant did not claim that plaintiff had any knowledge of these arrangements. The foregoing, of course, would be no defense against a holder in due course. . . .

We find that the proofs support the judgment in favor of plaintiff. As to defendant's claim that plaintiff did not receive the note "for value," it is clear from the evidence that the note was received by plaintiff in connection with the account of Home Specialists, Inc. It is settled law that a party taking a negotiable note in payment of, or as security for, an antecedent debt, is a holder in due course (cases cited). This is so even though satisfaction of the antecedent debt is conditioned on actual payment of the note (cases cited). . . .

Defendant's other point is that plaintiff did not prove the genuineness of the signature of the payee nor was there any proof of the authority of the president of the corporate payee to endorse and deliver the note to plaintiff. For these reasons, argues the defendant, the trial court erred in allowing the note to be marked in evidence. We do not agree. Plaintiff's witness testified that the note was delivered to him at the payee's office by the president and other officers of the payee corporation and that the president signed the endorsement on the back of the note in the presence of plaintiff's witness. We are in accord with the finding of the trial court that the "endorsement of the instrument was proved by direct testimony."

Defendant, however, claims that his mere denial of the corporate payee's endorsement puts plaintiff to its proof not only that the endorsing signature of the corporate officer is genuine but also that such officer was actually authorized to execute such endorsement. He cites *Van-Syckel v. Egg Harbor Coal and Lumber Co.*, 109 N.J.L. 604, 162 A. 627, 85 A.L.R. 300 (E. & A. 1932), in support of his argument. *Van-Syckel,* though, dealt with a situation where the note was payable to the order of an individual payee and the endorsement of the note purported to be signed by a third person under a power of attorney. There the court set aside a judgment for the plaintiff because it found there was no evidence that the signature upon the back of the note was the payee's, or that the agent purporting to sign the same was authorized to do so.

The New Jersey cases dealing with the authority of corporate officers to endorse checks or notes emphasize that they must be read in the light of the facts of the particular case (cases cited).

A corporation has the general power to make and endorse negotiable paper. *O'Connor v. First Bank & Trust Co.*, 12 N.J. Super. 281, 287, 79 A. 2d 687 (App. Div. 1951). The authority of the president to execute an endorsement of a promissory note on behalf of the corporation in the normal course of business must be presumed; otherwise the negotiability of the commercial paper would be seriously impaired. To become a holder in due course one is not required to satisfy himself of the actual authority of such officer. 10 C.J.S. Bills and Notes Section 506(h); 19

C.J.S. Corporations Section 1224(b). A corporate endorsement of a negotiable instrument will pass the property therein to the endorsee notwithstanding that from want of capacity the corporation may incur no liability thereon. R.S. 7:2–22, N.J.S.A.

It is to be noted that the Uniform Commercial Code, adopted in New Jersey (L. 1961, c. 120), effective January 1, 1963, in Article 3, revises and clarifies the Negotiable Instruments Law, R.S. 7:1 et seq., N.J.S.A. Section 3-307 thereof provides as follows:

(1) Unless specifically denied in the pleadings each signature on an instrument is admitted. When the effectiveness of a signature is put in issue

(a) the burden of establishing it is on the party claiming under the signature; but

(b) the signature is presumed to be genuine or authorized except where the action is to enforce the obligation of a purported signer who has died or become incompetent before proof is required.

The comment on this section made in Uniform Laws Annotated, Uniform Commercial Code, 1958 official text, includes the following:

The question of the burden of establishing the signature arises only when it has been put in issue by specific denial. "Burden of establishing" is defined in the definitions section of this Act (Section 1-201). The Burden is on the party claiming under the signature, but he is aided by the presumption that it is genuine or authorized stated in paragraph (b). "Presumption" is also defined in this Act (Section 1-201). It means that until some evidence is introduced which would support a finding that the signature is forged or unauthorized the plaintiff is not required to prove that it is authentic. The presumption rests upon the fact that in ordinary experience forged or unauthorized signatures are very uncommon and normally any evidence is within the control of the defendant or more accessible to him. He is therefore required to make some sufficient showing of the grounds for his denial before the plaintiff is put to his proof. His evidence need not be sufficient to require a directed verdict in his favor, but it must be enough to support his denial by permitting a finding in his favor. Until he introduces such evidence the presumption requires a finding for the plaintiff. Once such evidence is introduced the burden of establishing the signature by a preponderance of the total evidence is on the plaintiff.

Here, plaintiff is the holder of the note and produced testimony that the note was delivered to plaintiff by the officers of the payee-corporation before it was overdue in partial payment of a debt owed by the payee to plaintiff, that the note was delivered at the corporate office and that the president of the payee-corporation executed the endorsement. It is undisputed that the note is regular on its face and that defendant is the maker thereof. Under these circumstances, plaintiff has established that it is a holder in due course and is entitled to judgment. . . .

Affirmed. . . .

FIRST PENNSYLVANIA BANKING AND TRUST CO. v. DeLISE et al.
1958, 186 Pa. Super. 398, 142 A.2d 401

Gunther, J. This appeal is from an order of the court below discharging defendants' rule to open judgment.

The First Pennsylvania Banking and Trust Company confessed judgment against the defendants. The negotiable judgment note in question was made to Babco Aluminum Products, Inc., a home improvement contracting corporation, as payee, and endorsed to the plaintiff bank.

A petition to open the judgment was filed setting forth the following grounds:

1. The Babco Aluminum Products, Inc., obtained defendants' signature by fraud;
2. The consideration for the note failed;
3. The plaintiff bank had notice of dishonor before negotiation;
4. The plaintiff bank had notice that a valid defense existed before endorsement.

An answer was filed denying the above allegations and depositions were taken. The record discloses that on September 7, 1955, Babco Aluminum Products and defendants entered into an agreement for certain alterations to the order of Babco Aluminum Products in the amount of $2,320.66. The note was endorsed for value to the First National Bank of Philadelphia, predecessor to plaintiff.

Defendants, in their petition, claim that they were induced to sign the note by false representations as to the nature of the instrument by Babco Aluminum Products Co., Inc. It was also averred that plaintiff's predecessor in title had notice of dishonor prior to the date of the negotiation of the note.

Defendants testified that it was their impression that the legal size paper which they signed concerned the repairs only. They did not, according to their version, suspect that they were signing a judgment note. It was not until after Babco Aluminum Products, Inc., began the work that the defendants were advised that the legal size paper was a judgment note. The note in question is dated October 10, 1955, for $2,320.25 payable in thirty-six monthly installments of $64.46 each, beginning November 15, 1955. Defendants contend that they notified the bank that they would not honor the note because the repairs were not being made in a workmanlike manner and assert that the notice to the bank took place during the first week of October, 1955.

The bank, however, maintains that it first received notice from Mrs. DeLise, one of the defendants, on December 14, 1955, when she complained that the repairs were not satisfactory. Mr. Hanson, the bank supervisor, testified that the next time he heard from the defendants was on March 2, 1956, when Mr. DeLise complained that the work was unfinished. As to the instrument itself, the reverse side contains the following printed matter: "Pay to the Order of The First National Bank of Phila., Pa. Without Recourse except that the undersigned endorser warrants that the undersigned has furnished and installed all articles and materials and has fully completed all work which constitutes the consideration for which this note was executed and delivered by the maker. Babco Aluminum Products Co., Inc. Abe S. Mendelson."

The plaintiff bank introduced no testimony as to the date or circumstances of purchase of the note. There is evidence, however, that about the 9th or 10th of September the note was signed and that a few days later, when some disagreement arose over the straightening of the floor, Mrs. DeLise was requested to call the bank and informed the bank that she was not going to pay for the repairs unless the kitchen would be fixed the way it was promised.

After depositions were taken, the matter was submitted to Judge Lewis who has since retired from the bench. On July 11, 1957, the rule to open judgment was discharged and on March 6, 1958 an opinion was filed by Judge Carroll setting forth his reasons for refusing to open judgment. It is from this decree that the defendants filed the appeal.

It is our opinion that the judgment should be opened and defendants be allowed to present their defense. A holder in due course is a holder who takes the instrument without notice that it is overdue or has been dishonored or of any defense against it. Uniform Commercial Code, Act of April 6, 1953, P. L. 3, Section 3-302, 12A P.S. Section 3-302. Defendants contend that they were induced to sign the note by fraud and misrepresentation and that they notified the bank that they would not pay the note which Babco either intended to or did assign. Section 3-307 (3) of the Uniform Commercial Code, supra, provides that after evidence of a defense has been introduced a person claiming the rights of a holder in due course has the burden of establishing that he or some person under whom he claims is in all respects a holder in due course. Since the plaintiff introduced no testimony as to the circumstances under which the note was negotiated and since the endorsement is not dated, plaintiff has not met the burden placed upon it. See *Colonial Finance Co. v. Hoover* et al., 112 Pa. Superior Ct. 60, 170 A. 338. Where the makers of a negotiable instrument testify that it was fraudulently executed and used for a purpose not intended, a breach of faith is sufficiently established to require the endorsee to assume the burden of proving that he is a holder in due course. Here, evidence of a defense has been shown and the holder has the burden placed upon him by the Code.

Had plaintiff bank introduced evidence to the effect that it received the note for value before maturity and without notice of any claim or defense, a refusal to open judgment would have been warranted. However, the telephone call from Mrs. DeLise to the bank, advising it of her refusal to pay unless certain things were done, was sufficient. Notice may be given in any reasonable manner. It may be oral or written and in any terms which identify the instrument and states that it has been dishonored. Uniform Commercial Code, supra, Section 3-508 (3). As to the date of the notice, a question of fact has been raised, and this question is solely for the determination of the jury.

The other point in the appeal involves the question of fraud. The testimony of the defendants reveals that the Babco representatives gave them the impression that the instrument they were signing dealt with the matter of repairs only. Defendants aver that they never intended to sign a judgment note or any other negotiable instrument. On September 7, 1955, they entered into an agreement for repairs to be made in a workmanlike manner and to execute a promissory note at the completion thereof. Two days later Babco representatives called upon them to complete the details of repairs but instead had them execute a judgment note. This, if true, was an illegal imposition of liability on defendants. This misrepresentation induced them to sign the instrument without reasonable opportunity to obtain knowledge of its character.

It is urged, however, that [the fact that] some five months after the notice given to the bank, defendants voluntarily began payments on the note and continued to do so until October, 1956, operated as a waiver of rights accruing from the notice of dishonor. The testimony of defendants show that payments were made only after threats of foreclosure and sheriff's sale of their property were made. Such payments, under duress, cannot be considered as a waiver of anything nor a ratification of their acts. The relevant factors and circumstances surrounding execution of the judgment note lead us to conclude that justice will be served in opening the judgment and allowing the question to be determined by a jury.

Petition to open judgment granted.

Review Questions and Problems

1. *A* and *B* were co-makers of a note. *A* paid the balance due on the note to the payee. The payee then indorsed the note to *A* "without recourse." What is *A*'s status?
2. *A* purchased goods from *B* and accepted a trade acceptance for the amount of the purchase price. The acceptance stated that it was given in connection with goods to be delivered by *B*. *B* indorsed the instrument to Equitable Discount Corporation. *B* never delivered the goods. Equitable did not make inquiry from *A* as to whether the goods had been delivered. Can Equitable be a holder in due course?

3. The *X* Finance Co. furnished a dealer with printed forms of notes and contracts. The dealer, after making sales to customers and using these forms, would sell the paper to the finance company. On one such note the customer-maker of the note refused to pay contending that the merchandise he bought was defective. Is this defense good against *X* Finance Co.?
4. Allied Building Credits, a finance company, had been doing business with S, a builder, in financing his construction jobs. Allied prepared a completion certificate on a construction job; obtained the owner's signature; and granted a loan on the strength of the certificate. If you were the owner and were dissatisfied with the work done by the builder, what argument would you present that you had a defense to the note indorsed to the finance company by the builder?
5. *M* executed a note as a gift to *P*. *P* indorsed the note to *H* for value. Can *H* enforce the note against *M*? Would the result be different if *H* knew of the gift nature of the note when it was indorsed to him?
6. *A* fraudulently induced *B* to execute a check for $2495. *B* discovered the fraud and stopped payment on the check. In the meantime *A* cashed the check at Perfect's Market. The market seeks to recover from *B*. How would you decide?
7. What is the difference between "value" and "consideration"?
8. *M* drew a check to the order of *P* in payment for goods. The goods were defective and *M* stopped payment on the check. *P* indorsed the check to *A* in payment of an old debt. When the check was returned to *A* because of the stop order, *A* brought action against *M*. Should he prevail?
9. *O*, the owner of a motel, gave the contractor a judgment note which allowed confession of judgment at any time in payment for construction costs. The contractor indorsed the note to *A*. It developed that two subcontractors had not been paid and they had a lien upon the motel. *O* paid the subcontractors and wishes to set off these payments against the amounts due on the note. May he do so?
10. A judgment by confession was entered against Jacob and Bessie, husband and wife, on a note allegedly signed by both. Bessie denied that she signed the note and seeks to have the judgment set aside. Who has the burden of proving that Bessie's signature was genuine or forged?
11. Bearer government bonds were stolen from Bank of America. They were turned over to the First National Bank which collected the amount thereof from the Federal Reserve Bank and paid the proceeds to *P* and *R*. Bank of America seeks to recover the value of the bonds from *P*, *R*, and the two banks. What question must be decided in order to resolve this case?
12. *A* bought automatic automobile washing equipment on a conditional sales contract from *B* and executed a note. *B* indorsed the note to *C* after maturity. The equipment was faulty and cars of *A*'s customers were damaged. *A* informed *B* that he would have to remove the equipment. Can *C* collect on the note?
13. *A* drew a check in favor of *B* for $50 and presented it to *B* as a gift. *B* indorsed the check to *C* in payment of a debt that *B* owed *C*. *A* refused to honor the check. Can *C* recover from *A*?

14. *M* executed a note to *P* for siding which *P* agreed to furnish and install on *M*'s home. *M* delivered part of the siding but failed to deliver the balance and did no installation. *P* indorsed the note to *G* bank which had been placed on notice that precaution should be taken in purchasing notes from *P*. To what extent can the bank recover on the note?
15. *M* bought a truck from S Co. and gave a note secured by a chattel mortgage on the truck in payment. S Co. sold the note to a bank. *M* refused to pay the note because the truck was encumbered by a prior mortgage which had been concealed from him by S Co. Was the bank charged with knowledge of the prior mortgage?
16. *W*, president of *X* Corp. received checks payable to the corporation, indorsed them and deposited them to his personal account in *B* Bank. *W* drew checks against this deposit. Is *B* Bank liable to *X* Corp. for conversion of the checks?
17. *F*, a holder in due course of a check, transfers it to *H*, who has knowledge of a defense to the check. Is *H* a holder in due course? Would the result be the same if the transfer took place beyond a reasonable time after the check was issued?
18. *M* executed his note to *P* to pay for stock in the Geronimo Motor Co., but did so because of fraudulent representations of *P*. *P* sold and indorsed the note to *H* who sued and obtained a judgment, the court there holding *H* was a holder in due course. Then an assignment of the judgment was made to *P* for value. May *P* collect of *M*?
19. *A* held a check for $200 made payable to the order of *A*, agent of *P*. He indorsed the check to *H* in payment of a personal indebtedness. If *P* later claims the proceeds of the check, may *H* maintain that he took the instrument in good faith and so became a holder in due course?
20. *M* bought laundry machinery of Allied Machinery Co. and gave a series of notes therefor. The machinery company's president, *X*, went to Norbert Trading Co. and sold the notes thereto for 10 per cent less than their face value, telling the officer with whom he dealt that the machinery company was in a strained financial condition and needed the money rather than the notes. The notes were indorsed, "Allied Machinery Co., *X* Pres., *Y* Sec." On trial this was proved, but *M* still insisted that Norbert Trading Co. had not shown itself to be a holder in due course, specifically since there was no proof of the authority of *X* and *Y* to indorse. *M* offered no proof on these contentions. Should *M* prevail?

24

Liability of Parties

4-44. In general. The parties on negotiable paper may be divided into two groups—primary parties and secondary parties. The primary parties are the makers of notes and the acceptors of drafts. The secondary parties are drawers of drafts, drawers of checks, and indorsers. This classification is helpful in distinguishing the liabilities of the two types of parties. A primary party is primarily liable; that is, he is a person who, by the terms of the instrument is absolutely required to pay the same. A secondary party is secondarily liable; that is, he becomes liable only when the primary party fails to pay and the holder performs certain conditions precedent; namely presentment, notice, and dishonor, which will be discussed more in detail in Chapter 25.

The liability of the various parties to commercial paper will be discussed in the following sections.

4-45. Signature. The Code requires that an instrument, to be negotiable, must be in writing and signed by the maker or drawer. Section 3-401 provides:

> (1) No person is liable on an instrument unless his signature appears thereon.[1]
>
> (2) A signature is made by use of any name, including any trade or assumed name, upon an instrument, or by any word or mark used in lieu of a written signature.

It is not required that any particular type or kind of writing be used, nor is it necessary that the signature be at any particular place upon the instrument. The signature of the maker or drawer may be in any form: printed, written, or stamped. It may be a corporate name, partnership name, or assumed name.[2] A sign or any kind of written words is sufficient if it is clear that such method was intended to represent the signature

[1] In re Eton Furniture Co., page 570.

[2] Senor v. Bangor Mills, page 572.

of the party creating liability in the instrument. Parol evidence is admissable to determine who made the sign or symbol as his signature. When such identification is made the signature is legal. In some jurisdictions a signature by mark must be attested by a witness, although this is not required under common law.

A person signing a contract which gives rise to a negotiable instrument is liable on the contract, but his obligation is not measured by any negotiable instrument related thereto unless he signs such instrument. Drawees who orally accept, and purported indorsees who never sign the paper are not liable on the paper. Any liability that might arise by reason of warranties and breaches thereof, is not covered by this portion of the Code.

4-46. Signature in ambiguous capacity. The Code in revised language adopts the NIL which provided that where a signature is so placed upon the instrument that it is not clear in what capacity the person making the same intended to sign he is deemed to be an indorser.[3]

The Code states: "Unless the instrument clearly indicates that a signature is made in some other capacity it is an indorsement."

This provision applies in cases where the signer does not place his name on the paper in the usual place.[4] If the place of signature clearly indicates that the signer intended to be bound other than as an indorser, he will not be held as such, and parol evidence is not admissible to show that he intended to be an indorser. However, if the signer's name appears on the back of the paper or on the front thereof, after the word "indorser" the signer is an indorser even though he signed on the face of the paper. For example, a note stated: "We promise to pay *X*, *Y*, and *Z*" and then recited "the maker and indorser each hereby waive" various privileges, etc., and was signed by "*A* Corporation" by its president after which followed twenty names on the face of the paper. It was held that the twenty signators appearing on the face of the paper were indorsers.

The language on the paper must clearly indicate that the signer does not intend to be an indorser. Thus the signatures "John Jones, Maker," "Henry Brown, Acceptor," "Pete Smith, Surety" clearly indicate an intention to be bound, but not as indorsers. For example, where the back of an instrument contained a long list of notations of interest payments followed by an entry, "Int. paid to Aug. 1, 1963, J. B. Brown." Brown's indication of the purpose for which his signature was placed on the paper, namely, receipt for an interest payment, removes him from the application of the Code even though other names appeared upon the back of the paper as indorsers.

[3] Grange National Bank v. Conville, page 574.

[4] Fidelity-Philadelphia Trust Co. v. Rovner, page 576.

4-47. Signature by authorized representative. Most business is conducted by agents or representatives on behalf of principals. Principals may be individuals, partnerships acting under an assumed name, corporations, and other legal entities. The business relationship that exists between the principal and the agent in most cases presupposes that the acts and conduct of the agent bind the principal only. In creating negotiable commercial paper on behalf of the principal, an authorized agent may execute the instrument in many different ways. The Code prescribes methods by which an authorized agent may by proper signature release himself from liability, or how he may by ambiguous language subject himself to liability. Thus,

(1) A signature may be made by an agent or other representative, and his authority to make it may be established as in other cases of representation. No particular form of appointment is necessary to establish such authority.

(2) An authorized representative who signs his own name to an instrument

(a) *is personally obligated* if the instrument neither names the person represented nor shows that the representative signed in a representative capacity;

(b) except as otherwise established between the immediate parties, *is personally obligated* if the instrument names the person represented but does not show that the representative signed in a representative capacity, or if the instrument does not name the person represented but does show that the representative signed in a representative capacity.

(3) Except as otherwise established the name of an organization preceded or followed by the name and office of an authorized individual is a signature made in a representative capacity. (Emphases added)

A purchaser of a negotiable instrument is entitled to know by looking at the face of the paper whose obligation is evidenced by the paper. When a purchaser looks at an instrument and finds two or more names on the paper, it may not be easy from inspection of the paper to determine whether an agent relationship is created, or whether the purported agent intended to bind himself, or only his principal, or both.[5]

In all cases under the Code it is assumed that the agent has authority to bind the principal, however, the way the agent signs the paper may justify a purchaser in assuming that the agent intends to be jointly liable with the principal.[6] The problem is the same whether the kind of sig-

[5] Kiska v. Rosen, page 577.
[6] In re Laskin, page 578.

nature in question is that of an agent signing for a maker, drawer, indorser, or acceptor.

The different ways in which an agent may sign are numerous. The following examples will illustrate the problems involved.

1. An agent may sign only his own name, without showing the name of his principal and that he is signing in a representative capacity. Thus, he may sign simply, "John Doe." The agent here is personally liable and extrinsic evidence is not admissible to avoid liability. Since the principal's name does not appear on the paper, he cannot be liable.

2. An authorized agent may sign the name of his principal only. Thus, "Roy Roe." The principal here is personally liable. The authority granted by the principal to the agent, orally or by a separate agreement, relieves the agent in an action between the principal and agent.

3. An agent may sign the instrument, "John Doe, Agent." Here he has not disclosed a principal, but he has disclosed that he is acting in a representative capacity. Since the term, "agent," is merely descriptive, doubt is raised in the mind of a purchaser as to who is obligated. A holder in due course should be free from the burden of ascertaining for whom John Doe is an agent.

Introducing evidence to ascertain whose instrument has been created would impair negotiability. The mere addition of words describing the signer "as agent" does not exempt the agent from personal liability. Parol evidence is inadmissible to show that the agent did not intend to be bound. For example, corporate officers have been held personally liable as indorsers on a note signed in the corporate name as maker and indorsed by A, B, and C, identified as corporate officers such as president, secretary, director, on the theory that such signing merely described the indorsers, and did not disclose that they signed in a representative capacity.[7] Although such imposition of legal duty here imposes a burden on the corporate officers it nevertheless aids in the vendability of commercial paper. However the Code exonerates the agent by permitting him to use parol evidence in litigation between immediate parties if the paper on its face shows he signed in a representative capacity without naming the principal, or if the principal is named but the language does not show a representative capacity.[8]

The Code illustrates many ways by which an authorized agent may sign. No particular form of authorization is required.

The comment under the above section of the Code gives the following illustration:

[7] Grange National Bank v. Conville, page 574.
[8] Fidelity-Philadelphia Trust Co. v. Rovner, page 576.

Assuming "Peter Pringle" is a principal and "Arthur Adams" is his agent, an instrument might for example bear the following signatures affixed by the agent:

(a) "Peter Pringle" or
(b) "Arthur Adams" or
(c) "Peter Pringle by Arthur Adams, Agent" or
(d) "Arthur Adams, Agent" or
(e) "Peter Pringle
Arthur Adams" or
(f) "Peter Pringle Corporation
Arthur Adams"

The form set out in (a) does not bind the agent Arthur Adams, the signature in (b) does personally bind Adams even though he is the agent. He cannot introduce evidence to show he was such agent.

The most accurate way is to sign as in (c) where not only the principal is disclosed but also the agent's representative capacity is indicated.

In order to resolve conflicts the Code specifically provides, that where the agent signs his name only as in (b) or signs his name followed by descriptive terms, in litigation between immediate parties the principal is obligated, the agent having the right to introduce parol evidence to prove that he signed as an agent and in a representative capacity. As to all other persons the agent is personally liable.[9]

4-48. Unauthorized signatures. The Code revises the language of the NIL with regard to unauthorized signatures. Section 3-404 provides:

(1) Any unauthorized signature is wholly inoperative as that of the person whose name is signed unless he ratifies it or is precluded from denying it; but it operates as the signature of the unauthorized signer in favor of any person who in good faith pays the instrument or takes it for value.

(2) Any unauthorized signature may be ratified for all purposes of this Article. Such ratification does not of itself affect any rights of the person ratifying against the actual signer.

The term "unauthorized signature" encompasses not only forgeries but also signatures by agents who exceed their authority, actual or apparent. The person whose signature is forged is not bound on the instrument unless his conduct is such as to prevent him from asserting the forgery or other unauthorized signature as a defense.[10] However, the wrongdoer—forger or agent—is himself bound to the full amount of the instrument to a party who takes the instrument or pays it in good faith. In general this follows the NIL with the addition of the provision imposing liability on the forger or agent.

[9] Salitan v. Abington Tractor Co., page 580.
[10] Household Finance Corp. v. Newton Savings Bank, page 582.

Under the NIL, it was not clear as to whether a forgery could be ratified and the cases were in conflict. It is clear under the Code that a forged signature may be adopted and that such adoption is retroactive to the time when the forgery occurred. If the person whose name was forged retains the benefits of the transaction with knowledge of the forgery, the principle of ratification will apply. Likewise an estoppel may apply where there has been a representation to an innocent purchaser that the signature is genuine.

Of course, the actual signer or forger is liable to the person whose name was signed and he may also be subject to criminal action notwithstanding the ratification.

To illustrate the foregoing, suppose that *A*, an agent, executes an instrument and that he lacks the authority to do so. He signs the instrument in the name of his principal, *P*, by "*A*, agent." The principal, *P*, is not bound (absent ratification or estoppel), but *A* is liable to the holder.

Liability of banks. If a bank pays an instrument which is payable to the order of a person named therein, it is liable if it pays to the wrong person in the case of a forged or unauthorized signature or indorsement.[11]

In the case of a forged drawer's signature the so-called *"Rule of Price v. Neal"* precludes recovery by a drawee who honors a forged instrument. This is subject to the limitation that recovery may be had if the party who dealt with the forger was negligent.[12]

If a bank cashes a check indorsed by an agent who lacks authority, the bank will be held liable if it were charged with knowledge of the lack of authority and the principal can recover from the bank the amount paid out on such forged indorsement.[13]

The drawer can insist that the drawee recredit his account with the amount of any unauthorized payment.[14]

Liability of others. If the payee's employee wrongfully and without authority cashes checks payable to his employer, the person cashing such checks is liable to the payee for the amount of the checks.[15]

4-49. Impostors: Signature in name of payee. A situation which is comparable to forgery arises when an instrument is made payable to a fictitious person or where one person impersonates another and the instrument is made payable to the impostor. In each of these situations the drawer's signature may be genuine but the instrument is indorsed in the

[11] Provident Trust Co. of Phil. v. Interboro Bank & Trust Co., page 583.
[12] Mechanics Natl. Bank v. Worcester Trust Co., page 585.
[13] Huntingdon County v. First Grange National Bank, page 587.
[14] Stone & Webster Engineering Co. v. First National Bank & Trust Co., page 664.
[15] Gresham State Bank v. O. & K. Construction Co., page 591.

fictitious name or the name of the person who is being impersonated. Who should bear the loss under such circumstances?

The NIL provided that an "instrument is payable to *bearer* when it is payable to the order of a fictitious or nonexisting person . . ." Thus the loss was imposed on the drawer since he had created bearer paper which did not require any indorsement and could be negotiated by mere delivery. The Code reaches this result without resorting to the fiction of the NIL. Section 3-405 of the Code provides that an *indorsement by any person* in the name of a named payee is effective if:

(b) a person signing as or on behalf of a maker or drawer intends the payee to have no interest in the instrument; or
(c) an agent or employee of the maker of drawer has supplied him with the name of the payee intending the latter to have no such interest.

A typical situation is one in which a dishonest employee is either authorized to sign his employer's name to checks or draws checks which he presents to his employer for the latter's signature. The employee draws payroll checks or checks payable to persons with whom the employer would be expected to do business. He either signs them or obtains his employer's signature and then cashes the checks indorsing the name of the payee. If he is in charge of the company's books, he is able to manipulate the books when the cancelled checks are returned and may thus avoid detection for some time. The Code imposes this loss on the employer. The paper does not become bearer paper but the wrongdoer can effectively indorse in the payee's name.

Another fraudulent scheme is that in which a person poses as someone else and induces the drawer to issue a check payable to the order of the person who is being impersonated.[16] The Code provides in Section 3-405 (1) (a) that an indorsement in the name of a named payee is effective if:

an impostor by use of the mails or otherwise has induced the maker or drawer to issue the instrument to him or his confederate in the name of the payee;

The comment to this section states:

Subsection (1) (a) is new. It rejects decisions which distinguish between face-to-face imposture and imposture by mail and hold that where the parties deal by mail the dominant intent of the drawer is to deal with the name rather than with the person so that the resulting instrument may be negotiated only by indorsement of the payee whose name has been taken in vain. The result of

[16] Davis v. Western Union Telegraph Co., page 595.

the distinction has been under some prior law, to throw the loss in the mail imposture forward to a subsequent holder or to the drawee. Since the maker or drawer believes the two to be one and the same, the two intentions cannot be separated, and the "dominant intent" is a fiction. The position here taken is that the loss, regardless of the type of fraud which the particular impostor has committed, should fall upon the maker or drawer.

"Impostor" refers to impersonation, and does not extend to a false representation that the party is the authorized agent of the payee. The maker or drawer who takes the precaution of making the instrument payable to the principal is entitled to have his indorsement.

4-50. Negligence contributing to alteration or unauthorized signature—defenses. A customer of a bank signed and delivered to his clerk printed checks, blank as to payees and amounts. He authorized the clerk to fill in the name of the payees and the amounts of bills to be paid. The clerk caused one of the checks to be filled with the word, "fifty." The word commencing with a small letter was written some distance from the left side of the check. The figure, 50.00, was placed at a considerable distance from the $ sign. The clerk handed the check to a friend asking her to get cash at a super market. The friend inserted her name as payee, and in the blank space before the word, "fifty," wrote the words, "three hundred," and put the figure "3" between the dollar sign and the figures, "50.00." The drawee bank paid $350.00 on the check.

Such facts as here are related do occur, and as to the instrument, the loss is borne by the depositor-drawer. The Code has spelled out the drawer's liability as follows:

> Any person who by his negligence substantially contributes to a material alteration of the instrument or to the making of an unauthorized signature is precluded from asserting the alteration or lack of authority against a holder in due course or against a drawee or other payor who pays the instrument in good faith and in accordance with the reasonable commercial standards of the drawee's or payor's business.

In the example above, the drawer has so negligently controlled the check and by his agent so negligently executed the instrument as to facilitate material alteration. If checks are to pass current as money, the careless creator of paper should suffer the loss as against holders in due course and the innocent drawees and other payors who pay the instrument in good faith. How negligent and careless the drawer must be in creating the paper is a fact question. The improper execution must substantially contribute to the material alteration. What is a material alteration will be discussed in the next section. The relation of a depositor and the bank is that of debtor and creditor. The bank is under a duty to pay a check drawn by the depositor according to its tenor.

It is therefore proper that the depositor should be bound to exercise care in drafting checks in order to prevent the bank from being deceived. Drawing a check in a manner which facilitates fraud constitutes a breach of duty to the bank.

The Code declares that under fact situations like the above, a person negligently creating an instrument which facilitates alteration is estopped or barred from claiming a defense of "no contract and non-liability." A person placing current paper in the channels of business owes a duty to future users to so create paper that it cannot be altered. The holder, drawee, and other good faith takers should not be deterred in its use. The negligent drawers and makers must seek recovery from the wrongdoer. Of course when the instrument has been altered by a mechanical process or erasure or chemical change another instrument has been created, and no negligent conduct can be attributed to the issuer of the paper. A drawer of a check or a maker of a note who signs his name on blank paper is responsible for its completion by others; likewise he is liable for inadequate execution.

The Code not only imposes a duty on an issuer for negligent execution, but also imposes a duty for negligent conduct which contributes to forgery and the placing of another's signature and indorsement on paper without express or implied authority.[17] A forged or unauthorized signature is wholly inoperative, thus a real defense. However, under certain circumstances concerned with the law of agency, where paper has been inadvertently delivered, signatures may be legally effective.

A, as a course of conduct, has permitted his secretary to issue checks by means of a mechanical device and rubber stamps. Unauthorized checks issued and delivered by reason of the careless control and supervision of such equipment would prevent *A* from denying liability. *A* also would be precluded from setting up a defense of an unauthorized signature when, after knowledge that a forgery has occurred, he negligently makes no attempt to deny or prevent the use of his name. Inadvertency in mistakenly mailing checks, particularly to persons of the same name, is negligent conduct contributing to the use of an unauthorized signature, the loss of which must be borne by the issuer. The question is, what conduct is "negligent" so that it can be said that it has "substantially contributed to a material alteration" or to the making of "an unauthorized signature." It is believed that this section would not demand the use of sensitized paper, fast inks, and "checkographs" by drawers in order to avoid negligent conduct.

4-51. Material alteration—defenses. The Code not only deals with

[17] Gresham State Bank v. O. & K. Construction Co., page 591.

the conduct of the creator of paper who negligently executes it in such manner as to facilitate alteration, but also designates what constitutes a material alteration,[18] and declares the effect of such alteration on the rights of a holder in due course, and others not holders in due course.

Material alteration constitutes a change in the contract of the parties. The Code states that:

> (1) Any alteration of an instrument is material which changes the contract of any party thereto in any respect, including any such change in
> (a) the number or relations of the parties; or
> (b) an incomplete instrument, by completing it otherwise than as authorized; or
> (c) the writing as signed, by adding to it or by removing any part of it.

A person should not be charged on a contract he has not made. If a change in the contract does not affect the legal relation of the parties no material alteration has been made and such alteration will not discharge a party or give him a defense. Words may be added or deleted and not affect the paper. For example, addresses of parties may be changed; information about the parties added; none of which have any legal operative effect. Only the party whose legal relations are affected by the alterations can be exonerated; other parties on the paper cannot assert the defenses of the party entitled.

Changes in the amount of money due, adding persons as additional payees, changing the interest rate, unauthorized completion of blanks, mutilating or cutting away nonperforated related contracts are illustrations of material alterations which change the legal effect of the instrument and make a different contract than that originally intended.[19]

It is significant to note that an alteration to be material and discharge any party must be made by the holder. Interference with the paper by third party strangers can in no way affect the holder's rights nor impair the instrument in its original form. Such third parties gain no advantage by reason of alterations. Such third parties, however, may be liable in tort for injury to property. Commercial paper is often printed as part of formal written contracts. Such instrument may or may not provide for the detachment of the commercial paper. To evidence implied authority to detach, perforations or dotted lines are set out between the negotiable portion and the contract. In absence of authority to detach either ex-

[18] Poelcher v. Zink, page 595.
[19] Abercrombie Estate, page 596.

pressed or implied, unauthorized detachment from a formal written contract constitutes a material alteration. A holder in due course of a detached instrument, however, may recover according to the original tenor of the paper.

A provision of the Code changes a rule of the NIL by providing that a material alteration does not discharge any party unless it is made for a fraudulent purpose. If an alteration is made innocently with an honest belief that it is authorized or for the benefit of an obligor, the instrument is not discharged.

A holder in due course or a holder from a holder in due course is not affected regardless of the nature of the alteration. Thus such a holder may enforce the instrument according to its original tenor. Even though the instrument has been improperly completed it may be enforced as completed.[20] The old defense of nondelivery of an incompleted instrument has been abrogated by the Code.

A party whose original contract obligation is changed by the alteration is discharged to the extent of the change. If the alteration is not material or fraudulent, there is no discharge and the instrument is enforced according to its original tenor.

Since a delivered blank paper has no original tenor, such paper will be enforced according to the authority under which it was created.

Persons not holders in due course may also enforce the paper according to its original tenor, or as completed if completed as authorized provided the alterations are not material and fraudulent and are not made by a prior holder. Any subsequent party whose contract is affected thereby is discharged. A party whose contract would have been discharged by material alterations may however be bound if he has previously consented to the alterations or his conduct has been such as to estop him from asserting a defense.

4-52. Consideration. Negotiable instruments designated as commercial paper under the Code are contracts. Such paper evidences promises to pay money in the future. The basis for this liability—consideration—is the same as any other contract, except for the differences hereinafter set forth. Thus, consideration to make promises binding in commercial paper is essential and its want or failure is a defense as against all persons except holders in due course.[21] Thus,

> Want or failure of consideration is a defense as against any person not having the rights of a holder in due course (Section 3-305), except that no con-

[20] The First National Bank of Philadelphia v. Anderson, page 527.
[21] Umani v. Reber, page 599.

sideration is necessary for an instrument or obligation thereon given in payment of or as security for an antecedent obligation of any kind. Nothing in this section shall be taken to displace any statute outside this Act under which a promise is enforceable notwithstanding lack or failure of consideration. Partial failure of consideration is a defense pro tanto whether or not the failure is in an ascertained or liquidated amount.

In the law of negotiable paper another term, *value,* is used. Under the NIL, "value" was defined as "any consideration sufficient to support a simple contract." Under the NIL "consideration" and "value" were used as convertible terms. The Code distinguishes between these two terms. Consideration has significance only in determining whether a contractual binding obligation has been created. "Value" is used to determine whether a holder has given something in payment for the instrument. For a discussion of what constitutes taking for value, see Section 4-39, (U.C.C. Section 3-303.)

Although consideration is a requirement in the creation of contracts, it is not as rigidly applied in the law of negotiable paper. Negotiable instruments serve as important vehicles in business operations, and their function should not be impaired by the application of strict common law contract consideration. Thus the execution and delivery of a demand negotiable instrument by a debtor to his creditor in payment of a past debt is given for consideration.[22] The whole question of past consideration and antecedent debt as inadequate consideration is not an issue in "commercial paper." Accommodation parties who sign, or promise to sign, or who indorse, paper given in payment of an antecedent debt or as collateral security are bound.[23] Promises for the extension of time, promises to pay or payment of lesser sums than due, do not fail for want or inadequacy of consideration. Promissory estoppel and other substitutes for consideration are adequate.(See Section 2-29 for consideration in contract law generally.)

A holder in due course takes free from the failure or absence of consideration. However, want or failure of consideration is a defense between immediate parties and nonholders in due course. Partial failure of consideration is not a complete defense but may be set up pro tanto.

Local statutes should be examined to ascertain under what circumstances consideration is not required. Want and failure of consideration are defenses and must be affirmatively pleaded.

4-53. Draft not an assignment. The Code adopts in principle the law set out in section 127 of the NIL which states: "A bill of itself does not operate as an assignment of the funds in the hands of the drawee

[22] Insdorf v. Wil-Avon Merchandise Mart, page 599.
[23] Greater Valley Terminal Corp. v. Goodman, page 600.

available for the payment thereof, and the drawee is not liable in the bill unless and until he accepts the same." Section 189 of the NIL likewise provided "that a draft does not operate as an assignment of any funds to the credit of the drawer with the bank and the bank is not liable to this holder, unless and until it accepts or certifies the check."[24] The Code provides:

(1) A check or other draft does not of itself operate as an assignment of any funds in the hands of the drawee available for its payment, and the drawee is not liable on the instrument until he accepts it.

(2) Nothing in this section shall affect any liability in contract, tort or otherwise arising from any letter of credit or other obligation or representation which is not an acceptance.

Drawees of a draft or check occupy an unusual position. They are debtors, or potential debtors of the drawer. The drawer by the instrument orders the drawee to pay money to the payee or holder. Before such duty on the paper arises the drawee must accept the paper. Previous contracts between the drawer and drawee, such as a depositor-bank relationship, may give the drawer power to draw a check or draft on the drawee. Likewise, a future drawer-buyer might, by reason of a previous contract for the sale of goods, draw a draft on his purchaser-debtor-drawee by way of payment.

Even if the drawee by previous contract is under a duty to accept, such duty gives no cause of action to a holder upon refusal of the drawee to pay. The drawee's liability is to the drawer. The failure of the drawee to accept or his breach of other arrangements with the drawer, will expose the drawee to liability to the drawer, but not a holder. A drawee bank's refusal to pay or certify a check which impairs the credit of the drawer may subject the bank to tort liability for failure to promptly comply with letters of credit or other promises to pay or accept.

This does not mean that the drawee cannot become liable to a payee or holder. If the drawee is debtor in fact, the drawer-creditor by a contract of assignment may assign all or a part of his rights against the drawee to a third party. This process is governed by the law of contracts, not by the law of commercial paper. A payee or holder of a draft or check may have rights against a drawee by reason of a trust relationship or some contract made for the holder's benefit or otherwise; such rights rest on fact situations outside the law of commercial paper.

It is the acceptance of the paper by the drawee that gives rights to the holder. The acceptance makes the drawee-acceptor the primary obligor; the drawer and all other parties become secondary parties. By such

[24] Universal C.I.T. Credit Corp. v. Guaranty Bank, page 661.

method paper is created which can function freely in the channels of commerce as a substitute for money, whereas the assignment process as a means of transferring credit carries burdens against the title which limits its use as a substitute for money. (See Section 4-3, Transfer of claims for money.)

The next three sections are concerned with the definition, method, operation, and effect of the acceptance by the drawee of commercial paper, and how such acceptance facilitates negotiability.

4-54. Definition and operation of acceptance.

(1) Acceptance is the drawee's signed engagement to honor the draft as presented. It must be written on the draft, and may consist of his signature alone. It becomes operative when completed by delivery or notification.

(2) A draft may be accepted although it has not been signed by the drawer or is otherwise incomplete or is overdue or has been dishonored.

(3) Where the draft is payable at a fixed period after sight and the acceptor fails to date his acceptance the holder may complete it by supplying a date in good faith.

The acceptor of a bill of exchange is the primary party upon the paper. By accepting the instrument, he engages that he will pay it according to the tenor of his acceptance, and admits the existence of the drawer, the genuineness of his signature, his capacity and authority to draw the instrument, the existence of the payee, and his then capacity to indorse. Before accepting the bill of exchange, the acceptor is called the drawee. The instrument may be drawn by the drawer and negotiated before its acceptance by the drawee. The instrument may be accepted by the drawee before it is drawn or completed. As mentioned before, one who draws a bill of exchange (drawer) is usually a creditor of the drawee or has arranged with the drawee to draw on him. Some credit or contract right probably exists in the drawer against the drawee. For instance, John Doe enters into an agreement with the First National Bank whereby the latter agrees to accept bills of exchange for a certain amount drawn on the bank by John Doe. The bank is not liable to the payee of the bill until it accepts the bill. If it does not accept, it is only liable to John Doe for breach of contract to accept. After acceptance, the bank is liable to the payee as well as to the drawer.

The acceptance must be in writing on the draft and signed by the drawee-acceptor. Acceptance is usually made by the drawee's writing the word "accepted," with his name and the date, across the face of the instrument. The word "accepted" is not necessary; it is preferable, however, to write the word "accepted" across the face of the instrument above the signature of the drawee-acceptor. The acceptance is not completed until delivery of the instrument or notification of the acceptance by the acceptor to the person presenting it for acceptance.

It must be noted that the Code does not include either "collateral or constructive acceptances" as set out in the NIL. The Code specifically provides that "an acceptance is the drawee's signed engagement to honor the draft as presented. It *must be written on draft* and may consist of his signature alone." This excludes "promises to accept," and acceptances upon separate instruments and other collateral acceptances. Danger of separation from the draft or check, and ambiguous language leading to dispute as to whether an acceptance was or was not made dictate the necessity for certain and accurate evidence of the drawee's liability.

Present banking practice requires the paper to be forwarded to the drawee for acceptance either upon the paper, or upon the understanding that the obligation to pay has been previously secured by a letter of credit. (See U.C.C. Article 5, Letters of Credit.)

The usual form for an acceptance is the signature of the drawee on the face of the paper; however, he may sign in any convenient place. No additional words are necessary. The drawee's signature as acceptor on incompleted paper binds him to all subsequent parties to the extent of its completion as authorized. An acceptor is subject to all the risks and duties imposed by U.C.C. 3-406 and, if by his negligent conduct he contributes to materially altered paper which gets into the stream of commerce, he is liable for all loss caused by such negligence.

4-55. Certification of checks. When the bank upon which a check is drawn accepts or certifies it, such an act operates as an appropriation of as much of the drawer's deposit as is required to pay the instrument. Sufficient funds out of the drawer's account are set aside for the purpose of paying the check when it is later presented.

The certification of a check by the bank upon which it is drawn, at the request of a holder, is equivalent to an acceptance. The bank thereby becomes the principal debtor upon the instrument. The liability of the bank is the same as the liability of an acceptor of any other bill of exchange. The bank admits that the drawer's signature is genuine; that the depositor's account contains sufficient funds to pay the check; and that the money will not be withdrawn.

The certification must be in writing and signed by the proper officer of the bank. A certification adds much to the saleability of the paper, as it carries with it the strength and credit of the bank.

The certification may or may not change the legal liability of the parties upon the instrument. When the drawer has a check certified, such a certification merely acts as additional security and does not relieve the drawer of any liability. The holder of such an instrument, if it is dishonored after presentment, is still under a legal duty to satisfy the conditions precedent to charge the secondary parties. On the other hand, when the holder of a check secures certification by the drawee bank, he thereby accepts the bank as the only party liable thereon. Such an act discharges the drawer and all prior indorsers from liability. The effect of such certification is similar to a payment by the bank and redeposit by the holder.

The refusal of a bank to certify a check at the request of a holder is held not to be a dishonor of the instrument. The bank owes the depositor a duty to pay but not necessarily the duty to certify checks which are drawn on it, unless there is a previous agreement so to certify.

The Code continues the law as it existed under the NIL, but does give express recognition to banking practices in connection with certification of checks. Under the Code it is specified that a drawer cannot countermand a check after the bank has certified it.

Under Code Section 3-409 (2) a draft may be accepted although it has not been signed by the drawer or completed. A check may also come to the drawee bank incomplete without proper indorsement. The bank may under Section 3-411 (3) of the Code certify the check before returning the same through channels for indorsement, in order to relieve the drawer from liability that might arise because of loss occurring before the check is returned. Such certification discharges the drawer.

4-56. Acceptance varying draft. As previously stated, the right to draw a draft or check usually rests upon a previous contractual understanding between the drawer and drawee. The drawer is a creditor, the drawee a debtor. The depositor-bank contract gives the depositor the right to draw a draft-check upon the bank, which instrument as negotiable paper is used by the drawer to pay an obligation to the payee. The drawer orders the bank to pay by cash or accept the check in such manner as to discharge the drawer's obligation. The situations are numerous under which a creditor may draw a draft on his debtor. When such paper is created and placed in the channels of trade the payee and all future holders are entitled to an unqualified acceptance by the drawee. Any other acceptance changes the original contract between the parties. Thus "Where the drawee's proffered acceptance in any manner varies the draft as presented the holder may refuse the acceptance and treat the draft as dishonored in which case the drawee is entitled to have his acceptance cancelled." When the drawee offers an acceptance which in any manner varies or changes the direct order to pay or promise to pay money, the holder may refuse the acceptance. The paper is dishonored, and upon notice of dishonor or protest the holder may hold all prior parties on the paper back to and including the drawer. The attempted varied acceptance may be withdrawn by the drawee. An acceptance for part of the sum, payment at a different place, performance of service in payment of the debt, are all at variance from the duty to pay money as ordered by the drawer.

Tender of a different kind of acceptance by the drawee is an offer to give a substituted performance. If the holder wishes to accept such varied performance, he may do so. This however creates a new contract, and all prior parties including the drawer are discharged unless a consent for substituted performance has been given. If the drawee refuses to perform the varied acceptance, he is liable for breach of contract to the holder.

The Code provides that the draft is not varied by an acceptance to pay at a particular bank or place in the United States unless the draft specifically directs that payment is to be made at a particular bank. (See U.C.C. 3-504.)

4-57. Contract of maker, drawer, and acceptor. Section 3-413 of the Code does not substantially change the provisions of the NIL. It clearly establishes that the maker of a note and the acceptor of a draft are primarily liable. It provides: "(1) The maker or acceptor engages that he will pay the instrument according to its tenor at the time of his engagement or as completed pursuant to Section 3-115 on incomplete instruments." The incorporation of Section 3-115 makes it clear that if a maker signs and issues an incomplete note, such note when thereafter completed can be enforced against him. On the other hand if an instrument is materially altered after it is made or accepted, the maker or acceptor are only liable to pay the instrument according to its tenor at the time of their engagement. If the amount has been raised, they are only liable for the original amount. However, if negligence of the maker or acceptor is a material factor in contributing to the alteration, they may be held liable under Section 3-406 for the altered amount.

Subsection (2) which relates to the drawer's liability provides: "The drawer engages that upon dishonor of the draft and any necessary notice of dishonor or protest he will pay the amount of the draft to the holder or to any indorser who takes it up. The drawer may disclaim this liability by drawing without recourse." In effect the drawer assumes a conditional liability on the instrument—that he will pay if the instrument is dishonored and he is properly notified of this fact. Such liability can be disclaimed, however, if the draft is drawn "without recourse."

The party who makes a note, draws a draft or check, or accepts a draft admits as against all subsequent parties the existence of the payee and his then capacity to indorse. In the case of a draft or check the drawee is included within the protection of this provision.

4-58. Contract of indorser. Indorsers are secondarily liable on instruments by virtue of their contract of indorsement. The contract of indorsement is conditional, that is, if the instrument is properly presented to the primary party, is dishonored and any protest or notice of dishonor which may be necessary under Section 3-501 of the Code is given, the indorser will be required to pay the instrument. This obligation of the indorser runs to any holder and to any subsequent indorser who has reacquired the instrument. The engagement of the indorser is to "pay the instrument according to its tenor at the time of his indorsement." The indorser of an altered instrument thus assumes liability as indorser on the instrument as altered.

Basically section 3-414 of the Code which deals with the contract of indorsement follows the provisions of the NIL. The NIL provided specifically for a "qualified indorsement" whereby the indorser could disclaim this liability. The Code, while it does not use this terminology, provides for the same result. If an indorser adds the words "without recourse" to his indorsement, he thereby disclaims liability on the indorsement contract.[25]

Section 44 of the NIL, which provided that a person who indorsed in a representative capacity might indorse in such terms as to negative personal liability, has been omitted under the Code. It is felt that such right is included within the broader right to disclaim *any* liability.

It must be noted that in addition to his conditional liability an indorser, if he is a transferor, is liable for the warranties as stated in Section 3-417. Thus the indorser in addition to his conditional contract liability has unconditional liability as a warrantor.[26]

Subsection 2 of Section 3-414 provides: "Unless they otherwise agree indorsers are liable to one another in the order in which they indorse, which is presumed to be the order in which their signatures appear on the instrument." This is intended to clarify a similar provision in the NIL. Parol evidence is admissible to show that the indorsers did not actually indorse in the order in which their names appear or that they may have agreed among themselves as to the nature and order of their liability.

4-59. Contract of accommodation party. One who signs an instrument for the purpose of lending his name and credit to another party to the instrument is an "accommodation party."[27] Under the Code, an accommodation party is always a surety.

[25] The Union Bank v. Mobilla, page 601.
[26] *Ibid.*
[27] General Refrigerator and Store Fixture Co. v. Fry, page 603.

Section 3-415 of the Code defines the contract of an accommodation party as follows:

(1) An accommodation party is one who signs the instrument in any capacity for the purpose of lending his name to another party to it.
(2) When the instrument has been taken for value before it is due the accommodation party is liable in the capacity in which he has signed even though the taker knows of the accommodation.
(3) As against a holder in due course and without notice of the accommodation oral proof of the accommodation is not admissible to give the accommodation party the benefit of discharges dependent on his character as such. In other cases the accommodation character may be shown by oral proof.
(4) An indorsement which shows that it is not in the chain of title is notice of its accommodation character.
(5) An accommodation party is not liable to the party accommodated, and if he pays the instrument has a right of recourse on the instrument against such party.

The obligation of an accommodation party as a surety is determined by the capacity in which he signs. Thus an accommodation maker or acceptor is bound as a party to the instrument without the necessity of proceeding against the principal, the party accommodated, while an accommodation indorser may be liable only after presentment and notice of dishonor.

This section of the Code deals with the interrelations between the law of commercial paper and the law of suretyship. Generally, the Code favors the law of suretyship where the two branches of the law are in conflict. The accommodation party may take advantage of any defenses which are available to a surety and oral proof is admissible to show that he signed as an accommodation party. Oral proof, however, is not admissible against a holder in due course who had no notice of the accommodation and assumed that the party was a regular maker or indorser as the case may be.

The NIL required that in order to be an accommodation party one must have signed "without receiving value therefor." This requirement of gratuitous signing has been eliminated by the Code and a party may have the status of a surety-accommodation party even though he has been compensated for signing. The underlying concept is that the important element is whether the accommodation party is a surety—not whether he has been paid.

There are some decisions under the NIL which provided that an accommodation party, who signs a note after it is in the hands of a holder who gave value, is not bound because there is no sufficient consideration to support his obligation. Under the Code such party is clearly liable.

Since a surety's status is generally somewhat different from that of the contracting parties, it is important to note that an irregular or anomalous indorsement—one which is not in the chain of title—gives notice to all subsequent parties that such indorsement was for accommodation.

Some cases under the NIL had held that an accommodation indorser who paid the instrument could not maintain an action against the accommodated party. Subsection (5) above provides that the ordinary rules of suretyship apply and that the accommodated party who pays is subrogated to the rights of the holder with the right of recourse on the instrument.

As noted, the Code strikes a balance between the concepts of fostering negotiability and the rights of a holder in due course on one hand and of protecting the high-risk position of a surety on the other. The following examples illustrate some of the foregoing principles:

A borrows money from *C* and in return gives a note signed by *A* and *B* as co-makers. *C* negotiates the note to *D*, a holder in due course, who has no notice that *B* is an accommodation party. When the note falls due *C* gives *A* a 30-day extension of payment. Under suretyship law *B* would have been discharged by the extension. However, since *D* is a protected holder in due course, the law of commercial paper controls and *B* remains liable.

A buys a car from *C*. In payment *A* gives his note payable to the order of *C* and indorsed by *B* for *A*'s accommodation. *C* negotiates the note to *D*. The car turns out to be defective and is returned to *C* who refuses to make a refund. When the note falls due *D* presents it to *A* who is now insolvent. *D* now seeks to collect from *B*. Since failure of consideration is a defense available to the principal obligor, likewise the surety under the law of suretyship is entitled to such defense. In this case the accommodation party's (*B*'s) indorsement was not in the chain of title since it appeared before that of *C*, the payee, and *D* thus had notice of the accommodation character of the indorsement.

4-60. Contract of guarantor. The three preceding sections dealt with the contract of the maker, the drawer and acceptor, the indorser, and the accommodation party. There was no provision in the NIL expressly relating to a guarantor's contract, but such contract is covered by Section 3-416 of the Code. The Code expresses the commercial understanding attributed to words of guaranty.

If the words "Payment guaranteed" or their equivalent are added to a signature, the signer engages that if the instrument is not paid when due he will pay it without previous resort by the holder to other parties on the paper. If the words "Collection guaranteed" are added to a signature, the signer becomes secondarily liable on the instrument and can be required to pay only if the holder has obtained a judgment against the primary party and execution on the judgment has been returned unsatisfied, unless the primary party has become insolvent or "it is otherwise apparent that it is useless to proceed against him."

If words of guaranty are used but it is not specified whether "of payment" or "collection," they will be deemed to constitute a guaranty of payment.

Words of guaranty by a sole maker or acceptor are without effect; but if such words are added to the signature of one of two or more makers or acceptors such words create a presumption that the party who added such words signed for the accommodation of the others.

If an indorser guarantees payment, he waives the conditions precedent of presentment, notice of dishonor, and protest. The words of guarantee do not affect the indorsement as a means of transferring the instrument, but impose upon such indorser the liability of a co-maker. If the indorser guarantees collection, he likewise waives the performance of the conditions precedent.

4-61. Warranties on presentment and transfer. The preceding sections dealt with the *contract* liability of parties to instruments; this section deals with *warranty* liability. Contract liability and warranty liability often overlap. Both are imposed for the same basic purpose, to promote the free flow of commercial paper by giving assurance and protection to one who takes it.

A negotiable instrument not only represents contracts, but it is also a type of property which is sold and exchanged. Just as implied warranties with respect to title, description, and quality are made in the sale of chattels, such warranties also attach to the sale of negotiable instruments.

There are two basic types of warranties in the law of commercial paper; warranties on *presentment* and warranties on *transfer*. The Code distinguishes between the two types and clarifies and expands the NIL treatment of this subject. Presentment warranties set forth the undertaking of a person who receives *payment* or obtains *acceptance* of an instrument to the person who pays or accepts the instrument. Transfer warranties are given by one who transfers the paper, as distinguished from one who presents it for payment or acceptance.

Presentment warranties. Section 3-417 (1) of the Code enumerates the warranties which are made by persons in connection with the presentment of instruments for payment or acceptance. Thus, when the holder seeks to obtain payment or acceptance of an instrument, he is asserting that he is legally entitled to receive such payment or acceptance. After a drawee pays or accepts a draft or a maker pays a note, he may discover that his name was forged, that an indorser's name was forged, that the drawer's name was forged, or that the instrument had been materially altered. The payor or acceptor will then desire to recover his payment from either the party to whom payment was made or some other party to the paper. The rights of the payor and acceptor are governed by the warranties made upon presentment and the breach thereof.

Section 3-417 (1) provides:

> (1) Any person who obtains payment or acceptance and any prior transferor warrants to a person who in good faith pays or accepts that
>
> (a) he has a good title to the instrument or is authorized to obtain payment or acceptance on behalf of one who has a good title; and
>
> (b) he has no knowledge that the signature of the maker or drawer is unauthorized, except that this warranty is not given by a holder in due course acting in good faith
>
> (i) to a maker with respect to the maker's own signature; or
>
> (ii) to a drawer with respect to the drawer's own signature, whether or not the drawer is also the drawee; or
>
> (iii) to an acceptor of a draft if the holder in due course took the draft after the acceptance or obtained the acceptance without knowledge that the drawer's signature was unauthorized; and
>
> (c) the instrument has not been materially altered, except that this warranty is not given by a holder in due course acting in good faith
>
> (i) to the maker of a note; or
>
> (ii) to the drawer of a draft whether or not the drawer is also the drawee; or
>
> (iii) to the acceptor of a draft with respect to an alteration made prior to the acceptance if the holder in due course took the draft after the acceptance, even though the acceptance provided "payable as originally drawn" or equivalent terms; or
>
> (iv) to the acceptor of a draft with respect to an alteration made after the acceptance.

The warranty as to good title is breached if there is a forged indorsement in the chain of title. Since no title passes by a forged indorsement, the person who was in possession of the paper has no right to retain money paid to him. This is true even though he has no knowledge of the forged indorsement. The party whose name was forged as an indorser may recover from the party who collected on the paper or from the payor. The party who pays or accepts may recover the payment or avoid the acceptance on the theory that he is not in a position to verify the signatures of indorsers. On the other hand, if a *drawer's* signature is forged, a drawee who accepts or pays may not be allowed to recover his payment. As stated in the Comment to this section: "The justification for the distinction between forgery of the signature of the drawer and forgery of an indorsement is that the drawee is in a position to verify the drawer's signature by comparison with one in his own hands, but has ordinarily no opportunity to verify an indorsement."

In contrast to the warranty of good title, the warranty with regard to the signature of the maker or drawer is merely that the presenting party has no *knowledge* that such signatures are not genuine. This warranty has only limited application to a holder in due course, since the drawer and maker should be able to recognize their own signatures. The holder in due course does not warrant the genuineness of the signature of the drawer if he takes the instrument after the drawee's acceptance, or if he obtained the acceptance without knowledge that the drawer's signature was forged.

A person who pays a materially altered instrument can recover the payment in excess of the amount for which originally drawn, and a drawee who accepts such an instrument can disavow his acceptance. However, the warranty against material alteration is not imposed upon a holder in due course in favor of a maker or drawer. Such parties are presumed to know the provisions of the instrument as of the time when they signed. A holder in due course can recover from an acceptor if the alteration occurred prior to the acceptance, on the theory that the holder relied in good faith on the acceptance.

Even though a bank in certifying a check adds the words "Payable as originally drawn," it cannot avoid liability because such language does not impose the warranty of no material alteration on the holder in due course. If the alteration is made after acceptance, the holder in due course is also exempt from the warranty on the theory that the drawee could have checked its prior records before making payment. It is again to be noted that a holder who takes through a holder in due course will have the same rights as a holder in due course if he acts in good faith and otherwise satisfies the requirements of U.C.C. 3-201. The warranties in this section may be avoided by a disclaimer agreement between the immediate parties.

Transfer warranties. One who transfers an instrument is liable for warranties with regard to the nature and character of the instrument transferred. Section 3-417 (2) of the Code provides in part as follows:

> (2) Any person who transfers an instrument and receives consideration warrants to his transferee and if the transfer is by indorsement to any subsequent holder who takes the instrument in good faith that
> (a) he has a good title to the instrument or is authorized to obtain payment or acceptance on behalf of one who has a good title and the transfer is otherwise rightful; and
> (b) all signatures are genuine or authorized;[28] and
> (c) the instrument has not been materially altered; and
> (d) no defense of any party is good against him . . .

[28] Union Bank v. Mobilla, page 601.

These warranties are similar to those in the NIL. The warranty under the NIL that the instrument is "genuine and what it purports to be" is replaced by subsections 2(b) and 2(c) of the Code and subsection 2(a) imposes warranty liability on unauthorized agents. Subsection 2(d) is intended to make it clear that a transferor warrants that no defense is good against such indorser or transferor. One who transfers "without recourse" merely warrants that he has *no knowledge of a defense*. Except for this limitation the indorser "without recourse" has the same *warranty* liability as other indorsers. It will be recalled that an indorser "without recourse" effectively disclaims *contract* liability on his indorsement. Subsection 2(e) replaces the NIL provision "That he has no knowledge of any fact which would impair the validity of the instrument or render it valueless" with the following language: "he has no knowledge of any insolvency proceeding instituted with respect to the maker or acceptor or the drawer of an unaccepted instrument." This provision does not mean that a transferor warrants against collection difficulties but simply that if insolvency proceedings have been instituted against the primary party and the transferor has knowledge of such fact and conceals the same, a fraud has been perpetrated on the buyer.

The warranties upon transfer are made whether the transfer is by delivery, by qualified indorsement, or by unqualified indorsement. The Code imposes the full warranty liability that no defense of any party is good against him upon the transferor by delivery. In the case of delivery, warranties extend only to the transferee. If the transfer is by indorsement, warranties run to any subsequent holder who takes in good faith. An accommodation indorser is not liable on warranties since "only a person who transfers an instrument and receives consideration" is a warrantor.

The Code provides that a selling agent or broker who does not disclose his agency capacity is bound by warranties. However, if he discloses his capacity, he merely warrants his good faith and his authority to make the transfer.

4-62. Finality of payment or acceptance. As a counterpart of the preceding section, the Code in Section 3-418 provides:

> Except for recovery of bank payments as provided in the Article on Bank Deposits and Collections (Article 4) and except for liability for breach of warranty on presentment under the preceding section, payment or acceptance of any instrument is final in favor of a holder in due course, or a person who has in good faith changed his position in reliance on the payment.

Under this section a drawee who accepts or pays an instrument which bears the forged signature of the drawer is bound on his acceptance and is not permitted to recover his payment. The rationale of this rule is that "it is highly desirable to end the transaction on an instrument when it is paid rather than reopen and upset a series of commercial transactions at a later date when the forgery is discovered." The provisions of this section also apply to makers of notes and other parties who pay an instrument. The comments to this section state that it applies to overdrafts; and that it is restricted to good faith takers. The mere negligence of a holder in taking the paper justifies recovery from the holder by the paying party. The Code stresses the finality of the acts of paying or accepting an instrument.

This section requires reference to the warranties made by one who receives payment or acceptance and to the provisions of the Bank Collection Code, which permit a bank to recover payment of items which have been improperly paid.

4-63. Conversion of instrument. In tort law, a conversion is any act in relation to personal property inconsistent with the owner's interest in the goods. Under the NIL a drawee who refused to pay or return an instrument which had been delivered to him for acceptance or payment was said to have "constructively" accepted the instrument. The Code rejects this fictitious theory (see Section 3-410) but achieves substantially the same result by designating such refusal as a conversion in Section 3-419. This section further provides that refusal to return any instrument presented for payment, including a note, is a conversion. Likewise the payment of an instrument which bears a forged indorsement is a conversion of property belonging to the person whose indorsement was forged. The application of the concept of conversion in these three situations is predicated upon the fact that an instrument is property and a refusal to return an instrument after a demand therefor, or the payment of an instrument that belongs to someone else, is certainly inconsistent with the owner's interest in it. It is to be noted that the cause of action granted to the owner is not on the instrument itself but rather in tort for conversion. The measure of damages for the tort is the face amount of the instrument in an action against the drawee and is presumed to be the same as against other parties. Where an action is brought against someone other than the drawee, such party can introduce evidence that the instrument is worth less than face value because of insolvency, the existence of a defense, or for any other reason.

If an agent, such as a depositary or collecting bank or a broker, deals with an instrument on behalf of one who is not the owner, such representative is not liable in conversion to the true owner. The representative must have acted in good faith and "in accordance with the reasonable commercial standards applicable to the business of such representative. . . ." However, the representative may be required to account to the true owner for any proceeds remaining in his hands, or if he still has the instrument to return it to the true owner.

The purpose of these rules is to protect a party who is performing a service for his customer and assumes that such customer is honestly in possession of the item which is being collected. Such persons are insulated from liability because they are mere "funnels" to faciliate passage of the paper to the drawee.

An intermediary bank or a nondepositary payor bank will not be liable in conversion to the beneficial owner of an instrument "solely because of the fact that the proceeds of an item indorsed restrictively (Sections 3-205 and 3-206) are not paid or applied consistently with the restrictive indorsement of an indorser other than its immediate transferor." A payor bank is one upon which an instrument is drawn and an intermediary bank is one to which an item is transferred in the course of collection.

The payor bank is the drawee and items drawn on such bank by its customers may likewise be deposited in the same bank by other customers who are holders of such items. In this situation the payor bank is also a depositary bank. On the other hand many checks are drawn, for example, on *A* Bank and deposited by the holder in *B* Bank. *B* Bank sends the checks to *C* Bank in the process of collection. In this case *A* Bank is a nondepositary payor (drawee) bank and *C* Bank is an intermediary bank.

LIABILITY OF PARTIES CASES

IN RE ETON FURNITURE CO.

1961, 286 F. 2d 93

The general manager of the Eton Furniture Company, Huntington, on several occasions borrowed money from the bank, giving his personal note to the bank, and arranged for the proceeds to be credited to Eton's account. When Eton's deposits produced a balance deemed to be sufficiently ample, the bank appropriated Eton's funds to pay off the loans. On November 6, 1957, Eton was adjudged a bankrupt and the trustee in bankruptcy asked for a turnover order against the bank alleging that the bank had in its possession $6600 belonging to the bankrupt estate. The trustee contended that "the loans negotiated by Huntington from the bank, and for which he gave his personal notes to the bank were loans to him and not to Eton." The referee and the lower court held that the primary obligation was that of the company and ruled in favor of the bank.

BIGGS, C. J. . . . It was argued that Eton received the proceeds of the loans from Huntington and not from the Bank, and that therefore the satisfaction of the obligations from Eton's account with the Bank constituted an unjustified appropriation of Eton's funds by the Bank to pay the debts of another. . . .

The single issue which this court must determine is whether Eton was indebted to the Bank in the amounts of the loans negotiated by Huntington, its general manager. The trustee makes two arguments which we must consider. First, relying on Section 3-401 (1) of the Uniform Commercial Code, applicable in Pennsylvania, 12A P.S. Section 3-401 (1), he contends that since Huntington's signature alone appears on the notes given by him to the Bank, Huntington alone can be held liable by the Bank for repayment of the loans. Second, he argues that Huntington was not authorized to borrow money for Eton and that therefore, regardless of any understanding that may have existed between Huntington and the Bank, Eton, not being bound, could not be liable for repayment of the loans. . . .

Section 3-401 (1) provides that "[N]o person is liable on an instrument unless his signature appears thereon." On the basis of this provision the trustee contends that Eton, not having signed the notes given to the Bank, cannot be held liable for repayment of the loans. This argument finds no support in the words of the statute which provides merely that one who does not sign a note cannot be liable on the note. Contrary to the trustee's argument, the provision quoted cannot be read to mean that no person is liable on a debt whose signature does not appear on a note given as collateral security for that debt. Indeed, it has long been settled in Pennsylvania and elsewhere that the one to whom money is loaned or property advanced is liable for the debt regardless of the fact that his name may not appear on the security taken if that security was regarded by the parties purely as collateral. That Section 3-401 (1) was not intended to change this rule is demonstrated clearly by the comment to that section which states in pertinent part: "Nothing in this section is intended to prevent any liability arising apart from the instrument itself. The party who does not sign may still be liable on the original obligation for which the instrument was given—". . . .

In the present case, the evidence of Huntington, adopted "as verity" by the referee, similarly shows that the loans were for Eton's use, that the Bank, Eton and Huntington understood this to be so, and that the money was in fact used by the Company for its own benefit. We hold that the finding of the referee and that of the court below that the debts were incurred by Eton is supported by the evidence and that their rulings are in accordance with the applicable law. . . .

The judgment of the court below will be affirmed.

SENOR v. BANGOR MILLS
1954, 211 F. 2d 685

HASTIE, C. J. . . . This is a diversity case presenting a Pennsylvania controversy between a seller of certain goods and a purchaser of the same goods who did not deal with each other, but rather with a third person as a result of whose improper conduct and financial irresponsibility one of the present parties must bear a loss. The district court found that the defendant buyer was not liable to the plaintiff seller either for goods bought and sold or on a check given to the seller by the wrongdoer. The plaintiff has appealed.

These are the facts. At the time in question the demand for nylon yarn exceeded the supply which the sole producer of such yarn allocated among the members of the trade. This shortage had led to the development of a so-called "secondary" market in which some of those who purchased from the manufacturer resold yarn at a profit rather than using it themselves. Plaintiff Senor was such a seller. Defendant Bangor Mills, a very large user of nylon yarn in the manufacture of tricot, was able to maintain its production level only by frequent substantial purchases in the "secondary" market. But its known needs and economic position were such that it was asked to pay prices that were very high even for that market. Accordingly, it sought to get yarn cheaper through an intermediary.

Beginning in January, 1951, Bangor utilized William Shetzline as such an intermediary. . . .

However, Shetzline had no substantial credit of his own and thus had to make most of his purchases in the "secondary" market for cash. To enable him to proceed in this way in its interest Bangor established an account in the Peoples Bank of Langhorne, Pennsylvania, in both its name and Shetzline's, upon which Shetzline could draw without using Bangor's name. As to the actual purchase of yarn, the district court found that the agreement between Bangor and Shetzline was as follows:

> Shetzline had no authority to buy any yarn at all for Bangor, except as specified and agreed to from time to time by Bangor. Originally, each time that he was able to purchase yarn he had to get in touch with Bangor and advise it of the quantity and the price and gets its consent; otherwise there would be no sale. Later on, Bangor, in effect, gave its consent in advance by telling Shetzline how much yarn it would buy and at what price, but Shetzline had no more authority to buy more than the amount specified or to pay more than the price fixed than he had before.

The record further shows, and it is not disputed, that under this arrangement at the time of the transactions here in dispute Bangor had stipulated that Shetzline was not to buy yarn for Bangor at a price exceeding $10 per pound and that his purchases for its account should not exceed the unobligated balance in the bank account which Bangor had placed at his disposal. At the same time, again in the language of the district court, "Shetzline was under no obligation to buy any yarn at all for Bangor. He was entirely free to purchase as much as he wanted on his own account and sell it to manufacturers other than Bangor, or if he wished he could use it in his own manufacturing business." . . .

On June 19 Shetzline bought about 1250 pounds of nylon yarn from the plaintiff at $11.35 a pound and directed him to ship the yarn to River Lane, one of Shetzline's corporations, to whom Senor had shipped and billed goods on a number of prior occasions. The plaintiff sent the yarn as directed and [on June 29] received a check signed by Shetzline drawn, . . . upon the . . . account in the Peoples Bank. The yarn was delivered at Shetzline's place of business and was invoiced by Shetzline to Henry Mills [a dummy corporation for Bangor] at $10.00 a pound, but was delivered by him directly to Bangor. The check was returned unpaid because of insufficient funds.

The plaintiff knew nothing whatever of any relationship between Shetzline and Bangor. He intended to sell the yarn to River Lane, understood that River Lane was the buyer and made the sale entirely upon the credit of River Lane.

On all the facts one of the district court's conclusions was that "The result [of the arrangement between Shetzline and Bangor] was that a separate agency was created each time Shetzline bought yarn with Bangor's money." As we see it, this conclusion is both correct and in the present circumstances decisive against plaintiff on its claim against Bangor for goods sold and delivered. . . .

There remains the claim that Bangor is liable on the check which Shetzline gave Senor in payment for the yarn. Shetzline had not left sufficient funds on deposit to cover this item. The check was drawn on a bank account which had been established with Bangor's money as the account of "Bangor Mills Incorporated or William H. Shetzline, Jr." with either party authorized to draw on it. The check in suit had been drawn by Shetzline and signed "William H. Shetzline, Jr.," but with the further printed identification of the drawer on the face of the check as "William H. Shetzline, Jr., Division." It is undisputed that the bank had authorized the use of this style to distinguish this account from a private account standing in Shetzline's name.

These facts are relevant despite the general rule that an undisclosed principal is not liable as a party to a negotiable instrument. Restatement, Agency, Section 192. For under Section 18 of the Negotiable Instruments Law, 56 P.S., Section 23, "one who signs [a negotiable instrument] in a trade or assumed name" is liable thereon. And it is appellant's theory that "William H. Shetzline, Jr. Division" is an assumed or trade name of

Bangor Mills. The court, however, found that this was not the fact. And in the circumstances already outlined we think it was a reasonable and proper conclusion that "William H. Shetzline, Jr., Division" was a name designating Shetzline and not an assumed or trade name of Bangor.

The judgment will be affirmed. . . .

[Note that this case was decided under the NIL.]

GRANGE NATIONAL BANK v. CONVILLE

1956 (Pa.) Court of Common Pleas of Lycoming County, 8 D & C. 2d 616, 5 Lyc. 170

The plaintiff bank entered a judgment by confession against John P. Conville, Doris E. Conville, and the Hughesville Manufacturing Company, Inc. on two notes. The defendants sought to set aside the judgments against themselves as individuals and assert that liability should be assessed only against the Hughesville Manufacturing Company.

GREEVY, J. . . . John P. Conville and Doris E. Conville have petitioned this Court to open the judgments. In support of their petition they aver that by a mutual mistake of the Plaintiff and the Defendants the notes were improperly executed and signed as follows:

(No. 439, September Term, 1954)
John P. Conville
Doris E. Conville
Hughesville Mfg. Co. Inc. (Seal)
(No. 676, May Term, 1955)
Hughesville Mfg. Co.
John P. Conville
Doris E. Conville

Whereas, they should have been executed as follows:

(No. 439, September Term, 1954)
John P. Conville, President
Doris E. Conville, Secretary
Hughesville Mfg. Co. Inc. (Seal)
(No. 676 May Term, 1955)
Hughesville Mfg. Co. Inc.
John P. Conville, President
Doris E. Conville, Secretary

Plaintiff, in its answer, denies that there was any mutual mistake . . .

The Pennsylvania Uniform Commercial Code, Section 3-402, provides: "Unless the instrument clearly indicates that a signature is made in some other capacity it is an indorsement." 12 a P.S. 3-402. Under this section any ambiguity as to capacity in which a signature is made must be resolved that it is an endorsement. The question is to be determined from the face of the instrument alone and unless the instrument itself makes it clear that he has signed in some other capacity, the signer must be treated as an endorser.

Section 3-403 (2) provides: "An authorized representative who signs his name to an instrument is also personally obligated unless the instrument names the person represented and shows that the signature is made in a representative capacity. The name of an organization preceded or followed by the name and office of an authorized individual is a signature made in a representative capacity."

Under this section a representative is liable personally unless the instrument itself clearly shows that he signed only on behalf of another named on the paper. If he does not sign in such a way as to make that clear, the responsibility is his.

Under these sections any doubts are to be resolved against the representative and the Court is required to look to the four corners of the instrument and construe the writing, and the question is not for the jury. . . .

Evidence of a mistake must be clear, precise and indubitable, otherwise relief will not be granted. The mistake must be such that would warrant a court of equity to reform the contract and in the main it must be a mutual mistake as to a material fact. The remedy of reformation is never granted on a probability or mere preponderance of evidence. Relief, by the way of reformation, will be denied where the evidence is loose, equivocal, or contradictory, or where it is open to doubt or opposing presumptions.

From this record, being the depositions, we find that the testimony as to a mistake is not clear, precise and indubitable and is not of such weight and directness as to carry conviction to the mind, and that if there was a mistake it was not mutual but unilateral and was due to no fault of the plaintiff but to the petitioners' own negligence and reformation of the note would not be justified.

The testimony taken on the rule is insufficient to justify a chancellor reforming the note and likewise is insufficient to justify the submission of the question to a jury. In accordance therewith we find that petitioners do not have a meritorious defense to the claims upon which the judgments were based and the judgments should not be opened. See Henry on Pennsylvania Evidence, Vol. 2, Section 611. To reform a written document on the basis of such testimony as is before us would be contrary to law of Pennsylvania. See *Seaboard RB Corporation v. Yassky*, 176 Superior 453; *Weighman v. Weighman*, 342 Pa. 8.

We find, however, that the Hughesville Manufacturing Company, Inc. is not liable on the notes even though John L. Conville and Doris E. Conville may have been authorized to sign for the company, for the notes do not show that the signatures were made on behalf of the company. See Pennsylvania Uniform Commercial Code, Section 3-401, 12a P.S. 3-401. . . .

Judgment against individual defendants affirmed.

FIDELITY-PHILADELPHIA TRUST CO. v. ROVNER

1956, (Pa.) 43 Del. 288

DIGGINS, J. . . . This is a motion for judgment on the pleadings. The record shows that on March 22, 1954, the defendant in a representative capacity as president of a corporation known as 1415 Inc. executed as maker and drawer for legal consideration a negotiable promissory note to the order of the plaintiff, Fidelity-Philadelphia Trust Company, in the amount of $8,550.00, payable on demand, and on the reverse side of the note, in the space ordinarily used for endorsement, Laura Rovner and one Bernard Kimmel simply signed their respective names. A net of $250.00 has been paid to the plaintiff on the note but since May 24, 1954, no payment has been made and demand on the corporate maker having been refused, demand was made upon the defendant, Laura Rovner, who denies liability on the ground that she was signing as a maker in her capacity as an officer of the corporation, contending that she was directed by the plaintiff's officer or agent handling the transaction to sign the note on the face and on the reverse side, representing to her that both signatures were being affixed in one and the same capacity as an officer of the corporation.

At the time this instrument was executed, the NIL was in force and effect, and under Section 63 of the Negotiable Instruments Law of May 16, 1901, P.L. 194, any one signing at other than the place regularly provided for the maker or drawer is presumed to be an endorser unless he clearly indicates by appropriate words his intention to be bound in some other capacity (56 P.S. 154), and the liability of this defendant is to be determined not under the new Commercial Code but under the NIL.

Under the NIL Law, since the defendant signed on the back of the note, she is presumed to be an endorser, but it was frequently held under the NIL that this presumption was rebuttable. True, whereas here, the name is signed in the only proper place for an endorser, the burden on one seeking to avoid liability as such is great indeed and is almost irrebuttable against holders in due course, nevertheless where there was an ambiguity as to whether a name appears on a note in an official or individual capacity, and the litigation is between the original parties to the instrument, parol evidence is admissible to show the facts and circumstances attending its execution: *Dormont Savings & Trust Company v. Kommer and v. Philips,* 338 Pa. 548, cited with approval by Ervin, J. in *Merit Motors Inc. v. Bartholomew,* 179 Pa. Sup. Ct. 579.

While it is true the ambiguity here does not appear on the face of the instrument but arises because the defendant contends that she was misinformed and misled by the agent of the payee, this is nevertheless an ambiguity and seems to be the same situation pertaining in the *Dormont Savings & Trust Company v. Kommer* case, supra.

We are therefore of the opinion that since this is an action between the payee and the maker and the presumption is not irrebuttable, the issue is a question for a jury and accordingly we make the following:

The plaintiff's motion for judgment on the pleadings . . . is hereby dismissed. . . .

[Note. This case was decided under NIL.]

KISKA v. ROSEN

1956, 181 Pa. Super. 506, 124 A. 2d 468

ERVIN, J. . . . The plaintiff sued in assumpsit to recover the amount of $966.66 with interest, representing the balance due on a promissory note in the principal sum of $2,000 on which part payments had been made totalling $1,033.34. The note read as follows:

$2000 00/100 Feb. 4, 1950
One (1) year after date we promise to pay to the order of Anthony M. Kiska
Two thousand . . . . 00/100 Dollars
Payable at 936 N. Newmarket St., Phila.
Without defalcation, for value received
@ 6% per annum.
Jos. Rosen & Sons
Joseph Rosen—Milton Rosen
No. 59 Due Feb. 4, 1951 Atty. . . .

The court below in its opinion succinctly states: "Construing the complaint as a whole, the plaintiff's position evidently is that the signature 'Milton Rosen, Atty.' has a dual effect, to wit: (1) effectively binding Joseph Rosen as principal by the description of Milton Rosen as attorney, (2) binding Milton Rosen in his individual capacity." The plaintiff in his complaint clearly recognized that Milton Rosen was acting as the authorized agent of Joseph Rosen. Acting in that capacity, he was not liable to the plaintiff. Section 20 of the Negotiable Instruments Law, Act of May 16, 1901, P.L. 194, 56 P.S. Section 25, provides: "Where the instrument contains or a person adds to his signature words indicating that he signs for or on behalf of a principal, or in a representative capacity, he is not liable on the instrument if he was duly authorized; but the mere addition of words describing him as an agent or as filling a representative character, without disclosing his principal, does not exempt him from personal liability." However, a person known to be acting as an agent in signing a contract may still incur personal liability if in signing the contract he purports to act as a principal. As stated in *Horwath v. Simon*, 95 Pa. Super. 410, 414: "A person contracting as agent will be personally liable, whether he is known to be agent or not, in all cases where he makes the contract in his own name or voluntarily incurs a personal responsibility either expressed or implied: . . . See *Brunetto v. Ferrara*, 167 Pa. Super. 568, 76 A. 2d 448. It is true the instrument in the instant case sets forth in the body that "we" promise to pay. However, there is no testimony that Milton Rosen expressly assumed any personal liability. Nor is there any testimony that Milton Rosen was a part owner of the business registered in the name of Joseph Rosen and Sons. Moreover, according to his own testimony the plaintiff questioned defendant's authority to sign his father's name to the instrument and defendant thereupon added the designation "Atty." after his signature. It was thus obvious that defendant was acting in a representative capacity only.

We agree with the conclusion of the court below that the plaintiff failed to sustain his burden of proof.

The order granting a new trial is affirmed. . . .

[This case was decided under the NIL as the note was executed before the U.C.C. was adopted in Pennsylvania.]

IN RE LASKIN

1962, 204 F. Supp. 106

GRIM, S. D. J. The problem here presented is the construction of a promissory note:

> $15,426.50 March 31, 1959
> Sixty days after date . . . . promise to pay to the order of INDUSTRIAL RAYON CORPORATION Fifteen Thousand Four Hundred Twenty-Six and 50/100 . . . . Dollars payable at Cleveland, Ohio with interest at 6% per annum. Value received.
> LASKIN BROS. OF PHILA. INC.
> Harold Laskin
> K-71730 Due May 30, 1959

Harold Laskin being bankrupt, the question here is whether this note constitutes the holder, Industrial Rayon Corporation, a creditor of the bankrupt. The referee held that the bankrupt was not liable on the note and that the holder was not his creditor. The holder has petitioned for review of the referee's action.

The question is governed by Section 3-403 of the Uniform Commercial Code, 12-A P.S. Section 3-403:

> (1) A signature may be made by an agent or other representative, and his authority to make it may be established as in other cases of representation. No particular form of appointment is necessary to establish such authority.
>
> (2) An authorized representative who signs his own name to an instrument is also personally obligated unless the instrument names the person represented and shows that the signature is made in a representative capacity. The name of an organization preceded or followed by the name and office of an authorized individual is a signature made in a representative capacity.

It is helpful as well as proper (12-A P.S. Section 1-102(3) (f)) to refer to the Uniform Code Comment on Section 3-403 prior to the 1959 amendments.

> . . . The rule here stated is that the representative is liable personally unless the instrument itself clearly shows that he has signed only on behalf of another named on the paper. If he does not sign in such a way as to make that clear the responsibility is his . . .

Clearly and obviously, the signature "Harold Laskin" on the Industrial Rayon note, without one word to indicate that it was affixed to the note in a representative capacity, makes him individually liable on the note.

Section 20 of the Negotiable Instruments Law, 56 P.S. Section 25, in effect prior to the Code, provided:

> Where the instrument contains or a person adds to his signature words indicating that he signs for or on behalf of a principal, or in a representative capacity, he is not liable on the instrument if he was duly authorized . . .

Pennsylvania was one of the jurisdictions which admitted parol evidence to show that the instrument was signed in a representative capacity although this fact did not appear on the instrument. See *Dormont Savings & Trust Co. v. Kommer*, 338 Pa. 548, 13 A. 2d 525 (1940).

The 1959 amendment to Section 3-403 of the Uniform Commercial Code provides:

> (2) An authorized representative who signs his own name to an instrument . . .
>
> (b) *except as otherwise established between the immediate parties*, is personally obligated if the instrument names the person represented but does not show that the representative signed in a representative capacity. (emphasis added)

The Pennsylvania Annotation to the Code's 1959 amendment states:

> Section 3-403. Signature by Authorized Representative.
> Subsection (2). This subsection of the 1953 Code has been divided into two subsections. The revised subsection (2) changes the rule of the 1953 Code that a signing agent was personally liable unless the instrument both named the principal and disclosed the agency relationship. Under the revised Code it is open to the agent who has complied with one of the two requirements to show the other by evidence aliunde the instrument, as between the immediate parties. Insofar as the 1953 Code appeared to change the rule in Pennsylvania, the revised subsection is a reversion to the pre-Code rule (cases cited) . . .

Since the note is dated prior to the 1959 amendment and evidence outside of the note is not admissible to show that Laskin was not liable personally on the note, and since the acts and orders of the Referee were based on the premise that such evidence was admissible, those orders will be all vacated and the record returned to the Referee for proceedings consistent with this opinion. . . .

And now, April 17, 1962, the orders of the Referee sustaining objections to Industrial Rayon Corporation's claim, permitting the bankrupt to file an amended schedule A-3 deleting Industrial Rayon as a creditor, dismissing the specifications of objection to the bankrupt's discharge, and granting the bankrupt his discharge, are vacated, and the record in this matter will be returned to the Referee for proceedings not inconsistent with this opinion.

SALITAN et al. v. ABINGTON TRACTOR CO. & IMPLEMENT CO., et al.

1954, (Pa.) 55 Lack. Jur. 25

HOBSON, P. J. . . . Plaintiffs are factors and dealers in commercial paper, who purchased before maturity, for value, three trade acceptances purporting to be paper of the corporation defendant. The trade acceptances were dishonored on presentation.

Ohmlac Paint & Manufacturing Company, Inc., a New York firm, drew on Abington Tractor & Implement Company, a Pennsylvania corporation. The acceptances in each instrument were identical as follows: (Italicized words engraved on the commercial form)

Accepted at	Chinchilla, Pa. *on* 8/25 *1949*
Payable at	Abington Natl *Bank*
Bank Location	Clarks Summit, Pa.
Buyers Signature	(blank)
By Agent or Officer	P. J. Mills

It was conceded that the acceptances were insufficient to bind the corporation defendant and judgment in its favor will, therefore, be entered. The sole question remaining is whether or not P. J. Mills is liable individually on the instrument.

There is no question but that P. J. Mills signed the instrument, that the name of Abington Tractor & Implement Company appears in the body of the instrument, and it is therefore a disclosed principal, and that the signature of P. J. Mills was entered as that of an agent or officer. At the trial paragraph 11 of the amended complaint and the corresponding paragraph of the answer of P. J. Mills were offered in evidence. The Trial Judge refused the offer. If the exclusion of this evidence was proper, we are left with this factual situation. The document was signed only by an agent without any other effective signature of the principal. In such a situation the agent is not liable, providing that the agent has power to bind the principal. Section 20, Negotiable Instruments Law, 56 P.S. 25. But no proof has been offered by Mills that he had power to bind the principal. Failing such proof, he ought to be held responsible, for it is clear that he is the person who has put that instrument in course of trade, and if a bona fide holder for value received it, he should not suffer as against the one who is primarily responsible for uttering a negotiable instrument.

If, on the other hand, the Trial Judge was in error in failing to accept as evidence paragraphs 11 of the amended complaint and answer and these paragraphs are now accepted as part of the evidence of facts, this situation would arise. Mills signed the document but notified the agent of Ohmlac that another signature would be required before the trade acceptances would be valid. Ohmlac was, therefore, on notice that the signature of Mills alone not only would not bind the corporation but was being offered in a representative capacity as but one of two authorized co-signers. If the action were by Ohmlac against Mills, clearly we would have to enter judgment for Mills. But the plaintiffs as purchasers for value before maturity were holders in due course without notice of any defect unless a defect appeared on the face of the instrument. Such a defect, if any, can only be read from the description of Mills as an agent or officer.

Again, we are faced with the fact that the agent is subject to liability to a subsequent holder in due course who does not know that the agent lacked authority to bind the principal, and Mills has offered no evidence to prove such knowledge.

The case seems to fall squarely within the principle of Section 324 of the Restatement of Agency. See particularly Comment a. Under any view of the facts Mills is liable.

[This case was decided under the NIL.]

HOUSEHOLD FINANCE CORP. v. NEWTON SAVINGS BANK

1957, 14 Mass. App. Dec. 173

O'Connell owed a balance to plaintiff on a loan. He signed a note to defendant bank for a loan of $450 and forged his wife's name to the note. The bank gave him a check for $450 payable to him *and* his wife. He forged his wife's indorsement and indorsed the check to plaintiff in payment of a $154.27 obligation and received the balance in cash. Plaintiff deposited the check in another bank and when it was presented to defendant bank—drawee—payment was refused. The defendant bank did not verify Mrs. O'Connell's signature on the note; plaintiff did not verify her indorsement on the check. The plaintiff sought to recover the amount of the check from defendant. The lower court found for defendant.

BROOKS, J. . . . The plaintiff claims to be aggrieved by the denial of its request for ruling No. 2, "that there is no evidence to warrant a finding for the defendant," and further claims to be aggrieved by the court's rulings; that the plaintiff was not a holder in due course of the check but that it took the same for value in good faith and without knowledge of any infirmity; that the defendant was not precluded from setting up as a defense the forged endorsement of the payee, Mary G. O'Connell, and by the further ruling that the plaintiff was in no way misled by the defendant either by what it did or failed to do and that there was no causal connection between the signing of the note and endorsement of the check upon which to predicate any finding of negligence on the part of the defendant.

The plaintiff further claims to be aggrieved in the ruling of the court that the plaintff itself was lacking in the exercise of due care and was negligent in not satisfying itself, and in not making certain, that the wife's endorsement was genuine and not a forgery.

The plaintiff also claims to be aggrieved in the court's ruling that the plaintiff assumed the risk of honoring the check without such definite proof and that it honored the endorsement at its peril. . .

This case was ably argued. Much law was cited by counsel on both sides. The case falls within G. L. c. 107, Section 45 which provides:

> Where a signature is forged or made without authority of the person whose signature it purports to be, it is wholly inoperative, and no right to retain the instrument, or to give a discharge therefor, or to enforce payment thereof against any party thereto, can be acquired through or under such signature, unless the party against whom it is sought to enforce such right is precluded from setting up the forgery or want of authority.

The question then arises whether, under the last lines of the above section, defendant is precluded from setting up Mr. O'Connell's forgery of his wife's endorsement on the check received by him from defendant and negotiated by him to plaintiff. The determining factor in this issue is whether defendant was negligent in failing to verify Mrs. O'Connell's signature on the note before issuing the check. This was primarily a question of fact in which the court found that defendant was not negligent.

On the other hand the court found also as a fact that plaintiff was negligent in failing to verify Mrs. O'Connell's signature endorsing the check issued by the bank. These findings of fact are not to be disturbed unless plainly wrong. *Herman v. Sadolf*, 294 Mass. 358, 360; *Bridges v. Hart*, 302 Mass. 239, 242; *Hannon v. Hayes-Bickford Lunch System, Inc.*, 336 Mass. 268.

It would seem more logical to have found none or both of the parties negligent under these circumstances. If neither was negligent, defendant was not precluded from setting up the forgery as a good defense to this action. On the other hand, if both parties were negligent, plaintiff is hardly in a position to call the kettle black. Such circumstances might well call for application of the familiar maxim, "Let the loss lie where it falls,"—in this case on plaintiff.

We have considered plaintiff's argument that defendant's negligence precipitated subsequent events. We have also considered the argument that defendant's delay in notifying plaintiff of the forgery should entitle plaintiff to recover. These arguments seem to us to have little weight. . . .

Affirmed.

[This case was decided under the NIL.]

PROVIDENT TRUST CO. v. INTERBORO BANK & TRUST CO.

1957, 133 A. 2d 515, 389 Pa. 548

MUSMANNO, J. . . . On June 28, 1951, Arthur Benson obtained from Mrs. Cora V. Savidge, whom he had known for 25 years, a power of attorney to sell her Lansdowne property, manage the business of her deceased husband, invest funds, negotiate loans and accomplish other business matters not necessary to relate here. On July 6, 1951, he endorsed Mrs. Savidge's name without her knowledge to a judgment note and borrowed $6,000 on it from the Interboro Bank & Trust Company. With this money he opened an account in that bank in her name. He then withdrew from the account $5,049.63.

A week later he attended the settlement closing of the sale of Mrs. Savidge's Lansdowne property at the office of the Commonwealth Title Company, which turned over to him its check payable to Mrs. Savidge in the amount of $9,300.32 due her as grantor. The check was drawn on the Provident Trust Company of Philadelphia, the plaintiff in this lawsuit. Benson endorsed (again without her knowledge) the name of Mrs.

Savidge to this check and deposited it in the account he had opened in her name in the Interboro Bank. The Interboro Bank negotiated, transferred, and delivered the check to the Federal Reserve Bank of Philadelphia which delivered it to the Provident Trust Company and received from the Provident Trust the amount of the check which the Reserve Bank then turned over to Interboro. Provident then charged the account of Commonwealth Title with the amount of the check.

When Benson deposited the $9,300 check in the Interboro Bank on August 1, 1951, Mrs. Savidge's account at that time was already overdrawn in the amount of $35.12. With the depositing of the $9,300, Interboro collected the $6,000 it had loaned to Benson on the assumption it was going to Mrs. Savidge. By the end of August, 1951, the entire amount deposited by Benson had been withdrawn, save $33.17.

It was not until April, 1952, that Mrs. Savidge became aware of Benson's duplicities and illegal transactions. In that month Benson began serving a prison sentence for an unrelated Federal offense. Mrs. Savidge now employed counsel to represent her and she learned, inter alia, of the existence of the account in her name in Interboro, of the $6,000 and $9,300 deposits made in her name, and the ensuing withdrawals. She brought suit against the Commonwealth Title Company for the proceeds from the sale of her property, asserting that the Title Company had no authority to pay to Benson the money due her. The Title Company settled this lawsuit upon payment of $7,500 to Mrs. Savidge who then assigned to the Title Company all her rights to proceeds in the Lansdowne property transaction as well as her rights to the $9,300 check issued by the Title Company. The Title Company reassigned these rights to the Provident Trust Company which, in its dual position as assignee of Mrs. Savidge's rights, and as drawee bank, brought suit against the Interboro Bank for the amount it had paid to the Federal Reserve Bank, it having reimbursed its depositor's (Title Company) account for the amount charged against it.

Upon filing of Answer, the case was heard by the Court of Common Pleas of Delaware County without jury and verdict was rendered in favor of the plaintiff in the sum of $11,981.82. The defendant appealed.

It is the position of the plaintiff, Provident Trust, that the Interboro Bank, as the collecting bank, which, by its endorsement guaranteed all prior endorsements, was liable to Provident for the $9,300 paid by Provident. This position is a sound one. We said in the case of *Land Title Bank & Trust Co. v. Cheltenham National Bank*, 362 Pa. 30, 66 A.2d 768, 770:

> The applicable rule of law is so firmly settled that it needs no eleborate citation of authorities to support it. If a check is made payable to the order of a person named therein the absolute duty of a bank honoring the check is to pay

only to that payee or according to his order, and no amount of care to avoid error will protect it from liability if it pays to a wrong person; it must ascertain and act upon the genuineness of the indorsement at its peril. Section 23 of the Negotiable Instruments Law of 1901, P.L. 194, 56 P.S. § 28, provides that 'When a signature is forged or made without the authority of the person whose signature it purports to be, it is wholly inoperative, and no right to retain the instrument, or to give a discharge therefor, or to enforce payment thereof against any party thereto, can be acquired through or under such signature, unless the party against whom it is sought to enforce such right is precluded from setting up the forgery or want of authority.'

Finally, Interboro contends that in any event the plaintiff's recovery must be limited to $7,500, the amount of the loss actually sustained by the plaintiff's depositor, Commonwealth Title. But it is to be remembered that the Provident Trust Company, in addition to suing as the drawee bank, is suing also as the assignee of the rights possessed by Mrs. Savidge to recover the $9,300 withdrawn from her account in Interboro without her authority. In *Coffin v. Fidelity-Philadelphia Trust Co.*, 374 Pa. 378, 97 A.2d 857, 863, 39 A.L.R.2d 625, we said:

The basic principle of law relied on by the plaintiffs is not disputed by the defendant bank to the effect that a bank by accepting a deposit guarantees that it will not pay the depositor's money except (1) to the depositor or (2) to the payee named by the depositor in checks drawn on the bank or (3) to the person who by reason of a valid endorsement from the payee becomes entitled to such payment. This undertaking by the bank is contractual in nature, the relationship of depositor to bank being that of creditor and debtor, and the liability of the bank in the event of a breach of its guarantee is aboslute; ". . . no amount of care to avoid error will protect it from liability if it pays to a wrong person; it must ascertain and act upon the genuineness of the endorsement at its peril . . ."

In the instant case, Mrs. Savidge testified that the withdrawals were not made with her authority nor made in her behalf. This was not contradicted by the defendant.

Affirmed.

[This case was decided under the NIL.]

MECHANICS NAT. BANK v. WORCESTER COUNTY TRUST CO.

1960, (Mass.) 170 N.E. 2d 476

The plaintiff (drawee bank) brought action against the defendant (presenting bank) to recover back money paid out on a forged check. The check for $3940 had been taken by the presenting bank for deposit in the name of one of its depositors, and apparently indorsed by him, to the extent of $340. The balance of $3600 had been paid "over the counter" in cash to the person representing himself to be the depositor. The teller had required no identification although in addition to the request for such a large amount of cash there were other suspicious circumstances. The check was paid through a clearinghouse and was charged to the account of the alleged drawer by the drawee bank before the forgery was discovered. Both the drawer's signature and the indorsement were forged. The lower court ruled in favor of the plaintiff, drawee bank.

SPALDING, J. This action of contract or tort is brought to recover funds paid to the defendant bank as holder of a forged check. The declaration is in four counts: (1) negligence, (2) money had and received, (3) account annexed, and (4) warranties arising from the defendant's indorsement of the check. The case was tried to a judge who found for the plaintiff on the negligence count and declined to make findings on the other counts. . . .

The general rule is that money paid under a mistake of fact can be recovered. An important exception to this rule is that, where the equities are equal, a drawee of a check bearing a forged drawer's signature cannot recover from the person who has presented the check to the drawee and has received payment. This is the doctrine of *Price v. Neal,* 3 Burr. 1354, which is law in this Commonwealth (cases cited). The reason for the rule was stated in *First Nat. Bank of Danvers v. First Nat. Bank of Salem,* 151 Mass. 280, at pages 282–283, 24 N.E. 44, at page 45, where it was said, "It is presumed that the bank knows the signature of its own customers, and therefore is not entitled to the benefit of the rule [permitting a party to recover back money paid under a mistake of fact]."

For the *Price v. Neal* exception to apply, however, it is necessary that the party presenting the check does not contribute to the deception of the drawee. . . .

Here the trial judge expressly found that the defendant was negligent in cashing a check of the size of the one involved without making further inquiry. And there was the added circumstance of the defendant's teller calling the plaintiff and learning that there was no account standing in the name of the purported drawer. . . .

We turn now to the question of whether the conduct of the plaintiff with respect to the check is a bar to recovery. The judge found that the plaintiff erred in "receiving the check upon the clearing house balances." He found, however, that this error was not the cause of the loss, for if the plaintiff had disclaimed the check the defendant "would have been the party damaged by the . . .[conduct] of its own teller." The judge also found that the plaintiff erred in debiting the amount of the check to the conservator's account. He found, however, that this mistake was not harmful to the defendant. In support of this conclusion the judge said, "It is true that upon discovery of the fraud . . . the plaintiff would be under a duty to notify indorsers and all other persons interested of its discovery to reduce any loss that they might entail. But the plaintiff . . . performed this duty with immediate dispatch to the defendant. . . . As to the claim that if the plaintiff had returned the check to the clearing house instead of debiting it to the conservator's account, the defendant would be in a better position to more quickly investigate and ascertain who the impostor was for any possible recovery, it appears that this is only in the realm of possibility and not of probability since the teller could only give a very inadequate description of the imposter . . . [who] has never been located despite much effort. . . . The damage was done . . . when the impostor walked out of the bank with the money." The judge "concluded that there was no contributory negligence on the part of the plaintiff," and, "Particularly, there was no contributory negligence on the part of the plaintiff . . . that had any causal relation with the acts that eventually led to the damages sustained." Whether the defendant was prejudiced by the plaintiff's conduct was essentially a question of fact. We cannot say that the conclusions of the judge on this issue were erroneous or tainted by error of law. . . .

Exceptions overruled. . . .

[Note: This case was decided under the NIL. It is suggested that a different result would obtain under the Commercial Code.]

HUNTINGDON COUNTY v. FIRST GRANGE NAT. BANK OF HUNTINGDON

1959, (Pa.) Court of Common Pleas of Huntingdon County, 20 D. & C. 2d 418

Edward Kenneth Fox was employed as chief clerk to the County Commissioners and also served as clerk to the Commissioners in their capacity as commissioners of county institutions. He cashed approximately 500 checks belonging to the county or the county institution district and converted the proceeds to his own use. The county commissioners now seek to recover the amount so converted from the banks which cashed the checks.

SHEELY, P. J. . . . The present case arises from the fact that all parties placed confidence in a person who did not merit that confidence. The question presented is, who is to lose as the result of his defalcations? There are no substantial disputes in the testimony. . . .

Fox was authorized by the commissioners to endorse all checks belonging to the county or to the institution district for the purpose of delivering them to the county treasurer. He was furnished with a rubber stamp for this purpose, and for the deposit of money in the two accounts above referred to, which contained the words "Huntingdon County Commissioners, Huntingdon, Pennsylvania, ..., Clerk." He was not authorized to cash checks belonging to the county, but the rubber stamp contained no words limiting the endorsement for deposit only.

Fox's defalcations were accomplished by endorsing checks coming to the commissioners' office and cashing them at defendant banks. This included the checks made payable to guests at the county home and endorsed by them in blank and delivered to the commissioners, other checks coming to the commissioners' office payable to the county or to the institution district, and checks drawn by the commissioners on their account at the First National Bank in Mapleton and made payable to the county institution district. The proceeds of these checks were converted to his own use.

The commissioners did not know that Fox was cashing checks and had never authorized him to do so, his authority being limited to endorsing checks for deposit by the county treasurer or in the two bank accounts carried by the commissioners as above noted. . . .

Under Section 3-404 of the Uniform Commercial Code of April 6, 1953, P. L. e, 12A P.S. Section 3-404, it is provided:

> Any unauthorized signature is wholly inoperative as that of the person whose name is signed unless he ratifies it or is precluded from denying it; but it operates as the signature of the unauthorized signer in favor of any person who in good faith pays the instrument or takes it for value.
>
> "Unauthorized signature" means a signature made without actual, implied or apparent authority and includes a forgery: Section 1-201, 12A PS Section 1-201.
>
> Under the Uniform Commercial Code Comment, under 12A PS Section 3-404, it is stated that the term "unauthorized signature . . . includes both a forgery and a signature made by an agent exceeding his actual or apparent authority."

In section 23 of the Negotiable Instruments Law of May 16, 1901, P. L. 194, 56 P.S. Section 28, it is provided that: "When a signature is forged or made without the authority of the person whose signature it purports to be, it is wholly inoperative, and no right to retain the instrument, or to give a discharge therefor, or to enforce payment thereof against any party thereto can be acquired through or under such signature, unless the party against whom it is sought to enforce such right is precluded from setting up the forgery or want of authority."

Relying upon these statutes, it is the position of plaintiffs that the endorsements upon the checks in question by Fox were unauthorized and that, therefore, defendant acquired no title thereto but title remained in plaintiffs, and that defendant's act in assuming control over the checks and the proceeds thereof constituted a conversion of plaintiffs' property for which it is liable to plaintiffs: *Lindsley v. First National Bank of Philadelphia,* 325 Pa. 393 (1937).

Defendant contends that, since Fox had authority to endorse the checks in plaintiffs' names, the endorsements were not forgeries and his act in cashing the checks instead of depositing them was merely an unauthorized diversion of funds. Defendant relies upon a number of theories. It contends that Fox had actual authority to cash checks; authority implied from his position as chief clerk in charge of all operations of the commissioners' office; apparent authority from the fact that the commissioners' account at defendant bank was carried in his name as clerk, and he was authorized to use a rubber stamp for endorsement which was not restricted for deposit only; estoppel from the fact that the commissioners created the situation which made it possible for Fox to misappropriate the funds, and that it was a purchaser for value of the checks without notice of Fox's lack of authority.

It seems to us that all of these contentions overlook the one controlling fact of this case. All the cases relied upon by defendant are cases involving business or banking corporations or individuals. The present case involves public funds and public officers, as to which there are specific statutory provisions and limitations. . . .

These statutes provide a definite and carefully worked out system for the handling of county funds using serially numbered receipts, vouchers and checks as safeguards. Accounts and records are required to be kept in the offices of county commissioners and of the county treasurer and operate as a check against each other. The statutes contemplate no cash transactions and do not permit the expenditure of county funds by either the commissioners or the treasurer without the concurrence of the other. There is no authority whatever for the maintenance of a bank account in the name of the commissioners or of the institution district from which the commissioners themselves, or their chief clerk acting under their authority, may expend county funds without having such funds pass through the hands of the treasurer.

Since all moneys are required to be deposited in the officially named depository and disbursements may be made only by checks signed by the commissioners and the treasurer, there is not authority in anyone, the treasurer, the commissioners or the chief clerk to endorse checks and to receive cash therefor. And, since the commissioners themselves could not cash checks belonging to the county or to the institution district, they could not delegate such authority to their chief clerk, either expressly or apparently, or be estopped to deny the existence of such authority. Officials can ratify only those acts which they themselves are empowered to make: *Whiteside v. United States,* 93 U.S. 247, 23 L. Ed. 882. Nor could such authority exist by implication by reason of the chief clerk having control of all operations of the commissioners' office. The control of the operations of that office is limited to the proper functions of the office which do not include the cashing of county checks or the expenditure of county funds.

It must be borne in mind that we are not here dealing with individuals in their individual capacity. We are dealing with governmental officials whose authority and duty is prescribed and limited by statute. All persons dealing with such officials are bound to recognize the limitations of authority of such officials. . . .

In 8 Am. Jur. Section 411, p. 149 it is stated:

> Knowledge or notice, actual or constructive, that commercial paper is public property requires one dealing in it to act accordingly, and one purchasing such an instrument from a public officer is chargeable with notice of the lack of authority of the officer to use it for his private purpose.

It follows that defendant bank in this case, although it had no actual notice that Fox was not authorized to cash checks and had no intention of aiding him in perpetrating a fraud on the county, was bound to know that the county treasurer was the only official authorized to receive money due or accruing to the county or the institution district, and that neither the county commissioners nor their chief clerk had authority to cash checks belonging to the county or to the institution district. It, therefore, was bound to know that Fox's endorsement, and its payment of the proceeds of the checks to Fox was a conversion of funds belonging to the county and to the institution district.

The fact that the practice of the commissioners in maintaining a bank account in their own names, and in permitting Fox to draw checks on one of said accounts, continued for a long period of time does not relieve the bank. . . .

As to the checks payable to guests of the county home and endorsed by them in blank, defendant contends that such checks thereby become bearer instruments and that, since it paid value for the checks without notice, Fox was appropriating the proceeds to his own use, it has a complete defense as to these items. There might be some merit to this contention if the bank did not have knowledge that the checks were the property of the county or of the institution district, but the contention overlooks the fact that before cashing these checks Mr. Fox affixed the rubber stamp endorsement of the county commissioners thereon thereby giving the bank actual notice that the checks were county property. . . .

Judgment for plaintiff.

GRESHAM STATE BANK v. O & K CONSTRUCTION CO.

1962, 231 Or. 106, 370 P. 2d 726 (Rehearing denied, June 13, 1962, 372 P. 2d 187)

F. C. McKenna was employed by O & K Construction Company as a bookkeeper. In addition, he performed other office duties. He was authorized to receive checks payable to the company and to deposit these checks in the First National Bank of Gresham. The company furnished him with a rubber stamp, "For deposit only at the First National Bank." The office supplies also included another stamp, "O & K Construction Co., Route 1, Gresham, Oregon," which was intended to be used in marking statements and other items. During the years 1957, 1958, 1959, McKenna indorsed 30 checks which had been made payable to the company and cashed them at Zimmerman's store. He indorsed the checks with the latter rubber stamp followed by his own name and the designation, "Office Manager" or "Bkpr." Zimmerman's store deposited the checks in its account in the plaintiff bank. The checks were sent through the regular banking channels and paid by the drawee banks. In May, 1959, McKenna's defalcations were discovered. The construction company obtained the cancelled checks from the various drawers and made a demand for payment from all of the drawee banks. These banks in turn made demand upon the plaintiff bank. As these demands were made on it the plaintiff withdrew from the account of Zimmerman's Store an amount equal to the check and placed it in a "suspense account." After the last check had been presented, the bank filed an interpleader suit naming O & K Construction Co. and Zimmerman's Store as defendants. The bank paid the money represented by the checks into court and was discharged from liability. The lower court entered a judgment for Zimmerman's Store.

O'CONNELL, J. . . . The defendant O and K Construction Company relies upon the rule that one who makes payment upon an unauthorized endorsement of the payee's name is liable to the payee for conversion.

Defendant Zimmerman contends that the loss falls upon the defendant construction company on the basis of any one of the following grounds: (1) that McKenna had implied or apparent authority to endorse the checks and to present them to Zimmerman's for payment on behalf of the construction company; (2) the construction company is precluded from recovery by its negligence; (3) where one of two innocent parties must suffer the loss should fall upon the one whose acts made the loss possible.

The third contention adds nothing to the first two. There is no legal principle which places the loss upon one of two innocent parties merely because one acted and the other did not. The law makes the choice upon the basis of fault or some other consideration warranting the preference. In the present case we must decide upon some such rational ground which of the two defendants should be favored.

We begin with the well established rule that one who obtains possession of a check through the unauthorized endorsement of the payee's name acquires no title to it and is liable to the payee for the amount of the check unless the payee is precluded from setting up the want of authority. . . .

The mere fact that an employee has charge of a company's office does not entitle third persons dealing with the employee to assume that he has the authority to execute or endorse the company's negotiable paper. We find no evidence to support a finding that McKenna was clothed with apparent authority.

The contention that defendant O and K Construction Company was precluded from recovery because of its negligence presents a more difficult legal problem. There was evidence to support a finding that Osburn and Kniefel were negligent in failing to scrutinize the records of the company over the three-year period during which the defalcation occurred. They made little individual effort to examine their books during that period and no audit was made. . . .

It is our conclusion that, although under the circumstances it does not appear that Osburn and Kniefel were seriously at fault in not discovering McKenna's deception, their conduct can be regarded as constituting negligence. To so conclude does not, however, solve the problem in this case. The conduct of both defendant Zimmerman and defendant O and K Construction Company contributed to the successful forgery—Zimmerman in failing to make inquiry as to McKenna's authority to endorse the checks in question, and O and K Construction Company in failing to examine its records. The question is: Who should bear the loss under these circumstances?

In a considerable number of cases it has been held that the negligence of an employer in detecting the dishonest conduct of his employee does not preclude recovery against the payor of an instrument forged by the employee. In some cases this conclusion is reached on the theory that the employer's negligence is not the proximate cause of the loss; the payor's failure to inform himself as to the employee's authority being regarded as the sole cause of the loss.

On the other hand, a substantial number of cases recognize that the payor's duty to ascertain the authority of the employee-endorser is not absolute and that the employer's negligence may bar his recovery against the payor.

It seems evident that the O and K Construction Company's negligence was a causal factor contributing to the forgery. Each of the parties had a duty to exercise due care in connection with the checks in question. Each failed to perform its duty. The question is how to allocate the loss under such circumstances. The conduct of each could be described in terms of negligence. Applying the accepted rule in other negligence cases, the defendant construction company would be barred from recovery because of its contributory negligence. But it is not necessary or desirable to extend the doctrine of contributory negligence beyond its present scope and there are special reasons why we should not do so in the law of commercial paper.

The pattern for decision in cases such as the one before us is found in Section 3-406 of the Uniform Commercial Code which was adopted by the enactment of Oregon Laws 1961, Ch. 726, Section 73.4060, to be effective on September 1, 1963. That section (Or. Laws 1961, Ch. 726, Section 73.4060; U.C.C. Section 3-406) provides as follows:

> Any person who by his negligence substantially contributes to a material alteration of the instrument or to the making of an unauthorized signature is precluded from asserting the alteration or lack of authority against a holder in due course or against a drawee or other payor who pays the instrument in good faith and in accordance with the reasonable commercial standards of the drawee's or payor's business.

Although this section is not operative until September 1, 1963, it expresses the legislative view as of the time of its enactment. There is no existing Oregon statute or adjudicated case which announces a contrary principle. As we have already indicated the cases in other jurisdictions are in conflict. We are, therefore, free to adopt the principle which, in our opinion, will comport with the needs of the business community in dealing with commercial paper under circumstances such as we have here. We believe that Section 3-406 of the Uniform Commercial Code expresses the appropriate principle. We therefore adopt it. We believe that it is particularly appropriate to do so because it conforms to the view taken, at least tentatively, by the 1961 Legislative Assembly in adopting Oregon Laws 1961, Ch. 726 with a postponed effective date.

It is apparent that this section requires a weighing process in choosing between the owner of the forged instrument and the payor in allocating the loss. Translating the section in terms of the factual situation before us, the O and K Construction Company is not precluded from asserting McKenna's lack of authority unless two conditions exist: (1) that O and K Construction Company's negligence "substantially contributes" to the making of the unauthorized signature and, (2) that Zimmerman made payment on the instrument in good faith "and in accordance with the reasonable commercial standards of the . . . payor's business."

The requirement that the negligence "substantially contributes" to the making of the unauthorized signature is necessary to satisfy the test of factual causation; it is the equivalent of the "substantial factor" test applied in the law of negligence generally. See *Restatement, Torts* Section 433, p. 733 (Supp. 1948); *Prosser on Torts,* Section 44, pp. 218–223 (2d ed. 1955).

There was sufficient evidence to establish the negligence of the O and K Construction Company in failing to check its records and that this negligence substantially contributed to the making of the unauthorized signatures (at least with respect to those checks which were cashed after there was sufficient time for the company to examine its records and discover the depletion of its funds).

This leaves for our consideration the conduct of Zimmerman in cashing the checks. Defendant O and K Construction Company is not precluded from recovery unless Zimmerman's conduct was "in accordance with the reasonable commercial standards" of its business.

Ordinarily the customary practices of a business must be established by evidence. However, it has been judicially recognized in many adjudicated cases that one who cashes a check endorsed by an agent has the duty to inquire as to the agent's authority to make the endorsement. We can, therefore, take judicial notice of this duty to make inquiry as a part of the "reasonable commercial standards" of a business. . . .

In testing Zimmerman's conduct by the standard of ordinary commercial practice, it is to be noted that the checks were not cashed by McKenna in connection with any purchase of items in the store on behalf of the construction company. McKenna received the whole amount of the check. Moreover, the amounts paid to him were substantial, including several checks for $300 or more.

Ordinarily, it is the usual practice for a company to deposit checks received by it and to pay for its expenditures by checks drawn on its own account. . . .

We hold that, as a matter of law, Zimmerman did not make payment of the checks in accordance with the reasonable commercial standards of his business. . . .

We hold that, because of defendant Zimmerman's negligent failure to act in accordance with the reasonable commercial standards of its business, the defendant O and K Construction Company, although negligent, is not precluded from recovering upon the forged checks. Oregon Laws 1961, Ch. 726, Section 73.4060 indicates that the payor's failure to act in accordance with reasonable commercial standards might bar him from setting up the owner's negligence no matter how gross it might be. It is not necessary for us to decide whether the statute will be so interpreted. In the present case the negligence of the O and K Construction Company was clearly outweighed by that of Zimmerman.

We hold that, under these circumstances, Zimmerman cannot rely upon the construction company's negligence to bar the latter's recovery. . . .

Reversed and remanded.

[The U.C.C. became effective in Oregon on September 1, 1963.]

DAVIS v. WESTERN UNION TELEGRAPH CO.

1954, (Pa.) 4 D. & C. 2d 264

The plaintiff, Davis, received what purported to be a request from his son in California for money. He wired the money and it was paid over to a person who posed as the son. The imposter had a Marine Corps identification card which had been stolen from the son. The plaintiff did not ask for a "test question" or other method to identify the person entitled to the money. The plaintiff seeks to collect the money from defendant.

CUMMINS, J. . . . In *Real Estate Land Title & Trust Company v. United Security Trust Company,* 303 Pa. 273 (1931), the Supreme Court said (page 278): "The characteristic feature of these cases was . . . that the money was in fact paid to the person to whom the plaintiff by its actions showed it intended the money should be paid. . . ."

. . . The Supreme Court termed this line of cases cited hereinabove as the so-called impostor cases, defining such as those "which hold that a bank is not liable for the payment of a check on a forged indorsement where the person who committed the forgery and received the money was in fact the person to whom the drawer delivered the check and whom he believed to be the payee named." . . .

It is interesting to note that this will still be the law under the Pennsylvania Uniform Commercial Code. See Section 3-405 (1) (a).

. . . It is immaterial that the impostor posed through the mail is one of these cases.

Judgment for defendant.

[This case was decided under the NIL.]

POELCHER v. ZINK

1954, 375 Pa. 539, 101 A. 2d 628

The plaintiff was holder of a note executed by Peter Poelcher. The plaintiff entered a judgment against the maker who died thereafter. Poelcher's daughter sought to have the judgment set aside on the ground of material alteration. The lower Court ruled in favor of the plaintiff.

Horace Stern, C. J. . . . The main alteration which appeared on the note consisted of a chemical erasure in the upper left-hand corner opposite the dollar sign. There was also some writing-over of three letters in the body of the note, but without any change whatever in the words themselves, and even defendant's own expert witness admitted that these write-overs were wholly innocent and innocuous. It is, of course, true that when it clearly appears on the face of a writing that it has been altered in a material part it is incumbent on the party producing it to account for the alteration, and until this is done it is not admissible in evidence (cases cited). But an alteration is not material if it does not effect any change in the legal obligation of the maker of the instrument. The Negotiable Instrument Act of May 16, 1901, P.L. 194, Section 17, par. 1, 56 P.S. Section 22, provides that "Where the sum payable is expressed in words and also in figures, and there is a discrepancy between the two, the sum denoted by the words is the sum payable; . . . ." Section 125, 56 P.S. Section 278, enumerates the alterations of a note which are material, but, consistently with Section 17, there is not included in the list an alteration of the figures which state the sum payable if that sum is also denoted by words in the body of the note. It has therefore been consistently held that an alteration in the figures in the upper left-hand corner of a note is not a material alteration if the words clearly denote the sum payable (cases cited). The words in the present note do show the amount payable, namely, "Three thousand three hundred Dollars," and therefore the erasure in the upper left-hand corner did not constitute a material alteration, as the court below properly held. . . .

Judgment affirmed. . . .

[This case was decided under the NIL.]

ABERCROMBIE ESTATE

1959. (Pa.) 20 D. & C. 2d 496.

Rahauser, J. Decedent, Samuel M. Abercrombie, died intestate January 25, 1958, a resident of the City of Pittsburgh, Allegheny County. . . .

Ruth Marshall, the original administratrix in this estate, also submitted a claim against the estate in the amount of $10,000. Her claim was based on a check which she produced. The check purported to be payable to her order and signed by decedent, Samuel M. Abercrombie. There was no positive testimony as to the signature on the check although an official of the bank on which the check was drawn testified:

"I am not testifying as a handwriting expert. I am now testifying as to what we would accept in the ordinary course of business. We would accept that as being his signature."

The check on which Ruth Marshall's claim is based bears a blurred date of the month of January 1958, above which is written the figure "24." More important, there is an obvious erasure in the space in which the name of the payee appears, and because of the extent of this erasure it is impossible to say what originally appeared in the space which now contains the name of Ruth Marshall as payee. In addition to these alterations the check appears to have had its form altered, as though a pair of scissors was used to trim something off it. When such an instrument is produced as the basis of a claim against a decedent's estate it is the object of a just suspicion. In *Poelcher v. Zink*, 375 Pa. 539, 546, the court said:

It is, of course, true that when it clearly appears on the face of a writing that it has been altered in a material part it is incumbent on the party producing it to account for the alteration, *and until this is done it is not admissible in evidence: Cornog v. Wilson*, 231 Pa. 281, 80A. 174; *Miners Savings Bank of Pittston v. Naylor*, 342 Pa. 273, 280, 20 A. 2d 287, 291. (Italics supplied.)

In *Cornog v. Wilson*, above cited, in speaking of the above rule as to admissibility in evidence of written instruments bearing alterations, the court said, on page 284:

This rule is more stringent when applied to *negotiable paper* than to other written instruments, and in *relation to it there is no presumption of innocence and the burden of explaining* any apparent material alteration is cast on the holder thereof: (citing cases) . . . (Italics supplied.)

See also *Nagle Estate*, 134 Pa. 31, imposing the duty of explaining an erasure on a check on the holder.

We do not believe that the law as to the burden of explaining the alteration of a negotiable instrument was changed by the provisions of Section 3-307 or of Section 3-407 of the Commercial Code of April 6, 1953, P. L. 3, cited by claimant. Section 3-307, Subsection (2), provides:

When signatures are admitted or established, production of the instrument entitles a holder to recover on it unless the defendant establishes a defense: 12 A PS Section 3-307.

This section does not refer to an instrument bearing a material alteration on its face. Furthermore, it refers to signatures which are admitted or established; here the signature was not admitted and it is questionable if the signature was established since there was not positive testimony that the signature was that of decedent.

Section 3-407, Subsection (1), defines a material alteration as including any alteration which changes the contract of any party thereto in any respect, including any such change in the writing as signed by adding to it or removing any part of it. This would appear to include any erasure in the name of the original payee and the addition of another name, as well as a change in the date of the instrument or the scissoring of the instrument.

Section 3-407, subsection (2), provides:

> As against any person other than a subsequent holder in due course
> (a) alteration by the holder which is both fraudulent and material discharges any party whose contract is thereby changed unless that party assents or is precluded from asserting the defense;
> (b) no other alteration discharges any party and the instrument may be enforced according to its original tenor, or as to incomplete instruments according to the authority given: 12A. PS Section 3-407.

This section does not refer to the burden of proof where the instrument bears obvious material alterations on its face. In this state of events it seems logical to place that burden on the holder as the person in the best position to explain it. . . .

If arguendo, it is conceded that the signature to the check was adequately established, thus establishing a presumption of delivery of the check for consideration, and if it further conceded that the burden was on defendant to show a fraudulent alteration of the check, and that this burden was not met by defendant, it still appears that claimant assumed the burden of showing consideration for the check and failed to meet that burden, and her claim should accordingly be rejected. See *Calanno Estate*, 14 D. & C. 2d 153, 156. The only testimony as to services rendered to decedent by claimant was given by Mrs. Anne Growshok. She did not testify as to any specific contract, nor did she testify in detail as to the services rendered by claimant, the period for which they were rendered and the reasonable value of such services. She related a number of general conversations with decedent, and loose declarations by him, but there was no clear and convincing evidence of the type required to fix liability against a decedent's estate. Claims of his character are the subjects of just suspicion and the courts have consistently indicated that they must be established by testimony which is clear, precise and indubitable. See *Consentino v. Vittoria*, 394 Pa. 538, and cases cited therein. The testimony of Mrs. Growshok did not meet the high standards set by the courts. Her loose and rambling testimony was plain evidence that she could not distinguish between fact and fiction, nor between decedent's jests and reality. The auditing judge gives no credence to the testimony of this witness.

For the reasons hereinbefore set forth the auditing judge is of the opinion that the claim of Ruth Marshall against this estate, whether based on the said $10,000 check, or on a contract or quantum meruit basis for services rendered to decedent in his lifetime, must be rejected. . . .

UMANI v. REBER

1959, 191 Pa. Super. 185, 155 A. 2d. 634

Umani leased a hotel to Reber and also transferred the hotel liquor license with the understanding that the license would be returned upon termination of the lease. Later Reber threatened to surrender the license for cancellation unless Umani reimbursed him for losses resulting from operation of the hotel. He claimed that the amount of past revenue had been misrepresented in order to induce him to lease. He set his losses at $5000 and demanded this sum for return of the license. Umani executed two checks to Reber for a total of $5000 and placed them in escrow pending approval of the license transfer by the Liquor Control Board. Approval was forthcoming but Umani immediately told the escrow agent not to deliver the checks to Reber. The escrow agent deposited the checks with the court and the court awarded a judgment in favor of Reber.

ERVIN, J. . . . Appellant also argues that it was error for the trial court to enforce an oral agreement which lacked consideration because the parties were already obligated to perform under a prior agreement. The $5,000, represented by the two certified checks deposited by Mrs. Umani with Parke in escrow, was being paid to Reber, not for the retransfer of the liquor license but to compensate Reber for losses which he claimed to have sustained because of false information given to him by Joseph Umani concerning the previous money revenue from the operation of the hotel under Umani. Reber claimed these representations were false and induced him to enter into a bad bargain. The checks were to be turned over to Reber upon the retransfer of the license but they were actually given to settle his claim for losses. The testimony of Parke on this subject is quite clear. There was, therefore, a new and good consideration for the payment of the $5,000 and the cases cited by the appellant in this connection are not applicable to the facts in the present case. . . .

Orders affirmed. . . .

INSDORF v. WIL-AVON MERCHANDISE MART, INC.

1958 Court of Common Pleas of Chester County, Pa., 8 Ches. Co. Rep. 341

The defendant executed a check payable to the order of the plaintiff in settlement of accounts owing to the plaintiff. The check was made and delivered on January 11, 1958, but dated January 23, 1958. The plaintiff presented the check after January 23, but the bank refused payment because the defendant had stopped payment. The plaintiff attempted to recover the amount of the check and the defendant resisted claiming that the plaintiff's complaint failed to allege with particularity the accounts between the parties for which the check was allegedly given in payment.

GAWTHROP, J. . . . Defendant's second contention is without merit. Under the Negotiable Instruments Law, 1901, P. L. 194, Section 24, every negotiable instrument was deemed, prima facie, to have been issued for valuable consideration. There was no necessity to plead in detail the terms of the contract in connection with delivery of a check: *Caldwell, etc. v. Crown Avenue Silk Co.*, 45 D. & C. 45. The Uniform Commercial Code, 1953, P. L. 3, Section 3-408, supplies and replaces, inter alia, Section 24 of the Act of 1901, (see 12-A, P. S. 3-408, and Comment thereunder) and by its terms provides that "no consideration is necessary for an instrument or obligation given in payment of or as security for an antecedent obligation of any kind." We cannot conclude that the enactment of the Code has altered the law or the practice to require Plaintiff to aver the details of the contract which gave rise to making the check. Moreover, Section 3-408 of the Code, by making consideration unnecessary where the instrument is given for an antecedent obligation, makes it equally unnecessary to plead consideration in such circumstances. Therefore, the averment may be regarded as surplusage.

Furthermore, the same section of the Code makes want or failure of consideration a matter of defense as between the original parties. Both such defenses must, under Rule 1030, Pa. R. C. P., be pleaded under New Matter in Defendant's Answer, and if not so pleaded are waived under Rule 1032. In our view the detailed nature of the consideration pleaded need not be set forth, especially since Defendant must make any defense of want or failure of consideration by pleading it affirmatively as New Matter.

The preliminary objection is dismissed. Defendant is allowed twenty days to file an answer.

GREATER VALLEY TERMINAL CORP. v. GOODMAN

1962, 405 Pa. 605, 176 A. 2d 408

COHEN, J. ABC Federal Oil & Burner Co. (ABC) owed substantial debts to Greater Valley Terminal Corporation (plaintiff) and P. J. Goodman (defendant) for unpaid oil deliveries. Plaintiff was exerting pressure upon ABC for payment and had refused to sell any more oil to that firm unless paid for on delivery and unless the past debt was liquidated.

Defendant recognized that if plaintiff proceeded to enforce collection of the debt owed plaintiff by ABC, ABC would not be able to pay and its credit position would be so endangered that it would be forced to discontinue operations. Consequently, numerous meetings were held by parties representing plaintiff, defendant and ABC. As a result of these meetings, ABC gave plaintiff its note for $325,306.92 payable in eighteen weekly installments. Executed contemporaneously was defendant's signed statement written on the bottom of the note: "For value received, the undersigned hereby guarantees payment of the within Note." Defendant at the same time also delivered to plaintiff his personal financial statement indicating thereon the said statement was given by the defendant to induce plaintiff to accept defendant's guarantee of the note given by ABC to plaintiff. ABC defaulted in the terms and payment of the note and plaintiff brought this action on defendant's guarantee.

Since an inference of consideration may be drawn where surety is given contemporaneously with the principal obligation, the plaintiff could have properly rested its case after having proved, in addition to the principal agreement, defendant's contemporaneous endorsement and nonpayment. . . .

Judgment affirmed.

THE UNION BANK v. JOSEPH MOBILLA

1959, Court of Common Pleas of Erie County, Pa., 43 Erie Co. Leg. J. 45

LAUB, J. This is a complaint in assumpsit for breach of warranty to which the defendant filed an answer containing new matter and a counterclaim. The plaintiff filed a reply, then moved for judgment on the pleadings. It is this latter action which is before us now.

On January 15, 1958, the defendant, a used car dealer, represented to the plaintiff bank that he had sold a used Ford automobile to one Theresa Piotrowski of 650 East 24th Street. For finance purposes, he exhibited an installment sales contract and a judgment note allegedly signed by Theresa Piotrowski as maker. There was nothing on the face of either instrument to indicate that the signatures had not been placed there by the maker or that either had been signed by someone else acting in the maker's behalf. . . . The note which was payable to defendant was endorsed by him "without recourse," and the security agreement, which was in defendant's favor as a seller of a chattel, was assigned to the bank. Both instruments, as well as the title to the vehicle in question, were turned over to the bank as part of the finance transaction.

. . . After default the bank importuned both the purported maker and the defendant to discharge the obligation but without avail, the maker having denied executing either document or having bought the vehicle from the defendant. In consequence, plaintiff instituted this action, alleging that defendant is guilty of a breach of warranty, and as part of its action, alleging a written warranty in the security agreement "that the above instrument is genuine and in all respects what it purports to be." Plaintiff also claims upon an implied warranty of the genuineness of the note.

The defendant in his answer admits that he endorsed the note and assigned the security agreement to the plaintiff. He also admits that the maker did not sign either document. It is his defense, however, that Theresa Piotrowski's signature was affixed by an authorized agent named Edward Rogalia and that he (the defendant) is not liable in any event because his indorsement of the note was "without recourse." He also contends that plaintiff may not recover, as an item of damage, the fifteen per cent collection or attorney's fees provided for in the warrant to confess judgment.

We can see no merit whatever in the defenses offered and consider that plaintiff is entitled to the judgment which it seeks. The defendant's conception of the litigation as being a suit against an endorser who signed "without recourse," misses the point. Plaintiff is not suing on the note, but, as noted above, is claiming upon a breach of warranty. If it were true that the suit was against the defendant on the sole basis that he was an endorser, there might be some value to the defenses offered, but the pleadings reveal an entirely different situation. As the pleadings now stand, it is admitted on the record that the defendant in writing warranted the security agreement to be all that it purported to be, and it is clear that it was not. Further, the admission that defendant endorsed the note as part of his finance dealings with the plaintiff and that the note was not signed by the maker is a clear admission of a breach of the implied warranty which accompanies situations of this character. While no statute is required to establish the common sense conclusion that one who presents a document for discount or otherwise, impliedly warrants its genuineness when he accepts a consideration for its transfer, the Uniform Commercial Code has such a provision. In Section 3-417 (2) (a) of that Act (Act 1953, April 6, P.L. 3, 12A PS 3-417 (2) (a) it is provided that the transferor of an instrument for consideration warrants, among other things, that all signatures are genuine or authorized. This certainly does not imply that a transferor, with knowledge that a signature is not that of the person it purports to belong to and there is no qualifying or descriptive language indicating that the signature was made by someone other than the maker, may remain silent and suppress such knowledge to the detriment of the transferee.

Warranting the signature, or warranting that an instrument is all that it purports to be are important elements for the protection of a transferee in situations of this kind. The confession of judgment clause in the note was a very real and substantial element in the transaction. If there was an impediment to the entry or judgment, not disclosed to the transferee, it suffered material harm when it accepted the note on faith. A judgment note, not of sufficient validity to support a judgment obtained under its warrant, would, under such circumstances, be no security to the plaintiff; particularly where the endorsement was without recourse. . . .

Judgment for the plaintiff.

GENERAL REFRIGERATOR AND STORE FIXTURE COMPANY v. FRY

1958, 393 Pa. 15, 141 A. 2d 836

MUSMANNO, J. Edward Mueller of Philadelphia sought a loan of $5,000 from David Fogel, owner of the General Refrigerator and Store Fixture Company of the same city. When Fogel refused to lend the money unless Meuller could supply surety, Mueller prevailed upon a friend, Wm. O. Fry, to sign, with him, a judgment note in the sum of $6,750. Mueller then asked Fogel to make out two checks, one for $2,504.50 payable to Mueller and the other payable to Mueller and Fry in the amount of $2,495.50. Later, Mueller returned to Fogel with the two checks, the $2,495.50 one purportedly having been endorsed by Fry. Mueller asked Fogel to sign his name to the checks so they could be cashed since the bank knew Fogel but did not know Mueller. Fogel so signed the checks and Mueller cashed them but gave none of the proceeds to Fry, his signature, as well as that of his wife's, having been forged.

Fogel recorded the judgment note, Mueller absconded, and Fry was left holding the fi fa.

Fry refused to pay the amount of the note, which was assessed at $7,777.85. Later, by stipulation, the amount was reduced to $6,114.28. Fry contended that, since he was a payee on one of the checks but received none of the $5,000, a failure of consideration resulted and he, therefore, was not liable on the note. He accordingly filed a petition in the Court of Common Pleas of Philadelphia to open the judgment. The petition was granted but later rescinded by the Court and judgment confirmed in the name of Fogel in the amount indicated. Fry appealed.

From the time that man learned to communicate thought by means of writing, he has been expressing approval of things which he later repudiated. Whether he chiseled his name to a stone, scribbled it on parchment, or penned it to twentieth century bond paper, he has found reasons to regret his signature and has appealed to some tribunal to be excused from the obligation he voluntarily assumed. Thus William Fry asserts that he is not liable under the judgment note because he signed as an obligor and not as a surety. But the Court below found, from depositions which were taken, that Fry never expected to receive any of the proceeds of the two checks. Therefore, it was of no consequence that his name had been unauthorizedly added to one of the checks as payee. The Court concluded, from all the evidence, that Fry signed the judgment note as an accommodation maker and was responsible for the face value of the note since the original obligor had failed to honor the primary obligation.

Fry asserts on this appeal that he had many defenses to the note: (1) that he did not know what he was signing; (2) that the judgment note was blank when he signed it; (3) that in any event he could not be regarded as an accommodation maker since his name appeared on one of the checks as payee and his name was forged to the check; (4) that Fogel was negligent in the entire transaction. . . .

Although Fry did not dispute his signature to the judgment note, he testified that he was unaware that the paper he signed was a judgment note. At first he asserted that the blank lines on the note had not been filled in when he attached his signature to the document but later he declined to say "positively" that the blanks had not been filled in. The most that he could assert with assurance was that the note carried no date. He admitted that though he could read, he had not read the instrument but merely "glanced" at it. This is rather thin ice on which to skate to the shores of non-liability. We said in *Commonwealth, to Use of Liberty Nat. Bank of Pittston v. Gudaitis*, 323 Pa. 110, 111, 186 A. 82, 83:

> As long ago as when Shephard's Touchstone was written (1648), the law was as follows (page 56): "If a party that is to seal the deed can read himself and doth not, or being illiterate or blind, doth not require to hear the deed read or the contents thereof declared, in these cases albeit the deed is contrary to his mind, yet it is good and unavoidable." In language not quite so quaint, we repeated this principle in *Re Greenfield's Estate*, 14 Pa. 489, 496, adding that one who so signs a document "is guilty of supine negligence which . . . is not the subject of protection, either in equity or at law." We have never deviated from this ruling, one of our latest cases being *O'Reilly v. Reading Trust Co.*, 262 Pa. 337, 343, 105 A. 542.

The whole business structure of America would become a shambles if signers were to be allowed to repudiate their obligations on the basis that they did not know what they were signing. The ever-constant possibility of such a disavowal would turn into water the adhesive mortar of legal responsibility holding together the bricks of every contractual wall; such an accepted possibility would wreck every business dealing at the slightest touch of the repudiator.

And then, it was not established in the case at bar that Fry did not know what he was signing. He testified that when he signed the note he took for granted that "it was a *reference for a loan*." (Emphasis supplied.) He testified further:

(Q) What was the reference supposed to be for? (A) To borrow money. (Q) Why was he borrowing money? (A) I don't know. (Q) Are you related to him? (A) No. (Q) Are you a friend of his? (A) Yes.

When asked if he was seeking a loan from Fogel, Fry replied:

No. If I wanted to get a loan—it was my corporation—I could go to a bank and make a loan as far as that goes. As I said, I never heard of this Mr. Fogel or the General Refrigerator and Store Fixtures Company, and I am sure I would not have gone there. I know other people who I could go to to get a loan if I needed one.

As the lower Court indicated, Fry has not averred any fraud. A review of the entire record establishes quite clearly that Fry got himself into his present troubles through what this Court has already well denominated as "supine negligence." The person who willingly lies down so that others may step on him will have a difficult time convincing the world that he has not contributed in large measure to his own misfortune.

Even so, we believe that since the Frys were only sureties and received no part of the loan of $5,000, the costs in the case should be divided equally between the appellants and the appellee. *Thus, with that qualification, the judgment is affirmed.* . . .

Review Questions and Problems

1. A note was signed "Keystate Ins. Agency, Inc. (SEAL), Harry Ostroff (SEAL)." Is the insurance agency bound on this note?
2. Bregman signed an instrument acknowledging that he owed $23,000 to Berke. It provided for weekly payments and contained a stipulation that it was "without recourse." Berke sues Bregman on the note. What result?
3. Notes were executed in the name of *X* Company followed by the names of two persons who were officers of the company but did not indicate this in their signatures. Is *X* Company liable on the note?
4. *M*, the bookkeeper for *X* Corporation prepared payroll checks to the order of persons not on the payroll. The checks were presented to the company's treasurer who signed them as a matter of course. *M* indorsed the checks in the name of the purported payees and cashed the checks at various stores. The checks were honored by the drawee bank. *X* Corporation seeks to recover from (1) the stores which cashed the checks (2) the drawee bank. How would you decide this case?

5. Smith introduced himself to Brown as "Professor Weinstein," a noted psychologist and claimed to be raising funds for a study of juvenile delinquency. Brown drew a check for $10,000 payable to the order of "Professor Weinstein." Smith (alias Weinstein) indorsed the check in the name of Weinstein and cashed it at the bank. Is the bank liable to Brown?
6. *A* entered into a written contract for the installation of a heating system and on the same day signed an application for credit and a judgment note. The note was to be used to raise money for payment of the contract price. When the work was completed *A* signed a completion certificate at the request of the bank, holder of the note. The heating system was inadequate and a judgment was confessed on the note which authorized "entry of judgment at any time." The court held that *A* would have to pay the full amount of the note to the bank. Was this decision correct?
7. *A* drew a check in such fashion that enough room was left at the left margin to insert the words, "One thousand" in front of the word "Fifty" (the actual amount of the check). A person who obtained possession of this check thus altered it to read "One Thousand Fifty and no/100 Dollars." The check was then negotiated to *H*. How much can *H* recover on the check?
8. In question 7 above what would your answer be if the wrongdoer used chemicals to erase the word "Fifty" and then proceeded to fill in the amount of "One Thousand Dollars"?
9. *M* made a note payable to the order of *P* and delivered it blank as to amount. *P* agreed to fill in the amount which his books would show as the balance owed by *M*. Instead, he filled in the amount for 10 times the obligation and indorsed the note to *H*. How much can *H* recover from *M*?
10. *D* drew a check payable to the order of *P*. *P* indorsed to *A*, *A* indorsed to *B*, and *B* indorsed to *H*. *H* obtained certification of the check after which the drawee bank failed. What are *H*'s rights against *D*, *P*, *A*, and *B*?
11. *M* was induced by the fraud of *P* to execute a note payable to the order of *P* as an accommodation to *P*. *P* indorsed the note to *H*. Can *M* introduce evidence that he was induced by fraud to enter into the transaction and that he is only an accommodation party?
12. *D*'s signature is forged to a bill of exchange drawn in favor of *P* on drawee *Y*. *P* takes the bill to *Y* and has it accepted and then negotiates it to *H*, a holder in due course. *H* presents it for payment to *Y*, who refuses to pay because he has learned of the forgery. May *H* recover from *Y*?
13. *A* determines to make a gift to his son *P*, but not having the "ready cash" he makes a note for $1,000 to *P*. *P* immediately negotiates the note to *H*, a holder in due course. May *A* set up the defense of lack of consideration against *H*?
14. *M* sought to have a new furnace installed in her house and signed several papers, including a note, at the request of *P*, a heating contractor, without knowledge or reason to believe that any one of the papers was a note. *P* indorsed the note to *X* bank who indorsed it to *H*. *M* never received the furnace. Must *M* pay?

15. *H* holds a note which, unknown to him, has been forged. He, by a qualified indorsement, indorses it to *A*, a holder in due course. It is presented and payment is refused. *A* desires to hold *H* liable on his indorsement. May he do so?
16. *M* owed money to *P* for lumber sold and gave a note to evidence the debt. When it became due, a renewal note was executed, but *P* required an additional indorser. *P* stated, "We will want to use the note as collateral for a loan, and the bank will require the credit of some other person." *M* asked *A*, a businessman of substance, to indorse. *A* did so after *P* explained to him the purpose of his indorsement. *A* received no value for his indorsement. On *M*'s default, is *A* liable to *P*?
17. *M* signed the following note, leaving it on his desk:

   "Seattle, Washington.
   May 4, 1964.

   On or before six months from date I promise to pay to the order of ....
   ....
   .... Dollars ....
   (Signed) *M*."

   A, an agent, stole and completed the instrument. He then negotiated the note to *Y*, who endorsed to *P*. *P* sues *M*, who sets up the defense of nondelivery. What is the result?
18. *M* gave *P* a note for a debt owed. Three months later *F*, *M*'s father, signed on the face of the note below *M*'s name. The note was not then due, and *F* had had no part in the prior transactions. Can *P* collect from *F* if *M* doesn't pay at maturity?
19. *M* conducts a used car business. *X* came to *M*'s car lot with a Chevrolet sedan he had stolen from *P*. *X* had the registration certificate in *P*'s name and *P*'s driver's license. Upon the strength of the papers and *X*'s oral representations that he was *P*, *M* drew a check payable to "*P* or order" and handed it to *X*. X indorsed the check in *P*'s name and presented it to the drawee bank and received payment. Can *M* recover from the drawee bank for paying the check out of his account?
20. *M* bought a car from *X* at a price of $2995. *M* was allowed $1195 as a trade-in on his old car leaving a balance of $1800, to be paid in installments at 6% interest. *M* signed a note in blank and contends that it was later filled in for $2300. *X* sold the note to *A*. Does *M* have a good defense against *A*?

25

Presentment, Notice of Dishonor, and Protest

4-64. Introduction. In the preceding chapter we discussed the liability of the secondary parties, namely, drawers and indorsers of negotiable paper. It was pointed out that their conditional (contractual) liability to the holder does not arise until the performance of certain conditions precedent, namely, due presentment for payment, dishonor by the primary party, and the giving of due notice of dishonor to the drawer or indorser. In this connection it must be remembered that these conditions may be waived by the parties to a negotiable instrument. A waiver set forth in the body of a note is effective as to all parties whose names appear on the instrument, while a waiver which is part of an indorsement applies only to the indorser, unless the language used is broad enough to cover later indorsers. Protest is a very formal act or procedure for complying with the conditions precedent.

The NIL prescribed definite rules with regard to the manner of presenting an instrument for payment or acceptance; the methods of giving notice of dishonor and the time within such notice must be given in order to impose liability on the secondary parties. The Code continues these basic requirements but makes certain changes designed to make it easier to satisfy these conditions precedent.

The importance of this chapter should be stressed—failure to comply may result in either the complete or partial discharge of the secondary parties. Thus, a holder who fails to properly present a note to the primary party—maker—will have thereby discharged the indorsers from their conditional liability. If the maker does not pay, the holder will not have recourse against the indorsers.

It must be remembered that secondary parties also have unconditional liability which stems from warranties which they make. Such warranty liability exists without regard to the performance of conditions precedent. Likewise it must be noted that even though a secondary party is discharged from his liability as a secondary party, he may be liable on the underlying obligation which caused either the transfer or issuance of the instrument as the case may be. It is therefore appropriate at this point to mention the provisions of U.C.C. 3-802 which deal with the effect of an instrument on the obligation for which it is given. (See Section 4-78 for a discussion of this concept.) Thus there are cases in which a secondary party may incur liability on his contract as indorser or drawer (Sections 4-57 and 4-58); his warranty contract (Section 4-61) or the underlying obligation. (Section 4-78)

Performance of conditions precedent is not necessary in most cases to impose liability on a primary party—maker or acceptor. The secondary parties, however, engage to pay only upon presentment, dishonor, "and any necessary notice of dishonor or protest."

Attention will now be given to the various conditions precedent that normally must be fulfilled to establish secondary liability. It is necessary to carefully distinguish drawers from indorsers and also to differentiate between drawers of drafts as compared to drawers of checks. Also a distinction is to be noted as between indorsers of notes on one hand and indorsers of checks and drafts on the other.

4-65. When presentment, notice of dishonor and protest necessary or permissible. An instrument may be presented for payment (in the case of a note or draft) or may be presented for acceptance (in the case of a draft). Thus there are two basic types of presentment—for acceptance and for payment. Section 3-501 of the Code expressly provides that performance of conditions precedent "is necessary to charge secondary parties" unless excused.

Presentment for acceptance. Presentment for acceptance is not applicable to promissory notes, but it is often required in the case of drafts. The drawee of a draft is not bound upon the instrument as primary party until he accepts it. The holder may, in most cases, wait until maturity and present his draft to the drawee for payment, or he may present it to the drawee for acceptance before maturity in order to give credit to the instrument during the period of its term. The holder may present the draft to the drawee for acceptance at any time. The drawee is under no legal duty to the holder to accept; but if he refuses, the draft is dishonored by nonacceptance and a right of recourse arises immediately against the drawer and the indorsers, and no presentment for payment is necessary.

For example, the holder of a draft due in six months may present it for acceptance to the drawee immediately upon receipt of the instrument; or he may wait until the maturity date of the paper and present it for payment on that date. If the drawee dishonors when the instrument is presented for acceptance, the holder, after giving due notice, may immediately sue the drawer or any other secondary parties thereon.

When presentment for acceptance required. In most instances it is not necessary to present an instrument for acceptance. Although presentment for acceptance is not required in all cases, it is a desirable practice to present for acceptance all drafts that are payable at a future day. It is thus possible to determine whether the draft will be honored and to establish the liability of the drawee. Presentment for payment alone is usually sufficient, but in the following cases presentment for acceptance must be made to charge the drawer and indorsers of a draft:

1. Where the draft expressly stipulates that it must be presented for acceptance.

2. Where the draft is payable elsewhere than at the residence or place of business of the drawee. Otherwise the drawee may not know of his obligation to be present at the place designated for payment.

3. Where the date of payment depends upon such presentment. Where the draft is payable after sight, for example, "Thirty days after sight pay to the order of *X*," the draft must be presented to the drawee for acceptance in order to determine the maturity date of the instrument.

The foregoing rules were also contained in the NIL. The NIL had generally been construed as giving to the holder of a time draft the option of presenting for acceptance if he desired to do so. If he did present for acceptance and acceptance was refused, the holder had to give notice of dishonor. He was not required to wait until the maturity date and then present again, this time for payment. The privilege of presenting for acceptance does not apply to a demand draft for it is contemplated that the holder is entitled to immediate payment and there is no need for acceptance. This rule is codified in the Code which provides: "The holder may at his option present for acceptance any other draft payable at a stated date."

Presentment for payment. The Code continues the NIL requirement that presentment for payment is required to charge "*any indorser*" and a drawer. However, with regard to discharge of the drawer the Code makes an important change. Under the NIL the drawer of a draft other than a check was discharged completely by failure to present, but drawers of checks were discharged only to the extent of the loss caused by the delay in presenting. Thus, the liability of the drawer of a check to pay was absolute rather than conditional insofar as presentment and notice of dishonor are concerned, unless the drawer is damaged by the delay. If the drawee bank fails after the time when presentment is due, the drawer is discharged, but only to the extent that his funds were impaired by the failure. For example, suppose that on March 1, 1964, *A* draws his check on *D* Bank, payable to *B*. *B* negotiates the check to *C*. *C* does not present the check for payment within a reasonable time as specified. The check is dishonored by *D* Bank. *C* gives notice to *A*, the drawer, and *B*, the indorser. Although the check has been presented for payment after an unreasonable time, *A* is still liable, because he suffered no loss on account of the delay. However, if, between the date when presentment should have been made and the date of presentment by *C*, the bank had become insolvent and *A* had lost 60 per cent of the money he had on deposit in the bank, *A* would be discharged on the check held by *C* to the extent of 60 cents on the dollar. *B*, the indorser, is discharged in either case. The Code basically continues the NIL rule as to presentment of checks but extends it to apply to the following as well:

1. Any drawer.
2. The acceptor of a draft payable at a bank.
3. The maker of a note payable at a bank.

Under the Code drawers of drafts other than checks are not completely discharged as under the NIL, but receive a discharge only to the extent of any loss they may suffer. The Code requires that presentment be made to charge primary parties to instruments other than checks if they are payable at a bank. Some cases under the NIL have held that such parties are not discharged to any degree by failure to make a timely presentment. The Code gives such parties a discharge to the extent of the loss suffered. The Code continues the rule of the NIL that presentment is not necessary to charge primary parties (makers and acceptors of notes and drafts) where such instruments are not payable at banks. Notes and drafts payable at banks are called "domiciled paper."

Notice of dishonor. The Code continues the NIL rule that notice of dishonor is necessary to charge indorsers, but changes the law with respect to drawers of drafts. Whereas the NIL gave a complete discharge if proper notice of dishonor was not given to drawers, the Code grants only a *pro tanto* discharge—to the extent of the loss occasioned by the failure to give proper notice. The Code makes it clear that drawers of checks are likewise discharged pro tanto as in the case of slow presentment.

The makers and drawers of "domiciled paper" are entitled to notice of dishonor under the Code but are released only to the extent that they are injured by the failure of the holder to give prompt notice of dishonor.

Protest. Protest is a certificate which sets forth that an instrument was presented for payment or acceptance, that it was dishonored, and the reasons, if any, given for refusal to accept or pay. It is a formal method for satisfying the conditions precedent. The NIL required protest of "foreign" drafts and checks—instruments which are drawn in one state or country and payable in another state or country. The Code confines the requirement of protest to drafts which are drawn or payable outside the United States. The comment to the Code states that the protest requirement was retained as to international drafts "because it is generally required by foreign law which this Article cannot affect." In other cases protest is optional with the holder.

Indorsers after maturity. The NIL provided that an instrument indorsed when overdue became payable on demand as to an indorser after maturity. The Code has eliminated this provision and provides instead (U.C.C. 3-501 (4)): "Notwithstanding any provision of this section, neither presentment nor notice of dishonor nor protest is necessary to charge an indorser who has indorsed an instrument after maturity." The reason for this change is that few people thought to present an overdue instrument for the purpose of charging an indorser and the NIL provision had become "little more than a trap for those not familiar with the Act." (U.C.C. 3-501 Comment 8.)

Accordingly, indorsers after maturity are not entitled to performance of conditions precedent. Like primary parties they remain liable for the period of the statute of limitations.

4-66. Unexcused delay; discharge. As under the NIL, an unexcused delay in making any necessary presentment or in giving notice of dishonor discharges secondary parties—indorsers and drawers. The Code follows the rule that indorsers are completely discharged by such delay. As noted in the previous section, however, drawers, makers of notes payable at a bank, and acceptors of drafts payable at a bank receive only a pro tanto discharge. The NIL confined this concept to drawers of checks only, whereas the Code includes all drawers as well as makers and acceptors of domiciled paper. The NIL provided that the drawer of a check would be discharged from liability "to the extent of the loss caused by the delay." In practice this provision was not satisfactory because of the long delay and difficulty in proof of the amount of loss caused by failure of a bank. Accordingly, the Code provides for a more workable arrangement to give a discharge to drawers and to makers and acceptors of instruments payable at a bank. Section 3-502 (1) (b) provides: "any drawer or the acceptor of a draft payable at a bank or the maker of a note payable at a bank who because the drawee or payor bank becomes insolvent during the delay is deprived of funds maintained with the drawee or payor bank to cover the instrument may discharge his liability by written assignment to the holder of his rights against the drawee or payor bank in respect of such funds, but such drawer, acceptor or maker is not otherwise discharged." The drawer, acceptor, or maker has the privilege of assigning to the holder (where there has been an unexcused delay) his rights against the drawee or payor bank. Until a written assignment is made, however, a discharge is not effected. The assignment gives to the holder the rights which the drawer, maker, or acceptor had against the drawee or payor as to the funds covered by the particular instrument.

The rationale of the provision which grants a discharge is simply that if the holder had acted properly and presented the instrument promptly it would have been paid and the obligor would have been discharged. If during the delay the drawee or payor bank becomes insolvent, the resulting loss is caused by the holder and should be borne by him. The secondary party is not likely to be in a good position to prevent the loss for he feels obliged to leave his funds with the drawee or payor bank to cover the instrument. On the other hand, it is equally clear that there should be a limit on his discharge. The drawer, acceptor, or maker has not yet paid anything by virtue of having given the instrument and he has probably received some benefit because of his engagement. For example, *A* gives a check to *B* in payment for a new automobile and *B* delays unreasonably in presenting the check to the bank upon which it is drawn. When *B* presents the check it is dishonored because the bank in the meantime has become insolvent. It would be unfair to let *A* keep the automobile while giving nothing to *B*. Consequently the Code provides that *A* will be discharged if he makes an assignment to *B* of his rights against the drawee bank.

The Code provides as did the NIL that where *protest* is necessary, if it is delayed beyond the time when due, *any drawer or indorser* is discharged. Thus a complete discharge is given to all drawers and indorsers.

4-67. Presentment. Three sections of the Code deal with the details of presentment. These sections simplify the rules and procedures with respect to how and when presentment is to be made but do not radically change the law as it existed under the NIL.

How presentment is made. Presentment is defined by Section 3-504 of the Code as a "demand for acceptance or payment made upon the maker, acceptor, drawee or other payor by or on behalf of the holder." Unlike the NIL, the Code does not make exhibition of the instrument an essential element of a proper presentment. Under the Code it does not matter where or how the demand for payment is made. Presentment may be made by mail,[1] by telephone or in any other way. If the presentment is made by mail, it is effective on the date when the mail is received. Presentment may be made through a "clearing house." It may be made to any person who has authority to make or refuse the payment or acceptance. If there are two or more makers, acceptors, drawees or other payors, presentment can be made to any one of them. The NIL provided that unless the two or more makers, acceptors, drawees, or other payors are partners, or one has authority to act for the others, presentment must be made to all of the parties.

The place of presentment is usually immaterial, but a draft accepted or a note made payable at a bank must be presented at such bank. If the place of payment or acceptance is specified in the instrument, presentment may be made at such place. If no place is specified, it may be made at the place of business or residence of the party who is to accept or pay. If there is no one authorized to accept or pay "present or accessible" at the place

[1] Batchelder v. Granite Trust Co., page 624.

of payment specified, or at the place of business or residence of the party to accept or pay, presentment is excused. Ordinarily, presentment would be made at the primary party's place of business, but the Code is extremely liberal both as to place of presentment and mode of presentment.

Though the Code in most cases does not require that presentment be made at any particular place and does not require that the person making the presentment exhibit the instrument to the party who is to pay or accept, it does provide a safeguard for the rights of the latter. Section 3-505 (1) (c) provides: "The party to whom presentment is made may without dishonor require that the instrument be produced for acceptance or payment at the place specified in it, or if there be none at any place reasonable in the circumstances." Thus the party to pay or accept may not be imposed upon by a holder who presents at an unusual or inconvenient place.

Section 4-210 of Article 4—Bank Deposits and Collections provides further rules with respect to the manner of presentment with particular reference to the rights and duties of banks. (See Chapter 27.)

Time of presentment. Section 3-503 of the Code provides definite rules much like those under the NIL with respect to time of presentment for (a) payment and (b) acceptance.

The time of presentment depends upon several factors including the nature of the instrument. There are two basic rules, however, which apply to any presentment: "Where any presentment is due on a day which is not a full business day for either the person making presentment or the party to pay or accept, presentment is due on the next following day for both parties. Presentment to be sufficient must be made at a reasonable hour, and if at a bank during its banking day." (U.C.C. 3-503 (3) and (4)). These provisions are new. The related provisions in the NIL called for presentment prior to noon at the option of the holder if the instrument fell due on a Saturday. The Code gives recognition to the increasing practice of closing businesses on Saturday. The NIL allowed presentment at a bank "at any hour before the bank is closed. . . ." This meant that a person could make presentment after the close of the banking day. The Code rejects this concept as being inconvenient to banks and not in keeping with their efficient operation.

If the instrument expresses the time for presentment, such expression controls. Otherwise, the time for presentment is determined by certain specific provisions in the Code.

1. Where an instrument is payable at, or a fixed period after, a stated date, it must be presented for acceptance on or before such date.

2. When an instrument is payable after sight, the Code requires that it either be presented for acceptance or negotiated within a reasonable time

after date or issue whichever is later. This is similar to the NIL provision that the holder of a bill which is required to be presented for *acceptance* "must either present it for acceptance or negotiate it within a reasonable time. If he fails to do so, the drawer and all indorsers are discharged." (NIL, Section 144).

3. Where an instrument shows the date on which it is payable it is to be presented for *payment* on that date. This follows the NIL rule.

4. "Where an instrument is accelerated presentment for *payment* is due within a reasonable time after the acceleration." (U.C.C. 3-503 (1) (d)). This is a new provision. There was a conflict in the cases under the NIL but the majority followed the rule set forth in this subsection. This presumably means that the specified maturity date is controlling where the holder was not aware that payment had been accelerated. Persons who have not received notice of the occurrence of the event which accelerated payment are not charged with knowledge of the earlier maturity of the paper.

5. "With respect to the liability of any secondary party presentment for *acceptance or payment* of any other demand instrument is due within a reasonable time after such party becomes liable therein." (U.C.C. 3-503 (1) (d)). This also is a new provision under the Code. It encompasses demand instruments such as demand notes and demand drafts which do not fall within any of the prior classifications. The NIL provided that a demand instrument must be presented for payment "within a reasonable time after its issue, except that in the case of a bill of exchange, (draft and check) presentment for payment will be sufficient if made within a reasonable time after the last negotiation thereof." Under this NIL rule the liability of all of the indorsers of a demand note expired at the same time i.e., an unreasonable time after the note was issued whereas the liability of indorsers of all demand drafts and checks continued indefinitely by continuous negotiation. This unusual result is avoided by the above Code provision which is applicable to all demand instruments including demand notes. Under the Code a secondary party is discharged if the presentment is not made within a reasonable time after he issued or transferred the instrument.

The Code requires presentment within a "reasonable time" in those situations where a definite maturity date is not included in the instrument –i.e., sight and demand instruments. The Code like the NIL provides certain rules to be applied in determining what constitutes a "reasonable time." "A reasonable time for presentment is determined by the nature of the instrument, any usage of banking or trade and the facts of the particular case." (U.C.C. 3-503 (2)). Though this is of some help in resolving the question of reasonableness–and possibly as much as can be accomplished by statute—it is felt that more definite rules should be established for checks. Most of the problems arising under the NIL concerned the ordinary (uncertified) check. Accordingly, the Code provides in Section 3-503 (2):

> In the case of an uncertified check which is drawn and payable within the United States and which is not a draft drawn by a bank the following are presumed to be reasonable periods within which to present for payment or to initiate bank collection:
> (a) with respect to the liability of the drawer, thirty days after date or issue whichever is later; and
> (b) with respect to the liability of an indorser, seven days after his indorsement.

Thus the drawer must "back up" a check for a longer period than an indorser, but the drawer having issued the check is not being imposed upon by the requirement that he keep funds on hand for thirty days to cover it. Thirty days is also the period after which a purchaser has notice of the staleness of a check. But an indorser is in a different position and is entitled to more prompt notice so that he may take adequate steps to protect himself against his transferor and prior parties. It must be remembered, also, that the drawer receives only a pro tanto discharge while the discharge of indorsers is complete. In addition the drawer of a check is protected as to funds on deposit by Federal Deposit Insurance.

The old rule as to presentment of checks was evolved by the courts and required that all checks be presented or collection be initiated one day after receipt of the instrument. If this limit were not complied with, the loss occasioned by a bank failure was shifted to the holder. This proved in practice to be too short a time for many persons and the change wrought by the Code is in keeping with the needs of commerce. It is an interesting example of the way in which the law adjusts to the economic and commercial needs of those affected by the law. This is brought out in the Comment to Section 3-503 of the Code which provides: "The court-made time limit of one day after the receipt of the instrument found in decisions under the original Act has proved to be too short a time for some holders, such as the department store or other large business clearing many checks through its books shortly after the first of the month, as well as the farmer or other individual at a distance from a bank."

Rights of party to whom presentment is made. Since the Code discontinues the requirement of Section 74 of the NIL that "the instrument must be exhibited to the person from whom payment is demanded . . ." it was necessary to give some protection to the primary party. Under the Code a mere demand for payment or acceptance is sufficient and if payment or acceptance is refused, nothing more is required. The primary party may justifiably ask for assurance that the presenting party actually has the instrument and is entitled to collect it. In addition he will want a receipt marked on the instrument, or a surrender of the instrument, if he is making final payment. Likewise, he is entitled to have the instrument presented at a place where he has funds to make the payment. The Code in Section 3-505 (1) meets these needs by establishing the rights of the party to whom presentment is made as follows:

> (1) The party to whom presentment is made may without dishonor require
> (a) exhibition of the instrument; and
> (b) reasonable identification of the person making presentment and evidence of his authority to make it if made for another; and
> (c) that the instrument be produced for acceptance or payment at a place specified in it, or if there be none at any place reasonable in the circumstances; and
> (d) a signed receipt on the instrument for any partial or full payment and its surrender upon full payment.

If the primary party does not avail himself of these rights, the presentment is perfectly valid no matter how the presentment is made or where it is made. If he does require that the presentment be made in accordance with the above provisions, a failure to comply invalidates the presentment and the instrument is not dishonored. However, the time for presentment is extended to give the person presenting a reasonable opportunity to comply.

The requirement of identification of the presenting party applies to bearer paper as well as order paper.

4-68. Dishonor. The party who presents an instrument is entitled to have the instrument paid or accepted as the case may be. If the party to whom the instrument is presented refuses to pay or accept (except as stated in the preceding section), the instrument is dishonored. The presenting party then has recourse against indorsers or other secondary parties provided he has given proper notice of such dishonor.

Time allowed for acceptance or payment. Section 3-506 of the Code specifies the amount of time allowed to a party to whom an instrument is presented within which to accept or pay it. Section 136 of the NIL was limited to presentment for acceptance and allowed the drawee twenty-four hours after presentment in which to decide whether or not he would accept the bill. The Code covers both the time allowed to the primary party on presentment for payment, and presentment for acceptance, as follows:

> (1) Acceptance may be deferred without dishonor until the close of the next business day following presentment. The holder may also in a good faith effort to obtain acceptance and without either dishonor of the instrument or

discharge of secondary parties allow postponement of acceptance for an additional business day.

(2) Except as a longer time is allowed in the case of documentary drafts drawn under a letter of credit, and unless an earlier time is agreed to by the party to pay, payment of an instrument may be deferred without dishonor pending reasonable examination to determine whether it is properly payable, but payment must be made in any event before the close of business on the day of presentment.

It will be noted that the Code provides a more realistic and flexible treatment to this problem than did the NIL. The holder may allow one extra day in an effort to obtain acceptance, but he may not otherwise extend the time for payment without discharging secondary parties. The reference to letters of credit means that the time allotted is determined by Article 5—Letters of Credit—Section 5-112 which controls as to documentary drafts drawn under a letter of credit.

As to payor banks, Section 4-301 of Article 4—Bank Deposits and Collections—controls with regard to the bank's right to recover tentative settlements made by it on the day an item is received. (See Chapter 27).

Dishonor; holders right of recourse; term allowing representment. Section 3-507 (1) of the Code provides that an instrument is dishonored:

1. When presentment is duly made and acceptance or payment is refused or cannot be obtained within the prescribed time. In case of bank collections if the instrument is seasonably returned by the midnight deadline it is dishonored. The foregoing applies to both optional and necessary presentment.
2. When presentment is excused and the instrument is not duly accepted or paid.

Upon dishonor, the holder has an immediate right of recourse against secondary parties subject to any necessary notice of dishonor or protest. These provisions as to what constitutes dishonor and recourse against secondary parties are basically the same as the NIL provisions. A new provision in the Code provides: "Return of an instrument for lack of proper indorsement is not a dishonor." This is in keeping with general banking and commercial practices. The return of the instrument under these circumstances does not indicate an intention to dishonor.

The Code also makes provision for drafts which contain a provision for *representment* following an initial dishonor. Thus a draft or an indorsement thereon may allow the presenting party to present the draft to the drawee *again* if it is dishonored upon the first presentment. The requirement is that a stated time must be set forth within which such representment may be made. This provision is limited to (1) dishonor by nonacceptance if it is a time draft; (2) dishonor by nonpayment if it is a sight draft.

The Code in Section 3-507 (4) states that when such a provision is found in a draft or indorsement the holder may waive the initial dishonor, and present it again within the specified time without thereby discharging any secondary party upon whom the provision for representment is binding.

4-69. Notice of dishonor. In the preceding sections two of the conditions precedent to the enforcement of liability against secondary parties have been discussed—presentment and dishonor. This section deals with the third requirement.

When an instrument has been dishonored, the holder must give prompt notice of the dishonor and by so doing has an immediate right of recourse against the secondary parties who have been notified. The Code continues this basic requirement as it existed under the NIL, with some modifications as to the length of time allowed in which to give the notice, and the parties entitled to give notice. Section 3-508 of the Code sets forth the rules with regard to notice of dishonor.

By whom and to whom notice may be given. Generally, notice is given by the holder to secondary parties or by an indorser who has himself received notice. The Code permits any party who may be compelled to pay the instrument to notify any party who may be liable on it. The NIL essentially limited the parties who may give notice of dishonor to holders and secondary parties who have a right of recourse against the party notified. Under the Code an indorser may give notice to another indorser who is *not* liable to the one who gives notice. The Code provides: "Notice of dishonor may be given to any person who may be liable on the instrument by or on behalf of the holder or any party who can be compelled to pay the instrument."

If the party presenting the instrument is an agent of the owner or a bank, such agent or bank upon dishonor can "give notice to his principal or customer or to another agent or bank from which the instrument was received." (U.C.C. 3-508 (i)).

Time within which to give notice. The Code has substantially simplified the rules regarding the time within which to give notice of dishonor. It provides simply that except for banks, notice must be given before midnight of the third business day after dishonor. In the case of a person who has received notice of dishonor and wishes to notify other parties, notice must be given by him before midnight of the third business day after receipt of the notice of dishonor.

In the case of banks any necessary notice must be given before its "midnight deadline"—before midnight of the next banking day following the day on which a bank receives the item or notice of dishonor.

Section 4-212 of Article 4 provides further exceptions with respect to collecting banks. (See Chapter 27.)

In the case of individuals, the one day time limit imposed by the NIL proved too short in many cases. The Code provision is intended to give a person sufficient time to determine what he is supposed to do and then get out a business letter in relation thereto.

How notice is given. The Code follows the NIL with respect to the method of giving notice of dishonor. It provides that notice may be given in any reasonabe manner, which would include oral notice, notice by telephone and, notice by mail. Such notice must identify the dishonored instrument and state that it has been dishonored. The Code approves the general banking practice of returning the instrument bearing a stamp that acceptance or payment has been refused as a sufficient notice of dishonor.

The Code provides that written notice is given when sent although it is not received.[2] This follows Section 105 of the NIL which stated: "Where notice of dishonor is duly addressed and deposited in the post-office, the sender is deemed to have given due notice, notwithstanding any miscarriage in the mails." Note that under 3-504 (2) (a) time of *presentment* is determined by time of *receipt* of mail.

Notice to one partner is deemed to be notice to the firm even though the firm has been dissolved. When any party is dead or incompetent notice may either be sent to his last known address or given to his personal representative.

If a party to whom notice is to be given is involved in insolvency proceedings, e.g., assignment for benefit of creditors, the notice may be given either to such party or the representative of his estate.

Effect of notice. Proper notice preceded by any necessary presentment and dishonor imposes liability upon secondary parties to whom such notice of dishonor is given. Like the NIL, the Code provides that proper notice operates for the benefit of all parties who have rights on the instrument against the party notified. Thus it is only necessary to notify a party once for his liability to be fixed. For example, if *A, B, C,* and *D* are indorsers in that order, and the holder gives notice to *A* and *C*, *C* will not be required to give additional notice to *A* and if *C* is compelled to pay, he would have recourse against *A*.

4-70. Protest. The Code has practically eliminated the requirement of protest. Though the NIL required it in case of bills drawn in one state and payable in another, the Code requires it only in respect to drafts drawn or payable outside the United States. "A protest is a certificate of dishonor made under the hand of a United States consul or vice consul or other person authorized to certify dishonor by the law of the place where dishonor occurs. It may be made upon information satisfactory to such

[2] Durkin v. Siegel, page 625.

person." (U.C.C. 3-509). The Code further provides that the protest must:

1. Identify the instrument.

2. Certify that due presentment has been made (or the reason why it is excused).

3. Certify that the instrument has been dishonored by nonacceptance or nonpayment.

The protest *may* also certify that notice of dishonor has been given to all parties or to specified parties.

Protest is usually forwarded with the notice of dishonor. Any necessary protest must be made within the time required for notice of dishonor. However, the officer is permitted to note the protest on the instrument and extend the protest formally at a later date.

Protest is no longer of great importance in states which have adopted the Code. However, it is to be noted that a holder at his option may make protest of dishonor of any other instrument. Protest might thus be used as evidence of dishonor, but even the evidentiary utility of protest is weakened by other provisions of the Code which simplify proof of dishonor.

4-71. Evidence of dishonor and notice of dishonor. Section 3-510 of the Code is intended to simplify proof of dishonor and remove the need for formal protest. Cases under the NIL held that protest was admissible in evidence and created a presumption of the dishonor which it certified. This is only a presumption and can be rebutted by evidence that there was, in fact, no dishonor or that notice was not given. The Code codifies this rule and extends it. It recognizes two other types of admissible evidence which create a presumption of dishonor and notice of dishonor. One is "any book or record of the drawee, payor bank, or any collecting bank kept in the usual course of business which shows dishonor. . . ." The second is "The purported stamp or writing of the drawee, payor bank or presenting bank on the instrument or accompanying it stating that acceptance or payment has been refused for reasons consistent with dishonor." A stamp "Indorsement missing" or "Forgery" is not evidence of dishonor. However, a stamp "N.S.F." (insufficient funds) or "Payment stopped" is consistent with dishonor and creates a presumption of dishonor. If any of these types of evidence—protest, stamp or writing, or book or record—indicate that notice of dishonor has been duly given, it creates a rebuttable presumption that such notice was in fact given.

4-72. Presentment, protest, notice of dishonor—waiver, excuse, delay. The Code continues many of the NIL rules with respect to waiver of the conditions precedent necessary to charge secondary parties; excuses for failure to perform such conditions; and excuses for delay in complying with the conditions. Section 3-511 of the Code sets forth (1) those situations in which satisfaction of the conditions is "Excused" and (2) those in which performance is "Entirely excused."

Delay in performance of conditions precedent excused. Section 3-511 (1) of the Code provides:

(1) Delay in presentment, protest or notice of dishonor is excused when the party is without notice that it is due or when the delay is caused by circumstances beyond his control and he exercises reasonable diligence after the cause of the delay ceases to operate.

Delay in making presentment, in giving notice of dishonor, or in making protest is excused when the holder has acted with reasonable diligence and the delay is not due to any fault of the holder. He must, however, comply with these conditions or attempt to do so as soon as the cause of the delay ceases to exist. Also, delay in complying with the conditions precedent is excused if the holder did not know that the time for compliance had arrived. Thus, if an instrument has been accelerated but the holder did not know of this fact, his late presentment would be excused. Likewise, where a demand had been made by the party from whom he received the instrument immediately before his purchase, the holder's delay in presenting would be excused. He would not in either case know that the time for presentment had arrived.

Performance of conditions precedent entirely excused. Subsection (2) sets forth those situations in which presentment or notice or protest are entirely excused.

1. If the party to be charged, e.g. the indorser, upon whom liability is sought to be imposed, has waived the condition either before or after it is due. The waiver may be express as where it is set forth in the instrument or in the indorsement or it may be by implication. Where such waiver is stated on the face of the instrument it is binding on all parties; where it is written above the signature of the indorser it binds him only.

Implied waivers are not defined so that the cases under the NIL would appear to provide the test under the Code. Generally, the test evolved by the courts is whether the secondary party's conduct was such as to induce the holder to forego the usual procedures to fix liability on the indorser or was such as to otherwise indicate an intention to waive.

The Code further provides that the words "Protest Waived" contained in an instrument mean that presentment, notice of dishonor, and protest are waived. This is true even though protest is not required. The provision is in keeping with recognized commercial usage.

2. The performance of the conditions precedent is entirely excused if "the party to be charged has himself dishonored the instrument or has countermanded payment or otherwise has no reason to expect or right to require that the instrument be accepted or paid." (U.C.C. 3-511 (2) (b)).

This provision is illustrated by the situation in which a drawer of a check has stopped payment on the check. Such drawer is aware that the bank will dishonor the check in accordance with his order and certainly is not in a position to complain about slow presentment or any lack of notice of dishonor. Similarly, the rule applies to an accommodated party who has broken the accommodation agreement. For example: *M*, as maker, executes a note to *P* as an accommodation to *P* and *P* then indorses to *C* in order to obtain funds which *C* would not have loaned to *P* on the strength of the latter's own note. *C* indorses to *H*. *H* presents the note to *P* and *P* dishonors it. Although *P* is nominally an indorser he is in reality the primary party and *M* is a surety. *P* is not entitled to demand presentment or notice of dishonor.

3. Finally, performance of the conditions precedent is entirely excused if "by reasonable diligence the presentment or protest cannot be made or the notice given." (U.C.C. 3-511 (2) (c)). This means that if the circumstances which gave rise to the "excuse" persist, the performance of the conditions is "entirely excused."

The foregoing rules relate to dispensation with the requirements of any or all of the conditions precedent. The Code sets forth, in addition, two new rules which relate to *presentment* only.

1. If the maker, acceptor, or drawee of any instrument is dead or is involved in insolvency proceedings instituted after the issue of the instrument presentment is not required. (This provision does not apply to documentary drafts.) The rule is predicated upon the theory that there is no reason to require a useless thing to be done. The holder is permitted to have immediate recourse upon the drawer or indorsers leaving to them the right to file a claim against the estate in probate or in the insolvency proceedings.

2. Presentment is dispensed with in the situation where "acceptance or payment is refused but not for want of proper presentment." (U.C.C. 3-511 (3) (b)). Here again if the primary party has definitely refused to pay for reasons which do not relate to presentment it would be a useless ceremony to make a later presentment.

Draft dishonored by nonacceptance. The Code continues the rule of the NIL by providing: "Where a draft has been dishonored by *nonacceptance* a later presentment for payment and any notice of dishonor and protest for nonpayment are excused *unless in the meantime the instrument has been accepted.*" (Emphasis supplied. U.C.C. 3-511 (4)). This means that a holder who has presented a draft for acceptance is not, if acceptance is refused, required to make a subsequent presentment for payment. The refusal to accept is in itself a dishonor of the instrument. Of course a different result obtains if the drawee accepts the draft after his earlier refusal to do so.

PRESENTMENT, NOTICE OF DISHONOR, AND PROTEST CASES

BATCHELDER v. GRANITE TRUST CO.

1959, 339 Mass. 224, 157 N.E. 2d 540

The plaintiff was the holder of a note which it placed in the defendant's hands for collection. Plaintiff alleged that the defendant failed to make proper presentment to the maker (now bankrupt) and that a financially responsible indorser was thereby discharged. The bank had sent notice by mail ten days prior to maturity, notifying the maker that the note would become due and that the bank held it for collection. The lower Court ruled in favor of the defendant.

SPALDING, J. . . . The questions for decision arise out of exceptions taken by the plaintiff to certain rulings on evidence and to the denial of his fourth request for ruling.

The fourth request asked the judge to rule that the defendant did not make proper presentment of the third note. Inasmuch as the facts relating to presentment were agreed this presents a question of law. The request was rightly denied.

Since this case arose prior to the adoption of the Uniform Commercial Code the rights of the parties must be governed by the negotiable instruments law, G.L. c. 107, Sections 94-97. Section 96 of that statute provides that "Where no place of payment is specified, and no address is given" "[p]resentment for payment is made at the proper place" when "the instrument is presented at the usual place of business or residence of the person to make payment." And Section 97 requires that the instrument must be exhibited at the time payment is demanded. The plaintiff argues that this case is governed by these provisions, and since the defendant did not strictly comply with them, it failed to make proper presentment.

Prior to the adoption of the negotiable instruments law in 1898, it was well settled in this Commonwealth in situations similar to this that a written demand mailed by a bank to the maker of a note to pay the note at the bank on the due date was sufficient to make the offices of the bank the place of payment (cases cited). And it has been said that "such previous notice to the promisor, and neglect on his part to pay the note at the bank, are a conventional demand and refusal, amounting to a dishonor of the note" (cases cited). . . .

It could be argued that a strict construction of Section 96 would call for different presentment procedure than that employed by the defendant.

But we are not disposed to construe that section as abrogating a rule which has been so deeply embedded in our law. Our common law rule arose from the custom of merchants, the development of which was described by Chief Justice Shaw in these terms: ". . . the custom of the banks of Massachusetts, of sending a notice to the maker of a note to come to the bank and pay it, and treating his neglect to do so during bank hours, on the last day of grace, as a dishonor, and all parties acquiescing in, and consenting to, such neglect as a dishonor, has become so universal and continued so long, that it may well be doubted, whether it ought not now to be treated as one of those customs of merchants, of which the law will take notice, so that every man, who is sufficiently a man of business to indorse a note, may be presumed to be acquainted with it, and assent to it, at least, until the contrary is expressly shown. . . ." See *Mechanics' Bank of Baltimore v. Merchants' Bank*, 6 Metc. 13, 23–24. If conformity to custom need be shown, it was not lacking. The bank followed its usual practice in dealing with this note. Its practice was similar to that of the other local banks. The payee, maker and indorsers of this note were acquainted with this practice, since it was followed in making demand for payment of the two earlier notes, and they acquiesced in its use with regard to them.

It is worthy of note that the Uniform Commercial Code, which became law in this Commonwealth on October 1, 1958, although not applicable here, would sanction the presentment procedure followed by the defendant (cases cited). . . .

Exceptions overruled. . . .

[This case was decided under the NIL.]

DURKIN v. SIEGEL

1960, (Mass.) 165 N.E. 2d 81

CUTTER, J. . . . Promissory notes signed by one Browne were indorsed by the defendant. They were protested for nonpayment and notice of dishonor was sent on January 17, 1957, "by the plaintiffs' attorney by certified mail, return receipt requested, properly stamped and addressed to the defendant at his home . . . [in] Brookline. . . . The letter, unopened, was returned by the post office . . . with the notation 'refused' . . . across the face of the envelope. The defendant testified that he was in Canada at the time." The defendant in each of these two actions presented a motion for a directed verdict, which was denied. Certain of the defendant's requests for instructions were also denied. There were verdicts for the plaintiffs. The only question argued raised by the bill of exceptions is whether it was good notice of dishonor of promissory notes under G.L.

c. 107, sections 119 and 128 (both now repealed), to send a letter, otherwise in order, by certified mail, return receipt requested, rather than regular mail, where the letter was returned unopened and undelivered, marked "refused," with the blank form of post office receipt unsigned.

The Negotiable Instruments Law (G.L. c. 107) applies to this case, because these events occurred prior to October 1, 1958, the effective date of the Uniform Commercial Code, G.L. c. 106, as appearing in St. 1957, c. 765, Section 1. See also Section 21. The holder of a dishonored negotiable instrument must give prompt notice of dishonor to those secondarily liable. G.L. c. 107, Section 112. Giving this notice is governed by G.L. c. 107, Sections 119, 125-128, 131. The provision here controlling is G.L. c. 107, Section 128 (Section 105 of the original uniform act), which reads, "Where notice of dishonor is duly addressed and deposited in the post office the sender is deemed to have given due notice, notwithstanding any miscarriage in the mails." Registered and certified mail, return receipt requested, are usually regarded by careful people as preferred methods of ensuring delivery. No exception is made in Section 128 with respect to these or other types of first class mail. The section has been carried over into the Uniform Commercial Code in somewhat different language but without attempt to change its meaning. See G.L. c. 106, Section 3-508, which in par. (3) provides that "[n]otice may be given in any reasonable manner" and that "[i]t may be oral or written," and in par. (4) states, "Written notice is given when sent although it is not received." The comments of the draftsmen show that no changes in Sections 96 and 105 of the Negotiable Instruments Law (G.L. c. 107, Sections 119 and 128) were intended (cases cited). . . .

In the light of the foregoing considerations, we hold that Section 128 makes reasonable use of any form of first class mail (not excluding registered or certified mail) for a properly addressed notice of dishonor the equivalent of actual notice. Section 128 is not merely an application of the principle that the "mailing, postage prepaid . . . of a properly addressed letter is prima facie evidence of its receipt by the addressee" (cases cited). . . .

Persons who become secondarily liable upon negotiable instruments are not unfairly burdened if they are held bound by notices sent to them by any generally used form of first class mail at a usual address. They can protect themselves by stipulating (see Section 131) that a particular address be used and by arranging at that address during any absence to have their mail received, opened, forwarded and collected (in the event of the receipt of a notification from the postal authorities that it has not been possible to deliver to them a piece of registered or certified mail). That use of ordinary mail might have ensured delivery (see *Fields v. Western Millers Mut. Fire Ins. Co.*, 182 Misc. 895, 897–898, 50 N.Y.S. 2d 70) is completely irrelevant in view of Section 128. Refusal of a registered or certified letter, of course, would not protect an indorser from the effect of notice (case cited).

Certain decisions in other States, dealing with different types of notices, have held that use of registered mail may have obstructed delivery of a notice, thus making the notice insufficient. We put to one side cases arising under statutes or court rules requiring actual receipt of a notice or document (cases cited). . . .

Although some cases (see *Saffold v. Fellows,* 128 Misc. 422, 424, 220 N.Y.S. 200; but see Id., 219 App. Div. 865, 221 N.Y.S. 197) intimate that the senders of certain types of notice are not entitled to require a receipt, it is not unreasonable for the holder of a dishonored negotiable instrument to ask for a postal receipt when he gives notice of dishonor to one who has become secondarily liable on that instrument.

The defendant's motions for directed verdicts could not have been granted. *His requests for instructions were properly denied.* . . .

[This case was decided under the NIL.]

Review Questions and Problems

1. *M* executed a note containing an acceleration clause to *P*. *P* indorsed to *H*. *H* wrote to *M* requesting that interest in arrears be paid. *M* did not reply and *H* brought suit on the note. *M* claims that he was entitled to notice of election to accelerate prior to suit. Decide.
2. *D* gave two checks to *P*, one dated August 28, 1957 and the other October 7, 1957. The checks were deposited January 8, 1958 but were returned because of insufficient funds. The checks were given in payment for beer and defendant seeks a credit for beer returned in January and March, 1958. *D* contends that he was discharged from obligation on the checks. Decide.
3. *H*, the holder of a note executed by *M* made a demand for payment on the date of maturity. *M* refused to pay. Thereupon *H* notified *X*, the indorser. *X* denies liability because *H* did not have the note in his possession when the demand was made—it having been established that *H* had lost the note. Is *X* relieved of liability?
4. *A* drew a check in favor of *B* as payee. *B* delayed in presenting the check to the drawee bank and upon presentation the check was returned to him marked "insufficient funds." Can *B* hold *A* liable on the check? Would *B* be required to give notice of dishonor to *A*?
5. *M* draws a demand bill of exchange upon *D* in favor of *P*. *P* holds the bill for six months and then negotiates it to *A*. *A* holds the bill for a year and then negotiates it to *H*, who immediately presents it to *D*. *D* is insolvent and unable to pay. Upon giving proper notice of dishonor, may *H* recover from either *P* or *M*?

6. *A* is the holder of a bill of exchange drawn by *X* on *Y*. *A* presents the instrument to *Y* for the acceptance and *Y* refuses to accept. What should *A* do to protect his rights? May he wait until the bill matures before taking any action?
7. C.I.T. undertook to finance an automobile dealer's business and promised the dealer's bank verbally that the dealer was authorized to draw upon C.I.T. for amounts represented by contracts attached to the drafts. Accordingly the bank treated the drafts as cash when received from the dealer directly, credited his account, and permitted immediate withdrawals. The dealer went bankrupt. Must C.I.T. honor the drafts on C.I.T. which the bank had credited to the dealer's account and permitted him to check out?
8. Hardware Co. sold goods to Construction Co. and drew a draft payable to its own order on Construction Co., drawee. The drawee accepted the draft and Hardware Co. then indorsed and discounted it with Olympia Bank. May *H*, who purchased the draft from the bank five years after the due date, collect from the Hardware Co.? Why?
9. *A*, an officer of *X* Bank, executed a note in his own name but for the benefit of the bank. The note was indorsed by other officers of the bank. The note was not presented to *A* for payment. Can the holder require the indorsers to pay?
10. A bill of exchange comes into *X* Bank for collection. The bank calls the drawee on the telephone, demands payment, and is refused. Has there been sufficient presentment to charge secondary parties?
11. *A* executed a note in favor of *B*. The note was indorsed by *B* to the holder. Prior to the maturity of the note *A* became insolvent and for this reason the holder did not present the note to *A* for payment. Is *B* relieved of his liability as an indorser?
12. The holder of a note prior to the maturity date gave notice to the makers of the pending date and reminding them of their obligation to pay on that date. The makers defaulted and two months later notice of dishonor was sent to the indorsers. Can the holder require the indorsers to pay?
13. *M* executed a note in the sum of $3,000 in return for a loan. The note was made to the bank, payable in ten semiannual installments at set dates. *I* indorsed for accommodation under a statement that he waived "presentment, demand, protest and notice of protest of this note at the time of maturity." *M* paid nothing after 1961, and although the last installment was due in 1964, the payee did nothing until 1963, at which time *M* was not available. Is *I* discharged for failure to give notice of dishonor or delay in enforcement?
14. *A* drew a check for $400 in favor of *B* on June 10. *B* indorsed the check on June 16 and mailed it to *C*. *C* indorsed the check to *X* Bank on July 14. *X* Bank mailed the check to the drawee bank on July 14 and it was received on July 18 at which time it was dishonored. Notices of dishonor were sent to all parties. Can *X* Bank recover from the indorsers?
15. *A* executed a note in favor of *B*, the note containing an automatic acceleration clause. Several days after the event which accelerated payment had occurred the holder of the note presented it to *A* for payment. Payment was refused. Can the holder look to *B* as indorser?

16. A time bill of exchange was presented to the drawee for acceptance prior to the maturity date. The drawee refused to accept. Can the holder wait until the maturity date and again present the bill, this time for payment?
17. Contractor mailed a check to Subcontractor in payment for work performed. Subcontractor contended that check was not in proper amount and so notified Contractor. After repeated efforts to contact Contractor, Subcontractor mailed the check back, but the letter was returned unopened. Contractor claims that failure to promptly present the check for payment discharged his liability. Is this correct?

26

Discharge

4-73. Introduction. Section 3-601 of the Code provides that the discharge of *any party* to a negotiable instrument may be accomplished in a variety of ways. The NIL spoke in terms of acts which discharged an instrument on one hand and those which discharged secondary parties from liability on the other. The Code, however, classifies the grounds for discharge in terms of whether (1) an individual party to an instrument receives a discharge or whether (2) all of the parties to the instrument are discharged. The Code proceeds on the theory that an instrument is simply a piece of paper—that strictly speaking, it cannot itself be discharged. Rather the parties are discharged from their liability on the instrument. The basic discharge provisions, however, were much the same under the NIL as under the Code.

Discharge of "any party": The following are methods whereby "any party" may be discharged from liability on an instrument.

1. By payment or satisfaction.
2. By tender of payment.
3. By cancellation or renunciation.
4. By impairment of right of recourse or collateral.
5. By reacquisition of the instrument by a prior party. (Section 4-35)[1]
6. By fraudulent and material alteration. (Section 4-51)
7. By certification of a check. (Section 4-55)
8. By acceptance varying a draft. (Section 4-56)
9. By unexcused delay in presentment or notice of dishonor or protest. (Section 4-66)

In addition to the foregoing "any party is also discharged from his liability on an instrument to another party by any other act or agreement with such party which would discharge his simple contract for the payment of money." (U.C.C. 3-601 (2)). This is in recognition of the fact that insofar as the discharge of any one party is concerned a negotiable instrument differs from other contracts only in the special rules arising out of its character (as enumerated above) and in the effect of a discharge on a subsequent holder in due course. As provided in Section 3-602 of the Code: "No discharge of any party provided by this article is effective against a subsequent holder in due course unless he has notice thereof

[1] Dieringer v. Loutsion, page 635.

when he takes the instrument." Thus the defense of discharge is only a personal defense which is cut off when a subsequent holder in due course takes without notice. For example, if an instrument is paid without surrender and is then negotiated to a holder in due course, such a subsequent purchaser cuts off the defense of payment.[2]

Discharge of all parties. As to those situations in which the liability of *all parties* to an instrument is discharged the Code provides:

(3) The liability of all parties is discharged when any party who has himself no right of action or recourse on the instrument
  (a) reacquires the instrument in his own right; or
  (b) is discharged under any provision of this Article, except as otherwise provided with respect to discharge for impairment of recourse or of collateral (Section 3-606).

When no party is left with rights against any other party on the paper, it follows as a basic principle that all parties to an instrument are discharged. A person who reacquires in his own right is discharged from his own liability and any intervening party to whom he was liable is also discharged. If he has no right of action against any prior party and intervening parties are discharged, it is obvious that all parties are discharged. However, it is to be noted that the instrument is not "dead"—if the instrument were thereafter negotiated to a holder in due course the liability of intervening indorsers would be revived for such holder would not be aware of the prior discharge.

4-74. Payment or satisfaction. A perplexing problem under the NIL was the one confronting a payor to whom an instrument was presented for payment where the payor was aware that a third party had an adverse claim to the instrument. Can he safely pay the holder or must he refrain from paying until the adverse claim is settled? The Code resolves this problem by providing that the obligor can safely pay the holder even though he is aware of an adverse claim. This is subject, however, to the privilege of the adverse claimant to (1) bring court action to enjoin the payment or (2) to supply the obligor with indemnity against double liability. If either of these steps is taken the obligor is protected in his refusal to pay the holder. If the adverse claimant does not take either course of action, the obligor is protected in paying the holder.

There are two exceptions to the foregoing rule:

1. A party who in bad faith pays a holder who acquired the instrument by theft is not protected. Likewise the obligor is not protected if he in bad faith pays a holder (unless he has the rights of a holder in due course) who holds *through* a thief.

2. A party, with the exception of certain banks, will not be discharged

[2] Newark Trust Co. v. Birchler, page 636.

from liability if he pays the holder of a restrictively indorsed instrument in a manner not consistent with the terms of the restrictive indorsement.

The Code contains a new provision with respect to payment by a "stranger to an instrument." Payment may be made with the consent of the holder by any person, including one who is not a party to the paper. Thus a third party may intervene to protect the drawer's credit and at the same time preserve his own rights. When the instrument is surrendered to the third party, he obtains the rights of a transferee.

4-75. Tender of payment. A tender is an offer to pay or perform a contractual obligation. A tender does not discharge the debt or obligation, but it does stop the running of interest. If the creditor thereafter brings legal action to recover the amount of the debt, the costs of suit and attorney's fees will be imposed on him.

This generally accepted rule of tender is adopted by the Code to give a limited discharge to the obligor on an instrument. If he tenders to the holder full payment when or after it is due, "he is discharged to the extent of all subsequent liability for interest, costs and attorney's fees." (U.C.C. 3-604 (1)).

The Code further provides that where the maker or acceptor is ready and able to pay at every place of payment specified in the instrument (when the instrument is due), an equivalent of tender has been made. This does not apply to demand instruments. Thus makers and acceptors of notes and drafts payable at a bank have made a proper tender if they maintain an adequate balance in the bank as of the due date of the instruments. As previously noted, failure to make a proper presentment in the case of "domiciled paper" results in a pro tanto discharge of drawers and makers in the event of the insolvency of the bank.

If the holder refuses to accept a proper tender, indorsers and other parties who have a right of recourse against the party making the tender are discharged.

4-76. Cancellation and renunciation. Both the NIL and the Code provide for discharge by cancellation and renunciation. The NIL provide that such discharges did not apply to holders in due course. The Code as previously noted, states that all discharges, including the above, are only personal defenses and cannot, therefore, be asserted against a holder in due course.

The Code section, which is self-explanatory, provides:

(1) The holder of an instrument may even without consideration discharge any party

(a) in any manner apparent on the face of the instrument or the indorsement, as by intentionally cancelling the instrument or the party's signature by destruction or mutilation, or by striking out the party's signature; or

(b) by renouncing his rights by a writing signed and delivered or by surrender of the instrument to the party to be discharged.

(2) Neither cancellation nor renunciation without surrender of the instrument affects the title thereto.

4-77. Impairment of right of recourse or of collateral. It will be recalled that certain principles of the law of suretyship are significant in the law of negotiable instruments with reference to discharges. These principles are: a surety is discharged if the creditor releases the principal debtor; a surrender by the creditor of security furnished by the principal debtor discharges the surety; a binding agreement by the creditor to extend the time of payment by the principal debtor discharges the surety. These suretyship concepts are based upon the rationale that a surety is assuming liability to the creditor for the failure of the principal debtor to perform his obligation to the creditor. If the creditor increases the surety's risk by extending the time for the principal debtor's performance, or deprives the surety of the benefit of collateral, the surety is discharged. If the creditor releases the principal debtor he must also intend to release the surety—otherwise the creditor could sue the surety who in turn could demand reimbursement from the principal debtor.

Placed in the context of the law of negotiable instruments a holder is a creditor; the primary party—maker or acceptor—is the principal debtor; and the secondary party—indorser or drawer—is the surety. In the case of an accommodation party who is a maker, the rules for discharge would be applicable since such a party is a surety. The "suretyship defenses" are not limited to parties who are secondarily liable.

Another basic principle of suretyship law is that a creditor may release the principal debtor or grant him a binding extension of time without thereby discharging the surety if the surety consents to the release or extension.[3] Also the creditor who releases or grants a time extension to the principal debtor can preserve his rights against the surety by "reserving his rights" against the surety. If rights are reserved, the surety is privileged to satisfy the obligation to the creditor and then proceed against the principal debtor for reimbursement. The application of this concept to commercial paper is set forth in Section 3-606 (2) of the Code which provides:

(2) By express reservation of rights against a party with a right of recourse the holder preserves

(a) all his rights against such party as of the time when the instrument was originally due; and

(b) the right of the party to pay the instrument as of that time; and

(c) all rights of such party to recourse against others.

[3] Morrissey v. Ottman, page 638.

It would appear that timely notice of reservation of rights should be given to the parties against whom such rights are reserved.

4-78. Discharge of underlying obligation. In most situations involving the issuance or transfer of an instrument, there is an obligation involved for which the instrument was issued or transferred. It is the usual understanding of the parties that the obligation itself is not discharged until the instrument is paid and that action on the debt or obligation is simply held in abeyance pending the exhaustion of efforts to collect on the instrument.[4] By the same token the parties *could* agree otherwise—that is, that the instrument is received as final payment. However, it is not often that the parties spell out their intention in this regard and over the years the courts have enunciated certain presumptions as to what the parties expected. Thus an instrument is said to be only conditional payment—the person who receives it gives up the right to sue on the obligation until the paper is due, but if it is not paid upon proper and timely presentment, the right to sue on the obligation is reinstated.[5] (See Section 2-00, P. in the Book on Contracts).

While it is generally true that the underlying debt is not discharged by the execution of a negotiable instrument, both the NIL and the Code recognize one basic exception. If the instrument is one executed by a third party—someone other than the person who transfers it in payment of the obligation—it is presumed that such instrument was given and received in payment of the underlying debt.

The Code in Section 3-802 (1) retains this presumption but limits it substantially:

> Unless otherwise agreed where an instrument is taken for an underlying obligation
>
> (a) the obligation is pro tanto discharged if a bank is drawer, maker or acceptor of the instrument and there is no recourse on the instrument against the underlying obligor. . . .

Section 3-802 (1) (b) of the Code provides that where an instrument is taken for an underlying obligation the obligation is *suspended* until the instrument is due; and if it is dishonored, action can be brought either on the instrument or the obligation.[6]

Under the NIL there was some question as to the position of the parties where an instrument had been indorsed to another and the holder was late in presenting the instrument or in giving notice of dishonor. Here the holder initially had rights against the indorser on the indorsement con-

[4] Alden Estate, page 639.
[5] Doodan v. Szawlinsky, page 641.
[6] Visnov et ux v. Levy, page 642.

tract and the underlying debt. If because of slow presentment the indorser is discharged from the former is he also discharged from the latter? The Code provides that "discharge of the underlying obligor on the instrument also discharges him on the obligation." (U.C.C. 3-802 (1) (b)). As noted previously, failure to satisfy the conditions precedent discharges indorsers irrespective of any injury to them. On the other hand, *drawers* are discharged on the instrument only to the extent of injury caused by the delay —presumably this limitation would also extend to their liability on the underlying obligation.

4-79. Lost, destroyed or stolen instruments. The Code contains a provision not found in the NIL which provides a method of recovering on lost, destroyed, or stolen instruments. The Code in Section 3-804 provides:

> The owner of an instrument which is lost, whether by destruction, theft or otherwise, may maintain an action in his own name and recover from any party liable thereon upon due proof of his ownership, the facts which prevent his production of the instrument and its terms. The court may require security indemnifying the defendant against loss by reason of further claims on the instrument.

Since it is possible that the instrument might at a later date actually turn up in the hands of a holder in due course, the court may require security to indemnify the obligor against double liability.

DISCHARGE CASES

DIERINGER v. LOUTSION
1960 (Pa.) 39 Wash. 31.

WEINER, J. . . . The complaint avers that the defendant, George T. Loutsion, on or about June 25, 1952, delivered a postdated check to the order of Mike Pankas in the amount of $850.00, drawn on the First National Bank of Canonsburg, Pennsylvania; that the said Mike Pankas endorsed the check in blank and delivered the same to the plaintiffs who presented the check for payment and it was dishonored. The complaint also avers that one of the plaintiffs, by mistake and under a misapprehension that the check had been paid, delivered the said check to the defendant, George T. Loutsion; the mistaken impression being the result of false representations of the defendant.

In support of the defendant's contention that the check sued upon has been discharged by its delivery to him, his counsel relies upon Section 119 (5) of the Negotiable Instruments Law, 56 P.S. 271, which provides "that an instrument is discharged when the principal debtor becomes the holder of the instrument, at or after maturity, in his own right."

However, the point overlooked by the defendant's counsel is that the defendant did not become the holder of the instrument by virtue of any negotiation of the same, and therefore he does not come within the provision of the section mentioned. If the averments of the complaint are sustained, the defendant did not become the holder of the instrument in his own right.

Under the allegations of the plaintiffs, they are still the legal holders of the instrument in question, both in law and in equity, and they therefore have the capacity to maintain this action. This check was not delivered to the defendant in the sense contemplated by the Negotiable Instruments Law or in the sense contemplated by the present Uniform Commerical Code, Sections 3-601 (12A P. S. 601) and 3-208 (12A P. S. 208).

Judgment for plaintiff.

NEWARK TRUST CO. v. BIRCHLER
1954, (Pa.) 54 Lanc. L. Rev. 265

SCHAEFFER, P. J. This is a rule to show cause why a confessed judgment should not be opened and defendants let into a defense. Judgment was entered by the Newark Trust Company, as holder of the note, for $850.00 and a collection fee of 15%, or a total of $977.50. In the affidavit of default and amount due filed by Newark Trust Company it is averred that the "defendants have paid the sum of $300.00 on account of said note, but are in default for the monthly payments from May 31, 1953, to the present time."

It is not denied that the defendants made the following payments: June 6, 1952–$100.00; June 27, 1952–$300.00; July 18, 1952–$100.00 and October 6, 1952–$300.00. The plaintiff has given credit for the last payment on October 6, 1952, of $300.00, but it appears that the three prior payments totaling $500.00 were made to the payee of the note. General Sales and Service, Inc., or its agents prior to the negotiation of the note to the plaintiff. These payments on account, or the greater portion thereof, should have been credited on account of the note and such payments should have been made known to the present holder thereof. It is neither pleaded nor proven that plaintiff had either express or implied knowledge or notice of such prior payments. In *Newark Trust Company v. Herr*, 54 Lanc. 31, it was decided that the negotiation of an installment judgment note, similar to the one involved in this case, before maturity to one who takes it in good faith, for value, and without notice of any infirmities in the note, made such party a holder in due course under the Uniform Negotiable Instruments Act of both Pennsylvania and Delaware.

It is not definitely shown when the note in controversy was transferred by the payee, General Sales and Service, Inc., to Newark Trust Company. However, according to the evidence, it must have been about September 13, 1952. The defendants contend that the balance due on the note is only $375.00, which they have tendered in the past to the plaintiff and are still willing to pay to the plaintiff, but it has been refused by plaintiff. In *International Finance Company v. Magilansky et ux.*, 105 Pa. Superior Ct. 309, the note in question was a negotiable instrument payable in installments, containing a clause that a failure to pay any installment when due will make the whole note due. It was decided that plaintiff was entitled to the presumption that it was the holder in due course until evidence was produced showing its title to be defective. There is no such evidence in the instant case and it is not so pleaded. The only defense is payments not credited. In *Harbaugh's Estate*, 320 Pa. 209, 211, it is said: "The law is uniform that payment to the payee of a negotiable instrument when title and possession of the instrument has passed to another before maturity will not protect the maker."

The Negotiable Instruments Act of May 16, 1901, P. L. 194, Art. VI, Section 88, provides that "payment is made in due course when it is made at or after the maturity of the instrument, to the holder thereof, in good faith, and without notice that his title is defective."

This case presents an unfortunate situation. The defendants have admittedly paid $800.00 on a contract for painting the exterior of their residence. The contract price was $1,175.00. Defendants are willing to pay the alleged balance of $375.00, but plaintiff is demanding the principal sum of $850.00. Apparently defendants made the payments in good faith first to the payee of the note, or its agents, and later to the plaintiff, who had no knowledge of the prior payments. The court is bound to follow the law on negotiable instruments, but feels that an injustice may have been done to the defendants by those who received the prior payments and failed to make it known to the present holder of the judgment note. The legal remedy, if any, is against them. However, more caution should be exercised and further inquiry made in many of these financing cases. In *Stroudsburg Security Trust Company Case*, 145 Pa. Superior Ct. 44, it was decided that under the Negotiable Instruments Act of May 16, 1901, P. L. 194, one who receives negotiable paper for value is a holder in due course if, but only if, the circumstances under which he receives the paper do not put him upon notice that the person from whom he received the obligation was not the owner, or upon inquiry which would have led to knowledge of that fact.

. . . *The rule to open the judgment and let the defendants into a defense is discharged.*

[This case was decided under the NIL.]

MORRISSEY v. OTTMAN

1961, 23 Conn. Sup. 109, 177 A. 2d 223

ALEXANDER, J. This appeal is from a judgment in favor of the plaintiffs allowing recovery for the balance due on a promissory note. The defendant has been held liable in his capacity as guarantor.

The defendant was president of General Sand & Stone Corporation, the maker of the note. The plaintiffs are insurance agents who had paid sums of money for insurance premiums on behalf of the corporation. The indebtedness thus created was represented by the note, which called for periodic payments to plaintiffs. The corporation was in poor financial condition. At the time in question, it was under the personal care of the defendant, who was its president and who negotiated and signed the note, not only as president but also individually as guarantor.

The defendant has pleaded as a special defense that, as guarantor, he was released of personal liability because the maker was granted extensions of time to make payment of some of the periodic installments. The finding states that the extensions of time were mutually agreed upon by the plaintiffs and the corporation; that they were acquiesced in by the defendant in his capacity as an officer of the company; and that there was no direct evidence that the defendant agreed to the extensions in his personal capacity as guarantor, although he agreed to the extensions. The defendant has pleaded specially that the extensions of time were granted by the plaintiffs to the maker of the note without his assent in his capacity as a guarantor.

The statute, General Statutes, Section 39-121, provided in part: "A person secondarily liable on the instrument is discharged: . . . (6) by any agreement binding upon the holder to extend the time of payment or to postpone the holder's right to enforce the instrument, unless made with the assent of the party secondarily liable. . . ." There may be some question as to whether the defendant, in negotiating the extensions of time, tacitly gave his assent to them in his capacity as a guarantor. However, in our view of the case, the resolution of that issue is not necessary. This is so because, in order to prevail on his special defense, the defendant must establish that there was an agreement "binding upon the holder to extend the time." This phrase has been construed to mean that there must be legal consideration for the promise to extend the time. (cases cited) To the same effect, see *Lockwood v. Crawford,* 18 Conn. 360 [361] 376, where it was stated that "[a] mere indulgence given to the maker of a note, by the holder, will not discharge indorsers." The testimony in this case is barren of any evidence showing that there was consideration for the extension of time. Hence, the defendant's special defense must fail.

Error is also assigned in the court's finding that the defendant was an "absolute guarantor." Exhibit A reveals the following as the language of the guarantee: "For value received I hereby guarantee the payment of principal interest and chargeable costs of the attached note, waiving demand, notice of payment and payment."

"An absolute guaranty is 'an unconditional undertaking on the part of the guarantor that the maker will pay the note.'" *Beardsley v. Hawes*, 71 Conn. 39, 42, 40 A. 1043, 1044. "A guaranty of the payment of an obligation without words of limitation on condition is construed as an absolute or unconditional guaranty" (cases cited). "A conditional guaranty contemplates, as a condition of liability on the part of the guarantor, the happening of some contingent event other than the default of the principal debtor" (case cited). "The word 'protested' implies demand, nonpayment and consequent dishonor of the note." *Annville National Bank v. Kettering*, 106 Pa. 531. The unqualified language of the guarantee signed by the defendant indicates the correctness of the conclusion that the nature of his guarantee was absolute rather than conditional. Accordingly, the action against the guarantor will lie. Where a guarantee is absolute, no demand upon the maker of the note is necessary before bringing suit upon it. *Tyler v. Waddingham*, 58 Conn. 375, 20 A. 335, 8 L.R.A. 657.

There is no error. . . .

[This case was decided under the NIL.]

ALDEN ESTATE

1958, (Pa.) 13 D. & C. 2d 158

The petitioner, administratrix of the estate, sought to establish a credit of $110.53, representing a discount of 5 per cent on payment of a $2100 inheritance tax. The discount is allowed by statute if payment is made within three months of death. Decedent died on March 29, 1956 and petitioner delivered her check on June 29, 1956. The figures on the check appear as $2,1 00 (there being a slight extra space between the figure 1 and the first 0). The check was treated as being for $21. Subsequently, the petitioner delivered a check for the balance of $2079.

Roberts, P. J. . . . We must determine whether the taxpayer in the present instance earned the discount. The statute provides that discount shall be allowed if the tax is "paid" within the specified period. The required payment is not made merely by delivery of a check by taxpaper to the register of wills and its acceptance or receipt by the register. The check does not, at the moment of delivery, complete payment of the tax obligation. It is merely a step towards payment. Delivery of the check and its acceptance by the register is only conditional payment, subject to actual payment of the check by payor bank upon presentation. Conditional payment by check becomes absolute only upon actual payment by drawee bank or divested by nonpayment: *Wedmore v. McInnes,* 69 Pa. Superior Ct. 220. Payment is not accomplished until the check is honored and paid by drawee bank, and constitutes payment only to the extent that it is so paid upon presentation.

"It is elementary law that where a . . . check is received by a creditor from his debtor for an existing debt, the presumption is, in the absence of an agreement to the contrary, that it is received as conditional and not absolute payment, and the burden of proving the existence of such an agreement is upon the debtor": *Diskin v. Philadelphia Police Pension Fund Association,* 367 Pa. 273, 276.

On presentation of the check payor bank paid $21. This then is the amount of the conditional payment (made June 29, 1956, within the statutory period) that became absolute payment. It is therefore on this amount alone that taxpayer has established eligibility for discount. It is, of course, regrettable that only $21 was paid by drawee bank when the check was presented, rather than $2,100 which was directed by the words of the check, particularly since words control figures, and sufficient funds were on deposit to pay that amount. Neither this circumstance nor error, if any, on the part of the Commonwealth's agent, authorizes this court to allow the discount. . . .

It seems clear that a taxpayer to be entitled to the statutory discount must affirmatively bring himself within its provisions by full compliance with its terms. If the taxpayer, for any reason, fails to meet the requirements he is not entitled to the discount; we are without authority to relax any requirement or to extend the discount period. Nor may we accord to the delivery of the check on June 29, 1956, a conditional payment status, broad enough to include the final payment of $2,079 by drawee bank on August 15, 1956, so that it relates back to date of delivery. The wholly unreasonable lapse of approximately 45 days between delivery of check to the register, its presentation for payment in due course and the second payment by drawee bank precludes such a judicial determination. To hold otherwise would be completely contrary to long and well-established commercial practice and in direct conflict with the rules of law governing business transactions. See *Wendkos v. Scranton Life Insurance Co.,* 340 Pa. 550; also Uniform Commercial Code of April 6, 1953, P. L. 3, Commercial Paper, 12 A PS Section 3-102.

We are not required to nor do we fix responsibility for the result which none of the parties desired or intended. Perhaps a taxpaper who assumes to deliver a check so very near the end of the discount period, assumes whatever risks may be involved in accomplishing absolute payment of the check within the required period.

DOODAN v. SZAWLINSKY

1962, 197 Pa. Super. 623, 179 A. 2d 661

The plaintiff, a lawyer from Philadelphia, represented the defendant, Szawlinsky, in a trespass action which resulted in a verdict for $10,000. The Empire Mutual Insurance Co. had insured the defendant in the trespass action against liability in the sum of $5,000. The insurance company issued its check in the amount of $5,348.35, the face amount of the policy plus interest and costs. The check was made payable to Doodan and Szawlinsky jointly. The defendant Szawlinsky felt that the insurance company should pay more and refused to indorse the check. (Other facts appear in the opinion.)

FLOOD, J. . . . The defendant, being dissatisfied because he was not getting the full amount of his verdict in the trespass action, refused to indorse the check, despite the efforts of his attorney and of the trial judge to persuade him that he could not get anything more from the insurance company. After all efforts to persuade the defendant to indorse the check had failed, the plaintiff brought suit against him and obtained judgment by default in the amount of $3,329.98, later reduced, by an assessment of damages filed, to $3,053.40.

The plaintiff issued an attachment against the insurance company as garnishee and filed and served interrogatories. To the interrogatory asking whether it owed the defendant any money or was liable to him on account of the judgment obtained in the trespass action, the garnishee answered: "No, subject to the following qualifications. Judgment was paid by check from Garnishee No. 45831, issued April 28, 1961, in the sum of $5,348.35 payable to Michael Szawlinsky and plaintiff. Check has not yet been cashed."

The question before us is whether the garnishee is relieved from responding to the plaintff in these attachment proceedings because it has issued a check under its policy, which has never been cashed.

It is clear that the garnishee has funds in its hands due to the defendant in this action which the plaintiff is entitled to reach by attachment. The issuance of the check itself does not remove those funds from the hands of the garnishee until the check is cashed. A check is not legal tender and is not payment unless it is accepted by the creditor. 70 C.J.S. Payment Section 24, pp. 233 et seq. Even then unless the creditor agrees to accept it as absolute payment, it is only conditional payment, and becomes absolute payment only when it is paid by the drawee bank in due course. Ibid. Here there was no acceptance by the defendant and, although a year has gone by since the check was issued, it has not been paid or presented for payment. At this late date the drawee bank is not obligated to pay the check and normally will not do so without consulting the depositor: Uniform Commercial Code, Section 4-404 and Comment, 12A P.S. Section 4-404. See *Lancaster Bank v. Woodward,* 18 Pa. 357 (1852).

At the argument before us the plaintiff's counsel stated that the plaintiff, who has possession of the check, tendered its return, but the garnishee refused to accept it. But irrespective of who has possession of the check, the garnishee may, and undoubtedly will, order the drawee bank to stop payment on the check upon the entry of judgment against it. Uniform Commercial Code, Section 4-403, 12A P.S. Section 4-403. Since there has been no legal payment, the garnishee is still indebted to the defendant, and the plaintiff is entitled to judgment.

The order is reversed and the record is remanded with direction to grant the plaintiff's motion for judgment on the pleadings. . . .

VISNOV ET UX v. LEVY
1955, (Pa.) 2 D. & C. 2d 686

Flood, J. Judgment was entered in ejectment for the leased premises in the above case for failure to pay rent when due. The lease, dated June 1, 1953, provided that the rent should be payable in lawful money of the United States on the first of each month and that time was of the essence. The rent due April 1, 1954, was paid by check dated that day and received by plaintiff on April 2nd. The check was deposited by plaintiffs in their own bank on April 6th. On April 13th they received from their bank a notice, dated April 12, 1954, that the check had been returned marked "N.S.F." On April 18th defendant received a letter from plaintiff, dated April 16th, giving defendant 90 days' notice to quit under the lease for failure to pay rent as required under the lease.

The rent had been paid by check consistently from the beginning of the lease and therefore any requirement to pay in cash had long since been waived by the course of performance between the parties.

All of the checks commencing with that for June 1, 1953, were received by plaintiffs later than the first day of the month (ranging from the second to the sixth) until the rent due January 1, 1954. The March check was received on March 2, 1954. Under these circumstances it appears clear that the provision that time was of the essence also is inoperative because of the course of performance acquiesced in by plaintiffs.

This reduces the question before us to whether the facts set forth constitute so substantial a breach as to warrant a forfeiture of the lease, carrying with it defendant's option to purchase. We do not believe that it was. A check was received by plaintiffs on the second day of the month and was not deposited in their own bank until the sixth. We have no information in the stipulation as to the status of defendant's account with the drawee bank between April 2nd and April 6th. There is a serious question as to whether the drawer of the check would not have been discharged by the delay in presentation. It was plaintiff's duty as the law stood in April 1954, to present the check promptly to the drawee, although Section 3-503 (2*a*) of the Uniform Commercial Code of April 6, 1953, P. L. 3, which became effective thereafter, provided that presentation within 30 days is presumed to be within a reasonable time. It is clear that defendants' obligation to plaintiffs would have been completely discharged if anything had happened during that period which made it impossible for drawee to pay the check through no fault of defendant. While we do not hold that it is necessarily negligent on the part of the holders not to present the check within the period when it would have operated as a discharge in the case of failure of the drawee, yet it has some bearing upon plaintiff's right to declare a forfeiture when the check was dishonored.

We do not know when the check was dishonored, except that it was sometime between April 6th when the check was deposited at plaintiff's bank and April 12th when plaintiffs' bank wrote to the plaintiffs that the drawee had returned the check marked "N.S.F." It is to be noted that it is now the law under the code, section 3-802, that where a check is taken for an underlying obligation, here the obligation to pay the rent in cash, the obligation is suspended pro tanto until the presentation of the check. This presumably was law in Pennsylvania before the code. See Pennsylvania Bar Association notes, Section 3-802 of the code, 12-APS Section 3-802. This would indicate that the crucial date is not earlier than April 12th since on the question of forfeiture we must take all intendments in favor of defendant. It may have been on any date up to April 11th for all we know. When we add to this the fact that a new and good check was forthcoming promptly upon notice, we do not believe that forfeiture should be decreed. This is a situation in which plaintiff's position is not even as strong as it was in *Feinstein v. Siskin et al.*, 69 D. & C. 90 (1949), where the judgment of forfeiture was opened. We think the matter should be fully explored and the facts determined after a full hearing before a default judgment of forfeiture should be allowed to stand.

And now, January 27, 1955, the rule to open judgment is made absolute.

[This case was decided under the NIL.]

Review Questions and Problems

1. *M*, the maker of a note, made several payments on the note to *P*, the payee. *P* thereafter indorsed the note to *H* who was not aware that

the payments had been made. *H* now seeks to recover the entire amount of the note from *M*. Should he succeed?

2. *X* Corporation borrowed money from *Y* and the president of *X* Corporation indorsed the note. When the note fell due, *Y* extended the time of payment. Thereafter *X* Corporation became bankrupt and *Y* sought to recover from the president. Should he succeed?
3. *D* gave his check in payment for a new car, took possession, and died before the check was presented to the drawee bank in the dealer's home town, four days later. The check was not paid because the drawer was deceased. May the automobile be kept by *D*'s next of kin?
4. *A* is the accommodation maker of a note drawn in favor of *B*, the accommodated party. *B* indorsed the note to *C*. Does payment by *B* discharge the note?
5. *A* is the maker of a note, and *B* is the payee. *B* indorses to *C*, and *C* indorses to *D*. *D* orally renounces his rights against *A*. Is the note discharged? Would the result be different if the renunciation were in writing? If *D* negotiates the note to *H*, a holder in due course, after renouncing his rights against *A*, what are the rights of *H*?
6. *A* Bank sued *C*, accommodation indorser, on a renewal note. *C* contended that there was no consideration for the note because the bank had not cancelled the old notes. Is *C*'s contention correct?
7. *A* is the maker of a note drawn in favor of *B*. *B* indorses to *C*, and *C* indorses to *H*. *H* presents the note to *A* and receives a worthless check in payment. Is the note discharged?
8. *A* received from *M* a note for $200. In an attempt to recover an additional amount, *A* added a clause calling for the payment of 7 per cent interest. How much, if any, may he recover on the note? Assuming that the note was given for a debt, may he recover the amount of the original debt?
9. *H* is the holder of a negotiable bill of exchange upon which there are six indorsers. *H* desires to release the fourth on the list. If he does, what will be the effect?
10. *H* holds a negotiable note upon which there are three indorsers. The maker is unable to pay it at maturity and desires additional time. *H* consents to give him an additional thirty days in which to make payment. At the end of thirty days the note is not paid. Assuming that *H* made proper presentment and gave notice of dishonor at the maturity date, may he recover from the indorsers?
11. *A* is a co-maker with *M* of a negotiable note, although he is merely acting as surety. This fact is known to the holder. Do the rules of suretyship apply?
12. At the office of a real estate broker *X*, *M* gave his negotiable note and mortgage to *P* in return for the conveyance of land. *M* paid annual interest on the note to the broker *X* under *P*'s instructions. A year later *P* assigned the note to *H* but did not deliver the same. Thereafter *M* paid all the principal and interest in a lump sum to *X*, *X* retaining possession of the note. *X* absconded with the payments. Whose loss?
13. *M*, in securing a loan for $640.20 on stored corn, executed his note on March 16, 1950, payable to the First National Bank. On July 27, 1950, the bank indorsed the note to the Commodity Credit Corpo-

ration. When sued on the note, *M* set up the defense of payment. At the trial *M* testified that at maturity he had mailed his check in the sum of $664.20 payable to the Commodity Credit Corporation to the County Office that serviced such loans. *M*'s check was lost in the County office and was never cleared by the drawee bank. Does *M* have a defense?

14. *P*, the payee of a check, presented it for payment six months after issue. Is the drawer discharged from liability?

27

Bank Deposits and Collections

4-80. Introduction. Article 4 of the Uniform Commercial Code is entitled "Bank Deposits and Collections." It is not possible in this text to consider in detail the numerous provisions of this Article. Attention is directed rather to those provisions which most closely relate to the law of commercial paper, particularly checks.

Article 4 provides uniform rules to govern the collection of checks and other instruments for the payment of money. It also sets forth rules which govern the relationship of banks with depositors in the collection and payment of "items." (An item is any instrument for the payment of money whether it is negotiable or not). This Article covers items which are also within Article 3—Commercial Paper, and Article 8—Investment Securities. In the event of a conflict the provisions of Article 4 govern those of Article 3, but the provisions of Article 8 govern those of Article 4.

The significance of Article 4 is set forth in the comment to Section 4-101:

> The tremendous number of checks handled by banks and the country-wide nature of the bank collection process require uniformity in the law of bank collections. Individual Federal Reserve banks process as many as 1,000,000 items a day; large metropolitan banks average 300,000 a day; banks with less than $5,000,000 on deposit handle from 1,000 to 2,000 daily. There is needed a uniform statement of the principal rules of the bank collection process with ample provision for flexibility to meet the needs of the large volume handled and the changing needs and conditions that are bound to come with the years.
>
> The American Bankers Association Bank Collection Code, enacted in eighteen states, has stated many of the bank collection rules that have developed, and more recently Deferred Posting statutes have developed and varied further rules. With items flowing in great volume not only in and around metropolitan and smaller centers but also continuously across state lines and back and forth across the entire country, a proper situation exists for uniform rules that will state in modern concepts at least some of the rights of the parties and in addition aid this flow and not interfere with its progress.
>
> This Article adopts many of the rules of the American Bankers Association Code that are still in current operation, the principles and rules of the Deferred Posting and other statutes, codifies some rules established by court decisions and in addition states certain patterns and procedures that exist even though not heretofore covered by statute.

Article 4 does not substantially change the law in this area. In the main it codifies existing case law, statutes, and banking and commercial practices. Article 4 is flexible in that, within certain limits, the provisions of the Article can be varied by agreement between the depositor and his bank. Likewise the banks in the chain of collection of an item can make special agreements. The Code specifies that Federal Reserve Regulations and operating letters, clearing house rules and the like are part of each agreement.

Definitions. Article 4 defines certain terms which can best be illustrated by considering a typical banking transaction. *D* owes $100 to *P* for an article of merchandise which he has purchased from *P*. *D* draws a check on the bank ("payor bank") of which he is a "customer" and mails it to his creditor in another city. The creditor ("depositor") deposits the check in his own bank ("depositary bank"). *P*'s bank then forwards the check to *X* Bank which may in turn forward it to *Y* Bank. *X* Bank and *Y* Bank are called "intermediary banks" and along with the depositary bank are called "collecting banks." *Y* Bank ("presenting bank") presents the check to the payor bank. The payor bank honors the check, charges it to the customer's account and finally returns it to the customer along with his other cancelled checks and monthly statement. Even a simple transaction such as this involves a multiplicity of legal relationships.

The usual practice is for the depositary bank to credit the account of the depositor at the time of deposit. Each collecting bank likewise credits the account of the previous collecting bank (or remits to that bank) and finally when the check reaches the payor bank that bank debits the drawer's account. The payor bank then credits the account of the presenting bank, remits to it, or, if both the presenting bank and payor bank belong to the same "clearing house," includes the check in its balance at such clearing house. A clearing house is defined as "any association of banks or other payors regularly clearing items."

Provisional settlements. Each of the foregoing transactions is referred to as a "provisional settlement" because until final settlement it is not known whether or not the check is good. If the payor bank honors the check, the settlement is final; if it dishonors the check, each provisional settlement is revoked and the depositary bank which had given provisional credit for the deposit cancels the credit.

Deposit of items. It is provided in Article 3, as previously noted, that a check must be presented to the payor bank within a reasonable time after date of issue. The presumed reasonable time in order to charge the drawer is thirty days while seven days is the period in which presentment must be made to charge an indorser.

A significant term in connection with bank deposits, "banking day" is defined in Section 4-104 (c) as "that part of any day on which a bank is open to the public for carrying on substantially all of its banking functions." The Code permits a bank to establish a "cut-off" hour of 2 P.M. or later in order that the bank may have an opportunity "to process items, prove balances and make the necessary entries to determine its position for day . . ." (U.C.C. 4-107 (1)). If an item is received after the cut-off hour, if one be fixed, or after the close of the banking day, it may be treated as having been received at the opening of the next banking day.

If a customer deposits an item for collection without indorsing it, the depositary bank may supply the missing indorsement. If the bank states on the item that it was deposited by a customer or credited to his account, such a statement is effective as the customer's indorsement. This is a practical rule intended to speed up the collection process by making it unnecessary to return to the depositor any items he may have failed to indorse.

4-81. Collection of items: Depositary and collecting banks. Like the Bank Collection Code the Uniform Commercial Code provides that unless a contrary intent clearly appears, a collecting bank is an agent[1] or subagent for the owner of the item and that any "settlement" given for the item is a provisional one. The Code defines "settle" as meaning to pay in cash, by clearing house settlement, in debit or credit entries in accounts between banks, or by forwarding remittance instruments. A settlement may be either provisional or final. The bank is an agent until the settlement is or becomes final even though the bank allows immediate withdrawal against the deposit or withdrawal has in fact been made. As a practical matter the continuing agency status of the bank until its settlement is or becomes final is important in that the depositor bears the risk of loss as owner in the event of nonpayment of the check or insolvency of one of the collecting banks before final settlement. The original depositor thus continues to be the owner of the check until it is paid by the bank upon which it is drawn and final settlement is made to the depositary bank.

Responsibility for collection. When a bank has received a check for collection, the Code imposes upon it the duty to use ordinary care in performing its collection operations. These operations include presenting the check or forwarding it for presentment, sending notice of dishonor or nonpayment or returning the check after learning that it has not been paid, and settling for the check when it receives final payment. Also the bank must notify its transferor of any loss or delay in transit within a reasonable time after discovery thereof.

The Code also contains provisions with reference to the time within

[1] First Trust & Savings Bank v. Fidelity-Philadelphia Trust Co., page 658.

which the collecting bank should perform the above mentioned operations. If the bank takes proper action before its "midnight deadline" following receipt of an item, notice, or payment, it has acted seasonably. The "midnight deadline" of a bank is midnight of the bank's next banking day following the banking day on which the bank received the particular item or notice. Thus if a collecting bank receives a check on Monday and presents or forwards to the next collecting bank any time prior to midnight Tuesday, it has acted seasonably. Later action may be "seasonable" under some circumstances, but the burden of proof is on the bank to establish this.

Should the collecting bank fail to use ordinary care in handling a check or other item the depositor can recover damages from such bank. In the absence of bad faith on the part of the bank the amount of damages recoverable is limited to the depositor's actual loss. This is measured by "the amount of the item reduced by an amount which could not have been realized by the use of ordinary care . . ." (U.C.C. 4-103 (5)). Thus, if the loss would have occurred in spite of the exercise of ordinary care by the collecting bank, no recovery would be allowed.

The Code provides for a limited extension of the time limits which are stipulated in the Code. A collecting bank may allow a period not in excess of one additional banking day in a good faith effort to obtain payment of an item. Such extension does not discharge secondary parties nor does it impose any liability to its transferor or any prior party. Delay by a collecting or payor bank is excused "if caused by interruption of communication facilities, suspension of payments by another bank, war, emergency conditions or other circumstances beyond the control of the bank provided it exercises such diligence as the circumstances require." (U.C.C. 4-108 (2)).

Transfer between banks. As previously noted an item may pass through the hands of several banks in the collection process. The Code provides that any method agreed upon which identifies the transferor bank is sufficient for the transfer of an item to another bank. It is not necessary to use language such as "prior indorsements guaranteed" in transfers between banks as the transfer itself implies warranties of title and authorization to obtain payment.

Warranties of customer and collecting bank. The Code provides that each customer or collecting bank who obtains *payment or acceptance* of an item makes certain warranties to the payor bank or other payor who pays or accepts the item in good faith. Warranties are also made by each customer or collecting bank which *transfers* an item. These warranties made by customers and collecting banks are in general the same as those provided in Article 3—Commercial Paper. (See Section 4-61.)

Security interest of collecting bank. A security interest is an interest in personal property which secures payment or performance of an obligation. The Code recognizes the right of a bank in the collection process to claim a security interest in an item or its proceeds to protect the bank, with respect to advances and payments it has made, as against the depositor and his creditors.

Where an item has been deposited in an account the bank has a security interest to the extent that withdrawals have been made against the credit. This is true even though the depositary bank does not own the item—it may nevertheless be able to hold the item against the depositor or his creditors.

Where the item has not been deposited in an account but has, for example, been discounted and the bank has given to the transferor credit available for withdrawal as of right, the bank also has a security interest. The security interest exists even though the credit is not actually drawn upon and the bank has a right to charge back.

Likewise, a security interest is given when the bank makes an advance against an item.

Where a single credit is given for several items, the security interest on all of the deposited items continues though only a part of the credit is withdrawn. In determining whether there has been a withdrawal against a credit the Code provides that "credits first given are first withdrawn." This is often referred to as the "first in, first out rule."

The security interest continues until the bank receives a final settlement or surrenders the instrument for purposes other than collection.

Collecting bank as holder in due course. The Code provides that for purposes of determining the status of a bank as a holder in due course, a security interest constitutes value.[2] Thus, if a bank satisfies the other requirements as set forth in U.C.C. 3-302, it can qualify as a holder in due course and can enforce an instrument even though its depositor or other transferor could not. In this connection it is to be noted that an intermediary bank or a payor bank which is not a depositary bank, is not affected by a restrictive indorsement except that of the bank's immediate transferor. Otherwise, notice of claim or defense is not imparted by such indorsement. Depositary banks, however, may be liable to the owner of an item who had indorsed it restrictively.

Media of remittance. The Code specifies that a collecting bank may take the following in settlement of an item:

1. A check of the remitting bank or of another bank on any bank except the remitting bank.
2. A cashier's check or other primary obligation of a remitting bank.

[2] Universal C.I.T. Credit Corporation v. Guaranty Bank & Trust Co., page 661.

The remitting bank must be a member of or clear through a member of the same clearing house or group as the collecting bank.

3. Appropriate authority to charge an account of the remitting bank or of another bank with the collecting bank.

4. If the item is drawn upon or payable by a person other than a bank, a cashier's check, certified check, or other bank check or obligation. Thus, a nonbank payor, such as a business concern, can remit by check.

The foregoing list is not exclusive and other methods of settlement such as through a clearing house are recognized. The types of remittance listed may be received by a collecting bank in a settlement for an item, without such bank being responsible if the form of remittance itself is not paid. This risk lies with the owner of the item and not the collecting bank.

Right of charge-back or refund. If an item has been dishonored, the presenting bank may revoke its provisional settlement and charge the item back to the account of the next prior collecting bank or obtain a refund from that bank. Likewise, other banks in the chain of collection may charge back. The final step is a charge-back to the customer's account by the depositary bank. Each of the collecting banks must return the item or send notification of the facts by its midnight deadline. The right to charge back is not affected by the fact that the depositor may have drawn against the provisional credit.

Final payment of item by payor bank. The Code in Section 4-213 (1) sets forth the rules for determining the point of time at which an item is finally paid by a payor bank. Other subsections provide the rules for the related questions of (1) when provisional debits and credits become final and (2) when credits become available for withdrawal. As stated in the Comment to this section: ". . . final payment of an item is the 'end of the line' in the collection process and the 'turn around' point commencing the return flow of proceeds."

A depositor may not draw against uncollected funds. Accordingly, he is not entitled to draw against an item payable by another bank until the provisional settlement which the depositary bank has received becomes final.

Where the deposit is an item on which the depositary bank is itself the payor ("on us" items), the credit becomes final on the second banking day following receipt of the item.

Insolvency and preference. Section 4-214 sets forth provisions relating to insolvency and preferences. This section is applicable only to state banks. Practically, the Federal Deposit Insurance Regulation that each owner of a collection item for the payment of which a closed bank has become obligated will be recognized as a depositor of the closed bank, has greatly diminished the significance of this problem.

4-82. Collection of items: Payor banks. The previous section has dealt with depositary and collecting banks in the collection process. This section treats payor banks.

Deferred posting: recovery of payments by return of items: time of dishonor. When an item is presented to a payor bank for payment over the counter, it must be paid or dishonored before the close of business on the day of presentment. Most items will be presented through a clearing house or by mail and the payor bank will make a provisional settlement for them on the day they are *received.* In this event, it has until final payment of the check or its midnight deadline on the following day to decide whether or not the item is good. Within this time the bank may revoke the settlement and return the item or, if this is not possible, send written notice of dishonor or nonpayment. This enables the bank to defer posting as described in the comment to Section 4-301:

> 1. Deferred posting and delayed returns is that practice whereby a payor bank sorts and proves items received by it on the day they are received, e.g. Monday, but does not post the items to the customer's account or return "not good" items until the next day, e.g. Tuesday. The practice typifies "production line" methods currently used in bank collection and is based upon the necessity of an even flow of items through payor banks on a day by day basis in a manner which can be handled evenly by employee personnel without abnormal peak load periods, night work, and other practices objectionable to personnel. Since World War II statutes authorizing deferred posting and delayed returns have been passed in almost all of the forty-eight states. This section codifies the content of these statutes and approves the practice.

Likewise, where a check drawn by one customer of a bank is deposited by another customer for credit on its books, the bank may return the item or send notice of dishonor and may revoke any credit given or recover the amount thereof withdrawn by its customer. This likewise may be done at any time on the following day. Thus, if the payor bank decides that a check should not be paid, it has a sufficient time in which to return the check to its customer.

Responsibility for late return. The preceding section dealt with the time limits within which a bank must take action when it receives an item payable by it—this section relates to the rights of the customer if the bank fails to take action within the prescribed time limits. A payor bank may be held accountable for a check to the person who deposited it although the check is not paid and the drawer of the check did not have sufficient funds to cover it. This liability is imposed if (1) the bank retains a check presented to it by another bank beyond midnight of the day of receipt without settling for it or (2) does not pay or return the check or send notice of dishonor within the period of its midnight deadline. If the payor bank is also the depository bank, i.e., the check deposited by the customer is one which is drawn on his bank, settlement on the day of receipt is not required, but the bank must return the check or send notice of dishonor before its midnight deadline. Thus failure on the part of the payor bank to take the necessary action within the proper time renders it liable to the depositor even though the check was not properly payable.

Notice, stop orders, legal process or set-off, order of payment. Following the receipt of a check the payor bank must process it. This involves a series of acts which are initiated by receipt of the check from the clearing house, by mail, or over the counter. The check passes to the sorting and proving departments after which it may be photographed. It then moves to the bookkeeping department where it is examined as to form and signature. Here it is determined also whether the drawer's account is sufficient to cover it. If it is found to be proper in all respects it will be posted to the drawer's account. The entire process may require considerable time and may extend into the next banking day.

During the period of processing or prior thereto, the payor bank may receive knowledge or notice concerning the check or other item. Such knowledge or notice may be that the drawer has filed a petition in bankruptcy; that the drawer has stopped payment on a check; that the drawer's account has been attached by a creditor. These circumstances raise questions as to (1) when does a stop order become effective so that the bank is under a duty to refuse to pay the check and (2) when is an attachment effective so as to preclude the bank from paying checks which are drawn on the account. The payor bank is in somewhat of a dilemma because if it disregards the attachment or other legal proceedings or stop order and honors the checks, the attaching creditor or trustee in bankruptcy may seek to impose liability upon the bank or the customer who placed the stop order may seek to do the same. By the same token, if the bank refuses to honor the checks, the owners may claim that payment was effected prior to the time when the stop order, attachment, or other legal notice became effective. A related problem is that of a set-off by a bank whereby the bank charges its customer's account to satisfy an obligation owed by the customer to the bank. When does the set-off (or stop order, legal process, or notice) come too late to prevent the payment of a check and its charge to the customer's account? Under prior law the position of a bank was uncertain due to the fact that the court decisions on this subject were in conflict.

The Code provides definite rules to govern situations involving any notice, stop order, legal process, or any set-off exercised by the bank. In Section 4-303 (1) it is provided that any notice or stop order received by a bank, or any legal process such as attachment served on it, or any set-off exercised by the bank, comes too late to prevent payment of a check by the bank if the bank has done any one of the following:

(1) accepted or certified the item,

(2) paid the item in cash,

(3) settled for the item without reserving or having the right to revoke the settlement,

(4) completed the posting of the check to the customer's account or otherwise has evidenced its *decision* to pay the check by examining the customer's account and has taken some action to indicate an *intention to pay,*

(5) become liable for the check or other item because of failure to settle for or return the check in time.

It should be noted that while clearly if a bank had paid a check in cash an attachment, for example, would come too late, that such attachment may also come too late if the bank has prior thereto indicated its *decision* to pay the check or completed its posting process. Thus a check may well be considered as beyond the reach of an attachment or stop order even though it has not yet been "paid" for the purpose of returning the check because of insufficient funds. The check may still be subject to return by the payor bank to the collecting bank.

Still another problem relates to the order of payment of checks. The Code provides that there is no priority as among checks presented to a bank on any particular day. The account on which the checks are drawn may not have a sufficient balance to pay all of these checks. As a result some of the checks will be dishonored and others will be paid and charged to the customer's account. The checks and other items ". . . may be accepted, paid, certified or charged to the indicated account of its customer in any order convenient to the bank." (U.C.C. 4-303 (2)).

4-83. Relationship between payor bank and its customer. Several important problems arise in connection with the rights, duties, and obligations as between a bank and its customer.[3] Previous sections have treated the collection of items with reference to the relationships between depository and collecting banks and the role of payor banks. This section deals with the relationships between *payor bank* and customer.

When bank may charge customer's account. It is basic to the banking function that upon proper payment of a draft the drawee may charge the account of the drawer. This fundamental proposition applies even though the check or draft is an overdraft since the check itself authorizes the payment for the drawer's account and carries with it an implied promise to reimburse the drawee.[4] The Code specifically grants the bank the right

[3] Stone & Webster Engineering Corp. v. First National Bank & Trust Co., page 664.
[4] National Bank of Slatington v. Derhammer, page 667.

to charge its customer's account with any check otherwise properly payable even though such charge creates an overdraft.

It will be recalled that Article 3—Commercial Paper contains a provision protecting a holder in due course against discharge by reason of alteration and permits him to enforce the instrument according to its original tenor. Likewise, protection is afforded to a drawee who pays a completed instrument in good faith according to the instrument as completed. These concepts are applied to the banking situation in Section 4-401 (2) wherein it is provided that if a bank in good faith makes payment to a holder it may charge the indicated account of its customer according to (1) the original tenor of the altered check or (2) the tenor of a completed item. Thus, if a check is raised, the bank can charge its customer's account with the original amount of the check. Likewise, if a person signs his name to a check in blank and loses it, after which an unauthorized person completes it and it is paid by the drawee bank, the bank may charge the customer's account if it pays in good faith and does not know that the completion was improper.

Wrongful dishonor—bank's liability to customer. A bank is under a duty to honor checks drawn by its customers when there are sufficient funds in his account to cover the checks. If a bank wrongfully dishonors a check, it is liable in damages to its customer for damages proximately caused by the wrongful dishonor.

The Code both defines the extent of a bank's liability to its customers for wrongful dishonor and specifies the damages which may be recovered. When the dishonor occurs by mistake, as distinguished from malicious or willful dishonor, liability is limited to the actual damages proved. Provision is also made for *consequential* damages proximately caused by the wrongful dishonor and may include damages for arrest or prosecution of the customer. The Code rejects decisions which have held that if the dishonored item were drawn by a merchant he is defamed in his business because of the reflection on his credit and accordingly could recover substantial damages on the basis of defamation *per se* without proof of actual damage. Under the Code the merchant or trader must prove actual damages.

Customer's right to stop payment. The Code provides that a customer has the right to stop payment on checks drawn on his account. Only the drawer has this right—it does not extend to payees or indorsees. In order to be effective such order must be "received at such time and in such manner as to afford the bank a reasonable opportunity to act on it prior to an action by the bank with respect to the item. . . ." (U.C.C. 4-403 (1)).

If a check has been certified, the depositor cannot stop payment whether he, or the payee, procured the certification.

The Code provides that an oral stop order is binding on the bank for only 14 days unless confirmed in writing within that period.[5] A written order is effective for only six months unless renewed in writing.

If a bank pays a check upon which payment has been stopped, it will be liable to its customer for resulting damages. However, the burden is on the customer to prove the fact and amount of loss. If the customer cannot prove that he has suffered a loss he cannot recover against the bank for paying the check.

If the stop order agreement contains a provision relieving the bank from responsibility for negligently disregarding a stop order, such provision is invalid under the Code.

Stale checks. The Code provides that a bank is not obligated to pay a check that is over six months old. The bank, however, is entitled to pay a check which has been outstanding more than six months and may charge it to the customer's account.

Certified checks do not fall within the six months rule—they are the primary obligation of the certifying bank and the obligation runs direct to the holder of the check.

Death or incompetence of customer. As a general proposition the death or incompetency of a person terminates the authority of others to act on his behalf. If this principle were applied to banks, a tremendous burden would be imposed upon them to verify the continued life and competency of drawers. Accordingly, the Code provides that the death of a customer does not revoke the bank's authority to pay checks drawn by him until the bank knows of the death and has a reasonable opportunity to act on it. The same rule applies to an adjudication of incompetency.

The Code also provides that even though the bank knows of the death of its customer it may pay or certify checks for a period of ten days after the date of his death. This is intended to permit holders of checks drawn and issued shortly after death to cash them without the necessity of filing a claim in probate. This is subject to the proviso that a stop order may be made by a relative or other person who claims an interest in the account.

Duty of customer to bank. A bank generally makes available to its customer a statement of his account and his cancelled checks. The customer is under a duty to examine his bank statement and cancelled checks for forgeries of his signature and for raised checks within a reasonable time after they are returned to him or made available to him. He is further obligated to report any irregularities to the bank. While the bank does not have the right to charge his account with forged checks, the customer's failure to examine and notify will prevent him from asserting the forgery (or alteration) against the bank, if the bank can establish that it suffered a loss because of his failure. Thus, the bank may be able to prove that a

[5] Dinger v. Market Street Trust Co., page 669.

prompt notification would have enabled the bank to recover from the forger.

The Code does not specify the period of time within which the customer must report forgeries or alterations but it does specify that if the same wrongdoer commits successive forgeries or alterations, the customer's failure to examine and notify within a period not to exceed fourteen days after the first item and statement were available to him, will bar him from asserting the forgeries or alterations of subsequent checks paid by the bank in good faith. This rule is intended to prevent the wrongdoer from having the opportunity to repeat his misdeeds.

If the customer can establish that the bank itself was negligent in paying a forged or altered item, the bank cannot avail itself of the customer's failure to promptly examine and report. A customer is precluded from asserting a forged *signature* or *alteration* on a check after one year from the time the check and statement are made available to him even though the bank is negligent. If the customer does not discover and report any forged *indorsement* within three years from such time, he is precluded from asserting such forged indorsement against the bank.

If a payor bank as a matter of policy or public relations waives its defense of slow notification by its customer, it cannot thereafter hold the collecting bank or any prior party for the forgery.

Subrogation rights of payor bank. In some situations a payor bank is subrogated to the rights of other parties in order to prevent unjust enrichment and to prevent loss to the bank by reason of its payment of a check or other item. This arises in those cases where the bank has made an improper payment such as a payment in violation of a stop order. There are three aspects of a payor bank's subrogation rights.

(1) The bank is subrogated to the rights of any *holder in due course* on the item against the *drawer.* When a bank is sued for wrongful payment over a stop order, it can assert the defense that the drawer did not suffer a loss because he would have been liable to a holder in due course whether the stop order was obeyed or not. Thus, even if payment had been stopped, the drawer would have had to make good to a holder in due course. The Code recognizes this and to the extent necessary places the bank in the position of such holder as against the drawer.

(2) The bank is subrogated to the rights of the *payee* or any other holder of the item against the *drawer.*[6] This relates to rights in the check or item or to rights under the transaction out of which the item arose. Again, assuming payment of a check over a stop order, the payee may have received the check in payment for defective goods. If the drawer retains the goods he is obliged to pay part of the agreed price. If the bank

[6] Universal C.I.T. Credit Corp. v. Guaranty Bank & Trust Co., page 661.

has paid the check, it is subrogated to the payee's claim against the drawer for a portion of the contract price.

(3) The bank is subrogated to the rights of the *drawer* against the *payee* or any other holder in connection with the transaction which gave rise to the item. Here the bank, having improperly paid a check, takes over the rights of its own customer—the drawer—against the payee. If the drawer had been defrauded by the payee, the bank, upon reimbursing the drawer, is subrogated to the latter's right to get back his money from the fraudulent payee.

BANK DEPOSITS AND COLLECTIONS CASES

FIRST TRUST & SAVINGS BANK v. FIDELITY-PHILADELPHIA TRUST CO.

1954, 214 F. 2. 320

The defendant bank had received for safekeeping notes of a distiller secured by whiskey warehouse certificates. The plaintiff bank purchased the notes which later were revealed to be spurious. It now seeks to recover from the defendant bank for the loss suffered and contends that the defendant was a seller, and thus made warranties, within the meaning of the Securities Act of 1933. The lower Court ruled for defendant. (Other facts are set forth in the opinion.)

GOODRICH, C. J. This case presents the often recurring situation of two people who, doing business in the ordinary course, have been fooled by a swindler. The swindler disappears or goes to jail. Which of the two parties is to bear the loss his rascality has occasioned?

The trial court made very full findings of fact on the history of the dealings among the parties and also the facts of the immediate transactions out of which this suit arose. Those extensive findings need not be repeated here. See D.C.E.D. Pa. 1953, 112 F. Supp. 761.

Our set of operative facts gets down to this comparatively simple case. A bank's customer (the bank being the defendant, Fidelity-Philadelphia Trust Company) brings to the bank what purports to be the negotiable promissory note of a whisky distiller. This note is accompanied by what purports to be a negotiable warehouse receipt evidencing a deposit of whisky, which is to be collateral security for the note. Both the note and the warehouse receipt are, in fact, spurious. The customer (Philadelphia Acceptance Corporation, hereafter called PAC) does two things. First, it deposits with the bank in its trust department the purported warehouse receipt, for which the bank issues a safekeeping receipt and puts the document in a file. This is a bailment for the benefit of PAC and the purchaser of the promissory note. The charge made by Fidelity for the service is barely sufficient to cover its expenses in connection therewith. Second, the customer, PAC, leaves with the collection department of the bank a draft drawn by itself in its own favor on the plaintiff, The First Trust and Savings Bank of Zanesville, Ohio, (Zanesville), which is to be the purchaser of the note. Forthwith defendant Fidelity credits its customer with the amount of the draft and charges PAC interest until the transaction is closed. It is closed by Fidelity's forwarding the draft, note and safekeeping receipt to Zanesville. This bank in turn sends Fidelity a check payable to Fidelity's order and drawn on the Chase Bank in New York. In due course of time this check clears and Fidelity is thus reimbursed for the credit it has made to its customer.

The first problem is: Does this transaction make Fidelity a seller within the terms of the Securities Act of 1933? It should be noted that what was done here is very similar to what goes on in thousands and thousands of cases where a bank advances funds to its customer upon having endorsed to it the customer's draft on a third party, accompanied by a negotiable bill of lading or warehouse receipt. The only addition here is the keeping of the purported warehouse receipt in the files of Fidelity, not because Fidelity wanted it, but because of the arrangement made between PAC and Zanesville. . . .

Furthermore, it can hardly be denied that when a bank takes a document for collection advancing to its customer credit prior to the actual collection being made, the bank then becomes at least a security owner. *Maryland Casualty Co. v. National Bank of Germantown & Trust Co.*, 1936, 320 Pa. 129, 182 A. 362. And see Note, 22 A.L.R. 2d 479 (1952). And when it endorses the instrument, on which it thus advanced credit, to another bank by the general endorsement "pay any bank, banker or trust company," and gets its money, has it not passed its interest in that document along to him who pays the draft and gets the supposedly valuable bill of lading, warehouse receipt or note accompanying the draft? And if that is so, why have we not been pushed into the startling conclusion that every bank that makes an advance on an instrument left with it for collection, and passes that instrument on to someone else, has become a seller under the terms of the federal statute, if the transaction is one in interstate commerce?

We think that we do not need to reach this startling conclusion, at least on the facts of this case. In this we are supported by the clearly established law of Pennsylvania with regard to the relation of a bank and its depositor. It is true that in construing the federal statute we are not, of course, bound by state law concepts. But in deciding whether Fidelity has done things which bring it under the terms of a federal statute, we look to the law of Pennsylvania to see the state law consequence of business dealings between PAC, a Philadelphia customer, and Fidelity, a Philadelphia bank.

In the case of each of the worthless notes involved in this litigation, PAC, as stated above, had drawn a draft in its own favor upon Zanesville. These drafts were endorsed to the order of Fidelity, without qualification. Such endorsement is a special endorsement under Section 34 of the NIL* and is in no sense a restrictive endorsement. Ordinarily when a person is given physical possession of a negotiable instrument thus specially endorsed to him he becomes the owner. But in Pennsylvania this matter is expressly covered by a statute of 1931 and that statute is important enough to quote here:

Except as otherwise provided by agreement and except as to subsequent holders of a negotiable instrument payable to bearer or indorsed specially or in blank, where an item is deposited or received for collection, the bank of deposit shall be agent of the depositor for its collection and each subsequent collecting bank shall be subagent of the depositor but shall be authorized to follow the instructions of its immediate forwarding bank, and any credit given by any such agent or subagent bank therefore shall be revocable until such time as the proceeds are received in actual money or an unconditional credit given on the books of another bank, which such agent has requested or accepted. Where any such bank allows any revocable credit for an item to be withdrawn, such agency relation shall, nevertheless, continue, except the bank shall have all the rights of an owner thereof against prior and subsequent parties to the extent of the amount withdrawn. . . ." Purdon's Pa. Stat. Ann. tit. 7 Section 213.

A later section of the same statute provides:

"Where a deposited item is payable to bearer or indorsed by the depositor in blank or by special indorsement, the fact that such item is so payable or indorsed shall not change the relation of agent of the bank of deposit to the depositor, but subsequent holders shall have the right to rely on the presumption that the bank of deposit is the owner of the item. . . ." Purdon's Pa. Stat. Ann. tit. 7, Section 215**. . . .

The judgment of the district court will be affirmed. . . .

[* Purdon's Pa. Stat. Ann. tit. 56, Section 85; to be superseded by the Uniform Commercial Code, effective July 1, 1954, 12A P.S. Section 1-101 et seq.

** These two sections will be superseded by the Uniform Commercial Code, which becomes effective July 1, 1954 in Pennsylvania. The Code provision reads as follows: "Unless a contrary intent clearly appears, a depositary bank takes an item for collection regardless of the form of indorsement or lack of indorsement and even though credit for the item is subject to immediate withdrawal as of right." Purdon's Pa. Stat. Ann. tit. 12A, sec. 4-201. See also the comment to that section. The rule likewise represents the case law in Pennsylvania. See *Lipschutz v. Philadelphia Savings Fund Soc.*, 1933, 107 Pa. Super. 481, 164 A. 74, and cases cited therein; *Foster v. Federal Reserve Bank of Philadelphia*, D.C.E.D. Pa. 1939, 29 F. Supp. 716, affirmed 3 Cir., 1940, 113 F. 2d 326.]

UNIVERSAL C.I.T. CREDIT CORP. v. GUARANTY BANK & TRUST CO.

1958, 161 F. Supp. 790

WYZANSKI, D. J. This case, falling within this Court's diversity jurisdiction, arises under that version of the Negotiable Instruments Law now embodied in Mass. G.L. (Ter. Ed.), c. 107. The only problem of any difficulty is whether under Massachusetts law as it now stands, that is, before the effective date of what is commonly called the Commercial Code, adopted by c. 765 of the Massachusetts Acts of 1957 effective October 1, 1958, when a bank receives from its depositor a check endorsed without restriction but deposited pursuant to the usual deposit slip wherein the bank agrees merely to act as a collection agent, but nonetheless, the bank, before collecting the check allows the depositor to draw from the bank an amount equivalent to both his entire balance and the amount of that uncollected check, the bank is a holder for value of that uncollected check.

An abbreviated statement of the facts will suffice in view of what this Court concludes are the governing principles of law.

C.I.T. (more fully described as Universal C.I.T. Credit Corporation, a New York corporation, plaintiff herein) had an account with Guaranty (more fully described as Guaranty Bank and Trust Company, a Massachusetts corporation, defendant and third-party plaintiff herein). McCarthy (more fully described as McCarthy Motor Sales, Inc., a Massachusetts corporation, not a party to this case) had an account with Worcester (more fully described as Worcester County Trust Company), a Massachusetts corporation, third-party defendant.

On October 1, 1955 C.I.T. drew on Guaranty payable to the order of McCarthy two checks (hereinafter called *A* and *B*) in the amounts respectively of $10,886 and $880 (or a total of $11,766). The same day McCarthy deposited in Worcester these checks endorsed without restriction but accompanied by and in accordance with the usual bank deposit slip reciting that the item was received by the bank for collection only. At 9:10 A.M. October 2, 1956 C.I.T.'s representative presented to Guaranty a written stop-payment order covering checks *A* and *B*. Nonetheless, at the clearing later that same day when Worcester presented to Guaranty checks *A* and *B* for payment, Guaranty gave Worcester a final credit for the $11,766 stated therein. Later Guaranty asked Worcester to take back checks *A* and *B*, but Worcester refused. Guaranty debited C.I.T.'s account for $11,766. C.I.T. claims that this was an unauthorized debit.

On October 1, 1956 McCarthy's balance at Worcester was $18.22. After McCarthy on October 1, 1956 had deposited checks *A* and *B*, before Guaranty sought to return to Worcester checks *A* and *B* and before Worcester had any reason to know that checks *A* and *B* would be subject to any difficulties, Worcester during business hours on October 2, 1956 paid or settled at the clearing a check drawn on September 24, 1956 by McCarthy on Worcester payable to C.I.T. in the amount of $11,297.04 (hereinafter called check *X*) together with other checks which in combination exhausted both McCarthy's October 1 cash balance of $18.22 and the provisional credit of $11,766, attributable to checks *A* and *B*.

Upon the foregoing facts, the initial question relates to the effect of C.I.T.'s order to Guaranty to stop payment upon checks *A* and *B*. C.I.T., as the drawer of the checks, had an absolute right to order payment stopped; Guaranty, the drawee bank making payment thereon, acted at its peril. Since a check is merely an order to a bank to make payment in the manner set forth, the customer has the right to revoke such order before it is carried out. That was the rule of the common law (cases cited). It is the present rule under the Massachusetts version of the N.I.L. (cases cited). It will be the law when the Commercial Code becomes effective in Massachusetts (cases cited). And reference to this code is appropriate because the Massachusetts court regards it less as a novel enactment than as largely a restatement and clarification of existing law which has the approval of American scholars (cases cited). . . .

But although under the principles just stated C.I.T. has established against Guaranty a claim arising out of the unauthorized debiting by Guaranty of C.I.T.'s account in the amount of $11,766, the next issues are whether Worcester was a holder in due course of checks *A* and *B* amounting to $11,766, and whether, to avoid circuity of action, Guaranty is subrogated to Worcester's claim against C.I.T. . . .

Indeed, the majority of courts have ruled, pursuant either to the N.I.L. or to the common law, that a bank in Worcester's position is a holder in due course to the extent of its advances (cases cited). So have the draftsmen of the (as yet inoperable in Massachusetts) provisions of the Commercial Code. Section 4-208 (a) thereof will provide:

> Section 4-208. Security Interest of Collecting Bank in Items, Accompanying Documents and Proceeds.
>
> (1) A bank has a security interest in an item and any accompanying documents or the proceeds of either
>
> (a) in case of an item deposited in an account to the extent to which credit given for the item has been withdrawn or applied; . . .

And Section 4-209 "When Bank gives Value for Purposes of Holder in Due Course" will provide:

> For purposes of determining its status as a holder in due course, the bank has given value to the extent that it has a security interest in an item provided that the bank otherwise complies with the requirements of Section 3-302 on what constitutes a holder in due course (1957, 765, Section 1; effective Oct. 1, 1958).

Authority apart, there is fairness in this majority rule to the effect that there is a presumption that where a bank advances credit to a customer on his drawings after that customer has deposited with the bank for collection a check endorsed unrestrictively both parties intend that the bank may look to the collection item for security up to the amount of the bank's advances. In this country it is unusual for a bank to allow a customer to draw except against funds theretofore deposited or upon a formally established credit. Where the bank allows a customer to draw against an uncollected item, particularly in the face of a contract recognizing that the depositor has no right to demand such a privilege, both parties would ordinarily view this allowance not as an unsecured loan upon the customer's general credit but as a bank loan buttressed by the security of the uncollected item. This view is strengthened when, as in the case at bar, the bank's allowance to the customer is within the financial limits of the face amount of the uncollected item. In short, barring some clear agreement by both parties that the bank will not claim any such security rights, when the bank gives the customer the exceptional privilege of drawing against an uncollected item, a privilege to which under his contract the depositor has no right, the bank, while not purchasing the item is entitled to security to the extent of its advances, and is to that extent a holder in due course—that is, a person who has given value. . . .

This Court having concluded that under Massachusetts law, as indeed under the law in most other states, under the NIL, and under the Commercial Code, Worcester was a holder in due course for the amount of its advances, which were in fact the same as the amount of checks *A* and *B*, it follows that Guaranty (in responding to C.I.T.'s claim that Guaranty could not properly have debited C.I.T.'s account for checks *A* and *B* which were covered by C.I.T.'s timely order to stop payment) is subrogated to Worcester's rights against C.I.T. on checks *A* and *B*. Cf. *Usher v. A.S. Tucker Co.*, 217 Mass. 441, 443, 105 N.E. 360, L.R.A. 1916F, 826. [Compare Section 4-407 of the Commercial Code adopted by c. 765 of the Massachusetts Acts of 1957, effective October 1, 1958.] It is usually said that to avoid circuity of action, C.I.T. is not allowed to recover from Guaranty. But perhaps (see comment to Commercial Code Section 4-407) a sounder way of stating the matter is that C.I.T. is not allowed to recover because it has not borne its burden of showing that it suffered loss from Guaranty's disregard of the stop payment order; C.I.T. suffered no loss because it would have been liable to Worcester as a holder in due course in any event. Whichever form of statement is used, judgment must enter for defendant Guaranty in the action brought against it by C.I.T. Guaranty having prevailed against C.I.T., Guaranty's third-party action against Worcester is without foundation, and in that third-party action judgment must enter for Worcester. . . .

[This case was decided under the NIL.]

STONE & WEBSTER ENGINEERING CORP. v. FIRST NATIONAL BANK & TRUST CO. OF GREENFIELD

1962, (Mass.) 184 N.E. 2d 358

Between January 1, 1960, and May 15, 1960, plaintiff was indebted at various times to Westinghouse Electric Corp. for goods and services. Plaintiff drew three checks on its checking account in the First National Bank of Boston payable to Westinghouse in the total amount of $64,755.44. Before delivery of the checks to Westinghouse an employee of the plaintiff in possession of the checks forged the indorsement of Westinghouse and "cashed" the checks at the defendant bank. The defendant forwarded the checks to the First National and received full payment. The latter bank charged the account of the plaintiff and has refused to recredit the plaintiff's checking account. The drawer, Stone and Webster, sued the "cashing bank," defendant. The lower court sustained a demurrer to the complaint.

WILKINS, C. J. . . . The plaintiff contends that "First National paid or credited the proceeds of the checks to the defendant and charged the account of the plaintiff, and consequently, the plaintiff was deprived of a credit, and the defendant received funds or a credit which 'in equity and good conscience' belonged to the plaintiff."

In our opinion this argument is a non sequitur. The plaintiff as a depositor in First National was merely in a contractual relationship of creditor and debtor. *Forastiere v. Springfield Inst. for Sav.*, 303 Mass. 101, 103, 20 N.E. 2d 950; *Drinsky v. Pilgrim Trust Co.*, 337 Mass. 401, 405, 149 N.E. 2d 665. The amounts the defendant received from First National to cover the checks "cashed" were the bank's funds and not the plaintiff's. The Uniform Commercial Code does not purport to change the relationship. See G.L. c. 106, Sections 1-103, 4-401 to 4-407. Section 3-409 (1) provides: "A check or other draft does not of itself operate as an assignment of any funds in the hands of the drawee available for its payment, and the drawee is not liable on the instrument until he accepts it." This is the same as our prior law, which the Code repealed. See, formerly, G.L. c. 107, sections 150, 212. Whether the plaintiff was rightfully deprived of a credit is a matter between it and the drawee, First National.

If we treat the first count as seeking to base a cause of action for money had and received upon a waiver of the tort of conversion—a matter which it is not clear is argued—the result will be the same. In this aspect the question presented is whether a drawer has a right of action for conversion against a collecting bank which handles its checks in the bank collection process. Unless there be such a right, there is no tort which can be waived.

The plaintiff relies upon the Uniform Commercial Code, G.L. c. 106,

Section 3-419, which provides, "(1) An instrument is converted when . . . (c) it is paid on forged indorsement." This, however, could not apply to the defendant, which is not a "payor bank," defined in the Code, Section 4-105 (b), as a "bank by which an item is payable as drawn or accepted." See Am. Law Inst. Uniform Commercial Code, 1958 Official Text with comments, Section 4-105, comments 1-3; G.L. c. 106, Sections 4-401, 4-213, 3-102 (b).

A conversion provision of the Uniform Commercial Code which might have some bearing on this case is Section 3-419 (3). This section implicitly recognizes that, subject to defenses, including the one stated in it, a collecting bank, defined in the Code, Section 4-105 (3), may be liable in conversion. In the case at bar the forged indorsements were "wholly inoperative" as the signature of the payee, Code Sections 3-404 (1), 1-201 (43), and equally so both as to the restrictive indorsements for deposits, see Section 3-205 (c), and as to the indorsement in blank, see Section 3-204 (2). When the forger transferred the checks to the collecting bank, no negotiation under Section 3-202 (1) occurred, because there was lacking the necessary indorsement of the payee. For the same reason, the collecting bank could not become a "holder" as defined in Section 1-201 (20), and so could not become a holder in due course under Section 3-302 (1). Accordingly, we assume that the collecting bank may be liable in conversion to a proper party, subject to defences, including that in Section 3-419 (3). See *A. Blum Jr.'s Sons v. Whipple,* 194 Mass. 253, 255, 80 N.E. 501, 13 L.R.A., N.S., 211. But there is no explicit provision in the Code purporting to determine to whom the collecting bank may be liable, and consequently, the drawer's right to enforce such a liability must be found elsewhere. Therefore, we conclude that the case must be decided on our own law, which, on the issue we are discussing, has been left untouched by the Uniform Commercial Code in any specific section. . . .

We state what appears to us to be the proper analysis. Had the checks been delivered to the payee Westinghouse, the defendant might have been liable for conversion to the payee. The checks, if delivered, in the hands of the payee would have been valuable property which could have been transferred for value or presented for payment; and, had a check been dishonored, the payee would have had a right of recourse against the drawer on the instrument under Section 3-413 (2). Here the plaintiff drawer of the checks, which were never delivered to the payee (see *Gallup v. Barton,* 313 Mass. 379, 381, 47 N.E. 2d 921), had no valuable rights in them. Since, as we have seen, it did not have the right of a payee or subsequent holder to present them to the drawee for payment, the value of its rights was limited to the physical paper on which they were written, and was not measured by their payable amounts (cases cited).

The enactment of the Uniform Commercial Code opens the road for the adoption of what seems the preferable view. An action by the drawer against the collecting bank might have some theoretical appeal as avoiding circuity of action. See *Home Indem. Co. v. State Bank,* 233 Iowa 103, 135–140, 8 N.W. 2d 757. Compare 36 Harv. L. Rev. 879. It would have been in the interest of speedy and complete justice had the case been tried with action by the drawer against the drawee and with an action by the drawee against the collecting bank. See *Nichols v. Somerville Sav. Bank,* 333 Mass. 488, 490, 132 N.E. 2d 158. So one might ask: if the drawee is liable to the drawer and the collecting bank is liable to the drawee, why not let the drawer sue the collecting bank direct? We believe that the answer lies in the applicable defences set up in the Code.

The drawer can insist that the drawee recredit his account with the amount of any unauthorized payment. Such was our common law (cases cited). This is, in effect, retained by the Code Sections 4-401 (1), . . . 4-406 (4). But the drawee has defences based upon the drawer's substantial negligence, if "contributing," or upon his duty to discover and report unauthorized signatures and alterations. Sections 3-406, 4-406. As to unauthorized indorsements, see Sections 4-406 (4). . . . Then, if the drawee has a valid defence which it waives or fails upon request to assert, the drawee may not assert against the collecting bank or other prior party presenting or transferring the check a claim which is based on the forged indorsement. Section 4-406 (5). . . . See Am. Law Inst. Uniform Commercial Code, Official Text with comments, Section 4-406, Comment 6, which shows that there was no intent to change the prior law as to negligence of a customer. See *Jordan Marsh Co. v. National Shawmut Bank,* 201 Mass. 397, 407–411, 87 N.E. 740; *Blacker & Shepard Co. v. Granite Trust Co.,* 284 Mass. 9, 13–14, 187 N.E. 53. If the drawee recredits the drawer's account and is not precluded by Section 4-406 (5), it may claim against the presenting bank on the relevant warranties in sections 3-417 and 4-207, and each transferee has rights against his transferor under those sections.

If the drawer's rights are limited to requiring the drawee to recredit his account, the drawee will have the defences noted above this and perhaps others; and the collecting bank or banks will have the defences in Section 4-207 (4) . . . and Section 4-406 (5), and perhaps others. If the drawer is allowed in the present case to sue the collecting bank, the assertion of the defences, for all practical purposes, would be difficult. The possibilities of such a result would tend to compel resort to litigation in every case involving a forgery of commercial paper. It is a result to be avoided. . . .

Order sustaining demurrer affirmed. . . .

THE NATIONAL BANK OF SLATINGTON v. DERHAMMER

1958, Court of Common Pleas of Lehigh County, Pa., 16 D. & C. 2d 286

The plaintiff alleged that on March 4, 1957, the defendant opened a joint account at the plaintiff bank with one Paul M. Barry; that the only deposit to the account was a check drawn by Eli J. Brannon in favor of Paul M. Barry on a New York Bank; that plaintiff paid defendant or her cosignatory $150 in cash, and that on March 6, 1957, $2800 was paid to the "account owners" on a check signed by "one of the joint makers." It is further alleged that the check was drawn on a fictional bank and plaintiff therefore, sought to recover the deficit of $2950.

HENNINGER, P. J. . . . Defendant filed preliminary objections (1) by way of demurrer and (2) by way of motion for a more specific pleading in that (a) deposit slip not attached (b) failure to state whether defendant was a party to any of the instruments involved (c) whether the $4950 check was legally credited to the account and (d) on what theory defendant is being sued.

In passing upon a demurrer, we are limited to the facts as pleaded by plaintiff and we must accept them as verity. . . .

We find then from the facts pleaded and from the exhibits attached that, in addition to the above stated facts, the joint account was in the joint names of defendant and one Paul M. Barry, that, of the two, Barry's name alone appears on the invalid check upon which the deposit and subsequent withdrawals were based, but that the signature card states that the initial deposit was the joint property of both.

At the argument, defendant assumed that all of the chicanery was the work of Barry and that he reaped all of the fruits of it. That may well prove to be the case, but it is not the state of facts upon which we must decide the demurrer. We have no doubt of defendant's innocence of wrongdoing, but the complaint pleads that *she* deposited the invalid check and that *she* received the proceeds of the withdrawals against it.

If that be true, or if defendant participated even innocently in negotiation of the $4950 check, she might be sued for the money lost by reason of the dishonored check. This would be true although, as we know, it was only Barry who endorsed the invalid check and although, as we have been informed, it was only he who signed the $2800 check. Whether or not plaintiff, through any act of its own, has forfeited its right to recover or whether or not defendant actually received any of the money is a matter of defense.

In the light of the motion for a more specific pleading, it becomes necessary for us to rule upon the proposition advanced by plaintiff that every cosignatory to an account is answerable out of his own funds over and above those entrusted to the joint account, for transactions made by his cosignatory which may result in an overdraft. If that were the law, plaintiff's complaint would be sufficient; if it is not the law, other facts must be specifically pleaded to impose liability upon defendant.

While Article 4 of the Uniform Commercial Code of April 6, 1953, P.L. 3, 12A P.S. 4-101 to 4-407, is entitled "Bank Deposits and Collections," it deals almost exclusively with collections of checks and drafts. To rule as plaintiff would have us rule would endanger not only the cosignatory's balance in the account—to which he has consented—but all of his other assets as well—to which he has not consented. Every cosignature would constitute a partnership without limits as to the liability of one partner for the machinations of the other.

Although in Pennsylvania an overdraft is considered an involuntary loan to the one causing it (*F.D.I.C. v. Ciaffoni,* 176 Pa. Superior 91, 94), our attention has not been called to any Pennsylvania case, which holds that the cosignatory can be held beyond the balance in the account or that the joint deposit makes each cosignatory the agent of the other to borrow money from the bank in this irregular manner. See *Pittsburgh v. First National Bank of Sheraden,* 230 Pa. 176, 183.

We are not convinced that Article 4 of the Code intended to impose this new and additional responsibility upon the shoulders of a cosignatory or to change the law of agency, despite the language of Section 4-212 (12A P.S. 4-212) subjecting a customer to refund upon dishonor of an item for collection and Section 4-104 (12A P.S. 4-104) defining a customer as "any person having an account."

Exactly the same situation as in this case was ruled adversely to the bank in *Faulkner v. Bank of Italy.* . . . In that case, however, there was no allegation that the proceeds of charges against the invalid check had been received by the cosignatory.

When we come to the motion for a more specific complaint, it is clear that a litigant need not plead the *theory* upon which he sues. It is enough that he pleads facts which in law entitle him to a recover. Pleading theory might be helpful to Court and adversary, but we cannot demand it.

Plaintiff's complaint is obviously drawn so as to avoid showing that Barry and not defendant perpetrated the fraud. In our opinion, plaintiff's case must stand or fall upon some showing of defendant's responsibility for negotiation of the $4950 check or upon her enrichment through Barry's fraud.

Under these circumstances, we believe that the complaint is not sufficiently specific. Defendant's signature does not appear upon the invalid check. We should know, therefore, what acts on her part, besides the mere fact of cosignature, are relied upon by plaintiff to fasten liability upon this defendant. If, on the other hand, she is to be held because she received monies based upon a dishonored check, we should have a full frank statement naming by name the person or persons who received the money.

. . . *defendant's preliminary objections by way of demurrer are overruled and her preliminary objections by way of motion for a more specific complaint are sustained and it is ordered that plaintiff file, within twenty (20) days after service of this order on its counsel, a more specific complaint in accordance with this opinion. . . .*

DINGER v. MARKET STREET TRUST CO., et al
1956, (Pa.) 7 D. & C. 2d 674

SOHN, J. This suit, as originally brought between the plaintiff and defendant, is based upon the alleged failure of the trust company to honor the stop payment orders which the defendant says were not given. The liability of the defendant turns primarily on whether such stop payment orders were given as required by law. By its preliminary objection, the defendant first asks for a more specific complaint giving it the detailed circumstances as to what person or persons, representing the trust company, were given the notices.

The complaint sets forth that on or about September 30, 1953, the plaintiff executed and delivered to Harold Gross, additional defendant, six instruments in the form of checks on his account in the defendant trust company payable to the order of Harold Gross. Prior to their having been honored by the defendant trust company, plaintiff avers that "Sometime during the Spring of 1954 and before July 21, 1954 (the exact date being now unknown to Plaintiff)," he delivered a stop payment order to the bank covering the six checks. Plaintiff avers that on July 21, 1954, the defendant bank paid five of the six checks and that the sixth check was paid on or about July 27, 1954, even though as to this sixth check a second stop payment order was delivered to the bank. The plaintiff sues for the amount of six instruments which total $1500.00.

Paragraph 5 of the complaint, which the defendant asserts is not sufficiently specific, reads as follows:

5. Sometime during the Spring of 1954 and before July 21, 1954 (the exact date being now unknown to Plaintiff) and while said instruments were still held by the said Harold Gross and unpaid by the bank, Plaintiff orally informed Defendant not to pay said instruments or charge them or any of these to his account if, as and when they were presented for payment. At the request of one of Defendant's employees, Plaintiff thereupon executed and gave to Defendant a "stop payment order" on a form

provided for that purpose by Defendant. On the said form Plaintiff identified the instruments by payee and amount and directed Defendant not to charge them or any of them to his account since they were intended to be merely promissory notes. Plaintiff handed said stop payment order to Defendant's bookkeeper who accepted the same on behalf of Defendant without any objection as to its form or sufficiency. Plaintiff was not furnished with a copy of said stop payment order.

The defendant objects that the complaint is not sufficiently specific because it does not set forth the exact date when plaintff gave it the original stop payment order, because it does not identify the employee to whom plaintiff gave the oral order, or the employee who told him to execute a written order. Under Section 403 (2) of the Uniform Commercial Code, adopted April 6, 1953, P.L. 3, 12A P.S. Section 4-403, we find the following provision:

(2) An oral order is binding upon the bank only until the customer has had reasonable opportunity to send the bank a written confirmation if the bank requests such a confirmation. A written order is effective for only six months unless renewed in writing.

(3) The burden of establishing the fact and amount of loss resulting from the payment of an item contrary to a binding stop payment order is on the customer.

Under the pleadings complained about here, the time of the delivery of the stop payment order is described as "Sometime during the Spring of 1954 and before July 21, 1954 (the exact date being now unknown to Plaintiff)." Such a pleading contemplates a relatively long period of time, to wit: part of March, all of April, May and June, and the greater part of July. We think that the plaintiff must aver a more specific date and give the necessary facts, especially here where the defendant denies receiving any such stop payment orders. A complaint must state the date of the agreement or a reasonably specific date on which the plaintiff relies. This, we believe, is hornbook law. The plaintiff merely sets forth that "Plaintiff orally informed Defendant not to pay said instruments." He does not identify the person to whom his oral notice was given, and it is only reasonable for the defendant bank to require the identity of this person with particularity in order that it can answer and properly prepare its defense. It is a well known fact that a bank has numerous bookkeepers, especially one as large as the Market Street Trust Company, so that it is vitally necessary for the defendant in preparing its defense to know to whom the stop payment order was delivered. To simply aver that it was handed to a bookkeeper is of no help whatsoever to the defendant.

Also, the plaintiff avers that "at the request of one of defendant's employees," he executed the stop payment order. Again we say that it is only reasonable to require the plaintiff to name and identify such employee in order that it may prepare its defense.

In his depositions, the plaintiff admits that he was not a stranger in the bank in which he dealt. He and Gross both dealt there. He was asked on cross examination to describe the bookkeeper with whom he said he dealt. He could not describe her; he could not say whether she was tall or short, heavy or slight, whether she was a brunette or a blonde; he could give no information, he said, about her whatsoever. After he learned that the five checks had been cashed, he put through another stop payment order with respect to these six checks. When asked to whom he gave the stop payment order on this second occasion, he again was unable to describe the girl and only said that it was not the same bookkeeper he had dealt with the first time. Again he was unable to describe the second girl; whether she was tall or short, blonde or brunette, whether or not she wore glasses, or give any particulars whatsoever regarding her appearance. It seems rather strange that the plaintiff did not request the defendant bank for permission to view and interrogate its bookkeepers and other employees, and to let him have an opportunity to identify the specific persons with whom he dealt. We feel that the defendant bank is entirely within its rights in requesting specific information as to whom the stop payment orders were given, and that the complaint as filed must be amended before any other further proceedings can be had in this case.

Review Questions and Problems

1. *P*, the payee of checks drawn on *X* Bank, indorsed the checks on the same day they were drawn and deposited the checks in *Y* Bank. *P* then drew checks against the deposit and depleted the entire balance of his account. Unknown to *X* Bank, the drawer had stopped payment on the checks. The drawee, *X* Bank, paid the *Y* Bank and debited the drawer's account. What are the respective rights of *X* Bank and *Y* Bank?
2. *H*, the holder of a note which did not specify the place of payment, delivered the note to *X* Bank for collection. *X* Bank mailed a letter to *M*, the maker, notifying him that the bank held the note for collection. *M* did not pay and *H* seeks to recover from *A* and *B*, indorsers. Are *A* and *B* liable?
3. *A* and *B* maintained a joint account at *X* Bank. *A* issued a large check which created an overdraft in the joint account. *X* Bank seeks to recover from *A* and *B*. Should *B* be held liable?
4. *P* drew a check in favor of *X* Co. for materials purchased. *A*, an employee of *P*, stole the check from *P*'s office; forged the indorsement of *X* Co. and cashed the check at *C* Bank. *C* Bank forwarded the checks to the drawee, *Y* Bank, and received payment from that bank. What are *P*'s rights against *C* Bank? Against *Y* Bank?
5. *H* received a check by indorsement from *A* on June 1, 1964. On June 10 *H* deposited the check in his bank. The check was returned by the

drawee bank marked "Insufficient Funds." Can *H* recover from *A*, the indorser?

6. A check drawn on *Y* Bank was deposited in *X* Bank. The depositor did not indorse the check. The check was honored by *Y* Bank and charged to the drawer's account. The drawer challenged the payment. What result?
7. A check was sent to *X* Bank for collection. *X* Bank, through the negligence of one of its employees, delayed in forwarding the check to the drawee bank. When the check was finally forwarded, the drawer's account was overdrawn and the check was returned. Would the *X* Bank be liable to the depositor of the check?
8. *A* Bank forwarded checks to its correspondent *B* Bank for collection. While the checks were in the possession of *B* Bank, it became insolvent. Is *A* Bank liable to the owners of the checks?
9. *C* Bank, a collecting bank, received a collection item on Tuesday morning. It sent the item on to the next bank for collection on Thursday morning. The item failed to clear. Is *C* Bank liable?
10. The Federal Reserve Bank sent an item to *E* Bank, the payor bank, on Wednesday. When must *E* Bank give a provisional credit to the Federal Reserve Bank? What would be the result if the credit were delayed?
11. *B* drew a check in favor of *X* on *F* Bank. *B* entered a stop order after the remittance payment for the check had been deposited in the mail. The letter containing the check was still at the local post office when the stop order was given. What is *F* Bank required to do?
12. The drawer's signature to a check was forged. Neither the depositor nor any of the collecting banks has knowledge of the forgery. The payor bank honored the check. Against whom does the payor bank have recourse?
13. *A* draws on *D* Bank a check for $150 in favor of *P*. *P* holds the check for ninety days, and, when he presents it, he finds that *A* has no money in his account. At the time the check was drawn, *A* had more than sufficient funds there to meet it. May *P* recover from *A* on the check?
14. *M* drew a check on *D* Bank in favor of *P*. *P* presented the check to the bank, but the bank refused to make payment, although they had sufficient funds belonging to *M* to do so. Has *P* an action against the bank?
15. *M* gave his check to *P* in payment of merchandise, but when the merchandise failed to arrive, stopped payment on the check. The stop order which he signed contained language to the effect that the bank was to be relieved in case it paid the check through error or mistake. The check was paid at the lunch hour by an assistant to the teller. Will the loss fall upon *M* or the bank?
16. *M* owed his bank a note for $1,500, which matured on August 1, 1959. The bank charged it to his account of that day, the result being that several of *M*'s checks were dishonored. Does *M* have a cause of action against his bank?
17. *A* drew a check on *X* bank in favor of *B* in payment for merchandise. The merchandise was to be delivered ten days later and *A* postdated the check so that he would have an opportunity to receive and examine the merchandise before the date of the check. *B* presented the

check to *X* bank immediately and received payment. What are *A*'s rights against *X* bank?

18. *M*'s name was forged by *B*, his bookkeeper, to a $750 check. When the cancelled checks were returned, they were handed to the bookkeeper and, as a consequence, the bank was not notified of the forgery. Six months later the forgery was discovered, and the bank was notified, but other checks amounting to $7,500 have been forged in the meantime. Will the loss fall upon *M* or the drawee bank?
19. *M* drew a check in favor of *P* for $5. *P* altered the check to read $500 and indorsed it to *A*. *A* indorsed to *H* who presented the check to the drawee bank and received payment of $500. Is *M* liable to the drawee bank? What are the drawee bank's rights against *A*? Against *H*?
20. *D* purchased from *P* 517 lbs. of longhorn cheese that became spoiled. After a dispute about payment and responsibility for spoilage, *D* sent a check to *P* for $146.00, which was considerably less than the original price. *D* wrote on the check the words, "This pays my account in full to date." *P* accepted the check and had it certified by the drawee bank. Is *D* liable for the original price?
21. *A*, the drawer of a check, has it certified by the drawee bank and delivers it to *B*, the payee. *B* indorses to *C*, and *C* indorses to *H*. The bank fails before the check is presented for payment. What are *H*'s rights against *A*? What must *H* do to preserve his rights against *B* and *C*?

BOOK V

BUSINESS ORGANIZATIONS

PART ONE / PARTNERSHIPS

28

Characteristics and Distinctions

5-1. History and definition. In general, organizations for the conduct of business are of four distinct types—individual proprietorships, partnerships, corporations, and business trusts. Partnerships are mentioned and probably have their source in the Roman law. They were well known among the merchants of the Middle Ages. Like the law of negotiable instruments, cases involving questions of partnership are not found in the early common-law reports of England, because such cases were tried in the mercantile courts. The law of partnership was introduced into the common law from the law merchant. The Uniform Partnership Act defines a partnership as an association of two or more persons to carry on, as co-owners, a business for profit. This definition has been adopted by a majority of the states. In most respects the Act has codified the common law; the attention of the reader will be directed to those instances where it differs from the common law.

A partnership is the result of an agreement. The agreement is not required to be in writing but good business judgment dictates that a partnership agreement should be most carefully prepared and reduced to writing.

One important section that should be included in a partnership agreement is a "buy and sell" provision. Many problems arise upon the death or withdrawal of a partner and there are many possibilities of litigation and economic loss to all concerned. Many of these problems can be avoided by providing a method whereby the surviving partner can purchase the interest of the deceased partner or the remaining partner can purchase the interest of the withdrawing partner. A method of determining the value of such interest should be provided, and it is desirable that the partnership agreement provide for a periodic valuation by the partners. The time and method of payment should be stipulated and the buy and sell agreement should specify whether a partner has an option to purchase the interest or a duty to do so. As will be noted in a later section, partners can provide for life insurance on each other's lives and in the event of a partner's death the proceeds of the life insurance policy may be utilized to purchase the deceased partner's interest. A stipulation to this effect may be included in the agreement.

As between themselves, the existence of a partnership depends upon the intention of the parties, manifested either by an interpretation of their words, spoken or written, or by their conduct.[1] The basic question is whether they intend a relationship which includes the essential elements of a partnership as defined above.

If the essential elements of a partnership are present, the mere fact that the parties did not think they were becoming partners is immaterial. If the parties agree upon an arrangement that is a partnership in fact, it is immaterial that they call it something else or that they declare that they are not partners.[2] On the other hand, the mere fact that the parties themselves call the relation a partnership will not make it so if they have not, by their contract, agreed upon an arrangement which by the law is a partnership in fact.

5-2. Partnerships distinguished from a corporation. The distinguishing features between a partnership and a corporation are twofold. First, a partnership is the result of an agreement between two or more parties, whereas a corporation comes into existence not by reason of a contract, but by reason of an act of the state. A partnership, therefore, is a creature of contract, whereas a corporation is a creature of the state. Second, the liability of the partners is unlimited; that is, each partner is individually liable for all the obligations of the organization created in pursuit of the partnership business because each partner is an agent for the partnership entity and for each individual partner; whereas the liability of a member of a corporation is limited to the extent of any unpaid balances due upon stock owned by him. Persons contemplating the formation of a business organization should consider, also, certain other differences between partnerships and corporations. For example, a corporation must pay an income tax upon its net profits, and the stockholders must also pay an individual income tax upon the dividends which they receive. However, the federal income tax laws provide that a taxpayer may exclude from his income a specified portion of dividends received from qualifying domestic corporations during the taxable year. In a partnership organization the partnership itself pays no income tax, but the individual partner pays a personal income tax upon his share of the profits. The partnership must, however, file an income tax return showing the net profit of the firm and the amount allocated to each partner. Each partner must pay an income tax on his share of the profits, even though the income is not distributed to the partners. This is true even if the partnership agreement provides

[1] Worden Co. v. Beals et al., page 681.
[2] Constans et al. v. Ross et al., page 682.

that profits cannot be withdrawn but must remain in the partnership capital.

Thus, the partnership is generally not treated as a taxable entity, although the corporation is so treated. The tax laws now provide, however, that certain partnerships can elect to be treated as corporations for tax purposes. Likewise, the shareholders of small business corporations may, by unanimous consent, elect to pay taxes on the corporate income in the same way as if it had been received by them instead of the corporation. In a "tax option" corporation each shareholder pays a tax upon his proportionate share of the earnings, whether distributed or not, and the corporation itself does not pay a tax.

Other distinctions between partnerships and corporations will become apparent as the law of corporations is studied.

5-3. Partner by estoppel. Where a person by words spoken or written, or by conduct, represents himself or consents to another's representing him to be a partner in an existing partnership or a partner with other persons not in a partnership, he is liable to any party to whom such representation has been made. Such liability, created by estoppel, does not arise, however, unless the third party gives credit to the firm or other persons in reliance upon such representation.

The first essential in partnership liability by estoppel lies in the fact that the party sought to be held has either held himself out as a partner or knowingly permitted others to do so.[3] Under such circumstances, to relieve him would work an injustice on those who have relied upon such representations.

The cases are not in accord as to whether a person is under a duty affirmatively to disclaim a reputed partnership where the representation of partnership was not made by or with the consent of the person sought to be charged as a partner. Some cases hold that if a person is held out as a partner and he knows it, he should be chargeable as a partner unless he takes all reasonable steps to give notice that he is not, in fact, a partner. Other cases indicate that there is no duty to deny false representations of partnership where the ostensible partner did not participate in making the misrepresentation.

The second essential consists of a reliance by the party who extends the credit. If the facts in any particular case indicate that such party knew the true facts, or should reasonably have known them, no partnership relation is created.[4]

Estoppel may also arise when one of the partners in an existing partnership is acting outside the scope of his authority. For example, if one partner, with knowledge of the other partner, uses the firm name for the

[3] Brown & Bigelow v. Roy, page 617.
[4] West Side Trust Co. v. Gascoigne et al., page 618.

purpose of giving credit on negotiable instruments for other persons on matters outside the scope of the partnership business, and this course of conduct is allowed by the other partner to continue for a long time, the firm will be bound on the indorsement of the negotiable paper, under the doctrine of estoppel.

5-4. Who may become partners. A partnership is composed of two or more persons. A person, as defined by the Uniform Partnership Act, includes individuals, partnerships, corporations, and other associations. The members of most partnerships are individual human beings. Corporations cannot be partners unless authorized by their articles of incorporation or by statute. Subject to agreement, unincorporated associations may become members of a partnership.

An infant's partnership agreement is voidable and may be disaffirmed by him as against the other partner. An infant upon disaffirmance is entitled to recover his contribution to capital without loss. Some authorities, however, subject the infant's capital contribution to the claims of unpaid creditors and to whatever losses have been sustained by the firm.

5-5. To carry on as co-owners a business for profit. The essential attributes of a partnership are a common interest in the business and management and a share in the profits and losses. The presence of a common interest in property and management is not enough to prove a partnership. Also, an agreement to share the gross returns of a business, sometimes called gross profits, does not of itself prove an intention to form a partnership.[5] The Uniform Partnership Act provides that the receipt by a person of a share of the real or net profits in a business is prima facie evidence that he is a partner in the business.[6] The presumption that a partnership exists by reason of sharing net profits may be overcome by evidence that the share in the profits is received for some other purpose. Accordingly, no such inference shall be drawn if such profits are received in payment of a debt by installments, as wages of an employee, as rent to a landlord, as an annuity to a widow or representative of a deceased partner, as interest on a loan, or as the consideration of a sale of the good will or other property of a business by installments. Payment of wages to employees in amounts determined by net profits does not make such employees partners. Payment of rent from profits does not change the relationship of landlord and tenant to that of partners. Evidence of the control by the landlord of the tenant's business may be of such character as to impose partnership liability for the benefit of creditors. Upon the death of a partner the continuation of the partnership by agreement for the benefit of a dependent or a widow of the deceased partner by way of annuities derived from a share of the profits does not

[5] Olive et al. v. Turner, page 686.
[6] Troy Grain & Fuel Co. v. Rolston et al., page 687.

create a partnership relationship. A loan to the partnership under an agreement for the payment of interest out of profits does not make the creditor a partner.

CHARACTERISTICS AND DISTINCTIONS CASES

WORDEN CO. v. BEALS et al.

1926, 120 Or. 66, 250 Pac. 375

The defendant Beals, owner of a large tract of timber, entered into a written agreement with the defendant Bennett whereby the latter was given the right to cut the timber thereon and manufacture it into lumber. The agreement provided that Bennett would pay Beals $4 per thousand feet for the timber cut and in addition one third of the profits arising from the sale of the lumber produced from the timber. The profits were defined as the sales price in excess of $21 per thousand feet of lumber, that amount being the estimated cost of manufacturing. The plaintiff, Worden Co., sold goods, wares and merchandise to Bennett in connection with his logging and sawmill operations. Bennett failed to pay and the plaintiff brought this action against Bennett and Beals alleging that the agreement made them partners. The lower court held that Beals was a partner and entered a judgment against both defendants. Beals appealed contending that under the terms of the agreement he was not chargeable as a partner of Bennett.

RAND, J. . . . It is obvious that no partnership between Beals and Bennett could result either from the making or the performance of this contract. They were to share only in the gross earnings of the business after deducting a specified sum fixed arbitrarily as the cost to be incurred by Bennett in the purchase of the timber and the manufacture and sale of the lumber. Under this contract Beals was not to have any charge or control over the management of the business. He could not make contracts, incur liabilities, manage the business, or dispose of the entire property for any purpose. All that he was to receive under the contract was $4 per thousand feet, and one third of such gross earnings as should remain after deducting an estimated cost of $21 per thousand feet, which sum was to be allowed Bennett as the cost of operation. And since Beals had no community of interest in the business, and no common control thereover, no partnership could be created, for, where both of these elements are lacking, the sharing of the profits of the business is not sufficient to constitute a partnership.

. . . A careful reading of this contract will disclose that it was not the purpose of either of these contracting parties to submit the control of his interest under the contract to the other, but that each intended to leave himself free to act as an individual and solely for himself as an individual. Under this contract, the money which Beals was to receive was to be paid to him as compensation for property sold. Neither party had power to bind the other in respect to anything that he was to do in performing the contract, and each party was to act individually and look after his own interest, and not act as the agent of the other. In carrying out the contract, the only relation that could arise was that of debtor and creditor. There was to be no division of net profits, no community of interest in the capital of the business, or in the property resulting from the performance of the contract, and no common control of the business. Since all of these elements were lacking, no partnership was formed, and, since the contract itself conferred no express authority upon Bennett to bind Beals in the purchase of goods, and no partnership being formed, Bennet could have no implied authority to incur any liability binding upon Beals.

For these reasons, the judgment against Beals must be reversed, and it is so ordered.

CONSTANS et al. v. ROSS et al.

1951, 106 Cal. App.2d 381, 235 P.2d 113

The plaintiffs, Robert Q. Constans and Edith M. Constans, partners under the firm name of Live Oak Lumber Co., brought this action to recover the value of building materials furnished to Davidson, a building contractor. The defendants who were real estate brokers had entered into a written agreement with Davidson whereby the defendants would obtain purchasers for houses which were to be built by Davidson. The defendants were to arrange the financing, pay for all plans and specifications, and furnish nails, hardware and venetian blinds. The purchasers procured by the defendants were to contract directly with Davidson and defendants were to retain $1,000 of the monies paid under the building contracts, the balance to be paid to Davidson. Davidson did not pay for the materials furnished by the plaintiffs and the plaintiffs are seeking to hold the defendants liable upon the theory that they were partners of Davidson. The defendants denied the existence of any partnership contending that the agreement was simply to act as agent for Davidson in obtaining building contracts for him. The trial court held in favor of the plaintiffs and the defendants appealed.

WHITE, Presiding Justice. . . . The question of the existence of a partnership depends primarily upon the intention of the parties ascertained from the terms of the agreement and from the surrounding circumstances. (Cases cited)

It is the intention as evidence by the terms of the agreement, and not the subjective or undisclosed intention of the parties, that controls. As was said by this court in *Associated Piping, etc. Co., Ltd., v. Jones*, 17 Cal. App.2d 107, 110, 61 P.2d 536, 538. "The parties did intend to create exactly the relationship as shown by the contract, but did not intend that relationship to be called that of partnership. However, their intention in this respect is immaterial . . . and if the contract by its terms establishes a partnership between the parties, even the expressed intent that it should not be so classed would be of no avail. It is the intent to do the things which constitute a partnership that usually determines whether or not that relation exists between the parties."

. . . Considering the terms of the agreement here involved and the conduct and activities of the parties thereto in carrying on the business, the conclusion is impelled that a partnership existed. The agreement discloses an association for the purpose of carrying on a business and dividing the profits. And the agreement for division of profits implies an agreement also to bear the losses.

Judgment for plaintiffs, building materials dealers, affirmed.

BROWN & BIGELOW v. ROY

1955, (Ohio App.) 132 N.E.2d 755

MILLER, J. This is a law appeal from the judgment of the Municipal Court rendered in favor of the plaintiff-appellee for the sum of $413.66 and interest and costs. The action was one on an account for goods and merchandise sold and delivered to the F. & M. Truck Stop, an alleged partnership consisting of Clarence F. Roy, the appellant, and H. Fay Lucas, who was not a party to the action.

The answer was a general denial. Upon request being made the court filed separate findings and conclusions of law and fact. Those pertinent to the issues presented are:

(1) The merchandise was "purchased by the partnership, and sold to it."

(2) That the defendant-appellant "held himself out or permitted himself to be held out as a partner in the F. & M. Truck Stop."

(3) That the defendant-appellant is estopped from denying such partnership; and

(4) That no notice or publication pertaining to termination or dissolution of said partnership was made by the defendant.

All of the errors assigned relate to the sufficiency of the evidence to sustain the judgment, the appellant urging that his motion to dismiss at the close of plaintiff's case and again at the conclusion of all of the evidence, should have been sustained.

No direct proof of a partnership was offered, but the same was based upon the conduct of the appellant at the place of business; that a sum of money was advanced by the appellant which he testified was a loan to the other alleged partner and upon the further fact that a vendor's license was secured from the State of Ohio in the name of "Henry F. Lucas and Clarence F. Roy, DBA F. & M. Truck Stop." The application for this license was signed by both of the alleged partners and the license issued in response thereto was posted at the place of business of the alleged partnership. It is urged that the evidence does not disclose that the appellee had any knowledge of the information contained in the license and therefore there could have been no reliance placed on the statements it contained; that the doctrine of estoppel has no application. We concur with counsel for the appellant upon his factual conclusion and are of the opinion that his views as to the law would be correct were it not for the fact that our statutory law modifies the common-law rule. Section 1775.15 of the Revised Code provides:

When a person, by words spoken or written or by conduct, represents himself, or consents to another representing him to any one, as a partner in an existing partnership or with one or more persons not actual partners, he is liable to any such person to whom such representation has been made, who has, on the faith of such representation, given credit to the actual or apparent partnership, and if he has made such representation or consented to its being made in a public manner he is liable to such person, whether the representation has or has not been made or communicated to such person so giving credit by or with the knowledge of the apparent partner making the representation or consenting to its being made.

Clearly the defendant represented that he was a partner in the business when he signed the application for a vendor's license and the posting of the license at the place of business was notice to the public of the nature of the business being conducted on the premises. The Court did not err in holding that the defendant was a partner.

Affirmed.

WEST SIDE TRUST COMPANY v. GASCOIGNE et al.

1956, 39 N.J. Super. 467, 121 A.2d 441

The plaintiff bank brought action to recover on promissory notes alleged to represent obligations of the defendants Gascoigne and Jackson, trading as partners under the name Jackson Contractors. The defendant Jackson denied the existence of a partnership at the time when the notes were executed. The evidence disclosed that a partnership had existed from 1946 to 1949 but that it had been dissolved in 1949. In 1952 when Gascoigne applied for a loan from the bank he filled out a financial statement listing Jackson as a "special partner." Jackson testified that in 1952 Gascoigne by a subterfuge obtained his signature to an account card at the bank and on a trade name certificate as a partner of Jackson Contractors. The new certificate was filed by Gascoigne and a copy of it was given to the bank. The lower court ruled that Jackson was liable by virtue of the filing of the trade name certificate bearing Jackson's signature. Jackson appealed.

FRANCIS, J. A. D. . . . N.J.S.A. 42:1–16 (Uniform Partnership Law, 7 U.A.L. § 16, at 94) provides:

> 1. When a person, by words spoken or written or by conduct, represents himself, or consents to another representing him to anyone, as a partner in an existing partnership . . . he is liable to any such person to whom such representation has been made, who has, on the faith of such representation, given credit to the actual or apparent partnership, and if he has made such representation or consented to its being made in a public manner he is liable to such person, whether the representation has or has not been made or communicated to such person so giving credit by or with the knowledge of the apparent partner making the representation or consenting to its being made.

. . . Clearly the filing of the business name certificate under N.J.S.A. 56:1–1 constituted a representation of partnership "in a public manner." But § 16 of the act quoted does not create a conclusive estoppel in every situation and under all circumstances. If the person who extends credit knows, in spite of the representation, that there is in fact no partnership, or if he is made aware of facts which call for inquiry as to the verity of the representation and he fails to make a reasonably diligent investigation, the bar of the statute ought not to be applied.

. . . Was there a duty on the bank here to inquire into Jackson's relationship with Gascoigne? The trial court's opinion advances the view that the duly executed and filed trade name certificate conclusively negatived such obligation. We cannot agree.

On July 23, somewhat over five months prior to one of the notes in dispute and eight months prior to the other, the bank had notice in response to a specific question on the subject, that Jackson was a "special" partner and that the partnership agreement was a verbal one. Yet it ignored the requirement on its own form for a statement of the extent to which the special partner was responsible for partnership debts and for the signatures of all partners. No information was sought even from Gascoigne as to the nature of Jackson's interest.

Insistence on Jackson's signature would have revealed the true state of affairs. A telephone call or a letter would have produced his disclaimer or a consent to the transactions. The disregard of plaintiff's own rule for signatures of all partners cannot be ignored.

In our judgment the facts brought to the attention of the plaintiff called for reasonable inquiry as to Jackson's association with Gascoigne, and the burden of doing so was not removed as a matter of law because of the subsequent signing by Jackson at Gascoigne's behest of the bank account card of Jackson Contractors or the trade name certificate.

. . . Under the circumstances, we feel that it is for the jury to say whether the duty to make reasonable inquiry was eliminated by the presentation of the signature card and trade name certificate.

The judgment is reversed and the matter is remanded for trial.

OLIVE et al. v. TURNER
1954, 120 F. Supp. 478

The plaintiffs leased land to the defendant under an agreement whereby the defendant agreed to farm the land and share equally with the plaintiffs in everything raised on the farm. The plaintiffs also agreed to share expenses with the defendant. The plaintiffs contend that the agreement shows an intent to establish a partnership between the parties and not merely an agricultural lease. They are asking for a partnership accounting.

WALLACE, District Judge. . . . Although in the abstract theory of the law it is comparatively easy to define the component parts of a general partnership, often it is very difficult to apply the facts of an individual case to the applicable law; this is particularly true where, as here, the alleged partners are litigating between themselves, as distinguished from where a third party asserts that a partnership exists.

The general test applicable in the instant case is found in *Municipal Paving Company v. Herring*, 1915, 50 Okla. 470, 150 P. 1067, 1069:

> . . . No definite rule has ever yet been laid down which can be said to be a conclusive test as to whether or not a partnership exists *inter sese* from a given state of facts, but there must be, to constitute the same: (a) An intent on the part of the alleged partners to form a partnership; (b) there must be a participation generally in both profits and losses; (c) there must be such a community of interests as enables each party to make contracts, manage the business, and dispose of the whole property.

. . . A mere community of interest as owners of specific personal property, or the sharing of profits of a particular venture or business does not, in and of itself, constitute a partnership and such community of interest and income sharing is all that the plaintiffs have convincingly established by the adduced evidence; there is no showing that as between the parties there was ever any intent to enter into a general partnership agreement. The absence of such an intent is most strongly implied from the fact that nowhere in the record is there evidence that all parties to this agreement were understood to have joint authority or right in the administration and control of the property in which the community of interest lay, thus making all parties co-principals and agents for the other parties to the agreement. Naturally, where the litigation is between the parties themselves the actual intent must be controlling and ordinarily in such case a partnership should not be ruled to exist by implication or operation of law. . . . Although there is some fragmentary evidence which patently tends to prove that the defendant has by his own admissions and actions recognized the existence of a partnership the weight of the evidence is clearly against such a finding; the isolated items of evidence urged by the plaintiffs are not sufficiently persuasive to alter the impact of the evidence in its entirety. At most the word "partnership" which was used by the defendant for the first time several years after the contract in question came into existence, was employed to identify and distinguish this venture's personalty from property individually owned; the word was in nowise used with its legal connotation and cannot be relied upon to overrule the clear effect of all the evidence.

Inasmuch as the plaintiffs have failed to prove the existence of a general partnership they are not entitled to an equal voice in the management of the business venture in question and of course are not entitled to a decree of dissolution.

The defendant is entitled to judgment.

TROY GRAIN & FUEL CO. v. ROLSTON et al.

1950, (Mo. App.) 227 S.W.2d 66

The plaintiff, Troy Grain & Fuel Co. brought this action against Miller Howard and Jackson Rolston, as partners, for the unpaid balance due for corn and oats delivered. Howard owned two trucks and it was agreed that he would furnish the trucks and Rolston the labor in hauling grain. The profits from the operation were to be divided equally. A judgment was rendered in favor of the plaintiff and defendant Howard appealed.

SPERRY, Commissioner. . . . Howard stated that he and Rolston verbally agreed that Rolston should furnish the labor and use his trucks in hauling grain; that Rolston should keep books on the transactions, pay all expense of operation, and give Howard half of the profits as rent on the trucks; that Rolston kept books and delivered same to him, which he then had in court (but they were not offered in evidence); that Rolston kept the bank account in his own name and wrote all checks thereon; that they operated under this arrangement until shortly after these transactions occurred. He denied the existence of a partnership or that he was to bear any losses occurring in the operation.

The evidence made a submissible case on the question of partnership between Howard and Rolston. Partnership is a relation arising out of contract expressed or implied whereby two or more parties agree to engage in a common enterprise, each contributing capital or services and each sharing in the profits and losses. 47 C.J. 648 *et seq*. In the absence of proof of an express contract a partnership may be proved by evidence of the entire transaction, and construed from that, in the light of surrounding circumstances. *Willoughby v. Hildreth,* 182 Mo. App. 80, 91, 167 S.W. 639. The testimony of both Howard and Rolston was to the effect that they agreed that Howard should furnish his trucks, Rolston furnish the labor, and that Rolston should buy, transport, and sell grain, the profits thereof to be equally divided after payment of expenses. Sharing the profits of a business venture, where one furnishes capital and the other labor, constitutes prima facie evidence of the existence of a partnership. *Willoughby v. Hildreth, supra,* 182 Mo. App. *loc. cit.* 91, 167 S.W. 639. While an agreement to share profits in such a venture is not conclusive proof of the existence of a partnership, it is prima facie proof thereof and raises a presumption of partnership. If such presumption is not overcome by other evidence tending to prove that, in fact, the parties intended there to be no partnership, such prima facie proof of the existence of a partnership becomes conclusive. It is true that there was no direct proof that the partners were to share the losses accruing in the venture, nevertheless their agreement to share profits implies a sharing of loss; and that presumption can only be overcome by evidence tending to prove the contrary. While a partnership relationship necessarily rests on contract, as between the parties themselves, the contracting parties are not required to know and fully understand all of the legal incidents flowing therefrom. Parties "entering into agreements and transactions which, by the law of the land constitute them partners, whatever they may please to say or think about it, or by whatever name they may choose to call it," will be held to be partners. *Meyers v. Field,* 37 Mo. 434, 439. We hold that there was substantial evidence tending to prove that Howard and Rolston were partners; and the determination of that question was for the jury.

. . . *The judgment should be affirmed.*

Review Questions and Problems

1. Securities were loaned to a stock brokerage partnership comprised of *A, B,* and *C,* for use as collateral. The lenders were to receive 40 per cent of the profits of the firm in return for the loan. The lenders retained the right to veto business ventures of the partnership. Were the lenders partners with *A, B,* and *C*?
2. *A* and *B* as partners rented a cannery for one season. They entered into a contract with *P*, a broker, whereby it was agreed to label all products with *P*'s label, to allow *P* the exclusive right to sell their entire output and to pay him 5 per cent of gross sales. *P* guaranteed the cannery a supply of cans and other material and promised to ad-

vance money for operating expenses and payroll. For this advance *P* was to receive as "extra compensation" one half of the net profits of the cannery for the season. *P* had the right to control wages and payroll for the cannery. Is *P* a partner?

3. *A*, an infant, and *B*, an adult, formed a partnership. Has *A* the right to disaffirm? Has *B* the right to disaffirm? Can *A* recover his contribution? If both *A* and *B* were infants could they form a valid partnership?
4. *A* is hired to operate a store owned by *P*. It is agreed that *A* shall receive for his services one third of the net profits. No profits result, but losses are incurred. Must *A* share in these losses? Is he a partner?
5. *M* wished to purchase a tract of land, plat it, and sell the lots. He needed capital, and *P* loaned him $6,000. *M* gave *P* a note and it was understood that when the lots were sold the proceeds would first be used to pay the $6,000 to *P*. Any profits above the $6,000 would be divided equally. Was there a partnership?
6. *P* and *D* entered into an agreement for trading in grain futures. *P* furnished the funds for margin requirements and profits and losses were to be shared. No partnership income tax return was ever filed. The authorization for *D* to trade on *P*'s account with the brokerage company referred to *D* as *P*'s "agent." Do these last two facts prevent a holding that a partnership existed?
7. *A* and *B* are co-owners of a large office building. Does this ownership indicate a partnership? How do the rights of partners differ from those of tenants in common of property?
8. *A* leased a theater building to *B*. It was agreed that the gross receipts from *B*'s play which was performed in the building would be apportioned 40 per cent to *A* and 60 per cent to *B*. Are *A* and *B* partners? Would they be partners if the division were 50 per cent to each?
9. *A*, a grain broker, and *B*, his brother, a farmer, entered into an agreement whereby each was to pay to the other annually for three years one half of the profits of his business, and also to make good one half of the losses that might be suffered by the other. The ownership of each individual business was to be distinct. *B* became bankrupt. To what extent, if any, could *A* be made to satisfy the claims of *B*'s creditors?
10. *A* agreed to loan money to *P* and to indorse notes for him in order that *P* might operate a lumber mill. For this consideration, *A* was to receive one third of the profits. Was there a partnership?
11. The crew of a fishing vessel were to receive shares of the profits of the voyage. A member of the crew was injured during the voyage. Could he bring a tort action against the owners of the fishing boat?

29

Partnership Property

5-6. What constitutes partnership property. What constitutes partnership property is determined by the agreement between the partners. In absence of an express agreement, what constitutes partnership property is ascertained from the conduct of the parties and from the purpose for and the way in which property is used in the pursuit of the business. The mere use of property by a partnership is not sufficient to justify a conclusion that it is partnership property.[1] Such property may be owned by a third person or by the partners individually, the partnership possessing only the right to use the property. The partners may own, as tenants in common, joint tenants, or tenants by the entireties, real estate used in the firm business, yet such property may not be firm assets. There are several situations in which it is important to determine whether a particular item of property is partnership property or is, rather, the separate property of the partners. As will be noted in Section 5–45, this question is significant in determining how property is to be apportioned among creditors of the firm as distinguished from separate creditors of the individual partners.

The Uniform Partnership Act in general terms states: (1) All property originally brought into the partnership stock, or subsequently acquired by purchase or otherwise on account of the partnership, is partnership property. (2) Unless the contrary intention appears, property acquired with partnership funds is partnership property.

5-7. Firm name and good will as firm property. In the absence of statutory requirements a partnership may carry on its business under any name the partners choose to use. In some states, by statute, restrictions are placed upon the adoption of a firm name in that the firm must not, by the use of the words "and Company," lead the public to believe that it is a corporation; but such words may be used if they represent an actual partner or partners. In some states, partners doing business under a fictitious or an assumed name must file a certificate with the county clerk setting forth the name under which the business is to be conducted and the true and real names of the parties conducting the business. Failure to comply with this statute does not make contracts with third parties void,

[1] Sanderfur v. Ganter, page 696.

but a partnership that has not registered its name cannot sue on such contracts.

A firm is a collection of individuals, and the partnership name is used primarily in identifying the group. A firm name is an asset of the firm, and as such will be protected by law. It may also be sold, assigned, or disposed of in any way that the parties agree upon.[2]

Good will is based upon the justifiable expectation of the continued patronage of old customers and the probable patronage of new customers resulting from good reputation, satisfied customers, established location, and past advertising. It must be considered in evaluation of the assets of the business, and is capable of being sold and transferred. Upon dissolution caused by the death of one of the partners, it must be accounted for by the surviving partner to the legal representatives of the deceased partner.

The purchaser of the good will of a business, in the absence of an agreement to the contrary, secures the right to advertise to the public generally that he is a successor of the old firm and is carrying on its business. For example, he may advertise "Brown and Smith, successors of Smith, Watson and Company." In some jurisdictions the purchaser of the good will does not acquire the name of the business, and the use of the name may be enjoined if injury is caused thereby.

In the absence of an agreement, the vendor of the good will may establish a new business of like character in the same locality, but he cannot advertise that he is carrying on the old business. In many jurisdictions he is under a duty to refrain from active solicitation of business from old customers.[3] This is particularly true where the dissolution sale is a voluntary one. Such business of the old firm as comes to him from general advertisements or ordinary business activity, he is free to accept. The vendor may not use his own name in the establishment of a new business, if, by doing so, the public is led to believe that he is continuing the old business.

5-8. Partnership capital. In the eyes of the law, partnership capital consists of the total credits to the capital accounts of the various partners, provided the credits are for permanent investments made in the business. Such capital represents that amount which the partnership is obligated to return only at the time of dissolution, and it can be varied only with the consent of all the partners. Undivided profits which are permitted by some of the partners to accumulate in the business do not become part of the capital. They, like temporary advances by firm members, are subject to withdrawal at any time.

The amount which each partner is to contribute to the firm, as well as

[2] O'Hara v. Lance et ux., page 697.
[3] Bergum v. Weber, page 699.

the credit he is to receive for assets contributed, is entirely dependent upon the partnership agreement. Even though a person makes no capital investment, it is still possible for him to be a partner. His services or standing in the community may, for income purposes, balance the capital investment of others. Such a partner, however, has no capital to be returned at the time of liquidation. Only those who receive credit for capital investments—which may include good will, patent rights, and so forth, if agreed upon—are entitled to the return of capital when dissolution occurs.

As suggested, investments may be made in forms other than money. In cases of this kind, as soon as the particular asset is contributed, it no longer belongs to the contributing partner. He has vested the firm with title and he has no greater equity in the property than any other party. At dissolution he recovers only the amount allowed to him for the property invested.

TITLE TO PARTNERSHIP PROPERTY

5-9. Personal property. For the purpose of conducting business the title to personal property may be contracted for, acquired, held, and transferred in the firm name. This is true even though the firm name is other than the names of the individuals within the firm. Such an artificial name is merely representative of the individuals making up the partnership entity. Legal documents such as bills of sale, chattel mortgages, warehouse receipts, and bills of lading used in the ordinary course of business involving personal property may be effectively executed in the firm name by any partner acting as an agent of the firm.

5-10. Real property. A partnership, for many purposes heretofore discussed, is a distinct entity, separate from its members. This is particularly true with reference to the title to personal property, to taxing statutes, and to some extent to bankruptcy law.

The extent to which a partnership is to be treated as a legal person or entity has been the subject of much discussion.[4] Some courts have stated that a partnership is a legal person and others have stated that it is not. The general mercantile conception is that a partnership is a legal entity distinct from and independent of the persons composing it. The courts appear to be favoring this concept.

The Uniform Partnership Act recognizes such entity for the purpose of taking, holding, and conveying title to real property in the partnership name. Title so acquired can be conveyed in the partnership name; and a conveyance to a partnership in the partnership name, though without words of inheritance, passes the entire estate of the grantor, unless a con-

[4] Eule v. Eule Motor Sales, page 700.

trary intent appears. Where title to real property is in the partnership name, any partner may convey title to such property by a conveyance executed in the partnership name. To be effective such a conveyance must be within the terms of the partnership agreement or within the pursuit of the partnership business.

In those jurisdictions still controlled by the common law and which have not adopted the Uniform Partnership Act or do not recognize the entity idea, the method of taking title to real property rests upon a different footing. The common law requires that the title to real property rest in a person, either natural or artificial. A partnership as such, therefore, at common law, cannot hold title to real estate in its own name. In these states, a deed containing the name of a partnership as a grantee is a nullity for want of a person to receive legal title. If the grantee in the deed includes the names of all the partners in the firm, the legal title rests in the individual partners as tenants in common. If the firm name used as grantee includes the name of one of the partners, the whole legal title vests in him, as trustee, for the benefit of the firm. The same is true where title is expressly taken in the name of one of the partners for the benefit of the partnership.

PROPERTY RIGHTS OF A PARTNER

5-11. Partner's rights in specific partnership property. The Uniform Partnership Act enumerates the property rights of a partner as, (1) his rights in specific partnership property, (2) his interest in the partnership. A partner is a co-owner with his partners of specific partnership property and subject to any agreement between the partners, a partner has an equal right among his partners to possess partnership property for partnership purposes. He has no right to possess specific partnership property for other purposes without the consent of the other partners. A partner has a right that the property shall be used in the pursuit of the partnership business and to pay firm creditors. A partner does not own any particular part of the partnership property. He, therefore, has no right in specific partnership property that is assignable, and any sale by him, as an individual, of a particular part of the partnership property does not pass title to the specific property. He has no right to use firm property in satisfaction of his personal debts[5] and he has no interest in specific partnership property that can be levied upon by his personal creditors.[6] For example, *A, B,* and *C* are partners and the firm owns three trucks of about equal value. *A* does not own one of the three trucks, nor does he

[5] Windom National Bank et al. v. Klein et al., page 702.
[6] R. A. Myles & Co. v. A. D. Davis Packing Co., page 703.

own one third of the three trucks. He has no power to sell any of the trucks except in the pursuit of the partnership business, and a personal creditor of *A* could not, after obtaining a judgment against him, levy upon and sell any of the trucks. The trucks are owned by the firm and are to be used in its business or in the satisfaction of firm obligations.

When a partner dies his right in specific partnership property passes to the surviving partner or partners who possess the property only for partnership purposes. The surviving partner may sell the property, real and personal, of the partnership in connection with the winding-up of the business.

5-12. Partner's interest in the partnership. As noted above, the Uniform Partnership Act draws a distinction between a partner's rights in specific partnership property and a partner's interest in the partnership. A partner's interest in the firm consists of his rights to share in the profits which are earned and, after dissolution and liquidation, to the return of his capital and such profits as have not been distributed previously. This assumes, of course, that his capital has not been absorbed or impaired by losses.

The Uniform Partnership Act provides that a partner can assign his interest in the partnership and that such an assignment will not of itself work a dissolution of the firm. The assignee is not entitled to interfere in the management of the business or to require that the books of the firm be made available for his inspection. The only right of the assignee is to receive the profits to which the assignor would otherwise have been entitled and in the event of dissolution to receive his assignor's interest. The right of a partner to assign his interest also existed at common law but the effects thereof were not as clearly defined.

At common law a partner's interest could be levied upon by his separate creditors and sold at public sale. Under the Uniform Act a separate creditor of a partner is provided a remedy by way of a charging order.

The Act provides that a judgment creditor of a partner may apply to the court for an order charging the interest of the debtor partner with the unsatisfied amount of the judgment debt. The court will ordinarily appoint a receiver who will receive the partner's share of the profits and any other money due or to fall due to him in respect of the partnership. Likewise, the court may order that the interest charged be sold. Neither the charging order nor the sale of the interest will cause a dissolution of the firm.

5-13. Partnership insurance. A partner has an insurable interest in partnership property and may carry insurance to secure him personally against loss. Similarly, the firm may carry insurance against various hazards, and in the latter case the proceeds are payable to the firm.

Where life insurance is carried on a member of a firm, numerous problems develop. If the surviving partner is the beneficiary, does he keep the proceeds or hold them in trust for the firm; if payable to the firm, must they be used to purchase the interest of the deceased partner; and, if so, must the estate of the deceasd partner accept the proceeds of the insurance in full payment of the deceased partner's interest? Since the answers to these questions are not clear, the partnership agreement should cover all questionable matters relating to partnership life insurance. If insurance is carried upon the life of a partner and the premium is paid by the firm, it would seem that the proceeds should belong to the business, even though the named beneficiary is the surviving partner, although there are cases to the contrary. If the premiums are paid by a partner for a policy upon the life of another partner, it follows that the partner paying the premiums should be entitled to the proceeds of the policy. If the partnership is the beneficiary, the surviving partner is not obligated to use the insurance for acquiring the interest of the deceased partner. Provision for such procedure should be made in the partnership contract or in the policy of insurance, preferably in the former. If the survivor is to use the funds to purchase the interest of the deceased partner, he must pay the full value of the interest, unless some contract establishes the amount which will be paid to the estate of the deceased.

The basic question is whether or not the proceeds of the policy were intended to be firm property. Where the premiums are paid by the firm and the firm is designated as the beneficiary, the intent that the proceeds should belong to the firm is quite apparent.[7] Likewise, where the wife of a partner was named as beneficiary, it was held that the proceeds were not firm assets even though the premiums had originally been paid out of partnership funds.[8]

POWERS WITH RESPECT TO PROPERTY

5-14. Power to sell personal property. Each partner has implied authority to sell to good-faith purchasers personal property that is held for the purpose of resale and to execute such documents as are necessary to effect a transfer of title thereof. Of course, if his authority in this connection has been limited and such fact is known to the purchaser, the transfer of title will be ineffective or voidable. A partner has no power to sell the fixtures and equipment used in the business unless he has been duly authorized. Such acts are not a regular feature of the business and a prospective purchaser of such property should make certain that the particular partner has been given authority to sell. The power to sell,

[7] Block v. Mylish et al., page 638.
[8] Price v. McFee, page 640.

where it is present, gives also the power to make such warranties as normally accompany similar sales.

5-15. Power to sell realty—wrongful conveyance. As said in a previous section, the right to sell firm real property is to be inferred only if the firm is engaged in the real estate business. In other cases, there is no right to sell and convey realty, except where such sale has been authorized by a partnership agreement.

Under the Uniform Partnership Act, title may be taken in the firm name, and any member of the firm has power to execute a deed thereto by signing the firm name. In such a case, what is the effect of a wrongful transfer or real estate that has been acquired for use in the business and not for resale? The conveyance may be set aside by the other partners since the purchaser should have known that one partner has no power to sell without the approval of the others. However, if the first purchaser has resold and conveyed the property to an innocent third party, the latter takes good title.

If the title to firm property is not held in the firm name, but is held in the names of one or more of the partners, a conveyance by those in whose names the title is held passes good title, unless the purchaser knows or should know that title was held for the firm. There is nothing in the record title in such a situation to call the buyer's attention to the fact that the firm has an interest in the property.

5-16. Power to pledge or mortgage firm property. The power to mortgage or pledge firm property is primarily dependent upon the power, later discussed, to borrow money and bind the firm. A partner with authority to borrow may, as an incident to that power, give the security normally demanded for similar loans. Since no one partner, without the consent of the others, has the power to commit an act that will destroy or terminate the business, the power to give a mortgage on the entire stock of merchandise and fixtures of a business is usually denied. Such a mortgage would make it possible, upon default, to liquidate the firm's assets and thus destroy its business. Subject to this limitation, the power to borrow carries the power to pledge or mortgage.

PARTNERSHIP PROPERTY CASES

SANDERFUR v. GANTER

1953, (Ky. Ct. App.), 259 S.W.2d 15

The plaintiff, Dr. Fred Ganter, is seeking to recover possession of office space from the defendant Dr. B. D. Sanderfur. Plaintiff's father had secured a 10 year lease on the space for the practice of optometry. Plaintiff was called into military service and during his absence the father entered into a partnership agreement with the defendant which gave the latter an option to purchase an interest in the office equipment, but which did not mention the lease or the office space. The office space was actually used for partnership purposes. Plaintiff's father died and the executrix assigned all interests in the lease to the plaintiff. The defendant continued in possession claiming under the right of a surviving partner. The trial court ruled in favor of the plaintiff and defendant appealed.

Cullen, C. This is an appeal by Dr. B. D. Sanderfur from a judgment which held that Dr. Fred Ganter is entitled to the exclusive possession of certain office space in a building in Glasgow, and which mandatorily enjoined Dr. Sanderfur to surrender possession of the office to Dr. Ganter.

. . . The only basis upon which Dr. Sanderfur claims to be entitled to occupy the offices is that the lease (or at least Dr. George Ganter's interest in the lease) was a partnership asset. The trial court found that it was not, so our concern is with the correctness of that finding.

. . . The question of whether property which was owned by a partner prior to the formation of the partnership has been contributed by him to the firm so as to become partnership property, is a question of the intention of the parties, and the mere fact that the property is used in the firm business will not of itself show that it is firm property. (Cases cited) As concerns real estate owned by a partner, it has been held that there is a presumption against its inclusion in the partnership, and in order that it be treated as belonging to the partnership, the intention must be clearly manifested. While a lease is technically not real estate, we think that the reasons behind the rule with respect to real estate may be equally as applicable to a lease.

We find nothing in the partnership agreement here, or in the conduct of the parties, to show that the lease was intended to be contributed by Dr. George Ganter to the partnership as an asset. The agreement shows clearly that Dr. Ganter was not contributing his equipment, and there is no reason to conclude that he intended to contribute or donate the lease, which, as evidenced by this lawsuit, was a valuable item of property.

It is our opinion that the trial court correctly found that the lease was not a partnership asset, and therefore Dr. Sanderfur has no basis for his claim of right to occupy the office.

O'HARA v. LANCE et ux.

1954, 77 Ariz. 84, 267 P.2d 725

The defendant, General W. Lance, established a business known as the Ace-Lance Refrigeration Company in Phoenix in 1942. In 1946 the defendant and the plaintiff entered into a partnership agreement and continued in the same business as "Ace-Lance & O'Hara Refrigeration Company." In 1949 the partnership was dissolved, Lance selling all partnership assets, including goodwill, to O'Hara. Lance agreed not to compete for a period of two years and granted to O'Hara the exclusive right to the firm name except for the condition that after December 21, 1950, O'Hara might not further use Lance's name without his consent. In 1951 the plaintiff sued to enjoin the defendant from competing and to restrain him from using the word "Ace" in the firm name of any refrigeration business in Arizona. The lower court denied this relief and held that the defendant alone had the right to use the word "Ace." The plaintiff appealed.

Tullar, J. . . . The first and primary step is to determine what was bought and sold at the time of the dissolution of the partnership. Happily, the agreement of the parties is explicit. Lance, "the retiring partner," is being paid, "for his share in the business and the capital, stock, equipment, effects and good will thereof." The agreement recites that valuations and estimates have been placed upon these items, and agreed to, specifically including the good will, and a balance has been struck.

In the law of partnership, it is the rule that, in the absence of agreement to the contrary, a sale of assets and good will of a commercial partnership carries with it the right to use the partnership name. (Cases cited.) We are not here dealing with a "professional" partnership (see, e.g., *Hunt v. Street*, 182 Tenn. 167, 184 S.W.2d 553), wherein the law is quite different.

A conveyance of the good will of a business carries with it an implied covenant to do nothing which would derogate from the grant. If the vendor of the good will re-engage in business, it is his duty to conduct his new business in such a way that it will not appear to be a continuation of the business that he has sold. The vendor has a duty not only to his vendee, but to the public, not to confuse or deceive the customer into thinking he is in one place of business when he is in another. This type of confusion and deceit is the keystone of unfair competition. And, we have previously pointed out, this is the universal test for the presence of unfair competition; Is the public likely to be deceived? (Cases cited.)

So in this case, when Lance included in his sale the good will of the business, he sold to O'Hara the right to the use of the firm name, Ace-Lance & O'Hara Refrigeration Company. And, as the agreement recites, this was "to hold the same unto O'Hara absolutely."

This does not necessarily mean, in law, that Lance has parted with the right henceforth to use his own personal name. Indeed, there is a presumption that no one intends to part with this right, and that an assignment of good will does not, ipso facto, confer upon the assignee the exclusive right to the use of assignor's personal name. While one may sell his own name as a trade name servient to the business to which it is attached, the intent so to divest oneself must clearly be shown.

Lance . . . sold to O'Hara the exclusive use of his personal name as a trade name in the refrigeration business, but only for a limited time. The time limit having expired, there is now no restraint upon Lance's use of his personal name for any lawful purpose he may desire, so long as he does not transgress his obligation not to interfere with O'Hara's right to receive the benefits of his purchase.

. . . Fact and law conclusively show O'Hara's right in and to the use of the word "Ace," in the refrigeration business in his trade area. Lance does not have the same right.

O'Hara has prayed for state-wide restraint. He is, however, entitled to protection only in the territory from which he received business or might reasonably be expected to receive business in the future. His protection should extend as far as his business reputation and his goods have become known.

The judgment of the trial court is reversed with directions to dissolve the restraining order and enter judgment in favor of plaintiff, Richard O'Hara and against the defendants, General W. Lance and Vera Lance, his wife, granting to plaintiff the right to use the name, "Ace," and granting to plaintiff an injunction restraining the defendants, General W. Lance and Vera Lance, his wife, or either of them, and all persons acting for them or under them, from using the name, "Ace," in any refrigeration business within the area served by the Phoenix metropolitan area telephone directory.

BERGUM v. WEBER

1955, 136 Cal. App.2d 389, 288 P.2d 623

Plaintiff, Bergum, bought the entire interest of defendant, his former partner, in the partnership including goodwill. The defendant thereafter solicited business from customers of the old partnership and the plaintiff sought to enjoin such solicitation. The trial court dismissed the action and plaintiff appealed.

NOURSE, Justice pro tem. . . . Did the defendant, by the contract alleged in the complaint, impliedly covenant not to directly solicit the customers of plaintiffs who had been customers of the business he had sold to them[?]

We have come to the conclusion that this question must be answered in the affirmative.

The goodwill of a business is property and may be transferred. The customers of a business are an essential part of its goodwill. In fact, without their continued custom goodwill ceases to exist, for goodwill is the expectation of continued public patronage.

When the goodwill of a business is sold, it is not the patronage of the general public which is sold, but that patronage which has become an asset of that business. It follows that one who has sold his interest in the goodwill of a business can no more act directly to destroy that asset than he could to destroy or make useless any other asset which he had for value transferred to the purchaser.

The law implies in every contract a covenant that neither party will do anything that will deprive the other of the fruits of his bargain.

The direct solicitation by the seller of the customers of the business, the goodwill of which he has sold, is a violation of this covenant.

This implied covenant does not prevent the seller from engaging in a competing business and by fair means soliciting the business of the public generally. It does prevent him from directly soliciting the patrons of the business he has sold.

Relief sought by plaintiff was granted.

EULE v. EULE MOTOR SALES
1960, (N.J.) 162 A.2d 601

Foley, J. A. D. . . . Plaintiff suffered personal injuries when a motor vehicle owned by Eule Motor Sales, a partnership, and operated by her husband Joseph Eule, collided with an automobile owned and operated by Russell A. Boertzel in Fairlawn, New Jersey. Joseph Eule was a general partner in Eule Motor Sales.

Plaintiff instituted this action against Eule Motor Sales and Boertzel; the partners, Joseph Eule and Arthur McKeever, were not joined as defendants. The answer filed in behalf of Eule Motor Sales denied that Joseph Eule was driving on the business of the patrnership at the time of the accident and alleged affirmatively that the husband and wife relationship precluded a recovery against the partnership. . . .

After the case had been pretried and discovery completed, Eule Motor Sales moved for summary judgment under R.R. 4:58. Both the nonagency and interspousal immunity defenses were argued in a memorandum which accompanied this motion. The motion was granted by the trial court "for the reasons set forth in the oral arguments and supported by the brief of said defendant." Plaintiff appealed. . . .

The basic attack upon the judgment, as it appears in plaintiff's brief, is that plaintiff should be permitted by "decisional law" to maintain an action against the partnership notwithstanding the fact that her husband was a member thereof . . .

The theme espoused by plaintiff is that since her action is against the partnership entity as distinguished from the individual members thereof, her right of action should be viewed as if the partnership were a corporation, in which case the action would be maintainable. Cf. 1 Fletcher, *Corporations,* § 33 (1931). This contention is founded on the premise that in a case such as this a partnership is regarded as a jural entity.

The philosophy of *Mazzuchelli v. Silberberg,* 29 N.J. 15, 148 A.2d 8 (1959) is otherwise. There the court, after an extensive review of authorities, concluded that for the purposes of the Workmen's Compensation Act a partnership may not be deemed a jural entity. Id., 29 N.J. at pp. 19–24, 140 A.2d 8. In so holding the court made reference to what might be interpreted as a contrary view expressed in *Felice v. Felice,* 34 N.J. Super. 388, 112 A.2d 581 (App. Div. 1955). In Felice the Appellate Division permitted a recovery on a workmen's compensation claim by an employee against a partnership, of which her husband was a member, upon the theory that in the purview of the Workmen's Compensation Law, having in mind the beneficent social intention of the Legislature, the employee-wife's contract of employment was with a jural entity and not with her husband individually. The Supreme Court in Mazzuchelli approved the result in Felice but said:

> We add that there is no conflict with the actual holding in *Felice v. Felice,* 34 N.J. Super. 388, 112 A.2d 581 (App. Div. 1955). * * * The result was a fair adjustment between a wife's ancient inability to sue her husband for tortious injury and the statutory policy that the consequences of industrial injury be deemed to be a business expense. The observations there made with respect to the relationship btween the partners and an employee were unnecessary for the decision. * * * 29 N.J., at p. 24, 148 A.2d at page 12.

We find that the rationale of Mazzuchelli applies to the case sub judice and accordingly hold that for the purposes of this action the partnership is not a jural entity.

This inevitably brings into focus the relationship between the husband's interest in the partnership and the statutory immunity from suit for tortious injuries brought by the wife. . . .

Since . . . maintenance of this action by the wife would in effect deprive the husband of the benefits of the interspousal immunity granted by R.S. 37:2–5, N.J. S.A. we hold that for the purposes of conforming with the public policy implicit in the statute the husband must be regarded as a "litigant" and a real party in interest, and consequently that the action falls within the interdiction of the statute.

Lastly, plaintiff argues that, independent of the issue of interspousal immunity, a factual question was presented as to whether Joseph Eule was on the business of the Eule Motor Sales at the time of the accident.

In view of our determination of the partnership's nonliability the agency of its driver is a moot question.

Affirmed.

WINDOM NATIONAL BANK et al. v. KLEIN et al.

1934, 191 Minn. 447, 254 N.W. 602

Four brothers owned and operated as partners a dairy farm under the firm name of Bender Bros. The plaintiff bank had an unsatisfied personal judgment against two of the brothers and in conformity with the provisions of the Uniform Partnership Act had a receiver appointed over all the right and interest of the two brothers in the partnership. The court also gave an order charging *their interest* in the firm with payment of the judgment debt. The two brothers had mortgaged certain specific partnership property to the defendants, Klein and others, and this action by the bank was for the purpose of annulling these mortgages. The defendants demurred and the lower court sustained the demurrer. Plaintiffs appealed.

Stone, J. . . . The tenancy in partnership created by the statute is an innovation on the common law. Its genesis was in the "inequitable results" of the long established judicial habit of applying to partnership property the analogies of joint tenancy. Some of them (particularly a joint tenant's unrestrained power of disposition) did not fit. The result was "very great confusion" where separate creditors of a partner tried to reach specific partnership property or where a partner attempted to dispose of it for his own purposes. "Commissioners' Note," 7 U.L.A. 33. Thus it appears that tenancy in partnership is a restricted adaptation of common-law joint tenancy to the practical needs of the partnership relation. One of those needs arose from the formerly conflicting claims to specific partnership property of (1) separate creditors of a partner and (2) assignees of a partner's share in an aliquot part of the firm assets. To meet that need, two simple "incidents" have been attached to the tenancy in partnership: (1) Expressly, the interest of each tenant or partner in specific partnership property is put beyond reach of his separate creditors; and (2) it has been made nonassignable. That means simply that the partner owner is deprived of all power of separate disposition even by will.

All a partner has now, subject to his power of individual disposition, and all that is subject to the claims of his separate creditors, is his interest, not in specific partnership property, but in the partnership itself. Plain is the purpose that all partnership property is to be kept intact for partnership purposes and creditors. The statutory incidents of the partnership cotenancy are attached thereto for that purpose, which will be pro tanto thwarted as effect is given to an attempted disposition of a partner's interest in specific partnership property. The aim of the statute is to prevent such an assignment.

. . . Dean William Draper Lewis, one of the commissioners who drafted the Uniform Partnership Act, has said, in explanation of its purpose to "avoid the consequences of regarding partners as joint tenants" that "while any partner has an equal right with his copartners to possess partnership property for partnership purposes" and while he "may assign partnership property for a partnership purpose, . . . if he attempts to assign the property for his own purposes he makes no assignment at all, because the act destroys the quality of assignability for any but a partnership purpose."

. . . It follows that a receiver, such as plaintiff Gillam, of a partner's "share of the profits," acting under a charging order and § 28 (Mason's Minn. St. 1927, § 7411), has the right in a proper action to have adjudicated the nullity of any mortgage or other assignment by some but not all of the partners of their interest in specific property of the partnership less than the whole. Such a receiver is entitled to any relief under the language of the statute "which the circumstances of the case may require" to accomplish justice under the law. Obviously, a part of such relief is the avoidance of any unauthorized attempt to dispose of partnership property. Such a receiver is entitled to the "share of profits and surplus" (§ 26, Mason's Minn. St. 1927, § 7409) of the partner who happens to be the judgment debtor. While he is not entitled to share in the management of the firm as a partner, the receiver would be of little use if he could not protect "profits and surplus" by preventing such unauthorized and illegal dissipations of firm assets as the complaint alleges in this case.

The complaint states a cause of action. It was error to sustain the demurrer.

The order sustaining the demurrer was reversed because the partners could not lawfully mortgage partnership property to secure personal indebtedness.

R. A. MYLES & CO. v. A. D. DAVIS PACKING CO.

1919, 17 Ala. App. 85, 81 So. 863

This is an action by Myles & Co., a partnership, to recover the value of ten cows that were owned by the partnership and were levied upon and sold by the defendant under a judgment against R. A. Myles personally. The plaintiff firm operated a meat market and R. A. Myles was one of three partners.

SAMFORD, J. . . . It is undoubtedly the law of this state that under a *fieri facias* against the goods of one member of a partnership his interest in the tangible assets of the partnership may be levied on and sold, but only such interest as he has; the right acquired by such purchase is the right of the partner whose interest was sold and only his right, subject to all the liens, encumbrances, or infirmities affecting it as assets of the partnership. It is not a separate and exclusive right to any part or portion of it, or any right of any kind to any one part rather than to any other part, or any other right or interest than was held by the execution debtor as a member of the partnership. The ownership of each partner is subject to the ownership of all the other partners, and all the partners together hold the property subject to the right of the partnership to apply all of its funds to the payment of the partnership debts. The real ownership of all the chattels is vested in the firm, and the interest of each partner is merely a right to share in the profits of the business during its continuance, or in a division of the property upon dissolution after all the partnership obligations have been satisfied. No one partner has a separate ownership of or right to possess exclusively any part of the partnership assets, and a successor to his interest by purchase at an execution sale can acquire no greater interest than he has. . . .

And while the interest of a partner in the partnership may be levied upon and sold, if the sheriff, in total disregard and denial of the rights of the partnership, levies upon and sells the partnership property as the property of one of the individual partners under an execution against such member, the sheriff is a trespasser as to the partnership, and his act is a conversion of the partnership property. . . . And the partnership can maintain an action against him to recover the damages resulting from such conversion. . . .

Such sale being illegal and rendering the officer a trespasser *ab initio*, the action may properly be brought in the names of the partners, and they will be entitled to recover the full value of the goods sold.

Judgment for the plaintiff.

BLOCK v. MYLISH et al.

1945, 351 Pa. 611, 41 A.2d 731

The partnership composed of Mylish, Mann, and Drucker took out separate policies of insurance on the lives of each partner in the amount of $60,000. The partnership was named beneficiary in all of the policies and paid the premiums thereon with partnership funds. The partnership agreement contained provisions giving the surviving partners an option to purchase a deceased partner's interest in the business. Mann died and the plaintiff, Block, is the executor of his estate. Mylish and Drucker exercised their option to purchase Mann's interest but a dispute arose among the interested parties with respect to the extent to which the value of the business should be affected on account of the policies of insurance on Mann's life. His executor maintained that the life insurance proceeds became an asset of the partnership contemporaneously with Mann's death and should, therefore, be reflected in toto in a valuation of the business, while Mylish and Drucker contended that only the cash surrender value of the policies on Mann's life was a partnership asset at the date of his death and that the proceeds of the insurance were available to them under the partnership agreement for their personal use in purchasing Mann's interest in the business. The court below decided the controversy in favor of the deceased partner's estate and entered judgment accordingly from which the surviving partners have appealed.

JONES, J. The matter in dispute is to be determined in accordance with the intent and purpose of the partnership agreement.

. . . The presently material portions of the partnership agreement are contained in par. 7 thereof and the three ensuing unnumbered paragraphs from which the following excerpts or summaries are taken:

In par. 7 it is provided that "In the event of the termination of the partnership by the death of any one of the partners, a complete inventory of the assets of the business shall be ascertained as soon after the death of said partner as possible, . . ." by appraisers to be selected as provided in the agreement.

The next succeeding paragraph provides that "From the gross assets of the business so ascertained, the liabilities shall be deducted which shall show the net worth of the business. The surviving partners shall have the right and are hereby granted the option of purchasing the deceased partner's interest in the partnership for the sum so arrived at as to his share (good-will not to be included).

. . . The next paragraph provides that "In the event that the proceeds of life insurance on the deceased partner's life shall be paid to the co-partnership and is free and clear, or is partially so, then in that event the entire proceeds, or such portion thereof as is free and clear of the said life insurance, shall be turned over and paid by said partnership on account of the purchase price and applied against the above payments insofar as it can be."

. . . the surviving partners would have the agreement interpreted so as to mean that the proceeds of the insurance on the life of a deceased partner were to be the property of the surviving partners in their individual and personal right and not the property of the partnership. Such a construction is not admissible under any fair interpretation of the written agreement.

That the insurance policies on the lives of the partners were assets of the business, and as such partnership property, is not open to reasonable dispute.

. . . The purpose and intent of the provision respecting the use to be made of the proceeds of the insurance is readily apparent.

. . . In short, to the extent of the insurance money received by the partnership upon the death of a partner, his representatives were to receive (on account of the purchase price for his interest in the business) cash instead of notes of the surviving partners. That is the clearly expressed meaning of the provision. It was not intended to advantage the surviving partners pecuniarily at the expense of their deceased associate.

. . . The fact is that the partnership policies on the lives of all of the partners had asset value—cash surrender while they lived—face value (less any encumbrances) as to any of them who died. Consequently, at the instant of Mann's death, the life insurance assets on the books of the partnership would properly show the net proceeds payable on the matured policies on Mann's life and the cash surrender value of the policies on Mylish and Drucker.

The judgment is affirmed.

PRICE v. McFEE

1950, 196 Md. 443, 77 A.2d 11

DELAPLAINE, J. The question on this appeal is whether the insurance of $15,000 paid to Gertrude A. McFee as the beneficiary of a life insurance policy which had been held by her husband, Robert A. McFee, now deceased, is an asset of a partnership which consisted of Thomas J. Price and her husband and traded as Atlas Wiping Cloth Company and T. J. Price and Company.

. . . Mrs. McFee upon qualifying as administratrix of her husband's estate, asked Price for her husband's share in the partnership assets. Price claimed that he was entitled to deduct $15,000, the amount of the insurance which the Equitable Life Insurance Company had paid to Mrs. McFee as the beneficiary of her husband's policy. Mrs. McFee disputed that claim, and on March 25, 1949, Price and Mrs. McFee entered into a stipulation agreement admitting McFee's interest in the partnership assets to be $28,558.43, and providing that if it should be determined that Mrs. McFee is entitled to the additional sum of $15,000, Price would pay her that amount and interest thereon at 6 per cent from March 15, 1949. In accordance with the agreement, Price paid her $13,558.43 without prejudice to any right she might have to collect the additional sum of $15,000.

Mrs. McFee, as administratrix, entered this suit in the Court of Common Pleas to recover from Price the sum of $15,000 which she claimed was the balance due on account of her husband's interest in the partnership. The Court, sitting without a jury, found that the insurance policy was not an asset of the partnership, and accordingly entered a judgment in favor of Mrs. McFee for $15,849.60, this amount being the balance withheld by Price plus interest from March 15, 1949. From that judgment Price took this appeal.

Defendant relied chiefly upon the fact that the premiums were paid prior to 1946 out of the partnership account. It is undeniable that the use of partnership funds for the purchase of property is strong evidence tending to show that the partners considered the property as belonging to the partnership. But that fact alone is by no means conclusive. The Uniform Partnership Act, which has been in effect in this State since 1916, provides (1) that all property originally brought into the partnership stock or subsequently acquired, by purchaser or otherwise, on account of the partnership is partnership property; and (2) that unless the contrary intention appears, property acquired with partnership funds is partnership property. Laws of 1916, ch. 175, Code 1939, art. 73A, § 8. The criterion for determining whether property held in the name of one partner is to be considered as partnership property is the intention of the partners to devote it to partnership purposes at the time the property was acquired, as shown by the facts and circumstances surrounding the transaction of purchase considered in connection with the conduct of the parties toward the property after the purchase. Thus the United States Circuit Court of Appeals held in *Hays v. Harris*, 8 Cir., 78 F.2d 66, 70, that insurance on the life of a partner was not intended to be partnership property notwithstanding that the partnership was named as the beneficiary of the policy and the premiums were paid for a certain period of time out of the partnership fund and later charged against the accounts of the several partners. In the opinion in that case the Court took occasion to explain that the life insurance "was never included as a partnership asset in any financial report made by the company."

First, it is undeniable that neither Price nor McFee took out life insurance in pursuance of any written agreement.

. . . Secondly, the firm's accountant testified that he had never received any instructions as to how to charge the premiums on the books. It is true that the premiums were paid out of the partnership account prior to 1946, but that was admittedly done by the accountant on his own initiative; and after the agent of the Internal Revenue Bureau notified him that the premiums could not be charged to the partnership for tax purposes, Price and McFee, without comment, immediately ordered that the premiums be charged to their individual accounts.

Thirdly, no entries were ever made on the books of the firm to show that any life insurance policies were carried as assets of the partnership under the first, second or third agreements. The accountant testified that the cash surrender value of the insurance policies was never carried as an asset on the books of the partnership "during all the period of the years that the premiums were paid."

Fourthly, the fact that the insurance policy was not kept among the partnership assets, but was kept in McFee's home on Enfield Road, is still another significant fact showing the intention of the parties.

As the evidence sustained the conclusion that Price and McFee intended their life insurance policies to belong to them individually and not to be assets of the partnership, we will affirm the judgment entered in favor of plaintiff.

Judgment affirmed, with costs.

Review Questions and Problems

1. *A* owned a flour mill. Later he and *B* formed a partnership for the manufacture of flour, and the mill was used in the business. No rent was paid to *A* for the use of the mill, but all repairs were paid for by the firm. In a dispute between firm and individual creditors the question arises as to whether the property is firm or individual property. What is your opinion?
2. *A* and *B* formed a partnership, and *A* contributed an unpatented invention. He later took out the patent in his own name. To whom does the patent belong upon dissolution?
3. *A* invests $10,000 and *B* $5,000 in a certain business for profit. With the investment they purchase 15 pianos. What is the interest of each one in the pianos?
4. *A* and *B* were equal partners in the transfer and drayage business. They owned six trucks with which they conducted their business. *C*, a creditor of *A*, levied on three of the trucks and had them sold to *H*. Did *H* obtain good title to the trucks?
5. *A* and *B* are partners. *A* dies, and *B* continues the business in his own name. In accounting for the firm assets, he refuses to make any allowance for good will. May the executrix of *A* recover an additional sum for the good will of the business? Give a definition of good will.
6. *A*, *B*, and *C* were partners doing business as the Arkansas Machinery and Supply Co. They sold machinery to *X* and took back a chattel mortgage in the name of the partnership. *Y*, a creditor of *X*, took possession of the machinery and claimed that the chattel mortgage was invalid since a partnership cannot be a mortgagee. Who will prevail? Would the result be different if a real property mortgage were involved?
7. *A*, *B*, and *C* formed a partnership to purchase and develop a subdivision of suburban real estate. Title to some of the property was taken in the name of College Crest Realty Company, other portions of the realty were taken in the name of *A*, *B*, and *C* jointly, and some in *C*'s name. In each of the above situations what will be necessary to convey proper legal title to a purchaser?
8. A partner assigned his interest in the partnership to *X* as collateral security. The partner continued to be active in the partnership affairs. What are the rights of the assignee, *X*?

9. *A* and *B* are partners. *A* without authority sold firm real property to *C* and executed a deed in the partnership name. Can *B* set aside the conveyance? If *C* had conveyed to *D*, an innocent purchaser, could *B* set aside the conveyance to *D*?
10. In order to procure loans for carrying on their partnership, *A* and *B* took out life insurance on their respective lives. Partnership funds were used to pay the premiums. The partners told the insurance man that they wished to name the firm as beneficiary. He said that this would not be possible and they accordingly named their respective estates as beneficiaries. *A* died. How should the proceeds of the policy on *A*'s life be distributed?
11. *A* owned a tract of land upon which was a sawmill that *A* had operated for several years. *A* and *B* then formed a partnership to operate the mill and subsequently acquired a matching machine and planing machine of standard design. These were placed upon the land in a shed built to protect them from the weather. May *A* transfer the land to *X*? If so, is *X* also entitled to the machines?
12. *C*. Jones and *H*. Jones owned land and buildings as tenants in common. They operated a business on these premises as partners. *C* died and in his will left his one-half share of the land and buildings to *F*. Jones. *H*. Jones and *F*. Jones continued to operate the business as partners. The partnership was dissolved on account of insolvency and creditors of the firm sought to reach the land and buildings as firm property. Should they be allowed to do so?
13. *A* purchased an automobile business from *B* and the latter agreed that he would not thereafter compete with *A*. Subsequently, *A* formed a partnership with *X*. Could the partnership enforce *B*'s covenant not to compete?
14. *A* and *B* were partners in the operation of a grocery business. They purchased shares of stock in a railroad corporation and the certificate was issued in the partnership name. Was the stock partnership property?

30

Rights and Duties of Partners Among Themselves

RELATIONS OF PARTNERS TO ONE ANOTHER

5-17. In general. The rights that a partner has as against his copartners, as well as his duties to them, may in a very large measure be defined by the partnership agreement. The amount of his investment, his right to interest thereon, and the share of the profits to be credited to him, along with his right to share in the management of the business or to receive compensation for such, are matters one might well expect to see controlled by the articles of copartnership. When the agreement is silent on these matters, the rules found in the following sections control.

5-18. Partner's rights to indemnity and repayment of contribution. The Uniform Partnership Act provides that in the absence of any specific agreement between the partners, their rights and duties shall be determined by the following rules:

Each partner shall be repaid his contributions, whether by way of capital or advances to the partnership property and share equally in the profits and surplus remaining after all liabilities, including those to partners, and satisfied; and must contribute towards the losses, whether of capital or otherwise, sustained by the partnership according to his share in the profits.

The partnership must indemnify every partner in respect of payments made and personal liabilities reasonably incurred by him in the ordinary and proper conduct of its business, or for the preservation of its business or property.

5-19. Sharing of profits and losses. Subject to an agreement among themselves, each partner has a right to share equally in the profits of the enterprise. In absence of a different agreement, each partner is under a duty to contribute equally to the losses. Capital contributed to the firm, in the absence of an agreement to the contrary, is a liability owing by the firm to the contributing partners. If, on dissolution, there are not sufficient assets to repay each partner his capital, such amount is considered as a loss and must be met like any other loss of the partnership. For example, a partnership is composed of *A*, *B*, and *C*. *A* contributed $20,000,

B contributed $10,000, and *C* contributed $4,000. The firm is dissolved, and upon the payment of firm debts there remains only $10,000 of firm assets. Since the total contribution to capital was $34,000, the operating loss is $24,000. This loss must be borne equally by *A*, *B*, and *C*, so that the loss for each is $8,000. This means that *A* is entitled to be reimbursed to the extent of his $20,000 contribution less $8,000, his share of the loss, or net of $12,000. *B* is entitled to $10,000, less $8,000, or $2,000. Since *C* has contributed only $4,000, he must now contribute to the firm an additional $4,000 in order that his loss will equal $8,000. The additional $4,000 contributed by *C*, plus the $10,000 remaining will now be distributed so that *A* will receive $12,000 and *B* $2,000.

Occasionally articles of copartnership specify the manner in which profits are to be divided, but neglect to mention possible losses. In such cases, the losses are borne in the same proportion that profits are to be shared. In the event that losses occur when one of the partners is insolvent and his share of the loss exceeds the amount owed him for advances and capital, the excess must be shared by the other partners. They share this unusual loss, with respect to each other, in the same ratio that they share profits.

Thus in the above example, if *C* is insolvent, *A* and *B* would each bear an additional $2,000 loss.

5-20. Partner's right to interest. Contributions to capital, in the absence of an agreement, are not entitled to draw interest. The partner's share in the profits constitutes the earnings upon his capital investment. In absence of an expressed provision for the payment of interest, it is presumed that interest will be paid only on advances above the amount originally contributed as capital. Advances in excess of the prescribed capital, even though credited to the capital account of the contributing partners, are entitled to draw interest.

The Uniform Partnership Act provides in § 18 that a partner who, in aid of the partnership, makes any payment or advance over the amount of capital that he agreed to contribute shall be paid interest from the date of the advance. A partner is entitled to interest on capital contributed by him only from the date when repayment should be made.

Unwithdrawn profits remaining in the firm are not entitled to draw interest. Such unwithdrawn profits are not considered advances or loans by the mere fact that they are left with the firm. However, custom, usage, and circumstances may show an intention to treat such unwithdrawn profits as loans to the firm.

5-21. Right to participate in management. In the absence of an agreement, all partners have equal rights in the management and conduct of the firm business. The partners may, however, by agreement, place the management within the control of one or more partners. The right to an equal voice in the management and conduct of the business is not determined by the share that each partner has in the business.

In the absence of an agreement, in regard to ordinary matters arising in the conduct of the partnership business, the opinion of the majority of the partners is controlling. If the firm consists of only two persons, and they are unable to agree, and the articles of partnership make no provision for the settlement of disputes, dissolution is the only remedy.

The majority cannot, however, against the consent of the minority, change the essential nature of the business by altering the partnership agreement or by reducing or increasing the capital of the partners; or embark upon a new business; or admit new members to the firm.

There are certain acts other than those enumerated above which require the unanimous consent of the partners, in order to bind the firm, namely: (1) assigning the firm property to a trustee for the benefit of creditors; (2) confessing a judgment; (3) disposing of the good will of the business; (4) submitting a partnership agreement to arbitration; (5) doing any act which would make impossible the conduct of the partnership business.

5-22. Partner's right to be compensated for services. It is the duty of each partner, in absence of an agreement to the contrary, to give his entire time, skill, and energy to the pursuit of the partnership affairs. No partner is entitled to payment for services rendered in the conduct of the partnership business, unless an agreement to that effect has been expressed or may be implied from the conduct of the partners.[1] Often one of the partners does not desire to participate in the management of the business. The partnership agreement in such case usually provides that the active partners receive a salary for their services in addition to their share in the profits. A surviving partner is entitled to reasonable compensation for his services in winding up the partnership affairs.

5-23. Right to information and to inspection of books. Each partner, whether active or inactive, is entitled to full and complete information concerning the conduct of the business and may inspect the books to secure such information. The partnership agreement usually provides for a bookkeeper and each partner is under a duty to give the bookkeeper whatever information is necessary efficiently and effectively to carry on the business. It is the duty of the bookkeeper to allow each partner access to the books and to keep them at the firm's place of business. No partner has a right to remove the books without the consent of the other partners. Each partner is entitled to inspect the books and make copies therefrom, provided he does not make such inspection or copies to secure an advantageous position or for fraudulent purposes.

5-24. Fiduciary relation of the partners. Section 21 of the Uniform

[1] Waagen v. Gerde et ux., page 714.

Partnership Act provides: Every partner must account to the partnership for any benefit, and hold as a trustee for it any profits gained by him without consent of the other partners from any transaction connected with the formation, conduct, or liquidation of the partnership, and account for any use by him of the partnership property. This duty also rests upon representatives of deceased partners engaged in the liquidation of the affairs of the partnership.

The partnership relation is a personal one, and each partner is under duty to exercise good faith, and to consider the mutual welfare of all the partners in his conduct of the business.[2] If one partner attempts to secure an advantage over the other partners, he thereby breaches the partnership relation, and he must account for all benefits that he obtains. Where a partner, in the transaction of the partnership business, obtains a secret commission from a third person without the consent of the partners, he must share such commission or profit with his partners. A partner cannot buy commodities for the firm at one price and sell them to the firm at another price. Likewise, one partner cannot sell his interest in the partnership to another partner without disclosing all facts concerning the value of the interest sold. One partner cannot use information secured by him in the pursuit of the partnership business for any purpose which would compete with the firm, without accounting to the firm for any profits obtained by the use of such information. Neither may a partner, while a member of a firm, engage in a competing business, unless such conduct is approved by the other members of the firm.

5-25. Partner's right to an accounting. The partners' proportionate shares of the partnership assets or profits, when not determined by a voluntary settlement of the parties, can only be ascertained by a bill in equity for an accounting. A partner cannot maintain an action at law against other members of the firm upon the partnership agreement, because, until there is an accounting and all the partnership affairs are settled, the indebtedness between the firm members is undetermined.[3] Therefore, in order that a partner may determine his interest in the firm, he is entitled to an accounting in equity. Partners ordinarily have equal access to the partnership books, and there is no reason why they should be subject to formal accountings to determine their interest. An accounting will not be permitted to settle incidental matters of disputes between the partners, however, unless the disputes are of such a grievous nature as to make impossible the continued existence of the partnership.

In all cases a partner is entitled to an accounting upon the dissolution of the firm. In addition he has a right to a formal accounting without a dissolution of the firm in the following situations:

[2] Hamilton Company v. Hamilton Tile Corporation, page 715.
[3] Jeffries v. Moore et al., page 716.

1. Where there is an agreement for an accounting at a definite date.
2. Where one partner has withheld profits arising from secret transactions.
3. Where there has been an execution levied against the interest of one of the partners.
4. Where one is in such a position that he does not have access to the books.[4]
5. Where the partnership is approaching insolvency and all parties are not available.

Upon an agreement between themselves, the partners may make a complete accounting and settle their claims, without resort to a court of equity.

RIGHTS AND DUTIES OF PARTNERS CASES

WAAGEN v. GERDE et ux.

1950, 36 Wash.2d 563, 219 P.2d 595

The plaintiff and the defendants were partners in the ownership and operation of a fishing vessel. The plaintiff brought this action for an accounting and alleged that the defendants had wrongfully withheld partnership earnings from the plaintiff. The defendant Karl Gerde perfected a new type of net for catching sharks and contended that he was entitled to compensation for the time and effort expended in constructing the shark nets. The lower court held in favor of the plaintiff and the defendants appealed.

DONWORTH, J. . . . Appellant's final assignment of error is that the trial court erred in refusing to allow appellant any credit for work done by him in constructing the shark nets.

The evidence shows that appellant with some help from his two sons designed and built the shark nets. Respondent did not in any way assist him in this job. According to appellant, the value of this work was $2,500 and he claims that he should be compensated for this work.

The general rule is clear that one partner is not entitled to extra compensation from the partnership, in the absence of an express or an implied agreement therefor. Each case must depend largely upon its own facts, and thus other cases are generally of little or no assistance in deciding the case at hand.

The exception to the general rule is well stated in 1 Rowley, Modern Law of Partnership 412, § 354, as follows: "Where it can be fairly and justly implied from the course of dealing between the partners, (or) from circumstances of equivalent force, that one partner is to be compensated

[4] Giordano v. Kleinmaier, page 717.

for his services, his claim will be sustained." *Emerson v. Durand*, 64 Wis. 111, 24 N.W. 129, 54 Am. Rep. 593. The partnership may be of such a peculiar kind, and the arrangements and the course of dealing of the partners in regard to it may be such as pretty plainly to show an expectation and understanding, without an express agreement upon the subject, that certain services of a copartner should be paid for. Such cases, presenting unusual conditions, are exceptions to the general rule. *Hoag v. Alderman*, 184 Mass. 217, 68 N.E. 199.

While appellant's ingenuity and industry were largely responsible for the success of the Princess in shark fishing, we cannot find anything in the record from which an agreement to pay him special compensation could be implied. Appellant did inform respondent that he was busy getting the nets ready and that it would "be lots of work to fix" them, but never at any time did he inform respondent what the work actually entailed or that he expected any compensation for it. Since respondent had so little knowledge of the conduct of the net operations, there could not be any implied agreement for compensation. The trial court found no factual basis for such an allowance, and we can find none in the record.

Affirmed.

HAMILTON COMPANY v. HAMILTON TILE CORPORATION

1960, 197 N.Y.S.2d 384

Owen McGivern, Justice. In this non-jury action, the plaintiff, the remaining partner of a partnership called The Hamilton Company, seeks an accounting from his quondam partner, Sidney Goldman, and also from the latter's wife and two other defendants, all of whom, in concert, formed the Hamilton Tile Corporation.

From the evidence developed at the trial, it became manifest that the plaintiff Rosner and his wife, together with the defendants Goldman (husband and wife) formed the subject partnership, The Hamilton Company, on August 2, 1955. The purpose of the venture was the importation of plumbing supplies and other related merchandise, such as tile, into the United States for sale; the partners were to contribute money, share profits and upon dissolution, receive a return of the capital and divide the resultant profits.

. . . With indifferent success, the partnership struggled along until April of 1956, when the early beauty of the partners' friendship began to fade. Hot words ensued, if not altercations, and then on May 10, 1956, the defendants Goldman, together with the defendants Weisberg (also husband and wife, the latter a sister of Mrs. Goldman) surreptitiously formed the Hamilton Tile Corporation for the purpose of importing and selling tile and other products in this country. The plaintiff contends that these defendants clandestinely formed this rival corporation in order to take advantage of the prospects already developed by the plaintiff-partnership, and that it was the intent of the corporate group to euchre the partnership out of the profits about to be realized from the importations financially arranged through Stratford Factors. The sequency of events as unfolded at the trial sustains this contention and the court is persuaded to adopt the plaintiff's version of the evidence.

In any event, on May 22, 1956, the plaintiff received a letter from Mrs. Goldman informing him that The Hamilton Company was "dissolved." . . . The court feels that implicit in the conduct of the defendants was the concealed purpose to deflect profits realized from the merchandise orders previously obtained by the plaintiff-partnership away from it and into the hands of the new corporate group, which Goldman had covertly joined, without making a disclosure to the plaintiff and before a winding up of this partnership relationship had been achieved.

The letter of Mrs. Goldman, dated March 22, 1956, informing plaintiff that the partnership was "dissolved" did not accomplish a cut-off of the partnership relationship. The good faith and full disclosure exacted of partners continues even after a unilateral notice of intent to dissolve and assuredly during the winding up period. (*Mitchell v. Reed*, 61 N.Y. 123; *Holmes v. Gilman*, 138 N.Y. 369, 34 N.E. 205, 20 L.R.A. 566). "The only manner in which a partnership or joint venture can be wound up is through an accounting." *Toeg v. Margolies,* 280 App. Div. 319, 113 N.Y.S.2d 373, 375. Even pursuant to section 61 of the Partnership Law, on dissolution a partnership is not terminated, but continues until the winding up of the partnership affairs has been completed.

Being a partnership at will, Goldman may have had the right to dissolve and to request a winding up of the partnership affairs; he could even then go off to another new venture, but he could not secretly become part of a venture that looks for its profits to the accounts and fruits of the former partnership still in a process of being wound up.

The court places the improper profits realized by the Hamilton Tile Corporation as a result of Goldman's connivance in the sum of $5,500 and directs that the defendants account to the plaintiff-partnership in that amount.

JEFFRIES v. MOORE et al.

1951, 219 La. 692, 53 So.2d 898

Plaintiff Jeffries and defendants Moore and others, were partners in the sawmill business. The partnership had ceased operations and the plaintiff in an action at law before an accounting is seeking to recover his capital contribution to the firm. He contended that the defendant Moore had not contributed the agreed amount and that the court should order him to make such a contribution. The lower court ruled in favor of the plaintiff.

McCaleb, J. . . . It seems patent, from the foregoing statement of the pleadings and issues in this case, that the judgment rendered below is not only irregular but, we think, not sustainable. The suit was for the liquidation and settlement of the partnership known as "Frierson Lumber Company," the individual liabilities of the partners to each other for causes of action arising out of the partnership relation being ancillary to the principal object and could not be satisfactorily determined until the dissolution and liquidation of the partnership was accomplished. It is axiomatic in Louisiana, and the rule is the same in practically all courts of last resort of the several States and those of the United States, that an action "is not maintainable between partners with respect to partnership transactions, unless there has been an accounting or settlement of the partnership affairs." See 21 A.L.R. 34 with numerous authorities there cited, including twenty-seven decisions of this court.

In *Martin v. Seabaugh*, 128 La. 422, 54 So. 935, 937, it was said: "Nothing is better settled in our law than that a partner has no cause of action against his partner for any definite sum as representing his share of the profits of the partnership, but only for a settlement of the partnership." [Cases cited.]

Obviously, then, it was improper to consider the individual demands of plaintiff and Moore in advance of a settlement of the partnership affairs. The reason for this is stated in *Quintero v. Caffery*, 150 La. 1054, 108 So. 87, 99, to be that, "Partners, *inter sese*, are not liable as they would be to third persons, each for his share of the debt, but each partner is liable to the firm for what he has overdrawn, and the firm is liable to the other partner or partners for the balance due him or them."

Hence, plaintiff is not indebted to Moore, or vice versa. Either one or the other may be ultimately found to be debtors or creditors of Frierson Lumber Company, as the case may be. But that cannot be ascertained until there has been a full liquidation of the affairs of the partnership. It appears from the record that Frierson Lumber Company owns a mill and other assets which must first be disposed of and the liabilities of the partnership paid before the accounts of the partners are finally settled.

Judgment set aside.

GIORDANO v. KLEINMAIER

1954, 210 Ga. 766, 82 S.E.2d 824

The plaintiff Giordano and the defendant were partners in a business known as Piedmont Reweaving Company. The defendant who was operating the business did not account for any profits and plaintiff did not have access to the books and records of the firm. The plaintiff brought this suit for an accounting. A demurrer by the defendant was sustained and the plaintiff appealed.

ALMAND, J. . . . It is true that in a case of this character, where there is no contractual duty resting upon the defendant to furnish an accounting of the affairs of a partnership, a petition for an accounting must aver facts sufficient to indicate that something will be due on an account by the defendant, (Cases cited) but where, as in this case, the defendant is under a contractual duty to furnish an accounting of the affairs of the partnership, and has the books and records in his office and refuses to produce them, the plaintiff is entitled to seek an accounting, so that she may know what profits were made or losses sustained. In our opinion, the instant case falls with the ruling in *Floyd v. Farish*, 195 Ga. 70, 23 S.E.2d 258, which holds: "Where it appears from the petition that a contractual duty rests upon a party defendant to furnish an accounting of the affairs of a partnership, and such party has the books and records in his possession and refuses to produce them, the plaintiff is entitled to bring a petition in equity, seeking an accounting." Under the contract between the parties in the instant case, Kleinmaier agreed to operate for the plaintiff the business known as Piedmont Reweaving Company for a specified period, and from the income of the business, after payment of all expenses, he would receive one-half of the net profits for his services, and at the end or termination of the contract he would pay the balance of the net profits to the plaintiff. It is alleged that Kleinmaier took over the operation of the business under this contract, and refused to pay or account to the plaintiff for any part of the profits of the business, her part of which she estimated to be $3,000 or more. During the contract period, Kleinmaier had charge of the business, and all the records appurtenant to its operation were kept by him, and it would be necessary to have the records and information appurtenant to the operation of the business in order to show either that profit or loss was sustained. As against a general demurrer, these allegations were sufficient to state a cause of action for an accounting.

Judgment reversed.

Review Questions and Problems

1. *A* and *B* entered into a partnership for the purpose of conducting a grocery business. *A* invested $10,000 and *B* $5,000. At the end of the first year, no profits had been made and all capital had been lost. *A* desires to recover $2,500 from *B*. In the absence of any agreement concerning the division of profits and losses, is he entitled to recover?
2. *A* advances to a partnership, for a period of 60 days, the sum of $19,000 in addition to his agreed capital. Is he entitled to interest on the advance?
3. A partnership composed of several partners has operated at a profit but these profits have been retained in the business. One of the

partners being in need of funds requested a distribution. The other partners refused on the ground that the funds were needed in the business. Does the partner have any remedy?

4. *X*, *Y* and *Z* entered into a partnership agreement to conduct a business of buying and selling cotton seed. It was agreed that *Z* was to have the exclusive authority to buy and sell for the firm. *Z* contracted to sell seed to a company on credit. If *X* and *Y* believe the buyer will be unable to pay may they prevent the sale and sell elsewhere over *Z*'s objection? Suppose *X* and *Y* decide to buy and operate a cotton gin rather than buy and sell seed. What may *Z* do if he objects?
5. *A* and *B* were partners engaged in the operation of a jewelry business. *A* ran the business while *B* engaged in other activities not related to the firm business. Is *A* entitled to compensation for his services?
6. A partnership conducted its business on leased premises. Prior to the expiration of the lease one of the partners made an arrangement with the landlord whereby the latter would not renew the lease to the partnership; instead, the partner, and the landlord would take over the business and operate it together. Is any remedy available to the other partners?
7. *P* and *D* are partners to conduct a U-Drive business. Through the partnership connection with a national U-Drive Corporation that gave the partnership its franchise, *P* learned of an available franchise in the area which he took out individually. Despite a provision in the partnership that neither partner would transfer his interest or assist a third party in obtaining an interest, *D* attempted to force his brother into the partnership. Although the business is operating profitably, the partners refuse to talk with each other on any subject. What may be done?
8. *A* was a partner in a retail grocery business and acted as the purchasing agent for the firm. He was also a partner in a certain milling industry. He purchased flour from the mill for the grocery, purchases that, because of his interest in the mill, netted him $500 during the year. Assuming that his partners were unaware of his interest in the mill, but later ascertained the true facts, should *A* be allowed to retain his profits?
9. *A* and *B* have been partners for a number of years. Upon *A*'s death, *B* spent considerable time in winding up the partnership affairs. Is he legally entitled to compensation for his services?
10. Mining Co., a partnership, rented equipment from *X* Co. under a written agreement signed on behalf of the partnership by *A*, one of the partners. The agreement contained a clause providing for a confession of judgment against the partnership. Can a valid judgment be obtained against Mining Co. under the terms of this clause?
11. *A*, *B*, and *C* were partners operating a store under the name of Eufaula Cash Store. The store being in need of funds, *A* borrowed money from the bank and executed a note in the name of the firm. The note was not paid and the bank obtained a judgment against *A* and the firm. *A* paid the note and now wishes to bring action against his partners to require them to contribute their proportionate share. Should he succeed?

31

Powers and Liabilities of Partners in Relation to Persons Dealing with the Partnership

5-26. Powers of partners in general. The extent of the power of partners to bind the firm is determined by the law of agency. Section 9 of the Uniform Partnership Act provides as follows:

> Every partner is an agent of the partnership for the purpose of its business, and the act of every partner, including the execution in the partnership name of any instrument, for apparently carrying on in the usual way the business of the partnership of which he is a member binds the partnership, unless the partner so acting has in fact no authority to act for the partnership in the particular matter, and the person with whom he is dealing has knowledge of the fact that he has no such authority.
>
> An act of a partner which is not apparently for the carrying on of the business of the partnership in the usual way does not bind the partnership unless authorized by the other partners.[1]
>
> Unless authorized by the other partners or unless they have abandoned the business, one or more but less than all the partners have no authority to:
>
> (a) Assign the partnership property in trust for creditors or on the assignee's promise to pay the debts of the partnership,
> (b) Dispose of the good will of the business,
> (c) Do any other act which would make it impossible to carry on the ordinary business of a partnership,
> (d) Confess a judgment,
> (e) Submit a partnership claim or liability to arbitration or reference.
>
> No act of a partner in contravention of a restriction on authority shall bind the partnership to persons having knowledge of the restriction.

Section 13 of the Uniform Partnership Act provides:

> Where by any wrongful act or omission of any partner acting in the ordinary course of the business of the partnership or with the authority of his co-partners, loss or injury is caused to any person, not being a partner in the partnership, or any penalty is incurred, the partnership is liable therefor to the same extent as the partner so acting or omitting to act.

Thus a partner has the power to bind the partnership both in tort and in contract.

[1] Bole v. Lyle et al., page 656.

5-27. Express and implied powers. By express agreement, authority that cannot be exercised by any of the other partners may be given to a particular partner. This authority may be limited to a particular act, it may be general, or it may be authority which would seem to go beyond the scope of the usual authority of an agent not specially authorized. The limitation of the authority of a partner as an agent does not bind third persons who have no knowledge of the limit of authority.[2]

In the absence of an express agreement describing the powers of the partners, each partner has implied power to do all acts necessary for carrying on the business of the partnership. The nature and scope of the business and what is usual in the particular business determines the extent of the implied powers.

5-28. Trading and nontrading partnerships. Partnerships for the purpose of determining the limit of a partner's powers may be divided into two general classes—trading and nontrading partnerships. A trading partnership is one which has for its primary purpose the buying and selling of commodities. In such a trading firm, each partner has an implied power to borrow money and to extend the credit of the firm, in the usual course of business, by signing negotiable paper.[3]

A nontrading partnership is one that does not buy and sell commodities, but that has for its primary purpose the production of commodities or is organized for the purpose of selling services, such as professional partnerships. In such partnerships a partner's powers are more limited and a partner does not have implied power to borrow money or to bind the firm on negotiable paper. However, where the act is within the scope of the partnership business, a member of a nontrading partnership may bind the firm by the exercise of implied authority just the same as a partner in a trading partnership.

5-29. Notice and admissions. Each partner has implied authority to receive notice for all of the other partners concerning matters within the pursuit of the partnership business; and knowledge, held by any partner in his mind, but not revealed to the other partners, is notice to the partnership. Knowledge of one partner is knowledge of all. This knowledge, however, must be knowledge obtained within the scope of the partnership business. If the partner could have and should have communicated knowledge to the other partners and fails to do so, his failure would be chargeable to the firm. This rule does not apply, however, if fraud is perpetrated on the partnership by the partner having such knowledge.

Admissions or representations, pertaining to the conduct of the partnership business and made by a partner, may be set up as evidence against the partnership.

[2] Picone v. Commercial Paste Co., page 723.
[3] Holloway v. Smith et al., page 724.

5-30. Ratification. Acts of the partners with respect to third parties, which have been committed without authority express or implied, may be ratified by the copartners, thus binding the firm. Whether there is a ratification is always a question of fact in each particular case, and such question is determined by the general law of agency.

POWERS AND LIABILITIES CASES

BOLE v. LYLE et al.

1956, (Tenn. App.), 287 S.W.2d 931

Lyle, Peters, and Barton were partners operating a business of manufacturing packing crates and other wood products. The partnership had purchased a tract of timber and were cutting it into lumber to supply their needs. Barton, the managing partner, entered into a contract to sell lumber to the plaintiff and received payment therefor. The lumber was never delivered to plaintiff and Barton never acounted to the partnership for the money received. Plaintiff sought to hold the partnership accountable. The lower court held that Lyle and Peters were not liable. The plaintiff appealed.

McAmis, Presiding Judge. . . . The general rule is that each partner is a general agent of the firm but only for the purpose of carrying on the business of the partnership. Any sale by a partner to be valid must be in furtherance of the partnership business, within the real scope of the business or such as third persons may reasonably conclude, from all the circumstances, to be embraced within it. If the act is embraced within the partnership business or incident to such business according to the ordinary and usual course of conducting it, the partnership is bound regardless of whether the partner, in performing the act, proceeds in good faith or bad faith toward his copartners.

Sales made by a partner in a trading firm are, of course, not viewed with the same strictness as in nontrading firms such as here involved because in trading firms sales are usually within the scope of the business while in nontrading firms they are exceptional and only incidental to the main business. A priori, in determining whether an act is within the scope of the business it is of importance, first, to determine the character of the partnership operations. (Cases cited.)

We think the case here presented is simply that of a nonresident, unfamiliar with the partnership operations, being defrauded by one of the partners acting in a matter beyond both the real and apparent scope of the business and beyond the real or apparent scope of the agency. There was nothing in the firm name to suggest that it was in the business of selling lumber. Complainant chose to deal with one of the partners without knowing anything of the nature of the partnership operations and we agree with the Chancellor that the nonparticipating partners were in no way responsible for his loss and that recovery should be against Barton alone.

Affirmed.

PICONE v. COMMERCIAL PASTE CO.

1952, 215 Miss. 114, 60 S.2d 590

The plaintiff, Commercial Paste Co., brought this action against Mrs. Picone and Martin Cox, partners in a floor covering business operated under the name of Gulfport Linoleum Mart. The plaintiff had sold and delivered merchandise upon order of Cox. Mrs. Picone contended that Cox had no authority to bind her to pay for the merchandise. The lower court ruled in favor of the plaintiff and Mrs. Picone appealed.

ROBERDS, Presiding Judge. On June 18, 1948, the parties executed written articles of partnership containing this provision:

> Neither of the partners is to become surety, drawer, acceptor, or endorser, in any case whatever, except in and for affecting the partnership, without the consent of his copartner, and neither of the partners shall have the right to buy or contract for or on account of the partnership without the consent of his copartner; that is, both of said partners shall act co-jointly and be consulted and agree on each transaction affecting the business of the partnership. This agreement is to be binding on the partners and the public generally, and for such purpose these articles of copartnership shall be recorded in the office of the Chancery Clerk of Harrison County, Mississippi.

. . . Mrs. Picone testified she did not give her assent to this order and did not know about it at the time given. She, therefore, says the quoted provision of the articles of partnership relieves her of any liability. In support of her contention she relies upon the rule that a partnership may be limited and if those dealing with it have notice of the limitation, then the partners are not liable for acts beyond such limitation. Of course, that rule is well established. . . . However, it has no application to the facts of this case. It is not contended appellee had any actual notice of limitation of the powers of the partners. It is said the written agreement was recorded and this gave constructive notice to appellee. But the written order to appellee by Cox was given June 4, before the written agreement was had between the parties. Cox then had full power to bind the partnership within the scope of the partnership business—at least, as to appellee, he apparently had such power. If he did not as a fact have that power appellee had no notice of the limitation. The fact that a written agreement was later made between the parties and recorded some nineteen days after the order was given could not reach back and nullify the power and authority possessed by the partners on June 4th.

Affirmed.

HOLLOWAY v. SMITH et al.

1955, 197 Va. 334, 88 S.E.2d 909

The defendants Smith and Ten Brook were partners in the automobile business under the name of Greenwood Sales and Service. Defendant Ten Brook borrowed $6,000 from the plaintiff and gave a partnership note in return. It is contended by the Smiths that Ten Brook borrowed the money to make his initial capital contribution to the partnership and that the obligation to repay was solely that of Ten Brook. They also contended that Ten Brook lacked the authority to bind the partnership on the note. The lower court held that the Smiths were not liable on the note.

SPRATLEY, J. Greenwood Sales & Service was a trading or commercial partnership, and in the course of its business, it borrowed money for carrying on its business in the usual way.

. . . It is settled law in Virginia, both by statute and in numerous decisions that a partner is an agent of the firm for the purpose of the partnership business, and may bind all partners by his acts within the scope of such business. It is of no consequence whether the partner is acting in good faith with his copartners or not, provided the act is within the scope of the partnership's business and professedly for the firm, and third persons are acting in good faith.

. . . Pertinent here is this statement from 40 Am. Jur., Partnership, § 11 at p. 134:

> The character and nature of partnerships ordinarily determine the powers and liabilities of different classes of partners. In this connection, the most important distinction exists between trading or commercial partnerships and those which are not organized for the purpose of trade or commerce. Greater powers are impliedly given to members of the former as compared with the second type of partnerships, such as in the matter of drawing or endorsing negotiable instruments.

The Smiths selected Ten Brook as their partner. The partnership was a going concern when the $6,000 note was executed. In the absence of a restriction on his authority, known to Mrs. Holloway, Ten Brook had the same power to bind the partnership as his copartners had. Ten Brook, as the agent of the partnership, solicited the loan professedly for the firm, and executed the note evidencing it, for "apparently carrying on in the usual way the business of the partnership" of which he was a member.

The court held that the Smiths as well as Ten Brook were liable on the note.

Review Questions and Problems

1. *A* and *B* are partners in the hardware business. It is expressly agreed in the partnership agreement that the full duties of management shall be entrusted to *A* and that he shall be the only purchasing agent of the firm. Despite this fact, *B* orders from the *X* Company certain hardware for the firm. *A* refuses to accept the goods for the firm. Is the firm liable in damages to the *X* Company?
2. *A*, *B*, and *C* were partners in a garage business. Parts necessary to the repair of a customer's car were not in stock and *A* suggested that the customer pick them up from a supply firm. While en route to obtain the parts the customer was involved in an accident and *X* was injured. Is the partnership liable to *X*?
3. *A* and *B* are partners in the retail clothing business. Being short of funds in the business, *A*, without the consent or knowledge of *B*, borrowed $500 from *C* and gave him a chattel mortgage upon the fixtures. Is the mortgage good?
4. *X*, a partner, was driving a vehicle owned by the partnership for his own purposes. He had the permission of the other partners to use the vehicle. His negligent operation resulted in an injury to *Y*. Is the partnership liable to *Y*?
5. *A*, *B*, and *C* are partners. The firm owes *X* $500 for goods furnished to it. *X* obtains a joint judgment against *A* and *B* for the amount. They are unable to pay the judgment. May *X* recover in another action against *C*? Suppose *X* had released *C* from all liability upon the debt, what would have been the effect upon *A* and *B*?
6. *A* and *B* conducted a partnership business called Union Wallpaper Co. *X* came to the partnership store and stepped into an unlighted, unguarded elevator shaft where no warnings were posted. *B* was solely in charge of the store. *X* obtained a judgment against the Union Wallpaper Co. Assuming the partners and the partnership are all solvent, from whom may the judgment be collected?
7. *A* and *B* were partners in the business of buying and selling stocks and bonds. *B* sold some bonds to *X* and guaranteed on behalf of the firm that the bonds would be paid. The obligor on the bonds defaulted. Can *X* recover from both *A* and *B*?

32

Dissolution

5-31. Nature. Dissolution of a partnership is effected when the partnership relation is destroyed by any partner's ceasing to be a member of the firm. Under the Uniform Partnership Act, dissolution may occur without violation of the partnership agreement: (a) by the termination of the stipulated term or particular undertaking specified in the agreement; (b) by the express will of any partner when no definite term or particular undertaking is specified; (c) by the express will of all the partners who have not assigned their interests or suffered them to be charged for their separate debts either before or after the termination of any specified term or particular undertaking; or (d) by the expulsion, in good faith, of any partner from the business, in accordance with such a power conferred by the partnership agreement.

5-32. Dissolution by act of partner in violation of the partnership agreement. A partnership agreement originally created to continue for a definite term, in which no provision is made for dissolution prior to the expiration of the period, may be dissolved before the expiration of such period by the acts of one of the partners "in contravention of the partners' agreement." By reason of the partnership agreement there exists between the partners a principal and agency relationship. As in the law of agency, each partner has the power, but not the right, to revoke such relationship and in so doing is liable for damages. A partnership may always be dissolved. Because of the peculiar personal relationship necessary in the formation and carrying out of a partnership agreement, a court of equity will not grant specific performance for the continuance of a partnership, even though the agreement provides that such partnership shall continue for a long period of time. As a consequence of such breach the withdrawing partner becomes liable for the damages sustained by the other parties.

5-33. By operation of law. If during the period of the partnership, events occur that make it impossible or illegal for the partnership to continue, it will be dissolved. Such events or conditions are: death or bankruptcy of one of the partners or a change in the law which makes the continuance of the business illegal.

A partnership is a personal relationship existing by reason of contract. Therefore, when one of the partners dies, the partnership is dissolved. The former partners cannot bind the estate of the deceased partner by a new contract, even though it was expressly intended by the decedent that the partnership be continued. Although partnership agreements occasionally provide for the continued existence of the partnership after the death of the partner, the agreement does not bind the legal representatives of the deceased partner to continue the firm in existence. Occasionally articles of partnership provide that a deceased partner's interest in the firm may be retained by the survivors for a limited period. Such provision may be enforced and the partnership extended beyond the death of a partner. Although the authorities are not unanimous, it has been held that the estate of a deceased partner is liable for further transactions.

If, during the period of a partnership, a law is passed which makes continuance of the business illegal, the partnership will be dissolved. Also a partnership composed of residents of different countries could not legally continue, upon the declaration of war between such countries, because such parties would be enemies.

The bankruptcy of a partner will dissolve the partnership, because the control of his property passes to his assignee or trustee for the benefit of the creditors in somewhat the same way that the control of the property passes to the legal representatives upon the death of a partner. The mere insolvency of a partner will not be sufficient to justify a dissolution, unless there has been an assignment of his assets. The bankruptcy of the firm itself is a cause for dissolution, as is also a valid assignment of all the firm assets for the benefit of creditors.

5-34. Dissolution by court decree. Where a partnership, by its agreement, is to be continued for a term of years, circumstances may arise which might make the continued existence of the firm impossible and unprofitable. Therefore, upon the application of one of the partners to a court of equity, the partnership may be dissolved. The following are the circumstances and situations that will give a partner a right to go into a court of equity for dissolution:

Where a partner becomes totally incapacitated to conduct business and to perform the duties required under the contract for partnership, the court of equity will, upon application by any of the partners, declare a dissolution. Insanity of one of the partners does not necessarily dissolve the partnership. If, however, a partner is declared insane by a judicial process, the partnership is dissolved.

Where a partner is guilty of gross misconduct and neglect or breach of duty to such an extent that it is impossible to carry out the purposes of the partnership agreement, a dissolution will be decreed at the request of the remaining partners. The court will not interfere and grant a decree of dissolution for mere discourtesy, temporary inconvenience, differences of opinion, or errors in judgment.[1] The misconduct must be of such gross nature that the continued operation of the business would be unprofitable. Where a partner willfully and persistently commits a breach of the partnership agreement, misappropriates funds, or commits fraudulent acts, the partnership will be dissolved. A partnership that was entered into by reason of fraud may be dissolved on the application of an innocent party. But, if the defrauded partner continues in the partnership with the knowledge of the fraud, no decree of dissolution will be granted.

EFFECT OF DISSOLUTION BETWEEN THE PARTNERS

5-35. Effect of dissolution on powers of partners. Upon dissolution, a partnership is not terminated, but continues in existence for the purpose of winding up the partnership affairs. The process of winding up involves the liquidation of the partnership assets so that cash may be available to pay creditors and to make a distribution to the partners. Dissolution terminates all the authority of any partner to act for the partnership, except insofar as it may be necessary to create liability to complete unfinished transactions, or to liquidate the assets of the firm in an orderly manner.

In the event of dissolution resulting from the death of a partner, title to partnership property remains in the surviving partners for purposes of liquidation. Should death of one of the partners occur, both real and personal property is, through the survivors, made available to creditors. If all of the realty is not required to satisfy firm obligations, the disposition to be made of the remaining real estate depends on whether the firm operates under the common law or the Uniform Act. Under the Act, all realty is treated as though it were personal property,[2] the surviving partners finally accounting, usually in cash, to the personal representative of the deceased partner for the latter's share in the proceeds of liquidation. In those states which have not adopted the Uniform Act, the surviving partners are authorized to sell only that portion of the realty which is needed for the payment of debts. The unsold portion, to the extent of the deceased partner's interest therein, passes directly to the latter's heirs and is subject to widow's dower and the ordinary incidents of real property that passes by descent.

5-36. Right to contribution for liabilities incurred after dissolution. Under the Act, if the dissolution is caused by the act, death, or bank-

[1] Lunn v. Kaiser, page 733.
[2] Cultra et al. v. Cultra et al., page 734.

ruptcy of one of the partners, each partner will be liable, just as if no dissolution had taken place, upon any contracts entered into by one of the partners after the dissolution. However, if the contracting partner had knowledge or notice of the dissolution he has no right to bind the other partners or the estate of the deceased partner. In those states where the Uniform Partnership Act has not been adopted, and the partnership is dissolved by death or bankruptcy, each person, including the partners, must take notice of such death or bankruptcy whether or not they have actual knowledge of the fact. Therefore, if *A*, a partner in the firm of *A*, *B*, and *C*, enters into a contract after the death or bankruptcy of *C*, he must assume the entire liability of the contract, although he or the other partner is ignorant of the death or bankruptcy of *C*. Under the Uniform Partnership Act, however, *A* may call upon *B* and the estate of the deceased partner to assume their proportionate share of the liability and to contribute to any loss which may be sustained on account of such contract.

5-37. Right of partners after dissolution. Where the dissolution is caused by any act other than the breach of the partnership agreement, each partner, as against his copartners or their assignees, has a right to insist that all the partnership assets be used first to pay firm debts. After firm obligations are paid, remaining assets are used to return capital investments, proper adjustments for profits and losses having been made. All of the surviving partners, except those who have caused a wrongful dissolution of the firm, have the right to participate in the winding up of the business. The majority may select the method or procedure to be followed in the liquidation, but the assets, other than real estate, must be turned into cash unless all the partners agree to distribution in kind. Under the Uniform Act, realty is treated as personal property the same as any other asset and should be liquidated. Should the last surviving partner die prior to the final accounting, it becomes the duty of his legal representative to complete the liquidation.

5-38. Continuation of the business after dissolution. If a partnership which is to continue for a fixed period is dissolved by the wrongful withdrawal of one of its members, the remaining members may continue as partners if they have settled with the withdrawing partner for his interest in the partnership. The remaining partners, in determining the interest of the withdrawing partner, have the right to pay him his share in cash, less damages. In the calculation of his share, the good will of the business is not taken into consideration. Under the Uniform Partnership Act, if no accounting is made at the time that the partner withdraws, the remaining partners may continue the business for the agreed period by securing the payment of such withdrawing partner's interest by a bond approved by the court, covering not only the partner's interest at the time of the withdrawal, but also indemnifying him against any future liabilities of the continuing partnership.

The right of the partners to expel one of their number is determined entirely by the partnership agreement. Thus, the right to continue after expulsion, as well as the amount which the expelled partner is to receive, depends exclusively upon the articles of copartnership.

EFFECT OF DISSOLUTION AS TO THIRD PARTIES

5-39. Liability existing prior to dissolution. Although the dissolution of a partnership terminates the authority of the partners to create future liability, it does not discharge the existing liability of any partner. An agreement between the partners themselves that one or more of the partners will assume the partnership liabilities does not bind the firm creditors. However, upon dissolution, a partner may be discharged from any existing liability by an agreement to that effect in which he, the partnership creditors, and the remaining partners join. Such an agreement must satisfy all the requirements for a novation. If upon dissolution of a partnership, an incoming partner or the remaining partners promise to assume the liabilities of the dissolved partnership, such liabilities will be discharged as to the withdrawing partner if any creditor of the partnership, knowing of the agreement, changes or alters the character of the liability or the time of its payment by agreement with the new firm.

The individual estate of a deceased partner, where firm assets are insufficient to pay firm debts, is liable to third parties for all debts created while he was a partner, subject, however, to the payment of his separate debts.

5-40. Notice to the creditors of the firm. Transactions entered into with former creditors of the firm who have not received actual knowledge of the dissolution continue to bind any partner who has withdrawn. Notice of the dissolution is not necessary at common law, where the dissolution has been caused by the operation of the law. If the dissolution has been caused by agreement or an act of the parties, notice that carries knowledge to all persons who are creditors to the firm is required, as in the revocation of agency.[3] Therefore, a retiring partner who fails to give notice of dissolution to those who have extended credit to the old firm, assuming that knowledge of the dissolution has not been acquired in some other manner, will be liable on contracts of the new firm. Under the Uniform Partnership Act, notice of dissolution is required even though

[3] Letellier-Phillips Paper Co. v. Fiedler et al., page 735.

the dissolution is caused by operation of law, except where a partner becomes bankrupt. In the latter case notice is not required.

5-41. Notice to the public generally. Where the dissolution is caused by an act of the parties, the partners will continue to be liable to all persons who formerly dealt with the firm, unless notice of such dissolution is given to the public at large. This does not mean that notice of the dissolution must be brought to the attention of all third parties. Notice by publication in a newspaper in the community where the business has been transacted or notice of the dissolution by a properly addressed envelope placed in the mailbox is sufficient.

The duty to impart notice is broadened by the Uniform Act to include those situations where dissolution results from operation of law. Thus, in states operating under these laws, it becomes the duty of the legal representative of a deceased partner to see that notice is given. Should the continuation of the business become illegal, however, notice is not required, since all are presumed to be aware of the illegal nature of the enterprise.

Where a partner has not actively engaged in the conduct of the partnership business and creditors had not learned that he was a partner and have not extended credit to the firm on the faith of such partner, he is under no duty to give notice to either of the groups mentioned above.

5-42. The liability of an incoming partner. Under the common law an incoming partner causes a change in the personnel of the partnership to the extent that a new firm is formed, and he is, therefore, not liable as a member of the new firm to creditors of the old firm. He may make himself liable, however, to old firm creditors by assuming the liability. This agreement may take the form of a novation, a contract of suretyship, or a mere contract for the benefit of third parties. Under the Uniform Partnership Act, however, a person admitted as a partner into an existing partnership is, as a member of the firm, liable to the extent of his investment for all obligations created before his admission, as though previously he had been a partner. His separate estate is not liable for such obligations, and the creditors of the old firm can look only to the firm assets and to the members of the old firm.

5-43. Creditors of the old firm and the new firm. Under the Uniform Partnership Act, if the business is continued without liquidation of the partnership affairs, creditors of the first, or dissolved, partnership are also creditors of the partnership continuing the business. Likewise, if the partners assign all their interest to a single partner, who continues the business without liquidation of the partnership affairs, creditors of the dissolved partnership are also creditors of the single person so continuing the business. Likewise, when all the partners or their representatives assign their rights in the partnership property to one or more third persons who promise to pay the debts and to continue the business, the creditors of the dissolved partnership are also creditors of the person or persons continuing the business.

DISTRIBUTION OF FIRM ASSETS AND LIABILITIES OF PARTNERS ON DISSOLUTION

5-44. Distribution of firm assets where firm is solvent. Upon the dissolution of a partnership and a winding up of its business, an accounting is had to determine its assets and liabilities. Before the partners are entitled to participate in any of the assets, whether firm creditors or not, all firm creditors other than partners are entitled to be paid. After firm creditors are paid, the assets of the partnership are distributed among the partners, as follows:

1. Each partner who has made advances to the firm, or has incurred liability for or on behalf of the firm, is entitled to be reimbursed.
2. Each partner is then entitled to the return of the capital which he has contributed to the firm.
3. Any balance is distributed as profits, in accordance with the partnership agreement.

5-45. Firm creditors against firm assets. When the firm is insolvent and a court of equity has acquired jurisdiction because of a bill for accounting, a petition by creditors, or an insolvency proceeding, etc., over the assets of the partnership, together with the assets of the individual partners, the assets are distributed in accordance with certain well-defined rules.

Persons entering into a partnership agreement, by virtue of the contract itself, impliedly agree that the partnership assets shall be used for the payment of the firm debts before the payment of any individual debts of the partners. Consequently, a court of equity, in distributing firm assets, will give priority to firm creditors in firm assets as against the separate creditors of the individual partners and will give priority to private creditors of individual partners in the separate assets of the partners as against firm creditors. This principle is called "marshalling assets." Each class of creditors is not permitted to use the fund belonging to the other until the claims of the other have been satisfied. Since the firm creditors have available two funds out of which to seek payment—firm assets and the individual assets of the partners—and individual creditors of the partners have only one fund, equity compels the firm creditors to exhaust firm assets before having recourse to the partners' individual assets.[4]

[4] Casey et al. v. Grantham et al., page 736.

Hence the rule, "firm creditors in firm assets and separate creditors in separate assets." This rule does not apply, however, if a partner conceals his existence and permits the other member of the firm to deal with the public as the sole owner of the business. Under these circumstances the dormant partner by his conduct has led the creditors of the active partner to rely upon firm assets as the separate property of the active partner, and by reason of his conduct the dormant partner is estopped from demanding an application of the equity rule that firm assets shall be used to pay firm creditors in priority and individual assets to pay individual creditors. Thus the firm assets must be shared equally with firm creditors and the individual creditors of the active partners. Since the firm assets may not be sufficient to pay all the firm debts when depleted by payments to individual creditors, there may be unpaid firm creditors, and dormant partners will be personally liable. Since the firm creditors' right to firm property rests upon the partners' right that firm assets be used to pay firm debts, the conduct that estops a dormant partner also denies the creditors such a preference. Furthermore, the creditors who relied upon the assets in the hands of the sole active partner cannot claim a preference when later they learn such assets were partnership assets.

5-46. Firm creditors against individual assets. Just as the individual creditors are limited to individual assets, firm creditors are limited to firm assets. Therefore, firm creditors are not entitled to payment out of the individual assets of the partners until the individual creditors have been paid. This rule applies, even though the firm creditors may, at the same time, be individual creditors of a member of the firm. There are two main exceptions to this general rule. (1) Where there are no firm assets and no living solvent partners. The rule for the limit of firm creditors to firm assets applies only where there are firm assets. If no firm assets or no living solvent partner exists, the firm creditors may share equally with the individual creditors in the distribution of the individual estates of the partners. (2) If a partner has fraudulently converted the firm assets to his own use, it follows that the firm creditors will be entitled to share equally with individual creditors in such partner's individual assets.

DISSOLUTION CASES

LUNN v. KAISER

1955, (S.D.) 72 N.W.2d 312

Plaintiff and defendant were partners in the farming and livestock business. They became involved in a series of arguments over matters of a trivial nature and plaintiff brought this action to dissolve the partnership. The lower court ruled in favor of the plaintiff and the defendant appealed.

RUDOLPH, Presiding Judge . . . The evidence also discloses several minor incidents such as arguments about walking across the lawn, the amount of cream furnished plaintiff, the pounding on the house being remodeled while defendant's children were asleep, and perhaps other similar incidents.

It may be conceded that the relationship between the parties was not that of bosom friends but nevertheless the purpose for which the contract was entered into succeeded and the personal animosity, if such it may be called, existing between the parties did not detract from the successful conduct of the business.

. . . We find nothing in the record to support any determination that plaintiff was deprived of any right of direction he had under the contract. The real dispute here relates to discord over trivial matters, for which both parties were responsible. No doubt the bringing of this action only added to the discord, as plaintiff testified the parties were only on speaking terms during the two months preceding the trial, but defendant cannot be charged with commencing these proceedings.

The agreement expires by its own terms on March 1, 1956. It does not clearly appear that the plaintiff will suffer any loss by the continuation of the relationship during the existence of the agreement. The trial court stated in his memorandum opinion, "I am unable to determine that one is more responsible for this situation than the other. . . ." Under these circumstances we believe the harsh remedy of dissolution is unnecessary. We are inclined to agree with the Pennsylvania court, "Differences and discord should be settled by the partners themselves by the application of mutual forebearance rather than by bills in equity for dissolution. Equity is not a referee of partnership quarrels. A going and prosperous business will not be dissolved merely because of friction among the partners; it will not interfere to determine which contending faction is more at fault."

Reversed.

CULTRA et al. v. CULTRA et al.

1949, 188 Tenn. 506, 221 S.W.2d 533

Four people (Cultras) were partners doing business under the trade name "Morning Star Nursery." The partnership acquired several tracts of land. Two of the partners have died. A controversy arose as to the rights of a child of one of the deceased partners in the partnership real property. The lower court held that the interest of the deceased partners was personalty and that the surviving partner had a right to sell this land and then distribute the proceeds as other partnership property.

BURNETT, J. This case presents the question of whether or not the real estate owned by a partnership, purchased by said partnership with partnership funds for partnership purposes, and not needed to pay partnership debts, descends to the heirs of a deceased partner or continues to be personalty and subject to the laws of distribution.

. . . Courts of other states, in construing the Uniform Partnership Act, adopt the rule of "out and out" conversion, that is, that when the property is acquired by the partnership, from the partnership fund, for partnership purposes, it becomes personalty for all purposes. The most notable of these cases is *Wharf v. Wharf*, 306 Ill. 179, 137 N.E. 446, 449.

These cases, and the holdings last above referred to, in effect adopt the English rule. This rule is that partnership realty must be regarded as personalty for all purposes, including descent and distribution. Real estate purchased and used for partnership purposes is an "out and out" conversion to personalty so that it will be distributed as such.

. . . It is true that in the *Wharf* case the partnership was solely for the purpose of dealing in real estate and that the general rule is that real estate partnerships are considered as personalty, and must be distributed as such. We consider the reasoning in the *Wharf* case, that is, that the rule is changed as to all partnerships, whether real estate or otherwise, by reason of the passage of the Uniform Partnership Act, is the most reasonable rule and is one that we should adopt and do adopt as the applicable rule in this State.

In this construction and application of the Uniform Partnership Act, we are meeting and reaching the intent of the Legislature in passing this Act. By so doing the conversion of real estate into personalty for certain purposes and then when those purposes have been met, reconverting the real estate back into realty is done away with by this Act. By this construction when a partnership once acquires real estate, with partnership funds and for partnership purposes, it then becomes personalty for all purposes and can be conveyed according to the terms of the Act as other partnership property. This seems a sound rule to apply and we are applying it here.

From what has been said above, it results that the decree of the Chancellor must be affirmed.

LETELLIER-PHILLIPS PAPER CO. v. FIEDLER et al.

1949, 32 Tenn. App. 137, 222 S.W.2d 42

The plaintiffs brought this action to recover from the defendants as individuals and members of a partnership for merchandise sold and delivered to them. A corporation had been formed by the defendants which took over their individual and partnership assets. The plaintiffs alleged that they were not aware that the partnership had been converted into a corporation. From a judgment in favor of the plaintiffs, defendants appealed.

SWEPSTON, J. The suit is on account for merchandise sold and delivered and the essential question in the trial below was whether there was partnership liability or corporate liability, the partners having operated as such for about a year and having later formed a corporation.

. . . The bill alleges that about December 24, 1945 complainant agreed to extend credit to defendants, Fiedler & Sullivan, individually and as partners trading as Fied-Sul Paper Mills. That upon the pledge of the individual credit of the defendants complainant began shipping them merchandise.

That the account about January 1, 1947 was current and amounted to $6,855.26. That subsequently the balance began to grow larger until on August 1, 1947, it amounted to $26,890.70, which later upon demand was reduced to $24,060.74 at which figure it has remained, because all purchases lately have been for cash.

That about August 1, 1947 complainant learned for the first time that a corporation had been formed by defendants and that it had taken over certain assets of the individuals and of the partnership all without notice to complainant.

That it had never dealt with the corporation and had relied upon the credit of the partnership and the individuals composing it and that said transfer of assets was fraudulent, etc.

. . . The cases show that the notice may be an express notice or may be implied from sufficient circumstances. However obtained, it must be sufficient to amount to actual knowledge where one who has been dealing with the firm before dissolution is involved. The knowledge may be constructive as to those who have not dealt with the firm before dissolution.

Affirmed.

CASEY et al. v. GRANTHAM et al.

1954, 239 N.C. 121, 79 S.E.2d 735

The plaintiff, Casey, brought this action against the defendant Harold J. Grantham, his partner in the sawmill and cotton gin business, for a partnership accounting and against the defendant Clarence Grantham to enjoin the foreclosure of a deed of trust on partnership property and on the home and farm of the plaintiffs until a partnership accounting is had. The deeds of trust had been given to secure a loan made to the partnership by the defendant Clarence Grantham. The plaintiffs contend that the partnership property is well worth the amount of the debt owed by the partnership to Clarence Grantham. The lower court sustained a demurrer to the complaint and the plaintiffs appealed.

PARKER, J. . . . G.S. § 59–68 (1) reads:

When dissolution is caused in any way except in contravention of the partnership agreement, each partner, as against his copartners and all persons claiming through them in respect of their interest in the partnership, unless otherwise agreed, may have the partnership property applied to discharge its liabilities, and the surplus applied to pay in cash the net amount owing to the respective partners.

. . . It is said in 68 C.J.S., Partnership, § 185, p. 639, "The right, in equity, to have the partnership and individual assets marshaled is for the benefit and protection of the partners themselves, and, therefore, the equity of a creditor, to the application of this doctrine, is of a dependant and subordinate character, and must be worked out through the medium of the partners or their representatives"—citing in support of the text *Dilworth v. Curts,* 139 Ill. 508, 29 N.E. 861, 865, where it is said "the right in equity to have the partnership and individual assets marshaled is one resting in the hands of the partners, and must be worked out through them."

Each partner has the right to have the partnership property applied to the payment or security of partnership debts in order to relieve him from personal liability.

It appears that under the general rule as to marshaling partnership and individual assets, or under the application of a principle of equity similar to that rule, the rule that partnership debts may be paid out of individual assets is subject to the modification that the individual assets may be so applied where, and only where, there are no firm assets, or where the firm assets have become exhausted. It would seem that the rationale for this modification to the rule rests upon the fact that the partners occupy the position of sureties in respect to their individual property being liable for the payment of partnership debts.

. . . It may be that the property of the partnership conveyed in the deed of trust may not sell for enough at a forced sale to pay Clarence Grantham's debt in full—though the demurrer admits that it will—but that Harold J. Grantham may be indebted to the partnership in an amount to make up such deficiency, if such a deficiency should exist. How can that be determined, until there is an accounting between the parties of the partnership affairs?

Under the rules laid down above it would seem to be plain that the plaintiffs have alleged sufficient facts to enjoin a foreclosure sale under the deed of trust until there has been an accounting and settlement of the partnership affairs between the partners, Casey and Harold J. Grantham. Under such circumstances it is the rule with us that an injunction should be granted where the injury, if any, which the defendant Clarence Grantham, would suffer from its issuance would be slight as compared with the irreparable damage which the plaintiffs would suffer from the forced sale of their home and farm from its refusal, if the plaintiffs should finally prevail.

Reversed.

Review Questions and Problems

1. *A*, *B*, and *C* are partners, and by the terms of the agreement the partnership is to continue for a period of five years. At the end of the third year conditions have arisen that indicate that the firm cannot continue except at a loss. *B* and *C* refuse to quit, and *A* files a bill to obtain an order for dissolution. Should he succeed?
2. The majority of the partners in a partnership agreed to dissolve the firm prior to the date of termination specified in the partnership agreement. A minority of the partners wished the business to continue for the balance of the term. Can the majority work a dissolution? Would they be guilty of breach of contract in so doing?
3. A partnership employed *X* as its general manager. One of the partners died. Is *X*'s contract of employment terminated?
4. *A* and *B* formed a partnership to operate a restaurant. *A* contributed a building and fixtures worth $8,500, and *B* contributed $3,000 cash. *A* obtained a dissolution of the firm on account of *B*'s wrongful withholding of *A*'s share of the profits in the amount of $5,500. After dissolution but before final judgment on the accounting and termination of the partnership, *A* formed another partnership with *X* and *Y* which made a profit operating the restaurant. Is *B* entitled to a share therein?
5. *A*, *B*, and *C* are partners under an agreement whereby the firm is to continue in business for ten years. *A* causes a wrongful dissolution of the partnership and demands his interest therein. May he demand that firm assets be liquidated? Is there any asset in which he is not entitled to share?
6. *A* withdraws from a firm under an agreement with the surviving partners that they shall assume and pay all outstanding liabilities. *A* notified all creditors of his withdrawal from the firm. The surviving partners failed to pay the debts. Has *A* avoided liability therefor?
7. *A*, *B*, and *C* take a new partner, *D*, into their business. He invests $3,000. What is the extent of his liability, if any, to creditors of the old firm? What are the rights of creditors of the old firm, in comparison with creditors of the new firm, in the firm assets?
8. *A* contracted to perform a vaudeville act for a partnership which owned a theater. Prior to the performance one of the partners died. Is *A*'s contract terminated?
9. *X*, one of the partners in a business firm, retired and the remaining partners continued to operate the business. They did not pay for goods which had been ordered before *X*'s retirement but delivered subsequently. Does *X* have any liability for this purchase?
10. An insurance company issued a policy of fire insurance on partnership property. Thereafter one of the partners retired. Would the insurance policy be effective subsequent to the retirement?

11. *A* and *B* were partners. By mutual agreement *A* retired and *B* continued to operate the business. *B* agreed to assume the obligations of the firm existing at the time of *A*'s retirement and notice to this effect was sent to all the firm creditors. If *B* does not pay these bills, can the creditors look to *A*?
12. *A*, *B*, and *C* are partners. The firm is insolvent and is being wound up in a bankruptcy court. The firm assets amount to $40,000, its liabilities to $80,000. *A* has personal property worth $12,000; his personal liabilities are $6,000. *B* has personal property worth $20,000; he owes personal creditors $15,000. *C* has no personal property and owes personal creditors $5,000. Marshal the assets of the firm and make the proper distribution between firm and individual creditors.
13. *A*, *B*, and *C* are partners. *A* contributed $10,000, *B* contributed $4,000, and *C* contributed his services. Upon dissolution it was found that the firm had assets of $50,000 and liabilities to outside creditors of $20,000. *C* had loaned the firm $1,000 and had paid $300 in taxes and $450 insurance. Make the proper distribution of the firm assets.
14. *A* retired from a partnership in which he was associated with *B*. *A* authorized *B* to continue to use his name (*A*'s), but later withdrew this authority. Thereafter *B* borrowed money from *X* bank in the firm name. If *B* does not pay will the bank have a cause of action against *A*?
15. *A* agreed with B to share the profits and losses of a farming operation. *B* was to supervise and also to furnish a tractor and $2,500. *B* failed to furnish the tractor or money and was insolvent. There were no other joint funds available for harvest. *A* had already contributed more than he had agreed to contribute. What may *A* do?
16. *A* and *B* formed a partnership under written articles which provided that if either partner desired to dissolve the firm he was to give written notice to the other partner. The notice was to include a statement of the amount the partner was willing to pay for the interest of the other partner. The partner who received the notice was then to have his option of selling his interest for the sum so stated or else of buying the interest of the notifying partner for the same amount. *A* gave notice to *B*, and *B* elected to sell. *A* then attempted to withdraw the notice. What result?
17. *A*, *B*, *C*, and *D* formed a partnership to drill oil and gas wells. In 1950 it was dissolved by mutual consent. In 1951 still during the period of liquidation of partnership assets, *A*, who was in charge of liquidation, signed a note purporting to bind the partnership. This note was payable to *X*, who knew of the dissolution, and was given for an insurance premium payment that had become due in 1949. Against whom may *X* obtain a judgment on the note if it is not paid when due?
18. *A* and *B* formed a partnership by written agreement which provided that upon the death of either partner all partnership property is to be transferred to a trustee who will have five years to make disposition of the partnership property, to pay all its debts and then pay one half of the proceeds to the surviving partner and one half to the heirs of the deceased partner. Is such an agreement enforceable? What effect will a statute requiring two witnesses to attest all wills have?

PART TWO / CORPORATIONS

33 Characteristics of Corporations

5-47. Essential features. The corporation is the most effective vehicle yet discovered to manage and control modern business enterprises. It permits, with the minimum risk of loss to investors, the combination of capital and skill for vast business operations. No other method has been found by which large amounts of capital are so easily assembled for huge business control. A great portion of the business today is conducted by means of the corporate organization.

A corporation is a collection of individuals, but in law is treated primarily as an entity. Generally speaking, statutes provide that three persons are necessary for membership in a corporation. Even though one person owns virtually all the stock and dominates the corporation, a corporate entity exists.

Since a corporation is regarded in the law as a person for the purpose of convenience, there is a limitation with respect to what it can do, in that it has only those rights and powers which are given to it by the state. In order that it may function as a person, a legal entity separate and distinct from its members, it has certain inherent rights and powers: a corporation may sue and be sued in its own name; it has the capacity of perpetual succession, although there may be a change in its members by death or withdrawal; it may take, hold, and transfer property, both real and personal, in its own name as a legal entity, separate and distinct from its members; it may enter into contracts with its own members; it may take and convey property from its own members; and it may sue and be sued by them as a distinct person.

A corporation is a resident and a citizen for jurisdictional purposes of the state which creates it.[1] Wherever the word "person" or "persons" is used in constitutional and statutory provisions, corporations "are deemed and considered persons when the circumstances in which they are placed are identical with those of natural persons expressly included within such statute." Thus, a corporation is a person within the meaning of the

[1] Compania Embotelladora Carty, S.A. v. Seven-Up Co., page 747.

Fourteenth Amendment to the Federal Constitution, which provides that "no state shall make or enforce any law which shall abridge the privileges or immunities of citizens of the United States; nor shall any state deprive any person of life, liberty, or property without due process of law, nor deny to any person within its jurisdiction the equal protection of the laws." Also, the Fifth Amendment, providing that no person shall be deprived of liberty or property without due process of law, has been held to apply to corporations.

However, a corporation is not included within the word "person" under the Fifth Amendment to the Constitution, which pertains to rights of natural persons in criminal proceeding; also, a corporation is not a "citizen" within the meaning of section 2, article IV of the Constitution of the United States, which provides that "the citizens of each state shall be entitled to all privileges and immunities of citizens in the several states."

Private corporations, according to the character of their organization, may be either stock corporations or nonstock corporations. In stock corporations the membership is represented by shares of stock. In nonstock corporations there are no shares of stock, but the membership is determined by rules and regulations set out in the by-laws. The stock corporations are organized for the purpose of profit, whereas the nonstock corporations are organized as not-for-pecuniary-profit corporations, such as mutual benefit associations, fraternal organizations, clubs, and the like.

5-48. Entity disregarded. Occasionally, the courts feel free to look behind the corporate entity and take action as though no entity separate from the members existed.[2] However, the corporate entity may not be disregarded simply because all of the stock is owned by the members of a family or by one person.[3] One of the basic advantages of the corporate form of business organization is the limitation of liability. Frequently, a corporation is formed for the express purpose of limiting one's risk to the amount of his investment in the stock.[4]

There are certain distinct situations in which the entity is often disregarded. First, if the use of the corporation is to defraud or to avoid an otherwise valid obligation, the court may handle the problem as though no corporation existed. To illustrate, let us assume that *A* and *B* sold a certain business and agreed not to compete with the buyer for a given number of years. Desirous of re-entering business, in violation of the contract term, they organize a corporation, becoming the principal stockholders and managers. The buyer may have the corporation enjoined from competing with him as effectively as he could have enjoined *A* and *B*

[2] Mayrand v. Packaged Homes Mfg., Inc., page 748.
[3] Marks v. Green, page 749.
[4] Ramey v. Koons et al., page 751.

from establishing a competing business. If the corporate device is used to evade a statute, the corporate entity may be disregarded.[5]

A parent corporation, owning a controlling interest in a subsidiary, often completely dominates the activity of the latter so that it becomes purely an agent or arm of the parent company. Under such circumstances, the courts have often held the parent company liable for torts committed by the subsidiary. Occasionally, if the finances of the two companies have been used somewhat indiscriminately to meet the obligations of either company, ordinary contract creditors of the subsidiary are permitted to sue the holding company.

5-49. Foreign corporations. A corporation organized under the laws of a particular state or country is called within that particular state or country a "domestic corporation." A corporation has a residence that remains fixed in the state of its creation, although it may carry on a substantial part of its business in another state. A corporation doing business within another state or country is called a "foreign corporation." Nearly all corporations transact business across state lines, and in order to do so must satisfy the requirements of the particular state in which the business is conducted as to right of admission, service of process, and taxation, and must comply with such other restrictions as the state may see fit to impose.[6]

A corporation is a creature of the state which grants it a charter, and it has no existence beyond the boundaries of the state creating it. "It must dwell in the place of its creation and cannot migrate into another sovereignty." It may, however, like a natural person, enter into contracts, hold title to property, have agents, and engage in business in other states, subject to such limitations as those states prescribe. The Constitution of the United States provides that "the citizens of each state shall be entitled to all privileges and immunities of the citizens in the several states." Under this constitutional provision a citizen of one state has a right to go into another state for the purpose of engaging in lawful commerce, trade, or business. Likewise, a partnership would be privileged to engage in a trade or business in another state. However, a corporation has been held by the Supreme Court of the United States not to be a citizen entitled to the rights or protection of this particular constitutional provision. Therefore, the states have the power to impose conditions upon foreign corporations even though domestic corporations are not so burdened.

5-50. Conditions under which foreign corporations may "do business." Since a state may prescribe the conditions under which a foreign corporation may do business within its territorial limits, many states have taken

[5] New Hampshire Wholesale Bev. Assn. v. New Hampshire State Liquor Comm., page 753.

[6] Boney v. Trans-State Dredging Co., page 754.

advantage of this power by enacting statutes requiring foreign corporations to register by filing a copy of their articles with the secretary of state, to appoint an agent upon whom service of process may be served, to pay license fees, to designate and maintain an office in the state, to keep books and records, and to deposit bonds or securities with the treasurer of the state for the purpose of protecting any individual who might suffer loss by reason of the corporation's conduct. Refusal or failure by a foreign corporation to comply with these requirements justifies the state in denying the corporation the right to engage in business. Contracts of noncomplying foreign corporations are void and unenforceable by the corporation, because such corporations are denied the use of the courts by the state in which they are doing business without authority. But noncompliance cannot be used as a defense by the corporation when sued by a third party. If a contract is fully performed, neither party may seek restitution. Transacting business within the state without complying with the statute subjects the corporation or its officers to penalties.

A state cannot impose arbitrary and unreasonable requirements, particularly after having once admitted a foreign corporation to do business within the state. Such state cannot deny the corporation the equal protection of the law granted under the Fourteenth Amendment to the Federal Constitution. Discriminatory license taxes on capital stock, denial of the right of appeal to the federal courts, regulations interfering with interstate commerce by imposing taxes and license fees on the right to transport goods into or through the state from another state, are illustrations of unconstitutional restrictions upon "foreign corporations."

5-51. What constitutes "doing business" by a foreign corporation. The term "doing business" is not reducible to an exact and certain definition. State statutes do not define the term "doing business." In order to aid in determining whether a corporation is "doing business" within a state, the Model Foreign Corporation Act was drafted. It sets forth basic principles heretofore established by the courts. The Act in § 2 defines the term to mean that a foreign corporation is "doing business" when "some part of its business substantial and continuous in character and not merely casual or occasional" is transacted within a state.[7] Section 2, II of the Act states that a corporation is not "doing business" in a state merely because:

(a) It engaged in a single or isolated transaction in this state where its action in engaging in such single or isolated transaction indicates no intent or purpose of continuity of conduct in that respect; or . . .

(e) It does any act or acts which is or are merely preliminary to or looking toward the future transaction of business in this state, or

(f) It does any act or acts in this state relating solely to the management or control of the internal affairs of the corporation, such as the holding of corporate

[7] Frazier v. Ornamental Iron Works Company, page 756.

meetings, issuance of stock certificates, authorization of issue of bonds, making of calls on stock, or other acts of like nature; or

(g) It acquires and holds stock of domestic corporations and exercises in this state the incidents of such ownership unless through such stock ownership the domestic corporation is controlled by the foreign corporation and is in reality acting as the agent of the foreign corporation and doing business in this state for it and in its behalf . . .

Section 6 of the Act states that a foreign corporation shall not be required to obtain a license to do business or to file amended articles by reason of the fact that:

(a) It is in the mail order or a similar business, receiving orders by mail or otherwise, in pursuance of letters, circulars, catalogs or other forms of advertisement, or solicitation, accepting such orders outside this state and filling them with goods shipped into this state from without same direct to the purchaser thereof, or his agent; or

(b) It employs salesmen, either resident or traveling, to solicit orders in this state, either by display of samples or otherwise (whether or not maintaining sales offices in this state), all orders requiring approval at the offices of the corporation without this state, and all goods applicable to such orders being shipped in pursuance thereof from without this state to the purchaser; provided that any samples kept within this state are for display or advertising purposes only, and no sales, repairs, or replacements are made from stock on hand in this state . . .

A foreign corporation licensed to do business, doing business without a license, or whose license has been canceled, is subject to suit even though the corporation itself is denied access to the courts.

5-52. De jure and de facto corporations. A corporation de jure is a corporation which has been formed in compliance with the law authorizing such a corporation. A corporation de facto is one which operates as a corporation for all practical purposes, but has failed to comply with some provision of the law with respect to its creation and has no legal right to its corporate existence. Its corporate existence can be challenged only by the state itself, and not by third parties. Where persons have attempted in good faith to organize a corporation under a valid statute, but have failed in some particular and thereafter have assumed to exercise corporate power, a corporation de facto is said to exist. It must be clear that the three following situations are present: (1) a valid law authorizing such a corporation; (2) a bona fide attempt to organize and comply with the statute; (3) the exercise of corporate power. The corporation de facto can make contracts, purchase and hold real estate, sue and be sued in its corporate name, and do any and all things necessary to its corporate existence that a de jure corporation may do. The mere illegalities in the organization can be questioned only by the state itself.[8]

If persons hold themselves out as a corporation and create liability,

[8] Baum et al. v. Baum Holding Co. et al., page 691.

and such organization is less than a de facto corporation, they are generally held liable as partners. In some jurisdictions the stockholders even of a de facto corporation are held personally liable like partners for debts incurred by the corporation.[9] Some courts, however, hold that the liability rests not upon partnership relationship but upon the theory that such persons are agents for the other members of a pretended corporation. A few jurisdictions and authorities maintain that shareholders of a defectively organized corporation less than de facto should not be held individually liable on contracts, because the persons dealing with the pretended corporation contracted for corporate liability instead of for individual liability. For example, *A, B,* and *C* represent to *X* that they are a corporation, whereupon *X* purchases stock. *X* takes no part in the management of the pretended corporation. The pretended corporation contracts with *Y,* and *Y,* upon learning the fact that *A, B,* and *C* are not a corporation, sues *X* as a partner. Under these circumstances it would seem that *Y*'s claim should be merely a corporate one and *X*'s cause of action should be against *A, B,* and *C* individually.

PROMOTERS

5-53. Who are promoters. A promoter is one who usually performs the preliminary duties necessary to bring a corporation into existence. He calls together and supervises the first meeting of the organizers; enters into pre-corporation contracts with brokers, bankers, and subscribers; draws the preliminary articles of incorporation; and provides for registration and filing fees. He prepares the advertising, usually called a prospectus, which has for its purpose the informing of the public as to the character of the investment, so that they may be induced to subscribe for stock or other securities created by the company when organized. The above services of a promoter are applicable in the formation of large corporations. In organizing a small corporation the services of an attorney are usually adequate.

5-54. Corporate liability on contracts of promoters. The corporation, after its creation, may become bound by "adoption" upon contracts made by its promoter.[10] The term "adoption" does not mean ratification as applied in the law of agency, because, at the time the contract was made by the promoter with a third party, the corporation as principal was not in existence. More accurately, what occurs is a novation. When the corporation assents to the contract, the third party agrees to discharge the

[9] Burks et al. v. Cook et al., page 760.
[10] Knox et al. v. First Security Bank of Utah et al., page 762.

promoter and to look to the corporation. The discharge of the promoter by the third party is consideration to make binding the corporation's promise to be bound upon the contract.

In the absence of evidence to show that such a novation has occurred, the promoter will continue to be personally liable on the contract. Since the contract made with the promoter was made in anticipation of the formation of a corporation, the acceptance of the contract by the corporation after its creation is some evidence from which to draw an inference that a novation has occurred, but usually both the promoter and the corporation are liable, since the latter merely assumes, by implication, the obligation of the promoter without any agreement as to his release.

From the standpoint of the promoter, it is desirable that contracts entered into by him on behalf of the proposed corporation be so worded as to relieve him from personal liability. Thus it is possible in the contract to express an intent that the promoter shall not have personal liability.[11]

5-55. Corporate liability for expenses and services of promoters. Corporations are generally not liable for expenses and services of promoters, unless specifically made so by statute or by charter. However, a promise made after incorporation by the directors to pay for expenses and services of promoters will be binding and supported by sufficient consideration, on the theory of services previously rendered. It is held in some jurisdictions that corporations are liable by implication for the necessary expenses and services incurred by the promoters in bringing them into existence, and such expenses and services inure to the benefit of the corporation.

5-56. Duty of promoters to corporation ana stockholders. Promoters occupy a fiduciary relationship toward the prospective corporation and have no right, therefore, to secure any benefit or advantage over the corporation itself or over other stockholders, because of their position as promoters. A promoter cannot purchase property and then sell it to the corporation at an advance, nor has he a right to receive a commission from a third party for the sale of property to the corporation. In general, however, he may sell property acquired by him prior to the time he started promoting the corporation, provided he sells it to an unbiased board of directors after full disclosure of all pertinent facts.

5-57. Procedure for incorporation. A general law authorizing the formation of a corporation defines the purposes for which corporations may be formed, and prescribes the steps to be taken for the creation of the corporation. Such general law usually prescribes that any number of adult persons, usually not less than three, who are citizens of the United States and at least one of whom is a citizen of the state of incor-

[11] Ajouelo v. Wilkerson, page 764.

poration, may file an application for a charter. The application usually requires the names and addresses of the incorporators; the name of the corporation; the object for which it is formed; its duration; the location of its principal office; the total authorized capital stock, preferred and common; the number of shares, with their value; and, if the statute provides for stock without par value, the number of shares of such stock. It also requires the names and addresses of the subscribers to the capital stock, and the amount subscribed and paid in by each subscriber. It further requires the amount and the character of capital stock proposed to be issued at once, and whether the stock is paid for in cash or in property. This application, signed by all the incorporators and acknowledged by a notary public, is usually forwarded to a state official. This official then issues a charter which contains all the information on the application, and usually sets out the powers, rights, and privileges of the corporation as prescribed by the general incorporation act. The law usually requires that, upon the receipt of the charter, it be filed in the proper recording office located in the same community as the principal office of the corporation. A fee is usually charged, payable in advance, for filing an application for a charter, and no charter will be issued until such fee is paid. Where the application is for a corporation not for pecuniary profit, no detailed information is required relative to issues of stock, shares, and so forth. The requirements for securing a charter vary greatly in the different states and in different types of business in the same state. The requirements of the statute must be satisfied and complied with in detail for the formation of a de jure corporation.

After the charter has been received and filed, the board of directors and stockholders meets, drafts by-laws, and elects officers. The receipt of the charter and its filing are the operative facts that bring the corporation into existence and give it authority and power to operate.

The charter of a corporation is a contract and cannot be repealed or amended by the legislature unless such power has been reserved by the state when the charter was granted. The charter may be amended, however, by the consent of all of the stockholders or a certain portion thereof, as provided by the statute of the state.

CHARACTERISTICS OF CORPORATIONS CASES

COMPANIA EMBOTELLADORA CARTY, S.A. v. SEVEN-UP CO.

1960, 279 F.2d 175

Per Curiam. This appeal presents the question whether service of process on the Seven-Up Bottling Co. of Miami, Inc. as the alleged agent of the defendant, the Seven-Up Company, a Missouri corporation, is adequate service so as to confer jurisdiction on the District Court for the Southern District of Florida. The District Judge held that service on the Miami dealer was not service on the defendant and dismissed the suit.

The defendant has its principal place of business in St. Louis, Missouri and is the sole owner of trademarks, copyrights, and formula relating to a soft drink called "7-Up." The Seven-Up Bottling Company of Miami, Inc. bottles and sells the drink, using an extract or syrup purchased from the defendant under a contract giving the dealer the exclusive right to sell "7-Up" in Miami. The local dealer supplies its own bottles, crowns, and ingredients other than the extract. The Missouri company exercises no control over the local bottler except in the sense that unless the local bottler complies with certain standards, common to Seven-Up dealers, it may lose its franchise. The Miami dealer had no power to bind the Missouri corporation. The bottling company's sales were for its benefit; the Missouri company benefited only from the sales of the extract to the dealer.

We have carefully considered the pleadings, the depositions, and the exhibits, especially the "Territory Agreement" between the Seven-Up Company of Missouri and its Miami dealer. We agree with the district court that in the circumstances of this case service on the local dealer, the Seven-Up Bottling Company of Miami, Inc. cannot be said to be adequate service upon the Seven-Up Company of Missouri. . . .

Affirmed.

MAYRAND v. PACKAGED HOMES MFG., INC.

1960, 350 P.2d 862

The plaintiff, Mayrand, entered into a contract with Schultz whereby the latter agreed to remodel plaintiff's home for $7500. After partial performance Schultz abandoned the job on March 18, 1957. The plaintiff completed the remodeling at an expense in excess of $7,500 and brought this action for damages against defendant corporation which had been subsequently formed by Schultz and one Perry to engage in the building business. The trial court granted a judgment against the corporation.

OTT, Judge. . . . Appellant Packaged Homes Mfg., Inc., assigns error to the entry of judgment against it. Schultz abandoned the contract on March 18, 1957. The corporation was not formed until March 28, 1957. The trial court found that:

> . . . The only substantial asset or obligation of said defendant Schultz in said business not specifically and explicitly transferred to or assumed by said corporation was his abandoned contract with plaintiff which said corporation refused to perform.

The court held the corporation liable upon the authority of *Zander v. Larsen*, 1952, 41 Wash.2d 503, 250 P.2d 351. In that case, a corporation was formed for the purpose of taking over a business that had formerly been conducted as a partnership. The former partners were the only shareholders of the new corporation. All of the partnership assets became assets of the corporation, for which stock was issued to the former partners. All of the shareholders were individually liable on the obligation prior to incorporation. We held, in the cited case, that the corporation was merely a continuation of the partnership and was therefore bound to pay its debts. The partners, by incorporating, had simply "put on another coat."

The Zander case is not here apposite. Mrs. Mayrand contracted with Schultz only. The corporation was formed by Schultz and Perry (Herald A. O'Neill owned only a qualifying share). Perry contributed $4,100 in cash and $900 in services to the corporation. The corporation did not assume the abandoned Mayrand-Schultz contract. Perry was not obligated on the Mayrand-Schultz contract prior to the incorporation. Under these facts, the corporation was not a continuation of the Schultz business, but was a new entity. The new entity could assume any part of the former Schultz business it believed to be profitable. It was under no obligation to engage in unprofitable contracts or contracts which Schultz had abandoned.

. . . *The court erred in entering judgment against appellant corporation, and that judgment is reversed.*

MARKS v. GREEN

1960, (Fla.) 122 So.2d 491

The plaintiff is the sole owner of all the outstanding shares in Sa-Rey-Mar, Inc., a Florida corporation whose assets consist principally of intangible property. The corporation paid an intangible tax on this property but the defendant did not include his stock in Sa-Rey-Mar in his personal return. The taxing authorities ordered him to do so. He refused to do so and brought this suit for equitable relief against imposition of the tax. The defendants include the State Comptroller, the County Tax Assessor and the County Tax Collector. From a judgment in favor of the defendants plaintiff appealed.

WIGGINTON, Chief Judge. . . . The principal ground for relief is predicated upon the premise that the intangible tax assessment against appellant's ownership of all outstanding shares of stock in the corporation duplicated the tax assessment in the same amount levied against the corporation based upon the value of the intangible property owned by it, and as such amounted to a four mill levy on intangible property within the prohibition of the Constitution and laws of Florida. . . .

Appellant does not dispute that the capital stock owned by him in Sa-Rey-Mar Inc., falls within the classification of Class B intangible property as defined by the statute. He contends, however, that since he is the sole owner of the corporation and the corporation has already paid the intangible tax assessed against it on its capital assets, that he should be relieved of the burden of again paying an intangible tax on the value of the same property for which the corporation has already once paid the identical tax. Such reasoning falsely assumes that there exists an identity between the property owned by appellant as represented by his shares of stock in Sa-Rey-Mar, and the property owned by the corporation on which it has already paid the intangible tax. Appellant asks the court to indulge in this assumption on the theory that for tax purposes the separate identity of the corporation should be disregarded, and he as an individual should be adjudged the owner of the intangible property held by the corporation on which the tax has already been paid.

Appellant fortifies his position by citing a number of decisions in which courts of equity have under particular circumstances disregarded the corporate entity, pierced the corporate veil, or regarded the corporation as the alter ego of its stockholders. Such principles, when properly applied, are sound and entitled to respect. The cited authorities indicate, however, that such course has been followed as a matter of necessity only for the purpose of promoting justice or preventing injustice or fraud. We do not conceive that such principles may logically be applied in resolving the issue raised by this appeal. . . . It is our judgment that a sounder concept of the principles which should be followed in making an equitable distribution of the tax burden among the property owners of this state requires that for purposes of taxation, the identity of the corporate entity must be kept separate and distinct from the identity of its stockholders, unless otherwise provided by statute. . . .

Appellant has seen fit to organize a domestic corporation and own all its outstanding capital stock. He has elected to do business through this corporate entity. The benefits of conducting one's business in such manner are obvious and too numerous to mention in this opinion. Having so elected, appellant is in no position to claim all benefits accruing to him by virtue of doing business as a corporation, and at the same time seek to disregard the existence of the corporate entity in order to avoid payment of a tax otherwise chargeable to him. If payment of the intangible tax on the value of his stock in the corporation is considered to be an onerous burden, appellant . . . may dissolve the corporation and distribute to himself in kind the intangible property held by it.

. . . In adopting the latter course appellant would lose the many benefits he now enjoys by conducting his business through a fictitious legal entity. The choice of alternatives is the appellant's, but he cannot eat his cake and have it too.

Affirmed.

RAMEY v. KOONS et al.

1956, 230 F.2d 802

JONES, Circuit Judge. The appellant, Alex Ramey, by a written instrument dated October 8, 1954, and effective November 15, 1954, leased for ten years certain specifically described lands in Palm Beach County, Florida, to Charles A. Koons & Company, a partnership of which Charles A. Koons was a partner.

. . . As rental for the first three years, $5,000 was paid on the execution of the lease, $165,000 was payable on November 15, 1954, and $40,000 was to be paid when the landlord had completed some unfinished construction of canals, roads and bridges. On November 15, 1957, and semi-annually thereafter for the remainder of the term rental payments of $50,000 were to be made. Par. 13 of the sixteen numbered paragraphs of the instrument reads thus:

> It is understood that the Tenant will assign this lease and upon such assignment and the assumption by Assignee of the obligations hereunder, the Tenant shall be released from all obligations hereunder.

The landlord, appellant here, brought an action against Charles A. Koons individually and as a partner in a co-partnership doing business as Charles A. Koons & Company, and against Ramie Fiber Products, Inc., a Delaware corporation.

. . . The defendant, Charles A. Koons, as a partner of the original Tenant, executed an assignment of the lease in its entirety to Ramie Fiber Products, Inc. the corporate defendant, which appended to the assignment an assumption of the lease in which it agreed to make the stipulated payments and to carry out the terms, provisions and obligations thereof.

. . . The assignment was executed by Charles A. Koons as a partner and the assumption was signed in the name of the corporation by him as its President. The landlord averred that he had no knowledge of the assignment until November 30, 1954, when an attorney for Charles A. Koons delivered a copy to him with the advice that the contract would have to be renegotiated.

In his complaint it is stated by the plaintiff that . . . the corporation has no assets, is not legally responsible, is a mere "straw," and the "alter ego" of Charles A. Koons. The landlord charges that the assignment was made for the express purpose of attempting to relieve Charles A. Koons and the partnership from the lease liability. Refusal by Charles A. Koons to pay the $165,000 installment and advise to him that the lease was in default were pleaded. It was stated that the individual defendant, Charles A. Koons, told the landlord to go ahead and sue as the corporation had no assets. The landlord asserted he had sustained damages of one million dollars and the ad damnum of his complaint is laid in that amount. The defendants filed a motion to dismiss on the ground that the complaint fails to state a claim upon which relief can be granted. The court granted the motion and dismissed the complaint as to Charles A. Koons, individually and as a partner. The motion was denied as to Ramie Fiber Products, Inc. From the order dismissing the complaint against Charles A. Koons, individually and as a partner, an appeal has been taken.

. . . the appellant urges that the assignment is fraudulent because the corporate assignee is a "straw," the alter ego of the appellee, Charles A. Koons, and that the assignment was made for the purpose of relieving Koons and his partnership from liability on the lease. As a guide toward a decision on this question, we look to the Florida Supreme Court and find the following:

> The law is well settled that the organization of a corporation for the purpose of evading an existing personal liability on the part of those who became its stockholders will not be allowed to achieve that purpose, for in such case the courts will "pierce the veil of the corporate fiction" and hold the stockholders of the corporation to their personal liability, even though the corporation was regularly organized in accordance with the statutes. Not that the law deems it reprehensible to form a corporation in order to limit one's risk to the amount of his investment in the stock, so far as future liabilities of the corporation are concerned; for this is legitimate and an everyday occurrence.
>
> Thus Prof. Wormser, in the book referred to (*The Disregard of the Corporate Fiction and Allied Corporate Problems*) (p. 18), says:
>
> "Such a decision is entirely correct, because, if the corporation has been validly organized in its inception, the use of the corporation to prevent the incurring of personal obligations in the future is entirely proper and legitimate. The policy of our law to-day sanctions incorporation with the consequent immunity from individual liability. It follows that no fraud is committed in incorporating for the precise purpose of avoiding and escaping personal responsibility. Indeed, that is exactly why most people incorporate, and those dealing with corporations know, or at least are presumed to know, the law in this regard." *Bellaire Securities Corporation v. Brown*, 124 Fla. 47, 168 So. 625, 633.

In the case before us the parties agreed that the tenant would assign the lease and upon the assumption of its obligations by the assignee the tenant would be released. As said in the foregoing quotation from Professor Wormser, "no fraud is committed in incorporating for the precise purpose of avoiding and escaping personal responsibility." To hold otherwise "would completely destroy the corporate entity as a method of doing business and it would ignore the historical justification for the corporate enterprise system." *Advertects, Inc. v. Sawyer Industries,* Fla., 84 S.2d. 21, 23.

Viewing the complaint in the light most favorable to the appellant, we find no claim stated upon which relief can be granted against Charles A. Koons, individually or as a partner of the co-partnership doing business as Charles A. Koons & Company. We are not now concerned with the claim of the appellant against the corporation, Ramie Fiber Products, Inc.

The judgment appealed from is affirmed.

NEW HAMPSHIRE WHOLESALE BEVERAGE ASSN. v. NEW HAMPSHIRE STATE LIQUOR COMM.

1955, (N.H.) 116 A.2d 885

The plaintiff is an association of individuals who hold wholesaler's liquor permits issued by the defendant commission under authority of a statute (R.C.L. 170). Sec. 76 of the statute provides, "No person shall directly or indirectly hold more than two off-sale permits at one time." The plaintiff alleges that the defendant has violated the statute by issuing one or two off-sale permits to each of certain corporations with knowledge that such corporations are owned, operated or controlled by the same person or the same group of persons. The plaintiff seeks an injunction and a declaratory judgment. The trial judge referred the case to the Supreme Court.

Goodnow, J. . . . In applying this limitation to a corporation, the commission has treated the corporation as a separate entity, without regard to whether the person or persons who own or control it are the owners or in control of other corporate off-sale permittees. The plaintiffs contend that the same person or group of persons have thereby been permitted to hold "directly or indirectly . . . more than two off-sale permits at one time," in violation of § 76.

The fiction that the corporation is a being independent of those who are associated as its stockholders is not favored in this state.

It is to be disregarded "when justice demands it." In this case, it is not entitled to recognition as the basis for the issuance of off-sale permits if a means is thereby provided of avoiding a clear legislative purpose.

The defendants, relying on the fact that § 58 specifically authorizes the issuance of off-sale permits to corporations and that the word "person" in the statute in question should be construed as "corporation" in accordance with § 1, subd. III, contend that the Legislature did not intend that the issuance of off-sale permits to a corporation should in any way depend upon the identity of its stockholders. They further urge that if such had been the legislative purpose, that fact could have been spelled out as it is in the prohibitions concerning interlocking stock ownership between the holder of a wholesaler's permit and the holder of an on-sale or off-sale permit. We are unable to adopt this view of the Legislature's intention.

Chapter 170 has repeatedly been construed by this court as "intended to provide a complete and well-rounded system for the regulation and control of all intoxicating liquors."

By its terms, manufacturers, wholesalers and retailers of alcoholic beverages are separated into classes and "no control, direct or indirect and no interest, financial or otherwise, shall be exercised by one over the other." The statute now in question was designed to impose a similar regulation within one class of retailers.

The maximum number of off-sale permits is not only fixed at two but the limitation is to be applied so that "no person" shall hold more than that number either "directly or indirectly." By so limiting the number of off-sale permits we believe that the Legislature intended to prevent a concentration of such permits in the hands of the same persons. Not every case of interlocking stock ownership results in an indirect holding of an off-sale permit. Before the issuance of such permits to a corporation the facts must be determined by the commission as to whether the person or persons owning or controlling the corporation are also the holders of other off-sale permits, either individually or as the owners or those in control of other corporate off-sale permittees.

The relief sought by plaintiffs was granted.

BONEY v. TRANS-STATE DREDGING CO
1960 (S.C.) 115 S.E.2d 508

The plaintiff was injured when a boat in which he was traveling was upset by a cable used by the defendant corporation in connection with its dredging operations. The defendant is a Florida corporation and had not qualified as a foreign corporation doing business in South Carolina. The plaintiff brought his action in the South Carolina court and made a substituted service of process on the defendant. The defendant claims that the court does not have jurisdiction as the corporation was not "doing business" in South Carolina. The facts showed that the dredging operations brought the defendant in contact with both Georgia and South Carolina along the Savannah River. The lower court ruled that the service of process was ineffective and the plaintiff appealed.

LEGGE, Justice. . . . The crucial issue here is: Was the defendant doing business in this State at the time of the accident? If that issue be resolved in the affirmative, the substituted service under Section 12–722 was good. . . .

No universal formula has been, or is likely to be devised for determining what constitutes "doing business" by a foreign corporation within a state in such sense as to subject it to the jurisdiction of the courts of that state. The question must be resolved upon the facts of the particular case. *Jones v. General Motors Corporation,* 197 S.C. 129, 14 S.E.2d 628; *State v. Ford Motor Co.,* 208 S.C. 379, 38 S.E.2d 242.

Recent decisions of both federal and state courts have tended to discard older concepts whereby jurisdiction was accorded on the fictional premise of the corporation's implied consent or on the theory that the corporation is "present" wherever its activities are carried on, and to substitute therefor, as the jurisdictional test, the requirement that the corporation have such contact with the state of the forum "that the maintenance of the suit does not offend 'traditional notions of fair play and substantial justice.'" *International Shoe Co. v. State of Washington,* 326 U.S. 310, 66 S.Ct. 154, 158, 90 L.Ed. 95, 161 A.L.R. 1057. . . .

That this principle is in itself nebulous is evident from its statement. But in its application we are directed by the authorities just cited to certain considerations that are of help in the solution of the problem in most cases, and seem important here. Among them are the duration of the corporate activity in the state of the forum; the character of the acts giving rise to the suit, and the circumstances of their commission; and the balancing of the inconvenience to the parties, respectively, of a trial in that state on the one hand and in the state of the corporate domicile on the other.

It is evident that the criteria by which we mark the boundary line between those activities which justify the subjection of a corporation to suit, and those which do not, cannot be simply mechanical or quantitative. The test is not merely, as has sometimes been suggested, whether the activity, which the corporation has seen fit to procure through its agents in another state, is a little more or a little less. * * * Whether due process is satisfied must depend rather upon the quality and nature of the activity in relation to the fair and orderly administration of the laws which it was the purpose of the due process clause to insure. That clause does not contemplate that a state may make binding a judgment in personam against an individual or corporate defendant with which the state has no contacts, ties or relations * * *.

But to the extent that a corporation exercises the privilege of conducting activities within a state, it enjoys the benefits and protection of the laws of that state. The exercise of that privilege may give rise to obligation; and sofar as those obligations arise out of or are connected with the activities within the state, a procedure which requires the corporation to respond to a suit brought to enforce them can, in most instances, hardly be said to be undue. [*International Shoe Co. v. State of Washington. . . .*]

We are of opinion that the defendant's said operations, although not continuously performed in South Carolina, constituted corporate activity

within that state sufficient to meet the test before referred to and therefore to render the defendant subject to the jurisdiction of its courts. . . .
Reversed and remanded.

FRAZIER v. ORNAMENTAL IRON WORKS COMPANY
1958, 188 N.Y.S.2d 102

HUDSON, Justice. The motion in this case is made by the defendant, appearing specially to set aside the service of a summons on the ground that the defendant is a foreign corporation not doing business in this State and having no representative upon whom service is proper and is not subject to the jurisdiction of the Court. Affidavits have been submitted by both parties supporting their contentions as to the extent of the defendant's business and the duties of its employee upon whom service was made.

It is urged by the defendant that it is a corporation organized under the laws of Ohio; that its only place of business is in that State and that all of its operations are conducted therefrom. It is also urged that all of its work is directed from its Akron, Ohio offices and that all of its employees are paid by check issued therefrom and that it has no officer, director or managing agent in the State of New York nor any office for the conduct of business therein. It is also contended that its employee, Victor Nowlan, upon whom the summons was served, was merely a foreman; that he is employed under Union contract requirements and has no managerial duty or authority.

It is contended by the plaintiff in opposition to the motion that Victor Nowlan is in fact a job superintendent or supervisor for the defendant; that he has charge of the defendant's work in this state and that he supervises and directs the employees of the defendant in the carrying on of their duties under numerous subcontracts in which the company is engaged in this state. . . .

I am satisfied from the affidavits that the defendant is a corporation organized and existing under the laws of Ohio; that it has no certificate filed in the State of New York authorizing it to do business here; that it has done business within the State of New York to the extent that of 568 contracts performed in the past three and one half years, fourteen were done in New York State but that those fourteen constituted ten per cent of the total volume of business done by the defendant; that the defendant engaged in such contracts; that service of process was made upon one Victor Nowland, the foreman in charge of the work of the defendants in New York, he having authority to supervise the work, employ and direct workmen on the job and represent the company on the job in its dealings with prime contractors. I am, therefore, of the opinion that it is clearly established by the moving papers as a fact that Victor Nowland is a managing agent of the defendant within the meaning of that expression as used in section 229, subdivision 3 of the Civil Practice Act.

As has been repeatedly held by the Courts in this State, there is no precise formula by which to measure the nature or extent of local business activities which render foreign corporations amenable to process in this state. Each case must be determined on its own particular facts. *Tauza v. Susquehanna Coal Co.*, 220 N.Y., 259, 115 N.E. 915; *Palmer v. Pennsylvania Co.*, 35 Hun 369, at page 371; *Halpern v. Pennsylvania Lumber Industries*, 137 Misc. 688, 244 N.Y.S. 372, at page 374; *Sterling Novelty Corp. v. Frank & Hirsch Distributing Co.*, 299 N.Y. 208, 210, 86 N.E.2d 564, 565, 12 A.L.R.2d 1435. The proper and reasonable rule to be applied is set forth in the landmark case of *International Shoe Co. v. State of Washington, Office of Unemployment Compensation & Placement*, 326 U.S. 310, 66 S.Ct. 154, 90 L.Ed. 95, that jurisdiction exists where the foreign corporation has such contacts within the state of the forum as make it reasonable and just and inoffensive to traditional notions of fair play to require the corporation to defend the particular suit which is brought. The criteria applied should neither be mechanical nor quantitative but simply that a foreign corporation should be held to the obligation of responding to an action to the extent that it has exercised the privilege of conducting activities within a state. *International Shoe Co. v. State of Washington, Office of Unemployment Compensation & Placement, supra.* Such activities exercised in this forum must be an essential and integral part of its business but need not be the principal part thereof. *Pomeroy v. Hocking Valley R. Co.*, 218 N.Y. 530, 113 N.E. 504.

The defendant has submitted numerous authorities including two very recent decisions: *Miller v. Surf Properties*, 4 N.Y.2d 475, 176 N.Y.S.2d 318; *Hardaway v. Illinois Cent. R. Co.*, 9 Misc.2d 705, 170 N.Y.S.2d 584. In my opinion these cases involve an entirely different set of circumstances than those in the present case. I am also of the opinion that under the cases cited herein, Vincent Nowland exercised and performed duties on behalf of the defendant which would qualify him to be a managing agent within the meaning of section 229, subdivision 3 of the Civil Practice Act. The motion is, therefore, denied with ten dollars ($10.00) costs. Order accordingly.

BAUM et al. v. BAUM HOLDING CO. et al.

1954, 158 Neb. 197, 62 N.W.2d 864

A corporation known as the Baum Realty Company was incorporated in 1922 by the members of the Baum family who were the owners of a business building and adjoining garage in Omaha. 1,237 shares of stock were issued to the family in proportion to their interests in the property. Shortly thereafter four of the Baums, including David A. Baum, owning a total of 620 shares in the realty company, organized the holding company and assigned to it the shares in the realty company. David A. Baum had a majority of the holding company stock and the plaintiffs, stockholders in the realty company, claim that David A. Baum can completely control both corporations though he was in fact a minority stockholder in the realty company. The plaintiffs contend that at the time the holding company was organized, corporations in Nebraska were not permitted to hold and own stock in another corporation. The plaintiffs seek a declaratory judgment declaring the rights, status and other legal relations of the Baum Realty Company, and the Baum Holding Company and the stockholders of each. The lower court sustained defendants' demurrer and plaintiffs appealed.

CARTER, J. . . . It is the contention of the defendants [by way of demurrer] that plaintiffs, as stockholders in the holding company, cannot question the validity of the holding company as a corporation. The answer to this question turns on whether or not the holding company is a corporation, either de jure or de facto. If the holding company has no existence, either de jure or de facto, it is subject to collateral attack and plaintiffs can properly question it as a legal entity in the manner here sought. But if the holding company is a corporation, de jure or de facto, a suit to destroy it must be by direct attack by the state by quo warranto proceedings.

It is urged by the plaintiffs that corporations in this state were not permitted to hold and own stock in another corporation at the time the holding company was organized. We assume, without deciding the question, that this was true. In 1941, however, the Legislature enacted Chapter 41, § 77, Laws 1941, now § 21–1–141, R.S. 1943, which provides: "Any corporation operating or organized under this article may . . . purchase . . . the shares of the capital stock . . . created by any other corporation or corporations of this state."

. . . The defendants contend that with the adoption of § 21–1, 141, R.S. 1943, the power to organize a corporation to hold the stock of another was specifically granted and from and after that enactment, a de jure corporation could exist. The petition shows that the holding company carried on as a corporation many years after 1941. Officers were elected and dividends were paid. Plaintiffs recognized the holding company as a corporation until the difficulties arose which brought about this suit. We agree with the defendants that the enactment of § 21–1, 141 R.S. 1943, was sufficient authority to organize a de jure corporation for the holding of stock in another corporation and, consequently, it affords a sufficient basis for a holding that the holding company was a de facto corporation after its enactment.

. . . It is a fundamental principle that there cannot be a corporation de facto where there are no laws authorizing a corporation de jure. Assuming that there were no laws authorizing a corporation de jure prior to the enactment of Chapter 41, Laws 1941, such authorization clearly existed after the adoption of that act. A purported corporation was in existence which could have been organized pursuant to the 1941 corporation act. A colorable compliance with the act subsequent to 1941 was had. There was an actual user of the authority granted by the act in which the plaintiffs participated and acquiesced. The holding company carried on business in full compliance with Chapter 41, Laws 1941, for many years before plaintiffs undertook to question its validity and powers. In discussing the nature of de facto corporations this court has said: "But, ofttimes, an association may not be able to justify itself when called on by the state to show by what authority it assumes to be, and acts as, a corporation. It may, however, be so far a corporation that, for reasons of public policy, no one but the state will be permitted to call in question the lawfulness of its organization. Such is what is termed a corporation de facto; that is, a corporation from the fact of its acting as such, though not in law or of right a corporation."

A substantial compliance will create a corporation de jure. But there must be an apparent attempt to perfect an organization under the law. There being such apparent attempt to perfect an organization, the failure as to some substantial requirement will prevent the body being a corporation de jure; but, if there be user pursuant to such attempted organization, it will not prevent it being a corporation de facto.

The holding company being a de facto corporation it cannot be attacked collaterally and its legality as an entity may be called into question only by direct attack by the state. "The reason a collateral attack by a third person will not avail against a corporation de facto is that, if the rights and franchises have been usurped, they are the rights and franchises of the state, and it alone can challenge the validity of the franchise. Until such interposition, the public may treat those in possession and exercising corporate powers under color of law as doing so rightfully. The rule is in the interest of the public and is essential to the safety of business transactions with corporations. It would produce disorder and confusion, embarrass and endanger the rights and interests of all dealing with the association, if the legality of its existence could be drawn into question in every suit in which it is a party or in which rights were involved springing out of its corporate existence." *Thies v. Weible*, 126 Neb. 720, 254 N.W. 420, 423.

. . . Plaintiffs urge that in any event the right of one corporation to own and hold stock in another as permitted by the 1941 act is not an unlimited one, but merely a power to be exercised incidentally by a corporation organized for some purpose other than the mere holding of stocks. The statute bears no such construction and the articles themselves cannot be so limited where the only purpose, as here, is the holding of stocks in a named corporation. Cases which interpret the objects and purposes of a corporation as stated in its articles with respect to the holding of stocks of other corporations are not pertinent to the construction to be placed upon the statutory provision relating thereto in the 1941 act. Such act, § 21–1, 141, R.S. 1943, contains no language from which it can be inferred that the right to own and hold stock of another corporation is an incidental as distinguished from an independent power.

. . . For the reasons stated, that part of the petition which questions the existence of the holding company as a corporation does not state a cause of action on the part of these plaintiffs.

The demurrer was properly sustained.

BURKS et al. v. COOK et al.
1955, (Ark.), 284 S.W.2d 855

The plaintiffs, Cook and others, partners, brought this action to recover for merchandise sold and charged to the Motor Truck Rentals System, during the period from October 29, 1953, to December 12, 1953. The defendants are the incorporators and stockholders of the Motor Truck Rentals System, articles of incorporation of which were filed in the office of the Secretary of State on August 26, 1953. The Statute requires that the articles also be filed in the office of the County Clerk. This was not done until June 18, 1954. The court ruled in favor of the plaintiffs and defendants appealed.

WARD, J. The question for decision in this case is: When are the organizers of a purported corporation individually liable for debts contracted in the name of such corporation? No oral testimony was taken in the trial court, and this case is presented to us on the pleadings, stipulations and the record.

. . . On June 14, 1954, appellees filed this suit against appellants (the original incorporators named above) to recover judgment for the articles above mentioned. It was alleged that the articles of incorporation and the amendment thereof had never been filed in the office of the Pulaski County Clerk as required by Ark. Stats. § 64–103; that the Motor Truck Rentals System, Inc., is a de facto corporation, and that the stockholders or original organizers were individually liable as partners.

On June 18, 1954, the aforementioned Articles of Incorporation and the Amendment were filed in the office of the Pulaski County Clerk.

On April 22, 1955, the above factual situation was submitted to the trial judge, sitting as a jury, and he rendered a joint and several judgment against all appellants.

The judgment of the trial court must be affirmed in part on the authority of the *Gazette Publishing Company v. Brady*, 204 Ark. 396, 162 S.W.2d 494, and *Whitaker v. Mitchell Manufacturing Co.*, 219 Ark. 779, 244 S.W.2d 965.

It is earnestly contended that the judgment of the trial court should be reversed insofar as it held appellant, Willis V. Lewis, liable. Lewis was one of the original organizers of the National Truck Leasing System, Inc., the name of which was later changed to Motor Truck Rentals System, Inc. In the *Gazette* case, *supra* (204 Ark. 396, 162 S.W.2d 496) this court approved a statement made in the case of *Garnett v. Richardson*, 35 Ark. 144, that "in order to exempt the organizers of a corporation from personal liability for the debts of the concern the articles of incorporation must be filed in both the office of the secretary of state and the office of the county clerk." It is undisputed that in the present case neither the articles of incorporation nor the amendment had been, at the time suit was instituted, filed in the office of the County Clerk of Pulaski County. Thus it would seem from the above that Lewis must be held liable in this instance. However we do not think that, under the facts and circumstances of this case, the above conclusion correctly follows.

We have present in this case a fact situation which was not present in the *Garnett* and *Gazette* cases, *supra*, in that here credit was extended after Lewis ceased to be a member of the purported corporation. This fact question not being present in the cited cases we can feel sure that no special consideration was given to it. The *Garnett* opinion is short and certainly no consideration was given to the point under question in that case. The gist of the opinion in that case is found in the last sentence which reads as follows: "for purchases made by them before then they were personally liable as partners." From this it appears that the court was considering a case where the original incorporators made the purchases for which they were held liable. In this case Lewis had of course withdrawn from the purported corporation some two months before the purchases were made.

In this instance Lewis and the other original incorporators are placed in the role of partners by operation of law since they did not file articles of incorporation in the office of the County Clerk. Considering them as partners we have concluded that Lewis is not liable on the debt herein sued upon under the decisions of this court pertaining to a partnership. In the case of *Rector v. Robins*, 74 Ark. 437, 86 S.W. 667, 669, a creditor sought to hold liable Robins, a member of a partnership, who withdrew from the partnership before the debt was contracted. This court there approved an instruction which stated that Robins would be liable if the creditor "extended the credit for the claim sued on in the faith of his belief that W. H. Robins was such a partner." The court again indicated in 74 Ark. on p. 443, 86 S.W. 667, that before Rector could hold Robins liable he must have extended credit upon the faith of Robins' partnership in the firm.

It cannot be said in the case under consideration that appellees extended credit to the Motor Truck Rentals System, Inc., because of their reliance on Lewis' financial responsibility. No evidence was taken in this case and therefore there is no showing that appellees extended credit because of Lewis.

. . . It cannot, of course, be said in the case under consideration that Lewis' conduct in any way misled appellees, since no evidence was introduced. Neither did the "partnership" bear the name of Lewis.

Based upon the above observations it is our conclusion that the trial court erred in holding Lewis liable and the judgment is hereby reversed to that extent, but it is affirmed as to the other appellants.

Affirmed in part and reversed in part.

KNOX et al. v. FIRST SECURITY BANK OF UTAH et al.

1952, 196 F.2d 112

The plaintiffs as surviving heirs of Frank Knox brought this action against the bank as executor of the estate of A. C. Milner, deceased, and the Milner Corporation as defendants to recover damages for breach of contract. In 1909 Milner as a promoter entered into an agreement with the deceased Frank Knox whereby it was stipulated that the Milner Corporation would be organized and that when chartered the corporation would pay to Knox $25,000 from the first net profits derived by the corporation from the sale of the mining properties involved in the agreement. The corporation was subsequently organized and in 1924 Milner as president of the defendant corporation wrote a letter to the plaintiff, DeWitt Knox, stating that the corporation would live up to the terms of the agreement made with his father. The lower court sustained defendant's motion to dismiss and the plaintiffs appealed.

BRATTON, Circuit Judge. . . . The first contention urged by plaintiffs is that the complaint stated a cause of action against the defendant Milner Corporation, and that the court erred in dismissing the action as against that defendant. It is argued in support of the contention that the original undertaking entered into in 1909 was a promoters contract; that it was accepted and adopted by the defendant Milner Corporation; and that therefore such defendant is liable. It is well settled law in Utah that promoters or those contemplating the organization of a corporation do not have power to enter into a contract with binding effect upon the corporation after it is organized. They lack that power, either as agents or otherwise. But promoters or those contemplating the formation of a corporation may make a contract in furtherance of the corporation and for its benefit; and if the corporation after it comes into existence accepts or adopts the contract, it thereupon becomes the contract of the corporation and may be enforced against it. (Cases cited)

Under the law of Utah, a contract made by and with promoters which is intended to inure to the benefit of a corporation about to be organized is to be regarded as an open offer which the corporation may after its formation accept or adopt, as it chooses. And if it does in the exercise of its own judgment accept or adopt the contract and retain the benefits of it, it cannot reject liability under it. In the absence of acceptance or adoption of a contract of that kind, the corporation is not liable even though it may have been entered into with the understanding that the corporation would be bound. But it is not necessary that acceptance or adoption of a contract of that kind be by express action of the corporation entered in the minutes of the directors, or that it be effectuated in any other like formal manner. It may be inferred from acts, conduct, and acquiescence.

The original undertaking was an agreement in the nature of a promoters contract. And from what has been said it is manifest that defendant Milner Corporation is not bound by it to make payment of the $25,000 unless it was accepted or adopted in an effective manner. Assuming for the moment that Milner, in his capacity as president of the corporation, was clothed with authority to act for it in accepting and adopting the undertaking, there can be little doubt that the letter written in 1924 constituted an effective acceptance and adoption. The letter referred at the beginning to the undertaking to pay $25,000 from the sale of the property or from profits derived from its operation. It stated in clear terms that the time when liquidation of the obligation would begin was dependent upon the volume of business done and the payment of advances made to an operating company. And it further stated without condition or qualification that the agreement was being kept in mind and would be reached at the proper time. Plainly, the last statement was intended to mean that the obligation would be reached for payment at the proper time. The letter constituted recognition of the original undertaking as an obligation on the part of the corporation to pay the amount specified in the contract at the proper time. And in the circumstances, that recognition amounted to an effective acceptance and adoption of the undertaking.

The judgment insofar as it dismissed the action against the defendant Milner Corporation is reversed.

AJOUELO v. WILKERSON

1952, 85 Ga. App. 397, 69 S.E.2d 375

The plaintiff, an inventor, entered into a contract with the defendant, promoter, providing for the manufacture of certain patented devices and the employment of the plaintiff. It was further provided that the corporation which was to be formed for the purpose of manufacturing and selling the devices, shall have the promoter's rights under the contract and assume his obligations. The corporation was organized and the promoter assigned to it the contract. The plaintiff then entered into a new contract with the corporation which contract provided that the new contract "is to supersede and take the place of all prior contracts entered into by the parties hereto or their predecessors." The plaintiff thereafter sued the defendant promoter for the salary agreed upon in the first contract. The lower court ruled in favor of defendant and plaintiff appealed.

SUTTON, Chief Judge. The plaintiff's suit was for damages for breach of the contract between the parties dated June 30, 1932. It was undisputed that the plaintiff, Ajouelo, had offered to go to work for either Wilkerson, the defendant, or the Auto-Soler Company on June 1, 1933, and at intervals thereafter, and that neither the defendant nor his company had ever employed Ajouelo or paid him wages or salary, as provided for in the contract sued upon. It was undisputed that the defendant had formed a corporation, the Auto-Soler Company, on August 26, 1932; that he transferred and assigned to that corporation his rights under the contract or contracts with Ajouelo and received stock in the company therefor; and that the company had accepted these rights and assumed his obligations under said contract. It clearly appears from the contract sued on that it was within the contemplation of the parties thereto that such a corporation would be formed by Wilkerson to succeed to and take his place under said contract with Ajouelo.

. . . The plaintiff's main contention is that the contract sued upon was severable into parts, one part providing for the payment of royalties and another for the employment of Ajouelo by the defendant, and that the jury would have been authorized to find, under the evidence, that the latter part of the contract had never been superseded or extinguished by any of the later contracts between Ajouelo and the company formed by the defendant. However, under the undisputed evidence in the case and by the terms of the written contracts, there was no such issue for submission to the jury.

A novation of debtors is constituted by the release of the original debtor and the substitution of a new debtor in his place. This release and substitution may be by express terms, or may be inferred from the acts of the parties or by necessary implication from a construction of the subsequent agreement. *Loftis Plumbing & Heating Co. v. American Surety Co.*, 74 Ga. App. 590, 593, 40 S.E.2d 667, and citations. The contract of November 4, 1932, expressly provided that: "This contract and agreement is to supersede and take the place of all prior contracts and agreements entered into by and between the parties hereto or their predecessors and this contract contains the full and complete agreement between the parties." In the contract sued upon, Wilkerson "or his successors or assigns" was to employ the plaintiff, and the Auto-Soler Company was the assignee and successor of the defendant, Wilkerson. Therefore, a "predecessor" of the Auto-Soler Company was its promoter, Wilkerson, and the provision above quoted was effective to extinguish his obligations under the contracts between him and the plaintiff, Ajouelo, entered into prior to the formation of the Auto-Soler Company, including his promise in the contract of June 30, 1932, to employ the plaintiff.

Wilkerson and Ajouelo both signed the contract of November 4, 1932, and although Wilkerson signed it in his capacity as secretary of the company, it is apparent that both he and Ajouelo thereby assented to the execution of the new contract by which Wilkerson was released, and the Auto-Soler Company substituted for him. See, in this connection, *Acree v. Kay*, 188 Ga. 783, 4 S.E.2d 820.

The plaintiff also contends that there were ambiguities in the contracts which created issues of fact as to the intent of the parties which should have been submitted to the jury. But the contract of June 30, 1932, as above stated, shows plainly that the plaintiff and the defendant both contemplated that the defendant was to be succeeded by a corporation to be formed by him to carry on the exploitation of the plaintiff's inventions, and the contract of November 4, 1932, between Ajouelo and the Auto-Soler Company, shows without ambiguity the intent of the parties that said contract should supersede all contracts entered into by Ajouelo and the company or its predecessor, namely, the defendant.

Since the contract sued upon, as to both its employment and royalty features, was expressly superseded by the contract of November 4, 1932, which introduced a new party and new obligations, the trial judge did not err in directing a verdict for the defendant.

Judgment affirmed.

Review Questions and Problems

1. A corporation was engaged in the operation of a drive-in theater. The stockholders in the corporation were all members of one family. The corporation entered into a contract with the labor union calling for the employment of two union projectionists. Subsequently *A*, a stockholder and member of the family, took over the post of one of the union projectionists. The union picketed the theater and suit was brought to enjoin the picketing. What should be the result?

2. A bank was chartered under the laws of Tennessee. The bank financed the operations of an automobile dealer in Mississippi and discounted notes received from the dealer's customers. A fire destroyed the dealer's place of business and the bank brought suit to impound the insurance money for the satisfaction of the dealer's obligation to the bank. The dealer contended that the suit should not be allowed because the bank had not qualified to do business in Mississippi. Should the bank be allowed to sue in the Mississippi court?
3. A Massachusetts manufacturing corporation leased property in Arizona with a view toward conducting an operation there. The lease was cancelled by the owner who contended that the lease was invalid because the corporation had not qualified as a foreign corporation doing business in Arizona. Is this contention correct?
4. *A* and *B*, partners, incorporated their business but continued to operate it as though they were partners. The business was undercapitalized. Should *A* and *B* be held to partnership liability?
5. *A*, *B*, and *C* operated a bus line. They filed a certificate of incorporation and sold their buses to the corporation. After they completed the certificate but before it had been recorded a passenger on one of the buses was injured in a collision. Would *A*, *B*, and *C* be personally liable to the passenger?
6. The promoters of a corporation agreed that the corporation when organized would engage the services of *A*, an accountant, to install a bookkeeping system. They further agreed that *A* would receive 25 shares for his services. The corporation was formed and *A* performed the services but did not receive the stock. *A* brought suit against the corporation. Should he prevail?
7. *A*, *B*, and *C* petitioned for a corporate charter for the purpose of conducting a retail shoe business. All the statutory provisions were complied with, except that they failed to have their charter recorded. This was an oversight on their part, and they felt that they had fully complied with the law. They operated the business for three years, after which time it became insolvent. The creditors desire to hold the members liable as partners. May they do so?
8. The promoters of a corporation engaged the services of *A* prior to incorporation. After incorporation the company promised to pay *A* for his services. Is this promise enforceable?
9. *A* and *B* obtained an option upon a building which had been used for manufacturing pianos. They acted as the promoters for the corporation and turned over the building to the new corporation for $100,000 worth of stock. As a matter of fact, their option on the building called for a purchase price of only $60,000. The other stockholders desire to have $40,000 of the common stock canceled. Can they succeed in an action to have it canceled?
10. *A*, the promoter of a corporation gave an order for goods signed in his name on behalf of the corporation. The seller was aware that the corporation had not been formed. After the corporation was formed the goods were delivered but the entire price was not paid. The corporation became insolvent and the seller sued *A*. The trial court held in favor of the seller. Was this correct?

11. The Maxwell Café was a corporation holding a state liquor license in the corporate name. *A, B,* and *C,* brothers, purchased all the stock in the corporation. Thereafter the liquor license was revoked for violations occurring before the brothers bought the stock. The brothers contend that the revocation should be set aside, that the court should look behind the corporate entity to the stockholders and that *A, B,* and *C* as stockholders should not be held for conduct of the corporation before they bought all the stock. Should they succeed in setting aside the revocation?
12. *A, B,* and *C* operated a spoke and handle factory as partners. They ordered a machine from *X* and then formed a corporation to continue the business. *X* accepted some payments for the machine from the corporation. Are *A, B,* and *C,* who are now major stockholders in the corporation, liable individually for the amount due?

34

Powers of Corporations

5-58. In general. The corporation has only such powers as are expressly conferred upon it by the state. The state may grant any power to a corporation that it desires, if such grant is not limited by the state or federal constitution. The express powers of a corporation are found within its corporate charter and the statute that created it. It can do no acts that are not specifically set forth in the charter, unless such acts are impliedly inferred as reasonably necessary and proper for carrying out the express powers granted.[1]

In the application for a charter the incorporators usually state very broad powers; these statements of power are generally included in the charter.

5-59. Incidental powers. Under general incorporation acts now in force in most states, the powers incidental to corporate existence are generally enumerated. The following incidental powers have at various times been said to exist, as necessary for corporate existence: (1) to have a corporate name, to control, to own, to convey property, to sue and to be sued therein; (2) to have continued existence during the period for which created; (3) to have a common seal; (4) to make by-laws; (5) to purchase and to hold real estate for the purpose of the corporation, unless forbidden by its charter or statute; (6) to borrow money when necessary to carry out the corporate purpose.

The corporate name may not be deceptively similar to those of other business enterprises and by the law of many states must conclude with either the word "Company," "Corporation," or "Incorporated." The name may be changed by charter amendment at any time without affecting corporate contracts or title to corporate property in any way.

5-60. Power to purchase and hold property for corporate purposes. A corporation has implied power to take and to hold title to real and personal property for all purposes that are not foreign to the objects for which it is created. Such power is usually expressly given by statute or in

[1] Elward v. Peabody Coal Co. et al., page 771.

its charter. If the property purchased by the corporation is not to be used in connection with the chartered purposes of the corporation, the transaction is ultra vires.[2] In the absence of express restriction, it has implied power to purchase any real or personal property that is reasonably necessary for carrying on its business. For example, a manufacturing corporation has implied power to purchase all the materials necessary for the production of the article which it is to manufacture. But it cannot buy material for the purpose of resale. Likewise, a railroad owning animals for the purpose of carrying out its business may purchase grain, but it cannot purchase grain for the purpose of transportation and sale.

5-61. Power to take and to give mortgages or to pledge property. A corporation has implied power to take a mortgage on real estate to secure a debt, or to hold personal property as a security. Likewise, a corporation has implied power to mortgage or to pledge its own property when necessary in order to borrow money or to secure debts which have been created in accomplishing its corporate object. The officers may, with the consent of a majority of the stockholders, when the corporation is insolvent, make an assignment of all the property for the benefit of creditors. In the absence of statutory authority, a corporation cannot sell or mortgage its franchise or charter.

Corporations vested with the public interest, such as public utilities, cannot mortgage or sell their property without authority from the state creating them.

5-62. Power to borrow money when necessary to carry out the corporate purpose. In order to secure money for the purpose of carrying out its corporate objects, a corporation, in the absence of express restrictions, has power, with the consent of the stockholders, to issue bonds. The statute usually specifies the procedure necessary for issuing such bonds, and if the statute is not complied with, the bonds are invalid.

A corporation likewise has implied power to take or to indorse promissory notes and to accept or to indorse bills of exchange in the usual course of its business. A corporation has no implied power to loan money or become a surety or guarantor, in absence of express authority, unless it is strictly necessary for the purpose of carrying out the objects of the corporation. Statutes in some states authorize a corporation to enter into contracts of guaranty when the corporation has a direct interest in the subject matter of the contract guaranteed.[3]

5-63. Power to enter into partnership agreements. A corporation is without power to enter into a partnership or combination with other corporations for the purpose of bringing the management of the partner-

[2] Zion's Savings Bank & Trust Co. v. Tropic & East Fork Irrigation Co., page 772.
[3] Choctaw Lumber Co. v. Atlanta Band Mill, Inc., page 774.

ship or corporations under one control. A corporation does not have authority to share its corporate management with natural persons in a partnership because it would expose the stockholders to risks not contemplated by the stockholders' contracts, although it may enter a joint-venture. A corporation may, however, provide in its charter, when authorized by statute, that it has authority to become a partner.

5-64. Power of a corporation to subscribe and to hold stock in another corporation. A corporation, in absence of statutory authority, has no implied power to subscribe to, purchase, or hold the stock of another corporation whose chartered purpose is totally foreign to its own. To permit such action would subject the stockholders to risks not anticipated by them. By court decision or statute, the corporations of most states are now empowered to subscribe for, or purchase, the stock of other corporations for the purpose of furthering their own objectives. It may invest idle funds in the stock of other corporations or accept such shares in settlement of an indebtedness owing to it. A certain phase of its business may be transacted by means of a subsidiary for whose organization it is responsible or whose control it has acquired by stock purchase.[4] In such cases, the parent company may, or may not, be a holding company organized for the express purpose of acquiring stock of other corporations. A corporation is forbidden, however, to acquire the stock of a competing corporation for the purpose of eliminating or restraining competition.

5-65. Power to hold its own stock. A corporation is somewhat restricted in its power to purchase its own stock, because the purchase of its own stock might effect a reduction of its capital to the detriment of creditors and stockholders. In most states a corporation is permitted to purchase shares of its own stock only out of accumulated profits or surplus.[5] This retains an investment in the corporation by stockholders equivalent to the original capital as a protective cushion for creditors in case subsequent losses develop. A few states, however, permit a corporation to acquire treasury stock as long as the corporation is not insolvent. A corporation may also acquire its own stock in payment of, or in security for, an antecedent debt due the corporation. It may also take its own stock for nonpayment of an authorized assessment made by the company on the stock or it may take it as a gift. A corporation that has issued preferred stock has the power to redeem such stock, where there is no injury to, or objection by, creditors. Here again, many of the states require the preferred stock to be redeemed out of surplus or demand that authority to reduce the capital stock be obtained from the state.

Treasury stock—stock of its own issue acquired by a corporation—is not automatically canceled. It lies dormant in the treasury of the corporation

[4] Durham v. Firestone Tire & Rubber Co., page 775.
[5] Jarroll Coal Co., Inc. v. Lewis et al., page 776.

without the right to vote or to share in dividends until it is again sold and transferred to a stockholder. The capitalization of a corporation can be reduced only with the authority of the state that approved the original capital, and the procedure outlined in the state corporation laws must be followed in effecting the reduction.

POWERS OF CORPORATIONS CASES

ELWARD v. PEABODY COAL CO. et al.

1956, 9 Ill. App.2d 234, 132 N.E.2d 549

The plaintiff, a stockholder in the defendant corporation, brought this suit against the corporation and its seven directors for a declaratory decree that a stock option was invalid and for injunctive relief. The directors by resolution gave one of the employees of the corporation an option to purchase 40,000 shares at $3 per share. On the day that the option was given the market price of the common was $3 per share; in June, 1955, it was $8 per share. The plaintiff contended that under the corporate laws of Illinois the corporation was not authorized to grant the option. The lower court dismissed the complaint and plaintiff appealed.

BURKE, J. . . . The plaintiff asserts that the Business Corporation Act does not empower a corporation to issue a stock option; that this power is not granted in express terms or by implication; that a shareholder is entitled under the common law to preemptive rights; and that the Act should be construed strictly so as not to impair the preemptive rights of stockholders. The public policy of this state is found in the Constitution, the statutes and the decisions of the courts. Plaintiff cites cases pointing out the distinction between the power to sell and the power to give an option. The preemptive right of shareholders to share pro rata in any new issue of corporate stock so that their interest will not be diluted but continue proportionately, is part of the common law of this State. Section 24 of the Business Corporation Act, reads:

> The preemptive right of a shareholder to acquire additional shares of a corporation may be limited or denied to the extent provided in the articles of incorporation. Unless otherwise provided by its articles of incorporation, any corporation may issue and sell its shares to its employees or to the employees of any subsidiary corporation, without first offering the same to its shareholders, for such consideration and upon such terms and conditions as shall be approved by the holders of two-thirds of its shares entitled to vote with respect thereto or by its board of directors pursuant to like approval of the shareholders.

The first sentence of § 24 provides that the charter of an Illinois corporation may limit or deny the preemptive right of a shareholder to acquire additional shares of stock. The second sentence of the section allows a corporation which does not have an express charter denial or limitation of preemptive rights, to issue and sell stock to its employees free of preemptive rights for such consideration and upon such terms and conditions as shall be approved by the holders of two-thirds of its shares entitled to vote with respect thereto or by its board of directors pursuant to like approval of the shareholders. Plaintiff inquires that, keeping in mind the doctrine that corporate powers are to be construed strictly and that no power is to be implied unless reasonably necessary to an express power, under what section or sections could the power to issue stock options be regarded as implied? Section 5 of the Business Corporation Act states that each corporation shall have power to make contracts and incur liabilities, to elect or appoint officers and agents of the corporation, to define their duties and fix their compensations, and to exercise all powers necessary or convenient to effect any or all of the purposes for which the corporation is formed. It cannot be doubted that Illinois corporations are empowered to enter into contracts relating to employment. The implied powers which a corporation has in order to carry into effect those expressly granted and to accomplish the purposes of its creation are not limited to such as are indispensable for these purposes, but comprise all that are necessary in the sense of appropriate and suitable, including the right of reasonable choice of means to be employed. 13 Am. Jur., Corporations, § 740. We are of the opinion that there is ample implied power in §§ 5 and 24 of the Business Corporation Act and in Article 9 of the amended charter to sustain the action of the defendant corporation in entering into a valid contract with an officer or employee for a stock option.

Reversed and remanded however, for other reasons.

ZION'S SAVINGS BANK & TRUST CO. v. TROPIC & EAST FORK IRRIGATION CO.

1942, 102 Utah 101, 126 P.2d 1053

The plaintiff bank brought this action to recover from the defendant upon a promissory note. The defendant's articles of incorporation provide: "The object of this corporation is to construct a canal from the East Fork of the Sevier River to Tropic and to keep the same in repair for the conducting of the water of said stream to the town of Tropic. . . ." The defendant had executed the note in question to one Holt in return for a quitclaim deed of his interest in certain waters of the Sevier River. The defendant made payments on the note for six years and then refused further payments. The defendant pleaded ultra vires. The lower court gave judgment to the defendant and plaintiff appealed.

LEVERICH, District Judge. . . . The court concluded that the respondent had no power to purchase or contract for the purchase of water rights nor to execute the note; that the promissory note was therefore ultra vires and void ab initio; that plaintiff and its predecessors, the Holts, were charged with notice of the lack of power of defendant corporation and that the defendant was not estopped to assert the defense of ultra vires.

The first question to be determined is whether or not the Irrigation Company, in purchasing the water rights of Holt and executing its note therefor, was acting beyond the privileges conferred by its charter. It is stated in the Articles of Incorporation: "The object of this corporation is to construct a canal from the East Fork of the Sevier River to Tropic and to keep the same in repair for the conducting of the water of said stream to the town of Tropic also to control the waters of Bryce Canyon for culinary and irrigation purposes for said Town."

Article XII, § 10 of the Constitution of the State of Utah places a limitation upon all corporations organized under and pursuant to the laws of Utah in the following words: "No corporation shall engage in any business other than that expressly authorized in its charter, or articles of incorporation."

Several cases decided in this court have held that a strict interpretation must be given articles of incorporation in view of this constitutional limitation. In the case of *Tracy Loan and Trust Company v. Merchants' Bank*, 50 Utah 196, 167 P. 353, 355, the court, in passing upon the interpretation of articles of incorporation, after quoting Article XII, § 10 of the Utah Constitution, makes the following statement: "This court, in an early case under statehood . . . adopted the rule that a corporation in the management of its affairs and conduct of its business is limited to the purposes provided and enumerated in the object clause of its article of incorporation. In fact under the provisions of the Constitution . . . it would seem that no other rule or construction was permissible in this jurisdiction."

And further on in the opinion it is stated: "Implied powers of a bank, or of any corporation for that matter, are those incidental to and connected with the carrying into effect or the accomplishing of the general purposes of the corporation, as expressed in the object clause of its articles. When it has been determined that the acts done, or attempted to be done, are not within the powers of the corporation to do, no implied powers can validate such acts."

From the wording of the Articles of Incorporation of the Tropic and East Ford Irrigation Company it is clear that the only expressed purpose of the company is to construct canals between certain points and to keep them in repair. There is no express authority to purchase water or water rights. By the express limitations of authority, all other powers beyond those given are, by implication, excluded.

We therefore hold that the corporation and its officers and directors were acting beyond the privileges conferred upon the corporation by its charter and the laws of the State of Utah.

CHOCTAW LUMBER CO. v. ATLANTA BAND MILL, INC.

1953, 88 Ga. App. 701, 77 S.E.2d 333

The plaintiff corporation filed suits on two contracts of guaranty against the defendant-guarantor, Atlanta Band Mill, Inc. The defendant had guaranteed payment of the notes issued by the Atlanta Band Mill Sales Inc. The resolution passed by the Board of Directors of the defendant corporation read in part as follows: "Whereas, Atlanta Band Mill Sales, Inc. is a sales agency for Atlanta Band Mill, Inc. and whereas, it is to the financial advantage of Atlanta Band Mill, Inc. that Atlanta Band Mill Sales, Inc. meet its obligations and maintain its financial integrity; Now, therefore, be it resolved that Atlanta Band Mill, Inc. authorize and direct its officers to execute a Guarantee in usual terms guaranteeing the payment of the following note." The case proceeded to trial and at the conclusion of the plaintiffs' evidence a motion to nonsuit was granted. Plaintiff appealed.

Townsend, J. . . . Prior to the Corporation Act of 1938 Ga. L. 1938, p. 214, the law, as stated in Code, § 22-701, was as follows: "Corporations created under Chapter 22-3 may exercise all corporate powers necessary to the purpose of their organization, but shall make no contract, or purchase or hold any property of any kind, except such as is necessary in legitimately carrying into effect such purpose, or for securing debts due to the company." Following such Act, Code Ann. Supp. § 22-1828 (c) gives to corporations the power "to guarantee, become surety upon or indorse the contracts or obligations of any other corporation, firm or individual as to matters in which the corporation guaranteeing has a direct interest but shall not have the right to enter into any contract of guaranty, suretyship or indorsement where the corporation guaranteeing has no direct interest in the subject matter of the contract guaranteed or to make any purely accommodation guaranty, indorsement or contract of suretyship, unless such right . . . is contained in the charter of the corporation or an amendment lawfully made thereto."

The latter Code section certainly enlarged the meaning of the former to some extent as to the power of corporations to enter into guaranty contracts executed upon a valid consideration. The contract here had such consideration. (Cases cited.) The question of the extent to which such powers were enlarged must be determined. It is no longer necessary to prove that the contract was "necessary in legitimately carrying into effect such purpose (of the corporate organization), or for securing debts due to the company," but it must be shown that the guarantor corporation has a "direct interest in the subject matter of the contract guaranteed." The contract guaranteed was one granting an extension of time to the sales agency to pay a debt, for the purpose of avoiding a lawsuit which would have the effect of injuring the credit of the defendant. The term direct interest has previously been the subject of judicial construction. It is defined in Black's Law Dictionary as meaning "not contingent or doubtful." An employee seeking unemployment compensation is "directly interested" in a labor dispute which would affect the amount of wages received by himself and other employees similarly situated, under an unemployment compensation statute.

Applying this definition to the proof offered by the plaintiff on the trial of the case, it appears that the defendant guarantor whose owners had created the sales agency for its convenience was financially involved in the latter's credit, to the extent that a failure of the debtor corporation would seriously impair both the guarantor's credit and the distribution of its products; that it entered into the contract to prevent a lawsuit being filed against the sales company, and that the sales company was either insolvent at that time or became so between the date of the contract and the date of the filing of this suit, approximately five months later.

. . . It follows, therefore, that the evidence in this record is sufficient to authorize the finding that the defendant corporation had a direct interest in the subject matter of the contracts guaranteed within the meaning of Code Ann. Supp. § 22-1828. The trial court erred in granting a nonsuit and in overruling the motion to reinstate the case.

Judgment reversed.

DURHAM v. FIRESTONE TIRE & RUBBER CO. OF CALIFORNIA

1936, 47 Ariz. 280, 55 P.2d 648

The plaintiff, Firestone Tire and Rubber Company of California, brought action against Durham, the defendant, to recover on a promissory note executed by the defendant. The note was given in payment for stock in Firestone Service Stores, Inc. of Phoenix, an Arizona corporation. The incorporators of the Phoenix corporation included the California Corporation which by agreement was always to own at least 51 per cent of the stock. The defendant contended that one corporation may not organize or subscribe to the original stock of another and that the organization of the Phoenix Company was void, and its stock worthless so that there was no consideration for defendant's note. The lower court gave judgment to the plaintiff and defendant appealed.

LOCKWOOD, Chief Justice. . . . There is undoubtedly considerable conflict in the authorities as to whether one corporation may participate in the organization of another. Among those cases holding that it may not are found such as *Nebraska Shirt Co. v. Horton,* 3 Neb. (Unof.) 888, 93 N.W. 225; *Denny Hotel Co. v. Schram,* 6 Wash. 134, 32 P. 1002, 36 Am. St. Rep. 130; *Moore v. Los Lugos Gold Mines,* 172 Wash. 570, 21 P.2d 253; *Schwab v. E. G. Potter Co.,* 194 N.Y. 409, 87 N.E. 670, and others. Apparently this is based, although not always so expressed, upon the idea set forth in *Nebraska Shirt Co. v. Horton, supra,* in the following language: "Corporations have quite enough power without allowing them to incorporate themselves in new companies." Stated as a general proposition, there may be merit in this theory, but we think there is at least one well-grounded exception thereto. Where the obvious purpose of the new corporation is merely to act as a subsidiary for the parent one, and to carry out the purposes for which the parent itself was formed, we see no reason why, in the absence of a statute forbidding it, a corporation, as a matter of principle, should not be permitted to participate in the organization of its subsidiary. Unless prohibited by law, if its articles are broad enough, it can purchase stock in another such corporation after the latter is organized, and, through such purchase, control the operations of the other company, and, if it may do this, it would be extremely technical to say that it may not, through its duly authorized agents, organize the new company in the beginning. If the new company were organized for the purpose of evading limitations placed on the rights and authority of the parent company, the situation might be veiy different, but in the present case there can be no doubt that the Phoenix company was organized for the purpose of assisting in the better and more profitable disposition of the very product which the California company was engaged in producing and distributing.

. . . We hold, therefore, that under the law of Arizona a corporation is not prohibited from subscribing to or holding the stock of a new corporation whose purpose is naturally subsidiary to, and in aid of, the business of the old corporation.

JARROLL COAL CO., INC., v. LEWIS et al.

1954, 210 F.2d 578

On March 1, 1949, E. L. Jarroll, Sr. and the members of his family owned all of the stock of the mining company, defendant in this action. On that day he entered into a contract with the company by the terms of which the company purchased all of the stock from him paying him $4,000 in cash and giving him its note in the sum of $20,000. There was testimony that the note was to be secured by a chattel deed of trust but this was not executed until two years later. In March, 1949, the assets of the company, exclusive of good will, exceeded its liabilities, exclusive of the note by less than $15,000.

The plaintiffs, trustees of the United Mine Workers Welfare and Retirement Fund, had obtained a judgment against the company on a contract of March 1, 1949, whereby the company agreed to pay into the Welfare and Retirement Fund a certain amount per ton on coal mined by the company. This matter was brought before the court at the instance of the United States Marshal to have the court determine the conflicting claims to property of the coal company upon which he had levied execution. The trustees claimed it under their judgment and Mr. Jarroll claimed it under his trust deed.

. . . From a judgment in favor of the plaintiffs, execution creditors, holding the note and chattel deed of trust void as against them because violative of the West Virginia statute, Code of 1949, § 3051 (31–1–39), forbidding a corporation to use its funds to purchase its own stock, where this results in an impairment of capital, the coal company has appealed.

PARKER, Chief Judge. . . . The pertinent portion of § 3051 of the West Virginia Code of 1949 (31–1–39), which was taken from the general corporation law of the State of Delaware is as follows:

> Every corporation organized under this chapter, or existing under the laws of this State, shall have the power to purchase, hold, sell and transfer shares of its own capital stock: Provided, that no such corporation shall use its funds or property for the purchase of its own shares of capital stock when such use would cause any impairment of the capital of the corporation.

Accepting, as we think we should, the finding of the trial judge that the good will of the company was without value, there can be no question but that payment of the $4,000 in cash and the execution of the $20,000 note on March 1, 1949, not only impaired the capital of the corporation but rendered it insolvent. Appellant contends that, even so, the trustees of the welfare and retirement fund were not creditors at that time and cannot complain of the transaction for that reason. It appears, however, that the contract under which the claim of the trustees arises was executed on the very day that the note was given and that the indebtedness had been incurred before the execution of the chattel deed of trust, two years later, transferring the assets of the corporation to secure the note. It was the transfer under this deed which was relied upon to defeat the levy under the execution; and there can be no question but that such transfer, made at a time when the corporation was insolvent and made to secure stockholders for the purchase price of stock theretofore purchased from them, is void as to claims of creditors existing at the time it was made. *Boggs v. Fleming*, 4 Cir., 66 F.2d 859, 860. As said by this court in the case cited:

While, in the absence of charter or statutory prohibition, it is well settled that a corporation may purchase its own stock, it can only do so provided the act is in good faith and without intent to injure its creditors. . . . The authorities are unanimous to the effect that, even though a corporation be solvent when it contracts to purchase its own stock, it may not later, upon insolvency, pay for it, until after the existing creditors have been paid . . .

We think, also, that, even though the trustees be regarded as subsequent creditors, they are in position to attack the transaction here under consideration. It is a fraud on subsequent as well as upon existing creditors for the stockholders of a corporation to cause it to purchase their stock at a price rendering it insolvent, take an unrecorded lien upon all of its assets and allow it to continue doing business in its corporate name as if nothing had happened. Such creditors are unquestionably entitled to treat as void, because in fraud of their rights, a transaction which in effect gives stockholders a secret lien on corporate assets. . . . *There was no error and the judgment appealed from will be affirmed.*

Review Questions and Problems

1. *T* & Company is incorporated for the purpose of manufacturing and selling jewelry. It is incorporated as a manufacturing concern. Has *T* & Company a right to purchase jewelry manufactured by others and to sell it?
2. A corporation is formed under the name of Maybe Butter Company. Promoters for another concern desire to incorporate under the name of Mayby Butter Company. Will those responsible for granting charters grant them one under that name?
3. A medical insurance corporation, *A* & Co., is being formed under the name of "Family Doctor Plan." However, the Superintendent of Insurance has not yet approved the plan. His approval is required before certificate of incorporation can be issued by the state. Pending the approval of the application, *X* insurance company commenced using the name "Family Doctor Plan," for one of its various group policies. Can *A* & Co., as a corporation, obtain an injunction against *X*'s use of the same name?
4. A literary society was incorporated for the purpose of "advancing the mental development of its members by means of literary exercises, debates and lectures, and to foster sociability among its members." Later, the members adopted by-laws which pledged their support to a certain presidential candidate. Can a member who refuses to support that candidate be expelled?
5. *A*, the treasurer of the *X* Company, borrowed $5,000 from *Y* Bank and gave a mortgage on the property of the *X* Company as security. The stockholders contend that the mortgage is ineffective, because they had not authorized the officers to issue or to sign any mortgage. Are the stockholders correct?
6. The *X* Company was incorporated for the purpose of conducting a lumbermill. *A*, its president, desired to borrow money, and caused the

company to become surety upon his obligation. Assuming the contract of suretyship to be signed by the treasurer of the *X* Company, the proper officer, is the company liable?

7. A corporation entered into an agreement with *A* to engage in a joint venture. Is such an agreement valid?
8. International Silver Corp. issued all shares of its authorized stock for the par value thereof. A considerable amount was purchased by United Silver Co. Later, to prevent the owners of United Silver from obtaining control of International by buying more International stock, International purchased all the stock of United. Then it dissolved United, taking unto itself all its own shares previously owned by United. What are these shares now called? What may International do with these shares? Was it proper for International to buy the stock of United?
9. The *X* Company, which was engaged in motion picture business, entered into a contract with *D* Company whereby the latter agreed to furnish costumes to *X*. The *X* Company also entered into a contract with *P* Lumber Company, which was to furnish lumber and materials. The *X* Company defaulted in its payments to *P*. *D* Company guaranteed payment by *X* if *P* would continue to furnish lumber to *X*. Can *P* enforce this guaranty against *D*?

35

Ultra Vires Acts

5-66. In general. Any acts of a corporation that are beyond the authority given to it by the state are said to be *ultra vires* acts. No liability attaches to the corporation upon contracts outside the scope of its corporate powers, because the corporation has capacity only to do those things expressly authorized within its charter or which are incidental thereto.[1] This does not mean, however, that the corporation is free from liability for wrongful acts, such as torts and criminal liability, simply because such acts would be outside the scope of its authority. Like natural persons, a corporation has power to do wrong, and is liable therefor. There are certain exceptions to the above rules as to liability of the corporation, depending upon the nature of the acts and whether the contracts involved are executed, partially executed, or executory.

5-67. Who may object to them. If a corporation performs acts or enters into contracts to perform acts which are ultra vires, the state creating such corporation may forfeit its charter for misuse of its corporate authority. The extent of the misuse is controlling in determining whether the state will take away its franchise or merely enjoin the corporation from carrying out the ultra vires acts. A third party has no right to object to the ultra vires acts of a corporation. A stockholder or member, however, may enjoin a corporation from performing an ultra vires act. In addition, the corporation may recover from the directors who are responsible for the ultra vires contracts any losses or damages sustained because of the ultra vires venture. When they exceed corporate powers, they may become personally liable for resulting losses.

5-68. Effect of an ultra vires contract. The courts are somewhat in conflict concerning the rights arising out of an ultra vires contract. In general, however, the following rules are applicable:

1. Since a corporation has only that authority expressly conferred upon it by the state, any contracts made in excess of such authority are ultra vires and in essence illegal.

[1] Brinson et al. v. Mill Supply Co., Inc., page 783.

2. An ultra vires contract which is purely executory cannot be enforced by either party to the agreement.

3. A contract in excess of charter powers, which is fully executed by both parties, will not be disturbed by the courts.[2]

4. If an ultra vires contract has been fully performed by one of the parties thereto, so that it becomes inequitable and unjust for the other party to retain such performance and to refuse to perform on its part, the majority of the courts will enforce the ultra vires contract. A strong minority of the courts refuse to enforce the contract even in such cases. They do, however, compel the other party to the agreement to pay the reasonable value of what he has received or to return it. The only essential difference between these two views is that the majority of the courts enforce the agreement, while the minority allow recovery for the reasonable value of the benefit received unless the benefit is returned.

The statutes, in providing for the procedure for creating a corporation, require that its charter be filed for the purpose of giving public notice of its object and purpose and limitation of powers. Persons dealing with a corporation, therefore, are charged with notice of the extent of its corporate powers, and cannot set up a defense that they had no knowledge that the corporation entered into contracts in excess of such power. However, if persons enter into a contract with a corporation, which is in excess of its corporate powers and under circumstances in which it would be impossible for such persons to have knowledge of the limitations of the corporation, the corporation may be held liable. In other words, if the contract involves a subject matter that may fall within the scope of the business, but, because of the improper use to be made of the subject matter in this particular instance, the contract is outside the corporate powers, the contract is enforceable unless the other party had knowledge of the intended use. A corporation may purchase such real estate as is needed in its business, but has no right to purchase it for other purposes. A contract to purchase real estate for speculative purposes is ultra vires, but such a contract would be binding unless the seller knew of the improper use to be made of it. A corporation has power to take title to real estate in excess of its needs, and once acquired, the corporation's title may not be questioned. Although it may not have the right to purchase and sell real estate, it has the power to do so until it has been enjoined.

The Uniform Business Corporation Act adopted by some states provides that all ultra vires contracts are enforceable. Neither party to such a contract may use ultra vires as a defense. In these states ultra vires conduct on the part of the corporation may be enjoined by the state or any stockholder, but contracts previously made are binding whether they be wholly executory, partially executed, or fully performed. In such cases, the direc-

[2] Temple Lumber Co. v. Miller, page 785.

tors are liable for losses suffered as a result of engaging in ultra vires activities.

5-69. Ratification of ultra vires contracts by officers and stockholders. As a general rule an ultra vires contract cannot be ratified by the stockholders of a corporation. However, some courts hold that all the stockholders may ratify the ultra vires acts of the corporation, where the rights of the public in general or the rights of creditors are not involved.

5-70. Liability for tort and contract. A corporation, being an artificial person and impersonal, cannot personally commit a tort. But a corporation is liable under the laws applicable to principal and agent for the torts of its agent committed in the pursuit of the corporate business.[3] Although a corporation has no authority to act outside of the statute creating it or its charter, it has the capacity through its agents to do acts that may cause injury to others; therefore, it is liable for every wrong committed, by its agents, acting within their authority, even though the injury arises out of an act which is ultra vires.[4] A few courts hold, however, that a corporation is not liable for the torts of its employees in ultra vires transactions, even if it has authorized the ultra vires act—but the weight of authority is otherwise. A corporation is liable for fraud committed by its officers or agents within the scope of their authority. It is also liable if the act is apparently within the general authority of the agents. Corporations are not only liable for acts committed by their agents in the pursuit of the corporate business, but they are likewise liable for injury caused by their agents omitting to perform duties of the corporation. A corporation is liable for the negligence of an agent in failing to keep its property in safe condition.

Although a corporation is liable for injuries caused by its agents, even though acting ultra vires, it is not liable in contract. However, if a corporate agent acts in excess of his authority, the corporation is liable when the transaction is within corporate power and the agent is acting within his apparent authority.[5]

5-71. Liability for crimes. A corporation cannot commit crimes which involve intent or personal violence. However, a corporation may be criminally liable for the violation of a law which imposes a duty upon the corporation to do, or not to do, an act. For example, a corporation may be fined for failure to comply with some statute that specifies certain things to be done by the corporation—such as supplying protection for employees and making reports—and for the violation of regulatory statutes under the police power of the state.

A corporation may be indicted for improperly performing an act that

[3] Poledna v. Bendix Aviation Corporation, page 786.
[4] Massa v. Wanamaker Academy of Beauty Culture, Inc., page 787.
[5] Petition of Mulco Products, page 788.

it may lawfully do. For example, a corporation may be indicted for conducting a perfectly legal business in such a manner as to be guilty of maintaining a nuisance. Corporations cannot be held liable for criminal acts involving personal violence, but may be held criminally responsible for failure to comply with statutes which have prohibited certain acts. Corporations have been criminally liable for unlawful conspiracies to restrain trade, for knowingly and fraudulently concealing property under the Bankruptcy Act, for giving rebates to shippers in violation of federal statutes, and for violations of other statutes.[6] Corporations may also be held for contempt of court by reason of acts or omissions of their agents where they have violated an injunction. The court may punish such corporations by the levy of a fine, the same as against a natural person.

ULTRA VIRES ACTS CASES

BRINSON et al. v. MILL SUPPLY CO., INC.

1941, 219 N.C. 499, 14 S.E.2d 505

W. T. Brinson, one of the stockholders of the Mill Supply Company, brought an action to have a receiver appointed for the company alleging the company's insolvency. A receiver was appointed and a claim was presented to him for the balance due on a note executed by the president of the corporation in favor of Harriet L. Hyman. The note was guaranteed by the corporation. The receiver denied the claim and the lower court affirmed his action upon the ground that the contract of guaranty was ultra vires.

Barnhill, J. . . . Was the act of the officers of the defendant corporation, in authorizing and executing the contract of guaranty, ultra vires as contended by the receiver? The court below so concluded. In this conclusion we concur.

For a contract executed by the officer of a corporation to be binding on the corporation it must appear that (1) it was incidental to the business of the corporation; or (2) it was expressly authorized; and (3) it was properly executed. . . .

The contract of guaranty was no part of a transaction in which the corporation was borrowing or raising money for the purposes of its incorporation. It was clearly and exclusively an act in aid and for the accommodation of its president as an individual. From it the corporation received no benefit.

[6] Old Monastery Co. v. United States, page 789.

Hence, it appears that the undertaking of the corporation was not directly "necessary, suitable, convenient or proper for the accomplishment of" either of these or of any other purpose authorized by the charter.

Was the contract of guaranty incidental to, or in furtherance of, the powers expressly granted? If not, it was ultra vires and unenforceable.

A corporation is an artificial being, created by the State, for the attainment of certain defined purposes, and, therefore, vested with certain specific powers and others fairly and reasonably to be inferred or implied from the express powers and the object of the creation. Acts falling without that boundary are unwarranted—ultra vires. 7 R.C.L. 673, 19 C.J.S., Corporations, par. 1286, p. 965.

"A corporation . . . being the mere creature of law, . . . possesses only those properties which the charter of its creation confers upon it, either expressly, or as incidental to its very existence." Marshall, C. J., in *Dartmouth College* Case, 4 Wheat. 518, 636, 4 L.Ed. 629. "An incidental power exists only for the purpose of enabling a corporation to carry out the purposes expressly granted to it—that is to say, the powers necessary to accomplish the purposes of its existence—and can in no case avail to enlarge the express powers and thereby warrant it to devote its efforts or capital to other purposes than such as its charter expressly authorizes, or to engage in collateral enterprises, not directly, but only remotely, connected with its specific corporate purposes. . . .

Ordinarily, the power to endorse or guarantee the payment of negotiable instruments for the benefit of a third party is not within the implied powers conferred upon a private business corporation. The general rule is that no corporation has the power, by any form of contract or endorsement, to become a guarantor or surety or otherwise lend its credit to another person or corporation. . . .

A corporation is without implied power to guarantee for accommodation the contract of its customers with third persons on the ground that it may thus stimulate its own business. Such use of its credit is clearly beyond the power of an ordinary business corporation. . . . It has no authority to use its credit for the benefit of a stockholder or officer. . . .

The contract of guaranty was executed for the benefit of an individual. No part of the consideration moved to the defendant corporation. It was not either expressly or impliedly authorized by its charter to enter into contracts for the accommodation of a third party. To permit the payment of the claim would clearly result in an invasion of the assets of the defendant corporation in the hands of the receiver as a trust fund for the payment of legitimate creditors. See 7 R.C.L. 198. The defendant's plea of ultra vires must be sustained.

The judgment below is affirmed.

TEMPLE LUMBER CO. v. MILLER
1943, (Tex. Civ. App.) 169 S.W.2d 256

The plaintiff, Miller, sued the defendant Temple Lumber Company, a corporation, for damages resulting from defective workmanship and the use of defective material in the construction of a house for the plaintiff. The defendant contended that it could not be held liable on the contract because it was ultra vires. The corporation's charter set out the purposes of the corporation as that of "manufacturing lumber and the purchase and sale of material used in such business and doing all things necessary and incident to such lumber business." The lower court ruled in favor of the plaintiff and defendant appealed.

SPEER, J. . . . It is insistently urged that since defendant's charter only authorized it to buy and sell lumber and building material, it could not be held to have made a contract to construct a building, as contended by plaintiff.

. . . It appears that the early English cases, as well as some by federal courts, and even the early cases decided by our state courts, are not in complete harmony with respect to the extent a corporation may go and bind itself. But the trend seems to be that even though the charter provisions do not, in so many words, authorize an act, the corporation may bind itself to do many things when not against public policy and are not forbidden by law. There is a clear distinction between acts which are void because of legal inhibitions, and those which are not prohibited but are those which are not enumerated in the purpose clause of the charter. In the latter class are to be found instances which include acts which are appropriate, convenient and suitable in carrying out the purposes for which the charter was expressly granted. These are termed implied powers and authority. (Cases cited)

To our minds, the contract involved here was one not prohibited by law nor by any principle of public policy. No good reason exists why defendant could not contract with plaintiff to sell him the materials to go into his house. We think it would logically follow that as an inducement to plaintiff to buy the materials from it, defendant could agree and bind itself to deliver the materials at its own expense, although its charter did not expressly authorize it to haul building materials. If it could deliver, then could it not even cut the lumber into desired lengths? Carrying the thought further, it could with propriety obligate itself to do many things not expressly mentioned in its charter, when "appropriate," "convenient" and "suitable" in the prosecution of the line of business expressly mentioned in the charter. An act of a corporation is said to be ultra vires when beyond the scope either of the express or implied powers of its charter. If the acts are within the scope of the implied powers of the corporation, they cannot be said to be ultra vires, yet some of our courts deem them such if they are not within the express terms of the charter. We think that if the act is not one prohibited by law or public policy, and it inures to the direct benefit of the corporation, and is executed, it is not, strictly speaking, ultra vires, and this is apparently the view taken by the trial court.

. . . The court found as a fact (and there is an abundance of evidence to support it) that the house was in fact erected by defendant, and that plaintiff had paid to defendant the entire original contract price—the contract was fully executed on both sides; the controversy here being over defective workmanship and materials. It would appear that in such circumstances, defendant would be estopped to plead and rely upon ultra vires, and at the same time receive and retain the direct benefits of the contract it seeks to avoid. Such contention does not appeal to our sense of justice and equity. Estoppel was pleaded by plaintiff; the court found the facts as indicated, and concluded that defendant was estopped to rely upon its plea of ultra vires. In this we think he was correct.

. . . *We have concluded that no reversible errors are presented by any of the points raised, and we therefore order that the judgment of the trial court should be and is accordingly affirmed.*

POLEDNA v. BENDIX AVIATION CORPORATION

1960 (Mich.) 103 N.W.2d 789

EDWARDS, Justice. Plaintiff Robert Poledna brought a libel and slander action against defendants Bendix Aviation Corporation and Walter Bare for certain allegations of theft made against him. After trial before Berrien County Circuit Court, the jury returned a verdict of $10,000 "past damage" and $2,500 "punitive" damage. . . .

Defendants appeal claiming . . . that defendant corporation may not be held responsible for slander by an employee. . . .

The action was occasioned by the circumstances of plaintiff's discharge from the employment of defendant Bendix Aviation Corporation by defendant Walter Bare, at that time the employment manager for Bendix' plant at St. Joseph, Michigan.

. . . The next of appellants' issues pertains to the claim that defendant corporation is not liable for the actions of defendant Bare. In support of this contention, they cite *Robertson v. New York Life Ins. Co.*, 312 Mich. 92, 19 N.W.2d 498, and *Flaherty v. Maxwell Motor Co.*, 187 Mich. 62, 153 N.W. 45. In this latter case, 187 Mich. at page 67, 153 N.W. at page 46, the Court said:

Our examination of the cases satisfies us that the great weight of the authorities holds that a corporation is not liable for slander uttered by its servants unless it affirmatively appears that the agent was expressly authorized to speak the words in question or the corporation subsequently ratified the utterance.

The facts in our current record leave no doubt that Bare was functioning in his official capacity as employment manager of defendant corporation on the occasion of the slanderous utterance. The trial judge's charge included these words:

And by the way, the defendant, Bendix Aviation Corporation, is responsible for any act of its personnel officer, who is the other defendant, Walter Bare, in this case.

Whatever the state of the law of libel and slander when Flaherty was decided, it seems apparent that the trial judge's charge comes far closer to representing the majority rule today.

There is no longer any doubt that a corporation may be held liable for slander uttered by an agent while in the discharge of his duty as agent, and in relation to the matter about which his duty as agent permits or requires him to act, in the same way and to the same extent as an individual could be held liable for the same slander. *Priest v. Central States Fire Ins. Co.*, 1928, 223 Mo.App. 122, 9 S.W.2d 543). . . .

Fletcher's *Cyclopedia Corporations* (Perm. Ed.) § 4888, says:

The doctrine of nonliability based on the proposition that there can be no agency in slander has long been exploded.

See, also, 55 A.L.R.2d 828.

We approve the charge of the trial judge on this issue and overrule any language in the Flaherty and Robertson cases, supra, which conflicts with the views expressed herein.

The corporation was held to be liable.

MASSA v. WANAMAKER ACADEMY OF BEAUTY CULTURE, INC.

1948, 80 N.Y.S.2d 923

The defendant operates and maintains a beauty culture school. One of the teachers at the school performed services upon the plaintiff whereby the plaintiff sustained scalp burns which she attributed to the negligent manner in which the work was done. Plaintiff brought this action to recover damages for the injuries which she sustained.

CAPOZZOLI, J. . . . The defendant contends that it is forbidden by the state authorities to do any beauty work for the public at large. It argues further that the students alone are permitted to serve members of the public and then only for the purpose of acquiring experience. As a result of these contentions the defendant argues that the act of the teacher in working on the plaintiff was ultra vires and, therefore, not binding upon the defendant.

The contention of the defendant is untenable. The doctrine of ultra vires is applicable to contractual relations, and is not pertinent to torts. The doctrine of ultra vires cannot be invoked to defeat liability for an injury through negligence. This principle was clearly illustrated in the case of *Hannon v. Siegel-Cooper Co.*, 167 N.Y. 244, 60 N.E. 597, 52 L.R.A. 429 where a corporation operating a department store was held liable for the malpractice of a dentist held out by the defendant to be its employee, in spite of the fact that the practice of dentistry by the defendant was ultra vires.

. . . The jury further found that this teacher's work was performed within the scope of her employment in the business of her employer and that the plaintiff did not contribute to the occurrence of the accident by any negligence on her part.

Judgment for plaintiff.

PETITION OF MULCO PRODUCTS

1956, (Del.) 123 A.2d 95

This proceeding was instituted by the corporation to set aside a judgment entered by confession upon a note executed by the corporation. The general manager of the corporation, Welch, had executed the note to Black, the lender. Welch credited the proceeds of the loan to his personal account. The corporation contends that Welch did not have authority to borrow money on behalf of the corporation.

TERRY, J. . . . It is axiomatic that a corporation by structural necessity must act, if it acts at all, through its agents.

Consequently, in any situation where the power of an agent to bind his principal is put in issue, the agent's authority becomes a matter of paramount importance.

The authority of an agent may fall generally into two categories, actual and apparent. The actual authority of an agent of a private corporation in turn lends itself to dichotomy. It may consist of express authority granted the agent either by statute, corporate charter, by-law or corporate action by the stockholders or Board of Directors. Or it may amount to implied authority, another way of saying that certain powers spring by necessary inference from those expressly granted.

A second broad category of authority is not actual authority, being neither express nor implied. This class is commonly labeled apparent authority. In nature and effect, when a private corporation is the principal, it amounts to that authority which, though not actually granted, the principal knowingly or negligently permits the agent to exercise or which it holds him out as possessing. Thus in respect to apparent authority, when an agent of a corporation possesses such authority, the corporation is bound by the act of the agent within the scope of his apparent authority as to any person who believes and has reasonable ground to believe that the agent has such authority and in good faith deals with him. In such a case the corporation will be bound to the same extent precisely as if the apparent authority were real or actual authority.

. . . Although the words used to describe apparent authority vary somewhat, it is most widely defined as "that (authority) which, though not actually granted, the principal knowingly (or negligently) permits the agent to exercise or which he holds him out as possessing." 2 *Fletcher Corp.* (1954 Ed.) § 449.

. . . Although apparent authority is not actual authority, once the authority of the agent has been established, and it is shown that the third party relying on the apparent authority did so rely in good faith and was justified from all the circumstances in so relying, the corporation is bound to the same extent as though actual authority had existed. *Thompson on Corporations* (3rd Ed.) § 1800.

A review of the testimony establishes beyond any doubt whatsoever that Welch was endowed with all the necessary elements of apparent authority, as hereinabove defined, in his dealing with Black. I find that Welch possessed apparent authority on June 29, 1953, to give to Black the corporation's note for $25,000. I further find that Black had reasonable ground to rely upon Welch's apparent authority in accepting the note from Welch and that his acceptance was in good faith.

. . . *For the reasons hereinabove indicated the corporation's petition must be dismissed.*

OLD MONASTERY CO. v. UNITED STATES

1945, 147 F.2d 905

The defendant, Old Monastery Corporation, was indicted for conspiring to violate the terms of the Emergency Price Control Act of 1942. The jury found the defendant guilty as charged. The defendant appealed.

DOBIE, Circuit Judge. The final contention of Monastery is "there was a total failure of evidence to show that the defendant corporation was to receive any benefit from the conspiracy. . . . The government's case, instead of showing benefits to the corporation growing out of the personal acts of its then president, demonstrates conclusively that the acts attributed to him by Davis, if true, were definitely to its detriment." We do not accept benefit as a touchstone of corporate criminal liability; benefit, at best, is an evidential, not an operative, fact.

The generally accepted rule is thus laid down: "A corporation may be held criminally responsible for acts committed by its agents, provided such acts were committed within the scope of the agents' authority or course of their employment." 19 C.J.S. Corporations, § 1362. In *New York Central & Hudson River R. Co. v. United States,* 212 U.S. 481, 492–493, 29 S.Ct. 304, 306, 53 L.Ed. 613, Mr. Justice Day quoted with approval this extract from *Bishop's New Criminal Law,* § 417: "Since a corporation acts by its officers and agents, their purposes, motives, and intent are just as much those of the corporation as are the things done."

Affirmed.

Review Questions and Problems

1. The L & S Lumber Co. was a corporation operating a mill in the woods. A highline used in the mill extended across a road and had fallen. This highline had fallen once before, and *B*, who was a stockholder-director and officer of the corporation and who worked at the mill, knew this and the continuing danger that the line might fall again. The line fell again, and *X* was struck. Is *B* liable to *X*? Is the corporation liable to *X*?
2. *M* gave *P*, a bank, a note as security for a loan made to *X*. A writing executed by the bank's vice-president stated that the note would never be collected but was merely needed to satisfy the bank inspectors that there was security for the loan. May the bank collect on the note?
3. The *X* Company had no power under its charter to purchase land. It did upon one occasion purchase a small tract of land, but later sold it. May the state cause a forfeiture of the charter of the *X* Company? What are the rights of stockholders where ultra vires acts are being committed?
4. The *X* Company purchases real estate in excess of its needs, but obtains title thereto. Assuming the purchase to be ultra vires, may the grantor have the transaction set aside?
5. A corporation received, under an ultra vires contract, property that it is unable to return. May the unpaid vendor of such property recover for the property sold? On what theory, if any?
6. *X* corporation was organized to operate an amusement park. The corporation entered into a contract to sell stone to the United States and began the operation of a quarry. After some of the stone had been delivered the United States cancelled the contract. What are the rights of *X* corporation?
7. *X* corporation operated a market. The manager of the market falsely accused *A*, a customer, of taking groceries from the store without paying for them. *A* sued *X* corporation for false arrest, false imprisonment, and slander. Should he recover judgment?
8. *X* Company was by its charter authorized to sell fire insurance. Without amendment of its charter, it accepted the premium and issued a policy of hail insurance to *A*. After a loss from hail, *A* sued *X* Company and was met with the defense of ultra vires. Will *A* be able to recover from *X* Company?
9. *A* Company was incorporated for the purpose of manufacturing and selling ice cream. *B* Company was chartered to buy and sell milk at

retail and wholesale. *B* Company, without altering its charter, began to manufacture and sell ice cream. *A* Company started an injunction suit against *B* Company, requesting the court to enjoin the latter from manufacturing and selling ice cream. Should the injunction be issued?

10. *A* corporation was engaged in manufacturing and leasing railroad sleeping cars. It had a 99-year charter from the state. *B* corporation was in the same business. May *A* corporation lease all its cars and assets to *B* corporation for 99 years and promise not to manufacture or compete further?

36

Membership in Corporations

5-72. Membership in nonstock corporations. Where the corporation is a nonstock company, membership is regulated by the by-laws. No one can become a member of such corporation, except in compliance with the method prescribed by the by-laws.

5-73. Membership in stock companies. Membership in a stock corporation is acquired by a contract with the corporation; this membership is evidenced by a certificate showing ownership of shares of stock. The right to membership may be acquired by a stock subscription before the corporation is created, or by a purchase of shares of stock from the corporation after it is organized, or by a transfer of shares from some person who owns the stock.

5-74. Capital stock and capital. Much confusion has arisen by reason of the different meanings attributed to the terms "capital stock" and "capital."[1] Strictly speaking, from the viewpoint of the corporation, its capital stock is the expressed equity of the stockholders in corporate assets resulting from their investments before the latter have been influenced by profits or losses. It should equal the amount of money, services, and property paid in or subscribed by the stockholders for the purposes of carrying on the corporate business. However, if the subscriber pays more than par to the corporation for his stock, the excess is usually credited to capital surplus rather than capital stock. Capital stock is also said to be the sum fixed in the corporate charter. The capital stock would therefore always remain the same unless changed by an amendment of the charter.

The term capital stock has also been used to mean the representative interest of the shareholders in the total assets of the corporation, measured by its tangible and intangible property, franchise, and good will.

The term capital stock, as used in some statutes for taxation purposes, refers to the total value of the property owned by the corporation. The first of these three views is generally considered to express correctly the true meaning of capital stock.

[1] Fontainebleau Hotel Corp. v. Rosenberg, page 805.

On the other hand, capital means the net assets of the corporation, including not only the original investment, but also all gains and profits realized from the conduct of the corporate business. For example, if a corporation is incorporated with a capital stock of $50,000, fully paid, and it makes a profit of $20,000, which is kept in the business and is not distributed as dividends, it has a capital of $70,000. Its capital stock, however, is the $50,000 originally placed in the business.

5-75. Shares of stock. A share of stock is said to consist of a number of rights that the owner acquires in the corporation. These rights are primarily three in number: the right to share in profits, to participate in the control of the corporation, and to receive a portion of the assets at time of dissolution. A share of stock is representative of an investment made in the corporation, but it gives the holder no right to share in the active management of the business. A share of stock is personal property and in its nature a chose in action, even though the corporation owns nothing but real estate. Like other personal property it falls under the Statute of Frauds, which requires a memorandum in writing to evidence a sale or a contract to sell that involves more than a certain sum of money. Like other personal property a share passes, on the death of a shareholder, to his legal representatives and not to the heirs.

By statute, a share of stock is subject to execution and attachment by creditors of the stockholder. The statutes usually provide the method by which a levy and a sale of a share of stock for the payment of debts are made. A levy or an attachment by a sheriff of a share of stock is not good, unless the sheriff seizes actual possession of the certificate.

5-76. A certificate of stock. A certificate of stock is a written evidence of the ownership of a certain number of shares of stock of a corporation. The certificate itself is not property, but is merely evidence of the stockholder's right in the corporation. The certificate of stock shows upon its face the character and the number of the shares that it represents and the method of transfer, and may state a part of the contract existing between the shareholder and the corporation, or the other shareholders. A subscriber often becomes a stockholder before the certificate is issued. The certificate merely indicates that the corporation recognizes a certain person as being a stockholder.

5-77. Bonds and shares. A bond is an obligation of the corporation to pay a certain sum of money in the future at a specified rate of interest. It is comparable to a promissory note in which the corporation is the maker. Corporate bonds are often secured by a mortgage on the assets of the corporation but many corporate bonds called debentures do not have such security. A bondholder is a creditor of the corporation, whereas a stockholder is not. A stockholder has a right to receive dividends if declared by the board of directors and to participate in the assets of the corporation after all creditors have been paid. A bondholder has no right to vote or to participate in the management and control of a corporation, unless, upon insolvency, such rights are given by contract; whereas a shareholder, in the absence of contractual limitations, has a right to participate in the corporate control.

There are certain contracts with corporations which are difficult to classify. Is the holder of a preferred share of stock, which guarantees a dividend at a given rate and contains a promise of redemption at a given time, but which carries no right to vote, a shareholder or a creditor? Similarly, is a bondholder, whose bond draws interest payable only out of profits, and who is subordinated to the claims of general creditors in case of insolvency, and whose bond gives the holder the right to vote in case interest payments are not made, an investor in a corporation or a creditor? The law in regard to these questions has not been made clear at the present time. The answers are determined largely by the terms of the agreement.

5-78. Stock warrants. A stock warrant is a certificate which gives to the holder thereof the right to subscribe for a given number of shares of stock in a corporation at a stated price. It is usually issued in connection with the sale of other shares of stock, or of bonds, although the law of some states permits the issuance of stock warrants entirely separate and apart from the sale of other securities. Usually the warrants are transferable, although in some cases they are personal only. The option to purchase contained in the warrant may or may not be limited as to time. The warrant has value and can readily be sold on the market only when the option to purchase is at a price that is below the market price of the stock covered by the stock warrant.

STOCK SUBSCRIPTIONS

5-79. Stock subscriptions before incorporation. Where a number of persons subscribe for stock in a corporation to be formed in the future, there is generally no contract between the various subscribers. The subscription is regarded as an offer made to the corporation to be formed. Unless provided otherwise by statute, it stands as a mere continuing offer by each subscriber to the corporation to take stock when the corporation is formed, and may be revoked at any time before acceptance by the corporation.[2] However, in some jurisdictions a subscription paper signed by a number of persons, prior to the formation of a corporation, constitutes a binding, irrevocable offer to the corporation, by reason of the mutual

[2] Collins v. Morgan Grain Co., page 806.

promises of the parties, and amounts to a subscription when the corporation is formed.[3]

Subscriptions for shares are often made subject to the happening of certain conditions precedent. The subscriber agrees to take shares conditioned upon the promoter's securing certain other persons to take shares, or upon a certain number of shares being subscribed. Until these conditions are met, the subscriber neither is liable for his subscription nor does he become a stockholder. However, if creditors of the corporation and third parties will be prejudiced thereby, the nonperformance of these conditions will not relieve the subscriber of liability. Unless conditions precedent are written in the subscription contract, the breach of the conditions cannot be used as a defense by the subscriber in an action by the corporation, and oral testimony may not be used to prove the breach.

A distinction must be made between a subscription on a condition and a conditional delivery of a subscription contract. In an action against the subscriber, oral evidence may be admitted that the subscription contract was conditionally delivered and that in absence of the happening of the condition no subscription contract was to come into existence. Such evidence, however, cannot be introduced to show that the subscription was a conditional one if other parties have been misled thereby.

Certain conditions are inherent in the subscription contract. The subscriber will not be liable unless the corporation is completely organized as a de jure corporation, the full amount of the capital stock has been subscribed in absence of an express agreement to the contrary, and the purpose, articles, and by-laws of the corporation are as originally stated. Conditions express or implied are often waived by the subscriber who, with knowledge of the nonperformance, participates in stockholders' meetings, pays part or all of his subscription, or acts as an officer or director of the corporation.

5-80. Subscriptions after incorporation. A subscription to stock of a corporation already in existence is a contract between the subscriber and the corporation, and such a contract may come into existence by reason of an offer either made by the corporation and accepted by the subscriber or made by the subscriber and accepted by the corporation. If the corporation opens subscription books and advertises its stock, it is seeking for an offer to be made by the subscriber. The corporation may, however, make a general offer to the public, which may be accepted by the subscriber in accordance with the terms of the general offer.

One must exercise care in distinguishing between a present subscription to stock, by which contract the subscriber immediately becomes liable as a stockholder, and a contract to purchase stock. Where the contract is for the purchase of stock, the purchaser does not become a stockholder

[3] Hoppe v. Rittenhouse, page 808.

until a certificate of stock has been delivered to him. Upon the breach of such contract and the tender of the stock certificate by the corporation, recovery is limited to damages for failure to purchase. Under a present subscription contract, however, the subscriber is liable upon his promise to pay for the full amount of the stock subscribed, even though the corporation has not tendered the stock certificate.

An underwriter's contract to place a certain block of stock, or, if unable to dispose of it, to purchase it himself, is not a subscription contract. Such an underwriter may, however, be held liable for as much of the stock as he guaranteed to dispose of but was unable to place. For his services in this connection, the underwriter receives a certain commission on stock sold.

KINDS OF STOCK

5-81. Common stock. Common stock is the simplest type of corporate stock, and entitles the owner to share in the profits and assets of the corporation in proportion to the amount of common stock he holds. Such a stockholder has no advantage, priority, or preference over any other class of stockholders.

5-82. Preferred stock. Preferred stock is stock that has a prior claim to dividends, or to assets on dissolution, over other classes of stock. The most important right given to a preferred stockholder is the right to receive a certain specified dividend, even though the earnings are not sufficient to pay a like dividend to common stockholders.

Preferred stock may be provided for by the charter; but, if no provision is made for the issuance of preferred stock by the charter or statute, such stock cannot be issued without the unanimous consent of the common stockholders.

Preferred stock may be cumulative or noncumulative. If the certificate of the preferred stock evidencing the contract provides that the preferred shares shall be entitled to a dividend of a certain per cent annually when earned, and that the arrears, if any, in one year or more, are payable out of the earnings of the subsequent years, the dividends are said to be cumulative. If the dividends are to be paid out of current profits only, the preferred stock is said to be noncumulative. Whether preferred stock is cumulative or noncumulative usually depends upon the statute or the contract on the face of the certificate of stock. However, if nothing is said about the payment of the dividends, the preferred stock is cumulative,[4]

[4] Arizona Power Co. v. Stuart, page 809.

and preferred dividends and all arrears thereon must be paid before a dividend is declared on common stock.

Preferred stock may be participating or nonparticipating. If the preferred stock is given the right to share in dividends equally with other classes of stock, after the payment of the preferred dividends, it is generally designated as participating preferred stock. Such participating preferred stock is entitled to dividends, however, only after the common stock has had an equal dividend for the current year. If, however, it is limited in its dividend to a fixed amount, it is designated as nonparticipating preferred stock.[5] The term "participating preferred stock" is also used to designate a preferred stock which gives a preference in the assets on dissolution and liquidation of the corporation and may give the holder a future right to share with other classes of stock in the assets that remain after the common and preferred stock have been fully satisfied on the original investment. To determine whether preferred stock has equality in the participation in dividends with other classes of stock, after the payment of its fixed dividend, it is necessary to examine, not only the contract evidenced by the stock certificate, but also the articles of incorporation, the by-laws, and the statute. In the absence of an agreement, preferred stock has no preference in corporate assets at dissolution.

5-83. Watered stock. Watered stock is stock that has been issued as fully paid, when in fact its full par value has not been paid in money, property, or services.[6] The capital stock of a corporation represents the total par value of all the shares of the corporation, and the public has a right to assume that the capital stock issued has all been paid in full, so that the corporation will have assets sufficient to meet liabilities equal to its issued capital stock. If stock is issued in excess of the actual assets in money value of the corporation, it is said to be watered stock, and original holders of such stock are liable to creditors for its par value.

In suits by creditors against stockholders to force payment on watered stock, it is maintained by many jurisdictions that the capital stock is a "trust fund" for the payment of the corporate debts and that the law implies a promise by the original stockholders to pay their stock in full when called upon by the creditors.

Another basis upon which creditors seek recovery against holders of such stock is called the "holding out" theory. Under this doctrine the right of creditors to compel the holders of bonus stock to pay for it, contrary to their actual agreement with the corporation, rests not upon an implied contract or upon any trust fund doctrine but simply upon the ground of fraud. This right applies only to those creditors who have relied upon the stock as representing actual capital paid in; therefore, payment

[5] Miller et al. v. James F. Powers Foundry Co. et al., page 810.
[6] Bing Crosby Minute Maid Corp. v. Eaton, page 812.

cannot be enforced against stockholders in favor of those creditors who became such before the bonus stock was issued. In either case, only the original purchaser of the stock is liable. One who acquires it in good faith from the original stockholder has no additional liability.

5-84. No par stock. The statutes of some states provide that a corporation may issue stock with no par value, the value of the stock being determined by its sale value in the open market. Stockholders and the public will not be injured by this type of stock, because there is no holding out that the stock has any particular face value, and all persons dealing in such stock are under a duty to investigate the corporation's assets and its financial conditions. Stock with no par value represents on its face what proportionate part it is of the total assets of the corporation, but does not indicate the monetary value of the share. The law usually permits the directors to determine what portion of the amount received from the sale shall be credited to the capital stock account and how much, if any, shall be credited to capital surplus.

5-85. Treasury stock. Treasury stock is that which has been issued by the corporation for value and returned by gift or purchase to the corporation, or to trustees for the corporation to sell. It may be sold below par and the proceeds returned to the treasury of the corporation for working capital. It differs from stock originally issued below par, in that the purchaser is not liable for the difference between par and the sale price. It may be sold at any price the company sees fit to charge.

TRANSFER OF STOCK AND OTHER INVESTMENT SECURITIES

5-86. In general. A share of stock is personal property and the owner has a right to transfer his stock, just as he may transfer any other personal property. It is a marketable commodity and is bought and sold daily on the market. A share of stock is generally transferred by an indorsement and delivery of the certificate of stock. A share may be transferred or assigned by a bill of sale or by any other method that will pass title to a chose in action or other intangible property. Whenever a share of stock is sold and a stock certificate issued, the name of the owner is entered on the stock book of the corporation. In a small corporation the secretary of the corporation is capable of handling all transfers of stock and the canceling and reissuing of new certificates. This method, however, is inadequate in large corporations where the business of transferring stock has become enormous and complicated. For the purpose of meeting this situation transfer agents are now established and employed by corporations.

The transfer agents transfer stock, cancel old certificates, issue new ones, prepare and keep up-to-date the names of the stockholders of the corporation, distribute dividends, mail out stockholders' notices, and perform many of the functions normally performed by a corporation secretary. The New York Stock Exchange rules provide that corporations listing stock for sale must maintain a transfer agency and registry, operated and maintained under the rules of the Stock Exchange; similar rules are necessary for stock listed on the American Exchange. The registrar of stock is an agent of the corporation whose duty is to see that no stock certificates are issued in excess of the authorized capitalization of the corporation. For every share of stock transferred, the old certificate must be canceled and a new certificate issued.

The transfer of stock is an assignment, and in order to make a complete transfer a novation is necessary. A novation is executed when the old stock certificate is surrendered and canceled and a new certificate issued to the transferee and his name entered on the corporate stock book by the corporation through the transfer agent. Consequently, there are two distinct steps necessary to make a perfect transfer of the stock.

First, the certificate is assigned by the transferor to the transferee when the transferor signs his name in a blank provided on the back of the certificate, and delivers it to the transferee. Second, the transferred certificate is delivered to the corporation or transfer agent and the corporation enters upon the corporate stock transfer book that the transferee has acquired the stock, after which the corporation issues a new certificate of stock, certifying that the newly recorded stockholder owns the specified amount of stock. The corporation then cancels the old certificate of stock.

As between the transferor and the transferee, the registration of the transfer is not necessary. As between the stockholder and the corporation, a registration is necessary, in order that the corporation may know who is entitled to the rights of a stockholder.

Article 8, in the main, provides for the method of transfer indicated above.

Article 8—Investment Securities, of the Uniform Commercial Code "may be likened . . . to a negotiable instrument law dealing with securities." The Article deals with bearer bonds formerly covered by the NIL, and with registered bonds which were not previously encompassed by any Uniform Law. In addition, the article covers stock certificates which were previously the subject of the Uniform Stock Transfer Act. Additional types of investment paper which have not been covered by any Uniform Act are included within the coverage of Article 8.

It has been held that the Code does not apply to a sale of a corporation and its subsidiaries where the sale was accomplished by the buyer's purchase of all issued and outstanding capital stock of the corporation and its subsidiaries.

The Code defines a "security" as an instrument which is:

1. issued in bearer or registered form, and
2. is of a type commonly dealt in upon securities exchanges and markets or is commonly recognized as a medium for investment, and
3. evidences a share, participation or other interest in property or in an enterprise or evidences an obligation of the issuer.

Security instruments are governed by Article 8 even though they also meet the requirements of Article 3—Commercial Paper.

Registered form is defined as a security which specifies the name of the owner and which may be transferred by registration upon books maintained by or on behalf of the issuer.

Section 8-102 (d) provides: "A security is in bearer form when it runs to bearer according to its terms and not by reason of any indorsement."

It is to be noted that the definition of "security" is functional—based upon its use as a medium for investment—rather than formal as in the case of commercial paper. Transferable warrants (rights to subscribe for shares in a corporation) will usually satisfy the requirements of a security. The size of the organization issuing the securities is not significant—even the stock in small "closed" or family corporations is encompassed by Article 8. Stock certificates, bonds, debentures, script, certificates and other instruments which evidence a share, participation, or other interest in property or an enterprise, or evidence an obligation of the issuer, are included within the coverage of Article 8.

If an instrument is issued payable to order rather than payable to bearer or registered, it is not within Article 8 although it might qualify under the formal test of negotiable instruments under Article 3—Commercial Paper.

Negotiability is not affected under Article 8 by expressions that the instrument is "subject to" another agreement.

Overissue. The power of a corporation to issue securities is controlled by statute, and the charter limits the number of shares that can be issued. The issue of securities in excess of the authorized amounts is prohibited. An "overissue" is defined as the issue of securities in excess of the amount which the issuer has the corporate power to issue. If a person is entitled to securities and the issue exceeds the authorized limit, he may insist that the corporation purchase the shares, where identical shares are reasonably available on the market, or are available by purchase from other shareholders. As an alternative, the party entitled to the shares can recover damages for failure to provide the shares.

Securities negotiable. Section 8-105 of the Code provides that securities are negotiable instruments and that bona fide purchasers thereof have greater rights than they would have "if the things bought were chattels or simple contracts." The particular rules of Section 3-307 for commercial paper are applied to securities. Defenses of the issuer are in general not effective against a purchaser for value who has taken without notice of the particular defense.

5-87. Issuer. The issuer may impose restrictions on the transfer of stock—that is, limiting the right to dispose of the stock. Such restrictions even though lawful are ineffective against a person unless he has actual knowledge of the restriction. If the restriction is not noted, the issuer can be compelled to register the transfer. In most jurisdictions, corporations are authorized to impose restrictions on transfer to the extent that the corporation or stockholders of the issuing corporation have the option to purchase the stock at a specified price before it is offered to third parties. The right to transfer freely one's share in the ownership of the business is inherent in corporate organization. It is one of those features of corporate life which distinguishes it from a partnership. Unmindful of this principle, "closed" corporations often attempt by agreement or by-law to limit the group of potential purchasers. In this effort they are only moderately successful. A corporate by-law which provides that the shares of stock can be transferred only to the corporation or to those approved by the board of directors is unenforceable. It places too severe a restraint upon the alienation of property. Society is best protected when property may be transferred freely from hand to hand. However, an agreement or a by-law approved by all stockholders, to the effect that no transfer of stock shall be made until it has first been offered to the other members of the corporation, is generally enforced. Notice of the by-law or agreement should be set forth in the stock certificate, since an innocent purchaser without notice of the restriction on alienation takes free from it.

Occasionally an officer of a corporation is appointed upon the condition that he will purchase a certain amount of corporate stock. The agreement usually stipulates that, upon the termination of his official relationship, he will resell the stock at a stipulated price to the corporation. Such an agreement has generally been enforced, although, if it is clear that the *corporation promises* to purchase the stock, some courts suggest that the agreement is illegal. Since a corporation may acquire treasury stock only out of surplus, an agreement to purchase when no surplus exists is of doubtful validity.

Unauthorized signature on issue. A corporation may entrust its securities to an employee or transfer agent to prepare them for issue. This process includes affixing the corporate seal and adding a signature necessary for issue. If the person entrusted with the securities or who has access to them forges a signature or signs without authority "prior to or in the course of issue," such signature is ineffective except that "the signature is effective in favor of a purchaser for value and without notice of the lack of authority. . . ." (U.C.C. 8-205). The purpose of this section is to place upon the issuer the duty to avoid negligent entrusting of securities to employees or others in the course of issue. This section deals with signatures placed upon securities prior to or in the course of issue and does not apply to forged indorsements. A related problem is that of completion or alteration of an instrument. The Code provides that a purchaser for value without notice can enforce an incorrectly completed instrument and that a complete security which is wrongfully altered is enforceable but only according to its original terms. Nondelivery of an incomplete instrument is not a defense against a holder for value without notice.

Rights of issuer—registered owners. When a security in registered form is transferred, the new owner should present it to the issuer for registration of the transfer. Prior to such presentment, the issuer may "treat the registered owner as the person exclusively entitled to vote, to receive notifications, and otherwise to exercise all the rights and powers of an owner." (U.C.C. 8-207 (1)). Stock that is being paid for by installments that fall due at the demand or call of the board of directors may be sold before all of the calls have been made. In such cases the purchaser is deemed to have assumed responsibility for all future calls, and the transferor is relieved of liability. In other words, as soon as the transfer is recorded on corporate records, a novation has been consummated. This is not true when the transfer is made to a financially irresponsible person for the express purpose of eliminating the liability for stock of doubtful value.

As to the calls made previous to the transfer, but that remain unpaid at that time, the transferor remains liable. The liability of the transferee in such a case doubtless depends upon his knowledge or lack of knowledge of the unpaid calls. If the corporation issues a certificate prior to the time when all calls are made, it should not be marked "fully paid and nonassessable." An innocent purchaser of stock thus erroneously marked takes it free from any liability to the corporation for unpaid calls. The Code in Section 8-207 (2) provides: "Nothing in this Article shall be construed to affect the liability of the registered owner of a security for calls, assessments, or the like." Likewise, the Section does not preclude a holder of record from denying ownership when assessments are levied if he is otherwise entitled to do so under state law.

5-88. Purchaser. A "bona fide" purchaser is defined as one who purchases in good faith and without notice of any adverse claim "takes delivery of a security in bearer form or of one in registered form issued to him or indorsed to him or in blank." (U.C.C. 8-302). The Code provides that one who takes from a bona fide purchaser is given the rights of a bona fide purchaser. This is comparable to the "shelter provision" of Article 3—Commercial Paper. A bona fide purchaser takes free of "adverse claims" which include a claim that a transfer was wrongful or that some other person is the owner of, or has an interest in, the security.

5-89. Transfer. A person who transfers a security for value warrants that his transfer is effective and rightful; that the security is genuine and has not been materially altered; and that he knows of no fact which might impair the validity of the security. A broker makes all the warranties of a transferor.

A transfer is accomplished when the transferor delivers the security to the purchaser. Such transfer is complete upon delivery. If the security is in registered form and has been transferred without any necessary indorsement, the purchaser has a specifically enforceable right to have any necessary indorsement supplied. He does not attain the status of a bona fide purchaser until the indorsement is received.

Indorsement. The transfer may be accomplished by the signature of the transferor on the back of a security or by a separate document signed by the transferor. An indorsement may be in blank or special; an indorsement to bearer is a blank indorsement. A special indorsement specifies the person to whom the security is transferred. A holder may convert a blank indorsement into a special indorsement. The indorser does not assume any obligation that the security will be honored by the issuer unless the indorser has agreed to assume this obligation. Unlike commercial paper, an indorser may transfer only a part of a security representing units. Thus 50 shares may be transferred where the certificate represents 100 shares. There are two steps in the transfer—indorsement and delivery. The transfer is not accomplished until delivery has taken place. Since the concept of indorsement is applicable to registered securities, the indorsement of a security in bearer form is normally of no effect.

If an indorsement is forged, the owner may assert the ineffectiveness of the indorsement to deprive the owner of his ownership against the issuing corporation or any purchaser other than a bona fide purchaser who has in good faith received a new, reissued, or reregistered security on registration of transfer. The issuer who registers the transfer of a security upon a forged indorsement is subject to liability for improper registration.[7] Any person guaranteeing a signature of an indorser of a security makes certain warranties.[8]

[7] LeSavoy Industries v. Pennsylvania General Paper Corp., page 814.
[8] Love v. Pennsylvania R. R. Co., page 816.

5-90. Registration. Though a transfer, as between transferor and purchaser, is complete when a registered security is indorsed and delivered, the remaining step is to register the transfer. This means that the new owner's name is placed on the stock register and the transferor's name is removed. Registration is of vital importance to the purchaser. Section 8-401 (11) of the Code provides that where a security in registered form is presented to the issuer with a request to register transfer, the issuer is under a duty to do so provided the security is properly indorsed, reasonable assurance is given in a manner satisfactory to the corporation at the time of presentment that the indorsements are genuine, tax requirements have been satisfied, and the transfer is in fact rightful or is to a bona fide purchaser.

Lost, destroyed and stolen securities. Where a security has been lost, apparently destroyed or wrongfully taken, the owner must notify the issuer of such fact within a reasonable time. Should he fail to do so and the issuer registers a transfer, the owner is precluded from asserting the ineffectiveness of a forged indorsement and the wrongfulness of the registration of the transfer. If the lost security was indorsed by the owner the registration is not wrongful unless notice has been given to the issuer. Section 8-405 (2) (3) provides:

(2) Where the owner of a security claims that the security has been lost, destroyed or wrongfully taken, the issuer must issue a new security in place of the original security if the owner

(a) so requests before the issuer has notice that the security has been acquired by a bona fide purchaser; and

(b) files with the issuer a sufficient indemnity bond; and

(c) satisfies any other reasonable requirements imposed by the issuer.

(3) If, after the issue of the new security, a bona fide purchaser of the original security presents it for registration of transfer, the issuer must register the transfer unless registration would result in overissue, in which event the issuer's liability is governed by Section 8-104. In addition to any rights on the indemnity bond, the issuer may recover the new security from the person to whom it was issued or any person taking under him except a bona fide purchaser.

Right of transferee to dividends. Dividends on stock belong to the person who is owner of the stock at the time the dividends are declared. As to the corporation, the ownership of the stock is determined by the stock register, and the dividends will be paid to the person whose name appears upon the stock book. In the absence of an agreement to the contrary, dividends declared before a transfer of stock, although not payable until a future time, belong to the transferor. But dividends declared after the transfer of the stock, although earned before the transfer, belong to the transferee. However, by agreement between the transferor and the transferee, upon notice to the corporation, the corporation must pay the dividends in compliance with the agreement.

Dividends are often declared as of a certain date and payable to stockholders of record as of a later date. In such cases a transfer after declaration, but before the record date, carries the dividends to the transferee. There is also some authority to the effect that a stock dividend passes to the transferee unless the contract of sale provides otherwise. Dividends normally become a debt as of the time they are declared, but stock dividends may be rescinded, according to many courts, after they have been declared. Consequently, in the case of cash dividends, the debt is owed to the stockholder at the date of declaration, or record date, whereas in reference to stock dividends, no debt exists since the new issue of stock is transferred to the owner at the time it is issued.

In the comment to Section 8-207 (2), it is stated: "No interference is intended with the common practice of closing the transfer books or taking a record date for dividend, voting, and other purposes as provided for in by-laws, charters, and statutes."

MEMBERSHIP IN CORPORATIONS CASES

FONTAINEBLEAU HOTEL CORP. v. ROSENBERG

1960, (Fla.) 121 So.2d 675

HORTON, Chief Judge. . . . The defendant hotel corporation has appealed from a judgment in the total sum of $122,967.51, found to be due and owing by the defendant to the plaintiffs upon certain debentures issued by defendants. The final judgment entered in a nonjury trial recites in part as follows: . . .

> That under the terms of said debentures and the evidence taken before the Court, the Court finds that the said plaintiffs are entitled to the full relief which they seek in their complaint, and they are entitled to recover from the defendant the principal sums of said debentures. . . .

The debentures in question provide:

> The holders of debentures in this series shall be entitled to payment upon the occasion of dissolution of this corporation, or upon the occasion of a distribution of its assets, or upon the occasion of a reduction in its capital account, * * *

Pursuant to a contract with the Kirkeby Corporation, the hotel corporation purchased and retired to its treasury, certain of its stock held by the Kirkeby Corporation. The funds necessary for this purchase were secured by the issuance of a mortgage on the defendant's real property. The appellees, holders of the debentures in question, contended that the issuance of this mortgage and purchase of stock by the hotel corporation amounted to a reduction in the capital account of the corporation thereby entitling them, under the terms of the debentures, to payment.

The determinative question raised upon appeal is whether or not the plaintiffs sustained the burden of proof of necessary conditions precedent to establish a reduction in the capital account of the corporation. In support thereof, the appellant argues that in order to determine if the giving of the mortgage constituted a reduction in capital, it is necessary to determine the status of the capital account as of the date of the issuance of the debentures, and that this has not been established. . . . Both parties assert that the term "capital account" used in the debenture covenant must be construed as meaning the sum total of a corporation's assets over its liabilities. The appellant necessarily contends that the "capital account" is limited to that capital account of the corporation at the time the debenture was executed. It is apparent that the covenant in question, contained in the debenture, is to continue in effect for the life of the debenture, and at no time prior to their retirement, may the corporation occasion a reduction in its capital account. The natural meaning of this covenant would appear to be that no reduction was to be permitted regardless of the amount of the capital account, without entitling the debenture holder to payment. There is nothing in the language of the debenture to indicate an intention to limit the scope of the covenant to the capital account of the corporation at the time the debenture was executed. Compare *Chase National Bank of New York v. Sweezy,* Sup. 281 N.Y.S. 487, affirmed 261 N.Y. 710, 185, N.E. 803.

Undoubtedly, the appellees were justified in refusing to do any financing unless they were secured by the appellant's covenant not to reduce capital. . . .

Accordingly, the judgment (in favor of plaintiffs) appealed is affirmed.

COLLINS v. MORGAN GRAIN CO.

1926, 16 F.2d 253

Collins subscribed to stock in a corporation which was to be organized to take over the grain business of certain operators on the Pacific coast. Other subscribers also agreed to purchase stock in the proposed corporation, and the corporation was subsequently organized. The board of directors accepted the subscriptions and a certificate was tendered to Collins, who refused to accept or pay for it. The corporation brought action against Collins and he offered to prove that before the organization of the corporation he withdrew his subscription. The court below ruled that this evidence was incompetent and directed a verdict for the plaintiff.

RUDKIN, Circuit Judge. . . . The principal assignment of error is based on the ruling of the court excluding testimony tending to prove a revocation or cancellation of the subscription before the corporation was formed, and before the offer was accepted. Agreements to subscribe for stock of corporations to be formed in the future may assume different forms, with different results. For example, if an individual, acting singly and without co-operation with others, offers to take stock in such a corporation, all the authorities agree that the offer may be rescinded or revoked at any time before the corporation is formed and the offer accepted; this upon the familiar principle that it takes two parties to make a contract, and that, if one is not bound, the other is not, in other words, that a mere unaccepted offer cannot in the nature of things constitute a binding contract.

Again, such an agreement may assume a double aspect, as where a number of persons agree to form a corporation and to subscribe to its capital stock. Such an agreement constitutes a contract as between the subscribers themselves, operative at once, and it likewise constitutes a continuing offer to the proposed corporation, which, upon acceptance, becomes as to each subscriber a contract between him and the corporation. Some of the authorities hold that contracts of the latter class are irrevocable without the consent of all the parties thereto; but there is usually found in such cases some element of estoppel, which does not exist in the case at bar. But, without attempting to distinguish the present case from the cases so holding, we deem it sufficient to say that the cases relied on are not supported by the weight of authority.

According to the weight of authority, a subscription may be withdrawn at any time before it is accepted by the corporation, whether made before or after the formation of the corporation, for the reason that until such acceptance there is no binding contract, because, until then, there is no agreement and no mutuality of object, and hence no consideration, and, in the case of subscriptions made before the corporation is formed, for the additional reason that, until it is formed, the other contemplated party to the contract is not yet in existence; nor, where this rule obtains, is a subscriber deprived of the right to withdraw under such circumstances because other subscribers have acted upon the strength of his subscription, nor because he has induced others to subscribe. 2 Fletcher Cyc. Corp. 1225.

. . . The reason for the majority rule is well stated in *Hudson Real Estate Co. v. Tower,* 156 Mass. 82, 30 N.E. 465, 32 Am. St. Rep. 434:

At the time when the defendant signed the subscription paper declared on, it was not a contract, for want of a contracting party on the other side; but it has now been established that a subscription of this sort becomes a contract with the corporation when the corporation has been organized, and in this way the objection of the want of a proper contracting party is finally avoided, provided everything goes on as contemplated without any interruption. Until the organization of the corporation, the subscription is a mere proposition or offer, which may be withdrawn, like any other unaccepted offer. Unless the signer is bound upon a contract, he is not bound at all. It is open to him to withdraw. It is not on the ground that there was no sufficient consideration. The seal would do away with any doubt on that score. But it is on the ground that for the time being, and until the corporation is organized the writing does not take effect as a contract, because the contemplated party to the contract, on the other side, is not yet in existence, and for this reason, there being no contract, the whole undertaking is inchoate and incomplete, and since there is no contract the party may withdraw. . . .

For the foregoing reasons, we are of opinion that the court below erred in excluding the testimony tending to show a revocation or cancellation of the subscription before the corporation was formed and before the offer was accepted, and for this error the judgment is reversed, and the cause is remanded for a new trial.

HOPPE v. RITTENHOUSE
1960, 279 F.2d 3

The Trustee in Bankruptcy (Hoppe) challenged as a voidable preference a secured creditor's claim filed by one of the creditors. The creditor, Gamill, had assigned his claim to Rittenhouse. The bankrupt, Los Gatos Lumber Products, Inc., had been hampered by lack of adequate working capital. Morton, president of the bankrupt, had advanced substantial sums of money to it but this had not been sufficient. The creditor had also advanced money and had obtained a mortgage on the property of the bankrupt. The Trustee's contention was that the corporation was insolvent at the time the mortgage was given and that this was known to the creditors. The creditor contends that the corporation was not insolvent because Morton was not a creditor—that his advances were not "as loans but as equity capital in the form of subscriptions to the capital stock." The lower court ruled in favor of the creditor and the Trustee appealed.

KOELSCH, Circuit Judge. . . . The undisputed evidence is thus that the Mortons had orally agreed to exchange their notes for stock in the corporation on the condition that additional working capital be obtained from some outside source, and that the corporation, through its president, Carl Morton, not only agreed to this proposal but actively sought additional financing from prospective lenders by positively asserting that the apparent indebtedness of the corporation to the Morton family would be erased as a liability when additional financing was obtained. There is little doubt that the Mortons intended to and did enter into a conditional subscription agreement. The critical question, then, is whether this agreement was binding and enforceable, for on it hinges the validity of the referee's finding that the Mortons' advances were "subscriptions," not "loans." . . .

Under California law an agreement by prospective shareholders to purchase stock in a proposed corporation, or unissued shares in an existing corporation, is a binding and enforceable contract. . . . The proposal made by such subscribers must be accepted by the corporation before they are finally bound, and it is clear in the present case that Carl Morton, acting on behalf of the corporation, did so accept. . .

The trustee argues that because no stock was issued to the Mortons, they remained creditors and did not become subscribers of stock; but as in most cases, their status as subscribers is determined by the intention of the parties to the agreement. . . . Here the intention to convert notes into stock if additional capital was obtained is established by an abundance of testimony, and it is clear that the mere mechanical act of issuing stock certificates is not necessary to constitute the subscribers shareholders. . . .

It is true that the agreement was subject to a condition precedent, i.e., obtaining additional working capital, but that condition occurred when the Gammills began advancing considerable sums, which eventually exceeded $29,000.00, to the corporation. The condition thus having occurred, the contract became binding and constituted the Mortons shareholders instead of creditors, and as such "beneficial owners" of the corporate assets. . . .

Moreover, should we assume that the agreement was subject to some infirmity rendering it invalid, it is clear under California law that as between the Gammills and the Mortons, the latter would be estopped to deny their status as subscribers where, as here, the Gammills relied upon the agreement in making loans. . . .

The fact that the Mortons presented creditors' claims in the bankruptcy proceeding is not conclusive but at most creates a conflict in the evidence. Indeed, such behavior by subscribers follows a familiar pattern where efforts to continue the corporation in operation have failed: subscribers oftentimes endeavor to salvage something of their investment by attempting to qualify as creditors. . . .

Affirmed.

ARIZONA POWER CO. v. STUART

1954, 212 F.2d 535

The plaintiff corporation brought this action against the defendant, Collector of Internal Revenue, to recover income taxes allegedly overpaid. The question presented to the court was whether the plaintiff could deduct dividends paid on preferred stock for the purpose of computing the corporate surtax. This in turn depended upon whether the stock fell within the definition of preferred stock in the Internal Revenue Code as being stock the dividends of which are cumulative. The lower court ruled against the plaintiff and plaintiff appealed.

LEMMON, District Judge. . . . A preferred stockholder is not creditor of the corporation in which he holds his stock. The dividends thereon are not payable absolutely but only out of the net earnings or net assets in excess of capital and only when and as declared. A dividend is that which the corporation has set aside from its net earnings or profits to be divided among the stockholders. The preference is limited to profits when earned. The agreement to pay dividends on preferred stock is to be construed as an agreement to pay them from profits. This is the rule unless corporations are expressly authorized by statute to resort to capital in payment of such dividends.

Dividends on preferred stock are ordinarily regarded as cumulative.

. . . This brings into focus the distinction between a cumulative and a non-cumulative dividend. A cumulative dividend survives as a senior charge on earnings. A non-cumulative dividend disappears if not declared and ceases to be a preferential right.

. . . Appellee reminds us that there is no specific statement in the articles that the preferred stock is cumulative. But references are made in the articles to "accumulated and unpaid dividends" on the preferred stock.

. . . It is unnecessary that the word "cumulative" be used. It is sufficient if the stipulated preferences make it such.

. . . *Reversed and remanded with directions to enter judgment in favor of appellant.*

MILLER et al. v. JAMES F. POWERS FOUNDRY CO. et al.
1934, 166 Md. 590, 171 Atl. 842

The plaintiffs, Miller and Fenton, brought this suit as holders of preferred stock in the Foundry Company, for a decree against the two owners of all the common stock of the corporation for such sum as they had received as dividends on the common stock in excess of the rate of dividends paid on the preferred stock. In 1926 a dividend of 430 per cent had been paid on the common stock, a like amount in 1927, and 150 per cent in 1928. The lower court dismissed the bill against the defendants, common stockholders.

SLOAN, J. . . . Now, as to the contention of the plaintiffs that the defendants, William Sterling Evans and Standley Evans, should be required to refund such part of the common stock dividends received by them as would equalize the common and preferred stock dividends:

The only case in this court in which there has been a construction of a provision in a preferred stock certificate for the payment of a specified dividend with reference to a common stock dividend was *Scott v. Baltimore & O. R. Co.*, 93 Md. 475, 49 A. 327. In that case the holders of the 4 per cent preferred stock contended that they were not only entitled to the prescribed 4 per cent dividend, but that each share of preferred stock was entitled to share equally in any distribution by way of dividend with each share of common stock. The opinion is expressed 1 *Cook on Corporations* (6th Ed.) § 269, "that unless the contract expressly provides otherwise, preferred stockholders participate in the surplus profits remaining after the preferred dividend has been declared on the preferred and an equal dividend on the common stock." This view is supported by Mr. Machen in his *Modern Law of Corporation,* § 555. Mr. Cook then, after stating this to be the proper rule, said: "It has been held, however, in Maryland (*Scott v. Baltimore & O. R. Co.*, 93 Md. 475, 49 A. 327) that where preferred stock is entitled to dividends 'up to but not exceeding four per cent, before any dividends shall be set apart or paid on the common stock,' such preferred stock is not entitled to dividends in excess of four per cent, even though a larger dividend than four per cent is paid on the common stock, and even though the preferred dividends are not cumulative." In a note discussing the opinion, Mr. Cook said: "In this case the reasoning of the court went still further and was to the effect that preferred stock is never entitled to dividends in excess of the amount specified, even though the dividends are non-cumulative." And then he says: "Theoretically it is difficult to justify this conclusion, but practically it is true that the investing public assume and understand that preferred stock is never entitled to more than its specified and fixed dividends, even though the certificate is silent as to further dividends in case a higher dividend is paid on the common stock."

There can be no question that the popular rule, where there are no restrictions, is that the preferred stock is entitled only to be paid the fixed or prescribed dividend and that the things that appeal to the investor are the rate, regularity of payment and whether unpaid dividends are cumulative, and these are the factors which determine its marketability and value, and when these conditions are met, any additional earnings or profits are available to the common stockholders. The case here involves only a small local corporation, locally owned, but what we say with reference to its preferred stock will apply with equal force to larger corporations, the stock of which may be widely scattered among people who have no acquaintance or familiarity with its operations, charter, resolutions, and by-laws. Their only source of information is the stock certificate, if they read it, and they do not often see that until it is bought and paid for. In view of what we regard, and Mr. Cook says, is the common understanding of the investing public, it is the opinion of this court that the sound rule is, unless otherwise provided, that preferred stock dividends are limited to the rate prescribed by the charter of the issuing corporation and stated in the certificate.

. . . In this case, however, it is only necessary to resort to the amended charter to ascertain that there was not only no intention that the preferred stock should participate in the dividends with the common stock, but that its privileges and restrictions were exclusive of any rights which the common stock had except that of voting. It is entitled to "an annual dividend of not less than six per cent before any dividend shall be paid to the holders of the common stock." This is the usual and ordinary provision and, without anything further, is the foundation of the view expressed as the logical one in both Cook and Machen on Corporations, *supra.* It is cumulative though it does not use the word. The charter says the corporation shall "be bound to pay an annual dividend," and in the event of liquidation "the holders of the preferred stock shall be entitled to be paid in full both the par amount of their shares and all dividends unpaid thereon," before anything be paid the common stockholders. . . . Then the charter provides that after the payment of debts, preferred stock, and unpaid dividends, "The remaining assets and funds of the corporation shall be divided and paid to the holders of said common stock . . . according to their respective shares." If this last clause means anything, it means that after the preferred stockholders are paid par for their stock plus the unpaid dividends annually alloted to them, they are through, and any surplus earnings, profits, dividends, or property are, in the terms of the charter itself, the property of the common stockholders.

Affirmed.

BING CROSBY MINUTE MAID CORP. v. EATON
1956, (Cal.2d) 297 P.2d 5

The plaintiff corporation was a judgment creditor of a corporation in which the defendant Eaton was the principal stockholder. The judgment was not paid and the plaintiff brought this action to recover from the defendant. The defendant had received 4,500 shares of stock having a par value of $10 in return for consideration from the defendant of $34,780.83. The lower court rendered a judgment against the defendant in the amount of $10,219.17. The lower court granted a new trial and the plaintiff appealed.

Shenk, J. . . . In this state a shareholder is ordinarily not personally liable for the debts of the corporation; he undertakes only the risk that his shares may become worthless. (Cases cited.) There are, however, certain exceptions to this rule of limited liability. For example, a subscriber to shares who pays in only part of what he agreed to pay is liable to creditors for the balance.

. . . The plaintiff seeks to base its recovery on the only other exception to the limited liability rule that the record could support, namely, liability for holding watered stock, which is stock issued in return for properties or services worth less than its par value. Accordingly, this case calls for an analysis of the rights of a creditor of an insolvent corporation against a holder of watered stock. Holders of watered stock are generally held liable to the corporation's creditors for the difference between the par value of the stock and the amount paid in.

. . . The liability of a holder of watered stock has been based on one of two theories; the misrepresentation theory or the statutory obligation theory. The misrepresentation theory is the one accepted in most jurisdictions. The courts view the issue of watered stock as a misrepresentation of the corporation's capital. Creditors who rely on this misrepresentation are entitled to recover the "water" from the holders of the watered shares. (Cases cited.)

Statutes expressly prohibiting watered stock are commonplace today. In some jurisdictions where they have been enacted, the statutory obligation theory has been applied. Under that theory the holder of watered stock is held responsible to creditors whether or not they have relied on overvaluation of corporate capital.

. . . In his answer the defendant alleged that in extending credit to the corporation the plaintiff did not rely on the par value of the shares issued, but only on independent investigation and reports as to the corporation's current cash position, its physical assets and its business experience. At the trial the plaintiff's district manager admitted that during the period when the plaintiff extended credit to the corporation, (1) the district manager believed that the original capital of the corporation amounted to only $25,000, and (2) the only financial statement of the corporation that the plaintiff ever saw showed a capital stock account of less than $33,000. These admissions would be sufficient to support a finding that the plaintiff did not rely on any misrepresentation arising out of the issuance of watered stock. The court made no finding on the issue of reliance. If the misrepresentation theory prevails in California, that issue was material and the defendant was entitled to a finding thereon. Code Civ. Proc. § 632; see *Edgar v. Hitch*, 46 Cal.2d 309, 294 P.2d 3. If the statutory obligation theory prevails, the fact that the plaintiff did not rely on any misrepresentation arising out of the issuance of watered stock is irrelevant and accordingly a finding on the issue of reliance would be surplusage.

It is therefore necessary to determine which theory prevails in this state. The plaintiff concedes that before the enactment of § 1110 of the Corporations Code (originally Civ. Code, § 299) in 1931, the misrepresentation theory was the only one available to creditors seeking to recover from holders of watered stock.

. . . In view of the cases in this state adopting the misrepresentation theory, it is reasonable to assume that the Legislature would have used clear language expressing an intent to broaden the basis of liability of holders of watered stock had it entertained such an intention. In this state the liability of a holder of watered stock may only be based on the misrepresentation theory.

The plaintiff contends that even under the misrepresentation theory a creditor's reliance on the misrepresentation arising out of the issuance of watered stock should be conclusively presumed. This contention is without substantial merit. If it should prevail, the misrepresentation theory and the statutory obligation theory would be essentially identical. This court has held that under the misrepresentation theory a person who extended credit to a corporation (1) before the watered stock was issued, or (2) with full knowledge that watered stock was outstanding, cannot recover from the holders of the watered stock. These decisions indicate that under the misrepresentation theory reliance by the creditor is a prerequisite to the liability of a holder of watered stock. The trial court was therefore justified in ordering a new trial because of the absence of a finding on that issue.

. . . *The order granting the new trial is affirmed.*

LESAVOY INDUSTRIES v. PENNSYLVANIA GEN. PAPER CORP.

1961, 404 Pa. 161, 171 A.2d 148

The owner of all the stock in Lesavoy Industries, plaintiff, executed a general power of attorney to Allen Daniels. Plaintiff corporation was the owner of all the outstanding stock in the defendant corporation. Daniels entered into an agreement with one Price whereby Price was to receive 52 per cent of the stock in defendant corporation and a certificate was to be issued in the name of Price. Plaintiff corporation contends that it did not give the power to Lesavoy (its sole shareholder) or to Daniels to enter into this agreement. A certificate was issued to Price and is now in his possession. Plaintiff asked the court to declare null and void the transfer of shares from defendant corporation to Price and that defendant corporation be ordered to reassign and retransfer to plaintiff the shares of stock. The lower court ruled for plaintiff.

COHEN, J. . . . The lower court, in order to support its finding that the defendant corporation was a principal defendant, ruled that the plaintiff had alleged a proper cause of action against the defendant corporation on the theory that the defendant corporation breached its duty to protect its stockholder from an unauthorized transfer of shares.

It is generally accepted that a corporation owes its shareholders the duty to protect them from fraudulent transfers. *Pennsylvania Company, etc. v. Franklin Fire Ins. Co.*, 1897, 181 Pa. 40, 37 A. 191, 37 L.R.A. 780; *Egan v. United Gas Improvement Company*, 1935, 319 Pa. 17, 178 A. 683.

A corporation also owes its shareholders a duty to protect them from unauthorized transfers. See 12 Fletchers, Cyclopedia Corporations, Section 5537.1 (rev. vol. 1957). This court impliedly recognized such a duty where a corporation had been informed in advance of conflicting claims to the stock in question. *Leff v. N. Kaufman's, Inc.*, 1941, 342 Pa. 342, 20 A. 2d 786, 139 A.L.R. 267. We need not now decide if this duty extends beyond cases involving forgeries or notice to the corporation of irregularities, since here a wholly owned subsidiary relied upon a general power of attorney given to an agent by the parent corporation's sole shareholder. There can be no greater justification for a finding that the agent was clothed, at least, with apparent authority, thus effectuating an estoppel against the principal (plaintiff corporation). *Cf. Greene v. Nash*, 1892, 85 Me. 148, 26 A. 1114; 12 Fletcher Cyclopedia Corporations, Sections 5544, 5562 (rev. vol. 1957); Restatement, Agency, Sections 27, 31 (2d ed. 1958).

Plaintiff has failed to allege a cause of action against the defendant corporation and thus that defendant is only a passive party in a dispute between two claimants to the same stock. As such the defendant corporation is not a principal defendant (cases cited).

Since a principal defendant was not served in Chester County, we must now examine the second criterion for extra-territorial service; i.e., whether the subject matter of the action is property within the jurisdiction of the court. The situs of the stock in question is determined by the Uniform Stock Transfer Act (now embodied in the Uniform Commercial Code (12A P.S. Section 8-101), the policy of which is to make the certificate represent the shares of stock. See *Mills v. Jacobs*, 1939, 333 Pa. 231, 4 A.2d 152, 122 A.L.R. 333.

In *Crane v. Crane*, 1953, 373 Pa. 1, 95 A.2d 199, this court did consider the situs of stock to be that of the corporation and permitted an action against the corporation to transfer shares on its books. However, such actions will be permitted only where the outstanding certificates are either seized, surrendered or their transfer enjoined (See Restatement, Conflict of Laws, Sections 53 and 104) unless it is unnecessary to enjoin transfer; e.g., the defendant cannot convey title of the certificate without the joinder of the attaching creditor. See *Crane v. Crane*, supra. It is admitted that the outstanding shares in this case are located in New York and that they have not been seized or surrendered nor their transfer enjoined. We must therefore find that property which is the subject matter of the action is not within the jurisdiction of the court below.

Extra-territorial service upon Price, failing to qualify under either of the criteria set forth in Pa. R.C.P. 1504 (b), was unauthorized and ineffectual to subject him to the jurisdiction of the court below.

Decree reversed.

LOVE v. PENNSYLVANIA RAILROAD CO.
1961 (Pa.) 200 F. Supp. 563

The plaintiff and her father jointly owned stock, with the right of survivorship, in the Pennsylvania Railroad Company. The father prepared an assignment whereby the stock was transferred to him individually and forged plaintiff's name to the assignment. The railroad transferred the shares from the joint names of plaintiff and her father to the sole name of the father. Plaintiff sued the railroad and two banks were added as defendants on the basis that they had guaranteed the signatures of plaintiff and her father on a stock assignment and dividend request. Plaintiff seeks to amend her complaint to assert a claim against the additional defendants.

KRAFT, D. J. . . . Plaintiff relies in part upon Section 8-312 of the Uniform Commercial Code, 12A P.S. Section 8-312 as that section provided at the time of the guarantee:

Section 8-312. Effect of Guaranteeing Signature or Indorsement

(1) Any person guaranteeing a signature as being that of an indorser of a security warrants to any person taking or dealing with the security in reliance on the guaranteed signature that

(a) the signature is not forged; and
(b) the signer is the holder or has authority to sign in the name of the holder; and
(c) the signer has legal capacity to sign.

But the guarantor does not warrant the rightfulness of the particular transfer.

(2) . . .

(3) The guarantor of a signature or an indorsement shall be liable to any person, including an issuer who registers a transfer in reliance on the guarantee, for any loss resulting from breach of the warranties stated in this section but no issuer may require an indorsement guarantee as a condition to registration or transfer of a security.

Plaintiff emphasizes the phrase "to any person" in subsection (3), and contends that these words establish the third-party defendants' liability to her for her loss resulting from the breach of the warranty that "the signature is not forged." While a literal reading of the provision lends some support to the plaintiff's contention, we think it clear that its language must be read in conjunction with that contained in subsection (1). So read, the signature guarantor's liability "to any person" must be deemed co-extensive merely with his warranty, which runs only "to any person taking or dealing with the security in reliance on the guaranteed signature." That this was the real meaning of subsection (3) seems apparent from the fact that the subsection was amended in 1959 to express, in clear and unequivocal language, that precise meaning. Since, under the averments of the complaint, plaintiff did not take or deal with the security in reliance on the guaranteed signature, the third-party defendants' warranty did not extend to her, and they are not liable to her for any loss resulting from its breach.

The industry of counsel and our own research have disclosed a singular dearth of authority on the precise question. However, the few cases in point establish the principle that the guarantee of a signature does not run to the owner of the security unless the signature guarantor had actual knowledge of the impropriety of the transaction. It was so held in *Eulette v. Merrill, Lynch, Pierce, Fenner and Beane*, 101 So. 2d 603, 606 (Fla. App. 1958).

> The guarantee of the forged signature of the appellant (owner) on the stock certificate could not, in our opinion, afford the appellant any basis for recovery. The guarantee would run only to those persons who, subsequent to the guarantee, dealt with the stock in reliance upon the guarantee. There has been no showing that the appellant acted to his detriment, or, for that matter, acted at all, in reliance upon the appellee's guarantee.

It is the uniform rule in Pennsylvania that a person making a general guarantee to warranty is liable only to those parties who have acted in reliance thereon (cases cited).

We conclude, therefore, that the averments of the proposed amended complaint fail to state a legal claim against either third-party defendant, and the motion for leave to amend must be denied.

Review Questions and Problems

1. *A* bought stock in *X* corporation from the corporation. He did not receive certificates at the time, but did pay the price. Is *A* a stockholder if the transaction was entirely oral?
2. *A* is a bondholder in the *D* Company. Under ordinary conditions does he have any right to participate in the control of the business? Has a bondholder any security for his bond?
3. The *X* Company has both preferred and common stock. The preferred stock is 7 per cent stock. The company declares a 7 per cent dividend on the preferred stock and then declares a 10 per cent dividend on the common stock. Under such conditions, have the preferred stockholders a right to demand 10 per cent?
4. *A*, along with a number of others, subscribes for stock in anticipation that a corporation will later be formed. Before incorporation takes place, he notifies the incorporators that he withdraws his subscription. May he legally do so? Suppose the subscription had been made after incorporation?

5. The *X* Company purchased an invention from *A* and paid for it by the issuance of $100,000 of common stock. As a matter of fact the invention was worth only $50,000, but the directors honestly believed that it was worth $100,000. May the creditors recover an additional $50,000 from *A*?
6. *A* became a transferee of sixty shares of stock in a corporation which issued its stock marked fully paid and nonassessable upon the payment of 70 per cent of its par value. Assuming that *A* knew the conditions surrounding its issuance, is he liable to creditors in case of insolvency? Suppose he had been an innocent purchaser?
7. *A* held a certificate of stock for twenty shares in *X* Company, which was stolen. His indorsement was forged, and the certificate was transferred to *B*, an innocent purchaser. *B* obtained a new certificate from the company in his name and sold it to *H*, an innocent purchaser. What are the rights of *A*, *H*, and *X* Company?
8. *Y* Company on March 1 declared a cash dividend of 5 per cent, payable on June 1 to all stockholders of record on May 1. On April 10, *A* sold ten shares of stock in *Y* Company to *B*, although the transfer was not recorded on the corporation's books until May 15. To whom will the company pay the dividend? As between *A* and *B*, who is entitled to the dividend?
9. A corporation operated an apartment house. Its sole shareholders were its occupants. Each had one share which he purchased at the time of, and in conjunction with, the sale of an undivided interest in the building and grounds and the right to exclusively occupy one unit thereof. This was all in one contract. State Blue Sky laws require all securities offered for sale to be registered, including investment contracts. If the shares in the corporation were not registered would the sale outlined above violate state law?
10. *P* sold shares he owned in a corporation to *X* but the corporation refused to transfer ownership on its books to *X*. The corporation claimed it was holding the shares to answer for a debt *P* owed the corporation. May the corporation succeed in its attempt to collect in this way?

37

Rights of Stockholders

5-91. Right to inspect books. A stockholder of a corporation has the right to inspect the books and papers of the corporation for proper purposes at the proper time and the proper place. The inspection, however, must be made with a justifiable motive and not through idle curiosity or for purposes which in any way interfere with the corporate management. The business hours of the corporation are the reasonable and proper hours in which a stockholder is entitled to inspect the books. The right to inspect the books is sometimes expressly given by the statute, the constitution, the charter, or the by-laws of the corporation. This statutory privilege gives a stockholder an absolute right to inspect the books, but most courts hold that it cannot be exercised where its purpose is improper or unlawful or merely to satisfy one's idle curiosity. Other courts hold that the motive of inspecting the books is immaterial and that the corporation has no right to question the reason for which the books are being inspected.

5-92. Right to attend meetings and to vote. By virtue of the ownership of a share of stock, the stockholder has a right to attend meetings and to cast his vote for the election of directors and for the determination of corporate policies. A further treatment of this subject will be given under Chapter 37, "Management of Corporations."

5-93. Right to share in profits and dividends. A stockholder has a right to share pro rata with the other stockholders in the profits of the corporation when a dividend is declared. Whether or not a dividend is declared is within the discretion of the board of directors.[1] The stockholders of a corporation are not entitled to the payment of a dividend whenever an earned surplus exists. The board of directors, at its discretion, may see fit to continue the profits in the business for the purpose of extension and improvements. A board of directors, however, must act reasonably and in good faith. Where such is not the case and there are profits out of which dividends may be declared, the stockholders may

[1] Guttman v. Illinois Central R. Co., page 824.

compel the board of directors to declare dividends.[2] It must be clear, however, that the board of directors has, illegally, wantonly, and without justification, refused to declare a dividend before the stockholders have a right to interfere. In suits by stockholders against directors for improper conduct there is a conflict as whether a majority of the directors as defendants are necessary parties.[3]

When a dividend is declared, it becomes a debt of the corporation and will be paid to the person whose name appears on the corporate stock books as the owner of the share, unless the corporation has received notice of a transfer. A cash dividend, once its declaration has been made public, may not be rescinded, although there is some authority for rescinding a stock dividend.

5-94. When dividends may be declared. The statutes of the various states governing the declaration of dividends appear to follow two distinct patterns. The first group of states, apparently codifying the common law, provide that dividends can be declared only out of net profits. Under this rule it seems safe to say that dividends may be declared out of current profits, even though a deficit has arisen from the operation of previous years. Capital surplus or surplus arising from the appreciation of fixed assets would not appear to be available under the law of these states.

The other group of states, representing perhaps a majority, determine the legality of a dividend by its effect upon the capital stock.[4] A declaration of dividends is proper so long as it does not impair the capital stock. Any declaration, however, which reduces the net assets of the corporation below the outstanding capital stock is illegal. Under this view it would seem that capital surplus and surplus created by an appraisal of fixed assets might be available for dividends. The law in this regard is not at all definite, but the Uniform Business Corporation Act, which has accepted the majority view, makes capital surplus available for dividends. It limits the use of surplus arising from appreciation of fixed assets to stock dividends. Such a surplus is not available for other uses in those states which have adopted the Act.

In general, under either theory, dividends are permissible only after provision has been made for all expenses, including ample allowance for depreciation. In those industries dealing with wasting or depleting assets, such as mines and oil wells, it is not necessary to care for the depletion before declaring dividends.

The directors in many states are personally liable to creditors for dividends improperly declared in case the corporation later becomes insol-

[2] Knapp et al. v. Bankers Securities Corp. et al., page 827.
[3] Kroese v. General Steel Castings Corp. et al., page 828.
[4] Hamilton Mfg. Co. v. United States, page 831.

vent. The stockholders who receive such dividends may be compelled to return them. In a few of the states, statutes make the stockholders liable only if they received them in bad faith[5] and directors liable only if they acted carelessly or in bad faith.

KINDS OF DIVIDENDS

5-95. Cash dividend. It is customary to pay dividends in cash. The amount paid is usually a certain percentage of the outstanding stock of the particular class involved. The amount received by each stockholder varies with the amount of stock owned by him.

5-96. Scrip dividend. A scrip dividend is a certificate issued to the stockholder when the board of directors has declared dividends out of profits that are represented by property other than money. Such a dividend is issued where the directors anticipate the time when the property may be sold for cash and the cash distributed as a money dividend. The certificate gives the stockholder a right to share according to his stock in the cash derived from the sale of the property set aside as a dividend. These certificates sometimes draw interest and are occasionally convertible into bonds or stocks of the corporation. Such scrip certificates do not pass title to the property to stockholders, but merely give them the right to receive the proceeds from the sale of the property.

5-97. Property dividend. A property dividend is one made in property rather than in cash. A corporation owning stock in another corporation may issue such stock to its stockholders as property dividends. In some jurisdictions, however, a stockholder may insist upon the payment of his dividend in cash rather than in property. This is particularly true of a preferred stockholder. The dividend on preferred stock must usually be paid in cash if the stockholder demands it.

5-98. Stock dividend. A stock dividend is an issue of stock to the stockholders, based upon accumulated assets of the corporation over and above the capital stock. Instead of declaring a cash dividend, the stockholders may authorize an issue of additional stock out of the surplus and thus increase the capital stock of the corporation. This type of dividend payment is often resorted to where the corporation has used the earnings and profits for extensions and improvements of the business. In some states, the declaration of stock dividends is limited or prohibited by statute. It is improper in many states to declare a dividend of preferred stock on common stock or of common stock on preferred stock.

[5] Bartlett et al. v. Smith et al., page 834.

The stock dividend should be in stock of the class which is to receive it. Generally the purpose of a stock dividend is to capitalize the surplus profits of the corporation. If the stock dividend exceeds the surplus, it is an issue of bonus stock, and the holders will become liable to subsequent creditors for a sum equal to the par value. A stock dividend is not taxable as income of the stockholder. It is merely a subdivision of the property value to which the stockholder is already entitled. Where stock entitled to such a dividend is held by a trustee for the benefit of a life tenant, the remainder to be paid over to another after the death of the life tenant, a question arises as to who is entitled to the stock dividend. Under the general rule, if the stock dividend has been earned before the life estate was created, it is held to be principal, irrespective of the time when the dividend was declared. It thus belongs to the principal or corpus and is not an income for the benefit of the life tenant. If, however, the fund out of which the stock dividend is declared was earned after the creation of the life estate, it is held that the dividend is income and belongs to the life tenant. If it was earned partly before and partly after the creation of the life estate, an apportionment of the amount is usually made. Some courts, however, hold that stock dividends are part of the corpus itself, and do not belong to the life tenant, irrespective of when earned. Likewise, it is held that an apportionment between the life tenant and remainderman will not be made when based solely upon a corporate merger, and the stock is held as part of a trust. A distinction is also drawn between a stock dividend and a "stock split."[6]

5-99. Bond dividend. A corporation may issue dividends of its own bonds, if the capital stock is not impaired or the rights of creditors are not interfered with. Such a dividend, however, cannot be issued until after the corporate debts have been satisfied.

5-100. Right to preference upon the increase of capital stock. The capital stock of a corporation is fixed by the charter, and it cannot be increased except by express authority from the state creating the corporation. The stockholders and not the directors must authorize an increase in the capital stock. Such an authorization must be made by amendment of the charter in compliance with the statute providing for changes in the corporation.

When an increase in the capital stock has been properly authorized, the existing stockholders have a prior right against third parties to subscribe to the increased capital stock. This right is called the stockholder's *preëmptive* right and is based upon the stockholder's right to protect and maintain his proportionate control and interest in the corporation.[7] Thus,

[6] In re Trust Estate of Pew, page 835.
[7] Ross Transport Inc. et al. v. Crothers et al., page 836.

if a class of stock has no voting power and is nonparticipating, it is questionable whether such preëmptive right exists. This right may be limited or waived by contract and by provisions in the charter or by-laws of the corporation. It is not applicable to treasury stock.[8] It is applicable to new authorizations of stock and perhaps to new allotments of stock previously authorized, particularly if the new allotment of an original authorization takes place some time after the original issue. Some states approve the issuance of stock to employees without regard to the preëmptive right. Whether or not a stockholder must pay more than par value for the increased stock varies in the different states. Some states hold that he can be compelled to pay more, and other states hold that he cannot.

5-101. Right to sue for injuries to the corporation. A stockholder cannot maintain an action at law for injuries to the corporation, because the corporation is a legal entity and by law has a right to bring a suit in its own name. A stockholder cannot bring a suit at law for and in behalf of the other stockholders for injury to the corporation. Neither can a stockholder bring a suit in law against the directors or other officers of the corporation for negligence, waste, and mismanagement in the conduct of the corporate business, although such conduct is injurious to the stockholder. The right to sue for injuries to the corporation rests strictly with the corporation itself.

A stockholder may, however, bring a suit in equity to enjoin the officers of a corporation from entering into ultra vires contracts or from doing anything that would impair the stockholders' rights in the corporate assets. Likewise, the stockholder has a right to bring suit in equity for, or on behalf of, the corporation itself if the officers are acting outside the scope of their authority, are guilty of negligent conduct, or are engaging, or about to engage, in fraudulent transactions with other stockholders in such a way as to be injurious to the corporation itself.[9]

Before a stockholder may enter into a suit in equity for and on behalf of the corporation, he must show that he has done everything possible to secure action by the managing officers and directors and that they have refused to act. Any judgment received in such an action benefits the corporation and only indirectly the stockholder who initiates the action. He is permitted, however, to recover the expenses involved in the suit.

It has been held that mere dissatisfaction by some of the stockholders as to the management of the corporation will not justify the liquidation of the company.[10]

[8] Runswick et al. v. Floor et al., page 838.
[9] Ramsburg et al. v. American Investment Co. of Illinois et al., page 839.
[10] Hall v. John S. Isaacs & Sons Farms, Inc., page 840.

RIGHTS OF STOCKHOLDERS CASES

GUTTMAN v. ILLINOIS CENTRAL R. R. CO.

1951, 189 F.2d 927

The defendant's net income each year, from 1937 to 1947, inclusive, exceeded the annual dividend on the non-cumulative preferred stock, but no such dividends for those years were ever declared. Similarly, in each of the years 1948, 1949, and 1950, the net income exceeded the annual dividend on the preferred, but the directors declared a dividend on the preferred for each such year. In 1950, the directors also declared a dividend of $1.50 per share on the common stock.

The trial judge found as follows: "The decision of the directors of the defendant not to declare and pay dividends in any of the years 1937 to 1947, inclusive, was made in the exercise of sound business discretion and judgment by the directors, and in the interests of all the creditors, including the bondholders, and of all the preferred and common stockholders of the defendant, and of the public."

Plaintiff contends (1) that the directors abused their discretion in not declaring dividends on the preferred in the years 1942 to 1947, inclusive; (2) that, even if that is not true, the directors had power to declare those dividends subsequently, and abused their discretion when, without doing so, in 1950 they declared a dividend on the common stock.

Frank, Circuit Judge. The trial court's findings of facts establish that the directors acted well within their discretion in withholding declarations of dividends on the non-cumulative preferred stock up to the year 1948. In so holding, we assume, arguendo, that as plaintiff insists, the standard of discretion in weighing the propriety of the non-declaration of dividends on such preferred stock is far stricter than in the case of non-declaration of dividends on common stock. For, on the facts as found and on the evidence, we think the directors, in not declaring dividends on the preferred in the years 1937–1947, adopted a reasonable attitude of reluctant but contingent pessimism about the future, an attitude proper, in the circumstances, for persons charged, on behalf of all interests, with the management of this enterprise.

The issue then, is whether the directors could validly declare a dividend on the common stock in 1950 without directing that there should be paid (in addition to preferred dividends on the preferred for that year) alleged arrears of preferred dividends, the amount of which had been earned in 1942–1947 but remained undeclared and unpaid. To put it differently, we must decide whether (a) the directors had the power to declare such alleged arrears of dividends on the preferred and (b) whether they "abused" their discretion in declaring any dividend on the common without ordering the payment of those alleged arrears.

Our lode-star is *Wabash Railway Co. v. Barclay,* 280 U.S. 197, 50 S.Ct. 106, 74 L.Ed. 368, which dealt with the non-cumulative preferred stock of an Indiana railroad corporation. There were no controlling Indiana decisions or statutes on that subject. The United States Supreme Court was therefore obliged to interpret the contract according to its own notions of what the contract meant. We have a similar problem here, since there are no Illinois decisions or statutory provisions which control or guide us. Absent such decisions and statutes, we must take the Wabash opinion as expressing the correct interpretation of the rights of non-cumulative preferred stockholders of this Illinois company. For the difference between the language of the preferred stock here and that in Wabash seems to us to be of no moment.

In the Wabash case, plaintiffs, holders of non-cumulative preferred stock, sought an injunction preventing the defendant railroad company from paying dividends on the common stock unless it first paid dividends on the non-cumulative preferred to the extent that the company, in previous years, had had net earnings available for that payment and that such dividends remained unpaid. The Court decided against the plaintiffs. It spoke of the fact that, in earlier years, "Net earnings that could have been used for the payment were expended upon improvements and additions to the property and equipment of the road"; it held that the contract with the preferred meant that "if those profits are justifiably applied by the directors to capital improvements and no dividend is declared within the year, the claim for that year is gone and cannot be asserted at a later date." We take that as a ruling that the directors were left with no discretion ever to pay any such dividend. For if they had had that discretion, it would surely have been an "abuse" to pay dividends on the common while disregarding the asserted claim of the non-cumulative preferred to back dividends. Indeed, the plaintiff in the instant case contends that a payment of common dividends, whenever there is such a discretion, constitutes an unlawful "diversion" and such a "diversion" would be an "abuse" of discretion.

Plaintiff, however, seeks to limit the effect of the Wabash ruling to instances where the net earnings, for a given year, which could have been paid to the non-cumulative preferred, have once been expended justifiably for "capital improvements" or "additions to the property or equipment." He would have us treat the words "non-cumulative" as if they read "cumulative if earned except only when the earnings are paid out for capital additions." He argues that the Wabash ruling has no application when net earnings for a given year are legitimately retained for any one of a variety of other corporate purposes, and when in a subsequent year it develops that such retention was not necessary. We think the attempted distinction untenable. It ascribes to the Supreme Court a naïve over-estimation of the importance of tangibles (because they can be touched and seen) as contrasted with intangibles. Suppose the directors of a corporation justifiably invested the retained earnings for the year 1945 in land which, at the time, seemed essential or highly desirable for the company's future welfare. Suppose that, in 1948, it turned out that the land so purchased was not necessary or useful, and that the directors thereupon caused it to be sold. Plaintiff's position compels the implied concession that the proceeds of such a sale would never be available for payment of so-called arrears of unpaid non-cumulative preferred dividends, and that the directors would forever lack all discretion to pay them. We fail to see any intelligible difference between (1) such a situation and (2) one where annual earnings are properly retained for any appropriate corporate purpose, and where in a later year the retention proves wholly unnecessary. There is no sensible ground for singling out legitimate capital outlays, once made, as the sole cause of the irrevocable destruction of the claims of the preferred. We do not believe that the Supreme Court gave the contract with the preferred such an irrational interpretation. It simply happened that in the Wabash case the earnings had been used for capital additions, and that, accordingly, the court happened to mention that particular purpose. Consequently, we think that the Court, in referring to that fact, did not intend it to have any significance.

Here we are interpreting a contract into which uncoerced men entered. Nothing in the wording of that contract would suggest to an ordinary wayfaring person the existence of a contingent or inchoate right to arrears of dividends. The notion that such a right was promised is, rather, the invention of lawyers or other experts, a notion stemming from considerations of fairness, from a policy of protecting investors in those securities. But the preferred stockholders are not—like sailors or idiots or infants—wards of the judiciary. As courts on occasions have quoted or paraphrased ancient poets, it may not be inappropriate to paraphrase a modern poet, and to say that "a contract is a contract is a contract." To be sure, it is an overstatement that the courts never do more than carry out the intentions of the parties: In the interest of fairness and justice, many a judge-made legal rule does impose, on one of the parties to a contract, obligations which neither party actually contemplated and as to which the language of the contract is silent. But there are limits to the extent to which a court may go in so interpolating rights and obligations which were never in the parties' contemplation. In this case we consider those limits clear.

In sum, we hold that, since the directors did not "abuse" their discretion in withholding dividends on the non-cumulative preferred for any past years, (a) no right survived to have those dividends declared, and (b) the directors had no discretion whatever to declare those dividends subsequently.

From the point of view of the preferred stockholders, the bargain they made may well be of a most undesirable kind. Perhaps the making of such bargains should be prevented. But, if so, the way to prevent them is by legislation, or by prophylactic administrative action authorized by legislation, as in the case of the S.E.C. in respect of securities, including preferred stocks, whether cumulative or non-cumulative, issued by public utility holding companies or their subsidiaries. The courts are not empowered to practice such preventive legal medicine, and must not try to revise, extensively, contracts already outstanding and freely made by adults who are not incompetents.

Affirmed.

KNAPP et al. v. BANKERS SECURITIES CORPORATION et al.
1956, 230 F.2d 717

The plaintiffs, shareholders in defendant corporation, brought this action against the corporation and its directors to compel the declaration of dividends. The lower court held in favor of the plaintiffs.

Maris, Circuit Judge. . . . The present action was brought in the district court for the eastern district of Pennsylvania by shareholders, New York residents, against the Bankers Securities Corporation, a Pennsylvania corporation, and its directors, charging that Albert M. Greenfield, one of the directors and the majority shareholder, and the other directors were acting unreasonably in failing to eliminate accumulated arrearages of dividends of approximately $3,000,000 on the common stock in order that the preferred and common stockholders might participate in the earnings of the corporation, that the distribution of earnings was being arbitrarily withheld for the benefit of the majority shareholder.

. . . It is an elementary principle of corporation law that the declaration of dividends out of net profits rests in the discretion of the board of directors. However, there are circumstances under which shareholders may compel the declaration of dividends. If directors have acted fraudulently or arbitrarily in refusing to declare a dividend when the corporation has a surplus which it can divide among the shareholders without detriment to the business, a shareholder may invoke the equitable powers of a court for relief. It is just such equitable power which the plaintiffs seek to invoke in this case. The question then is whether in such an action the shareholder is seeking relief from a personal wrong done to him and thus is enforcing a primary or personal right of his own or is seeking to redress a wrong done to the corporation and thus is enforcing a secondary right derived from the corporation.

. . . The right to dividends is an incident of the ownership of stock. The fact that the distribution of profits cannot ordinarily be enforced until after a dividend has been declared does not detract from the shareholders' fundamental right to share in the net profits of the corporation. This right is the basis of his suit to compel the declaration of dividends. If the directors have wrongfully withheld the declaration of dividends the shareholder is the injured party. He shows an injury to himself which is quite apart from any which the corporation might be thought to suffer. Even if the corporation might under some circumstances have a right of action that fact would not affect the authority of its shareholders to enforce by suit their personal and individual rights to the declaration of a dividend.

It is suggested that the right here asserted must be regarded as one vested in the corporation because the mechanics of relief have to be worked out by a decree against the directors rather than against the corporation. Our answer to this proposition was made by Judge Goodrich in *Kroese v. General Steel Castings Corporation*, 3 Cir., 1950, 179 F.2d 760, 763–764, 15 A.L.R.2d 1117, when he said:

> It is to be observed that when a court steps in and orders the payment of a dividend, the corporate affairs have reached the point where the judgment of the directors is no longer controlling. The set of facts presented is such that the court substitutes its judgment, based on a rule of law, for the ordinary business judgment of those in charge of the business enterprise. . . .
>
> In such a case, even though the individual directors are joined as parties, they are not called upon to exercise any business discretion. The case has passed that point. As said before, the court is declaring rights protected by a rule of law, not calling upon the directors to exercise judgment. . . . The duty of a corporation to pay dividends then and there has been imposed by the judgment of the court, not by the ayes and nays of the members of the board. The situation becomes in substance the same as that in which any corporate creditor sues the enterprise in the corporate name to recover from it what it owes him; he does not need any meeting of the corporation's board to make his judgment good. Nor does a shareholder whose claim to dividends is based on his showing of fiduciary mismanagement need a directors' meeting to make his rights good. The judgment of a court is enough in either case.

. . . *The order of the district court will be affirmed.*

KROESE v. GENERAL STEEL CASTINGS CORP. et al.

1950, 179 F.2d 760

GOODRICH, Circuit Judge. Are a majority of a corporation's board of directors indispensable parties to an action by a shareholder to compel the declaration of dividends? That is the question before us in this case. The district judge, on motion, dismissed the complaint; he thought the directors were indispensable parties and that the court was powerless to grant relief in their absence. D.C.E.D. Pa. 1949, 9 F.R.D. 273.

There has been no trial of facts; not even an answer by the defendants. All we have is the plaintiff's complaint, plus a motion to dismiss. On this state of the record we must assume, ad hoc, the truth of the allegations of the complaint. It is also to be observed, preliminarily, that the case is in federal court on grounds of diversity of citizenship only. We recognize rights and interests, therefore, as a Pennsylvania court would recognize them, including reference to the foreign law in the same fashion as a Pennsylvania court would make it. Pennsylvania law was not briefed by either party in the argument, but we have made our own investigation. There is no Pennsylvania decision either directly in point or anywhere near it, but we will refer hereafter to such Pennsylvania authority as we find helpful in considering the general question.

On the basis of the plaintiff's statement, these facts may be assumed for the purpose of our consideration. The corporate defendant is a Delaware corporation whose principal office is in Ridley Township, Delaware County, Pennsylvania. It operates plants in Pennsylvania and Illinois for the manufacture of steel castings for locomotives and railway cars. The plaintiff is a resident of New York. The corporation has outstanding 456,576 no-par common shares, 92 per cent of which are held by four large users of the products manufactured by it.

Dividend arrearages on the preferred shares amounted to $5,850,000 when the complaint was filed, or $57.75 per share. The corporation's net worth on December 31, 1947, was $28,000,105. It had a capital surplus of $4,133,449 and an earned surplus of $13,410,080. There were "net current assets" of $12,114,409, and a ratio of current assets to current liabilities of approximately 7 to 1. From 1940 through 1947 the corporation earned net profits totaling $18,278,617, and had accumulated out of earnings a reserve of $17,411,310 against plant facilities which had an original cost of $33,000,000.

The plaintiff further alleges that in refusing to declare preferred dividends the directors are "unreasonable and arbitrary" and acting primarily in the interest of the four major common shareholders they represent. He says that "in violation of their duties as fiduciaries to the holders of said preferred stock" the directors are expanding the corporation's production facilities in order to assure the four major common shareholders of an adequate supply of its products. The relief demanded is payment to the preferred shareholders of the arrearages.

The plaintiff has not served the majority of the board of directors of this corporation in the Eastern District of Pennsylvania. When he started his lawsuit he named no directors at all. The District Court on December 13, 1948, held that a majority of the directors were necessary parties and ordered them joined as defendants. But only three out of the twelve were served in Pennsylvania and the plaintiff says that there is no one state or federal district in which a majority of the board may be served.

We are faced squarely with the question, then, whether the action can proceed in the absence of personal jurisdiction over at least sufficient directors to make up the majority of the board. The defendants understandably support the result reached by the District Court in holding that the action could not go on without personal jurisdiction over the directors. If that holding results in the complaining shareholder being unable to bring his suit either in any federal court or, for that matter, in any state court the result may disappoint the plaintiff, but the defendants will bear up under it pretty well.

The defendants' argument is simple and easy to understand. Dividends are payable, they say, only when the directors vote them. To make the directors vote them there must be before the court the human beings, that is the directors, who are to be made subject to the decree. Like any other situation where the chancellor is asked to act against an individual because of alleged violation of a legal duty, there must be personal jurisdiction over the individual before he can be affected by the order. . . . It is to be observed that when a court steps in and orders the payment of a dividend, the corporate affairs have reached the point where the judgment of the directors is no longer controlling. The set of facts presented is such that the court substitutes its judgment, based on a rule of law, for the ordinary business judgment of those in charge of the business enterprise. The court says, in effect, to the directors, "You have abused your office. You have withheld earnings of this enterprise from those who, by the rules of law governing it, are entitled to be paid those earnings. You go ahead and pay them."

In such a case, even though individual directors are joined as parties, they are not called upon to exercise any business discretion. The case has passed that point. As said before, the court is declaring rights protected by a rule of law, not calling upon the directors to exercise judgment. If formal action is to be recorded, following a court decree, on a minute book of a directors' meeting, that formal action is nothing but a ministerial act. The duty of a corporation to pay dividends then and there has been imposed by the judgment of the court, not by the ayes and nays of the members of the board. The situation becomes in substance the same as that in which any corporate creditor sues the enterprise in the corporate name to recover from it what it owes him; he does not need any meeting of the corporation's board to make his judgment good. Nor does a shareholder whose claim to dividends is based on his showing of fiduciary mismanagement need a directors' meeting to make his rights good. The judgment of the court is enough in either case. It follows that directors are not indispensable parties to a lawsuit by a defrauded shareholder to recover dividends in a proper case."

. . . The necessity of formal action by the directors is not a matter of federal law, as we stated earlier. It is a matter of Pennsylvania law, which in this case would make reference to the law of Delaware, the state which chartered the defendant corporation.

It is surprising how little direct authority there is on the precise point of this case. We admit a Sixth Circuit case squarely against the conclusion here reached. *Schuckman v. Rubenstein*, 6 Cir., 1948, 164 F.2d 952, certiorari denied, 333 U.S. 875, 68 S.Ct. 905, 92 L.Ed. 1151. While the court in that case does not say anything about it, we take it that it must have been giving its views on Ohio law. Since we are declaring Pennsylvania law, as best we can, our conflicting decision brings nothing more than an expressed difference on the law of two states. There is an Indiana appellate case which is in accord with the result we are reaching, but it must be admitted that the corporation there was a one-man corporation and not the kind of business enterprise with which we are confronted in this litigation.

The absence of an "all-fours" decision need not dismay us, however. There must always be a first time for every legal rule. That is the way the law grows. If the rule thus declared is bottomed solidly upon principles worked out before hand we can call its formulation not "dangerous innovation" but "healthy growth." Courts are understanding rules governing corporate activity better than they did a few decades ago. It has not been long since the question was fought out whether a corporation could sue or be sued in federal court. Likewise, corporations used to be successful in maintaining the view that they could not be sued outside the state where they were chartered.

What the merits of the plaintiff's case are, we have no idea. If, on the facts, he cannot prove that he is right, the inconvenience to the corporation will be no more than that of any other litigant who successfully defends a lawsuit. If, on the other hand, the plaintiff proves his case he is only getting what the law says he is entitled to have. It would be most unjust if he could not prove that claim for the lack of a proper forum.

The judgment of the District Court will be reversed and the case remanded for further proceedings not inconsistent with this opinion.

HAMILTON MFG. CO. v. UNITED STATES

1954, 214 F.2d 644

LINDLEY, Circuit Judge. Plaintiff, a Wisconsin corporation, brought suit in the District Court to recover undistributed profits tax, assessed and paid for the year 1936 under the Revenue Act of that year, 26 U.S.C. § 14, which imposed a surtax on retained corporate net income earned but not distributed to the stockholders. The statute was amended in 1942 in order to provide retroactive relief for taxpayers who had been taxed, even though prohibited by state law from paying dividends. 26 U.S.C. § 501 (a). Plaintiff averred that it had a deficit in its earnings account, i.e., its earned surplus, at the beginning of 1936 of $106,134.89; that its net profits for the year were $121,515.96; that the remainder of $15,381.07, after deducting from the earnings the existing deficit, was the only amount legally subject to tax as undistributed profits, instead of the entire amount of net earnings for the year of $121,515.96, as the commissioner had held, and on which it had paid the protested tax. It sought to recover the alleged overpayment of $23,672.61.

. . . As the Supreme Court announced, in *United States v. Ogilvie Hardware Co.*, 330 U.S. 709, 67 S.Ct. 997, 91 L.Ed. 1192, and as observed by the District Court, the statute was intended to provide relief to corporations which had paid taxes under duress of conflicting state and federal compulsions. In *Seiberling Rubber Co. v. U.S.*, D.C., 115 F. Supp. 798, 801, affirmed 6 Cir., 207 F.2d 585, the court added the additional thought that ". . . The 1942 amendment was not an exemption measure,—it was a congressional acknowledgment of the punitive character of the 1936 provision, and afforded an opportunity of securing relief from the unjust consequences of the law. . . ." Consequently the crucial question confronting us is whether the trial court correctly ruled that plaintiff, under the Wisconsin law, was not "prohibited by a provision of a law" from paying dividends in 1936 under the circumstances alleged to be then existing.

The pertinent Wisconsin statute, following a provision in § 182.08 for stockholders' liability in case of derogation of creditors' rights, in § 182.19, provides that: "(1) No dividend shall be paid by any corporation until at least fifty per cent of the authorized capital stock has been fully paid in, and then only out of new profits properly applicable thereto, and which shall not in any way impair or diminish the capital. . . . (2) But any corporation which has invested net earnings or income in permanent additions to its property, or whose property shall have increased in value, may declare a dividend either in money or in stock to the extent of the net earnings or income so invested or of the said increase in the value of its property. . . ." The parties disagree sharply as to the correct meaning of the words "net profits," plaintiff insisting that a deficit in earned surplus, resulting from deficiencies or losses in corporate operations over a protracted period, is the opposite of net profits, and that until current earnings increase sufficiently to extinguish the losses, i.e., the deficits, they may not properly be designated "net profits," while defendant asserts that the correct interpretation of the term is that dividends can be declared and paid from current earnings, despite the over-all deficit in earnings or profits.

We are of the opinion that, under the circumstances which plaintiff avers existed here, the Wisconsin statute did not authorize dividends out of plaintiff's current earnings in view of the fact that at that time there had been no earnings but only losses resulting in a deficit, which inevitably impaired the corporate capital. Wisconsin treats capital investment as a trust fund, primarily to protect creditors. *Goetz v. Williams*, 206 Wis. 561, 240 N.W. 181. Obviously operating losses necessarily reduce or impair this trust fund. The logical result, it seems to us, is that subsequent current earnings may not be turned over to the stockholders by way of dividends before restoring the trust fund. Such conclusion, we think, is the only one consistent with the general intent of the Wisconsin theory of a capital trust fund.

Furthermore the import of the language of the specific statute in question is to the same effect. It forbids dividends from anything other than "net profits." This can mean only a surplus over expenses incurred and paid in producing earnings. Here, at the beginning of the year, instead of there having been such a surplus, there was a substantial deficit, an accumulated loss, which impaired and reduced the capital investment.

We find no merit in the contention that the legislature of Wisconsin included in the words "net profits" only annual net earnings. We think it can be said reasonably only that by net profits is meant the net profits upon the business from its organization, and that the net profits are such as appear from the entire business of the company from its inception, and are not to be confined to one period and made synonymous with annual profits. (Cases cited) We approve the language of *Lich v. United States Rubber Co.*, D.C., 39 F. Supp. 675, 681, as follows: "What are 'net profits' within the meaning of the statute? The statute is devoid of any definitive answer. The term, however, is one of common usage and the ordinary acceptation must be adopted. The term connotes the clear pecuniary gain remaining after deducting from the gross earnings of the business the expenses incurred in its conduct, the losses sustained in its prosecution and the capital invested. It is a prerequisite to the existence of net profits that the assets of a corporation exceed the liabilities, including the liability on the capital stock. Where the capital is impaired, annual net earnings, if insufficient to offset the impairment, do not constitute net profits. . . . The term net profits is not synonymous with the term annual net earnings. Annual net earnings may be productive of net profits, or, as in the instant case, reductive of the deficit." As the Supreme Court said in *Willcuts v. Milton Dairy Co.*, 275 U.S. 215, 217, 48 S.Ct. 71, 72 L.Ed. 247: " 'There can of course be no earned surplus or undivided profits until any deficit or impairment of paid-in capital due to depletion, depreciation, expense, losses or any other cause has been made good.'"

In view of Wisconsin's established theory of a trust fund, and its express limitation of dividends to "net profits," plaintiff was in no position to declare dividends. In the preceding years there were no net profits but only accumulated losses, to the reduction of which current earnings must necessarily be applied until the deficit is wiped out and net profits have actually come into existence. There was here no fund within the meaning of the words "net profits"; to have paid dividends would have been in violation of the statue.

The judgment is reversed and the cause remanded to the District Court for further proceedings not inconsistent with this opinion.

BARTLETT et al. v. SMITH et al.

1932, 162 Md. 478, 160 Atl. 440

The plaintiffs are the receivers of the First National Company, a Delaware corporation, and the defendants are the executors of the estate of a deceased stockholder of the corporation. The plaintiffs are seeking to recover the amount of a dividend paid to the decedent which was allegedly not paid out of earnings but out of the capital of the corporation to the impairment thereof. A demurrer to the complaint was sustained and plaintiffs appealed.

ADKINS, J. . . . The important questions are: Can an innocent stockholder be required to refund dividends seemingly declared in regular course of business out of profits, but actually declared and paid out of capital? When the corporation was not insolvent at the time the dividends were paid, but subsequently became insolvent? When the corporation was insolvent at the time the dividends were paid?

The first question has been answered in the negative by the Supreme Court of the United States and by the federal courts generally. These courts have repudiated the trust fund doctrine as applied to capital stock.

There is substantial authority on the other side in jurisdictions other than federal.

. . . In this situation we are disposed to follow the federal decisions as being more in accord with modern conditions and with the realities of life. In these days stocks of corporations are so widely held that it would be practically impossible for stockholders generally to know whether or not each semi-annual dividend paid in regular course was earned. Whatever their position may be theoretically, practically they are in no better position than creditors to know the condition of the company, and it would be an unfair and unreasonable burden to require them to pay back, years after they have been spent, dividends received in good faith from a solvent corporation in regular course of business.

. . . As to the second question, there is but little conflict in the authorities. It is generally held that dividends paid when the corporation was insolvent may be recovered for the benefit of creditors.

. . . A sufficient and satisfactory ground is that money so paid after insolvency was taken from a fund held in trust for creditors and did not belong to the corporation; and it could give no title in the money it paid to one who did not receive it bona fide, and for value.

Judgment reversed and case remanded to determine whether the corporation was or was not insolvent at the time the dividend was paid.

In re TRUST ESTATE OF PEW

1960, (Pa.) 158 A.2d 552

The deceased, Mary C. Pew, created an inter vivos trust to which she transferred 40,000 shares of common stock of the Sun Oil Company. The settlor provided that the net income would be paid to a grandson during his lifetime and that the corpus, upon the grandson's death, would be distributed to the grandson's child or children. The Sun Oil Company's directors in 1954 adopted the following resolution:

> . . . the Board of Directors . . . declare that it is advisable that each four (4) shares of Common Stock, without nominal or par value, now issued, and outstanding, shall be equal to and are hereby changed into five (5) shares of Common Stock, without nominal or par value, and the holders of said Common Stock, without nominal or par value, now outstanding, shall be entitled to receive one (1) additional share of said Common Stock, without nominal or par value for each four (4) shares of Common Stock held. . . . After stockholder approval of this resolution, the directors adopted another resolution: . . . the additional shares of Common Stock, without nominal or par value, to which holders of said Common Stock are entitled as a result of the split-up of said Common Stock . . . shall be issued on December 30, 1954 to common stockholders of record. . . . November 29, 1954 . . .

As a result of this action the trust received additional shares of common stock. No transfer was made on the corporate books from earned surplus to the capital stock account. When the trustees filed their customary report the additional shares were not apportioned to income and the grandson filed objections.

BENJAMIN R. JONES, Justice. This appeal presents a problem in the field of apportionment: does a common stock distribution in 1954 by the Sun Oil Company to its stockholders, including this trust, unaccompanied by a contemporaneous capitalization of earnings, constitute an apportionable event under the Pennsylvania Rule of Apportionment?

. . . If this 1954 stock distribution was a "stock split" it did not constitute an apportionable event. Appellant's attempt at an equation of a "stock split" and a "stock dividend" in that both result in a "proliferation" of book value was well answered by the court below:

> It must be conceded that the income beneficiary's example outlined above does illustrate that the stock split effects, in a sense, a division of earnings from the stockholder's point of view. However, this result does not appear to be the type of division and distribution of earnings contemplated by the apportionment cases. After the occurrence of the stock split the earnings of a corporation remain intact in an accumulated earnings account, undisturbed, unaltered, and available for future stock dividends or cash dividends. It is true that more shares of stock represent these identical earnings after a stock split has occurred; but it is only the stock certificates representing the earnings that undergo a split or division, and not the earnings themselves.

A substantial and conclusive difference exists between a stock split and a stock dividend: in the former, a division of the shares of stock, not of the earnings or profits of the corporation, takes place without any change in or impingement upon the then existing status on the corporate books of the earned surplus and capital accounts; in the latter, an addition of shares of stock and a division of, at least, some of the earnings or profits of the corporation take place, such division being reflected on the corporate books by an irreversible allocation of corporate funds from the earned surplus to the capital account. Although this Court has not directly passed upon the apportionability of a stock split, the rationale which justifies an apportionment between a life tenant and a remainderman is conspicuously absent in a stock split situation, i.e. a division of corporate earnings and profits . . . "The fundamental principle involved in these questions is whether there has been a distribution or division of the earnings, profits, or accumulation of the corporation. Until there has been such division, the life tenant is not entitled to any increase in the value of the principal of the trust fund, or the capital assets of the corporation, shares of which constitute the trust fund." . . . A stock split represents neither a division of corporate earnings or profits nor a recognized apportionable event and, therefore, is not apportionable. . . .

Decree affirmed at appellant's costs.

ROSS TRANSPORT INC. et al. v. CROTHERS et al.

1946, 185 Md. 573, 45 A.2d 267

The plaintiff Crothers and other stockholders brought this action against the corporation, its directors and certain stockholders to set aside the issuance of certain shares of stock. The stock was sold to a director and to the family of the president and director. The lower court decreed that the stockholders who had received the additional stock must repay to the corporation the dividends received by them and the stock declared to be illegally issued and ordered cancelled. The defendants appealed.

MARBURY, Chief Judge. . . . The sale of this additional stock to a director and to the family of the president and director . . . without opportunity to buy given to other stockholders, is sought to be justified on the ground that it was originally planned, and that the money was needed to purchase additional buses at a cost of about $16,000. The facts, however, show no such need. The company was an immediate financial success.

. . . The appellees give two reasons for their contention that the stock sales of August 26th were void: First, because they deprive them and the other original stockholders of their pre-emptive rights to purchase a proportionate amount of the remaining shares, and, second, because, in selling to themselves and their nominees, Williams and Ross have abused their trust as officers and directors. They claim to be injured in two ways. Their voting powers have been proportionately lessened, and the control of the company has passed to Williams and Ross. And the amount paid in dividends has to be divided among 365 more shares of stock to the consequent financial loss of the holders of the original shares.

. . . The doctrine known as the pre-emptive right of shareholders is a judicial interpretation of general principles of corporation law. Existing stockholders are the owners of the business, and are entitled to have that ownership continued in the same proportion. Therefore, when additional stock is issued, those already having shares, are held to have the first right to buy the new stock in proportion to their holdings. This doctrine was first promulgated in 1807 in the case of *Gray v. Portland Bank*, 3 Mass. 364, 3 Am. Dec. 156. At that time, corporations were small and closely held, much like the one before us in this case. But in the succeeding years, corporations grew and expanded. New capital was frequently required. New properties had to be acquired for which it was desirable to issue stock. Companies merged, and new stock in the consolidation was issued. Stock was issued for services. Different kinds of stock were authorized—preferred without voting power but with prior dividend rights—preferred with the right to convert into common—several classes of both common and preferred with different rights. Some stock had voting rights. Other stock did not. Bonds were issued, convertible into stock. All of these changes in the corporate structure made it impossible always to follow the simple doctrines earlier decided. Exceptions grew, and were noted in the decisions.

Only one of these exceptions is involved in the present case. It has been held that pre-emptive rights do not exist where the stock about to be issued is part of the original issue. This exception is based upon the fact that the original subscribers took their stock on the implied understanding that the incorporators could complete the sale of the remaining stock to obtain the capital thought necessary to start the business. But this gives rise to an exception to the exception, where conditions have changed since the original issue. The stock sold the Williams family and Ross was part of the original issue and it is claimed by the appellants that it comes within the exception, and the appellees and the other stockholders have no pre-emptive rights.

The appellees, on the other hand, contend, and the chancellors found that changed conditions made it unnecessary to use the remaining unsold stock to obtain capital, and pre-emptive rights exist in it just as they would exist in newly authorized stock.

It is unnecessary for us to decide which of these two conflicting points of view applies to this cause, because another controlling consideration enters. The doctrine of pre-emptive right is not affected by the identity of the purchasers of the issued stock. What it is concerned with is who did not get it. But when officers and directors sell to themselves, and thereby gain an advantage, both in value and in voting power, another situation arises, which it does not require the assertion of a pre-emptive right to deal with.

It has long been the law in this State that trustees cannot purchase at their own sale, and trustees, in this sense, include directors of corporations.

. . . *The decree will be affirmed.*

RUNSWICK et al. v. FLOOR et al.

1949, 116 Utah 91, 208 P.2d 948

The plaintiff and other stockholders of the New Quincy Mining Company, a corporation, brought this action against Floor and other defendants to set aside the sale of treasury stock to the defendant Floor. The lower court ruled in favor of the defendants and plaintiffs appealed.

LATIMER, J. . . . The principal issue to be decided by this court is as to the validity or invalidity of the sale of the treasury shares to defendant Floor. In proceeding to determine this question, it should initially be pointed out that the shares of stock involved had been once fully paid for and had been returned to the treasury of the company. Officers of a corporation may reissue this type of stock for value and in good faith without first offering it pro rata to existing shareholders. (Cases cited) We quote from *Borg v. International Silver Co.*, D.C.S.D.N.Y., 11 F.2d 143, 11 F.2d 147: "The distinction may appear tenuous, but rests upon the effect which a new issue has upon the voting control of the company. When a person buys into a company with an authorized capital, he accepts that proportion of the voting rights which his purchase bears to the whole. This applies certainly so far as the other shares are issued at the same time, and perhaps, also, though they are issued much later. But treasury shares have by hypothesis once been issued, and have diluted, as it were, the shareholder's voting power *ab initio*. He cannot properly complain that he is given no right to buy them when they are resold, because that merely restores the status he originally accepted. All he can demand is that they shall bring to the corporate treasury their existing value. If they do, his proportion in any surplus is not affected. However, when the capital stock is increased beyond the original amount authorized, the voting power is diluted along with it; the shareholders who had not originally bought into so large an issue may insist that the old proportions be observed. To deprive them of their right of pre-emption is to change their contract. At any rate it is only on this theory that any right of pre-emption exists, and since the shares at bar were never bought to be retired, and the capital was not increased, the right does not exist."

Hence, the sale of the 150,000 shares to Floor was not objectionable by reason of the fact that the shares were not first offered to existing shareholders on a pro rata basis.

Affirmed.

RAMSBURG et al. v. AMERICAN INVESTMENT COMPANY OF ILLINOIS et al.

1956, 231 F.2d 333

The plaintiffs as stockholders of defendant Domestic Finance Corporation brought this suit for an injunction to restrain a proposed merger of that Company with defendant American Investment Company of Illinois. Both are incorporated under the laws of Delaware. The complaint averred that American had, through divers means, obtained some 80 per cent of the common stock of Domestic thereby gaining control; that American had utilized its stock to effectuate election of a board of directors of Domestic composed of officers of American, who were serving as Domestic's officers, and that American, through its control, had so operated Domestic as to reduce its effective position as a competitor of American in various cities and states where both corporations transact business. On August 17, 1955, Domestic mailed to its stockholders a notice of a special meeting to be held September 15, 1955, to consider and vote on a proposed merger of the two corporations. The complaint herein was filed September 7, 1955, charging that the merger would constitute a violation of § 7 of the Clayton Act, in that its effect would be to lessen substantially competition in commerce. It was further averred that Domestic would be seriously injured by the proposed action.

The complaint prayed a preliminary injunction restraining American from voting its Domestic stock in favor of the merger at the September 15 meeting or at any other time, and that, after hearing on the merits, the temporary injunction be made final, and a decree entered directing American to divest itself of the Domestic stock it owns and granting such other and further relief as to the court might seem just. The lower court denied the injunction and plaintiffs appealed. The defendants moved to dismiss the appeal on the ground that the cause was moot since the merger had been accomplished.

LINDLEY, Circuit Judge. . . . The question before us is reduced to an inquiry as to whether a stockholders' derivative suit will lie under § 7 of the Clayton Act. We frame our answer to that question on the teachings contained in a recent opinion by the Court of Appeals for the Second Circuit in *Fanchon & Marco, Inc. v. Paramount Pictures, Inc.*, 202 F.2d 731, 36 A.L.R.2d 1336, which involved an appeal from a judgment dismissing a stockholders' derivative, antitrust suit for treble damages and injunctive relief. The court held that the action would lie and reversed the judgment of dismissal, saying, 202 F.2d at p. 734: "Now there does not seem real doubt but that an antitrust derivative suit will lie; indeed, that seems to follow from the nature of such suits. '. . . Equity . . . traditionally entertains the derivative or secondary action by which a single stockholder may sue in the corporation's right when he shows that the corporation on proper demand has refused to pursue a remedy, or shows facts that demonstrate the futility of such a request. . . . The cause of action which such a plaintiff brings before the court is not his own but the corporation's. . . .' Mr. Justice Jackson in *Koster v. (American) Lumbermen's Mutual Casualty Co.*, 330 U.S. 518, 522, 523, 67 S.Ct. 828, 91 L.Ed. 1067." After discussing the applicable authorities, the court continued, 202 F.2d at p. 735: "There is an occasional flat statement . . . that no derivative antitrust suit will lie, as in *Kalmanash v. Smith*, 291 N.Y. 142, 157, 51 N.E.2d 681, 688; but, as indicated, the precedents actually look the other way and we can see no reason for such a view." We agree with this reasoning and hold that plaintiffs were competent parties when this suit was brought and have remained so throughout pendency of the litigation.

Motion to dismiss appeal denied.

HALL v. JOHN S. ISAACS & SONS FARMS, INC.

1960, (Del.) 163 A.2d 288

WOLCOTT, Justice. The plaintiffs, stockholders in family corporations, brought suit for the appointment of liquidating receivers based upon alleged mismanagement of these corporations. The defendants are four corporations and two individuals who together owned 50% of the stock of the four corporations. The litigation followed an intra-family squabble and dissension among the stockholders. The lower court denied the plaintiffs the relief which they sought and the plaintiffs appealed.

. . . These corporations for which the plaintiffs ask the appointment of liquidating receivers are all solvent. Under some circumstances courts of equity will appoint liquidating receivers for solvent corporations, but the power to do so is always exercised with great restraint and only upon a showing of gross mismanagement, positive misconduct by the corporate officers, breach of trust, or extreme circumstances showing imminent danger of great loss to the corporation which, otherwise, cannot be prevented. (Cases cited.) . . . Mere dissension among corporate stockholders seldom, if ever, justifies the appointment of a receiver for a solvent corporation. The minority's remedy is withdrawal from the corporate enterprise by the sale of its stock. *Drob v. National Memorial Park, Inc.*, 28 Del. Ch. 254, 41 A.2d 589.

Review Questions and Problems

1. The *X* Company was engaged in the business of manufacturing patent medicines. *A*, who was a stockholder in the company, was engaged in a competitive business. *A* desired to inspect the books of the *X* Company for the purpose of obtaining a list of the customers. Had he a right to do so?
2. Stock in the Texas Company was held in trust whereby the income was to be paid to *A* for life and upon his death the stock would pass to *B*. The Company declared a stock dividend. Should this dividend be paid to *A* or held for the benefit of *B*?
3. The *X* Company had a surplus of $5,000,000 and had made plans for extensions and improvements which would require the expenditure of $3,000,000. Assuming that the directors could not show a need for further improvements, might *A*, a minority stockholder, by proper action, have forced the directors to declare a dividend?
4. The directors of the *X* Company declared a dividend when there were insufficient profits and surplus to pay it, although, at the time, the remaining assets were more than sufficient to pay liabilities if stock was not regarded as a liability. The corporation soon became insolvent. Could the creditors have recovered the amount of the dividend from the directors?
5. The directors of *X* Corporation declared a dividend but at a later meeting rescinded this action. Are the stockholders entitled to the dividend?
6. The directors of a corporation, by reason of misconduct and negligence, have wasted the assets of the corporation. May a stockholder of the corporation recover from them in the name of the corporation for the losses caused by the director's negligence? What should he do first?
7. *X* Corporation declared and paid a dividend at a time when a divi-

dend could not legally be declared. Can the stockholders be required to return these dividends?

8. *P* was a stockholder in *X* Corp. He desired to obtain a list of stockholders so that he could contact them before the annual stockholders meeting to persuade them to vote for a corporate merger to which the board of directors of *X* Corp. was opposed. If the clerk required by the by-laws to keep the books refuses *P* the opportunity to inspect them, what may *P* do?

9. *A* owned all the preferred stock of the Cotton Belt Railroad. *B* and *C* owned all the common. The Cotton Belt declared and paid a $5.00 dividend on preferred and then declared a dividend of $1.00 per share on all stock. A dispute arose as to whether the preferred stock was entitled to participate in the $1.00 per share dividend. Can the Cotton Belt cancel the $1.00 dividend inasmuch as it has not yet been paid? Is there a legal method by which the Railroad corporation may protect itself from making the wrong choice as to which class of shareholders are entitled to a dividend?

10. *A* became a stockholder in a non-profit corporation previously formed for the maintenance and construction of streets in a residential development as its charter provided. The by-laws stated that there would be assessments levied against the stockholders in accordance with the cost of streets built. Does *A* have any standing to prevent construction of streets and levies therefor when the streets concerned will be of no use to him?

38

Management of Corporations

5-102. In general. Regulation and control of a corporation rest in the stockholders. The majority of the stockholders, by vote, have a right to bind the corporation and all its members in any transaction or proceeding within the scope of the corporate powers as authorized by the corporate charter.

The charter may, however, vest control and management of the corporation exclusively within the board of directors. The power of the stockholders is then limited to the extent of securing a new board of directors, if they are not satisfied with the acts of the present board.

The extent of the powers of the corporation is defined by the statute creating it and by its charter. The by-laws regulate the conduct and define the duties of the officers and the members between themselves and the corporation, with respect to carrying out the powers given to the corporation by the state.

5-103. By-laws. A by-law is a rule of conduct which regulates and defines the duties of the members and the officers of a corporation among themselves. Every corporation has implied power to enact by-laws for the purpose of carrying out the powers conferred upon it by the state. These by-laws must not violate any rules of law; they must be general in their nature and must not be directed toward the conduct of any particular individual. The by-laws are binding upon all the stockholders. They must be consistent with the purpose and objects for which the corporation is created and are not binding upon third persons unless third persons have knowledge of such rules.

The stockholders have power to amend, to add to, and to repeal the by-laws to the same extent as they have power to create by-laws in the first instance. They cannot, however, repeal, amend, or add to the by-laws, where such change will affect the vested rights of a stockholder.

The stockholders may delegate to the board of directors the right to adopt new by-laws, or to repeal or to add to them. The board of directors, however, cannot change the by-laws with respect to limitation of power or duty given to them by the stockholders.

The by-laws usually provide for the number of officers and directors, the method of electing them, and the enumeration of their duties. They also specify the time and place of the meetings of the directors and the stockholders. If the corporation is a nonstock corporation, the by-laws specify the requirements and the method for membership.

5-104. Stockholders' meetings. Action by the stockholders normally binds the corporation only when taken in a regular, or properly called, special meeting, after such notice as is required by the by-laws or statute has been given. However, it is generally conceded that action approved informally by all stockholders will bind the corporation. Unless otherwise provided by statute, notice of regular meetings need not be given if the by-laws provide for a definite place and time of meeting. Most by-laws and many state statutes provide that notice must be given of regular as well as special meetings.

Notice of a called meeting must include a statement concerning the matters to be acted upon at the meeting, and any action taken on other matters will be ineffective. If unusual action, such as a sale of corporate assets, is to be taken at a regular meeting, notice of the meeting must call attention to that fact.

Failure to give proper notice of a meeting generally invalidates the action taken at the meeting. A stockholder who, having failed to receive notice, attends and participates in a meeting is said to waive the notice by his presence.

A quorum of stockholders must be present in order to transact business, such quorum being a majority of the voting shares outstanding, unless some statute or the by-laws provide for a smaller percentage. Affirmative action is approved by majority vote of the shares present at a meeting, providing a quorum exists. There are certain unusual matters, such as merger or sale of all corporate assets, which, at common law, required unanimous vote. Today, statutes usually provide that such action can be taken by vote of two thirds or three fourths of the stockholders. Many of these statutes also provide that the dissenting shareholders have the right to surrender their shares and receive their fair value in case they disapprove of the action taken.

5-105. Voting. Every member of a corporation is entitled to vote. In nonstock companies the members are entitled to one vote. In stock companies the members are entitled to as many votes as they own shares of stock. The stockholder whose name appears upon the corporate record is usually designated by the by-laws as the person entitled to vote. Preferred stockholders, by their contract with the corporation, may not be entitled to a vote. All jurisdictions hold, however, that every stockholder, whether preferred or not, is entitled to vote unless agreed otherwise. A stockholder cannot be deprived of a right to vote by a by-law. However, unless expressly prohibited by statute, the corporation may issue stock in the future, either common or preferred, and specify that the holder shall not vote.

The statutes of some states provide that a stockholder, in the election of directors by cumulative voting, may cast as many votes for one candidate for a given office as there are offices to be filled, multiplied by the number of his shares of stock; or he may distribute this same number of votes among the candidates as he sees fit.

A stockholder is entitled to vote only by virtue of his ownership in the stock, and, under the common law, this right can only be exercised in person. However, by statute, or the charter, or the by-laws, a stockholder may specifically authorize another to vote his stock. This authorization is made by power of attorney and must specifically state that the agent of the stockholder has power to vote his principal's stock. This method of voting is called voting by proxy. It is a personal relationship, and may be revoked at any time by the stockholder before the authority is exercised. The laws relative to principal and agent control this relationship.

A stockholder, unlike a director, is permitted to vote on a matter in which he has a personal interest. In certain respects he represents the corporation welfare in his voting, whereas in other respects he votes in such a manner as he thinks will best serve his interest. The majority of stockholders may not take action, however, that is clearly detrimental to the corporation and minority interests. This becomes particularly significant when the majority of the shareholders also own most of the stock of an allied or related enterprise and seek to operate the first corporation in such a manner as to profit the second at the expense of the first. If it is clear that the affairs of the first corporation are being mishandled in order to benefit the second, such action may be enjoined by the minority interests.

5-106. Voting pools and trust agreements. Various devices have been used whereby minority interests or a group of stockholders may effectively control a corporation. The creation of a holding company, the issuance of non-voting shares or the issuance of shares with voting rights, but with a small or nominal par value, voting pools and voting trusts, have all been utilized for this purpose, and in general all of them are effective means for obtaining control. A voting pool arises whenever a number of stockholders agree to vote their stock as a unit in accordance with a certain plan. Such an agreement is enforceable unless the purpose to be accomplished is improper.

A voting trust develops from the transfer of title of their shares by various stockholders to a trustee for the purpose of voting the stock. The stock is then registered in his name, he votes at the meetings of shareholders, and receives dividends as they are declared. He issues to each stockholder, whose stock he holds, a certificate of beneficial interest which entitles the owner thereof to have his shares returned at the termination of the trust and to receive dividends within a given time after they are paid. Some courts have held voting trust unenforceable because they tend to separate ownership from control and management. Many of the courts, including most of those rendering recent decisions, enforce the trust agreement unless its objectives are improper or the period of its continuance unreasonably long.[1] The Uniform Business Corporations Act sets a limit of ten years upon voting trusts.

DIRECTORS

5-107. Qualifications and powers. The directors of a corporation are, with the possible exception of the first board, elected by the stockholders. In a few states, the corporate charter names the first board of directors. In the absence of a provision in the charter, by-laws, or statute, it is not essential that directors hold stock in the corporation. Since they are to supervise the business activities, select key employees, and plan for the future development of the enterprise, they are presumably elected because of their business ability.

The directors have power to take such action as is necessary in the ordinary business activities of enterprises of the type being managed. They may not exceed the power granted to the corporation by its charter, amend the charter, approve a merger, or bring about a consolidation with another corporation. Charter amendments, consolidations, and mergers require the approval of a rather large percentage of the stockholders.

Directors are presumed to be free to exercise their independent judgment upon all matters presented to them. Consequently, their management of the business cannot be interfered with by action on the part of the stockholders.[2] Similarly, any contract made by a director with a stockholder concerning a particular matter before the board is contrary to public policy and unenforceable. Free and independent action by directors is required for the best interests of the corporation itself as distinct from the interests of a few stockholders.

5-108. Meetings. The statute, charter, and by-laws usually provide for the number of directors. In most cases, not less than three directors are required. Since the board of directors must act as a unit, it is neces-

[1] Alderman et al. v. Alderman et al., page 848.
[2] Petition of Avard, page 781.

sary that it assemble at board meetings.[3] The by-laws usually provide for the method of calling directors' meetings and for the time and the place of meeting. A record is usually kept of the activities of the board of directors, and the evidence of the exercise of its powers is usually stated in resolutions kept in the corporate record book. A majority of the members of the board of directors is necessary to constitute a quorum. Special meetings are proper only when all directors are notified or are present at the meeting. Directors may not vote by proxy, having been selected as agents because of their personal qualifications.

5-109. Liabilities of directors. Directors are said to stand in relation to the corporation as trustees, for both the corporation and the stockholders.[4] However, they are not trustees in the strict sense. They are agents with more than the usual authority of an agent. Therefore, a director occupies a position of trust and confidence with respect to the corporation, and cannot, by reason of his position, directly or indirectly derive any personal benefits that are not enjoyed by the corporation or the stockholders.[5] All secret profits obtained by a director in the pursuit of the corporate business must be accounted for to the corporation.

A director may contract with the corporation that he represents, but he is subject to the same limitations that an agent is in dealing with his principal. He is required to disclose his interest in all contracts and, because of his fiduciary relation, to volunteer all pertinent information regarding the subject matter involved. Furthermore, he is forbidden to vote as a director on any matter in which he has a personal interest. Even though his vote is not necessary to carry the proposition considered, most courts consider the action taken to be voidable. Some courts go so far as to hold that, if he is present at the meeting, favorable action will not be binding. Clearly, if his presence is required to make a quorum, no transaction in which he is interested should be acted upon. These rather severe rules are enforced so that directors will not be tempted to use their position to profit at the expense of the corporation.

Directors are personally liable when they willfully misuse their power and misapply the funds of the corporation. They are also personally liable where they issue stock as fully paid when it is not paid in full. directors are required to perform the duties of their office in a reasonable manner and in good faith. The standard of care required of directors cannot be exactly defined. It is generally held that directors are bound to exercise that degree of care which men of prudence exercise in the management of their own affairs. The standard of care varies with the size and type of the corporation. In large corporations many duties must be

[3] Tuttle v. Junior Bldg. Corp., page 852.
[4] Mardel Securities, Inc. v. Alexandria Gazette Corp., page 853.
[5] Vulcanized Rubber & Plastics Company v. Scheckter, page 854.

delegated, thus intimate knowledge of details by the directors is not possible. In corporations invested with a public interest such as insurance companies, banking, building and loan, and public utilities, rigid supervision and specific obligations are imposed upon directors. If a director fails to exercise the requisite degree of care and skill, the corporation will have a right of action against him for resulting losses. When directors by their negligent misconduct involve the corporation in an ultra vires transaction which causes a loss, the directors may be liable to the corporation. They are not liable, however, for accidents and mistakes of judgment or for losses, if they have acted in good faith and have exercised ordinary care, skill, and diligence.

The directors, although holding a fiduciary relation to the corporation, have no such relationship with the individual stockholders. In a sale of stock by a stockholder to a director, they deal at arm's length. The director who, because of his relation to the corporation, is in a position to know many factors which affect the value of the stock, is not obligated to volunteer such information to the stockholder. There is a strong minority view and a tendency in recent decisions to support a fiduciary relationship.

5-110. Compensation. In the absence of a stipulation in the charter or by-laws, directors receive no compensation for their services as such. If they do work not recognized as falling within the duties of a director, they may recover for the reasonable value of their services. Directors who are appointed as officers of the corporation should have their salaries fixed at a meeting of the shareholders or in the by-laws. Since directors are not supposed to vote on any matter in which they have a personal interest, it is difficult for director-officers of small corporations to fix their rate of compensation. Any action to determine salaries should be ratified by the stockholders in order to insure the validity of the employment contracts.

MANAGEMENT OF CORPORATION CASES

ALDERMAN et al. v. ALDERMAN et al.

1935, 178 S.C. 9, 181 S.E. 897

The plaintiffs had assigned their stock in the D. W. Alderman & Sons Company to the defendants R. J. and Paul R. Alderman in a voting trust. The plaintiffs sought to have the trust declared null and void. The lower court ruled in favor of the defendants and the plaintiffs appealed.

Baker, J. . . . It is a universally known fact to lumbermen that the operation of a sawmill and lumber plant, small or large, is a business in which one can lose heavily unless well managed. Indeed, this is so well recognized that it has become an adage among lumbermen, "Never to wish an enemy in torment but wish such enemy owned a sawmill."

Realizing, no doubt, that the success of the corporations, especially D. W. Alderman & Sons Company, depended upon the management, D. W. Alderman, Sr., requested that upon his death R. J. and Paul R. Alderman should be continued in the active management and control of the corporations in order that his well-known policies would be continued, and therefore, in deference to the wishes of the said D. W. Alderman, Sr., and having little if any experience with the operation and management of the business of said corporations, Mrs. Rice, Mrs. Shaw, Miss Martha Alderman, and D. W. Alderman, Jr., severally executed trust deeds or contracts conveying their stock in trust in the said corporations to the said R. J. and Paul R. Alderman.

. . . The position of appellants is that the instruments placing R. J. and Paul R. Alderman in the control of the corporations constituted what is known to the law as "voting trusts"; that they are void and voidable; being without consideration, illegal, and against public policy.

Therefore, the natural approach to a decision is to first inquire what constitutes a voting trust. There are various definitions of a voting trust given by the textbook and text-writers, among such definitions being as follows:

> A voting trust agreement is an agreement which cumulates in the hands of a person or persons the shares of several owners of stock in trust for the purpose of voting them in order to control the corporate business and affairs. [14 C. J. 915]
>
> A voting trust may be comprehensively defined as one created by an agreement between a group of the stockholders of a corporation and the trustee, or by a group of identical agreements between individual stockholders and a common trustee, whereby it is provided that for a term of years, or for a period contingent upon a certain event, or until the agreement is terminated, control over the stock owned by such stockholders, either for certain purposes or for all, shall be lodged in the trustee, with or without a reservation to the owner or persons designated by them of the power to direct how such control shall be used. [Fletcher's *Cyclopedia of Corporations*, No. 1705, vol. 3.]

The definitions given by the various leading text-writers are practically in accord, and the whole theory of voting trusts is built up on the idea that a group or a portion of the stockholders of a corporation unite and execute an instrument to a trustee for the purpose of voting and controlling the policies of the corporation, but in no definition, nor reported case, do we find the entire stock of the corporation pooled in the same trustee or trustees. The instruments executed in the case at bar, while containing practically every element going to make up what is commonly known as a voting trust, in fact go farther, and constitute in addition thereto a managing trust and trust deed, and the voting power given under the instruments has been treated as only one of the many powers conveyed by the instruments and as incidental to governing the management of the corporations. The instruments before the court convey the certificates of stock in the corporations to these trustees with full power and authority to control the corporations, and for a definite time, the lifetime of the trustees or the survivor. On their face, the instruments have all the earmarks of a complete contract. The parties thereto were competent to contract. There was a subject-matter, there was a legal consideration, and there was mutuality of agreement and mutuality of obligation.

We come then to the question first if the instruments before the court are void or voidable as being against public policy.

. . . If the instruments create nothing more than voting trusts, are they void as against public policy? There are two distinct lines of cases, the one holding that the separation of the voting power in stock from its beneficial ownership is contrary to public policy and void, the other, that any voting trust which is entered into in good faith and for the promotion and good of the corporation, and thereby necessarily for the welfare and good of all of the stockholders, is valid and enforceable.

> . . . It is very generally held or said that voting trusts are not per se unlawful; and one of the most familiar illustrations of a voting trust which may be lawful is where the object is to carry out a particular policy, with a view to promote the best interest of all the stockholders. It is said that the validity of the trust is to be determined by the propriety and justness of the ultimate purposes sought to be accomplished; . . . 14 C. J. 915.

The instruments herein sought to be declared null and void are not against the public policy of the state, not contravening any statute, and there being a total lack of evidence that they were entered into to serve any illegal purpose, but, to the contrary, to better serve the interests of all of the stockholders and benefit them and the corporations.

Judgment affirmed.

PETITION OF AVARD
1955, 144 N.Y.S.2d 204

The petitioners, minority stockholders of Oneita Knitting Mills, a corporation, brought this action against the corporation to recover the value of their stock in the corporation. The corporation, which manufactured knit goods, was operating at a loss in its plant in New York and it desired to shift its operations to a low-cost plant in South Carolina where it was believed that the business could be profitably conducted. The petitioners contended that the sale by the company of its property in New York could not be made without the consent of two thirds of the stockholders. The lower court dismissed the petition and the stockholders appealed.

GORMAN, J. . . . Section 20 of the Stock Corporation Law in substance requires the approval of two-thirds of the stockholders entitled to vote if a corporation desires to sell or convey its property, rights, privileges and franchises, or any interest therein or any part thereof, if such sale, lease or exchange is not made in the regular course of its business and involves all or substantially all of its property, rights, privileges and franchises, or an integral part thereof essential to the conduct of the business of the corporation. Section 21 of the same law prescribes the procedure to be followed by duly objecting stockholders. If, in view of the purposes and objects of a corporation, a particular sale may be regarded as within the regular and normal course of the business of the corporation and as not involving an integral part thereof, it is not within the purview of the statute. If the sale is such as to deprive the corporation of the means of accomplishing the ends for which it was incorporated; that is, if the business, and assets sold were essential to the ordinary conduct of the business, it is within the statute.

The present controversy squarely poses the question of whether the conduct of the respondent was such as to bring it within the scope of § 20. The management of a corporation is entrusted to its board of directors. It is well established that the directors have power, in the ordinary course of business, to do any act permitted by the charter or certificate of incorporation. There is no serious suggestion that the actions of the board of directors were tainted by fraud, deceit or bad faith in any of the contested transactions. Although the statute has been held inapplicable to the actions of a corporation pursuing a business advantage, *Matter of Leventall,* 241 App. Div. 277, 271 N.Y.S. 493, the courts have rarely been called upon to construe the applicability of its terms to the actions of a solvent corporation motivated by business conditions to pursue somewhat far-reaching measures in the manipulation of its assets in an effort to continue its business.

If corporate management determines that a business is unprofitable, it may dispose of the property or business to eliminate further loss without the consent of its stockholders.

The time-honored test to determine the need for stockholder consent "is not the amount involved, but the nature of the transaction, whether the sale is in the regular course of the business of the corporation and in furtherance of the express objects of its existence, or something outside of the normal and regular course of the business."

The instant transactions do not involve the investment of respondent's assets in a substantially different business of a kind in which it was not authorized to engage, nor the exchange of its stock for the stock of another corporation, nor were they pro tanto going out of business in any vital department or branch of respondent's business.

"What in the instance of one corporation may be a sale or lease of all its assets requiring consent of stockholders, may, in the case of another corporation, depending upon its purposes, methods of operation and past history, and the industry practices and pattern, represent usual, normal and ordinary activity which does not require consent." *Schreiber v. Butte Copper & Zinc Co.*, D.C., 98 F. Supp. 106, 111. Respondent has shown that it has long been the custom in the knit goods industry in general and its own operations in particular to discontinue unprofitable production and to sell equipment and machinery no longer needed in the ordinary course of its business. Subsequent to 1920, respondent found it expedient to reduce the production of men's and, particularly, women's heavy-weight underwear, the volume of which had previously been much greater than the aggregate of all its other production. This procedure constituted a normal operation of its business and was affected without specific stockholder approval. Respondent's present decision to concentrate upon the profitable production of light-weight underwear, T-shirts and outerwear would seem to be in accord with accepted business practice. Respondent has not relinquished any of its franchises nor has it prohibited itself from engaging in any branch of the knitted goods business which may now, or in the future, prove acceptable to consumers and profitable to it. None of the acts of the respondent can practicably be called acts of complete or partial self-destruction. It has not deprived itself of its ability to carry out its corporate purposes as exemplified in its amended charter by alienating an integral part of its business and has not altered the avowed purpose of the corporation—to manufacture, process, sell and otherwise deal in knit goods of any character. Since the charter further specifically provides that the corporate purpose is to do all acts and things as may be necessary, convenient or incidental to the foregoing, the board of directors may not be held to have acted in excess of their declared powers.

Affirmed.

TUTTLE v. JUNIOR BLDG. CORPORATION

1948, 228 N.C. 507, 46 S.E.2d 313

The directors and stockholders of the defendant Junior Building Corporation met informally and discussed plaintiff's offer to purchase the building owned by the corporation. It was informally agreed to sell to the plaintiff, and the defendant's attorney, who was also a director, was instructed to prepare a deed. There was no formal vote and no record of the meeting was entered in the corporate minutes. The deed was delivered to the bank in escrow and later withdrawn without the consent of the plaintiff and before he tendered the balance of the purchase price. The plaintiff brought this suit to compel specific performance of the contract of purchase and sale. From a judgment for defendant, plaintiff appealed.

BARNHILL, J. . . . A corporation is bound by the acts of its stockholders and directors only when they act as a body in regular session or under authority conferred at a duly constituted meeting. "As a rule authorized meetings are prerequisite to corporate action based upon deliberate conference, and intelligent discussion of proposed measures." *O'Neal v. Wake County*, 196 N.C. 184, 145 S.E. 28, 29.

. . . "The separate action, individually, without consultation, although a majority in number should agree upon a certain act, would not be the act of the constituted body of men clothed with corporate powers." Angel & Ames on Corporations, § 504. "Indeed, the authorities upon this subject are numerous, uncontradicted, and supported by reason." *Duke v. Markham*, 105 N.C. 131, 10 S.E. 1017, 18 Am. St. Rep. 889.

. . . If stockholders and directors cannot bind the corporation by their individual acts and declarations, *a fortiori* an unauthorized act performed in the name of the corporation by its officers cannot thereafter be ratified by such acts or declarations. Hence the court below properly excluded the evidence of declarations made by stockholders and directors after the sale had been repudiated and the deed withdrawn from escrow.

Affirmed.

MARDEL SECURITIES, INC. v. ALEXANDRIA GAZETTE CORP.

1960, 183 F.Supp. 7

WALTER E. HOFFMAN, District Judge. Mardel Securities, Inc. has instituted this secondary action in its capacity as a 48% minority stockholder of the Alexandria Gazette Corporation, publishers of a newspaper advertised as "America's Oldest Daily Newspaper," against the Gazette and its principal officer, Charles C. Carlin, Jr., the latter being the owner of 52% of the outstanding stock issued by the Gazette. Plaintiff contends that Carlin is indebted to the Gazette in substantial amounts allegedly occasioned by reason of Carlin's ownership and operation of a newspaper known as the "Arlington Daily Sun," hereinafter referred to as the "Sun," which said newspaper Carlin caused to be printed at, and partially operated from, the physical plant of the Gazette at Alexandria, Virginia, only a few miles from Arlington where the Sun had its principal office but possessed no facilities for printing the newspaper. Plaintiff contends that the amounts charged to the Sun by the Gazette resulted in substantial losses to the Gazette for which Carlin, by reason of his fiduciary capacity, is liable to the Gazette. In short, the action, while maintained by the minority stockholder, is actually for the use and benefit of the Gazette corporation.

. . . We have no difficulty applying the controlling principles of law to the facts here presented. As was said in *Rowland v. Kable,* 174 Va. 343, 6 S.E.2d 633, 642:

> The authorities are agreed that a director of a private corporation cannot directly or indirectly, in any transaction in which he is under a duty to guard the interests of the corporation, acquire any personal advantage, or make any profit for himself, and if he does so, he may be compelled to account therefor to the corporation. This does not mean that he may not deal with his corporation or sell his property to the corporation if the transactions are open, fair and honest, and the corporation is represented by competent and authorized agents. The unbending rule is that the director must act in the utmost good faith, and this good faith forbids placing himself in a position where his individual interest clashes with his duty to his corporation. The purpose of the law is to secure fidelity in the director. If, in violation of the general rule, he places himself in a position in which he may be tempted, by his own private interest, to disregard that of the corporation, his transactions are voidable at the option of the corporation and may be set aside without showing actual injury. One who is entrusted with the business of another cannot be allowed to make that business an object of interest to himself.

To the same effect will be found . . . *Wight v. Heublein,* 4 Cir., 238 F. 321, 324. In the last cited case, the Court pointed out that directors are:

> . . . (precluded) from doing any act, or engaging in any transaction in which their own private interest will conflict with the duty they owe to the stockholders and from making any use of their power or of the corporation property for their own advantage.

In *Solimine v. Hollander,* 128 N.J.Eq. 228, 16 A.2d 203, 217, we are told that

> a director or officer of a corporation cannot use corporate assets to acquire, finance, or develop his own individual business project or venture and insist that either the venture or the profits thereof are his own property.

It is clear that Carlin, in his fiduciary capacity as officer and director of the Gazette, has violated the cardinal rules applicable to his position.

VULCANIZED RUBBER & PLASTICS COMPANY v. SCHECKTER

1960 (Pa.) 162 A.2d 400

Cohen, Justice. On August 20, 1959, the appellee corporation moved for and was granted a temporary order restraining the appellants, two of whom had been both lawyers and accountants of the appellee and a third a former director, from voting any of appellee's stock owned, held or controlled by appellants at any future stockholder's meeting. After holding several hearings, the chancellor, finding that certain stock was acquired by appellants in breach of their fiduciary responsibilities, decreed that the restraining order be continued as a preliminary injunction pending final hearing and determination of the case. From this order appellants have taken these appeals.

The instant suit involves another round in the struggle between the present management group of the appellee, Vulcanized Rubber & Plastics Company, and a group headed by the individual appellants, Scheckter, Fish and Redland, for managerial control of the appellee corporation. . . .

The chancellor found that from about March 1, 1956, until approximately the commencement of this action, a Weatherly Steel Castings Company and its successor, the appellant Dutron Plastics, Inc., made numerous purchases of the appellee's common stock, causing the price of the stock to increase from about $25 per share to more than $60 per share. Throughout this period, appellants Scheckter and Fish held majority control of both Weatherly Steel Casting Company and Dutron Plastics. They did not reveal their interest in these companies to the appellee. . . .

. . . Generally speaking, a corporation as such has no interest in its outstanding stock, or in dealings by its officers, directors, or shareholders with respect thereto. *Howell v. McCloskey*, 1953, 375 Pa. 100, 99 A.2d 610; *Bisbee v. Midland Linseed Products Co.*, 8 Cir., 1927, 19 F.2d 24. As a result, in and of itself, there can be nothing improper so far as the corporate entity is concerned with one of its fiduciaries, be he officer, director or otherwise, buying up a controlling number of shares. . . . Nor can it be of any consequence, therefore, if the control is secretly acquired (which as a practical matter will usually be the case, for to do so otherwise will result in a rise in the market price).

On the other hand, if there should exist some reason or necessity for the corporation to purchase its outstanding shares, the situation is necessarily altered. There is no doubt that the relationship between a corporation and its officers and directors, as well as its lawyers and accountants, is such that these "fiduciaries" cannot act contrary to or compete with the interests of the corporation. Predominantly for the protection of shareholders, there has developed in corporation law a doctrine of "corporate opportunity" under which a corporation has the right to legal redress where one of its fiduciaries has in some way usurped some advantageous opportunity in which the corporation has an existing interest or where the opportunity is necessary for corporate existence or prosperity. . . .

It becomes evident that the basis of appellee's action here must be that the appellant fiduciaries, in purchasing the stock in issue, regardless of the secrecy in doing so, have acted in competition with some existing corporate interest in the stock, or have pre-empted a corporate purchase which was necessary for the appellee's prosperity or existence. . . . Upon an examination of the record, and upon analysis of the applicable doctrines of corporate law, we find that the appellee corporation, as a corporate entity separate and apart from its management group, had no interest in purchasing the stock in issue . . . which could result in the appellee being legally harmed by the conduct of the appellants. . . .

There being no indication in the record that the board of directors as a body ever considered purchasing any stock, there could not be any existing corporate interest therein. Accordingly, it cannot be held that appellants' purchases were in competition with the corporation itself. . . .

The order granting the preliminary injunction is reversed.

Review Questions and Problems

1. A majority of the stockholders of a corporation happen to meet at the corporation offices. While there, they hold a meeting and transact certain corporate business. Are their actions effective?
2. A state statute provided that a corporation could not issue preferred stock unless the certificate of incorporation provided for such issue. The stockholders by unanimous vote adopted a by-law which provided for the issuance of preferred stock although the certificate of incorporation did not so provide. Upon dissolution of the corporation *A*, a preferred stockholder, claimed the right to receive full par value plus dividends in arrears, before any distribution should be made to common stockholders. Should the court uphold *A*'s contention?
3. *A* holds a certificate of stock for five shares in the *X* Company. How many votes is he entitled to cast at a stockholders' meeting? Does a preferred stockholder have a right to vote?
4. *A* owned 100 shares in *X* corporation and gave his proxy to a director with his initial but not his signature upon the proper line for signing. The director presented the proxy at the opening session of the annual shareholders' meeting. If *A*'s 100 shares were not counted there would be no quorum. At the beginning of the second session, *A* withdrew his proxy. Was the business conducted at the first session valid? At the second?
5. *A*, a director and officer of *X* Corporation purchased shares of the corporation from a shareholder, *B*. *A* realized a substantial profit on the transaction. Must *A* account to the corporation for this profit?
6. *A*, a stockholder in a corporation, desires to sell certain real estate to the corporation. He is present at the meeting of the stockholders when the matter is considered and votes in favor of the purchase. Assuming that a majority favors the purchase, has a minority stockholder any right to object? Suppose *A* had been a director and the matter had been before a meeting of the board of directors?
7. A corporation was in need of additional money. *B* bank was willing to loan the money upon the pledge of all the preferred stock except

for the fact that the preferred did not have voting control. The bank feared that the common stockholders would take action which could lessen the security value of the preferred stock. What device might be used to insure that the common shareholders could not take such action?

8. *X* desired to buy all of the stock of *Y* Corporation. He approached the officers and directors of the corporation and offered to pay them a certain price for the shares which they held. The officers and directors persuaded the stockholders to sell for a price less than that which the officers and directors would receive. Do the stockholders have a cause of action against the officers and directors?
9. *A*, *B*, and *C* are directors of a small corporation and, as such, appoint themselves as officers of the corporation at fabulous salaries. May they later be made to account to the corporation for any amount received in excess of the reasonable value of their services?
10. *A* was elected director of a certain corporation by the majority interests upon his promise to vote for *B* as the general manager. Was *A*'s promise enforceable?
11. *A* is a director of a corporation operating an automobile dealership. The corporation owes him $21,000. It also owes *X*, a third party creditor, $50,000. Both debts cannot be paid and insolvency is imminent. *A* persuades the other directors to join him in authorizing payment to himself. May *X* require *A* to pay over to him the amount received?
12. *P* was the general manager and president of *C*, a corporation operating a cannery business. *P* also owned 73 per cent of the stock. *P* signed a $5,000 pledge to *X*, a non-profit corporation engaged in soliciting money for, and constructing, a general hospital in the community in which the cannery was situated. *P* signed the pledge in behalf of the corporation in his capacities as president and general manager. No resolution of the board authorized him to do so. However *P* had signed pledges of the corporation to the Red Cross and Community Chest for several hundred dollars in the past. May *X* collect from the corporation?

39

Dissolution of a Corporation

5-111. Expiration of charter. Corporate existence may be terminated by the expiration of its charter through dissolution by the attorney general, by consolidation, or by action of the stockholders.

Where the charter provides that the corporation shall exist for a definite period, it automatically terminates at the expiration of the period. However, upon application, a rule for the continued existence of the corporation may be made.

5-112. Dissolution by attorney general. The attorney general of the state is the only person authorized to forfeit a charter. The state, having brought the corporation into existence, has a right to forfeit the charter. Neither a stockholder, a corporate creditor, nor any other governmental agency can bring a suit to forfeit a corporation charter. If a corporation misuses its power, or enters into illegal acts, such as combinations in restraint of trade, or ceases to perform its corporate functions for a long period of time, the attorney general may institute a suit for the purpose of forfeiting the corporate charter. A suit by the state to forfeit a corporate charter is called a quo warranto proceeding. The Attorney General may also, without charter forfeiture, by proper proceedings enjoin a corporation from engaging in a business not authorized by its charter.[1]

5-113. Consolidation and merger. Consolidation is the uniting of two or more corporations, by which a new corporation is created and the old entities are dissolved. The new corporation takes title to all the property, rights, powers, and privileges of the old corporations, subject to the liabilities and obligations of the old corporations.

In a merger, however, one of the corporations continues its existence, but absorbs the other corporation, which is merged into it. The continuing corporation may expressly or impliedly assume and agree to pay the debts and liabilities of the absorbed corporation. If so, such creditors become third party creditor beneficiaries. By statutes in many states the surviving corporation is deemed to have assumed all the liabilities and

[1] State v. Zale Jewelry Company of Wichita, page 860.

obligations of the absorbed corporation.[2] The statutes of the various states provide the methods for corporate consolidation and merger.

5-114. Dissolution by the stockholders. A corporation can be dissolved by the consent of all the stockholders and by less than all of the stockholders if it is insolvent. If the corporation is insolvent, it may be dissolved upon application to the state that created it. Under these circumstances, a court usually appoints a receiver to marshal the assets and to make distribution to the creditors.

Upon dissolution, all the corporate property, both personal and real, is first used to pay corporate debts. After the debts are paid, the remainder is to be distributed among the stockholders in proportion to the capital stock they own. The liability of the stockholders, upon dissolution, ceases as to any further business. Where a receiver has been appointed and it is necessary to carry out contracts not yet completed, the corporation still remains liable for the performance of its executory contracts.

RIGHTS OF CREDITORS

5-115. Right against corporate assets. The corporation stands in the same position as a natural person, with respect to creditors. A suit may be brought against it, and upon judgment being obtained, an execution may be levied against its property, which may then be sold. Likewise, corporate assets may be attached, and if the corporation has no property subject to execution, its assets may be traced by a bill in a court of equity.

The creditors have no right, because they are creditors, to interfere with the management of the business. A creditor who has an unsatisfied judgment against a corporation, because there is no corporate property upon which a levy can be made, may bring a bill in equity to set aside conveyances and transfers of corporate property which have been fraudulently transferred for the purpose of delaying and hindering creditors.[3] Creditors may also, under the above circumstances, ask for a receiver to take over the assets of the corporation and to apply them to the payment of debts.

5-116. Right against stockholders. Stockholders are not liable for the debts of the corporation. This distinction is the essential feature in which a corporation differs from a partnership. Each member of a partnership is liable for the debts of the firm. The members of a corporation, on the other hand, are not liable for the debts of the firm.[4]

[2] State ex rel. Safeguard Ins. Co. v. Vorys, page 863.
[3] State et al. v. Simmer Oil Corp. et al., page 864.
[4] Shaw v. Bailey-McCune Company, page 865.

If the members of a corporation have not paid their stock in full, however, the creditors, after exhausting the assets of the firm, may look to the stockholders for their unpaid balance. This is the limit of the liability of the members of a corporation.

But the statutes of many states have increased the liabilities of stockholders to corporate creditors. That is, the statutes provide that the stockholders shall be liable for a sum in addition to the par value of their stock. This additional liability is known as the statutory liability of stockholders. A few states by statute attach additional liability to stockholders of manufacturing corporations. Some attach liability equal to the par of the shares in banking and trust companies. The stockholders will be liable to the creditors if the capital stock has been distributed among the stockholders before the creditors have been paid, and the creditors can reach the assets of the corporation in the hands of the stockholders on the theory that the assets have been transferred in fraud of creditors.

DISSOLUTION OF A CORPORATION CASES

STATE v. ZALE JEWELRY COMPANY OF WICHITA
1956, (Kan.) 298 P.2d 283

SMITH, C. J. This is an original action in quo warranto brought by the state on the relation of the attorney general wherein the state asks that the defendant corporation be ousted from engaging in the practice of optometry. Plaintiff also asks that the charter of the corporation be forfeited and a receiver appointed. Our commissioner found in favor of the defendant. The state asks us to read the record and make findings of fact and conclusions of law in its favor. The cause has been submitted on the merits.

The petition alleged that Zale was a corporation and had forfeited its corporate rights by practicing optometry in the state within the meaning of G.S. 1949, 65-1501 and 65-1502; that it had never been licensed to so practice optometry; that it had further violated G.S. 1949, 65-1510, relating to optometry, by unlawful acts set out.

The petition further alleged that unless the defendant corporation should be ousted from unlawfully exercising the right and privilege to practice optometry it would continue to so engage; that the acts described amounted to a forfeiture of its corporate rights.

The prayer was that it be ousted from practicing optometry and it should be dissolved and a receiver appointed to close out its business, and for costs.

. . . We appointed a commissioner who proceeded to hear and receive evidence. He made findings of fact and conclusions of law.

. . . What are the facts and circumstances we must consider? The defendant is a domestic corporation with its stock all owned by a Texas corporation. It is engaged in the main in the retail jewelry business. In Wichita it operates a jewelry store in a two-story store building. Its jewelry business is transacted on the ground floor. The second story is used for storage purposes. In the rear of the first floor is a balcony reached by stairs from the floor. On this balcony Dr. Marks and The Douglas Optical Company carried on their activities. Each had a lease with defendant, both leases executed on April 1, 1952. Dr. Marks rented a room about 8 x 20 feet for a refracting room and a room adjoining for a waiting room. The rent was $100 a month. Defendant agreed to service and handle the accounts receivable of Marks, including his collections, bookkeeping and clerical work. Marks agreed not to engage in any business in competition with defendant. Douglas Optical leased the entire balcony except what was leased to Marks. It agreed to pay defendant 20% of its gross sales to be paid on the 10th of every month. Defendant agreed to service and handle at its own expense the accounts receivable of Douglas, including collections, bookkeeping and clerical work. It should be pointed out here that the business of Marks, the optometrist, was to test eyes and to ascertain what glasses, if any, the patient needed. That of the optical company was to grind the lenses according to the optometrist's prescription and to furnish frames for the lenses. The lenses were all ground in Dallas, Texas.

In the early stages of the case there was in the rear corner of defendant's store near the stairway to the balcony a neon sign reading "Optical Dept." After this action was commenced this was changed to "Douglas Optical."

There is no dispute about how business was carried on. When a customer entered the store a clerk would ask what he wanted. When he answered he had come to get some glasses he was directed to the stairs at the back of the optical department. On arriving at the balcony he would be met by a young lady who would ask him some questions. Dr. Marks then proceeded to examine his eyes. A prescription by Marks was then handed to the optical company. He was shown frames, informed of the price of glasses and made arrangements how he wanted to pay, whether cash or in payments. The fact is the glasses could be paid for in payments. The customer would be taken downstairs then to defendant's cashier, where credit arrangements on payments were made. Payments were made to defendant's cashier and correspondence as to delinquent accounts was on defendant's stationery.

In the front of defendant's store are display windows. One is devoted exclusively to the display and advertising of eye glasses. Above the front of the store is a large projecting neon sign bearing the words "Zale's Jewelers." Below these words appeared the replica of a pair of glasses and the words "Glasses Fitted." After this action was commenced the replica of the pair of glasses was removed and the words "Glasses Fitted" were omitted. There were no signs in the window or on the balcony that made any reference to Dr. Marks or Douglas Optical except the sign on the stairs that was changed from "Optical Dept." to "Douglas Optical" after this action was begun.

Defendant carried on an extensive advertising campaign in the local newspapers. These were usually rather large display ads. They would devote considerable space to the jewelry business of defendant but always a portion would be devoted to the optical business.

. . . A corporation can act only through its agents or employees. Since it is clear that Dr. Marks is practicing optometry our inquiry is narrowed to the question whether Marks is an agent or employee of defendant. If he is, we must find as a matter of fact that defendant is practicing optometry. Our commissioner found that neither Dr. Marks nor Douglas Optical was an employee of Zale. There was testimony that Zale had no control over either Marks or Douglas Optical and that neither the defendant corporation nor the parent corporation had ever employed him. We may believe circumstantial evidence and disbelieve direct evidence. See *Brothers v. Adams*, 152 Kan. 675, 107 P.2d 757. In the consideration of the entire record it is our duty to draw our own inferences and indulge our own presumption and to draw our own conclusions from the proven facts as long as they are reasonable inferences, presumptions and conclusions. Defendant relies in the main on the two leases already mentioned to establish that the relationship between it and Marks and it and Douglas was strictly that of lessor and lessee. Our commissioner adopted that view. There are some features of the two leases, however, that cause us to be a little skeptical of that view. The two leases were entered into the same day. They each had the provision about defendant handling the business and financial affairs of both Marks and Douglas Optical. A reasonable inference is that such provision was in the lease so as to permit defendant to exercise control over both.

. . . In practically every authority we have examined on the question the courts have been compelled to examine and consider a course of dealing such as we have here. They have universally held that a lease arrangement such as these parties entered into was a subterfuge.

. . . We have examined the record before the commissioner. Perhaps we have not set down all the facts and circumstances that have caused us to reach the conclusion we have reached as to the facts. Triers of facts very seldom do. At any rate, we find as a matter of fact that the relationship between defendant and Dr. Marks is that of employer and employee. Dr. Marks is practicing optometry. He is employed to do so by defendant —hence defendant is practicing optometry, which it cannot do.

Judgment is in favor of plaintiff ousting defendant from the practice of optometry in the state. Plaintiff asks us to order the dissolution of defendant and the appointment of a receiver to wind it up. We find the record does not warrant such a drastic measure. (The injunction against practicing optometry was granted but the charter of the defendant was not forfeited.)

STATE ex rel. SAFEGUARD INS. CO. v. VORYS
1960, (Ohio) 167 N.E.2d 910

The relator (Safeguard Ins. Co.) brought an action in mandamus against Vorys, Superintendent of Insurance, to require the latter to release to relator $53,000 in securities which had been deposited by an insurer which had since merged into relator. Safeguard had deposited with the Superintendent for the security and benefit of all its policy holders the requisite amount of securities required. The relator filed a demurrer to the Superintendent's answer.

TAFT, Judge. . . . Generally, where there is an assumption by one legal entity of the liability or obligation of another legal entity, such assumption will not represent a payment or an extinguishment of such liability or obligation. However, the extent of the liability or obligation of a corporation may be dependent upon and measured by the law which establishes its existence as a legal entity. Thus, that law may authorize the substitution, for the liability and obligation of a corporation that it has created as a corporate entity, of the liability of another solvent legal entity into which it lawfully merged. . . .

Certainly, a creditor who voluntarily deals with such a corporation in the light of constitutional provisions such as those found in Section 2 of Article XIII of the Ohio Constitution ("corporations may be formed under general laws: but all such laws may, from time to time, be altered or repealed") is in no position to complain where the law which created the corporation provides that (on the happening of certain events and without interfering with any pending legal proceedings) such corporation's obligations and liabilities shall cease to be the obligations and liabilities of such corporation and instead shall become the obligations and liabilities of a solvent legal entity into which said corporation merges. . . .

Thus, after the merger, any obligations and liabilities secured by the $53,000 deposits made with the respondent superintendent by the indemnity company, which were not the subject of pending legal proceedings (none apparently were) were no longer obligations and liabilities of the indemnity company as a legal entity separate from relator but were obligations and liabilities of relator, although still secured by those $53,000 of deposits; and those deposits belong to relator, subject to any claims or liens against such deposits in favor of those to whom the indemnity company had been before the merger and to whom relator was thereafter obligated or liable. . . .

It follows that relator's demurrer to the amended answer must be sustained. . . .

Writ allowed.

STATE et al. v. SIMMER OIL CORPORATION et al.
1942, 231 Iowa 1041, 2 N.W.2d 760

The plaintiff, State of Iowa, obtained a judgment against the defendant corporation. This judgment was not paid and the plaintiff is seeking to set aside certain transfers of property made by the corporation in order that the property may be made available to satisfy the plaintiff's claim. The corporation deeded the property to Leonard Simmer and his wife, the principal stockholders of the defendant corporation. The trial court ruled that the transfer would not be set aside and the plaintiff appealed.

SAGER, J. . . . Appellants insist that they are entitled to have these properties subjected to the unpaid debts of the oil corporation. Appellees deny, urging that they legally have claim to these properties because transfers were made in satisfaction of money advanced by them to the corporation; and they say that even though the corporation deeded to Leonard, president and director, this was a valid legal transaction. The trial court took this view and we think therein erred. It must be admitted that some of our earlier cases tend to support the decision below. (Cases cited)

These cases do declare generally the right to give such preference but our later cases, while not overlooking the prior decisions, have limited their apparent scope. In discussing the so-called "trust fund" doctrine we said in *Luedecke v. Des Moines Cabinet Co.*, 140 Iowa 223, 118 N.W. 456, 458, 32 L.R.A., N.S., 616:

> We do not recognize the trust-fund doctrine to the extent that it has obtained in some of the courts; but are of opinion that corporate creditors are entitled in equity to the payment of their debts before any distribution of corporate property is made among the stockholders, and recognize the right of a creditor of a corporation to follow its assets or property into the hands of any one who is not a good-faith holder in the ordinary course of business.

Certainly the appellees Simmer are not good-faith holders "in the ordinary course of business." We do not wish to be understood as charging that they were guilty of any actual or intentional fraud. The record excludes this. Agnes Simmer put into this corporation upwards of twenty thousand dollars even mortgaging the homestead to keep the business going. If there be any fraud in the transaction it is in a strictly legal sense and not actual fraud with which we are dealing.

. . . Under the authorities cited the properties above described should be made subject to the debts held by appellants and other creditors, if any there be.

. . . As to these, any equities there may be above existing mortgages should be applied to the payment of unpaid creditors of the Simmer Oil Corporation.

It follows that the cause must be and it is remanded for further proceedings in accordance herewith. Other creditors, if there are any, should be brought in as parties so their interests may be protected.

SHAW v. BAILEY-McCUNE COMPANY

1960, (Utah) 355 P.2d 321

The defendant, Bailey-McCune Company, leased real property from the plaintiffs and also purchased certain items of merchandise on credit. The individual defendants are stockholders in the corporation. The corporation failed financially and the plaintiffs contending that the corporate structure is a sham, seek to hold the stockholders personally liable for the unpaid rent and merchandise. The plaintiffs contend that the corporation was under-capitalized. The lower court dismissed the action against the individual defendants. The plaintiffs appealed.

Callister, Justice. . . . The mere relation of being a stockholder in a debtor corporation does not under the law make a stockholder liable for the debts and obligations of the corporation. A corporation is a statutory entity which is regarded as having an existence and personality distinct from that of its stockholders even though the stock is owned by a single individual.

Under some circumstances the corporate entity may be disregarded in the interest of justice in such cases as fraud, contravention of law or contract, or public wrong. However, great caution should be exercised by the courts in disregarding the entity.

Moreover, the conditions under which the corporate entity may be disregarded or the corporation be regarded as the alter ego of the stockholders vary according to the circumstances in each case inasmuch as the doctrine is essentially an equitable one and for that reason is particularly within the province of the trial court.

The lower court found that the corporation was not a sham or the alter ego of the Baileys and refused to disregard the corporate entity. These findings of the trial court should not be overturned unless the evidence clearly preponderates against them. We have carefully examined the record and find no reason to reverse the trial court's determination.

Affirmed.

Review Questions and Problems

1. *X* Corporation entered into a contract to purchase linseed oil from *Y*. Subsequently, *X* Corporation merged with *Z* Corporation and the latter refused to purchase linseed oil from *Y*. Does *Y* have a cause of action against *Z* Corporation?
2. *X* Corporation merged with *Y* Corporation. At the time of the merger accrued dividends were owing to the preferred stockholders of *X* Corporation. What effect will the merger have upon the rights of these preferred stockholders?
3. The majority of the stockholders of a corporation, being interested in a rival concern, vote to dissolve the corporation. Can it be dissolved without the consent of the minority? Suppose the corporation had been insolvent?
4. The directors of *X* Corporation took action to bring about the dissolution of the corporation. *A*, a minority stockholder, is dissatisfied with this action and seeks to enjoin the dissolution. Should he succeed?
5. A corporation had not made a profit for 20 years and no dividends had been paid for that period. The preferred stockholders brought suit to obtain a decree of dissolution. Should they succeed?
6. The stockholders of a corporation sell some of the corporation property and divide it equally among the stockholders. Later, the corporation becomes insolvent. Can the creditors force the stockholders to return the amount which they received?
7. *A* owned a minority of the stock in *X* corporation. He could not agree with the majority on the way they desired to conduct the business. Specifically they desired to merge with another corporation over his vehement objection. What may be done? If *A*'s stock is ordered sold to the majority how will the price be fixed?

PART THREE / MISCELLANEOUS BUSINESS ORGANIZATIONS

40

Noncorporate Associations

5-117. Introduction. Most of our business is conducted by individual proprietorships, partnerships, and corporations. A few of the other types should, however, be given some consideration. The most important of these are the limited partnership, the joint stock company, and the business trust. In the sections that follow, it is proposed to consider briefly their organization and the extent to which the owners have personal responsibility for obligations which are incurred.

LIMITED PARTNERSHIPS

5-118. History. A limited partnership is one which comes into existence by virtue of an agreement. A limited partnership, like a corporation, is authorized by statute. Limited partnerships are so called because the liability of one or more of the partners, but not of all, is limited to the amount of capital contributed at the time of the creation of the partnership. It is similar to a corporation in that its right to exist is accorded by statute, and that the limited partners, like stockholders, are liable only to the extent of their original investment. The English common law originally looked with disfavor upon any arrangement to limit the liability of one who engaged in business. As expressed in *Grace v. Smith* (1774) it was felt that "Every man who has a share of the profits of a trade ought also to bear his share of the loss." However, in modern times recognition is given to the business need for forms of business organization wherein liability is limited. The statutes providing for limited partnerships recognize this need.

The common-law rule prevented a person desiring to invest in a noncorporate enterprise from limiting his liability for the debts of the business to the amount invested, where the return upon his investment was not to be limited by a fixed rate of interest, but was to be determined by a share of the profits of the business. In effect these investors were treated as though they were partners to the extent that liabilities for trade debts were imposed upon them. In 1822 New York enacted a statute enabling the organization of what was called a "limited partnership," patterned upon the lines of a similar type of business organization recognized by the French Commercial Code. Subsequently, other states adopted similar statutes. Thus, there was legislative recognition of the commercial need for this type of business organization to encourage trade by making it possible to invest capital without running the risk of partnership liability.

5-119. How formed; statutory requirements. A limited partnership may be formed by two or more persons, having one or more general partners and one or more limited partners. Under the Uniform Limited Partnership Act, which has been adopted by most of the states, with variations, two or more persons, to create a limited partnership, must sign and swear to a certificate containing the following information: the name of the partnership; the character of the business; the location; the name and place of residence of each member; those who are to be the general and those who are to be the limited partners; the term for which the partnership is to exist; the amount of cash or the agreed value of property to be contributed by each partner; the additional contributions, if any, to be made from time to time by each partner; the time that any such contributions are to be returned to the limited partner; the share of profit or compensation which each limited partner shall receive; the right that a limited partner has to substitute an assignee of his interest; the right to admit additional limited partners; the right given to one or more of the limited partners to priority over other limited partners as to contributions, and compensation by way of income; the right of a limited partner to demand property rather than cash in return for his contribution; and the right of the remaining general partners to continue the business on the death, retirement, or incapacity of other partners.

5-120. Filing and publication of certificate. The certificate must be recorded in the county where the partnership has its principal place of business, and a copy must be filed in every community where it conducts business or has a representative office. To determine the requirements of recording, it is necessary to consult the statutes of the various states.

In nearly all the states, it is required that the certificate be published in some newspaper during a specified period of time before the beginning of business. It is also required in some states that proof of publication be made by affidavit of the publisher, and filed with the certificate. If such certificate is not filed and recorded, with the affidavit relative to publication, a limited partnership is not considered as organized.

Upon the expiration of the partnership, a new certificate must be filed in compliance with the statutory requirements for a new organization. Likewise, if there is any alteration in the original certificate, such as a change in the name of the partnership, the capital, or other matters, a new certificate must be filed. If such a certificate is not filed and the partnership continues, the limited partners immediately become liable as general partners.

5-121. Name of partnership. The statutes of most states require the partnership to conduct its business in a firm name which does not include the name of any of the limited partners or the word "Company." Some states specify that the word "Limited" shall be added. In some jurisdictions no liability will attach to the limited partners unless creditors are misled or injured by the failure of the firm to use the word "Limited" or by the use of the word "Company." Some states also provide that the partnership shall post in some conspicuous place the name of the firm, including the names of all the members therein.

5-122. Liability of limited partner. A limited partner is not liable beyond his contribution to creditors created by the partnership in the pursuit of the partnership business, unless the limited partner participates in the management and control of the business.[1]

5-123. Dissolution. A limited partnership cannot be dissolved voluntarily before the time for its termination as stated in the certificate, without the filing and publication of the notice of the dissolution. Upon dissolution, the distribution of the assets of the firm is prescribed in the statute, and priority among partners with respect to their share in the assets is controlled by the statutory requirements in the several states which have adopted the Uniform Limited Partnership Act.

JOINT STOCK COMPANIES AND BUSINESS TRUSTS

5-124. Joint stock companies. A joint stock company is a business arrangement which provides for the management of the business to be placed in the hands of trustees or directors. Under the constitution or by-laws of the organization, shares represented by certificates are issued to the various members who are joint owners in the enterprise. These shareholders elect the board of directors or trustees. The shares are transferable, the same as the shares of a corporation, and such transfer does not cause dissolution. Likewise, the death of one of the shareholders does not dissolve the organization as in a partnership.[2] It exists for the period of time designated in the by-laws. Such an association is a partnership, even though the primary purpose of such an arrangement is to secure many of the advantages of a corporation. Unlimited liability

[1] Silvola v. Rowlett, page 871.
[2] Hammond et al. v. Otwell et al., page 873.

continues, but in many other respects the features of a corporation are present. In many states by statute a suit may be brought against a joint stock company as an entity.

5-125. Business trusts. The business trust is an organization formed by trustees under a contract, called a declaration of trust, executed by the trustees. Under the agreement, the trustees issue certificates of beneficial interest, which are sold to investors.

The trustees take the capital in compliance with the agreement and operate the business, whatever it may be, as principals, for the benefit of the shareholders. Such an organization has many of the characteristics of a corporation, in that the trustees elect officers from among themselves, and in some states the shareholders at stated meetings, by virtue of the trust agreement, are permitted to elect the trustees.

Such an organization avoids the statutory regulations of a corporation, in that it is not a creature of the state, and seeks as well to avoid partnership liability on the part of the investors. The courts in most of the states, however, have held that if the investors under the trust agreement have a right to exercise some control over the management of the business, by way of election of trustees or otherwise, such shareholders are liable as partners.[3] It is clear, on the other hand, that if such shareholders have no control over, or no right to interfere in any way with, the management of the business, they are beneficiaries under a trust agreement and are not liable as partners.[4] This business organization has been called different names, such as "Business Trust," "Massachusetts Trust," and "The Common Law Trust." As a substitute for a corporation, it has lost many of its advantages, owing to statutory regulation by the various states; as a method to avoid partnership liability, it is ineffective, in that a shareholder whose money is being risked in a business venture naturally desires to have some control over the policy and conduct of the business, and such reservations carry with them the obligation of partnership.

The trustees are usually held to have unlimited liability for all obligations of the business trust unless the contracts restrict the rights of the creditors to the assets of the trust. It is customary for business trusts to place this limiting clause in all contracts, particularly if there is any possible question about the solvency of the trust.[5] Generally those organizations known as "Business Trusts" engage in the investment business. Investors purchase shares or certificates which entitle the holders to income from and increased value of stocks and bonds purchased by the trustees or directors of trust.

[3] First National Bank v. Chartier et al., page 875.
[4] Commercial Casualty Insurance Co. v. North et al., page 876.
[5] Pennsylvania Co. v. Wallace et al., page 877.

5-126. Nonprofit organizations. Nonprofit unincorporated associations arise, like partnerships, out of a contract.[6] Such associations are organized for social, educational, philanthropic, and fraternal purposes. These organizations have many of the characteristics both of the corporation and of the partnership in that they have by-laws, directors or trustees, and the usual officers, namely, president, secretary, and treasurer. In their method of functioning and their form they are much like corporations. To the extent that they are less formally organized, it may be said that such associations resemble partnerships. As a general rule, the liability of the members in such associations does not rest upon the theory of partnership, but on the theory of principal and agent, the officers of the association being the agents and the members the principals.[7] Since no entity exists by either a partnership or corporate organization, the officers are not agents of an entity, but those members of the organization who approve of a particular contract are liable as principals.

5-127. Joint adventure. A joint adventure is quite similar to a partnership but falls short of being one because its activities do not go far enough to be called a business. It is usually limited to one transaction or a series of transactions relating to a particular property. If two people buy a specific piece of real property for the purpose of resale at a profit, they become parties to a joint adventure.

The law controlling their individual relationship is essentially the same as found in the partnership. They have a fiduciary relationship and share profits or losses as is done in a partnership. They have much the same relation to third parties as partners have, particularly when the limited nature of the undertaking is considered.

NONCORPORATE ASSOCIATIONS CASES

SILVOLA v. ROWLETT

1954, 129 Colo. 522, 272 P.2d 287

The plaintiff, an accountant, brought this action against the defendant for the value of services rendered to a partnership in which the defendant and one McRea were partners. The defendant contended that he was a limited partner and therefore not personally liable for the firm debts. The defendant served as shop foreman in the firm's auto repair shop. The lower court ruled in favor of the defendant and the plaintiff appealed.

ALTER, J. . . . It is here conceded by counsel for plaintiff that the

[6] Chicago Grain Trimmers Ass'n. v. Murphy, Director of Labor, page 879.
[7] Stone v. Guth, page 880.

partnership was duly formed in substantial compliance with our statute governing the formation of limited partnerships, and that this case is one of first impression in our state on the question involved; but it is contended that the evidence demonstrates conclusively that the intent and conduct of the defendant here was that of a general partner because: 1. He contributed services to the business in violation of § 47, chapter 123, '35 C.S.A. Said section reads as follows: "The contributions of a limited partner may be cash or other property, but not services." . . .

It further is contended by plaintiff's counsel that § 50, chapter 123, '35 C.S.A., was violated by defendant, thereby imposing upon him the liability as a general partner. Said § 50 reads: "A limited partner shall not become liable as a general partner unless, in addition to the exercise of his rights and powers as a limited partner, he takes part in the control of the business."

The court found, and there was evidence to support its finding, "That at all times alleged in the Complaint the sole control and management of the firm rested with the said L. D. McRea and that the activities of the defendant, E. F. Rowlett, were at all times subject to such control."

The evidence discloses that after the formation of the partnership and for a period of time, defendant acted as foreman in the repair shop operated by the partnership; as such foreman he purchased necessary parts from an adjoining place of business without consulting McRea with respect thereto; when parts were needed from sources outside of Colorado Springs, he made out the order and gave it to McRea, who attended to the purchasing thereof. Further, that when there were important business transactions to be determined, McRea sometimes mentioned them to Rowlett; also, that as shop foreman all extensions of credit for repair work or parts thereon had to be approved by McRea, excepting only those persons known to defendant, and as to those he was authorized to extend credit under his agreement to pay the account if the creditor failed to do so. Defendant, being interested in the success of the partnership business, did not thereby forfeit his right to make suggestions or express opinions as to the advisability of transactions when his suggestion or opinion was sought by the general partner.

Both plaintiff and defendant have cited many decisions of our Court and others in support of their respective positions. We have read and considered all thereof without finding one that parallels the factual situation in the instant case, and none are helpful in our determination.

We hold that the services rendered by defendant after the formation of the limited partnership were not included in the "contributions" as that term is used in § 47, *supra;* we further hold that defendant's services rendered as foreman in the repair shop of the partnership did not deprive him of protection as a limited partner; and, further, that § 50, *supra,* does not impose silence on a limited partner who has a material interest in the success of the partnership business, especially so when his opinion and suggestions are sought by the general partner.

The judgment is affirmed.

HAMMOND et al. v. OTWELL et al.
1930, 170 Ga. 832, 154 S.E. 357

The plaintiffs, Hammond and others, brought this action against the defendants who were allegedly members of a joint stock association, People's Bank. The plaintiffs all have claims against the now defunct bank. The defendants contended that the bank was a partnership which had been dissolved by the prior death of some of the partners. The lower court granted a non-suit as to all of the defendants except one, and the plaintiffs excepted.

HINES, J. . . . The question whether a joint-stock company can be legally created in this state by agreement of parties, without legislative action, has been discussed by counsel for the defendants; but in the view which we take of this case we deem it unnecessary to pass upon this question. The controlling question is whether the articles of association, the substance of which is above set out, created a partnership or a joint-stock company. It is difficult to frame an exact definition of a joint-stock company, one sufficiently comprehensive to embrace every essential element, and sufficiently exclusive to exclude every irrelevant factor. It has been held that at common law joint-stock companies are regarded as partnerships. It has been said that unincorporated joint-stock companies are governed by the same general principles as are applicable to partnerships. It has been said that such companies are partnerships except in form. It has been held that they are partnerships with some of the powers of corporations. But such companies are not entirely controlled by the legal rules and principles which govern ordinary partnerships. *Spotswood v. Morris,* 12 Idaho 360, 85 Pac. 1094, 6 L.R.A. (N.S.) 665. In a joint-stock company there is no delectus personae as in the ordinary partnership. It has been declared that one distinction between a joint-stock company and a partnership is that the death of a member of the former does not ordinarily dissolve a joint-stock company, whereas it does have that effect in an ordinary partnership. Another distinction is that in a partnership each member speaks and acts as the agent of the firm, while this is not true in a joint-stock company. It has been declared that a joint-stock company at common law lies midway between a corporation and a partnership, and partakes of the nature of both. The changeability of membership or transferability of shares is often used as a determining criterion between ordinary partnerships and joint-stock companies. *Haiku*

Sugar Co. v. Jonstone (C.C.A.) 249 Fed. 103. "The fundamental distinction between ordinary partnerships and joint-stock companies is that the partnership consists of a few individuals known to each other, bound together by ties of friendship and mutual confidence, and who therefore are not at liberty, without the consent of all, to retire from the firm, and substitute other persons in their places, and the decease of a member works a dissolution of the firm; whereas, a joint-stock company consists of a large number of individuals not necessarily or indeed usually acquainted with each other at all, so that it is a matter of comparative indifference whether changes are made among them or not, and consequently the certificates and shares in such associations may be transferred at will, without the consent of other members, and the decease of a member does not work a dissolution of the association or entitle the personal representative to an accounting. In joint-stock companies there is no delectus personae."

In view of these fundamental distinctions between ordinary partnerships and joint-stock companies, in which class does the association with which we are dealing fall? The answer to this question is not entirely free from doubt. We cannot say that this association consisted of such a large number of individuals as to hold that it falls within the class of joint-stock companies. The articles of association limit the transferability of the shares of the members of the association. In the first place, a member desiring to withdraw from the business must give 60 days notice in writing of his intention to do so. In the second place, a member can only sell, transfer, and convey his interest in the bank to some individual, corporation, or firm who is acceptable to the finance committee in charge of said business, as a shareholder in the bank. Here the right of delectus personae is reserved to the members composing the association. In joint-stock companies the members have no right to decide what new members shall be admitted; on the other hand, the right of delectus personae is an inherent quality of an ordinary partnership. The provision that the shares shall be of the par value of $100, and that certificate shall be issued to the members, indicating the amount paid and the amount of interest that each subscriber has in the business of the bank, is not conclusive of the fact that the association is a joint-stock company. Such provision is consistent with the formation of a partnership. The shares are issued to indicate the amounts paid in by the members and the amount of interest the subscriber has in the bank. Of course, this provision can be looked to in determining the character of the association. Again, the provision that the business shall be conducted by a finance committee to be elected or appointed by the subscribers, and that each subscriber shall be entitled to one vote for each $100 or for each share paid in by him, does not conclusively establish the character of the association as a joint-stock company. It can be looked to in the solution of this question. All of the above provisions are consistent with the view that the association established by this agreement was a partnership and not a joint-stock company. The articles of association expressly declare that it is the purpose of the members signing the same to establish a partnership. Again, the articles of association declare that the committee appointed to conduct the business of the bank shall select a cashier and general manager who shall "be in charge of disbursing the funds belonging to the partnership hereby formed."

. . . We hold that under the articles of association a partnership was formed by the defendants for the purpose of conducting a banking business.

Having reached the conclusion that the association formed by the defendants under the articles of agreement constituted a partnership, we are next to consider the question whether the death of three of the members of the partnership dissolved it; these deaths occurring prior to the contraction of the debts upon which the plaintiffs sue in this case. Every partnership is dissolved by the death of one of the parties. A dissolution puts an end to all the powers and rights resulting from the partnership. As to third persons, it absolves the partners from all liability for future contracts and transactions, but not for transactions that are past. Civil Code 1910, § 3162, 3164. After dissolution, a partner has no power to bind the firm by a new contract, or to revive one already for any cause extinct, nor to renew or continue an existing liability. § 3188. When one of the partners dies, it is not necessary that notice should be given to third persons or to the world of the dissolution of the partnership. *Bass Dry Goods Co. v. Granite City Mfg. Co.*, 116 Ga. 177, 42 S.E. 415. The death of a partner supplies such notice. So, when the debts sued on in this case were contracted, the partnership doing business as the People's Bank had been dissolved by the death of several of its members; and members of the partnership who had no part in creating these debts could not be held liable by reason of their membership in the dissolved partnership.

Applying the principles above ruled, the trial judge did not err in granting a nonsuit as to all the defendants except M. W. Webb.

FIRST NATIONAL BANK v. CHARTIER et al.

1940, 305 Mass. 316, 25 N.E.2d 733

The plaintiff bank was the holder of a promissory note issued by the Textile Loan Company, a business trust. The bank brought this action against the fifty-seven certificate holders of the Textile Loan Company to hold them personally liable on the note. The lower court held that the defendants were not liable and the plaintiff appealed.

DONAHUE, J. . . . In order to pass upon the question of liability of the defendants upon the note given to the plaintiff, it is necessary to determine whether the relationship of the parties defendant was one of partnership, as the plaintiff contends, or whether they were merely beneficiaries under a trust, as some of the defendants suggest. As there was no formal trust deed or agreement of co-partnership, their relationship must be determined from the by-laws adopted, a copy of which was introduced in evidence by the plaintiff. If, under the by-laws the ultimate control of the affairs of the company was in the shareholders, and not in the directors or trustee, the relationship created was in the nature of a partnership, and not a trust.

. . . The by-laws of the Textile Loan Company contain provisions which in other similar cases have been held to indicate control in the shareholders over the affairs of such a company. In the present case the by-laws required that the officers and directors be elected by the shareholders annually for the term of one year. The shareholders had the right, for cause, to remove any officer and to expel any member, and to fill a vacancy occurring in any office.

. . . An annual meeting of the shareholders was required and a special meeting must be called on the written request of five shareholders.

The by-laws contained the provision that "These By-Laws may be altered, amended or repealed at any annual or special meeting of the stockholders duly called by the affirmative vote of two-thirds of the stockholders present, and voting thereon," if the proposed change was stated in the call for the meeting and the amendment had been recommended by a vote of the board of directors.

We think that under our decisions above cited the agreement of the parties as expressed in the by-laws, viewed as a whole, constituted the directors and the trustee agents of the company, but left in the shareholders the ultimate power of control of its affairs with the result that the relationship of partnership and not that of a trust was created. A provision in the by-laws that "no member shall be individually liable for debts" was not in itself sufficient to make the association a trust.

As the defendant members of the Textile Loan Company voluntarily adopted a form of agreement of association which created a partnership, their obligations as shareholders for the debts of the company must be determined by the rules of law applicable to ordinary partnerships.

Reversed.

COMMERCIAL CASUALTY INSURANCE CO. v. NORTH et al.

1943, 320 Ill. App. 221, 50 N.E.2d 434

The plaintiff brought this action against the defendants, who were the beneficiaries of a business trust in the construction business. The plaintiff had furnished a performance bond for the business trust and had been required to defend a legal action for an alleged breach of the construction contract. The plaintiff seeks to recover the expenses incurred in defending the suit. The lower court ruled in favor of the defendants and the plaintiff appealed.

Dove, J. . . . Appellant invokes the rule that when the beneficiaries of an alleged trust are given control over the management of the trust property, the so-called trust agreement, as a matter of law, creates a partnership.

. . . In *Schumann-Heink v. Folsom,* 328 Ill. 321, 327, 159 N.E. 250, 253, 58 A.L.R. 485, the court sets out in the opinion the well-established rule in such cases, in the following language: "There are also essential differences between a business trust and a partnership, but there are times when it is difficult to determine whether the declaration of trust relieves the trustees and shareholders from liability as partners. A partnership is, in effect, a contract of mutual agency, each partner acting as a principal in his own behalf and as agent for his copartner. Where, under the declaration of trust, the unit holders retain control over the trustees and have authority to control the management of the business the partnership relation exists. On the other hand, where the declaration of trust gives the trustees full control in the management of the business of the trust and the certificate holders are not associated in carrying on the business and have no control over the trustees, then there is no liability as partners."

We agree with the claim of appellees that the trust agreement in this case goes further than a positive vestiture of powers in the trustees, and negatives any right of control in the beneficiaries. After generally and in detail vesting complete control of the business and the property in the trustees, too voluminously set out to be repeated here, Paragraph Fourth (F) concludes with these words: "and the right of said Trustees to manage, control and administer the said trust estate shall be absolute and unconditional, free from the control or management of the Certificate Holders." And Paragraph Ninth (C) provides: "The ownership of interests hereunder shall not entitle the Certificate Holder to any title in or to the trust property whatsoever, or . . . for an accounting, or for any voice or control whatsoever of the trust property or of the management of said property or business connected therewith by the trustees."

. . . Our conclusion is that the trust agreement is valid, and appellees are not liable to appellant individually or as partners for any of the reasons urged. *Affirmed.*

PENNSYLVANIA CO. v. WALLACE et al.
1943, 346 Pa. 532, 31 A.2d 71

The plaintiff insurance company brought this action to recover from the defendants a deficiency judgment upon a bond given to secure a mortgage on real estate. The defendants are the trustees of the Lancaster Apartment Company, a Massachusetts trust, the mortgagor. The lower court ruled that the defendants were not liable and the plaintiff appealed.

MAXEY, C. J. . . . The issue resolves itself into a factual question: Did the insurance company when it entered into this contract know that the other party to the contract was a Massachusetts trust, the trust instrument of which provided that neither the trustees nor the certificate holders shall be personally liable on the obligations of the trust? The court below found from the evidence that it did.

. . . Nor is there any reason of public policy which makes it obligatory on the courts of Pennsylvania to refuse to recognize the fact that there are associations of individuals which are characterized as "Massachusetts trusts" and in which associations it is customary for the associates to agree that they will not be personally liable for the debts of the association. This agreement affects no third parties except those who deal with these associations "with their eyes open" and who either expressly or by clear implication agree that they will not hold the members of that association personally liable on the association's contracts. The legal nature of the dealings third persons have with such associations relate chiefly to the law of contracts. The members of such associations can by contract protect themselves against personal liability on the association's contracts exactly as can the members of a partnership.

9 American Jurisprudence at p. 296 states: "In the absence of a prohibitory or controlling statute, business trusts of the character known as 'Massachusetts' trusts, which carry on a business for profit in the interest and for the benefit of the certificate or shareholders, are, generally speaking, legal and valid. Business trusts as such are not against public policy." In *Hess et al. v. Werts*, 4 Serg. & R. 356, 361, Justice Gibson said: "I see no reason to doubt, but they (the members of an unincorporated banking association) may limit their responsibility, by an explicit stipulation, made with the party with whom they contract, and clearly understood by him at the time. . . ." See also *McCarthy v. Parker et al.*, 243 Mass. 465, 138 N.E. 8.

From the evidence in this record which we have cited and from other evidence which could pertinently be cited we are convinced that the court below was fully warranted in making the following findings of fact: "35. The New York Life Insurance Co. did not make said loan on the basis of the personal liability of the trustees, but impliedly agreed that the liability on said bond and mortgage was limited to the trust property."

Affirmed.

CHICAGO GRAIN TRIMMERS ASS'N v. MURPHY, DIRECTOR OF LABOR

1945, 389 Ill. 102, 58 N.E.2d 906

This is an action by the State of Illinois to collect an assessment made under the Unemployment Compensation Act against the Chicago Grain Trimmers Association. The Association was made up of several grain trimmers whose work consists of loading and unloading bulk grain in barges and ships, their secretary and treasurer making contracts with those desiring their services and dividing the income on the basis of the number of hours worked during the week by each member. For his services the secretary received a share of the income the same as the other members. The Association denies that the members are employed by them and has refused to pay the assessment.

SMITH, J. In a general sense, an association is a body of persons acting together, without a charter, for the prosecution of a common enterprise. . . . The term does not have, in law, a fixed meaning such as is accorded to partnerships or corporations, but is used to indicate a collection of persons who have joined together for a certain object. Our statute does not contain a definition of an association. It has, however, been defined in Vol. 1 *Bouv. Law Dict.* (p. 269) as persons uniting together for some purpose. Black's Law Dictionary defines "association" as the act of a number of persons who unite or join together for some special purpose or business: "the union of a company or business for the transaction of designated affairs or the attainment of some common object."

Some associations may be incorporated under applicable statutes, in which event they are legal entities having such attributes as the statute may give them. In the absence of a statute empowering it to do so, an unincorporated association having no legal existence independent of the members who compose it, is ordinarily incapable, as an organization, of taking or holding either real or personal property in its associate name. . . . In the absence of statutory authority, an unincorporated association has no capacity to enter into contracts in its associate name. However, the officer who makes such a contract and the members who assent to it may be personally bound. The dealing with an association as a legal entity may, under certain circumstances, cause it to be estopped from denying its right to contract. . . .

It is argued by appellee that the Chicago Grain Trimmers Association is engaged in a business for profit and must be treated as a legal entity and an employer under the Unemployment Compensation Act.

In the instant case the members of the association have only one source of income, and that is derived from the capacity of its members to labor. The association is not in business for the purpose of acquiring profit upon the use of the capital contributed by its members or upon the labor of its members. The obvious and real purpose of the common enterprise is to provide a practical means of disposing of the services of its members and of dividing the earnings of the working members. It appears grain trimming is an occupation which must be conducted by a group of men in order to satisfactorily handle a job. A shipowner requires the services of such a group only during the comparatively short interval necessary for the loading and unloading of a ship. In all probability it would be expensive or impracticable to continuously employ the number of grain trimmers necessary to load or unload the ship with reasonable dispatch. Thus from the very nature of the occupation it would appear some workable arrangement is necessary for the calling of the proper number of men at the proper times to effectually do the work.

We are of the opinion the association is not the employer of its members, but merely a convenient device for allocating work among its members in groups which can efficiently perform the various loading jobs as they present themselves, and which can in a convenient and practical manner divide the earnings of the members in accordance with their individual efforts.

Judgment for defendant.

STONE v. GUTH

1937 (Mo. App.) 102 S.W.2d 738

The business manager of the Associated Electrical Contractors, Inc., an association formed to combat an electrical workers union, brought action against a member of the association to recover for services rendered in the publication of a magazine which the association sponsored. Plaintiff's theory of the case was that the members of the association were partners.

SUTTON, C. A voluntary unincorporated association as recognized and defined in the books, strictly speaking, is neither a partnership nor a quasi partnership. The members thereof, whatever may be their relations and liability to third persons dealing with the association, are not partners *inter sese,* since the death or withdrawal of a member does not of necessity work a dissolution of the association, and there exists no authority in a single member to bind the others. . . .

It is broadly stated as a general rule that an unincorporated association organized for profit is in legal effect a mere partnership so far as the liability of members to third persons is concerned, and that accordingly each member is individually liable as a partner for all debts contracted by the association within the scope of its object. But an association not engaged in business enterprises and the objects of which do not contemplate profit and loss is not a partnership, and the liability of its members for debts contracted in behalf of the association is governed not by the principles of partnership but by those of agency. Membership as such imposes no personal liability for the debts of the association, but to charge a member therewith it must be shown that he has expressly or impliedly authorized or ratified the contract upon which the liability is predicated. As a rule nonparticipating members are not liable.

The association involved here is not a partnership. There is absolutely no evidence of an agreement among the members to share profits. The objects of the association do not contemplate profits. The sole function and purpose of the association is to regulate certain affairs of its individual members connected with and related to their individual business enterprises as affected by the demands of the electrical workers' union, and its principal purpose appears to have its source in the advisability of united action in opposition to the united action of the electrical workers' union.

Manifestly the plaintiff here failed to make out a submissible case against the Guth Company. It was a mere nonparticipating member of the association. It had nothing to do with the employment of the plaintiff. . . .

Judgment for defendant.

Review Questions and Problems

1. Ten doctors formed a limited partnership to operate a clinic. Dr. *A.* was the sole general partner. A contractor, *C*, was hired to construct a building for the clinic and was paid $9,000 in advance, but he failed to construct it. The partnership sued *C* for the money. *C* attempted to assert a counterclaim based on the fact that Dr. *X*, one of the ten, owed him that much for construction of a private cabin in the mountains. Will *C* be allowed to balance this claim against Dr. *X* over against the claim of the limited partnership to which Dr. *X* belongs?
2. A limited partnership was dissolved and the contribution of *A*, limited partner, was returned to him before the partnership creditors were paid. Is *A* obligated to restore the sum received in order to meet the claims of creditors?
3. A business trust agreement provided that the trustees would "consult" with an advisory committee of beneficiaries in connection with the operation of the trust. However, the trustees were not required to follow the advice of this committee. Would the beneficiaries be personally liable for debts of the trust?
4. A restriction was placed upon the transferability of the shares of *X* Company, a joint stock association. *A*, one of the shareholders, died. Would this bring about a dissolution of *X* Company?
5. *A*, *B*, and *C* invest money in a joint enterprise and place this money in the hands of certain trustees. From time to time they offer suggestions to the trustees and at times they elect new trustees. What are the liabilities of the investors?

6. *A, B, C, D, E, F, G,* and *H* form a reading club. *H,* the secretary, orders twenty books from a certain bookstore and charges them to the club. Under what conditions may the bookstore recover from the members of the club?
7. A labor union picketed a ship after an injunction had been issued. The ship owner sued in tort and obtained a judgment. May he collect it from the assets of the union if it is unincorporated?

BOOK VI

PERSONAL PROPERTY

41

Nature of Personal Property

6-1. Definition. Property is deemed to be any object, corporeal or incorporeal, capable of being reduced to exclusive possession. Property, for most purposes, is classified as either real or personal. Generally speaking, *real property* is considered to be land or anything permanently attached thereto. All other property is said to be *personal property*.

6-2. Types of personal property. There are three distinct kinds of personal property: chattels real, chattels personal in possession, and chattels personal in action. *Chattels real* are those interests in land that at one's death do not pass directly to the heirs, but pass first to the administrator or executor for administration, as provided for by law. Usually, leases of land for a period of years are considered chattels real.

Chattels personal in possession are those tangible and movable objects which may be transferred from hand to hand. This class of personal property is the kind with which most of us are quite familiar.

Chattels personal in action, often called "choses in action," include those things to which one has a right to possession, but concerning which it may be necessary to bring some legal action in order eventually to enjoy possession. Any contract action may be said to be a chose in action. The most common form of a chose in action is a negotiable instrument. It evidences a right to the money provided for therein, but it is possible that an action may have to be maintained to reduce the money to possession.

6-3. Methods of acquiring title. Title to personal property may be acquired through any of the following ways: original possession, transfer, accession, or confusion.

6-4. Original possession. Personal property which is in its native state and over which no one as yet has taken full and complete control belongs to the first person reducing such property to his exclusive possession. Although most property today may be said to belong definitely to someone, there are still some kinds of property, especially wild animals, fish, and other property of like kind, that are still available for appropriation by any individual. Property once reduced to ownership, but later discarded, belongs to the first party taking possession.[1]

In addition to the above, it might be said that property created through mental or physical labor belongs to the creator unless he has agreed to create it for someone else, being induced to do so because of some compensation that has been agreed to by the interested parties. Under this heading might be included such items as books, inventions, and trade-marks. This kind of property is usually protected by the government through means of copyrights, patents, and trade-marks.

6-5. Transfer. Property may be transferred through sale, gift, will, or operation of law. The law relating to a transfer by sale will be taken up in more detail in a subsequent chapter, as it forms an important branch of our law today. A transfer by gift may be made effective with the consent of the owner by an actual physical change in possession of the property. Normally, the gift is not complete until the change in possession has been effected. In the case of choses in action, the transfer of possession usually takes place by means of an assignment, the exception being negotiable instruments, which may be transferred either by assignment or by negotiation.

At a person's death, all his property, either real or personal, may be disposed of by will. The person taking personal property under the terms of a will is called a legatee, and the property is spoken of as a legacy or a bequest.

Where the deceased leaves no will, the property descends as provided by the laws of descent in the particular state involved. The laws of the different states vary greatly in this particular but operate to transfer intestate property to those persons stipulated in the law as being entitled to it. Foreclosure sale offers another illustration of transfer of title by operation of law.

In most cases of transfer of property, the transferee takes no better title than his transferor had. This is true even though the transferee believes that his transferor has a good title. Thus, an innocent purchaser from a thief obtains no title to the property purchased, and no subsequent purchaser stands in any better position. However, if the transferor of the property has a voidable title, and he sells the property to an innocent transferee, the transferee may obtain good title to the property. This topic is discussed in more detail under the heading "Voidable Title" in Chapter 41, "Sales."

6-6. Accession. *Accession*, taken literally, means "adding to." Property permanently added to other property and forming a minor portion of the finished product becomes part and parcel of the larger unit.[2] In such

[1] Huggins v. Reynolds, page 889.
[2] Eaton v. Munroe, page 890.

case, title automatically passes to the party holding title to the larger mass. This rule applies when the minor unit is stolen, as well as when it is purchased. The original owner may recover damages from the party who first converted the property to his own use, but may not recover the property. Another type of accession may arise when personal property owned by one person is increased in value by skill or material added by another. Generally, the increased value passes to the one who retains title to the raw material.

6-7. Accession to stolen property. An important problem arises where property wrongfully taken is greatly increased in value, after the taking, by the expenditure of labor and materials. In accordance with the law of the previous section, the benefit of such increase in value would pass to the one having title to the raw material. Such is not always the result arrived at by the courts. An increase in value by an intentional wrongdoer through the expenditure of labor and materials always passes to the true owner of the property, and he may successfully bring suit to reduce it to his possession, although the raw material has been enhanced in value many times.[3] A sale of the property in its improved state by the wrongdoer does not affect the right of the true owner. He may recover his property from the bona fide purchaser. The person who has wrongfully taken possession of personal property may never receive or pass title to it, regardless of how much he has increased its value.

Property purchased from a wrongdoer and increased in value by the bona fide purchaser follows a different rule. An innocent purchaser of stolen goods, who greatly increases the property in value by the expenditure of skill and materials, becomes liable to the true owner for the value of the goods in their original state only. In effect, title passes to the bona fide purchaser, provided he pays to the original owner the former value of the property. The original owner, however, may reclaim the property unless the bona fide purchaser has greatly increased its value—at least two or three times its original value.

An unintentional wrongdoer who greatly improves the value of the property wrongfully taken, if sued for the value of the property, is always liable for the original value of the property. If he has improved the value of the property to a great extent by the expenditure of skill and labor, the original owner may not replevin the article from him. There are a few courts, however, which seem to permit the original owner to recover the improved article.

6-8. Confusion. Property of such a character that one unit may not be distinguished from another unit and that is usually sold by weight or measure, is known as fungible property. Grain, hay, logs, wine, and other similar articles afford illustrations of property of this nature. Such prop-

[3] Sligo Furnace Co. v. Hobart-Lee Tie Co., page 890.

erty, belonging to various parties, often is mixed by intention of the parties, and occasionally by accident or by the misconduct of some wrongdoer. Confusion of fungible property belonging to various owners, assuming that no misconduct is involved, results in an undivided ownership of the total mass. To illustrate: grain is stored in a public warehouse by many parties. Each owner holds an undivided interest in the total mass, his particular interest being dependent upon the amount stored by him. Should there be a partial destruction of the total mass, the loss would be divided proportionately.

Confusion of goods which results from the fraudulent conduct of one of the parties causes the title to the total mass to pass temporarily to the innocent party. If the wrongdoer is unable to show that the resultant mass is equal in value per unit to that of the innocent party, he loses his interest in the resulting mass. Where the new mixture is worth no less per unit than that formerly belonging to the innocent party, the wrongdoer may claim his portion of the new mass by presenting convincing evidence of the amount added by him.

6-9. Abandoned and lost property. Property is said to be abandoned whenever it is discarded by the true owner, who, at that time, has no intention of reclaiming it. Such property belongs to the first individual again reducing it to possession.

Property is lost whenever, as a result of negligence, accident, or some other cause, it is found at some place other than that chosen by the owner. Title to lost property continues to rest with the true owner. Until the true owner has been ascertained, the finder may keep it, and his title is good as against everyone except the true owner.[4] The rights of the finder are superior to those of the person in charge of the property upon which the lost article is found. Occasionally, state statutes provide for newspaper publicity concerning articles which have been found. Under these statutes, if the owner cannot be located, the found property reverts to the state or county if its value exceeds an established minimum.

Mislaid or misplaced property is such as is intentionally placed by the owner at a certain spot in such a manner as to indicate that he merely forgot to pick it up. In such a case the presumption is that he will later remember where he left it and return for it. The owner of the premises upon which it is found is entitled to hold such property until the true owner is located.

6-10. Extent of ownership. Title to personal property may be held in common with others. Normally, in such a case, the owners are entitled to an equal use of the property or to their portion of the income derived from its use. In the event of the death of one of the co-owners, his share in the property passes to the executor or administrator of his estate.

[4] Hamaker v. Blanchard, page 891.

Under the laws of many states, personal property, as well as real estate, may be held in joint tenancy.[5] The interest of a deceased owner passes automatically to his joint owner without the necessity of probate. Because of this fact, husband and wife in many cases hold personal property jointly in order to avoid the expense of administration of an estate in the event of the death of either. Joint tenancy of personal property does not arise unless a contract between the co-owners states clearly that such is the case and that the right of survivorship is to apply.

NATURE OF PERSONAL PROPERTY CASES

HUGGINS v. REYNOLDS

1908, 51 Tex. Civ. App. 504, 112 S.W. 116

Connor, C. J. Appellee (Reynolds) was a tenant of appellant, and instituted suit, in the justice court, upon an account aggregating $96. Among other items specified was one of $40 for three fourths of two bales of cotton less cost of picking. . . . Appellee's lease terminated January 1, 1907, and appellant Huggins testified, in substance, that, on or about the 15th day of January, 1907, he went to see appellee, who had then removed from the witness' place, in order to get the unobstructed use of the rented premises for pasturage, and that appellee then directed him "to go ahead and turn in, that he (appellee) was not going to pick any more cotton"; that it was after this that appellant caused to be picked and sold the cotton, the proceeds of which was sued for in this case.

It seems to be well settled in the authorities that a party may abandon and relinquish his right to property. If the owner sees proper to abandon his property, and evidences his intention by an act legally sufficient to vest or divest ownership, why may he not do so? In *McGoon v. Ankeny*, 11 Ill. 558, it is said, quoting from the headnote: "A party considering an article entirely worthless casts it away, intending to abandon it; he loses his title to it." And on the same subject, the case of *Wyman v. Hurlburt*, 12 Ohio 81, 40 Am. Dec. 461, the Supreme Court of Ohio says, again quoting from the headnote: "abandonment of property divests the owner of his title therein, and the finder who reduces the same to possession after such abandonment is not guilty of conversion. . . ." So that it would seem that appellant would not be liable for the "three fourths of two bales of cotton," for which appellee sued, if he in fact, as appellant in substance testified, wholly abandoned it.

Judgment for defendant.

[5] Park Enterprises, Inc. v. Trach et al., page 892.

EATON v. MUNROE
1862, 52 Me. 63

WALTON, J. This is an action (by Eaton) of replevin. It appears from the evidence that the plaintiff let one Hall have canvas for the foresail of a gondola; that Hall procured the sail to be made at an expense of about ten dollars for labor, and from five to eight dollars for materials; that the canvas cost $40.63; that it was agreed the plaintiff should own the sail; and that it should remain his property till paid for; that Hall never paid for the sail, but afterwards sold it to one Chase, and that Chase sold it to the defendant.

The defendant contends that the plaintiff acquired no property in the materials furnished by Hall; that, inasmuch as the plaintiff consented that his canvas should be inseparably connected with Hall's property, and the plaintiff cannot now hold what was his own, without also holding what was the property of Hall, the action cannot be maintained.

But we are of the opinion that the action can be maintained. . . . If this was not sufficient for the purpose, we think the plaintiff became the owner of the materials furnished by Hall, upon the principle of accession. Title by accession applies not only to what is produced by one's own property, as the increase of animals, but also to that which is united to it, either naturally or artificially.

In *Pulsifer v. Page,* 32 Me. 404, this court held that a right of property, by accession, may occur when materials belonging to several persons are united by labor into a single article; and that the ownership of an article, so formed, is in the party, if such there be, to whom the principal part of the materials belonged. In respect to the sail, it is clear the canvas formed the principal part of it, and the plaintiff being the owner of the canvas, he would, within the authority of this case, be the owner of the sail when it was completed.

Judgment for plaintiff.

SLIGO FURNACE CO. v. HOBART-LEE TIE CO.
1911, 153 Mo. App. 442, 134 S.W. 585

Action by Sligo Furnace Company to recover the value of certain railroad ties alleged to have been converted. The evidence was conflicting as to whether defendant was a wilful or an unintentional trespasser. The court finally found that he was a wilful trespasser.

COX, J. Appellant insists, first, that the measure of damages was the value of the ties regardless of the question of good faith in cutting them from plaintiff's land. . . .

In our judgment the true rule for fixing the measure of damages is that, if the timber was taken by honest mistake, then the value of the timber before being cut is the measure of damages, but if the party taking the timber knew he had no right to it, and thus became a wilful trespasser in the first instance, then in a suit against him the measure of damages is the value of the timber in its improved condition without reduction for labor bestowed, or expense incurred by the wrongdoer. . . .

The law is not only careful to compensate the owner for the loss of his property, but it is also careful to see that a wilful wrongdoer shall not profit by his own wrong, and by requiring him to respond in damages for the value of the property in its improved state both these purposes are accomplished. To fix the measure of damages at the value of the property in its improved condition when the party had taken it by honest mistake would be as harsh as to fix it at the value in the tree when taken by a wilful trespasser would be unjust. In the former case, the owner would be profiting by the labor of an honest man mistakenly bestowed upon his property, and in the latter case, a wilful trespasser would be profiting by his wrong. . . .

It is conceded by all the authorities that in the case of a wilful trespasser the owner may follow and retake the property in his hands notwithstanding it may have been largely increased in value by the labor of the trespasser. . . .

Judgment for plaintiff.

HAMAKER v. BLANCHARD

1879, 90 Pa. St. 377, 35 Am. Rep. 664

Sophia Blanchard, plaintiff, was a domestic servant in a hotel of which defendant Hamaker was the proprietor. She found in the public parlor three twenty-dollar bills. She handed them to defendant upon his assumption that they belonged to a certain transient guest. They did not, but defendant refused to surrender them.

Trunkey, J. It seems to be settled law that the finder of lost property has a valid claim to the same against all the world, except the true owner, and generally that the place in which it is found creates no exception to this rule. But property is not lost in the sense of the rule, if it was intentionally laid on a table, counter, or other place, by the owner, who forgot to take it away. . . . Whenever the surroundings evidence that the article was deposited in its place, the finder has no right of possession against the owner of the building. . . .

An article casually dropped is within the (lost property) rule. Where one went into a shop, and as he was leaving picked up a parcel of bank notes, which was lying on the floor, and immediately showed them to the shopman, it was held that the facts did not warrant the supposition that the notes had been deposited there voluntarily, they being manifestly lost by some one, and there was no circumstance in the case to take it out of the general rule of law, that the finder of a lost article is entitled to it as against all persons, except the real owner. *Bridges v. Hawksworth*, 7 Eng. L. & Eq. R. 424. . . .

When money is found in his house, on the floor of a room common to all classes of persons, no presumption of ownership arises; the case is like the finding upon the floor of a shop. . . . If the finder be an honest woman, who immediately informs her employer, and gives him the article on his false pretense that he knows the owner and will restore it, she is entitled to have it back and hold it till the owner comes.

Judgment for plaintiff.

PARK ENTERPRISES, INC. v. TRACH et al.

1951, (Minn.) 47 N.W.2d 194

LORING, C. J. In this case plaintiff, Park Enterprises, Inc., sued defendant, Benedict B. Trach, in the municipal court of Minneapolis to enforce payment of rent under an oral lease between the parties. In proceedings ancillary to this action, plaintiff garnisheed a joint bank account standing in the name of defendant and his wife, Dorothy Trach. Mrs. Trach was permitted to intervene in the garnishment proceedings. The Northwestern National Bank of Minneapolis is the garnishee.

Plaintiff obtained a default judgment for $143.45 against defendant in the main action. . . .

The facts as stipulated are as follows: At the time the garnishment summons was served, defendant and intervener had a "joint bank account" with the garnishee in which the deposit credit was $327.38. This account was opened and maintained subject to the following terms and conditions, which are printed on the reverse side of a joint account signature card:

"The account listed on the reverse side hereof is a joint and several account. All funds now or hereafter deposited in said account by either or any of the depositors shall be the property of the depositors jointly with the right of survivorship. Each depositor shall have complete and absolute authority over said account during the joint lives of the depositors and may withdraw all or any part of such funds on checks or other withdrawal orders signed by either or any of the depositors and by the survivor or survivors in case of death of any thereof."

Defendant and intervener had independent incomes. Each of them, from time to time, has deposited portions of his or her individual funds to the credit of this joint account and from time to time has withdrawn funds from the account for family or individual purposes. It is impossible to determine on an evidentiary basis the exact amount of funds each of them has contributed to the joint account.

The trial court made findings in conformity with the facts stipulated, and, having concluded that defendant and intervener should be presumed equal owners of the garnisheed account in the absence of proof establishing the amount each has contributed to it, ordered judgment against the garnishee for $143.45, together with interest and costs, the entire judgment not to exceed $163.69, that being one-half the joint account. Judgment was entered accordingly.

Intervener's sole allegation and claim in the garnishment proceeding is that she and defendant are joint owners of the garnisheed bank account, and therefore that the account is not garnishable for defendant's individual debt to plaintiff. Defendant's contentions are the same as those of intervener. These contentions having been rejected by trial court, defendant and intervener have appealed from the judgment against the garnishee.

This type of account is difficult, if not impossible, to classify under traditional categories of legal ownership. The account is distinguished from a joint tenancy because of the fact that it is joint and several, whereas in a joint tenancy there is joint ownership only.[6] The survivorship feature of the account readily distinguishes it from a tenancy in common, and is not sufficient alone to make it a joint tenancy. "Joint and several," when used to designate a type of ownership, is somewhat of a legal anomaly notwithstanding that the term appears in M.S.A. § 48.30. By definition several ownership is a denial of joint ownership. Since the type of ownership which the bank and its depositors have created by their contract defies classification under traditional concepts of property ownership, we are forced to treat this case as presenting a contract question and must decide what the incidents of this type of ownership are primarily by reference to the terms of the contract creating it.

By the deposit agreement here involved, each depositor has given the other depositor in the account complete and absolute authority to withdraw all or any part of the account. By the terms of the agreement, the bank is likewise obliged to pay any part or all of the account to either depositor upon demand.

Since in purpose and legal effect a garnishment proceeding is virtually an action brought by defendant in plaintiff's name against the garnishee, resulting in the subrogation of the plaintiff to the right of the defendant against the garnishee, we have concluded that plaintiff here may not only garnishee this joint account, but also that it would be entitled to recover judgment against the garnishee for the entire amount of the account if its

[6] It is well settled that a joint tenancy is characterized by the four unities of time, title, interest, and possession, and if any of these elements is lacking the estate is a tenancy in common.

judgment against the defendant were sufficient to exhaust it. Defendant is entitled to withdraw any part or all of the account, and plaintiff, in effect is subrogated to that right. . . .

The peculiar features of a joint bank account, such as this case presents, makes it difficult, if not impossible, in most cases, to determine what portion of the account belongs to each depositor. A long series of deposits which cannot be traced to their source, and a similar series of withdrawals which cannot be traced to their destination, are normally involved. This defect is inherent in the severalty feature of such bank accounts wherein each depositor is allowed to treat joint property as if it were entirely his own. Like any loose system of dealing with money, joint bank accounts sacrifice precision to convenience and becloud the respective rights of the depositors. The courts should not encourage parties to do their bookkeeping in court when, by their private contract, they have virtually declared that they do not wish to be inconvenienced by any strict accountability as between themselves. A joint bank account of this kind is a creature of contract between parties avowedly indifferent to the exact percentage of ownership between themselves. The law should take them at their word and give effect to their contract without making detailed and belated evidentiary inquiries to establish factual ownership. Any presumption, whether conclusive or rebuttable, that part or all of these joint accounts are immune from garnishment has the effect of either creating or tending to create a nonstatutory exemption for the parties using them, and any attempt to base the extent of garnishment upon the respective amounts of the account owned by each depositor will compel courts and juries to grope with problems which the depositors themselves have declared to be of no consequence. Let them abide the results which flow from their own declared purposes.

Although the trial court's order limiting judgment against the garnishee is erroneous so far as it limits judgment against the garnishee to one-half the account, plaintiff has not complained of the error in this proceeding, and we accordingly affirm the judgment entered pursuant to the trial court's order.

Affirmed.

Review Questions and Problems

1. *A*, a farmer, learns that another party killed a number of rabbits which were running at large upon his farm. To whom do the rabbits belong?
2. *A* desires to present an automobile to his son, and, on January 1, he purchases and delivers a car to the son, telling him that it is a belated Christmas gift. Shortly thereafter, the father demands the car. Is the father entitled to it?
3. *A* installed a replacement motor in *B*'s automobile. *C* had sold the automobile to *B*, but *B* had not paid *C* in full. In the event that *C*

should reclaim the automobile from *B*—which he has a right to do under the sales contract for nonpayment of the purchase price—does *C* or *A* have a better right to the new motor?

4. *A* owned a farm, a house in the city, and a bank account. He died without making a will. A sister and two sons survived him. Who should get the property?
5. *A* intentionally took corn belonging to *B* and distilled it into whisky. *B* had the sheriff seize the whisky, but *A* contends that the whisky belongs to him because of the great increase in its value. Is *A* correct?
6. What is *fungible* property? *A* owns some lumber which he fraudulently mixes with lumber owned by *B*. The quality of the two piles of lumber was entirely different, but the contents of the two amounts cannot now be distinguished. May *B* retain title to both amounts?
7. *O* gave *M* a chattel mortgage on certain sheep as security for an indebtedness, but *O* later commingled the sheep with other sheep that he owned. Since *O* is in default, *M* seeks to foreclose, and *O* insists that *M* must identify the particular sheep that have been mortgaged. Is *O* correct?
8. *A*, employed by *P* Hotel Company to paint certain rooms, lifted a rug and found $750 in old bills. Being told by the hotel that the owner was known, he surrendered the money to *P* Company. The hotel was unable to locate the owner, and *A* demands the money. Is he entitled to it?

42

Sales Noncode States

TRANSFER OF TITLE

6-11. Introduction. Many of the legal difficulties of the average businessman revolve around the sale and purchase of merchandise. The legal relations concerning these activities are largely controlled by the law of sales. A contract to sell personal property, like all other agreements, must satisfy the requisites for a binding contract. There must be offer and acceptance, consideration, competent parties, and legal object. Contracts for the sale of personal property of a certain value come within the provisions of the Statute of Frauds. (For discussion of the Statute of Frauds, see Book Two on "Contracts.") In addition, there is a special body of legal rules concerned with the sale of personal property, known as the law of sales, which forms a specialized branch of the law of contracts. Many of the terms of a contract for the sale of merchandise are implied rather than expressed, and most of the states have codified applicable rules of law by adoption of the Uniform Sales Act. The rules as found in this act form the basis for most of the discussion in this chapter.

6-12. Distinction between contract "to sell" and contracts "of sale." The risk of possible loss brought about by the theft or destruction of property, the rights of creditors of buyer or seller, and the rights of buyer and seller as between themselves, often depend upon whether or not title to goods that are the subject matter of sale has passed from seller to buyer at the time the issue is raised. An agreement *to sell* evinces an intention to transfer title to personal property at some subsequent date. A contract *of sale* has for its purpose the present transfer of title to the property in question. Only property that is in existence and title to which rests with the seller may be the subject of a present sale. On the other hand, a contract to sell may relate to property not yet in existence or to property the title to which is possessed by some third party. The undertaking in such a case is that of bringing the property into existence or of acquiring title prior to the date set for delivery. Any attempt to transfer present title to such property is, at best, an agreement to sell rather than a sale. Property not yet owned by the seller is often known as *future goods.*

6-13. Risk of loss. Normally, the risk of loss as related to personal property rests with the person holding title, although it is possible in a contract of sale to stipulate that risk of loss shall rest with the seller until delivery takes place, even though title may have passed earlier. It is also possible, in a contract to sell, to provide that the risk of loss shall be borne by the buyer prior to the time when title is to pass. In most instances, however, title is the decisive factor in determining where the loss shall fall.[1]

A default in meeting contract terms may shift the loss from the one normally expected to bear it to the person in default. Thus, in a contract *of sale,* a delay in delivery beyond the time provided for in the contract because of the fault of the seller, and which makes the loss possible, often causes the loss to fall upon the seller. Similarly, in a contract to *sell,* any unreasonable delay on the part of the buyer in giving shipping instructions may result in his absorbing the loss.

Where goods that form the basis of a contract to sell, as differentiated from a contract of sale, are only partially destroyed before title has passed, the buyer has an option of accepting the balance of the goods or of rescinding the agreement. If he elects to receive the portion of the goods that remains, he must pay the full contract price, unless they are sold by number, weight, or measure. In the latter case, he pays only the unit price established in the agreement. In this situation, the same rules would apply if this were a contract of sale, except for the fact that the goods would have been partially destroyed prior to the time the contract was made.

As was indicated earlier in the study of contracts, the destruction of the particular thing that is to be sold relieves the seller of his duty to perform, whereas the destruction of goods out of which he expects to make delivery—or the destruction of the source from which he usually obtains his supply—merely makes the contract more burdensome for the seller to perform. Failure on his part to deliver in the latter case constitutes a breach of contract.

To illustrate: *A* contracts to sell to *B* a certain used speedboat for $800. The boat is destroyed by fire prior to the date set for delivery and passage of title. The loss falls upon *A,* but he is relieved of his duty to deliver the boat. If we assume that, instead of a boat, *A* agrees to deliver 500 bushels of apples at $1 a bushel, he is not relieved of his duty to perform even though the apples in his orchard are all destroyed by an early freeze. If he fails to provide apples from some other source, he is liable to pay such damages as *B* suffers as a result of the breach.

[1] Miller v. Seaman et al., page 906.

6-14. Title passes according to intention of parties. Title to personal property that is the basis of a sale, passes from seller to buyer at the time intended by the parties.[2] If the agreement either states or clearly implies at what time title is to pass, the terms of the agreement govern. In the absence in the agreement of any stipulation to the contrary, or of any conduct that indicates a contrary intention on the part of the parties, title passes in accordance with the rules set forth in the sections that follow.

6-15. Cash sales. Contracts that call for delivery and payment to take place as concurrent acts are usually called cash sales and indicate an intention that title shall not pass until the goods are paid for and delivery takes place.

In those cases in which a check or draft is offered in payment of goods obtained under a cash sale, the check or draft is usually accepted as conditional payment only, and if the check fails to clear at the bank or if the drawee of the draft fails to honor it, the buyer obtains only a voidable title to the goods. The seller may demand the return of the goods from the buyer but may not repossess them from an innocent purchaser who has obtained them from the buyer.

6-16. Sale on trial. When goods are delivered to the buyer on approval, trial, or other similar terms, title remains in the seller until the buyer evidences in some manner an intention to adopt the transaction. This intention may be evidenced by express notice to the seller, or by any conduct which indicates an acceptance of the goods. Retention of the goods beyond a reasonable time or beyond the time established by the agreement indicates an intention to keep the property.

A sale on trial must be distinguished from a transaction in which goods are delivered "on sale and return." Whenever the agreement indicates an intention to make a present sale, but also gives the buyer an option to return the goods, title passes with a right on the part of the buyer to revest title in the seller by returning or tendering the goods. Such return or tender must take place within a reasonable time, provided that no limit has been prescribed in the contract.

Ascertained goods. An unconditional contract to sell specific goods in a deliverable state passes title to the property at the time of the agreement. In other words, where the specific articles to be delivered are identified, the goods are said to be ascertained. In such a case, articles of like kind cannot be substituted; the particular goods upon which the minds of the parties met are to be delivered. Under such circumstances, title

[2] Plummer v. Kingsley, page 907.

passes at the time the contract is formed. The fact that the date of delivery or payment is postponed beyond the time of the agreement does not delay the passing of title.

Where ascertained goods form the basis of a sale and the seller is to do something to them for the purpose of putting them in a deliverable condition, title does not pass until such thing is done. Thus, if he is to repair, measure, or weigh the property, the title passes only after he has completed his task.

6-17. Fungible goods. Fungible goods are those that are sold, not by the individual unit, but by weight or measure—goods in which one unit is like any other unit. A sale of a certain quantity of fungible goods passes title at the time of the agreement to an undivided interest in the total mass, if the particular mass out of which it is to be delivered has been agreed upon. However, if the seller is to weigh, sack, or do something to the goods to place them in a deliverable condition, title passes only after he has completed his work.

6-18. Unascertained goods. A contract to sell unascertained or future goods by description or sample causes title to pass only when goods corresponding to the description or sample have been unconditionally appropriated to the contract by one of the parties with the assent of the other. Title passes whenever the seller appropriates specific property with the assent of the buyer, or when the buyer appropriates it with the assent of the seller. The assent may be either express or implied and may be given either before or after the appropriation. Both the appropriation and the assent must combine, however, to pass title.

6-19. Delivery to carrier. Delivery of goods to a carrier for the purpose of transmission to the buyer or to some bailee of the buyer constitutes an appropriation of the goods by the seller. If the contract to sell requires the seller to deliver the goods to a certain destination or to pay the delivery charges, the title does not pass until the goods have been delivered. If the buyer is to pay delivery charges, title passes as soon as the goods are delivered to the carrier.

Title does not pass unless the goods shipped correspond in both quality and quantity to those ordered. If those delivered to the carrier are not of the kind or the amount ordered, the buyer is not required to accept them. Therefore, any loss arising during their carriage must be borne by the seller. Likewise, failure to follow shipping instructions given by the buyer or, in the absence of any, to make the customary contract for the protection of the buyer, shifts the risk of loss during transit to the seller.

6-20. C.O.D. shipments. The mere fact that goods are shipped C.O.D., which, taken literally, means cash on delivery, does not affect passing of title. Such a provision in the bill of lading merely indicates that the shipper is retaining a lien and the right to possess the goods until payment is made. Title passes to the buyer, if he is to pay transportation charges, at the time the goods are received by the carrier; but the seller reserves a lien, evidenced by his right to possession, until the price is paid by the buyer.

When goods are shipped under a bill of lading denoting that the goods are to be delivered to the seller or his order, the seller retains title. But if, except for the form of the bill of lading, title would have passed to the buyer, it is presumed that title is retained for security only, and the risk of loss is carried by the buyer from the moment the goods are delivered to the carrier. Since title is reserved for security only, it passes to the buyer when he obtains the order bill of lading properly indorsed. The bill of lading is usually accompanied by a draft or bill of exchange, drawn by the seller on the buyer, both being sent to a bank or other agent of the seller. After the buyer accepts or pays the draft or bill, the buyer receives the bill of lading. When the order bill of lading, properly indorsed, is sent by the seller directly to the buyer along with a bill of exchange for his acceptance or payment, he obtains no right or title to the goods until acceptance or payment. However, a third party who—in good faith—purchases from the buyer the bill of lading or goods, obtains good title, although the original buyer's title was defective.

To illustrate these rules, let us assume that *A* ships *B* goods on an order bill of lading which designates *A* as consignee. *A* mails the bill of lading, indorsed in blank, to *B*'s bank, accompanied by a bill of exchange drawn on *B* for $500, payable at sight. The agreement calls for payment of the freight by *B*. If the goods are damaged in shipment by some act of God, the loss must be borne by *B*, since title is retained as security only.

6-21. Voidable title. Where the seller has a title that may be voided by some third party, the buyer acquires a good title to the property, provided he purchases it in good faith without knowledge of the right of the third party. Thus, a party who has a right to rescind an agreement because of fraud has no right to do so after his buyer has resold the property to an innocent purchaser.

In addition, a seller who sells goods, but retains possession of them, and then resells, delivers, and receives payment therefor from an innocent third party who does not know of the previous sale, passes good title to the third person. The buyer who obtains title to property but leaves it in the possession of the seller makes it possible for the seller to perpetrate a fraud. In the event of such misconduct, any loss must be suffered by the original buyer, unless he can recover from the seller.

WARRANTIES

6-22. Express warranty. A warranty is an affirmation of fact or a promise by the seller, relating to the goods, which acts as an inducement for the buyer to purchase.[3] Warranties are of two kinds: express and implied. An express warranty is one which becomes part of the sale agreement because of a direct statement or promise made by the seller; an implied warranty attaches itself to the contract by reason of the nature of the agreement.

Two distinct factors combine to bring about an express warranty. First, the seller must make a statement of fact or a promise of future conduct concerning the property sold; second, the statement or promise must be such as to induce, in some measure, the buyer to act. Statements of fact should be clearly distinguished from statement of opinion. Any representation qualified by "I think" or "I believe" clearly expresses an opinion and does not form any part of a warranty. Statements referring to the value of an article are usually considered matters of opinion. Ideas concerning the value of property must necessarily vary with the individual. Any reference to the quality of the article, however, is usually considered a statement of fact.

Any conduct on the part of the buyer which indicates that he is relying on his own judgment or investigation rather than on the statement of the seller negatives the idea of a warranty. Furthermore, any general statement made by the seller, where the property is available and is being inspected by the parties does not cover obvious defects. Thus, *A* sold *B* a horse, the horse being present and subject to inspection at the time of the sale. *A* made a statement that the horse was sound "in every particular." It was held that the statement did not operate as a warranty against blindness, which was apparent to anyone upon casual inspection.

6-23. Implied warranty of title. The seller of personal property warrants, as an implied term of his contract of sale, that he has the right to sell and that no one having a paramount title will interfere with the quiet enjoyment of the property by the buyer. In addition, he warrants that the property is free from all liens, except those of which the buyer has knowledge.[4] If the agreement be one to sell rather than one of sale, he warrants that he will have title to the specified property before the time it is to be transferred.

[3] Logue et al. v. Hill, page 909.
[4] Ward v. Hickerson, page 910.

6-24. Warranty of fitness for a particular purpose. Where the buyer expressly or impliedly indicates to the seller the particular purpose for which he desires the goods and relies upon the skill or judgment of the seller, there arises an implied warranty that the goods will prove fit for the purpose. In such instances it is presumed that the seller is more familiar than the buyer with the results to be obtained from the use of particular property. Property purchased by its trade or patent name carries with it no implied warranty of fitness for a particular purpose since it is plain the buyer relies upon his own judgment and not that of the seller.

6-25. Warranty that goods are merchantable. A sale of goods by sample or description usually carries an implied warranty that they shall be merchantable. Goods are merchantable whenever they are free from hidden defects and are fit for the use to which they are ordinarily placed.[5] When goods are inspected by the buyer, there is no implied warranty against defects which the examination should have revealed. However, a warranty arises against defects which are hidden and not apparent upon an examination of the goods.

At one time, only the grower, packer, or manufacturer warranted goods to be merchantable. The Uniform Act has broadened the rule so that it includes anyone regularly engaged in selling such goods. Thus, the warranty of merchantability forms an implied part of all sales, except casual sales made by people not regularly engaged in selling the articles involved.

Implied warranties, as well as express warranties, may be provided against in the contract of sale. Waiver of implied warranties must be clearly expressed to be effective. A statement that only those warranties written into the contract shall attach to a sale does not have the effect of eliminating the implied warranties, more definite language being required to attain that end.

In addition to being merchantable, goods ordered by sample must conform to the sample. Where ordered by both sample and description, the goods must correspond to the description as well as to the sample. It is not enough for the bulk of them to be like the sample; compliance with the description is also necessary.

6-26. Extent of implied warranties. Warranties associated with a contract of sale are usually applicable only between the seller and the buyer.[6] Purchasers from the buyer have no contractual agreement with the original seller, and warranties are normally dependent upon there

[5] Ryan v. Progressive Grocery Stores, Inc., page 911.
[6] Smith v. Ford Motor Company, page 912.

being privity of contract between the parties involved. Thus, when a consumer purchases an article from a retailer, and a hidden defect in that article then appears, the consumer has no right of recovery against the manufacturer, packer, or grower. The only recourse of the consumer is to look to the retailer upon express or implied warranties.

There is one generally recognized exception to the rule just stated. If the article or product sold is one that, if defective, would prove dangerous to human life while being used in the normal way, many courts permit the ultimate consumer to recover from the manufacturer, packer, or grower, as well as from the retailer. This exception is most usually applied in cases where the product sold consists of food, beverages, or drug preparations, although some decided cases involve other products. Different theories have been used in permitting such recovery. Many courts permit recovery in tort based upon negligence in the preparation of the product. Other courts take the position that warranties, express or implied, extend to the consumer irrespective of privity of contract. This theory appears frequently, especially in the more recent decisions. In effect, this means that the warranty runs with the goods. Other theories have been resorted to at times to reach the same result.[7]

REMEDIES

6-27. Remedies of seller where buyer refuses delivery. Whenever the seller properly performs by tendering delivery of the quality and quantity of goods ordered by sample or description, he is entitled to have the purchaser accept the goods and make payment. Delivery and payment are presumed to take place contemporaneously unless a different time for payment has been provided in the agreement. A refusal by the buyer to accept the goods and to pay for them gives a seller a right to recover damages only. His damages are dependent upon the correct market price of the goods at the time of the buyer's refusal. In case the agreement relates to goods for which there is no available market, a tender of delivery gives to the seller a right to recover the full contract price. This rule applies particularly to goods manufactured especially for the buyer.

Where title has passed to the buyer before delivery, as in the case of ascertained goods, and he refuses to pay, action may be maintained for the full purchase price. The same remedy is also available where the buyer, regardless of delivery or the passing of title, is to make payment at a certain time, and the buyer wrongfully does not make payment.

[7] Swift & Co. v. Wells, page 914.

6-28. Unpaid seller's lien. The unpaid seller of goods, who is in possession of the goods although title may have passed to the buyer, is entitled to retain possession, under a lien, until payment of the purchase price where the goods are to be paid for when delivered; the period of credit has expired; or the buyer has become insolvent. In other words, the unpaid seller has a lien upon the goods until such time as they are delivered or paid for unless the period of credit previously agreed upon has not expired. The unpaid seller who has delivered a part of the goods called for by the contract, may maintain his lien on the undelivered portion of the goods remaining in his possession, unless his action in making partial delivery indicates that he is giving up his lien on all the goods.

Insolvency as used in the law of sales means the inability of the buyer to meet his current demands as they fall due. Failure of the debtor to satisfy his obligations in the ordinary course of business makes him insolvent and gives a seller the right to invoke an unpaid seller's lien or to stop goods in transit.

6-29. Stoppage in transitu. An unpaid seller who has parted with possession of the goods to some transportation agency may, in the event of the insolvency of the buyer, stop the goods in transit, even though title may have passed to the buyer. The insolvency of the buyer gives the seller a right to demand a return of the goods as long as they have not been delivered to the buyer. He must, however, pay the necessary transportation charges to the carrier. As long as the carrier is still in possession, unless it has wrongfully refused delivery or holds the goods in storage under a subsequent agreement with the buyer, the seller's right to demand a return of the goods continues.

Notice must be given to the carrier in ample time so that the carrier may, by the use of reasonable diligence, communicate with its agent in charge of the goods. Delivery of the goods to the buyer, before notice can reach the agent in charge, terminates the lien of the seller.

6-30. Right of resale. The unpaid seller who has a lien upon the goods is entitled to resell them within a reasonable time after the buyer has been in default in payment of the purchase price. If the goods are of a perishable nature, the right to resell arises immediately upon the default of the buyer. The seller is under no duty to notify the buyer of his intention to resell, although a failure to give notice is relevant in determining whether a reasonable time elapsed prior to the resale. If a loss results from the resale, the buyer must make good the loss, but if a profit results, the seller is under no obligation to account to the buyer for it.

If the buyer has been in default for an unreasonable time, the seller may, instead of reselling the property, merely rescind and look to the buyer for any damages suffered. Rescission will not be considered as having taken place unless he has given notice to the buyer or has in some other way definitely indicated his intention to rescind.

Once delivery of the goods has been made to the buyer, the only remedy of the unpaid seller is to bring suit for the purchase price. He may not rescind and demand the return of the property.

6-31. Remedies of the buyer. Where title to the goods has passed to the buyer, and the seller wrongfully neglects or refuses to deliver the goods, the buyer may bring suit to recover damages resulting from conversion, or initiate an action of replevin to gain possession of the property.[8] If the agreement consists of a mere contract to sell unascertained goods and the seller defaults, the buyer may bring suit for damages. In the absence of extenuating circumstances showing special damages, the buyer is limited in his recovery to the difference between the current market price and the price which he has agreed to pay.

Remedies for breach of warranty. Any warranty made by the seller that proves to be false gives to the buyer a choice of four remedies. He may accept or keep the goods and set up the breach of warranty as a partial extinction of the purchase price, or he may accept or keep the goods and recover for the damages sustained. He may refuse to accept the goods where title has not passed and maintain an action against the seller for damages arising from the breach of warranty; or he may rescind the agreement, and, if the goods have been delivered, return them and recover any part of the purchase price which has been paid.

6-32. Inspection of goods. Upon receipt of goods the buyer has the right to inspect them before acceptance. If the inspection discloses that they do not conform to the description, sample, or warranties, or that the quantity is greater or less than ordered, the buyer may reject the property. An acceptance of the goods by the buyer, after an inspection has revealed a defect of some character, constitutes a waiver of the right to rescind and limits the buyer to his remedy for damages. Thus, if *A* orders from *B* a gross of cut-glass tumblers which are described as having certain markings, and those received have entirely different markings, the buyer may either return them, or keep them and deduct from the purchase price the damages occasioned by the breach.

If the buyer accepts or retains a shipment of goods containing less than the amount ordered, when he knows the seller does not expect to ship the balance, he is obligated to pay at the contract rate. For those goods received and used or disposed of before it is known that the seller does not expect to perform in full, the buyer is obligated to pay only for their reasonable value to him. The buyer who receives more than he has or-

[8] Abraham v. Karger, page 916.

dered may accept the correct amount and reject the excess, or he may accept the full amount, in the latter case being liable for all at the contract rate. These rules relating to under- and over-contract shipments, however, are subject to trade custom or previous dealings between the parties.

The buyer has no right to inspect goods which are shipped C.O.D. until after he has paid the purchase price. If defects are revealed by a later inspection, however, he may return the goods and demand his purchase price.

SALES CASES

MILLER v. SEAMAN et al.
1896, 176 Pa. St. 291, 35 Atl. 134

Action by Miller to recover for some lumber alleged to have been sold to the defendant, but which had been borne away by a flood before delivery. The lumber had been delivered only in part when the flood occurred.

WILLIAMS, J. . . . The object of this action is to determine whether the plaintiff or the defendant must bear the loss so occasioned, and this must depend on which of them held title at the time the flood came. The provisions of the contract . . . amount to an agreement to sell all the lumber in the eleven piles, not in a lump or for a gross price, but by the 1,000 feet, at the price of $8.25 per 1,000 feet. The quantity is not to be estimated or ascertained at once, but is to be obtained by actual measurement, when, and as often "as the lumber is loaded, measured, and inspected by Mr. Sam Aurand, upon the order of the purchaser." The actual delivery is not made when the lumber is loaded in the yard, but [when] the seller delivers it to the purchaser "F.O.B. cars Williamsport." The price is to be paid within thirty days after shipment, on the quantity contained in each shipment ordered, and shipments are to be made only as ordered by the purchaser until June 1, 1894. . . .

It is clear that the defendants had no right to take possession of these piles as piles of lumber. If they had attempted it, Miller could have proceeded, either by replevin or trespass, against them. They could not have sold the lumber in a lump, and delivered it to a purchaser. . . . The lumber swept away by the flood had not been ordered by the purchaser; it had not been inspected, measured, or loaded by the seller, and delivered at Williamsport for the buyer. When the time came for ascertaining its quantity, it was not in the yard of the Dent Lumber Co. to be inspected and measured or estimated, and delivery was therefore impossible. The title had left the plaintiff only as orders had been filled and shipped, and, as to all that remained on the yard, it had never left him.

Judgment for defendant.

PLUMMER v. KINGSLEY

1951, 190 Oregon 378, 226 P. 2d 297

Plummer brings this action of replevin to recover a certain automobile. The car in question was sold for $800 cash to one Davis, the latter giving his check in settlement with the understanding that there was no deal until the check cleared. Possession of the car was surrendered to the buyer and the certificate of title, properly indorsed in blank by a former owner of the car, was placed in his hands. Davis, whose check was returned N.S.F., sold the car to the defendant. The plaintiff contended that Davis received no title and could pass none to the defendant. The lower court gave judgment for the plaintiff, and the defendant appealed.

BRAND, J. . . . Williston, in his work on sales, writes: "Sometimes after a bargain for a cash sale the buyer gives in payment of the price a worthless check, and it has been held that such a false check is no payment; and that not only does no title pass to the fraudulent buyer, but that the seller may assert his title against an innocent purchaser from the buyer." 2 Williston on Sales, Revised Ed. Section 346a, p. 343. . . . Williston argues at length that these decisions are unsound. He concedes, however, that the parties could agree that title should not pass unless the check is paid, although he believes that in the ordinary case, a seller for cash, receiving an N.S.F. check, assents to transfer of ownership in the goods. We quote: ". . . If a seller should say 'you must not deal with these goods, though I have put them in your hands, until I collect the check,' that would show an intent not to transfer the property to the buyer. . . ." 2 Williston on Saes, Revised Ed., Section 346a, p. 344.

In view of the findings and the undisputed evidence that there was to be "no deal" until the check was cashed, we think the learned author would agree with our conclusion that no title passed from the plaintiff to Davis in the case at bar.

The more serious question for decision is whether the defendant can successfully claim title by estoppel as against the claim of ownership by the plaintiff. Since the car was in Oregon at the time of the transaction between Davis and the defendant, the law of this state should determine the issue. Restatement, Conflict of Laws, Sections 255 to 257. This principle is conceded by the plaintiff.

The plaintiff relies upon the familiar general rule stated in American Jurisprudence:

> The general rule that a purchaser can acquire no better title than that possessed by his vendor finds application in replevin actions. So, the rightful owner of property purchased from a trespasser may recover the same in an action of replevin against the purchaser, irrespective of good faith . . .
>
> . . . The owner of personal property may, by placing it in the power of another to defraud innocent purchasers by an apparently valid transfer of the property, bar himself from claiming it, and it has been said that he thereby divests the title from himself. . . . 46 Am. Jur., Sales, Section 463, p. 626.

Concerning the particular situation in which a bad check is knowingly given in payment for chattels on a cash sale, we read the following:

> Although as between the parties to a sale of personal property, a check or draft given by the buyer and accepted by the seller constitutes only a conditional payment and title does not pass until the paper is paid, if there has been an actual delivery of the goods to the buyer by the seller, according to the weight of authority, a bona fide purchaser from the buyer without notice of the equities of the seller obtains a title which protects such purchaser against the demand of the seller to be repossessed of the goods or to have a trust declared in his favor in the proceeds thereof. Such result has been justified on the theory of an estoppel against the seller arising out of his act in delivering the property to the buyer, and also upon the principle that where one of two innocent persons must suffer for the fraud of a third person, the loss should fall on him who, by his imprudence, enabled such third person to commit the fraud. Other authority takes the position that since title does not pass where the check or draft is accepted as a conditional payment only, the goods may be reclaimed from a subsequent purchaser upon the dishonor of the check or draft when presented for payment, if the seller has not been guilty of such conduct or laches as will create an estoppel against him. This result has been reached in reliance upon the provision of the Uniform Sales Act that where goods are sold by a person who is not the owner thereof, and who does not sell them under the authority or with the consent of the owner, the buyer acquires no better title to the goods than the seller had, unless the owner of the goods is by his conduct precluded from denying the seller's authority to sell. . . . 46 Am. Jur., Sales, Section 478, p. 644.

. . . We limit our decision to the facts of the instant case in which the owner expressly retained title until cash payment should be made but in which he did deliver to the fraudulent purchaser both the car and the certificate of title. We hold that when an owner voluntarily clothes the fraudulent or criminal purchaser with indicia of title and delivers to him the possession of the chattel, he will be estopped to assert his title as against one who for value and in good faith and without notice, purchases the chattel in reliance upon the apparent ownership of the one so entrusted with possession and indicia of title. . . .

Judgment for defendant.

LOGUE et al. v. HILL
1951, (Ark.) 238 S.W. 2d 753

Action by Hill against Logue and others for the purchase price of a used tractor, the sale price being $1,400. The defendant claimed breach of express warranty and denied any liability. The evidence indicated that Hill induced the sale by stating the tractor was "in first class shape," and that "it was in A-1 shape." The lower court held this to be an express warranty and allowed recovery for the sum of $1,159.65, allowing $240.35 deduction for the breach of warranty. Both parties appealed.

McFADDIN, J. . . . Section 68-1412, Ark. Stats., is a part of the Uniform Sales Act adopted by Act 428 of the 1941 Arkansas Legislature and says: "Any affirmation of fact or any promise by the seller relating to the goods is an express warranty if the natural tendency of such affirmation or promise is to induce the buyer to purchase the goods, and if the buyer purchases the goods in reliance thereon. No affirmation of the value of the goods, nor any statement purporting to be a statement of the seller's opinion only shall be construed a warranty."

That the tractor was not in "first class shape," or "A-1 shape," when sold to Logue is established by an abundance of evidence. It needed some new rings, connecting rods, and other parts to be "in first class shape" for the work contemplated by the parties. Logue produced paid receipts for $240.35 covering various repairs, and testified to other items for which he had no receipt. Even when we disregard—as we do—the repairs necessitated by the damage to the tractor caused by Logue's son, nevertheless, we cannot say that the amount of $240.35 allowed by the Chancery Court is shown to be excessive: particularly when Hill's brother testified that the tractor was not in good running condition; and the witness, Goins, testified that the cylinders were so worn that some of the rings broke.

Logue claims that he rescinded the purchase contract as soon as he found the tractor to be defective; and therefore he says he is not liable for any part of the purchase price. He claims rescission under Section 68-1469, Ark. Stats., which provides in subdivision (1) (d): "Where there is a breach of warranty by the seller, the buyer may, at his election . . . rescind the contract to sell or sale and . . . if the goods have already been received, return them or offer to return them to the seller. . . ."

But in making this claim for rescission, Logue has failed to bring himself within the requirement of subdivision (3) of the same Statute, which reads: "Where the goods have been delivered to the buyer, he cannot rescind the sale . . . if he fails to notify the seller within a reasonable time of the election to rescind. . . ."

The evidence in the case at bar shows that Logue kept the tractor, used it all during the spring and summer of the crop year, and made no offer to return it until after he had gathered his cotton crop in the fall of the year. Logue's own witnesses placed a value of several hundred dollars on the tractor independent of the value of the attachments. From the evidence, it is apparent that Logue did not rescind within the time and manner required by the Statute. Thus, all the relief that Logue can claim is that provided in subdivision (1) (a) of the same Section, which says: "Where there is a breach of warranty by the seller, the buyer may, at his election . . . keep the goods and set up against the seller, the breach of warranty by way of recoupment in diminution . . . of the price."

The Chancery decree allowed Logue such relief in the sum of $240.35, as previously stated.

We affirm on both direct appeal and cross-appeal.

WARD v. HICKERSON
1950, (Tenn.) 236 S.W. 2d 993

This was a suit by Ward against Hickerson to recover the amount paid to the defendant for a 1942 Ford Sedan. Recovery was had in the court below and the defendant has appealed.

HOWELL, J. . . . There was ample competent evidence to justify the jury in finding for the plaintiff. The record discloses that on November 10, 1945, C. E. Hickerson sold this car to the plaintiff Ward, doing business as the Ward Motor Company, for $1,015 paid in cash. On that day the defendant Hickerson wrote a memorandum of sale in his own handwriting on a piece of scratch paper which is as follows:

> For & in consideration of $1,015.00 cash, receipt of which is hereby acknowledged I hereby sell transfer & convey to Ward Motor Co. one 1942 Ford Sedan M No. 45288 Lic. 1-36629.
>
> This Nov. 10-45
> C. E. Hickerson

About thirty days thereafter Ward sold this same automobile to Thomas J. Hughes of California, and thereafter it was replevied from Hughes by the Security Investment Company of Nashville, which company had a valid title thereto, and Hughes filed a bill in the Chancery Court of Nashville and by a final decree entered in Minute Book 162 at page 466, on April 15, 1948, a judgment was entered in that case against Ward in favor of Thomas J. Hughes and wife for $1,163.11 and the costs. This judgment was paid. Certified copies of the decrees in that case were filed and are a part of the record in this case. A certified copy of the original Chattel Mortgage on this car to the Securities Investment Company, duly registered in the Register's Office of Warren County, Tennessee, is also filed as an exhibit herein.

It is also insisted for the defendant that he made no warranty as to the title of the automobile involved and therefore is not liable. It is true that in the bill of sale there is no express warranty of title, but in a case of this kind the law will presume a warranty of title.

The defendant had the automobile in his possession as owner thereof and when he sold it for cash and delivered it to the plaintiff the law will import in the contract of sale a warranty of title by the seller. This subject is fully discussed in an opinion by Felts, Judge in the case of *Rundle v. Capital Chevrolet, Inc.*, reported in 23 Tenn. App. 151, 129 S.W. 2d 217, 220. In that case after citing a number of cases this Court said:

> Where one in possession of goods sells them as owner, the law, in order to discourage dishonesty and fraud, will import into his contract of sale a warranty of title by him.

The Court then said:

> Such was the common law of this State upon the subject of warranties of title by the vendor in sales of personalty when the Uniform Sales Act (Code, Sections 7194-7270) was enacted. This act we think, was but declaratory of the common law on this subject. It provides (Section 7206):
>
> In a contract to sell or a sale, unless a contrary intention appears, there is
>
> (1) An implied warranty on the part of the seller that in case of a sale he has a right to sell the goods, and that in case of a contract to sell he will have a right to sell the goods at the time when the property is to pass.
>
> (2) An implied warranty that the buyer shall have and enjoy quiet possession of the goods as against any lawful claims existing at the time of the sale.
>
> (3) An implied warranty that the goods shall be free at the time of the sale from any charge or encumbrance in favor of any third person, not declared or known to the buyer before or at the time when the contract or sale is made. . . .

A judgment will be entered here in favor of the plaintiff W. B. Ward and against the defendant C. E. Rickerson for the sum of One Thousand and Fifteen Dollars ($1,015.00) with interest from March 9, 1950, and the costs of the case.

Affirmed.

RYAN v. PROGRESSIVE GROCERY STORES, INC.

1931, 255 N.Y. 388, 175 N.E. 105

CARDOZO, C. J. The action is for breach of warranty. Plaintiff through his wife, who acted as his agent, bought a loaf of bread at the defendant's grocery. The loaf had concealed in it a pin, which hurt the plaintiff's mouth. There has been a judgment for the damage. . . .

The plaintiff did not rely on the seller's skill or judgment. His wife stated to the salesman that she wished to have a loaf of "Ward's Bread." The salesman gave her what she asked for, wrapped in a sealed package as it had come from the Ward Baking Company, the baker. She made her own choice, and used her own judgment. . . .

The award of damages, if it is to be upheld, must rest upon some other basis than the imputation of reliance.

"Where the goods are bought by description from a seller who deals in goods of that description (whether he be the grower or manufacturer or not), there is an implied warranty that the goods shall be of merchantable quality." Personal Property Law, Section 96, subd. 2. . . .

Loaves baked with pins in them are not of merchantable quality. The dealer is thus charged with liability, though the buyer selects the brand, just as he would be liable for concealed defects upon a sale of wool or silk. Assume that the sale had been made by a manufacturer or a grower, and that there had been a request for a special brand. There would then be no warranty of fitness for any "particular" purpose. Would anyone dispute, however, that a defect of this order, destroying value altogether would be covered by the warranty of merchantable quality? The question carries its own answer. The rule is different, to be sure, upon a sale of specific goods, not purchased by description. *Hight v. Bacon*, 126 Mass. 10, 30 Am. Rep. 639. It may even be different, though the purchase is by description, if the goods are subject to inspection and the defects are of such a nature that inspection will reveal them. Williston, Sales, Section 234; Personal Property Law, Section 96, subd. 3. Here the sale was by description, the defect was wholly latent, and inspection was impossible. In such circumstances the law casts the burden on the seller, who may vouch in the manufacturer, if the latter was to blame. The loss in its final incidence will be borne where it is placed by the initial wrong. . . .

The facts proved without objection make out a breach of warranty under subdivision 2. In such circumstances the plaintiff ought not to lose the benefit of his judgment because he fancied that he had brought himself under subdivision 1. . . .

The judgment should be affirmed, with costs.

SMITH v. FORD MOTOR COMPANY
1959, (Mo.) 327 S.W. 2d 535

Plaintiff sued defendant motor company for breach of implied warranty. Plaintiff had purchased from a dealer a new car manufactured by defendant. Defendant had warranted the car to the dealer against defects for 4,000 miles or 90 days, and the dealer gave a similar warranty to plaintiff. Plaintiff alleged a number of defects had appeared in the car within the warranty period, and the dealer being unable to correct the defects, plaintiff offered the car to defendant and sought recovery from defendant for the cost of the car, extra equipment, repairs and loss of use to the extent of $6971.09. Defendant denied any contract or liability with or to plaintiff, alleging it had sold the car to the dealer who had paid defendant for it and that, by agreement, the dealer was not an agent of defendant.

The lower court dismissed the plaintiff's action and plaintiff appealed.

WOLFE, P. J. . . . Plaintiff seems to base his petition on an implied warranty in the first place, and he later follows this with an averment that the defects complained of "were present at the time of the purchase or developed within ninety days or 4,000 miles of travel of said automobile. . . ." This unquestionably has reference to the dealer's written warranty mentioned in the dealer's contract. The burden of plaintiff's argument, however, is directed to the theory that there was an implied warranty by the defendant manufacturer that none of the defects of which he complains were present. He contends that this implied warranty is not defeated by lack of privity between the plaintiff and the manufacturer. He bottoms this view chiefly upon two cases by this court, *Worley v. Proctor & Gamble Mfg. Co.*, 241 Mo. App., 1114, 253 S.W. 2d 532, and *Williams v. Coca-Cola Bottling Company*, Mo. App., 285 S.W. 2d 53.

[1] The general rule of law is that only the person in privity with the warrantor may recover on a warranty. The exception to the rule is that goods intended for human consumption carry to the ultimate purchaser an implied warranty of fitness. This rule was extended in the case of *Worley v. Proctor & Gamble Mfg. Co.* to include packaged soap products which were alleged by the plaintiff to have caused skin irritation. The case of *Williams v. Coca-Cola Bottling Company* falls within the exception mentioned. In that case the plaintiff drank some impure Coca Cola and became ill from the effects of it.

[2] It is argued that we should extend this exception to facts alleged in the petition, citing *Baxter v. Ford Motor Co.*, 168 Wash. 456, 12 P.2d 409; 15 P.2d 1118, 88 A.L.R. 521, and *Bahlman v. Hudson Motor Car Co.*, 290 Mich. 683, 288 N.W. 309. Both of these cases were actions to recover damages arising out of personal injuries. In the Baxter case the manufacturer had advertised a shatter-proof windshield, which did shatter when struck by a pebble and put out the eye of its purchaser. In the Bahlman case the offending and injuring portion of the automobile was a seam in the top of a car that had been advertised as having a seamless

top. The qualities advertised and stated were definite, fixed, and ascertainable qualities in both instances. In both instances they were falsely stated, and the parts in question caused injury. In these cases where recovery has been allowed upon an implied warranty to the purchaser there has been an injury and an element of tort present as recognized in the *Worley case.* It is to such situations that an implied warranty to the ultimate purchaser may be relied upon. *Dotson v. International Harvester Company,* 365 Mo. 625, 285 S.W. 2d 585; *Dennis v. Willys-Overland Motors,* D.C., 111 F. Supp. 875; *Turner v. Edison Storage Battery Co.,* 248 N.Y. 73, 161 N.E. 423.

[3] The only warranty that the plaintiff received was an incident of the sale. He bought the car from the Goodwin Motor Company. This company was not an agent of the manufacturer under the terms of its contract as a dealer. It has been consistently so held in construing similar contracts. *Burkhalter v. Ford Motor Co.,* 29 Ga. App. 592, 116 S.E. 333; *S. B. McMaster, Inc., v. Chevrolet Motor Co.,* D.C., 3F. 2d 469; *Westerdale v. Kaiser-Frazer Corp.,* 6 N.J. 571, 80 A.2d 91.

[4] It therefore follows that there was no privity between the plaintiff and the manufacturer, and under the facts pleaded no warranty, either expressed or implied, could exist.

The judgment dismissing the petition is affirmed. . . .

SWIFT & CO. v. WELLS

1959, (Va.) 110 S.E. 2d 203

Plaintiff's husband purchased a smoked pork shoulder from a supermarket. The meat had been processed, wrapped in cellophane, and labeled by the defendant. The plaintiff became ill as a result of eating the meat and sued the defendant for damages. The trial court held for the plaintiff and the defendant appealed.

SPRATLEY, J. . . . The precise question whether a nonnegligent manufacturer of food, who supplies the same to a retailer for resale for human consumption, is liable to the ultimate consumer for injuries sustained by him as a result of eating such food, shown to be unwholesome at the time it left the manufacturer's possession, has not heretofore been presented to this Court.

The authorities are in conflict. There is a great contrariety of opinion and reasons. Many courts have denied recovery by the ultimate consumer against the manufacturer, insisting strictly on the requirement of privity where the action is for a breach of the warranty. Other courts, however, disregard the requirement of privity and hold the manufacturer liable directly to the consumer, although there is no contractual relation between them. *Decker & Sons, Inc. v. Capps,* 139 Tex. 609, 164 S.W. 2d

828, 142 A.L.R. 1479; 22 Am. Jur., Food, Section 104, page 890; 36 C.J.S. Food Section 58, p. 1106. See also 77 C.J.S. Sales Section 305 (b) 3, p. 1127.

Many of the courts in order to circumvent the privity rule have done so by indulging in legal fictions, such as fraud; deceit; assignment of cause of action from dealer to consumer; third party beneficiary contract; and agency of the buyer for the consumer. Jeanblanc, "Manufacturer's Liability to Persons other than their immediate Vendees," 24 Va. L. Rev. 134, 158. Other courts have imposed on the manufacturer and vendee an implied warranty, which is said to run with the article. *Coca-Cola Bottling Company of Ft. Worth v. Smith*, Tex. Civ. App., 97 S.W. 2d. 761.

Some courts reason that the remedies of injured customers ought not to depend upon the intricacies of the law of sales, nor the obligation of the manufacturer based only upon privity of contract; but should, because of the demands of justice and social welfare, rest upon the ground of a warranty and soundness imposed by law as a matter of public policy. *Decker & Sons, Inc. v. Capps*, supra; Annotation, 142 A.L.R. 1490, and prior annotations therein cited. . . .

The facts in *Decker & Sons, Inc. v. Capps*, supra, are similar to those in the present case. There the defendant manufactured sausage, advertised being suitable for human consumption under the trade name "Cervalet." The sausage, wrapped in a cellophane package, was sold by it to a retail grocer, who in turn sold it three days later to C. K. Capps. Members of Capps' family, including the plaintiff, Mrs. Capps, ate it, and as a result were poisoned. The jury found that although the manufacturer was free from negligence, the sausage had become contaminated before it left its hand.

In a well reasoned opinion in the above case, Chief Justice Alexander, after reciting the historical background of and the reason for the rule that in sales of food for domestic use there is an implied warranty that it is fit and wholesome for human consumption, concluded that such warranty is imposed by operation of law as a matter of public policy for the protection of health and life. He pointed out that the manufacturer of food occupies a better position of knowledge, or opportunity for knowledge, of the contents of its cans and sealed packages and, the processes of its manufacture. Then said he:

". . . A party who processes a product and gives it the appearance of being suitable for human consumption, and places it in the channels of commerce, expects some one to consume the food in reliance on its appearance that it is suitable for human consumption. He expects the appearance of suitableness to continue with the product until someone is induced to consume it as food. But a modern manufacturer or vendor does even more than this under modern practices. He not only processes the food and dresses it up so as to make it appear appetizing, but he uses the newspapers, magazines, billboards, and the radio to build up the psychology to buy and consume his products. The invitation extended by him is not only to the housewife to buy and serve his products, but to the members of the family and guest to eat it. In fact, the manufacturer's interest in the product is not terminated when he has sold it to the wholesaler. He must get it off the wholesaler's shelves before the wholesaler will buy a new supply. . . ." 139 Tex. at page 619, 164 S.W. 2d at page 832, 142 A.L.R. at page 1487. . . .

[2, 3] For the reasons above expressed, we are of the opinion that where a manufacturer of food for human consumption sells such food, in sealed containers or packages, to a retailer, who in turn sells it to a consumer, and the consumer upon eating it suffers damage in consequence of impurities in the product, shown to have existed therein before it left the manufacturer's hands, the manufacturer is liable to the consumer on its implied warranty of wholesomeness of the food, and the consumer may recover against the manufacturer for damages suffered, irrespective of a lack of privity of contract between the manufacturer and the consumer. This permits the placing of the loss occasioned upon the manufacturer who is in the best position to prevent the production and the sale of unwholesome food. We are not here concerned with the question of the liability of a manufacturer for impurities or deterioration in food which occurs after the commodity has left the manufacturer's possession. . . .

The judgment of the trial court is affirmed.

ABRAHAM v. KARGER

1898, 100 Wis. 387, 76 N.W. 330

Clara Abraham brought an action of replevin for a specified lot of merchandise alleged to have been purchased from Karger. The evidence disclosed that plaintiff was to give in payment $2,000 in cash and a negotiable note of one Meyer for $500. The defendant refused to accept the note, claiming that he had not agreed to do so. After a proper tender and a refusal to surrender the goods, this action was brought. The defendant requested the lower court to instruct the jury that under the evidence an action of replevin could not be maintained. The court refused the instruction and this appeal is prosecuted.

PINNEY, J. . . . There is nothing to show that the contract was executory, so far as anything remaining to be done to the goods was concerned. The evidence shows that they were ready for delivery, and set apart, and the price agreed upon, and a partial delivery made before the tender of the $500 note. The goods were in the sight of the parties, and were pointed out in the presence of Karger, the defendant. . . . There can be no doubt but that, under the circumstances stated, the title to the goods and the right of possession as well, passed to the plaintiff, and, if afterwards they were wrongfully detained, she might maintain replevin for them.

Review Questions and Problems

1. *A* contracted to sell and deliver to *B* 2,000 cords of wood, at $5.50 a cord, from a certain timber plot. A fire destroyed all the timber except 500 cords. *B* refused to accept the 500 cords, and *A* sued for damages. Did *A* have a right to recover?
2. *A* sells *B* a certain used automobile. Before the car is delivered, it is destroyed by fire. Who must bear the loss? Does the fact that it is not paid for have any bearing on the result?
3. *A* made an agreement with *B* whereby *A* took possession of a radio for a 30-day trial period, *A* making a part payment on the radio. Within the 30 days' period, *A* decided not to keep the radio. Is *A* entitled to return the radio and get back his payment?
4. *A* sold *B* a horse and warranted it to be sound. The horse proved to be unsound, and *B* desires to rescind. *A* desires to introduce evidence which indicates that he made the statement in good faith. Is such evidence pertinent?
5. *A* sold goods to *B* on credit and put them on board a carrier for delivery to *B*. Before the goods reached *B* and before the credit period expired, *A* learned that *B* was unable to pay other current debts. *A* notified the carrier to return the goods to him. Is *A* entitled to the goods?
6. *A*, an automobile dealer, bought some automobiles from *X*, the manufacturer, under agreement that the title to the automobiles should remain with *X* until *A* paid for them. *A* put the cars in his display room and sold one of them to *P*, a bona fide purchaser. Could *A*, who has not paid *X* for the cars, convey a good title to *P*?
7. *C* agreed with *D* to manufacture and put in place some roofing planks according to plans and specifications. *C* installed the planking but it was unsatisfactory and the roof sagged. *D* had to install additional support for the roof, at additional cost. Could *D* recover damages for breach of warranty from *C*?
8. *A* sold goods to *B* for a stipulated price. Nothing was stated in the contract as to allowing *B* credit. May *A* keep possession of the goods until *B* pays for them?
9. *A* shipped, C.O.D., $500 worth of groceries to *B* in accordance with an order from the latter. The goods arrived at their destination, but *B* refused to accept or pay for them without first inspecting them. The carrier refused to permit the inspection, and before the groceries could be sold elsewhere some of the fresh vegetables were badly damaged. Was *B* entitled to inspect the goods before payment? Who bore the loss?
10. *B* desired a tractor and trailer for a specific purpose he had in mind and informed S, the seller, of his purpose. Relying upon the selection of the seller, he purchased the items, but the written contract said, "no warranties have been made to the buyer unless written herein."

The items were not suitable for the purpose *B* had in mind, and he sued *S* for breach of the implied warranty of fitness. Should he have recovered?

11. A consumer bought canned fruit juice from a retailer and became ill after drinking it. Should the consumer be allowed to recover from the manufacturer?
12. *P* purchased a car from *G*, receiving possession of the car in return for a check for the purchase price. *P* sold the car for cash to *T*, a good faith purchaser. *P*'s check was not paid by the drawee bank because *P*'s account was not large enough to cover the amount of the check. May *G* recover the car from *T*?

43

Sales: Uniform Commercial Code States

6-33. Introduction. Article 2 of the Uniform Commercial Code has made extensive changes in the law of sales of personal property. The states that have adopted the Uniform Commercial Code have repealed their Uniform Sales Act.

Article 2 of the Code represents a modern approach to the law of sales. Many of the technical, and sometimes conflicting, interpretations of the Uniform Sales Act developed by the courts are either eliminated or simplified by the Code. This has been accomplished by the rewriting of many sections of the Uniform Sales Act, as well as by the introduction of new definitions and new concepts—at least in some instances.

In certain areas of the law of sales, articles of the Code other than Article 2 apply and will be referred to where appropriate to the discussion. Since a contract to sell personal property involves the law of contract as well as the law of sales, many of the provisions of the Code concerned with the formation of a contract for the sale of goods are discussed in Book Two on Contracts.

6-34. Contracts for sale and goods covered. The Code uses the comprehensive term *contract for sale* to mean both a present sale and a contract to sell goods at a future time. A sale is defined as the passing of title from the seller to a buyer for a price. A *present sale* occurs when the making of the contract accomplishes a sale. The seller must, in general, tender goods strictly in compliance with his obligations under the contract before the buyer need accept them but the Code permits a seller to *cure* a tender, rejected for nonconformity with the contract, if the time for performance by the seller has not expired and the seller notifies the buyer of his intention to *cure,* and, within the proper time, makes a conforming delivery.

The Code defines goods as being all things movable at the time of identification to the contract, except the money in which the price is to be paid, investment securities, and things in action. The term includes specially manufactured goods and the unborn young of animals. Growing crops and other identified things attached to real property are included if they are to be severed from the realty.

Goods must be both existing and identified before any interest in them can pass, but there may be a present sale of a part interest in such goods. If they are not both existing and identified, they are future goods, and any purported present sale of them constitutes a *contract to sell.*

The identification of goods to the contract can be made at any time and in any manner explicitly agreed to by the parties. In absence of such agreement, the identification of the goods takes place when the contract is made, if the goods are in existence and identified. If future goods are involved, the identification occurs when the seller ships, marks, or otherwise designates particular goods as fulfilling the requirements of the contract. If the contract refers to growing crops or to the unborn young of animals, the identification takes place when the crops are planted or when the young are conceived.

If identification of existing goods has occurred, the buyer receives a special property in them which gives him an insurable interest, even though the goods designated do not conform to the contract, and the buyer, therefore, would be entitled to return or reject such goods. Further, the buyer may, by valid tender of the unpaid portion of the purchase price and if he has made a previous partial payment, recover the goods from the seller should the seller become insolvent within ten days after the first payment has occurred. Thus, if the buyer actually wants the goods, he is to this extent given priority over creditors of the seller. If the buyer has the right to make the identification, however, the goods he designates must conform to the contract or he will have no right to recover them. This limitation prevents the buyer from claiming goods which might be superior to the goods he was entitled to receive under his contract.

The seller retains an insurable interest as long as he has title to, or a security interest in, the identified goods. If the seller alone has made the identification, he may substitute other goods for the ones he originally designated, unless he is insolvent, has defaulted, or has notified the buyer that his original designation was final.

Fungible goods are goods that are sold, not by individual unit, but by weight or measure because one unit is similar to any other unit. A sale may be made of an individual share of fungible goods—provided the bulk is identified—whether the quantity of the bulk is known or not. The seller and buyer become owners in common of proportionate shares of the bulk.

6-35. General obligation of the contract. The obligations that the seller and the buyer assume are determined by their agreement. In general, the Code attempts to protect each party to a fair agreement so that each one is entitled to the benefit of the stipulated performance of the other. However, the parties may agree to change the risks or burdens imposed by the Code upon one or the other of the parties, provided that the resulting agreement, or any part thereof, is not unconscionable. It is recognized that in a given situation the parties to the agreement might prefer to modify the normal protections offered them by the Code; they are free to do so.

6-36. Price of the goods sold. The price of the goods sold may be payable in money, goods, or other value, including an interest in real property, as the parties agree. The parties may form a contract containing an "Open Price Term," in which case the price is not now stated, and will be determined by an amount that is reasonable at the time of delivery. If the contract provides that the price is to be determined by agreement of the parties, or by a third party, and if the parties do not agree, or the third party does not act, whatever price is judged to be a reasonable one will prevail. The agreement may allow either the seller or the buyer to fix the price, and in such a case the price set by the party thus authorized becomes the price to be paid provided the party setting the price acts in good faith. If the price is to be set other than by agreement of the parties, and if the price is not so set because of the fault of one of the parties, the remaining party may set a reasonable price of his own or he may treat the contract as cancelled, as he elects. If it is clear that the parties intend to be bound only if the price is determined by a stated method, and if the price is not so determined, the contract is not formed. The buyer must then return any goods already delivered, or pay a reasonable price as of the date of delivery if he cannot return them, and the seller must return any payments made by the buyer.

6-37. Delivery of the goods sold. In the absence of any other agreement, the proper place for delivery of the goods is the seller's place of business or, if he has none, his residence. If the parties are aware at the time they enter into the contract that the specific goods involved are located at some other place, that place is the proper place for delivery. If documents of title are involved in the transaction, they may be delivered through usual banking channels. In the absence of a contrary agreement, the goods involved in the contract are to be shipped or delivered within a reasonable time.

The seller properly tenders delivery by holding conforming goods for the buyer and by giving him any notification reasonably necessary to enable him to take delivery. If documents of title are involved, the seller must tender correct documents directly to the buyer or through customary banking channels. Proper tender of goods must be made at a reasonable hour and the goods must be kept available for a period reasonably necessary to permit the buyer to take possession. In the absence of a contrary agreement, the buyer must provide reasonable facilities for the delivery of the goods.

6-38. Payment for the goods sold. In general, the buyer is required to pay for the goods at the time and place of delivery; but if delivery is to be made by the tender of documents of title, payment is due at the time and place of delivery of the documents irrespective of when the goods are to be delivered. The contract may permit the buyer to inspect the goods before payment is required. If the seller ships goods on credit pursuant to the contract, the credit period starts with the time of shipment; but a delay in sending the invoice covering the goods, or in postdating the invoice, delays accordingly the start of the credit period.

6-39. Incomplete terms. The Code clearly adopts the concept that a fair bargain should be enforceable although some of the terms of performance are not definite. The contract may allow either one of the parties to specify these terms, and if the right is exercised in good faith and the result is commercially reasonable, the contract will be enforceable accordingly. Reference has been made before to the use of this procedure in setting the price. In general, the buyer may specify the assortment of the goods, and the seller may specify the terms of shipment. If the specifications by either party materially affect the performance of the other, or if the cooperation of both parties is necessary and one of the parties prevents action from being taken within a reasonable time, the injured party may be excused for any delay in his own performance which is caused by the inaction. In addition, the injured party may perform as best he can, or treat such failure to act as a breach of the contract.

In the absence of contrary provisions, any required performance under the contract shall take place within a reasonable time. If the contract contemplates successive performances by the parties, but provides no definite time limits, the contract is valid for a reasonable time only. Either party, upon giving reasonable notice to the other, may terminate such a contract at any time.

6-40. Warranties. The Code provides that both express and implied warranties may be present in a sale or contract for sale. An express warranty is created when the seller makes statements of fact concerning the goods sold. Implied warranties arise as an incident of the sale and are created by operation of law. If the buyer is induced to purchase the goods as a result either of the seller's statements or the circumstances of the sale, and the goods sold do not meet the standard set by the warranty, the buyer may recover damages from the seller—or he may, in some instances, rescind the contract. The Code has retained many of the concepts of warranties as developed under the Uniform Sales Act, but it also has resolved many of the conflicting interpretations found in the court decisions on warranty problems.

6-41. Warranty of title. The seller warrants that he conveys a good title to the buyer and that the goods will be delivered free of any encumbrance on the title which was not known to the buyer when the contract was made. This warranty may be excluded only by specific language; however, if the buyer is aware that the seller is not claiming title in himself, or that he is selling only such rights as he or some third party may have in the goods, the warranty does not apply.

6-42. Warranty against infringement. The warranty of title, just discussed, is broadened by the Code to include a warranty that the goods delivered by the seller will be free of any rightful claim by a third party that such third party's rights have been infringed. This warranty against infringement is made only by a merchant who deals regularly in goods of the kind sold. However, if the goods have been prepared or manufactured to the buyer's specifications, the buyer warrants to the seller that the goods so manufactured will not infringe on the rights of a third party, and the buyer must indemnify the seller in event such infringement occurs. For example, if the goods sold or manufactured, as the case may be, violate a patent right held by a third party, this warranty would be breached. Thus, either the seller or the buyer may be liable to the other contracting party for breach of the same warranty, depending upon which party is at fault.

6-43. Express warranty. The seller expressly warrants to the buyer that the goods involved in the bargain conform to any statement of fact, promise, or description, made or given by him to the buyer, if any of these become part of the basis of the agreement between the parties.

If a model or sample has been shown, and such model or sample is part of the basis of the bargain, the seller warrants that all of the goods sold conform to the model or sample. The warranty is created whether or not the seller uses specific words of warranty, and whether or not he intended making a specific warranty.

Statements of the seller's opinion or commendation of goods are not matters of fact and do not result in express warranties that the statements made are true, if it is clear that the statements are only matters of opinion. Statements concerning the value of the goods are deemed to be statements of opinion.

6-44. Warranty of merchantability. An implied warranty of merchantability arises in a contract for the sale of goods if the seller is a merchant in goods of the kind called for under the contract. Merchantability, as defined by the Code, means that the goods sold are at least of such quality that they are fit for the ordinary purposes for which such goods are used. If fungible goods are involved, they must be of fair average quality as designated by their description in the contract. Should the sale involve packaged goods, the goods must be properly packaged and labeled, and must conform to any statements which are made on the label or container concerning their quality. Thus, the warranty may be said to extend to both container and contents. Other warranties may arise from a course of dealing or usage of trade. If food or drink is served for consumption, either on the premises or elsewhere, the transaction is a sale and is covered by this warranty. This last provision of the Code determines an issue upon which many of the present court decisions are in conflict.

6-45. Warranty of fitness for a particular purpose. An implied warranty of fitness for a particular purpose is created if the seller is aware of the purpose which the buyer has in mind, and knows that the buyer is relying on him to select goods suitable for the purpose. The buyer need not specifically tell the seller his purpose if the seller is otherwise aware of the facts.[1] If these two requirements are present, the seller need not be a merchant for this warranty to apply; nor is the warranty necessarily eliminated by a sale of an article under a trade name if the seller has recommended it for the buyer's purpose.

6-46. Extent of warranty. A seller's warranty, express or implied, is specifically extended by the Code to run in favor of members of the buyer's family and guests in his home if any such person could reasonably be expected to use the product purchased and is in person injured by breach of the warranty. To this extent, the more modern view that many of the courts have been adopting on this problem has been followed by the Code.

6-47. Exclusion of warranties. Warranties can be negatived or limited providing this is done in such a conspicuous way that it is certain that the buyer is not misled. Also, in the absence of such exclusion, warranties are, as far as possible, to be construed as being cumulative and consistent as to each other, unless the situation reasonably demands a different interpretation.

6-48. Shipment and delivery terms. The Code defines the meaning of many terms commonly used in commercial practice with respect to the shipment and delivery of goods via carrier. The apparent purpose is to clarify and standardize the meaning of these terms, and to remove conflicts which have arisen from varying court decisions as to the exact meaning to be given to such terms. For example, F.O.B. (free on board) at a designated place is a delivery term of the contract which requires

[1] Kirk v. Stineway Drug Store Company, page 934.

the seller, if the designated place is the point of shipment, to put the goods into the carrier's possession at the seller's risk, and to promptly notify the buyer of the shipment. If the stipulated place is the destination, the seller must, at his own expense and risk, transport the goods to that place and properly tender delivery. If the F.O.B. term refers to a vessel, car, or vehicle, the seller must, at his own expense and risk, load the goods on board the vehicle.

The seller may reserve a security interest in the goods shipped by taking a negotiable bill of lading from the carrier and making it deliverable to his own order, or to the order of a third party, financing agency, or buyer. The purpose of this procedure is to keep control of the goods in the seller until the buyer performs his duties under the contract. Frequently the buyer is required, under the terms of the contract, to pay for the goods before receiving delivery. When payment is made, the buyer receives the bill of lading, properly endorsed if necessary, and he may then obtain the goods from the carrier.

The term F.A.S. (free alongside) vessel at a named port, is a delivery term which requires the seller, at his own expense and risk, to deliver the goods alongside the vessel in the manner usual in that port; or to make delivery on a dock provided by the buyer. The seller is required to obtain a receipt for the goods in exchange for which the carrier is required to issue a bill of lading.

The term, C.I.F. means that the price includes the cost of the goods plus insurance and freight charges to the destination. The seller is required, at his expense and risk, to put the goods in the carrier's possession for shipment, load the goods, obtain a proper insurance policy (including any usual war risk insurance) payable to the buyer, and to obtain and forward all documents promptly in order to protect the buyer. The term C.F. (or C. & F.) imposes the same duties on the seller except the need for procuring insurance. The buyer is required to make payment upon tender of the proper documents. The meaning of all these terms can be varied by agreement between the parties.

6-49. Sale on approval. In a sale on approval the goods are delivered to the buyer for his use, but the title and risk of loss remains with the seller until the buyer indicates his intention to retain the goods. Use of the goods by the buyer, consistent with the purpose of the trial, is not acceptance; but failure to notify the seller of the buyer's election to return the goods within the trial period, or within a reasonable time if no trial period is stipulated, is acceptance. If the goods conform to the contract, acceptance of any part is an acceptance of all. Unless otherwise agreed, this type of sale arises where the goods are delivered primarily for use, i.e., delivered to a consumer. Unless and until the buyer finally accepts the goods, his creditors may not subject the goods to their claims.

If the buyer gives proper notification to the seller of his election to return the goods, the return is at the seller's risk and expense.

6-50. Sale or return. In a sale or return, the goods are delivered to the buyer, and the property and risk of loss then pass to the buyer. The agreement permits the buyer to return the goods, or some portion of them, to the seller if he so elects; the returned goods again become the property of the seller. However, the buyer must act reasonably, and the return is at his own risk and expense. In the absence of an agreement to the contrary, this type of sale occurs if the goods are delivered primarily for resale, i.e., delivered to a merchant. The goods, so long as they are in the buyer's possession, are subject to the claims of his creditors.

6-51. Consignments. When goods are delivered to a person who deals in goods of the kind delivered, and he maintains a place of business under a name other than the name of the person delivering the goods, it is a sale or return so far as the claims of creditors of the person in possession are concerned. The delivered goods are subject to the claims of such creditors, even though the agreement under which the goods are delivered purports to reserve title in the person delivering the goods, until payment or resale. This rule is broad enough to include goods delivered "on consignment" or "on memorandum." The purpose of the rule is to protect creditors of the buyer who are unaware of the terms of the delivery to him and might reasonably assume the goods belong to him since he has possession and customarily deals in such goods.

The one delivering the goods may protect himself against the claims of the creditors of the person in possession if he complies with an applicable law providing for his interest to be shown by a sign. He is also protected where the creditors know that the person in possession is substantially engaged in selling the goods of others, or if he complies with the filing provisions of Article 9 (Secured Transactions) of the Code. In these instances, the creditors should not be misled by the mere possession of the goods by their debtor.

6-52. Passing of title. It should be emphasized that the "title" concept, as used in the Uniform Sales Act, has little importance under the Code. The rights, remedies, and obligations of the parties, are controlled by provisions of the Code irrespective of title to the goods. It is only where a Code provision refers to title, that the title concept is applicable.[2] However, it is specifically provided that, assuming no agreement to the contrary, the title to goods passes when the seller has made physical delivery of proper goods in accordance with the contract. Delivery may be at the point of shipment or at the point of destination, depending on the requirements of the contract. If the contract concerns identified goods which are to be delivered without moving the goods, the title passes

[2] Girard Trust Corn Exchange Bank v. Warren Lepley Ford, Inc., page 936.

at the time and place of sale, unless the seller is to deliver a document of title, in which case the title passes at the time and place of delivery of the document.

6-53. Voidable title and power to transfer. The Code contains several provisions which are designed to protect a good faith purchaser when he purchases from a seller who has only a voidable title to goods. For example, if goods are sold and delivered in return for a worthless check, or delivery is obtained by fraud, and then, the original buyer—the wrongdoer—resells the goods to a good faith purchaser, the good faith purchaser obtains a good title. Further, any entrusting of goods to a merchant who deals in such goods, gives the merchant power to transfer to a buyer, in the ordinary course of business, all rights of the one so entrusting.[3] This is true regardless of any stated conditions between the entruster and the merchant. This provision seems broad enough to allow such a merchant to sell and to transfer good title to goods entrusted to him solely for repair or safe keeping.

6-54. Risk of loss. The risk for the loss of the goods rests with the buyer as soon as the goods are delivered by the seller to the carrier, provided the seller is not required by the contract to deliver the goods to a specific place. If the contract requires the seller to deliver the goods to a specific place, the risk of loss passes to the buyer as soon as the goods are there tendered to the buyer. These rules assume that the seller has properly observed the requirements of the contract and that the parties have not otherwise provided in the agreement.

If the goods are in the possession of a bailee, and are to be delivered without being moved, the risk of loss passes to the buyer when he receives a document of title representing the goods, or the bailee has acknowledged the buyer's right to possession.

If the seller is a merchant and the goods are to be delivered to the buyer at the seller's place of business, or at some place where the goods are situated, the buyer assumes the risk of loss only when he has received the goods. The seller is in control of the goods until the buyer has received them, and can still protect himself by proper insurance. However, if the seller is not a merchant, the risk of loss passes to the buyer when delivery is offered to him, whether he has actually received the goods or not. The parties may change these rules by agreement.

6-55. Destruction of the goods. When specific goods have become identified to the contract, and the goods are totally destroyed without fault of either party, if the risk of loss has not passed to the buyer, the contract is avoided. If the destruction to the goods is partial rather than total, the buyer may inspect them and either avoid the contract or accept

[3] Independent News Co. v. Williams, page 937.

the goods with proper deduction from the contract price, as he may desire. The buyer is entitled to the same choice where the goods have deteriorated to the extent that they no longer conform to the requirements of the contract.

The contract may contain a "no-arrival, no sale" term. This provision would be appropriate where both parties are aware that the specific goods covered by the contract are to be received by the seller from a third party who is not under the seller's control. In such a case, the seller is obligated to ship only such goods as he receives, and if he receives no goods, he has no liability on the contract to the buyer. If only part of the goods are received by the seller, or if any or all of the goods received have so deteriorated that they do not conform to the contract, the buyer has the option to accept the goods or to avoid the contract.

6-56. Inspection. In general, the buyer has the right to inspect the goods before payment or acceptance unless the contract otherwise provides. If it is so provided in the contract, the buyer may be required to pay for the goods before inspection. However, his rights and remedies are not affected if the subsequent inspection discloses that the contract has not been performed properly by the seller. In such a case, his payment does not constitute acceptance of the goods.

Unless the contract provides otherwise, the buyer has the right, before payment or acceptance, to inspect the goods at any reasonable time and place in any reasonable manner. This right arises when the goods are tendered or delivered to the buyer, or when they are identified to the contract. When the seller sends the goods to the buyer, the inspection may take place after the arrival of the goods.

The parties may stipulate the place or method of inspection without affecting the risk of loss, the place for delivery, or the identification of the goods. If the stipulated procedure becomes impossible, the buyer may follow the rules of the Code as to the time, place, and manner of inspection, unless it is clear that the stipulated method was intended to be an indispensable condition. If the latter is the case, failure to follow the agreed method avoids the contract.

The buyer is required to pay the expenses incurred in the inspection but if the goods do not conform to the contract and are rejected by the buyer, he may recover his expenses from the seller.

6-57. Remedies of the seller. The Code broadens the remedies of the seller while retaining those remedies previously given under the Uniform Sales Act. For example, the seller may refuse further deliveries to an insolvent buyer unless the buyer pays cash for such deliveries and pays for all goods previously delivered.

6-58. Stoppage in transit. If the seller entrusts the goods to a carrier or other bailee for delivery to the buyer, the seller may, upon proper notification to the bailee, stop delivery when he discovers the buyer to be insolvent. In such a case, the bailee must hold the goods subject to the further orders of the seller. This right of stoppage ends when the buyer has obtained the goods or when the bailee has acknowledged that he holds the goods for the buyer. If the bailee is a carrier, the acknowledgment occurs only after the carrier has performed its contract as a carrier and is holding the goods as a warehouseman, or has reshipped the goods for the buyer. If a negotiable document of title has been issued for the goods, a bailee need not follow a stop order unless the document is surrendered to him. The costs incurred by the bailee in following the stop order must be paid by the seller, and this duty would extend to the repayment of any damages paid by the bailee to the buyer if the stop order violates the buyer's rights.

In large deliveries such as by carload, truckload, and the like, the seller may exercise the right of stoppage in transit for reasons other than the buyer's insolvency, including the buyer's failure to make a payment due before delivery, or his repudiation of the contract. This represents an enlargement of the right of stoppage in transit given the seller under the Uniform Sales Act.

6-59. Reclaiming goods. The seller is entitled to reclaim goods from an insolvent buyer where the buyer has received such goods on credit, provided he demands the goods within ten days from the time that the buyer receives them. If the buyer has made a misrepresentation of solvency in writing to the seller within three months of receiving the goods, the ten day limit does not apply. This right to reclaim by the seller is inferior to the rights of a good faith purchaser from the buyer and, under some circumstances, to the rights of other lien creditors. Should the seller pursue the right to reclaim successfully he has no other remedy with respect to the goods.

6-60. Cancellation and resale. In the event the buyer refuses to accept the goods, repudiates wrongfully, or otherwise violates the contract, the seller is given certain additional rights.

He may cancel the contract if he sees fit. If goods have not already been identified to the contract, he may identify proper goods to the contract provided such goods are in his possession at the time he learns of the buyer's breach. He may complete the manufacture of unfinished goods and identify them to the contract or cease the manufacture of such unfinished goods and resell them for scrap value. In any of these cases, he may resell the identified goods in a commercially reasonable manner and recover from the buyer the difference between the resale price and the contract price plus any reasonable incidental damages.

6-61. Action for the price. If goods have been identified to the contract and the seller is unable to resell them, he may sue the buyer for the price but must then hold the goods for the buyer. If resale later becomes possible, the seller may resell them at any time before he collects his judgment. If the seller does so, the proceeds of the resale are credited to the buyer and payment of the balance of the judgment entitles the buyer to any goods not so resold.

If the buyer fails to pay the contract price, as it falls due, for goods which he has accepted, or for conforming goods damaged within a reasonable time after risk of loss has passed to him, the seller may sue for the contract price.

If the seller is denied a judgment for the price, he is given a judgment for damages without the necessity of bringing another action against the buyer.

6-62. Remedies of the buyer. Where the seller fails to make delivery or repudiates, or the buyer rightfully rejects the goods, the buyer is permitted to cancel the contract. He may recover damages from the seller for nondelivery or he may choose to "cover" by purchasing substitute goods from some other source. As long as the new purchase is made in good faith and without undue delay, the buyer may recover from the seller the difference between the cost of "cover" and the contract price and, in addition, any incidental damages resulting to the buyer from the seller's breach.

A buyer who has paid part or all of the price of the goods and has them in his possession is given a security interest to the extent of his payment, if the goods are properly rejected. He may resell the goods to obtain repayment for any reasonable expenses he has incurred in the inspection, care, transportation, and receipt of the goods, as well as for the payments he has made on the goods. The buyer may have a decree of specific performance if the goods involved in the contract are unique, or other proper circumstances entitle him to this special remedy. He may maintain an action for replevin for goods identified to the contract if he is unable to effect "cover." If the goods are shipped under a security interest reserved to the seller, and the buyer has satisfied, or offered to satisfy, the security interest, he may bring an action for replevin.

6-63. Conclusion. The student is again referred to Book Two on Contracts for other Code provisions which apply to Contracts as well as Sales. Rules pertaining to liquidated damages, anticipatory breach, fraud, the Statute of Limitations, and similar problems are discussed there and have not been repeated here.

Within certain limits, the parties are free to provide in the sales contract for remedies in addition to, or as substitutes for, those given in the Code. If the provisions are too broad, they will be ignored and the courts will grant the parties the remedies given by the Code.

6-64. Bulk transfers. Article 6 of the Code adopts the terminology of *bulk transfers* rather than the perhaps more familiar term *bulk sales.* A bulk transfer is defined as any transfer in bulk of a major part of the materials, supplies, merchandise, or other inventory—including equipment if made in connection with a bulk transfer of inventory—of an enterprise whose principal business is the sale of merchandise from stock (this includes enterprises which sell what they manufacture), so long as the transfer is made in other than the transferor's ordinary course of business. Certain types of bulk transfers, such as security transactions and judicial sales, are excepted from the Code.

The purpose of this legislation is to prevent the defrauding of the seller's creditors. This protection is given by the purchaser's requiring the seller (transferor) to furnish a sworn statement of his existing creditors, including their names, addresses, and the amount owed each.

The transferor is responsible for the accuracy of the list of creditors and, unless the transferee is aware of errors in the list, he may rely upon it.

The parties also must prepare a schedule of the property involved in the transfer. These documents are to be kept for six months by the purchaser (transferee) or publicly recorded by him. Under either procedure, the information is made available for the creditors of the transferor who may inspect the documents at reasonable times.

The transferee is further required to give personal notice, or notice by registered mail, to all creditors listed by the transferor, and to all other persons known by the transferee, if any, to hold or assert claims against the transferor. This notice shall state that a bulk transfer is about to be made and shall be given at least ten days before the transferee takes possession of the goods, or pays for them, whichever event is first.

The notice also must list the names and addresses of the transferor and transferee, and a full statement as to how and when the transferor's creditors are to be paid and the address to which the creditors should send their bills.

An optional section of the Code, which some states may not adopt, puts the burden on the transferee, in effect, to see that the creditors are paid either in full or pro rata, from the consideration received by the transferor.

If the required procedure has been followed, the transferor's creditors will have had ample opportunity to take any steps required to protect their interests. If the Code has not been followed, the transfer is ineffective as to the creditors, and they may use any appropriate remedy for the payment of their debts. The creditors must then act within six months after the transferee took possession unless the transfer was concealed, in which case they must act within six months after they learn of the transfer. A purchaser who buys for value and in good faith from the transferee obtains the property free of objection based on noncompliance with the Code.

6-65. Documents of title. Article 7 of the Uniform Commercial Code revises the law as to Warehouse Receipts and Bills of Lading primarily, although it also applies to other documents of title.

A document of title is defined as one which, in the regular course of business or financing, represents the goods covered by the document and entitles the person holding it to receive, hold, and dispose of the document and the goods represented by it. It is issued by, or addressed to, a bailee in possession of the goods, which goods are either identified or are fungible portions of an identified mass. The document may be negotiable or nonnegotiable. It is negotiable if it provides for the delivery of the goods to bearer or to the order of a designated person. If the document is negotiable and properly negotiated, the holder may have better rights than his transferor. If it is nonnegotiable the holder is in no better position than his transferor.

6-66. Negotiation. If the instrument is originally drawn to bearer, no indorsement is required to pass title to it. When it is drawn to a certain person or order, that person's indorsement must appear on the instrument. In this latter case, if the document is delivered to the transferee without indorsement, he has the right to obtain the transferor's indorsement, but until he does so the transferee can have no better rights than the transferor. A forged indorsement passes no title to the purchaser of the document. An instrument properly indorsed in blank becomes payable to bearer and may thereafter be negotiated by delivery, whereas a special indorsement to a certain person requires that it again be indorsed, if further negotiation is to take place.

A public warehouse which issues a negotiable receipt is not at liberty to surrender the goods to the original bailor unless he surrenders the receipt for cancellation. The receipt represents the goods and must be surrendered before the goods may be obtained. The warehouse that surrenders goods without the return of the receipt may be called upon for the goods by someone who has purchased the document. The goods should be delivered only to the person in possession of the receipt and then only if it has been properly indorsed when such indorsement is required. Much the same can be said of a common carrier or any other organization which issues a negotiable document of title.

However, the bailee may refuse to deliver the goods called for by the document until the payment of his just charges have been made, if the bailee requests such payment to be made, or where applicable law prohibits delivery without payment.

6-67. Rights of purchaser. A bona fide purchaser of a negotiable document of title takes it free of certain equities of ownership. A bona fide purchaser of a negotiable document payable to bearer, or indorsed in blank, takes good title thereto. Thus, a thief or a finder of such an instrument can sell it to an innocent party and pass good title. The holder of a bearer document, or of one which has been indorsed to him, may transfer good title to an innocent third party, although the holder violates a trust in so doing. If he holds it as an agent for a certain purpose and wrongfully disposes of it, the purchaser obtains good title to it.

One who is persuaded to dispose of a negotiable document of title by reason of fraud, mistake, or duress cannot recover it from a bona fide purchaser. To illustrate, let us assume that *A*, upon delivery of goods to a public warehouse, receives a negotiable warehouse receipt. *B*, by misrepresenting his financial standing, induces *A* to sell the goods to him on credit. The warehouse receipt is indorsed to *B*, who indorses it and sells it to *C*, an innocent purchaser. It is clear that *C*'s claim to the goods is superior to *A*'s, whose only recourse would be to recover from *B* for his fraud.

It should be borne in mind that if the original bailor of the goods—the one who delivered them to the carrier or warehouse—had no title to them, a subsequent purchaser of the document of title could get no title to the goods. A negotiable document of title is valuable only where its first possessor had title to the goods represented thereby. A thief cannot pass title to stolen property by delivering it to a public warehouse and then selling the negotiable warehouse receipt which he receives therefor.

A bailee is responsible for documents which are issued when no goods are delivered. Thus, an agent who fraudulently issues a negotiable document of title without receiving any goods makes it possible for an innocent purchaser thereof to recover from the bailee.

If a warehouse receipt has been issued without filling in all blanks in the document, and the blanks are later filled in without authority, an innocent purchaser of the now complete receipt may hold the warehouseman according to the completed terms. If the receipt was complete when issued, but was later altered without authority, the warehouse's liability is determined by the original term of the document. However, either an unauthorized alteration or the filling in of a blank in a bill of lading leaves the bill enforceable according to its original terms.

A warehouse receipt, even though it has been properly negotiated, will, in one situation, be inferior to the rights of a buyer of the goods represented by the receipt. The Code provides that a buyer in the ordinary course of business, who buys fungible goods from a warehouseman who also is engaged in the business of buying and selling such fungible goods, takes the goods free of any claim under the receipt. The official comments to this section of the Code point out that a typical case would involve the purchase of grain from an elevator by a farmer. In such a case, the holder of the receipt would have no claim against the grain purchased.

It will be recalled that this same concept is consistent with the result in a similar situation, previously discussed in the Section on Voidable Title, involving the sale of goods, entrusted to him for some other purpose, by a merchant who deals in such goods.

6-68. Liability of indorser or transferor. The indorser or transferor of a document of title makes three warranties to his immediate purchaser.

(1) He warrants that the document is genuine. One who purchases a forged document of title may, upon discovery of the forgery, recover from the person who sold it to him.

(2) He warrants that he has no knowledge of any facts which would impair its validity or worth.

(3) He warrants that his sale of the document is rightful and fully effective with respect to the title to the document and the goods it represents. However, unless he also has sold the goods, he does not make any additional warranties as to the goods. If he is also the seller of the goods, he makes the warranties previously presented in the discusssion on sales contracts. The indorser of a document of title does not warrant performance by the bailee or against default by any previous indorser.

His warranties are satisfied when the purchaser obtains a good right against the warehouseman or carrier. If the bailee has misappropriated the goods or refuses to surrender them, the holder of the document has, as his only recourse, an action against the bailee who issued the document.

If a bank or other person has been authorized to deliver a document of title, acting as an agent for this purpose, the delivery of the document creates no warranty by the agent as to the document itself. The bank or other agent does, however, warrant that it is acting in good faith and has the authority to deliver the document. Thus, no liability would be assumed by any such agent if the document were not genuine.

SALES
UNIFORM COMMERCIAL CODE CASES

KIRK v. STINEWAY DRUG STORE COMPANY
1963, (Ill. App.) 187 N.E. 2d 307

SCHWARTZ, J. This is an appeal from a judgment on a directed verdict entered in favor of defendant at the close of plaintiff's evidence in a suit for personal injuries sustained as a result of a fall from a household stepladder purchased from defendant. . . .

On April 28, 1960, plaintiff, a 67 year old woman, was in the process of moving and had need of a stepladder. She entered one of the stores of defendant and asked a sales clerk whether they had any small ladders. He solicited the help of another clerk and one of them went to see if they had such a ladder in the stockroom. Some time thereafter one of the clerks came to plaintiff with an open carton and pulled out of it approximately one-third of a red and white metal stepladder, the color plaintiff had said she wanted. Plaintiff said it was satisfactory, bought it, and took it home, keeping it in the carton until she moved. On May 5, 1960, having moved, she used the ladder twice, without incident. On the third instance the ladder collapsed and plaintiff fell. It is apparent from an examination of the ladder, which was placed in evidence and is part of the record, that there are imperfections in its construction, which the trial court described as follows:

> The condition in this case indicates that the rivet hole's loose because it is not hooking that step now, but in that point where it is not hooking that step, there is no safety cleat hook on that and that is the only one missing; so they apparently failed to put the safety cleat on there.

Trial counsel for defendant said: "The rivet broke; that's what caused the step to give away." In addition there were other apparent defects. . . .

The factual requirements of an implied warranty of fitness for a particular purpose are that the buyer makes known to the seller the purpose for which an article was purchased and that it appears that he relied on the seller's skill or judgment. Plaintiff did not expressly state to the seller the precise purpose for which she purchased the ladder. However, a stepladder is purchased for the purpose of elevating a person in order that he may perform a task or reach an object. As the trial court said, it might be used for the purpose of a flowerpot stand, but certainly no one would buy it for such purpose. The degree of particularity which should be required in such a case is dependent on the nature of the article and its general purpose. A household ladder is in particularity a ladder to be used for a purpose within the house. That purpose must be considered to have been impliedly made known to the seller by the very nature of the article and by the circumstances surrounding the transaction. . . .

The next question is whether there was evidence to show that plaintiff here relied on the seller's skill or judgment. As to this there is no direct evidence. There seldom is when reliance is involved. The issue of reliance involves an inquiry into a state of mind. It cannot be proved by direct evidence, except as a witness might testify that he did so rely, and such testimony has been permitted. In *Michaelson v. Hopkins,* 38 Wash. 2d 256, 228 P.2d 759 (1951), the trier of facts received such testimony but held otherwise, as a jury might do in the instant case. Plaintiff in the case before us did not herself directly testify that she relied upon defendant. We consider better proof to be found by the inferences drawn from circumstances surrounding the transaction. Plaintiff testified that in her conversation with defendant's sales clerks she specified no requirements except that the ladder should be a small one and that she wanted it to be red and white. She asked no questions as to its structure, nor did she inspect it. She was 67 years old, as we have said, and used a ladder only in connection with her household requirements. The trial court apparently thought the evidence supported the conclusion that plaintiff relied upon defendant, saying: "I think under these circumstances where you have a woman of this age that undoubtedly has no training in mechanics she has to rely on the seller." There was adequate evidence on this point for submission of the issue to the jury. . . .

Judgment reversed and cause remanded with directions.

[This case was decided under the Uniform Sales Act, but the result should be the same under the Code.]

GIRARD TRUST CORN EXCHANGE BANK v. WARREN LEPLEY FORD, INC.

(No. 1) 1957, 12 Pa. D. & C. 2d. 351

Ford Motor Company delivered via carrier five cars to Lepley Ford, Inc., under an agreement that until the cars were paid for, the title should remain with Ford Motor Company with the right reserved to retake possession and resell the cars until title passed to the dealer. The carrier delivered the cars to Lepley despite instructions not to deliver the cars until payment in full was made either in cash or certified checks. Lepley gave uncertified checks in payment for three of the cars, and made no payment at all for the other two. Lepley is now in receivership and plaintiff demands that the receivers return the five cars since title to the cars is still in the plaintiff and that plaintiff is entitled to the cars under the agreement. The Girard Bank and the receivers of Lepley Ford opposed this demand of Ford Motor Co., Inc., who is the actual plaintiff in this action.

MILNER, J. . . . There can be no doubt that this matter comes within the scope of the Uniform Commercial Code . . . which is intended to encompass commercial transactions within this Commonwealth. After a careful study of the Code, we conclude that we are compelled to find against the petitioner. [Plaintiff]

The Code is an attempt to codify all existing law governing commercial transactions and reference should not be made to one section alone. The Code must be considered as a whole, and each section should be read in conjunction with others in order to ascertain the intent of the legislature.

One of the changes brought about by the Code is in reference to title to property. The common law and The Sales Act of May 19, 1915, P.L. 543, 69 P.S. Section 1 et seq., made the rights of the parties to a transaction depend upon the location of the legal title. The Code, however, provides for the rights of parties irrespective of the location of legal title: Introductory Comment, Pennsylvania Bar Association Notes, 12A PS page 62. The first sentence of Section 2-401 of the Code provides:

> Each provision of this Article with regard to the rights, obligations and remedies of the seller, the buyer, purchasers or other third parties applies irrespective of title to the goods except where the provision refers to such title.

The reason for the rule is to be found in the Uniform Commercial Code Comment, 12A PS page 63, wherein it is stated:

> The arrangement of the present Article is in terms of contract for sale and the various steps of its performance. The legal consequences are stated as following directly from the contract and action taken under it without resorting to the idea of when property or title passed or was to pass as being the determining factor. The purpose is to avoid making practical issue between practical men turn upon the location of an intangible something, the passing of which no man can prove by evidence and to substitute for such abstractions proof of words and actions of a tangible character.

The article on secured transactions removes any doubt of the lack of importance of where legal title rests. Section 9-202 provides: "Each provision of this Article with regard to rights, obligations and remedies applies whether title to collateral is in the secured party or in the debtor."

[Here the court points out that the only interest Ford Motors had was a security interest in the cars, and that Ford Motors had not taken the required steps to perfect the security interest under the Code–Article 9. Since it was also true that the receivers were unaware of the interest of Ford Motors, the court held that the receivers took priority over the security interest and need not return the cars.]

INDEPENDENT NEWS CO. v. WILLIAMS
1961, 293 F. 2d 510

McLaughlin, C. J. Can a second-hand periodical dealer who purchases cover-removed comics from waste paper dealers be enjoined . . .

from marketing them as reading material? . . . Plaintiff, Independent News Co., Inc., is the distributor of the comics. . . . The defendant, Harry Williams, is a Philadelphia distributor of second-hand books and magazines.

The critical facts involve the distribution system used in marketing the comics. The distributor, Independent, pursuant to a written contract, sells the comics to the wholesaler. The comics are to be offered for sale during a period specified by the publisher. The wholesaler then sells them to the various retail outlets with the same restriction. At the end of the sales period, the wholesaler reacquires from the retail outlets all unsold comics and gives the retailer full credit. In turn, the wholesaler is entitled to full credit from Independent. However, instead of returning the entire comic, the agreement provides that unless otherwise directed, the wholesaler need only return the covers. As to the remaining portion of the comic, the wholesaler is obligated to, ". . . destroy or mutilate the remaining portions so as to render them unsalable as publications.". . .

[Here the court points out that the contract required that the destroyed or mutilated copies were to be disposed of or sold only as waste paper, and that the wholesaler should obtain a written agreement from a purchaser of such copies that he would use them only for waste, and not resell them. The defendant purchased cover-removed comics from waste paper dealers and resold them. No written commitment not to resell was obtained from the waste paper dealers, and it appeared that the defendant had no knowledge that the waste paper dealers were required to sell the coverless comics as wastepaper only. This action is brought to enjoin defendants from selling these comics as reading material.]

. . . Under the Uniform Commercial Code, adopted in Pennsylvania, Section 2-403 (2), . . . provides "(2) Any entrusting of possession of goods to a merchant who deals in goods of that kind gives him power to transfer all rights of the entruster to a buyer in ordinary course of business."

That section of the Code has broadened the protection of buyers in the ordinary course of business and has changed prior Pennsylvania law. . . . In the case at bar, plaintiffs ". . . conceded that plaintiffs have 'entrusted' the magazines in question to the Wholesaler—Agent." However, they dispute the applicability of Section 2-403 (2) stating: "(a) Wholesaler-Agent is not a 'merchant who deals in goods of that kind' . . . and "(b) neither the waste paper house nor the defendant is a 'buyer in the ordinary course of business' as defined by the Code."

The first assertion seeks to distinguish between the Wholesaler ". . . selling new publications prior to or during the publication period," and the wholesaler selling the cover-removed magazines. The argument is specious. The wholesaler deals in comics, and the fact that the covers are present, or not is irrelevant. His regular business is dealing with comics and as such he is a "merchant who deals in goods of that kind."

The interrelated second contention, namely, that neither the waste paper dealer nor the defendant are buyers in the ordinary course of business is equally without merit. . . . Section 1-201 (9) of the Code, . . . provides: "(9) 'Buyer in ordinary course of business' means a person who in good faith and without knowledge that the sale to him is in violation of the ownership rights or security interest of a third party in the goods buys in ordinary course from a person in the business of selling goods of that kind. . . ."

. . . There is no evidence in the record . . . that shows that the waste paper dealers had any notice of any restriction whatsoever on the cover-removed comics purchased from the wholesaler. It follows, that when the wholesaler sold these coverless comics to the waste paper dealer, the waste paper dealer, under Section 2-403 (2) of the Code, obtained the totality of property rights in the comics, which included the right to use or sell them as reading material. . . .

The judgment of the district court will be affirmed.

Review Questions and Problems

1. What is meant by the term "conforming goods"?
2. If the price of goods sold is, by the agreement, to be fixed by the seller, and he fails to do so, what option does the buyer have?
3. A merchant contracted to sell goods to a buyer but specifically told the buyer that he was not certain that he himself owned the goods as another party also claimed them. The buyer was willing, nevertheless, to purchase the goods. It turned out that the third party's title was indeed good. Has the merchant breached a warranty?
4. *A* went to a dealer in hardware and told the dealer that he wanted to buy a spade, describing in detail the particular purpose he wished to accomplish. The dealer then sold him a spade which was of a well known make carrying a trade name. The spade was not suitable and failed to accomplish *A*'s purpose. The dealer contends that he made no warranty of fitness for a particular purpose since he sold the spade under a trade name. Is this correct?
5. *A* shipped ten radios to *B*, a dealer in radios. *C*, a judgment creditor of *B*, wishes to levy on all the radios in *B*'s store, not knowing about the ten radios held by *B* on consignment from *A*. Could *C* have a better right in the ten radios than *A*?
6. *X* took his nearly new television set to *Y*, who sold both new and used television sets, and left it in *Y*'s store for minor repairs. The repairs were made and the television set was ready for *X* to pick up. *Z* came into *Y*'s store and saw this particular television set. *Z* purchased it from one of *Y*'s employees who sold it believing it to be one properly held for sale. *Z* took the television set home. Does *X* or *Z* have the better right to the television set?

7. If a sales contract involves wheat not yet planted, when would the wheat become identified goods?
8. *A* offered to deliver proper goods to *B*, pursuant to a contract between the parties. What are *A*'s rights against *B*, assuming there is no specific contract provision requiring any further action on *A*'s part?
9. *X* contracted to buy goods from *Y*. Under the agreement, *Y* delivered proper goods to *Z* carrier. Assuming no further contract requirement, does *X* or *Y* bear the loss if the goods are now destroyed?
10. If in the question above, *Y* had not delivered the proper goods to the carrier, would the result be the same?
11. Pursuant to a contract between *A* and *B*, *A* shipped goods to *B*. The contract provided that *B* was to pay for the goods on delivery. *B* demanded the right to inspect the goods before he paid for them. Does *B* have this right?
12. *D* sold goods to *B* under a contract which required *B* to pick up the goods at *D*'s place of business. The contract also provided that *B* would have thirty days to pay for the goods. When *B* came to get the goods, as had been properly agreed upon by the parties, *D* refused to let *B* have them unless *D* paid cash. *D*'s reason for his refusal was that he had discovered *B* to be insolvent. Is *D*'s action justified?
13. *A* had contracted to sell and deliver goods to *B* at a contract price of $1000. *A* refused to go ahead with the contract because the price of similar goods had risen twenty-five per cent since the contract was made. *B* then contracted with *C* to buy similar goods at a price of $1,300, and wants to recover $300 from *A*. May he do so?
14. *A* sold his entire inventory to *B* and gave *B* a sworn list of all his creditors. He omitted *C*'s name from the list, and *C* upon learning of the transfer, contends the transfer is ineffective as to him and that he has the right to obtain judgment against *A* and levy on the goods, if necessary. Is *C* correct in his contention?
15. *F* stored one hundred bushels of shelled corn in *T*'s public grain elevator and received a negotiable warehouse receipt covering the stored corn. *F* properly negotiated the receipt to *H*, a good faith purchaser. *B* bought fifty bushels of this corn from *T*—from whom he had purchased grain on previous occasions—intending to use the corn as feed for his livestock. Could *H* reclaim the corn from *B*?

44

Bailments of Personal Property

GENERAL RULES

6-69. Definition of bailments. Possession of property is often temporarily surrendered by the owner. In such cases the person taking possession may perform some service pertaining to the goods, after which he returns them to the owner. Upon many occasions one person borrows or rents an article which belongs to another. A contract whereby possession of personal property is surrendered by the owner with provision for its return at a later time forms a *bailment.*[1] The owner of the goods is known as the *bailor,* whereas the one receiving possession is called the *bailee.* From the foregoing definition it appears that three distinct requisites of a bailment exist. If these essentials are thoroughly understood, the student should encounter no difficulty in distinguishing a bailment from other contractual relationships. The three requisites are: (1) retention of title by bailor; (2) possession and temporary control of the property by the bailee; (3) ultimate possession to revert to the bailor unless he orders it transferred to some designated third person.

6-70. Distinguished from a sale. It often becomes important to determine whether a particular transaction is a bailment or a sale. To illustrate: *A* surrenders possession of 50 sheep to *B,* who, by the terms of the agreement, is to return to *A,* at the end of a three-year period, 50 sheep of like kind, age, and weight. Is this transaction a sale of a certain 50 sheep for 50 other sheep? Or is it a bailment? If it is a sale and one half of the sheep die, the loss falls upon *B* rather than upon *A.* Furthermore, creditors of *B* may levy upon the sheep, provided it is a sale; whereas, if a bailment has been created, only the creditors of *A* may assert an interest in the sheep. A purchaser may pass title to goods purchased to a third party, whereas a bailee has no right to pass title to goods of the bailor unless he also happens to be acting as the bailor's agent. The test used in the foregoing illustration to determine the nature of the transaction is the application of the third requisite of a bailment. Are the identical articles delivered to be returned to the bailor? A close

[1] Drybrough v. Veech, page 946.

analysis of the terms of the particular agreement shows that a delivery of 50 other sheep of like kind and character would satisfy all requirements. Thus, a sale of 50 sheep for 50 sheep to be delivered later has taken place; and *B* is a purchaser rather than a bailee.

A mere change in the form of the property while in the hands of the bailee does not affect the relationship. Thus, *A* floats logs downstream to *B*, to be sawed into lumber by the latter. *B* is as much a bailee of the lumber as he was of the logs.

6-71. Types of bailment. Bailments group naturally into three classes: bailments for the benefit of the bailor; bailments for the benefit of the bailee; and bailments for the mutual benefit of the bailor and the bailee. Typical of the first group are those cases in which the bailor leaves goods in the safekeeping of the bailee under circumstances that negative the idea of compensation. Inasmuch as the bailee is not to be paid in any manner, the bailment is for the exclusive benefit of the bailor. A bailment for the benefit of the bailee is best exemplified by a loan of some article. Thus, *A* borrows *B*'s watch to carry for the day. The bailment is one for the sole benefit of *A*.

The most important type of bailment is the one in which both parties are to benefit. Contracts for repair, carriage, storage, or pledge of property fall within this class. The bailor receives the benefit of some service; the bailee benefits by the receipt of certain agreed compensation; thus both parties profit as a result of the bailment.

6-72. Degree of care required. Provided that proper care has been exercised by the bailee, any loss or damage to the property bailed follows title and consequently falls upon the bailor. Each type of bailment requires a different degree of care. In a bailment for the benefit of the bailor, the bailee is required to exercise only slight care, while, in one for the benefit of the bailee, extraordinary care is essential. A bailment for the mutual benefit of the parties demands only ordinary care on the part of the bailee. *Ordinary care* is defined as that care which the average individual usually exercises over his own property.[2] Slight care and extraordinary care vary from ordinary care in that the one is a lower, and the other a higher, degree of care than ordinary care.

Furthermore, the amount of care demanded varies with the nature and value of the article bailed. The care found to be sufficient in the case of a carpenter's tool chest would probably not be ample for a diamond ring worth $10,000. A higher standard of protection is required for valuable articles than for those less valuable.

Property leased by the bailor to the bailee must be reasonably fit for the service desired. For this reason it is the duty of the bailor to notify

[2] Kassvan v. Thomas E. McElroy Co., page 948.

the bailee of all defects in the property leased, of which he might reasonably have been aware. The bailor is responsible for any damage suffered by the bailee as the result of such defects, unless he notifies the bailee of them. This rule holds true even though the bailor is not aware of the defect if, by the exercise of reasonable diligence, he could have discovered it. If, on the other hand, the article is merely loaned to the bailee—a bailment for the benefit of the bailee—the bailor is in duty bound to notify the bailee only of known defects.[3] A bailor who fails to give the required notice of a defect is liable to any person who he might anticipate would be using the defective article as a result of the bailment. Employees of the bailee and members of the bailee's family might well recover of the bailor for injuries received as a consequence of the defect.

6-73. Contracts against required care. Certain classes of bailees have found it desirable to provide in the bailment agreement against any liability resulting from their negligence or that of their employees. Such a provision found in the contract of a quasi-public bailee, such as a railway or a hotel, is illegal and, therefore, ineffective. The ordinary private bailee, however, may insert in the contract any provision which he desires, as long as the bailor is willing to enter into the agreement under the particular terms.[4] If the latter is unwilling to accept the particular terms, he is at liberty to contract elsewhere. Where the provision is such as to defeat the real purpose of the contract and to shock the sense of justice of the court, the provision will not be enforced. Thus, *A* stored apples in *B*'s private warehouse to protect them against the winter weather. The agreement provided that they were left at the owner's risk. *B* failed to heat the building, and the apples were frozen. It was held that such a provision did not relieve *B* from liability.

6-74. Effect of exceeding the bailment contract. The bailment agreement governs the duties and rights of the bailee. Should he treat the property in a different manner, or use it for some purpose other than that contemplated by the contract, he becomes liable for any loss or damage to the property in the interim.[5] This result appears to be true, although the damage can in no sense be attributed to the conduct of the bailee. To illustrate: Let us assume that *A* stores his car in *B*'s public garage for the winter. *B*, because of a crowded condition, has the car temporarily moved to another garage without the consent of *A*. As the result of a cyclone, the car is destroyed while at the second location. The loss falls upon *B*, as he exceeded the terms of the bailment contract. In a restricted sense, the bailee is guilty of conversion of the bailor's property during the period in which the contract terms are being violated.

[3] Gagnon v. Dana et al., page 949.
[4] Samelson v. Harper's Furs, page 950.
[5] McCurdy v. Wallblom Co., page 951.

6-75. No right to deny title of bailor. The bailee has no right to deny the title of the bailor unless he has yielded possession to one having paramount title. In other words, the bailee has no right to retain possession of the property merely because he is able to prove that the bailor does not have title. In order to defeat the bailor's right to possession, the bailee must show that he has returned the property to someone having better title, or is holding the property under an agreement with the true owner.

COMMON CARRIERS

6-76. Definition. A common carrier of freight is defined as one who holds himself out as being ready and willing to carry goods for anyone who presents them. A common, or public, carrier is distinguished from a private carrier in that the former stands ready to serve anyone desiring the service, while the latter operates under a contract only. A common carrier usually operates between definite termini or over a definite route. A private carrier transports freight from point to point, as demanded by his contract with the shipper. A private carrier becomes a public one as soon as it begins to cover definite territory at somewhat regular intervals and carries goods for anyone desiring to ship them. An ordinary drayman is a private carrier, but the operator of a truck between two cities on a regular schedule would, under most circumstances, be a common carrier.

A common carrier rests under a duty to accept goods for transportation whenever they are presented. It may, however, limit its business to a particular kind of property. The mere fact that a truck owner limits his business to the transportation of milk does not render him a private carrier if he stands ready to carry milk for anyone. An express company is not bound to accept any or all personal property presented. Its business is limited to somewhat small and valuable articles.

6-77. Care required of the common carrier. The contract for carriage of goods constitutes a mutual benefit bailment, but the care required of the carrier greatly exceeds that of the ordinary bailee. A common carrier is an absolute insurer of the safe delivery of the goods to their destination. This rule is subject to only five exceptions. Any loss or damage which results from (1) an act of God, (2) action of an alien enemy, (3) order of public authority, (4) inherent nature of the goods, or (5) misconduct of the shipper must fall upon the one possessing title. Thus, any loss which results from an accident or the wilful misconduct of some third party must be borne by the carrier. For example, A, in order to injure a certain railway company, sets fire to several boxcars loaded with freight. Any damage to the goods falls upon the carrier. On the other hand, if lightning, an act of God, had set fire to the cars, the loss would have fallen upon the shipper.

Any damage to goods in shipment which results from the very nature of the goods or from the failure properly to crate or protect the property must be suffered by the shipper. Thus, the damage to a shipment of fresh strawberries, caused by excessive heat during the period of shipment, must be borne by the shipper, provided the carrier has offered proper refrigeration.

Goods may be damaged while in the possession of either the receiving or a connecting carrier. Damages arising while goods are being transported by a connecting carrier may be recovered by the shipper from either of the two carriers. If the shipper files his claim against the original carrier, it, in turn, demands restitution from the connecting carrier.

6-78. Contract against liability of carrier. A common carrier may not contract away its liability for goods damaged in shipment by the negligence of its employees. Such a provision in a bill of lading is illegal. It may, however, where lower rates are granted, relieve itself from the consequences of causes or of conduct over which it has no control. Thus, a provision which relieves a carrier from damage caused by fire is effective, where the fire is not caused by any misconduct on the part of employees.

Furthermore, the company may limit its liability to an agreed valuation. The shipper is limited in his recovery to the value asserted in the bill of lading. The rate charged for transportation may vary with the value of the property shipped. It is for this reason that the agreed valuation is binding.[6]

6-79. Beginning of the relation. The liability of the carrier attaches as soon as the goods are delivered to it. The receipt of the goods is usually acknowledged by a bill of lading, which sets forth the terms and conditions of shipment. The carrier becomes responsible for a carload shipment as soon as the car has been delivered to it. If the car is loaded while located upon railroad property, the carrier becomes liable at the moment the car is fully loaded.

6-80. Termination of the relation. The extreme degree of care required of the carrier may be terminated before the goods are actually delivered to the consignee. Three views prevail in this country as to when the relationship of carrier ceases. Some states hold that the duties of the carrier end and those of a warehouseman begin as soon as the local shipment is unloaded from the car into the freight house. Others hold the carrier to strict liability until the consignee has had a reasonable time in which to inspect and remove the shipment. Still other states hold that the consignee is entitled to notice and that he has a reasonable time after notice in which to remove the goods before the liability of the carrier as a

[6] Tilson v. Terminal R. Ass'n. of St. Louis, page 952.

carrier is terminated.[7] To illustrate: Let us assume that goods arrive at their destination and are unloaded in the freight house. Before the consignee has had time to take them away, the goods are destroyed by fire, although the carrier has exercised ordinary care. Under the first of these views, the loss would fall upon the shipper, as at the time of the fire the railway was no longer a carrier but a warehouseman. Under the other two views, the loss would fall on the carrier, as the extreme liability had not yet terminated, inasmuch as no time had been given for delivery.

The carload shipment is delivered as soon as it is placed on the private switch of the consignee or "spotted" at the unloading platform. Any subsequent loss, unless it results from the negligence of the carrier, must fall upon the owner of the goods.

6-81. Rates. Rates charged by common carriers must be reasonable. Carriers engaged in interstate business are subject to the regulation of the Interstate Commerce Commission and all tariffs or rate schedules must be filed with it. Almost all the states have railroad commissions for the purpose of establishing rates for intrastate business. These commissions also require tariffs to be filed with them. Any rate either higher or lower than that shown in the tariff is illegal. Discriminatory rates by the use of rebates are also forbidden, and the giving or receiving of rebates constitutes a crime.

A railway may insist upon the payment of the charges at the time it accepts the delivery. Since it has a lien upon the goods as security for the charges, however, it customarily waits until the goods are delivered, before collecting. The carrier usually refuses to surrender the goods unless the freight is paid, and, if the freight remains unpaid for a certain period of time, it may advertise the property for sale. Any surplus, above the charges, realized from the sale reverts to the owner of the goods.

Any undue delay on the part of the consignee in removing the goods from the warehouse or the tracks of the railway permits the carrier to add a small additional charge known as demurrage.

[7] Walters et al. v. Detroit United Ry. Co. page 882.

BAILMENTS OF PERSONAL PROPERTY CASES

DRYBROUGH v. VEECH

1951, (Ky.) 238 S.W.2d 996

MILLIKEN, J. This is an appeal from an order of the trial court overruling defendant's (Drybrough's) motion for judgment notwithstanding a verdict against him for $214. . . .

The plaintiff, Ray F. Veech, filed her petition stating that she had parked her automobile at the parking lot of the defendant, F. W. Drybrough, on South Fourth Street, Louisville, paid fifty cents for the privilege, and that the defendant, Drybrough, "and his agents and servants so negligently managed and conducted said parking lot . . . as to cause and permit the plaintiff's fur coat to be stolen from the automobile while parked on said lot." The petition alleged that "as a direct and proximate result of said negligence" the plaintiff suffered damages amounting to the value of the fur coat.

The defendant, Drybrough, filed no demurrer to the petition, but simply filed an answer stating "that he is without knowledge or information sufficient to constitute a belief and therefore specifically denies each and every additional allegation, word, and figure of the plaintiff's petition." Upon a verdict being rendered for the plaintiff, the defendant moved the court for judgment notwithstanding the verdict upon the ground that the petition did not state a cause of action. When the trial court overruled this motion, appeal was taken directly from this ruling. . . .

The petition in the case at bar alleges a bailment of the automobile, but no bailment of the contents of the car or the fur coat. The only way the petition can be considered adequate as imposing a duty on the bailee in regard to the fur coat is for us to conclude that the bailment of the automobile implies a bailment of the contents of the car. As stated in appellant's brief: "Here it is claimed an automobile was bailed and a coat was stolen." In the one Kentucky case upon the subject, *Barnett v. Latonia Jockey Club*, 1933, 249 Ky. 285, 60 S.W.2d, 622, 624, we said: "Moreover, this action complains of no dereliction with reference to the automobile, but only of what happened to its contents, and the law recognizes well-settled distinctions between liability of a bailee for a bailed vehicle and liability for its contents, the latter existing only in special cases which it is the duty of the loser (the alleged bailor) to both allege and prove before recovery may be had."

There being no allegation of a bailment of the coat or its presence in the car being called to the attention of the parking lot attendants in any way, we conclude there was no duty as to the coat imposed upon the appellant or his agents at the parking lot and as a consequence they could not be negligent as to it. It is not necessary for us to discuss cases involving obligations of gratuitous bailees because here there was no bailment of the coat, gratuitous or otherwise. Where a petition fails to state a duty owed by the defendant, as in the case at bar, a judgment notwithstanding the verdict should be entered for the defendant. *Helton v. Louisville & N. R. Co.*, 313 Ky. 693, 233 S.W.2d 401.

The judgment is reversed with directions for the trial court to enter judgment for the defendant in accordance with his motion notwithstanding the verdict against him.

KASSVAN v. THOMAS E. McELROY CO.
1950, 179 F.2d 97

The plaintiff, Kassvan, shipped certain furs to defendant, valued at $3,950, for inspection and purchase if they were the kind and quality desired. They were sent by Railway Express and valued at $400. The defendant returned them by the same express agency, placing a value of $50 on them. They were lost in transit during the return, and the Railway Express was limited in liability to $50. This is an attempt to recover the balance from the defendant on the theory of negligence by the bailee.

MAJOR, C. J. . . . From the above findings, the court concluded, as alleged in count 3 of the complaint, that the defendant in returning plaintiff's furs acted negligently in declaring a value of $50.00, and as a result plaintiffs were deprived of a right of action against the express company when the furs were lost by the latter. Judgment in favor of the plaintiffs was for the full value of the furs. The court also concluded that the fact that both plaintiffs and defendant carried insurance against loss did not affect the question of defendant's liability.

In addition to the facts found by the court, others shown by the stipulation appear to be material. Plaintiffs gave defendant no verbal or written instructions in regard to the return shipment or the valuation to be placed upon the furs. Plaintiffs made no offer to pay any part of the carrier charges on the return shipment. The express company's charges were based largely upon the declared value of the shipment, and if they had been valued in excess of the $50.00 minimum, an extra charge would have been made. The charge was 70¢ on a $50.00 valuation of the furs, and $4.00 on a full valuation.

Plaintiffs were insured against loss of the furs in transit. Their policy contained, among others, the following provisions: "It is understood and agreed that in respect to shipments by Railway Express Agency, the assured will declare to the Express Agency a valuation of 10% of the amount of each shipment," and "This policy also includes return shipments made by Railway Express Company only."

We need not cite cases for the proposition that the burden was upon the plaintiffs to establish the defendant's negligence as a prerequisite to its right of recovery. While perhaps immaterial, we also need not cite cases in support of the proposition that defendant's delivery of the furs to the express company terminated the bailment and that it had no proprietary interest in the goods while in transit. Defendant's liability as epitomized by the judgment rests solely on the premise that it was negligent in placing a value of $50.00 on the furs rather than their actual value.

We are unable to discern in what respect defendant acted other than a reasonably prudent person would have acted under similar circumstances.

It can hardly be claimed that defendant had any greater or different duty to protect the plaintiffs from loss during shipment than plaintiffs had to protect themselves. True, plaintiffs placed a higher valuation on the furs for the purpose of the outgoing shipment than the defendant did for their return, but even so, plaintiffs' valuation was only 10% of their actual value and it is obvious that this valuation was not for the purpose of protecting them against loss while the goods were in transit but because of a requirement contained in their insurance policy. The effect of plaintiffs' valuation was to relieve the express company of all damages for loss on the outgoing shipment in excess of $400.00. Such being the case, why should the defendant as their bailee be held liable because in returning the goods it relieved the express company of all liability in excess of $50.00? To so hold is to require of the defendant as consignee the exercise of a higher degree of care in the handling of plaintiffs' property than plaintiffs were willing to exercise on their own behalf.

If defendant had fixed the same valuation on the return of the goods as plaintiffs fixed on their original shipment, the question would, of course, be more simple. There is no contention, however, that defendant was negligent in fixing a $50.00 valuation rather than one of $400.00, but the claim is that the defendant was negligent in fixing a $50.00 valuation rather than a full valuation of $3,950.00. While the record does not specifically show, we think it properly inferable that defendant had knowledge that plaintiffs were relying upon their insurance rather than on the express company in the event of loss of goods in shipment. Certainly plaintiffs' valuation of 10% would so indicate. It also seems that if plaintiffs expected to rely upon the express company for loss sustained during the return shipment that they were under a duty to so advise the defendant, with the request that it place a valuation upon the goods which would permit such result. Particularly is this so when their valuation on the outgoing shipment indicated that they were not so relying.

While the question is not free from doubt, we are of the view that it cannot be held as a matter of law that the defendant was negligent in the respect relied upon. And this is so irrespective of the testimony relied upon by the defendant as to the custom and usage relative to valuation.

The judgment is, therefore, reversed and the cause remanded, with directions that the complaint be dismissed.

GAGNON v. DANA et al.

1898, 69 N.H. 264, 39 Atl. 982

This action was brought by Frank Gagnon against Dana & Provost for personal injuries resulting from a fall of staging while working at the

Sacred Heart Hospital, in Manchester, occasioned by the breaking of an unsound and decayed bracket. The plaintiff was employed by one Gay, who borrowed this bracket, along with others, from the defendant. There was some slight evidence that the defendants knew the brackets were defective, although the evidence was conflicting on this point. The lower court instructed the jury that it was the defendants' duty to notify the plaintiff's employer of any known defects, or defects of which they ought to have known. The correctness of this instruction is in dispute, the defendants contending that it was improper.

BLODGETT, J. The brackets having been loaned by the defendants for the use of the borrower, without any reward or compensation to be received by them from him, their only duty in respect to defects was to inform him of any of which they were aware, and which might make the use of the loan perilous to him or to his servants, one of whom was the plaintiff. "The ground of this obligation is that, when a person lends, he ought to confer a benefit, and not to do a mischief. . . ." But the obligation of a mere lender goes no further than this, and he cannot, therefore, be made liable for not communicating anything which he did not in fact know, whether he ought to have known it or not. . . .

It would be the greatest injustice as well as extending the law beyond any recognized principle, to subject him to liability for defects of which he is not aware; and especially in a case like this, where the defect complained of was apparently as open to ascertainment by the plaintiff as it could possibly have been to the defendants. . . . While in many respects the duties and liabilities of the parties are materially different in the case of a gratuitous bailment and one for hire, it is enough for the present purpose to observe that while in the former the benefit is exclusively to the bailee, and therefore the liability of the bailor for defects in the thing loaned extends only to those which are known to him and not communicated to the bailee, in the latter, the bailment being for the mutual benefit of both alike, the bailor's obligation is, and of right ought to be, correspondingly enlarged; and it is therefore his duty to deliver the thing hired in a proper condition to be used as contemplated by the parties, and for failure to do so he is justly liable for the damage directly resulting to the bailee or his servants from its unsafe condition.

Judgment for defendants.

SAMELSON v. HARPER'S FURS

1955, (Conn.) 120 A.2d 429

Plaintiff's intestate delivered a mink jacket to defendant's employee for storage with defendant who was engaged in the storage business. She signed a receipt, issued in duplicate, and paid the storage charge of $3.00. The receipt contained a blank for valuation of the jacket, which was filled in for $100.00. A provision, among others, on the other side of the receipt provided in essence that defendant would not be liable for loss or damage to the goods for more than the stated value. When plaintiff presented the receipt to defendant, the defendant was unable to find a duplicate receipt or the jacket. It was found that defendant's employee had stolen the jacket and had not given the duplicate receipt to defendant. Defendant admits the bailment of the jacket but denies liability. The plaintiff, in the lower court, sued on grounds of negligence and breach of contract. The court found no negligence but allowed recovery for breach of contract. Appealed.

FITZGERALD, J. . . . On the ground of public policy the declared Connecticut rule is that a bailee cannot limit his liability by special contract so as to be relieved against his own negligence. *Malone v. Santora,* 135 Conn. 286, 293, 64 A.2d 51. However, in the case at bar, the imposed limitation is referable only to what purports to be a stipulation as to the agreed value of the subject of the bailment. In 6 Am. Jur. 304, § 186, appears this statement of the law:

"(A) bailee for hire (as was the defendant), without contravening the principle, that he cannot contract for exemption of limitation from liability on account of his own negligence, may, by reasonable provisions, contract to limit his liability to an agreed value of the article received, provided the rate charged is based, bona fide, upon the value of the article and the stipulation does not amount to a mere arbitrary limitation designed to apply in all cases."

It is found that the declared value of the mink jacket was that made by Mrs. Samelson. The amount was not an arbitrary sum fixed in advance by the defendant, as appears in *Nothnagle v. New York, N. H. & H. R. Co.,* 139 Conn. 278, 280, 93 A.2d 165. It was open to discussion and could have been revised within five days thereafter. Moreover, Mrs. Samelson signed the receipt directly under the provision appearing in bold type as described. In doing so she accepted all terms and conditions. . . . Damages awarded to the plaintiff under the prevailing count are limited to $100 in view of the sustained special defense.

McCURDY v. WALLBLOM CO.

1905, 94 Minn. 326, 102 N.W. 873

This was an action of trover brought by McCurdy to recover the value of certain household furniture. The plaintiff stored furniture with the defendant, while the latter conducted business at a certain location. Later the defendant, without the consent or knowledge of the plaintiff, moved his business to a new location nearby. While at the new location the goods were destroyed by fire, no question of negligence being involved.

JAGGARD, J. . . . Where goods which have been removed by the bailee from an agreed to another place of storage without notice to or consent of the bailor are destroyed by fire, the bailee is liable in an action at law for the reasonable market value of the goods. Schouler, Bailments, 106. Such a state of facts makes out "a case of the defendant having taken the plaintiff's goods to a place where he had no right to take them; therefore he must pay the loss. . . ." The bailor is entitled to the safety, to the convenience, and to any and every advantage of the agreed location. He is entitled to unchanged hazards as to things priceless to him personally, as well as to things only merchantable. . . .

Any other rule here applied would serve no useful purpose, but would easily conduce to misappropriation and fraud, put a premium on craftiness, jeopardize the property of the ordinary prudent man, and wholly fail to afford adequate protection to the community in general.

Judgment for plaintiff.

TILSON v. TERMINAL R. ASS'N OF ST. LOUIS

1951, (Mo., St. Louis App.) 236 S.W.2d 42

This is an action brought by Tilson to recover damages for the loss of certain articles taken from her luggage while it was in the possession and control of the defendant. She had given two pieces of hand luggage to one of defendant's redcaps and received two claim checks. Other facts appear in the opinion.

BENNICK, J. . . . After turning the bags over to the redcap, plaintiff walked back to the waiting room, where the redcap shortly came to her and informed her that while he had been occupied in rendering service to another person, the bags had disappeared from his truck and could not be located. Plaintiff was thereupon taken to the station master's office, where she gave a description of the contents of her bags, and then boarded her train and went on to Kansas City without them. A few days later her bags were delivered to her in Kansas City with all their contents intact except for certain articles of jewelry valued at $2,885.

The whole question in the case was one of the amount that plaintiff was entitled to recover.

At the time in question there was a tariff in effect (Local Passenger Tariff No. 9), which had been issued by the Interstate Commerce Commission, and which prescribed the charges that defendant's redcaps might make for the handling of hand baggage and other personal effects of passengers. Under the terms of such tariff it was provided that the redcap's charge for his service would be at the rate of ten cents for each piece of luggage handled, and that defendant's liability would be limited to $25 for each bag or parcel unless a greater value was declared in writing by the passenger. In the event a greater value was declared, an additional charge of ten cents per bag or parcel would be made for each $100 or fraction thereof above the $25 so declared.

Defendant offered in evidence a copy of the tariff duly certified by the Secretary over the seal of the Interstate Commerce Commission. While the tariff was excluded at the trial, there was no question of its existence, but instead the exclusion was put upon the ground that the matters involved in the particular transaction were purely intrastate so as to have rendered the tariff inapplicable.

This was in accord with plaintiff's theory that the transaction between herself and the redcap was a mere contract of bailment which was not only made but intended to be wholly performed in Missouri, and which was entirely separate and distinct from plaintiff's contract for her own interstate transportation.

Defendant contended, on the other hand, that plaintiff was bound, and the case governed, by the provisions of the tariff, and that in the absence of a greater declared valuation, its liability was limited to $25 each for the two bags and their contents, or to a total of $50.

The court submitted the case upon plaintiff's theory, and a verdict was returned in favor of plaintiff, and against defendant, in the sum of $2,885. In due time defendant filed its motion for judgment in accordance with its motions for a directed verdict for plaintiff for $50, or, in the alternative, for a new trial. The court overruled the motion for judgment, but sustained the motion for a new trial upon the ground of error in the exclusion of the tariff and in the submission of the case upon plaintiff's theory of recovery. Plaintiff thereupon gave notice of appeal from the order sustaining the motion for a new trial, and by proper successive steps has caused the case to be transferred to this court for our review.

It could be no ground for denying the application of the tariff that plaintiff had no actual knowledge of its existence. Once a regulation limiting liability is filed with the Interstate Commerce Commission in compliance with law, it becomes binding on the carrier and the passenger alike, whether or not the latter is aware of the limitation. In other words, where the carrier, as in this instance, files a tariff giving a choice of rates based on a difference in declared valuation, the passenger is to be charged with notice that the risk which the carrier assumes will be based on the rate he pays for the service rendered. . . .

The question of whether the tariff is controlling in the case at bar is therefore reduced to one of whether, in undertaking to handle plaintiff's luggage, the redcap was engaged in the furtherance of interstate commerce. Of this there would seem to be no room for doubt. That plaintiff's journey was interstate is of course conceded. In making her journey plaintiff had the right to carry the two pieces of hand baggage with her in the cars of the successive trains upon which she rode; and the service of the redcap in transferring her luggage from the one train to the other for the completion of her journey was, by both reason and precedent, so closely related to her own physical transportation in the cars as to have been essentially a part of such transportation. Indeed it is upon such precise theory that the charges for such service as the redcap rendered on the occasion in question are subject to regulation by the Interstate Commerce Commission. *Stopher v. Cincinnati Union Term. Co., Inc.*, 246 I.C.C. 41; *Williams v. Jacksonville Terminal Co.*, 315 U.S. 386, 397, 62 S.Ct. 659, 86 L.Ed. 914. There is actually nothing to be retried, and the order granting the new trial should therefore be reversed and the cause remanded with directions to the trial court to enter final judgment in favor of plaintiff, and against defendant, in the sum of $50. It is so ordered.

WALTERS et al. v. DETROIT UNITED RY. CO.

1905, 139 Mich. 303, 102 N.W. 745

CARPENTER, J. On the 7th of April, 1903, plaintiffs (Walters and another) . . . placed property in the custody of defendant's agent at Trenton, with instructions to ship the same over defendant's railway—defendant is a common carrier of merchandise—to them at Pontiac, Oakland county, on Friday, April 10th. . . . The goods were in fact shipped on the 8th and arrived in Pontiac on the 9th. They were placed in defendant's warehouse, and were there destroyed by fire, Tuesday, April 14th, before notice of their arrival was given to plaintiffs. Plaintiffs brought suit and recovered judgment upon the ground that defendant's liability as common carrier continued at the time the goods were destroyed. Defendant insists that a verdict should have been directed in its favor.

There was no evidence of negligence. If, at the time the goods were destroyed by fire, defendant continued to hold them under its responsibility as a common carrier, it was liable. If it did not so hold them, it was not liable. Jurists have not agreed as to the obligation of a carrier who holds goods after transit, awaiting delivery. Respecting this question,

"three distinct views have been taken: First, that when the transit is ended, and the carrier has placed the goods in his warehouse to await delivery to the consignee, his liability as carrier is ended, also, and he is responsible as warehouseman only; second, that merely placing the goods in the warehouse does not discharge the carrier, but that he remains liable as such until the consignee has had reasonable time after their arrival to inspect and take them away in the common course of business; third, that the liability of the carrier continues until the consignee has been notified of the receipt of the goods, and has had reasonable time, in the common course of business to take them away after such notification" *McMillan v. M.S. & N.O.R. Co.*, 16 Mich. 102....

We have no hesitancy in declaring that the carrier's obligations continue until the lapse of a reasonable time after he has notified the consignee of the arrival of the goods... In stating this conclusion, we have not overlooked defendant's contention that the rule does not apply where, as in this case, plaintiffs knew the probable date of shipment, and the probable time of arrival of the goods. To insist that this circumstance exempts the carrier from liability is to deny the existence of the rule we have just declared. To be more precise, it is to insist that the second, and not the third, of the rules heretofore stated, is the correct one.

Judgment affirmed.

Review Questions and Problems

1. A bill of lading of a common carrier contains a clause relieving it of liability for all loss to property in transit caused by fire. A fire, caused by the negligence of the carrier's agent, destroyed goods in shipment belonging to *B*. Has *B* an action against the carrier?
2. Miss *J* went to *M*'s restaurant to eat dinner and to watch a style show. She deposited her coat in *M*'s check room paying no fee for the service. The cloak room attendant also acted as hostess in the restaurant. When Miss *J* went to get her coat, it was gone, apparently stolen by some unknown third party. What type of bailment was this? Was *M* liable to Miss *J* for the value of the coat?
3. *A* brought some ore to be assayed and returned to *A*. *B* learned that the ore did not belong to *A* and refused to return it. *A* brought an action of replevin to recover the ore. Should he succeed?
4. *A* takes to *B*'s mill certain wheat to be ground into flour. After the wheat is ground into flour, but before the flour is returned to *A*, creditors of *B* levy upon the flour. Are their rights superior to those of *A*?
5. *B* was injured while using a defective wrench, furnished by *A* for consideration. *A* knew, or should have known, that the wrench was defective. Is *A* liable to *B* for the injury?
6. *A* accepted a truckload of eggs from *B* as a common carrier. *B* had entrusted the eggs to *A* without proper precautions as to their refrigeration. *A*'s driver learned during the journey that the eggs were not at proper temperature, but completed the delivery to *C*, who refused to accept them. Is *A* or *B* liable for the loss?
7. *B* employed *A*, a trucker, to transport several bales of cotton. The cotton was destroyed by fire while on *A*'s truck, the cause of the fire being unknown. *A* did not hold himself out to carry goods for the public and did not operate his truck on a regular schedule. If *A* was not negligent, could *B* recover from *A* for the cotton?
8. Goods shipped over the *B* Railway are stolen after they reach their

destination and are placed in the warehouse. Under what conditions may the carrier be held liable?

9. *W* parked *A*'s car in *W*'s parking lot. The car was unlocked and the keys were left in the glove compartment of the car. Some boys found the keys, stole the car and wrecked it. *A* brings action for damages against *W* who defends that leaving the keys, as he did, was his usual procedure with his own cars and that he was, therefore, not liable. Is *W* liable for the damage to the car?
10. *B* entered into a bailment with *A*, leaving his car in a parking lot operated by *A*. The car was stolen and when recovered, some articles of property, which had been left on the back seat and in the trunk, were gone. The court refused to allow recovery for these articles which consisted of sporting goods and architectural plans, on the ground that these articles were not part of the bailment since their presence was not known to the bailee and hence were not accepted by him. Would you agree with this reasoning and result?
11. *T* parked his car regularly in *P*'s garage. He locked his car and retained the keys. The car and valuable contents were stolen and when the car was found by the police, the contents were missing. *T* sued *P* contending *P* had violated a bailment contract by failing to return the car and contents. The court held that no bailment existed but only a lease for parking. What do you believe induced the court to reach this result?

BOOK VII

SECURED TRANSACTIONS

45

Security Devices Noncode States

7-1. Introduction. Prior to the enactment of the Uniform Commercial Code, several different devices were developed to give a creditor security rights in personal property. These devices are still used in states which have not adopted the Code to protect creditors where the debtor is in a position to offer such protection. These security devices fall into two categories: (1) those in which the creditor has a lien on personal property which is created by a bailment or similar relationship or by a mortgage and (2) those in which the creditor retains actual legal title to the property until payment is made. The basic principles of these various security devices will be discussed in this chapter for the purpose of supplying the historical background for the secured transaction provisions of the Code.

7-2. Consignments. A consignment consists of a shipment of goods by the owner, called the consignor, to an agent, called the consignee or factor, for the purpose of having them sold by the agent who receives a commission for his services. The device is often used by a manufacturer who considers the retailer a poor financial risk, or by a producer with a new product. It is used in these situations because the consignee holds the proceeds of the sale in trust for the consignor giving the consignor a preferred claim to the proceeds. It should be noted that a consignor who allows a consignee to treat the proceeds as his own may waive his preferred claim to the proceeds. A consignment is a bailment in which title and risk of loss is retained by the consignor and possession reverts to him unless the goods are sold by the consignee as agent to a third party or the consignor gives other directions.[1] The consignee has a lien against the goods for amounts owed to him by the consignor for commissions or advancements for such items as freight or insurance.

7-3. Artisans lien. From a very early date, the common law permitted one who expended labor or material upon the property of another to retain possession of such property as security for his compensation. The right arose when the task was completed and was not assignable since it was personal. The lien did not arise in a credit transaction. The lien also existed in favor of public warehousemen and common carriers of goods entrusted to their care; it has been extended by statute in many states to cover all cases of storage or repair.

[1] Harris v. Coe et al., page 964.

The artisans lien is subject to prior liens of record or the claim of a conditional vendor. Since it is based on possession, surrender of possession terminates the lien forever, unless the surrender is only temporary with an agreement that the property will be returned.[2] Even here, if the rights of a third party arise while the lienholder is not in possession, the lien is lost. Surrender of part of the goods will not affect the lien on those remaining. In some states, surrender of possession will not terminate the lien if a notice of lien is recorded.

At common law, the lienholder retained the property until a judgment was obtained at which time he levied execution on the property. Modern statutes, however, permit the lienholder to sell the property and to pay the surplus proceeds to the owner of the property.

7-4. Pledges. A pledge is a bailment of property by the owner to the pledgee as security for a debt. The lien is created when the pledgee takes actual or constructive possession of the property.[3] A person is in constructive possesion if his dominion is such that third persons may learn of his interest in the property. A temporary surrender of possession by the pledgee effects a temporary release of the security.

While any personal property may be pledged, such evidences of property rights as stock certificates, notes, bonds, warehouse receipts, and bills of lading form the basis of most pledges. Delivery of the property to the pledgee is sufficient to create the lien without any necessity of indorsement. Of course, a pledgee cannot be a holder in due course of unindorsed order paper thus an indorsement should be obtained if the pledgee is to be free of personal defenses. On the other hand, the pledgor by indorsing allows the pledgee the opportunity to transfer the paper to someone else in violation of the pledge agreement.

A pledgee may retain any increase in the property pledged, such as dividends or interest, as additional security, but the increase must be accounted for on termination of the pledge. Most pledge agreements provide that in addition to the debt for which the pledge was created, the collateral may be used to secure other obligations to become due or to be created by the pledgor. The right to use the collateral for other debts may be limited to the payee or it may extend to other holders. A pledgee may tranfer possession of the property upon negotiation of the underlying obligation without incurring any liability for misconduct of the indorsee in respect to the collateral. A pledgee does not guarantee the genuineness of the collateral security to the indorsee of the principal debt.

A pledgee has no right to sell pledged property until after maturity of the debt nor does he have the right to repledge or mortgage the property. Such action would constitute a conversion for which the pledgee

[2] North End Auto Park v. Petringa Trucking Co., page 965.
[3] Abraham Heilbron et al. v. Guarantee Loan & Trust Co., page 967.

would have liability for the value of the property at the time of the conversion or at the time of his demand for the property, whichever value is greater. In the case of default, the pledged property is sold and any surplus proceeds are paid to the pledgor. In the event of a deficiency, the pledgee of course has a course of action against the pledgor to recover the same.

7-5. Hypothecation of accounts receivable. Accounts receivable may be used to obtain operating capital either by a sale of the accounts or by hypothecation. When an account is sold, the finance house collects the debt and absorbs the bad debts. Though the procedure may vary from state to state,[4] hypothecation is usually accomplished by a mere written assignment of existing accounts receivable without recording the assignment. The accounts are collected by the borrower and the account debtor is usually not notified of the assignment. For a valid lien in bankruptcy, strict accounting of the proceeds is required, since the right of the borrower to control the proceeds acts as a waiver of the lien both on the amounts collected and the remaining accounts.

7-6. Trust receipts. A trust receipt indicates that money has been advanced to a businessman, usually a retailer, and that he holds certain goods in trust for the lender as security for the loan. Trust receipts are used for financing businessmen, such as automobile dealers, where a chattel mortgage is unsuitable. The entruster authorizes the trustee to sell the goods as a means of obtaining funds to liquidate the loan; in the ordinary course of business, a purchaser obtains good title to the goods. The entruster's lien is transferred from the goods to the proceeds, including commercial paper, still in the trustee's possession. However, one who purchases other than in the ordinary course of business, or who is a judgment creditor of the trustee, is subject to the equity of the lender. Under the Uniform Trust Receipts Act, which governs in most states which have not adopted the Code, the agreement between the entruster and the trustee to use trust receipts must be filed annually with the Secretary of State if the entruster is to be protected.[5] When so filed, the lien of the entruster is good on all items on which a trust receipt is issued. An entruster has the right to take possession of the goods on default or as provided in the contract after which he may sell them at public or private sale and apply the proceeds on the indebtedness. Expenses of selling are added to the indebtedness but the surplus goes to the trustee.

7-7. Inventory factoring. Some states also have a Factors Lien Act which permits a lender to contract for a lien on the borrower's merchandise consisting of raw material, semifinished or finished goods. Its oper-

[4] Taylor et al. v. New Line Industries, page 967.
[5] In the Matter of AA Appliance & TV Center, Inc., Bankrupt, page 969.

ation is similar to a trust receipt in that the borrower can sell the goods in the ordinary course of business with the lien carrying over to the proceeds. Local filing of the agreement is usually required instead of the central filing used in trust receipts. The applicability of the Act is usually limited to actual loans on an inventory and is not available to an unpaid seller.[6]

7-8. Chattel mortgages. A chattel mortgage is a contractual lien as security for a debt on personal property in possession of the mortgagor. On default, the mortgagee must foreclose his mortgage in accordance with the statute or his contract terms in order to secure his money. Some states allow repossession under a chattel mortgage, but strict requirements as to notice, the method of conducting the sale, and for accounting for the proceeds are usually included also. Property must be in existence and be acquired by the mortgagor before it can be mortgaged.[7] A clause in mortgage which purports to cover after-acquired property is not effective as against innocent third parties. Some states have adopted a rule that allows a mortgage on merchandise to cover after-acquired inventory.

A chattel mortgage which allows the mortgagor to retain possession of the property is good against third parties only when properly executed and recorded or filed. The law varies from state to state as to filing and recording with some states providing that if the mortgage is recorded or filed within a given period, its effect relates back to its execution, but that failure to record or file within the period voids the mortgage.

The mortgage must describe the goods with sufficient clarity to identify the property and if growing crops are involved, the real estate must also be described.[8] A change in the form of the property does not affect the validity of the mortgage. A mortgage may cover future advances of money as well as existing debts if the agreement so provides. If the mortgagor fails to pay the obligation secured by the mortgage, the mortgagee is entitled to foreclose the mortgage and to have the property sold with the proceeds applied to the debt to the extent required with the surplus being paid to the mortgagor. In the event of a deficiency, the mortgagor has liability therefor. Many states allow private as well as public sales if the agreement so specifies.

7-9. Conditional sales contracts. A conditional sales contract is one in which title to the property under sale does not pass to the vendee until some specified condition, usually payment, has been satisfied. This device is generally used in installment sales as a method of securing the purchase price for the article sold, it being agreed that the buyer may

[6] Freeman v. International Shoe, page 971.
[7] Townsend Brick & Contracting Co. v. Allen et al., page 975.
[8] Baldwin v. Boyce, page 976.

have possession, but not title, until the purchase price is paid. At common law and in several states, recording or filing of the agreement is not required to protect the security against third parties, the only requirement being the contract provision that title is retained by the vendor.[9] However, some states have recently enacted legislation which does require either recording or filing of the contract to establish rights of the conditional vendor superior to those of other parties.

A conditional sales contract by its nature can not be used as a general security device since it must grow out of a sale. It cannot be used after the buyer has title, and it is not effective to protect a vendor, such as a manufacturer or wholesaler, who sells to a vendee who is a retailer. In the latter case, the retention of title is not good against those who purchase from the retailer. The retention of title is good against attaching creditors of the conditional vendee, and purchasers other than in the ordinary course of business. The basis of these rules is found in the implied waiver of title on resale as the expected source of proceeds for payment. However, the conditional vendor has no interest in the proceeds and is only a general creditor if the retailer fails to pay his obligation.

A conditional vendor has two remedies in the event of default by the vendee. He may rescind the agreement and repossess the goods after demanding payment. In the absence of a statute or agreement, the vendor on repossession may retain all payments previously made and, in addition, all of the proceeds from resale.[10] However, in the event of a deficit, the vendee has no further liability. Many states have, by statute, authorized provisions in conditional sales contracts which allow the vendor to collect any deficit on resale and which require the payment of any surplus to the vendee.

The vendor's other remedy is an action for the unpaid balance on the contract. These remedies are mutually exclusive; a conditional vendor who elects to take a judgment for all installments has waived his right to repossess and title passes to the buyer upon rendition of the judgment.[11]

The conditional vendee has the right to possession until the vendor elects to rescind upon proper cause. All warranties of a usual sale extend to him just as if he had title. Unless the contract prohibits it, the conditional vendee may assign his rights and dispose of his interest in the property. He is, of course, still liable on the agreement. The risk of loss is on the conditional vendee since the conditional vendor's sole interest in the property is for security.

[9] Fairbanks-Morse & Co. v. Parker et al., page 977.
[10] Nuttall v. Baker, page 977.
[11] Woods v. Bournes et al., page 978.

SECURITY DEVICES NON-CODE STATES—CASES

HARRIS v. COE et al.

1898, 71 Conn. 157, 41 Atl. 552

An action of replevin to recover certain property levied on by defendant Coe, a deputy sheriff, in favor of Taylor. The property in question was shipped by plaintiff to one Mamory for sale by the latter. It was levied on as property of Mamory.

HALL, J. . . . Was the contract in question one of sale or bailment? . . . What were, then, the terms of the parol contract which we are asked to construe, and under which the goods in question were delivered to Mamory? For the period of one month, the plaintiff, from his store, was to furnish to Mamory certain goods, which the latter was to select and to sell for the former on consignment, accounting each week for all goods sold, at prices designated by the plaintiff, and marked upon the goods.

At the expiration of the month, there was to be a final settlement, when Mamory was to receive for his services 15 per cent of the prices fixed by the plaintiff, upon all goods sold. Transportation charges were to be paid by Mamory. The trial court found that there was no intention of a sale of any kind to Mamory, but that it was intended that he should receive the goods and sell them as agent of the plaintiff, on consignment. . . . By the express terms of the agreement, the goods were delivered to him upon consignment. It was expressly provided that he was to receive and sell them as the plaintiff's agent, and that each week he should account for all goods sold at the plaintiff's fixed price, including his commission of 15 per cent, which was to be paid to him by the plaintiff on final settlement at the end of the month. A consignment of goods for sale is ordinarily a bailment. The word "consignment" does not imply a sale. The very term imports an agency, and that title is in the consignor.

But the defendant claims that notwithstanding it appears by the terms of the contract to have been the real intention of the parties that Mamory should receive and sell the goods as plaintiff's agent, and receive a commission from him, yet, because the consignee, though bound to account to the consignor at a fixed price, might himself sell at any price, the contract is in law one of sale. We do not think that the absence of a limitation upon the price at which goods may be sold by a consignee, who is to account to his consignor at a fixed price, will transform an agreement made in good faith, and clearly intended by both parties to be one of agency, into a contract of sale. . . . It has been distinctly held in this state that such power in the consignee does not of itself render a contract intended to be one of consignment a contract of sale. . . .

Judgment for plaintiff.

NORTH END AUTO PARK v. PETRINGA TRUCKING CO.

1958, (Mass.) 150 N.E. 2d 735

SPALDING, J. This is a petition to enforce a garage keeper's lien under G.L. c. 255, Sections 25 and 26. The case was submitted on a statement of agreed facts, amounting to a case stated.

The petitioner operates a public garage in Boston. During the period from August 1, 1955, to August 2, 1956, the respondents Mary Petringa and Petringa Trucking Co., Inc., were the owners of all of the motor vehicles (consisting of trucks, trailers and tractors) on which a lien is claimed. In this period the petitioner stored the vehicles, supplied them with gasoline and oil, and repaired them. During part of this period (from August 1, 1955, to April 30, 1956) the respondents used all of the vehicles in their trucking business, taking them away each day from the petitioner's garage with its knowledge and consent. On April 30, 1956, the petitioner refused to allow the respondents to remove the vehicles, and from that date to August 2, 1956, they remained in the uninterrupted possession of the petitioner under a claim of lien. On the latter date the vehicles were sold and the proceeds, under a stipulation executed by all of the interested parties, were placed in escrow, "pending judicial determination of the rights of the petitioner in . . . (the fund) under the claim of lien."

As of April 30, 1956, the unpaid balance due the petitioner in connection with the vehicles was as follows: for gasoline and oil $3,425.21; for repairs $464.47; for storage $2,250. These charges, amounting to $6,-139.68 in the aggregate, were incurred during the period from August 1, 1955, to April 30, 1956.

After the commencement of the present proceedings both respondents were adjudicated bankrupts, and their trustees in bankruptcy were substituted as parties.

The trial judge ruled that for the period up to April 30, 1956, the petitioner had no lien because it did not retain uninterrupted possession of the trucks. He further ruled that by reason of the petitioner's uninterrupted possesion of the trucks for the period between April 30, 1956, and August 2, 1956, the petitioner was entitled to have its lien established in the amount of $750, the storage charges for three months. A report to the Appellate Division was dismissed and the petitioner appealed.

The petitioner is asserting a lien for storage, gasoline, oil, and repairs. The questions for decision are whether, for the period during which the vehicles were taken daily from the garage, any lien exists, and, if so, to which of the foregoing items it extends.

Section 25 of c. 255 provides: "Persons maintaining public garages for the storage and care of motor vehicles brought to their premises or placed in their care by or with the consent of the owners thereof shall have a lien upon such motor vehicles for proper charges due them for the storage and care of the same." At common law the garage keeper had no lien for storage and it is only by Section 25 that he acquired one. . . .

We are of opinion that both on principle and authority the petitioner's lien here was not defeated by the owner taking the trucks out daily and returning them to the garage each night. A contrary conclusion would render the lien of little value; it would be limited to charges accruing after the last return of the vehicle. Except for vehicles in "dead storage" such charges would be comparatively small. We think that the Legislature in enacting Section 25 intended to give the garage keeper a more substantial right.

Of course, the rule just stated is subject to the qualification that if a bona fide purchaser acquires the rights in the vehicle while it is temporarily out of the garage his rights will prevail over those of the garage keeper. *Vinal v. Spofford,* 139 Mass. 126, 29 N.E. 288. And doubtless an attaching or levying creditor who has no knowledge of the lienor's interest would have rights superior to the lienor if he acquired them while the vehicle was out of the lienor's possession. *Restatement: Security, Section* 80.

The lien under Section 25 is for "storage and care." We must now determine what items, beyond that of storage, are covered by these words. We are of opinion that they do not cover the items for gasoline and oil. A more difficult question is whether "care" is limited to that care which is incident to the storing of automobiles, or whether it is used in a more general sense to include repairs made to an automobile. This question, however, we need not decide, because we think that the petitioner can secure its charges for repairs with a common law lien. At common law a mechanic or artisan who, with the consent of the owner, does work or adds materials to a chattel has a lien. . . .

It follows that the petitioner is entitled to recover for repairs in the amount of $464.47, and storage in the amount of $3,000 or $3,464.47 in the aggregate. Accordingly the order of the Appellate Division is reversed and judgment is to be entered for the petitioner in the sum of $3,464.47.

So ordered.

ABRAHAM HEILBRON et al. v. GUARANTEE LOAN & TRUST CO.
1896, 13 Wash. 645, 43 Pac. 932

Respondents, plaintiffs in the court below, as executors of the estate of George H. Heilbron, brought this action to recover possession of two insurance policies. It appeared that Heilbron was the manager of the appellant bank and also a heavy borrower. A question arose about the security for these loans, and he told the secretary of the bank that, if anything happened to him, he desired the secretary to place the policies with the other collateral as security. He told the secretary where to find the policies—among Heilbron's private papers—but they remained undisturbed and were never entered on the books as collateral. After Heilbron's death the secretary removed them, placing them with other collateral.

Gordon, J. . . . We think it clearly shows that the policies were not pledged by the deceased. His conduct and conversation were not sufficient for that purpose. There was neither possession nor right of possession in the appellant during the lifetime of the deceased, and as possession was lacking no pledge resulted. The bank, therefore, never, during the lifetime of George H. Heilbron, had possession of the policies in dispute. His death revoked the authority upon which appellant relied when thereafter it went by its secretary, Mr. Downing, to his private papers and took said policies therefrom.

"To constitute a pledge, the pledgee must take possession; and to preserve it he must retain possession. An actual delivery of property capable of personal possession is essential." Jones, *Pledges*, 23. . . . Of course a symbolical delivery is sufficient where the property is incapable of manual delivery and that is the extent to which the cases . . . go.

Judgment for Heilbron, plaintiff.

TAYLOR et al. v. NEW LINE INDUSTRIES
1955, (N.J. Sup.) 117 A. 2d 643

Haneman, J. S. C. This matter is before the court on the return of two orders to show cause, obtained by the Millville National Bank, and Wheaton Die Casting Corporation, in which Maurice Risley, receiver for New Line Industries, Inc., is directed to show cause why he should not turn over to the Millville National Bank and Wheaton Die Casting Corporation all payments he has received or may receive on accounts receivable theretofore assigned to them by New Line Industries, Inc., as collateral security for loans or the payment of sums due for the sale of merchandise. Incidentally, he is also required to show cause why he should not turn over to them all records of New Line Industries, Inc., pertaining to said assigned accounts, and notify account debtors that payments thereof should be made directly to them. The Millville National Bank also seeks to hold the receiver liable in connection with an assignment of an alleged receivable account due from Consolidated Bottle Company. A succint statement of the three questions here involved is as follows:

1. Does an assignment of accounts receivable as collateral security, where no security interest in merchandise is taken, have to be recorded under the Factor's Lien Law in order for the assignment to be valid?

2. Is an assignment of an account receivable effective if the books of the assignor are not marked to indicate the assignment?

3. If the receiver of an assignor of an account receivable accepts the return of merchandise from an account debtor, in lieu of the moneys owed on the account, is the assignee of the account, who did not authorize this action, entitled to hold the receiver liable for the loss sustained?

The solution of the primary problem in this matter turns upon the question of whether the provisions of the Factor's Lien Law, N.J.S. 2A; 44-178 et seq., N.J.S.A., require a recordation of an assignment of accounts receivable where there was never created nor did there ever exist a lien upon the goods, the sale of which gave rise to the accounts receivable.

Generally, under our common law, the delivery of an assignment of accounts receivable, without anything more, gave the assignee a valid title, at least as between the assignor and assignee. . . .

The statue here involved is in derogation of the common law insofar as it concerns assignment of accounts receivable, and hence must be strictly construed. . . .

The Factor's Lien Law, when adopted, provided a new type of security for the lender. It created a lien upon certain goods of the borrower and upon the sale of those goods said lien was automatically transferred to the receivable resulting from the sale.

The cited statute does not basically concern itself with an assignment of accounts receivable unaccompanied by a lien on the goods, the sale of which gave rise to such accounts.

That this is what the Legislature contemplated is borne out by the very verbiage of the act. See N.J.S. 2A; 44-178, N.J.S.A., where a factor is defined as those who "lend upon the security of merchandise"; N.J.S. 2A; 44-180, N.J.S.A.; which requires that notice of lien shall be filed where "the merchandise subject to the lien . . . shall be located"; N.J.S. 2A; 44-181, N.J.S.A., where provision is made for the effectiveness of the lien "as against all claims of creditors in or against such merchandise"; and N.J.S. 2A; 44-182, N.J.S.A., where provision is made for the discharge of the lien on "the said merchandise."

This statute was adopted in New Jersey and is largely patterned after the New York statute of 1911.

In construing the comparable New York statute it has been held that it applies only where a loan is made on the security of the merchandise of which the borrower will retain possession, and that it does not apply where there is simply an assignment of accounts as security. . . .

In the light of the foregoing, it is here held that the assignments to the Millville National Bank and Wheaton Die Casting Corporation are valid.

What has been stated above disposes as well of the second propounded question. There being no statutory provision for any indication on the books of the assignor of an assignment, since such notice was not required under the common law, an assignment, even absent such notice, is valid, especially where, as here, no third parties suffered any detriment resulting from the failure to so stamp.

Insofar as the third question is concerned, which involves the alleged act of Consolidated Bottle Co., the merchandise was consigned to said Consolidated Bottle Co. The transaction was not a complete sale and there never arose any account receivable, the merchandise having been returned to the consignor. The alleged assignment of this so-called account receivable was invalid and ineffectual. The proceeds held by the receiver resulting from the subsequent sale of the merchandise is not subject to any lien.

Judgment will be entered accordingly.

IN THE MATTER OF AA APPLIANCE & TV CENTER, INC., BANKRUPT

1959, 271 F. 2d 800

KNOCH, J. Marshall and Ilsley Bank of Milwaukee, Wisconsin, filed, with the Wisconsin Secretary of State, a statement of the Bank's financing and anticipated financing (by means of trust receipt transactions) of acquisition of "Television, Appliances and Other Similar Equipment" by AA Appliance & TV Center, Inc.

Subsequently the President of the AA Appliance delivered to the bank three trust receipts on refrigerators, washers, dryers, and a freezer. When AA Appliance was adjudicated a bankrupt, the trustee in bankruptcy took possession of all assets including the unsold merchandise enumerated in the trust receipts. The referee denied the bank's petition to reclaim these items on the ground that the statement filed with the Secretary of State insufficiently described the goods, and that they were, therefore, not subject to any security interest of the bank.

On review District Judge Tehan reversed the referee and this appeal followed.

The applicable statute, 241-43 (1), reads:

(1) Any entruster undertaking or contemplating trust receipt transactions with reference to documents or goods is entitled to file with the secretary of state a statement, signed by the entruster and the trustee, bearing the correct name of the sole trader, copartnership or corporation of the entruster and trustee, as well as the correct trade name of the sole trader, copartnership or corporation of the entruster and trustee, as well as the correct trade name, if one is used; and have plainly printed or typewritten thereon the names of the parties executing the same; the statement shall further contain:

(a) A designation of the entruster and the trustee, and of the chief place of business of each within this state, if any, including street and post-office address; and if the entruster has no place of business within the state, a designation of his chief place of business outside the state, including street and post-office address; and

(b) A statement that the entruster is engaged, or expects to be engaged, in financing under trust receipt transactions the acquisition of goods covered or to be covered by such financing.

(2) The following form of statement (or any other form of statement containing *substantially* the same information) shall suffice for the purposes of Sections 241.31 to 241.50:

Statement of trust receipt financing

The entruster, ..., whose chief place of business within this state is at .... Street, in the city of .... and state of .... (or who has no place of business within this state and whose chief place of business outside this state is at .... Street, in the city of .... and state of ....), is or expects to be engaged in financing under trust receipt transactions the acquisition by the trustee, ..., a sole trader ( ), a copartnership ( ), or corporation ( ), whose chief place of business within this state is at .... (Street or Rural Route No.), and whose P. O. address is ...., of goods of the following description: coffee, silk, automobiles or the like.

....

(Signed) .... Entruster
(Signed) .... Trustee

Section 241.39 expressly provides that entrusters are subordinated to bona fide purchasers for value and that filing of the statement under Section 241.43 shall not constitute notice of the entruster's interest to such bona fide purchasers for value other than to transferees in bulk.

In his closely reasoned opinion, D. C., 170 F. Supp. 103, the District Judge agreed with the referee that certain portions of this statute, such as statement of names and places of business, which are clearly known at the time the statement is filed, are susceptible of strict compliance (citing cases) but that the statute itself calls only for "substantially" the same information as set out in the sample form of Section 241.43 (2) with its suggested broad descriptive terms.

The trustee argues that the word "appliances" is a less specific term than the examples in the statute. He sees "appliances" as analogous to "groceries" and "fabric" rather than "coffee" and "silk." He states that he knows of no other cases in point, but fears that the District Court's decision, if affirmed, will establish a policy adverse to the uniformity which would be desirable in connection with trust receipt financing.

Here the name of the bankrupt provides a clue. The statute calls for no statement of the amount or terms of the loan. We are constrained to agree with the distinguished District Court Judge, that (170 F. Supp. 104):

In respect of notice therefore, we can only conclude that the framers of the act contemplated providing only for the first step of a two-step process to be undertaken by a prospective creditor in order to discover the exact status of the goods he is concerned with.

Rather than have to resort to exercises in semantics in each case, it seems to us that the intent of the Act in respect of notice is met if the descriptive words used would inform an experienced and sophisticated creditor that goods in the possession of the trustee could not be relied on and that he should investigate further.

Affirmed.

FREEMAN v. INTERNATIONAL SHOE
1961, 294 F. 2d 126

FORMAN, C. J. International Shoe Company (International) claimed the security of a factor's lien in the bankruptcy of Samuel Freeman, trading as Pedi-Tred Shoes (the bankrupt). The lien was contested by the trustee. The referee held the lien void as a secured obligation and the United States District Court for the District of New Jersey affirmed the referee. This appeal followed.

The parties to the litigation are not in disagreement as to the basic facts. The bankrupt conducted a retail shoe business in Newark, New Jersey. In June 1959 he was indebted to International in the sum of fifteen hundred dollars for previously acquired merchandise. He desired to obtain a larger inventory from International but neither his credit rating nor his business to that date warranted a further extension of credit. International describes the events that followed thus:

After meetings with International's agent, it was agreed that the bankrupt would be allowed to draw on International for its merchandise up to a maximum amount of Eight Thousand Five Hundred ($8,500.00) Dollars, during a three year period, in return for which International was to be secured by a factor's lien on inventory, proceeds and accounts receivable from the sale thereof during the existence of the lien. This agreement for the factor's lien was entirely separate and apart from the purchases which bankrupt had made on credit previously, of approximately Fifteen Hundred ($1500.00) Dollars. A "Factor's Lien Agreement" was entered into, . . . and a proper notice of lien . . . was duly filed. . . .

Subsequently, the bankrupt drew on International as provided in the "Factor's Lien Agreement" . . . for merchandise to the stated maximum amount of Eight Thousand Five Hundred ($8,500.00) Dollars. In the meantime, his credit purchases remained at approximately Fifteen Hundred ($1500.00) Dollars.

The relevant portion of the factor's lien agreement provides:

(2) *Amount and Duration of Loan or Credit*—International has presently extended a loan or credit to the Borrower in the amount of approximately Fifteen Hundred Dollars ($1500.) on open account and/or installment notes and, while International shall not be obligated to furnish the Borrower future credit in any specific amount, all such further advances, loans or credits as may be extended by International to the Borrower from time to time in the future during the ensuing three (3) years (if requested by the Borrower), to the maximum amount of Eighty-five Hundred Dollars ($8500.), shall, nevertheless, be subject to the provisions of this agreement and secured by the factor's lien herein created. . . .

On June 28, 1960, the bankrupt filed a voluntary petition in bankruptcy. A receiver was appointed on June 28, 1960. Upon his application, returnable July 25, 1960, an order, consented to by International, was made by the referee for a public sale of the bankrupt's assets free and clear of encumbrances, but providing that the lien of International, if valid was to be transferred to the proceeds of the sale. The merchandise brought $5,997.60.

After the public sale the respondent trustee presented further legal argument as to the validity of International's lien and the referee, on September 14, 1960, entered an order declaring the lien invalid because "the Factor's Lien Act of the State of New Jersey was applicable only to loans and advances of money and not to the extension of credit for goods and merchandise. . . ."

The Factor's Lien Act of the State of New Jersey (Act) N.J.S.A. 2A:44-178 et seq. was adopted in 1942. Laws, 1942, c. 182. It defines a factor in the following language:

The terms "factor" and "factors" wherever used in this article include persons, firms, and corporations, and their successors in interest, engaged in the business of factoring or financing sales of merchandise or of purchasing or lending on the security of receivables arising out of such sales who as part of or incidental to such business lend upon the security of merchandise, and any consignee or consignees, pledgee or pledgees, who advance money on goods consigned to or pledged with them, whether or not such consignee or pledgees are employed to sell such goods, and their successors in interest. N.J.S.A. 2A:44-178.

It further provides:

If so provided by any written agreement all factors shall have a continuing general lien upon all goods and merchandise from time to time consigned to or pledged with them, whether or not in their constructive, actual or exclusive occupancy or possession, and upon any accounts receivable or other proceeds resulting from the sale or other disposition of such goods and merchandise, for all their loans and advances to or for the account of the person creating the lien (hereinafter called the borrower), . . . N.J.S.A. 2A:44-179.

International contends that:

". . . the statutory factor is one who is, among other things, "financing sales of merchandise" and is in no way prevented by the Act from financing the sale of his own merchandise. The phrase "advance money" which was found to be a prerequisite to the acquisition of the statutory lien in the proceedings below . . . appears only in the latter part of this definitional section quoted above. (N.J.S.A. 2A:44-178).

It further contends that the word "advances" as used in N.J.S.A. 2A:44-179 should not be restricted to money but should be interpreted as credit advanced for merchandise as in this case and that in N.J.S.A. 2A:44-185 liberal construction is called for "to secure the beneficial interests and purposes thereof."

At the common law a factor was an agent employed to sell goods for a principal and receive a commission thereon. The factor had a lien on the goods for any advances made by him and for his commissions. The common law factor's lien was founded on the possession of the goods of his principal and served the function of securing him for the advances owed by the principal (citing cases).

The modern factor, however, is a financier who generally lends monies and takes in return an assignment of accounts receivable or some other security. He is not a selling agent. In re *Tele-Tone Radio Corp., supra.; 4 Collier, op. cit. supra.* It is the modern factor who is the primary beneficiary of the factors' lien statutes of the various states. They were enacted to foster his growth and function. Those statutes authorize a floating lien on inventory giving the modern factor a lien without the necessity of taking and maintaining possession of the pledged property (citing cases). . . .

No case has been cited to us nor have we found one in which a seller of his own merchandise has obtained a lien under a factor's lien statute. The cases reveal that where a lien has been obtained under such statutes the factor was an independent financing agency that had loaned or advanced money to a borrower. Neither is there reason to believe that the courts of New Jersey would extend the umbrella of its factors' lien law to the transaction involved in this case.

In the instant case International was neither a common law nor a modern factor. It was not a factor as that term is defined in N.J.S.A. 2A:44-178. It was not a corporation engaged in the business of factoring or financing sales of merchandise or of purchasing or lending on the security of receivables arising out of such sales which, as part or incidental to such business, loaned upon the security of such merchandise. Nor was it a consignee or pledgee who advanced money on goods consigned or pledged with it. Here it was engaged in the business of selling shoes on credit. To hold that International had a lien under the Act obviously would be contrary to the purpose of the Act which was to facilitate financing agencies in making loans and advances of money on the security of goods not in their possession.

International submits many definitions of the terms "loans" and "advances" to support its position that in *advancing credit* to the bankrupt under the circumstances of this case it brought itself within the purview of the Act. It suggests that if it had given the bankrupt its check for $8500 and he had endorsed it back to it "in payment of the credit or indebtedness involved" it would be a compliance with the Act. It concedes that such an exercise would be a technical and meaningless compliance. It would be meaningless, indeed, and not a compliance. . . .

The word "advance" as used in N.J.S.A. 2A:44-179 refers to an advance of money. This is made clear when the above noted section and N.J.S.A. 2A:44-178 are viewed together. N.J.S.A. 2A:44-178 defines the term factor. The first class of factors there defined "lend(s) upon the security of merchandise" while the other class "advance(s) money on goods consigned to or pledged with them" for all their advances. In both instances, however, "loans and advances" refer to money. Cf. *People ex rel. James Talcott, Inc. v. Goldfogle,* 1925, 213 App. Div. 719, 211 N.Y.S. 122.

Moreover the use of the term "borrower" in N.J.S.A. 2A:44-179 to describe the person who creates the lien fortifies the proposition that the framers of the law had in mind a lien to protect a loan or advance in terms of money. It is difficult to conceive of the bankrupt as a "borrower" of the merchandise in question notwithstanding the same term was carried over into the purported lien agreement between him and International. . . .

International contends that the small business community would benefit from a construction of the Act which would hold its lien valid, since such an interpretation would provide an expanded source of credit. This may be true but that is a task for the Legislature of the State of New Jersey and not for the courts.

The order of the District Court will be affirmed.

TOWNSEND BRICK & CONTRACTNG CO. v. ALLEN et al.

1900, 62 Kan. 311, 62 Pac. 1008, 52 L.R.A. 323

John W. Allen, James P. McGuire, John H. Barry, and T. J. Emlen, who owned six acres of land, upon which there were machinery and appliances for the manufacture of bricks, leased the same to John Gaffney for one year. The agreement provided that the lessors should have and retain a lien on the clay and material taken from the premises, and upon brick manufactured there to secure the payment of rent. Gaffney manufactured large quantities of brick, and on Nov. 10, 1894, Townsend Brick & Contracting Co. purchased a large quantity of the brick. At the time this controversy arose $250 were due for rent and plaintiffs, Allen and others, maintain they are entitled to a lien on the bricks sold to the defendant.

JOHNSTON, J. . . . It may be assumed that the lease created a lien on any brick that had been made and were in existence when the lease was executed and filed in the office of register of deeds, but can it be held to create a lien on brick made long afterwards? None of the brick in controversy had been made when the lease was executed, and even the clay and shale from which brick were subsequently made were then in the bank and in a natural state. . . . The clay and shale in the bank have peculiar qualities, necessary for the manufacture of vitrified brick—qualities which ordinary clay does not contain; but no portion of the same which ultimately became an element in the brick in controversy was in any manner set apart by severance or by the marking of the place from which it should be taken. . . . The lessee, Gaffney, had the right to take clay and shale for the purpose of making brick from any portion of the six-acre tract leased to him. Certainly the brick in controversy were not in actual existence when the chattel mortgage was made, and the clay and shale which entered into the manufacture could not be identified in any manner.

The general rule is that no one can mortgage property which does not exist or which does not belong to him. It is true, parties may make contracts with reference to afterwards acquired property which will be upheld as between themselves, but such contracts are not to be considered as chattel mortgages. The contention here is that the clay and shale used in producing the brick in controversy were in existence; that these constituted the principal elements which entered into the making of the bricks of controversy, and therefore they had a potential existence, to which the lien might attach. . . .

Other elements and forces were employed in the manufacture, so that the identity of the clay was entirely lost; and the product, as we have seen, is worth about 40 times more than the clay which entered into it.

It having been held that the instrument was insufficient to constitute a lien on the brick in controversy it is unnecessary to consider (other) points.

Judgment for defendant.

BALDWIN v. BOYCE
1898, 152 Ind. 46, 51 N.E. 334

Action by Mary Baldwin to foreclose a mortgage against Sarah Herman. The defendant intervened and claimed title to the property, which raised a question concerning the validity of the mortgage. The property mortgage was described as:

> All and singular the restaurant and hotel furniture and fixtures located in and situated in and about the 1st, 2nd, and 3rd stories of No. 313 East Main Street.

Then followed a statement of the articles such as chairs, desks, shelves, coffee urn, etc. The mortgage further indicated that the mortgagor was in possession. The description is questioned because the town was inadvertently omitted, although the county is indicated.

JORDAN, J. . . . Appellee virtually concedes that, if the instrument contained anything by which the property might be identified, then, in that event, it might be held sufficient. The insistence is that the instrument states but one thing that would, if certain, afford means of identification, and that is that the mortgaged goods are situated at "No. 313 East Main St." but as to where "East Main Street" is located, it is asserted, is left wholly indefinite by the mortgage. The rule is well settled in this jurisdiction, as well as elsewhere, that the description in a chattel mortgage must be reasonably certain; and a description of the property which will enable third persons, aided by inquiries which the instrument itself indicates or suggests, to identify the mortgaged property is sufficient. . . .

Cobbey, Chat. Mortg. Section 188, states the rule as follows:

> The general rule seems to be that, as between the parties, any description is good if the parties at the time knew and understood what the mortgage covered; that as to third parties, where the property intended to be mortgaged was identified at the time, any description which points out the particular property, or suggests inquiries by which it can be identified outside of the instrument, is good against the world.

Applying the principles to which we have referred to the mortgage in the case at bar, and testing it thereby, we are of the opinion that the description therein must be held sufficient.

Judgment for plaintiff.

FAIRBANKS-MORSE & CO. v. PARKER et al.
1925, 167 Ark. 654, 269 S.W. 42

Appellant, Fairbanks-Morse & Co., brought this action against appellees, to recover three gasoline engines. It appears that these engines were sold from time to time to J. C. Shepherd. Notes were accepted in settlement, and the contract provided that title was to be retained by appellant. Shepherd, without the consent or knowledge on the part of the appellant, sold these engines to defendant, who has now been in possession of them for three years. He claims title by a three year adverse possession. The plaintiff did not know of the adverse possession. Judgment of the lower court was given for defendant.

HART, J. We think the decision of the circuit court was wrong. There is no showing in the record that appellees claimed the property adversely to the rights of appellant, or that the latter waived his right to retake the property under his contract, for failure to pay the purchase money. The contract in each case was in writing and in express terms stated that the title to the property should remain in the seller until it was paid for. The fact that the original purchaser sold the engines did not give the second purchaser any greater rights than the original purchaser possessed, in the absence of notice to the seller, or of facts equivalent to notice, that the second purchaser claimed the property adversely to the rights of the seller. In conditional sales of personal property where the title is retained by the vendor until the purchase price is paid, the vendee acquires an interest that he can sell or mortgage without the consent of the vendor; but the vendor's right to recover the property, if the purchase price of the property is not paid, is not prejudiced by such sale or mortgage. . . .

Judgment for plaintiff.

NUTTALL v. BAKER
1958, (Md.) 143 A. 2d 500

Baker sold to Nuttall, plaintiff, a tractor and trailer for $7,165 on conditional sale contract. After several installments had been paid, the defendant repossessed the items because of a substantial default. The plaintiff sued for loss of income resulting from the repossession and for payments made on the contract. The lower court gave judgment for defendant and the plaintiff appealed.

PRESCOTT, J. . . . In the absence of contractual or statutory provisions, the authorities are not in agreement as to whether a conditional seller of goods must restore to the buyer the purchase money paid on a retaking of the property on the buyer's default. . . . Many states have held that the buyer, having broken his contract, forfeits his payments on the purchase price. . . . We think the weight of authority is to this effect. . . .

On the other hand, apparently based on the rescission theory, some courts have held, in cases not affected by statutes, that the purchaser is entitled to a return of his payments, either in full, or subject to deductions for the value of the use of the goods, or for depreciation, or both. For a collection of the cases so holding, see 2A U.L.A. *op. cit.* p. 183. In other decisions it is intimated that while the purchaser has no right at law to demand a recovery of his part payments, he may have equitable rights. . . .

We see no sound reason for holding that the appellant is entitled to recover his part payments on the purchase price under the circumstances of this case. Such a holding would mean that the vendee in every similar conditional sales contract in existence in this State could simply default in his contract, and, if the seller repossessed, collect all of the payments made by him. Neither justice nor reason calls for such a result. We agree with the majority rule that generally, in the absence of contractual or statutory provisions, a conditional vendee, after a repossession of the property due to his substantial default, has no right to recover payments made by him upon the purchase price. The appellant has offered no evidence to show why this general rule should not apply to his case, which, of course, means that he is not entitled to recover the payments made by him upon the purchase price.

We recognize that, under certain circumstances, there might arise a case where the doctrine of unjust enrichment would be held to be available to a conditional vendee (*Cf. Quillen v. Kelley, supra*); but, we do not reach the question in this case and leave it open.

Judgment affirmed with costs.

WOODS v. BOURNES et al.
1958, (Ark.) 309 S.W. 2d 309

Woods, plaintiff, sold to Bournes a tractor at a price of $1,250 and retained title as security for two annual payments of $625 each. The obligation was also secured by a mortgage on certain farm land. The tractor was repossessed by the plaintff because neither payment had been made when due and, the tractor not having been resold, this is a suit to foreclose the mortgage. The lower court gave judgment for the defendant and the plaintiff has appealed.

McFADDIN, J. . . . The note for $1,250 signed by Augustine Bournes recited:

> This note is given for the purchase of property, to-wit: Massey Harris 22 Tractor Serial No. 22G3106-2-14 B. Plow 5-ft. Disk Harrow and it is agreed that the title thereof shall remain in the said Woods Equipment Company, his successors or assigns, until the purchase price or judgment for same is paid in full.

In a long line of cases on conditional sales, this Court has recognized that on default of payment by the maker, the holder of such note has a choice of two remedies: (a) he may disaffirm the sale and repossess the property; or (b) he may affirm the sale and sue on the debt. . . .

If the holder of the note disaffirms the sale and repossesses the property, he cannot thereafter sell the property and claim a deficiency judgment. . . .

When the indebtedness secured by Woods' mortgage had been satisfied, the mortgage could not be foreclosed. . . .

Judgment for defendant affirmed.

Review Questions and Problems

1. *A* shipped *B* goods on consignment. They were to be sold at prices established by *A*, and the consignee, *B*, was to account at the end of each week for the goods sold, less a certain amount for his commission. While the goods were in *B*'s possession, they were destroyed by fire. Who must bear the loss, assuming that *B* exercised proper care?
2. *S* sold a truck to *B*, retaining title as security for the unpaid balance. *B* later towed the truck to *G*'s garage for repairs and was unable thereafter to pay either *S* or *G*, who is still in possession of the truck. Who has the better claim to the truck, *S* or *G*?
3. *X* Co., a wholesaler of plumbing fixtures and fittings, pledged to *Y* Co. a large stock of such supplies, the merchandise being segregated, placarded, and an agent of *X* Co. being made the agent of *Y* Co. to retain intact the pledged inventory. *C* obtained a judgment against *X* Co. and levied on the goods, maintaining there was no effective pledge. Was the pledge good?
4. *G* held a chattel mortgage on a certain automobile as security for a debt, the mortgage being properly recorded. The owner later took his car to *H*'s garage for repairs. The owner has paid neither obligation, the car being in the possession of *H*. *G* seeks possession in order to foreclose and *H* claims his lien is superior. The court held in favor of *H*. Does this decision appear sound to you?

5. Bank loaned *A* $29,000 and accepted trust receipts on certain automobiles as security. *A* died, having sold the cars without accounting for them, though the day before *A*'s death the bank demanded settlement. Assets of $18,000 were identified as proceeds from sale and the bank claimed these assets and a prior lien of $11,000 on other assets of the deceased. *A*'s estate was insolvent but the courts allowed both claims of the bank. Was this decision sound?
6. *A*, desiring to purchase two trucks, gave to a bank a mortgage on the trucks to obtain the money with which to purchase them. He then purchased the trucks. He later sold one of these trucks to *C*, an innocent purchaser. Assuming the mortgage to be properly recorded, whose claim to the truck is superior?
7. *O* borrowed $10,000 of *M* and on June 1 executed a chattel mortgage on certain personal property as security. *M* neglected to have the mortgage recorded until July 5, although the statute required recording within 20 days. On July 20, *O* borrowed $5,000 of *X* and gave him a chattel mortgage on the same equipment. Is his mortgage better than the mortgage of *M*, if *X* recorded his mortgage on July 21?
8. *A* gave *B* a chattel mortgage upon certain leather. This leather, unknown to *B*, was converted into shoes and sold to *C*. Does *C* take the shoes subject to the mortgage?
9. *O*, a resident of Wyoming, took a trip into Colorado, and while there, borrowed money of *M* and gave him a chattel mortgage on the car that *O* was driving. *M* recorded the mortgage in the county where he resided and where *O* and the car were at the time the mortgage was given. *O* returned to Wyoming and sold the car to *B*. If *B* knew nothing about the mortgage, is his title better than *M*'s lien?
10. *M* sold to *R* farm machinery and retained title as security, *R* being a retailer of such machinery. *R* sold three machines for cash and deposited the money in his bank account. If *C* gets a judgment against *R* and seeks to take the bank account, has *M* a superior claim to it? Did the buyer of the machines obtain good title?
11. A conditional vendor obtains a judgment for the unpaid purchase price of certain goods. The judgment not being paid, he desires to take possession of the goods. Is he free to do so?
12. *S* sold to *B*, a consumer, a refrigerator and retained title as security for a price of $240. Before making all payments, *B* resold the machine to *T*, an innocent purchaser. May *S* repossess the machine of *T* if *B* defaults in his payments?
13. *D* owed *C* $500 for money previously borrowed. He gave *C* a new note for that amount, which stated that *C* was retaining title to certain property owned by *D* until the note was paid. This property that had at all times been in the possession of *D* was later sold by *D* to an innocent purchaser. Did the innocent purchaser obtain good title?
14. S sold a car to *B*, the price being payable in installments and title being retained as security. *B* was behind three installments in his payments, and S, without notice or demand, repossessed the car. *B* sued S for conversion of his property. Is S liable?

46

Secured Transactions Uniform Commercial Code

7-10. Introduction. The preceding chapter dealt with the various security devices used to give a creditor security in personal property in those states which have not adopted the Code and in Code states prior to its adoption. In those states which have adopted the Code, there is a single security device known as a security interest. A security interest is created by a security agreement between the creditor, known as the secured party, and the person giving the collateral, known as the debtor. The security interest concept is applicable to all transactions where the parties intend to create a security interest in personal property as payment for a debt, except certain specified exceptions. Though such terms as pledge, chattel mortgage, conditional sales contract, or trust receipt may still be used, all of those concepts come within the definition of a security interest and are subject to the provisions of the Code. Under the Code, distinctions based on the form of the contract are eliminated and the remaining distinctions between various agreements relate to substantive matters such as the intended use of the goods which controls the method of perfecting the security interest.

Not only does the Code simplify the law of secured transactions; the security interest is capable of possessing the desirable characteristics of each of the former security devices. For example, a security interest may be created and perfected by the secured party taking possession of the property in the same manner as a pledge. The filing or recording concept of the chattel mortgage has been adopted to create an interest with priority over third persons. The favored treatment formerly available to a vendor under a conditional sales contract is now available to all creditors who advance purchase money for personal property. The security agreement may cover future advances of money and after-acquired property may be part of the collateral just as in the case of financing under the Trust Receipts Act or the Factors Lien Act. The strict requirement of tracing proceeds, as was required in the case of consignments and hypothecation of accounts receivable, has been eliminated. Thus, the Code has taken the best of the various security devices and has provided business with a system for handling secured transactions that is not only greatly simplified, but is also capable of serving the demands of modern business.

In addition to the typical security devices discussed in the preceding chapter, the Code provisions are applicable to sales of contract rights and sales of chattel paper, except for isolated sales. Contract rights are those resulting from a contract in which the work has not been done. Chattel paper includes both a money obligation and a security interest.

7-11. Creation and attachment of the security interest. A security interest is created by agreement. Unless the secured party takes possession of the collateral (a possessory security interest), the agreement must be in writing to be enforceable. The security agreement must describe the collateral and if the collateral relates to land, it must also contain a description of the land. A description is sufficient if it reasonably identifies the collateral and the real estate. Although not required, a security agreement will usually include (1) a statement of the debt, (2) the debtor's duties in respect to the collateral such as insuring it, (3) rights of the secured party on default, and (4) other matters on which the parties have agreed.

It is not sufficient to merely create a security interest, it must attach to the collateral. A security interest attaches only after three events have occurred: (1) the security agreement has been executed, (2) the secured party has given value, and (3) the debtor has rights in the collateral. They may occur in any order. A debtor has no rights: in crops, until they are planted or become growing crops; in livestock, until conceived; in fish, until caught; in oil, gas or minerals, until extracted; or in timber, until it is cut. A security interest that has attached establishes the rights and liabilities as between the secured party and the debtor. However, other persons may also claim an interest in the property. To have priority over third persons or to be able to collect from a bankrupt estate, the secured party must perfect his security interest. Perfection of the security interest is discussed in the next section.

7-12. Perfection of the security interest. A possessory security interest, one that is created by possession, is also perfected by the secured party or his agent taking possession of the collateral. Possession of property imparts notice to the world that the bailee thereof may be claiming some interest in property held by him. This is the only method whereby a security interest in negotiable instruments may be perfected. It is also the only way that a security interest in negotiable documents of title and chattel paper may be protected against those who buy them or loan on them in good faith and in the ordinary course of business. The security interest in instruments and documents, however, is good for 21 days without possession unless someone has advanced new value against them and takes possession in good faith. Thus, a secured party may temporarily release a warehouse receipt or securities to the debtor to enable him to sell the collateral to pay off the loan without losing his security for the 21-day period.

For other classes of property, such as accounts receivable, contract rights, negotiable documents of title and chattel paper—not sold in regular course of business—and goods, a security interest may be perfected by filing a financing statement. All financing statements will in some states be filed with a central state officer while in other states there will be provisions for both central and local filing. In those states which have both central and local filing, the actual place of filing will be determined by the classification of the collateral or the relationship between the secured party and the debtor. The Code establishes four classifications of goods—tangible personal property. They are as follows:

1. *Consumer goods*—goods for personal, family, or household use.
2. *Equipment*—goods used in one's business, in farming, in a profession, or by a nonprofit corporation.
3. *Farm products*—such items as crops, livestock, supplies used or produced in farming, or products of crops or livestock in unmanufactured state—such as wool clip, maple syrup, eggs or milk, as long as they are still in the possession of a debtor who is engaged in farming or raising, grazing, or fattening livestock.
4. *Inventory*—such items as are held for sale or lease or furnished under a contract of service, whether they be raw material, work in process, completed goods, or material consumed in business.

Generally, those states with both local and central filing will require local filing, in the office of the debtor's residence, where the agreement involves consumer goods, farm equipment, or farm products, and central filing if the collateral is inventory or nonfarm equipment. If the debtor is a nonresident, the local office where the items are kept is used for local filing. In the case of crops, the financing statement is filed where a mortgage on the real estate would be filed. Some states require dual filing in the case of inventory and nonfarm equipment. Generally, in these states only one filing is required where the debtor is a farmer or a consumer but dual filing is required where the debtor is a businessman involved in a commercial transaction.

The financing statement describes the property, parties, and indebtedness; the lien is perfected only when the interest has attached and filing has taken place, except as indicated below.

1. A purchase money security interest—an interest retained at time of sale or lease or one taken for money advanced for and used to purchase property—is good for ten days without filing or possession as against lien creditors and bulk purchasers.
2. A purchase money security interest in consumer goods and farm equipment costing $2,500 or less, except motor vehicles, is perfected with-

out taking possession or filing. However, filing or possession must occur to protect the lien against those who buy in good faith for personal or family use or for farming operations.

Natural increases, interest, and dividends are subject to the lien. Any money payments received by the secured creditor, if retained, must immediately be applied on the indebtedness.

7-13. Extent of the security interest. The Code has greatly expanded and liberalized the use of personal property as collateral for a debt. Security agreements may provide that the security interest covers after-acquired property and future advances of credit.[1] In addition, it allows a debtor to have absolute control over the collateral without eliminating the lien of the secured party.[2] Thus, a debtor may have the right to use, commingle, or dispose of the collateral, or to compromise claims and allow repossessions without voiding the lien of the secured party. These three provisions provide the basis for the so called "floating lien" concept. The amount of the debt and the actual collateral can be constantly revolving if the security agreement is so worded as to include after-acquired property and future advances of money. The use of after-acquired property as collateral does not extend to crops which become such more than one year after the execution of the security agreement, or to consumer goods, unless the debtor within ten days after the giving of value by the secured party acquires rights in the goods. Businessmen can pledge property to be obtained in the future but consumers cannot.

The security interest may also extend to proceeds of the sale of collateral. Those situations in which it does so extend are discussed in the next section.

In addition, a security interest in raw materials can pass to the finished product as well as to the proceeds of a sale. For example, a security interest in lumber will pass to furniture manufactured by the debtor and then to the proceeds of a sale of the furniture.

7-14. Proceeds. A debtor in possession of collateral may or may not be in a business which sells such property in the ordinary course of business. In any event, if the collateral is sold by the debtor, the lien of the creditor carries over to the proceeds. Thus, if the creditor has a lien on the inventory of a retailer, his normal source of recovery would be from the proceeds received from the sale of the goods. This lien on the proceeds carries over indefinitely if the security contract called for the lien to cover the proceeds. If the contract includes no such provision, however, the lien on the proceeds is lost ten days after the sale unless a new agreement covering the proceeds is perfected. If the collateral is sold by the debtor, but not in the regular course of business—the sale being rather, an iso-

[1] Industrial Packaging Prod. Co. v. Fort Pitt Pack. Int., page 987.

[2] Benedict v. Ratner, page 990.

lated sale by an owner—the secured creditor may elect to recover the collateral from the purchaser or to take the proceeds as seems best to him.

If proceeds take the form of cash and identity of the cash is lost by commingling it with other cash or by depositing it in a bank, the secured creditor has a lien on all cash or bank balances to the extent of unaccounted cash proceeds received within the last ten days prior to insolvency or bankruptcy proceedings. Thus, the lien on cash proceeds continues only for a limited time, while the lien on other proceeds realized from the sale of collateral continues indefinitely unless sold in the ordinary course of business. In order for this security interest in the proceeds to continue, it is not essential that strict accounting be required, as is quite often true under common law. Permitting the debtor to use some of the collateral or proceeds for his personal use does not affect the security interest in the remaining collateral or proceeds.

To illustrate these principles, let us assume that Finance Company holds a perfected security interest in Retailer's stock of electric appliances and that some have been sold for cash, checks, used appliances, and chattel paper. The security contract would doubtless provide that the lien carry over to the proceeds. Should Retailer become insolvent, Finance Company, to the extent of the unpaid remaining appliances, has a lien on all of the proceeds, except that the lien on cash which has been commingled will continue for a relatively short time only. Likewise, any interest in chattel paper would be lost if Retailer had disposed of it in the ordinary course of business. Furthermore, it should be clear that those who purchased appliances in the ordinary course of business from Retailer take good title to them.

7-15. Purchasers in the ordinary course of business. In previous sections, creation, perfection, and extent of the security interest were discussed. However, just as a security interest may include after-acquired property, there are certain situations in which the security interest will cease upon a sale by the debtor.

A creditor may have a security interest in the inventory of his business debtor, but whenever the debtor is regularly engaged in the business of selling such personal property, a purchaser who buys in the ordinary course of business takes title free from the security interest of the creditor.[3] This is true, even though the purchaser knows of the security interest, unless he also knows that the seller is violating his security contract in making the sale.

To illustrate, let us assume that Russell is engaged in selling electrical appliances at retail and that Farnham has loaned money on the stock of appliances, holding a perfected security interest. Parsons, who purchases an electric range from Russell, will take good title unless he knows that

[3] Weisel v. McBride et al., page 993.

Russell had agreed not to sell it without the consent of Farnham. If Parsons merely knows that Farnham holds a security interest in the range, the sale passes good title.

A secured creditor who leaves his collateral with his debtor who is regularly engaged in selling such items impliedly consents to the sale, relying upon the proceeds realized therefrom to satisfy the secured obligation.

There can be no sale in the regular course of business by one not regularly engaged in the sale of such items. Casual sales between individuals made in good faith are made subject to any perfected security interest. One who is engaged in farming is not deemed to sell farm products in the ordinary course of business.

In the field of business, it should be emphasized that negotiable paper, negotiable documents of title, chattel paper, and other nonnegotiable paper are regularly sold in the normal course of business and an innocent buyer or one who loans money will take title free from an outstanding security interest in them if he takes possession in good faith.

7-16. Priorities between security holders. Occasionally, because of the misconduct of the debtor or other circumstances, a conflict of interest may develop within the collateral, or affecting some object of which the collateral has become a part. The Code has attempted to particularize priorities under a number of given situations.

1. If two parties claim a security interest in the same property and filing is used to perfect the interest, the one who files first has the better lien even though he knew of an earlier interest when he secured his. First filing takes priority over first security interest, thus emphasizing the value of prompt filing of any present or potential security interest.

2. As was discussed in Section 7-13, it is possible to have a continuing security interest in a floating stock of merchandise. In other words, future stock may be the subject of a security contract. The Code provides that a purchase-money security interest in inventory is better than the after-acquired clause contained in an earlier security agreement, provided that the purchase-money creditor perfected his interest before the debtor took possession and, in addition, notified prior parties known to have an interest or who had filed their security agreement. For collateral other than inventory, the purchase-money security interest is superior if filed at the time when, or within ten days after, the debtor takes possession. No notice need be given.

3. When several items subject to different security interests combine to make the finished product, the holders share in the new product or proceeds from its sale in proportion to the cost of their materials used.

4. Goods sold are occasionally returned or repossessed. In such a case, any lien on the goods prior to sale will revive, but if the buyer had given

chattel paper, such as a conditional sale contract, which the retailer has sold, the one holding the collateral paper has a better claim than the one having a lien on the inventory. This does not seem to be true, however, of one who acquired the resulting account receivable. The holder of the lien on the inventory gets the better claim to the inventory as against the one to whom the account was assigned.

5. One who sells fixtures often retains a security interest in them. If they are later attached by the purchaser to real estate, the seller of the fixture may remove it from the realty, even though it be mortgaged before or after the fixture is attached. If he repossesses and any person other than the debtor has an interest in the real estate, such as a mortgage, the lienholder must restore the property to its former position; that is, correct any damage done by installation or repossession.

6. The common-law lien on goods allowed for repair, improvement, storage, or transportation is superior to a perfected security holder as long as the lien claimant retains possession of the property. The common-law lienholder is thus given better protection than he had at common law in many states although some courts allowed a repairman priority until he could easily remove his additions to the property.[4] Even though his lien is second in point of time, it is granted priority, presumably because the service rendered by the lienholder has added to or protected the value of the property.

UNIFORM COMMERCIAL CODE CASES

INDUSTRIAL PACKAGING PROD. CO. v. FORT PITT PACK. INT.
1960, (Pa.) 161 A. 2d 19

JONES, J. The Provident Trust Company of Pittsburgh, pursuant to Section 9-403 of the Uniform Commercial Code (Act of April 6, 1953, Section 9-403, 12A P.S. Section 9-403) filed the following financing statement in the office of the Prothonotary of Allegheny County on August 18, 1955:

15110 of 1955
Financing Statement

This financing statement is presented to a filing officer for filing pursuant to the Uniform Commercial Code.

1. Debtor (or assignor)—Fort Pitt Packaging Co., Inc., 5615 Butler Street, Pittsburgh 1, Pa.

2. Secured Party (or assignee)—Provident Trust Co., 900 East Ohio St., Pittsburgh 1, Pa.

3. Maturity date of obligation____________________.

[4] Havas Used Cars Inc. v. Lundy, page 995.

4. The financing statement covers the following types of property: All present and future accounts receivable submitted.

Fort Pitt Packaging Co., Inc.
Leo A. Levy, Treas.
Provident Trust Company
A. W. Charlton
Executive Vice Pres.

Under Section 9-403 of the Code such a statement remains effective for a period of five years. On August 19, 1955, Provident Trust Company filed a similar statement in the office of the Secretary of the Commonwealth in Harrisburg.

On February 4, 1957, Fort Pitt Packaging International Inc. entered into a written contract with the United States Government for the maintenance, repair, and overhaul of vehicles. On March 26, 1957, Fort Pitt entered into a contract with Empire Commercial Corporation wherein Empire agreed to lend Fort Pitt $140,000 and Fort Pitt agreed to assign to the Provident Trust Company as Empire's agent its contract with the United States Government and any and all payments due or to become due thereunder. On the same day, March 26, Fort Pitt sold and assigned to the Provident Trust Company, the payments due or which may become due under the government contract. Notice of the assignment was given to the Contracting Officer of the Department of the Army, pursuant to the provisions of the Federal Assignment of Claims Act of 1940, as amended, 31 U.S.C.A. Section 203.

One year later, on March 27, 1958, Fort Pitt was placed in receivership and on May 27, 1958, upon petition of creditors, Robert Mellin, Esquire, was appointed receiver. On June 10, 1958, the said receiver petitioned the Court of Common Pleas of Allegheny County for a rule upon Empire to show cause why the assignments of the proceeds for Fort Pitt's services performed under the government contracts should not be declared null, void, and ineffective as against the receiver. After hearing held and argument, the court below dismissed the receiver's petition. From that order this appeal was taken.

Empire contends that the laws of New York should govern because under paragraph 16 of Fort Pitt's letter to Empire dated March 26, 1957—the contract between them—it is provided "that (the) agreement and performance thereof shall in all respects be governed by, and in accordance with, the laws of the state of New York." Empire cites Section 1-105 (6) of the Uniform Commercial Code which provides "whenever a contract, instrument, document, security, or transaction bears a reasonable relationship to one or more states or nations in addition to this state the parties may agree that the law of any such other state or nation shall govern their rights and duties. In the absence of an agreement which meets the requirements of this subsection, this Act governs." However, the Uniform Commercial Code also provides, in Section 9-103, "if the office where the assignor . . . keeps his records . . . is in this state, the validity and perfection of a security interest . . . is governed by this Article." We agree with the court below that "as between parties it is lawful for them to agree as to what law shall apply; but where, as here, we are dealing with the rights of creditors in the property of one of the contracting parties, then the law of the state of such party's domicile or place of business shall apply. Otherwise, it would be possible for two parties to render nugatory as to third parties an act of Assembly passed for the benefit of such third parties." The laws of Pennsylvania, not New York, govern this controversy.

Appellant Mellin contends that the filing of the financing statement in 1955 was not sufficient to secure the amounts due under Fort Pitt's contract with the United States Government which was executed in 1957. The filing of the financing statement pursuant to Section 9-403 was entirely proper. The Uniform Commercial Code does not require that the secured party as listed in such statement be a principal creditor and not an agent. In this case, apparently, the Provident Trust Company filed the financing statement as a principal creditor, but in 1957, it became the collecting agent for the Empire Commercial Corporation. Neither the Provident Trust Company nor Empire had any reason to believe that it would be necessary to file a second financing statement which would in all respects duplicate the 1955 statement with the exception that the Provident Trust Company would be listed as an agent for Empire. The purpose of filing this financing statement is to give notice to potential future creditors of the debtor or purchasers of the collateral. It makes no difference as far as such notice is concerned whether the secured party listed in the filing statement is a principal or an agent, and no provision in the Uniform Commercial Code draws such a distinction.

The financing statement covered "all present and future accounts receivable submitted." Section 9-110 of the Uniform Commercial Code provides that "for the purposes of this Article any description is sufficient whether or not it is specific if it reasonably identifies the thing described." There is no doubt that the description in the financing statement reasonably identifies the collateral security. It is difficult under the circumstances to imagine how the description could be more complete without filing new and amended descriptions each time a new account receivable falls within the purview of the financing statement. Nowhere in the Uniform Commercial Code is such a requirement set forth.

Section 9-204 (3) provides that "except as provided in subsection (4) (which deals with crops and consumer goods) *a security agreement may provide that collateral, whenever acquired, shall secure any* advances made or other *value given at any time* pursuant to the security agreement. (Emphasis added.)

In the 1957 agreement between Fort Pitt and Empire, Fort Pitt agreed to assign to Provident Trust Company all payments to be received as they became due from the United States Government under Fort Pitt's contract of February 4, 1957 with the Government. These amounts due fell within the clause "future accounts receivable submitted" contained in the 1955 financing statement filed by Provident Trust Company. Comment 2 to Section 9-303 of the Code states that the "secured party is entitled to have his security interest recognized in insolvency proceedings instituted against the debtor." Therefore, the interest of the secured party, Provident Trust Company is superior to that of the receiver in bankruptcy and any funds which have been placed in the hands of Provident Trust Company pursuant to the Assignment by Fort Pitt need not be turned over to the receiver. These funds are properly being held by the Provident Trust Company for the benefit of its principal, Empire Commercial Corporation.

Order affirmed.

BENEDICT v. RATNER
1925, 268 U.S. 353

The Hub Carpet Company on May 23, 1921, to secure an existing loan of $15,000 and further advances not to exceed $15,000, assigned all of its accounts receivable then outstanding, and all which should thereafter accrue in the ordinary course of business, to Ratner. On July 1, 1921, Ratner advanced the additional $15,000. A list of creditors was delivered on May 23 and a new list was delivered on the 23rd day of each month. The receivables were collected by the company. On Septemebr 26, 1921, the Hub Carpet Company was adjudged bankrupt in involuntary proceedings and Benedict was appointed receiver and trustee in bankruptcy. Benedict collected the accounts receivable. Ratner filed a petition claiming the receivables under the assignment. Benedict contended that the assignment was void as a fraudulent conveyance and filed a cross petition for all amounts collected by Ratner prior to the bankruptcy proceedings. The District Judge held for Ratner ruling that an assignment of future accounts was valid upon delivery of the list of the accounts on September 23, 1921. The Circuit Court of Appeals affirmed the order. The Supreme Court of the United States granted certiorari.

BRANDEIS, Justice . . . It may be assumed that, unless the arrangement of May 23 was void because fraudulent in law, the original assignment of the future acquired accounts became operative under the state law, both as to those paid over to Ratner before the bankruptcy proceedings and as to those collected by the receiver, and that the assignment will be deemed to have taken effect as of May 23. . . .

The receivables were to be collected by the company. Ratner was given the right, at any time, to demand a full disclosure of the business and financial conditions; to require that all amounts collected be applied in payment of his loans; and to enforce the assignment although no loan had matured. But until he did so, the company was not required to apply any of the collections to the repayment of Ratner's loan. It was not required to replace accounts collected by other collateral of equal value. It was not required to account in any way to Ratner. It was at liberty to use the proceeds of all accounts collected as it might see fit. The existence of the assignment was to be kept secret. The business was to be conducted as theretofore. Indebtedness was to be incurred, as usual, for the purchase of merchandise and otherwise in the ordinary course of business. The amount of such indebtedness unpaid at the time of the commencement of the bankruptcy proceedings was large. Prior to September 17, the company collected from accounts so assigned about $150,000, all of which it applied to purposes other than the payment of Ratner's loan. The outstanding accounts enumerated in the list delivered September 23 aggregated $90,000.

Under the law of New York a transfer of property as security which reserves to the transferor the right to dispose of the same, or to apply the proceeds thereof, for his own uses, is, as to creditors, fraudulent in law and void. This is true whether the right of disposition for the transferor's use be reserved in the instrument or by agreement in pais, oral or written; whether the right of disposition reserved be unlimited in time or be expressly terminable by the happening of an event; whether the transfer cover all the property of the debtor or only a part; whether the right of disposition extends to all the property transferred or only to a part thereof; and whether the instrument of transfer be recorded or not.

If this rule applies to the assignment of book accounts, the arrangement of May 23 was clearly void; and the equity in the future acquired accounts, which it would otherwise have created, did not arise. Whether the rule applies to accounts does not appear to have been passed upon by the Court of Appeals of New York. But it would seem clear that whether the collateral consist of chattels or of accounts, reservation of dominion inconsistent with the effective disposition of title must render the transaction void. Ratner asserts that the rule stated above rests upon ostensible ownership, and argues that the doctrine of ostensible ownership is not applicable to book accounts. That doctrine raises a presumption of fraud where chattels are mortgaged (or sold) and possession of the property is not delivered to the mortgagee (or vendee). The presumption may be avoided by recording the mortgage (or sale). It may be assumed, as Ratner contends, that the doctrine does not apply to the assignment of accounts. In their transfer there is nothing which corresponds to the delivery of possession of chattels. The statutes which embody the doctrine and provide for recording as a substitute for delivery do not include accounts. A title to an account good against creditors may be transferred without notice to the debtor or record of any kind. But it is not true that the rule stated above and invoked by the receiver is either based upon or delimited by the doctrine of ostensible ownership. It rests not upon seeming ownership because of possession retained, but upon a lack of ownership because of dominion reserved. It does not raise a presumption of fraud. It imputes fraud conclusively because of the reservation of dominion inconsistent with the effective disposition of title and creation of a lien.

The nature of the rule is made clear by its limitations. Where the mortgagor of chattels agrees to apply the proceeds of their sale to the payment of the mortgage debt or to the purchase of other chattels which shall become subject of the lien, the mortgage is good as against creditors, if recorded. The mortgage is sustained in such cases "upon the ground that such sale and application of proceeds is the normal and proper purpose of a chattel mortgage, and within the precise boundaries of its lawful operation and effect. It does no more than to substitute the mortgagor as the agent of the mortgagee to do exactly what the latter had the right to do, and what it was his privilege and his duty to accomplish. It devotes, as it should, the mortgaged property to the payment of the mortgage debt." The permission to use the proceeds to furnish substitute collateral "provides only for a shifting of the lien from one piece of property to another taken in exchange." . . .

On the other hand, if the agreement is that the mortgagor may sell and use the proceeds for his own benefit, the mortgage is of no effect although recorded. Seeming ownership exists in both classes of cases because the mortgagor is permitted to remain in possession of the stock in trade and to sell it freely. But it is only where the unrestricted dominion over the proceeds is reserved to the mortgagor that the mortgage is void. This dominion is the differentiating and deciding element. . . .

The results which flow from reserving dominion inconsistent with the effective disposition of title must be the same whatever the nature of the property transferred. The doctrine which imputes fraud where full dominion is reserved must apply to assignments of accounts although the doctrine of ostensible ownership does not. There must also be the same distinction as to degrees of dominion. Thus, although an agreement that the assignor of accounts shall collect them and pay the proceeds to the assignee will not invalidate the assignment which it accompanies, the assignment must be deemed fraudulent in law if it is agreed that the assignor may use the proceeds as he sees fit.

In the case at bar the arrangement for the unfettered use by the company of the proceeds of the accounts precluded the effective creation of a lien and rendered the original assignment fraudulent in law. Consequently the payments to Ratner and the delivery of the September list of accounts were inoperative to perfect a lien in him, and were unlawful preferences.

Reversed.

WEISEL v. McBRIDE et al.

1959, (Pa. Super.) 156 A.2d 613

HIRT, J. The plaintiff on June 6, 1957, bought a Studebaker Station Wagon from the defendant James McBride trading as McBride Motor Sales, who at the time was an authorized distributor or dealer for Studebaker cars. He paid this defendant the sale price in full, including the Pennsylvania Sales Tax and the fee for registration of title in his name. Thereupon, on the above date, possession of the automobile was given to the plaintiff and he then signed an application for title to the car in his name and delivered the application to McBride for forwarding to the proper authorities. Notwithstanding he had been paid the full consideration for the sale, McBride subsequently, on June 12, 1957, executed a collateral mortgage in favor of the County Trust Company under an existing floor plan agreement which McBride had with that bank. The mortgage covered the identical car sold and delivered to the plaintiff. Accompanying the mortgage McBride gave his note to the bank for $2,411.66, the amount of his debt as stated in the collateral mortgage. McBride then sent in his own application for title to the car, instead of the plaintiff's and a certificate of title was issued by the Commonwealth of Pennsylvania in the name of McBride Motor Sales with an encumbrance of $2,411.66 in favor of County Trust Company noted thereon. The Trust Company, subsequently, on May 1, 1958, assigned the above note and the collateral mortgage to the defendant John P. McNelly. Title to the car with the encumbrance noted thereon was also assigned to McNelly by McBride. In this action in equity the plaintiff sought a mandatory injunction directing McNelly to deliver to him, Charles A. Weisel Jr., a certificate of title in his name for the Studebaker Station Wagon, free and clear of all encumbrances, and without further cost to him. The court after hearing, refused relief and dismissed the complaint; hence this, the plaintiff's appeal.

On August 16, 1956, a financing statement had been filed by McBride Motor Sales in the Prothonotary's office of Somerset County under Section

9-302 of the Uniform Commercial Code of April 6, 1953, P.L. 3, 12A P.S. Section 9-302 for the wholesale "floor planning" of Studebaker and Packard automobiles not to exceed four cars at any one time, at factory delivered prices. Plaintiff has recently traded the Studebaker in on a new automobile in one of the Western States and it is important that he assign to the new owner his title to the station wagon here involved.

The Uniform Commercial Code in Section 9-307, 12A P.S. Section 9-307 provides: "(1) In the case of inventory, and in the case of other goods as to which the secured party files a financing statement in which he claims a security interest in proceeds, a buyer in ordinary course of business takes free of a security interest even though perfected and even though the buyer knows of the terms of the security agreement." And under the heading: "Power to Transfer; Good Faith Purchase of Goods; 'Entrusting'" the Code in Section 2-403, 12A P.S. Section 2-403 provides: "(1) A purchaser of goods acquires all title which his transferor has or has power to transfer except that a purchaser of a limited interest acquires rights only to the extent of the interest purchased. A person with voidable title has power to transfer a good title to a good faith purchaser for value. (2) Any entrusting of possession of goods to a merchant who deals in goods of that kind gives him power to transfer all rights of the entruster to a buyer in ordinary course of business. (3) 'Entrusting' includes any delivery and any acquiescence in retention of possession regardless of any condition expressed between the parties to the delivery or acquiescence and regardless of whether the procurement of the entrusting or the possessor's disposition of the goods have been such as to be larcenous under the criminal law." In the comment on this section it is said in 12A P.S. Section 2-403: "The many particular situations in which a buyer in ordinary course of business from a dealer has been protected against reservation of property or other hidden interest are gathered by subsections (2)-(4) into a single principle protecting persons who buy in ordinary course out of inventory. Consignors have no reason to complain, nor have lenders who hold a security interest in the inventory, since the very purpose of goods in inventory is to be turned into cash by sale." The instant case presents one of "the many situations" in which the Commercial Code intends to protect "persons who buy in ordinary course out of inventory" as did the plaintiff in this case. It was the obligation of McBride when he received the entire consideration for the sale from Weisel, to satisfy any outstanding "security interest" against the Studebaker Station Wagon. Instead, McBride fraudulently created a new debt with the identical automobile as security in an accompanying mortgage. The fraud was inexcusable on any ground for notwithstanding the appearance of regularity, he used the property of another—the automobile which had been sold to Weisel—as security for his debt. A transaction, even such as this, may be good between the parties but in this case the mortgage was wholly void as to Weisel under the above sections of the Commercial Code. . . .

The order is reversed and the action is remanded to the lower court for the entry of a mandatory decree directing the defendants James McBride and John P. McNelly to deliver to the plaintiff the title to the 1957 Studebaker Station Wagon engine number 12223680 free and clear of all encumbrances and without further cost to him.

HAVAS USED CARS INC. v. LUNDY
1954, (Nev.) 276 P. 2d 727

Plaintiff sold a Hudson automobile by a conditional sales contract to Grimes. Grimes, without the plaintiff's knowledge or consent, delivered the car to the defendant for installation of a new engine.

After installing the new engine, defendant retained possession of the car because of nonpayment of the repair bill. Grimes defaulted and plaintiff claimed the car including the new motor. The trial court found that the engine could be removed without material injury to the car and held that the plaintiff was guilty of converting the defendant's engine.

BADT, Justice. Where an automobile repairman has installed a rebuilt engine in a car at the request of a conditional sale vendee lawfully in possession, with the understanding that the repairman shall retain title to the engine and possession of the engine and car till payment of his bill, and the engine thus installed can be readily removed without damage to the other parts of the car, is such repairman entitled to remove the engine, or entitled to a judgment for its value, in a claim and delivery action brought by the conditional sale vendor upon the conditional vendee's default in payments?

We answer this question in the affirmative, as did the trial court, against the contention of the conditional sale vendor, plaintiff below and appellant here, that by reason of the doctrine of accession it became entitled to the new engine so united to the car as to constitute a part of the vehicle. . . .

Appellant concedes that the trial court found a reservation of title to the engine by the defendant, but contends that, although there is a division of authority as to the effect of such reservation, the better view is that the same is not good as against a chattel mortgagee or a conditional seller of the principal property to which it is attached . . . *Clarke v. Johnson,* 43 Nev. 359, 187 P. 510 . . . , one Crumley had installed upon two trucks, for the contracting vendee, \$339.40 repairs and \$477 new tires. Under claim and delivery by the contracting vendor, the contracting vendee defaulted as in the present case. The trial court had found that the repairs item represented value that could not be removed from the trucks.

This court, upon such finding, held that it was error to render judgment for the repairs item, but affirmed the judgment for the value of the tires. It is true that the court there construed a provision of the sale contract as a recognition that the tires were separable and severable distinct parts. This however does not weaken the court's rejection of the contention that the tires were accession. The conclusion of separability and severability in *Clarke v. Johnson* may indeed have been aided by the terms of the contract. Here such conclusion is supported by the finding of the trial court based on undisputed evidence.

Under the trial court's finding of the retention of title to the engine by the defendant and the ready removability of the engine without damage to the car, neither of which findings is questioned, we are led to the conclusion, under *Clarke v. Johnson*, supra, that the engine did not become an accession. The distinction between the installation of a new set of tires and the installation of a new engine is, after all, one of degree only. The car could no more be operated without tires than it could without an engine. Each case in which the doctrine of accession is advanced must be decided on its own facts.

. . . To like effect as *Clarke v. Johnson* is *Atlas Assurance Co. v. Gibbs*, 121 Conn. 188, 183 A. 690, 692, which also involved the installation of an engine claimed to have become part of the chassis by accession, although it was readily detachable without damage to the automobile. The court said: "If, as appears here, the engine can be readily detached from the car without damage to the rest of it, to permit the plaintiff to take the engine which lawfully belongs to the defendant would be to impose an unjust loss upon the latter and give to the former an enhancement of value to which he is not entitled."

The judgment is affirmed with costs.

Eather, C. J., and Merrill, J., concur.

Review Questions and Problems

1. *F*, a farmer, borrowed $10,000 of *L* and secured the loan by a security interest in growing crops. The lien was perfected by filing, but the crops were harvested and sold to *X* Co., who paid *F* for them. Does *L* have a claim against *X* Co., for the value of the crops as security for the $10,000, *F* being unable to pay?
2. *X* Co., a manufacturer of bicycles, borrowed money from time to time from a bank and gave as security its inventory of raw material, semi-processed or processed goods, then on hand or to be found on hand from time to time in the future. Proper filing took place. Later *X* Co. became bankrupt. Is the bank's lien superior to that held by the trustee in bankruptcy on inventory acquired after the loan was made by the bank?
3. *R*, a retail automobile dealer, at times borrowed money from *X* Co. and *Y* Co., each of whom had filed the necessary statements, *X* Co.

being first to file. Thereafter on October 1, *R* borrowed \$10,000 of *Y* Co. and used four cars as security. He later borrowed \$8,000 of *X* Co. and used the same cars as security. *R* is now insolvent and *X* Co. took possession of the cars. Is his lien superior to that of *Y* Co.?

4. *R*, a retail farm implement dealer, sold a used tractor to *F*, a farmer, for \$2,200, payable in installments, and retained a security interest in the tractor to secure the payments. After *F* had reduced the indebtedness to \$1,800, he became a bankrupt. *R* had not perfected his lien by filing. Is *R*'s security interest good as against the trustee in bankruptcy?
5. *F* Co. loaned *M* Co. money, taking a security interest in an inventory as security, the security contract providing that the lien carry over to the proceeds. If *M* Co. becomes a bankrupt after selling several items of the inventory, having on hand notes receivable, checks, and accounts receivable growing out of the sales, does the lien of *F* Co. carry over to these items, assuming proper filing had taken place?
6. *A*, an automobile dealer, by a valid security agreement retained a security interest in an automobile which he sold *B* on credit. No financing statement was filed and *B* was given both the automobile and the certificate of title which failed to show *A*'s interest. *B* resold the car to *C*. If *A*'s claim is not paid, may he possess the car?
7. *A*, a furniture dealer, by a valid security agreement retained a security interest in a \$750 sofa sold to *B* on credit. No financing statement was filed. *B* resold the sofa to *C*, another consumer. If *A* is unpaid, may he repossess the sofa?

47

Suretyship

NATURE

7-17. Introduction. Although security often takes the form of a lien on property, credit may be extended upon the combined financial standing of the debtor and some third person. The agreement whereby the third party extends his financial standing as security for the debtor is known as a contract of suretyship or guaranty.

Since much of business today is conducted by agents, it becomes necessary for the principal to exact the utmost honesty and good faith of his agent in the performance of his duties. Whenever the principal is unwilling to repose such confidence in the agent alone, he usually obtains what is known as a *bond* for faithful performance that is signed by the agent and some third party. This bond also amounts to a *contract of suretyship.* A contract of suretyship, therefore, appears to have for its objective, security either for the payment of money or for the faithful performance of some other duty, in the latter case often being known as fidelity insurance.

The person primarily bound to perform is known as the *principal* or *principal debtor;* the party secondarily liable is called the *surety* or *guarantor;* and the party entitled to performance is customarily spoken of as the *creditor.*

7-18. Nature of relation. Whenever, as between two parties, one of them is primarily liable and the other secondarily or collaterally liable for the faithful performance of an obligation, in the broad sense a suretyship relation exists. As soon as interested third parties learn of it, they are bound to treat it as such. To illustrate, let us assume that Jones sells his retail lumber business to Smith with the latter assuming and agreeing to pay, as part of the purchase price, all outstanding liabilities. It is clear as between Smith and Jones, that Smith has now become the primary debtor with Jones being collaterally liable. As soon as the creditors are notified of the change, they are obligated to respect the new relationship that exists. This does not mean, as is indicated later, that the creditors must first attempt to recover of Smith before looking to Jones.

7-19. Distinction between guarantor and surety. In a general way the term suretyship is broad enough to encompass both guaranty and suretyship, and for the purposes of this chapter the term surety will be considered to include both surety and guarantor except as otherwise indicated. The courts have, however, in some cases made a technical distinction between the two.

A *surety*, in the technical sense, is liable on the same obligation with the principal debtor. His promise is made jointly or jointly and severally with the principal debtor to the creditor.[1] Thus an accommodation comaker of a note is a surety rather than a guarantor.

A *guaranty* is by language a secondary promise, a promise to pay or perform if the principal debtor defaults—a promise that another will perform, but if he fails, the guarantor will perform. It is separately made, but impresses a duty on the guarantor to perform as soon as the principal defaults. Since he has not joined in the principal's promise to perform, his liability is secondary, but effective as soon as the principal defaults. A guaranty of collectibility guarantees the solvency of the debtor at the time the obligation matures. In such a case, the guarantor is not liable unless the creditor first sues the debtor and is unable to collect or presents convincing evidence it would have done no good to do so. The creditor is also obligated to notify such a guarantor, usually called a conditional guarantor, of a default. Failure to do so releases the guarantor to the extent he is injured by failure to receive prompt notice of default.

Although in a few states all guarantors are entitled to notice, in most of the states absolute guarantors and sureties are not entitled to notice of default. It becomes their duty to keep informed and to make good where the principal fails unless their contract with the creditor has provided for notice.

7-20. Contract of suretyship. Although suretyship may result by operation of law because of a change in the relationship of parties, as was indicated in the previous illustration, it most often develops as a result of an express contract between the surety and the creditor whereby the former assumes a secondary responsibility for the principal's performance. He agrees that he may be called upon to perform in case the principal defaults. Like all other contracts, the agreement consists of offer and acceptance supported by consideration, although in the majority of instances the consideration is the same as that received by the principal. Thus, one who promises to pay for goods supplied to *A* in case *A* fails to pay for them gets no beneficial consideration. The creditor who supplies the goods to *A* on the strength of *A*'s promise to pay and the surety's secondary promise supplies the needed consideration to both by delivery of goods to *A*. In reliance upon the two promises, the creditor did an act he was not otherwise obligated to do. However, if the goods had been delivered before the surety made his promise, some new consideration would have been essential to bind the surety.

[1] Edward Corporation of Miami v. Woolin & Son, Inc., page 1007.

As indicated in the study of contracts, contracts of suretyship—agreements to become secondarily liable for the debt or default of another—are required by the Statute of Frauds to be evidenced by writing. As suggested at that point, if the debt really becomes that of the promisor—let *P* have goods and I will pay for them—no writing is required. Likewise, if the main purpose of the surety's promise is to derive some substantial benefit for himself from the performance of the creditor, no writing is necessary in most states. The benefit in such a case must be something other than mere consideration for becoming a surety.

The duties assumed by the surety are largely determined by the contract terms as expressed by the parties, but, in the interpretation of ambiguous language, historically the courts have favored the voluntary or accommodation—unpaid—surety at the expense of the creditor. Currently, the courts incline so far as possible to give words their normal meaning even though it works a hardship on the surety, but, where the meaning is uncertain, courts construe ambiguous language against the person who used it. Since in the case of unpaid sureties, the language is usually framed by the creditor and signed by the surety, this serves to benefit the surety.

7-21. Fiduciary relation. A suretyship relation is, within limits, fiduciary in character, involving special trust and confidence between the parties. As a consequence, a creditor in possession of extremely vital information affecting the risk should volunteer such information to the surety at the time the contract is made. This applies only to information so significant and unusual that the surety normally would not think to inquire concerning it.

Since the contract is between the surety and the creditor, any misconduct of the principal which induces the surety to become such does not permit the surety to avoid the contract.[2] However, if the creditor is aware, when the contract is being formed, of the principal's misconduct, he is obligated to inform the surety.

Because of these rules, an employer who is aware of past defalcations of an employee and who seeks a bond assuring faithful performance by the employee of his duties is bound to notify the surety at the time the contract is being formed of such misconduct. Similarly, a creditor who learns that the principal has misrepresented his financial condition to a prospective surety is obligated to warn the surety that he is assuming a risk not anticipated. Otherwise, the creditor will not be able to enforce the surety's promise.

An employer who discovers that his employee has been guilty of misappropriation of funds should immediately discharge him unless the surety

[2] Watkins Co. v. Brund et al., page 1009.

assents to his continued employment. To continue the employee at his task subjects the surety to a risk not contemplated, so if a second opportunity to make good is to be offered the employee, it should be done with the approval of his surety.

7-22. Immediate recourse to surety. As indicated in an earlier section, the surety or absolute guarantor becomes liable to the creditor as soon as the principal defaults in the performance of his obligation, and the creditor need not exhaust his remedies against the principal before looking to them. This rule seems to apply even though the creditor is in possession of collateral provided by the principal debtor. He may resort to the surety without disposing of the collateral unless the surety requests the sale of the collateral in order to avoid unreasonable hardship. In a case of extreme hardship the surety may require the creditor to dispose of the collateral before looking to him.

Where several sureties are jointly or severally liable, they may be joined in one action and, after obtaining judgment, the creditor may recover the entire amount from any one of them. If these obligations are several, he may sue any one for the full amount unless it exceeds the particular surety's maximum liability. The claim, unless the creditor has agreed otherwise, is entire and need not be divided for the benefit of the sureties.

7-23. Duration of liability. A guarantor or surety for a particular debt naturally continues liable until the obligation has been satisfied unless released by the Statute of Limitations. Similarly, one who agrees to be liable for the default of an employee or an elected official continues liable as long as the employee works under his original contract or the official remains in office, unless the contract sets its own period of liability.

Ambiguous language often causes difficulty where a guarantor guarantees payment of goods supplied a principal debtor. "Let bearer have what leather he needs and if he fails to pay for it, I will," may be construed to apply to a single purchase or to be a continuous guaranty of credit. Usually in the absence of a time or an amount limitation, the courts tend to limit the liability to one transaction unless it is clear from other evidence that the parties intended otherwise. Where there is a limit as to time the courts tend to construe the guaranty as continuous for that period up to any reasonable amount, and when a limit on amount is indicated the guaranty is likewise continuous,[3] with the maximum liability being the figure established. In the latter case, the guaranty of credit continues on various obligations until it is withdrawn, being much like a continuing offer. Receipt of the withdrawal notice or death of the guarantor terminates liability for credit thereafter extended to the principal. Difficulty in all these cases could be eliminated by a careful phrasing of the contract terms relating to liability.

[3] Frell v. Dumont-Florida, Inc., page 1010.

Confusion exists as to whether a creditor who relies upon a letter of guaranty is obligated to notify the guarantor that he accepts, that he has acted or will act in reliance upon it. If it is a general letter addressed "to whom it may concern," the better view is that the creditor must notify the guarantor within a reasonable time after credit has been extended. Because of existing uncertainty, it is a wise business policy in all cases to give notice that the guaranty has been or will be relied upon. Although the offer is unilateral and accepted by the act of extending credit, if the act is one knowledge of which when performed is not readily available, notice of performance should be given.

7-24. Subrogation. Literally, subrogation means the substitution of one person in place of another, and as used in this section it refers to the creditor's right to step into the shoes of the surety so far as they relate to the surety's right against the principal. Security of any kind given to the surety by the principal for the protection of the former in case the latter defaults may be available to the creditor. To the extent of his claim, the creditor may substitute his position for that of the surety, with reference to the securities. Thus, it has been held that, in the event of the return of securities by the surety to the principal, the creditor is entitled to follow them into the hands of the debtor and subject them to a lien in his favor. This rule applies only where the rights of innocent third parties have not intervened. He may also secure an injunction against their return to the principal, thus having the securities impounded by the court until the principal debt falls due, at which time they may be sold for the benefit of the creditor.

Collateral posted with a surety to protect him against loss on any one of several obligations upon which he is surety does not necessarily give a particular creditor the right of subrogation. In the event of the surety's insolvency, the collateral is apportioned among the various creditors to whom the surety was obligated.

The right of subrogation does not exist where the securities are left with the surety by some third party. The theory is that securities placed with the surety form a trust of that portion of the estate of the principal which he sets aside for the payment of his debt. Securities belonging to third parties do not form part of the principal's estate, and, therefore, are not subject to subrogation.

RIGHTS OF SURETIES

7-25. Extension of time. The creditor should be careful not to extend the time for performance without the consent of the surety. A contract between the principal and the creditor, which definitely extends the time within which performance may be demanded, releases the surety. The reason for this rule is that the financial status of the principal may become less sound during the period of the extension. Such a change in his financial condition would work to the disadvantage of the surety. The court does not consider in each case whether the position of the surety has been injured by the extension, but merely applies the general rule that an extension of time releases the surety.

Mere indulgence upon the part of the creditor or passively permitting the debtor to take more time than the contract calls for does not release the surety. The latter is in no sense injured by such conduct, because he is free at any time to perform on his part and immediately start suit against the principal. The surety is not discharged unless there is a binding agreement between the principal and the creditor for a definite period of extension.

The consent of the surety may be obtained either before or after the extension has been granted. Consent given after the extension amounts to a waiver of the right to rescind and is valid, although it is not based upon any new consideration. Notice to the surety that an extension has been granted or a failure on the part of the surety to reply to a request seeking permission to extend is not equivalent to consent. In the latter case, silence should act as a warning not to grant the extension since the surety is apparently unwilling to extend the risk.

7-26. Extension with rights reserved. An extension of time by the creditor, in which the extension agreement stipulates reservation of rights against the surety, does not release the surety. Such an extension binds only the creditor. It does not bind the surety. He is free at any time to complete performance for the principal and immediately to sue him for damages suffered, since to him the arrangement is quite similar to mere indulgence. To illustrate: *S* becomes surety for *P* on a note in favor of *C*. The note falls due on a certain date, and *P* requests from *C* an extension of ninety days. The extension is granted with the express stipulation that *C* reserves all rights against *S*. *S* is not released, although he receives no notice of the extension. His right to pay the debt at any time he desires and to turn to *P* for reimbursement is not impaired.

To the extent that a surety is protected by securities placed with him by his principal debtor, an extension of time does not effect a discharge. An extension of time cannot injure a fully secured surety, and one who is only partially secured is released to the extent the security is inadequate.

A paid surety—one who has received some compensation for the risk that he assumes—is not released unless he is damaged as a result of the extension of time granted to the principal.[4] In such a case the surety is

[4] Murray City v. Banks et al., page 1011.

released only when he can show that the ability of the principal to perform has perceptibly weakened during the period of extension.

An extension of time on an obligation arising out of a continuous guaranty does not release the guarantor except that the maximum liability is not thereby extended. To illustrate, let us assume that *G* guaranteed payment of goods sold to *P* by *C* up to a maximum of $10,000. If a claim for $3,000 falls due, an extension of time by *C* will not release *G*. *C* is still protected by the $10,000 maximum liability of *G*.

7-27. Change in contract terms. Any material change in the terms of the contract between the principal and the creditor, without the consent of the surety, discharges him.[5] Inasmuch as the principal contract governs the surety's liability, any change in its terms must be assented to by him.

A discharge of the principal debtor, or any one of them if there are two or more, unless assented to, releases the surety. This rule is subject to those exceptions existing in the case of an extension of time; that is, the surety is not released if the principal debtor is discharged with reservation of rights against the surety, or if the surety is protected by securities or is a paid surety and is not injured.

7-28. Payment. Payment of the principal obligation by the debtor or someone in his behalf discharges the surety, although a payment later avoided causes the surety's liability to revive. This situation is likely to occur in bankruptcy, where a creditor may be compelled in certain cases to surrender a preference received.

A valid tender of payment by either the principal or the surety that is rejected by the creditor releases the surety. In such a case it is not necessary that the tender be kept good or continuously available in order for the surety to be released. Since the creditor has had an opportunity to receive his money, the surety is no longer liable.

Whenever payment is made by a debtor who owes several obligations to the creditor, unless the debtor has indicated where it is to be applied, the creditor is free to apply it on any matured obligation. However, if the money is in reality supplied by the surety, and this fact is known to the creditor, he must apply it on the one for which the surety is liable. If the creditoı makes no specific application, in court the money will be applied where the court feels it is equitable, but a tendency to apply it on the unsecured obligations is reasonably clear from court decisions.

The mere receipt of a note or check of the principal debtor by the creditor does not release the surety, as the debt is not paid until the note or check is honored. If a new note is given in settlement of an old one, the old one being canceled and returned, an extension of time has taken place, which releases the surety. Where both notes are retained by the

[5] Magazine Digest Pub. Co., Limited v. Shade et al., page 1011.

creditor, the courts hold that the second is merely collateral to the first and the surety is not released.

7-29. Defenses of principal. Many of the defenses available to the principal may be asserted by the surety against the creditor, particularly where the principal is willing to have the defenses so used. Such defenses as mutual mistake, fraud, illegality, lack or failure of consideration, or undue influence, if available to the principal, may be used by the surety. Infancy and bankruptcy form exceptions to the rule, and may not be used by the surety, since he is employed in the first instance to protect the creditor against the inability of the debtor to perform.

Although a minor may avoid his contract and return the consideration he received, the surety is, in perhaps the majority of the states, required to make up any deficiency between the value of the item returned and the amount of the indebtedness. Other states hold that avoidance by the minor releases the surety.

Generally, if the debtor is insolvent or the principal and surety are jointly sued, the surety is entitled to use set-offs that are available to the principal debtor.

Similarly, the surety may set off against the creditor any claim which the creditor owes him if the debtor is insolvent or the creditor is solvent. If the creditor calls upon the surety to pay the principal's obligation of $500, the surety may deduct any amount which is due him from the creditor. Thus, it may be said that the surety can interpose either his own or his principal's defenses against the creditor.

The Statute of Limitations available to the principal debtor may not be used by the surety.[6] Each has his own period after which he is no longer liable to the creditor, and the period may be longer for one than the other. Thus, the debtor may be liable on an oral contract while the surety is liable on a written contract, or the debtor may have made a part payment which extends the period of his liability but which has no effect upon the liability of the surety.

7-30. Subrogation. The surety who fully performs the obligation of his principal is subrogated to the creditor's rights against the principal. The surety who pays his principal's debt becomes entitled to any securities which the principal has placed with the creditor to secure that particular debt. Likewise, if the creditor has obtained a judgment against the principal, the surety receives the benefit of the judgment when he satisfies the principal's debt. Where the creditor has collateral as general security for a number of obligations, the surety's right of subrogation does not arise unless all of the obligations are satisfied. It should be noted that subrogation applies only to rights of the creditor against the principal. If some third person, to secure the principal's debt, also pledges collateral

[6] Bomud Company v. Yockey Oil Company and Osborn, page 1012.

to the creditor, the surety has no equity in the security although the creditor calls upon him to satisfy the debt.

A creditor in possession of collateral given to him by the principal is not at liberty to return it without the consent of the surety. Any surrender of securities releases the surety to the extent of their value, his loss of subrogation damaging him to that extent. Failure of the creditor to make use of the securities, however, does not relieve the surety, since the latter is free to pay the indebtedness and to obtain the securities for his own protection. However, if the creditor loses the benefit of collateral by inactivity—failure to record a mortgage or notify an indorser—the surety is released to the extent he is injured.

7-31. Recovery from principal. One who becomes a surety at the request, or with the approval, of the principal is entitled to reimbursement for any loss caused by the principal's default. Normally, the surety is not permitted to add any attorney's fees that he has been compelled to pay on his own behalf by way of defense or fees paid to the creditor's attorney. All attorney's fees can be avoided by performance of contract terms; when the principal fails to perform, it becomes the immediate duty of the surety to act. Attorney's fees incurred in a bona fide attempt to reduce the amount of the recovery form an exception to this general rule.

The surety may recover only the amount paid by him. Thus, if he settles a claim for less than the full amount owing the creditor, his right to recover is limited to the sum paid under the settlement. Furthermore, bankruptcy on the part of the principal, although it takes place before the surety is called upon to perform, releases him from further liability to the surety.

Any securities falling into the possession of the surety at the time he settles his principal's obligation may be disposed of as far as is necessary to extinguish the surety's claim for indemnity.

The surety also possesses the right to be exonerated, which makes it possible for him to go into court and compel the principal to perform in order to save the surety harmless. Naturally, this right of exoneration has little value where the principal is financially unable to make payment or to take such other action as his contract requires.

7-32. Cosureties' liability. Whenever two or more sureties become secondarily liable for the same obligation of the principal, they become cosureties whether they know of each others' liability or not at the time they become sureties. If the creditor compels one surety to meet the obligation in full, that particular surety takes on the burden of recovering from his cosureties the portion they should contribute.

An extension of time to or a release of one surety releases other sureties only to the extent the released surety would have been obligated to contribute. There is an implied contract between cosureties that they will share any loss equally unless they have agreed otherwise or have fixed different maximum amounts for their liability. In the latter event, they are assumed to have agreed to share in proportion to their maximum liability. This right to contribution from cosureties provides initially for a sharing between solvent cosureties within the state. Each contributing surety then possesses an independent action against the insolvent or nonresident surety for the amount which he paid on behalf of the insolvent or nonresident surety.

So long as the balance of a claim remains outstanding and unpaid, a cosurety has no right to contribution unless he has paid more than his share of the claim, and then only to the extent of the excess. This he may recover from any cosurety unless it compels the latter to pay more than his full share.

No surety has a right to profit at the expense of a cosurety. Neither has he a right to reduce his personal risk by secretly procuring collateral from the principal debtor. Any such collateral, obtained either before or after he became a surety, must be held for the benefit of all the sureties.[7] It is possible, of course, for all the sureties at the time they become such to agree that one of them may be favored by receiving collateral for his protection, but in the absence of such an arrangement, all have a right to share in the collateral held by one.

SURETYSHIP CASES

EDWARD CORPORATION OF MIAMI v. WOOLIN & SON, INC.

1959 (Fla. App.) 113 S.2d 252

HORTON, J. This is an appeal from a final judgment dismissing the plaintiff's second amended complaint. The trial judge found the contract sued upon one of suretyship rather than guaranty, thus requiring the addition of the principal as party-defendant.

The facts, as disclosed by the complaint, reveal that Edward Corporation of Miami refused to deliver goods to Medley Industries without the joinder of the appellee in the obligation. After receipt of the order, the supplier, Edward Corporation of Miami, submitted the folowing "Order Confirmation" to Medley Industries:

Gentlemen:

We confirm having entered your above order as follows, subject to conditions on the reverse side hereof:

We confirm herewith having sold to you approximately 40 tons of bar-size

[7] Hoover et al. v. Mowrer et al., page 1013.

angles and smooth rounds as per your specifications and 5 tons of flats, squares and beams.
It is understood between us that the price for the first item will be 8¢ a lb., and the 2nd item 9¢ a lb.
The purpose of this contract note is also to receive a confirmation by Messrs. David Woolin & Sons, Inc., that they authorize you to draw this merchandise from us on their behalf and that they will be responsible for payment of your invoices up to the total amount of approximately $8,000.00.
We would appreciate your acceptance of this contract note on the attached copy which acceptance should be countersigned by Messrs. David Woolin & Sons, Inc.

Accepted:
By: /s/ M. Thomas
Medley Industries

Edward Corporation
of Miami
Edward Tohari,
President

Accepted:
By: /s/ David M. Woolin
David Woolin & Sons, Inc.

After unsuccessful attempts to recover the unpaid balance on this order from Medley Industries, the plaintiff brought suit against David M. Woolin and Sons, Inc., on their promise in the "Order Confirmation." The defendant moved to dismiss, incorporating, as one of the grounds for the motion, the failure to join an indispensable party. The trial judge dismissed the second amended complaint, finding only that the contract was one of suretyship rather than guaranty. The plaintiff refused to further amend its complaint, final judgment was entered, and this appeal followed.

Both appellant and appellee appear to be in basic agreement on the proposition that the distinction between guaranty and suretyship is merely academic and not essential to a final determination of the obligation created by the contract. In this respect we agree. The determinative point is whether Medley Industries and David M. Woolin and Sons, Inc., were bound jointly, or jointly and severally.

From the wording of the contract, it appears that David M. Woolin and Sons, Inc. and Medley Industries promised to pay for the goods ordered. Thus, we have two promises for the same act, i.e., payment of the goods ordered and delivered. Generally, under such circumstances, the contract is a joint obligation unless the wording contained in the agreement requires a contrary construction. Restatement of Contracts, § 112; 4 Corbin, Contracts, § 925; 17 C.J.S. Contracts, § 349 et seq.

The facts presented herein are analogous to the illustration in Corbin, *supra*, § 926, p. 705:

* * * [T]he dealer replies to the order saying that he will ship no goods to *B* unless *A* assures payment for them, and that *A* replies that he will do so. * * * With respect to the goods shipped to *B*, the dealer can get judgment against *B;* and he can get judgment against *A*. For the goods shipped to *B*, both *A* and *B* have promised to pay. * * * [T]hese two promises are for one single performance, the payment of the price of *B*'s goods. Under modern procedure there should be no difficulty in joining *A* and *B* as co-defendants in an action for the price of *B*'s goods, even though they would not be described by the old common law as "jointly" bound, and even though *B* is principal debtor and *A* his surety.

We feel the trial judge correctly treated the contract as a joint obligation in dismissing the complaint for failure to join an indispensable party. The dismissal being without prejudice would not preclude the right of the appellant to bring an action against both parties.

Affirmed.

WATKINS CO. v. BRUND et al.

1931, 160 Wash. 183, 294 Pac. 1024

Action by J. R. Watkins Company against Joseph Buerkli, one of the defendants, the latter having signed a bond which guaranteed the payment by one Brund of $988.54 to plaintiff and such additional sums as arose out of a certain sales agreement between the plaintiff and Brund. The bond was signed by Buerkli with the definite understanding between him and Brund that it was not to be delivered to the plaintiff until the signature of one Kalb had been obtained. Disregarding this agreement, Brund procured Heim, financially irresponsible, to sign the agreement, and mailed it to the plaintiff. Brund defaulted and plaintiff seeks to recover from Buerkli. The lower court gave judgment for the plaintiff.

BEELER, J. . . . The trial court found, which finding is supported by the record, that respondent knew nothing whatever of the understanding or agreement between Brund and Buerkli, and furthermore, that it had no means of obtaining any knowledge concerning the negotiations between them. . . . It was wholly a secret understanding between appellant and Brund. [Here he quotes the rule as found in 21 R.C.L. 968.]

Hence, the rule sustained by the great weight of authority is that the agreement of a surety with his principal that the latter shall not deliver a bond until the signature of another be procured as a cosurety will not relieve the surety of liability on his bond although the cosurety is not obtained, where there is nothing on the face of the bond, or in the attending circumstances, to apprise the taker that such further signature was called for in order to complete the instrument. In such cases the surety, having vested his principal with apparent authority to deliver the bond, is estopped to deny his obligation to the innocent holder, on the principle that where one of two innocent persons must suffer, the loss must fall upon him who puts it in the power of a third person to cause the loss.

The judgment is affirmed.

FRELL v. DUMONT-FLORIDA, INC.
1959, (Fla. App.) 114 S.2nd 311

PEARSON, J. The appellant [Frell] was defendant in an action on a written guaranty. He appeals from a final judgment for the plaintiff which was based upon a jury verdict. The letter of guaranty contained the following:

> You have been requested to open a line of credit not to exceed Ten Thousand Dollars ($10,000.00), in favor of: Best Appliance Sales & Service Ltd.
> You have indicated that you are unwilling to extend this line of credit to this dealer without other, and further, security of payment thereof.
> In consideration of this agreement to extend this dealer a line of credit in question, the undersigned, hereby undertakes to, and does guarantee payment of. any, and all, credit granted by you not to exceed Ten Thousand Dollars ($10,000.00), * * *.

The appellant contends first that the guaranty was, by its terms, limited to $10,000 and after that total amount had been purchased the guaranty did not cover new purchases even though the indebtedness was not as much as $10,000. This argument overlooks the ordinary meaning of "a line of credit," which is a limit of credit to cover a series of transactions. *Pittinger v. Southwestern Paper Co.*, Tex. Civ. App. 1941, 151 S.W.2d 922.

It is further argued that the guaranty was rendered ineffective as to purchases from the plaintiff after the date that the principal-debtor changed its name and one of the partners withdrew. The trial judge correctly found that the appellant as guarantor was estopped to claim this defense because the guarantor 1) participated in the change of name, 2) participated in the profits (if any) of the original debtor after the change, which business both before and after the name change was dependent upon the purchases made under the continuing guaranty, and 3) the guarantor at no time disclaimed responsibility under the guaranty until suit. See *Wilson & Toomer Fertilizer Co. v. American Cyanamid Co.*, 5 Cir., 1929, 33 F.2d 812.

The appellant also assigns and argues certain other alleged errors. They have been considered and are found not well taken. The judgment of the trial court is therefore affirmed.

Affirmed.

MURRAY CITY v. BANKS et al.

1923, 62 Utah 296, 219 Pac. 246

Banks was an officer of the plaintiff city, and the American Surety Company signed Banks' official bond. A shortage in Banks' accounts was discovered and certain officers of the plaintiff took a note from him for the amount of the shortage, bearing 6 per cent interest and falling due in six months. This action was instituted to recover the shortage from Banks and his surety.

CHERRY, J. . . . The trial court made findings of fact to the effect that the note had been executed and delivered to the plaintiff, and a payment made and credited on it, and concluded that the plaintiff, by accepting the note, thereby extended the time of payment of the amount due until September 1, 1920, without the knowledge or consent of the surety, and the surety was thereby relieved from liability. . . .

Does an agreement of the obligee of a bond, extending the time of payment to the principal, without the consent of the surety of itself and without a showing of prejudice, discharge the surety when the latter is engaged in the surety business for hire, and as such has executed the undertaking? The law of suretyship, of late years, has undergone a change. In the interpretation of the surety's liability a distinction is made between a voluntary gratuitous surety and one who makes suretyship a business for compensation. . . .

The same distinction is made, and the corresponding rule is applied, to both the determination of the surety's liability in the first instance and the sufficiency of the grounds by which he may be later discharged from liability. The courts generally hold that a compensated surety can be relieved from its obligation for suretyship only where a departure from the contract is shown to be a material variance, and that it must show some injury done before it can be absolved from its contract. . . . There was no sufficient ground appearing to justify the discharge of the surety. The trial court erred in granting the nonsuit and entering judgment for the surety.

The judgment is reversed.

MAGAZINE DIGEST PUB. CO., LIMITED v. SHADE et al.

1938, 330 Pa. 487, 199 Atl. 190

DREW, J. This suit in assumpsit was brought [by Magazine Digest] to recover money alleged to be due under a contract between plaintiff and Mutual Magazine Distributors, Inc., on which contract defendants were guarantors. In their affidavit of defense defendants denied liability on the ground that they were discharged by a subsequent oral agreement which altered the original contract without their knowledge or consent. . . .

Under its original contract Mutual Distributors agreed to buy plaintiff's magazines at 14½¢ a copy for resale to retailers at 16½¢. Defendants guaranteed Mutual's obligation to pay plaintiff, with the additional stipulation that:

> . . . the publisher (plaintiff) may in his absolute discretion and without diminishing the liability of the guarantors (defendants), grant time or other indulgence to the distributor and may accept or make any composition or arrangements when and in such manner as the publisher may think expedient.

The parties continued under this contract until September 19, 1933, when Mutual was in arrears to the extent of $1,162.12. On that date it was orally agreed between plaintiff's president and the president of Mutual that if plaintiff refrained from terminating the contract, Mutual would pay the increased price of 15¢ a copy for the magazines. . . .

We cannot agree that defendants are liable for Mutual's debts under the substituted agreement of September 10, 1933. Even compensated guarantors—and defendants are not shown to be such—are not liable when the original contract on which their undertaking was made is materially changed without their assent. *Sall B. & L. Ass'n v. Heller*, 314 Pa. 237, 171 Atl. 464. A gratuitous or accommodation guarantor is discharged by any change, material or not, and "even if he sustains no injury by the change, or if it be for his benefit, he has a right to stand upon the very terms of his obligation and is bound no farther." 100 Pa. 500, 505. But there can be no doubt here the alteration was material. To the distributor it meant 25 per cent less in its sale profit, to the plaintiff it made the difference between the terminating and continuing contractual relations with the distributor, and to the defendants it meant an increase in their obligation of $1,118.05 on 223,609 magazines received from the publisher after the new contract was in force. . . . Nor can the legal effect of alteration be escaped by limiting recovery against guarantors to the rate set in the original contract. The very theory of their defense is that after the change there is a new contract on which the guarantor has not agreed to be liable to any extent. . . .

Defendants are not relieved, however, from Mutual's debts which accrued while the original contract remained in force. The subsequent variation of that contract had no effect upon the liability that had already become fixed. Consequently defendants were not discharged as to it.

BOMUD COMPANY v. YOCKEY OIL COMPANY AND OSBORN

1958, (Kan.) 142 2nd 148

Osborn in a letter guaranteed payment by Yockey of oil well supplies which the plaintiff, Bomud, in reliance on the letter sold to Yockey on credit. Yockey is no longer liable because of the short Statute of Limitations for oral agreements but the five year statute applying to written accounts has not run. Osborn contends that he is released because Yockey is no longer liable and the lower court awarded judgment in favor of Osborn, against whom the plaintiff has taken this appeal.

FATZER, J. A guarantor, to be relieved from his obligation to pay, must establish one of three facts: (1) the debt has been paid or extinguished; (2) a valid release or discharge; or (3) the bar of the statute of limitations as to himself. It is conceded that the debt has not been paid. The fact that the statute bars recovery against Yockey does not extinguish the debt. . . . It is also conceded that the statute of limitations has not run as to Osborn's individual liability on his written contract if he has not been released or discharged. Did the failure to bring the action upon the open account, until the statute had run in favor of Yockey, release or discharge Osborn from his guarantee to pay under his written contract? We think it did not. . . . The contract of a guarantor is his own separate contract. It is in the nature of a warranty by him that the thing guaranteed to be done by the principal shall be done, and is not an engagement jointly with the principal to do the thing. A guarantor, not being a joint contractor with the principal, is not bound like a surety to do what the principal has contracted to do, but answers only for the consequence of the default of the principal. . . . When default occurs on the part of the principal, the guarantor's liability becomes primary and is absolute. . . .

Osborn's contract with Bomud was based upon a valid consideration. It was a separate undertaking to pay if Yockey defaulted. When Osborn's liability became primary and absolute, the open account was then enforceable against Yockey, and it is of no consequence to Osborn if since that time the statute has run in Yockey's favor. Osborn's liability was fixed and determined by his written guaranty and that obligation has not been discharged. That the statute of limitations, G.S.1949, 60–306, *First*, had not run in Osborn's favor when suit was filed, is conceded. The debt has not been paid. Bomud is entitled to recover from Osborn in accordance with the terms and conditions of his contract.

The judgment is reversed with directions to set aside the order entering judgment for Osborn on the pleadings, and to proceed in accordance with the views expressed in this opinion. It is so ordered.

HOOVER et al. v. MOWRER et al.

1891, 84 Iowa 43, 50 N.W. 62

This was an action on a promissory note. It appears that the note was made by one Mowrer to R. W. Adams, E. O. Craig, C. Hoover, and James

Hoover and by them indorsed to the plaintiff for the accommodation of Mowrer, the four indorsers thus becoming sureties. It further appears that Mowrer became insolvent, but that Adams and Craig took a chattel mortgage on some stock in trade to protect them. Hoover & Hoover are now attempting to force them to share the proceeds from a sale of the mortgaged goods.

BECK, C. J. . . . We are first required to determine whether Craig & Adams may appropriate the proceeds of the mortgaged property to their exclusive benefit, or whether the mortgage should be regarded as security for all the indorsers of the note. Counsel for the appellees state quite correctly, we think, the rule of law, "that securities obtained by one surety inure to the benefit of all. . . ." The rule exists for the protection of the sureties, and not for the good of the creditors or the principal debtor. By the contract of sureties, they became severally bound for the debt of the principal. But it is plain that each should contribute equally in case they are called upon to pay the debt. One cannot in any way escape the burden while his cosurety is not relieved. . . . Each surety is authorized to rely upon this rule to protect himself from imposition and fraud which his cosurety and principal might practice upon him. The principal, by indemnifying one of the sureties, would relieve him of the burden of suretyship which the other still carried. This would be unfair and inequitable. In case it is done with the knowledge and consent of the other surety, it would thereby be relieved of objection, for the surety could not complain of that to which he assents.

Judgment for plaintiffs.

Review Questions and Problems

1. *S* wrote a letter to *C*, a material man, saying he would be liable for "any bill my son makes for material." A dispute arose later as to whether this covered one purchase or a series of purchases. What is your answer?
2. Suppose *S* signs a statement to the effect that he will be secondarily liable for groceries, not exceeding $300, furnished to *X*. How long will such a guaranty continue?
3. *G*, by contract, guaranteed prompt payment of a certain note owing by *P* to *C*. The note fell due at a time when the maker was solvent, but *C* made no attempt to collect and gave *G* no notice of the default. Later *P* became insolvent and *C* desires to collect of *G*. May he do so?
4. Davis was surety for his brother on a $1,152 note in favor of Bank, the brother giving Davis a mortgage on real property to protect him against loss. Davis and his brother are insolvent and are thinking about releasing the mortgage. The court held Bank could have the mortgage impounded for its benefit. Why?
5. *S* was surety upon *P*'s obligation to *C*. Some time after the debt fell due, *P*, with the knowledge and consent of *S*, made a payment on the

obligation. Did this payment toll the statute of limitations for *S* as well as *P*?

6. *C* held an obligation of *P*'s upon which *S* was surety. *C* permitted the obligation to run several years past its maturity date, although the interest was always paid. No definite extension period was ever agreed upon between *P* and *C*. After a number of years, although within the period required by the Statute of Limitations, *C* attempted to recover from *S*. Should he have been allowed to recover?
7. *C*, *A*, *E*, and *M* were sureties upon a $4,000 obligation of *B* to *W*. The obligation provided for attorney fees of 10 per cent if placed with an attorney for collection. *B* defaulted and *C*, upon demand, paid the $4,000 note to *W*. He then sued *A*, *E*, and *M* for $3,000 and attorney fees in an action against them jointly. The court refused to allow any attorney fees and refused to give a joint judgment against the three. Why?
8. *A* and *B* are sureties upon an obligation of *P*. At the time *A* became a surety, he obtained a mortgage from *P* upon certain personal property to protect himself in case *P* defaulted. *P* failed to perform, and *A* and *B* were compelled to carry out the agreement. Did *A* hold the mortgage for his own protection alone or for the mutual protection of the sureties? If you were *A*, how would you arrange the matter to protect yourself only?
9. The mother and wife of *P* became cosureties on *P*'s note for $5,000, the note being secured by a chattel mortgage on *P*'s household furniture. The wife settled the claim for $3,500 and released the chattel mortgage on furniture worth $2,500. She now seeks contribution from the mother, her mother-in-law. How much should she recover?
10. *C* Co. loaned *J* Co. $68,000, $59,280 of the amount being guaranteed in writing by *W* and his wife. As security for the guaranty, they pledged a note for $59,280 owing to them as joint tenants by *X*. The $68,000 debt fell due and in settlement a new note for a lesser amount and a different rate of interest was given *C* Co. by *J* Co. *W* guaranteed the new debt and repledged the $59,280 note as security, his wife not joining in the guaranty or pledge. *J* Co. is again in default and *C* Co. proposes to use the $59,280 note as a means of collection, when *W*'s wife claims one-half of it because she did not join in the pledging. Was her original pledge still good?
11. *A* and *S* signed a mortgage note in favor of *P* for $15,000, it being known to *P* that *S* was merely a surety. Some time later, *A* became insolvent, and *P* accepted $7,000, discharging *A* from further liability. May *P* recover the $8,000 balance from *S*?
12. *S* wrote a letter to *C* in which he promised to be liable as a continuous guarantor on all goods sold to *P* until the guaranty was withdrawn by notice. Before any goods had been sold, *S* died, but this fact being unknown to *C*, he sold goods to *P* on credit. Since *P* has failed to pay for the goods, *C* seeks to recover of the estate of *S*. Is the estate liable?

48

Insurance

7-33. Introduction. Insurance plays an important role in our national economy. Security in every area of life appears to be desired by most people, and, in many ways, insurance readily adapts itself to the satisfaction of this desire. It offers a method whereby possible losses may be borne by numerous individuals, rather than by the particular person upon whom the loss chances to fall in the first instance. The insurance company acts as a sort of collecting agency and clearing house for the purpose of distributing the risk, charging a fee for its services.

The subject of insurance is treated under security relations because it is often used as a security device or is closely associated with other security which is given. Buyers who purchase on credit are often required to keep the property insured against fire loss. A borrower who gives a mortgage on real property as security for an indebtedness is generally compelled to keep the property insured, in favor of the mortgagee, against loss from windstorm and fire. A person to whom credit has been extended often protects his creditor by procuring a policy of life insurance equal to the indebtedness, naming the creditor as the beneficiary. Insurance is thus used to protect both the creditor and the debtor against loss resulting from abnormal events or premature death.

7-34. Types of insurance. Numerous types of insurance have been originated in an attempt to meet as many as possible of the risks faced by businessmen and their employees. Protection can be procured for almost any risk if the one subject to the risk is able and willing to pay the required premium. Many forms of insurance are familiar to all of us, among them life, health and accident, fire, theft, windstorm, workmen's compensation, and public liability insurance. Unemployment compensation and old-age benefits paid by state or federal governments are closely akin to insurance.

Since insurance is treated at this point primarily as a protective device for creditors, further mention will be made only of those legal principles which relate to fire and life insurance. It can be said in general, however, the law governing health and accident insurance follows closely that which controls life insurance. The other types of insurance—often spoken of as casualty insurance—are in large measure subject to the same rules of law which govern fire insurance.

7-35. Formation of contract—fire insurance. The formation of a contract of insurance differs little from that of any other agreement. When an offer has been made and accepted, a contract exists. Neither the delivery of the policy by the insurer nor the payment of the premium by the insured is required to give protection to the insured. There is nothing in the Statute of Frauds which requires such an agreement to be in writing. The insured may sign a formal written application for insurance in which he describes the risk to be covered and the premium to be paid, but he may well handle the matter by telephone.

It is customary in the fire insurance field for insurance companies to authorize the local agent to accept risks and to issue policies. Because of this fact the protection becomes operative from the moment he indicates if it is made clear what insurer he intends to bind.[1] The issuance of a policy may take place some time after the risk is approved, but an agent who represents several companies and who accepts the risk orally should at that time indicate in some manner to the insured or by memo which company is to assume the risk. Otherwise, the one desiring insurance may find himself without protection if a loss occurs before a policy is issued.

The policy of insurance when delivered contains the controlling contract terms and if the terms vary from those requested, the policy is considered a counter offer accepted by the insured upon its retention if he is made aware of the change. Where the terms are so flagrant a violation of the insured's request as to leave him substantially without protection, such terms are said to be waived by the mere issuance of the policy, thus giving the insured the desired protection.

An insurance broker, as distinct from an agent, has no authority to accept risks. He is an agent of the insured for the purpose of obtaining insurance, after which his agency terminates unless he is retained as an insurance consultant or supervisor.

Fire insurance policies customarily run for a definite period—one, three, or five years—and expire at the end of the period unless a new contract is made.[2] It is common practice for local agents, shortly before a policy expires, to forward a new policy to the insured for a similar term and to bill him for the premium. Since payment of the premium in fire insurance is not a condition precedent to effective insurance, a question arises as to when the new contract is formed. When the insured retains the new policy with intent to benefit from its protection, his silence acts as an acceptance, thus making him liable for the premium and the insurer liable for any loss following the date of the policy.

7-36. Contract—life insurance. The point at which a contract of life insurance becomes effective depends in large measure upon the custom

[1] Dubuque Fire & Marine Ins. Co. v. Miller et al., page 1029.
[2] Luther v. Coal Operators Casualty Co., page 1031.

of particular companies and the nature of the receipt issued at the time the first premium is paid.[3] Nearly all companies provide that the insurance is not effective until the first premium has been paid, although an occasional company accepts a note for the initial payment. A note given to a local agent who agrees personally to pay the premium is not payment unless the agent remits.

Where a physical examination is required and the first premium is paid, most old-line companies authorize the local agent to issue a receipt which in effect may be a binder giving immediate protection. The receipt often states that the insurance dates from the time of the physical examination provided that the insured is then an acceptable risk according to company standards. Consequently, if the insured dies or is killed between the time of the examination and the issuance of the policy, the right of the beneficiary to collect turns upon insurability of the insured at the date of the physical.

A second type of contract frequently used provides that it becomes effective when the policy is delivered to the insured at a time he is in good health. Delivery in such a case dates from the time the policy is mailed from the home office, even though sent to a local agent for manual delivery. However, if the local agent is entrusted with discretion concerning ultimate delivery, protection begins at the time he finally surrenders possession of the policy to the insured. Good health means freedom from serious illness as distinct from minor ailments which may or may not later become serious. A policy of this type delivered to one in bad health becomes good if premiums are paid and the policy retained until after the contestable period—usually two years—has expired.

7-37. Misrepresentation. Since the willingness to insure and the size of the premium to be charged depend primarily upon the nature of the risk to be assumed, any misrepresentation of a fact which materially affects the risk makes the contract voidable. Whether the statement is made intentionally should be unimportant, because if the risk varies from that thought to be assumed, the company should be granted recission. Several of the states, however, permit rescission only when the misrepresentation was intentional. Since most of the states have provided by statute that misrepresentation cannot be used as a defense unless included in the application and made a part of the policy,[4] the essential terms of the application are set forth in the policy or a photostatic copy is attached.

Because the insured is in a much better position to know vital and unusual elements of risk than the insurer, failure to communicate such information, where such failure would virtually amount to fraud, makes the contract voidable by the company. To illustrate, let it be assumed that

[3] National Life & Accident Ins. Co. v. Moore, page 1032.

[4] Acacia Mutual Life Ins. Co. v. Weissman, page 1033.

a general fire existed in an area and that one was without fire insurance. Clearly, an applicant for insurance under such circumstances would be obligated to volunteer information concerning the nearby fire.

Occasionally an agent of the insurer is given correct information, but inserts the wrong answers to questions in the application. Unless collusion between the agent and the applicant exists, the company is generally held liable even though the applicant has signed the application.

Representations by the insured relate to matters existing at the time the contract is made and are not to be treated as warranties that such facts will continue to be true in the future. Thus, a statement by an applicant for life insurance that he is a salesman is not a warranty that he will continue to be so employed.

7-38. Incontestable clause. Most states by statute and most companies by provision in the policy provide that a life insurance policy may not be contested after a certain period of time, except for nonpayment of premiums or violation of the military or airplane clauses found in the policy. Thus, fraud on the part of the insured at the inception of the policy may not be raised by the company after the policy has been outstanding for two years; two years represents the usual period provided in which the company is given a right to rescind. To illustrate: an applicant for life insurance materially misrepresents to the insurer the condition of his health at the time has application is filed. Three years later he dies from tuberculosis, with which he was afflicted at the time he made the application. His beneficiary is entitled to recover on the policy, because the incontestable clause bars the insured's fraud as a defense. Misstatement of the applicant's age gives no right of rescission to the company, but the face of the policy is correspondingly reduced.

A policy which has lapsed and is again reinstated is subject to the two-year period again. Fraud involved in the reinstatement may be used to avoid the policy only if discovered during the contestable period following the reinstatement.

The clauses of a life insurance policy calling for double indemnity in case of accidental death or for payments in case of disability may be contested after the contestable period has expired. The courts have felt that these clauses are not essentially a part of life insurance, and, consequently, are not subject to the provision or statute concerning incontestability. Of course, the contract can be so drawn as to make the policy incontestable on these points, if the company desires.

A mere statement by the company that the policy is no longer in effect and that future premium payments will be returned is not an effective contesting of the policy. Only some legal action taken by the insurance company to set aside the policy will stop the running of the contestable period. Such action must be instituted within the two-year period or such other period as the statute prescribes.

7-39. Insurable interest. Since insurance possesses some of the elements of a gambling contract, to avoid the evil effects that might develop from wagers concerning the life or property of others, the courts require the insured to have an insurable interest in the person or property insured by him. Thus, one who secures a policy of fire insurance upon property cannot recover in case the property is damaged by fire unless he holds some legal or equitable interest in it, in which case a destruction of the property could involve him in a pecuniary loss. If the destruction of the property or person insured is likely to or may well result in a financial loss to the person obtaining the insurance, an insurable interest exists. Thus, an owner, lessee, mortgagee, bailee, trustee, or purchaser has an insurable interest in property, while an employer, employee, business associate, creditor, or dependent relative may legally insure the life of a person. In a few cases, mere close blood relationship has been held to create an insurable interest in the life of another. In addition to having an insurable interest for life insurance the consent of the insured must be had except in the case of the parent who procures insurance upon minor children.[5]

In fire insurance, it is clear that the insurable interest must exist at the time the fire loss occurs, and there is some authority to the effect that it must also exist at the time the policy is issued. Consequently, if fire insurance is taken out on a residence before the insured purchases it but a fire occurs after he acquires title, the insurance is effective in many of the states, although recovery in other states is doubtful.

In life insurance it is sufficient if the insurable interest exists at the date the policy is issued. A subsequent change in the relation of the party securing the insurance to the one whose life is insured does not terminate the insurance. In this connection, it should be pointed out that a person who procures insurance upon his own life may make anyone he desires his beneficiary if a company is willing to issue such a policy. Inasmuch as the insured has an interest in his own life, the beneficiary is not required to have such an interest. It is only where one takes out insurance upon the life of another that an insurable interest is required.

RISKS ASSUMED BY INSURER

7-40. Life insurance. The policy of insurance contains many provisions inserted for the benefit of the various parties. Its terms, considered in the light of the application, govern largely the rights of the parties.

[5] Volunteer State Life Ins. Co. v. Pioneer Bank, page 1035.

There are, therefore, many types and variations of life insurance policies, but they may be divided generally into three classes: term, whole life, and endowment. Upon the death of the one whose life is insured under any of these policies, the insurance company becomes liable for the face of the policy.

A term policy calls for the payment of premiums for a relatively short period with the company carrying the risk only for that period unless the insured reaches a later agreement with the insurer to substitute another type of policy within the term or to renew the term. The rate on term insurance is lower than on other types since the protection is to run only for a limited period of time and results in a lower probability of death.

The whole life insurance policy calls for payment of premiums as long as the insured lives, unless it is modified by a paid-up provision, which requires the payment of premiums only for a certain specified number of years. Thus, a twenty-year paid-up policy would require the payment of premiums for only twenty years, although the amount of the premium would be somewhat larger than the premium on a general life policy.

An endowment policy provides for the payment of the face of the policy upon the death of the insured or at the end of a certain specified number of years. Thus, a twenty-year endowment policy calls for payment of the policy at the end of twenty years, unless the insured dies sooner. Such an insurance policy serves the double purpose of insurance and investment, and requires an annual premium still larger than either of the other types of policies.

A few companies, for a slight addition to the premium, insert a clause which provides for a monthly payment to the insured in case he becomes permanently disabled. Another provision often included calls for double indemnity if the insured dies as the result of an accident. In addition to the policies enumerated, there are various combinations and variations which take care of unusual situations, but those mentioned constitute by far the largest portion of total insurance written.

7-41. Fire insurance. The object of fire insurance is to protect the insured against loss to particular property which results directly or proximately from an unfriendly or hostile fire.[6] A hostile fire is one that is not confined to its proper container. In other words, as soon as a fire leaves the place where it is expected to burn, it ceases to be friendly and becomes hostile. To illustrate: *A* has his furniture insured against fire. By accident, a valuable piece of furniture is placed so near an open fireplace as to be materially damaged, although it never actually catches fire. The insurer is not liable for the resulting damage. However, if the furniture takes fire and burns, the company is liable, for at that time the fire

[6] Lipshultz v. General Insurance Co., page 1036.

is said to become unfriendly; it has ceased to burn in its customary receptacle.

The insurance company is liable for any loss caused directly or proximately by the fire. Thus, loss from smoke, water, theft, removal damage, or falling walls is covered, as well as any direct loss from the fire itself, assuming an unfriendly fire. The fact that the unfriendly fire is confined to another building does not preclude one whose property has been damaged by smoke, water, or falling walls from recovering on his policy of fire insurance. It is not necessary that the fire enter his premises in order to permit recovery.

In the past, the courts have not been in harmony concerning certain types of loss. Loss caused by an explosion or a resulting fire gave rise to controversy. Today the matter is largely controlled by policy provisions. It is customary in fire insurance policies on residence property to cover all loss from explosions, except those involving steam pipes and boilers. At common law, it was an open question whether loss from lightning unaccompanied by a fire was covered, but today special policy provisions usually give coverage in event of such a loss.

To obtain protection against many risks not covered by the ordinary fire insurance policy, "extended coverage," or "broad form," clauses are made available. Under them the company assumes responsibility for losses resulting from explosions, hail, windstorms,[7] damage from airplanes, and numerous other causes.

The fact that a fire originates through the carelessness of the insured, his agent, or a member of his family does not affect the right to recover. One of the chief purposes of insurance is to protect against loss resulting from such causes. At the time of a fire, however, it is the duty of the insured to remove goods, where possible, from the path of a fire in order to keep the loss of the insurance company to a minimum.

7-42. Property insured. Only property which is definitely described in the policy is protected. Furthermore, the policy often limits its application to property owned by the insured, unless the applicant clearly states his desire to have other property in his care protected by the insurance. The interest of the insured in the property should be clearly set forth where such is pertinent according to policy terms. Thus, a policy which covers the goods of the insured located at a certain place does not cover goods held on consignment, unless the agreement is expressly so drawn.

A policy may be issued that covers property regardless of where it is located, although most insurance contracts protect property only so long as it remains at a certain location, the particular location being one of the

[7] Alexander v. Firemen's Insurance Company, page 1038.

elements of the risk. In this latter situation, a removal of the property without notice to the insurer terminates the protection.

7-43. Mortgage clause. The destruction of mortgaged property by fire gives the mortgagee no interest in the proceeds recovered under a fire insurance policy unless the mortgage required the mortgagor to insure the property for the benefit of both parties. Since the vast majority of mortgages require insurance, insurance companies have formulated various mortgage clauses for insertion when insurance is issued on mortgaged property.

One of these clauses provides that in case of loss, payment shall first be made to the mortgagee until his debt is satisfied, any balance being paid to the insured. Such a provision is a simple loss-payable clause and gives the mortgagee no greater rights against the insurer than those possessed by the mortgagor. Thus, if property mortgaged for $7,000 is fully insured, and a $9,000 loss occurs, $7,000 is payable to the mortgagee and $2,000 to the mortgagor. The amount paid to the mortgagee effectively reduces the amount owed by the mortgagor. In this manner both parties are adequately protected by a single policy.

In many states the insurer, when requested, inserts in the policy what has become known as the "standard mortgage clause." In effect, a policy with such a clause creates two contracts, one with the mortgagor and one with the mortgagee.[8] Consequently, if for any reason the policy is not enforceable by the mortgagor, it nevertheless is enforceable by the mortgagee to the extent of his interest. Misconduct or violation of policy terms by the mortgagor does not destroy the mortgagee's protection unless he is aware of such conduct and fails to report it to the insurance company. To terminate the policy as to the mortgagee, ten days' written notice is required. However, if at any time the insurer pays the mortgagee when under no duty to the mortgagor, the latter having violated some policy term, the mortgage debt is not reduced. To the extent payment is made to the mortgagee under these conditions, the insurer takes over that portion of the claim against the owner under the doctrine of subrogation.

7-44. Coinsurance. A coinsurance clause in a fire insurance policy requires the insured to carry insurance equal to a certain percentage of the value of the property or to bear part of any fire loss. Thus, an 80 per cent coinsurance clause requires the insured to carry fire protection equal to 80 per cent of the then value of the property or, to the extent he is deficient, to bear a portion of the fire loss. Because most fire losses are small, one who carries this rather full protection is given a substantially lower rate. The inclusion of such a clause is optional with the insured and is not available for ordinary residence property, being available only for the larger risks. A formula to determine the amount of recovery under

[8] Syracuse Savings Bank v. Yorkshire Ins. Co., page 1039.

coinsurance runs as follows: Recovery equals the insurance carried divided by the amount of insurance which should be carried times the loss, the recovery never exceeding the amount of the loss or the face of the policy. $R = \frac{I}{.8\,V} \times L$ is the formula for 80 per cent coinsurance.

7-45. Termination of policy. Fire insurance companies have incorporated a provision in their policies which gives the insurance company a right to terminate the risk by giving five days' written notice, which notice states that the unearned premium is available upon request.

The notice does not begin to run until it has been received by the insured unless the policy reads otherwise. However, the policy may provide that the notice begins as soon as mailed to the last known address of the insured. Cancellation by the insurer entitles the insured to the return of a proportionate amount of the premium paid.

The insured likewise has the right to terminate the insurance by notice and return of the policy. In return, he receives a portion of the unearned premium, somewhat less than that represented by the unexpired period covered by the policy, being charged the short rate for the time the policy was in effect.

Notice of termination by the company must be mailed to the insured or his agent. Notice to his broker or to the company's local agent is not an effective termination.[9]

7-46. Lapsed policies—life insurance. Statutes require life insurance companies, a certain number of days before a premium is due, to mail notice that the premium falls due on a certain date. The companies must then give the insured a certain grace period, usually 30 days, in which to pay the premium after it is due. If the premium is not paid within the allotted grace period, the policy is said to lapse or be forfeited, and can be reinstated within a given time—usually three years—only by presenting evidence of insurability and payment of back premiums plus interest.

The mere mailing of a check within the grace period in good faith keeps the policy from lapsing. If it is lost in transit or the bank dishonors it improperly, the policy does not lapse provided that the insured promptly offers to make good.

Lapsed policies of life insurance, other than term policies, are by statute and policy provision made valuable in that the insured may obtain the cash-surrender value or obtain paid-up insurance. Most or all of the reserve set aside to protect the life insured is made available in one form or another. Unless the insured has taken the cash-surrender value or fully borrowed against it, he is within 60 days given a choice of extended term insurance for the full face of the policy, as long as the reserve will carry

[9] Kinney v. Rochester German Ins. Co., page 1040.

it, or a paid-up policy for a lesser amount, the amount being dependent upon the size of the reserve and the age of the insured. If no choice is made within 60 days, the policy specifies which of the two prevails, it usually being extended-term insurance.

7-47. Provisions that benefit the insurer. A fire insurance policy contains numerous provisions that, if not adhered to by the insured, may excuse the company from performing.

Since insurance companies are regarded by the courts much like public utilities—in that many features of their business can be regulated by the state—it is possible for the state to prescribe a standard policy for use in the state or merely to stipulate that any policy used must include certain provisions and exclude others. Because of this, the number and content of clauses contained in a policy vary materially from state to state and careful reading of the terms of the policy used in a particular state is imperative. Some of the more usual provisions are discussed below.

It is customary to include a clause that the policy shall be suspended if the property is vacant or unoccupied beyond a stated time and the company has not waived the provision by a rider attached to the policy. The policy is automatically reinstated when the property again becomes occupied, assuming the policy has not expired. Another common clause provides that the insurance shall be suspended while the risk is materially increased by any act within the control or knowledge of the insured.[10] This clause usually refers to matters on the property of the insured over which he has control, not including factors of risk arising out of the use made of adjoining property.

In policies covering a changing stock of merchandise it is customary to provide that the insured shall keep adequate records of account, take an annual inventory, and have a fireproof safe in which the records are kept when the business house is closed. If no inventory has been had within a year, the insured is required to take one within 30 days. Other clauses of one kind or another are included in certain instances, and if not adhered to, offer the company an opportunity to avoid payment in case of loss.

The policy provides that the insured shall give immediate notice of loss to the insurer. Furthermore, unless the loss is settled in the interim, within 60 days he must make a sworn statement of loss to the company, detailing the nature and extent of the fire loss.

7-48. Subrogation. The purpose of fire insurance is to indemnify the insured if a loss results from fire. If the insured suffers no loss as a result of fire, the insurer should suffer none. For this reason, any right of action possessed by the insured against some third party that would compensate the former for the loss automatically passes to the insurer upon settlement

[10] Standard Marine Ins. Co. v. Peck, page 1041.

in full for the loss suffered. This right of substitution of the insurer to the position of the insured is known as *subrogation*. Thus, a mortgagee who takes out insurance to protect only his interest, if allowed to recover insurance in case the mortgaged property is destroyed, must assign his mortgage debt to the insurer. The latter then has a cause of action against the mortgagor, just as the mortgagee would have had. Insurance taken to protect only the mortgagee affords the mortgagor no protection. In case of a fire loss the liability of the mortgagor for the debt merely runs to the insurance company to the extent it has paid the mortgagee for the fire loss.

Where subrogation is involved, the insured should be careful not to release some third party responsible for the loss. A release of the third party releases the insurer of liability to the owner, since the latter has robbed the insurer of his right of subrogation.

The right of subrogation does not apply to life or health and accident insurance unless special provision is made for it in the policy, inasmuch as it is not directly the purpose of such insurance to compensate for the actual loss sustained.

7-49. Loss and division of loss. If a fire occurs, the insurance company, in the absence of a valued policy—one making the company liable for the face of the policy in the event of total destruction—is liable only for the actual loss suffered. In case of total loss, this is the actual cash value of the property providing it does not exceed the face of the policy. If the property is only partially destroyed, cost of restoration is usually the basis of recovery. The policy provides that it may restore the property rather than make payment if it desires, and it further provides for arbitration where agreement on the amount of the loss is in dispute.

At one time fire policies provided that in case other insurance was obtained on the same property without approval by the insurer, the policy became void. Today most policies provide that other insurance may be carried but stipulate that any loss must be borne pro rata, without any one company being liable for the share of another.

To illustrate: Jones carries on certain property a $10,000 policy in Beech Co. and a $5,000 policy in Pine Co. If the property is worth only $12,000, a total loss permits recovery of that amount only. Of this, only $8,000 can be recovered of Beech Co., even though Pine Co. is insolvent and unable to pay its $4,000 liability.

RIGHTS OF BENEFICIARY IN LIFE INSURANCE

7-50. Rights vest at the time policy is issued. Such rights as are given the beneficiary named in a life insurance policy vest at the time the policy is issued. The insured possesses no power to alter or amend effectively the terms of the contract, without the consent of the beneficiary, unless the right has beeen specifically reserved in the policy. However, the policy is customarily drawn so as to permit the insured to borrow of the insurer on the strength of the policy or to surrender it and obtain the cash surrender value or to change the beneficiary.

Nearly all policies provide that, in case the beneficiary dies before the insured and no substitute beneficiary is named, the proceeds are payable to the estate of the insured. Where the right to change the beneficiary is expressly reserved in the policy, the change dates from the time it is indorsed on the policy, but in cases where the insured has done everything possible on his part to effect the change, and dies before the indorsement is made, the new beneficiary is protected. Delay on the part of the mail or in the conduct of the company employees after receiving the policy and a request for change will not injuriously affect the right of the newly named beneficiary.

7-51. Rights of creditors. The creditors of the insured have almost no rights in the proceeds of his life insurance. Upon the death of the insured, the money is paid directly to the designated beneficiary, who is in no sense responsible for the debts of the insured, except that in some community property states, unless husband and wife join in naming the beneficiary, only one half the proceeds go to the beneficiary, the balance to the surviving spouse. Should the insurance be payable to the estate of the insured, then, like any asset, the amount may be used to satisfy the debts of the deceased. Of course, in any event where the payment of premiums constitutes a transfer in fraud of creditors, the creditors may reach the proceeds to the extent of the premiums improperly paid.

During the lifetime of the insured, a policy has a loan or cash surrender value, and creditors often seek to reach this as one of the assets of the insured. If the insured has not reserved the right to change the beneficiary, the rights of the beneficiary are not affected by the insolvency or bankruptcy of the insured. Since the rights under such a policy are vested in the beneficiary at the time the policy is issued, the cash-surrender value of the policy cannot be touched by the creditors or by the trustee in bankruptcy. Where the right to change beneficiaries has been reserved, the bankruptcy of the insured permits the trustee in bankruptcy to claim the cash-surrender value for the benefit of the creditors. In order to protect the families of those carrying insurance, many states have enacted legislation exempting the cash-surrender value from claims of creditors or exempting a portion ol insurance proceeds payable to the estate of the insured. Reference must be made to the statute of a particular state to determine the extent of this protection. Life insurance companies obligate themselves to loan, up to the cash-surrender value of the policy, to the insured at a given rate of interest unless the insured has not reserved control over the policy. The borrowing is not considered a debt of the borrower, but an advance which need not be repaid. Consequently, the estate of the insured is not obligated to pay the debt, the beneficiary receiving the face of the policy less the outstanding claim against it.

An insurance policy may be used as collateral for a loan. In case the right to change beneficiaries has been reserved, in most states the insured may effectively pledge the policy without consent of the beneficiary, the pledge constituting in effect a partial change of beneficiary.[11] If no right to change the beneficiary exists, a pledge is effective only when joined in by the beneficiary. In either case, it is customary for lender to require both insured and beneficiary to join in the pledge agreement.

A policy of insurance, taken out upon the life of a debtor by his creditor, is enforceable for the face amount, despite the fact that the debt is reduced below the face of the policy. In some states the courts compel the creditor to turn the excess above the indebtedness over to the estate of the debtor. Similarly, where the debtor carries the insurance and has named the creditor as beneficiary, the right of the creditor to retain the proceeds extends only to the amount of the indebtedness, unless the insurance was plainly a gift to the creditor and entirely unrelated to the indebtedness.

7-52. Absolute assignment. A life insurance policy in which the insured is also the beneficiary may be sold to a third party, although the assignee is a stranger and has no insurable interest in the life of the insured. The absolute assignment binds the company as soon as it receives notice thereof. If the assignee continues to pay the premium, he is entitled to the face of the policy upon the death of the insured. Certain fraternal insurance provides that the policy of life insurance may be made payable only to certain members of the family. In such cases the policy may not be assigned, being payable only to the estate of the insured or to the members of his family indicated in the policy.

One may make a gift of a life insurance policy as readily as he can sell it. If it is clear that he places the policy in absolute control of the donee, the gift is completed.[12] When the policy is sold or transferred by way of gift, if a beneficiary is named in the policy, it should be changed to the new owner or made payable to the estate of the insured before it is assigned. The courts are in conflict as to whether an absolute assignment is effective without the change of beneficiary.

A fire insurance policy may not be assigned without the consent of the insurer. Such a policy gives a personal right, and, as the risk varies

[11] Antley v. St. Mathews National Bank, page 1043.
[12] Prudential Ins. Co. v. Deyerberg et al., page 1044.

in many cases with the person protected, the right may not be assigned. If the insured no longer needs protection, he may assign the policy, provided the company consents; or, if the company refuses, the insured may cancel the policy and demand a return of a portion of the premium previously paid.

After a fire loss has occurred, the right to the proceeds may be assigned, and the assignment becomes effective as soon as the insurance company receives notice of it. Only where an attempt is made to assign the policy protection is the assignment ineffective unless it is assented to by the insurer.

INSURANCE CASES

DUBUQUE FIRE & MARINE INS. CO. v. MILLER et al.

1951, (S.C.) 64 S.E.2d 8

This action was instituted to cancel a policy of fire insurance. The defendants, Miller and another, were about to open a new restaurant, so they called the Wilson Insurance Agency for fire protection and were told that $25,000 in fire insurance was effective as of that date, although no particular company was named as the insurer. The Wilson agency, receiving the call on Friday, executed no policy immediately and the restaurant in question was totally destroyed by fire on Sunday. Thereafter Wilson contacted the ten companies which it represented and suggested that policies for $2,500 each be delivered. The plaintiff failed to give any definite answer immediately, but the general agent indicated that likely the company would reject the proposal because it had very little business from Wilson. However, Wilson did execute ten policies and sent the fire abstract sheet with the premium for its policy to the general agent of the plaintiff company. The premium was retained, but the company denies liability and seeks to have the policy cancelled. The lower court held that no contract was made when Wilson originally accepted the risk because no specific company was specified, but held that receipt and retention of the premium was a ratification of the agent's act in later delivering the policy.

L. D. Lide, J. . . . Referring now to the applicable law, we are in full accord with the ruling of the trial Judge in regard to the alleged oral "binder" arising from the telephone agreement between the Wilson Agency and the defendants on January 24, 1947, to the effect that the failure to designate any company or companies is fatal to its validity, as applied to the Dubuque Company, or incidentally any other company. The authorities on this point, we think are conclusive. . . .

Judge Baker also held that the subsequent delivery by the Wilson Agency to the defendants of the policy in question here, bearing date January 24, 1947, which was prior to the date of the fire, was an independent act on the part of the local agency; and that clearly the Wilson Agency had no authority to execute and deliver the same; although we may add that the policy was delivered prior to the letter of the Timmons Agency, dated February 17, 1947, actually forbidding the delivery of the Dubuque policy; but there was a previous letter stating that unprotected restaurants were on the prohibited list for this company. However, Judge Baker upon due consideration of the testimony as to the acceptance and retention of the premium by the insurer held that the plaintiff "waived its right for a cancellation of the policy, even though in its inception the contract was void."

It is true that some contracts absolutely void ab initio may not be subject to waiver or ratification, where such a contract is forbidden by law; or perhaps where it violates some established rule of public policy. 26 C.J. 66; 44 C.J.S., Insurance, § 273. But we do not think that principle is apposite here, because the insurance policy in question was void ab initio *solely* because the Agency issuing and delivering it had no authority to do so. It is elementary that lack of authority *can be supplied by express ratification.* And in the case at bar it was testified, without objection, that seven of the companies involved had paid in full. This is mentioned merely for the purpose of illustrating express ratification and not to indicate that the payment by other companies imputes any liability to the plaintiff. And it may be observed that the Pennsylvania Fire Insurance Company case tried with the case at bar was decided in its favor by Judge Baker.

If an unauthorized contract or policy of insurance may be ratified *expressly*, it follows that there may be an *implied* ratification by the acceptance and retention of the premium.

The words "waiver," "estoppel," and "implied ratification" appear rather frequently in insurance cases and are sometimes used interchangeably, although distinguishable in some respects. The principle expressed by the use of these terms is recognized in the law as tending to the furtherance of justice. The rule is succinctly and correctly stated in the following quotation from 45 C.J.S., Insurance, § 672, p. 610: "An insurance company may waive, or be estopped to assert, a ground for avoidance or forfeiture of an insurance policy, and the courts are prompt to seize on any circumstances which indicate a waiver on the part of the company or which will raise an estoppel against it. . . ."

Judgment of lower court affirmed.

LUTHER v. COAL OPERATORS CASUALTY CO.
1954, (Pa.) 108 A.2d 691

This action was instituted by Luther to recover on an implied insurance contract. He obtained a policy for one year, and the defendant through its brokers voluntarily renewed it each year for the next three years. It was not renewed the fourth year and the plaintiff overlooked the matter. The lower court gave judgment for defendant.

STERN, C. J. . . . It will be noted that the complaint alleged that defendants "voluntarily undertook" to reissue the policy each year as it expired. The nature or form of such "undertaking" is not set forth, but such allegation is obviously based solely upon the proposition—and indeed it is so argued by plaintiff—that by reason of defendants having renewed or reissued the policies for three successive years without notification to or request by him, an obligation on their part thereby arose to continue issuing such renewals from year to year indefinitely thereafter.

Plaintiff has cited no authority, and our research discloses none, which holds that the rendering of such service by defendants created a duty on their part to continue it. It may well be asked, if such a duty did arise, when did it come into being,—after the first, the second, or the third renewal? It is interesting to note that plaintiff dates defendants' "voluntary undertaking" as "on or about November 22, 1946," which was the time of the first renewal. True, it is the law that where an insurance agent or broker promises, or gives some affirmative assurance, that he will procure or renew a policy of insurance under such circumstances as to lull the "insured" into the belief that such insurance has been effected, the law will impose upon the broker or agent the obligation to perform the duty which he has thus assumed. But here no such promise or assurance was given, nor was there any arrangement between the parties or any instruction given by plaintiff to keep up the insurance at all times or for any particular year. During the period of nine months from November 23, 1949, to the time when, August 14, 1950, the accident to plaintiff's employee occurred, plaintiff had not made any request for a renewal of the policy, and he must certainly have been aware of the fact that he had not received a new policy or any certificate of renewal of the old policy, or that he had paid any premium or been billed for one. It is perfectly clear that if at any time either during that period or thereafter defendants had made a claim upon him for payment of a renewal policy, he might, with perfect legal propriety, have refused to meet such a demand on the ground that the renewal had been made without his knowledge or request, and if, therefore, defendants could not have enforced any alleged contractual obligation against him he obviously could not now impose such a liability upon them since contractual obligations must be mutual and co-existent. The fact is that plaintiff was merely assuming that defendants would continue to look after him without his giving any further attention to the matter. . . .

Judgment for defendants affirmed.

NATIONAL LIFE & ACCIDENT INS. CO. v. MOORE

1951, 83 Ga. App. 289, 63 S.E.2d 447

Mrs. Fay Moore sued the National Life & Accident Ins. Co. to recover the face of a $1,000 policy of life insurance alleged to have been executed by them. Her husband made application for the policy, paid the first monthly premium for $2.15, and obtained the following receipt:

Received of Ernest L. Moore a deposit of 2.15 Dollars to cover all of the first monthly premium on proposed insurance, if issued for $1,000.00 on the life of App for which an application numbered as below is this day made to The National Life and Accident Insurance Company. Such deposit will be returned (a) if application is declined or (b) if a policy is issued other than as applied for and applicant declines to accept it. No insurance is in force on such application unless and until a policy has been issued thereon and delivered in accordance with the terms of such application, except that when such deposit is equal to the full first premium on the policy applied for and such application is approved at the Home Office of the Company for the Class, Plan and Amount of insurance and at the rate of Premiums as so applied for, then without affecting the issue date and anniversaries as set forth in the policy, the amount of the insurance applied for will be in force from the date of this receipt, but no obligation is assumed by the company unless and until such application is so approved. If a policy is offered by the Company that is not in all respects the same as the policy applied for, such policy will not take effect unless, and until it has been accepted by the applicant and the additional premium therefor, if any, has actually been paid to and accepted by the Company during the lifetime of the applicant.

Date 6/10 1949 No 468919 D P. L. Langston Agent District Rome, Ga.

If policy is not delivered to you within 60 days from date, this receipt should be presented at the District Office, or the Home Office in Nashville, Tenn., for redemption.

It is alleged that the company did approve the application but failed to deliver the policy because the insurer was killed in an automobile accident two days after the application was made.

Sutton, C. J. . . . If the application was approved at the home office of the defendant as alleged, then under the terms of the premium receipt the insurance became effective from the date of the receipt. Was the application so approved? This is the controlling question in the case. The binder and the approved application for insurance would constitute a valid contract of insurance. This would be true, although the applicant died before the application was approved, since the insurance became effective from the date of the receipt and not from the date of the approval of the application. The receipt was a binder, conditioned only upon the approval of the application by the company at its home office. "A binder is a contract of insurance in praesenti, temporary in its nature, intended to take the place of an ordinary policy until the same can be issued. It is a short method of issuing a temporary policy for the convenience of all parties, to continue, unless sooner canceled, until the execution of a formal policy." *Fort Valley Coca-Cola Co. v. Lumbermen's Mutual Casualty Co.*, 69 Ga. App. 120(3), 24 S.E.2d 846, 847. It was held in *New York Life Ins. Co. v. Babcock*, 104 Ga. 67(1, 2), 30 S.E. 273, 42 L.R.A. 88, that

A contract of life-insurance is consummated upon the unconditional written acceptance of the application for insurance by the company to which such application is made.

Actual delivery of the policy to the insured is not essential to the validity of a contract of life-insurance, unless expressly made so by the terms of the contract.

The intention of the parties to a life insurance contract controls as it does in other contracts, and we think it was the intention of the parties here for the insurance in question to become effective from the date of the binder receipt, upon the approval of the application therein referred to, for this is exactly what the binder receipt states. In 29 Am. Jur. 160, Insurance, § 144, it is stated:

Usually, when an insurance agent procures an application for life, health, or accident insurance, he accepts payment of the first premium from the applicant. Quite commonly, there is a provision in the receipt given to the applicant, which, in some instances, is duplicated in the application, to the effect that the insurance shall be considered as in force from the date of the receipt or the date of the medical examination, provided the application is approved and accepted at the home office of the insurer. Such receipts are known in the insurance business as "conditional receipts," or, less frequently, as "condition binding receipts. . . ." Upon the acceptance of the application, the insurer becomes obligated notwithstanding the policy is not delivered, and the receipt protects the applicant against the contingency of sickness or disability rendering him uninsurable intervening the date of the receipt and the delivery of the policy. In other words, the vitality of such a receipt is retroactively derived from the acceptance of the application. . . .

Judgment for plaintiff affirmed.

ACACIA MUTUAL LIFE INS. CO. v. WEISSMAN

1955, 164 Ohio 82, 128 N.E.2d 34

The insurance company, plaintiff, brought this action to obtain the cancellation of a policy of life insurance. The policy had lapsed, but an application for reinstatement was made and accepted. The plaintiff seeks to cancel the policy because the insured's answers contained in the application for reinstatement were fraudulent. The lower court gave judgment for defendant beneficiary, the insured having died shortly after reinstatement. No copy of the application was attached to the policy, so defendant contended fraud could not be used as a basis for rescission.

WEYGANDT, C. J. This court is of the view that the lower courts were correct in holding that the failure of the plaintiff company to furnish the insured a copy of the application for reinstatement estopped the company from denying the truth of the application.

Section 9389, General Code, Section 3911.04, Revised Code, reads as follows:

> Every company doing business in this state shall return with, and as part of any policy issued by it, to any person taking such policy, a full and complete copy of each application or other document held by it which is intended in any manner to affect the force or validity of such policy. A company which neglects so to do, so long as it is in default for such copy, shall be estopped from denying the truth of any such application or other document. In case such company neglects for thirty days after demand made therefor, to furnish such copies, it shall be forever barred from setting up as a defense to any suit on the policy, any incorrectness or want of truth of such application or other document.

The plaintiff company contends that these statutory provisions apply alone to the original application for the policy and not to the application for reinstatement. However, that is not the comprehensive language of the statute. Not only must the company furnish a complete copy of "each" application but also of any "other document" affecting the force or validity of a policy. It is not the province of the courts to read into this sweeping language a limitation that "each" means merely some applications or the original application.

While, of course, the terms of the particular statutes are controlling, it is commented generally in 44 C.J.S., Insurance, § 268, p. 1074, that such a statute "is applicable, not only to an application for the original policy, but also to an application for the restoration or revival of a policy which has lapsed for the nonpayment of premiums, and to an application for the renewal of a policy."

The company claims further that it complied with the requirement of the statute by supplying the defendant widow with a copy of the application when a request therefor was made after the death of the insured, since the insured himself made no such demand. Again this contention finds no support in the statute. The simple, unambiguous language is that the company "*shall return with, and as part of any policy,* issued by it, to *any person taking such policy,* a full and complete copy of each application." The company reinstated the policy on August 14, 1950. The death of the insured did not occur until April 23, 1952—more than a year and eight months later—and still the company had not furnished him a copy of the application.

Hence, it is the opinion of this court that the plaintiff company is not entitled to a cancellation of the policy. Furthermore, the lower courts were not in error in rendering a judgment for the defendant widow on her cross-petition.

Judgment affirmed.

VOLUNTEER STATE LIFE INS. CO. v. PIONEER BANK

1959, (Tenn. App.) 327 S.W.2d 59

One Steiner and his wife took a child from Family Service Agency expecting, if the situation remained favorable, to adopt the child. The child could be returned at any time prior to adoption, but while the child was in their custody, they agreed to treat him as if he were their own. During this uncertain period, Steiner took out a $5,000 policy of life insurance on the child and named himself as beneficiary. The policy was later assigned to others. This is an action because of lack of an insurable interest to set aside the policy by the plaintiff insurance company. The lower court gave judgment for the plaintiff, canceling the policy and the defendant appealed.

HOWARD, J. . . . Notwithstanding previous decisions by the appellate courts of this state that a policy of insurance taken out on the life of another, without the latter's consent, is void as against public policy, *Branson v. National Life & Acc. Ins. Co.*, 4 Tenn. App. 576; *Interstate Life & Acc. Ins. Co. v. Cook*, 19 Tenn. App. 290, 86 S.W.2d 887, the complainant tacitly concedes that it is now the prevailing rule in most states, including Tennessee, that parents may insure the lives of their infants who are unable to give their consent, though we have been unable to find in our reports a decision to this effect. Obviously the latter rule has been generally approved, because the Courts were compelled either to deny the possibility of insuring infants at all, or in the alternative permitting them to be insured under certain conditions, without their consent, as where the person procuring the policy has a recognized insurable interest, other than a pecuniary interest in the life of the infant, and is a parent or, as in the instant case, stands in loco parentis to the infant. . . . In 29 Am. Jur., it says:

> While all the authorities are agreed that an insurable interest of some sort must exist in the case of life insurance, the authorities are not exactly agreed on

the question of what constitutes a requisite interest. There are cases which hold that the interest must be a pecuniary one and that near relationship is not per se enough. The weight of authority, however, is to a different effect. The general rule supported in substance by most of the cases is that any reasonable expectation of benefit or advantage from the continued life of another creates an insurable interest in such life; the advantage or benefit need not be capable of pecuniary estimation, but an insurable interest may be predicated upon any relation which is such as warrants the conclusion that the person claiming an insurable interest has an interest, whether pecuniary or arising from dependence or natural affection, in the life of the person insured. * * *

In all cases, however, there must be a reasonable ground, founded on the relations of the parties to each other, either pecuniary or of blood or affinity, to expect some benefit or advantage from the continuance of the life of the insured. Otherwise, the contract is a mere wager by which the party taking the policy is directly interested in the early death of the insured. * * * *The essential thing is that the policy shall be obtained in good faith, and not for the purpose of speculating on the hazard of a life in which the insured has no interest.* The existence of an insurable interest in the final analysis, therefore, depends upon the inherent nature of the financial, beneficial, or personal relationship that exists between the parties involved, and is not dependent upon who pays the premiums or upon the consent of the insured. [Sec. 353, pp. 309, 310, 311.] (Emphasis supplied.)

In line with the foregoing authorities, we are constrained to hold that the original beneficiary stood in loco parentis to the infant at the time the policy was issued, for the following reasons: Prior to taking the child from the Welfare Agency, the Steiners signed an agreement "that while this child is in our custody, we will treat him in all respects as if he were our own child, will give him the care and attention of a parent, and the full advantage of educational and religious facilities of our community. ****We will give this child a free home, assuming complete responsibility for his care and maintenance* with the intention of adopting him if we find him*** to be a child whom we want to make permanently ours." (Emphasis supplied.) And standing in loco parentis, it follows that the original beneficiary had an insurable interest in the child, said interest, under our decisions, being fixed at the inception of the policy. . . .

Decision for defendant.

LIPSHULTZ v. GENERAL INSURANCE CO.

1959, (Miss.) 96 N.W.2d 880

Lipshultz, the plaintiff, carried fire and extended coverage insurance on the contents in a certain building. The extended coverage provision included direct loss resulting from windstorm. There was a heavy windstorm in the area which knocked down power lines, and breaks in the lines leading to plaintiff's building left him without power to operate his refrigeration units, resulting in loss or damage to perishable foodstuffs in the amount of $1,080.02. The defendant claimed the loss was not the direct result of a windstorm. The lower court gave judgment for the plaintiff and defendant appealed.

Nelson, J. . . . In the instant case the chain of events culminating in the loss to the contents in plaintiff's store was set in motion by a windstorm which struck the area or community in which the insured property is located. It would hardly seem reasonable to say that a break such as occurred due to windstorm in the 13.8 kilovolt supply lines supplying the power company's Snelling substation located about ½ mile from plaintiff's store and the failure of the 4 kilovolt distribution lines serving the area in which plaintiff's store is located were not in the contemplation of the parties at the time the policies were issued. Similar results due to windstorms have occurred heretofore in many communities and constitute a hazard familiar to both insurer and insured. We are unable to find wherein the policies contain a limitation of coverage excluding this type of loss, one which the insurers might have inserted if deemed advisable by an appropriate exclusionary clause in the insurance contracts. It is not unreasonable to assume that such a peril was well within the contemplation of both insurer and insured when insuring the stock in trade consisting of many perishable foodstuffs requiring refrigeration. Adopting the contention of defendants would in our view, as was said by the Iowa court in the Jordan case, be "entirely too narrow a construction."

The manner in which the refrigeration equipment was powered by electric current furnished by the Northern States Power Company and the probability of interruption by windstorm was not beyond the common knowledge of both insurer and insured.

If under all the circumstances revealed by a stipulation of the facts the parties could have reasonably foreseen that a complete interruption in the supply and distribution lines furnishing the necessary electric power for refrigeration purposes might occur and cause damage to the contents in plaintiff's store in the manner and to the extent stipulated, such contingency was an element in the risk covered by the insurance policies.

Since we have concluded from an examination of the policies issued that the word "direct" as used in said policies means merely "immediate" or "proximate," as distinguished from "remote," we are compelled to hold under the stipulation of facts, constituting the evidence in this case, that the cause of the damage was a question of fact and that the evidence clearly sustains the decision of the trial court.

It is our conclusion that the loss which the plaintiffs suffered following the windstorm comes within the fair meaning of the term "direct loss" in the policies and that the judgments appealed from must be affirmed.

Affirmed.

ALEXANDER v. FIREMEN'S INSURANCE COMPANY

1958, (Tex. Civ. App.) 317 S.W.2nd 752

Alexander, plaintiff, carried fire and extended coverage insurance on a warehouse which he contends was destroyed as a result of the sonic boom caused by an airplane flying over the building at supersonic speed. The extended coverage provisions covered loss from explosions and loss by airplanes which shall include "loss by falling aircraft or objects falling therefrom." The lower court withdrew the case from the jury and gave judgment for the defendant, and the plaintiff appealed.

McDONALD, C. J. . . . The record reflects that plaintiff's building was constructed in 1954 of frame and metal, that it was well constructed and there was no visible evidence that it was unsafe or had deteriorated in any manner prior to the loss; that it was used as a warehouse for storing lumber; that it had a capacity of seven or eight boxcars of lumber and had been filled to capacity several times; that on 17 November 1956 it had 2½ or 3 boxcars of lumber stored therein; that on such date a terrific blast or sonic boom occurred over Hico (the loudest ever heard by one witness); that the plaintiff's building immediately thereafter collapsed and was extensively damaged. It is common knowledge that when an airplane exceeds the speed of sound that a report is heard which is commonly called a sonic boom, and that some concussion or air pressure accompanies the sound. . . .

The aircraft coverage provision of the policy is not limited to loss by falling aircraft, or objects falling therefrom. The terms *"shall include,"* being words of enlargement and not of limitation, by their use in the instant policy, do not restrict the coverage to loss by falling aircraft or objects falling therefrom. Since plaintiff alleged a loss occasioned by aircraft, he is entitled to recover if he can prove that he has a loss which was proximately caused by aircraft. In our view the loss complained of was covered by the instant policy provision.

Plaintiff contends that his loss is further covered by the *"Explosion"* coverage of his policy. His allegation and proof were to the effect that a sonic boom caused by an airplane proximately caused his damage and loss. Defendant denied that a sonic boom was an explosion. The Trial Court found that the plaintiff tendered no proof that a sonic boom was an explosion. Plaintiff contends that the court can take judicial knowledge of scientific phenomenon and that a sonic boom is an explosion. It is true that the doctrine of judicial notice is applied to scientific facts and principles as are generally recognized and ought to be known by men of ordinary understanding and intelligence. *English v. Miller*, Tex. Civ. App., 43 S.W.2d 642, W/E Ref.; McCormick & Ray on Evidence, Sec. 202. Here, however, the Trial Court refused to take judicial notice of what a sonic boom is or if it is an explosion, presumably because he did not know such to be a fact; and this court cannot take judicial knowledge of such for the same reason. For such reason proof was necessary that a sonic boom is an explosion and it was plaintiff's burden to adduce such proof. Failing to do so, he cannot now complain of the Trial Court's ruling in this regard. It may be that a sonic boom is an explosion. Indeed, an article in the March 1958 *American Bar Association Journal* at p. 216 (Vol. 44, No. 3), cited to this court in defendant's brief, asserts that a sonic boom is an explosion, and it may be that in future times our courts can take judicial knowledge of such fact. See Sec. 211, McCormick & Ray on Evidence. As of this date, however, this court (nor the Trial Court which preceded us) has not the requisite "verifiable certainty" to take judicial knowledge of such matter.

The judgment of the trial court was reversed and the case remanded for new trial.

SYRACUSE SAVINGS BANK v. YORKSHIRE INS. CO.

1950, 301 N.Y. 403, 94 N.E.2d 73

The plaintiff bank had a $44,000 mortgage on property owned by one Blumberg, the mortgage requiring the owner to keep the property insured for the benefit of both. The defendant, along with other insurance companies, issued a policy containing a standard mortgage clause and which also provided for arbitration in event the parties were unable to agree upon the amount of loss. A fire loss occurred, a disagreement developed as to the amount of the loss, and arbitration procedure initiated to which the mortgagee was not a party. The plaintiff, having rejected the arbitration amount, sued to recover the actual damages and the lower court gave judgment to defendant. Plaintiff appealed.

Dye, J. . . . The controversy turns on the meaning of the standard mortgagee clause as used in the policy when read in connection with the appraisal provisions, viz.:

> Loss or damage, if any, under this policy, shall be payable to Syracuse Savings Bank, as first mortgagee (or trustee), as interest may appear, and this insurance, as to the interest of the mortgagee (or trustee) only therein, *shall not be invalidated by any act or neglect of the mortgagor or owner*. (Emphasis supplied.)

It is well settled in this and most other States that a mortgagee clause in a standard form policy creates an *independent* insurance of the mortgagee's interest just as if he had received a separate policy from the company but without any inconsistent or repugnant conditions imposed upon the owner and free from invalidation by the latter's "act or neglect." *Savarese v. Ohio Farmers Ins. Co.*, 260 N.Y. 45, 182 N.E. 665, 91 A.L.R. 1341; . . .

This principle of the mortgagee's separate independent interest in the proceeds of the policy has been conclusive of earlier problems arising under this and similar clauses. Thus, failure of the owner to render proof of loss as required by provisions of the policy within the policy time limit, may not prevent a mortgagee's recovery, *McDowell v. St. Paul Fire & Marine Ins. Co., supra,* the interest of the mortgagee and owner being regarded as distinct subjects of insurance, *Heilbrunn v. German Alliance Ins. Co., supra.* The mortgagee, we have held, is a necessary party to any suit to recover for a fire loss brought by the owner against the company, *Lewis v. Guardian Fire & Life Assur. Co.,* 181 N.Y. 392, 74 N.E. 224, 106 Am. St. Rep. 557, if a judgment rendered in such an action is to be binding upon the mortgagee, see *Steinbach v. Prudential Ins. Co. of America,* 172 N.Y. 471, 65 N.E. 281; Civil Practice Act, § 193. Nor is the mortgagee to be bound in any manner by the owner's proof of loss or any admission by an owner after a fire concerning either the sound value of the property or the amount of damage in an action by the mortgagee against the insurer for there is no relationship of principal and agent—their interest being separate and distinct, *Browning v. Home Ins. Co., supra.* We thus come to the further conclusion that no settlement between the owner and the insurer can operate in any way to the detriment of a mortgagee, *Hathaway v. Orient Ins. Co.,* 134 N.Y. 409, 32 N.E. 40, 17 L.R.A. 514; *McDowell v. St. Paul Fire & Marine Ins. Co., supra.* It necessarily follows that a mortgagee in his own right is entitled as a principal in any appraisal proceedings which will actually determine the amount due him by reason of the mortgage.

Upon principle and precedent then, we hold that a standard mortgagee clause, creating as it does, a separate and independent insurance of the mortgagee's interest, must operate to free the latter from any act or neglect by the owner, despite the fact that the latter may be, in his own right, proceeding strictly in accordance with the policy terms and conditions applicable to him when the loss occurs, *cf. Savarese v. Ohio Farmers Ins. Co., supra; Eddy v. London Assur. Corp., supra.* The owner has no greater power to affect the mortgagee's security interest by sanctioning an appraisal proceeding without his knowledge and participation than he has by entering into a settlement with the insurer or by procuring a judgment in an action to which the mortgagee was not a party. . . .

Judgment reversed and new trial ordered.

KINNEY v. ROCHESTER GERMAN INS. CO.

1908, 141 Ill. App. 543

Action by Kinney to recover on a fire insurance policy.

The plaintiff, through his agent McCrague, who in turn acted through

Cummings & Co., insurance brokers, obtained a policy of fire insurance for $1,500 through defendant's local agents, Hermann & Co. On October 19, 1906, Hermann & Co. notified Cummings & Co. that they desired to cancel the policy and that it would continue only until October 24 at noon. In some manner Cummings & Co. were in possession of the policy and they returned the same to the defendant's agent. A fire occurred early on October 25. The previous day Hermann & Co. figured the rebate and the day of the fire they credited the account of Cummings & Co. for the proper amount, still unaware of any fire. Cummings & Co. maintained an open account with Hermann & Co.

BROWN, J. . . . Mr. Kinney testified:

I never received any notice from the Rochester German Insurance Company or its agents of any intention on their part to cancel this policy. Neither the defendant nor George Hermann & Co. ever paid or offered to pay me any portion of the return premium.

This statement of the evidence is sufficient to show, we think, that no proper notice under the cancellation clause in the policy was given to the plaintiff nor the requisite repayment of premiums to him made. H. D. Cummings & Co. were simply the insurance brokers for the plaintiff. It does not appear that they had or assumed to have any authority to receive either notice of cancellation or premium rebate for him. It is very probable that if this fire loss had not unfortunately occurred when it did, a few days later the cancellation would have been properly accomplished by the assent of the assured. Cummings & Co. would probably have notified the plaintiff. . . .

Their employment by Mr. Kinney through his agent to procure the insurance gave them no authority to surrender or cancel the policy, or to receive the return premium or cancellation. . . . "The insured does not have to tender his policy in order to entitle him to receive back the unearned premium, but it is for the company desiring cancellation to seek the assured and tender the money to him, and until it does so, the cancellation has not been effected." No such tender was shown here. The "crediting" Cummings & Co. "with the unearned premium for the unexpired term" was not such a return or tender.

Judgment for plaintiff.

STANDARD MARINE INS. CO. et al. v. PECK
1959, (Colo.) 342 P.2d 661

The plaintiff, Peck, and his wholly owned corporation, Lawn and Garden Supply and Equipment Company, seek to recover for fire loss. The lower court gave judgment for plaintiffs and defendants appealed.

DAY, J. . . . Among several defenses interposed by Standard Marine was the existence in its insurance contract of a clause suspending its insurance during any period in which an increase in hazard existed in the premises. The particular paragraph provided as follows:

> Conditions suspending or restricting insurance.—Unless otherwise provided in writing added hereto this Company shall not be liable for loss occurring (a) while the hazard is increased by any means within the control or knowledge of the insured, * * * . . .

In support of their contention that the insurance coverage had been suspended at the time of the fire, the defendant insurance companies proved that plaintiff, the Lawn and Garden Supply Company, stocked a display of fireworks openly on tables in its store. Three boys came into the store on a Sunday afternoon about 2 o'clock and from one of the display tables picked a toy gun which emitted sparks when the trigger was pulled. The boy said he was playing "rockets" which he explained as aiming the sparks at various of the fuses protruding from the fireworks to see if they would orbit. The boy succeeded in igniting a pyrotechnic device called a "fountain," whereupon the display, like some politicians, went off in all directions, and the ensuing fire destroyed the store and contents. . . .

QUESTIONS TO BE DETERMINED:

First: Did the court err in holding that there was no increase in hazard? This question is answered in the affirmative.

Regardless of the academic question as to where the burden of proof lies, the defendant did establish by the evidence, uncontradicted, that the fireworks in fact did increase the hazard. The evidence disclosed that the fire originated as the result of such increase of hazard and from the very merchandise which was added to the stock. The ordinary merchandise carried by the establishment was of the hardware variety consisting of garden and lawn tools, mowers, etc. The court concluded because "there was on the premises gasoline contained in demonstrator lawnmowers and in cans on the premises; that there was also carried in stock an inflammable fluid in the nature of kerosene for the purpose of starting charcoal fires and to be sold for that purpose, and also matches were carried in stock; that the carrying of the fireworks did not in fact in view of the foregoing facts increase the hazard;***"

The evidence discloses that the gasoline was not for sale and was not exposed for sale but was kept in two cans in the basement for the purpose of demonstrating lawnmowers. There was also gasoline in the demonstrator lawnmower. The charcoal lighter fluid was contained in screw-type cans. This being the usual merchandise normally carried in the type of business being conducted, it is not to be compared with the hazard of an open display of fireworks. The fireworks by demonstration to the court were conclusively shown to be highly inflammable and explosive in character. That they have a particular appeal to children is a matter of common knowledge, explicitly demonstrated in this case. The evidence, therefore, does not support the conclusion of the court that there was no actual increase in the hazard. If the offering and display of a stock of fireworks was not an increase in the ordinary hazards of a hardware store, it is difficult to conceive what would be. Where the provisions of a policy are couched in plain and unambiguous language and do not contravene some principle of public policy, we have no right to relieve one of the parties to the contract from its disadvantageous terms by a forced construction or interpretation of its provisions. It must be given the meaning which a person of ordinary intelligence would attach to them. . . .

The judgments are reversed. Decision for defendants.

ANTLEY v. ST. MATHEWS NATIONAL BANK
1927, 139 S.C. 23, 137 S.E. 199

This is an action to determine the right to the proceeds of a policy of insurance. The plaintiff Antley was the beneficiary and the defendant was the pledgee, to whom the $2,000 policy had been pledged to secure an indebtedness of approximately $2,100. The pledge was made without the consent of the beneficiary, although the right to change beneficiaries had been reserved. No formal change of beneficiary had been made at the time of the insured's death. The lower court gave judgment for the plaintiff.

Cothran, J. . . . "The contract may reserve to the insured the right to change the beneficiary at will; and, when this is done, the nominated beneficiary acquires no vested interest in the policy or its proceeds, and until the death of the insured has a mere expectancy." *Merchants Bank v. Garrard,* 158, Ga. 867, 124 S.E. 715.

The case last named is in exact parallel with the case at bar, and it is there held that the assignment was in effect a change of the beneficiary, what our court practically held in the Deal Case. . . . In 37 C.J. 581, it is said:

On the other hand, where the right to change the beneficiary has been reserved in the policy so that the beneficiary does not have a vested right or interest, it is held that the insured has complete control and domination of the policy; that his right to change the beneficiary includes the lesser right partially to affect the rights of the beneficiary by assigning or creating a lien on the policy; and that he may do directly what he might do after having changed the beneficiary to himself or his estate. . . .

The judgment of this court is that the decree of the Circuit Court be reversed, and that the case be remanded to that court for the purpose of rendering judgment in favor of the defendant St. Mathews National Bank.

PRUDENTIAL INS. CO. v. DEYERBERG et al.

1927, 101 N.J. Eq. 90, 127 Atl. 785

This is a contest for money paid into court by the Prudential Ins. Co. on a policy of insurance for $500 issued by it on the life of Herman H. Deyerberg, payable to his "administrators, or assigns." One Helene Elschepp claims the proceeds by reason of an assignment. The policy was delivered to her as a gift, but later returned to the insured for safekeeping, whereupon he gave her a written statement indicating that the policy was to be paid to her. Herman F. Deyerberg claims as administrator, inasmuch as there was no change of beneficiary. The policy contained a provision that an assignment must be written, and notice given before it would bind the company.

Fielder, V. C. . . . As a general rule, the interest of an individual designated as beneficiary in a policy of insurance is a vested property right, payable to him if he outlives the insured, which right can only be divested by the insured making a change in beneficiary in the manner provided by the policy contract. Consequently an assignment of such a policy by the insured, even if made in full compliance with terms similar to those contained in the policy now under consideration, is ineffectual as against such beneficiary. . . . But where the sole beneficiary named in the policy is the executors, administrators or assigns of the insured, the policy, in effect, is made payable to the insured himself, or in the event of an assignment by him, to his assignee, and such is the situation with respect to the policy now under consideration. Although the insured could have made it payable to a new beneficiary only in the manner provided in the policy, he could make a valid assignment of it and of the money to become due thereon because no individual beneficiary had any interest therein. . . . Failure of the insured to comply with the policy provision that any assignment must be in writing cannot avail the administrator, because such provision was an agreement between the insured and the insurer alone, which the latter waived by paying the proceeds of the policy into court.

[*Judgment was for Helene Elschepp.*]

Review Questions and Problems

1. *A*'s life insurance policy had lapsed, but could be reinstated if he was in good health. On May 6, he made application for reinstatement, stating he was in good health. On May 17, he consulted a doctor for headache and bad vision, dying on May 19. Reinstatement was then denied. The beneficiary insisted that *A*'s good faith in stating he was in good health and an unreasonable delay in acting on the application made the company liable. What result?
2. *A* applied for fire insurance on certain property, stating it was occupied but, unknown to him, the tenant had recently moved. Shortly thereafter, a fire developed and the insurance company refused to pay. Is it liable?
3. *A* made an offer to purchase realty from *X* Co., but before his offer was accepted, he covered the property against fire by a policy from *P* Co. He later obtained title to the property and still later, it was damaged by fire. The company refused to pay, stating no insurable interest when policy was issued. The court held *P* Co. liable. Why?
4. *B* obtained a fire insurance policy on a house he was building for himself on his mother's land, the mother having promised to convey the land to him when the house was completed. A fire damaged the house and the company urged *B* had no insurable interest. The court held *B* had an interest. Was this sound?
5. *C* Co. insured *O*'s residence against fire and explosion. *W* installed for *O* an air conditioning unit which, being defective, exploded. *C* Co. paid *O* for the loss and sued *W* to recover its loss. The court held *W* liable. Can this be justified?
6. *Y* owned a valuable ring which she wrapped in paper and laid on a dresser. A maid carried the paper to a trash container and burned it. The ring was badly damaged by the fire and *Y* seeks recovery from her fire insurance company. The court held in favor of the insurer. Why?
7. *B* made application for life insurance which stated it was to be effective when delivered to *B* in good health. It was approved and mailed to the company's agent for delivery. While it was in the mail, *B* was killed and his servant, to obtain the policy, told the agent, in response to a question, that *B* was not sick. *B*'s beneficiary sought to recover on the policy and the court allowed recovery. Was this a sound decision?
8. A fire department was called because of smoke in a certain business area and firemen entered through the skylight but found no fire there, it being discovered and extinguished in a nearby building. Later *O*'s property was badly damaged by rain because the firemen replaced the skylight improperly. May *O* recover on his policy of fire insurance?
9. What is meant by the term "coinsurance?" What is its purpose?
10. *S*, who held a $10,000 policy of fire insurance on insured property, contracted to sell it to *B* for $32,500. Before the transfer had been completed a fire loss occurred. *B*, expecting to demolish the building in any event, paid *S* the full price. May *S* recover for the fire loss? Has *B* any equity in the insurance?
11. The plaintiff placed the ingredients for making soap in a pan and

lighted a fire under it. She forgot it, and went out to do some shopping. While away, smoke damage of $500 resulted, there being evidence that the ingredients in the pan had been on fire. Is the damage covered by her fire insurance policy?

12. Assume that a policy contains a two-year incontestable clause. *A* in his application states that he does not use intoxicating liquors. Three years after the policy is issued, he dies from excessive use of such liquors. The evidence clearly shows that he was a user of intoxicants at the time he filed his application. May his beneficiary recover?
13. What is a standard mortgage clause? To whom is a fire loss paid when a policy includes a standard mortgage clause? If the insured violates the terms of the policy, does this fact relieve the insurer of its duty to the mortgagee?
14. *A* carried a $10,000 life insurance policy in which *B*, his wife, was named the beneficiary. If *A* dies while he is insolvent, must *B* use the proceeds of the insurance to pay *A*'s obligations?
15. The insured desired to change the beneficiary in a policy of life insurance from his wife to his mother. The policy provided that he might do so by making the request, surrendering the policy, and having the change indorsed thereon. He made the request for change but failed to return the policy for indorsement. At the time of his death, was his wife or mother entitled to the insurance? If his wife had possession of the policy and refused to surrender it, would this affect your decision?
16. *A* carried a policy of life insurance for $5,000, which was payable to his estate. Shortly before his death, he mailed the policy to his fiancée, telling her that he wanted her to have it in case anything happened to him. At his death, will the money be paid to his estate or to his fiancée?
17. *S*, an insured in *X* Company, mailed his check for his life insurance premium during the grace period, but the bank by mistake returned the check n.s.f. Before *S* had an opportunity to correct the matter he died, the grace period having expired. Is his life insurance effective?
18. *A* borrowed $15,000 of *B* and as security procured a policy of life insurance for that amount and named *B* as the beneficiary. *A* died at a time when the debt had been reduced to $7,000. Determine the rights of *A* and *B*. Would the result be the same if *B* had taken out the insurance on *A*'s life?
19. *F* Co. operated a bakery and carried fire insurance on plant and equipment in *P* Ins. Co. The thermostatic control on the gas ovens failed to function one night. As a result the flames increased, the heat became intense in the ovens, they became red hot, so as to char and burn the adjoining floor to the extent that smoke was coming from it. The court held this to be an unfriendly fire. Since there was no flame outside the oven, do you agree with the decision?

BOOK VIII

REAL PROPERTY

49

Principles of Real Property

8-1. Introduction. Before studying the material presented here, the student is advised to review Section 1-5, Chapter 1, Book I, on the Basic Legal Concepts of Property. The material to follow in this part of the text deals with particular rules of law concerning real property. These rules may consider property as "a thing" or property as "the subject matter of relationships." Whichever meaning is intended, will be manifested by the purposes sought to be accomplished, through the use and application of particular rules.

A comprehension of the basic concepts behind what is meant by real property will aid in understanding how a particular rule has been developed and why the court has applied the rule in reaching its decision.

8-2. Fixtures. There are many definitions of the terms *fixtures.* In a broad sense, a fixture is an article that formerly had the characteristic of personal property, but upon becoming attached, annexed, or affixed to real property becomes a part of the real property. In order to determine in a particular case whether personal property attached to realty has become part of the realty the following rules and tests have been developed by the courts:

1. *Actual annexation to the realty.* The old English law required the chattel to be "let into" or "united" to the land, or to some substance that is a part of the land. A chattel that lies upon the ground is not attached by force of gravity. The test of annexation alone is inadequate, for many things attached to the soil or buildings are not fixtures and many things not physically attached to the soil or buildings are considered fixtures. For example, articles of furniture or plumbing substantially fastened but capable of easy removal are not necessarily fixtures. Physical annexation may be only for the purpose of more convenient use. On the other hand, machinery that has been annexed, but detached for repairs or other temporary reason, may still be considered a fixture although severed.

Keys, doors, windows, window shades, screens, storm windows and the like, although readily detachable, are generally considered fixtures because they are an integral part of the building and pertain to its function. The mode and degree of attachment and whether the article can be removed without material injury to the article, the building, or land are often important considerations in determining whether the article is a fixture. Electric ranges connected to a building by a plug or vent pipe under the material injury test are not fixtures, but the removal of wainscoting, wood siding, fire place mantels, and water systems, including connecting pipes, would cause a material injury to the building and land.

2. *Adaptation test.* Since the annexation test alone is inadequate to determine what is a fixture, there has been developed the adaptation test. Adaptation means that the article is used in promoting the purpose for which the land is used. Thus, if an article is placed upon or annexed to land to improve it, make it more valuable, and extend its use, it is a fixture. Windmills, pipes, pumps and electric motors for irrigation systems, and fruit dryers are examples of chattels which may be so adapted as to become fixtures. This test alone is not adequate because rarely is an article attached or placed upon land except to advance the purpose for which the land is to be used.

3. *Intention test.* Annexation and adaptation as tests to determine whether a chattel has become realty are only part of the more inclusive test of intention. Annexation and adaptation are evidence of an intention to make a chattel a fixture. In addition to annexation and adaptation as evidence of an intention, the following situations and circumstances are also used from which intention is deduced: (1) the kind and character of the article affixed; (2) the relation and situation of the parties making the annexation; for example, the relation of landlord and tenant suggests that such items as show cases and machinery, acquired and used by the tenant, are not intended to become permanently part of the real property. Such property called trade fixtures is generally intended to be severed at the end of the term; (3) the structure, degree, and mode of annexation; (4) and the purpose and use for which the annexation has been made.

An article that upon annexation does not lose its identity and removal of which will not materially injure it or the freehold may continue by agreement of the parties after annexation to be personal property. Thus, under a conditional sale contract, the reservation of title by the vendor for security, as between the vendor and vendee, is regarded as an agreement that the property retains its personalty character. Subsequent purchasers and mortgagees of the realty to which the chattel is attached with notice of the agreement take subject to the rights of the conditional vendor. But purchasers, lienees, and mortgagees who have no notice of the conditional sale agreement will not be affected, and as to them the article will be treated as a fixture. In some jurisdictions it is provided by statute that all conditional sales contracts or leases of personal property that are to be attached to the real estate so as to become a fixture shall be void as to any purchaser or mortgagee of the real property, unless, within ten days after the personal property is placed in and becomes part of the realty, a memorandum of the contract is filed by the vendor with the county recorder.

8-3. How title to real property is acquired. Title to real property may be acquired in several different ways: (1) by original entry, called title by occupancy; (2) by transfer through, and with the consent of, the owner; (3) by transfer upon sale by a sheriff; (4) by possession of a party under claim of title for the period of the Statute of Limitations, usually 20 years, called adverse possession; (5) by will; (6) by descent, regulated by statute; and (7) by accretion, as when a river or a lake creates new land.

8-4. Original entry, or title by occupancy. Except in those portions of the United States where the original title to the land was derived from grants that were issued by the King of England and other sovereigns who took possession of the land by conquest, title to all the land in the United States was derived from the United States government. Private individuals who occupied land for the period of time prescribed by federal statute and met such other conditions as were established by law acquired title by patent from the federal government.

8-5. Transfer with the consent of the owner. The title to real property is most commonly transferred by the owner's executing a deed to his transferee. A deed is generally a formal instrument under seal. The deeds most generally used are warranty and quit claim. A warranty deed conveys the fee simple title to the grantee, his heirs, or assigns and is so called because of the covenants on the part of the grantor by which he warrants: (1) that, at the time of the making of the deed, he has fee simple title therein and right and power to convey the same; (2) that the property is free from all encumbrances, except those encumbrances enumerated therein; (3) that his grantees, heirs, or assigns will have the quiet and peaceful enjoyment thereof and that he will defend the title to the property against all persons who may lawfully claim it. In most states it is not necessary that the above warranties be written in the deed. Such a deed is substantially as in the form shown on page 1112.

There may be circumstances under which the grantor would not wish to make warranties with respect to the title, and under such conditions he may execute a quitclaim deed. Such a deed merely transfers his existing legal and equitable rights in the premises described in the deed to the grantee. A quitclaim deed would be used under circumstances where an heir, owning an undivided interest in real property, wished to make a conveyance of his rights in the land, or where the interest of a person in land is questionable, a quitclaim deed would be used to clear the title. In the latter case, if he had title, he has parted with it, and if he had none, no injury has been done to him by the execution of the deed. The usual form of a quitclaim deed is shown on page 1113.

8-6. Transfer upon sale by sheriff. Title to land may be acquired by a vendee at a sale conducted by a sheriff or other proper official. Such sale is one made under the jurisdiction of a court having competent authority to order the sale. In order to secure the money to pay a judgment secured by a successful plaintiff, it may be necessary to sell the property of the defendant. Such a sale is called a judicial sale. A tax sale is a public sale of land, owned by a delinquent taxpayer, for the collection of unpaid taxes. The purchaser at such sale acquires a tax title. A mortgage foreclosure sale is a proceeding in equity by which a mortgagee secures by judicial sale money to pay the obligation secured by the mortgage. The word foreclosure is applied to the proceedings for enforcing other types of liens such as mechanics liens, assessments against realty to pay public improvements, and other statutory liens. The character of title acquired by a purchaser at such judicial sale is determined by statute.

8-7. Title acquired by adverse possession. Title to land may be acquired under a principle known as adverse possession. Thus one who enters into actual possession of land and remains thereon openly and notoriously for the period of time prescribed in the Statute of Limitations, claiming title thereto in denial of, and adversely to, the superior title of another, will at the end of the statutory period acquire legal title.[1] A person may acquire title to land even though he is not in actual possession of all the land claimed under what is called the doctrine of constructive adverse possession. Such a person must assert in good faith as evidence of his title, a writing describing the total property claimed and purporting to convey the land to the claimant. Such writing, although defective and imperfect, may be adequate as some evidence of ownership if it is a sign, semblance, token, or color of title. Before possession of a part of the land is sufficient to sustain a valid claim to the whole, the area claimed must have some relation in size, proximity, and use to that portion actually occupied. Actual knowledge by the true owner that his land is occupied adversely is not essential. However, the possession must be of such a nature as to charge a reasonably diligent legal owner with

[1] Hibbard v. Robert G. Fromkin Woolen Corporation, page 1058.

knowledge of the adverse claim. It has also been held that adverse possession will not run against a municipal corporation.[2]

8-8. Title by will or descent. A person may make disposition of his property after death by an instrument in writing called a will. One who dies leaving a will is said to die *testate*, and in speaking of such a person after death he is called the *testator*. The person who carries out the provisions of the will is called an *executor*. The words "last will and testament" are usually used together. When personal property is involved, the word *testament* is used, and the beneficiary in the will is called a *legatee*. When the will operates to transfer real property, it is often called a devise, and the beneficiary a devisee. Who may make a will, how it may be executed, who may or may not be excluded as beneficiaries, how a will may be revoked, and what rules are to be used in construing a will are controlled by state statute. The student is directed to read the Statute of Wills found in the code of his state.

A will is effective only when it has been drawn by one of sufficient mental capacity to realize fully the nature and effect of his act. The law requires that the signature to the will be witnessed by at least two, and in some states three, persons who are not interested in the estate. In a few states, a will written entirely in the handwriting of the deceased is probated even if it has not been witnessed. It should be understood that a will has no effect on the right of the owner to dispose of property during his lifetime. A will takes effect only at death and only then if it has not been revoked by the testator prior to his death.

If a person dies without making a will his real property will pass to his heirs or those entitled to receive the same according to the Statute of Descent. The student is directed to read the Statute of Descent found in the code of his state. When a person dies without making a will he dies *intestate*. The person who probates the estate is called an *administrator*.

8-9. Title acquired by accretion. An accretion is the accumulation of land to the land of an owner by action of water. If land is added to that of an owner by reason of an imperceptible gradual deposit by water, so that the shore or bank is extended, such increase is called alluvion. If a gradual increase in the land of an owner is caused by the receding of water, such increase is called reliction. If an addition to an owner's land be caused suddenly by reason of a freshet or flood, even though boundaries are changed, no change in ownership occurs. However, if such change in boundaries is slow and gradual by alluvion or reliction, the newly-formed land belongs to the owner of the bed of the stream in which the new land is formed. If the opposite bank of a

[2] Messersmith v. Mayor & Common Council of Riverdale, page 1059.

private stream belongs to different persons, it is a general rule that each owns the bed to the middle line of the stream. In public waters, such as navigable streams, lakes, and the sea, the title of bed of the water, in absence of special circumstances, is in the United States. Thus accession to the land would belong to the government.

8-10. Covenants and conditions. Quite often the grantor places restrictions upon the use that may be made of the land conveyed. He may, for instance, provide that the land shall be used exclusively for residential purposes, that the style and cost of the residence meet certain specifications, that certain fences and party walls shall be maintained, that building lines shall be established, that ways and roads shall be open and parks established. These restrictions inserted in the deed are covenants or promises on the part of the grantee to observe them and are said to run with the land. Even though the grantee fails to include them in a subsequent deed made by him, the new owner is nevertheless subject to them. They remain indefinitely as restrictions against the use of the land.[3]

Most of these covenants are inserted for the benefit of surrounding property and may be enforced by the owners of such property. This is particularly true where the owner of land which is being divided into a subdivision inserts similar restrictions in each deed. The owner of any lot which is subject to the restrictions is permitted to enforce the restrictions against the other lot owners located in the same subdivision. Occasionally a covenant is inserted for the personal benefit of the grantor, and will not run with the land. If a grantee *A* as part of the consideration covenants to repair a dam on land owned by the grantor *B*, such covenant will not run with the land and place a duty upon a grantee of *A*. The promise does not touch and concern the land granted from *A* to *B*, but is only a personal covenant for the benefit of *B*.

An estate on condition is an estate in fee, for life or for years, but its beginning or its continuation is dependent upon the happening of or the doing of an act by some person. If before an estate can begin, an event must occur, the event is a condition precedent. Thus, if *A* is to have an estate in land upon his marriage and his arrival at 25 years of age, such event is a condition precedent. If an estate may be terminated by the grantor or his successors, upon the happening of an event (a condition), an estate subject to a condition subsequent has been created. Thus, if *A* conveys to *B* and his heirs land on condition that if liquor is sold upon the premises conveyed, *A* may enter and terminate the estate, *B* has a fee simple estate, subject to a condition subsequent.

8-11. Execution of deeds. The statutes of the various states provide the necessary formal requirements for the execution and delivery of

[3] Arlt et al. v. King et al., page 1060.

deeds. A deed must be signed, sealed, acknowledged, and delivered. A deed is not effective until it is delivered to the grantee: that is, placed entirely out of the control of the grantor. This delivery usually occurs by the handing of the instrument to the grantee or his agents. Where property is purchased on installment contract and occasionally in other cases, the deed is placed in the hands of a third party to be delivered by him to the grantee upon the happening of some event, usually the final payment by the grantee. Such delivery to a third party is called delivery in escrow and takes control over the deed entirely out of the hands of the grantor. Only if the conditions are not satisfied is the escrow agent at liberty to return the deed to the grantor. The owner of land may deed it to another, but reserve to himself certain rights as, for example, mineral rights.[4]

8-12. Recording of deeds. In order that the owner of real estate may notify all persons that he has title to the property, the statutes of the various states provide that deeds shall be recorded in the recording office of the county in which the land is located. Failure to record a deed by a new owner who has not entered into possession makes it possible for the former owner to convey and pass good title to the property to an innocent third party, although the former owner has no right to do so and would be liable to his first grantee in such a case.

8-13. Abstracts of title. Every deed, mortgage, judgment, lien, or estate proceeding that affects the title to real estate is required by statute to be filed and recorded in the recording office of the county within which the real estate lies. In order for an owner to know the history and nature of the title to be obtained by him, title companies examine such records and prepare abstracts of the record. A purchaser of real estate should demand such abstract of title and have it examined in order to determine whether there are any existing claims against the property, or any outstanding interests that might in any way affect his title. The abstract of title must be supplemented from time to time, in order to show the chain, so that all court proceedings, such as foreclosures, partitions, transfers by deed, and probate proceedings, may be shown. Title companies are organized for the purpose of preparing such abstracts, and, after their preparation, examination of them should be made by a competent attorney before a purchaser accepts the title from the grantor. In many communities title companies are now organized as title insurance companies and upon the purchase of land, the grantor usually secures for the grantee from the title insurance company a land-title insurance policy which has for its purpose the protection of the grantee from claims against the title.[5]

[4] Fleming Foundation v. Texaco, page 1061.
[5] Udell v. City Title Insurance Co., page 1063.

ESTATE IN REAL PROPERTY

8-14. Estates in fee simple. A person who owns the entire estate in real property is said to be an owner in fee simple.

8-15. Life estates. An owner of land may create, either by will or by deed, a life estate therein. Such a life estate may be for the life of the grantee or it may be created for the duration of the life of some other designated person. Unless the instrument that creates the life estate places limitations upon it, the interest can be sold or mortgaged like any other interest in real estate. The buyer or mortgagee takes into consideration the fact that he receives only a life estate and that it may be terminated at any time by the death of the person for whose life it was created. For full protection, the mortgagee should carry insurance upon the life of the life tenant.

The life tenant is obligated to use reasonable care to maintain the property in the condition in which it was received, ordinary wear and tear excepted. It is his duty to repair, to pay taxes, and out of the income received, to pay interest on any mortgage that may have been outstanding at the time the life estate was created. The life tenant has no right to make an unusual use of the property if such a use tends to deplete the value of the property, unless the property was so used at the time the estate was created. For instance, a life tenant would have no right to mine coal or to cut and mill timber from land in which he held only a life estate unless such operations were being conducted or contemplated at the time the life estate was created.

8-16. Remainders and reversions. After the termination of a life estate, the remaining estate may be given to someone else, or it may revert to the original owner or his heirs. If the estate is to be given to someone else upon the termination of a life estate, it is called an estate in remainder. If it is to revert back to the original owner, it is called a reversion. If the original owner of the estate is dead, the reversion comes back to his heirs. A remainder or a reversionary interest may be sold, mortgaged, or otherwise disposed of in the same manner as any other interest in real property.

8-17. Dower and curtesy. At common law, a wife is entitled, upon the death of her husband, to a life estate in one third of any real property that her husband owned at the time of his death. The common law provided that, if there was a child born alive, upon the death of the wife the husband was entitled to a life estate in the whole of the wife's property. This was known as curtesy.

Curtesy has quite generally been abolished by statute, although in some of the states the husband is given a right comparable to the wife's dower. Some of the states have also abolished dower, making some other provision for the surviving wife or husband. In those states where dower or curtesy is provided for, the husband or wife cannot defeat the other by conveying his or her property prior to his or her death. A purchaser acquires good title only if the wife and husband join in the deed, unless the statute makes some other provision. Dower and curtesy are now generally controlled by statute. The student is advised to investigate the statute of the state, in order to ascertain the extent of the wife's dower interest.

8-18. Easements. An easement is a right, granted by the grantor to the grantee, to use real property. For example, the grantor may convey to the grantee a right of way over his land, the right to erect a building that may shut off light or air, the right to lay drain tile under the land, or the right to extend wires over the land. If these rights of easement are reserved in the deed conveying the property, or granted by a separate deed, they pass along with the property to the next grantee and are burdens upon the land. Such easements may be made separate and distinct by contract and are binding only on the immediate parties to the agreement. If such right to use another's land is given orally, it is not an easement but a license, and the owner of the land may revoke it at any time; unless it has become irrevocable by estoppel; whereas an easement given by grant cannot be revoked or taken away, except by deed, as such a right of way is considered a right in real property. An easement, like title to property, may be acquired by prescription which is similar to adverse possession.

8-19. Tenancies—joint tenancy and tenancy in common. An estate in land may be owned by several persons. Such persons may hold the real estate, either as tenants in common or as joint tenants, according to the nature of the granting clause in the deed by which the title is transferred. In a joint tenancy each person owns an undivided interest in the real property. Upon the death of any one of the owners, the remaining owners take the property, and upon the death of all the owners except one, the entire property passes to such survivor if the joint tenancy has not been terminated by some act of the parties.[6] In tenancies in common, however, upon the death of one of the several owners, the title to his share passes to his heirs, and the heirs, therefore, become tenants in common with the surviving tenants in common. A joint tenancy can be created only by a specific statement in the granting clause of the deed, which usually states that the grantees shall hold title to said premises as joint tenants with the right of survivorship, and not as tenants in common. In the absence of such clause, grantees are tenants in common.

[6] Van Antwerp v. Horan et al., page 1064.

8-20. Tenancy by entirety and community property. Since at common law a husband and wife are considered as one person, a conveyance of land to a husband and wife, in absence of words to the contrary, creates presumably an estate called a "tenancy by the entirety." To the extent that upon the death of either the survivor takes the entire estate, a tenancy by the entirety is similar to a joint tenancy. Tenancy by the entirety, however, differs from a joint tenancy in that the estate by entirety cannot be determined without the consent of both parties. A joint tenancy, however, can be destroyed by either cotenant transferring his interest to a third party, thus making the transferee a tenant in common with the other owner.

Several of the southwestern and western states have what is known as community property, having inherited it in part from their French and Spanish ancestors. In these states all property acquired after marriage other than by devise, bequest, or from the proceeds of noncommunity property becomes the joint property of husband and wife. Control of the property is vested primarily in the husband, and he is authorized, in most states, to sell or to mortgage it. The proceeds of the sale or mortgage in turn become community property. Upon the death of one of the parties, title to at least half of the community property passes to the survivor. In most of the states, the disposition of the remainder may be by will or under the rules of descent.

PRINCIPLES OF REAL PROPERTY CASES

HIBBARD v. ROBERT G. FROMKIN WOOLEN CORPORATION
1960, (Maine) 165 A.2d 49

The plaintiff and defendant were in dispute as to the boundary line between their respective premises. The plaintiff brought suit to recover possession of the disputed area. The plaintiffs' predecessor in title had entered into possession in 1914 and thereafter had maintained certain small buildings on the premises in connection with a plumbing business and had kept the bushes cut on much of the area. The lower court held in favor of the plaintiff.

WEBBER, Justice. . . . the premises comprising cleared land were in proximity to a populous community and every act of occupancy was obvious and apparent. The possession which will ripen into title must be actual, open, notorious, hostile, under claim of right, continuous, and exclusive for a period of at least twenty years. *Shannon v. Baker,* 145 Me. 58, 71 A.2d 318. The nature of the posession must be such as to give implied notice to the true owner who thereafter is presumed to acquiesce in the claim of the intruder. The overt acts must be such as to leave no question as to the intention to oust the owner from possession and ownership. *Roberts v. Richards*, 84 Me. 1, 10, 24, A. 425. We think that the acts shown to have been done in the instant case supported a jury finding that all of the foregoing requirements for title acquisition by adverse possession were fully satisfied. . . . The acts of dominion openly performed upon the property were such as would ordinarily be performed by a true owner on premises of this character. . . .

Affirmed.

MESSERSMITH v. MAYOR & COMMON COUNCIL OF RIVERDALE

1960, (Md.) 164 A.2d 523

The owners of a subdivision granted a parcel of land to a municipal corporation with a limitation to a use "as public parks and parking for the use of the public and especially for lot owners of the town of Riverdale." The town did not make any use of this property and the plaintiffs enclosed a portion of it by a low hedge. They landscaped and cut the grass for a period of more than 20 years. The plaintiffs brought this suit to quiet title to the land in question. The lower court dismissed the complaint.

HORNEY, Judge. . . . The contention with respect to adverse possession is . . . without merit. The claim is that the plaintiffs' action in maintaining the lot for more than twenty years constitutes a sufficient basis for adverse possession. And, although conceding that in ordinary circumstances adverse possession will not run against a municipal corporation, the argument is that since there has been nonacceptance, if not an abandonment, the rights of the public are not affected by the adverse possession. The argument is not sustainable.

By its charter, the town of Riverdale, among other common corporate powers, is authorized to "purchase and hold real and personal property or dispose of the same for the benefit of said town." Code P.L.L., Art. 17 (Prince George's County), § 864 (Everstine (1953) § 1276). The powers thus conferred, however, refer only to property in which the town holds absolute title, and not to property it holds as a public trust.

The general rule as to alienability of municipally held property was clearly stated in *Montgomery County v. Metropolitan District*, 1953, 202 Md. 293, at page 303, 96 A.2d 353, where it was said:

> A distinction is frequently drawn between property held by a county in its proprietary (or business) capacity and that held by it in its governmental capacity. Property which is held in a governmental capacity or is impressed with a public trust, cannot be disposed of without special statutory authority.

. . . There can be little doubt that the lot in question is impressed with a public trust. . . .

It is equally clear that property held as a public trust may not be privately acquired by adverse possession. . . .

Under the circumstances in this case, it is not possible for the plaintiffs to acquire the lot in question by adverse possession. It may be that the town could obtain authority to sell the lot to the plaintiffs, but that is a matter for the legislature to decide, not the courts.

For the reasons expressed herein, the decree must be affirmed.

Decree affirmed; appellants to pay costs.

ARLT et al. v. KING et al.

1950, 328 Mich. 645, 44 N.W.2d 195

Boyles, C. J. . . . The lots involved in this litigation are in block *A* of said subdivision. At least 24 of the 33 lots in said block have been sold by the plattors. In each conveyance from the common grantors a restriction has been included to the effect that the property is restricted to residence purposes only. Most of them also contain a provision that there should not be more than one residence on a lot. The conveyances were recorded. Plaintiff Arlt and his wife acquired a lot in said block in 1940 or 1941, with the above restrictions. Subsequently, plaintiffs Bolton, Rose, Ryckeman, and Adamson became owners of lots by deeds from the common grantors, with the same restrictions (Adamson's lot is in Block *B*). It is conceded that the other conveyances of the 24 lots in block *A*, sold by the common grantors, contain the same restriction of use for residence purposes only, and that many of them also add "with but one residence on any lot." Defendants became owners of lots 15-16-17-18 in said block *A* in 1945, the conveyance containing a restriction that the property was to be used for residence purposes.

While there is no general uniformity of expression in the language used in the conveyances, all contained a restriction of use to residential purposes, and a large percentage also with the added restriction as to only one residence on a lot. The conveyances were recorded, the defendants not only had constructive notice of the restrictions, but also had actual knowledge, from their grantors and others. The record is convincing that defendants' lots were burdened with a reciprocal negative easement as to use for residence purposes only, limited to one residence on each lot. The trial court did not err in finding from the testimony and the conveyances that block *A* was restricted to use for residences, with only one on each lot, was intended for substantial summer homes, with commercial use of said lots prohibited. See *Sanborn v. McLean,* 333 Mich. 227, 206 N.W. 496, 60 A.L.R. 1212.

The defendants divided their lots 15 and 16 and part of lot 17 into 6 smaller lots, consisting of 3 lots north and south, and 2 lots east and west. They proceeded to erect a cabin or cottage on each of the 6 smaller lots, to be rented to tourists and resorters. When defendants started the foundations they were repeatedly notified of the restrictions by the protests of other lot owners. Furthermore, the restrictions of record in many other conveyances were sufficient notice to the defendants, when considered in connection with the other circumstances in the instant case, although some part of the restriction was inadvertently left out of their conveyance from one who was not the common grantor. *Nerrerter v. Little,* 258 Mich. 462, 243 N.W. 25.

The defendants used their residence on their property as an office from which to rent and operate their cabins and cottages as a tourist court business, renting them by the week, for week ends, or overnight.

Defendant King admitted: "At the present time, I am renting such cottages to people who come to me. I have a sign at the road, "Cottages for rent. . . . I rent the cottages near the road for $45 a week. I get $55 a week for the cottages near the lake. The longest period of time I have had any of these cottages rented to one person was 2 weeks."

The record supports the conclusion of the trial court that the defendants use their lots for business and commercial purposes.

The decree as entered enjoins the defendants from using their lots for business or commercial purposes or renting the same "for any period not less than 1 year." Said limitation as to the rental period is gratuitous relief, not conforming to the prayer, and will be eliminated. The provision against having more than one cottage upon any one lot is proper, as is the provision which permits the defendants to convert the cottages in excess of one on each lot into garages, or otherwise requires their removal. The decree also restricts the use of defendants' cottages to persons of the Caucasian race, conforming to some restrictions in some of the conveyances of lots in said block. Such provision must be deleted. *Shelley v. Kraemer,* 334 U.S. 1, 68 S.Ct. 836, 92 L.Ed. 1161, 3 A.L.R. 2d 441, reversing *Sipes v. McGhee,* 316 Mich. 614, 25 N.W.2d 638. A decree may be entered in this Court affirming the decree as entered, with the above exceptions, with costs to appellees.

FLEMING FOUNDATION v. TEXACO

1960, (Tex.) 337 S.W.2d 846

The plaintiffs, owners of land in Texas, sold the land but reserved the rights to oil, gas and other minerals. A portion of the land was leased to Texaco which was given the right to drill for water. Texaco drilled several wells and produced and used considerable water from these wells. The plaintiffs brought suit to recover for the water which had been taken from the land. The lower court ruled in favor of the defendants.

NORTHCUTT, Justice. . . . We have not been cited a Texas case determining the exact meaning of the terms here in question in cases of this kind and neither have we found one.

. . . The intention of the parties to a deed is the paramount consideration, and their intention is to be gathered from a consideration of the entire instrument taken by its four corners. A deed will be construed most strictly against the grantor. *City of Stamford v. King*, Tex. Civ. App., 144 S.W.2d 923 (writ refused). A deed will be construed to confer upon grantee the greatest estate that the terms of the instrument will permit. *Waters v. Ellis*, 158 Tex. 342, 312 S.W.2d 231 by the Supreme Court.

. . . we think, it may be said, generally, that a conveyance of the surface only in a tract of land with a reservation of the minerals vests in the grantee such rights to the use thereof as are usually exercised by owners in fee subject only to the right of the grantor to remove the minerals reserved. Then we must determine if water was one of the minerals reserved by appellants.

What we have said above about the intention of the parties to a deed being the paramount consideration will apply also in determining what is intended by the term "other minerals." In construing a reservation of minerals in a deed regard must be had, not only to the words used to describe the things reserved, but to the relative portion of the parties interested, and to the substance of the transaction or arrangement which such deed embodies. There is no question in this case but what the real intention of the appellants was to retain the minerals. Neither is there any doubt about water being technically a mineral. We think the question whether a given substance is or is not a mineral within the meaning of the deeds in which the reservations are made is a question of fact to be decided according to the circumstances of the particular case. For example, were the terms such as to constitute a like substance? The rule in Texas seems to be where specific things are followed by some general term such general term must refer to things of the same kind; but when the general term precedes the specific it is different. . . .

We do not think water is a thing of like kind to oil and gas. . . .

We approve the holding of the Oklahoma Court in the case of *Vogel et al. v. Cobb*, Okl., 141 P.2d 276, 148 A.L.R. 774, where it held "other minerals" referred to minerals of the same generic class as oil and gas and did not include water. We think the holding in the *Vogel v. Cobb* case should be the rule in this state and we hold that the reservation of oil, gas and other minerals does not include the sub-surface water.

We think the trial court rendered the proper judgment and overrule all of appellants' assignments of error.

Judgment of the trial court is affirmed.

UDELL v. CITY TITLE INSURANCE CO.

1960, 208 N.Y.S.2d 504

RABIN, Justice. The plaintiff contracted to purchase a six story loft building and shortly thereafter retained the defendant-title company to search the title and issue a policy of title insurance. The defendant prepared the customary title report which contained a description of the property. This description revealed the presence of a party wall on the westerly side but failed to show a party wall on the easterly side of the building. Thereafter, plaintiff took title to the premises and in due course received a title policy from the defendant. Some 16 months later the building adjoining on the east was demolished and a party wall was disclosed. It is for damages allegedly suffered by reason of the undisclosed existence of such party wall that the plaintiff here seeks recovery.

The plaintiff brings suit upon two causes of action. The first is in contract based upon the title policy and the second in negligence based upon defendant's alleged negligence in failing to report the existence of the party wall. . . .

The report of the title company showed a party wall on the westerly side of the premises. The plaintiff apparently did not consider that of any consequence because he took title with knowledge of that fact. It might very well be that had the title company turned up a party wall on the easterly side of the premises the plaintiff would likewise have had no objection to taking title. Be that as it may, the plaintiff is entitled to take advantage of any claimed delinquency on the part of the defendant and, if the defendant exposed itself to any liability, to seek a recovery.

Before the plaintiff may recover, however, it must be shown, with respect to the negligence cause of action, that the plaintiff suffered some injury, and, with respect to the contract cause of action, that he is entitled to a recovery under the terms of the policy. With respect to the latter, the mere existence of the party wall without disclosure does not create liability in and of itself. There must be found a breach of some obligation assumed by the defendant on which the plaintiff must rely. What obligations did the defendant assume by the issuance of its policy? Pertinent to this case we find that the defendant only obligated itself (1) to defend the plaintiff against adverse claims of title or claims of encumbrances; (2) to pay damages where there has been an adjudication ousting plaintiff from all or a portion of the premises; (3) to pay damages where there has been an adjudication adverse to title upon a lien or encumbrance; (4) to pay damages upon proper notice where plaintiff shall have contracted to sell and title is rejected because of defect in title or of an encumbrance; (5) to pay damages where plaintiff transfers title with warranties and there is an adjudication against plaintiff on such warranties because of defect in title or of an encumbrance. Giving the plaintiff the benefit of the broadest interpretation of this policy, there is nothing shown to indicate any breach on the part of the defendant with respect to any of these obligations assumed by it. The policy is a contract. The rights of the parties are limited to the terms thereof. Therefore, the first cause of action cannot be sustained.

The second cause of action is based upon the defendant's alleged negligence in failing to discover and report the existence of the party wall. While it would appear that a triable issue is presented as to whether the defendant, in the exercise of reasonable care, should have discovered the existence of the party wall, a resolution of such issue in plaintiff's favor, without more, would not entitle him to recover. The plaintiff must show injury. There must be demonstrated damage proximately resulting from the negligence of the defendant. The plaintiff contends that the mere existence of the party wall constitutes an infirmity in title and that in consequence damage naturally follows. An existing party wall, even without a party wall agreement, may well constitute an infirmity of title, but we need not be detained to determine that question here. The demolition of the adjoining building, prior to the commencement of the action, relieved the plaintiff's property of such infirmity, if indeed there was one (*357 East Seventy-Sixth Street Corp. v. Knickerbocker Ice Co.*, 263 N.Y. 63, 188 N.E. 158).

Case dismissed.

VAN ANTWERP v. HORAN et al.
1945, 390 Ill. 449, 61 N.E.2d 358

The question presented for the court's consideration is whether a joint tenancy is severed by a levy made under an execution upon the share of one of the joint tenants, no sale having taken place at the time of the death of the tenant against whom the levy was made.

THOMPSON, J. . . . The characteristics of a joint estate are derived from its unity, which are the unity of interest, the unity of title, the unity of time, and the unity of possession. It is the destruction of one or more of the four unities that severs and destroys the joint tenancy and this may be done by a conveyance, voluntary or involuntary, of the interest of one of the joint tenants, and the unity of title and interest being destroyed, the interest severed is changed into a tenancy in common. . . . It is recognized that the interest of the joint tenant in real estate is subject to levy and sale upon execution. . . .

The appellants urge, however, that the making of the levy destroys the identity of interest in that this is such an act in reduction of the interest of the joint tenant as to destroy the unity of interest and to bring about a severance of the joint tenancy. This court has previously considered the question of the effect of a judgment lien on the interest of a joint tenant and has held that the judgment lien does not sever the joint tenancy and that by the taking of the judgment nothing was done to sever this estate. *People's Trust & Savings Bank v. Haas,* 328 Ill. 468, 160 N.E. 85. This presents to us for consideration the effect of the levy upon the interest of the judgment debtor holding as a joint tenant. To be specific, does a levy made under an execution upon the share or interest of one of the joint tenants, sever or terminate, before final sale, the joint tenancy? This presents a new proposition and we have been cited no authority in which this exact and precise question has been passed upon in this or any other court. . . .

The taking of a judgment gives to the judgment creditor a lien upon the property of the judgment debtor, and we have held before that the attaching of a judgment lien upon the interest of a joint tenant does not sever the joint tenancy. *People's Trust & Savings Bank v. Haas,* 328 Ill. 468, 160 N.E. 85. By following this decision, it is clear that if the attaching of a judgment lien upon the interest of a joint tenant does not sever the joint tenancy, the making of a levy upon the interest of the joint tenant debtor would not be such act as would sever the joint estate, because of the fact that the levy gives no greater interest than that which the judgment creditor already possessed. . . .

Judgment for the surviving joint tenant.

Review Questions and Problems

1. *A* owned an office building which was mortgaged to *X*. *B* sold to *A*, and *W* installed in the building movable, standard-design air-conditioning units and placed on the roof a water tower to provide water for these units only. The units and tower were easily removable without damage. The office building had been previously used without air conditioning. On foreclosure of the mortgage, may *X* claim the tower and units as part of the real estate covered by the mortgage?
2. *A* owned 40 acres of land bounded by the Missouri River. On the side of *A*'s tract opposite the river there was an 80-acre tract owned by *B* that was separated from the river by *A*'s tract. All of *A*'s tract, except a strip 10 feet wide, was eroded away by the river. Then a revetment was constructed into the river upstream and silt was gradually deposited against this strip until a tract 60 acres in size was built up. To whom does it belong?
3. The owner of two adjoining buildings sold one of them to *A*. The

deed provided that *A* should have the privilege of passage from the other building to the one which he purchased. Subsequently, the owner sold the remaining building to *X*. *X* tore down the building and built a new one. Does *A* have a right of passage in the new building?

4. The A. & B. Grocery Co. desired to use a lot adjacent to its store for customer parking. The grocery company acquired the lot by a deed which stated that the lot was "subject to restrictions of record pertaining to this development." One such restriction prohibited building "more than one dwelling house—which shall be used for residence purposes only"—on each lot. By permission from the city zoning authority, may A. & B. Grocery Co. use the lot for parking purposes? Who may object, and why?
5. A power company cleared a right of way across *A*'s land and suspended a power line which had been constantly maintained. No poles or towers, however, were on the property. Many years later the company replaced the old power line with a new one and part of the installation was on *A*'s land. Can *A* require the company to remove the line?
6. In a state having a 10-year statute of limitations for actions involving real property, would *X* obtain title to land owned by *A* by closing a gap between two fence lines and keeping a cow on the property? Assume that *X* got quitclaim deeds from two of three cotenants of the land but not from the third, *A*. Assume also that the deeds contained a clause indicating *X* was to have all the property in the land through the deeds, and that *X* recorded the deeds and lived on the property for over 10 years, paying the taxes. If within the 10 years *A* died leaving *B* and *C* as his heirs, who would own the land? Who could contest this?
7. *H* murdered his wife and then claimed complete ownership of an apartment building owned by them as joint tenants. *X* purchased *H*'s interest with knowledge of the murder. Would the wife's heirs at law, *A* and *B*, have any claim to the property?
8. *H* died leaving a will which gave *W*, the wife, the "use during her lifetime" of a 400-acre farm and upon *W*'s death the farm to go to *X* and *Y*, a niece and nephew. Instead of putting half the income back into the farm in the nature of barns, ponds and fertilizer as had been previously done by *H*, her husband, she spent the entire income of the farm on herself. Who, if anyone, may object?
9. An outdoor advertising company ADCO signed an agreement with a hotel owner which granted ADCO "the exclusive right and privilege to maintain an advertising sign" on an exterior wall of the hotel. ADCO installed the sign. May the owner remove the sign during the period agreed? Is the privilege conferred a license or easement?
10. *A* willed certain land to *W* for life with the remainder to *W*'s minor children. *A* died, and sometime thereafter *W* leased the property to *X* Coal Company, which stripped the land of coal and destroyed it for other useful purposes. Have the children a good cause of action against the coal company?

50

Real Estate Mortgages

8-21. Nature of, and essential requirements under the early common law. A real estate mortgage is now generally considered a lien on land, created by contract, for the purpose of securing the performance of an obligation, usually the payment of money. The party who makes the mortgage is the mortgagor; the party to whom it is made—the one who lends the money—is the mortgagee. Under the common law, the early form of a mortgage on land consisted of an absolute conveyance of the title of the land by the owner to the mortgagee, upon a condition that the title would revert to the mortgagor when the obligation was performed or the money was repaid. The mortgagee secured the absolute right to the land and could take possession and collect the rents and profits. If the mortgagor failed to pay the money on or before the day set, the property would never revert to the mortgagor.

8-22. Growth of equitable theory. Under the common-law theory, the owner often lost his land if he was unable to repay a small loan on the due date, as required under his contract. In order to avoid the harshness of this rule, courts of equity began to allow the mortgagor to redeem his land after he had made a default. This right of the mortgagor, first recognized by a court of equity, is called his *equity of redemption.* Upon default, the mortgagee, by a process called a bill to foreclose the mortgage, asked the court to fix a date within which time the mortgagor must exercise his right to redeem his land. On the mortgagor's failure to redeem within the fixed time, the property became the absolute property of the mortgagee.

Also at common law, during the time that the land was encumbered by the mortgage, the mortgagee had the absolute right to take possession of the property and to secure the income from it. On account of these unjust advantages given to the mortgagee, courts of equity have taken the view that, since the transaction is intended by the parties only as a security transaction, such intention should be carried out. Under modern statutes regulating mortgages, the mortgagor is now regarded as the real owner of the land. He has the right to exercise all the powers of an owner, subject, however, to the limitations contained in the mortgage.

8-23. Legal and equitable theories of mortgages. Many of the states still hold to the old legal theory and regard the title and the right of possession as passing to the mortgagee. This theory is called the title theory of mortgages, since title passes to the mortgagee. In the states where the title theory prevails, courts of equity permit the mortgagor to have a right of accounting against the mortgagee for any income obtained from the property while it is in his possession. In the law courts in the title-theory states, the mortgagor today is regarded as the real owner as to everyone except the mortgagee.

In a majority of the states the equitable theory prevails; in these states the title remains in the mortgagor, and the mortgagee has only a lien against the property as a security for his loan. Such view is called the lien theory of mortgages.

8-24. Property capable of being mortgaged. In general, any interest in land, an equitable as well as a legal interest, can be mortgaged. The common interests subject to mortgage are fee simple estates, estates for life, estates for years, dower interests of widows, a mortgagee's interest, and a mortgagor's interest. Land may be mortgaged separately from its improvements, or the improvements may be mortgaged separately from the land, or both land and improvements may be mortgaged. Growing crops and various other interests in real estate may be mortgaged for the purpose of securing a loan.

Property that one does not own cannot be mortgaged, but a mortgage may be so drawn as to cover property to be acquired in the future. Although no mortgage exists at the time, equity will recognize a lien against the property as soon as it is acquired. This lien is good as to all persons who acquire rights in the property, except bona fide purchasers for value without notice.

A mortgage may be given prior to the time when the money is advanced to the mortgagor. It has been held that when the mortgagee makes the payment the mortgage is a valid lien as of the date when the mortgage was recorded.[1]

8-25. Form of mortgage. The form of mortgage in common use still reflects the title theory, and as in a deed, states that it conveys the property to the mortgagee, subject to the conditions set forth in the mortgage. Such a conveyance of real property must be in writing, under seal, and executed with all the formalities of a deed. The contract between the parties with respect to the loan need not be included in the deed of conveyance, but may be set forth on a separate sheet of paper. In the title-theory states, a mortgage is a very formal instrument. In the lien-theory

[1] Simpson v. Simpson, page 1077.

states, short forms of mortgages are usually authorized by statute and are not of such a technical nature.

8-26. Recording mortgages. In order that the mortgagee may give notice to third parties that he has an interest in the real estate covered by the mortgage, it is necessary that the mortgage be recorded in the recording office of the county where the real estate is situated. This recording protects the mortgagee against subsequent bona fide purchasers of the land from taking the real estate free from the mortgage. The statutes of the various states specify the requirements necessary for recording mortgages.

8-27. An absolute conveyance may be a mortgage. An absolute deed made by a landowner to a person may be shown by parol evidence to be a mortgage, if such evidence indicates that the intention of the parties was to make the transfer a security for a loan. The landowner must prove, however, by clear, precise, and positive evidence that it was the intention of the parties to draw up the deed for the purpose of securing a loan.[2]

Likewise, a landowner may sell his land and give an absolute deed, with an agreement that he retain the right to repurchase for a certain price within a specified time. Parol evidence may be introduced in such a case to establish that the deed was given for the purpose of securing a loan. If the evidence is convincing, a court of equity will declare such a deed to be a mortgage. For example, a man may convey his farm worth $30,000 for a consideration of $10,000. The so-called buyer then gives the seller an option to repurchase at a figure approximating $10,000 and interest. If the evidence is clear that the parties intended to make a loan, even though the option period has expired, it is not too late for the grantor to redeem his property, because the court will treat the deed as if it had been a mortgage.

8-28. Deed of trust in the nature of a mortgage. A deed of trust is often used as a substitute for a mortgage for the purpose of securing debts. The property is conveyed to a trustee to hold in trust for the benefit of the creditor. If the mortgage is paid at the time required by the contract, the trustee reconveys the property to the grantor. If there is a default in the payment, the trustee forecloses the mortgage and applies the proceeds to the payment of the debt secured. Deeds of trust are used where numerous notes are secured by the same property and are used to secure bondholders. For example, where it is desired to issue bonds secured by railroad or other corporate property, a trust deed may be executed to secure the entire bond issue. This method is necessary, because it would be impractical to execute a separate mortgage to secure each bond.

[2] Newport et al. v. Chandler, page 1078.

8-29. Purchase money mortgages. A purchase money mortgage is given for a part or the whole of the purchase price of land. For example, *A* wishes to purchase real estate worth $30,000. He has $10,000 in cash. Upon securing title from the vendor, he can complete his purchase by giving back to the vendor a mortgage on the real estate to secure the remaining purchase price of $20,000. This type of mortgage is normally used in the buying and selling of real estate. In many jurisdictions a deficiency decree obtained upon the foreclosure of a purchase money mortgage will not be enforced. See § 8-44.

8-30. Rights of mortgagor. The mortgagor is personally liable for the mortgage debt, not by reason of the mortgage, but because he makes a note, a bond, or other contract which evidences the debt secured by the mortgage. A mortgage may be made to secure the performance of an obligation other than the payment of money. The mortgagor under the lien theory of modern statutes is regarded as the owner of the land. He has the same right to control the property as he had before making the mortgage, and he may sell the land, lease it, or make other mortgages, subject, however, to the agreement creating the already existing mortgage.[3] Upon his death, interest in the real estate passes to his heirs, or, if he leaves a will, to his devisees under the will. His interest may be sold by a judgment creditor under an execution, subject to the prior right of the mortgagee. The mortgagor is entitled to retain possession of the property, cultivate the land, and secure the income therefrom. Since he is the owner of the mortgaged property, the mortgagor has an insurable interest in the property and can insure it for full value, regardless of the amount for which it is mortgaged. By the terms of the mortgage, the mortgagor is usually required to keep up the insurance for the benefit of the interest represented by the mortgage for, and on behalf of, the mortgagee. Upon a loss the insurance company pays the mortgagor and the mortgagee, as their interests may appear, if the insurance policy is so drawn as to protect both parties.

8-31. Rights and liabilities of the mortgagee. In the title-theory states, the mortgagee has legal title and theoretically the right to possess the mortgaged property during the period of the mortgage, unless the contract grants to the mortgagor the right to remain in possession. In the lien-theory states, the mortgagor is entitled to possession unless a different arrangement is provided for in the mortgage. In both the lien- and title-theory states, the mortgagee is protected against any person who commits waste or impairs the security. Even the mortgagor may not use the property in such a manner as to reduce materially its value. Mining ore, pumping oil, or cutting timber are operations which must be provided for in the mortgage agreement. Perhaps, if they were being con-

[3] Kehr v. Blomenkamp, page 1079.

ducted at the time the mortgage was created, the mortgagor might continue without authorization in the mortgage. Under either title or lien theory, the mortgagee who takes possession of the property is obligated to derive a revenue from its use and to account for the amount received.

A mortgagee has a right to pay off or to redeem from any superior mortgage in order to protect his security, and he can charge the amount so paid to the mortgagor. Likewise, he may pay taxes or special assessments, which are a lien on the land, defend suits which threaten the title of the mortgagor, and recover the sum so expended. The mortgagor is under a duty to protect the security, but, should he fail to do so, the mortgagee has the right to make any reasonable expenditures necessary to protect the security for a debt.

8-32. Transfer of mortgaged property. The mortgagor may sell, will, or give away the mortgaged property, subject, however, to the rights of the mortgagee. A transferee from a mortgagor occupies the position of a grantee; he stands in the same position as the mortgagor and has no greater rights. Such grantee of the mortgagor's interest may redeem the land and require the mortgagee, if the latter is in possession, to account for rents and profits. A grantee of mortgaged property is not personally liable for the mortgage debt, unless he impliedly or expressly assumes and agrees to pay the mortgage. Such obligation must be established by clear and conclusive evidence.[4] If he merely purchases "subject to" the mortgage, he pays the mortgage debt only when he deems the real estate to have a value greater than the amount of the mortgage, and he is not personally liable on the obligation. If he assumes the mortgage, he becomes personally liable for the debt, although the land is worth less than the mortgage. For example, if *A* purchases real estate worth $8,000 which is subject to a mortgage of $5,000 and assumes and agrees to pay the mortgage, he pays the former owner $3,000 and assumes responsibility for the ultimate payment of the mortgage. If he merely purchases the real estate subject to the mortgage, he again pays the owner $3,000, but pays the $5,000 mortgage only if the land is worth that much when the mortgage matures. Otherwise, he permits the land to be foreclosed without any personal liability on his part for the deficit: whereas, if he had assumed the debt, he would have been liable for it.

8-33. Liability of mortgagor after transfer. If the grantee of the mortgaged property assumes and agrees to pay the indebtedness, he thereby becomes the person primarily liable for the debt; as between himself and the mortgagor, by virtue of his promise to the mortgagor to pay the debt, he is the principal debtor and the mortgagor is the surety.[5] This assumption by the grantee, however, does not relieve the mortgagor

[4] Perkins v. Brown et al., page 1080.
[5] Stalcup v. Easterly, page 1081.

of his obligation to the mortgagee, and such mortgagor continues liable unless he is released from his indebtedness by the mortgagee. Such a release must comply with all the requirements for a novation. In those states which recognize the relationship of principal and surety between the mortgagor and his grantee, an agreement made by the mortgagee with the grantee, to extend the time of payment, will release the mortgagor from liability. If the grantee takes "subject to" the mortgage, the original debtor is not released, since suretyship is not involved directly. Many states, however, release the mortgagor of responsibility for any loss resulting from a decline in value of the mortgaged property during the period of extension.

TRANSFER OF DEBT AND MORTGAGE

8-34. Transfer of debt. A debt that is secured by the mortgage is a chose in action, usually evidenced by notes or bonds. If the notes or bonds are nonnegotiable, the assignee of such notes or bonds takes title subject to all defenses that are available against the assignor. If, however, the notes or bonds are negotiable instruments and are transferred by negotiation as required under the Law of Negotiable Instruments, the holder takes free of personal defenses that would have been available against the transferror. The holder of the negotiable instrument secured by the mortgage has the right, upon default, to enforce the mortgage for the purpose of securing payment of the debt, as evidenced by the notes or bonds. If the mortgagee transfers the note without any formal transfer or mention of the mortgage, the transferee of the note is entitled to the benefit of the mortgage, because the security follows the debt. Since a debt secured by the mortgage is the principal and the mortgage only an incident, it would appear that an assignment of the mortgage without the debt is a nullity. Since a mortgage without a debt is difficult to comprehend, an assignment of the mortgage without the assignment of the debt accomplishes nothing. The debt cannot be assigned to one and the mortgage security to another.

If an assignment of the mortgage is made, the assignment should be recorded in order to give notice of the rights of the assignee to all subsequent purchasers. However, failure to record the assignment will not aid a purchaser or later mortgagee who has notice of the assignment. Actual notice should also be given to the mortgagor; otherwise, payment by the mortgagor to the mortgagee may discharge the mortgage.

8-35. Payment before default. Payment of the mortgage debt terminates the mortgage. Upon payment by the mortgagor a release or satisfaction is secured from the mortgagee, and this release should be recorded in order to clear the title to the land. Otherwise, the unreleased mortgage will remain a cloud on the title. If the mortgagee refuses voluntarily to give a release, he can be compelled to do so in a court of equity by a bill to remove a cloud on the title or by other proceeding provided for by statute.

A tender of the principal by the mortgagor before the due date does not terminate the lien evidenced by the mortgage, because the mortgagee cannot be forced to lose his investment before maturity. However, a tender of principal and interest upon the due day terminates the lien, although such a tender does not discharge the debt, and the mortgagee may still enforce it personally against the mortgagor until absolute payment has taken place. Under the common-law title theory, a tender on the due date satisfies the condition and reinvests the title in the mortgagor, but a tender after the due day does not have such an effect. The condition not having been performed, a reconveyance by the mortgagee is necessary. Thus, in the title theory states, a tender at maturity reinvests the title in the mortgagor, although in the lien theory states, a ender at or after maturity terminates the lien. The mortgagor's only remedy in title theory states is that of placing his money in court and bringing a suit in equity for redemption. Such tender does, however, forestall recovery for interest and court costs.

8-36. Right to redeem before foreclosure sale. At any time after default, but before sale of the land on foreclosure, a mortgagor may exercise his right to redeem from the mortgage or foreclosure sale, unless this right has been barred by a period of time specified by the statute. The mortgagor or any person who has an interest in the mortgaged land is entitled to redeem from the mortgage before foreclosure sale; but, in order to do so, he must pay the entire mortgage debt, with interest, and all other sums, including costs, to which the mortgagee may be entitled by reason of the mortgage. If the mortgagee is in possession of the mortgaged property and refuses to consent to a redemption, the mortgagor or any party entitled to redeem may file a bill in equity for the purpose of redeeming the mortgaged property. Such person, however, must be ready and willing to pay whatever the court finds due, or tender to the court all moneys due on said mortgage.

8-37. Right to redeem after the foreclosure sale. By statute in most states, any person interested in the premises, through or under the mortgagor, may, within a specified period of time from the foreclosure sale of said property, redeem the real estate so sold. To do so, he must pay to the purchaser thereof, to the sheriff or to the court officer who sold the property for the benefit of the purchaser, the sum of money, with interest and costs, for which the premises were sold or bid off. The period of time allowed for redemption varies greatly from state to state.

MORTGAGE FORECLOSURES

8-38. Right to foreclose. If the mortgagor fails to perform his obligation—that is, to pay the debt when it falls due or to perform any of the covenants set forth in the mortgage, such as the payment of principal by installment, of interest, insurance, or taxes—or if he defaults in other obligations, the mortgagee may declare the whole debt due and payable, and foreclose for the purpose of collecting the indebtedness.

8-39. Types of foreclosure. The statutes of the various states specify the procedure by which mortgages are foreclosed. There are four types of foreclosure proceedings for the purpose of using the mortgaged property to pay the mortgage debt; strict foreclosure, foreclosure by suit in equity, foreclosure by exercise of the power of sale, and foreclosure by entry and writ of entry.

8-40. Strict foreclosure. Strict foreclosure is one by which the mortgagee gets the land free from the right of redemption after the date specified in the foreclosure decree; that is, the decree provides that, if the debt is not paid by a certain date, the mortgagor loses the realty and the mortgagee takes it free from the rights of junior mortgagees and lienholders. This is a harsh rule and is used only where it is clear that the mortgaged property is not worth the mortgage indebtedness, the mortgagor is insolvent, and the mortgagee accepts the property in full satisfaction of the indebtedness.

Strict foreclosure as a remedy for the mortgagee-creditor is not only used under limited circumstances in mortgages, but may also be used as a remedy by the vendor in installment land sale contracts. In many contracts for the sale of land, the vendee is put in possession by making a down payment of part of the purchase price with the remainder to be paid in stated installments. The title is reserved by way of security by the vendor with a deed placed in escrow. The contract usually provides that all payments must be promptly made, otherwise the vendor may declare all payments due, terminate the contract, and cause the vendee to forfeit all previous payments and improvements as liquidated damages or as rent for the use of the property.

That such strict foreclosure might work a hardship on a purchaser is apparent. Since the relationship created is similar to that of mortgagee-mortgagor, the courts upon proper application will not permit the vendee to lose his equity of redemption and will order a foreclosure and sale of the land. Whether a land sale contract will be strictly foreclosed lies within the discretion of an equity court. If the vendee has made only a small payment, is guilty of gross laches, or has been negligent in the performance of his contract and it is not inequitable to place the vendor in his original position, strict foreclosure will be permitted. However, if the vendee has made only a slight default as to the amount and time of payment, or has largely completed his payments, and the amount of the unpaid purchase price is much less than the value of the property involved, strict foreclosure will be denied.

8-41. Foreclosure by suit in equity. The usual method of foreclosing a mortgage is a proceeding in equity, such proceeding being provided for by statute. A bill for foreclosure is filed in a court of equity; this bill sets up the mortgagee's rights, as provided for in the mortgage, and shows such breaches of the covenants in the mortgage as will give a right of foreclosure. The court will issue a certificate of sale authorizing the master in chancery or some other officer of the court to sell the land at public auction. Following the sale, he gives the purchaser a deed to the land and accounts for the funds realized as a result of the sale. To the extent that funds are available, they are used to pay court costs, the mortgage indebtedness, and inferior liens in the order of their priority. If any surplus remains, it is paid to the former owner of the property. Foreclosure by a second mortgagee is made subject to all superior liens. The buyer at the foreclosure sale takes title, and the first mortgage remains a lien on the property. All inferior liens are cut off by foreclosure except as the holders thereof have an equity in a surplus if such exists. As stated in § 8–36, the statutes in many states provide a short period of time after the sale within which the mortgagor or other persons in interest are entitled to redeem the property. Where such statutes are in force, the purchaser is not entitled to his deed until after the expiration of the period within which redemption may be made.

8-42. Foreclosure by exercise of power of sale. The mortgage often provides that, upon default by the mortgagor, the mortgagee may sell the land without judicial process. This method of foreclosure can only be made in strict conformity with the terms of the mortgage. The power of sale makes the mortgagee the agent of the mortgagor to sell the land. In some states, however, a power of sale in the mortgage is expressly forbidden by statute, and foreclosures must be effected by judicial proceeding. A power of sale granted in a mortgage or a deed of trust is not revocable, since the agency is coupled with an interest; therefore, the death or insanity of the mortgagor will not revoke the power. In those states where the exercise of power is regulated by statute, the sale must be public after the prescribed notice is given. In the absence of statute or mortgage agreement, however, the sale may be private. Since a mortgagee, in selling the land under a power of sale, is acting as an agent for the mortgagor, he is not allowed to purchase at the sale, because an agent cannot himself purchase that which he has been given authority by his principal to sell. The purchaser at such a sale secures only such title as the mortgagor had when he made the mortgage.

When a deed of trust, in which the trustee is empowered to sell the land and to apply the proceeds to the mortgage debt, is given to secure the payment of a debt, the same rules apply as are set forth above.

8-43. Foreclosure by entry and by writ of entry. In a very few states, the mortgagee may foreclose by entry upon the land, after default, after publication of notice and advertisement, and in the presence of witnesses; or by the possession of the premises for a period of time. If, after a limited period, the mortgagor does not redeem, the foreclosure is said to be completed and the title to rest in the mortgagee.

8-44. Deficiency decree. Since the mortgage debt is usually represented by a bond or a note, the mortgagor is personally liable for such debt, and the mortgagee may sue the mortgagor for it. If the land that is the security for the debt does not sell for a sum sufficient to pay the mortgage indebtedness, by statute in most states the court may enter a deficiency decree for that part of the unsatisfied debt. This decree will stand as a judgment against the mortgagor, and his other property may be levied on to satisfy such judgment. For example: *A*, the mortgagee, owns a mortgage which is security for an indebtedness of $10,000 against *B's* land. If, on foreclosure and sale of the land, the sum of only $7,000 is secured, *A* may obtain a deficiency judgment against *B* for $3,000, which will be a lien against any other property that *B* may own. Such other property may then be levied on and sold to satisfy the $3,000 deficiency judgment.

In order not to impose too great a hardship on mortgagor-debtors, different schemes have been devised to limit the amount of deficiency decrees.[6] A revaluation of the property at the time of the foreclosure is sometimes used if its value is less than the total debt, and this amount is deducted from the judgment. Many states have statutes limited to purchase money mortgages that provide in part that when a decree is granted for the foreclosure of any mortgage given to secure payment of the balance of the purchase price of real property, the decree shall provide for the sale of the real property covered by such mortgage for the satisfaction of the decree, but the mortgagee shall not be entitled to a deficiency judgment if the property sells for less than the amount due on the debt. The elimination of deficiency decrees rests on several theories: that the mortgagee loaned his money on the security of the land and not the personal credit of the purchaser-debtor; that a mortgagee-creditor should share with the debtor the risk of declining land value; and that if the land is the limit of the security, fewer inflationary and sounder loans will be made.

[6] Handy v. Rogers, page 1082.

REAL ESTATE MORTGAGE CASES

SIMPSON v. SIMPSON
1960, (Fla.) 123 So.2d 289

M. C. Simpson, a single man, executed and delivered a $10,000 demand note to his mother and as security for the note executed a mortgage on a house which he owned. The mortgage was recorded in 1953. No money had actually been loaned but the mother had agreed to make it available whenever Simpson requested it. In 1956, Simpson married the defendant and the home owned by Simpson was established as their homestead. On January 2, 1957, Simpson requested his mother to pay over to him the sum of $10,000 which she did. Simpson died in May, 1957. The plaintiff brought foreclosure proceedings and the lower court ruled that the mortgage was a valid claim against the homestead property.

ALLEN, Chief Judge. This apparently is a case of first impression in Florida.

The appellee insists that the mortgage was for future advances valid at the time the mortgage was recorded, which was prior to the marriage of the mortgagor.

The appellant contends that there was no lien on the property until after the $10,000 was paid over to the mortgagor at his request, which was subsequent to his marriage to the appellant. . . .

Courts and text writers have expressed a diversity of opinion on the question of the validity of mortgages to secure future advances, and as to the rights of mortgagees under such mortgages against subsequent purchasers and incumbrancers. Although formerly such mortgages were looked upon with disdain, their validity is now fully recognized and established. In the United States the weight of authority supports mortgages made in good faith for the purpose of securing future debts or future obligations as creating liens from the time the debts thereunder accrue except where local law prohibits. *Thompson on Real Property,* Vol. 9, section 4747 (1958 Replacement).

The cases are not harmonious, however, on the issues involving the necessity that the advance be obligatory, whether the mortgage itself must indicate the future advance or the extent thereof and priorities as respects third parties. The cases in Florida have not always consistently followed the same view. . . .

The novel or unusual intervening factor of the property acquiring homestead status prior to the advancement and the effect thereof appears to present a problem that has not been discussed by the courts of this state. . . .

. . . The rule that a mortgage, deed of trust, or purchase money or vendor's lien is not subject, or subordinate, to rights arising through the subsequent creation of a homestead has been applied in numerous cases which are collected and discussed in Annotation 123 A.L.R. 427.

In *Ashdown Hardware Co. v. Hughes,* 1954, 223 Ark. 541, 267 S.W. 2d 294, the court cited the various authorities previously discussed herein and held that a mortgage for future advances becomes an effective lien from the time of its execution and recordation rather than from the time when each advance is made, where the making of the advances is obligatory upon and not merely optional with the mortgagee notwithstanding the fact that intervening claims have been filed against the property.

The appellant at the time of her marriage to M. C. Simpson and their move to their home was confronted with a homestead having thereon a recorded mortgage of $10,000 with an obligation on the part of Ethel May Simpson to pay $10,000 to M. C. Simpson on demand, which she subsequently did, thus the consideration would relate back to the time of the recording of the mortgage and become a valid lien against the homestead.

The lower court was correct in his decree and is affirmed.

NEWPORT et al. v. CHANDLER
1944, 206 Ark. 974, 178 S.W.2d 240

KNOX, J. The primary question presented by this appeal is whether under the circumstances disclosed by the record a warranty deed and a contract permitting the grantors to reacquire title constituted a mortgage. The contract was signed by appellant W. E. Newport and the appellee, and provides that appellants "have agreed to sell and have sold to the party of the second part (appellee) and the party of the second part has agreed to purchase and has purchased the following described property, to-wit": (Property description omitted).

. . . The trial court found that under the circumstances the transaction constituted an absolute conveyance and not a mortgage to secure a debt.

. . . The general doctrine prevails in this state that the grantor may show that a deed absolute on its face was only intended to be a security for the payment of a debt and thus is a mortgage. Since the equity upon which the court acts arises from the real character of the transaction, any evidence, written or oral, tending to show this, is admissible. If there is a debt existing with a loan of money in advance and the conveyance was intended by the parties to secure its payment, equity will regard and treat an absolute deed as a mortgage. However, the presumption arises that the instrument is what it purports to be; and, to establish its character as a mortgage, the evidence must be clear, unequivocal, and convincing. By this is meant, that the evidence tending to show that the transaction was intended as a security for debt, and thus to be a mortgage, must be sufficient to satisfy every reasonable mind without hesitation.

However, every case must, of necessity, depend upon its peculiar circumstances. No fixed rule can be laid down by which it can be ascertained with mathematical certainty whether the proof has met the test above described.

. . . One test which may be applied in determining the nature of the transaction is whether there exists mutuality and reciprocity of rights between the parties. In other words, it may be helpful to determine whether the grantee has the right to compel the grantor to pay the consideration named in the stipulation for reconveyance. If he can compel such payment the transaction is generally regarded as a mortgage, while if he cannot compel such payment the transaction is generally regarded as a conditional sale. 36 Am. Jur. Mtg. § 167.

. . . After a careful review of the testimony we are unable to say that the finding of the Chancellor that the transaction was a sale, and not a mortgage to secure a debt, is contrary to the preponderance of the evidence, and such findings, while not conclusive, are persuasive, and the decree is therefore, affirmed.

KEHR v. BLOMENKAMP

1960, (Neb.) 106 N.W.2d 179

Blomenkamp on Feb. 16, 1955, executed a note for $15,000 to Kehr secured by a mortgage. On November 14, 1956, a mortgage on the same real estate was given to Melville Investment Co. and on Dec. 3, 1956, a mortgage on the same property was given to Universal Surety Co. On June 1, 1956, when the balance on the note was $8000, the defendant executed another note to the plaintiff in this amount. Plaintiff sought to foreclose and the other mortgagees resisted. The lower court rendered a foreclosure decree and ruled that plaintiff had a first lien, Melville had a second, and Universal (appellant) a third.

HEAGER, Justice. . . . The court adopted the theory of the plaintiff and in effect found and decreed that the mortgage given to the plaintiff by the defendants Blomenkamp on February 16, 1955, to secure the $15,000 note of even date thereof remained as security for the note for $8,000 given as of June 1, 1956, and as such was a first lien on the real estate. The further effect of the theory was that the note for $8,000 was a renewal note for the balance due on the other note, in consequence of which the obligation and security of the mortgage remained in full force and effect.

The appellant on the other hand contends that the note for $8,000 was a new obligation and transaction which was not secured by the mortgage.

The principles of law on which this question must be determined were stated early in the decisions of this state. There has been no departure from the early statements. In *Davis v. Thomas*, 66 Neb. 26, 92 N.W. 187, 189, it was said: "Nothing but payment or a formal release will discharge a mortgage. The existence of a lien securing the original loan furnishes a presumption that any renewal was not a discharge of the original, where the renewal is not secured."

This principle was approved in *Auld v. Walker*, 107 Neb. 676, 186 N.W. 1008, 1009. The following was also said in this case: "The taking of a new note for an existing note is a renewal of the old indebtedness, and not a payment of the debt, unless there is a specific agreement between the parties that the new note shall extinguish the original debt." . . .

By what was said in these cases it is clear that the specific agreement that a new note will extinguish the original debt must be one between the parties to the transaction.

In the record before this court there is no evidence either direct or circumstantial in proof of a specific agreement between the plaintiff and the defendants Blomenkamp that the note for $8,000 should or would extinguish the original debt. . . .

The decree of foreclosure and the allocation of priority of liens was correct. The mortgage of the appellant is by its terms subject to that of the plaintiff and of the Melville Investment Company. On its face and as a part thereof it is stated that it is "subject to prior mortgages of record." The other two are prior mortgages of record.

The judgment of the district court is affirmed.

PERKINS v. BROWN et al.
1934, 179 Wash. 597, 38 P.2d 253

STEINERT, J. This is an action to recover upon a promissory note and to foreclose a real estate mortgage given as security therefor. Plaintiff obtained a decree of foreclosure and also a money judgment against the makers of the note and the grantee of the mortgaged property for the full amount thereof, with interest and costs, plus the amount of taxes paid by the mortgagee. The grantee has appealed from the money judgment.

. . . When the present action was instituted, appellant here was made a party, on the theory that by the contract above referred to it had assumed to pay the Brown mortgage.

The trial court held that, as a matter of law, the Brown note, herein sued on, had been assumed by appellant, by virtue of the terms of its contract with the storage company, and that therefore appellant was liable for the deficiency remaining after the sale of the mortgaged property. The one question presented by this appeal relates to the liability of appellant for any deficiency so remaining.

The principal dispute between the parties is with reference to the construction to be given to the word "reimburse" used in paragraph 1 (a) of the contract. (". . . for which mortgage the purchaser herein agrees to reimburse the vendor. . . .")

. . . We now come to the vital phase of the case. When the contract is read in its entirety and in connection with the deed that accompanied it, it becomes apparent, we think, that the word "reimburse" has an equivocal implication. The word itself, considered alone, is rather broad in its signification. According to Funk and Wagnall's Standard Dictionary, it is defined as follows:

1. To pay back as an equivalent for what has been abstracted, expanded, or lost; refund; repay; as, to reimburse one's expenses;
2. To make return of an equivalent to; indemnify.

. . . The rule undoubtedly is that the obligation of a grantee to assume and pay a mortgage debt must be established by evidence that is clear and conclusive, and cannot be established by inference. (Cases cited.) While the obligation need not be expressed in any particular language, yet the expression upon which reliance is placed must unequivocally show that the grantee has undertaken to pay the debt. If the language used in a written instrument is susceptible of different interpretations, extraneous evidence may be resorted to in order to ascertain the intention of the parties. *People's Savings & Loan Ass'n v. Cram*, 172 Wash. 117, 19 P.2d 667.

We are of the view that the language of the deed and contract does not show a clear and unequivocal assumption by appellant of respondent's mortgage, and that the trial court was, therefore, in error in holding, as a matter of law, that it did.

Judgment reversed.

STALCUP v. EASTERLY
1960, (Okl.) 351 P.2d 735

Berry, Justice. Plaintiffs sold city property to defendants. As of date of sale the property was subject to an insured FHA and a GI loan. It was provided in the deed from plaintiffs to defendants, and in a contract entered into in connection with the sale, that defendants assumed and agreed to pay the referred-to loans. Defendants failed to timely satisfy the provisions of the loans and the mortgages securing the loans were foreclosed. The proceeds of the sale based upon judgment foreclosing the mortgages were insufficient to satisfy the loan obligations. . . .

Following payment of the deficiency, plaintiffs instituted this action to recover the amount thereof. Their action is based upon defendants' breach of the agreement to pay the loans. . . .

Following trial of case to the court, the court dismissed plaintiffs' action. . . .

It is stated in the first paragraph of the syllabus to *State ex rel. Com'rs of Land office v. Pitts*, 197 Okl. 644, 173 P.2d 923, 924, that "Where a mortgagor conveys mortgaged land to a grantee who assumes and agrees to pay the mortgage, the relationship between the grantee and grantor is that of principal and surety, the grantee becoming the principal obligor of the mortgage debt and the grantor his surety." . . .

In *Johnson v. Davis*, 146 Okl. 170, 293 P. 197, it is pointed out in the third paragraph of the syllabus that "Where a mortgage debt forms a part of the consideration for the purchase of land, the purchaser is bound to indemnify the mortgagor upon his payment of the debt." In the body of the opinion it is stated that "the defendant (grantee) was liable as on a contract on indemnity. Plaintiff's (grantor's) cause of action against defendant did not accrue to him until he had paid the deficiency judgment on the mortgage debt." . . .

Reversed and remanded for new trial.

HANDY v. ROGERS

1960, (Colo.) 351 P.2d 819

The plaintiff (Rogers) sold a hotel to the defendant (Handy) for $40,000 of which $34,000 was paid by a note secured by a deed of trust on the hotel. $6000 was paid in cash. The defendant entered into possession and made repairs in the amount of $4400. The operation of the hotel was not financially successful and the defendant abandoned the premises and employed a realtor to sell the property. The defendant ceased to make payments on the note and the plaintiff brought an action to recover on the note and to foreclose the deed of trust. The court entered judgment for the plaintiff in the amount of $40,519. Special execution issued and plaintiff purchased the property at a sheriff's sale on a bid of $1,000. The defendant contends that the plaintiff had fraudulently induced the sale by misrepresentation of the income received from the operation of the hotel. . . .

DOYLE, Justice. The court awarded damages to the plaintiff in the amount of $40,519. This figure . . . included the $34,000 owing on the note, $4,552.20 interest, $466.80 for insurance paid for by plaintiff, and $1,500 for attorney's fees. The court also ordered that the property which was secured by a deed of trust to the public trustee be sold at special execution by the sheriff of Teller County after thirty days' prior publication of notice of such sale and that the proceeds be applied first to the costs of the sale and then the balance to the judgment debt. A deed of trust may be foreclosed in court under our authority. *Neikirk v. Boulder Nat. Bank,* 53 Colo. 350, 127 P. 137. A supplemental record filed by the defendant indicates that the sheriff's sale was held and that the property was purchased by the plaintiff Emma Rogers for $1000. The outcome then is that the plaintiff now has the hotel, the improvements to which alone cost $4,400, the down payment of $6,000 and in addition has an unsatisfied judgment in excess of $40,000. That such a result may have been obtained through strict adherence to legal procedures does not mitigate its obvious harshness. The words of Mr. Justice Bradley in *Graffam v. Burgess,* 1886, 117 U.S. 180, 186, 6 S.Ct. 686, 689, 29 L.Ed. 839 are applicable here.

> It is insisted that the proceedings were all conducted according to the forms of law. Very likely. Some of the most atrocious frauds are committed in that way. Indeed, the greater the fraud intended, the more particular the parties to it often are to proceed according to the strictest forms of law.

It is the traditional duty of a court of equity to safeguard the interests of a mortgagor in the foreclosure of his equity of redemption. This power has been summarized by the Supreme Court in these words:

> In the absence of legislation, courts of equity have exercised jurisdiction in suits for the foreclosure of mortgages to fix the time and terms of sale and to refuse to confirm sales upon equitable grounds where they were found to be unfair or inadequacy of price was so gross as to shock the conscience.

Home Building & Loan Ass'n v. Blaisdell, 290 U.S. 398, 446, 54 S.Ct. 231, 243, 78 L.Ed. 413. . . . Similarly a court of equity possesses the power to examine an execution sale in the ordinary manner and to set aside an unconscionable sale. . . . The power to require confirmation of a foreclosure sale is inherent in a court of equity. 3 Jones, *Mortgages,* Sec. 2103. The requirement of confirmation constitutes an essential difference between a foreclosure sale and an execution in the ordinary manner. 1 Glenn, *Mortgages,* Sec. 92 at 557. The employment of the sheriff to carry out the foreclosure sale has been approved by decision of this Court, *Scott v. Burlington State Bank,* 76 Colo. 582, 233 P. 835.

When, however, the sale is carried out through the sheriff, a result such as that found in the present case is possible. Therefore, in the face of such possibility, it is incumbent on a court of equity to supervise the sale in a manner such as that required by Rule 120, Rules of Civil Procedure.

By proceeding as she did, plaintiff obtained a decree which neither referred to the statutory right of redemption, *Denver Brick and Manufacturing Co. v. McAllister,* 6 Colo. 261, nor reserved the right of confirmation of the sale. The results which followed indicate that the failure of the trial court to supervise the sale has resulted in serious prejudice. In fairness to the trial judge, it should be noted that the then attorney for defendant did not move to set aside the sale. As we view it, however, this fact should not operate to permit plaintiff to obtain a double recovery and thus transform a claim for compensation into a highly profitable transaction. Although plaintiff is entitled to be made whole, she does not have the right to use the courts for the purpose of furthering an unconscionable enterprise.

The effect of our holding here is not to establish an invariable rule for the conduct of foreclosure sales. We merely recognize and apply traditional equitable principles to a shocking and unconscionable condition. Where a result such as the present one occurs or is threatened the Court should remedy it or raise safeguards to prevent it.

The sale of the property in question is hereby set aside and the case remanded. Upon remand, the decree should be amended so as to require the appointment of appraisers in connection with the foreclosure sale. It should also require a return and report of sale and approval thereof by the trial court. If the trial court deems it necessary, a hearing should be had so that the court can be apprised concerning the actual value of the property. It goes without saying that the trial judge should disapprove any sale at a price which bears no relationship to the actual value of the property.

The judgment is affirmed in part and reversed in part and the cause remanded for further proceedings consistent with the views herein expressed.

Review Questions and Problems

1. *A* loaned money to *B* and gave a note secured by a mortgage. It was provided that the mortgage would also be security for future advances which *A* might make to *B*, but *A* was not obligated to make any further advances. If *A* loaned additional amounts to *B* would the security of the mortgage extend to such amounts?
2. *A* mortgages to *B* certain land that *A* now owns and certain land that he shall acquire later. The latter land is subsequently purchased, but is sold to *C*, who has no knowledge of the mortgage. Determine the rights of *B* and *C*.
3. In April *M* gave *P* a note secured by a mortgage on his house. *P* on October 14 delivered the mortgage to the county recorder of deeds. On October 18 a mechanic's lien was filed with the recorder for materials furnished by *X* for improvement of the house over a period beginning August 31. On August 20 *Y* filed a lien for drilling an outside well that was begun on June 23. Which party has priority of lien assuming each was ignorant of the other? What effect would *P*'s recording of the mortgage in April have had? When did the mortgage

become effective to prevent claims of other creditors becoming precedent to it?

4. *A*, desiring to borrow $15,000, gives *B* an absolute deed as security for a loan of this amount. *B* executes an agreement to reconvey the property upon the payment of the debt and interest three years later. Is this a sale or a mortgage?
5. *A* mortgaged his hotel to *B*. The mortgage contained a provision that *A* would replace the furniture in the hotel as it became necessary and that the mortgage would cover any furniture thereafter purchased. *A* purchased furniture and gave a chattel mortgage to *X*. As between *B* and *X* who has a better claim to the furniture?
6. *A* sells *B* property which has a $10,000 mortgage on it in favor of *C*. *B* purchases the property subject to the mortgage. The property declines in value and, at the maturity of the mortgage debt, is foreclosed and sells for $8,000. May *C* recover the deficit from *B*? May he recover from *A*, assuming that *A* is the mortgagor? Would the result differ if *B* had assumed the mortgage debt?
7. *A* loaned $25,000 to *B* and received a note secured by a mortgage on real property. Thereafter *A* learned that *B* had obtained title to the mortgaged property from the former owners by fraud. Should *A* be allowed to foreclose the mortgage upon failure to pay the installments on the note?
8. *M* gave a negotiable note to *P* secured by a mortgage. *P* transferred the note to *H* by indorsement, but there was no mention of the mortgage. Who may foreclose? If the note was overdue when *H* received it, may *M* assert an equitable defense in the foreclosure proceeding?
9. *A* mortgaged property to *B* as security for a note. Thereafter *B* transferred the note to *X* but did not specifically transfer the mortgage. Would *X* obtain the benefit of the mortgage?
10. *A* was the holder of a promissory note secured by a mortgage on real estate. The note was not paid and 21 years after its due date the mortgagee brought suit to foreclose the mortgage. Should he succeed?
11. *M* gave *P* a note secured by a mortgage on realty. The note was payable in monthly installments with an option given to the payee-mortgagee to accelerate the due date of the entire sum upon a 15 day default. *M* paid several installments, then defaulted as to the April 11 payment. *M* sent payment by mail the 29th. Can *P* on May 2 accelerate the due date of the entire obligation and foreclose?
12. *A* holds a first mortgage on land of $15,000 and *B* has a second mortgage of $6,000. *A* forecloses, and the land sells for $18,000. What are the rights of the parties?
13. *A* purchased a house from *B* in 1941 and executed a contract calling for a $700 down payment and the balance of $5,450 with interest to be paid at the rate of $42.50 per month. It was further provided that any default by *A* would give *B* the right to declare a forfeiture of *A*'s interest. The checks for the June and August 1946 payments were dishonored by the bank. *B* declared a forfeiture and *A* immediately tendered the amount of the checks. Should *A*'s interest be forfeited?

51

Landlord and Tenant

8-45. Relation created by lease. The relationship of landlord and tenant is created as a consequence of a lease, either express or implied, oral or written, and arises only when the tenant takes possession of the premises leased. No particular form of words is necessary to create the lease or the relation of landlord and tenant. The language used must be sufficient to indicate an intent to divest the landlord of possession and to vest possession in the tenant. The person giving up possession under the lease is called the landlord, or lessor, and the one coming into possession by virtue of the conveyance is called the tenant, or lessee. The instrument which creates the relation is called a lease. It need not be in writing unless the period of time is such that it comes under the Statute of Frauds. The landlord, or lessor, grants possession of land or tenements in return for rent or other income on the part of the tenant, or lessee.

The particular classes of tenancy are terms for years, tenancy at will, tenancy from year to year, and tenancy at sufferance.

TYPES OF TENANCY

8-46. Tenancy for years. A lease for years is a conveyance between the lessor and the lessee by which the lessor grants the possession and enjoyment of property for a definite period of time and by which the lessee agrees to pay rent in money or other consideration, at the end of stated periods, during the term of the lease. The period of time must be certain and definite, or no estate for years is created. A lease for a period of time, depending upon a contingency which is not certain to happen, is not definite. Except when regulated by statute, a lease may be made for any period of time the parties may agree upon: it may be made for 99 years, for 999 years, or for one day.

8-47. Termination of lease. A lease for years terminates at the expiration of the period. Such lease does not terminate at the death of the lessee before the expiration of the term. A leasehold estate is personal property and passes to the personal representative of the lessee upon his death, and his estate is liable, as in any other contract, on the covenants in the lease for the payment of rent. If the property leased consists of rooms or apartments in a building, the destruction of the building by fire or otherwise terminates the lease and the liability of the tenant to pay rent. This is an exception to the general rule that a tenant remains liable for the rent on the premises, irrespective of injury or destruction by fire or other casualties. Where the tenant leases the land as well as the building, destruction of the building does not destroy all the premises; whereas, in a lease of rooms or of an apartment, the whole of the premises leased is destroyed and the enjoyment of the premises contracted for becomes impossible, because nothing remains upon which the lease can operate. It is customary in the ordinary lease of property to insert a clause which effects a termination of the lease in case an important building is destroyed or materially damaged.

8-48. Rights of tenant after term. In the case of a tenancy for a term of years, the interest of the lessee ceases at the end of the period, the landlord being under no duty to give him notice. During the term, the tenant has a right to remove those movable fixtures which he has installed, and, if they are not moved before the expiration of the term, such fixtures become a part of the realty and the property of the landlord. If, during the term, the tenant has sown crops which mature after the term, the right to such crops passes to the landlord with the reversion.

8-49. Tenancy at will. Where the lease is for no definite period, but at the will of the lessor or lessee, it is said to be a tenancy at will. A tenancy at will may be either express or implied, and, if the landlord-owner permits a person to occupy his premises an indefinite period of time, a tenancy at will is said to be created by implication. Such a tenancy may be terminated at any time by either the lessor or the lessee, and the death of either terminates such tenancy. Under some jurisdictions, it is necessary to give reasonable notice of such termination;[1] whereas, under others, the landlord may terminate the tenancy at any time. Where the landlord terminates a tenancy at will, the tenant is entitled to the unmatured crops and may enter upon the property for the purpose of harvesting them at maturity.

8-50. Tenancy from period to period. When a tenant holds over after the termination of a lease for a definite period and remains in possession, and the landlord accepts rent, a tenancy from period to period is created. Also, if a lease is invalid for failure to comply with the Statute of Frauds and if entry has been made and rent paid, a tenancy from period to period arises if annual rental has been paid. If the original lease calls

[1] Covina Manor v. Hatch, page 1095.

for a monthly rental, rather than an annual rental, or if the period of the original lease was for one month, a holding over creates only a month-to-month tenancy. If the original lease called for an annual rental, the tenancy becomes one from year to year. The two leases differ in regard to the notice that is required to terminate them. At common law, a lease from year to year could be terminated by either party only if notice of the desire to terminate was given at least six months before the year expired. Failure on the part of the landlord to give such notice made it possible for the tenant to remain another year. A month-to-month tenancy was terminable by giving at least 30 days' notice before the close of the particular month in which it was to be terminated. The customary written notice now provided for in state statutes, is 60 days for a year-to-year tenancy and 30 days for a period-to-period lease of less than a year.

A tenant of farm land who holds it under a lease from year to year has the right to return and harvest those crops that have been planted prior to the time notice of termination is received. Leases from period to period, like leases for years, are not terminated by the death of the tenant or landlord.

A lease from period to period may also result from an agreement at the time of letting. If the contract provides for a periodical payment of rental without any fixed duration, a tenancy from period to period arises.

8-51. Tenancy at sufferance. Where a tenant holds over without right after the expiration of a definite period, the landlord may treat him as a tenant at sufferance. Likewise, a tenant at sufferance is created if the original entry by the tenant was wrongful and otherwise than by lease, and if such person continues in possession at the option of the landlord. If the owner accepts the payment of rent due after the expiration of a term, the acceptance is evidence of his intention to treat the party in possession as a tenant, and such act creates a new tenancy from month to month or for a period for which the rent was received.[2] A tenancy at sufferance may be terminated at any time by the landlord.

8-52. Difference between a lease and a license. A license is a mere privilege granted by one person to another to use his land for some particular purpose, without the licensor passing to the licensee any interest or estate in the land. A license merely gives one the privilege of coming on another's land without committing a trespass. It is personal, can be enjoyed only by the party to whom the privilege is given, and may be revoked at any time by the person granting the license. A license is not assignable, and even though given for consideration, it cannot be exercised by any person other than the licensee. A demise or lease, however, is more than a license, in that it carries a present interest or estate in land

[2] Wingert v. Prince, page 1096.

for a definite period, and gives the right to the possession of the land and the exclusive occupation and enjoyment of it for all purposes set out in the lease. The granting of permission to place advertising signs and billboards upon land or buildings is an illustration of a license.

RIGHTS AND DUTIES OF THE LANDLORD

8-53. Right of landlord to enter upon premises. The estate of the landlord during the term of the lease is called a *reversion*. The lessee is the absolute owner of the premises for the purposes for which the lease is created. The tenant is in possession of the premises and the landlord has no right to interfere with the lessee's enjoyment and use of the land, except as provided by the lease. In the absence of an agreement, the lessee has the sole and exclusive right to the occupancy and control of the premises and may prevent the landlord from entering upon the premises or interfering in any way with the lessee's possession.

Most leases provide, however, that the landlord may enter on the premises and place "to let" and "for rent" signs thereon. The landlord has the right to enter the premises to make a demand for rent. If the tenant abandons the premises, the landlord may enter for the purpose of taking care of them, without incurring any liability to the tenant as a trespasser. Care must be exercised in such cases to make it plain that the landlord is not consenting to the abandonment of the premises by the tenant. If the landlord accepts the surrender of the premises without protest, the lease is terminated by the mutual agreement of the parties, and the tenant is relieved of responsibility for loss in case the landlord is unable to find a new tenant.

8-54. Right to recover for injuries to the premises. The landlord may recover from a third party who impairs the value of his reversionary interest, that is, the estate after the expiration of the lease. For example, the destruction of the premises, or uses of the estate likely to ripen into easements—such as the laying of water pipes across the premises, removal of part of the property, or construction of party walls—give the landlord a cause of action. The landlord has no right to recover for injuries to growing crops, as such an injury is an injury to the possession rather than to the reversion. However, an injury to trees or to standing timber, or the removal of line fences, would be an injury to the reversion, for which the landlord may recover.

8-55. Warranty of landlord as to condition of premises. In general, there is no implied warranty that the premises are suitable for the use for which they are leased by the tenant. The duty of the lessee is to examine the premises for defects, and, if he neglects to do so, or if he fails to provide against such conditions in his lease, he takes the premises at his peril. The landlord is under a duty to notify the lessee of unhealthful conditions of the premises, which may arise from latent defects; failure of the landlord to do so constitutes fraud and gives a right to the tenant to abandon the premises.

8-56. Duties and liabilities of landlord as to repairs of premises. In the absence of an agreement, the landlord is under no obligation to repair the leased premises.[3] Nor is there any implied covenant to rebuild or to repair property damaged by fire or other causes. The lessee takes the premises as they are and cannot bind the landlord for repairs without the latter's consent. A promise to repair on the part of the landlord after the lease has been executed is without consideration and cannot be enforced. However, in some states, if the premises are defective, a promise to repair is binding if the tenant notifies the landlord that unless such repairs are made, he will vacate the premises. In a few states it is provided, by statute, that the landlord, in renting houses for habitation, shall keep them in repair fit for occupancy by human beings. Otherwise, the tenant may vacate after notice, without incurring liability for future rent. If a building is rented to two or more tenants, the landlord is obligated to keep in repair the portion of the building used in common by the various tenants. The roof, common hallways, and the foundation must be cared for by him.[4]

8-57. Recovery from the landlord for injuries occasioned by defects. In general, it may be said that the landlord is not liable to the tenant, his family, or guests for defects existing in the rented property. Since the landlord makes no warranty as to its condition, the tenant and his guests use the property at their peril. Even in those cases where the landlord is obligated by contract to repair or where common property is involved, the landlord's liability is generally based on carelessness. Unless he has been notified of the defect or has been negligent in failing to discover it, his failure to correct it will ordinarily result in no liability.

The owner of business property, knowing that business invitees of the lessee will be constantly entering it to transact business, has an increased responsibility. The determination of this increased responsibility is a question for the jury. Whether the landlord is liable for injuries sustained by business invitees and employees of the lessee as a result of defects existing at the time the lease was created, or arising, thereafter, is a fact question. The jury must determine whether the condition of the premises was so dangerous as to subject persons using them to an un-

[3] Hoover v. Wukasch et al., page 1097.
[4] Holzer Displays, Incorporated v. 383 Lafayette Corporation, page 1098.

reasonable risk or whether the persons using them had knowledge of the danger and did not exercise due care.[5]

A similar principle attaches to owners of property concerning passersby. An injury occasioned to a person passing by property, and which results from either original or use defects, must be compensated for by the landlord.

REMEDIES FOR RECOVERY OF RENT

8-58. Landlords lien. At common law a landlord has no lien upon the property of a tenant for unpaid rent. However, if the landlord is receiving part of the crop or produce of a farm as rent by usage, in some states he is given a lien on the crops. The landlord and the tenant may, by express provision in any lease, provide that the landlord be given a lien upon personal property of the tenant that is present upon the leased premises. In many jurisdictions statutes have been enacted expressly giving a landlord a lien for rent. Such statutes specify the property subject to the lien. The statutes of the various states should be examined to determine the nature and extent of the lien. In some cases a lease that gives the landlord a lien on the personal property of the tenant for rent is in the nature of a chattel mortgage, and to be effective, the lease must be recorded, in order to protect bona fide purchasers and creditors.

8-59. Suit on the lease. The landlord may recover for rent in an action at law where the lease contains an express covenant to pay rent. The usual procedure for the recovery of rent is called distress for rent.

8-60. Distress for rent. This is a common-law remedy by which the landlord may, by obtaining a distress warrant, seize the personal property of the tenant to force payment of rent. In some states, it has been abolished by statute, and in other states, it has been adopted or changed by statute. Where a tenancy from year to year is ended by the landlord's giving notice to quit and the tenant holds over, no action for distress will lie—the only remedy being damages for the holding-over. In order for the landlord to distrain for rent, the tenant must owe him a certain definite sum of rent, payable in money or produce or other services as in arrears. The tenant has all the day on which the rent falls due in which to make payment, and suit cannot be brought until the morning after the day the rent is due. All the personal chattels of the defendant, which are not perishable, are subject to be distrained for rent. Usually book accounts of merchants and implements of trades or professions cannot be taken on distress; they are also exempt under the statutes. If the rent is paid prior

[5] O'Neill v. Sherrill et al., page 1099.

to an authorized sale, it is the duty of the landlord to return the property in the same condition as it was when it was distrained.

8-61. Place of distraining. Only property that is on the premises can be distrained or taken for rent. If, however, the tenant fraudulently removes his property from the premises in order to avoid seizure, the landlord may follow and seize such property, provided it was removed by the tenant after the landlord had actually come to distrain. By statute, the landlord is permitted to follow property removed from the premises, and to levy distress after the termination of the tenancy; and in some jurisdictions he has the right to distrain the tenant's property, even though it has not been on the leased premises.

8-62. Procedure for distress. Under the statutes of some of the states, the landlord must make an affidavit setting forth his right to distrain and to secure a warrant to be levied by the proper court officers. The statutes provide for the time when notice of sale must be given both to the tenant and to the public, and, if the distress has been wrongfully made, a purchaser at such sale will acquire no title. The purchaser will be liable for damages for trespass.

RIGHTS AND LIABILITIES OF THE TENANT

8-63. Estoppel to deny landlord's title. A tenant, by virtue of his possession, is estopped from denying his landlord's title. The actual possession of the premises gives an advantage to the lessee, and, by reason of this advantage, he has no right to question the title of the lessor. The lessee must surrender his possession before he may assert whatever title he has. He is then at liberty to recover the land if he can prove his right. Neither can the lessee claim title to the premises by reason of defects in the lease or by admissions on the part of the lessor.

8-64. Duty of lessee to redeliver at expiration of term. There is an implied covenant in every lease that the lessee will redeliver the premises to the lessor at the end of the term, and, if the lessee wrongfully withholds possession, the lessor may sue and recover damages. The lessee is also under duty, at the expiration of the lease, to remove his personal property and to return the premises in the same condition as they were when he received them at the beginning of the term. This provision does not bind the lessee, however, to make payment for ordinary wear and tear from reasonable use of the premises or for actual destruction beyond his control.

8-65. Duty of tenant as to care and repair of premises. In the absence of any agreement, the tenant is under duty to keep the premises in repair, such as replacing doors and broken windows, repairing fences, and making ordinary repairs that are not permanent in nature but are necessary to keep the premises from deteriorating and unduly depreciating. The tenant usually is under no obligation to make substantial and lasting repairs, such as putting on new roofs, rebuilding walls, and other permanent improvements. The landlord and tenant may make agreements as to the nature and character of repairs during the term; but, in the absence of such agreement, there is no implied liability on the part of the tenant to make such lasting repairs or to make repairs that were needed at the time he entered.

8-66. Improvements by lessee in the absence of an agreement. There is no implied covenant on the part of the lessor to pay the lessee for improvements placed on the premises during the term of the lease, although such improvements become part of the real estate and, upon the expiration of the term, revert to the lessor. If, however, the lessee makes improvements upon the land and wrongfully is denied the use and benefit of them by the landlord, he is entitled to recover for the reasonable value of such improvements. In general, such improvements are usually for the benefit of the lessee, and under such circumstances, he is not entitled to recover from the lessor for improvements made by him during the term. Neither can the lessee, upon the expiration of the term, remove permanent improvements, placed by him upon the premises, which have become a part of the realty.

8-67. Duty to pay rent. Where one party has the use, enjoyment, and possession of another's land, the law will imply an agreement on the part of such person to pay a reasonable rent for the premises, in the absence of an agreement to the contrary. In order to raise an implied promise to pay rent, it is necessary to show that the relation of landlord and tenant exists. Rent may be payable either in money or any other consideration agreed upon between the parties. The right to collect rent is a chose in action and may be assigned by the landlord, separate and distinct from his reversionary interest in the premises. In the absence of an agreement, the duty to pay rent arises at the end of a period, rather than at the beginning.

8-68. Defenses to liability for rent. A tenant may have a right to set up counterclaims against any action on the part of the landlord to recover rent, if the landlord has violated any of the covenants in the lease. That is, if the lessor has interfered with the possession of the lessee to the damage of the latter, the tenant may set off such damage against rent due. If the landlord has evicted the tenant of the whole of the premises, the tenant will be relieved of his duty of paying further rents. Eviction may be actual or constructive.[6] If the landlord, through failure to per-

[6] Gillingham v. Goldstone, page 1100.

form substantially the terms of his lease, causes the premises to become untenable, so that the tenant is forced to give up possession, the latter is said to be constructively evicted. If the tenant remains in possession of the premises, however, he waives his defense of constructive eviction and is bound for the payment of the rent. Where the landlord is under duty to furnish heat and fails to do so and the premises become uninhabitable, the tenant may surrender possession and escape liability for future rents.

ASSIGNMENT AND SUB-LEASE DISTINGUISHED

8-69. An assignment. An assignment of a leasehold by a lessee-assignor is a transfer of all the unexpired interest held by the lessee at the time of the assignment.[7] The assignee acquires the leased premises, whether he takes possession or not, on the same terms as those expressed in the head lease. By the assignment the lessee-assignor divests himself of privity of estate with the lessor, but does not divest himself of privity of contract. The assignment places the lessee in privity of estate with the lessor, entitles him to benefits of the lease, and subjects him to the burdens which run with the land. An assignee of a lease may bind himself to the landlord and the lessee-assignor, expressly or by implication, to perform the covenants in the lease.

Whether the transfer creates an assignment or sub-lease is not always clearly defined. Thus, if the landlord is seeking to enforce the covenants in the head lease against the person in possession, the courts often find an assignment has been made instead of a sub-lease. However, if the lessee is seeking to recover from his transferee, the situation may be a sub-lease.

In the absence of statutory restrictions and restrictive covenants prohibiting an assignment of a lease for a definite term, a tenant has a right to assign his interest, without the consent of the landlord. In order to prevent restraints on alienation and hardship, covenants forbidding assignments are strictly construed. In order to avoid the forfeiture of the lease because of the assignment of the lease by the lessee in violation of the restrictive covenant, the courts will often construe the transfer as granting a temporary interest, mortgaging the term, or executing a sub-lease. Such conduct is not in violation of the restrictive covenant.

8-70. The sub-lease. There are generally enumerated several important differences between the assignment of a lease and the subletting of the property. As stated above in § 69 by an assignment, the

[7] Baehr v. Penn-O-Tex Oil Corporation, page 1101.

lessee transfers his entire estate to the assignee. However, when a tenant-lessee sublets, he transfers to the sub-lessee only a part of his interest. By an assignment, the assignee is in privity of estate with the lessor under the same terms of the head lease and may become liable to the lessor for the performance of the lessee's covenants that run with the leasehold. A sub-lessee, however, is not in privity of estate with the original lessor, is not under the terms of the head lease, and is not entitled to its benefits or subject to its burdens.

In a sub-lease it is said there always remains some reversionary or other interest in the lessee. This interest remaining in the lessee makes the relation between the lessee and sub-lessee like that of landlord and tenant. The lease grants to the sub-lessee a part out of the estate held by the lessee under the head lease. The interest or part retained by the lessee may be a portion of time, that is, three years out of ten; a right to surrender or terminate the main lease; or a particular segment of the premises. A sub-lease creates a new estate taken out of the original head lease. The original estate out of which another estate may be created is necessarily for a term.

As in assignment of leases, a tenant may sublet without consent of the lessor, unless there are restrictive covenants to the contrary. These covenants, however, are strictly construed against the lessor. Since the restrictions are for the benefit of the landlord, he may waive such restrictions or by conduct be estopped to enforce them.

LANDLORD AND TENANT CASES

COVINA MANOR v. HATCH

1955, 133 Cal. App.2d 790, 284 P.2d 580

An action by Covina Manor in unlawful detainer to recover from Hatch possession of a dwelling house and damages to the premises. Judgment was given to the plaintiff for restitution and damages in the sum of $1,470, from which the defendant appeals.

Defendant Hatch was an employee of the plaintiff. As such employee he was granted oral permission to move into the premises in question. There was no agreement concerning rent, it appearing that his right to occupy the dwelling was to continue as long as he was in the plaintiff's employment.

When defendant's employment terminated, plaintiff demanded possession, or $200 per month rent. Defendant Hatch remained in possession, alleging as one element of defense that he was a tenant at will and entitled under statute to three days written notice before vacation.

PATROSSO, J. . . . "A tenancy at will is an estate which simply confers a right to the possession of premises leased for such indefinite period as both parties shall determine such possession shall continue. . . . The tenant at will is in possession by right with the consent of the landlord either express or implied, and he does not begin to hold unlawfully until the termination of his tenancy. His estate is a leasehold and he holds in subordination to the title of the landlord." 51 C.J.S. Landlord and Tenant, § 156, p. 762. And "a permissive occupation of real estate, where no rent is reserved or paid and no time agreed on to limit the occupation, is a tenancy at will." 51 C.J.S. Landlord and Tenant, § 159, p. 766. See also *Jones v. Shay*, 1875, 50 Cal. 508; *Hayden v. Collins*, 1905, 1 Cal. App. 259, 265, 81 P. 1120. It is equally well settled that "one who enters upon land by permission of the owner under a void parol contract, or under a void lease, or pending unexecuted negotiations for a written lease, is a tenant at will." (Cases cited.)

Thus, under the authorities cited, whether we accept the testimony adduced upon behalf of plaintiff to the effect that defendants were granted oral permission to occupy the premises without specification as to time and absent any agreement for the payment of rent, or whether we accept defendants' version that they entered into possession of the property under a verbal agreement—invalid under the statute of frauds—that the property was to be conveyed to them in consideration of services rendered or to be rendered by defendants, the status of defendants was that of tenants at will. . . . The plaintiff is not entitled in this action to damages for detaining the property unless is proves that it is entitled to possession. The action of unlawful detainer is a statutory proceeding and is governed solely by statute creating it. . . .

Judgment reversed.

WINGERT v. PRINCE
1960, (Fla.) 123 So.2d 277

In 1949, Prince leased land from Wingert for one year with the right to renew for another year. It was provided that Prince would erect a frame structure at his expense and that he could remove the same at any time or at the termination of the contract. After the term of the lease expired, Prince remained in possession, paying rent on a month to month basis. On May 8, 1959, the State Road Department filed condemnation proceedings against the land. The proceedings resulted in a judgment for $81,000. Prince brought this action claiming a right to a part of this sum as it included compensation for his buildings. The lower court granted him $2,993.68 and Wingert appealed.

Germany, John, Associate Judge. The Princes remained in possession after June, 1951, the term provided for in the written lease, paying rent from month to month to and including June, 1959. The trial judge construed this to be a tenancy from month to month while the attorneys for the appellant and appellees are both agreed that the Princes were tenants at sufferance. As no award was made for any leasehold interest, it becomes moot for this court to determine the question of tenancy.

. . . It is the contention of the appellant that the appellees were not entitled to any compensation for the value of the improvements on the premises. It is the further contention of the appellant that while the appellees may have had the right to remove the buildings and equipment "at any time or at the termination of their contract," such right terminated when the lease expired in June of 1951. The general rule seems to be that the tenancy arising from the tenants holding over with the consent of the landlord is presumed to be upon the same covenants and terms as the original lease so far as they are applicable to the new tenancy. See 32 Am. Jur., Landlord and Tenants, Section 948; see also *Rosamond v. Mann,* Fla. 1955, 80, So.2d 317, 318, 49 A.L.R.2d 476.

Statute providing that a holdover tenancy after written lease but without a written renewal shall be a tenancy at sufferance, but if such holding over be continued with written consent of lessor then tenancy is a tenancy at will, does not release either landlord or tenants from implied obligation that holding over is subject to all covenants and terms of original lease applicable to new situation.

The decree of the lower court is affirmed.

HOOVER v. WUKASCH et al.

1955, (Tex. Civ. App.), 274 S.W.2d 458

Archer, C. J. . . . The suit was instituted by the appellee as landlord against appellant as tenant for the recovery of rents accruing on a rental covenant contained in a contract to lease.

. . . The appellant seeks an avoidance from further performance of the rent covenant because of an alleged failure by appellee to perform an alleged covenant to repair the roof on the premises, which omission appellant asserts rendered the premises untenantable and alternatively that he should at least be entitled to an "offset or credit," because of the leaky condition of the roof.

These affirmative contentions of the tenant presented a law question of whether the contract contained a landlord's covenant to repair the roof.

. . . The trial court had a hearing on the motion for Summary Judgment and concluded that in view of the admitted fact that the landlord was never given any written notice of necessity for repairs to the roof, that the tenant did not have any legal excuse for his failure to fully perform his rent covenant, and rendered judgment for the amount both parties agreed should be paid if the trial court's judgment on such law question was correct.

We believe that the trial court was justified in granting the motion and in rendering the judgment that was entered, as there were no genuine disputed issues of fact.

A tenant takes rented premises as he finds them and there is no obligation upon the landlord to keep any part of them in repair unless expressly so covenanted, and any omission to repair will not excuse the tenant from performance of his rent covenant. 27 Tex. Jur., 250, § 141; 33 Am. Jur. 521, § 657; *Japhet v. Polemanakos,* Tex. Civ. App., 160 S.W. 416, er. dism.; 27 Tex. Jur. 253, § 143.

Paragraph 8 of the rental contract is as follows:

> Lessors shall not be liable for any damage that may result to any property of lessee or his tenants on account of failure to make repairs to the roof of said property until lessors shall have been given written notice of the necessity for such repairs and shall have had a reasonable time after receipt of such notice within which to make such repairs.

It is apparent that the parties covenanted that there would be no duty on the landlord to repair the roof until the tenant gave the written notice of the necessity for such repairs. (Cases cited.)

Judgment of the trial court affirmed.

HOLZER DISPLAYS INCORPORATED v. 383 LAFAYETTE CORPORATION
1960, 200 N.Y.S.2d 467

EDGAR J. NATHAN, JR., Justice. This motion by plaintiff-tenant for summary judgment in an action against the owner of the premises for property damage allegedly resulting from water leakage. It has been established that the damage was caused by a blockage of the drain on the roof which resulted from collection of waste material discharged from hoppers maintained on the roof by another tenant. It appears that the water, accumulated because of the blocked drain, seeped down from the roof to a floor occupied by the defendant and from there to plaintiff's floor. It has also been established that defendant had actual knowledge of this situation for about two weeks prior to the incident herein alleged and had written letters to the tenant responsible requesting them to take steps necessary to remove the cause of the condition. It also appears that landlord frequently over a considerable period of time had advised the tenant owning the hopper that escaping material fell on the roof and blocked the drain. It is settled law that defendant having retained control of the roof had the duty to maintain it in a reasonably safe condition (*Loucks v. Dolan*, 211 N.Y. 237, 105 N.E. 411). Therefore, absent any showing of contributory negligence, no matter how the blockage occurred, an owner of premises who fails to repair after ample notice of a defect must be held to be negligent (*Kuperschmid v. Tauszig*, 124 Misc. 548, 208 N.Y.S. 464). Defendant here does not deny knowledge of the defective situation. It merely contends that by notifying the offender it did all that was necessary under the circumstances. This as a matter of law was insufficient. The owner had the primary responsibility to repair. . . .

Motion for summary judgment is granted.

O'NEILL v. SHERRILL et al.

1953, (Mo. App.) 254 S.W.2d 263

ANDERSON, J. This is an action for damages for personal injuries alleged to have been sustained by plaintiff when she fell on the premises of defendants [landlord] located at the southwest corner of Maryland and Euclid Avenues in the City of St. Louis. The trial below resulted in a verdict and judgment for plaintiff in the sum of $3,600. From the judgment, defendants have appealed.

. . . Plaintiff was directed by her employer [lessee] to enter and leave the store by the rear door which led into the courtyard in question; and, in gaining access to the courtyard from the alley, it was necessary for plaintiff to enter the courtyard through the opening above mentioned.

Immediately to the north of the entrance way through the concrete wall, at the place one would step upon, in stepping down from the alley to the courtyard, there was a rough, broken place in the surface of the concrete paving. The upper edge of the step was also badly cracked and broken.

. . . In the case at bar, there was a rough, jagged and depressed area at the bottom of a twelve inch step-down from the alley. The condition was such that one attempting to step over it, as plaintiff tried to do in this case, could, without fault, suffer a loss of balance and fail to execute the step as intended. We believe that it was for the jury to say whether the condition was so dangerous as to subject persons using the entry to an unreasonable risk.

. . . An owner or possessor of land may not be held liable to his licensees, whether business visitors or gratuitous licensees, for bodily injuries sustained by them and caused by a dangerous condition of the premises, if said injured person knew of the condition and realized the risk involved. The right of such person to enter the land is derived solely from the possessor's consent, which he is free to give or withhold at will. Therefore, the one entering the land under such invitation is entitled to nothing more than knowledge of the dangerous condition which he may encounter, so that he may exercise an intelligent choice as to whether the advantage to be gained from accepting the invitation is sufficient to justify the risk which he knows is inseparable from it. Knowledge on the part of the invitee dispenses with the duty to warn, and where the evidence shows such knowledge, no breach of duty is shown; hence there is no actionable negligence.

This rule, however does not apply where the relation of landlord and tenant obtains. (Cases cited.) In such cases, the required standard of care to be exercised by the landlord toward a tenant, and those standing in his right, though defined as the exercise of ordinary care, affords greater protection in that actionable negligence may exist even though the injured party may be aware of the defect and its dangerous potentialities. This solicitude on the part of the courts in the interest of the tenant, and those on the premises in his right, springs from the nature of the relationship involved and the necessities of the case. In the balancing of convenience, it is thought undesirable to compel a tenant to abandon the use of that portion of the premises under the landlord's control which contains a dangerous defect, provided that in using it due care is exercised. The tenant has paid for the use of it and, under the decisions, he and his invitees may use it unless the defect is of such a dangerous character that no reasonable person in the exercise of due care would use it. *Roman v. King*, 289 Mo. 641, 233 S.W. 161, 25 A.L.R. 1263; Restatement of the Law of Torts, Vol. 2, § 360.

Judgment affirmed.

GILLINGHAM v. GOLDSTONE
1959, 197 N.Y.S.2d 237

ARTHUR WACHTEL, Justice. Plaintiffs sue the defendants for return of security in the amount of $200 which had been given to the defendants at the time the parties entered into a lease on December 5th, 1958. The lease provided that the security would be forfeited if the tenant vacated "before one year." The tenants vacated on or about June 28th, 1959.

The tenants contended that there was an actual eviction on June 28th, 1959, and that the defendants breached the implied covenant of quiet enjoyment. The contention of actual eviction was not sustained. However, in the Court's opinion the preponderance of all the credible evidence supports a finding of constructive eviction, on the authority of *Onward Construction Company v. Harris*, Sup., Appellate Term, 1st Dept., 144 N.Y.S. 318 and *Purcell v. Leon*, Appellate Term, 1st Dept., 83 Misc. 5, 144 N.Y.S. 348.

The Appellate Term, 1st Dept. has recognized that "The tenants should be protected from insult." Page J, *Manhattan Leasing Company v. Schleicher,* Sup., Appellate Term, 1st Dept. 1913, 142, N.Y.S. 545, at page 546. Where the landlord's conduct is "so grossly insulting and threatening in character as to seriously and substantially deprive the defendant of the beneficial enjoyment of the premises demised," and as a result, the tenant is forced to vacate the premises, there may be a constructive eviction and a breach of the covenant of quiet enjoyment (cf. Seabury, J., *Onward Construction Co. v. Harris, supra,* 144 N.Y.S. 2d at page 318). Whether or not there are sufficient facts to support a constructive eviction is a matter to be determined upon the circumstances of each case.

Upon termination of the lease by constructive eviction, the tenant need not await the expiration date of the lease to recover the deposit. *One Hundred and Forty-Two West Fifty-Seventh Street Company v. Trowbridge,* Appellate Term, 1st Dept. 88 Misc. 70, 150 N.Y.S. 538.

Accordingly, judgment for the plaintiffs $200 with interest from June 28, 1959.

BAEHR v. PENN-O-TEX OIL CORPORATION

1960, (Minn.) 104 N.W.2d 661

The plaintiff, Penn-O-Tex Oil Corporation, leased certain gasoline filling stations to one Kemp under written leases. Kemp was purchasing a business known as Webb Oil Company from the defendant, Baehr. Kemp became unable to meet payments due to defendant and on December 10, 1955, gave defendant an assignment of accounts receivable and to become receivable, including rentals from the service stations which Kemp had sub-let to various operators. Thereafter the defendant collected rents paid by the operators of the filling stations and installed its agent in the Webb Oil Company's office to run the business. No rent was paid to the plaintiff during the period December 1, 1955 thru June 2, 1956. This action was instituted to recover rent for that period. The lower court ruled in favor of the defendant.

LOEVINGER, Justice. . . . Plaintiff contends that defendant is liable for the rents pursuant to M.S.A. § 504.04 relating to the liability for rent of persons in possession of land. . . .

Apart from statute, the assignee of a leasehold in possession of leased premises is liable for the rent. There is a rebuttable presumption that one in possession of leased premises is there as an assignee of the lessee. Even without a formal assignment, one in possession may be an equitable assignee and subject to the covenants and obligations of the lease. An assignment occurs where, and only where, a lessee transfers his entire interest, without regard to the form of the transaction. However, the liability of an assignee arises by privity of estate, rather than privity of contract, and thus may be terminated by further assignment.

"Possession" is a chameleon-like term which takes its meaning from its context both in common speech and in legal terminology. The term is used interchangeably to denote the legal concepts of "actual possession" and "constructive possession." With reference to land, the legal concept of "actual possession" is substantially the same as "actual occupancy," which means physical presence upon and control of premises. "Constructive possession" is more difficult to define. It is usually said to mean the legal right to possession which follows from title without actual possession.

In any event, it is unnecessary in this case to attempt further refinement of these definitions. The mere assignment, as security for a debt, of the right to receive rents from a sublessee is not sufficient under the authorities to amount either to an assignment of the lease or to possession of the leased premises. The fact that defendant installed its agent in lessee's office to receive sums due lessee and assigned to defendant does not render defendant liable to pay lessee's rents to plaintiff. . . .

Affirmed.

Review Questions and Problems

1. *A*, an invalid, owned 100 acres. He permitted *B* to farm the land for a period of several years, in return for a yearly sum and the care for *A*. *B* provided seed, equipment, and all labor. There was no written agreement. What is the relation between *A* and *B*? If *B* mortgaged one year's crop after it was growing would *A* have a lien prior to that of the mortgagee? If *A* dies in the summer, may his heirs evict *B* and require him to release the year's crop?
2. *A* is a tenant at will on *B*'s farm. *B* terminates the tenancy after *A* has planted certain crops. May *A* return and harvest the crops? Suppose the lease had been for a definite period? Suppose it had been a tenancy at sufferance?
3. *A* was negotiating with *B* for the lease of premises owned by *B*. During the negotiations *A* moved into the premises. What is *A*'s status?
4. *A* leased premises to *B* and gave permission to *B* to sublet. *B* sublet to *C* who destroyed the building by fire. Can *A* recover the value of the building from *B*?
5. *A* leased to *B* certain premises for dwelling purposes. Unknown to *B*, there was a buried cesspool under the basement. The pool was not properly covered and the house became uninhabitable. Had *B* a right to terminate the lease?
6. During the period of a lease the ceiling in the leased premises required repair. The tenant contended that the obligation to repair rested with the landlord. Is he correct?
7. *L* claimed to own land upon which *T* entered with *L*'s permission, paying $45.00 monthly to *L*. If *L* does not own the land, may *T* defend on this ground if *L* seeks to evict *T*?

8. *O* leased certain business property to *T* for ten years at an annual rental of $18,000, payable in monthly installments of $1,500. At the end of three years *T* assigned the lease to *A*, who remained in possession for only two of the remaining seven years. Is *A* liable in damages to either *O* or *T*? Is *T* liable to *O*, assuming *O* assented to the assignment?
9. *O* leased property to *T* for one year at $1,500 a year, payable in monthly installments of $125 a month. After the termination of the lease, *T* remained in possession for twenty-three months and paid $125 a month to *O*. On the closing day of the twenty-third month, *O* gave *T* notice to vacate the property. What are the rights, if any, of *T*?
10. *L*, owner of certain land, leased it to *T* for seven years with a provision that at the expiration of the period "Lessor reserves the right to sell, lessee shall have first option to buy; but if lessor elects not to sell lessee is granted the privilege of renewing this lease." At expiration *L* offered to sell to *T* for $36,000 but the market value was only $9,000 which *T* offered to pay. There were no offers by others. If *L* won't sell for $9,000, what may *T* do?
11. *W* delivered furs to *A* for treatment. *A* was the tenant of *B* and had leased only a part of the building for his business. *W*'s furs were damaged as a result of the leaky roof in the building. Is *B* liable in damages to *W*?

52

Mechanics' Lien Laws

8-71. Nature. Mechanics' lien laws are the result of legislation that makes possible liens upon real estate where such real estate has been improved. The purpose of such legislation is to protect the laborer and materialman in the event of the insolvency of the owner or the contractor. The laws of the states vary slightly in the protection accorded and the procedure required to obtain it. For these reasons, the laws of the individual state should be consulted in a particular instance. The sections which follow relate to provisions which are generally found in the various state laws.

8-72. Persons entitled to lien. Those persons are entitled to a lien, who, by either express or implied contract with the owner of real property, agree: (1) to deliver material, fixtures, apparatus, machinery, forms, or form work to be used in repairing, altering, or constructing a building upon the premises; (2) to fill, sod, or do landscape work in connection with the same; (3) to act as architect, engineer, or superintendent during the construction of a building; or (4) to furnish labor for repairing, altering, or constructing a building.

Those parties who contract with the owner, whether they furnish labor or material, or agree to construct the building, are known as contractors. Thus, practically any contract between the owner and another that has for its purpose the improvement of real estate gives rise to a lien on the premises in favor of those responsible for the improvement. To illustrate: a contract to attach a permanent fixture to a building or one to beautify a lawn would create a lien in favor of the contractor.

In addition to contractors, anyone who furnishes labor, materials, or apparatus to contractors, or anyone to whom a distinct part of the contract has been sublet, has a right to a lien. These parties are customarily referred to as subcontractors. Their rights differ slightly from those of contractors, and some of these differences will be considered in later sections.

In order that a lien for materials may be maintained, the material must be furnished to the contractor or subcontractor.[1] In addition, a record of the material furnished on each job is usually required. This procedure is necessary for two reasons: first, the record is essential to accuracy in the determination of the amount of the lien; and, second, it is evidence that the contractor is not his own materialman. If the material is sold on the general credit of the contractor and no record of the deliveries is kept, title passes to the contractor, and he becomes his own materialman so that the original materialman is not entitled to the lien.[2]

The lien of a party furnishing building material arises as soon as the material is delivered to the premises. On the other hand, one who supplies equipment or machinery receives a lien only if he can show that the goods delivered have become a part of the completed structure.

8-73. Against whom does the lien arise. Any interest in real estate may be subjected to a lien. A fee simple, a life estate, or a lease for years may have a lien against it, depending on the nature of the contract. If the owner of the fee simple contracts for the construction, or authorizes or knowingly permits the improvement to be made, the lien is good against his interest as well as against the improvement. If a lessee, without the consent or knowledge of the owner, contracts for the construction or improvement of property, the lien arises only upon the interest of the lessee.[3] To illustrate: *A* leases a vacant lot from *B*, with the understanding that *A* is to construct a building on the premises. Any lien created will affect the interests of both *A* and *B*. If *A* had not obtained *B*'s consent to erect the building, the lien would have been created only against the interest of *A*.

The improvement of real property should not give to the lien holder a right to disturb or destroy a prior mortgage. At the same time, there is no occasion to increase the protection of the mortgagee at the expense of the lien holder. Consequently, an existing mortgage is always given a superior lien on the value of the property in its unimproved state. In many states, however, if the improvement, or its value, can be segregated, the mechanic's lien will be superior on the improvement. Where separation is not feasible, a method of appraisal is usually provided for, to determine what portion of the proceeds, at time of sale, are derived from the improvement.

8-74. Formalities required to perpetuate lien. Under the law of most states the contractor's lien arises as soon as the contract is entered into. In order to protect the contractor against claims of innocent third parties who might purchase the property or obtain a mortgage thereon, the law provides that the lien must be made a matter of record within a certain

[1] Dealers Supply Co. v. First Christian Church, page **1107**.
[2] Finney v. Story, page **1108**.
[3] Murray v. Zemon, page **1109**.

time, usually three to four months after all work is completed. Failure on the part of the materialman to register his claim as required by the statute will result in the loss of the lien as against subsequent bona fide purchasers or encumbrancers.[4] As between the owner and the contractor, however, the time limit may be extended somewhat beyond this period. During the four months' period, the lien is good against innocent third parties even though it is not recorded.

To establish their liens, the subcontractors—materialmen, laborers, and others—must, within a relatively short period of time after they have furnished the last of their materials or labor, either make the liens a matter of record, or serve written notice thereof on the owner, according to the particular state statute. The period most frequently mentioned by the various states is 60 days.

8-75. Protection accorded the owner. The mechanics' lien law usually states that the owner shall not be liable for more than the contract price, provided he follows certain procedure outlined in the law. The law further provides that it shall be the duty of the owner, before making any payments to the contractor, to obtain from the latter a sworn statement setting forth all the creditors and the amounts due, or to become due, to them. It is then the duty of the owner to retain sufficient funds at all times to pay the amounts indicated by the sworn statements, provided they do not exceed the contract price. In addition, if any liens have been filed by the subcontractors, it is the owner's duty to retain sufficient money to pay them. He is at liberty to pay any balance to the contractor. If the amount retained is insufficient to pay all the creditors, they share proportionately in the balance, except that most of the states prefer claims of laborers. The owner has a right to rely upon the truthfulness of the sworn statement. If the contractor misstates the facts and obtains a sum greater than that to which he is entitled, the loss falls upon the subcontractors rather than upon the owner. Under such circumstances, the subcontractors may look only to the contractor to make good their deficit. Payments made by the owner, without first obtaining a sworn statement, may not be used to defeat the claims of subcontractors, materialmen, and laborers. Before making any payment, it is the duty of the owner to require the sworn statement and to withhold the amount necessary to pay the claims indicated.

Where the contractor is willing, the owner may also protect himself by stipulating in the construction contract a waiver of the contractor's lien. A waiver of lien by the contractor also waives the lien of the subcontractors, as they derive their rights through those of the contractor. Certain states require the owner to record such a contract before subcontractors begin work, in order that the agreement may bar their right to a lien.

[4] Star Lumber & Supply Co. v. Mills, page 1110.

MECHANICS' LIEN LAW CASES

DEALERS SUPPLY CO. v. FIRST CHRISTIAN CHURCH

1954, (Tenn. App.) 276 S.W.2d 769

A bill to enforce a mechanics' lien for materials furnished in the construction of a church building. From a decree in favor of the Dealers Supply Co. the defendants appealed. The defendant church alleges that the complainant's lien must fail because the materials sold were shipped to the subcontracting place of business which was not on the church property, and that it was intermingled with other supplies of the subcontractor, and later moved from its warehouse and then to the job; also that the material was sold to the subcontractor on open account, and that there is no evidence that such materials were for this particular job. There was evidence introduced to show that the Dealers Supply Co. left plans with the subcontractor for the purpose of having a "take-off" made for special materials for the church.

McAmis, P. J. . . . We think the fact that the materials were furnished on a "take-off" from the plans for the church building is sufficient to show that the materials were furnished for that particular job and, while it is true they were not shipped directly to the job but were shipped to the subcontractor's place of business, there is no proof that they were intermingled in a general stock of supplies on hand in the storeroom of the subcontractor and all of the proof shows that the materials invoiced by complainant to the subcontractor and allowed by the Chancellor were used on the job.

. . . The case of *Mills v. Terry Mfg. Co.*, 91 Tenn. 469, 19 S.W. 328 is relied upon in defendants' brief filed in this case. In the *Mills* case the materials were sold to a contractor on open account with no specifications or intent as to whom they should be sold or where they would be used. Here the record clearly shows that they were sold by the furnisher and bought by the subcontractor to be used in the church building and that they were actually used in that building to the extent of the Chancellor's decree.

We think where a materialman, in good faith, sells and ships to a contractor or subcontractor materials intended for use on a particular improvement, if the proof shows that the materials were actually used on the job, it is of no consequence that the materialman did not himself deliver the materials at the site of the improvement. *Standard Lumber Co. v. Field,* 29 Wash.2d 327, 187 P.2d 283, 175 A.L.R. 309; 57 C.J.S., Mechanics' Liens, § 42, pp. 532, 533.

Our statute, Code, § 7913 defines "materialman" or "furnisher" as follows:

> Materialman or furnisher means any person who, under contract, furnishes material to the owner, contractor, or subcontractor of any degree, on the site of the improvement or for direct delivery to the site of the improvement, or who specially fabricates materials for the improvement, and who performs no labor in the installation thereof.

We think the statute contemplates that delivery of the materials may be made to the contractor or subcontractor at a place other than the site of the improvement, provided the delivery to the contractor or subcontractor is made with the intent that the materials will be later delivered to the job by the contractor or subcontractor and they are later so delivered. Where that operation has actually occurred and the materials actually have been used in the improvement, it hardly seems open to question that delivery was made to the contractor or subcontractor "for direct delivery to the site of the improvement."

Finding no error, it results that the decree is in all respects affirmed with costs and the cause remanded for enforcement of the lien and the decree generally.

FINNEY v. STORY
1960, (Ala.) 123 So.2d 129

Goodwyn, Justice. This is an appeal from a final decree of the circuit court of Etowah County, in equity, in a materialman's lien suit. Code 1940, Tit. 33, § 37 et seq.

The only question presented is whether the complainants (appellees) met the burden on them of proving their allegations that the respondent (appellant) "entered into an oral contract" with them whereby they "agreed to and did furnish the defendant building materials, lumber and fixtures for the erection, repairing, altering or beautifying a house, building or improvement" upon respondent's lot in Gadsden.

The cause was submitted to the trial court for final decree upon the pleadings and the testimony of witnesses taken orally before the register. In this situation we must weigh and consider the evidence de novo and arrive at a conclusion without the aid of any presumption in favor of the trial court's decision on the issues of fact presented. In other words, we must sit in judgment on the evidence as if at nisi prius. . . .

After a full consideration of the testimony, in the light of the foregoing rule of review, we are at the conclusion that the complainants failed to meet the burden on them of proving the alleged contract. While one of them testified that in a telephone conversation had with respondent,

respondent agreed to pay for the materials delivered to respondent's contractor, such agreement was denied by respondent. As we view the evidence, taken as a whole, it is insufficient to show "a positive agreement between the materialman and the owner of the property." See *Brewton v. Sessions,* 264 Ala. 123, 125, 84 So.2d 763, 764; *Lindsey v. Robers,* 260 Ala. 231, 234 69 So.2d 445, 447. As said in the last cited case:

> . . . It must be kept in mind that a materialman's lien is a statutory creation and is not "allowable in equity independently of statute." *Emanuel v. Underwood Coal & Supply Co., supra* (244 Ala. 436, 14 So.2d 154). In other words the lien must be perfected by compliance with statutory requirement that there be a valid contract of purchase between the materialman and the owner of the property. This may arise either by virtue of a positive agreement between the materialman and the owner of the property or where the statutory notice has been given by the materialman to the owner prior to the furnishing of the materials that the materialman will look to the owner for payment for the materials. (*Buettner Bros. v. Good Hope Missionary Baptist Church,* 245 Ala. 553, 18 So.2d 75, 76). . . .

The decree appealed from is due to be reversed and one rendered here dismissing the bill.

Reversed and rendered.

MURRAY v. ZEMON

1960 (Rehearing denied 1961), Pa. 167 A.2d 253

The defendant Zemon leased property from defendant Sperling, the owner of the premises. The lessee arranged to renovate the buildings on the leased premises and entered into a contract with the plaintiff-contractor. The work was completed but plaintiff was not paid. He now asserts a mechanic's lien against the interest of the defendant owner. The lower court held that no lien could be claimed.

EAGEN, Justice. The narrow question presented is whether the facts pleaded in support of the lien satisfy the requirements of the Mechanics' Lien Act of June 4, 1901, P.L. 431 § 2 (49 P.S. § 24), which provides as follows:

> Nor shall any claim be valid against the estate of an owner, by reason of any consent given by him to his tenant to improve the leased property, unless it shall appear in writing, signed by such owner, that said improvement was in fact made for his immediate use and benefit.

. . . We must always bear in mind that this is not a common law action, but rather a claim to assert a peculiar type of lien against real estate under the provisions of a statute, strict compliance with which has always been demanded. Such liens are purely creatures of statutes; they did not exist at common law. Consequently, they are available only on such terms as the Legislature saw fit to provide. . . . The right to the lien arises not from the act of furnishing the labor and materials, but rather from the debt arising therefrom. . . . The right to file a mechanics' lien must have a contract as its basis.

The written contract for the repairs involved herein was entered into between the claiming contractor and the tenant, Zemon. By its express terms, it manifests that the person agreeing to pay the bill was Zemon. No contractual relationship ever existed between the contractor and the owners whereby the latter agreed to pay the cost of the repairs or any portion thereof. No promise, by the owners, to pay for the repairs is asserted. The fact that the owners had knowledge of and consented to the repairs being made is not in itself sufficient.

. . . If the law were otherwise, the cost of almost every alteration made by a tenant could be the subject of a lien against the owner. In order for the claim to be valid against the estate of the owner, where he is not a party to the contract, his consent must appear in the form of a written statement, signed by him, and which shall also state that the improvement is made for his immediate use and benefit. This is a condition precedent. The claim filed must on its face show the existence of such consent to satisfy this requirement. Every mechanic's lien must be self-sustaining. . . .

. . . if the contractor desired to subject the estate of the owner to such a lien, it was his duty to inquire into the nature of the consent given, if any. His failure to do so is his fault alone. When consent, of the type required by statute as a prerequisite to such a lien, is lacking, no such lien may successfully be asserted.

Judgment for defendant affirmed.

STAR LUMBER & SUPPLY CO. v. MILLS
1960, (Kan.) 349 P.2d 892

FATZER, Justice. The plaintiff entered into a contract with one Mills whereby the plaintiff agreed to furnish lumber and materials and Mills agreed to construct houses on lots which he owned. The houses would then be sold and the plaintiff would be paid from the proceeds. After the houses were completed the plaintiff filed a mechanic's lien. The Statute requires that the lien statement be filed within four months from the time the last materials are furnished. The houses were completed on September 29, 1956, and the statement was filed on March 21, 1957. However, the plaintiff introduced in evidence two tickets in the amount of $3.74 and $5.62 respectively, charged to Mills by one McClaskey, the contractor, for materials to make repairs to some of the houses.

The plaintiff sought to foreclose the lien.

. . . a careful examination of the record discloses there was ample evidence to support the trial court's findings that the two orders were not a part of the original contract of the parties to furnish materials and supplies to build the houses, but were materials purchased by McClaskey on two independent contracts with Mills to perform minor repairs on the houses. The findings accord with the holdings of this court that trivial isolated orders, as the plaintiff relies upon in this case, cannot serve to extend the time within which to file a mechanic's lien. . . . (Cases cited.)

Not having complied with G.S. 1949, 60–1402 by filing its lien statement within four months from September 29, 1956, the time the last materials were furnished under the original contract between the parties, the plaintiff's lien statement when filed on March 21, 1957, was fatally defective and no lien was created on the property involved.

Review Questions and Problems

1. *A* entered into a contract to purchase two lots from *B*, the price to be paid upon delivery of the deed. *A* then contracted to purchase building supplies from *X* for the construction of a building on one of the lots. *X* commenced on that day to make deliveries. Thereafter *A* borrowed money from *Y* and gave him a deed of trust on the property. The money was used to pay *B* who then gave *A* a deed to the property. *A* failed to pay for the materials furnished by *X*. Would *X*'s mechanic's lien be superior to *Y*'s lien?
2. *A* agreed to furnish material and to install a heating plant for *B* at a cost of $300. *B* advanced to *A* $200 with which to buy the material. The material was purchased on credit, and *A* used the money for other purposes. *A* failed to complete the work, and *B* was compelled to pay *C* $150 for completing the job. May the materialman maintain his lien?
3. *A* rented a plot of ground from *B*, with the understanding that *A* might have buildings constructed thereon, such as were necessary to the operation of an amusement park. The buildings were constructed under contract with *A*, but the various contractors were not paid. May they maintain a lien against *B*?
4. *A* agreed with *C* to have the latter build a house at a cost of $4,000. The house was completed on January 15. On February 1 the property was sold to *B*, who had been informed by *A* that all contractors' bills had been paid. As a matter of fact *C* had received no money. May *C* file his lien as against *B*?
5. *A*, an architect, drew plans for a building for *B*. *A* did not receive payments for his services. May he claim a lien upon the building?
6. *M* gave *P* a note secured by a mortgage on his house in April. *P* on October 14 delivered the mortgage to the county recorder of deeds. On October 18 a mechanics' lien was filed with the recorder for materials furnished by *X* for improvement of the house over a period beginning August 31. On August 20 *Y* filed a lien for drilling an outside well starting June 23. Which party has priority of lien assuming each was ignorant of the other? What effect would *P*'s recording of the mortgage in April have had?

7. *L* leased several rooms of his office building to *T* for five years for restaurant purposes. *T* contracted with *C* for a complete remodeling including installation of coffee urns, steam chests, a soda fountain and a metal hood over the kitchen stove, all of which were attached to the building when installed. *C* filed a mechanic's lien against *T*'s leasehold interest for all work done without specifying what amount was allocated to the items just mentioned. Can *C* enforce such a lien on such an interest?

Glossary

Abandonment: The term applies to many situations. Abandonment of property is the giving up of the dominion and control over it with the intention to relinquish all claim to the same. Losing property is an involuntary act; abandonment is voluntary.

When used with duty, the word abandonment is synonymous with repudiation.

Abandonment of a child by its parents may be a criminal offense when such parents fail to perform their parental duty.

Abandonment in divorce law means the voluntary separation or desertion of one spouse from the other.

Abatement: The ending of a suit at law for want of proper parties.

Abatement of a nuisance: An action to end any act detrimental to the public, such as a suit to enjoin a plant from permitting the escape of noxious vapors.

Ab initio: Latin phrase meaning, "from the beginning." A person who enters upon the land of another by permission and thereafter abuses the permission becomes a trespasser ab initio; that is, he becomes a trespasser from the time he first entered upon the land.

Abscond: To fraudulently hide or conceal one's self for the purpose of avoiding legal process.

Absolute: Unconditional or unrestricted. That which is without relation to another person or thing. The promise in a negotiable note is absolute or unconditional.

Action ex contractu: An action at law to recover damages for the breach of a duty arising out of contract. There are two types of causes of action; those arising out of contract, ex contractu, and those arising out of tort, ex delicto.

Action ex delicto: An action at law to recover damages for the breach of a duty existing by reason of a general law. An action to recover damages for an injury caused by the negligent use of an automobile is an ex delicto action. Tort or wrong is the basis of the action. See *Action ex contractu.*

Actionable: The breach of any legal duty that will form the basis of a remedy by action.

Ad damnum clause: A clause in a declaration or complaint of the plaintiff that makes the demand for damages and sets out the amount.

Ad hoc: Latin words meaning, "for this." An ad hoc refers to a limited or particular situation. An ad hoc decision means, for this purpose only. An ad hoc committee is one limited to a special purpose. An ad hoc attorney is one appointed to do a special task in a particular case.

Adjective law: The rules of procedure used by and in courts for enforcing the duties and maintaining the rights defined by the substantive law. Adjective law primarily involves matters of evidence, procedure, and appeals. It is also called remedial law.

Adjudicate: The exercise of judicial power by hearing, trying, and determining the claims of litigants before the court.

Administrator: A person to whom letters of administration have been issued by a probate court, giving such person authority to administer, manage, and close the estate of a deceased person.

Adverse possession: To acquire, by adverse possession, the legal title to another's land, the claimant must be in continuous possession during the period prescribed in the statute. This possession must be actual, visible, known to the world, with an intention by the possessor to claim the title as owner as against the rights of the true owner. The claimant usually must pay the taxes and liens lawfully charged against the property. Cutting timber or grass from time to time on the land of another is not such adverse possession as to confer title.

Affidavit: A voluntary statement of facts formally reduced to writing, sworn to, or affirmed before, some officer authorized to administer oaths. Such officer is usually a notary public.

A fortiori: Latin words meaning "by a stronger reason." The phrase is often used in judicial opinions to say that, since specific proven facts lead to a certain conclusion, there are for this reason other facts that logically follow which make stronger the argument for the conclusion.

Agency coupled with an interest: When an agent has possession or control over the property of his principal and has a right of action against interference by third parties, an agency with an interest has been created. *A*, an agent, advances freight for goods sent him by his principal. He thus has an interest in the goods.

Agent: An agent is a person authorized to act for another (a principal). The term may apply to a person in the service of another, but in the strict sense an agent is one who stands in place of his principal. *A* works for *B* as a gardener and is thus a servant; but he may be an agent. If *A* sells goods for *B*, he becomes more than a servant. He acts in the place of *B*.

Aliquot: A subdivision or portion of the whole. An aliquot part.

Alter ego: Latin words literally meaning, "the other I." In law an agent is the alter ego or other person for his principal. When members of a corporation misuse the corporate entity, the courts look behind the entity that is the alter ego of the members.

Annuity: A sum of money paid yearly to a person during his lifetime, which sum arises out of a contract by which the recipient or another had previously deposited sums in whole or in part with the grantor—the grantor to return a designated portion of the principal and interest in periodic payments upon the arrival of the beneficiary at a designated age.

A priori: A generalization resting on presuppositions and not upon proven facts.

Architect's certificate: A formal statement signed by an architect that a contractor has performed under his contract and is entitled to be paid. The construction contract provides when and how such certificates shall be issued.

Arguendo: A Latin word which means to make the case by way of argument or in an argument.

Artisan's lien: One who has expended labor upon or added to another's property is entitled to the possession of such property as security until reimbursed for the value of labor or material. *A* repairs *B*'s watch. *A* may keep the watch in his possession until paid by *B* for such repairs.

Assignee: An assign or assignee is one to whom an assignment has been made.

Assignment: An assignment is the transfer by one person to another of a right that usually arises out of a contract. Such rights are called choses in action. *A* sells and assigns his contract right to purchase *B*'s house to *C*. *A* is an assignor. *C* is an assignee. The transfer is an assignment.

Assignment for the benefit of creditors: *A*, a debtor, has many creditors. An assignment of his property to *X*, a third party, with directions to make distribution of his property to his creditors is called an assignment for the benefit of creditors. See *Composition of creditors.*

Assignor: An assignor is one who makes an assignment.

Assumpsit: An action at common law to recover damages for the breach of contract. Historically it was based upon an implied undertaking (the word "assumpsit" is a Latin word meaning, "undertaking") to properly perform a duty.

Attachment: A legal proceeding accompanying an action in court by which a plaintiff may acquire a lien on a defendant's property as a security for the payment of any judgment which the plaintiff may recover. It is provisional and independent of the court action, and is usually provided for by statute. *A* sues *B*. Before judgment, *A* attaches *B*'s automobile in order to make sure of the payment of any judgment that *A* may secure.

Attorney at law: A person who has been granted a license by the state giving him the privilege of practicing law.

Attorney in fact: A person acting for another under a grant of special power created by an instrument in writing. *B*, in writing, grants special power to *A* to execute and deliver for *B* a conveyance of *B*'s land to *X*.

Auction: A method of conducting a public sale of property, personal or real, by an auctioneer who asks for bids and who, upon receipt of the highest bid, completes the sale either by receipt of the bid or upon the fall of the hammer.

Auctioneer: A person who conducts a public competitive sale called an auction. He calls for bids and closes a bargain for the sale of the goods either by receipt of the highest bid or by the fall of the hammer.

Authority: The power of government as evidenced by an executive order, by legislation, or by the decision of a court.

Bad faith: The term means "actual intent" to mislead or deceive another. It does not mean misleading by an honest, inadvertent, or careless misstatement.

Bail (verb): To set at liberty an arrested or imprisoned person upon security's being given to the state by himself or at least two other persons that will appear at the proper time and place for trial.

Bailee: A person into whose possession personal property is delivered.

Bailment: A bailment is the delivery of personal property to another for a special purpose. Such delivery is made under a contract, either expressed or implied, that upon the completion of the special purpose, the property shall be redelivered to the bailor or placed at his disposal. *A* loans *B* his truck. *A* places his watch with *B* for repair. *A* places his furniture in *B*'s warehouse. *A* places his securities in *B* Bank's safety deposit vault. In each case, *A* is a bailor and *B* is a bailee.

Bailor: One who delivers personal property into the possession of another.

Bank: An institution for the custody of, and the lending of, money; for the exchange and transmission of money by means of checks and drafts; and, if authorized by the federal government, for the issuance of bearer notes to be used as currency. Banks are regulated by federal and state legislation, and, if so authorized, may act as trustees in the administration of decedent's estates, and engage in the investment of trust funds.

Bench: A term often used to designate a court or the judges of a court. Sometimes used to name the place where the judges sit. The term "bench and bar" means the judges and attorneys of the profession.

Beneficiary: A person (not a promisee) for whose benefit a trust, an insurance policy, a will, or a contract promise is made.

Bequest: A term used in a will to designate a gift of personal property. It is used synonymously with "devise" and often is construed to include real property.

Bet: An understanding between two or more persons to place money or property with a third person, ultimate ownership of such money or property to be determined either by the happening of an uncertain future event, not within the control of the parties concerned, or, upon the ascertaining of the truth of a disputed fact.

Bid: An offering of money in exchange for property placed for sale. At an ordinary auction sale a bid is an offer to purchase. It may be withdrawn before acceptance is indicated by the fall of the hammer.

Bill for specific performance: The name given to a paper filed in a court of equity to compel the promisor of a contract to perform specifically that which he has promised. It will lie only when money damages as a remedy for breach of a promise would be inadequate and unjust. A promisor, having promised to convey land, may be compelled by the court to do so. The land and its title is what the promisee wanted, not money damages.

Bill of credit: An evidence of debt that circulates as money or is used in discharge of obligations in any given commercial community. Warrants issued by public bodies are examples.

Bill of lading: A contract signed by a carrier or his agent to deliver goods described in the contract to the person or persons designated by the shipper. The person to whom the goods are to be delivered is called a consignee and the shipper a consignor.

Order bill of lading—A contract of carriage made to the order of the consignee or bearer. It controls the right to the goods. The carrier is under no duty to deliver the goods until the bill of lading has been surrendered. This bill of lading is negotiable.

Straight bill of lading—A contract of carriage only. The carrier may deliver the goods to the consignee without receipt of the bill of lading. It is nonnegotiable.

Bill of sale: A written evidence that the title to personal property has been transferred from one person to another. It must contain words of transfer and be more than a receipt.

Binder: A memorandum evidencing temporary insurance issued by the insurer to the insured to cover a period of time during which the insured is considering formal application for a policy. Although incomplete as to specific terms, it is understood to include the normal provisions found in regular policies of insurance.

Bond: A promise under seal to pay money. The term is generally used to designate the promise made by a corporation, either public or private, to pay money to bearer. U.S. Government Bonds; Illinois Central Railroad Bonds.

The term also describes an obligation by which one person promises to answer for the debt or default of another—a surety bond.

Book account: A record of the debits and credits between persons evidenced by entries in a book. The record usually contains detailed statements of the transactions between the parties. It indicates rights and duties and is an assignable chose in action.

Boundary: A term used to indicate the line of demarcation between two parcels of land. Boundaries of land are fixed by known markers or monuments. Whatever the computed distance may be, the known markers fix the boundary.

Breach of contract: The failure of a promisor to perform his promise, thus giving a remedy to the promisee by way of damages; by an excuse for nonperformance; or by specific performance in equity. If the promisee has partly performed at the time of the breach, he is entitled to restitution.

Broker: A person employed to make contracts with third persons on behalf of his principal. Such contracts involve trade, commerce, buying and selling for a fee (called brokerage or commission).

By-laws: The rules adopted by the members or the board of directors of a corporation or other organization for its government. These rules must not be contrary to the law of the land, and they affect only the rights and duties of the members of the corporation or organization. They are not applicable to third persons.

Call: An assessment upon a subscriber for partial or full payment on shares of unpaid stock of a corporation. The term may also mean the power of a corporation to make an assessment, notice of an assessment, or the time when the assessment is to be paid.

Call-in pay: Pay guaranteed by contract to workers called for work, who report and are ready, but to whom no work is made available. Sometimes used to designate pay for "featherbedding." See *Featherbedding.*

Cancellation: The striking out of a signature or the destruction of a written instrument with the intention on the part of the person so acting to discharge either the party whose signature was stricken or the instrument or both.

Capital: The net assets of an individual enterprise, partnership, joint stock company, corporation, or business institution, including not only the original investment, but also all gains and profits realized from the continued conduct of the business.

Carelessness: A word sometimes used synonymously with "negligence." It means lack of ordinary care; i.e., lack of such care as a man of diligence and care would exercise under the particular circumstances.

Cargo: Between merchants, the word means the entire load of merchandise upon a ship.

Carrier: A natural person or a corporation who receives goods under a contract to transport for a consideration from one place to another. A railroad, a truck line, a bus line, an air line.

Carry on business: The phrase is used to define conduct or acts of persons, associations, or corporations which occupy their time and attention, wholly or in part, for the purpose of making a living or profit, or both. The acts or conduct must be continuous or successive. Doing a single act of a particular business is usually not considered as carrying on a business.

Case: The term used to name a cause of action in a court of law or equity. Any issue which is to be heard, tried, and decided by a judicial tribunal may be called a case.

Case (action on): The term distinguishes between a common-law action used as a remedy for damages resulting from the indirect consequences of a tort and a cause of action used to collect damages resulting from the direct result of a tort. Damages caused by a patent infringement would be a basis for "action on the case." The immediate damages caused by *A* striking *B*'s car would give rise to a remedy in trespass, not case.

Case law: The law as found in cases decided by the courts. Through what is called "common law judicial process," the courts, by deciding cases, evolve legal principles that become law. This law is called "unwritten law," as distinguished from laws passed by Congress, state legislatures, and city councils.

Cash: The word generally carries the idea of current coins—dollars, half-dollars, quarters, dimes, nickels, and pennies. It also includes paper money—United States silver certificates, and Federal Reserve bank notes. Legal tender as defined by the federal statute is cash. A check may be considered cash by the parties concerned, and if so tendered and accepted, will discharge a debt. Usually, however, a check is only conditional payment. The debt is not paid until the holder of the check receives the money at the drawee bank.

Cash sale: A present exchange of goods for money.

Cashier's check: A bill of exchange drawn by the cashier of a bank, for the bank, upon the bank. After the check is delivered or issued to the payee or holder, the drawer bank cannot put a "stop order" against itself. By delivery of the check, the drawer bank has accepted, and thus becomes the primary obligor. Note that an ordinary depositor after drawing a check, but before it is paid by the drawee bank, may countermand the same with a "stop order."

Cause of action: When one's legal rights have been invaded either by a breach of a contract or by a breach of a legal duty toward one's person or property, a cause of action has been created.

Caveat emptor: These words express an old idea at common law—"let the buyer beware"—and mean that when goods are sold without an express warranty by the vendor as to their quality and capacity for a particular use and purpose, the buyer must take the risk of loss as to all defects in the goods. The rule of caveat emptor applies at judicial sales. The buyer takes no better title than that held by the debtor or defendant.

Caveat venditor: These words mean "let the seller beware" (in contradistinction to caveat emptor—"let the buyer beware"). Caveat venditor means that unless the seller by express language disclaims any responsibility, he shall be liable to the buyer if the goods delivered are different in kind, quality, use, and purpose from those described in the contract of sale.

Certiorari: An order issuing out of an appellate court to a lower court, at the request of an appellant directing that the record of a case pending in the lower court be transmitted to the upper court for review.

Cestui que trust: A person who is the real or beneficial owner of property held in trust. The trustee holds the legal title to the property for the benefit of the cestui que trust.

Charter: As to a private corporation, the word "charter" includes the contract between the created corporation and the state, the act creating the corporation, and the articles of association granted to the corporation by authority of the legislative act. The word is also used to define the powers and privileges granted to the corporation by the legislature. The states have enacted general laws for the purpose of the creation and organization of corporations. Formerly many corporations were created by special acts of legislatures.

As to municipal corporations, charter does not mean a contract between the legislature and the city created. A city charter is a delegation of powers by a state legislature to the governing body of the city. The term includes the creative act, the powers enumerated, and the organization authorized.

Chattel: The word "chattel" is derived from the word "cattle." It is a very broad term and includes every kind of property that is not real property. Movable properties, such as horses, automobiles, choses in action, stock certificates, bills of lading, and all "goods, wares, and merchandise," are chattels personal. Chattels real concern real property, such as a lease for years—in which case the lessee owns a chattel real. A building placed on real property by a lessee is a chattel real.

Chattel mortgage: A formal instrument executed by a debtor called the mortgagor transferring an interest in a chattel to a creditor called a mortgagee, for the purpose of giving security for a debt. If the debt is not paid, the mortgagee may sell the chattel and use the proceeds to pay the debt. This proceeding is called a foreclosure.

Chose in action: Words used to define the "right" one person has to recover money or property from another by a judicial proceeding. Such right arises out of contract, claims for money, debts, and rights against property. Notes, drafts, stock certificates, bills of lading, warehouse receipts, insurance policies are illustrations of choses in action. They are called tangible choses. Book accounts, simple debts, and obligations not evidenced by formal writing are called intangible choses. Choses in action are transferred by assignment.

Circumstantial evidence: If from certain facts and circumstances, according to the experience of mankind, an ordinary, intelligent person may infer that other connected facts and circumstances must necessarily exist, the latter facts and circumstances are considered proven by circumstantial evidence. Proof of fact *A* from which fact *B* may be inferred is proof of fact *B* by circumstantial evidence.

Civil action: A proceeding in a law court or a suit in equity by one person against another for the enforcement or protection of a private right or the prevention of a wrong. It includes actions on contract, ex delicto, and all suits in equity. Civil action is in contradistinction to criminal action in which the state prosecutes a person for breach of a duty.

Claim: A claim in a legal sense is a request by one person against another for the recovery of money or property. Such request must arise out of a right one person has against another, to do, or forbear to do, some act or thing as a matter of duty. A debt is a claim for money. A true owner claims the right to title and possessions of property. *A* claims damages because of an injury to his person by *B*.

Claim and delivery: A statutory remedy for the purpose of recovering specific personal property claimed to be unlawfully withheld. If the property cannot be returned, the action permits a remedy for money to the extent of the value of the property.

Claimant: One who makes a claim. One who files a claim against a deceased person's estate. A creditor who files a claim against an insolvent debtor's estate. A material man who files a claim under the mechanics' lien law is a claimant.

Client: A person who applies to or contracts with a lawyer for legal advice and services.

Cloud on title: Words used to express the idea that there is some evidence of record which shows a third person has some prima facie interest in another's property.

Code: A collection or compilation of the statutes passed by the legislative body of a state. Such codes are often annotated with citations of cases decided by the State Supreme Courts. These decisions construe the statutes. Examples—Oregon Compiled Laws Annotated, United States Code Annotated.

Codicil: An addition to or a change in an executed last will and testament. It is a part of the original will and must be executed with the same formality as the original will.

Codify: To make a concise, systematic statement of the law. A compilation of legislation is called a Code. Thus the Oregon Revised Statutes are called the Oregon Code.

Cognovit: The name of a plea by which the defendant for the purpose of avoiding a trial admits the right of the plaintiff. It is an answer to the complaint often called a "narr" in a confession of judgment action. This remedy is often used to secure judgments on promissory notes.

Co-insurer: A term in a fire insurance policy that requires the insured to bear a certain portion of the loss when he fails to carry complete coverage. For example, unless the insured carries insurance which totals 80 per cent of the value of the property, the insurer shall be liable for only that portion of the loss that the total insurance carried bears to 80 per cent of the value of the property.

Collateral: With reference to debts or other obligations, the term "collateral" means security placed with a creditor to assure the performance of the obligator. If the obligor performs, the collateral is returned by the creditor. *A* owes *B* $1,000. To secure the payment, *A* places with *B* a $500 certificate of stock in *X* Company. The $500 certificate is called collateral security.

Commercial law: That branch of the law used to designate the rules that determine the rights and duties of persons engaged in trade and commerce. The Law of Negotiable Instruments, the Law of Partnership, and the Law of Sales are examples of commercial law.

Commission: The sum of money, interest, brokerage, compensation, or allowance given to a factor or broker for carrying on the business of his principal.

Commission merchant: An agent or factor employed to sell "goods, wares, and merchandise" consigned or delivered to him by his principal, for a compensation called a commission.

Commodity: "Goods, wares, and merchandise" that are the objects of sale within the channels of commerce.

Common carrier: One who is engaged in the business of transporting personal property from one place to another for a compensation. Such person is bound to carry for all who tender their goods and the price for transportation. A common carrier operates a public utility and is subject to state and federal regulations.

Community property: All property acquired after marriage by husband and wife other than separate property acquired by devise, bequest, or from the proceeds of noncommunity property. Community property is a concept of property ownership by husband and wife inherited from the civil law. The husband and wife are somewhat like partners in their ownership of property acquired during marriage.

Company: The term "company" may apply to an unincorporated association engaged in a trade or business, or it may apply to a corporation. In the construction of statutes, the term may be synonymous with corporation. Or it may refer to persons, a partnership, a joint stock company, or associations.

Complaint: The first paper a plaintiff files in a court in a law suit. It is called a pleading. It is a statement of the facts upon which the plaintiff rests his cause of action.

Composition of creditors: An agreement between creditors and their debtors by which they agree that the creditors will take a lesser amount in complete satisfaction of the total debt due. *A* owes *B* and *C* $500 each. *A* agrees to pay *B* and *C* $250 each in complete satisfaction of the $500 due each. *B* and *C* agree to take $250 in satisfaction. Such agreement is called a composition of creditors.

Compromise: An agreement between two or more persons, usually opposing parties in a law suit, to settle the matters of the controversy without further resort to hostile litigation. An adjustment of issues in dispute by mutual concessions before resorting to a law suit.

Condemnation proceedings: An action or proceeding in court authorized by legislation (federal or state) for the purpose of taking private property for public use. It is the exercise by the judiciary of the sovereign power of eminent domain.

Condition: A clause in a contract, either expressed or implied, that has the effect of investing or divesting the legal rights and duties of the parties to the contract. In a deed, a condition is a qualification or restriction providing for the happening or nonhappening of events that on occurrence will destroy, commence, or enlarge an estate. "A grants Blackacre to *B* so long as said land shall be used for church purposes." If it ceases to be used for church purposes, the title to Blackacre will revert to the grantors.

Condition precedent: A clause in a contract providing that immediate rights and duties shall vest only upon the happening of some event. Securing an architect's certificate by a contractor before he (the contractor) is entitled to payment is a condition precedent.

A condition is not a promise; hence, its breach will not give rise to a cause of action for damages. A breach of a condition is the basis for a defense. In the above illustration, if the contractor sues the owner without securing the architect's certificate, the owner has a defense.

Conditions concurrent: Conditions concurrent are conditions that are mutually dependent and must be performed at the same time by the parties to the contract. Payment of money and delivery of goods in a cash sale are conditions concurrent. Failure to perform by one party permits a cause of action upon tender by the other party. If S refuses to deliver goods in a cash sale, *B*, upon tender, but not delivery of the money, places S in default and thus may sue S. *B* does not part with his money without getting the goods. If S sued *B*, *B* would have a defense.

Condition subsequent: A clause in a contract providing for the happening of an event that divests legal rights and duties. A clause in a fire insurance policy providing that the policy shall be null and void if combustible material is stored within ten feet of the building is a condition subsequent. If a fire occurs and combustible material was within ten feet of the building, the insurance company is excused from its duty to pay for the loss.

Conditional acceptance: Words used in an attempted acceptance that vary the legal effect of the offer. It is a counter offer. *A* offers *B* his house for $10,000. *B* replies, "I will buy it if my lawyer approves the title." *B*'s reply is a conditional acceptance or counter offer. *A* must accept *B's* condition to close the bargain. Also, a conditional acceptance may be made by the drawee of a bill of exchange.

Confession of judgment: A voluntary submission to the jurisdiction of the court by a debtor permitting judgment to be taken against him without a formal trial. Such permission often appears in promissory notes giving consent that the judgment may be taken immediately upon default. See *Cognovit.*

Consideration: An essential element in the creation of contract obligation. A detriment to the promisee and a benefit to the promisor. One promise is consideration for another promise. This creates a bilateral contract. An act is consideration for a promise. This creates a unilateral contract. Performance of the act asked for by the promisee is a legal detriment to the promisee and a benefit to the promisor.

Consignee: A person to whom a shipper usually directs a carrier to deliver goods. Such person is generally the buyer of goods and is called a consignee on a bill of lading.

Consignment: The delivery, sending, or transferring of property, "goods, wares, and merchandise" into the possession of another, usually for the purpose of sale. Consignment may be a bailment or an agency for sale.

Consignor: The person who delivers freight to a carrier for shipment and who directs the bill of lading to be executed by the carrier is called a consignor or shipper. Such person may be the consignor-consignee if the bill of lading is made to his own order.

Constitution: The Constitution of the United States constitutes the rules of organization of the United States and enumerates the powers and duties of the federal government thereby created. The constitutions of the several states prescribe the organization of each of the states and in general enumerate those powers not delegated to the federal government.

Constructive delivery: Although physical delivery of personal property has not occurred, yet by the conduct of the parties, it may be inferred that as between them possession and title has passed. *A* sells large and bulky goods to *B*. Title and possession may pass by the act and conduct of the parties.

Contemplation of insolvency: A debtor who, at any time, considering the state of his financial circumstances, decides that he will not be able in the future to pay his debts, contemplates insolvency.

Continuing guaranty: An undertaking by one person to another person to answer from time to time for moneys to be loaned or goods to be sold to a third person. The term refers to the future liability of the principal for a series of future transactions. It is usually revocable upon actual notice as to all future transactions.

Convey: The transfer of the title to real property by means of a formal written instrument.

Conveyance: A formal written instrument usually called a deed by which the title or other interests in land (real property) is transferred from one person to another. The word expresses also the fact that the title to real property has been transferred from one person to another.

Corporation: A collection of individuals created by statute as a legal person, vested with powers and capacity to contract, own, control, convey property, and transact business within the limits of the powers granted.

Corporation de facto: If persons have attempted in good faith to organize a corporation under a valid law (statute) and have failed in some minor particular, but have thereafter exercised corporate powers, such is a corporation de facto. Failure to have incorporators' signatures on applications for charter notarized is an illustration of noncompliance with statutory requirements.

Corporation de jure: A corporation that has been formed by complying with the mandatory requirements of the law authorizing such a corporation.

Corporeal: Physical things that are susceptible to the senses are corporeal. Automobiles, grain, fruit, and horses are corporeal and tangible and are called "chattels." The word corporeal is used in contradistinction to incorporeal or intangible. A chose in action (such as a check) is corporeal and tangible; or a chose in action may be a simple debt, incorporeal and intangible.

Costs: Costs, in litigation, are an allowance authorized by statute to a party for the expenses incurred in prosecuting or defending a law suit. The word "costs," unless specifically designated by statute or contract, does not include attorney's fees.

Counter-claims: A claim of the defendant by way of cross-action that the defendant is entitled to recover from the plaintiff. It must arise out of the same transaction set forth in the plaintiff's complaint, and be connected with the same subject matter. *S* sues *B* for purchase price. *B* counter-claims that the goods were defective, and that he thereby suffered damages.

Countersign: To sign what has already been signed. A president of a corporation who signs checks previously signed by the treasurer, countersigns. To make official by an additional signature is to countersign.

County warrant: A nonnegotiable instrument in the form of a bill of exchange drawn by the proper officer of the county, upon the county treasurer, directing the treasurer to pay out of a particular fund a sum of money to the order of the payee or bearer. School warrants, city warrants, and state warrants are of the same character.

Coupon: Usually, interest certificates attached to term bonds. When the interest date is due, these coupons are cut off the original bond and cashed or sold. Such coupons may or may not be negotiable. The bonds to which such certificates are attached are called coupon bonds.

Course of business: A retail merchant in selling goods to a customer (the consumer) is acting in "due course of business," or in the "usual and ordinary course of business"; but a sale of his entire stock to one person from the point of view of his creditors, his insolvency, and his bankruptcy, is not a sale in due course of business. Such sale may be some evidence of a fraudulent transfer.

Covenant: A promise in writing under seal. It is often used as a substitute for the word contract. There are covenants (promises) in deeds, leases, mortgages, and other instruments under seal. The word is used sometimes to name promises in unsealed instruments such as insurance policies and conditional sale contracts.

Covenant (action on): The name of remedy at early common law for the breach of a promise under seal.

Craft union: A labor organization limited to members who have special skills, such as typesetters, die workers, carpenters, plumbers, bricklayers, and so forth.

Credit: The trust, confidence, or reputation a person has in the opinions of others, which permits such person to borrow money or obtain goods to be paid for in the future. *X* borrows money at the bank on his personal note. He has used his personal credit. *Y* sends goods to *W* on "90 days' credit."

Creditor: One to whom a debt is owed. The term may also be applied to one who is entitled to enforce any right by a legal action.

Creditor beneficiary: If a promisee is under a duty to a third party, and, for a consideration, secures a promise from a promisor which promise, if performed, discharges the promisee's duty to the third party, such third party is a creditor beneficiary. *A* owes *C* $100. *B*, for a consideration, promises *A* to pay *A*'s debt to *C*. *C* is a creditor beneficiary.

Creditor's bill: A bill filed by a judgment creditor in a court of equity to have set aside previous fraudulent conveyances, in order to find property upon which to levy execution.

Cumulative voting: A stockholder in voting for a director may cast as many votes for one candidate for given office as there are offices to be filled multiplied by the number of shares of his stock, or he may distribute this same number of votes among the other candidates as he sees fit.

Currency: The joint resolution of Congress of June 5, 1933, 48 Stat. 112 provides: ". . . all coins and currency of the United States (including Federal Reserve notes, and circulating notes of Federal Reserve banks and national banking associations) heretofore and hereinafter coined or issued shall be legal tender for all debts public and private. . . ." The terms "currency" and "current funds" now seem to include not only coin, silver, United States Notes, Treasury Notes, but also silver certificates, Federal Reserve notes, and National Bank notes. See *Cash.*

Curtesy: If a child, issue of the husband, has been born alive, then upon the death of the wife, the husband will be entitled to a life estate called "curtesy" in the whole of the wife's property. Such estates are now generally abolished by statute.

Custody (law): Property taken by virtue of legal process is in "the custody of the law." Thus, a sheriff taking property in satisfaction of a judgment has it in his custody. Property in the hands of a receiver is in the custody of the law.

Custody (person): One who is in jail or under the control of law enforcement officers is in custody.

Custody (personal property): The word custody and possession are not synonymous. Custody means in charge of, to keep and care for under the direction of the true owner, without any interest therein adverse to the true owner. A servant is in custody of his master's goods. See *Possession.*

Custom: The word custom is used interchangeably with "usage" and "course of trade," and means those rules and regulations which, by long practice and common consent, have become established as unwritten law. The silent assent over a long period of time of those affected constitutes the authority for the rules.

Damages: A sum of money the court imposes upon a defendant as compensation for the plaintiff because the defendant has injured the plaintiff by breach of a legal duty.

Dealer: One who makes a business of dealing; a merchant, broker, factor. One who buys and sells "goods, wares, and merchandise."

Dealing: A broad term that implies buying goods to sell, selling goods, trading in goods, stocks, or bonds, as an avocation or business. A wholesale grocery deals in groceries. A bond broker deals in bonds.

Debenture: A term used to name corporate obligations that are sold as investments. It is similar to a corporate bond. However, it is not secured by a trust deed. It is not like corporate stock.

Debt: Any obligation to pay money. Ordinarily the term debt means a sum of money due by reason of a contract expressed or implied. Broadly, the word may include obligations other than to pay money, such as the duty to render services or deliver goods.

Debt (action on): A common law remedy for the recovering of a sum certain in money.

Deceit: A term to define that conduct in a business transaction by which one man, through fraudulent representations, misleads another who has a right to rely on such representations as the truth, or, who by reason of an unequal station in life, has no means of detecting such fraud.

Decision (judicial): The word "decision" may mean a final judgment of a court of last resort, a conclusion of law or facts, the opinion of the court, or the report of the court. Generally speaking, a decision means the judgment of the court as to the disposition of the case—for the plaintiff, for the defendant, or for neither. Decision must be distinguished from opinion. An opinion of the court constitutes the reasons given for its decision or judgment. The report of the case is a printing of the opinion and decision.

Declaration: At common law, a word used to name the plaintiff's first pleading in which are set out the facts upon which the cause of action is based. The word "complaint" is used synonymously with declaration.

Decree: The judgment of the chancellor (judge) in a suit in equity. Like a judgment at law, it is the determination of the rights between the parties and is in the form of an order that requires the decree to be carried out. An order that a contract be specifically enforced is a decree.

Deed: A written instrument in a special form signed, sealed, and delivered, that is used to pass the legal title of real property from one person to another. See *Conveyance.* In order that the public may know about the title to real property, deeds are recorded in the Deed Record office of the county where the land is situated.

Deed of trust: An instrument by which title to real property is conveyed to a trustee to hold as security for the holders of notes or bonds. It is like a mortgage except the security title is held by a person other than the mortgagee-creditor. Most corporate bonds are secured by a deed of trust.

De facto: Arising out of, or founded upon, fact, although merely apparent or colorable. A de facto officer is one who assumes to be an officer under some color of right, acts as an officer, but in point of law is not a real officer. See *Corporation de facto.*

Defalcation: A person occupying a trust or fiduciary relation who, by reason of his own fault, is unable to account for funds left in his hands, has committed a defalcation. The word often means to embezzle or misappropriate funds.

Defamation: The use of words that are generally understood to impute some disreputable conduct or moral delinquency about the person of whom they are spoken.

Defendant: A person who has been sued in a court of law; the person who answers the plaintiff's complaint. The word is applied to the defending party in civil actions. In criminal actions, the defending party is referred to as the accused.

Defense: The word "defense" applies to all methods of procedure used by the defendant and to all facts alleged by way of denial by the defendant in his response to the plaintiff's complaint. Demurrers, set-offs, pleas in abatement, answers, denial, confession, and avoidance are procedural means of defense.

Deficiency judgment: If, upon the foreclosure of a mortgage, the mortgaged property does not sell for a sufficient amount to pay the mortgage indebtedness, such difference is called a "deficiency" and is chargeable to the mortgagor or to any person who has purchased the property and assumed and agreed to pay the mortgage. Illus.: *M* borrows $10,000 from *B*, and as security gives a mortgage on Blackacre. At maturity *M* does not pay the debt. *B* forecloses and at a public sale Blackacre sells for $8,000. There is a deficiency of $2,000, chargeable against *M*. If *M* had sold Blackacre to *C* and *C* had assumed and agreed to pay the mortgage, he would also be liable for the deficiency.

Defraud: To deprive one of some right by deceitful means. To cheat or withhold wrongfully that which belongs to another. Conveying one's property for the purpose of avoiding payment of debts is a transfer to "hinder, delay, or defraud creditors."

Del credere agency: When an agent, factor, or broker undertakes to guarantee to his principal the payment of a debt due from a buyer of goods, such agent, factor, or broker is operating under a del credere commission or agency.

Delectus personae: A Latin phrase used to designate a chosen or selected person. Partners are chosen persons—"a copartnership cannot be compelled to receive strangers . . ." since such "association is founded on personal confidence and delectus personarum." Delectus personae is absent in joint stock companies.

Delivery. A voluntary transfer of the possession of property, actual or constructive, from one person to another with the intention that title vests in the transferee. In the law of sales, delivery contemplates the absolute giving up of control and dominion over the property by the vendor, and the assumption of the same by the vendee.

Demand: A request by a party entitled, under a claim of right, that a particular act be performed. In order to bind an endorser on a negotiable instrument, a demand must first be made by the holder on the primary party and such person must dishonor the instrument. Demand notes mean "due when demanded." The word "demand" is also used to mean a claim or legal obligation.

Demurrage: Demurrage is a sum, provided for in a contract of shipment, to be paid for the delay or detention of vessels or railroad cars beyond the time agreed upon for loading or unloading.

Demurrer: A procedural method used in a law suit by which the defendant admits all the facts alleged in the plaintiff's complaint, but denies that such facts state a cause of action. It raises a question of law on the facts, which must be decided by the court.

Dependent covenants (promises): In contracts, covenants are either concurrent or mutual, dependent or independent. Dependent covenants mean the performance of one promise must occur before the performance of the other promise. In a cash sale, the buyer must pay the money before the seller is under a duty to deliver the goods.

Deposit (in general): A bailment by which a person receives property of another to be redelivered on demand.

Deposit (in banking): Special Deposit—A bailment relationship in which property is placed with the bank for safekeeping. Bonds in a safety deposit box.

Specific Deposit—Money or commercial paper left with the bank for a special purpose. The bank becomes an agent or trustee. Items for collection or payment of taxes are illustrations.

General Deposit—Money placed in the ordinary checking account or savings account, which creates a debtor-creditor relationship between the depositor and bank.

Descent: The transfer of the title of property to the heirs upon the death of the ancestor; heredity; succession. If a person dies without making a will, his property will "descend" according to the Statute of Descent of the state wherein the property is located.

Destination: The "destination of goods" is the place of delivery as provided for in the shipping contract. The carrier is under a duty to deliver the goods at such a place unless ordered otherwise by the consignee.

Detinue: A common law action to recover property. It is to be distinguished from trover, which is an action to recover damages for taking property, not the recovery of the actual property.

Detriment: Legal detriment that is sufficient consideration, constitutes change of position or acts of forbearance by a promisee at the request of a promisor. See *Consideration.*

Devise: A gift, usually of real property, by a last will and testament.

Devisee: The person who receives title to real property by will.

Dictum: An expression of an idea, argument, or rule in the written opinion of a judge that has no bearing on the issues involved and that is not essential for their determination. It lacks the force of a decision in a judgment.

Directed verdict: If it is apparent to reasonable men and the court that the plaintiff by his evidence has not made out his case, the court may instruct the jury to bring in a verdict for the defendant or himself direct a verdict for the defendant. If, however, different inferences may be drawn from the evidence by reasonable men, then the court cannot direct a verdict.

Discharge: The word has many meanings. A servant or laborer upon being released from his employment is discharged. A guardian or trustee, upon termination of his trust, is discharged by the court. A debtor released from his debts is discharged in bankruptcy. A person who is released from any legal obligation is discharged.

Discount: If a seller reduces the price of his goods to a buyer, upon payment of cash, he has sold the goods at a discount. Illus.: "Cash 10 days 10 per cent." In banking, the term is applied to the purchase of negotiable instruments.

Discretion: A privilege of a judge, in absence of a definite rule of law, to decide a case upon its merits in light of what is fair, right, just, and equitable under the circumstances of the particular case.

Dishonor: A negotiable instrument is dishonored when it is presented for acceptance or payment, and acceptance or payment is refused or cannot be obtained.

Disputed claim: A bona fide controversy between two persons over the amount of an indebtedness that is unliquidated.

Dissolution: Of a corporation—The termination of a corporation at the expiration of its charter, by the Attorney General of the state under proper statutory authority, by consolidation, or by the action of the stockholders, is dissolution.

Of a partnership—The termination of a partnership by the express will of the partners at a fixed or indefinite time, or by operation of law due to the incapacity, death, or bankruptcy of one of the partners, is dissolution.

Dividend: A dividend is a stockholder's pro rata share in the profits of a corporation. Dividends are declared by the board of directors of a corporation. Dividends are cash, script, property, and stock.

Domicile: That place that a person intends as his fixed and permanent home and establishment and to which, if he is absent, he intends to return. A person can have but one domicile. The old one continues until the acquisition of a new one; thus, while in transit the old domicile exists. One can have more than one residence at a time, but only one domicile. The word is not synonymous with residence. See *Residence*.

Dominion: As applied to the delivery of property by one person to another, the word means the separation by the transferor or donor from all control over the possession and ownership of the property and the endowing of the transferee or donee with such control of possession and ownership. See *Gift*.

Donee beneficiary: If a promisee is under no duty to a third party, but for a consideration secures a promise from a promisor for the purpose of making a gift to a third party, such third party is a donee beneficiary. *A*, promisee for a premium paid, secures a promise from the insurance company, the promisor, to pay *A*'s wife $10,000 upon *A*'s death. *A*'s wife is a donee beneficiary.

Dormant partner: A partner who is not known to third persons, but is entitled to share in the profits and is subject to the losses. Since credit is not extended upon the strength of such partner's name, he may withdraw without notice and is not subject to debts contracted after his withdrawal.

Dower: A right for life held by a married woman in part of the lands owned by her husband, which right becomes vested upon his death.

Due care: The words express that standard of conduct which is exercised by an ordinary, reasonable, prudent person. See *Negligence*.

Due process of law: The words have a broad meaning. The constitutions of the United States and the states create and guarantee to every person the right to life, liberty, and property. These rights cannot be denied by government, except by the exercise of a fair and impartial legal procedure that is proper and appropriate. Legislation that confiscates one's property without just compensation is in the absence of due process of law. Under due process, a person accused of a crime is entitled to a trial by jury.

Duress (of person): Duress means a threat of bodily injury, criminal prosecution, or imprisonment of a contracting party or his near relative to such extent that the threatened party is unable to exercise freely his will at the time of entering into or discharging a legal obligation.

Duress (of property): The seizure by force, or the withholding of goods by one not entitled, and the demanding by such person of something as a condition for the release of the goods.

Duty (in law): A legal obligation imposed by general law or voluntarily imposed by the creation of a binding promise. For every legal duty there is a corresponding legal right. By general law, *A* is under a legal duty not to injure *B*'s person or property. *B* has a right that *A* not injure his person or property. *X* may voluntarily create a duty in himself to *Y* by a promise to sell *Y* a horse for $100. If *Y* accepts, *X* is under a legal duty to perform his promise. See *Right*.

Earnest: "Earnest money" is a term used to describe money that one contracting party gives to another at the time of entering into the contract in order to "bind the bargain" and which will be forfeited by the donor if he fails to carry out the contract. Generally, in real estate contracts such money is used as part payment of the purchase price.

Earnings: Earnings as applied to a natural person are the rewards or income gained for labor and services. Earnings is a broader term than wages. The term "wages" is applied generally to compensation for manual labor, skilled and unskilled, paid at fixed times and determined by the day, week, or month. Earnings as applied to a corporation or business establishment may mean either the gross or net receipts of the ordinary business operation over a specified period. See *Profits*.

Easement: An easement is an interest in land—a right that one person has to some profit, benefit, or use in or over the land of another. Such right is created by a deed, or it may be acquired by prescription (the continued use of another's land for a statutory period).

Economic strike: A strike to compel an increase in wages or change in working hours and conditions as distinguished from a strike to object to an unfair labor practice.

Effects: The word is used synonymously with personal property.

Ejectment: An action to recover the possession of real property. It is now generally defined by statute, and is a statutory action. See *Forcible entry and detainer*.

Eleemosynary: A word used to classify corporations and institutions engaged in public charitable work, such as a hospital or children's home owned and operated by a church.

Embezzlement: The fraudulent appropriation by one person, acting in a fiduciary capacity, of the money or property of another. See *Conversion*.

Eminent domain: The right that resides in the United States, state, county, city, school, or other public body, to take private property for public use, upon the payment of just compensation. Eminent domain is to be distinguished from governmental power to take private property by limiting its use in order to eliminate nuisances. Abating a nuisance is the exercise of police power. No compensation is given for limiting the use of property under the police power.

Entire contract: A contract, which by its terms requires full and complete performance on one side in return for the full and complete performance on the other. The term "entire contract" is used in contradistinction to the term "divisible contract," wherein a part of the performance required may be set over against a part of the performance on the other side.

Entirety (estate by): Property acquired by husband and wife whereby upon the death of one, the survivor takes the whole estate. The estate is called "entirety" because the law regards the husband and wife as one. They are vested with the whole estate so that the survivor takes no new title upon death of the other but remains in possession of the whole as originally granted. Such estate must be distinguished from a joint tenancy. Neither the husband nor wife may by conveyance destroy the right of survivorship. The words in a deed, "To John Smith and Mary Smith, his wife, with the right of survivorship," and not as tenants in common, will create an estate by the entirety. For the legal effect of such estate, the state statute should be consulted. See *Joint tenants.*

Entity: The word means "in being" or "existing." The artificial person created when a corporation is organized is "in being" or "existing" for legal purposes; thus, an entity. It is separate from the stockholders. The estate of a deceased person while in administration is an entity. A partnership for many legal purposes is an entity. The marriage status is an entity.

Equitable action: In Anglo-American law there have developed two types of courts and procedures for the administraion of justice: law courts and equity courts. Law courts give as a remedy money damages only, whereas equity courts give the plaintiff what he bargains for. A suit for specific performance of a contract is an equitable action. In many states these two courts are now merged.

Equitable conversion: An equitable principle that, for certain purposes, permits real property to be converted into personalty. Thus real property owned by a partnership is, for the purpose of the partnership, personal property because to ascertain a partner's interest, the real property must be reduced to cash. This is an application of the equitable maxim, "equity considers that done which ought to be done."

Equitable mortgage: A written agreement to make certain property security for a debt, and upon the faith of which the parties have acted in making advances, loans, and thus creating a debt. Example: an improperly executed mortgage, one without seal where a seal is required. An absolute deed made to the mortgagee and intended for security only is an equitable mortgage.

Equity: Because the law courts in early English law did not always give an adequate remedy, an aggrieved party sought redress from the king. Since this appeal was to the king's conscience, he referred the case to his spiritual adviser, the chancellor. The chancellor decided the case according to rules of fairness, honesty, right, and natural justice. From this there developed the rules in equity. The laws of trusts, divorce, rescission of contracts for fraud, injunction, and specific performance are enforced in courts of equity.

Equity of redemption: The right a mortgagor has to redeem or get back his property after it has been forfeited for nonpayment of the debt it secured. By statute, within a certain time before final foreclosure decree, a mortgagor has the privilege, by paying the amount of the debt, interest, and costs, of redeeming his property.

Error: A mistake in fact or law committed by the court in the trial of a case that may be the basis of an appeal to a higher court. The admitting of improper evidence is "error of law occurring at the trial." Assumption that a fact exists when it does not is error of fact.

Escrow: An agreement under which a grantor, promisor, or obligor places the instrument upon which he is bound with a third person called escrow holder, until the performance of a condition or the happening of an event stated in the agreement permits the escrow holder to make delivery or performance to the grantee, promisee, or obligee. *A* (grantor) places a deed to *C* (grantee) accompanied by the contract of conveyance with *B* Bank, conditioned upon *B* Bank delivering the deed to *C* (grantee) when *C* pays all moneys due under contract. The contract and deed have been placed in "escrow."

Estate: A word used to name all the property of a living, deceased, bankrupt, or insane person. It is also applied to the property of a ward. In the law of taxation, wills, and inheritance, the word has a broad meaning. Historically, the word was limited to an interest in land: i.e., estate in fee simple, estate for years, estate for life, and so forth.

Estoppel: When one ought to speak the truth, but does not, and by one's acts, representations, or silence intentionally or through negligence induces another to believe certain facts exist, and such person acts to his detriment on the belief that such facts are true, the first person is estopped to deny the truth of the facts. *B*, knowingly having kept and used defective goods delivered by S under a contract of sale, is estopped to deny the goods are defective. *X* holds out *Y* as his agent. *X* is estopped to deny *Y* is not his agent. Persons are estopped to deny the legal effect of written instruments such as deeds, contracts, bills and notes, court records, judgments, and the like. A man's own acts speak louder than his words.

Et al.: Literally translated means "and other persons." Words used in pleadings and cases to indicate that persons other than those specifically named are parties to a law suit.

Et cetera—etc.: Literally translated means "and other things" or "and so forth." When a number of things of the same class have been listed and others exist, it is customary to add the word "etc." in order to avoid full enumeration. Example: "There are many items of junk, old cars, wagons, plows, etc."

Et uxor: The words mean "and wife." Sometimes used in the name of cases. Smith v. Jones et ux.

Eviction: An action to expel a tenant from the estate of the landlord. Interfering with the tenant's right of possession or enjoyment amounts to an eviction. Eviction may be actual or constructive. Premises made uninhabitable because the landlord maintains a nuisance is constructive eviction.

Evidence: In law the word has two meanings. First, that testimony of witnesses and facts presented to the court and jury by way of writings and exhibits, which impress the minds of the court and jury, to the extent that an allegation has been proven. Testimony and evidence are not synonymous. Testimony is a broader word and includes all the witness says. Proof is distinguished from evidence in that proof is the legal consequence of evidence. Second, the rules of law, called the law of evidence, that determine what evidence shall be introduced at a trial and what shall not; also what importance shall be placed upon the evidence.

Exception: An objection taken by an attorney at a trial because of some ruling made by the court upon a matter of law. It forms the basis of an appeal to a higher court.

Executed: As applied to contracts or other written instruments, means signed, sealed, and delivered. Effective legal obligations have thus been created. The term is also used to mean that the performances of a contract have been completed. The contract is then at an end. All is done that is to be done.

Execution: Execution of a judgment is the process by which the court through the sheriff enforces the payment of the judgment received by the successful party. The sheriff by a "writ" levies upon the unsuccessful party's property and sells it to pay the judgment creditor.

Executor (of an estate): The person, named or appointed in a will by a testator (the one who makes the will), who by authority of the will has the power to administer the estate upon the death of the testator and to dispose of it according to the intention of the testator. The terms executor and adminisrator are not synonymous. An executor is appointed by the deceased to administer an estate. An administrator is appointed by the court to administer the estate of a person who dies without having made a will. See *Intestate.*

Executory (contract): Until the performance required in a contract is completed, it is said to be executory as to that part not executed. See *Executed.*

Exemplary damages: A sum assessed by the jury in a tort action (over and above the compensatory damages) as punishment in order to make an example of the wrongdoer and to deter like conduct by others. Injuries caused by wilful, malicious, wanton, and reckless conduct will subject the wrongdoers to exemplary damages.

Exemption: The condition of a person who is free or excused from a duty imposed by some rule of law, statutory or otherwise. A workman against whom a judgment has been secured is by statute exempt from a writ of execution upon his working tools. A portion of a soldier's pay is exempt from the imposition of federal income tax.

Express warranty: When a seller makes some positive representation concerning the nature, quality, character, use, and purpose of goods, which induces the buyer to buy, and the seller intends the buyer to rely thereon, the seller has made an express warranty.

Face value: The face value of an interest-bearing instrument at any particular point of time is the principal plus the then-accrued interest.

Factor: A factor is an agent for the sale of merchandise. He may hold possession of the goods in his own name or in the name of his principal. He is authorized to sell and to receive payment for the goods. The law concerning factors is codified in some states by legislation, and is called "Factors' Acts." See *Agent.*

Factor's lien: A lien or right that a factor has to keep the possession of goods consigned to him for the purpose of reimbursing himself for all advances previously made to the consignor.

Facts in issue: Those facts in the particular case upon which the party, either plaintiff or defendant, rests his legal right to a remedy or defense.

Failure of consideration: A phrase used to describe the situation in which one party to a contract has failed to fulfill or comply with his promise, giving the other party either a cause of action for damages or an excuse for nonperformance.

Fair market value: Words used to express "that price which a seller would be willing to take for goods but who is not obliged to sell, and that price which a buyer would be willing to pay but who is not obligated to buy."

False pretense: A false representation of some circumstance or fact for the purpose of misleading. See *Fraud.*

F.A.S.: The abbreviation means the seller places goods on the wharf alongside the ship's tackle. Without evidence to the contrary, legal title and risk of loss passes to the buyer at the moment the goods are so placed. F.A.S. means literally "free alongside steamer."

Featherbedding: A term used in labor relations to describe the situation in which demand is made for the payment of wages for a particular service not actually rendered.

Fee simple estate: A term describing the total interest a person may have in land. Such an estate is not qualified by any other interest and passes upon the death of the owners to the heirs free from any conditions.

Fellow-servants: Persons working together at a common task and controlled by the same master or employer.

Felony: At common law, a felony was a criminal offense, and upon conviction the criminal forfeited his lands and goods to the crown and was subject to death. Today, by statute, the term includes all those criminal offenses that are punishable by death or imprisonment.

Fiction of law: An assumption, or supposition, that something is true and exists, that in actual fact does not exist. "It is used as a rule of convenience, but cannot be used to work a wrong." To say a corporation is a person is a fiction of law. It is of great public convenience to use the idea that a corporation may act as a person. If the corporation wrongfully uses this artificial or fictitious person, the courts will "look behind the corporate veil or person," to the natural persons using the fiction and hold them personally liable.

Fiduciary: In general a person is a fiduciary when he occupies a position of trust or confidence in relation to another person or his property. Trustees, guardians, and executors are illustrations of persons occupying fiduciary positions.

Fieri facias: Literally means "you cause it to be made." A writ or order issued by a court directing the sheriff to levy on goods or personal property of the defendant, in order to satisfy the judgment of the plaintiff.

Fine: A sum of money collected by a court from a person guilty of some criminal offense. The amount may be fixed by statute or left to the discretion of the court.

The term "fine" is to be distinguished from "penalty," which means a sum of money exacted for the doing of or failure to perform some act. Payment of a penalty of $5 for failure to secure a license to sell tobacco is different from paying a $5 fine for committing the offense of larceny.

Fiscal: The term applies to the money or financial affairs and management of institutions, public and private. Fiscal officer is the treasurer. Fiscal year is the period within which budgets operate and the time when books are closed. A fiscal year may be from July 1 to June 30.

Floating policy: An insurance policy that covers a class of goods located in a particular place that the insured has on hand at the time the policy was issued, but which goods at the time of fire may not be the identical items that were on hand at the time the policy was issued. A fire policy covering the inventory of a grocery store is an example.

F.O.B.: The abbreviation means the seller places goods without cost to the buyer on a ship, car, truck, or other conveyance ready to go forward. Without evidence to the contrary, legal title and risk of loss pass to the buyer at the time the goods are placed on the means of transportation. "F.O.B." literally means "free on board."

Forbearance: Giving up the right to enforce what one honestly believes to be a valid claim in return for a promise is called forbearance and is sufficient "consideration" to make binding a promise.

Forced sale: A sale of a debtor's property by public officials to secure money to pay the debtor's creditors is a forced sale. Sales by sheriff after judgment, foreclosure, and so forth, are illustrations.

Forcible entry and detainer: A remedy given to a landowner to evict persons unlawfully in possession of his land. A landlord may use such remedy to evict a tenant in default.

Foreign bill of exchange: A draft drawn by the resident of one state or country on a resident of another state or country is a foreign bill of exchange.

Forfeiture: Loss of money or property by way of compensation and punishment for injury or damage to the person or property of another or to the state. One may forfeit his citizenship upon the commission of a felony. One may forfeit interest earnings for charging a usurious rate.

Forgery: Forgery is the false writing or alteration of an instrument with the fraudulent intent of deceiving and injuring another. Writing, without his consent, another's name upon a check for the purpose of securing money, is a forgery.

Forthcoming bond: A bond given by a defendant in possession of property subject to a foreclosure proceeding that he will hold the property "subject to any order of the court that may be entered finally in the cause."

Franchise: A right conferred or granted by a legislative body. It is a contract right and cannot be revoked without cause. A franchise is more than a license. A license is only a privilege and may be revoked. A corporation exists by virtue of a "franchise." A corporation secures a franchise from the city council to operate a water works within the city. See *License*.

Franchise tax: A tax on the right of a corporation to do business under its corporate name.

Fraud: An intentional misrepresentation of the truth for the purpose of deceiving another person. The elements of fraud are: (1) false representation of fact, not opinion, intentionally made; (2) intent that the deceived person act thereon; (3) knowledge that such statements would naturally deceive; and (4) that the deceived person acted to his injury.

Fraudulent conveyance: A conveyance of property by a debtor for the intent and purpose of defrauding his creditors. Such conveyance is of no effect, and such property may be reached by the creditors through appropriate legal proceedings.

Freehold: An estate in fee or one for life is a "freehold." A freeholder is usually a person who has a property right in the title to real estate amounting to an estate of inheritance (in fee), or one who has title for life, or for an indeterminate period. A grant by a city to a corporation to use the sidewalks for 30 years is not a freehold. "Householder" is not synonymous with "freeholder." See *Householder.*

Freight: Freight, generally speaking, is the compensation received by a carrier for the transportation of goods. The word also applies to the goods that are transported.

From and to: Generally the word "from" is a word of exclusion, and the word "to" a word of inclusion. "From May 5 to May 10," in computing time means May 5 is excluded and May 10 included; thus, the period of time is 5 days.

Fund: The term in ordinary commercial transactions means money-cash. In its broader sense, the word may mean every kind of property, such as land, stocks, bonds, checks, notes. An "endowment fund" may include more than cash. "Corporate funds" may include all the resources of the corporation.

Funded debt: The term applies to a debt where provision is made for a method of paying off the debt and its interest at fixed periods. A funded debt of a municipality is one where provision is made for the annual raising by tax of the sum necessary to pay the interest and principal as they respectively mature.

Funding: The procedure by which the outstanding debts of a corporation are collected together and the re-issuing of new bonds or obligations for the purpose of paying the debts. Thus 10 year 3 per cent bonds may be called and paid by issuing 20 year 3 per cent bonds. This process is called funding.

Fungible goods: Fungible goods are those "of which any unit is from its nature of mercantile usage treated as the equivalent of any other unit." Grain, wine, and similar items, are examples.

Futures: Contracts for the sale and delivery of commodities in the future, made with the intention that no commodity be delivered or received immediately.

Gambling: An arrangement between two or more persons to risk money or other things of value in any type of contest or game of chance wherein one of the parties wins at the expense of another.

Garnishee: A person upon whom a garnishment is served. He is a debtor of a defendant and has money or property that the plaintiff is trying to reach in order to satisfy a debt due from the defendant.

Garnishment: A proceeding by which a plaintiff seeks to reach the credits of the defendant that are in the hands of a third party, the garnishee. A garnishment is distinguished from an attachment in that by an attachment an officer of the court takes actual possession of property by virtue of his writ. In a garnishment, the property or money is left with the garnishee until final adjudication.

General agent: An agent authorized to do all the acts connected with carrying on a particular trade, business, or profession.

Gift: A gift is made when a donor delivers the subject matter of the gift into the donee's hands, or places in the donee the means of obtaining possession of the subject matter, accompanied by such acts as show clearly that the donor intends to divest himself of all dominion and control over the property.

Gift causa mortis: A gift made in anticipation of death. The donor must have been in sickness and have died as expected; otherwise, no effective gift has been made. If the donor survives, the gift is revocable.

Gift inter vivos: A gift inter vivos is an effective gift made during the life of the donor. By a gift inter vivos, property vests immediately in the donee at the time of delivery; whereas, a gift causa mortis is made in contemplation of death and is effective only upon the donor's death.

Going business: "Going business" is a term applied to an insolvent corporation or firm, when it is "still carrying on with the apparent prospect and expectation of continuing to do so even though its assets are insufficient to meet its obligations."

Good and marketable title: In a contract to sell land, a title showing a complete and unbroken chain as evidenced by the record in the recording office is a marketable title.

Good title: A title free from incumbrance, such as mortgages and liens, as disclosed by a complete abstract of the title as taken from the records in the recorder's office.

Goods (1): Synonymous with the word "property." Specifically it means a "stock of goods," or articles of trade often called "goods, wares, and merchandise."

Goods (2): The word "goods" extensively used may mean real property. A statement in a will "all my worldly goods" includes realty. Cattle, stock certificates, money, notes, and mortgages are called "goods."

Grant: A term used in deeds for the transfer of the title to real property. The words "convey," "transfer," and "grant" as operative words in a deed to pass title are equivalent. The words "grant, bargain, and sell" in a deed, in absence of statute, mean the grantor promises he has good title to transfer free from incumbrances and warrants it to be such.

Grantee: A grantee is a person to whom a grant is made; one named in a deed to receive title.

Grantor: A grantor is a person who makes a grant. The grantor executes the deed by which he divests himself of title.

Gross earnings: Gross earnings are the total "receipts," "proceeds," or "income" derived from the pursuit of a trade, business, or profession.

Gross negligence: The lack of even slight or ordinary care.

Guarantor: One who by contract undertakes "to answer for the debt, default, and miscarriage of another." In general, a guarantor undertakes to pay if the principal debtor does not; a surety, on the other hand, joins in the contract of the principal and becomes an original party with the principal. See *Suretyship*.

Guardian: A person appointed by the court to look after the property rights and person of minors, insane, and other incompetents or legally incapacitated persons.

Guardian ad litem: A special guardian appointed for the sole purpose of carrying on litigation and preserving the interests of a ward. He exercises no control or power over property.

Habeas corpus: A writ issued to a sheriff, warden or official having custody of a person, directing the official to return the person, alleged to be unlawfully held, before a court in order to determine the legality of the imprisonment.

Hawker: An itinerant or traveling trader or peddler. Historically, one who sold his wares by crying them from the street.

Hearsay evidence: Evidence that is learned from someone else. It does not derive its value from the credit of the witness testifying, but rests upon the veracity of another person. It is not good evidence because there is no opportunity to cross-examine the person who is the source of the testimony.

Hedging contract: A contract of purchase or sale of an equal amount of commodities in the future by which brokers, dealers, or manufacturers protect themselves against the fluctuations of the market. It is a type of insurance against changing prices. A grain dealer, to protect himself, may contract to sell for future delivery the same amount of grain he has purchased in the present market.

Heirs: Those persons upon whom the statute of descent casts the title to real property upon the death of the ancestor. See Statutes of descent for the particular state. See *Descent*.

Hinder and delay creditors: The doing of any illegal act by a debtor that causes an obstacle or difficulty to be presented to his creditors in reaching his assets for the satisfaction of his debts. Transfer of property by a debtor for less than its value is an illustration of hindering creditors.

Holder: As applied to negotiable instruments, "a holder means the payee or endorsee in possession of a bill or note or the bearer thereof."

Holder in due course: "A person who takes a negotiable instrument under the the following conditions: (1) That it is complete and regular on its face; (2) That he becomes the holder of it before it was overdue and without notice that it had been previously dishonored, if such was the fact; (3) That he took it in good faith and for value; (4) That at the time it was negotiated to him he had no notice of any infirmity in the instrument or defect in the title of the person negotiating it."

Holding company: A corporation organized for the purpose of owning and holding the stock of other corporations. Shareholders of underlying corporations receive in exchange for their stock, upon an agreed value, the shares in the holding corporation.

Homestead: A parcel of land upon which a family dwells or resides, and which to them is home. The statute of the state or federal government should be consulted to determine the meaning of the term as applied to debtor's exemptions, federal land grants, and so forth.

Householder: The term has different meanings as applied to the right to serve on the jury, or to have property exempt from execution for personal debts. See *Freeholder*. Consult Statute of state.

Idem sonans: Absolute accuracy in spelling names is not required in legal documents. If a name spelled in a document is different from the correct name, it is still legally effective as sufficient name of a person, if, when pronounced, it sounds to the ear the same as the correct name. This is called the doctrine of idem sonans. For example: Smythe and Smith. Mackey and Macky.

If: the word "if" in legal documents, wills, and contracts imports a condition.

Ignorance of law is no excuse: This phrase expresses a rule of necessity for the preservation of law and order. If all persons could be immune from the law because of ignorance, it would be impossible to administer the criminal and civil laws.

Illegal: Conduct that is contrary to public policy and the fundamental principles of law is illegal. Such conduct includes not only violations of criminal statutes, but also the creation of agreements that are prohibited by statute and the common law.

Illusory: That which has a false appearance. If that which appears to be a promise is not a promise, it is said to be illusory. For example: "*A* promises to buy *B*'s horse, if *A* wants to," is no promise. Such equivocal statement would not justify reliance; thus, it is not a promise.

Immunity: Freedom from the legal duties and penalties imposed upon others. The "privileges and immunities" clause of the United States Constitution means no state can deny to the citizens of another state the same rights granted to its own citizens. This does not apply to office holding. See *Exemption*.

Impanel: The word means to list the persons who are to be drawn for jury service. It applies not only to the general list returned by the sheriff to serve for a term of court, but also to the list used by the clerk for a particular case.

Implied: The finding of a legal right or duty by inference from facts or circumstances. See *Warranty*.

In bulk: In large quantity, as distinguished from "package" or "parcel." The sale of all of a stock of goods would be in bulk.

In personam: A legal proceeding, the judgment of which binds the defeated party to a personal liability.

In rem: A legal proceeding, the judgment of which binds, affects, or determines the status of property.

In statu quo: The conditions existing at the time of the commencement of an action, or, in case of rescission of contract, the position of the parties just prior to the creation of the contract.

In toto: In the whole amount. All together. As the persons were liable in toto.

Inalienable: The words means not capable of transfer or sale. The right to sue for a tort is inalienable. Contracts for personal service are inalienable choses in action. The word means nonassignable.

Inchoate: Incomplete situations out of which rights and duties may later arise. It also means "as yet not perfect." For example: a wife's dower is inchoate until her husband's death.

Incidental beneficiary: If the performance of a promise would indirectly benefit a person not a party to a contract, such person is an incidental beneficiary. *A* promises *B*, for a consideration, to plant a valuable nut orchard on *B*'s land. Such improvement would increase the value of the adjacent land. *C*, the owner of the adjacent land, is an incidental beneficiary. He has no remedy if *A* breaches his promise with *B*.

Incontestable: As applied to insurance, a clause in an insurance policy which states that after a certain period of time the policy may not be contested except for nonpayment of the premiums.

Incorporeal: Not manifest to the senses. The right of an owner of land to take the water of a stream for irrigation is an incorporeal hereditament.

Incumbrance: A burden on either the title to land or thing, or upon the land or thing itself. A mortgage or other lien is an incumbrance upon the title. A right of way over the land is an incumbrance upon the land and affects its physical condition.

Indebtedness: To be under a duty to another, usually for the payment of money. It is not a contract, but it may be the result of a contract.

Indemnity: A duty resting on one perosn to make good a loss or damage another has suffered. *A* contracts to build a house for *B*. *B* contracts with *C* for a premium to answer for any loss *B* may suffer by reason of *A*'s default. If *A* defaults and *B* suffers loss, *C* will indemnify *B*.

Indenture: A deed executed by both parties, as distinguished by a deed poll that is executed only by the grantor.

Independent contractor: The following elements are essential to establish the relation of independent contractor in contradistinction to principal and agent. An independent contractor must: (1) exercise his independent judgment as to the means used to accomplish the result; (2) be free from control or orders from any other person; (3) be responsible only under his contract for the result obtained.

Indictment: An indictment is a finding by a grand jury that it has reason to believe the accused is guilty as charged. It informs the accused of the offense with which he is charged in order that he may prepare his defense. It is a pleading in a criminal action.

Indorsement: Writing one's name upon paper for the purpose of transferring the title. When a payee of a negotiable instrument writes his name on the back of the instrument, such writing is an indorsement.

Inequitable conduct: When applied to contracts, inequitable conduct means the doing of acts, omitting to do acts, and making deceptive representations concerning performances, any one of which defeats the justifiable expectations of the other party to the contract and which the court finds to be unconscionable.

Inference: A deduction or conclusion from known facts.

Information: An allegation made by a prosecuting officer to a magistrate that a person has committed a crime. See *Indictment*.

Infringement: Infringement of a patent on a machine is the manufacturing of a machine that produces the same result by the same means and operation as the patented machine. Infringement of a trademark consists in the reproduction of a registered trademark and its use upon goods in order to mislead the public to believe that the goods are the genuine, original product.

Inhabitant: The term is used to designate a person who has a place that is the principal place of his residence, his business, his attachments, and his political and municipal relationships. See *Domicile.*

Inherit: The word is used in contradistinction to acquiring property by will. See *Descent.*

Inheritance: An inheritance denotes an estate that descends to heirs. See *Descent.*

Injunction: A writ of judicial process issued by a court of equity by which a party is required to do a particular thing or to refrain from doing a particular thing.

Injunction pendente lite: A provisional remedy granted by a court of equity before a hearing upon the merits of a suit, for the purpose of preventing the doing of any act whereby the rights in the controversy may be materially changed.

Insolvent: An insolvent debtor is one whose property is insufficient to pay all his debts, or out of which his debts may be collected. Within the Bankruptcy Act, "Whenever the aggregate of his property . . . shall not at a fair valuation be sufficient in amount to pay his debts."

Insurable interest: A person has an insurable interest in a person or property if he will be directly and financially affected by the death of the person or the loss of the property.

Insurance: By an insurance contract, one party, for an agreed premium, binds himself to another, called the insured, to pay to the insured a sum of money conditioned upon the loss of life or property of the insured.

Intent: A state of mind that exists prior to or contemporaneous with an act. A purpose or design to do or forbear to do an act. It cannot be directly proven, but is inferred from known facts.

Interim certificate: An instrument negotiable by statute in some states payable in stocks or bonds, and given prior to the issuance of the stocks or bonds in which payable.

Interlocutory decree: A decree of a court of equity that does not settle the complete issue, but settles only some intervening part, awaiting a final decree.

Interpleader: A remedy available to a stakeholder whereby he can require rival claimants to the thing or fund, to litigate their rival claims and thus relieve him of the risk of being sued twice.

Inter sese: Between or among themselves.

Intestate: The intestate laws are the laws of descent or distribution of the estate of a deceased person. A person dies intestate who has not made a will.

Intrinsic value: The true or inherent value independent of place, person, or scarcity. The same value to different persons at different places and different times.

Inventory: An itemized list, usually showing kind and quantity, of articles composing part of the assets of an estate, institution, corporation, stock in trade, etc., with the value of each article enumerated.

Irreparable damage or injury: Irreparable does not mean such injury as is beyond the possibility of repair, but it does mean that it is so constant and frequent in occurrence that no fair or reasonable redress can be had in a court of law. Thus, the plaintiff must seek a remedy in equity by way of an injunction.

Issue (in a will): The word, as applied to a will, means descendants of whatever degree.

Issue (in pleading): The purpose of pleadings in a court proceeding is to find the "issue"; that is, a point which is affirmed on one side and denied on the other.

Issue (bonds and securities): As applied to bonds and securities, the word means those bonds and securities that are created and delivered at the same time.

Itinerant trader: A person who travels from place to place for the purpose of trading, either by samples or by display of his wares.

Jeopardy: A person is in jeopardy when he is regularly charged with a crime before a court properly organized and competent to try him. If acquitted, he cannot be tried again for the same offense.

Joint adventure: When two persons enter into a single enterprise for their mutual benefit without the intention of continuous pursuit, they have entered a joint adventure. They are essentially partners.

Joint contract: If two or more persons promise upon the same consideration for the same purpose to another party, they are joint obligors to the other party to the contract and have formed a joint contract.

Joint ownership: The interest that two or more parties have in property. Such interest has no existence in the absence of the interest of the other parties. The parties together own the total interest. *A*, *B*, and *C* as a unit own the property. See *Joint tenants*.

Joint tenants: Two or more persons to whom is deeded land in such manner that they have "one and the same interest, accruing by one and the same conveyance, commencing at one and the same time, and held by one and the same undivided possession." Upon the death of one joint tenant, his property passes to the survivor or survivors. Some states have abolished joint tenancy; other states make joint tenants, tenants in common.

The Statute of Descent does not apply to this type of estate so long as there is a survivor. See *Entirety*.

Joint tort-feasors: When two persons commit an injury with a common intent, they are joint tort-feasors.

Joint will: A joint will is a single will of two or more persons. A mutual will is one by which each testator makes a testamentary disposition in favor of the other.

Judgment (in law): A judgment is the decision, pronouncement, or sentence rendered by a court upon an issue in which it has jurisdiction.

Judgment in personam: A judgment against a person directing the defendant to do or not to do something, is a judgment in personam. See *In personam*.

Judgment in rem: A judgment against a thing, as distinguished from a judgment against a person. See *In rem*.

Judicial discretion: The freedom of a judge to apply rules and principles of law and to recognize such facts as are pertinent to the cause in coming to a decision of the case.

Judicial sale: A judicial sale is a sale authorized by a court that has jurisdiction to grant such authority. Such sales are conducted by an officer of the court. See *Sale*.

Jurisdiction: The authority conferred upon a court by the constitution to try cases and determine causes.

Jury: A group of persons, usually twelve, sworn to declare the facts of a case as they are proved from the evidence presented to them, and, upon instructions from the court, to find a verdict in the cause before them.

Kite checks: To execute and deliver a check in payment of a debt at a time when the drawer has insufficient money in the bank, but with the intention of making a deposit to cover the shortage before the check is presented for payment.

Label: The term is broader than "trademark" in that it particularly includes a general description of the goods and indicates the source of the chattel.

Laches: Laches is a term used in equity to name that conduct which is neglect to assert one's rights or to do what by the law a person should have done and did not do. Such failure on the part of one to assert a right will give an equitable defense to another party.

L.S.: The letters are an abbreviation for the Latin phrase "locus sigilli," meaning "place of the seal."

Latent defect: A defect in materials not discernible by examination. Used in contradistinction to patent defect which is discernible.

Lease: A contract by which one person divests himself of possession of lands or chattels and grants such possession to another for a period of time. The relationship where land is involved is called landlord and tenant.

Leasehold: The land held by a tenant under a lease.

Legacy: Personal property disposed of by a will. Sometimes the term is synonymous with bequest. The word "devise" is used in connection with real property distributed by will. See *Bequest, Devise*.

Legal holiday: Legal holidays are created by the legislature. On such days, —Sunday, the Fourth of July, Christmas, Labor Day, and so forth—statutes generally provide that no person shall be held to answer in court, no public elections shall be held, and no depositions taken. Also debts maturing on legal holidays are not collectible until the next business day. Consult Statute of state.

Legal incapacity: A person who has no power to sue except by a guardian, or a person such as an infant or insane person who has the power of avoidance of contract liabilities.

Legal right: Any claim that is enforceable in a court that has jurisdiction over the issue.

Legal tender: Any money which, if received, will discharge a debt. See *Money, Currency*.

Legatee: A person to whom a legacy is given by will.

Letter of credit: A letter of credit is a letter containing a request that the party to whom it is addressed pay the bearer or person named therein money, sell him commodities on credit, or give him something of value, with the intention that the addressee later seek payment from the writer of the letter. It is used by a buyer to secure goods without the necessity of having cash in hand.

Letters testamentary: The orders or authority granted by a probate court to an administrator or representative of an estate whereby such person has power to reduce to money the estate of a deceased and make proper disposition. There are two kinds of letters. "Domiciliary letters" are issued at the domicile of the testator. When property is found in places other than at the domicile of the testator, the courts of such places issue "ancillary letters." Examples: *A* lives in state *B*. At his death, he owned property in state *C*. "Ancillary letters" will be issued in state *C*.

Levy (taxes): The word as applied to taxation means to impose or assess, or to charge and collect, a sum of money against a person or property for public purposes.

Levy (writ of): The literal use refers to the seizure of the defendant's property by the sheriff to satisfy the plaintiff's judgment. The word sometimes means that a lien has been attached to land and other property of the defendant by virtue of a judgment.

Liability: In its broadest legal sense, the word means any obligation one may be under by reason of some rule of law. It includes debt, duty, and responsibility.

Libel: The malicious publication of a defamation of a person by printing, writing, signs, or pictures, for the purpose of injuring the reputation and good name of such person. "The exposing of a person to public hatred, contempt, or ridicule."

Liberty: The word "liberty" is generally defined with reference to the Constitution of the United States. In its broad sense, the word means, "The right of every person not only to be free from servitude, imprisonment, or restraint, but the right of every person to use his faculties in all lawful ways, to live and work where he will, to earn his living in any lawful calling, and to pursue any lawful trade or profession, to worship God according to the dictates of his own conscience," and to write and speak his opinion limited only by the law of libel and slander.

License (privilege): A license is a mere personal privilege given by the owner to another to do designated acts upon the land of the owner. It is revocable at will, creates no estate in the land, and such licensee is not in possession. "It is a mere excuse for what otherwise would be a trespass."

License (governmental regulation): A license is a privilege granted by a state or city upon the payment of a fee, which confers authority upon the licensee to do some act or series of acts, which otherwise would be illegal. A license is not a contract and may be revoked for cause. It is a method of governmental regulation exercised under the police power. Examples: license to keep dogs in the city, to sell commodities in the street.

Lien: A right one person, usually a creditor, has, to keep possession of or control the property of another for the purpose of satisfying a debt. There are many kinds of liens: judgment liens, attorneys' liens, innkeepers' liens, loggers' liens, vendors' liens. Consult Statute of state for type of liens. See *Judgment.*

Limitation of actions: Statutes of limitations exist for the purpose of bringing to an end old claims. Because witnesses die, memory fails, papers are lost, and the evidence becomes inadequate, stale claims are barred. Such statutes are called statutes of repose. Within a certain period of time, action on claims must be brought; otherwise, they are barred. The period varies from 6 months to 20 years.

Lineal descendant: A lineal descendant is one descended in a direct line from another person such as son, grandson, great-grandson, etc.

Liquidated: A claim is liquidated when it has been made fixed and certain by the parties concerned.

Liquidated damages: A fixed sum agreed upon between the parties to a contract, to be paid as ascertained damages by that party who breaches the contract. If the sum is excessive, the courts will declare it to be a penalty and unenforceable.

Liquidation: The process of winding up the affairs of a corporation or firm for the purpose of paying its debts and disposing of its assets. May be done voluntarily or under the orders of a court.

Lis pendens: The words mean, "pending the suit nothing should be changed." The court, having control of the property involved in the suit, issues notice "lis pendens," that persons dealing with the defendant regarding the subject matter of the suit, do so subject to final determination of the action.

Local agent: Statutes provide that foreign corporations doing business within a state shall designate a person upon whom service shall be had for the purpose of giving the local courts jurisdiction. Such person is often called a local agent. Consult local statutes.

Lottery: A scheme of gambling for the distribution of prizes, based upon chance, by which, among those persons who have paid, one or more may secure the prize. Three elements are essential: payment of money; offering of a prize; and distribution of the prize resulting from chance.

Lowest bidder: The phrase "lowest bidder" for public works does not mean the mathematical and grammatical "lowest," but the best, most practical and responsible "lowest bidder."

Magistrate: A public officer, usually a judge, "Who has power to issue a warrant for the arrest of a person charged with a public offense." The word has wide application and includes justices of the peace, notaries public, recorders, and other public officers who have power to issue executive orders.

Maintenance (in law suits): The assisting of either party to a law suit by a person who has no interest therein. An officious intermeddling in a law suit.

Mala in se: Acts that are "bad in themselves" and are void of any legal consequences. A contract to do immoral acts is illegal and void because mala in se. Such acts are in contradistinction to acts "mala prohibita," which means illegal because prohibited by statute.

Malice: Malice is a term to define a wrongful act done intentionally without excuse. It does not necessarily mean ill will, but it indicates a state of mind that is reckless concerning the law and the rights of others. Malice is distinguished from negligence in that in malice there is always a purpose to injure, whereas such is not true of the word "negligence."

Malicious: Possessed of a wilful and purposeful intent to injure another without just cause.

Malicious prosecution: The prosecution of another at law with malice and without probable cause to believe that such legal action will be successful.

Mandamus: A writ issued by a court of law, in the name of the state, directed to some inferior court, officer, corporation, or person commanding them to do a particular thing that appertains to their office or duty.

Mandatory: As applied to statutes, a mandatory provision is one, the noncompliance with which creates no legal consequences. For example, city bonds, issued in violation of statutory requirements that are mandatory, are void.

Mandatory injunction: An injunctive order issued by a court of equity that compels affirmative action by the defendant.

Margin: A sum of money deposited by a principal, buyer, or seller, with his broker to protect the broker against any loss due to price fluctuation in buying and selling.

Marital rights: The rights acquired by husband and wife by reason of the marriage status.

Maritime contract: A contract, the subject matter of which relates to transportation by sea and the employment of seamen. Litigation concerning such contracts is within admiralty jurisdiction.

Marketable title: A title of such character that no apprehension as to its validity would occur to the mind of a reasonable and intelligent person. The title to goods in litigation, subject to incumbrances, in doubt as to a third party's right, or subject to lien, is not marketable.

Marshaling assets: A principle in equity for a fair distribution of a debtor's assets among his creditors. For example, when a creditor of *A*, by reason of prior right, has two funds *X* and *Y* belonging to *A* out of which he may satisfy his debt, but *B*, also a creditor of *A*, has a right as to *X* fund, the first creditor will be compelled to exhaust *Y* fund before he will be permitted to participate in *X* fund.

Master in chancery: An officer appointed by the court to assist the court of equity in taking testimony, computing interest, auditing accounts, estimating damages, ascertaining liens, and doing such other tasks incidental to a suit, as the court may require. The power of a master is merely advisory and his task largely fact-finding.

Material alteration: Any alteration of a written instrument that affects the identity of the parties or changes the legal obligations and rights of the parties is material.

Maxim: A proposition of law that because of its universal approval needs no proof or argument, and the mere statement of which gives it authority. Example: "A principal is bound by the acts of his agent, when the agent is acting within the scope of his authority."

Mechanics' lien: A mechanics' lien is created by statute to assist laborers in collecting their wages. Such lien has for its purpose to subject the land of an owner to a lien for material and labor expended in the construction of buildings, which buildings having been placed on the land become a part thereof by the law of accession.

Mens rea: The term means "guilty mind." It is an element that has to be proven to sustain a verdict of guilty for a criminal offense. It is generally presumed from the proven facts.

Merger: Two corporation are merged when one corporation continues in existence and the other loses its identity by its absorption into the first. Merger must be distinguished from consolidation, in which case both corporations are dissolved, and a new one created which takes over the assets of the dissolved corporations.

Ministerial duty: The performance of a prescribed duty that requires the exercise of little judgment or discretion. A sheriff performs ministerial duties.

Minutes: The record of a court or the written transactions of the members or board of directors of a corporation. Under the certificate of the clerk of a court or the secretary of a corporation, the minutes are the official evidence of court or corporate action.

Misdemeanor: A criminal offense, less than a felony, that is not punishable by death or imprisonment. Consult the local statute.

Misfeasance: The improper performance of a duty imposed by law or contract which injures another person. It is distinguished from nonfeasance which means doing nothing of an imposed duty.

Misrepresentation: The affirmative statement or affirmation of a fact that is not true; the term does not include concealment of true facts or nondisclosure or the mere expression of opinion.

Mistake of fact: The unconscious ignorance or forgetfulness of the existence or nonexistence of a fact, past or present, which is material and important to the creation of a legal obligation.

Mistake of law: An erroneous conclusion of the legal effect of known facts.

Mitigation of damages: A plaintiff is entitled to recover damages caused by the defendant's breach, but the plaintiff is also under a duty to avoid increasing or enhancing such damages. Such is called a duty to mitigate damages. If a seller fails to deliver the proper goods on time, the buyer, where possible, must buy other goods, thus mitigating damages.

Money: Coined metal, gold, silver, or other metal upon which there is placed the stamp or seal of a government. Such stamp or seal indicates the value of the coin and gives it currency to discharge a debt. The word includes paper, such as bank notes, silver certificates, and Federal Reserve notes. See *Legal tender*.

Monopoly: The exclusive control of the supply and price of a commodity that may be acquired by a franchise or patent from the government; or, the ownership of the source of a commodity or the control of its distribution.

Moot case: A judgment in advance of a presumed controversy, the decision of which has no legal effect upon any existing controversy.

Mortgage: A conveyance or transfer of an interest in property for the purpose of creating a security for a debt. The mortgage becomes void upon payment of the debt, although the recording of a release is necessary to clear the title of the mortgaged property.

Motive: The reason or cause why a person does a particular act. Intent, on the other hand, is the purpose to use a particular means or to do a particular act to reach a particular result.

Mutual assent: In every contract each party must agree to the same thing. Each must know what the other intends; they must mutually assent or be in agreement.

Mutuality: A word used to describe the situation in every contract that it must be binding on both parties. Each party to the contract must be bound to the other party to do something by virtue of the legal duty created.

Negligence: The failure to do that which an ordinary, reasonable, prudent man would do, or the doing of some act which an ordinary, prudent man would not do.

Reference must always be made to the situation, the circumstances, and the knowledge of the parties.

Negotiate: To transfer an instrument from one person to another in such manner as to make the transferee the holder thereof.

Net: The word indicates that something has been deducted; charges, freight, storage, and the like.

Net assets: The property or effects of a firm, corporation, institution, or estate, remaining after all its obligations have been paid.

Net cash: As between buyer and seller, the term means the buyer shall pay to the seller a price which shall include all expenses.

Net earnings: A sum remaining from the operation of a business, trade, profession, institution, trust, fund, estate, etc., after the deduction of all necessary charges and expenses.

Nolle prosequi: A discharge of a particular indictment against the accused by the court upon request of the prosecuting officer. It is not an acquittal nor a pardon. The accused may be indicted again and tried for the same offense.

Nolo contendere: This plea by an accused in a criminal action is an implied confession of the offense charged. It virtually equals a plea of guilty. A judgment of conviction follows such plea.

Nominal damages: A small sum assessed as sufficient to award the case and cover the costs. In such case, no actual damages have been proven.

Non compos mentis: One who does not possess understanding sufficient to comprehend the nature, extent, and meaning of his contracts or other legal obligations.

Non obstante verdicto: A judgment given to the moving party notwithstanding the verdict already obtained. If upon re-examination, the court finds the plaintiff's pleadings demurrable, he will enter a judgment "non obstante verdicto" even though the plaintiff has a verdict.

Nonfeasance: The failure to perform a legal duty. See *Misfeasance.*

Nonresident: The citizen of another state.

Nonsuit: A judgment given against the plaintiff when he is unable to prove his case or fails to proceed with the trial after the case is at issue.

Notary: A public officer authorized to administer oaths by way of affidavits and depositions; also to attest deeds and other formal papers in order that such papers may be used as evidence and be qualified for recording.

Novation: The substitution of one obligation for another. When debtor *A* is substituted for debtor *B*, and by agreement with the creditor *C*, debtor *B* is discharged, a novation has occurred.

Nuisance: The word nuisance is generally applied to any continuous or continued conduct that causes annoyance, inconvenience, and damage to person or property. It usually applies to the unreasonable and wrongful use of property that produces material discomfort, hurt, and damage to the person or property of another. Example: Fumes from a factory.

Oath: A pledge given by a person that what he is about to say is true and that such statement is made under a responsibility to God. If taken before a court and the statements are not true, the oath-taker has committed perjury. If statements are untrue and the oath is not taken before a court, the oath-taker is guilty of false swearing.

Obligation: The term obligation is synonymous with duty.

Obligee: A creditor or promisee.

Obligor: A debtor or promisor.

Occupation: The term is synonymous with calling, trade, business, or profession.

Operating expenses: The value of the use of the property that is used but not consumed; the value of the labor and management; and the value of property consumed in performing the operation.

Opinion: An opinion is a conviction founded upon probable evidence. In a strict legal sense, the opinion of a court is the reason the court gives for its decision. See *Decision, Judgment.*

Option: A right secured by a contract to accept or reject an offer to purchase property at a fixed price within a fixed time. It is an irrevocable offer sometimes called a "paid-for offer."

Ordinance: An ordinance is, generally speaking, the legislative act of a municipality. A city council is a legislative body and passes ordinances that are the laws of the city.

Ordinary care: That care that a prudent man would take under the circumstances of the particular case.

Overt act: Overt means open. Overt act is any motion, gesture, conduct, or demonstration that evidences a present design to do a particular act that will lead to a desired result.

Par value: The words mean face value. The par value of stocks and bonds on the date of issuance is the principal. At a later date, the par value is the principal plus interest.

Pari materia: Latin words that mean "related to the same matter or subject." Statutes and covenants concerning the same subject matter are in pari materia, and as a general rule, for the purpose of ascertaining their meaning, are construed together.

Parole: The release of a convict from prison on certain conditions to be observed by him, as well as a suspension of his sentence while he is at liberty.

Partition: Court proceedings brought at the request of a party in interest, that real property be taken by the court and divided among the respective owners as their interests appear. If the property is incapable of division in kind, then the property is to be sold and the money divided as each interest appears.

Passbook: A book in which a bank enters the deposits made by a depositor, and which is retained by the depositor.

Patent ambiguity: An uncertainty in a written instrument that is obvious upon reading.

Payment: The discharge of a debt or other obligation.

Penal bond: A bond given by an accused, or by another person in his behalf, for the payment of money if the accused fails to appear in court on a certain day.

Penalty: The term has two different meanings. In criminal law it means the punishment imposed for the commission of a crime. It is used with the word "fine." In civil law, it may mean a sum agreed upon as payable for the breach of promise. The word is sometimes used as synonymous with "forfeiture." See *Liquidated damages.*

Pendente lite: A Latin phrase which means "pending during the progress of a suit at law."

Per curiam: A decision by the full court in which no opinion is given.

Peremptory challenge: An objection, by a party to a law suit, to a person serving as a juror, for which no reason need be given.

Perjury: False swearing upon an oath properly administered in some judicial proceedings. See *Oath.*

Perpetuity: The taking of any subject matter out of the channel of commerce by limiting its capacity to be sold for a period of time longer than that of a life or lives in being and 21 years thereafter plus the period of gestation.

Person or persons: In law, the term includes natural persons and artificial persons, such as corporations.

Persona ficta: The Latin phrase for a fictitious person which refers to the corporate entity or artificial legal person.

Personal property: The rights, powers, and privileges a person has in movable things such as chattels, and choses in action. Personal property is used in contradistinction to real property.

Personal representative: The administrator or executor of a deceased person. The term also means the heir, next of kin, or descendant of a deceased person. The meaning of the term must be ascertained from the context.

Personal service: The term means that the sheriff actually delivered to the defendant in person a service of process.

Picket: A workman, member of a trade union on strike, posted in front of a struck place of employment for the purpose of publicizing that the workmen are on strike.

Place of Business: The place where a person continues to conduct his calling, trade, business, or profession for the purpose of a livelihood, gain, and profit.

Plaintiff: In an action at law, the complaining party or the one who commences the action is called the plaintiff. He is the person who seeks a remedy in court.

Plea: An allegation or answer in a court proceeding.

Pleading: The process by which the parties in a lawsuit arrive at an issue.

Pledge: The deposit or placing of personal property as security for a debt or other obligation with a person called the pledgee. The pledgee has the implied power to sell the property if the debt is not paid. If the debt is paid, the right to possession returns to the pledgor.

Policy of insurance: In insurance law, the word policy means the formal document delivered by the insurance company to the insured, which evidences the rights and duties between the parties.

Polling jury: To poll the jury is to call the name of each juror and inquire what his verdict is before such is made a matter of record.

Possession: The method, recognized by law, of holding, detaining, or controlling by one's self or by another, property, either personal or real, which will exclude others from holding, detaining, or controlling such property.

Precedent: A previously-decided case that can serve as an authority to help decide a present controversy. The use of such case is called the doctrine of "stare decisis," which means to adhere to decided cases and settled principles. Literally, "to stand as decided."

Pre-emption: The right to make a first purchase. The privilege of being first. The word has many applications. At early common law the king had the right to buy provisions for his household in preference to others. In the United States, the government pre-empted land as against settlers.

Preference: The term is used most generally in bankruptcy law. Where a bankrupt makes payment of money to certain creditors enabling them to obtain a greater percentage of their debts than other creditors in the same class, and the payment is made within four months prior to the filing of a bankruptcy petition, such payment constitutes illegal and voidable preference. An intention to prefer such creditors must be shown. An insolvent person may lawfully prefer one creditor to another, if done in good faith and without intent to defraud others.

Preferred stock: Stock that entitles the holder to dividends from earnings before the owners of common stock can receive a dividend.

Premises: As applied to the occupancy of real property, the word includes a definite portion of land, the building and appurtenances thereto over which the occupant exercises control. As applied to a controversy, the word means the general statement of a proposition.

Preponderance: Preponderance of the evidence means that evidence which in the judgment of the jurors is entitled to the greatest weight, which appears to be more credible, has greater force, and overcomes not only the opposing presumptions, but also the opposing evidence.

Prerogative: Rights, powers, privileges, and immunities, which one person has that others do not possess. Ambassadors of foreign countries have certain prerogatives. A senator has the prerogative of making remarks that would be slanderous if used by an ordinary citizen.

Presumption: A presumption is an assumed fact. It may serve as evidence until actual facts are introduced. In absence of actual facts, the person in whose favor a presumption exists prevails. A holder of a negotiable instrument is presumed to be a holder in due course until facts are introduced to the contrary. A disputable presumption makes a prima facie case. See local statute for a list of rebuttable and nonrebuttable presumptions.

Prima facie: The words literally mean "at first view." Thus, that which first appears seems to be true. A prima facie case is one that stands until contrary evidence is produced.

Privilege: A legal idea or concept of lesser significance than a right. An invitee has only a privilege to walk on another's land because such privilege may be revoked at will; whereas, a person who has an easement to go on another's land has a right, created by a grant which is an interest in land and cannot be revoked at will. To be exempt from jury service is a privilege.

Privity: Mutual and successive relationship to the same interest. Offeror and offeree, assignor and assignee, grantor and grantee are in privity. Privity of estate means that one takes title from another. In contract law, privity denotes parties in mutual legal relationship to each other by virtue of being promisees and promisors. At early common law, third party beneficiaries and assignees were said to be not in "privity."

Probate: The word means proof of a will by the proper court.

Process: In court proceeding, a process is an instrument issued by the court in the name of the state before or during the progress of the trial, under the seal of the court, directing an officer of the court to do, act, or cause some act to be done incidental to the trial.

Proof: The legal effect of evidence; that which is established.

Property: All those rights, powers, privileges, and immunities which one has concerning tangibles and intangibles. The term includes everything of value subject to ownership.

Pro tanto: "For so much." Persons are liable pro tanto or for such an amount.

Proximate cause: The cause that sets other causes in operation. The responsible cause of an injury.

Proximate damage: Damages that are direct, immediate, and the natural result of negligence or wrong, and which might reasonably have been expected.

Proxy: Authority to act for another; used by absent stockholders or members of legislative bodies to have their votes cast by others.

Public business: A telephone company, a railroad, or any utility that operates under a franchise from a state or city to carry on a public business.

Public policy: There can be no strict definition for the term "public policy." Any conduct or any contract, the performance of which is against public morals or injurious to the public good, is in violation of public policy.

Punitive damages: Damages by way of punishment allowed for an injury caused by a wrong that is wilful and malicious.

Quantum meruit (in pleading): An allegation that the defendant owes the plaintiff for work and labor a sum for as much as the plaintiff reasonably is entitled.

Quasi contracts: The term "quasi contracts" is used to define a situation where a legal duty arises that does not rest upon a promise, but does involve the payment of money. In order to do justice by a legal fiction, the court enforces the duty as if a promise in fact exists. Thus, if *A* gives *B* money by mistake, *A* can compel *B* to return the money by an action in quasi contract.

Quit claim: A deed that releases a right or interest in land, but which does not include any covenants of warranty. The grantor transfers only that which he has.

Quo warranto: A proceeding in court by which the state, city, county, or other governmental body tests or inquires into the legality of the claim of any person to a public office, franchise, or privilege. It is a proceeding to oust persons from public office.

Quoad: "As to." To illustrate: quoad this agreement means as to this agreement.

Ratification: The confirmation of one's own previous act or act of another: e.g., a principal may ratify the previous unauthorized act of his agent. *B*'s agent, without authority, buys goods. *B*, by keeping the goods and receiving the benefits of the agent's act, ratifies the agency.

Ratify: To ratify means to confirm or approve.

Real property: The term means land with all its buildings, appurtenances, equitable and legal interests therein. The word is used in contradistinction to personal property which refers to moveables or chattels.

Reasonable care: The care that prudent persons would exercise under the same circumstances.

Rebuttal evidence: The evidence that is given to explain, repel, counteract, or disprove the testimony in chief given by the adverse party.

Receiver: An officer of the court appointed on behalf of all parties to the litigation to take possession of, hold, and control the property involved in the suit, for the benefit of the party who will be determined to be entitled thereto.

Recognizance: A recognizance is a contract of record or obligation made before a court by which the parties thereto obligate themselves to perform some act. It is different from a bail bond, in that a bail bond is under seal and creates a new debt. A recognizance is in the nature of a conditional judgment and acknowledges the existence of a present obligation to the state.

Recoupment: A right to deduct from the plaintiff's claim any payment or loss that the defendant has suffered by reason of the plaintiff's wrongful act. The words mean "a cutting back."

Redemption: To buy back. A debtor buys back or redeems his mortgaged property when he pays the debt.

Re-insurance: A contract of re-insurance is where one insurance company agrees to indemnify another insurance company in whole or in part against risks which the first company has assumed. The original contract of insurance and the re-insurance contract are distinct contracts. There is no privity between the original insured and the re-insurer.

Release: The voluntary relinquishing of a right, lien, or any other obligation. A release need not be under seal, nor does it necessarily require consideration. The words "release, remise, and discharge" are often used together to mean the same thing.

Remand: To send back a cause from the appellate court to the lower court in order that the lower court may comply with the instructions of the appellate court. Also to return a prisoner to jail.

Remedy: The word is used to signify the judicial means or court procedures by which legal and equitable rights are enforced.

Remise: The word means discharge or release. It is also synonymous with "quit claim."

Rent: Rent is compensation given to an owner either in money, chattels, or services for the use and occupancy of land.

Replevin: A remedy given by statute for the recovery of the possession of a chattel. Only the right to possession can be tried in such action.

Repudiation: Words or conduct by one of the parties to a contract indicating that he will not perform, or will not continue to perform, a contract is called "repudiation of the contract." Such conduct may be a breach or an anticipatory breach.

Requirements: If a party to a contract agrees to purchase his "requirements," he thereby agrees to purchase what he will need in his regular course of business and not what he may choose to order.

Res: A Latin word that means "thing."

Res adjudicata: The doctrine of "res adjudicata" means that a controversy once having been decided or adjudged upon its merits is forever settled so far as the particular parties involved are concerned. Such a doctrine avoids vexatious lawsuits.

Residence: The place where a person lives and has his abode. It is not synonymous with domicile. See *Domicile.*

Respondent: One who answers another's bill or pleading, particularly in an equity case. Quite similar, in many instances, to defendant in law cases.

Respondeat superior: Latin words that mean the master is liable for the acts of his agent.

Responsible bidder: The word "responsible," as used by most statutes concerning public works in the phrase "lowest responsible bidder," means that such bidder has the requisite skill, judgment, and integrity necessary to perform the contract involved, and has the financial resources and ability to carry the task to completion.

Restraining order: An order issued by a court of equity in aid of a suit to hold matters in abeyance until parties may be heard. A temporary injunction is a restraining order.

Restraint of trade: Monopolies, combinations, and contracts that impede free competition are in restraint of trade.

Retainer: The payment in advance to an attorney to cover future services and advice.

Return of a writ: A sheriff's return of a writ is an official statement written on the back of a summons or other paper that he has performed his duties in compliance with the law or a statement as to why he has not complied with the law.

Right: The phrase "legal right" is a correlative of the phrase "legal duty." One has a legal right if, upon the breach of the correlative legal duty, he can secure a remedy in a court of law.

Right of action: The words are synonymous with "cause of action"; a right to enforce a claim in a court.

Riparian: A person is a riparian owner if his land is situated beside a stream of water, either flowing over or along the border of the land.

Robbery: The stealing or taking away from a person his money or other property either by force and violence or by putting him in fear of force and violence.

Rule (as a noun): The regulation or direction of an administrative body is a rule. A rule of law is a general statement as to what the law is. "Every contract must be supported by consideration," is a rule of law. Rules of court are the rules for practice and procedure in a particular court.

Rule (as a verb): The act of a court issuing an order that a defendant file a pleading is called a rule or command of the court.

Sanction: The penalty for the breach of a rule of law. Redress for civil injuries is called civil sanction; punishment for violation of criminal law is called penal sanction. The word literally means "enforcement."

Satisfaction: The term "satisfaction" in legal phraseology means the release and discharge of a legal obligation. Such satisfaction may be partial or full performance of the obligation. The word is used with accord. Accord means a promise to give a substituted performance for a contract obligation; satisfaction means the acceptance by the obligee of such performance.

Scienter: Knowledge by a defrauding party of the falsity of a representation. In a tort action of deceit, knowledge that a representation is false must be proved.

Scintilla of evidence: A very slight amount of evidence which aids in the proof of an allegation. If there is a "scintilla of evidence," the court generally presents the case to the jury.

Scrip: As applied to corporation law, "scrip" is a written certificate or evidence of a right of a person to obtain shares in a corporation.

Seal: A seal is to show that an instrument was executed in a formal manner. At early common law sealing legal documents was of great legal significance. A promise under seal was binding by virtue of the seal. Today under most statutes any stamp, wafer, mark, scroll, or impression made, adopted, and affixed, is adequate. The printed word "seal" or the letters "L.S." is sufficient.

Security: Security may be bonds, stocks, and other property placed by a debtor with a creditor, with power to sell if the debt is not paid. The plural of the term, "securities," is used broadly to mean tangible choses in action such as promissory notes, bonds, stocks, and other vendible obligations.

Sell: The words "to sell" mean to negotiate or make arrangement for a sale. A sale is an executed contract. "Sell" is the name of the process in executing the contract.

Servant: A person employed by another and subject to the direction and control of the employer in performance of his duties.

Served or service: The delivery of a writ issued out of a court to a proper officer, usually the sheriff, by which a court secures jurisdiction over the defendant. See *Process.*

Set-off: A matter of defense, called a cross-complaint, used by the defendant for the purpose of making a demand on the plaintiff and which arises out of contract, but is independent and unconnected with the cause of action set out in the complaint. See *Counter-claims* and *Recoupment.*

Severable-contract: A contract, the performance of which is divisible. Two or more parts may be set over against each other. Items and prices may be apportioned to each other without relation to the full performance of all of its parts.

Several: A contract in which each promissor makes a separate promise and is separately liable thereon. There may be several promises. If the promissors make a single promise the obligation is joint. A joint and several promissory note consists of the joint promise of all and the separate promise of each. "We jointly and severally promise" is an illustration.

Share of stock: A proportional part of the rights in the management and assets of a corporation. It is a chose in action. The certificate is the evidence of the share.

Sheriff: A public officer whose authority and duties are created by legislation. His duties are to execute and administer the law.

Simulation: A word synonymous with "collusion" which means a fraudulent arrangement between two or more persons to give false or deceptive appearance to a transaction.

Situs: Situs means "place, situation." The place where a thing is located. The "situs" of personal property is the domicile of the owner. The "situs" of land is the state or county where it is located.

Slander: Slander is an oral utterance that tends to injure the reputation of another. See ***Libel.***

Sole ownership: In insurance contracts, ownership is "sole," when no other person has an interest in the insured property.

Solvent: A person is solvent when he is able to pay his debts.

Sovereignty: The word means the power of a state (organized government) to execute its laws, and its right to exercise dominion and authority over its citizens and their property subject only to constitutional limitations.

Special appearance: The appearance in court of a person through his attorney for a limited purpose only. A court does not get jurisdiction over a person by special appearance.

Special verdict: A special verdict is one in which the jury finds the facts only, leaving it to the court to apply the law and draw the conclusion as to the proper disposition of the case.

Specialty: The word "specialty" in commercial law means a promise under seal to pay money—a bond. In early law there were two kinds of "specialties." "Common law specialties" were formal instruments under seal—bonds and covenants; "mercantile specialties" included bills and notes, insurance policies, and other unsealed commercial papers.

Specific performance: A remedy in personam in equity that compels such substantial performance of a contract as will do justice among the parties. A person who fails to obey a writ for specific performance may be put in jail by the equity judge for contempt of court. Such remedy applies to contracts involving real property. In absence of unique goods or peculiar circumstances, damages generally are an adequate remedy for the breach of contracts involving personal property. See Specific Performance under the Uniform Sales Act.

Stand-by pay: A term used to define pay demanded for services which have not been performed or are not to be performed. For example, "to hire one orchestra and then pay for another stand-by orchestra which does no work."

Stare decisis: Translated, the term means "stand by the decision." The law should adhere to decided cases. See *Precedent.*

Statute: A law passed by the legislative body of a state is a statute.

Stock: The word has several meanings. When applied to "goods, wares, and merchandise," it means goods in a mercantile house that are kept for sale. As applied in corporation law, the word means the right of an owner of a share of stock to participate in the management and ownership of a corporation. See *Capital Stock.*

Stock dividend: The issue by a corporation of new shares of its own stock to its shareholders as dividends.

Stockholders: Those persons whose names appear on the books of a corporation as the owners of the shares of stock and who are entitled to participate in the management and control of the corporation.

Stock split-up: A type of readjustment of the financial plan of a corporation whereby each existing share of stock is split into such number of new shares as may be determined by the managers of the corporation.

Stoppage in transitu: The right of a seller of goods, which have not been paid for, upon learning of the insolvency of the buyer, to stop the goods in transit and hold the same as security for the purchase price. It is an extension of the unpaid seller's lien.

Subpoena: A process issued out of a court requiring the attendance of a witness at a trial.

Subrogation: The substitution of one person in another's place, whether as a creditor or as the possessor of any lawful right, so that the substituted person may succeed to the rights, remedies, or proceeds of the claim. It rests in equity on the theory that, where a party is compelled to pay a debt for which another is liable, such payment should vest the paying party with all the rights the creditor has against the debtor. For example: X insurance company pays Y for an injury to Y's car by reason of Z's negligent act. X insurance company will be subrogated to Y's cause of action against Z.

Substantial performance: The complete performance of all the essential elements of a contract. The only permissible omissions or deviations are those which are trivial, inadvertent, and inconsequential. Such performance will not justify repudiation. Compensation for defects may be substituted for actual performance. See *Breach.*

Substantive law: A word applied to that law which regulates and controls the rights and duties of all persons in society. It is used in contradistinction to the term adjective law, which means the rules of court procedure or remedial law which prescribe the methods by which substantive law is enforced.

Succession: The word means the transfer by operation of law of all the rights and obligations of a deceased person to those who are entitled to take.

Succession tax: This tax is not a burden on property, but a tax upon the privilege of taking property, whether by will or descent.

Suit: The term refers to any type of legal proceeding for the purpose of obtaining a legal remedy; the term "suit" generally applies to "suit in equity," whereas, at law, the term is "action at law."

Summons: A writ issued by a court to the sheriff directing him to notify the defendant that the plaintiff claims to have a cause of action against the defendant and that he is required to answer. If the defendant does not answer, judgment will be taken by default.

Surrender: The abandonment of leased premises by a tenant. If a landlord accepts the abandonment as a termination of the lease, a surrender has occurred.

Tacit: That which is understood from the nature of things. Those rules that are generally understood to be the law by reason of customs and mores.

Talisman: A juror summoned to fill up a panel for the trial of a particular case. Such person is not bound to serve the term.

Tangible: Tangible is a word used to describe property that is physical in character and capable of being moved. A debt is intangible, but a promissory note evidencing such debt is tangible. See *Chose in action, Chattel.*

Tax: A sum of money assessed by the government against a person or his property to be used for the support and needs of government.

Tenancy: The interest in property that a tenant acquires from a landlord by a lease is called a tenancy. It may be at will or for a term. It is an interest in land.

Tenant: The person to whom a lease is made. A lessee.

Tender: To offer money in satisfaction of a debt or obligation by producing the same and expressing to the creditor a willingness to pay. See *Legal tender.*

Tenement: The word has historical significance as applied to real property. In a broad sense it means an estate in land or some interest connected therewith, such as houses, rents, profits, and rights, to which a holder of the title is entitled. It is used with the word "hereditaments."

Tenure: The word is used to designate the means by which title is held to real property. For example, "tenure in fee simple," "tenure for life." It also is used to indicate the time limit of a person's right to public office. "Term" means limited time. "Tenure" means indefinite.

Term of court: That period of time prescribed by statute within which a court may legally hold its sessions and transact its business.

Testament: A testament is the declaration of a person's intention as to what disposition he desires to be made of his property after his death. The word is synonymous with will. The word is so used because a will is a testimonial of one's intention.

Testamentary capacity: A person is said to have testamentary capacity when he understands the nature of his business, the value of his property, knows those persons who are natural objects of his bounty, and comprehends the manner in which he has provided for the distribution of his property.

Testator: A male person who has died leaving a will. A female person is called a testatrix.

Testimony: Those statements made by a witness under oath or affirmation in a legal proceeding. See *Evidence.*

Title: This word has different meanings. It may be limited or broad in its meaning. When a person has the exclusive rights, powers, privileges, and immunities to property, real and personal, tangible and intangible, against all other persons, he may be said to have the complete title thereto. The aggregate of legal relations concerning property is the title. The term is used to describe the means by which a person exercises control and dominion over property. A trustee has a limited title. See *Possession.*

Tonnage: In marine insurance, registered tonnage means the vessel's carrying capacity as stated in the ship's papers at the date of the policy, and not the tonnage fixed by the law of the government under which the vessel is registered.

Tort: A wrongful act committed by one person against another person or his property. It is the breach of a legal duty imposed by law other than by contract. The word tort means "twisted" or "wrong." *A* assaults *B,* thus committing a tort. See *Right, Duty.*

Total disability: In a contract of insurance, these words do not mean "absolute helplessness." Their meaning is relative, depending on the circumstances of each case, the occupation, and capabilities of the insured.

Trade fixtures: Personal property placed upon or annexed to leased land by a tenant for the purpose of carrying on a trade or business during the term of the lease. Such property is generally to be removed at the end of the term, providing it can be so removed without destruction or injury to the premises. Trade fixtures include show cases, shelving, racks, machinery, and the like.

Trade-mark: No complete definition can be given for a trade-mark. Generally it is any sign, symbol, mark, word, or arrangement of words in the form of a label adopted and used by a manufacturer or distributor to designate his particular goods, and which no other person has the legal right to use. Originally, the design or trade-mark indicated origin, but today it is used more as an advertising mechanism.

Trade union: A combination of workmen usually (but not necessarily) of the same trade organized for the purpose of securing by united action the most favorable working conditions for its members.

Transfer: In its broadest sense, the word means the act by which an owner sets over or delivers his right, title, and interest in property to another person. A "bill of sale" to personal property is evidence of a transfer.

Treasury stock: Stock of a corporation that has been issued by the corporation for value, but that is later returned to the corporation by way of gift or purchase or otherwise. It may be returned to the trustees of a corporation for the purpose of sale.

Trespass: An injury to the person, property, or rights of another person committed by actual force and violence, or under such circumstances that the law will imply that the injury was caused by force or violence.

Trial: A proceeding by the properly authorized officials into the examination of the facts and for the purpose of determining an issue presented according to proper rules of law.

Trust: A relationship between persons by which one holds property for the use and benefit of another. The relationship is called fiduciary. Such rights are enforced in a court of equity. The person trusted is called a trustee. The person for whose benefit the property is held is called a beneficiary or "cestui que trust."

Trustee in bankruptcy: An agent of the court authorized to liquidate the assets of the bankrupt, protect them, and to bring them to the court for final distribution for the benefit of the bankrupt and all the creditors.

Trustee (generally): A person who is intrusted with the management and control of another's property and estate. A person occupying a fiduciary position. An executor, an administrator, a guardian.

Ultra vires: Literally the words mean "beyond power." The acts of a corporation are ultra vires when they are beyond the power or capacity of the corporation as granted by the state in its charter.

Undertaking: A so-called informal bond without a seal is called an "undertaking."

Unfair competition: The imitation by design of the goods of another for the purpose of palming them off on the public, thus misleading the public by inducing it to buy goods made by the imitator. It includes misrepresentation and deceit; thus, such conduct is fraudulent not only as to competitors but as to the public.

Unilateral contract: A promise for an act or an act for a promise; a single enforceable promise. *A* promises *B* $10 if *B* will mow *A*'s lawn. *B* mows the lawn. *A*'s promise now binding is a unilateral contract. See *Bilateral contract.*

Unlawful: An act is unlawful in the strict sense when it is in violation of a rule of law. A criminal act is unlawful. An act that is merely not authorized may be unlawful. Such act carries no punishment. It merely has no legal consequence. See *Void, Illegal.*

Usage: When conduct has been long continued and is of uniform practice, it will fall within the category of "usage." Usage is a fact, not opinion. In trade, it is a course of dealing. Customs are the rules of law that arise from usage. Customs rest on usage.

Usurious: A contract is usurious if made for a loan of money at a rate of interest in excess of that permitted by statute.

Utter: The word means to put out or pass off. To utter a check is to offer it to another in payment of a debt. The words "utter a forged writing" mean to put such writing in circulation, knowing of the falsity of the instrument with the intent to injure another.

Vacancy: As applied to a fire insurance policy, the words "vacancy," "vacant," or "unoccupied" mean, "that if the house insured should cease to be used as a place of human habitation or for living purposes, it would then be vacant or unoccupied." The period of time is unimportant. Vacant property increases the risk of the insurer, hence violates the policy.

Valid: That which is sufficient to satisfy the requirements of the law. A valid judgment is one lawfully obtained under the proper rules of procedure and evidence.

Valuable consideration: Any consideration that will support a simple contract. A classic definition is, "valuable consideration consists of some right, interest, profit, or benefit or value accruing to the promisor, and some forbearance, detriment, loss, or responsibility given or suffered by the promisee."

Value: The term has many meanings in law. Value is any consideration sufficient to support a simple contract. Although an antecedent debt would not be value to support a simple contract, it is considered adequate to support a negotiable instrument by the Law Merchant. A "bona fide purchaser," called a "B.F.P.," gives up something of value, either money, property, or services. Value in a business sense means market value. The money equivalent of property is value.

Valued policy: As used in fire insurance, a valued policy is one in which the sum to be paid in case of loss is fixed by the terms of the policy. No reference can be made to the real value of the property that is lost.

Vendee: A purchaser of property. The term is generally applied to the purchaser of real property. The word "buyer" is usually applied to the purchaser of chattels.

Vendor: The seller of property. The term is usually applied to the seller of real property. The word "seller" is applied to the seller of personal property.

Vendor's lien: An unpaid seller's right to hold possession of property until he has recovered the purchase price. See *Seller's lien.*

Venire: To come into court; a writ used to summon a jury. The word is used sometimes to mean jury.

Venue: The geographical area over which a court presides. Venue designates the county in which the action is tried. Change of venue means a move to another county.

Verdict: The decision of a jury, reported to the court, on matters properly submitted to it for its consideration.

Verify: To fix, determine, or establish a fact by a statement under oath. A corporate secretary verifies, by oath, that a statement is an exact copy of part of the minutes of a corporate meeting.

Vested: The word generally applies to the title to or interests in land. The word strictly means "there is an immediate right of present enjoyment, or a present fixed right of future enjoyment." A life estate is a vested interest. Dower right of a wife, however, is not vested until the death of the husband.

Vis major: The force of nature, sometimes called "act of God," which excuses persons from liability. If the ordinary exertion of human skill and prudence cannot avoid the effect of the force of nature, then an obligor may be excused under the doctrine of impossibility of performance.

Void: That which has no legal effect. A contract that is void is a nullity and confers no rights or duties.

Voidable: That which is valid until one party, who has the power of avoidance, exercises such power. An infant has the power of avoidance of his contract. A defrauded party has the power to avoid his contract. Such contract is voidable.

Voucher: A written instrument that bears witness or "vouches" for something. Generally a voucher is an instrument showing services have been performed or goods purchased, and is presented to a disbursing officer authorizing him to make payment and charge the proper account.

Wager: A relationship between persons by which they agree that a certain sum of money or thing owned by one of them will be paid or delivered to the other upon the happening of an uncertain event, which event is not within the control of the parties and rests upon chance. Consult state statutes.

Wages: Compensation or reward, usually money, paid at stated times for labor. If compensation is paid at completion of a job or task, or if compensation is earned as a profit from the labor of others, such compensation is not wages.

Waive (verb): To "waive" at law, is to relinquish or give up intentionally a known right or to do an act which is inconsistent with the claiming of a known right.

Waiver (noun): The intentional relinquishment or giving up of a known right. It may be done by express words or conduct which involve any acts inconsistent with an intention to claim the right. Such conduct creates an estoppel on the part of the claimant. See *Estoppel.*

Warehouse receipt: An instrument showing that the signer has in his possession certain described goods for storage, and which obligates the signer, the warehouseman, to deliver the goods to a specified person or to his order or bearer upon the return of the instrument. Consult Uniform Warehouse Receipts Act.

Warrant (noun): An order in writing in the name of the state and signed by a magistrate directed to an officer commanding him to arrest a person.

Warrant (verb): To guarantee, to answer for, to assure that a state of facts exists.

Warranty: An undertaking, either expressed or implied, that a certain fact regarding the subject matter of a contract is presently true or will be true. The word has particular application in the law of sales of chattels. The word relates to title and quality. The word should be distinguished from "guaranty" which means a contract or promise by one person to answer for the performance of another. See *Suretyship, Guarantor.*

Waste: Damage to the real property so that its value as security is impaired.

Watered stock: Corporate stock issued by a corporation for property at an over valuation, or stock issued for which the corporation receives nothing in payment therefor.

Wharfage: A charge against a vessel for lying at a wharf. It is used synonymously with "dockage" and "moorage."

Wholesale: The usual meaning of the word is the sale of goods in gross to retailers who, in turn, sell to consumers.

Will (testament): The formal instrument by which a person makes disposition of his property to take effect upon his death. See *Testament.*

Witness: A person who testifies under oath in a legal proceeding.

Working capital: The amount of cash necessary for the convenient and safe transaction of present business.

Writ: An instrument in writing under seal in the name of the state, issued out of a Court of Justice the commencement of, or during a legal proceeding, directed to an officer of the court commanding him to do some act, or requiring some person to do or refrain from doing some act pertinent or relative to the cause being tried.

Writing obligatory: These words refer to writings under seal.

Zoning ordinance: An ordinance passed by a city council by virtue of the police power which regulates and prescribes the kind of buildings, residences, or businesses that shall be built and used in different parts of a city.

INDEX

Index

Index